Roger Ebert's
Movie Yearbook
2009

Other Books by Roger Ebert

An Illini Century

A Kiss Is Still a Kiss

Two Weeks in the Midday Sun:
A Cannes Notebook

Behind the Phantom's Mask

Roger Ebert's Little Movie Glossary

Roger Ebert's Movie Home Companion
annually 1986–1993

Roger Ebert's Video Companion
annually 1994–1998

Roger Ebert's Movie Yearbook
annually 1999–2007

Questions for the Movie Answer Man

Roger Ebert's Book of Film: An Anthology

Ebert's Bigger Little Movie Glossary

I Hated, Hated, Hated This Movie

The Great Movies

The Great Movies II

Your Movie Sucks

Roger Ebert's Four-Star Reviews—1967–2007

Awake in the Dark: The Best of Roger Ebert

Scorsese by Ebert

With Daniel Curley
The Perfect London Walk

With Gene Siskel
The Future of the Movies: Interviews with Martin Scorsese, Steven Spielberg, and George Lucas

DVD Commentary Tracks
Citizen Kane
Dark City
Casablanca
Floating Weeds
Crumb
Beyond the Valley of the Dolls

Roger Ebert's Movie Yearbook 2009

Andrews McMeel Publishing, LLC
Kansas City

Roger Ebert's Movie Yearbook 2009

Printed in the United States of America.

For information write
Andrews McMeel Publishing, LLC,
an Andrews McMeel Universal company,
1130 Walnut Street,
Kansas City, Missouri 64106.

ISSN: 1532-8147
ISBN-13: 978-0-7407-7745-5
ISBN-10: 0-7407-7745-9

09 10 11 12 13 RR4 10 9 8 7 6 5 4 3 2 1

www.andrewsmcmeel.com

All the reviews in this book originally appeared
in the *Chicago Sun-Times.*

This book is dedicated
to Robert Zonka, 1928–1985.
God love ya.

Contents

Introduction

It was a year when animation and "comic book movies" both reached new heights. Animation, by entering unexpected narrative territory with films like *WALL-E*. Comic book movies, by finding a new depth in films like *The Dark Knight* and *Iron Man*—films you couldn't so easily keep an ironic distance from.

But the news was not so bright in straight narrative films, where several key indie distributors went out of business, and independent filmmakers found it was more difficult than ever to find sources of financing and distribution. When the windows between theatrical release, cable play, and DVD grew smaller, viewers enjoyed their increased choices but were threatened by the prospect of traditional movie theaters disappearing. The best way to see a movie is in a theater with good projection and sound and a sympathetic audience, and it always will be.

For me, this has been a time of health struggles, beginning with surgery in June 2006, followed by other surgeries and complications. There was no traditional *Yearbook 2008*, but we bridged the gap with a *special* "anniversary edition" titled *Roger Ebert's Four-Star Reviews—1967–2007*.

During my illness I had long periods of recuperation and mobility when I was able to see and review movies, including the past several months, so this 2009 volume contains a respectable cross section of the movies of two years, especially since I doubled back and reviewed some I had missed. It also has the customary Answer Man items, Glossary entries, and something new: Many of the entries I wrote for my new blog on rogerebert.com. The blog was a revelation for me, allowing a new kind of interaction with my readers, who astonished me with their writing, insight, knowledge of movies, and thoughtful comments.

After entries like "In Search of Redemption" and "When a Movie Hurts Too Much," I was moved by the personal revelations and thoughts so many readers shared. I must have a high-quality readership, because after thousands of comments I have not yet received even one example of that classic online riposte "You suck!"

I find I value movies more than ever these days. They are a lifeline for me. Deprived by necessary surgery of the power of speech, I can no longer appear on television or do many of the things I treasured. But I can still think, see, and review movies, in exactly the same way. And that is a comfort. That, and knowing you are there joining in the dialogue.

Roger Ebert

Acknowledgments

My editor is Dorothy O'Brien, tireless, cheerful, all-noticing. My friend and longtime editor Donna Martin suggested the yearbook approach to the annual volume. The design is by Cameron Poulter, the typographical genius of Hyde Park.

My thanks to production editor Christi Clemons Hoffman, who renders Cameron's design into reality. John Yuelkenbeck at Coleridge Design is the compositor who has worked diligently on the series for years. I have been blessed with the expert and discriminating editing of Laura Emerick, Miriam DiNunzio, Darel Jevins, Jeff Johnson, and Teresa Budasi at the *Chicago Sun-Times*; Sue Roush at Universal Press Syndicate; and Michelle Daniel and David Shaw at Andrews McMeel Publishing. For much advice and counsel, thanks to Jim Emerson and John Barry of www.rogerebert.com.

Many thanks are also due to Marsha Jordan at WLS-TV. My gratitude goes to Carol Iwata, my expert personal assistant, and to Gregory Isaac, who is a computer whiz and invaluable aide-de-camp. I must also thank those who have given me countless observations and corrections, including Peter Debruge, Jana J. Monji, and Troylene Ladner.

And special thanks and love to my wife, Chaz, who was always at my side during a difficult illness, helped see three books through the press during that time, and was a cheerleader for this one. I am so grateful to her as we once again, relieved, enter a period of good health.

Roger Ebert

Key to Symbols

★★★★ A great film
★★★ A good film
★★ Fair
★ Poor

G, PG, PG-13, R, NC-17: Ratings of the Motion Picture Association of America

G Indicates that the movie is suitable for general audiences

PG Suitable for general audiences but parental guidance is suggested

PG-13 Recommended for viewers 13 years or above; may contain material inappropriate for younger children

R Recommended for viewers 17 or older

NC-17 Intended for adults only

141 m. Running time

2006 Year of theatrical release

☞ Refers to "Questions for the Movie Answer Man"

Reviews

A

Across the Universe ★ ★ ★ ★

PG-13, 133 m., 2007

Jim Sturgess (Jude), Evan Rachel Wood (Lucy), Joe Anderson (Max), Dana Fuchs (Sadie), Martin Luther McCoy (JoJo), T. V. Carpio (Prudence), Bono (Dr. Robert), Eddie Izzard (Mr. Kite). Directed by Julie Taymor and produced by Matthew Gross, Jennifer Todd, and Suzanne Todd. Screenplay by Dick Clement and Ian La Frenais.

Here is a bold, beautiful, visually enchanting musical where we walk INTO the theater humming the songs. Julie Taymor's *Across the Universe* is an audacious marriage of cutting-edge visual techniques, heartwarming performances, 1960s history, and the Beatles songbook. Sounds like a concept that might be behind its time, but I believe in yesterday.

This isn't one of those druggy 1960s movies, although it has what the MPAA shyly calls "some" drug content. It's not grungy, although it has Joe Cocker in it. It's not political, which means it's political to its core. Most miraculous of all, it's not dated; the stories could be happening now, and in fact they are.

For a film that is almost wall-to-wall music, it has a full-bodied plot. The characters, mostly named after Beatles songs, include Lucy (the angelic Evan Rachel Wood), who moves from middle America to New York; Jude (Jim Sturgess), a Liverpool ship welder who works his way to New York on a ship; and Lucy's brother Max (Joe Anderson), a college student who has dropped out (I guess). They now all share a pad in Greenwich Village with their musician friends, the Hendrixian JoJo (Martin Luther McCoy), the Joplinesque Sadie (Dana Fuchs), and the lovelorn Prudence (T. V. Carpio), who has a thing for Max, although the curious cutting of one scene suggests she might have lesbian feelings as well.

Jude and Lucy fall in love, and they all go through a hippie period on Dr. Robert's Magic Bus, where the doctor (Bono) and his bus bear a striking resemblance to Ken Kesey's magical mystery tour. They also get guidance from Mr. Kite (Eddie Izzard), having been some days in preparation. But then things turn serious as Max goes off to Vietnam, and the story gets swept up in the antiwar movement.

Yet when I say "story," don't start thinking about a lot of dialogue and plotting. Almost everything happens as an illustration to a Beatles song. The arrangements are sometimes familiar, sometimes radically altered, and the voices are all new; the actors either sing or synch, and often they find a mood in a song that we never knew was there before. When Prudence sings "I Wanna Hold Your Hand," for example, I realized how wrong I was to ever think that was a happy song. It's not happy if it's a hand you are never, never, never going to hold.

Julie Taymor, famous as the director of *The Lion King* on Broadway, is a generously inventive choreographer, such as in a basic training scene where all the drill sergeants look like G. I. Joe, a sequence where inductees in jockey shorts carry the Statue of Liberty through a Vietnam field, and cross-cutting between dancing to Beatles clone bands at an American high school prom and in a Liverpool dive bar. There are underwater sequences that approach ballet, a stage performance that turns into musical warfare, strawberries that bleed, rooftop concerts, and a montage combining crashing waves with the Detroit riots.

But all I'm doing here is list making. The beauty is in the execution. The experience of the movie is joyous. I don't even want to know about anybody who complains they aren't hearing "the real Beatles." Fred Astaire wasn't Cole Porter, either. These songs are now more than forty years old, some of them, and are timeless, and hearing these unexpected talents singing them (yes, and Bono, Izzard, and Cocker, too) only underlines their astonishing quality.

You weren't alive in the 1960s? Or the '70s, or '80s? You're like the guy on the IMDb message board who thought the band was named the *Beetles,* and didn't even get it when people made Volkswagen jokes because he hadn't heard of VW Beetles either. All is forgiven. Jay Leno has a Jaywalking spot for you. Just about anybody else is likely to enjoy *Across the Universe.*

I'm sure there were executives who thought it was suicidal to set a "Beatles musical" in "the Vietnam era." But this is a movie that fires its songs like flowers at the way we live now. It's the kind of movie you watch again, like listening to a favorite album. It was scheduled for the Toronto Film Festival, so was previewed (as several Toronto films were) for critics in major cities. I was drowning in movies and deadlines, and this was the only one I went to see twice.

Now do your homework and rent the DVD of *A Hard Day's Night* if you've never seen it. The thought that there are readers who would get this far in this review of this film and never have seen that film is unbearably sad. Cheer me up. Don't let me down (repeat three times).

Adam & Steve ★ ★

NO MPAA RATING, 100 m., 2006

Craig Chester (Adam), Malcolm Gets (Steve), Parker Posey (Rhonda), Chris Kattan (Michael), Noah Segan (Twink), Sally Kirkland (Mary), Julie Hagerty (Sheila). Directed by Craig Chester and produced by Kirkland Tibbels and George Bendele. Screenplay by Chester.

Adam & Steve exerts a strange fascination with its balancing act between scenes that work and others so clunky that, I dunno, is it possible to be this awkward by accident? There is an underlying story here, and some comic ideas, that in the hands of a better director (or more ruthless editor) could have become an entertaining romantic comedy. But the couple in love is forced to enact so many directorial conceits that the movie trips over itself. The director, Craig Chester, is also the costar; as an actor, he has the wrong director.

Chester stars as Adam Bernstein, first seen in the 1980s with best pal Rhonda (Parker Posey), dressed as Goths and entering a gay disco on Glitter Night, the wrong night for them. Adam makes eye contact with a dancer named Steve (Malcolm Gets), and it's love at first sight, but, "We don't dance," they explain. "We're Goths. We're dead." Not too dead for Steve to give Adam his first hit of cocaine, which makes him instantly addicted. The coke is laced with baby laxative, leading to a scene in which so many bodily wastes and fluids are ejected or vomited that a serious plot miscalculation is involved, evoking such a strong "ewww!" reflex that it takes the audience five minutes and a "17 Years Later" subtitle to get back on track.

Adam and Steve meet again in their late thirties, neither one remembering their first meeting (or perhaps much else of the late 1980s). Adam is clean and sober now, a pet lover who accidentally stabs his dog while slicing sausage and takes him to a human emergency room, where Steve, a psychiatrist who "trained as a veterinarian" (does that make him a pet psychiatrist?), treats the wound. For the two men, it's love at second sight.

Their romance develops despite the usual plot convenience (fear of commitment), but there's a crisis when Steve realizes who Adam is and flees rather than confess he made the deposit on Adam's rug seventeen years ago. Will they reconcile? Can Rhonda and Steve's straight roommate, Michael (Chris Kattan), be the go-betweens? Before we can learn the answer to that question, we get a scene both bizarre and weirdly funny.

Remember those old musicals such as *Seven Brides for Seven Brothers,* where lumberjacks would stage dance duels for the favor of the girl? Steve and Adam face off in a disco where western line dancing and two-steps in cowboy boots are the dance style, and both men instantly acquire backup dancers for a meticulously choreographed confrontation that's as well-staged as it is dramatically inexplicable. That scene, and one where Steve serenades Adam by singing to him at brunch, show how the movie uses any genre that can be plundered for effect, and does it with humor and sometimes charm.

I liked, for example, the visit to Adam's parents, who are the nicest people in the world although they suffer from the "Bernstein curse" (mother in neck brace, father in wheelchair, sister bites tongue). I liked the deadpan way Posey plays the formerly fat Goth who has become a slender stand-up comic who still tells fat jokes. The scene where Adam, leading a bird-watching tour in Central Park, meets Steve again after a tragic duck shooting. And Sally Kirkland as an AA group leader shouting "no cross-talking!" during a verbal fight.

But what can we make of other scenes that

destroy any dramatic effect and all but shout, "This cumbersome scene is being committed to film by ham-handed amateurs"? I'm thinking of a conversation that is observed by a man in the center background who stares at the camera, reacts to the conversation, and closes the scene with an unintelligible comment. Who was that man? Friend of the director? Investor? In another scene a drunken girl, trying to pick up Michael in a bar, is so self-consciously awful in her awkward overacting that you can see Kattan, a pro, wishing himself elsewhere. Or a scene where Adam and Rhonda have a talk on a bench in a gay sculpture park, and in the last shot they awkwardly "happen" to take the same pose as the sculptures they're seated next to. What does a shot like that mean? Where does it go? How do we react?—Wow! They're in the same pose as the sculpture!

There is a gay-bashing montage in which Adam and Steve try to pursue their courtship while offscreen homophobes throw beer bottles at them. Far from funny, and it isn't saved by a pan up to the street sign: "Gay Street." And a scene where Steve gets fed up with a homophobic neighbor who screams insults at them and drags him, beaten and bloody, into a bar so that the gay-basher can get his arm twisted while he speaks for Steve in proposing marriage to Adam. This is an agonizingly bad idea.

The movie is one hundred minutes long. My guess is that by taking out maybe fifteen judicious minutes, it could be cut into a measurably better film—funnier, more romantic, more professional. The sad thing is to watch it finding a rhythm and beginning to work as a comedy, then running into a brick wall of miscalculation or incompetence. Any professional film editor watching this movie is going to suffer through one moment after another that begs to be ripped from the film and cut up into ukulele picks. Never mind the film editor: A lot of audiences, with all the best will in the world, are going to feel the same way.

The Adventures of Sharkboy and Lavagirl in 3-D ★ ★

PG, 94 m., 2005

Cayden Boyd (Max), David Arquette (Dad), Kristin Davis (Mom), Taylor Dooley (Lavagirl), Taylor Lautner (Sharkboy), George Lopez (Mr. Electricidad), Sasha Pieterse (Ice Princess), Jacob Davich (Minus). Directed by Robert Rodriguez and produced by Elizabeth Avellan and Robert Rodriguez. Screenplay by Racer Rodriguez and Robert Rodriguez.

The Adventures of Sharkboy and Lavagirl in 3-D is an innocent and delightful children's tale that is spoiled by a disastrous decision to film most of it in lousy 3-D. Fully three-quarters of the movie is in "3"-D, which looks more like 1-D to me, removing the brightness and life of the movie's colors and replacing them with a drab, listless palette that is about as exciting as looking at a 3-D bowl of oatmeal.

The 3-D process subtracts instead of adding. Ordinary 2-D movies look perfectly real enough for audiences and have for years; if it's not broke, don't fix it. Paradoxically, since it allegedly resembles our real-world vision, 3-D is less real than standard flat movies; 3-D acts as a distraction from character and story, giving us something to think about that during a good movie we should not be thinking about.

To be sure, there is a new 3-D process that is pretty good. That would be the IMAX process that uses oversized glasses and creates a convincing 3-D effect, as in James Cameron's *Aliens of the Deep.* That is not the process used in *Sharkboy and Lavagirl,* which settles for those crummy old cardboard glasses where the left lens is such a dark red that the whole movie seems seen through a glass, darkly.

What a shame. I assume the unaltered original color footage of the movie exists, and no doubt will be used for the DVD. My suggestion to Robert Rodriguez, who directed the movie from a screenplay by one of his sons and uses three of them as actors, would be to make a non-3-D version available theatrically as soon as possible. This is a movie aimed at younger kids, who may be willing to sit through almost anything, but they're going to know something is wrong and they're not going to like it.

The origin of the film makes a good story. Rodriguez's son Racer, then seven, told him a story about a boy who grew gills and a fin and became half-shark, and a girl who incorporated fiery volcanic elements. He encouraged his son to keep working on the story, in which the young hero, Max (Cayden Boyd), is a daydreamer. Max is mocked by Linus, the school bully, because of his Dream Journal, where he documents the adventures of Sharkboy and Lavagirl. Then a tornado appears out of a clear sky, bringing with it Sharkboy (Taylor Lautner) and Lavagirl (Taylor Dooley), who explain they have been created by Max's dreams and now need his help; the world he created for them, Planet Drool, will be destroyed by darkness in forty-five minutes. I may not have followed these details with perfect fidelity, but you get the drift.

Max, SB, and LG go on a journey that takes them on the Stream of Consciousness to the Sea of Confusion; they ride a Train of Thought, and eventually arrive at a Dream Lair. There they find the nasty Minus, played by the same actor (Jacob Davich) who was the bully in Max's classroom. Many adventures result, some of them involving an Ice Princess and a robot named Tobor, as well as an all-knowing character named Mr. Electric, who looks exactly like Max's teacher Mr. Electricidad (George Lopez).

Mr. Electric appears as a big, round smiling face in a frame outfitted with spindly arms and legs. He reminded me of someone, which was odd, since he looked like nobody I've ever seen. Nobody, I realized, except the Man in the Moon in Georges Melies's *A Trip to the Moon* (1902). Mr. Electric floats about like a busybody commentator, offering advice, issuing warnings, and making a general nuisance of himself; one of his peculiarities is that he won't allow the kids on the planet to stop playing—ever. One group is trapped on a roller coaster that never stops.

Sharkboy and Lavagirl has the same upbeat charm as Rodriguez's *Spy Kids* movies, and it must be said that the screenplay by Racer Rodriguez involves the kind of free-wheeling invention that kids enjoy; this is a movie where dream logic prevails. Their movie also resembles *Spy Kids* in having roles for parents, including Max's dad and mom (David Arquette and Kristin Davis).

Because the real-world scenes are in 2-D and the dream and fantasy scenes are in 3-D, we get an idea of what the movie would have looked like without the unnecessary dimension. Signs flash on the screen to tell us when to put on and take off our polarizing glasses, and I felt regret every time I had to shut out those colorful images and return to the dim and dreary 3-D world. On DVD, this is going to be a great-looking movie.

Akeelah and the Bee ★ ★ ★ ★

PG-13, 112 m., 2006

Angela Bassett (Tanya Anderson), Keke Palmer (Akeelah Anderson), Laurence Fishburne (Dr. Joshua Larabee), Curtis Armstrong (Mr. Welch), J. R. Villarreal (Javier), Sahara Garey (Georgia), Sean Michael Afable (Dylan), Erica Hubbard (Kiana Anderson). Directed by Doug Atchison and produced by Laurence Fishburne, Sidney Ganis, Nancy Hult Ganis, Daniel Llewelyn, and Michael Romersa. Screenplay by Atchison.

Akeelah Anderson can spell. She can spell better than anyone in her school in south central Los Angeles, and she might have a chance at the nationals. Who can say? She sees the national spelling bee on ESPN and is intrigued. But she is also wary, because in her school there is danger in being labeled a "brainiac," and it's wiser to keep your smarts to yourself. This is a tragedy in some predominantly black schools: Excellence is punished by the other students, possibly as an expression of their own low self-esteem.

The thing with Akeelah (Keke Palmer) is that she *can* spell, whether she wants to or not. Beating time with her hand against her thigh as sort of a metronome, she cranks out the letters and arrives triumphantly at the words. No, she doesn't have a photographic memory, nor is she channeling the occult, as the heroine of *Bee Season* does. She's just a good speller.

The story of Akeelah's ascent to the finals of the National Spelling Bee makes an uncommonly good movie, entertaining and actually inspirational, and with a few tears along the way. Her real chance at national success comes after a reluctant English professor agrees to act as her coach. This is Dr. Joshua Larabee (Laurence Fishburne), on a leave of absence after the death of his daughter. Coaching her is a way out of his own shell. And for Fishburne, it's a reminder of his work in *Searching for Bobby Fischer* (1993), another movie where he coached a prodigy.

Akeelah is not mocked only at school. Her own mother is against her. Tanya Anderson (Angela Bassett) has issues after the death of her husband, and she values Akeelah's homework above all else, including silly afterschool activities such as spelling bees. Akeelah practices in secret, and after she wins a few bees, even the tough kids in the neighborhood start cheering for her.

Keke Palmer, a young Chicago actress whose first role was as Queen Latifah's niece in *Barber Shop 2*, becomes an important young star with this movie. It puts her in Dakota Fanning and Flora Cross territory, and there's something about her poise and self-possession that hints she will grow up to be a considerable actress. The movie depends on her, and she deserves its trust.

So far I imagine *Akeelah and the Bee* sounds like a nice but fairly conventional movie. What makes it transcend the material is the way she relates to the professor and to two fellow contestants: a Mexican-American named Javier (J. R. Villarreal) and an Asian-American named Dylan (Sean Michael Afable). Javier, who lives with his family in the upscale Woodland Hills neighborhood, invites Akeelah to his birthday party (unaware of what a long bus trip it involves). Dylan, driven by an obsessive father, treats the spelling bee like life and death, and takes no hostages. Hearing Dylan's father berate him, Akeelah feels an instinctive sympathy. And as for Javier's feelings for Akeelah, at his party he impulsively kisses her.

"Why'd you do that?" she asks him.

"I had an impulse. Are you gonna sue me for sexual harassment?"

The sessions between Akeelah and the professor are crucial to the film, because he is teaching her not only strategy but also how to be willing to win. No, he doesn't use self-help clichés. He is demanding and uncompromising, and he tells her again and again, "Our deepest fear is that we are powerful beyond measure." This quote, often attributed to Nelson Mandela, is actually from Marianne Williamson but is no less true for Akeelah (the movie does not attribute it).

Now I am going to start dancing around the plot. Something happens during the finals of the national bee that you are not going to see coming, and it may move you as deeply as it did me. I've often said it's not sadness that touches me the most in a movie, but goodness. Under enormous pressure, at a crucial moment, Akeelah does something good. Its results I will leave for you to discover. What is ingenious about the plot construction of writer-director Doug Atchison is that he creates this moment so that we understand what's happening, but there's no way to say for sure. Even the judges sense or suspect something. But Akeelah, improvising in the moment and out of her heart, makes it airtight. There is only one person who absolutely must understand what she is doing, and why—and he does.

This ending answers one of my problems with spelling bees and spelling-bee movies. It removes winning as the only objective. Vince Lombardi was dead wrong when he said, "Winning isn't everything. It's the only thing" (a quote, by the way, first said not by Lombardi but in the 1930s by UCLA coach Henry "Red" Sanders—but since everybody thinks Lombardi said it, he won, I guess). The saying is mistaken because to win for the wrong reason or in the wrong way is to lose. Something called sportsmanship is involved.

In our winning-obsessed culture, it is inspiring to see a young woman like Akeelah Anderson instinctively understand, with empathy and generosity, that doing the right thing involves more than winning. That's what makes the film particularly valuable for young audiences. I don't care if they leave the theater wanting to spell better, but if they have learned from Akeelah, they will want to live better.

Aliens of the Deep ★ ★ ★

G, 45 m., 2005

With James Cameron, Pamela Conrad, Djanna Figueroa, Kevin Hand, Loretta Hidalgo, and Maya Tolstoy. A documentary directed by James Cameron and Steven Quayle and produced by Cameron and Andrew Wight.

The timing of *Aliens of the Deep* couldn't be better. Days after a space probe landed successfully on Saturn's moon Titan and sent back spectacular photographs of its surface, here is a movie that explores the depths of the seas of Earth and then uses animation to imagine a probe that would fly to Jupiter's moon Europa and drill through its ice layer to the liquid water thought to be below. By finding living creatures on Earth that live under extreme conditions—

no sunlight, no photosynthesis, incredible pressure, extremes of hot and cold—James Cameron convincingly argues that life could exist in the seas of Europa, or, for that matter, in any number of harrowing environments.

For Cameron, the film continues an obsession. When he wrote and directed *The Abyss* in 1989, his story involved scientists venturing into the deepest parts of the ocean. The movie was a box-office disappointment, not least because the director's cut reveals that the studio chopped crucial and amazing footage—and also, reportedly, because many potential ticket buyers did not know what an "abyss" was. For Cameron, it was an epiphany.

He returned to the sea bed for *Titanic* (1997), still the highest-grossing movie of all time, and essentially never came up for air. In 2002 his *Expedition: Bismarck,* made for the Discovery Channel, used deep-water submersibles to visit the grave of the doomed battleship, and in 2003 he made the 3-D IMAX movie *Ghosts of the Abyss,* which visited the wreck of the *Titanic* itself.

That was a movie with fascinating content, but I found the 3-D format unsatisfactory, and thought it might have been better to forget the gimmick and just give us the images. Now comes Cameron's *Aliens of the Deep,* also in IMAX 3-D, also fascinating, and with much-improved 3-D. After tinkering with the format for years, the IMAX technicians have devised oversized glasses that fit easily over existing eyeglasses and cover the entire field of vision. I saw the first 3-D movie, *Bwana Devil,* in 1952, and have been tired of the format ever since, but IMAX finally seems to be getting it right.

The movie is about expeditions to the deepest seas on Earth, where life is found to flourish under incredible conditions. We've read reports of some of these discoveries before—the worms that live around the sulphurous vents of hot water on the cold sea bottom, for example—but now we see them, photographed in lonely and splendid isolation, and the sights are magnificent.

What are these creatures? A good question, and one you might well still be asking after the movie, since it is high on amazement but low on information. His aquanauts, all real scientists or students, keep saying their discoveries are magnificent, beautiful, unbelievable, incredible, etc., and so they are, but only rudimentary facts are supplied about these life forms.

That didn't bother me as much as it might have, because *Aliens of the Deep* is not a scientific documentary so much as a journey to an alien world, and basically what we want to do is peer out the portholes along with the explorers. We see a vast, drifting, transparent creature, looking like nothing so much as a linen scarf, with a fragile network of vessels holding itself together. How does it feed? What does it know?

The tube worms are fascinating because they exist in symbiosis with bacteria that live inside of them. They have no digestive facility, and the bacteria have no food-gathering ability, but working together they both make a living. Astonishingly, we see shrimp, millions of them, darting endlessly through superheated vents of escaping lava-heated water, which is hundreds of degrees warmer than the icy water around it. How do these creatures move through such extremes of hot and cold so quickly, when either by itself would kill them?

Aliens of the Deep is a convincing demonstration of Darwin's theory of evolution because it shows creatures not only adapted perfectly to their environment but obviously generated by that environment. It drives me crazy when people say evolution is "only a theory," because that reveals they don't know what a scientific theory is. As *National Geographic* pointed out, a theory is a scientific hypothesis that is consistent with observed and experimental data, and the observations and experiments must be able to be repeated. Darwin passes that test. His rival, creationism, is not a theory, but a belief. There is a big difference.

Evolution aside, there are some wonderful images in *Aliens of the Deep,* even if the crew members say how much they love their jobs about six times too often. In a late segment of the film, Cameron uses special effects to imagine a visit to Europa, where a nuclear-heated probe would melt and drill its way down to the liquid seas thought to be three to fourteen miles below ice, and find there—well, life, perhaps. He even envisions an underwater city that belongs on the cover of *Amazing Stories,* circa 1940. It's not a million miles different from the one in the director's cut of *The Abyss.* That his city was astonishingly cut from the theatrical version of *The Abyss* to make more room for the love story is no doubt one of the several reasons Cameron has recently worked in documentary instead of fiction. It's tempting to say that Cameron should have stayed with the wonders of Earth and not created imaginary civilizations on Europa, but I was enthralled by those fictional sequences, unlikely as they are. I would suggest that if an advanced civilization has evolved on Europa, however, it is unlikely to have cities, since interior rooms and corridors would not occur naturally to swimming creatures. More likely, like dolphins, the Europans will fully exploit their given habitat. Or maybe they will all look like pond scum, which as discoveries go would also be quite amazing enough.

Alvin and the Chipmunks ★ ★

PG, 91 m., 2007

Jason Lee (Dave Seville), David Cross (Ian), Cameron Richardson (Claire), voice of Justin Long (Alvin), voice of Jesse McCartney (Theodore), voice of Matthew Gray Gubler (Simon). Directed by Tim Hill and produced by Ross Bagdasarian Jr., Janice Karman, and Steve Waterman. Screenplay by John Vitti, Will McRobb, and Chris Viscardi.

The most astonishing sight in *Alvin and the Chipmunks* is not three singing chipmunks. No, it's a surprise saved for the closing titles, where we see the covers of all the Alvin & C albums and CDs. I lost track after ten. It is inconceivable to me that anyone would want to listen to one whole album of those squeaky little voices, let alone ten. "The Chipmunk Song," maybe, for its fleeting novelty. But "Only You"?

There are, however, Alvin and the Chipmunks fans. Their latest album rates 4.5/5 at the iTunes store, where I sampled their version of "Only You" and the original by the Platters, and immediately downloaded *The Platters' Greatest Hits*. I imagine people even impatiently preorder the Chipmunks, however, which speaks highly for the drawing power of electronically altered voices by interchangeable singers. This film is dedicated to Ross Bagdasarian Sr., "who was crazy enough" to dream them up. I think the wording is about right.

Despite the fact that the film is set in the present, when the real (or "real") Chipmunks already have a back catalog bigger than Kimya Dawson's, the movie tells the story of how they become rock stars and almost get burned out on the rock circuit. Jason Lee stars as Dave Seville, who accidentally brings them home in a basket of muffins, discovers they can talk, and is soon shouting "Alvin!" at the top of his lungs, as Chipmunk lore requires that he must.

David Cross plays Ian, the hustling tour promoter who signs them up and takes them on the road, where they burn out and he suggests they start lip-synching with dubbed voices. Now we're getting into Alice in Wonderland territory, because of course they *are* dubbed voices in the first place. Indeed the metaphysics of dubbing dubbed chipmunks who exist in the real world as animated representations of real chipmunks is . . . how did this sentence begin?

That said, whatever it was, *Alvin and the Chipmunks* is about as good as a movie with these characters can probably be, and I am well aware that I am the wrong audience for this movie. I am even sure some readers will throw it up to me that I liked the Garfield movie better.

Yes, but Garfield didn't sing, and he was dubbed by Bill Murray. My duty as a reporter is to inform you that the chipmunks are sorta cute, that Jason Lee and David Cross manfully play roles that require them, as actors, to relate with empty space that would later be filled with CGI, and that at some level the movie may even be doing something satirical about rock stars and the hype machine.

I was also grateful that Alvin wears a red sweater with a big "A" on it as an aid to identification, since otherwise all the chipmunks seem to be identical, like mutant turtles or Spice Girls. It doesn't much matter which one is Theodore and which one is Simon, although Simon is always the one who seems a day late and a walnut short. ☞

American Dreamz ★ ★ ★

PG-13, 107 m., 2006

Hugh Grant (Martin Tweed), Dennis Quaid (President Staton), Mandy Moore (Sally Kendoo), Marcia Gay Harden (First Lady

Staton), Chris Klein (William Williams), Jennifer Coolidge (Martha Kendoo), Sam Golzari (Omer), Adam Busch (Sholem), Seth Meyers (Chet Krogl). Directed by Paul Weitz and produced by Rodney M. Liber, Andrew Miano, and Weitz. Screenplay by Weitz.

American Dreamz is a comedy, not a satire. We have that on the authority of its writer-director, Paul Weitz, who told *Variety*: "Satire is what closes on Saturday night. So it's a comedy." Actually, it's a satire. Its comedy is only fairly funny, but its satire is mean, tending toward vicious. The movie is more slapdash than smooth, more impulsive than calculating, and it takes cheap shots. I responded to its savage, sloppy zeal.

The movie has two targets, *American Idol* and President George W. Bush, not in that order. As it opens, a TV producer and star named Martin Tweed (Hugh Grant) is planning the new season of his hit show. On camera, he's Simon Cowell. Off camera, he's Machiavelli, scheming for contestants who get the highest ratings. The season will end in a three-way contest between a Hasidic Jew rapper (Adam Busch), a corn-fed Ohio blonde (Mandy Moore), and a theater buff from Iraq (Sam Golzari) who is secretly a terrorist.

Meanwhile, in the White House, President Staton (Dennis Quaid) awakens after his reelection victory and has an impulse: "I'm gonna read the newspaper!" He asks for the *New York Times*. "We can get one," an aide assures him uncertainly. He finds the paper instructive. "Did you know there are three kinds of Iraqistans?" he asks his chief of staff (Willem Dafoe), who looks uncannily like Dick Cheney. Surrounding himself with books and even the left-wing *Guardian* from England, the president isn't seen in public for weeks. "There is a lot of interesting things in the paper!" he marvels.

The plot chugs forward on two fronts. On the TV program, we see Sally Kendoo (Moore) playing the role of a screamingly delirious young contestant, pushed by her mother (Jennifer Coolidge) and superagent (Seth Meyers), and dumping her boyfriend (Chris Klein) because he's going nowhere and she's going up-up-up. As the godlike *American Dreamz* producer and judge, Grant does what he's curiously good at, playing an enormously likable SOB.

When the president is finally blasted out of his bedroom in the White House, he resumes public life with an earpiece so his chief of staff can dictate, word for word, his response in every situation. That many Americans believe Bush has used such earpieces, and that he rarely if ever reads a newspaper, brings a certain poignancy to these scenes. The first lady (Marcia Gay Harden) labors behind the scenes to counsel and advise him, and to explain stuff to him. Badgered by publicity about his "reclusive" chief executive, the chief of staff decides to book the president on the season finale of *American Dreamz* to show what a great guy he is. The terrorist, who seems headed for the final round, is ordered by his handlers to wear a bomb into the studio.

This is dark comedy in the spirit of *Dr. Strangelove*, a movie that thought the unthinkable. *American Dreamz* isn't nearly as good as *Strangelove*, perhaps because it lacks its merciless ironic detachment. But I was surprised at the movie's daring, at its frank depiction of the Bush-like president as the clueless puppet of his staff. His mom wanted him to run for president, he says, "to show my dad any idiot could do it." Quaid looks and sounds a little like Bush, and Dafoe looks a little and sounds a lot like Cheney. Grant, for that matter, could stand in for Simon Cowell.

Weitz was only thirty-three when he directed *American Pie*. It looked like a teenage sex comedy, played like a teenage sex comedy, and was a teenage sex comedy—and a lot more. He proved with *About a Boy* (2002) that he was a director of considerable gifts; working with his brother Chris, he adapted a Nick Hornby novel into the perfect setting for Grant's merger of selfishness and charm. *In Good Company* (2004), which he wrote and directed, starred Quaid as an aging executive bossed by a young hotshot who is also dating his daughter. Now Quaid, Grant, and Weitz are together on a project that lacks the polish and assurance of those earlier films but has a kind of reckless nerve. *American Dreamz* looks like a sitcom, plays like a sitcom, and is a sitcom—and is the riskiest political satire since *Wag the Dog*.

At a time when I am already receiving messages of alarm about Oliver Stone's forthcoming *World Trade Center*, does *American Dreamz* go too far? Is it in bad taste? That would depend on what you think satire is supposed to do. Satire by definition goes beyond the norm, exaggerates, is partisan, is unfair. It offends those who believe others (not themselves) are too stupid to know it's satire. And it alarms those who think some things are not laughing matters. To them I recommend Lord Byron: "And if I laugh at any mortal thing, 'tis that I may not weep."

The buried message of the film, perhaps, is that our political system resembles *American Idol*. Contestants are chosen on the basis of superficial marketability, and they go through a series of primaries and debates while the pollsters keep score. The winner is not necessarily the deserving contestant from an objective point of view but the one with the best poll numbers. A candidate from either party will be defeated if he is not entertaining. His intelligence and matters of right or wrong don't have much to do with it. In this scenario, satire plays the role in politics that Simon Cowell plays on TV.

Americanese ★ ★ ★ ½

NO MPAA RATING, 108 m., 2006

Chris Tashima (Raymond Ding), Allison Sie (Aurora Crane), Joan Chen (Betty Nguyen), Kelly Hu (Brenda Nishitani), Ben Shenkman (Steve), Sab Shimono (Wood Ding), Michael Paul Chan (Jimmy Chan). Directed by Eric Byler and produced by Lisa Onodera. Screenplay by Byler, based on a novel by Shawn Wong.

Americanese is the second feature I've seen by Eric Byler, who has a quiet confidence not only about film but about life. Byler deals with characters who have lived their years, have learned from them, and try to apply their values to their lives. Their romances are not heedless but wary and involve a lot of negotiation. Listen to Betty calmly tell Raymond, after their first date, "We can be friends, or we can be something more." The choice is theirs. But they must make it, and with their eyes wide open. And they have to start out knowing that.

There's none of the silliness of an Adult Teenager Movie where romance is a montage of candlelight and sailboats, and the characters never have a conversation of any substance. Don't these people know that you have to be able to *talk* with the other person for hours, days, and years, or the relationship is doomed? Watching *Americanese* after movies like *Failure to Launch*, I felt like I'd wandered into the grown-up cinema.

Raymond Ding (Chris Tashima) meets Betty Nguyen (Joan Chen) on a double rebound. He's a university professor in San Francisco whose first marriage ended in divorce. For three years he lived with Aurora Crane (Allison Sie), but they've broken up, in a strange, sad, subdued process that's not quite finished. They're still "friends." She kept their apartment. During the day, when he knows she's not at home, he enters it and pokes around, as if looking for clues to what went wrong. She knows he does this.

Raymond is Chinese-American. Aurora is half-Asian; her dad is white. Betty is from Vietnam. Before Raymond and Betty make love for the first time, she tells him he will find scars on her legs. Later, they talk about that. "Did you . . . get them all at once?" he asks her. "Yes, all the same time," she says quietly. And later: "It's not your job to heal me." In her sleep, she says the name "Amy." Amy is her daughter by her first marriage, to a long-haul trucker in Houston. She lost custody because she made mistakes. In a few words, Byler creates a character who was wounded in Vietnam, came to America, made a bad marriage, walked out on it, went to the University of Texas to start her life over again, is now in San Francisco, and is, as they say, strongest at the broken places.

But Betty is not even the central character in the movie. Byler establishes his characters with a few words or quick strokes, like a short-story writer. Nothing is hammered home. These lives are still being lived. One of the reasons Raymond and Aurora broke up, we learn, is that he never believed she accepted her Asian identity. There is a scene where Aurora goes home for a weekend with her white father, her Asian mother, and her sister. The sister is engaged to a black man, whom we meet and like. A good man. Her father doesn't want this man coming to his retirement party; he wants to save "possible embarrassment." He explains to Aurora: "I'm not a racist; otherwise, I wouldn't have married your mom." That's when Aurora realizes he's a racist.

Raymond tells Aurora, not making a big deal of it, that her father thinks of her as white. That in her father's mind, there is a difference between him marrying an Asian woman and a black man marrying his daughter. "When you let something slide," he tells her, "you're essentially passing as white." Until Aurora can accept both sides of herself, Raymond cannot feel accepted. It is perhaps no surprise that Aurora's new boyfriend is white. "When am I gonna meet your new guy?" Raymond asks her. "You've met, actually," she says. Those three words do the work of a scene in someone else's movie.

The film centers on the performance of Tashima, handsome but not thinking about it, playing an inward man whose view of race is not confrontational but observational. He wants to be a good man, and the breakup with Aurora hurts. He senses in the Vietnamese woman Betty another kind of gulf: She accepts her Asian identity, all right, but when she looks at him she sees not an Asian but an Asian-American, more American than Asian. This is true. "I don't read Chinese," Raymond casually reminds his father, Wood (Sab Shimono). He's startled when his dad, a widower, announces plans to go to China and find a wife. Just like that? Why not? To Raymond, marriage is a minefield of emotional and intellectual challenges. To his dad, it's a necessity: "It's not good to live without a wife."

I've been writing in such a way you'd think *Americanese* is a movie entirely about the theory and practice of race in America. Not at all, based on a novel by Shawn Wong, it is above all about people seeking love and happiness in their lives. I've spoken with Byler several times since seeing his *Charlotte Sometimes* (2002) for the first time, and I know that when he grew up in Hawaii he sometimes felt like an outsider because he, like Aurora, is half-Asian. Standing on the divide, he opens his arms and his artistic imagination to those who let it separate them. That they are Asian in one way or another is a reality of their search, but not a condition of it. It's a strange thing about characters in movies: The more "universal" they are, the more provincial. The more specific they are, the more they are exactly themselves, the more we can identify with them.

American Gangster ★ ★ ★ ★

R, 157 m., 2007

Denzel Washington (Frank Lucas), Russell Crowe (Det. Richie Roberts), Chiwetel Ejiofor (Huey Lucas), Cuba Gooding Jr. (Nicky Barnes), Josh Brolin (Det. Trupo), Ted Levine (Lou Toback), Armand Assante (Dominic Cattano), Carla Gugino (Laurie Roberts). Directed by Ridley Scott and produced by Scott and Brian Grazer. Screenplay by Steven Zaillian, based on an article by Mark Jacobson.

Apart from the detail that he was a heroin dealer, Frank Lucas's career would be an ideal case study for a business school. *American Gangster* tells his success story. Inheriting a crime empire from his famous boss, Bumpy Johnson, he cornered the New York drug trade with admirable capitalist strategies. He personally flew to Southeast Asia to buy his product directly from the suppliers, used an ingenious importing scheme to get it into the United States, and sold it at higher purity and lower cost than anyone else was able to. At the end, he was worth more than $150 million, and got a reduced sentence by cutting a deal to expose three-quarters of the NYPD narcotics officers as corrupt. And he always took his mom to church on Sunday.

Lucas is played by Denzel Washington in another one of those performances where he is affable and smooth on the outside yet ruthless enough to set an enemy on fire. Here's a detail: As the man goes up in flames, Frank shoots him to put him out of his agony. Now that's merciful. His stubborn antagonist in the picture is a police detective named Richie Roberts (Russell Crowe), who gets a very bad reputation in the department. How does he do that? By finding $1 million in drug money—*and turning it in.* What the hell kindofa thing is that to do, when the usual practice would be to share it with the boys?

There is something inside Roberts that will not bend, not even when his powerful colleague (Josh Brolin) threatens him. He vows to bring down Frank Lucas, and he does, although it isn't easy, and his most troubling opposition comes from within the police. Lucas, the student of the late Bumpy, has a simple credo: Treat people right, keep a low profile, adhere to sound business practices, and hand out turkeys on Thanksgiving. He can trust the people who work for him because he pays them very well, and many of them are his relatives.

In the movie, at least, Lucas is low-key and soft-spoken. No rings on his fingers, no gold around his neck, no spinners on his hubcaps, quiet marriage to a sweet wife, a Brooks Brothers image. It takes the authorities the longest time to figure out who he is because they can't believe an African-American could hijack the Harlem drug trade from the Mafia. The Mafia can't believe it either, but Frank not only pulls it off, he's still alive at the end.

When it was first announced, Ridley Scott's movie was inevitably called the black *Godfather.* Not really. For one thing, it tells two parallel stories, not one, and it really has to because without Richie Roberts there would be no story to tell, and Lucas might still be in business today. But that doesn't save us from a stock female character who is becoming increasingly tiresome in the movies, the wife (Carla Gugino) who wants Roberts to choose between his job and his family. Their obligatory scenes together are recycled from a dozen or a hundred other plots, and although we sympathize with her (will they all be targeted for assassination?), we grow restless during her complaints. Roberts's domestic crisis is not what the movie is about.

It is about an extraordinary entrepreneur whose story was told in a *New York Magazine* article by Mark Jacobson. As adapted into a (somewhat fictionalized) screenplay by Steve Zaillian *(Schindler's List)*, Lucas is a loyal driver, bodyguard, and coat holder for Bumpy Johnson (who has inspired characters in three other movies, including *The Cotton Club*). He listens carefully to Johnson's advice, cradles him when he is dying, takes over, and realizes the fatal flaw in the Harlem drug business: The goods come in through the Mafia after having been stepped on all along the way.

So he flies to Thailand, goes upriver for a face-to-face with the general in charge of drugs, and is rewarded for this seemingly foolhardy risk with an exclusive contract. The drugs will come to the United States inside the coffins of American casualties, which is apparently based on fact. It's all arranged by one of his relatives.

In terms of his visible lifestyle, the story of Frank Lucas might as well be the story of J. C. Penney, except that he hands out turkeys instead of pennies. Everyone in his distribution chain is reasonably happy because the product is high-quality, the price is right, and there's money for everyone. Ironically, an epidemic of overdoses occurs when Lucas's high-grade stuff is treated by junkies as if it's the usual weaker street strength. Then Lucas starts practicing what marketing experts call branding: It becomes known that his *Blue Magic* offers twice the potency at half the price, and other suppliers are forced off the streets by the rules of the marketplace, not turf wars.

This is an engrossing story, told smoothly and well, and Russell Crowe's contribution is enormous (it's not his fault his wife complains). Looking like a care-worn bulldog, his Richie Roberts studies for a law degree, remains inviolate in his ethical standards, and just keeps plugging away, building his case. The film ends (this isn't a spoiler, I hope) not with a *Scarface*-style shootout, but with Frank and Richie sitting down for a long, intelligent conversation, written by Zaillian to show two smart men who both know what the score is. As I hinted above: less *Godfather* than *Wall Street,* although for that matter a movie named *American Gangster* could have been made about Kenneth Lay.

American Gun ★ ★ ★

R, 95 m., 2006

Donald Sutherland (Carl), Forest Whitaker (Carter), Marcia Gay Harden (Janet), Linda Cardellini (Mary Anne), Tony Goldwyn (Frank), Chris Marquette (David), Arlen Escarpeta (Jay), Garcelle Beauvais-Nilon (Sara), Nikki Reed (Tally). Directed by Aric Avelino and produced by Ted Kroeber. Screenplay by Steven Bagatourian and Avelino.

American Gun tells three stories that are small, even quiet. The stories are not strident but sad, and one of them is open-ended. They are about people who find that guns in the hands of others have made their own lives almost impossible to live.

The first story involves a mother named Janet, played by Marcia Gay Harden, whose son shot and killed other students at his Oregon high school three years ago and then was shot dead. She carries on with her remaining son, David (Chris Marquette), who attends a private school. She needs money. She agrees to a paid interview with a local television station, during which she seems inarticulate about her older son's rampage. Well, what can she say? Like other parents, she lost a child in the shooting. Perhaps it is harder to be the parent of a killer than the parent of a victim. Then David has to leave the private school and enroll in the very same school where his brother did the shooting.

Also interviewed is a cop (Tony Goldwyn) who some people feel should have been able to save lives that day. He knows he followed department procedures but feels blamed for the deaths. Both the mother and the cop are at a loss for words when TV reporters ask them questions beginning with "How does it make you feel?" They're not glib and don't fall easily into the clichés of remorse and redemption.

The second story stars Forest Whitaker as Carter, the principal of an inner-city high school in Chicago. He moved to the big city from Ohio, thinking he could make a difference, but now his wife (Garcelle Beauvais-Nilon) feels she is losing him to his job. He is discouraged, weary beyond belief, despairing. One of his honor students, Jay (Arlen Escarpeta), is found with a gun near the school and faces expulsion. We follow Jay to his job inside a padlocked cashier's station at an all-night gas station where any customer might confront him with a gun. He needs to carry a gun, he feels, for protection, even though it isn't loaded.

The third story, the open-ended one, involves a gentle old man named Carl (Donald Sutherland) who runs a gun shop in Charlottesville, Virginia. His granddaughter Mary Anne (Linda Cardellini) enrolls at the university and works part time in the store. Carl is not a gun nut. He might as well be selling fishing tackle. Mary Anne feels uneasy working in the store, however, and then one of her friends is assaulted.

All three stories ask the same question: How do you lead a reasonable life in a world where a lot of your fellow citizens can and do walk around armed? Two answers seem to be possible: They should be disarmed, or you should be armed. A third answer, implied by some gun owners, is that they should be armed but many other categories of people should not be. They never include themselves in those categories. I am reminded of my friend McHugh, who was shown a gun by a guy in a bar. "Why do you carry that?" McHugh asked him. "I live in a dangerous neighborhood," the guy said. "It would be safer," McHugh told him, "if you moved."

At one point in the movie, the neighbors of Janet, the mother, observe the third anniversary of the high school massacre by planting flags on their lawns, including a black flag on hers. They are vindictive and revengeful. Did it occur to them to plant signs asking for a ban on handguns? No. Guns don't kill people. Janet's son does.

American Gun is a first feature by Aric Avelino, who cowrote it with Steven Bagatourian. He shows an almost tender restraint in his storytelling, not pounding us with a message but simply looking steadily at how guns have made these lives difficult. The mother's real answer to the TV interviewer could have been: "My son killed his schoolmates because he had a gun and he could." The Columbine shooters without weapons still would have been antisocial psychopaths, but they would not have been killers.

As for the Chicago school principal, his despair is easy to understand. During the same week I saw *American Gun,* two children were shot dead in Chicago just as a byproduct of guns. They were not targets, but accidental victims. The cost of guns is multiplied day after day, year after year, body after body, in our society. The rest of the world looks on in wonder. The right to bear arms is being defended by the sacrifice of the lives of their victims. That doesn't mean gun owners are all bad people. Sutherland's gun dealer seems like one of the nicest people you would ever want to meet. On the door of his store there is a sign: WE BUY USED GUNS. Just a sign. No big deal. It's the final image in the movie.

America the Beautiful ★ ★ ★

R, 106 m., 2008

A documentary written, directed, and narrated by Darryl Roberts and produced by Michele G.

Bluthenthal, Roderick Gatlin, and Stela Georgieva.

The documentary *America the Beautiful* is not shrill or alarmist, nor does it strain to shock us. Darryl Roberts, its director and narrator, speaks mostly in a pleasant, low-key voice. But the film is pulsing with barely suppressed rage, and by the end I shared it. It's about a culture "saturated with the perfect," in which women are taught to seek an impossible physical ideal, and men to worship it.

It opens with shots of a pretty girl named Gerren Taylor, who looks terrific in the skimpiest of bikinis and draws admiration at a topless pool party, although she keeps her top on. Gerren is twelve. Her life as a fashion model began when a woman handed her a card for a modeling agency. She is tall, has a good figure and a model's "walk," and an ambitious mother named Michelle.

Roberts will follow her career in a film that's also a general look at the media-driven worship of women whom the average woman may never resemble (or, if they have any sense, feel the need to). To establish the world Gerren enters, he calmly assembles facts and observations: (1) "Three minutes of looking at a fashion magazine makes 90 percent of women of all ages feel depressed, guilty, and shameful"; (2) three years after the introduction of television to the Fiji Islands, the culture's rate of teenage bulimia went from zero to 11 percent; (3) a model who is six feet tall and weighs 130 pounds is told she must lose fifteen pounds; (4) the "average woman" in those crypto-feminist Dove soap ads became "average" only after complex makeup and photo retouching.

Roberts watches as Gerren becomes, for a season, a sensational success. Her appeal is based largely on her age. Celebrity magazines are fascinated by a twelve-year-old who models adult fashions, and she conquers Fashion Week in New York. But a year later her novelty has worn off, she is rejected by the same casting directors who selected her earlier, and after learning her hips are "too wide" for Milan, she and her mother seek success in London and Paris. After becoming a cover girl and overnight success, Gerren and her mom, who seem to live prudently, are essentially broke. Yes, she gets paid in London: She gets to keep the clothes she wears.

Their quest leads to an unsettled personal life for the young girl. During an argument with her mother over wearing a padded bra to school, Gerren sobs that her mom is ruining her high school years, but those years are impacted in ways she doesn't yet understand. Her sensible Los Angeles middle school principal finds she has become a classroom problem and asks her to sign a "behavior contract." Insulted, Michelle moves her daughter to a more "understanding" school in Santa Monica, and finally opts for home schooling.

Talking to models about the profession that drives them to starvation, Roberts is tentative and quiet as he asks things like, "Do you ever think this might have an impact on your . . . health?" The one time his voice lifts in anger is after a photographer fights with an African-American woman who refuses to wear makeup that will lighten her skin by four or five shades. Roberts, black himself, listens incredulously as the photographer berates the model for being ignorant, "unable to listen," and "knowing nothing" about beauty, fashion, and society. The "problem" of the model's dark skin tone is simply one manifestation of the "problems" all women are told they have if they don't match the fashion ideal. Roberts knows women like the model, and the photographer doesn't, but as the man with the camera, the photographer ordains himself with authority.

Roberts has a powerful message here, but he includes too much material not really necessary for his story. We could have done without his own experiences on a Web site named beautifulpeople.net, where applicants are rated on a sliding scale to discover if they're beautiful enough to qualify. We don't need still more standard footage of Paris Hilton, Britney Spears, and other plastic creatures. Even more unnecessary is an interview with celebrity-gossip journalist Ted Casablanca, whose four-letter language earns an R rating for a film that might rescue the lives of some girls age twelve and up.

But *America the Beautiful* carries a persuasive message and is all the more effective because of the level tone Roberts adopts. The cold fact is that no one can look like a supermodel and be physically healthy. And in a film filled with astonishments, one of the most stunning is that designers like their models the skinnier the better because—are you ready for this?—they save money on the expensive fabrics they use.

Annapolis ★ ½

PG-13, 108 m., 2006

James Franco (Jake Huard), Tyrese Gibson (Lieutenant Cole), Jordana Brewster (Ali), Donnie Wahlberg (Lieutenant Commander Burton), Chi McBride (McNally), Vicellous Shannon (Twins), Roger Fan (Loo), McCaleb Burnett (Whitaker), Wilmer Calderon (Estrada), Brian Goodman (Bill Huard). Directed by Justin Lin and produced by Mark Vahradian and Damien Saccani. Screenplay by David Collard.

Here I am at Sundance 2006. Four years ago I sat in the Park City Library and saw a film named *Better Luck Tomorrow* by a young man named Justin Lin, and I joined in the cheers. This was a risky, original film by a brilliant new director who told the story of a group of Asian kids from affluent families in Orange County, who backed into a life of crime with their eyes wide open.

Now it is Sundance again, but I must pause to review *Annapolis,* which is opening in the nation's multiplexes. Let the young directors at Sundance 2006 set aside their glowing reviews and gaze with sad eyes upon this movie, for it is a cautionary lesson. It is the anti-Sundance film, an exhausted wheeze of bankrupt clichés and cardboard characters, the kind of film that has no visible reason for existing, except that everybody got paid.

The movie stars James Franco as Jake Huard, a working-class kid who works as a riveter in a Chesapeake Bay shipyard and gazes in yearning across the waters to the U.S. Naval Academy, which his dead mother always wanted him to attend. His father, Bill (Brian Goodman), opposes the idea: He thinks his kid is too hotheaded to stick it out. But Jake is accepted for an unlikely last-minute opening, and the movie is the story of his plebe year.

That year is the present time, I guess, since Jake is referred to as a member of the class that will graduate in 2008. That means that the Navy is presumably fighting a war somewhere or other in this old world of ours, although there is not a single word about it in the movie. The plebes seem mostly engaged in memorizing the longitude and latitude of Annapolis to avoid doing push-ups.

There is a subplot involving Jake's fat African-American roommate, nicknamed Twins (Vicellous Shannon). There is much suspense over whether Twins can complete the obstacle course in less than five minutes by the end of the year. If I had a year to train under a brutal Marine drill sergeant with his boot up my butt, I could complete the goddamn obstacle course in under five minutes, and so could Queen Latifah.

The drill sergeant is Lieutenant Cole (Tyrese Gibson), who is a combat-veteran Marine on loan to the academy. Where he saw combat is never mentioned, even when he returns to it at the end of the movie. I've got my money on Iraq. But this movie is not about war. It is about boxing.

Yes, *Annapolis* takes the subject of a young man training to be a Navy officer in a time of war and focuses its entire plot on whether he can win the Brigades, which is the academy-wide boxing championship held every spring. It switches from one set of clichés to another in the middle of the film, without missing a single misstep. Because Jake has an attitude and because Cole doubts his ability to lead men, they become enemies, and everything points toward the big match where Jake and Cole will be able to hammer each other in the ring.

I forgot to mention that Jake was an amateur fighter before he entered the academy. His father thought he was a loser at that, too. He tells the old man he's boxing in the finals, but of course the old man doesn't attend. Or could it possibly be that the father, let's say, does attend, but arrives late and sees the fight, and then his eyes meet the eyes of his son, who is able to spot him immediately in that vast crowd? And does the father give him that curt little nod that means, "I was wrong, son, and you have the right stuff"? Surely a movie made in 2006 would not recycle the Parent Arriving Late and Giving Little Nod of Recognition Scene? Surely a director who made *Better Luck Tomorrow* would have nothing to do with such an ancient wheeze, which is not only off the shelf, but off the shelf at the resale store?

Yes, the Navy is at war, and it all comes

down to a boxing match. Oh, and a big romance with another of Jake's superiors, the cute Ali (Jordana Brewster), who is twenty-five in real life and looks about nineteen in the movie. I have not been to Annapolis, but I think plebes and officers are not supposed to fraternize, kiss, and/or dance and do who knows what else with each other, in spite of the fact that they Meet Cute after he thinks she is a hooker (ho, ho). Ali and the academy's boxing coach (Chi McBride) help train Jake for his big bout.

Here is a movie with dialogue such as:

"You just don't get it, do you, Huard?"

"I don't need advice from you."

Or . . .

"You aren't good enough."

"I've heard that all my life."

Is there a little store in Westwood that sells dialogue like this on rubber stamps? There is only one character in the movie who comes alive and whose dialogue is worth being heard. That is the fat kid, Twins. His story is infinitely more touching than Jake's; he comes from a small Southern town that gave him a parade before he went off to the academy, and if he flunks out, he can't face the folks at home. When Jake's other roommates move out because they don't want to bunk with a loser, Twins stays. Why? His reason may not make audiences in Arkansas and Mississippi very happy, but at least it has the quality of sounding as if a human being might say it out loud.

Après Vous ★ ★

R, 110 m., 2005

Daniel Auteuil (Antoine), José Garcia (Louis), Sandrine Kiberlain (Blanche), Marilyne Canto (Christine), Michèle Moretti (Martine), Garence Clavel (Karine), Fabio Zenoni (André). Directed by Pierre Salvadori and produced by Philippe Martin. Screenplay by Benoît Graffin, David Léotard, and Salvadori

Daniel Auteuil, who seems to be the busiest actor in France, has that look about him of a man worried about whether he is doing the right thing. In *Après Vous* he does the right thing and it results in nothing but trouble for him. He rescues a man in the act of committing suicide, and then, in an irony that is probably covered by several ancient proverbs, he feels responsible for the man's life.

Auteuil plays Antoine, the maître d' at a Paris brasserie that, if the customers typically endure as much incompetence as they experience during this movie, must have great food. Taking a shortcut through a park late one night, Antoine comes upon Louis (the sad-eyed, hangdog José Garcia) just as he kicks the suitcase out from under his feet to hang himself from a tree. Antoine saves him, brings him home, introduces him to his uneasy girlfriend, Christine (Marilyne Canto), and cares more about Louis than Louis does.

Louis, in fact, wishes he had committed suicide. He is heartbroken over the end of his romance with Blanche (Sandrine Kiberlain), and suddenly remembers he has written a letter bidding farewell from life and mailed it to the grandmother who raised him. Antoine promptly drives through the night with him to intercept the letter, and finds himself living Louis's life for him.

Après Vous is intended as a farce, but lacks farcical insanity and settles for being a sitcom, not a very good one. One problem is that neither Louis nor his dilemma is amusing. Another is that Antoine is too sincere and single-minded to suggest a man being driven buggy by the situation; he seems more earnest than beleaguered.

Farces often involve cases of mistaken or misunderstood identities, and that's what happens this time as Antoine seeks out Blanche, finds her in a florist shop, and falls in love with her. That would be a simple enough matter, since after all, she has already broken up with Louis, but Antoine is conscientious to a fault, and feels it is somehow his responsibility to deny himself romantic happiness and try to reconcile Louis and Blanche. Since there is nothing in the movie to suggest they would bring each other anything but misery, this compulsion seems more masochistic than generous.

Much of the action centers on the brasserie, Chez Jean, where I would like to eat the next time I am in Paris, always assuming Louis and Antoine no longer work there. Antoine gets Louis the wine steward's job, despite Louis's complete lack of knowledge about wine; he develops a neat trick of describing a wine by its results rather than its qualities, recommending expensive labels because they will make the customer feel cheery. This at least has the advantage of making him less boring than most wine stewards.

Blanche meanwhile doesn't realize the two men know each other, and that leads of course to a scene in which she finds that out and feels betrayed, as women always do in such situations, instead of being grateful that two men have gone to such pains to make her the center of their deceptions. There are also scenes that I guess are inevitable in romantic comedies of a certain sort, in which one character and then another scales a vine-covered trellis to Blanche's balcony, risking their lives in order to spy on her. I don't know about you, but when I see a guy climbing to a balcony and his name's not Romeo, I wish I'd brought along my iPod.

There is a kind of mental efficiency meter that ticks away during comedies, in which we keep an informal accounting: Is the movie providing enough laughter to justify its running time? If the movie falls below its recommended laughter saturation level, I begin to make use of the Indiglo feature on my Timex. Antoine and Louis and Blanche make two or three or even four too many trips around the maypole of comic misunderstandings, giving us time to realize that we don't really care how they end up anyway.

Aquamarine ★ ★

PG, 109 m., 2006

Emma Roberts (Claire), JoJo (Hailey), Sara Paxton (Aquamarine), Jake McDorman (Raymond), Arielle Kebbel (Cecilia), Bruce Spence (Leonard). Directed by Elizabeth Allen and produced by Susan Cartsonis. Screenplay by John Quaintance and Jessica Bendinger, based on the novel by Alice Hoffman.

Aquamarine is another movie where an event of earthshaking astonishment takes place and is safely contained within a sitcom plot. In this case, a mermaid comes ashore at a Florida beach resort, makes friends with two thirteen-year-old girls, and dates a cute lifeguard. Oh, and of course there's a bitchy blonde with her posse to make life miserable for everybody.

And yet—well, the movie is awfully sweet. The young actresses playing eighth-graders look their age, for once, and have an unstudied charm. I know there's an audience for this movie just as surely as I know I am not that audience. It's clever in the way the two heroines get a crush on the lifeguard and then use the mermaid as their designated hitter; they coach her on how to win a boy's attention, and watch fascinated as she dazzles the boy they can only dream about.

The girls are Claire and Hailey, played by Emma Roberts and JoJo (aka Joanna Levesque). They're best friends, but when the summer ends in a few days, Hailey has to move to Australia with her mom. Meanwhile, they fantasize about Raymond (Jake McDorman), who is blond and muscular and awfully nice. They study his body language: how he shakes his hair and stretches his arms to flex his biceps.

One night there's a big storm, and the next day Claire, who is afraid of the water, falls into a swimming pool and glimpses a mermaid who washed up during the night. Soon the girls are best friends with Aquamarine (Sara Paxton), who despite having swum several times around the world and having a father who can create tsunamis, behaves like a Nickelodeon star. She explains her rules: Merpeople can speak all human languages and can grow legs on dry land, but the legs turn back into a tail after dark, or when they get wet. "We are not fictional," Aquamarine tells the girls. "We're discreet." She has nail polish that changes colors to reflect her moods.

Her mission on land is to prove that love exists. This is because her father has arranged a marriage for her. She doesn't love the proposed husband and has been given three days to prove to her dad that there is such a thing as love. Hailey and Claire coach her in the art of getting a boy's attention. Step One: Call him and hang up. Step Two: Walk past and don't seem to notice him. Soon Aquamarine and Raymond are holding hands and stuff like that, which enrages the scheming Cecilia (Arielle Kebbel). She snoops around trying to discover Aquamarine's secret, and what with one thing and another the mermaid is trapped overnight inside the big water tank outside town.

So you get the idea. Suspense builds as

Cecilia and Aquamarine compete to be Raymond's date for the Final Splash, a big block party on the last day of summer. Meanwhile, Hailey learns that mermaids can grant a wish and wonders if she can use hers to make her mother stay in Florida and forget about Australia. And gee, that's about it.

A movie like this does not engage the mind, but it engages the eyes. It shows pleasant and cheerful young people on screen looking as if it's still fun for them to be making movies. It stays so far away from specific sexual content that the PG rating, "for mild language and sensuality," seems severe. The plot is predictable, the emotions are obvious, and the mermaid reminds me of my friend McHugh explaining why lobsters make ideal pets: They don't bark, and they know the secrets of the deep.

Oh, I almost forgot Leonard (Bruce Spence), the beach handyman, who looks so ominous that one girl whispers to another, "He knows what you did last summer." I learn from IMDb.com that he stands 6 feet 7 inches tall, and his role as the Mouth of Sauron in *The Lord of the Rings: The Return of the King* was cut from the movie but has been restored in the extended edition. I tell you these things because when Leonard comes on the screen you will want to know more about him. He plays the only character of which that can be said.

Arctic Tale ★ ★

G, 84 m., 2007

Queen Latifah (Narrator). A documentary directed by Sarah Robertson and Adam Ravetch and produced by Adam Leipzig and Keenan Smart. Narration written by Linda Woolverton, Mose Richards, and Kristin Gore.

Arctic Tale journeys to one of the most difficult places on Earth for animals to make a living, and shows it growing even more unfriendly. The documentary studies polar bears and walruses in the Arctic as global warming raises temperatures and changes the way they have done business since time immemorial.

Much of the footage in the film is astonishing, considering that it was obtained at frigid temperatures, sometimes underwater, and usually within attacking distance of large and dangerous mammals. We follow two emblematic characters, Nanu, a polar bear cub, and Seela, a newborn walrus. The infants venture out into their new world of blinding white and merciless cold, and learn to swim or climb onto solid footing, as the case may be. They also get lessons from their parents on stalking prey, defending themselves against predators, and presumably keeping one eye open while asleep.

The animals are composites of several different individuals, created in the editing room from footage shot over a period of ten years, but the editing is so seamless that the illusion holds up. The purpose of the film, made by a team headed by the married couple of director Sarah Robertson and cinematographer Adam Ravetch, is not to enforce scholarly accuracy but to create a fable of birth, life, and death at the edge of the world.

It is said that the landmark documentary *March of the Penguins* began life in France with a cute sound track on which the penguins voiced their thoughts. The magnificence of that film is explained in large part by Morgan Freeman's objective narration, which was content to describe a year in the lives of the penguins; the facts were so astonishing that no embroidery was necessary.

Arctic Tale, on the other hand, chooses the opposite approach. Queen Latifah narrates a story in which the large and fearsome beasts are personalized almost like cartoon characters. And the sound track reinforces that impression with song: As dozens of walruses huddle together on an ice floe, for example, we hear *We Are Family* and mighty blasts of walrus farts.

They might also have been singing "we are appearing in a family film." The movie might be enthralling to younger viewers, and the images have undeniable power for everyone. The dilemma the movie sidesteps is that being a polar bear or a walrus is a violent undertaking. In a land without vegetation, evolution has provided that animals survive by eating each other. (Not that there aren't carnivores, including man, in temperate climates.) In one blood-curdling scene, Nanu's mother cautiously shepherds her cubs away from a male polar bear that would, yes, like to eat them. And the walrus with her baby is automatically issued (it seems) another female walrus, an "auntie," who volunteers to help protect the little family. This is all the more unselfish considering what happens to the auntie.

The film does not linger on scenes of killing or eating, preferring to make it clear that such events, and other tragedies, are happening not far offscreen. The eyes of little audience members are spared the gory details. But the comfy view of Arctic life, opening with two little bear cubs romping in the snow and snuggling under Mom for a snack, quickly descends into a struggle for survival.

It's hard enough for them to live in such an icy world but harder still when the ice melts. When ice grows scarce, so will polar bears and walruses, because although both species are accomplished swimmers, they are mammals and have to breathe and need to crawl up on ice floes. Queen Latifah's narration, coauthored by Al Gore's daughter, makes it clear that global warming is to blame. We see Nanu walking gingerly across ice that is alarmingly slushy, and we can only speculate about how that makes her feel.

The movie gives some attention to other northern life forms, including jellyfish, birds, and foxes who trail behind polar bears to eat the remains of their kills. We see no humans, not even the Inuit who assisted the filmmakers. I was reminded of the extraordinary 2002 film *The Fast Runner*, about the lives and loves of the Inuit, and of course of the classic Flaherty documentary *Nanook of the North* (1922). To live in this place is to constantly tempt death.

In the end, I'm conflicted about the film. As an accessible family film, it delivers the goods. But it lives in the shadow of *March of the Penguins*. Despite its sad scenes, it sentimentalizes. It attributes human emotions and motivations to its central animals. Its music instructs us how to feel. And the narration and overall approach get in the way of the visual material.

Are We There Yet? ★ ★

PG, 91 m., 2005

Ice Cube (Nick Persons), Nia Long (Suzanne Kingston), Aleisha Allen (Lindsey Kingston), Philip Bolden (Kevin Kingston), Jay Mohr (Marty). Directed by Brian Levant and produced by Matt Alvarez, Ice Cube, and Dan Kolsrud. Screenplay by Steven Gary Banks, Claudia Grazioso, J. David Stem, and David N. Weiss.

Ice Cube is an effortlessly likable actor, which presents two problems for *Are We There Yet?* Problem No. 1 is that he has to play a bachelor who hates kids, and No. 2 is that two kids make his life miserable in ways that are supposed to be funny but are mean and painful.

Mr. Cube plays Nick, owner of a sports memorabilia store, who one day is struck by the lightning bolt of love when he gazes upon Suzanne (Nia Long), who runs an event-management service across the street. There is a problem. She is the divorced mom of two kids. Nick hates kids. But one Dark and Stormy Night he passes Suzanne next to her stalled car and offers her a lift. There is chemistry, and it seems likely to lead to physics, but then she sadly observes that they can only be "good friends" because he doesn't really care for kids.

But . . . but . . . Nick cares so much for her that he's willing to learn. Suzanne is needed in Vancouver to coordinate a New Year's Eve party, her ex-husband breaks a promise to baby-sit the kids, and Nick agrees to bring the kids to Vancouver. That's when the trouble starts.

We've already seen what these kids are capable of. One of their mom's dates arrives on the front sidewalk, hits a trip wire, and is pelted with buckets of glue before losing his footing on dozens of marbles and falling hard to the ground. Hilarious, right?

Now it's Nick's turn. He attempts to take the kids north by plane and train before settling on automobile—in his case, a brand-new Lincoln Navigator, curiously enough the same vehicle that was used in *Johnson Family Vacation*. It's the SUV of choice for destruction in bizarre ways through family adventures.

Young Lindsey (Aleisha Allen) and younger Kevin (Philip Bolden) retain the delusion that their father will come back home someday, and have dedicated themselves to discouraging their mother's would-be boyfriends. This leads to such stunts as writing "Help us!" on a card and holding it to the car window so a trucker will think they're the captives of a child abuser. It also leads to several potentially fatal traffic adventures, a boxing match with a deer that stands on its hind legs and seems to think it's a kangaroo, and the complete destruction of the Navigator.

Nick displays the patience of a saint. Far from being the child-hater he thinks he is, he's gentle, understanding, forgiving, and empathetic. The kids are little monsters. What they do to him is so far over the top that it's sadistic, not funny, and it doesn't help when they finally get to Vancouver and Suzanne cruelly misreads the situation.

I would have loved to see a genuine love story involving Ice Cube, Nia Long, and the challenge of a lifelong bachelor dating a woman with children. Sad that a story like that couldn't get made, but this shrill "comedy" could. Maybe it's the filmmakers who don't like children. They certainly don't seem to know very much about them.

The Aristocrats ★ ★ ½

NO MPAA RATING, 92 m., 2005

Featuring Jason Alexander, Shelley Berman, Lewis Black, David Brenner, Drew Carey, George Carlin, Tim Conway, Andy Dick, Phyllis Diller, Joe Franklin, Judy Gold, Whoopi Goldberg, Gilbert Gottfried, Eric Idle, Eddie Izzard, Richard Lewis, Bill Maher, Howie Mandel, Merrill Markoe, Jackie "The Joke Man" Martling, Michael McKean, Larry Miller, Martin Mull, Kevin Nealon, the *Onion* editorial staff, Penn & Teller, Emo Philips, Kevin Pollak, Andy Richter, Don Rickles, Chris Rock, Bob Saget, Harry Shearer, the Smothers Brothers, David Steinberg, Jon Stewart, Larry Storch, Rip Taylor, Dave Thomas, Peter Tilden, Bruce Vilanch, Fred Willard, Robin Williams, Steven Wright. Directed by Paul Provenza and produced by Penn Jillette and Peter Adam Golden.

Two extremes in joke-telling:

Style No. 1. As tight as a haiku. Not one wasted word. Told with aggressive brutality. Ends with a punch line that ends with the punch word. The last word delivers the joke. Then, bang, it's over.

Style No. 2. The joke-teller's purpose is to sadistically control the time and attention of the other person by an elaborate and unnecessary recital of the setup. He lovingly adds irrelevant details. Uses one or more accents. Chuckles during the telling to prompt you that he's funny. Inverts the punch line, so the payoff comes at the start, not the end, of the final sentence, which then meanders in anticlimax. Then provides a helpful explanation of the joke. ("See, the bartender was talking to the duck, not the woman.") In the worst of all possible worlds, he finds his joke so funny that he actually repeats it, to be sure you properly appreciated it. Anyone who tells a joke this way should not be trusted in positions of authority.

The perfect joke in Style No. 1, as told by Henny Youngman, Rodney Dangerfield, Lou Jacobi:

Guy goes to a psychiatrist.

Psychiatrist says, "You're crazy!"

"I want a second opinion!"

"All right, you're ugly!"

Now for a joke in Style No. 2, which can easily go five minutes. I will mercifully condense it. A carpenter dies and goes to heaven, and he tells St. Peter he is looking for his son. His description of the son matches Jesus. The son appears. "Father?" says the son. "Pinocchio!" says the father.

I am constantly amazed that the people who tell this joke don't realize that *every single person in the English-speaking world has already heard this joke five hundred times.* The joke-teller relentlessly spins it out for minute after minute, while his captives stand there with glazed eyes and a rictus that he mistakes for a grin.

I will now describe two versions of another joke.

Style No. 1:

Guy goes into a talent agency to pitch his act.

"What do you do?" asks the agent.

"We come out and crap on the stage."

"What do you call yourselves?"

"The Aristocrats."

Style No. 2 now has an entire movie devoted to it. It is famous among professional comedians, we're told, as the dirtiest joke of all time. Here's how you tell it. After the talent agent asks, "What do you do?" the other guy describes a long series of the most depraved and disgusting words, images, and actions that he can string together. Absolutely nothing is off-limits. The act can involve incest, bestiality, matricide, bodily waste, vomiting and other sudden voidings, necrophilia, bondage, whatever. It is described in racist, sexist, and obscene terms. After the litany is complete, the agent asks, What do you call yourselves? and the guy replies, etc.

No less than one hundred comedians appear in *The Aristocrats,* according to someone who kept score. I think the editorial board of the *Onion* is counted as one. It's observed by several of them that professional comedians don't tell "jokes" onstage; they do an act, often involving their cosmic struggle with life. The dirtiest joke is reserved for when they hang out with each other. There's a competition: Who can make it longer and dirtier? Michael O'Donoghue once told a version that lasted ninety minutes.

I am an expert on joke-telling and often hold audiences spellbound with my mastery of the topic. I contend that this joke cannot be funny one-on-one or in a small group. It must be performed before a larger group, preferably in a situation where it is transgressive and dangerous. That's because it is not a funny joke, but it can potentially create a funny situation, or an interesting one. That explains why, with all the firepower in this movie (George Carlin, Andy Dick, Richard Lewis, Chris Rock, and ninety-six more), the funniest version ever told, everyone agrees, was by Gilbert Gottfried at a 2001 Friar's Club roast of Hugh Hefner.

Gottfried had a lot of things going for him. (1) Every comic in the room knew the joke and couldn't believe he was telling it. (2) Hefner was seated in a wingback chair next to the podium and seemed uncertain if he should laugh at its extreme political incorrectness. (3) The roast was held not long after 9/11, and from the audience there were shouts of "Too soon!" to warn that New York, in mourning, was not ready for it. (4) He tells it with breakneck, manic intensity, so that the point is not the joke, but the reckless, heedless performance. All the conditions are in place for Gottfried to have a big success, because at last the joke has found a setting in which it can actually offend.

In *The Aristocrats,* which was directed by Paul Provenza and coproduced by Penn Jillette, we hear the joke in many versions and styles. Sometimes we cut between takes of the same guy telling it two or three times. It is theorized about. It is marveled at. What's remarkable is that no one, except Dick Smothers and Phyllis Diller, thinks that it isn't funny. Everything depends on the risk involved in telling it; without risk, no joke.

The Aristocrats might have made a nice short subject. At ninety-two minutes, it's like the boozy salesman who corners you with the Pinocchio torture. I am left with three observations. (1) If Buddy Hackett were still alive, he could have told it better than Gilbert Gottfried. (2) Whatever happened to Andrew Dice Clay? (3) The punch line stinks. These are better:

"The Brothers Two."

"The Mellow Tones."

"Penn and Teller."

Art School Confidential ★ ★ ★

R, 102 m., 2006

Max Minghella (Jerome), Sophia Myles (Audrey), John Malkovich (Professor Sandiford), Anjelica Huston (Sophie), Jim Broadbent (Jimmy), Ethan Suplee (Vince), Matt Keeslar (Jonah), Joel David Moore (Bardo), Steve Buscemi (Broadway Bob). Directed by Terry Zwigoff and produced by Lianne Halfon, John Malkovich, and Russell Smith. Screenplay by Daniel Clowes.

I believe you can go to school to learn to be an accountant, a doctor, a physicist, an engineer, an astronaut. I am not sure you can learn to be an artist. Artists are born, not made, and the real reason to study the arts is to have fun, learn technical skills, network with other creative types, fall in love with people who are not boring, and do the work you probably would have done anyway. That said, I highly recommend college. I majored in English and journalism, and I wanted to be a graduate student forever.

I am writing this the morning after my wife and I attended the Head to Toe Gala, at which students of the School of the Art Institute of Chicago presented their spring fashion show. We saw about half of the work presented a week earlier at the school's 2006 Fashion Show at Marshall Field's, which sounds ever so much more upscale than the 2007 Fashion Show at Macy's. I was astonished. The creativity and wit in their designs would have made Fellini envious. These were not items of clothing; these were visual arts. I could imagine the same models, wearing the same designs, walking up the red carpet at the Cannes Film

Festival and sending the designers of Paris weeping and gnashing into the shadows.

Then we learned that the first third of the show, featuring white clothing, was all by freshmen. They didn't learn to create those fashions between September and May. Therefore, apparently, they always could design. I am not suggesting the school's faculty serves no purpose; indeed, as a teacher of film appreciation, I believe faculties in the arts are sainted. They must guide, advise, moderate, encourage, teach methods, provide a context, share secrets, and declare an informed opinion on the worth of the work. They create a world within which such work is possible and valued. What they cannot do, I suspect, is teach a student how to be original and creative.

Art School Confidential, the new comedy by Terry Zwigoff, seems to share these sentiments. It was written, like his *Ghost World,* by the artist Daniel Clowes and is based on one of Clowes's graphic novels. Zwigoff also made the great documentary *Crumb,* about another artist who is entirely his own creation. *Art School*'s hero is Jerome (Max Minghella), already an extraordinary draftsman when he enters the school; his drawings glow from the page with conviction and love. "I want to be the next Picasso," he claims, which indicates his vision is indeed inward and personal, since he does not know enough about Picasso to see that his work does not have a single line in common with that master. Perhaps he simply means he wants to be famous, make lots of money, and grow old while making love to beautiful women. Honorable goals.

There is a moment in the film when the students are asked to create a self-portrait. Jerome's work bears comparison with the pre-Raphaelites. The student whose self-portrait is most highly praised has created an assemblage of lines and squiggles that "looks like a Cy Twombly," someone says—in praise. I'm not saying a nineteenth-century representational style is superior to Twombly, but I do believe that in a freshman class the purpose of a self-portrait assignment is to draw something that looks like it might be you. Students have to learn to walk before they can crawl.

Jerome's teacher is Professor Sandiford (John Malkovich), who paces the classroom talking on his cell phone, trying to get a gallery to give him a show. Sandiford draws triangles. "I was one of the first," he says, to paint triangles—in his mind, perhaps second only to Euclid. Malkovich's character issues dire warnings about the future awaiting any would-be artist, conceals rage about his own neglect, and in general provides the kind of forbidding detachment that drives students crazy trying to please him.

Jerome falls in love with the artists' model Audrey (Sophia Myles). She likes the drawing he does of her, as who would not, and is kind to him, and as a nerd in high school he is thrilled that his talent at last has brought him the affection of a beautiful girl. Jerome's roommates are Vince (Ethan Suplee) and Bardo (Joel David Moore), who, like all roommates (in the words of John D. McDonald), deprive him of solitude without providing him with companionship. The Vince character is a wonderful creation, an unkempt underground filmmaker, making a work of enthusiasm and incoherence; much of his time is spent rearranging three-by-five cards describing hypothetical scenes. Bardo is helpful on practical stuff, explaining the politics of the Strathmore school of art and briefing him on his fellow students.

There is a wise and understanding teacher on the faculty, played by Anjelica Huston. Defending the work of Dead White Males, she sensibly observes that when they did their best work "they weren't dead yet." Even more wisdom and certainly more weariness come when Jerome visits the squalid apartment of the drunken old artist Jimmy (Jim Broadbent), who might once have been young and might once have had hopes but now festers in cynicism, anger, despair, and the need for a drink. There is something in the Zwigoffian universe that values such characters; having abandoned all illusions, they offer the possibility of truth. I also much enjoyed Broadway Bob (Steve Buscemi); his café is a hangout for the students, who hope he will hang their work on his walls. Bob at this point is more important to them than the art critic of the *New York Times.*

Now I regret to tell you that the plot also involves a serial killer who is stalking the campus and has claimed several victims. The police investigate, the students become paranoid, and some of the characters fall under suspicion. There is nothing particularly wrong with this subplot except that it is completely unnecessary and imposes a generic story structure on a film that might better have just grown from scene to scene like an experience. I wasn't interested in the killer and would have rather seen more of Jerome interacting with his professors, with Broadway Bob and old Jimmy, and with the beautiful Audrey, who will surely see that her future lies with the next Picasso, since she was born too late to lie with the previous one.

Ask the Dust ★ ★ ★

R, 117 m., 2006

Colin Farrell (Arturo Bandini), Salma Hayek (Camilla Lopez), Donald Sutherland (Hellfrick), Eileen Atkins (Mrs. Hargraves), Justin Kirk (Sammy), Idina Menzel (Vera Rivkin). Directed by Robert Towne, and produced by Tom Cruise, Paula Wagner, Don Granger, and Jonas McCord. Screenplay by Towne, based on the novel by John Fante.

Who is harder to portray in a movie than a writer? The standard portrait is familiar: the shabby room, the typewriter, the bottle, the cigarettes, the crazy neighbors, the nickel cup of coffee, the smoldering sexuality of the woman who comes into his life. Robert Towne's *Ask the Dust* is not the first film to evoke this vision of a writer's life, and not the first to find that typing is not a cinematic activity. Just the week before, *Winter Passing* starred Ed Harris in a version of the same kind of character at the other end of his career.

Still, in its wider focus, *Ask the Dust* finds a kind of poetry because although we may not find it noble and romantic to sit alone in a room, broke and hungover and dreaming of glory, a writer can, and must. The film stars Colin Farrell as Arturo Bandini, who lives in a Los Angeles rooming house during the Depression. He has sold one story to the *American Mercury,* edited by H. L. Mencken, the god of American letters, and now he tries to write more: "The greatest man in America—do you want to let him down?"

Arturo has one nickel, with which he buys a cup of coffee in a diner where Camilla (Salma Hayek) is the waitress. Something happens between them, but it is expressed curiously. One day she gives him a free beer, which he pours into a spittoon. She takes the magazine with his story, tears it up, and throws it into the same spittoon. Why this hostility, which is meant to mask lust but seems gratuitous?

The answer may be in the source of the material. *Ask the Dust* is a novel by John Fante, a writer of the generation just before Charles Bukowski, who saw to it that the book was reissued by his publisher, the Black Sparrow Press. It shares Bukowski's view of women who are attracted to a courtship consisting largely of hostility. In *Ask the Dust,* there is the additional element of racism; Camilla is wounded, as she should be, by prejudice against Mexicans in the city, and Bandini is uneasy about his Italian heritage. When they go to the movies together, Anglos pointedly move away from them, but the movie evokes racism without really engaging it, and the crucial scenes in their romance take place in a cottage on a deserted Laguna Beach, where they create a world of their own. There is also the mysterious Jewish woman, Vera (Idina Menzel), who comes into his life, makes a sudden and deep impression, reveals to him her scarred body, and then departs from the plot in a particularly Los Angeles sort of way.

What the movie is about, above all, is the bittersweet solitude of the would-be great writer. Whether Arturo will become the next Hemingway (or Fante or Bukowski) is uncertain, but Farrell shows him as a young man capable of playing the role should he win it. He could also possibly live a long and happy life with Camilla, but stories like this exist in the short run and are about problems, not solutions.

I did not feel a strong chemistry between Farrell and Hayek, but I have started to write the word "chemistry" with growing doubts. What is it, anyway? William Hurt and Kathleen Turner had it in *Body Heat,* and Nicolas Cage and Cher in *Moonstruck,* but *Ask the Dust* does not provide a setting for great, dramatic, towering lust and love: It is about poverty, fatigue, lives that are young but already old in discouragement. Perhaps what we are meant to feel between Arturo and Camilla is not chemistry but geometry: They could fit well together and provide each other's missing angles.

I enjoyed and admired the film without being grabbed or shaken by it. Where can such a story lead? I have been lucky enough to know a great writer in his shabby apartment, with his typewriter, his bottle, and his cigarettes, and I know he had a famous romance, and that later he hated the woman, and having achieved all possible success was perhaps not as happy as when it was still before him.

What immediately impressed me about *Ask the Dust* was its evocation of time and place. The cinematographer, Caleb Deschanel, creates Depression-era Los Angeles with the same love the 2005 *King Kong* lavished on New York at the same period, and although one is a smaller film about a writer and the other is an epic about an ape, the cityscapes are so evocative they take on a character of their own. In the case of *King Kong*, much of the city was special effects; in *Ask the Dust* there are some effects, but Deschanel in large part is working with reality.

Towne filmed on location in Cape Town, a city I lived in for a year, and I agree with him that it can double for prewar Los Angeles. Just keep Table Mountain out of the shot and you have storefront cafés, rooming houses built on hillsides with the front door on the top floor, palm trees, and a feeling in some neighborhoods of strangers who don't know what brought them together or why they wait. Such a person is Hellfrick (Donald Sutherland), Arturo's wise, weary neighbor, who shuffles onstage to provide the ghost of Arturo's possible future.

Ask the Dust requires an audience with a special love for film noir, with a feeling for the loneliness and misery of the writer, and with an understanding that any woman he meets will be beautiful. Such stories are never about understanding landladies. I am not sure the film achieves great things, but it achieves its smaller things perfectly.

The Assassination of Jesse James by the Coward Robert Ford ★ ★ ★ ½

R, 160 m., 2007

Brad Pitt (Jesse James), Casey Affleck (Robert Ford), Sam Shepard (Frank James), Mary-Louise Parker (Zee James), Paul Schneider (Dick Liddil), Jeremy Renner (Wood Hite), Garret Dillahunt (Ed Miller), Zooey Deschanel (Dorothy Evans), Michael Parks (Henry Craig), Ted Levine (Sheriff Timberlake), Sam Rockwell (Charley Ford). Directed by Andrew Dominik and produced by Jules Daly, Dede Gardner, Brad Pitt, Ridley Scott, and David Valdes. Screenplay by Dominik, based on the novel by Ron Hansen.

Few things have earned me more grief from readers than my suggestion that in the sport of sex, Captain Renault of *Casablanca* plays for both teams. I think I will get less disagreement when I focus on the homosexual undertones of *The Assassination of Jesse James by the Coward Robert Ford*. Jesse (Brad Pitt) is certainly not gay, but the Coward (Casey Affleck) is so powerfully mesmerized by him that hero worship shades into lust. Since sex between them is out of the question, their relationship turns into a curiously erotic dance of death; it is clear to both of them (and to anyone reading the title) what must happen at the end, and they move together toward that event with almost trancelike inevitability.

The movie has the space and freedom of classic Western epics. Like *McCabe and Mrs. Miller* and *Days of Heaven*, it was photographed in the wide open spaces of western Canada, where the land is so empty it creates a vacuum, demanding men to become legends. Jesse James is such a man, a ruthless killer and attentive father and husband, glorified in the dime novels that Robert Ford memorizes. If Ford is a coward, what does that make James, who led his efficient gang in stagecoach and bank robberies that involved the deaths of unarmed men and women? Yes, but he did it with style, you see, and Ford is only a callow squirt.

The story begins in 1881, after Jesse's legend is already part of the mythology and the James Gang has only one robbery left to go. The gang members are Jesse's older brother Frank (Sam Shepard), the Coward's older brother Charley Ford (Sam Rockwell), Jesse's cousin, Wood Hite (Jeremy Renner), and the outlaw Dick Liddil (Paul Schneider). Robert Ford, at nineteen, comes after them begging to be let in; his devotion is so intense that Jesse asks him at one point, "Do you want to be like me, or do you want to *be* me?"

The Coward is like a starstruck stalker, something all the gang members recognize. Why does Jesse tolerate him? Is there a buried message that James, having become a founding member of America's celebrity royalty, realizes that Robert is the price he has to pay? After their last train job, Frank has had enough and heads out. Jesse goes home to his wife (Mary-Louise Parker) and children, and unaccountably invites Robert to visit them. There are the usual lyrical passages of Jesse playing with his kids and loving his wife, and yet all the time he and the Coward have something deadly going on between them. If Robert cannot be the lover of his hero, what would be more intimate than to kill him?

In a quiet parlor one day in Jesse's home, Robert knows, and Jesse knows, and we know, that the time has come. Ford doesn't so much shoot him in the back as have the back presented to him for the purpose. If he did not pull the trigger at that moment, I think they would both feel an appointment had been missed. Does Jesse want to die? I think he is fascinated by the idea and flies too close to the flame.

The film was written and directed by Andrew Dominik, based on the novel by Ron Hansen. It is Dominik's second and has a great deal in common with his good first film, *Chopper* (2001). That was the story of Australia's most notorious prisoner, who at one point is stabbed by his best friend, ignores it, talks for a time, and then looks down at the blood pouring from him, as if disappointed in the other man. Both Chopper Read and Jesse James were savage murderers and both masochistically put themselves in harm's way.

Dominik filmed *Chopper* largely in prison, but here opens up his camera to the far horizons, showing how small a man might feel unless he did something to make his mark. The cinematography is by Roger Deakins, who in *No Country for Old Men* by the Coen brothers shows the modern West as also in need of hard, unforgiving men to stand up to the landscape. Brad Pitt embodies Jesse James's mythic stature as if long accustomed to it; Casey Affleck plays the kid like Mark David Chapman, a nobody killing the one he loves. The gang members are like sidemen for Elvis, standing by in subservience, keeping the beat, all except for Frank, whom Sam Shepard plays as the insider who understands it all.

There are things about men, horses, and horizons that are uniquely suited to the wide screen. We see that here. The Western has been mostly in hibernation since the 1970s, but now I sense it stirring in rebirth. We have a program to register the most-read reviews on my Web site, and for the month of September 2007 the overwhelming leader was not *Eastern Promises*, not *Shoot 'Em Up*, not *The Brave One*, but *3:10 to Yuma*. Now here is another Western in the classical tradition.

Yes, it is long, at 160 minutes. There is a sense that an epic must have duration to have importance. The time reaching ahead of us must be as generous as the landscape unfolding before us. On this canvas Dominik portrays his hero at a time when most men were so powerless, they envied Jesse James even for imposing his will on such as they. ☞

The Assassination of Richard Nixon ★ ★ ★ ½

R, 95 m., 2005

Sean Penn (Samuel Bicke), Naomi Watts (Marie Bicke), Don Cheadle (Bonny Simmons), Jack Thompson (Jack Jones), Mykelti Williamson (Harold Mann), Michael Wincott (Julius Bicke). Directed by Niels Mueller and produced by Alfonso Cuaron and Jorge Vergara. Screenplay by Kevin Kennedy and Mueller.

Baltimore, 1974. Sam Bicke explains and explains and explains. He has it all worked out, why he is right and the world is wrong, and he has a fierce obsession with injustice. "My name is Sam Bicke," he says at the beginning of one of the tapes he mails to Leonard Bernstein, "and I consider myself a grain of sand." He sells office supplies, very badly. His marriage is at an end. The Small Business Administration is not acting on his loan application. Nixon is still in the White House. The Black Panthers are being persecuted. It is all part of the same rage coiling within him.

Sean Penn plays Bicke as a man who has always been socially inept and now, as his life comes apart, descends into madness. His own frustration and the evils in the world are all the same, all somehow someone else's fault, and in the opening scene of *The Assassination of Richard Nixon*, we see him in an airport parking garage, concealing a pistol in a leg brace. He mails one last tape to Leonard Bernstein. He plans to hijack a plane and fly it into the White House.

There was a real Sam Bicke (spelled Byck), whose plan of course failed. Niels Mueller's movie is based on his botched assassination scheme, but many of the other details, including some scenes of mordant humor, are the invention of Mueller and his cowriter, Kevin Kennedy. This is a character study of a marginal man who goes off the rails, and Penn is brilliant at evoking how daily life itself is filled, for Bicke, with countless challenges to his rigid sense of right and wrong.

Consider his job as an office supply salesman. He is selling chairs covered in Naugahyde. The client asks if they are leather. He says they are not. His boss, Jack Jones (Jack Thompson), steps in and smoothly explains they are "Naugahyde-covered leather." Uh-huh. When Sam offers a client a discount to close a sale, Jack calls him into his office and screams at him for selling the desk at a loss. The client overhears. Later Sam finds out the joke was on him. Jack wants to help him, and recommends reading *The Power of Positive Thinking* and *How to Win Friends and Influence People.*

His sense of honesty offended by his job, Sam becomes obsessed with Nixon: "He made us a promise—he didn't deliver. Then he sold us on the exact same promise and he got elected again." He visits the local Black Panther office to make a donation and, as a Panther official (Mykelti Williamson) listens incredulously, shares his ideas about renaming the Panthers the Zebras and admitting white members—like Sam Bicke, for example.

Sam is separated from his wife, Marie (Naomi Watts), and two daughters. He dreams of saving his marriage. She can't make him understand it's over. He is served with divorce papers and protests, "We're supposed to be working this out!" In one of the movie's most painful moments, he talks to the family dog: "You love me, don't you?" The dog seems indifferent.

Sam dreams of starting a limousine company with his closest friend, Bonny Simmons (Don Cheadle). This depends on a small business loan. Sam and Bonny are a poor risk, the bank drags out the paperwork, and Sam explains and explains and explains how important the loan is, and how urgent it is that it comes quickly.

Sean Penn conveys anger through small, contained details. He is one of our great actors, able to invest insignificant characters with importance because their lives are so urgent to themselves. Was it Penn or the filmmakers who thought of the touch where Sam puts on a false mustache in the airport parking lot. What for? Nobody knows who he is or what he looks like, and if his plan succeeds there will be no Sam Bicke left, mustache or not.

Penn shows him always on the outside. Kept out of his house. Turned away by the bank. Ineligible for the Black Panthers. The outsider at the office, listening to his boss and a coworker snickering about him. The only person he can confide in is Leonard Bernstein, whose music he admires. (The real Bernstein, who received tapes from the real Byck, was mystified to be attached however distantly to a hijacking plot.)

The Assassination of Richard Nixon is about a man on a collision course; given the stark terms in which he arranges right and wrong, he will sooner or later crack up. He hasn't a clue about appropriate behavior, about how others perceive him, about what may be right but is nevertheless impossible. The movie's title has one effect before we see it, and another afterward, when we can see the grandiosity and self-deceit that it implies. What really happens is that Sam Bicke assassinates himself.

Does the film have a message? I don't think it wants one. It is about the journey of a man going mad. A film can simply be a character study, as this one is. That is sufficient. A message might seem trundled in and gratuitous. Certainly our opinions of Nixon, Vietnam, and the Black Panthers are irrelevant; they enter the movie only as objects of Bicke's obsessions. We cannot help but sense a connection with another would-be assassin from the 1970s, another obsessed loner, Travis Bickle. Travis pours out his thoughts in journals; Sam uses tapes. They feel the need to justify themselves, and lack even a listener.

Assault on Precinct 13 ★ ★ ★

R, 109 m., 2005

Ethan Hawke (Jake Roenick), Laurence Fishburne (Marion Bishop), Drea de Matteo (Iris Ferry), Brian Dennehy (Jasper O'Shea), John Leguizamo (Beck), Jeffrey "Ja Rule" Atkins (Smiley), Maria Bello (Alex Sabian), Gabriel Byrne (Marcus Duvall). Directed by

Jean-Francois Richet and produced by Pascal Caucheteux, Stephane Sperry, and Jeffrey Silver. Screenplay by James DeMonaco, based on the film by John Carpenter.

Assault on Precinct 13 is not so much a remake as a riff on an old familiar plot: The fort is surrounded, and the defenders have to fight off the attackers and deal with possible traitors in their midst. Howard Hawks did versions of this so often that after John Wayne starred for him in *Rio Bravo* (1959) and *El Dorado* (1966), he told Wayne he was sending over a script for *Rio Lobo*, and Wayne told him, "I'll make it, but I don't need to read it. We've already made it twice."

John Carpenter's 1976 film, made just before his famous *Halloween*, added some touches from George Romero's *Night of the Living Dead* and moved the action from a threatened sheriff's office in the Old West to a threatened police station in the inner city. Now French director Jean-Francois Richet takes essentially the same material and makes it work with strong performances and a couple of new twists.

Precinct 13, in this version, is scheduled to close forever at midnight. Burnt-out desk sergeant Jake Roenick (Ethan Hawke), still traumatized by the death of two partners, is on the graveyard shift with old-timer Jasper O'Shea (Brian Dennehy), who in a revelation fraught with omens announces he will soon retire. Also in the station is the buxom secretary Iris (Drea de Matteo).

There's basically nothing for them to do except for Jake to pop some more painkillers and chase them with booze from the office bottle. Then everything changes. An ubercriminal named Bishop (Laurence Fishburne) has been arrested and is being transported by police bus with some other detainees, including the motormouth Beck (John Leguizamo), a crew-cut girl crook (Aisha Hinds), and a counterfeiter named Smiley (Jeffrey Atkins, a.k.a. Ja Rule). It's New Year's Eve, a Dark and Stormy Night, the highway is blocked by an accident, the officers on the bus decide to dump the prisoners at Precinct 13, and then things get dicey when it appears that Bishop's men are determined to break him free. It's up to Jake to pull himself together and command the defense of the surrounded station; he can't call for help because the phones, cell phones, and radios are all conveniently inoperable—all because of the Dark and Stormy, etc., I think.

Turns out the forces surrounding the station are not quite who they seem, ratcheting up the level of interest and danger, and providing Gabriel Byrne with one of his thankless roles in which he is hard, taciturn, and one-dimensional enough to qualify for Flatland. Never mind; an interesting dynamic develops inside the station, especially after Jake's psychiatrist, Alex Sabian (Maria Bello), comes to visit, leaves for home, has to return to the station because of the Dark, etc., and ends up as part of the defense team. Also recruited are the prisoners, who must fight for their own lives alongside the cops who have imprisoned them.

All classic and airtight, and handled by Richet with economy and a sturdy clarity of action; he doesn't go overboard with manic action scenes. There are, however, a few plot points that confused me. One is the way a forest seems to materialize near the station, which seemed in an overhead shot to be in an urban wasteland. My other problem is with a character who, in order to be who he is and what he is, would have to have known that Bishop would end up at Precinct 13, even though Bishop clearly ends up there by accident. Oh, and a tunnel turns up at a convenient moment, as tunnels so often do.

Problems like these amuse me with the nerve shown in trying to ignore them. Everybody is in a forest in the middle of downtown Detroit? Okay, then everybody can hide behind trees. They're running down a long-forgotten sewage tunnel? Okay, but not so forgotten that it doesn't have electric lights. There's no way for that particular character to have prior knowledge of where Bishop would be, and no way for him to communicate plans that are essential to the outcome? Okay, then just ignore those technicalities, and concentrate on such delightful synchronicities as that John Wayne played characters named both Ethan and Hawk.

Asylum ★ ★

R, 90 m., 2005

Natasha Richardson (Stella Raphael), Ian McKellen (Peter Cleave), Marton Csokas (Edgar

Stark), Hugh Bonneville (Max Raphael), Sean Harris (Nick), Gus Lewis (Charlie Raphael), Joss Ackland (Straffen), Robert Willox (Archer). Directed by David Mackenzie and produced by David E. Allen, Laurie Borg, and Mace Neufeld. Screenplay by Patrick Marber and Chrysanthy Balis, based on the novel by Patrick McGrath.

Asylum is well titled, since everyone in it is more or less crazy, mostly more. It's an overwrought Gothic melodrama that has a nice first act before it descends into shameless absurdity. To care about the story you would have to believe it, which you cannot, so there you are. Yet the movie is well made, and the actors courageously try to bring life into the preposterous story. Perhaps the original novel by Patrick McGrath held up better, or perhaps imagined images have a plausibility that gets lost when a movie makes them literal.

The story is set circa 1960 in a vast old asylum built in the Victorian era—one of those buildings looking like an architectural shriek. Max Raphael (Hugh Bonneville) has arrived to become the new superintendent; he brings his wife, Stella (Natasha Richardson), and their son, Charlie (Gus Lewis). All is not well in this family, but, then, nothing is right in the asylum, where the long-serving Peter Cleave (Ian McKellen) resents being passed over for Max's job. He's expected to serve as Max's second-in-command, leading to acid one-liners that McKellen delivers like dagger thrusts:

Max: "May I remind you that I am your superior?"

Peter: "In what sense?"

Max and Stella seem separated by a vast emotional gulf. Charlie is not much loved by his parents. He finds a friend in one of the patients, Edgar (Marton Csokas), who becomes his buddy and sort of a father figure, which would be heartening if Edgar had not been declared insane after murdering his wife, decapitating her, and so on and so forth.

Edgar undertakes to rebuild a gardener's shed that Stella wants to make use of. Soon she is making use of it with Edgar. There is this to be said for Richardson: Required to play an asylum-keeper's wife who has sudden, frequent, and heedless sex with an inmate, she doesn't leave a heed standing.

Edgar's diagnosis is "severe personality disorder with features of morbid jealousy." With admirable economy, the movie eventually applies this diagnosis to just about everyone in it except little Charlie, who is way too trusting, and not just of Edgar. There are lots of scenes involving British twits who are well dressed but with subtly disturbing details about their haberdashery and styles of smoking. They sit or stand across desks from one another and exchange technical jargon that translates as, "I hate you and your kind." Meanwhile, the cinematographer, Giles Nuttgens, makes the asylum into a place so large, gloomy, and foreboding that we suspect maybe *Eyes with No Face* is being filmed elsewhere on the premises.

If I'm spinning my wheels, it's because we've arrived (already) at a point in the plot where major developments start to tumble over one another in their eagerness to bewilder us. In my notes I find many entries beginning with such words as:

"Yes, but . . ."

"Why would . . ."

"Surely they . . ."

"Yet he . . ."

"How could . . ."

And then several one-word entries followed by too many exclamation points, such as:

"Drowns!!!"

But I do not want to spoil these developments and so will not reveal who drowns, except to say it's not every movie that reminds you of *Leave Her to Heaven*. There is also a question, some distance into the film, of the plausibility of certain living arrangements. Also of their wisdom, of course, but wisdom at this point has been left so far behind, it's churlish to double back for it.

The director, David Mackenzie, made *Young Adam,* also the story of a married woman attracted to a young and possibly dangerous man. The screenplay is cowritten by Patrick Marber, who wrote *Closer,* a movie about four-way sexual infidelity involving characters who deserved one another. Certainly the characters in *Asylum* richly earn their fates, and by the end we are forced to reflect that although they are indeed mad, at least the villain is acting reasonably under the circumstances.

ATL ★ ★ ★

PG-13, 105 m., 2006

Tip Harris (Rashad), Evan Ross (Anton "Ant"), Mykelti Williamson (Uncle George), Lauren London (New-New), Keith David (John Garnett), Jackie Long (Esquire), Jason Weaver (Teddy), Albert Daniels (Brooklyn), Antwan Andre Patton (Marcus). Directed by Chris Robinson and produced by Dallas Austin, Jody Gerson, James Lassiter, and Will Smith. Screenplay by Tina Gordon Chism, based on a story by Antwone Fisher.

Since their parents died in a car crash, Rashad and Anton have been living with their Uncle George, or maybe he's been living with them, since it was their parents' house. Rashad is seventeen, a high school senior, working part time to save money for his kid brother "to make it out of here"—out of their poor black neighborhood in Atlanta. Anton, known as "Ant," sees a faster route, standing on a corner selling drugs for a local dealer.

But no, *ATL* isn't a drug movie, and it doesn't send its characters on a harrowing journey into danger. It's a film about growing up and working, about falling in love, about planning for your future, and about the importance of friends. For Rashad (Tip Harris), the best day of the week is Sunday because that's when he and three friends head for the Cascade, a roller rink where they show off with intricately choreographed moves on the floor.

Rashad's friends are Esquire (Jackie Long), Teddy (Jason Weaver), and Brooklyn (Albert Daniels). They're solid and will last for a lifetime. Esquire, who has top grades, is a waiter at a country club, where he meets the black millionaire John Garnett (Keith David). He needs a letter of recommendation to go with his Ivy League scholarship application. Garnett is happy to give him one and to invite the smart, polite kid to his mansion on the other side of town. And that's when . . .

But let's back up to New-New (Lauren London). Rashad meets her at the Cascade, they like each other, they start spending time together, and it looks like love. But there is something she doesn't tell him—although she almost does, before he interrupts her. I'm not going to reveal her secret, except to say that it threatens to sink their romance and their trust in each other. And for a while it looks like it may destroy Rashad's friendship with Esquire.

What this plot outline doesn't describe is the warmth and heart of *ATL*, which is about good kids more or less raising themselves. Uncle George is not a bad man, and at forty-one he has been a janitor long enough to plead with his nephews to get themselves an education. But when he finds out Ant (Evan Ross) is selling drugs, his immediate reaction is pragmatic: "We can always use some money in this house." Rashad is a lot more disturbed and takes action.

But even before that, the movie offers an unusual portrait of the fourteen-year-old as drug dealer. Yes, he works for a guy with a big, expensive car (the rumbles of the sound system are an advance warning system). But Ant's own job is to stand on a corner, hour after hour, lonely, cold, hungry, scared, not making much money and then getting that stolen. The movie is lacking the false sense of empowerment that sometimes seems to surround drugs in the movies.

Apart from its other qualities, which are real, the movie has a lot of music. The director, Chris Robinson, has made many music videos, and two of his actors are rap artists: Tip Harris records as T.I. (and did a lot of the sound track) and Antwan Andre Patton records as Big Boi. Their music, plus the mix at the Cascade, creates a sound track that drives the movie, especially in the roller-skating scenes, which are choreographed to make the rink look like a magical place. And yes, there is a Cascade in Atlanta and it's just as popular as it seems in the movie. I know this because my wife is visiting relatives there and they took her to the Cascade, and she called me half an hour ago and was having a great time. Small world.

The screenplay, by Tina Gordon Chism, is based on a story by Antwone Fisher, and do I have to say, yes, *that* Antwone Fisher? I doubt *ATL* is as autobiographical as his 2002 film, but it reflects lives of focus and determination; Rashad and his friends *are* young and sometimes foolish and like to party, but they're also smart and determined to survive and prevail. That's why Rashad can't understand it when . . . well, you'll find out if you see the film.

What I liked most was its unforced, genuine affection for its characters. Rashad likes his friends, and so do we. He realizes Uncle George is not a paragon, but Mykelti Williamson has a strong scene where he defends his life from his point of view. He's forty-one, no wife, pushing a broom, trying to hold a home together for two nephews he didn't ask for, and he's doing his best. I sense that somewhere in the film, if we know where to look, maybe in the support of Uncle George, the friendships involving Rashad, Esquire, and New-New, we can find clues about how Antwone Fisher evolved from a kid with a shaky future into a screenwriter with a big one.

Atonement ★ ★ ★ ★

R, 122 m., 2007

Keira Knightley (Cecilia Tallis), James McAvoy (Robbie Turner), Romola Garai (Briony, age eighteen), Brenda Blethyn (Grace Turner), Vanessa Redgrave (Older Briony), Saoirse Ronan (Briony, age thirteen), Patrick Kennedy (Leon Tallis). Directed by Joe Wright and produced by Tim Bevan, Eric Fellner, and Paul Webster. Screenplay by Christopher Hampton, based on the novel by Ian McEwan.

Atonement begins on joyous gossamer wings and descends into an abyss of tragedy and loss. Its opening scenes in an English country house between the wars are like a dream of elegance, and then a thirteen-year-old girl sees something she misunderstands, tells a lie, and destroys all possibility of happiness in three lives, including her own.

The opening act of the movie is like a breathless celebration of pure, heedless joy, a demonstration of the theory that the pinnacle of human happiness was reached by life in an English country house between the wars. Of course, that was more true of those upstairs than downstairs. We meet Cecilia Tallis (Keira Knightley), bold older daughter of an old family, and Robbie Turner (James McAvoy), their housekeeper's promising son, who is an Oxford graduate thanks to the generosity of Cecilia's father. Despite their difference in social class, they are powerfully attracted to each other, and that leads to a charged erotic episode next to a fountain on the house lawn.

This meeting is seen from an upstairs window by Cecilia's younger sister, Briony (Saoirse Ronan), who thinks she sees Robbie mistreating her sister in his idea of rude sex play. We see the same scene later from Robbie and Cecilia's point of view, and realize it involves their first expression of mutual love. But Briony does not understand, has a crush on Robbie herself, and as she reads an intercepted letter and interrupts a private tryst, her resentment grows until she tells the lie that will send Robbie out of Cecilia's reach.

Oh, but the earlier scenes have floated effortlessly. Cecilia, as played by Knightley with stunning style, speaks rapidly in that upper-class accent that sounds like performance art. When I hear it, I despair that we Americans will ever approach such style with our words that march out like baked potatoes. She is so beautiful, so graceful, so young, and Robbie may be working as a groundsman but is true blue, intelligent, and in love with her. They *deserve* each other.

But that is not to be, as you know if you have read the Ian McEwan best-seller that the movie is inspired so faithfully by. McEwan, one of the best novelists alive, allows the results of Briony's vindictive behavior to grow offstage until we meet the principals again in the early days of the war. Robbie has enlisted and been posted to France. Cecilia is a nurse in London, and so is Briony, now eighteen, trying to atone for what she realizes was a tragic error. There is a meeting of the three, only one, in London, that demonstrates to them what they have all lost.

The film cuts back and forth between the war in France and the bombing of London, and there is a single (apparently) unbroken shot of the beach at Dunkirk that is one of the great takes in film history, achieved or augmented with CGI although it is. (If it looks real, in movie logic it is real.) After an agonizing trek from behind enemy lines, Robbie is among the troops waiting to be evacuated in a Dunkirk much more of a bloody mess than legend would have us believe. In the months before, the lovers have written, promising each other the happiness they have earned.

Each period and scene in the movie is compelling on its own terms, and then compelling on a deeper level as a playing-out of the destiny that was sealed beside the fountain on that perfect summer's day. It is only at the end of the film, when Briony, now an aged novelist played by Vanessa Redgrave, reveals facts about the story, that we realize how thoroughly, how stupidly, she has continued for a lifetime to betray Cecilia, Robbie, and herself.

The structure of the McEwan novel and this film directed by Joe Wright is relentless. How many films have we seen that fascinate in every moment and then, in the last moments, pose a question about all that has gone before, one that forces us to think deeply about what betrayal and atonement might really entail?

Wright, who also directed Knightley in his first film, *Pride and Prejudice*, shows a mastery of nuance and epic, sometimes in adjacent scenes. In the McEwan novel he has a story that can hardly fail him, and an ending that blindsides us with its implications. This is one of the year's best films. ☞

August Rush ★ ★ ★

R, 114 m., 2007

Freddie Highmore (Evan Taylor/August Rush), Keri Russell (Lyla Novacek), Jonathan Rhys Meyers (Louis Connelly), Terrence Howard (Richard Jeffries), Robin Williams (Wizard Wallace), William Sadler (Thomas Novacek), Leon G. Thomas III (Arthur). Directed by Kirsten Sheridan and produced by Richard Barton Lewis. Screenplay by Nick Castle and James V. Hart.

Here is a movie drenched in sentimentality, but it's supposed to be. I dislike sentimentality where it doesn't belong, but there's something brave about the way *August Rush* declares itself and goes all the way with coincidence, melodrama, and skillful tear-jerking. I think more sensitive younger viewers, in particular, might really like it.

The story is a very free modern adaptation of elements from *Oliver Twist*. We meet Evan Taylor (Freddie Highmore), an eleven-year-old who runs away from his orphanage rather than be placed with a foster family. He has been told that his parents are still alive and were musicians, and he believes that through the power of music he can find them again. Do you begin to see what I mean about sentimentality?

As it happens, his parents *were* musicians, and they met through their music. Lyla (Keri Russell) was a cellist, and Louis (Jonathan Rhys Meyers) an Irish rock singer, and in a flashback we see them meeting in Greenwich Village, falling in love at first sight, and making love so very discreetly that they remain safely within the PG rating. They promise to meet again, but Lyla's stage-door father (William Sadler) forces her to leave town for career reasons and they have no way to contact each other. Young lovers, learn from the movies and always remember: *Exchange cell numbers!* Inevitably, she is pregnant (otherwise they wouldn't be Evan's parents, now would they be?), but her father tells her the baby died and ships Evan to an orphanage. Nothing must interfere with Lyla's career.

Back to the present. The runaway Evan sees some street musicians in Washington Square Park, picks up a guitar and, despite having had no training, turns out to be a naturally gifted musician. Another young musician (Leon G. Thomas III), who is not called the Artful Dodger but should be, hears Evan and takes him back to an abandoned theater, where he and other young lads live under the management of a character who is called the Wizard (Robin Williams), but could be called Fagin. He sends his little army out into the streets every day not as pickpockets but as buskers. Only in a movie like *August Rush* could the endless practical and legal problems suggested by this arrangement be considered plausible.

The Wizard, who dresses like a drugstore cowboy, spots Evan's talent and introduces him to the world as August Rush. August believes, really believes, that music has the power to bring people together, and finds a sympathizer when he comes upon a church choir where the preacher (Mykelti Williamson) turns out to have connections at Juilliard. And so, yes, August is discovered as a child genius, and quickly earns the right to conduct his own symphony at an outdoor concert in Central Park, where he proves himself an expert conductor and (gasp!) his mother is the cellist and his father is nearby, both of them still under the spell of their long-lost love, and . . .

I'm telling you, the ghost of Dickens would be applauding. The movie, directed by Kirsten Sheridan and written by Nick Castle and James

V. Hart, pulls out all the stops, invents new ones, and pulls them out too. But it has a light-footed, cheerful way about its contrivances, and Freddie Highmore (*Finding Neverland*) is so open and winning that he makes August seem completely sincere. One touch of craftiness would sink the whole enterprise.

Another quality about the movie is that it seems to sincerely love music as much as August does. If you're going to lay it on this thick, you can't compromise, and Sheridan doesn't. I don't have some imaginary barrier in my mind beyond which a movie dare not go. I'd rather *August Rush* went the whole way than just be lukewarm about it. Yes, some older viewers will groan, but I think up to a certain age, kids will buy it, and in imagining their response I enjoyed my own.

Awake ★ ★ ★

R, 78 m., 2007

Hayden Christensen (Clay Beresford), Jessica Alba (Sam Lockwood), Terrence Howard (Dr. Jack Harper), Lena Olin (Lilith Beresford), Christopher McDonald (Dr. Larry Lupin), Sam Robards (Clay Beresford Sr.), Arliss Howard (Dr. Jonathan Neyer). Directed by Joby Harold and produced by Jason Kliot, John Penotti, and Joana Vicente. Screenplay by Harold.

Do not believe anything you hear about *Awake*, do not talk to anyone about it, and above all do not even *glance* at the poster or ads, which criminally reveal a crucial plot twist. This movie, which was withheld from critics and has scored a pitiful 13 percent on the Tomatometer from those few who were able to see it, is a surprisingly effective thriller. I went to a regular theater to see it Friday afternoon, knowing nothing about it except that the buzz was lethal, and sat there completely absorbed.

The movie involves a very, very rich young man named Clay Beresford (Hayden Christensen), who lives with his loving but dominating mother (Lena Olin) and fears to tell her about his engagement with the beautiful Samantha (Jessica Alba). But "the clock is ticking," he is warned by his friend and surgeon Jack Harper (Terrence Howard). Jack saved Clay in the ER after he had a massive heart attack, and now Clay's on the waiting list for a transplant. "Marry that girl," Jack advises him, and even invites him into the operating room for a trial run to explain how dangerous the surgery is.

This and other medical procedures are highly unlikely, and the heart transplant itself involves an improbably small team, a last-minute replacement as the anesthesiologist, and an uninvited visitor allowed to put on a surgical gown and observe. But accuracy is not the point. Suspense is. And from the moment Clay realizes he is not fully under anesthesia and can hear and feel everything that is happening, the movie had me. The character does a voice-over in which he tries to force his eyes open and signal that he's conscious, and then a series of unexpected developments take place, which I will not even begin to reveal.

Since the movie involves a plot that cannot be discussed, let me just say that I may be the slowest tomato on the meter, but I did not anticipate the surprises, did not anticipate them piling on after one another, got very involved in the gory surgical details, and found the supporting soap opera good, as such things go.

It involves a rich kid who believes he can never live up to his father, a mother who believes she cannot surrender her son, and the beautiful Jessica Alba coming between them. It also involves Clay's determination to have the transplant performed by Dr. Jack, his trusted friend, instead of his mother's candidate (Arliss Howard), who boasts, "I have had my hands inside presidents." He wrote the book on transplants and will be the next surgeon general. "Well, I hope Jack has read your book," Clay replies.

All preposterous, I know, but this edges us into a consideration of why we are at the movies in the first place, and what works and what does not work. I got involved. I felt real suspense. I thought Lena Olin gave a nuanced performance as the mother, who is deeper than we first think, and that the tension between her and Alba was plausible. And I thought the scenes where Clay imagines leaving his body, roaming the hospital, and having psychic conversations were well handled.

So maybe I'm wrong. It has happened before. *Awake*, written and directed by first-timer

Joby Harold, clocks at only seventy-eight minutes, but that's the right length for what happens. The movie opened under a cloud on a weekend all other mainstream movies side-stepped, apparently because it was our duty to commence Christmas shopping. But I felt what I felt, and there you have it. ☞

Away from Her ★ ★ ★ ★

PG-13, 110 m., 2006

Julie Christie (Fiona Andersson), Gordon Pinsent (Grant Andersson), Olympia Dukakis (Marian), Michael Murphy (Aubrey), Kristen Thomson (Kristy), Wendy Crewson (Madeleine), Alberta Watson (Dr. Fischer). Directed by Sarah Polley and produced by Jennifer Weiss, Simone Urdl, and Daniel Iron. Screenplay by Polley, based on a short story by Alice Munro.

Away from Her is the fifth film I've seen about Alzheimer's in these opening years of the century, and the best, although only one of them has been disappointing. Using sympathy and tenderness for its characters, it tells the story of a marriage that drifts out of the memory of the wife and of the husband's efforts to deal with that fact. We have two Canadian women to thank for this film: the writer and director, Sarah Polley (born 1979), and the author of the short story that inspired it, Alice Munro (born 1931). In her short fiction, Munro has the ability to evoke a lifetime in images and dialogue of almost startling perception. Polley with her camera takes the material, finds an uncanny balance in her casting, and bathes the film in the mercy of simple truth.

Fiona and Grant Andersson (Julie Christie and Gordon Pinsent) have been married more than forty years, mostly happily despite some stumbles. They have the beauty in age they had in youth, although it is weathered now, as a park bench looks more inviting after some seasons in the sun. They have been told she has Alzheimer's disease. The movie spares us coy early scenes where she seems healthy and then starts to slip; she starts right out putting a frying pan into the refrigerator.

They're retired and live in a cottage overlooking fields that are perfect for cross-country skiing. They look robust in their cold-weather gear, and when they come inside from their daily skiing, they look so comfortable with each other that they make us feel cozy. Just as the models in plus-size catalogs always look thin, so the models in retirement ads always look like these two: youthful, athletic, foxy.

Fiona has too much respect for herself, and too much pity for Grant, to subject him to what seems her certain decay. She makes a decision on her own to check into a comfortable nearby nursing home, and Grant drives her there, remembering their younger adventures along the same route. An administrator explains that Grant will not be able to visit for thirty days; it's easier if new patients are cut off from family contact while adjusting to their new lives.

All of this is seen not in darkness and shadows and the gloom of winter and visions in the night, but in bright focus. Polley told Andrew O'Hehir of Salon: "For me the overriding palette that we were working with was the idea of this very strong, sometimes blinding winter sunlight that should infuse every frame. I didn't want the visual style to draw too much focus to itself. I felt like this needed to be an elegant and simple film, and that it had to have a certain grace."

How can you do that by limiting your palette, instead of making it more complex? I was reminded of Bergman's *Winter Light* (1962), which bathes despair in merciless daylight. The despair here is Grant's. When he returns after thirty days, he finds Fiona almost inseparable from another patient, the mute Aubrey (Michael Murphy). She tends him like her own patient and seems indifferent, even vague, about Grant. Is she getting even with him for cheating he did earlier in their marriage? That would almost be a relief, if the alternative is that she is forgetting him. He is deeply wounded.

One reason we get married is that we need a witness to our lives. So says the Susan Sarandon character in Audrey Wells's much-quoted dialogue for *Shall We Dance* (2004). With the death of every person we have known, our mutual memories become only personal, and then when we die the memories die. In a sense, those remembered events never happened. Death wipes the slate clean at once, which is a mercy compared to the light of recognition that slowly fades in the eyes of loved ones who have Alzheimer's. Remember the first time we made love? You don't? Who is "we"? What is "love"?

As it turns out, Aubrey has a wife named Marian (Olympia Dukakis), and Grant visits her, at first wondering if she could consider moving her husband to another place. Or whatever. They talk over her kitchen table, Dukakis imparting a sense of implacable truth. She regards reality without blinking. And that is enough about the plot.

The other recent Alzheimer's movies are Bille August's *A Song for Martin* (2002), Nick Cassavetes's *The Notebook* (2004), and Erik Van Looy's *Memory of a Killer* (2005). All very good, the third perhaps the best. And then there was Richard Eyre's *Iris* (2001), about the decline of the novelist Iris Murdoch, which struck me as cheating because it was too much about young Iris.

True, *The Notebook* also moved from present to past and supplied well-timed but unlikely moments when the patient's mind opened in perfect clarity and memory. But it proposed to be a romance, not a biography. *A Song for Martin* is about a couple who meet in later life, fall in love passionately, and then have the cloud fall between them. And *Memory of a Killer* stars Jan Decleir in an unforgettable performance as an aging Belgian hit man who wants to retire and undertakes one last job in which he fights against the fading of his light to bring about an extraordinary outcome. Rent it.

All of these films persist in linking Alzheimer's disease to a story. Sarah Polley, whose *Away from Her* is a heartbreaking masterpiece, has the courage to simply observe the devastation of the disease. Alzheimer's is usually like that. There are few great love stories replayed in the closing days, few books written, few flashbacks as enjoyable for the victims as they are for us. There is only the victim going far, far away, until finally, as if they have fallen into a black hole, no signs can ever reach us from them again.

The performances here are carefully controlled, as they must be, so that we see no false awareness slipping out from behind the masks; no sense that the Julie Christie character is in touch with a more complete reality than, from day to day, she is. No sense that Gordon Pinsent, as her husband, is finally able to feel revenge, consolation, contrition, or anything else but inescapable loss. No sense that the Olympia Dukakis character deceives herself for a moment. No sense that Michael Murphy's character understands his behavior.

The one aware character is Kristen Thomson as Kristy, the kind nurse who gives Grant practical advice. She has empathy for him, and pity, and she can explain routines and treatments and progressions to him, but she cannot do anything about his grief. She has worked in the home for a while. She knows how Alzheimer's is and must be. I have gotten to know some nurses well over the last year and have seen the sadness in their eyes as they discuss patients (never by name) whom they are helpless to help. Thomson finds that precise note.

Sarah Polley, still so young, always until now an actress (*The Sweet Hereafter, My Life Without Me*), emerges here as a director who is in calm command of almost impossible material. The movie says as much for her strength of character as for her skills. Anyone would could read Munro's original story and think they could make a film of it, and then make a great film, deserves a certain awe. ☞

B

Bad News Bears ★ ★ ★

PG-13, 111 m., 2005

Billy Bob Thornton (Morris Buttermaker), Greg Kinnear (Roy Bullock), Marcia Gay Harden (Liz Whitewood), Sammi Kane Kraft (Amanda Whurlitzer), Jeffrey Davies (Kelly Leak), Carter Jenkins (Joey Bullock). Directed by Richard Linklater and produced by J. Geyer Kosinski and Linklater. Screenplay by John Requa and Glenn Ficarra, based on a screenplay by Bill Lancaster.

Billy Bob Thornton stages a head-on collision between two previous roles in *Bad News Bears,* a movie in which he plays, and I quote, "a drunk who makes a living killing rats to live in a trailer." The movie is like a merger of his ugly drunk in *Bad Santa* and his football coach in *Friday Night Lights,* yet he doesn't recycle from either movie; he modulates the manic anger of the Santa and the intensity of the coach and produces a morose loser whom we like better than he likes himself.

The movie, directed by Richard Linklater, is a fairly faithful remake of the 1976 film starring Walter Matthau, which inspired sequels starring William Devane and Tony Curtis. They had strengths of their own, but following Matthau's boozy vulgarian was not one of them. Thornton's performance is obviously fond of the Matthau approach but finds a weary sadness in Coach Morris Buttermaker, who made it out of the minor leagues long enough to play in one major league game.

His team, the Bears, exists only because of a lawsuit filed by attorney Liz Whitewood (Marcia Gay Harden), who believes the Little League discriminates; she files a class-action suit demanding that the league accept all players. The Bears end up with bad players in several categories: a black kid, two Spanish speakers, an Indian, a kid almost too little to hold the bat, and another one in a motorized wheelchair. What they have in common is not their minority status, but their inability to play the game.

They revived my own childhood memories of Little League, which I hated; it was a meritocracy in which good players were heroes and I was pointed toward right field with the hope that I would just keep on walking. Well, of course it was a meritocracy. Sports involves winning, and winning involves skills. What I could never figure out was how some kids had always been good at sports and others would never be any good, no matter how hard they tried: Kids like me, so nearsighted that the approach of a ball had to be described to me by teammates.

If Matthau was a grumpy old drunk, Thornton descends still further into self-loathing; he's coaching only for the money, keeps his "nonalcoholic" beer can filled with bourbon, and recruits some of the kids to crawl under houses and spray dangerous chemicals. When Liz Whitewood thinks she smells booze on his breath, he uses the "nonalcoholic" line and points out he is driving. "That's right! Never drink and drive," she tells her son, Toby. Coach Buttermaker adds helpful details: "Stay away from crack, too. You'll wake up in prison married to some guy named Big Bear."

The progress of the story is predictable, as it is in all movies about underdogs. They are bad and will get better. In the case of the Bad News Bears, this process is aided when Buttermaker recruits his daughter, Amanda (Sammi Kane Kraft), from a failed marriage. She's a gifted pitcher. He also recruits a strong hitter named Kelly Leak (Jeffrey Davies), advises one kid to deliberately get hit by a ball in order to get on base, and another one to lie to his parents. Buttermaker is not a role model, and his private life is untidy; required to find a sponsor willing to pay for the Bears' uniforms, he recruits—well, it gets a big laugh.

The movie works on two levels. On the top level it's a dark but traditional PG-13 version of a kids' sports movie, with everything but the f-word in the dialogue. The plot leads inexorably up to the last inning of the final game; we know the routine.

On a more insidious level, the movie suggests that America has embraced a new approach to winning. Where sportsmanship and fair play once counted for something, success now often includes lying, cheating, and stealing, as demonstrated in criminal trials sending millionaire executives off to prison in chains.

Whether Coach Buttermaker develops better values by the end of the film, I will leave for you to discover. Thornton, in the opening and middle innings, displays a nice touch for cynical vulgarity. His archenemy in the league is Coach Bullock (Greg Kinnear), whose Yankees, like the real ones, usually win. Bullock, however, is not a paragon compared to Buttermaker, but vile in his own right, and really tough on his own kid. He's actually more in the tradition of Vince Lombardi ("Winning isn't everything; it's the only thing") than Buttermaker ("Baseball. Once you love it, it doesn't always love you back. It's like dating a German chick"). When he does finally edge toward a change of heart, it involves replacing false phony team spirit with real phony team spirit.

That the movie lacks the evil genius of *Bad Santa* is perhaps inevitable; you couldn't put a character as misogynistic and vulgar as Billy Bob's Santa in a movie where he's surrounded by kids. There's a limit. But Buttermaker does his best to be politically incorrect ("You guys are acting like Helen Keller at a piñata party"), and when it comes time for him to utter his big inspirational speech, it is grounded in dour reality.

What I liked most about the movie, I think, was that it undermines the self-congratulatory myths we cultivate about sports in America. It writes the obituary of good sportsmanship. Grantland Rice wrote, "It's not whether you win or lose; it's how you play the game," to which, according to the *Baseball Almanac,* celebrated baseball team owner Gene Autry replied: "Grantland Rice can go to hell as far as I'm concerned."

Note: The language in the movie pushes the limits of the PG-13 *rating.*

The Ballad of Jack and Rose ★ ★ ★

R, 111 m., 2005

Daniel Day-Lewis (Jack), Camilla Belle (Rose), Catherine Keener (Kathleen), Paul Dano (Thaddius), Ryan McDonald (Rodney), Jena Malone (Red Berry), Beau Bridges (Marty Rance). Directed by Rebecca Miller and produced by Lemore Syvan. Screenplay by Miller.

The Ballad of Jack and Rose is the last sad song of 1960s flower power. On an island off the East Coast, a craggy middle-aged hippie and his teenage daughter live alone in the remains of a commune. A generator is powered by wind. There is no television. Seaweed fertilizes the garden. They read. He homeschools her. They divide up the tasks. When Rose looks at Jack, her eyes glow with worship, and there is something wrong about that. When they lie side by side on the turf roof of their cottage, finding cloud patterns in the sky, they could be lovers. She is at an age when her hormones vibrate around men, and there is only one in her life.

Rebecca Miller's film is not about incest, but it is about incestuous feelings, and about the father's efforts, almost too late, to veer away from danger. Jack (Daniel Day-Lewis) is a fierce idealist who occasionally visits the other side of the island to fire shotgun blasts over the heads of workers building a housing development. Rose (Camilla Belle) admires him as her hero. "If you die, then I'm going to die," she tells him. "If you die," he says, "there will have been no point to my living."

This is not an academic discussion. He's had a heart attack, and he may die. She regularly takes away his home-rolled cigarettes, but out of her sight he's a chain-smoker, painfully thin, his idealistic serenity sometimes revealing a fierce anger just below the surface. He hates the developer (Beau Bridges) who is building the new homes on what Jack believes are wetlands: "That's not a house. It's a thing to keep the TV dry," he says, and, "They all want to live in places with people exactly like themselves, and have private police forces to keep their greedy little children safe."

Jack is being forced to think about the future. His daughter, he finally realizes, is too fixated on him. He visits the mainland, where for six months he has been dating Kathleen (Catherine Keener). He asks her to move with her two teenage boys out to the island and live with them: "It will be an experiment." Because he has a trust fund, he can write her a handsome check to make the move more practical. Kathleen, who lives at home with her mother, needs the money and is realistic about that, while at the same time genuinely liking Jack. But how much does she know about him? She has never been to the island.

The film's best scenes involve the introduction of these three outsiders into the solitude of Jack and Rose. The sons, by different fathers, are different creatures. Rodney (Ryan

McDonald) is an endomorphic sweetheart; Thaddius (Paul Dano) is a skinny pothead. "I'm studying to be a woman's hair dresser," Rodney tells Rose. "I wanted to be a barber, but men don't get enough pleasure out of their hair."

Having possibly fantasized herself as her father's lover, Rose reacts with anger to the newcomers and determines in revenge to lose her virginity as soon as possible. She asks Rodney to sleep with her, but he demurs ("I am sure my brother will be happy to oblige") and suggests a haircut instead. The short-haired Rose seems to have grown up overnight, and in reaction to her father's "experiment" offers him evidence of an experiment of her own.

The fundamental flaws in their idyllic island hideaway become obvious. As long as Jack and Rose lived in isolation, a certain continuity could be maintained. But the introduction of Kathleen as her father's lover, and the news that she is to start attending a school in town, cause Rose to rage against the loss of—what? Her innocence, or her ideas about her father's innocence?

Rebecca Miller, the writer and director, had a strong father of her own, the playwright Arthur Miller. She had a strong mother, too, the photographer Inge Morath. That she is now essentially the photographer (although the cinematography is by the visual poet Ellen Kuras) and her subject is a father and daughter may be less of a case of acting out her own childhood, as some writers have suggested, as identifying with her mother. It would be reckless and probably wrong to find literal parallels between Rebecca and Rose, but perhaps the film's emotional conflicts have an autobiographical engine.

Toward the end of the film, events pile up a little too quickly; there are poisonous snakes and sudden injuries, confrontations with the builder and medical concerns, and Jack resembles a lot of dying characters in the movies: His health closely mirrors the requirements of the story. By the end I had too much of a sense of story strands that had strayed too far to be neatly concluded, and there is an epilogue that could have been done without.

Despite these complaints, *The Ballad of Jack and Rose* is an absorbing experience. Consider the care with which Miller handles a confrontation between Jack and the home-builder. Countless clichés are sidestepped when Jack finally sees their conflict for what it is, not right against wrong, but "a matter of taste." Is it idealistic to want a whole island to yourself, and venal to believe that other people might enjoy having homes there? The movie has a sly scene where Jack and Rose visit one of the model homes, which to Jack is an abomination and to Rose a dream.

Balls of Fury ★ ★ ½

PG-13, 90 m., 2007

Dan Fogler (Randy Daytona), Christopher Walken (Mr. Feng), George Lopez (Agent Rodriguez), Maggie Q (Maggie), Tom Lennon (Karl Wolfschtagg), James Hong (Master Wong), Robert Patrick (Sgt. Pete Daytona). Directed by Robert Ben Garant and produced by Tom Lennon, Roger Birnbaum, Gary Barber, and Jonathan Glickman. Screenplay by Garant and Lennon.

Ping-Pong is to tennis as foosball is to soccer. I know it's on cable now, with lots of controversy over slower balls and faster paddles, but it retains for me only memories of rainy days at summer camp. I have never lost all affection for the sport, however, and am careful to play it at least once every decade. Thus it was with great eagerness that I attended *Balls of Fury*, which is, I believe, the first movie combining Ping-Pong and kung-fu and costarring Maggie Q. How many could there be?

Dan Fogler is the star, playing Randy Daytona, who in his youth was a Ping-Pong phenom but has been reduced in his twenties to working as a lounge act in Vegas, bouncing the ball off a board while flanked by two babes. That kind of lounge entertainment reminds me of an annual banquet of the Chicago Newspaper Reporters Association, at which the entertainment consisted of a man who came onstage with twelve of those paddles that have a bouncing ball attached with a rubber band, kept all twelve balls going at once, and then, one by one, got all twelve in his mouth.

Randy Daytona, now grown pudgy and in the early stages of a Curly Howard hairstyle, is discovered in Vegas by Rodriguez (George Lopez), an FBI agent who wants him to get back into training so he can compete undercover in an illegal global Ping-Pong and martial arts tournament run by the evil criminal weapons dealer Mr. Feng (Christopher Walken). Walken plays the role with makeup that makes him look Asian and clothes that look recycled from the wallpaper in a Chinese restaurant. Back in the days of Charlie Chan, Asians were rightfully offended when Caucasian actors portrayed them, but I doubt there is an Asian alive who will begrudge Walken this particular role.

Daytona's assignment: Get back in shape under the tutelage of blind Master Wong (James Hong) and his niece, played by Maggie Q (*Mission: Impossible III*). How can you be blind and play Ping-Pong? If you can't see, what other option do you have? Daytona thrives under his lessons, learns deadly martial arts moves from Maggie Q, and then he's ready for Mr. Feng's bizarre tournament.

Don't expect me to explain the rules and purposes of the tournament, if it has any. I was preoccupied with observing the sheer absurdity of everything on the screen, including Daytona's old Ping-Pong archenemy Karl Wolfschtagg (cowriter Tom Lennon), who will be a star if World Wrestling Entertainment ever sanctions this sport. All he needs is a leather mask and some spurs.

At some point in my study of the press releases, I came across the usual claims about how Fogler and the other actors became experts at the game and did many of their own scenes. Pure baloney. There are Ping-Pong games in this movie where the balls move faster than a quark on Saturday night. Fermilab should show *Balls of Fury* in its training program.

Now what else can I tell you? Well, I received a nice letter from Greg Packnett of Madison, Wisconsin, who enjoyed my "extremely qualified recommendation" for *Rush Hour 3*, remembering that while camping near the Wisconsin Dells, "it was so hot and so humid, that the people I was with decided to go to *Rush Hour 3* "just for an excuse to spend a few hours in air-conditioning." Substituting the movie title, here's the qualified recommendation Mr. Packnett enjoyed so much: "Once you realize it's only going to be so good, you settle back and enjoy that modest degree of goodness, which is at least not badness, and besides, if you're watching *Balls of Fury*, you obviously didn't have anything better to do anyway."

Balzac and the Little Chinese Seamstress ★ ★ ½

NO MPAA RATING, 111 m., 2005

Xun Zhou (Little Seamstress), Kun Chen (Luo), Ye Liu (Ma), Shuangbao Wang (Village Chief), Zhijun Cong (Old Tailor), Hong Wei Wang (Four Eyes), Xiong Xiao (Mother of Four Eyes). Directed by Sijie Dai and produced by Lise Fayolle. Screenplay by Dai and Nadine Perront, based on the novel by Dai.

Balzac and the Little Chinese Seamstress is artfully designed to appeal to lovers of romance and books, but by the end of the film I was not convinced it knew much about either. The romance is sincere but lacking in passion, and the books have the strange result of sending the heroine away from both men who love her, and toward an unknown future in the big city.

The story takes place in 1971, when two city boys are sent to a remote mountain area to be "reeducated" under the Cultural Revolution. Luo (Kun Chen) confesses to the village chief that his father is a "reactionary dentist" who committed the sin of once treating Chiang Kai-shek. Ma (Ye Liu) is the child of intellectuals. Enough said. In the rural vastness, surrounded by breathtaking scenery, they stagger up a mountainside with barrels of waste and work in a copper mine.

The chief (Shuangbao Wang) takes a hard line at first. He goes through the young men's possessions, throwing a cookbook into the fire because in the village they will eat not bourgeois chicken but proletarian cabbage and corn. Ma has a violin, which the chief thinks is a toy until Ma begins to play Mozart. Everyone in the village is enchanted by the music, which the chief allows after being informed the composition is in honor of Chairman Mao. Nearby lives the little seamstress (Xun Zhou), with her ancient grandfather, the tailor (Zhijun Cong). The boys are attracted to her beauty and grace, and Luo courts her while Ma feels the same way.

The movie has been cowritten and directed by Sijie Dai, based on his own best seller in which the young men find a cache of forbidden Western books and read them aloud to the seamstress. They also teach her to read and write. The novels are by Balzac, Dumas, and Flaubert, whose *Madame Bovary* perhaps inspires the seamstress to one day leave the village and set out alone to walk to the city. The boys protest, passively, and let her go. To be sure, by this time she's been through harrowing experiences and is no longer the innocent we first met, but still: Is this a success story about literacy, or a failure to communicate?

Some of my favorite episodes from the novel are well visualized in the movie, including the way Luo and Ma travel to a nearby town, watch Korean films, and return to describe them to the villagers with great drama (making up most of the details). There's also the drama of Luo's sudden departure for the city, and an emergency that Ma helps the seamstress survive. But somehow the principal characters seem oddly remote from their own lives. We're not sure what literature means to them (aside from the sentimental assumption that it is redemptive). And we're not sure how deep the love between Luo and the seamstress can possibly be, considering the way they eventually part.

When the movie violently yanks us twenty years into the future for the epilogue, it is an unsatisfactory one in which one character shows his video footage of how the mountain district was flooded after a new dam was built, but the two men are never really clear about their feelings for the seamstress, or each other. There should have been more urgency at the time, more powerful memories afterward, and less complacency about the way the seamstress disappears from the story.

I do believe that books are redemptive. I believe that no child who can read and has access to books and the time to read them is without hope. That alone can change a life. But in *Balzac and the Little Chinese Seamstress*, the city boys go through the motions of transforming the seamstress through books, without the how and why. What does she think—do any of them think—about the strange foreign worlds described by Balzac and the others?

I am reminded of the scene in Truffaut's *The 400 Blows* where the young hero has a shrine to Balzac; *Seamstress* has a sort of shrine, too, a hidden grotto, but without Truffaut's perception about how his character changes. And after some initial hardships, the lives of the boys seem to become easier and filled with free time; there's no sense that the village chief represents a real danger to them, and a scene where Luo treats his tooth is badly acted and seems awkward. The elements in the story push all the right buttons, but the buttons don't seem to be wired to anything.

The Band's Visit ★ ★ ★ ★

PG-13, 86 m., 2008

Sasson Gabai (Tewfig), Ronit Elkabetz (Dina), Saleh Bakri (Haled), Khalifa Natour (Simon), Imad Jabarin (Camal), Tarak Kopty (Iman). Directed by Eran Kolirin and produced by Eilon Ratzkovsky, Ehud Bleiberg, Yossi Uzrad, Koby Gal-Raday, and Guy Jacoel. Screenplay by Kolirin.

The eight men wear sky-blue uniforms with gold braid on the shoulders. They look like extras in an opera. They dismount from a bus in the middle of nowhere and stand uncertainly on the sidewalk. They are near a highway interchange, leading, no doubt, to where they'd rather be. Across the street is a small café. Regarding them are two bored layabouts and a sadly, darkly beautiful woman.

They are the Alexandria Ceremonial Police Orchestra, a band from Egypt. Their leader, a severe man with a perpetually dour expression, crosses the street and asks the woman for directions to the Arab Cultural Center. She looks at him as if he stepped off a flying saucer. "Here there is no Arab culture," she says. "Also no Israeli culture. Here there is no culture at all."

They are in a dorp in the middle of the Israeli desert, having taken the wrong bus to the wrong destination. Another bus will not come until tomorrow. *The Band's Visit* begins with this premise, which could supply the makings of a light comedy, and turns it into a quiet, sympathetic film about the loneliness that surrounds us all. Oh, and there is some comedy, after all.

The town they have arrived at is lacking in interest even for those who live there. It is seemingly without activity. The bandleader, named Tewfig (Sasson Gabai), asks if there is a hotel. The woman, Dina (Ronit Elkabetz), is amused. No hotel. They communicate in careful, correct English—she more fluent, he weighing every word. Tewfig explains their dilemma. They are to play a concert tomorrow at the opening of a new Arab Cultural Center in a place that has almost, but not quite, the same name as the place they are in.

Tewfig starts out to lead a march down the highway in the correct direction. There is some dissent, especially from the tall young troublemaker Haled (Saleh Bakri). He complains that they have not eaten. After some awkward negotiations (they have little Israeli currency), the Egyptians are served soup and bread in Dina's café. It is strange how the static, barren, lifeless nature of the town seeps into the picture even though the writer-director, Eran Kolirin, uses no establishing shots or any effort at all to show us anything beyond the café—and later, Dina's apartment and an almost empty restaurant.

Dina offers to put up Tewfig and Haled at her apartment, and tells the young layabouts (who seem permanently anchored to their chairs outside her café) that they must take the others home to their families. And then begins a long, quiet night of guarded revelations, shared isolation, and tentative tenderness. Dina is tough but not invulnerable. Life has given her little that she hoped for. Tewfig is a man with an invisible psychic weight on his shoulders. Haled, under everything, is an awkward kid. They go for a snack at the restaurant, its barren tables reaching away under bright lights, and Dina points out a man who comes in with his family. A sometime lover of hers, she tells Tewfig. Even adultery seems weary here.

When the three end up back at Dina's apartment, where she offers them wine, the evening settles down into resignation. It is clear that Dina feels tender toward Tewfig, that she can see through his timid reserve to the good soul inside. But there is no movement. Later, when he makes a personal revelation, it is essentially an apology. The movie avoids what we might expect, a meeting of the minds, and gives us instead a sharing of quiet desperation.

As Dina and Tewfig, Ronit Elkabetz and Sasson Gabai bring great fondness and amusement to their characters. She is pushing middle age; he is being pushed by it. It is impossible for this night to lead to anything in their future lives. But it could lead to a night to remember. Gabai plays the bandleader as so repressed, or shy or wounded, that he seems closed inside himself. As we watch Elkabetz putting on a new dress for the evening and inspecting herself in the mirror, we see not vanity but hope. And throughout the evening we note her assertion, her confidence, her easily assumed air of independence. Yet when she gazes into the man's eyes, she sighs with regret that as a girl she loved the Omar Sharif movies that played daily on Israeli TV, but play no more.

There are some amusing interludes. A band member plays the first few notes of a sonata he has not finished (after years). A band mate calls him "Schubert." A local man keeps solitary vigil by a pay phone, waiting for a call from the girl he loves. He has an insistent way of showing his impatience when another uses the phone. In the morning, the band reassembles and leaves. *The Band's Visit* has not provided any of the narrative payoffs we might have expected, but it has provided something more valuable: an interlude involving two "enemies," Arabs and Israelis, that shows them both as only ordinary people with ordinary hopes, lives, and disappointments. It has also shown us two souls with rare beauty. ☞

Basic Instinct 2 ★ ½

R, 113 m., 2006

Sharon Stone (Catherine Tramell), David Morrissey (Dr. Michael Glass), Charlotte Rampling (Milena Gardosh), David Thewlis (Roy Washburn), Hugh Dancy (Adam Towers), Indira Varma (Denise Glass), Heathcote Williams (Jakob Gerst). Directed by Michael Caton-Jones and produced by Moritz Borman, Joel B. Michaels, Mario Kassar, and Andrew G. Vajna. Screenplay by Leora Barish and Henry Bean.

Basic Instinct 2 resembles its heroine: It gets off by living dangerously. Here is a movie so outrageous and preposterous it is either (a) suicidal or (b) throbbing with a horrible fascination. I lean toward (b). It's a lot of things, but boring is not one of them. I cannot recommend the movie, but . . . why the hell can't I? Just because it's godawful? What kind of reason is that for staying away from a movie? Godawful and boring, *that* would be a reason.

I have here an e-mail from Adam Burke, a reader who says: "I'm tired of reading your reviews where you give a movie three stars but make sure we know it isn't a great movie. You always seem to want to cover your ass, making sure we know you're smarter than the movie." He has a point. Of course, I am smarter than most movies, but so are you. That doesn't always prevent us from enjoying them. What Burke doesn't mention is my other maddening tendency, which is to give a movie 1½ stars and then hint that it's really better than that.

Which brings us full circle to *Basic Instinct 2.* It has an audacious plot, which depends on (a) a psychopathic serial killer being able to manipulate everyone in her life, or (b) a woman who uncannily seems to be a psychopathic serial killer, while there is (c) an alternative explanation for everything. True, (a), (b), and (c) are equally impossible, but they're the only possibilities, I think. That leaves us feeling screwed at the end, which is how everyone in the film feels, so we cross the finish line together.

So much for the plot. Now for Sharon Stone. She may get some of the worst reviews in years, but she delivers the goods. Playing Catherine Tramell, a trashy novelist who toys with life, death, and sex while doing "research" for her next best seller, Stone brings a hypnotic fascination to her performance. You don't believe it, but you can't tear your eyes away. She talks dirty better than anyone in the movies. She can spend hours working her way through "every position in Masters and Johnson," she sighs wistfully, and forget all about it in a week, "but I'd remember it if a man died while having sex with me."

She says this, and lots of other things, to a shrink named Dr. Michael Glass (David Morrissey). He's appointed by the courts to evaluate her sanity after the car she is driving goes off a bridge at 110 mph and her passenger, a soccer star, drowns. In court we learn she has a "risk addiction" so severe that "the only limit for her would be her own death." They say that with any addiction you have to hit bottom. Death may be taking it too far.

Back on the street after unlikely legal technicalities, she comes salivating after Dr. Glass, who insanely accepts her as a client. Also involved in the tangled web are his ex-wife (Indira Varma); a gossip writer (Hugh Dancy) the ex-wife is currently bonking; a Freudian in a fright wig (Heathcote Williams); a fellow shrink (Charlotte Rampling) who warns Glass he is playing with fire; and a cop (David Thewlis) who sniffs around the case like a dog convinced that if liverwurst is not in the room at this moment, it was here not very long ago.

Some of these people die unpleasantly during the course of the film, possibly giving Tramell something to remember. Some of them are suspected of the murders. The details are not very important. What matters are the long scenes of dialogue in which Tramell mind-whacks Dr. Glass with speculations so detailed they rival the limerick about who did what, and with which, and to whom.

The Catherine Tramell role cannot be played well, but Sharon Stone can play it badly better than any other actress alive. The director, Michael Caton-Jones, alternates smoldering close-ups with towering dominatrix poses, and there's an extended Jacuzzi sequence in which we get the much-advertised full frontal nudity—which does not, somehow, manage to be full, frontal, and nude all at the same time. First a little nude, then a little full, then a little frontal, driving us crazy trying to load her simultaneously onto our hard drive.

Dr. Glass is played by Morrissey as a subdued, repressed basket case who listens to Tramell with a stony expression on his face. This is because he is either (a) suppressing his desire to ravage her in lustful abandon, or (b) suppressing delirious laughter. I'll bet there are outtakes of Stone and Morrissey cracking up. How else to respond to dialogue such as, "Don't take it so hard—even Oedipus didn't see his mother coming."

Basic Instinct 2 is not good in any rational or defensible way, but not bad in irrational and indefensible ways. I savored the icy abstraction of the modern architecture, which made the people look like they came with the building. I grinned at that absurd phallic skyscraper that really does exist in London. I liked the recklessness of the sex-and-speed sequence that opens the movie (and, curiously, looks to have been shot in Chicago). I could appreciate the plot once I accepted that it was simply jerking my chain. You can wallow in it.

Speaking of wallowing in the plot, I am reminded of another of today's e-mails, from Coralyn Sheridan, who tells me that in Parma they say, "The music of Verdi is like a pig: Nothing goes to waste." Those Parmesans.

Of Sharon Stone, what can I say except that there is within most men a private place that responds to an aggressive sexual challenge, especially when it's delivered like a lurid torch song, and Stone plays those notes like she worked out her own fingering.

Note No. 1: The last shot in the film is wrong. It should show only the eyes.

Note No. 2: My 1½–star rating is like a cold shower, designed to take my mind away from giving it four stars. I expect to hear from Adam Burke about this.

Batman Begins ★ ★ ★ ★

PG-13, 140 m., 2005

Christian Bale (Bruce Wayne/Batman), Michael Caine (Alfred Pennyworth), Liam Neeson (Henri Ducard), Katie Holmes (Rachel Dawes), Morgan Freeman (Lucius Fox), Gary Oldman (Lieutenant James Gordon), Cillian Murphy (Dr. Jonathan Crane), Tom Wilkinson (Carmine Falcone), Rutger Hauer (Richard Earle), Ken Watanabe (Ra's Al Ghul). Directed by Christopher Nolan and produced by Larry J. Franco, Charles Roven, and Emma Thomas. Screenplay by David S. Goyer and Nolan.

Batman Begins at last penetrates to the dark and troubled depths of the Batman legend, creating a superhero who, if not plausible, is at least persuasive as a man driven to dress like a bat and become a vigilante. The movie doesn't simply supply Batman's beginnings in the tradition of a comic book origin story, but explores the tortured path that led Bruce Wayne from a parentless childhood to a friendless adult existence. The movie is not realistic, because how could it be, but it acts as if it is.

Opening in a prison camp in an unnamed nation, *Batman Begins* shows Bruce Wayne (Christian Bale) enduring brutal treatment as a prisoner as part of his research into the nature of evil. He is rescued by the mysterious Henri Ducard (Liam Neeson), who appoints himself Wayne's mentor, teaches him sword-fighting and mind control, and tries to enlist him in his amoral League of Shadows ("We burned London to the ground"). When Wayne refuses to kill someone as a membership requirement, Ducard becomes his enemy; the reclusive millionaire returns to Gotham determined to fight evil, without realizing quite how much trouble he is in.

The story of why he identifies with bats (childhood trauma) and hates evildoers (he saw his parents killed by a mugger) has been referred to many times in the various incarnations of the Batman legend, including four previous films. This time it is given weight and depth.

Wayne discovers in Gotham that the family Wayne Corp. is run by a venal corporate monster (Rutger Hauer), but that in its depths labors the almost-forgotten scientific genius Lucius Fox (Morgan Freeman), who understands that Wayne wants to fight crime and offers him the weaponry. Lucius happens to have on hand a prototype Batmobile, which unlike the streamlined models in the earlier movies is a big, unlovely juggernaut that looks like a Humvee's wet dream. He also devises a Bat Cape with surprising properties.

These preparations, Gotham crime details, and the counsel of the faithful family servant Alfred (Michael Caine) delay the actual appearance of a Batman until the second act of the movie. We don't mind. Unlike the earlier films, which delighted in extravagant special-effects action, *Batman Begins* is shrouded in shadow; instead of high-detail, sharp-edged special effects, we get obscure developments in fog and smoke, their effect reinforced by a superb sound effects design. And Wayne himself is a slow learner, clumsy at times, taking foolish chances, inventing Batman as he goes along ("People need dramatic examples to shake them out of fear and apathy, and I can't do that as a human being").

This is at last the Batman movie I've been waiting for. The character resonates more deeply with me than the other comic superheroes, perhaps because when I discovered him as a child he seemed darker and more grown-up than the cheerful Superman. He has secrets. As Alfred muses: "Strange injuries and a nonexistent social life. These things beg the question, what does Bruce Wayne do with his time?"

What he does is create a high profile as a

millionaire playboy who gets drunk and causes scenes. This disappoints his friend since childhood, Rachel Dawes (Katie Holmes), who is now an assistant D.A. She and Lieutenant James Gordon (Gary Oldman), apparently Gotham's only honest cop, are faced with a local crime syndicate led by Carmine Falcone (Tom Wilkinson). But Falcone's gang is child's play compared to the deep scheme being hatched by the corrupt psychiatrist Dr. Jonathan Crane (Cillian Murphy), who in the tradition of Victorian alienists likes to declare his enemies insane and lock them up.

Crane's secret identity as the Scarecrow fits into a scheme to lace the Gotham water supply with a psychedelic drug. Then a superweapon will be used to vaporize the water, citizens will inhale the drug, and it will drive them crazy, for reasons the Scarecrow and his confederates explain with more detail than clarity. Meanwhile, flashbacks establish Wayne's deepest traumas, including his special relationship with bats and his guilt because he thinks he is responsible for his parents' mugging.

I admire, among other things, the way the movie doesn't have the gloss of the earlier films. The Batman costume is an early design. The Bat Cave is an actual cave beneath Wayne Manor. The Batmobile enters and leaves it by leaping across a chasm and through a waterfall. The early Bat Signal is crude and out of focus. The movie was shot on location in Chicago, making good use of the murky depths of Lower Wacker Drive (you may remember it from *Henry: Portrait of a Serial Killer*) and the Board of Trade building (now the Wayne Corp.). Special effects add a spectacular monorail straight down LaSalle Street, which derails in the best scene along those lines since *The Fugitive*.

Christian Bale is just right for this emerging version of Batman. It's strange to see him muscular and toned, after his cadaverous appearance in *The Machinist*, but he suggests an inward quality that suits the character. His old friend Rachel is at first fooled by his facade of playboy irresponsibility, but Lieutenant Gordon (destined to become in the fullness of time Commissioner Gordon) figures out fairly quickly what Batman is doing, and why. Instead of one villain as the headliner, *Batman Begins* has a whole population, including Falcone, the Scarecrow, the Asian League of Shadows leader Ra's Al Ghul (Ken Watanabe), and a surprise bonus pick.

The movie has been directed by Christopher Nolan, still only thirty-five, whose *Memento* (2000) took Sundance by storm and was followed by *Insomnia* (2002), a police procedural starring Al Pacino. What Warner Bros. saw in those pictures that inspired it to think of Nolan for Batman is hard to say, but the studio guessed correctly, and after an eight-year hiatus the Batman franchise has finally found its way.

I said this is the Batman movie I've been waiting for; more correctly, this is the movie I did not realize I was waiting for, because I didn't realize that more emphasis on story and character and less emphasis on high-tech action was just what was needed. The movie works dramatically in addition to being an entertainment. There's something to it.

The Baxter ★ ★

PG-13, 91 m., 2005

Michael Showalter (Elliot Sherman), Elizabeth Banks (Caroline Swann), Justin Theroux (Bradley Lake), Michelle Williams (Cecil Mills), Michael Ian Black (Ed), Peter Dinklage (Benson Hedges), Paul Rudd (Dan Abbott). Directed by Michael Showalter and produced by Daniela Taplin Lundberg, Galt Niederhoffer, Celine Rattray, and Reagan Silber. Screenplay by Showalter.

We are informed early in *The Baxter* that "the baxter" is a term for the guy in a movie who never gets the girl. This came as news to me, and I expect it will come as a shock to my friend Billy "Silver Dollar" Baxter, who always gets more or less what he wants, especially when he wants a good seat in a restaurant, which is usually harder to get than the girl.

The movie stars Michael Showalter as Elliot Sherman, who is the baxter, and has been told about baxters by his grandmother, which means baxters are entering their third generation of nobody ever having heard about them. Given the definition of a baxter, I guess that makes sense. The opening scene shows Elliot at the altar, about to marry a girl, when the man she truly loves bursts into the church and sweeps her away. That's the baxter: the guy left at the altar. I'm trying to think of the name of the baxter in *The Graduate.*

Elliot, it must be said, richly deserves to be a baxter. He is a certified public accountant who is engaged to a smart, hot, successful young woman named Caroline (Elizabeth Banks), who is playing well below her league. Maybe she wants to marry Elliot so she won't always be bothered by having a husband. But when her high-school honey, Bradley (Justin Theroux), turns up, she forgets all her reasons for wanting to marry Elliot, if there are any.

Actually, there aren't any. It is Showalter's misfortune to be releasing a movie about a boring and unlikable nerd only two weeks after the opening of *The 40-Year-Old Virgin,* which stars Steve Carell as a fascinating and lovable nerd. The thing you have to remember about movie nerds is that they're *movie* nerds; they're nerds for the convenience of the plot, but secretly fascinating. To be a good nerd in a movie, a nerd should resemble a baked potato, as I have so often heard them described by Billy "Silver Dollar" Baxter: "I've been tubbed, I've been scrubbed, I've been rubbed! I'm lovable, huggable, and eatable!"

There is, luckily, a baked potato in *The Baxter.* She is played by Michelle Williams, as Cecil Mills, the cute temp who is right there in Elliot's outer office and adores him and is perfect for him and is cuter than a button and almost as cute as two buttons. She glows in the movie. She glows so much, indeed, that I was waiting for her to dump Elliot, too. She's too good for a baxter.

There's also a hilarious supporting performance by Peter Dinklage as a wedding planner named Benson Hedges. His name reminds me of the year Edy Williams introduced me to her date on Oscar night: "I'd like you to meet Dean Witter." Dinklage, whom you may remember from *The Station Agent* (and if you don't, that is the next movie you should rent), plays a gay dwarf who not only steals every scene he's in but pawns it and buys more scenes and walks off with them, too. He has a little routine with cute guys on a city sidewalk that is like a meditation on hope and lust. Benson may be a Hedges, but he will never be a baxter.

The problem with *The Baxter* is right there at the center of the movie, and maybe it is unavoidable: Showalter makes too good a baxter. He deserves to be dumped. At some point everyone in the movie should have jilted him and gone off and started a movie of their own. If Elliot ever gets to the altar with Cecil, Benson Hedges the wedding planner should march in and sweep her away. Yes, he's gay, but maybe they could work out something. He could plan her into another wedding.

The Beat That My Heart Skipped ★ ★ ★

NO MPAA RATING, 107 m., 2005

Romain Duris (Thomas), Niels Arestrup (Robert), Linh-Dan Pham (Miao-Lin), Aure Atika (Aline), Emmanuelle Devos (Chris), Jonathan Zaccaï (Fabrice), Gilles Cohen (Sami), Anton Yakovlev (Minskov). Directed by Jacques Audiard and produced by Pascal Caucheteux. Screenplay by Audiard and Tonino Benacquista, based on the film *Fingers* by James Toback.

The first time we see Thomas, he's carrying a sack squirming with movement. It contains rats he will set loose in a building he wants to buy cheaply; he has to persuade the current tenants to leave. Later, with two sidekicks, he smashes windows and intimidates squatters in another desirable property. This is how the real estate business operates at his level in Paris. He learned it from his father, Robert, a seedy soak with a big gut, who has been an insidious influence in his son's life.

A more beneficent influence, his mother, is dead. She was a concert pianist, and as a young man Thomas studied the piano seriously. One day he meets the impresario who booked his mother's concerts, and the man remembers his talent and invites him to audition. Thomas is stirred, and torn. He is working at a job he loathes, doing things that make him despise himself, but is reluctant to defy his father. He loves classical music but doubts his ability to regain whatever talent he once had.

This story, told in Jacques Audiard's *The Beat That My Heart Skipped,* will sound familiar to anyone who has seen *Fingers* (1978), the first film directed by James Toback, who himself has always been torn between his good and bad angels. The Toback film, filled with fierce energy and desire, starred Harvey Keitel, torn between Bach and brutality, as the son of a mafioso (Michael V. Gazzo).

The French movie is not a remake so much as a riff on the same material, seen in a more realistic, less emotionally extreme way. Thomas, played by Romain Duris with self-contempt that translates into coiled energy, is fully capable of violence. His anger may be fueled by frustration at the piano keyboard.

He hires a coach. This is Miao-Lin (Linh-Dan Pham), a Chinese pianist, newly arrived in Paris and without a word of French. They communicate through the music. In her own way she is as demanding and unforgiving as his father, forcing him to repeat passages again and again. Thomas's whole life comes down to the inability to satisfy authority figures. After a long but unspecified period of practice, he is ready for his audition, but the impresario represents yet one more test he fears he will fail.

In a different kind of movie, Thomas and Miao-Lin would fall in love. There is certainly feeling between them, but unrealized; they are an intriguing mystery to each other. Thomas has an affair with the wife of one of his shady partners, but regards in puzzlement his father's new "fiancée," Chris (Emmanuelle Devos), who is deluded if she thinks she has a future with Robert. Yes, Robert (Niels Arestrup) exhibits her with pride, as proof that he is still the man he has always played for his son, but clearly he is a heart attack on hold, an overweight, florid-cheeked shambles with a yellow sport coat and tangled hair. He no doubt thinks his hair, probably dyed, preserves the dash he had in the 1960s, but it's a discouraged mop of worn-out bravado.

What hold does Robert have over his son? Why will Thomas do his dirty work? The times have bypassed Robert, as Thomas tries to explain when his dad has a deal that goes bad with a Russian mobster named Minskov (Anton Yakovlev). He tries to tell his father to stay clear of Minskov, to forget the bad deal and write off the loss; Minskov is dangerous and out of their league. But the father sits implacably in a series of shabby cafés, smoking and drinking and setting tests for his son.

The 1978 Toback film was crazier and edgier than this one; the young Keitel brought it a desperate energy, and Gazzo had a charisma that helped you understand why the son loved his father so. *The Beat That My Heart Skipped* is a darker and more downbeat enterprise, with a hero who is as conflicted, but not as mad, as the Toback original. There is nothing in this movie to match Toback's famous shot of Keitel crouched naked behind a piano, but there is a noir grunginess that is always convincing. The film seems to argue that a man who conducts his life like Thomas cannot successfully play classical music because he cannot feel its exaltation.

Audiard is a considerable filmmaker. His *Read My Lips* (2001), like this one cowritten with Tonino Benacquista, was a superb psycho-thriller involving a hearing-impaired office worker (again, Devos) who gets involved with an ex-con (Vincent Cassel) in a situation where lip-reading takes on a startling urgency. Both of these films occupy the meeting point between crime and middle-class respectability, and have central characters who are not prepared to live in both of those worlds, but cannot choose. *The Beat That My Heart Skipped* doesn't replace *Fingers,* but joins it as the portrait of a man reaching out desperately toward his dying ideals.

Beauty Shop ★ ★ ★

PG-13, 105 m., 2005

Queen Latifah (Gina Norris), Alicia Silverstone (Lynn), Andie MacDowell (Terri Green), Alfre Woodard (Miss Josephine), Mena Suvari (Joanne Marcus), Djimon Hounsou (Joe), Kevin Bacon (Jorge Christophe), Keshia Knight Pulliam (Darnelle), Paige Hurd (Vanessa), Bryce Wilson (James). Directed by Bille Woodruff and produced by Robert Teitel, George Tillman Jr., Queen Latifah, David Hoberman, Shakim Compere, and Elizabeth Cantillon. Screenplay by Kate Lanier and Norman Vance Jr.

Early in *Beauty Shop,* Queen Latifah asks her daughter if her pants make her butt look big. When the answer is "yes," she slaps it and says, "Good!" And means it. Latifah is profoundly comfortable with herself, and *Beauty Shop* is comfortable with itself. It isn't simply trying to turn up the heat under a *Barber Shop* clone, but to be more plausible (not a lot, but a little) in the story of a woman starting her own business. It's more of a human comedy than stand-up or slapstick.

Queen Latifah stars as Gina, recently arrived in Atlanta from Chicago (where she appeared briefly in *Barber Shop 2*). She's already the top stylist in an upscale salon run by the improbable Jorge Christophe, a streaked blond self-promoter who keeps Latifah from being the only queen in the movie. Jorge is over the top in every possible way, and you have to blink a couple of times before you realize he's being played by—Kevin Bacon?

It's very funny work, and sets up Gina for a big showdown where she walks out on Jorge and starts her own beauty shop. There's nothing terrifically original in the way she finds an old salon, remodels and repaints it, and staffs it with a shampoo girl from Jorge's (Alicia Silverstone) and an array of expert and verbal hairdressers, most notably Miss Josephine (Alfre Woodard) and Darnelle (Keshia Knight Pulliam, from *Cosby*). But consider the scene where she applies for a bank loan, and gets it after she shows the loan officer what she should be doing with her hair.

It is a convention of these movies that the shop is under threat from a landlord, a developer, or another ominous menace. This time it is the jealous Jorge, bribing a corrupt city inspector to put Gina out of business, and later taking more drastic measures. The movie wisely doesn't treat the threats as the whole plot, and it's refreshing how most of the movie is essentially about the characters, their stories, their lives.

Gina, for example, is a widow raising her daughter, Vanessa (Paige Hurd), a promising pianist. The man who lives upstairs over the beauty shop is Joe (Djimon Hounsou), an African who is both an electrician and a pianist. That sets up a sweet romance that isn't the usual bawdiness, but kind of touching, especially since Hounsou has so much warmth as an actor.

Just as *Barber Shop* had one white barber (Troy Garrity), *Beauty Shop* has one white beautician (Silverstone, promoted from shampoo). Andie MacDowell plays a customer from Jorge's shop who makes a crucial trip across town to follow Gina, her favorite hairdresser, and Mena Suvari is another customer from the old shop, not so nice. Some of the other employees, including the outspoken Miss Josephine, came with the old shop; others walk in through the door, including Bryce Wilson as James, an ex-con truck driver who knows so much about braids that Gina hires him on the spot, setting off intense speculation in the shop about his sexuality.

The beauty of the *Beauty* movies is that they provide a stage for lively characters. Countless plays have been set in bars for the same reason. The format almost works like a variety show, allowing each character to get a solo, as when Woodard's Miss Josephine takes the floor for a passionate recital of Maya Angelou's "Still I Rise."

Presiding like a den mother and emcee, Queen Latifah exudes a quiet confidence that sort of hugs the movie, making it feel warmer than the *Barber Shop* films. *Beauty Shop* doesn't shout at us, not even when catastrophe strikes; it's more about choosing a goal, being confident you can get there, and having some fun along the way.

Because of Winn-Dixie ★ ★

PG, 105 m., 2005

AnnaSophia Robb (Opal), Jeff Daniels (Preacher), Cicely Tyson (Gloria Dump), Dave Matthews (Otis), Eva Marie Saint (Miss Franny). Directed by Wayne Wang and produced by Trevor Albert and Joan Singleton. Screenplay by Singleton, based on the novel by Kate DiCamillo.

Because of Winn-Dixie tells the story of a lonely girl with a distant father, who is adopted by a dog. The dog changes her life, helps her make friends, and gives her someone to confide in for the first time. All without doubt sweet and warmhearted, but there is another film with a similar story that is boundlessly better, and that is *My Dog Skip* (2000). Also with the lonely kid. Also with the dog who makes friends. Also with the dad who thinks the dog should go back to the pound.

The difference between the two films is that *My Dog Skip* is made with a complexity that appeals to adults as much as children, while *Because of Winn-Dixie* seems pretty firmly aimed at middle school and below. Its portrait of the adult world comes from storybooks, not life, and its small town is populated entirely by (1) eccentric characters, and (2) anonymous people seen from a distance.

The little girl is named Opal (AnnaSophia

Robb). She is ten and lives in a house trailer supplied rent-free to her dad, who preaches in a church that uses the corner convenience store. When Opal was three, her mother ran away from the family for reasons unknown. Preacher (apparently his only name) has been depressed ever since, and spends long hours gazing out the window and "working on a sermon."

He sends Opal to the Winn-Dixie supermarket, and while she's there a dog runs up and down the aisles and is chased by countless clerks, who skid into piles of cans and knock over pyramids of boxes; destruction during a supermarket chase is the indoor shopping equivalent of the Fruit Cart Scene. Opal rescues the dog, claims it is hers, and names it Winn-Dixie.

Although both her dad and Mr. Alfred, the mean old man who runs the trailer park, want the dog to go to the pound, Opal stubbornly bonds with Winn-Dixie, and together they meet (1) Otis, played by Dave Matthews, who is the temporary clerk at the local pet store; (2) Gloria Dump, played by Cicely Tyson, who is blind and very wise; (3) Miss Franny, played by Eva Marie Saint, who is a fading southern belle with genteel airs; and (4) various local kids.

Otis takes out his guitar and sings her his story one day, in a nice scene. But is he really the clerk in the pet shop? What happened to the owner? And why, for that matter, does this pet shop stock ducks, chickens, pigs, and pigeons in addition to cats and dogs and hamsters? Is this a pet store, or an ark? Another local business, now defunct, once made Luttmuss Lozenges; when you put one in your mouth, you think it tastes like emotions. No surprise to me; I've always thought M&M's tasted like uncertainty, Peppermint Patties like sarcasm, and Tootsie Rolls like sweet revenge.

Although the movie has heartfelt conversations about the absence of Opal's mother, and scenes in which dog ownership is viewed as a great philosophical consolation, the picture mainly meanders until a big party scene at Miss Gloria's, to which all of the characters are invited—even Preacher, who, true to the ancient tradition of movie fathers, arrives late but then recognizes that his daughter has done a good thing.

It is one of those parties you see only in the movies, where the people may be poor, but they have an unlimited budget for candles. Hundreds of them. Thousands, maybe, all over the yard outside Miss Gloria's house. Covered dishes are uncovered, and meanwhile the stage has been set for drama.

"We have to be sure Winn-Dixie doesn't get out during a thunderstorm," Opal says. "He might run away." This makes it absolutely certain there will be a thunderstorm, right in the middle of the party, and that Winn-Dixie will run away, and have to be searched for all over town, with Opal's little voice piping, "Winn-Dixie! Winn-Dixie!" until . . . well, until the thunderstorm clears as quickly as it sprang up, and the party resumes, and so on.

Because of Winn-Dixie doesn't have a mean bone in its body, but it's dead in the water. It was directed by Wayne Wang, who usually (how can I put this?) makes films for grown-ups *(The Joy Luck Club, Smoke, The Center of the World, Maid in Manhattan).* Why did he choose this project? Why did he feel it had to be made? Did he screen *My Dog Skip* and realize he'd been dealt a weak hand? I don't know, and maybe I don't want to know.

Becoming Jane ★ ★ ★

PG, 120 m., 2007

Anne Hathaway (Jane Austen), James McAvoy (Tom Lefroy), Julie Walters (Mrs. Austen), James Cromwell (Rev. Austen), Maggie Smith (Lady Gresham), Laurence Fox (Mr. Wisley). Directed by Julian Jarrold and produced by Graham Broadbent, Robert Bernstein, and Douglas Rae. Screenplay by Kevin Hood and Sarah Williams.

Jane Austen wrote six of the most beloved novels in the English language, we are informed at the end of *Becoming Jane,* and so she did. The key word is "beloved." Her admirers do not analyze her books so much as they just plain love them to pieces. When I was very sick last year, there was a time when I lost all interest in reading. When I began to feel a little better, perhaps strong enough to pick up a book, it was Austen's *Persuasion.* Who else? And I entered again the world of that firm, fine intelligence, finding the humors and ironies of human existence in quiet domestic circles two centuries ago.

Becoming Jane is a movie every Janeite will

want to see, although many will not approve of it. The Jane Austen in the film owes a great deal more to modern romantic fancies than to what we know about the real Jane Austen, and if Austen had been as robust and tall in those days (circa 1795) as Anne Hathaway, the five-foot, eight-inch actress who plays her, she would have been considered an Amazon. Studying the only portrait drawn during her life, by her sister Cassandra, I think she looked more like Winona Ryder. But no matter. Patton was no George C. Scott.

My quarrel involves what this film thinks Jane is "becoming": a woman or a novelist? The action centers on a passionate romance between Jane at about twenty and a handsome, penniless young lawyer named Tom Lefroy (James McAvoy). What intimacies or decisions they arrive at, I will leave for you to discover, but surely few of Jane's contemporaries would have allowed themselves to be so bold. Jane, in any event, discovers love. And in the movie's sly construction, she also discovers a great deal of the plot of *Pride and Prejudice,* beginning with Mr. Lefroy as the original for Mr. Darcy. She even happily chances on what will become the novel's opening words: "It is a truth universally acknowledged, that a single man in possession of a good fortune must be in want of a wife."

Austen is already an author as the movie opens, although she will not for many years be a published one. We see her sitting at a beautiful desk in a beautiful chair, writing with a beautiful quill pen in a stylish script, and gazing out at a beautiful pastoral view, like an illustration for a Regency edition of the Levenger catalog.

Reader, it was not so. In her famous *A Room of One's Own,* Virginia Woolf writes: "A woman must have money and a room of her own if she is to write fiction." But Austen, a rector's daughter, had neither. Woolf writes: "The middle-class family in the early 19th century was possessed only of a single sitting room between them. If a woman wrote, she would have to write in the common sitting room. . . . Jane Austen wrote like that to the end of her days. 'How she was able to effect all this,' her nephew writes in his memoir, 'is surprising, for she had no separate study to repair to, and most of the work must have been done in the general sitting room, subject to all kinds of casual interruptions.'"

But in the movie, as always in the movies, writing flows easily and life is hard, when in reality life is hard and writing is harder. Jane learns this in one of the movie's best scenes, when she calls on Ann Radcliffe, one of the few women novelists then existing, who created the gothic novel.

The romance with Tom Lefroy is based on speculation in a recent biography by Jon Spence, but I suspect it has been much improved here. In her surviving letters to Cassandra, to whom she told everything, Jane mentions Mr. Lefroy the first time on January 9, 1796, and the last time on January 16 of the same year. Love could hardly have flowered so fast in those days, especially since rectors' daughters had to walk everywhere.

So followers of Austen will know they are watching a fiction. How good is it? Pretty good, in the same way that the movies based on Austen's books are good; in the movie version of Britain in those years, Laura Ashley seems to have dashed in to dress everyone, while Martha Stewart was in the kitchen. Hathaway is a stunning beauty, with big eyes and a dazzling smile, and James McAvoy as Mr. Lefroy seems to have modeled his dashing personality on Tom Jones, the hero of a scandalous novel he gives Jane, who much enjoys it.

Her parents are played by Julie Walters and James Cromwell, who have the good sense to stay under the blankets while indulging in hanky-panky that must not have been common in the vicarages of the day. And Maggie Smith plays the dowager Lady Gresham, one of those minor titled figures who believe they've been charged by heaven to pass judgment on everyone in the neighborhood, especially anyone who is young and has a breath of feeling.

Mr. Lefroy's problem is that he depends on an allowance from his uncle, who will cut him off cold should he marry a country girl. Austen has another suitor named Mr. Wisley (Laurence Fox), who has money but no charm or beauty. Austen feels keenly that she must help support her family but believes optimistically she can do so from her writings, still for the most part unwritten. Lefroy is desperate not to lose his allowance. Yet they are so much in love. But can they live in a dirt-floored cottage, with Jane plunging her fair skin into laundry water?

The way all of this plays out is acted warmly by the principals, and Eigil Bryld's photography (of Ireland) makes England look breathtakingly green and inviting. The director, Julian Jarrold (*Kinky Boots* and the TV version of *White Teeth*) is comfortable with the material, and it is comfortable with him. Maybe too comfortable. The coast is clear for the sequel, *What Jane Became.*

Be Cool ★ ½

PG-13, 112 m., 2005

John Travolta (Chili Palmer), Uma Thurman (Edie Athens), Vince Vaughn (Raji), Cedric the Entertainer (Sin LaSalle), Andre 3000 (Dabu), Steven Tyler (Himself), Christina Milian (Linda Moon), Harvey Keitel (Nicki Carr), Danny DeVito (Martin Weir), The Rock (Elliot Wilhelm). Directed by F. Gary Gray and produced by Danny DeVito, David Nicksay, Michael Shamberg, and Stacey Sher. Screenplay by Peter Steinfeld, based on the novel by Elmore Leonard.

John Travolta became a movie star by playing a Brooklyn kid who wins a dance contest in *Saturday Night Fever* (1977). He revived his career by dancing with Uma Thurman in *Pulp Fiction* (1994). In *Be Cool,* Uma Thurman asks if he dances. "I'm from Brooklyn," he says, and then they dance. So we get it: "Brooklyn" connects with *Fever,* Thurman connects with *Pulp.* That's the easy part. The hard part is, what do we do with it?

Be Cool is a movie that knows it is a movie. It knows it is a sequel, and contains disparaging references to sequels. All very cute at the screenplay stage, where everybody can sit around at story conferences and assume that a scene will work because the scene it refers to worked. But that's the case only when the new scene is also good as itself, apart from what it refers to.

Quentin Tarantino's *Pulp Fiction* knew that Travolta won the disco contest in *Saturday Night Fever.* But Tarantino's scene didn't depend on that; it built from it. Travolta was graceful beyond compare in *Fever,* but in *Pulp Fiction* he's dancing with a gangster's girlfriend on orders from the gangster, and part of the point of the scene is that both Travolta and Thurman look like they're dancing not out of joy, but out of duty. So we remember *Fever* and then we forget it, because the new scene is working on its own.

Now look at the dance scene in *Be Cool.* Travolta and Thurman dance in a perfectly competent way that is neither good nor bad. Emotionally they are neither happy nor sad. The scene is not necessary to the story. The filmmakers have put them on the dance floor without a safety net. And so we watch them dancing and we think, yeah, *Saturday Night Fever* and *Pulp Fiction,* and when that thought has been exhausted, they're still dancing.

The whole movie has the same problem. It is a sequel to *Get Shorty* (1995), which was based on a novel by Elmore Leonard just as this is based on a sequel to that novel. Travolta once again plays Chili Palmer, onetime Miami loan shark, who in the first novel traveled to Los Angeles to collect a debt from a movie producer, and ended up pitching him on a movie based on the story of why he was in the producer's living room in the middle of the night threatening his life.

This time Chili has moved into the music business, which is less convincing because, while Chili was plausibly a fan of the producer's sleazy movies, he cannot be expected, ten years down the road, to know or care much about music. Funnier if he had advanced to the front ranks of movie producers and was making a movie with A-list stars when his past catches up with him.

Instead, he tries to take over the contract of a singer named Linda Moon (Christina Milian), whose agent (Vince Vaughn) acts as if he is black. He is not black, and that's the joke, I guess. But where do you go with it? Maybe by sinking him so deeply into dialect that he cannot make himself understood, and has to write notes. Chili also ventures into the hip-hop culture; he runs up against a Suge Knight type named Sin LaSalle (Cedric the Entertainer), who has a bodyguard named Elliot Wilhelm, played by The Rock.

I pause here long enough to note that Elliot Wilhelm is the name of a friend of mine who runs the Detroit Film Theater, and that Elmore Leonard undoubtedly knows this because he also lives in Detroit. It's the kind of in-joke that doesn't hurt a movie unless you happen to know Elliot Wilhelm, in which case you can think of nothing else every second The Rock is on the screen.

The deal with The Rock's character is that he is manifestly gay, although he doesn't seem to realize it. He makes dire threats against Chili Palmer, who disarms him with flattery, telling him in the middle of a confrontation that he has all the right elements to be a movie star. Just as the sleazy producer in *Get Shorty* saved his own life by listening to Chili's pitch, now Chili saves his life by pitching The Rock.

There are other casting decisions that are intended to be hilarious. Sin LaSalle has a chief of staff played by Andre 3000, who is a famous music type, although I did not know that and neither, in my opinion, would Chili. There is also a gag involving Steven Tyler turning up as himself.

Be Cool becomes a classic species of bore: a self-referential movie with no self to refer to. One character after another, one scene after another, one cute line of dialogue after another, refers to another movie, a similar character, a contrasting image, or whatever. The movie is like a bureaucrat who keeps sending you to another office.

It doesn't take the in-joke satire to an additional level that might skew it funny. To have The Rock play a gay narcissist is not funny because all we can think about is that The Rock is not a gay narcissist. But if they had cast someone who was *also* not The Rock, but someone removed from The Rock at right angles, like Steve Buscemi or John Malkovich, then that might have worked, and The Rock could have played another character at right angles to himself—for example, the character played here by Harvey Keitel as your basic Harvey Keitel character. Think what The Rock could do with a Harvey Keitel character.

In other words: (1) Come up with an actual story, and (2) if you must have satire and self-reference, rotate it 90 degrees off the horizontal instead of making it ground-level. Also (3) go easy on the material that requires a familiarity with the earlier movie, as in the scenes with Danny DeVito, who can be the funniest man in a movie, but not when it has to be a movie other than the one he is appearing in.

Bee Movie ★ ★

PG, 100 m., 2007

With the voices of: Jerry Seinfeld (Barry B. Benson), Renee Zellweger (Vanessa), Matthew Broderick (Adam Flayman), Chris Rock (Mooseblood), John Goodman (Layton T. Montgomery), Patrick Warburton (Ken), Kathy Bates (Janet Benson), Barry Levinson (Martin Benson), Oprah Winfrey (Judge Bumbleton), Ray Liotta (himself), Sting (himself). Directed by Steve Hickner and Simon J. Smith and produced by Jerry Seinfeld and Christina Steinberg. Screenplay by Seinfeld, Spike Feresten, Andy Robin, and Barry Marder.

From each according to his ability, to each according to his need.

—Karl Marx

Applied with strict rigor, that's how bee society works in Jerry Seinfeld's *Bee Movie*, and apparently in real life. Doesn't seem like much fun. You are born, grow a little, attend school for three days, and then go to work for the rest of your life. "Are you going to work us to death?" a young bee asks during a briefing. "We certainly hope so!" says the smiling lecturer to appreciative chuckles all around.

One bee, however, is not so thrilled with the system. His name is Barry B. Benson, and he is voiced by Seinfeld as a rebel who wants to experience the world before settling down to a lifetime job as, for example, a crud remover. He sneaks into a formation of ace pollinators, flies out of the hive, has a dizzying flight through Central Park, and ends up (never mind how) making a friend of a human named Vanessa (voice by Renee Zellweger). Then their relationship blossoms into something more, although not very much more, given the physical differences. Compared to them, a Chihuahua and a Great Dane would have it easy.

This friendship is against all the rules. Bees are forbidden to speak to humans. And humans tend to swat bees (there's a good laugh when Barry explains how a friend was offed by a rolled-up copy of *French Vogue*). What Barry mostly discovers from human society is *gasp!* that humans rob the bees of all their honey and eat it. He and his best pal, Adam (Matthew

Broderick), even visit a bee farm, which looks like forced labor of the worst sort. Their instant analysis of the human-bee economic relationship is pure Marxism, if only they knew it.

Barry and Adam end up bringing a lawsuit against the human race for its exploitation of all bees everywhere, and this court case (with a judge voiced by Oprah Winfrey) is enlivened by the rotund, syrupy-voiced Layton T. Montgomery (John Goodman), attorney for the human race, who talks like a cross between Fred Thompson and Foghorn Leghorn. If the bees win their case, Montgomery jokes, he'd have to negotiate with silkworms for the stuff that holds up his britches.

All of this material, written by Seinfeld and writers associated with his TV show, tries hard, but never really takes off. We learn at the outset of the movie that bees theoretically cannot fly. Unfortunately, in the movie, that applies only to the screenplay. It is really, really, really hard to care much about a platonic romantic relationship between Renee Zellweger and a bee, although if anyone could pull if off, she could. Barry and Adam come across as earnest, articulate young bees who pursue logic into the realm of the bizarre, as sometimes happened on *Seinfeld.* Most of the humor is verbal and tends toward the gently ironic rather than the hilarious. Chris Rock scores best, as a mosquito named Mooseblood, but his biggest laugh comes from a recycled lawyer joke.

In the tradition of many recent animated films, several famous people turn up playing themselves, including Sting (how did he earn that name?) and Ray Liotta, who is called as a witness because his brand of Ray Liotta Honey profiteers from the labors of bees. Liotta's character and voice work are actually kind of inspired, leaving me to regret the absence of B. B. King, Burt's Bees, Johnny B. Goode, and the evil Canadian bee slavemaster Norman Jewison, who—oh, I forgot, he exploits maple trees. ☞

Bee Season ★ ★ ★

PG-13, 104 m., 2005

Richard Gere (Saul Naumann), Juliette Binoche (Miriam Naumann), Flora Cross (Eliza Naumann), Max Minghella (Aaron Naumann), Kate Bosworth (Chali), Justin Alioto (Kevin). Directed by Scott McGehee and David Siegel and produced by Albert Berger and Ron Yerxa. Screenplay by Naomi Foner Gyllenhaal, based on the novel by Myla Goldberg.

Bee Season involves one of those crazy families that cluster around universities: an intellectual husband who is clueless about human emotions, a wife who married him because she was afraid to be loved and he didn't know how to, a son who rebels by being more like his father than his father is, and a daughter who retreats into secret survival strategies. There are many movies about families sharing problems; in this one the members are isolated by them. They meet mostly at meals, which the father cooks and serves with a frightening intensity.

Like many families without centers, this one finds obsessions to focus on. Saul Naumann (Richard Gere) is a professor at Berkeley, specializing in Jewish theology and the Kabbalah. His wife, Miriam (Juliette Binoche), emotionally wounded by the early loss of her own parents, slips into the homes of strangers to steal small glittering things. Their teenage son, Aaron (Max Minghella), watches his father intimidate students with icy theological superiority and does the one thing best calculated to enrage him; he joins the Hare Krishnas. Their daughter, Eliza (Flora Cross), who is about twelve, seems to be trying to pass as unobserved and ordinary, but her inner life has a fierce complexity.

The father teaches Judaism and follows its forms, but his spiritual life is academic, not mystical. What no one in the family perceives is that Eliza is a genuine mystic, for whom the Kabbalah is not a theory but a reality. One of the things that Kabbalah believes is that words not only reflect reality but in a sense create it. God and the name of God are in this way the same thing.

How could this association enter into the life of a twelve-year-old in a practical way? Eliza finds out when she enters a spelling bee. Because she exists in the same world with words, because words create her world, she doesn't need to "know" how to spell a word. It needs merely to be evoked, and it materializes in a kind of vision: "I see the words." Although this gift gets her into the national finals, *Bee Season* is not a movie about spelling bees. It is a movie about a spiritual choice that calls everyone's bluff; it involves the sort of refusal and rebellion seen in that half-forgotten masterpiece *The Loneliness of the Long-Distance Runner* (1962).

Eliza is at the center of the film, and Cross carries its weight in a performance of quiet, compelling wisdom; the foreground character in the early scenes is Saul, the father. The members of his family swim in and out of focus. He is proud that Miriam is a scientist, in the sense that "my wife is a scientist," but does he know what enormous secrets she keeps from him? He is proud that his son is a gifted musician, and joins him in violin and cello duets. But Eliza is essentially invisible to Saul, because she has no particular accomplishments. Only when she wins a spelling bee does he start to focus on her, "helping" her train, pushing her to the next level, sitting proudly in the audience. He is proud not so much of her as of himself, for fathering such a prodigy.

The performance by Cross is haunting in its seriousness. She doesn't act out; she acts in. She suggests that Eliza has grown up in this family as a wise, often-overlooked observer, who keeps her own counsel and has her own values, the most important being her autonomy. In her father's manic kitchen behavior as he prepares and serves unwanted meals, she sees people-pleasing that exists apart from people who are pleased. In her fellow contestants in the spelling bees, she sees the same thing: Young people who are devoting their lives to mastering useless information for the glory of themselves and their parents. Yes, it is necessary to be able to spell in an ordinary sort of way, but to be able to spell every word is to aim for perfection, and perfection will drive you crazy, because our software isn't designed for it.

The movie, directed by Scott McGehee and David Siegel, is based on a novel by Myla Goldberg, unread by me. They made *Suture* (1993), a film about "identical" brothers played by actors of different races; you can deal with this apparent inconsistency by saying it doesn't matter—but in that case, why doesn't it? And their powerful *Deep End* (2001) starred Tilda Swinton as a mother scarcely less secretive than the Binoche character here.

Neither prepares us for *Bee Season*, which represents Eliza's decision to insist on herself as a being apart from the requirements of theology and authority, a person who insists on exercising her free will. This is a stick in the eye of her father. When people say they are "doing God's will," I am struck by the egotism of such a statement. What Eliza is doing at the end of *Bee Season* is Eliza's will. Does that make her God? No. It makes her Eliza.

Before the Devil Knows You're Dead ★ ★ ★ ★

R, 117 m., 2007

Philip Seymour Hoffman (Andy), Ethan Hawke (Hank), Albert Finney (Charles), Marisa Tomei (Gina), Rosemary Harris (Nanette), Bryan F. O'Byrne (Bobby), Amy Ryan (Martha). Directed by Sidney Lumet and produced by Michael Cerenzie, Brian Linse, Paul Parmar, and William S. Gilmore. Screenplay by Kelly Masterson.

Sidney Lumet's *Before the Devil Knows You're Dead* is such a superb crime melodrama that I almost want to leave it at that. To just stop writing right now and advise you to go out and see it as soon as you can. I so much want to avoid revealing plot points that I don't even want to risk my usual strategy of oblique hints. You deserve to walk into this one cold.

Yet that would prevent my praise, and there is so much to praise about this film. Let me try to word this carefully. The movie stars Philip Seymour Hoffman and Ethan Hawke as brothers—yes, brothers, because although they may not look related, they always feel as if they share a long and fraught history. Hoffman plays Andy, a payroll executive who dresses well and always has every hair slicked into place, but has a bad drug habit and an urgent need to raise some cash. Hawke plays Hank, much lower on the financial totem pole, with his own reasons for needing money; he can't face his little girl and admit he can't afford to pay for her class outing to attend *The Lion King*. Hank looks more like the addict, but you never can tell.

Andy suggests they solve their problems by robbing a jewelry store. And not just any jewelry store, but find out for yourself. He has it all mapped out as a victimless crime: They won't use guns, they'll hit early Saturday when the shopping mall doesn't have customers, the store's losses will be covered by insurance, and so on. Sounds good on paper, before everything goes wrong. And that's when the movie becomes intense and emotionally devastating.

These two brothers are capable of feeling emotions rare in modern crime films: grief and remorse. They cave in with regret. And they *still* need money; Andy learns that when you are heartbroken it is bad enough, but even worse when your legs may be broken, too. Meanwhile, their dozy father (Albert Finney) starts looking into the case himself, and that leads to a conversation with one son that Eugene O'Neill couldn't have written any better.

The movie fully establishes the families involved. Finney has been married forever to Rosemary Harris and still loves her to pieces. Hoffman is married to Marisa Tomei, who just keeps on getting sexier as she grows older so very slowly. Hawke is divorced from Amy Ryan, who would happily see him in jail for nonpayment of child support. And although the film opens with Hoffman and Tomei ecstatically making love in Rio (say what you will about the big guy, Hoffman looks to be an energetic and capable lover), their marriage is far from perfect.

The Japanese name some of their artists as Living Treasures. Sidney Lumet is one of ours. He has made more great pictures than most directors have made pictures, and found time to make some clunkers on the side. Here he takes a story that is, after all, pretty straightforward, and tells it in an ingenious style we might call "narrative interruptus." The brilliant debut screenplay by Kelly Masterson takes us up to a certain point, then flashes back to before that point, then catches us up again, then doubles back, so that it meticulously reconstructs how spectacularly and inevitably this perfect crime went wrong.

And it doesn't simply go wrong, it goes wrong with an aftermath we care about. This isn't a movie where the crime is only a plot, and dead bodies are only plot devices. Its story has deeply emotional consequences. That's why an actor with Albert Finney's depth is needed for an apparently supporting role. If he isn't there when he's needed, the whole film loses. As for Hoffman and Hawke, so seemingly different but such intelligent actors, they pull off that miracle that makes us stop thinking of anything we know about them and start thinking only of Andy and Hank. This is a movie, I promise you, that grabs you and won't let you think of anything else. It's wonderful when a director like Lumet wins a Lifetime Achievement Oscar at eighty and three years later makes one of his greatest achievements. ☞

Before the Rains ★ ★ ½

PG-13, 98 m., 2008

Linus Roache (Henry Moores), Rahul Bose (T.K. Neelan), Nandita Das (Sajani), Jennifer Ehle (Laura Moores), John Standing (Charles Humphries), Leo Benedict (Peter Moores). Directed by Santosh Sivan and produced by Doug Mankoff, Andrew Spaulding, Paul Hardart, Tom Hardart, and Mark Burton. Screenplay by Cathy Rabin, based on the film *Red Roofs* by Danny Verete.

Before the Rains tells the kind of story that would feel right at home in a silent film, and I suppose I mean that as a compliment. It's a melodrama about adultery, set against the backdrop of southern India in 1937. There's something a little creaky about the production, especially in its frequent use of large crowds of torch-bearing men, who can be summoned in an instant at any hour of day or night to blaze a trail, search for a missing woman, or group in front of the house of a possibly guilty man.

The movie comes from the Merchant-Ivory group, long associated with films made in English and filmed in India. It's directed by Santosh Sivan, originally a cinematographer, whose masterpiece *The Terrorist* (1999) involved a young woman committed to being a suicide bomber. That's the most thoughtful and empathetic film I've seen about the mind of a person who arrives at such a decision. It involves an assassination attempt; this one is set against the tide of Indian nationalism.

But it's not really a political film. It's driven by lust, guilt, and shame of a melodramatic sort that was right at home in the silent era. That doesn't mean it's old-fashioned, but that it's broadly melodramatic. It centers on the lives of a British landowner in India, his Indian right-hand man, and his affair with his beautiful young servant woman. Both the man and the woman are married, so there are problems in addition to the taboo against mixing the races and classes.

The man is Henry Moores (Linus Roache), who lives in a big, comfortable house with his wife, Laura (Jennifer Ehle), and young son, Peter (Leo Benedict). Next door lives his assistant, T.K. (Rahul Bose), who has abandoned his roots in the nearby village and cast his lot with the Brits. They run a tea plantation and discover cinnamon higher in the hills. That involves the construction of a road up a steep hillside that must zigzag its way to the top to avoid being washed away in the monsoons.

Laura and Peter are away at the beginning of the film, and Henry and his servant Sajani (Nandita Das) seek honey for their tea in a "sacred grove." They're seen by two talkative young boys and that leads, as it must, to tragedy. Laura and Benjamin return. Sajani is beaten by her husband, who has learned of her secret tryst (but not the identity of her partner). And that sets into motion a series of events involving whom she can trust, whom she can believe, and where she can turn.

This paragraph is a spoiler. Henry gives T.K. all the money he has on hand and asks him to send Sajani "away." T.K. reports, "I put her in a boat—for the North." But India is a big country, and the North is a distant destination for a woman in a small boat with one oarsman. Sajani, covered in blood, returns in the middle of the night to T.K.'s house, where Henry meets her. He's desperate. The village has reported her "missing," his wife is having suspicions, and when Sajani asks him, "Do you really love me?" he replies, "No." I think he says that for her own good. But she takes a handy pistol and kills herself.

It's in the details that a film reveals its origins. How does that pistol come into her hands? Henry gave it to T.K. in an early scene, and at the midnight meeting T.K. takes it out for no good reason and doesn't even seem to notice as he drops it where her hand can find it. All of this is explained in close-ups. Silent films knew just how to handle such prop deliveries.

Before the Rains is lushly photographed, as we would expect, by Sivan himself. It's told sincerely and with energy. It enjoys its period settings and costumes, and even its conventions. In a movie with plenty of room for it, there isn't a trace of cynicism. I am growing weary (temporarily, I think) of films that are cynical about themselves. Having seen several films recently whose characters have as many realities as shape-shifters, I found it refreshing to see a one-level story told with passion and romanticism.

But I can't quite recommend it. In a plot depending on concealment and secrecy, Henry and T.K. make all the wrong decisions, including a cover-up that almost seems designed to fail. And I didn't even mention the banker who pulls the plug on the financing of the road. That's part of the silent tradition, too: bankers who pull plugs.

Be Kind Rewind ★ ★ ½

PG-13, 101 m., 2008

Jack Black (Jerry), Mos Def (Mike), Danny Glover (Mr. Fletcher), Mia Farrow (Miss Falewicz), Melonie Diaz (Alma). Directed by Michel Gondry and produced by Georges Bermann and Julie Fong. Screenplay by Gondry.

whimsy (n.): Playfully quaint or fanciful behavior or humor.

Michel Gondry's *Be Kind Rewind* is whimsy with a capital W. No, it's WHIMSY in all caps. Make that all-caps italic boldface. Oh, never mind. I'm getting too whimsical. Maybe Gondry does, too. You'll have to decide for yourself. This is a movie that takes place in no possible world, which may be a shame, if not for the movie, then for possible worlds.

The place: Passaic, New Jersey. On a street corner stands a shop so shabby that only an art director could have designed it. This is *Be Kind Rewind*, a store that rents a skimpy selection of VHS tapes. Not a DVD in sight. It's owned by Mr. Fletcher (Danny Glover), who has convinced himself the store was the birthplace of Fats Waller (identified only as "some old-time jazz musician" on one Web site, which has plainly never heard of him). Behind in his rent, Mr. Fletcher faces eviction, and the store will be pulled down, no doubt to make way for Starbucks or Dunkin' Donuts.

Mr. Fletcher's faithful, long-suffering clerk is Mike (Mos Def), who is entrusted with the store while the owner goes undercover, hoping to scope out the success of the big competitor down the street, West Coast Video. Maybe it's because they rent DVDs? To be in the video rental business and not have heard of DVDs does not speak well for Mr. Fletcher's knowledge of the market, but then we suspect that when we see his store. I was once in a dirt-floored "store and bar" in a poor rural district of Ireland that had a stock of one (1) bottle of Guinness. Same idea.

One of the store's most loyal visitors and nuisances is Jerry (Jack Black), who works nearby in a garage. Paranoid about a power plant next door, he breaks in to sabotage it and is zapped with so much electricity he looks like a lightning strike during one of Victor Frankenstein's experiments. This does not turn him into a cinder, only magnetizes him, after which he visits the store and inadvertently erases all the tapes.

Crisis. What to do before Mr. Fletcher comes back? The tapes can't be replaced, because Mike and Jerry don't have the money and besides, how easy is it to get VHS tapes except on eBay? I take that back. Amazon lists six VHS tapes of *Ghostbusters*, one of the erased movies, for one (1) cent each. At that rate, you could build up a decent VHS library for a dollar. Anyway, the lads have a masterstroke: They will *reenact* the movies and rent them to unsuspecting customers like Miss Falewicz (Mia Farrow), who won't know the difference anyway. Costarring as their female leads in these movies is the fetching Alma (Melonie Diaz), who has the sexiest smile since Rosario Dawson.

The reenactments are not very skillful, to put it mildly, but they have the advantage, as Mike argues, of not taking up all your time because they're as short as twenty minutes. They explain that they import their versions from Sweden, which is why they call them *sweded.* You can see the works of Mike and Jerry on the Web, by the way, which might be about two-thirds as good as seeing the whole movie. One of the perhaps inevitable consequences of reenacting movies is that the exercise brings out all the latent manic excess within Jack Black, who when he is trying that hard reminds me of a dog I know named Mick Q. Broderick, who gets so excited when you come over you have to go to the dry cleaners after every visit.

Whether their scheme works, whether the store is saved, whether Hollywood considers their work homage or piracy, I will leave for you to discover. But you haven't read this far unless you hope to learn whether I would recommend the movie. Not especially. I felt positive and genial while watching it, but I didn't break out in paroxysms of laughter. It's the kind of amusing film you can wait to see on DVD. I wonder if it will come out on VHS?

Bella ★ ★ ★

PG-13, 91 m., 2007

Eduardo Verastegui (Jose), Tammy Blanchard (Nina), Manny Perez (Manny), Ali Landry (Celia), Angelica Aragon (Mother), Jaime Tirelli (Father), Ramon Rodriguez (Eduardo). Directed by Alejandro Monteverde and produced by Eduardo Verastegui, Leo Severino, Monteverde, and Denise Pinckley. Screenplay by Monteverde and Patrick Million.

Bella tells the story of two people who fall in love because of an unborn child. Winner of the Audience Award at Toronto 2006, it is a heart-tugger with the confidence not to tug too hard. It stars an actor named Eduardo Verastegui, whom I would describe as the next Antonio Banderas if I ever wrote clichés like that, which I do not. Tall, handsome, bearded, he plays Jose, the chef of his brother's Mexican restaurant in New York, until his life changes one day when his brother fires a waitress named Nina (Tammy Blanchard) for being late.

Jose and Nina are not a couple. All the same, he walks out of the kitchen, chases her into the subway, apologizes that his brother humiliated her in front of the staff, and finds out she was late because she is pregnant. Now what kind of a reason is that for being late? If I were in the habit of criticizing other critics, which I am not, I would quote Robert Koehler of *Variety,* who writes: "Nina, however, could easily have been to work on time, since her delay was due to her buying and using a home pregnancy test—something she rationally would have done after her shift was over." Uh, huh. And if Mr. Koehler feared he was pregnant, which would he do first? Buy and use a home pregnancy test or review *Bella*? I don't trust a review written by some guy who's wondering if he's pregnant.

Jose and Nina walk and talk, have lunch, share memories, and go to a restaurant where the owner, a friend of Jose's, offers to hire them both. Along the way, Jose tries to convince her to have the child. He is motivated by reasons that are fully explained in early premonitions and later flashbacks, which I will not reveal. Perhaps the clincher on his argument is provided by a visit to his mother and father (Angelica Aragon and Jaime Tirelli), whose warmth is a contrast to Nina's own wretched past.

Counterpoint is provided by Jose's brother, Manny (Manny Perez), who apparently was not as affected by the sunshine in his childhood home. He's a martinet and perfectionist, a taskmaster, heartless, and (as it turns out) incompetent to run his own kitchen. His attitude toward Nina's pregnancy is about as abstract as Robert Koehler's. Compare them to a man who is *bearing* a child. Remember Arnold Schwarzenegger in *Junior*, the movie where he was pregnant and said that merely scooping out the center of a honeydew melon gave him a *you know*.

I have failed to convey the charm of the movie. Eduardo Verastegui, despite sporting a beard so thick and black it makes him look like a nineteenth-century anarchist, has friendly eyes, a ready smile, and a natural grace in front of the camera that will soon have fans shifting their Banderas pinups to the bottom drawer. And Tammy Blanchard fits comfortably into the role of a woman who wants to do the right thing but feels alone, friendless, and broke. All she needs is someone to trust and she melts.

There is also a lot of cooking in the movie. Jungles of cilantro are chopped. The restaurant's staff luncheon features quail in a mole sauce. Verastegui looks like he knows what he's doing in the kitchen. His IMDb profile says he likes cooking, which I believe, although that's usually the desperation answer by people who can't think of anything they like. You sense a little of that, indeed, in his profile's next two sentences: He has a golden retriever; he likes golden retrievers. He stops short of liking to cook golden retrievers.

The movie is not deep and profound, but it's not stupid. It's about lovable people having important conversations and is not pro-choice or pro-life but simply in favor of his feelings—and hers, if she felt free to feel them. The movie is a little more lightweight than the usual Audience Award winner at Toronto (this year: Cronenberg's *Eastern Promises*), but why not? It was the best-liked film at the 2006 festival, and I can understand that.

Beowulf ★ ★ ★

PG-13, 114 m., 2007

Ray Winstone (Beowulf), Anthony Hopkins (King Hrothgar), John Malkovich (Unferth), Robin Wright Penn (Queen Wealthow), Brendan Gleeson (Wiglaf), Crispin Glover (Grendel), Alison Lohman (Ursula), Angelina Jolie (Grendel's mother). Directed by Robert Zemeckis and produced by Zemeckis, Steve Starkey, and Jack Rapke. Screenplay by Neil Gaiman and Roger Avary.

In the name of the mighty Odin, what this movie needs is an audience that knows how to laugh. Laugh, I tell you, laugh! Has the spirit of irony been lost in the land? By all the gods, if it were not for this blasted infirmity that the Fates have rendered me, you would have heard from me such thunderous roars as to shake the very Navy Pier itself down to its pillars in the clay.

To be sure, when I saw *Beowulf* in 3-D at the giant-screen IMAX theater, there were eruptions of snickers here and there, but for the most part the audience sat and watched the movie, not cheering, booing, hooting, recoiling, erupting, or doing anything else unmannerly. You expect complete silence and rapt attention when a nude Angelina Jolie emerges from the waters of an underground lagoon. But am I the only one who suspects that the *intention* of director Robert Zemeckis and writers Neil Gaiman and Roger Avary was satirical?

Truth in criticism: I am not sure Angelina Jolie was nude. Oh, her character was nude, all right, except for the shimmering gold plating that obscured certain crucial areas, but was she Angelina Jolie? Zemeckis, who directed the wonderful *Polar Express*, has employed a much more realistic version of the same animation technology in *Beowulf*. We are not looking at flesh-and-blood actors but special effects that look uncannily convincing, even though I am reasonably certain that Angelina Jolie does not have spike-heeled feet. That's right: feet, not shoes.

The movie uses the English epic poem, circa AD 700, as its starting point and resembles the original in that it uses a lot of the same names. It takes us to the Danish kingdom of King Hrothgar (Anthony Hopkins), where the king and his court have gathered to inaugurate a new mead hall, built for the purpose of drinking gallons of mead. The old hall was destroyed by the monster Grendel, whose wretched life consists of being the ugliest creature on earth and destroying mead halls.

To this court comes the heroic Geatsman named Beowulf (Ray Winstone), who in the manner of a Gilbert and Sullivan hero is forever making boasts about himself. He is the very model of a medieval monster slayer. (A Geatsman comes from an area of today's Sweden named Gotaland, which translates, Wikipedia helpfully explains, as "land of the Geats.") When the king offers his comely queen, Wealthow (Robin Wright Penn), as a prize if Beowulf slays Grendel, the hero immediately strips naked, because if Grendel wears no clothes, then he won't, either. This leads to a great deal of well-timed Austinpowerism, which translates (Wikipedia does not explain) as "putting things in the foreground to keep us from seeing the family jewels." Grendel arrives on schedule to tear down the mead hall, and there is a mighty battle, which is rendered in gory and gruesome detail, right down to cleaved skulls and severed limbs.

Now when I say, for example, that Sir Anthony plays Hrothgar, or John Malkovich plays Beowulf's rival Unferth, you are to understand that they supply voices and the physical performances for animated characters who look more or less like they do. (Crispin Glover, however, does not look a thing like Grendel, and if you are familiar with the great British character actor Ray Winstone, you will suspect he doesn't have six-pack abs.) *Variety* reports that Paramount has entered *Beowulf* in the Academy's best animated film category, which means nothing is really there, realistic as it may occasionally appear. I saw the movie in IMAX 3-D, as I said, and like all 3-D movies, it spends a lot of time throwing things at the audience: spears, blood, arms, legs, bodies, tables, heads, mead, and so forth. The movie is also showing in non-IMAX 3-D, and in the usual 2-D. Not bad for a one-dimensional story.

But I'm not complaining. I'm serious when I say the movie is funny. Some of the dialogue sounds like Monty Python. No, most of the dialogue does. "I didn't hear him coming," a wench tells a warrior. "You'll hear me," he promises. Grendel is ugly beyond all meaning. His battles are violent beyond all possibility. His mother (Jolie) is like a beauty queen in centerfold heaven. Her own final confrontation with Beowulf beggars description. To say the movie is over the top assumes you can see the top from here.

Now about the PG-13 rating. How can a movie be rated PG-13 when it has female nudity? I'll tell you how. Because Angelina Jolie *is not really there*. And because there are no four-letter words. Even Jolie has said she's surprised by the rating; the British gave it a 12A certificate, which means you can be a year younger and see it over there. But no, Jolie won't be taking her children, she told the BBC: "It's remarkable it has the rating it has. It's quite an extraordinary film, and some of it shocked me."

Here's the exact wording from the MPAA's code people: "Classified PG-13 for intense sequences of violence including disturbing images, some sexual material and nudity." How does that compare with a PG rating? Here's the MPAA's wording on *Bee Movie*: "Classified PG for mild suggestive humor and a brief depiction of smoking." I have news for them. If I were thirteen, Angelina Jolie would be plenty nude enough for me in this movie, animated or not. If I were twelve and British, who knows? ☞

The Best of Youth ★ ★ ★ ★

R, 366 m., 2005

Luigi Lo Cascio (Nicola Carati), Alessio Boni (Matteo Carati), Adriana Asti (Adriana Carati), Sonia Bergamasco (Giulia Monfalco), Fabrizio Gifuni (Carlo Tommasi), Maya Sansa (Mirella Utano), Valentina Carnelutti (Francesca Carati),

Jasmine Trinca (Giorgia), Andrea Tidona (Angelo Carati), Lidia Vitale (Giovanna Carati). Directed by Marco Tullio Giordana and produced by Angelo Barbagallo. Screenplay by Sandro Petraglia and Stefano Rulli.

Every review of *The Best of Youth* begins with the information that it is six hours long. No good movie is too long, just as no bad movie is short enough. I dropped outside of time and was carried along by the narrative flow; when the film was over, I had no particular desire to leave the theater, and would happily have stayed another three hours. The two-hour limit on most films makes them essentially short stories. *The Best of Youth* is a novel.

The film is ambitious. It wants no less than to follow two brothers and the people in their lives from 1963 to 2000, following them from Rome to Norway to Turin to Florence to Palermo and back to Rome again. The lives intersect with the politics and history of Italy during the period: the hippies, the ruinous flood in Florence, the Red Brigades, kidnappings, hard times and layoffs at Fiat, and finally a certain peace for some of the characters, and for their nation.

The brothers are Nicola and Matteo Carati (Luigi Lo Cascio and Alessio Boni). We meet their parents, Angelo (Andrea Tidona) and Adriana (Adriana Asti), their older sister, Giovanna (Lidia Vitale), and their kid sister, Francesca (Valentina Carnelutti). And we meet their friends, their lovers, and others who drift through, including a mental patient whose life seems to follow in parallel.

As the film opens, Nicola has qualified as a doctor and Matteo is still taking literature classes. Matteo, looking for a job, has been hired as a "logotherapist"—literally, a person who takes mental patients for walks. One of the women he walks with is Giorgia (Jasmine Trinca), who is beautiful, deeply wounded by electroshock therapy, and afraid of the world. On the spur of the moment, Matteo decides to spring her from the institution and take her along when he and Nicola take a summer trip to the "end of the world," the tip of Norway.

Giorgia is found by the police but has the presence of mind to protect the brothers. Nicola continues on his journey and gets a job as a lumberjack, and Matteo returns to Rome and, impulsively, joins the army. They are to meet again in Florence, where catastrophic floods have drowned the city. Nicola is a volunteer, Matteo is a soldier assigned to the emergency effort, and in the middle of the mud and ruins Nicola hears a young woman playing a piano that has been left in the middle of the street.

This is Giulia (Sonia Bergamasco). Their eyes meet and lock, and so do their destinies. They live together without marrying, and have a daughter, Sara. Giulia is drawn into a secret Red Brigade cell. She draws apart from her family. One night she packs to leave the house. He tries to block her way, then lets her go. She disappears into the terrorist underground.

Matteo meanwhile joins the police, takes an assignment in Sicily because no one else wants to go there, and meets a photographer in a café. This is Mirella (Maya Sansa). She wants to be a librarian, and he advises her to work at a beautiful library in Rome. Years later, he walks into the library and sees her for the second time in his life. They become lovers, but there is a great unexplained rage within Matteo, maybe also self-hatred, and he will not allow anyone very close.

Enough about the plot. These people, all of them, will meet again—even Giorgia, who is found by Nicola in the most extraordinary circumstances, and who will cause a meeting that no one in the movie could have anticipated, because neither person involved knows the other exists. Because of the length of the film, the director, Marco Tullio Giordana, has time and space to work with, and we get a tangible sense of the characters growing older, learning about themselves, dealing with hardship. The journey of Giulia, the radical, is the most difficult and in some ways the most touching. The way Nicola finally finds happiness is particularly satisfying because it takes him so long to realize that it is right there before him for the taking.

The film must have deep resonances for Italians, where it was made for national television; because of its politics, sexuality, and grown-up characters, it would be impossible on American networks. It is not easy on Italy. As he is graduating from medical school, Nicola is advised by his professor: "Do you have any ambition? Then leave Italy. Go to London, Paris, America if you can. Italy is a beautiful country. But it is a place to die, run by dinosaurs." Nicola asks the professor why he stays. "I'm one of the dinosaurs."

Nicola stays. Another who stays is his brother-in-law, who is marked for kidnapping and assassination but won't leave, "because then they will have won." There is a scene where he stands in front of windows late at night and we feel real dread for him. With the politics and the personal drama there is also the sense of a nation that beneath the turbulent surface is deeply supportive of its citizens. Some of that is sensed through the lives of the parents of the Carati family: The father busies himself with optimistic schemes; the mother meets a grandchild who brings joy into her old age.

It is a luxury to be enveloped in a good film, and to know there's a lot more of it—that it is not moving inexorably toward an ending you can anticipate, but moving indefinitely into a future that is free to be shaped in surprising ways. When you hear that it is six hours long, reflect that it is therefore also six hours deep.

Bewitched ★ ★ ½

PG-13, 100 m., 2005

Nicole Kidman (Isabel Bigelow), Will Ferrell (Jack Wyatt), Shirley MacLaine (Iris Smythson), Michael Caine (Nigel Bigelow), Jason Schwartzman (Richie), Kristin Chenoweth (Maria Kelly), Heather Burns (Nina), Steve Carell (Uncle Arthur), Stephen Colbert (Stu Robison). Directed by Nora Ephron and produced by Nora Ephron, Penny Marshall, Douglas Wick, and Lucy Fisher. Screenplay by Nora Ephron and Delia Ephron.

One of the many areas in which I am spectacularly ill-informed is prime-time television. You would be amazed at the numbers of sitcoms I have never seen, not even once. When you see 500 movies a year, you don't have a lot of leftover yearning for watching television. In the evenings, you involve yourself in more human pursuits. On TV you watch the news, talk shows, or old movies. You don't watch sports unless your team is in the finals. You can sense I am edging up to the admission that I have never seen a single episode of *Bewitched*. I knew it existed, however, because of my reading.

That makes me well prepared to review the movie *Bewitched*, since I have nothing to compare it with and have to take it on its own terms. It is tolerably entertaining. Many of its parts work, although not together. Will Ferrell and Nicole Kidman are funny and likable, but they're in a plot that doesn't allow them to aim for the same ending with the same reason. It's one of those movies where you smile and laugh and are reasonably entertained, but you get no sense of a mighty enterprise sweeping you along with its comedic force. There is not a movie here. Just scenes in search of one.

The joke is this: Will Ferrell plays Jack Wyatt, a movie star whose career has hit bottom. Sales of his last DVD: zero. In desperation he turns to television and finds himself considered for a starring role in a revival of *Bewitched*. He will play the Darrin role. At least that's what everyone says. I assume Darrin was a character on the original show. I know (from my reading) that the show's interest centered on Samantha, who was played by Elizabeth Montgomery. I know from the movie that Samantha had a way of twitching her nose that was very special, and that they can't find an actress with twitchability until Jack spots Isabel Bigelow (Nicole Kidman) in Book Soup on Sunset.

He insists on using her in the role because (a) he wants a complete unknown, so he'll get all the attention, (b) the twitch, and (c) already he is falling in love with her. What he doesn't realize, oh, delicious irony, is that Isabel is in fact a real witch. She has, however, just decided to move to the Valley, get a house with a VW Bug in the garage, live a normal life, and find a guy who loves her for herself and not because she put a hex on him. Her father (Michael Caine) warns her that this dream is not possible, and indeed she has a lot of trouble giving up witchcraft. It's so tempting to charge your purchases on a Tarot card.

The movie has been directed by Nora Ephron *(Sleepless in Seattle, You've Got Mail)*, and written by her with her sister Delia. They have a lot of cute scenes. I like the way they make Jack Wyatt an egotistical monster who wants three trailers, star billing, and cake every Wednesday. He's hysterically in love with himself. His ego is, of course, no match for Samantha, who can make him act in Spanish if she wants to. Occasionally when things go wrong she rewinds the arrow of time, although even after a rewind, it's a funny thing: Something magical happens anyway.

The movie has fun with Ferrell on the star trip, and fun with Kidman's love-hate relationship with magic. It has a lot of good supporting work, including Jason Schwartzman as Jack's desperate agent, and Shirley MacLaine as Samantha's mother (her theory on actors: "Sometimes, deep down, there is no deep down"). If you watch *The Daily Show* you'll enjoy cameos by Stephen Colbert and Steve Carell. It might have been a good idea to bring in Samantha Bee, too, and have her interview Jack Wyatt ("You're staring at my boobs!").

Will Ferrell has become a major star in almost no time at all. One moment he was a *Saturday Night Live* veteran who had played backup in a lot of movies, and the next moment he had made *Old School* and *Elf* and *Anchorman* and *Melinda and Melinda* and had *The Producers* on the way, and he was bigtime. One reason for that is, you like the guy. He has a brawny, take-no-prisoners style of comedy that suggests he's having a lot of fun.

Nicole Kidman, on the other hand, is an actor with more notes in her repertoire (maybe Ferrell could have played a role in *The Hours,* but that remains to be seen). Here, she is fetching and somehow more relaxed than usual as Samantha, and makes witchcraft seem like a bad habit rather than a cosmic force.

But what are they doing in the same movie? You have two immovable objects or two irresistible forces. Both characters are complete, right off the shelf. There's no room for them to move. Yes, Jack becomes a nicer guy after he falls in love, and yes, Samantha realizes that magic is sometimes just not fair. But they are separate at the beginning and essentially still self-contained at the end, and the movie never works them both into the same narrative logic. Still, that's a great moment when Jack shouts: "Guys! Make me 200 cappuccinos! Bring me the best one!"

Bigger, Stronger, Faster ★ ★ ★ ½

PG-13, 106 m., 2008

A documentary directed by Christopher Bell and produced by Alex Buono, Tasmin Rawady, and Jim Czarnecki. Screenplay by Bell, Buono, and Rawady

Midway through watching Chris Bell's *Bigger, Stronger, Faster,* I started to think about another film I'd seen recently. The Bell documentary is about the use of steroids in sports and bodybuilding. The other film is Darryl Roberts's *America the Beautiful,* about the guilt some women feel because they don't look like the models in fashion magazines. The steroid users want to be bigger. The weight-obsessed women want to be thinner. The Roberts doc focuses on Gerren Taylor, who at twelve achieved fame as a child who looked like an adult fashion model. A year later, she was dropped by those who cast for runway models, but she tried to make a comeback. At thirteen.

Bell is one of three brothers. They've all used steroids, and two still do. Mike ("Mad Dog") Bell had some success in pro wrestling but never as the star, always as the scripted loser. Wrestling has dropped him, but he's still in training, even though he's now "too old," he's told. "I was born to attain greatness," he tells Chris, "and I'm the only one that's holding myself back."

The third Bell brother, Mark ("Smelly") Bell, has promised his wife he will stop taking steroids after he achieves his dream of powerlifting seven hundred pounds. He attains it, but later tells Chris he will use steroids again. Chris tells him, "I'm afraid you'll lose your job, your wife, and yourself." Smelly replies, "If I lose my job and my wife, what else do I have but myself?" Both of Chris's brothers are remarkably frank in talking to him, as are his parents, who are "opposed to steroids" but are red-faced with cheering after Smelly lifts the weights.

Bell uses a clip from the movie *Patton,* in which the famous general addresses his troops: "Americans love a winner and will not tolerate a loser." That is the bottom line of *Bigger, Stronger, Faster.* We say we're opposed to steroids, but we're more opposed to losing. Steroids are not nearly as dangerous as amphetamines, he points out, but the United States is the only nation that *requires* its fighter pilots to use amphetamines. They may be harmful, but they work.

This movie is remarkable in that it seems to be interested only in facts. I was convinced that Bell was interviewing people who knew a lot about steroids, and the weight of scientific, medical, and psychological opinion seems to be that steroids are not particularly dangerous. Is the movie "pro-steroid"? Yes, but it is even more against the win-win mentality. We demand that our athletes bring home victories, and yet to compete on a level playing field, they feel they have to use the juice.

The movie goes against the drumbeat of anti-steroid publicity, news reports, and congressional hearings to say that steroids are not only generally safe but have been around longer and been used more widely than most people know. Bell and his brothers grew up pudgy in a Poughkeepsie family, were mesmerized by early heroes like Hulk Hogan, Rambo, and Conan the Barbarian, got into weight-lifting, and still have muscular physiques. They all used muscles as a powerful boost to their self-esteem.

But think for a second. *America the Beautiful* quotes this statistic: "Three minutes of looking at a fashion magazine makes 90 percent of women of all ages feel depressed, guilty, and shameful." I don't have similar statistics about bodybuilders, but I assume they study the muscle magazines with similar feelings. Those who cannot be too thin or too muscular are attracted to opposite extremes but use the same reasoning: By pursuing an ideal that is almost unattainable and may be dangerous to their health, they believe they will be admired, successful, the object of envy.

Bell interviews some bodybuilders who are over fifty, maybe sixty, and still "in training." The words "in training" suggest that a competition is approaching, but they're in training against themselves. Against their body's desire to pump less iron, eat different foods, process fewer proteins, and, in general, find moderation. Anorexia represents one extreme of this reasoning. At another extreme is Gregg Valentino, who has the world's largest biceps; they look like sixteen-inch softballs straining against his skin. He makes fun of himself: He walks into a club and no chick is gonna go for that, "but the dudes come over." There are men who envy him.

What's sad is that success in both fashion and bodybuilding is so limiting. For every Arnold Schwarzenegger, who used the Mr. Universe crown to catapult himself into movie and political stardom, there are hundreds, thousands who spend their lives "in training." When a model gets thin enough (few do, especially in their own minds), they must spend their lives staying that thin.

The question vibrating below the surface of both docs is, has America become maddened by the need for victory? When our team is in the World Series, do we seriously give a damn what the home run kings have injected? We are devout in Congress, but heathens in the grandstands. That is one of Bell's messages, and the other is that steroids have become demonized far beyond their actual danger to society. Which side do you vote on? Chris Bell marks his ballot twice: Steroids are not very harmful, but by using them, we reveal a disturbing value system.

Black Snake Moan ★ ★ ★

R, 116 m., 2007

Samuel L. Jackson (Lazarus), Christina Ricci (Rae), Justin Timberlake (Ronnie), S. Epatha Merkerson (Angela), John Cothran Jr. (R.L.). Directed by Craig Brewer and produced by John Singleton and Stephanie Allain. Screenplay by Brewer.

I had never really heard many half snorts before. Snorts, yes, and silence. But what do you make of an audience that has no idea how to react? *Black Snake Moan* is the most peculiar movie I've seen about sex and race and redemption in the Deep South. It may be the most peculiar recent movie ever except for *Road House*, but then what can you say about *Road House*? Such movies defy all categories.

The movie—I will try to be concise—stars Samuel L. Jackson as a broken-down blues musician and vegetable market gardener whose wife has just walked out. On the road leading to his property, he finds a battered young white girl, whose injuries hardly seem curable by the cough syrup he barters fresh vegetables for at the drugstore. The girl is Rae (Christina Ricci); it is no coincidence that Jackson's character is named Lazarus, and Lazarus determines to return her from near death or whooping cough, one or the other. No saint himself, he wants to redeem her from a life of sluttery.

His technique, with a refreshing directness, is to chain her to a radiator. Good thing he lives way out in the wilderness. Lazarus and Rae have no sex per se, but they do a powerful lot of slapping, cursing, and chain rattling, and the reaction of the blue-collar town on Market Day is a study. I think the point is that they somehow redeem each other through these grotesqueries, a method I always urge be used with extreme caution.

The performances are very good: hell-bent for leather and better than the material deserves. There is much hysteria and snot. The writer-director, Craig Brewer, made that other splendid story of prostitution and redemption, *Hustle and Flow,* with its Oscar-winning song ("It's Hard Out Here for a Pimp"). In fact, I pretty much enjoyed the whole movie, with some incredulity and a few half snorts.

Both *Black Snake Moan* and *Hustle and Flow* are about neglected characters living on the fringe who find a healing in each other. Both movies use a great deal of music to illustrate the souls of their characters.

We sense that the girl has never been treated other than in a beastly manner, and that the man, having lost his wife, is determined not to allow sex to betray his instincts to do good. Yes, I think it is probably against the law to chain a drifter to a radiator, but in a sense these people exist outside the law, society, and common or any kind of sense. Their society consists of the usual locals who seem clueless and remarkably unobservant, leading to remarkable non sequiturs.

There is another woman, the middle-aged pharmacist Angela, played by the sweet S. Epatha Merkerson, to provide Lazarus an alternative to a life of sluts and tramps. But, as for Rae—well, I gather that when compulsive nymphomania passes a certain point, you're simply lost.

After Rae says good-bye to her boyfriend Ronnie (played by Justin Timberlake), who has enlisted in the service for cloudy reasons, she immediately falls to the ground and starts writhing as if under attack by fire ants. This is her way of conveying uncontrollable orgiastic need. A girl that needy, you'd approach like Miss RoboCop.

I love the way that both Samuel Jackson and Christina Ricci take chances like this, and the way Brewer creates characters of unbelievable forbearance, like Ronnie, who is in a more or less constant state of panic attacks and compulsion. And I like the understated way the rural Tennessee locations are used. You have never seen a movie like this before. Then again, you may not hope to. Some good blues music helps carry the day.

I heard some days after the screening that Jackson considers this his best performance. Well, maybe it is. He disappears into the role, and a good performance requires energy, daring, courage, and intensity, which he supplies in abundance. Few actors could accomplish work at this level with this screenplay. As for Christina Ricci, she was the right actor for this role; she embodies this poor, mixed-up creature and lets you experience both her pain and her hope. Her work defines the boundaries of the thankless.

Blame It on Fidel ★ ★ ★ ½

NO MPAA RATING, 100 m., 2007

Julie Depardieu (Marie), Stefano Accorsi (Fernando), Nina Kervel (Anna), Benjamin Feuillet (Francois), Martine Chevallier (Grandmother), Olivier Perrier (Grandfather). Directed by Julie Gavras and produced by Sylvie Pialat. Screenplay by Gavras, based on the novel by Domitilla Calamai.

Anna is a privileged and happy child, until one day when her parents radically change their style of living. This does not suit her. Like all children, she is profoundly conservative—not in a political way, but by demanding continuity and predictability in her life. One day she lives in a big house with a lovely garden, and the next she and her little brother are suddenly yanked into a grotty flat filled with bearded, chain-smoking young men.

It is 1970 in Paris, at a time of social change. What has happened is that her middle-class parents have become radicalized. Her Spanish father, Fernando (Stefano Accorsi), sufferers from guilt because his family cooperates with Franco's fascist regime, but his sister and her husband are communists. After the husband is arrested and destined to who knows what terrors from the police, Fernando and his

French wife, Marie (Julie Depardieu), go to Spain, help his sister and niece escape, and come home as left-wing activists. Their idealism causes them to move into more humble working-class quarters and join forces with a group of Chilean exiles working for the election of the reformer Salvador Allende.

Anna (Nina Kervel) understands all of this only dimly. What she knows is that her world is out of order and her parents are acting oddly. She loves going to a Catholic school but is taken out of the religion class. She loves comic books but is informed that Mickey Mouse is a fascist. She doesn't like opening her bedroom door and seeing strangers at all hours of the day and night. She is very displeased, and young Kervel, who was around nine when the film was made, gives an astonishing performance, showing that in some ways she is more mature than her parents.

She has an instinctive logic that won't accept all their instructions. Lectured on *group solidarity,* she decides to practice it one day in school. When the nun asks a question and Anna knows the answer, she nevertheless raises her hand along with all the other students, who are wrong. She knows they are wrong, I think, and this is her way of pointing out a flaw in the solidarity theory. Another day she is more specific, asking innocently how group solidarity differs from the behavior of sheep.

In the scenes in which Anna figures, the film is shot almost exclusively from her eye level. This is particularly effective when her parents take her along on a political demonstration, and what she sees are blue jeans, running shoes, and tear gas. It is foolhardy to take a kid to a potentially violent demonstration and foolish of her parents to think she must be instantly radicalized. But they do love her, and so do her grandparents, and so do the nannies who seem to come and go. (One of them, a Cuban refugee, confides in Anna that the communists are barbarians.)

The movie involves the adult children of two famous filmmakers. Its director, Julie Gavras, is the daughter of the Greek director Costa-Gavras, who made *Z, State of Siege,* and other pro-revolutionary films. Interesting to speculate that the screenplay, although based on an Italian novel by Domitilla Calamai, may in some respects reflect the director's own girlhood. And Marie, Anna's mother, is played by Julie Depardieu, daughter of Gerard. Was Julie's father also mercurial, zealous, and changeable, but loving? And were the childhood homes of both women filled with wine-drinking strangers night after night?

It is a blessing that *Blame It on Fidel* doesn't pull back to answer such questions but focuses resolutely on the world as seen through nine-year-old eyes. Kids don't care if millions are starving in South America nearly as much as they care that three-course family meals have been replaced by weird-looking casseroles. They don't care if there is a God or not nearly as much as they like the nun who teaches divinity class. They're not thrilled that their parents are away in Spain or Chile fighting evil; they want them at home every night. And no matter what Anna is told, she knows these things are true and will not be swayed.

The film contains a surprising amount of understated humor. It is not a grim portrayal of a harsh upbringing, but an affectionate portrait of parents who will be able to change the world before they will be able to change their daughter. Anna and her parents continue to love one another above all, and so this is not an angry film but a wry and observant one. It could have been worse for Anna; consider Sidney Lumet's *Running on Empty* (1988), about the family of radical underground members in hiding. Anna's parents haven't bombed anyone, although they do circulate a lot of petitions.

Born into Brothels: Calcutta's Red Light Kids ★ ★ ★ ½

R, 85 m., 2005

A documentary directed and produced by Zana Briski and Ross Kauffman.

In a movie named *The Five Obstructions,* the Danish director Lars von Trier creates an ordeal for his mentor, Jorgen Leth. The older director will have to remake a short film in five different ways, involving five obstructions that von Trier will devise. One of the five involves making a film in "the most miserable place on Earth," which they decide is the red-light district of Mumbai. The director is unable to deal with this assignment.

Now here is a documentary made in a place that is by definition as miserable: the red-light district of Calcutta. I thought of the Danish film as I was watching this one, because the makers of *Born into Brothels: Calcutta's Red Light Kids* also find it almost impossible to make. They are shooting in an area where no one wants to be photographed, where lives are hidden behind doors or curtains, where with their western features and cameras they are as obvious as the police, and indeed suspected of working for them.

Zana Briski, an American photographer, and Ross Kauffman, her collaborator, went to Calcutta to film prostitution and found that it melted out of sight as they appeared. It was all around them, it put them in danger, but it was invisible to their camera. What they did see were the children, because the kids of the district followed the visitors, fascinated. Briski hit upon the idea of giving cameras to these children of prostitutes and asking them to take photos of the world in which they lived.

It is a productive idea and has a precedent of sorts in a 1993 project by National Public Radio in Chicago; two teenagers, LeAlan Jones and Lloyd Newman, were given tape recorders and asked to make an audio documentary of the Ida B. Wells public housing project, where they lived and where a young child had been thrown from a high window in a fight over candy. Their work won a Peabody Award.

The kids in *Born into Brothels* (which won the 2005 Oscar) take photos with zest and imagination, squint at the contact sheets to choose their favorite shots, and mark them with crayons. Their pictures capture life, and kinds of beauty and squalor that depend on each other. One child, Avijit, is so gifted he wins a week's trip to Amsterdam for an exhibition of photography by children.

Over a couple of years, Briski teaches photo classes and meets some of the parents of the children—made difficult because she must work through interpreters. Prostitution in this district is not a choice but a settled way of life. We meet a grandmother, mother, and daughter, the adults engaged in prostitution, and the granddaughter seems destined to join them. Curiously, the movie does not suggest that the boys will also be used as prostitutes, although it seems inevitable. The age of entry into prostitution seems to be puberty. There are no scenes that could be described as sexually explicit, partly because of the filmmakers' tact in not wanting to exploit their subjects, partly no doubt because the prostitutes refused to be filmed except in innocuous settings.

Briski becomes determined to get several of the children out of the district and into a boarding school, where they will have a chance at different lives. She encounters opposition from their parents and roadblocks from the Indian bureaucracy, which seems to create jobs by requiring the same piece of paper to be meaninglessly stamped, marked, read, or filed in countless different offices. She goes almost mad trying to get a passport for Avijit, the winner of the Amsterdam trip; of course with his background he lacks the "required" papers.

The film is narrated mostly by Briski, who is a good teacher and brings out the innate intelligence of the children as they use their cameras to see their world in a different way. The faces of the children are heartbreaking, because we reflect that in the time since the film was finished, most of them have lost childhood forever, some their lives. Far away offscreen is the prosperous India with middle-class enclaves, an executive class, and a booming economy. These wretched poor exist in a separate and parallel universe, without an exit.

The movie is a record by well-meaning people who try to make a difference for the better, and succeed to a small degree while all around them the horror continues unaffected. Yes, a few children stay in boarding schools. Others are taken out by their parents, drop out, or are asked to leave. The red-light district has existed for centuries and will exist for centuries more. I was reminded of a scene in Buñuel's *Viridiana*. A man is disturbed by the sight of a dog tied to a wagon and being dragged along faster than it can run. The man buys the dog to free it but does not notice, in the background, another cart pulling another dog.

Bottle Shock ★ ★ ★ ½

PG-13, 112 m., 2008

Alan Rickman (Steven Spurrier), Chris Pine (Bo Barrett), Bill Pullman (Jim Barrett), Rachael Taylor (Sam), Freddy Rodriguez (Gustavo Brambilia), Dennis Farina (Maurice), Bradley

Whitford (Professor Saunders), Miguel Sandoval (Mr. Garcia), Eliza Dushku (Joe). Directed by Randall Miller and produced by J. Todd Harris. Screenplay by Jody Savin, Miller, and Ross Schwartz.

In 1976, the year of the American bicentennial, the tall ships sailed from Europe to America and back again. But a smaller event was, in its way, no less impressive. In a blind taste-testing held in France, the wines of California's Napa Valley defeated the best the French had to offer—and all the judges were French! A bottle of the winning American vintage, it is said, now rests on exhibit in the Smithsonian Institution.

Bottle Shock is a charming fictionalized version of the victory, "based," as they love to say, "on a true story." Shot in locations near the locale of *Sideways* but set much closer to the earth, it tells the story of a struggling vineyard named Chateau Montelena, deeply in debt with three bank loans. It's run by the hard-driving Jim Barrett (Bill Pullman), who despairs of his layabout, long-haired son Bo (Chris Pine).

Meanwhile, in Paris, we meet a British wine lover named Steven Spurrier (Alan Rickman), whose tiny wine shop is grandly named The Academy of Wine. We never see a single customer in the shop, only the constant visits of a neighboring travel agent, Maurice (Dennis Farina, in full Chicago accent). Maurice encourages Steven by praising his wines, which he samples freely while passing out business advice.

Spurrier (yes, a real man) has been hearing about the wines of California and has an inspiration: His grand-sounding "academy" will sponsor a blind taste test between the wines of the two countries. That he is able to gather a panel of expert judges says much for the confidence of the French, who should have realized it was a dangerous proposition.

In Napa, we meet two other major players: A pretty summer intern named Sam (Rachael Taylor) and an employee of Jim's named Gustavo Brambilia (Freddy Rodriguez—yes, another real character). Gustavo has wine in his bones, if such a thing is possible, and would go on to found a famous vineyard. The two boys raise cash by Gustavo's (partially true) ability to identify any wine and vintage by tasting it, and of course they both fall in love with Sam, who lives for the summer in a shack out of *The Grapes of Wrath.*

The outcome is predictable; anyone who cares even casually knows the Yanks won, but the director milks great entertainment, if not actual suspense, out of the competition. Much of its effect is due to the precise, quietly comic performance by Alan Rickman as Spurrier. "Why do I hate you?" asks Jim Barrett, who resists the competition. "Because you think I'm an asshole," Spurrier replies calmly. "Actually, I'm not an asshole. It's just that I'm British, and, well . . . you're not."

We see him navigating the back roads of Napa in a rented Gremlin, selecting wines for his competition and getting around U.S. customs by convincing twenty-six fellow air travelers to each carry a bottle back for him. That the momentous competition actually took place, that it shook the wine world to its foundations, that it was repeated twenty years later, is a story many people are vaguely familiar with. But *Bottle Shock* is more than the story. It is also about people who love their work, care about it with passion, and talk about it with knowledge. Did you know that a thirsty, struggling vine produces the best wines? It can't just sit there sipping water. It has to struggle—just like Chateau Montelena.

Note: Read the credits to find out how the movie fudges a few names, facts, and vineyards—and what happened to Gustavo.

The Bourne Ultimatum ★ ★ ★ ½

PG-13, 115 m., 2007

Matt Damon (Jason Bourne), Julia Stiles (Nicky Parsons), David Strathairn (Noah Vosen), Scott Glenn (Ezra Kramer), Paddy Considine (Simon Ross), Edgar Ramirez (Paz), Albert Finney (Dr. Albert Hirsch), Joan Allen (Pam Lundy). Directed by Paul Greengrass and produced by Patrick Crowley, Frank Marshall, and Paul Sandberg. Screenplay by Tony Gilroy, Scott Z. Burns, and George Nolfi, based on the novel by Robert Ludlum.

Run, Jason, run. The Bourne films have taken chases beyond a storytelling technique and made them into the story. Jason Bourne's search for the secret of his identity doesn't involve me in pulsating empathy for his dilemma, but as a MacGuffin, it's a doozy. Some guy finds himself with a fake identity, wants to know who he really is, and spends three movies finding out at breakneck speed. And if the ending of *The Bourne Ultimatum* means anything at all, he may need another movie to clear up the loose ends.

That said, so what? If I don't care what Jason Bourne's real name is, and believe me, I sincerely do not, then I enjoy the movies simply for what they are: skillful exercises in high-tech effects and stunt work, stringing together one preposterous chase after another in a collection of world cities, with Jason apparently piling up frequent flier miles between them.

Ultimatum is a tribute to Bourne's determination, his driving skills, his intelligence in outthinking his masters, and especially his good luck. No real person would be able to survive what happens to him in this movie, for the obvious reason that he would have been killed very early in *The Bourne Identity* (2002) and never have survived to make *The Bourne Supremacy* (2004). That Matt Damon can make this character more convincing than the Road Runner is a tribute to his talent and dedication. It's not often you find a character you care about even if you don't believe he could exist.

This time Bourne is engaged in a desperate hunt through, alphabetically, London, Madrid, Moscow, New York, Paris, Tangier, and Turin, while secret CIA operatives in America track him by a perplexing array of high-tech gadgets and techniques. I know Google claims it will soon be able to see the wax in your ear, but how does the CIA pinpoint Bourne so precisely and yet fail again and again and again to actually nab him? You'd think he was bin Laden.

And why do they want him so urgently? Yes, he is proof that the CIA runs a murderous secret extra-legal black-ops branch that violates laws here and abroad, but the response to that is: D'oh! The CIA operation, previously called Treadstone, is now called Blackbriar. That'll cover their tracks. It's like if you wanted to conceal the Ford plant you'd call it Maytag. Seeking a hidden meaning in the names, I looked up Treadstone on Wiktionary.com and found it is a "fictional top-secret program of the Central Intelligence Agency in the Jason Bourne book and movie series." Looking up Blackbriar, I found nothing. So they are hidden again from the Wik empire.

In his desperate run to find the people who are chasing him, Jason hooks up in Madrid with the CIA's Nicky Parsons (Julia Stiles), who is given several dozen words to say with somber gravity before Jason is off to Algiers and running through windows and living rooms in the Casbah; I think I recognized some of the same steep streets from *Pepe le Moko,* which is a movie about just staying in the Casbah and hiding there, a strategy by which Jason could have avoided a lot of property damage.

Of course there are sensational car chases, improbable leaps over high places, clever double-reverses, and lightning decisions. The crashes all look fatal, but Bourne survives (funny; I don't remember any air bags being deployed). Sometimes we cut back to CIA headquarters (although surely a secret CIA black-op would not be hidden in its own headquarters) and meet agent Pamela Lundy (Joan Allen), who suspects maybe there is something to be said on Jason's behalf, and her boss, Noah Vosen (David Strathairn), who must have inherited hatred of Bourne as part of the agency's institutional legacy, since he wasn't in the first two movies. And then finally, that shadowy nightmare figure in Bourne's flashbacks comes into focus and, in the time-honored tradition of the Talking Killer, explains everything instead of whacking him right then and there. After which there is another chase.

The director, masterminding formidable effects and stunt teams, is Paul Greengrass (*United 93, Bourne Supremacy*), and he not only creates (or seems to create) amazingly long takes, but does it without calling attention to them. Whether they actually are unbroken stretches of film or are spliced together by invisible wipes, what counts is that they present such mind-blowing action that I forgot to keep track. There are two kinds of long takes: (1) the kind you're supposed to notice, as in Scorsese's *GoodFellas,* when the mobster enters the restaurant, and (2) the kind you don't notice because the action makes them invisible. Both have their purpose: Scorsese wanted to show how the world unfolded before his hero, and Greengrass wants to show the action without interruption to reinforce the illusion it is all actually happening. Most other long takes are just showing off.

But why, if I liked the movie so much, am I going on like this? Because the movie is complete as itself. You sit there, and the action assaults you, and using words to re-create it would be futile. What actually happens to Jason Bourne is essentially immaterial. What matters is that *something* must happen so he can run away from it, or toward it. Which leads us back to the MacGuffin theory. ☞

The Boys of Baraka ★ ★ ★

NO MPAA RATING, 84 m., 2006

Featuring Devon Brown, Darius Chambers, Richard Keyser, Justin Mackall, Montrey Moore, and Romesh Vance. A documentary produced and directed by Heidi Ewing and Rachel Grady.

Here is a movie that makes you want to do something. Cry, or write a check, or howl with rage. It tells the story of twenty "high-risk" inner-city black boys, twelve and thirteen years old, who are lifted out of the Baltimore school system and given scholarships to the Baraka School. Where is Baraka? In Kenya, in an area poorer than the ghettos of Baltimore. There's not even full-time electricity. Here they are told, "Fail one class and you go home."

Two boys who fight are taken on a hike to "base camp," given a two-man tent, and told to spend the night. How do you assemble the tent? They have to figure it out together. One boy refuses to do it. Fine, says the teacher. Sleep outdoors. We see a process at work. The tent gets assembled. The fights stop.

The movie, by Heidi Ewing and Rachel Grady, begins in Baltimore, where 76 percent of African-American boys do not graduate from high school. A recruiter for Baraka speaks at an assembly, telling potential students they have three choices: jail, death, or high school graduation. Despairing parents and grandparents embrace the idea of this strange school in Africa because nothing could be worse than the children's present reality. Two brothers apply. The school asks their mother what would happen if only one was selected. "Don't make one a king and the other a killer," she says. Both are given scholarships.

All the teachers we see at Baraka School are white; it is not an African school but one run by American volunteers who chose Kenya, among other reasons, because it is cheap, and because "boys can live the lives of boys"—running around, swimming in streams, seeing wild animals, climbing Mount Kenya. In Baltimore it can be dangerous for them to go outside, and they stare at television. The boys thrive at Baraka. Their behavior is transformed, their grades improve, and they think differently of themselves.

Then everything changes. Because of terrorist attacks and the closure of the American embassy in Nairobi, Baraka has to shut down at the end of the first of the boys' two years. In Baltimore that summer, they're told they won't be going back. One review actually complains that the movie is "unsatisfactory" because unforeseen events prevented the filmmakers from "completing" their story. Oh, it's complete, all right. "All our lives gonna be bad now," one tearful boy says. One parent on the terrorist threat: "They're more likely to be killed right here in Baltimore." Another parent: "If you send them to Baltimore, you're sending them to jail."

Some of the boys seem to return to the same aimless lives they were leading before. But a boy named Devon is elected president of his ninth-grade class, and we see him already beginning his life's work, as a preacher. Montrey, the boy with the worst attitude and behavior problems, is so changed by one year at Baraka that at the end of the next year he gets the top score in all of Maryland on a math test and is admitted to the most competitive high school in Baltimore. He speaks at the close of the film: "People think we ain't got a future. I'm gonna make a difference. I'm gonna be on the map."

In a simple, direct way, without a lot of filmmaking sophistication, *The Boys of Baraka* makes this argument: Many of our schools are failing, and many of our neighborhoods are poisonous. Individual parents and children make an effort, but the system is against them, and hope is hard to find. One of the mothers in the film goes back to drugs and is jailed during the Baraka year. Grandparents realistically look at the city and see a death sentence for their grandchildren. The recruiter for Baraka says, "Nothing's out there for them other than a new jail they just built." These children are born into a version of genocide.

If I were in charge of everything, and I certainly should be, I would divert billions of dollars into an emergency fund for our schools. I would reduce classroom size to fifteen or twenty. I would double teachers' salaries. I would fund boarding schools to remove the most endangered children from environments that are killing them. I would be generous and vigilant about school lunch programs and medical care for kids. I would install monitors on the television sets in the homes of these children and pay a cash bonus for every hour they are not turned on during homework time. I would open a storefront library on every other block. And although there are two sides to the question, I would consider legalizing drugs; illegal drugs are destroying countless lives, and legalizing them would destroy the profit motive for promoting and selling them.

All of this would cost a fraction of—well, of the cost of the government undertaking of your choice. It would pay dividends in one generation. There is something wrong when, as our own officials say, we depend on immigration to supply us with scientists. A kid like Montrey, who goes from a standing start to the top state score in math in one year, can supply us with an invaluable resource, but he has to be given a chance. We look at TV and see stories of drugs and gang bangers and despair, and we assume the victims bring it on themselves. If we had been born and raised as they were, in areas abandoned by hope and opportunity, the odds are good we would be dead, or watching TV in prison.

Brand Upon the Brain! ★ ★ ★ ½

NO MPAA RATING, 95 m., 2007

Sullivan Brown (Young Guy Maddin), Gretchen Krich (Mother), Maya Lawson (Sis), Erik Steffen Maahs (Older Bruno), Katherine E. Scharhon (Chance Hale). Directed by Guy Maddin and produced by Amy E. Jacobson and Gregg Lachow. Screenplay by Maddin and George Toles.

Guy Maddin's new film *Brand Upon the Brain!* exists in the world Maddin has built by hand over several features that seem to be trying to reinvent the silent cinema. Flickering, high-contrast black-and-white images, shot in 8 mm, tell a phantasmagoric story that could be a collaboration between Edgar Allan Poe and Salvador Dali. It's an astonishing film: weird, obsessed, drawing on subterranean impulses, hypnotic.

The film opens with a man named Guy Maddin in a rowboat. He is a housepainter, answering his mother's summons. She wants two fresh coats of paint on the family's lighthouse, an orphanage that is the only structure on the island of Black Notch.

Once Guy arrives on the island, he is cast back into flashbacks of the troubled childhood he had there with his sister and his sexually jealous mother. She stands fiercely atop the lighthouse, sweeping the island with a powerful searchlight and a phallic telescope, and issuing commands through an "aerophone," an invention of Guy's dad, which allows communication between any two people who love each other, although few seem to love the mother.

The plot, as it always does in a Maddin film, careens wildly in bizarre directions, incorporating material that seems gathered by the handful from silent melodrama. There is a murder mystery involving an orphan named Savage Tom, and an investigation by two teenage detectives named the Light Bulb Kids, who discover suspicious holes in the heads of some of the orphans.

Elements from mad scientist and black magic stories also creep into the plot, while the film hurtles headlong into an assault of stark images.

Guy Maddin, based in Winnipeg, Manitoba, is a pleasant, soft-spoken man who hardly seems a likely source for this feverish filmmaking. His world, his style, and his artistry are all completely original, even when they seem to be echoing old silent films. The echoes seem to come from a parallel universe. In films like *The Saddest Music in the World,* he creates haunting worlds that approach the edge of comedy but never quite tip over.

In a sense, you will enjoy *Brand Upon the Brain!* most if you are either an experienced moviegoer who understands (somehow) what Maddin is doing or a naive filmgoer who doesn't understand that he is doing anything. The average filmgoer might simply be frustrated and confused. For me, Maddin seems to penetrate to the hidden layers beneath the surface of the movies, revealing a surrealistic underworld of fears, fantasies, and obsessions.

The Brave One ★ ★ ★ ½

R, 122 m., 2007

Jodie Foster (Erica Bain), Terrence Howard (Sean Mercer), Naveen Andrews (David Kirmani), Nicky Katt (Detective Vitale), Mary Steenburgen (Carol). Directed by Neil Jordan and produced by Susan Downey and Joel Silver. Screenplay by Roderick Taylor, Bruce A. Taylor, and Cynthia Mort.

How many films have there been about victims of violence who turn into avengers? Charles Bronson made five. Kevin Bacon's *Death Sentence* was released two weeks ago. How are we supposed to respond to them? When Bronson's kill count got above fifty, why didn't the scales of justice snap? But now here is Jodie Foster, with a skilled costar and director, to give us a movie that deals, really deals, with the issues involved.

Foster is such a good actress in thrillers: natural, unaffected, threatened, plucky, looking like she means it. And Neil Jordan's *The Brave One* gives her someone strong to play against. Terrence Howard and Foster are perfectly modulated in the kinds of scenes it's difficult for actors to play, where they both know more than they're saying, and they both know it.

Foster plays Erica, a talk jock on a New York radio station. She's engaged to a doctor named David (Naveen Andrews), they're in Central Park late one night, they're mugged, he's killed, and she's badly injured. When Erica is discharged, she's shaking with terror. Her illusion of a safe city life is destroyed. And one day she buys a gun and practices on a shooting range where you can see fear turning into anger in her eyes.

Not long after, she's in a late-night convenience store (note: midnight strolls in Central Park rank second only to all-night stores in their movie crime rates). A holdup takes place, there's violence, she kills a guy to save her life, and she feels—well, how does she feel? Shaken, nauseous maybe, but certainly glad she's alive.

We've started with one of those admirable National Public Radio types whose voice is almost maddeningly sane and patient, and now we have a woman (narrating the movie, sometimes) who sounds more like she doesn't work upstairs over the saloon but she does own a piece of it. Erica has never seen herself as capable of killing, and now she grows addicted to it, offering herself as defenseless bait for criminals and then proving how terribly mistaken they were.

These are the general parameters of all vengeance movies. And often there's a cop on the case who grows curiously close to the killer. With Bronson, it was Vincent Gardenia. With Bacon, Aisha Tyler. With Foster, it's Terrence Howard, playing a detective named Mercer who is assigned to the original mugging, who chats with Erica, who observes there seem to be a lot of people in the city who would like to get even. "Yes," she says, "there must be a lot of us." Us. Curious word choice. Mercer hears it.

Now the movie becomes less about Erica's killings and more about how they make her feel. And about how she and Mercer begin to feel about each other—not in a romantic way, although that scent is in the air, but as smart, wary people who slowly come to realize they share knowledge they dare not admit they share.

Neil Jordan, the director (*The Crying Game, Michael Collins, Breakfast on Pluto, Mona Lisa, The Good Thief*), often makes movies about characters who are not who they seem, and about those who wonder if they can trust them. His characters are not deliberately deceptive but have been pushed into their roles by their lives and don't see a way out. Often you sense in them a desperate urge to confess.

That kind of psychological suspense is what makes *The Brave One* spellbinding. The movie doesn't dine out on action scenes, but regards with great curiosity how these two people will end up. The movie's conclusion has a slight aroma of a studio rewrite to it; I'm not saying Jordan and his writers did revise it, but that the strict logic of the story should lead in a different direction. Where did Hollywood get the conviction that audiences demand an ending that lets them off the hook? Foster doesn't let herself off the hook in *The Brave One,* and we should be as brave as she is.

Breakfast on Pluto ★ ★ ★ ½

R, 135 m., 2005

Cillian Murphy (Patrick "Kitten" Braden), Liam Neeson (Father Bernard), Stephen Rea (Bertie), Ruth Negga (Charlie), Laurence Kinlan (Irwin), Gavin Friday (Billy Hatchet), Bryan Ferry (Mr. Silky String), Brendan Gleeson (John-Joe). Directed by Neil Jordan and produced by Stephen Woolley, Alan Moloney, and Jordan. Screenplay by Jordan and Patrick McCabe, based on the novel by McCabe.

We'll fly to the stars . . .
Journey to Mars . . .
And find our breakfast on Pluto.

I heard this song performed in London by a blind man in a pub on Portobello Road in the early 1970s, and remembered it during Neil Jordan's new film. His hero, Patrick Braden, known as Kitten, would have heard it at about the same time, and needed to, because he needed all the cheering-up he could get, and usually breakfast, too. *Breakfast on Pluto* tells the story of an Irish orphan, left on the steps of a priest's rectory and raised by a strict foster mother. Patrick discovers his identity at an early age. One day the woman finds him trying on her dresses and shoes.

"I'll walk you up and down the streets before the whole town in disgrace!" she screams.

"Promise?" says Patrick.

He is then about ten. Too young to have such feelings and smart answers? Not if you have seen Jonathan Caouette's documentary *Tarnation,* which contains a home movie of Jonathan in drag at about the same age, with something of the same personality. Patrick decides that his name is Kitten, insists on being called by it, and is not a boy trapped in a girl's body but a boy trapped in a transvestite's body—or, more accurately, a boy trapped in a world he desperately wants to escape, using his imagination to reinvent himself and escape it. He is, as they say, not like the other boys.

The enchanting and hopeful *Breakfast on Pluto,* adapted by Jordan from a novel by Patrick McCabe, has a hero who is a little mad and a little saintly. Many saints insist on living in their own way regardless of what the world thinks. Some climb trees or pray in caves. Some work among the poor. Some, like Kitten, insist on optimism in the face of absolutely everything. In his case, it could be sainthood, could be denial, could be insanity. Whatever it is, Kitten so stubbornly insists on it that motorcycle gangs, London cops, and IRA killers all realize they can kill him but they can't change him.

The movie is like a Dickens novel in which the hero moves through the underskirts of society, encountering one colorful character after another. Kitten believes his birth mother may have moved to London. His only clue is that she looked like Mitzi Gaynor. Of course Kitten would know who that was. In the course of his journey to find her, he sings with a rock band, becomes a magician's assistant, is a suspected IRA bomber, and is reduced to street prostitution, although he handles it with a kind of dreamy denial. The movie becomes a series of seductions, with the goal not sex but acceptance.

Consider that Kitten is unluckily in a London pub when it's bombed by the IRA. The cops suspect him as a cross-dressing bomber and interrogate him for a week, not gently. At the end of that time they give up and accept him for who and what he says he is. A little later, one of the same cops who beat him sees him working the streets, knows Kitten is no match for the life, drives him to Soho, drops him outside a peep show, and says, with real concern, "Get a job here. It's safe and it's legal."

Kitten depends on the kindness of strangers. Played by Cillian Murphy with a bemused and hopeful voice, he meets such characters as Billy (Gavin Friday), leader of the scruffy rock band Billy Hatchet and the Mohawks, and soon Kitten is onstage as a squaw, helping out during the performance of *Running Bear.* Billy falls in love with him, but eventually "the band thinks the squaw is not working out," and Kitten finds a job being sawed in two by a magician named Bertie (Stephen Rea). In Jordan's *The Crying Game,* Rea fell in love with a cross-dressing hairdresser. But no one is deceived by Kitten, who doesn't care if you think he's male or female, as long as you think he's Kitten.

That's the part of the story Dickens would have agreed with. His heroes, from Pip to Oliver Twist to Nicholas Nickleby to David Copperfield, travel bleak landscapes of gruesome betrayal and disappointment and meet villains of every description but never lose their innocence. Dickens also would have enjoyed the story's use of melodrama and improbable coincidence, and the way the hero befriends and is befriended just when it's needed the most.

Consider Father Bernard (Liam Neeson), whose rectory steps are Kitten's first home. The priest is one of those good souls bumbling through, doing what good he can. And John-Joe (Brendan Gleeson), a streetwise hobo who shares what he has. And Charlie (Ruth Negga), a black girl who becomes Kitten's closest friend. And consider the story of how Kitten does, or does not, find his mother, or Mitzi Gaynor, or whoever, and what he finds out then.

Breakfast on Pluto is being included in earnest analytical articles about this being the season of homosexuals *(Brokeback Mountain)*, transsexuals *(Transamerica)*, transvestites (this movie), or all three *(Rent)*. As a "trend," this means absolutely nothing, although as a coincidence it is worth notice, however slight. What these titles have in common with many other good current films are characters who are given the challenge to be true to their own natures and either rise to the occasion or descend into misery.

Kitten has less to do with sexual unorthodoxy than knowing what you must be and do, and being and doing it: characters like those played by Terrence Howard in *Hustle and Flow*, Anthony Hopkins in *The World's Fastest Indian*, Amy Adams in *Junebug*, Naomi Watts in *Ellie Parker*, Miranda July in *Me and You and Everyone We Know*, Tommy Lee Jones in *The Three Burials of Melquiades Estrada*, Charlize Theron in *North Country*, and King Kong. This drive toward individualism is an encouraging counterforce to the relentless team spirit that seems to drive so much unhappiness in our society. Although it is true that in some times and places Kitten would be murdered (the fear that haunts Ennis in *Brokeback Mountain*), it is also true that Kitten might be given a pass by dangerous characters who either recognize a kindred independence, or envy it.

The Break-Up ★ ★

PG-13, 106 m., 2006

Vince Vaughn (Gary Grobowski), Jennifer Aniston (Brooke Meyers), Joey Lauren Adams (Addie), John Michael Higgins (Richard Meyers), Jon Favreau (Johnny O), Vincent D'Onofrio (Dennis Grobowski), Justin Long (Christopher), Cole Hauser (Lupus Grobowski), Judy Davis (Marilyn Dean), Ann-Margret (Wendy Meyers), Jason Bateman (Riggleman). Directed by Peyton Reed and produced by Vince Vaughn and Scott Stuber. Screenplay by Jeremy Garelick and Jay Lavender.

The Break-Up hints that the broken-up couple will get back together, but that doesn't make us eager for a sequel. The movie stars Vince Vaughn and Jennifer Aniston as Gary and Brooke, a steady couple who have many reasons to break up but none to get together, except that they fall in love. Since the scenes where they're together are so much less convincing than the ones where they fall apart, watching the movie is like being on a double date from hell.

Gary is obsessed with the Chicago Cubs and video games, and thinks if they moved the dining table into the living room, that would make space for a pool table. He and his brothers run a Chicago tour bus company, and he is the tour guide. Brooke works in a high-powered Chicago art gallery. They break up because she says he never listens to her, or appreciates all the work she does around the house or how she cooks his meals and picks up his laundry. All true, but these are not merely faults; they are his essential nature, and he will never, ever be interested in her world. Not when he thinks Michelangelo painted the ceiling of the "Sixteenth Chapel."

True, their arguments are funny, at least while they're still getting along. They have a fight right at the beginning that had me nodding my head and recognizing my own shortcomings. At the thirty-minute mark, I thought the movie had a chance, but it grew dreary and sad, especially when they both receive spectacularly bad advice from their best friends (Joey Lauren Adams and Jon Favreau). There's a stretch when Gary's sleeping on the sofa surrounded by dirty underwear, and she's trying to make him jealous by being picked up at home by a series of handsome studs. Would any woman really do this? The way to make a guy jealous is by seeming to really like someone else, not acting like first prize on Match.com.

Gary, on the other hand, tries to make Brooke jealous by hiring hookers to join his buddies in a strip poker game. Believe it or not, this doesn't work, either. By the time they have a heart-to-heart, it's way too late because both hearts are broken, and it isn't a pretty sight. What the movie lacks is warmth, optimism, and insight into human nature. I point you to *Fever Pitch* (2005), with Jimmy Fallon as a schoolteacher and Red Sox fan, and Drew Barrymore as a business executive. It begins by showing them really and truly falling in love, and then baseball season starts, and she realizes that he is two guys: the guy she fell in love with, and the Red Sox fan. If she can accept both of these personalities and he can accept her needs, they can repair their problems.

The problem with Gary is that he has only the one personality, and even if he starts listening to her and thanking her for picking up his dirty socks, they still will be profoundly incompatible. For the movie to work, we would have to like the couple and want them to succeed. Despite some sincere eleventh-hour soul-searching by Vaughn, we're sorry, but we don't want them back together. We want them to end their misery.

The supporting cast adds variety, to be sure, but of a strange kind. Occasionally, supporting actors will be so effective you want the movie to be about them. *The Break-Up* is filled with actors who seem to be auditioning for that role. John Michael Higgins, as Brooke's brother, is the leader of a men's choir and tries to turn a family dinner party into a sing-along; this scene might be funny in theory, but in practice, it's ungainly. Favreau and Adams, as the best friends, get whiplash from a plot that requires them to give one kind of advice at the beginning and another kind toward the end, as if they hadn't been listening to themselves. And Judy Davis, as the art gallery owner, behaves as if she should be carrying a whip. The best supporting performance is by Vincent D'Onofrio, as Gary's older brother: He does exactly what is required, finds the right notes, and is so convincing we hardly notice he is cleaning his ears with separate handkerchiefs.

That Aniston and Vaughn are such likable actors compounds the problem. They're not convincing as sadistic meanies, and when the movie makes them act that way, we feel sorrier for them than for their characters. Their problems start in the first scene, at Wrigley Field, where Gary is a jerk who forces Brooke to accept a hot dog she doesn't want and then insults her date. Why would a girl end up with a guy who acts like that the first time she meets him? We never find out. The next time we see them, they're living together. Must have been some courtship.

Brick ★ ★ ★

R, 110 m., 2006

Joseph Gordon-Levitt (Brendan Frye), Nora Zehetner (Laura Dannon), Lukas Haas (The Pin), Noah Fleiss (Tugger), Matt O'Leary (The Brain), Emilie de Ravin (Emily Kostach), Noah Segan (Dode), Richard Roundtree (Mr. Trueman), Meagan Good (Kara), Brian White (Brad Bramish). Directed by Rian Johnson and produced by Ram Bergman and Mark G. Mathis. Screenplay by Johnson.

You have preserved in your own lifetime, sir, a way of life that was dead before you were born.

—the butler in Elaine May's *A New Leaf* (1971)

You will forgive me for reaching back thirty-five years for a quotation to open this review of *Brick*, since the movie itself is inspired by hard-boiled crime novels written by Dashiell Hammett between 1929 and 1934. What is unexpected, and daring, is that *Brick* transposes the attitudes and dialogue of classic detective fiction to a modern Southern California high school. These are contemporary characters who say things like, "I got all five senses and I slept last night. That puts me six up on the lot of you." Or, "Act smarter than you look, and drop it."

What is the audience for this movie? It is carrying on in its own lifetime a style of film that was dead before it was born. Are teenage moviegoers familiar with movies like *The*

Maltese Falcon? Do they know who Humphrey Bogart was? Maybe it doesn't matter. They're generally familiar with black-and-white classics on cable and will understand the strategy: The students inhabit personal styles from an earlier time.

This mixing of styles and ages has been done before. Alan Parker's *Bugsy Malone* (1976) was a 1930s gangster movie cast with preteen kids (including Jodie Foster). Once you accepted the idea, it worked, and so does *Brick*. The crucial decision by writer-director Rian Johnson is to play it straight; this isn't a put-on, and the characters don't act as if they think their behavior is funny.

The movie opens in James Ellroy territory, with the hero, Brendan (Joseph Gordon-Levitt), finding the dead body of his onetime girlfriend in a drainage ditch. From the mouth of a tunnel comes the sound, perhaps, of her murderer escaping. The victim is Emily (Emilie de Ravin), who called him earlier for help; from a lonely phone booth (itself a relic of pre-cellular movies) he sees her being taken past in a car, possibly a captive.

Brendan turns into a classic 1930s gumshoe, tracing Emily's movements back through a high school drug ring and ignoring threats from a high school principal who tries to pull him off the case (this is the role police captains filled in old private-eye movies). True to the genre that inspired it, the movie has tough and dippy dames, an eccentric crime kingpin, some would-be toughs who can be slapped around like Elisha Cook Jr. in *The Maltese Falcon*, and an enigmatic know-it-all. This last character was, in the old days, an informer, bookie, or newspaper reporter often found in the shadows of a bar; in *Brick*, he apparently exists permanently sitting against a back wall of the high school, from which vantage point he sees and knows, or guesses, everything.

Does the movie work on its own terms as a crime story? Yes, in the sense that the classic Hollywood noirs worked: The story is never clear while it unfolds, but it provides a rich source of dialogue, behavior, and incidents. Then, at the end, if it doesn't all hold water, who cares as long as all the characters think it does? *The Big Sleep* is famous for the loophole of a killer who is already dead when he commits his crime. At the Madison Film Festival this year, I saw *Laura* again and was reminded that it is entirely a movie about atmosphere, dialogue, and acting styles, in which the very realities of murder are arbitrary. It makes no difference who committed the central killing; what's important is that everyone acts as if it does.

Brick is a movie reportedly made with great determination and not much money by Johnson, who did the editing on his Macintosh (less impressive than it sounds, since desktop machines are now often used even on big-budget movies). What is impressive is his absolute commitment to his idea of the movie's style. He relates to the classic crime novels and movies, he notes the way their mannered dialogue and behavior elevate the characters into archetypes, and he uses the strategy to make his teenagers into hard-boiled guys and dolls. The actors enter into the spirit; we never catch them winking.

The movie has one inevitable point of vulnerability: Because we can't believe in the characters, we can't care about their fates. They have lifestyles, not lives. The same can be said of many (not all) noir films, and it is because of style that we treasure them. This movie leaves me looking forward to the director's next film; we can say of Johnson, as somebody once said about a dame named Brigid O'Shaughnessy, "You're good. You're very good."

Brick Lane ★ ★ ★ ½

PG-13, 101 m., 2008

Tannishtha Chatterjee (Nazneen), Satish Kaushik (Chanu), Christopher Simpson (Karim), Naeema Begum (Shahana), Lana Rahman (Bibi), Zafreen (Hasina). Directed by Sarah Gavron and produced by Alison Owen and Christopher Collins. Screenplay by Abi Morgan and Laura Jones, based on the novel by Monica Ali.

Brick Lane tells a story we think we already know, but we're wrong: It has new things to say within an old formula. It begins with a young woman from Bangladesh, whose mother's suicide causes her father to arrange her marriage with a man now living in London, older than her, whom she has never met. Nazneen (Tannishtha Chatterjee) is a stunning beauty, seventeen when she marries

Chanu (Satish Kaushik), who is fat, balding, and easily twenty years older. So this will be a story of her servitude to this beast, right?

Not exactly. Chanu is not a hateful man. He is not a fountain of warmth and understanding and has few insights into his wife, but he is an earnest citizen, a hard worker, and there is sometimes a twinkle in his eye. He likes to sing little songs to himself. The two have three children; their first, a son, is a victim of crib death. The next two are daughters, Shahana (Naeema Begum) and Bibi (Lana Rahman). Time passes. Sex for Nazneen is a matter of closing her eyes and dreaming of her village back home and the sister she receives regular letters from.

Her husband is so unwise as to take loans from the usurer who works their council flat in East London; these loans apparently can never quite be repaid and delay their dream of returning "home." Meanwhile, Chanu pursues his dream of becoming a properly educated Brit, which for him means familiarity with Thackeray, Hume, and other authors not much read anymore, alas, by Brits. He dreams such knowledge will win him a promotion at work, but it doesn't; he loses his job and starts working as a minicab driver. And Nazneen does what other women in the public housing estate do—she buys a sewing machine and does piece work, finishing blue jeans.

That's how Karim (Christopher Simpson) comes into her life—young, handsome, charming, the delivery man for the unfinished jeans. Yes, they fall in love, have sex, talk of her divorce and their marriage. Chanu walks into the flat at times when he must be blind not to understand what's happening—but he doesn't, or at least he doesn't say anything; his method is to remain jolly at all times, as if everything's fine. The performance by Kaushik makes him almost impossible to dislike, although he's no doubt an ordeal to live with.

Now comes the part of the story that caused controversy when Monica Ali's best-selling novel was announced for filming. The attacks of 9/11 take place, anti-Muslim sentiment increases in London, community meetings are held, Karim starts growing a beard and becomes more militant, and then Chanu, of all people, turns into a spokesman against extremist militancy and in favor of a faith based not in politics but in the heart.

His sentiment aroused so much opposition among Muslims in London that the novel could not be filmed on Brick Lane (the center of London's Bangladeshi population), but in fact what Chanu says is deeply felt and seems harmless enough. Without getting into the politics, however, let me say that the film's story surprised me by being less about the illicit love affair and more about the marriage, Nazneen's deepest feelings, and the two daughters—the young one docile, the older one scornful of her father.

"Tell him you don't want to go home," says Shahana. "I've never once heard you tell him what you really feel." But what Nazneen really feels is a surprise even to herself, and the final notes of the film are graceful and tender. Watching it, I was reminded of how many shallow, cynical, vulgar movies I've seen in this early summer season, and how few that truly engage in matters of the heart. *Brick Lane* is about characters who have depth and reality, who change and learn, who have genuine feelings. And it keeps on surprising us, right to the end.

Bride and Prejudice ★ ★ ★

PG-13, 110 m., 2005

Aishwarya Rai (Lalita Bakshi), Martin Henderson (Will Darcy), Naveen Andrews (Balraj), Indira Varma (Kiran Bingley), Nitin Chandra Ganatra (Mr. Kholi), Daniel Gillies (Johnny Wickham), Anupam Kher (Mr. Bakshi), Nadira Babbar (Mrs. Bakshi), Namrata Shirodkar (Jaya Bakshi), Meghna Kothari (Maya Bakshi), Peeya Rai Chowdhary (Lucky Bakshi), Marsha Mason (Will's Mother). Directed by Gurinder Chadha and produced by Deepak Nayar and Chadha. Screenplay by Paul Mayeda Berges and Chadha, inspired by Jane Austen's *Pride and Prejudice.*

Bollywood musicals are the Swiss Army knives of the cinema, with a tool for every job: comedy, drama, song and dance, farce, pathos, adventure, great scenery, improbably handsome heroes, teeth-gnashing villains, marriage-obsessed mothers and their tragically unmarried daughters, who are invariably ethereal beauties.

"You get everything in one film," my friend Uma da Cuhna told me, as she took me to see *Taal* in Hyderabad. "No need to run around here and there, looking for a musical or an action picture." The movie lasted more than three hours, including an intermission, which Uma employed by correctly predicting everything that would happen during the rest of the film.

Bollywood, is, of course, Bombay—or Mumbai, as it is now called, although there has been no movement to rename the genre Mumblywood. Although western exhibitors aren't crazy about a movie they can show only twice a night, instead of three times, Bollywood has developed a healthy audience in London, where the Bollywood Oscars were held a year ago. Now comes *Bride and Prejudice,* which adds the BritLit genre to the mix.

Directed by Gurinder Chadha, whose *What's Cooking?* (2000) and *Bend It Like Beckham* (2002) make you smile just thinking about them, this is a free-spirited adaptation of the Jane Austen novel, in which Mr. Darcy and the unmarried sisters and their family are plugged into a modern plot that spans London, New York, Bombay, and Goa. Darcy is an American played by Martin Henderson, and Lizzie Bennett becomes Lalita Bakshi, second of four daughters in Amritsar, India—true to Austen, a country town.

Lalita is played by Aishwarya Rai, Miss World of 1994, recently described by at least one film critic (me) as not only the first but also the second most beautiful woman in the world. According to the Internet Movie Database, "The Queen of Bollywood" is so popular she was actually able to get away with appearing in ads for both Coke and Pepsi. I also learn she carried the Olympic Torch in 2004, has a puppy named Sunshine, and was listed by *Time* as one of the 100 most influential people in the world. If this review is not accompanied by a photograph of her, you have grounds for a lawsuit.

Aishwarya (ash-waar-e-ah) Rai exudes not the frightening seriousness of a woman who thinks she is being sexy, but the grace and ease of a woman who knows she is fun to look at and be around. What a smile. What eyes. Rai is not remotely overweight, but neither is she alarmingly skinny; having deliberately gained twenty pounds for this role, she is the flower of splendid nutrition.

Sorry, I got a little distracted there. Gurinder Chadha, who was born in Kenya, was raised in London, and is married to a Japanese-American, seems attracted to ethnic multitasking. Her *What's Cooking?* is set in Los Angeles and tells parallel stories about families with Vietnamese, African-American, Mexican, and Jewish roots. *Bend It Like Beckham* was about a London girl from a Kenyan family with Punjabi roots, who wants to play soccer.

In *Bride and Prejudice* Chadha once again transcends boundaries. This is not a Bollywood movie, but a Hollywood musical comedy incorporating Bollywood elements. Her characters burst into song and dance at the slightest provocation, backed up by a dance corps that materializes with the second verse and disappears at the end of the scene. That's Bollywood. So is the emphasis on the mother and father; the lovers in most American romantic comedies seem to be orphans. And she employs the Bollywood strategy for using color, which comes down to: If it's a color, use it.

Will Darcy (Henderson) is a rich young New York hotel man, visiting India because his old friend from London, Balraj (Naveen Andrews), is the best man at a wedding. The Bakshi family is friendly with the family of the bride, and Mrs. Bakshi (Nadira Babbar) hopes her four daughters can meet eligible husbands at the event. That strategy works immediately for Balraj and Jaya Bakshi (Namrata Shirodkar), Lalita's older sister. For them, it's love at first sight. For Darcy and Lalita, it's not.

Darcy makes tactless remarks, disagrees with the custom of arranged marriages, seems stuck-up, is distracted by business, and creates the possibility that Lalita may have to follow her mother's instructions and marry the creepy Hollywood mogul Mr. Kholi (Nitin Chandra Ganatra). Things could be worse; Harvey Weinstein is also visiting India. We know Lalita won't really marry Mr. Kholi, since he is never provided with a first name, but in stories of this sort it's necessary for Darcy and Lalita to rub each other the wrong way so that later they can rub each other the right way.

This plot, recycled from Austen, is the clothesline for a series of dance numbers that, like Hong Kong action sequences, are set in unlikely locations and use props found there; how else to explain the sequence set in, yes, a Mexican restaurant? Even the most strenuous dances are intercut with perfectly composed close-ups of Aishwarya Rai, never sweaty, never short of breath. What a smile. Did I say that?

Brokeback Mountain ★ ★ ★ ★

R, 134 m., 2005

Heath Ledger (Ennis Del Mar), Jake Gyllenhaal (Jack Twist), Michelle Williams (Alma Del Mar), Anne Hathaway (Lureen Twist), Randy Quaid (Joe Aguirre), Linda Cardellini (Cassie Cartwright), Anna Faris (LaShawn Malone). Directed by Ang Lee and produced by Diana Ossana and James Schamus. Screenplay by Larry McMurtry and Ossana, based on the short story by E. Annie Proulx.

Ennis tells Jack about something he saw as a boy. "There were two old guys shacked up together. They were the joke of the town, even though they were pretty tough old birds." One day they were found beaten to death. Ennis says: "My dad, he made sure me and my brother saw it. For all I know, he did it."

This childhood memory is always there, the ghost in the room, in Ang Lee's *Brokeback Mountain.* When he was taught by his father to hate homosexuals, Ennis was taught to hate his own feelings. Years after he first makes love with Jack on a Wyoming mountainside, after his marriage has failed, after his world has compressed to a mobile home, the Laundromat, the TV, he still feels the same pain: "Why don't you let me be? It's because of you, Jack, that I'm like this—nothing, and nobody."

But it's not because of Jack. It's because Ennis and Jack love each other and can find no way to deal with that. *Brokeback Mountain* has been described as "a gay cowboy movie," which is a cruel simplification. It is the story of a time and place where two men are forced to deny the only great passion either one will ever feel. Their tragedy is universal. It could be about two women, or lovers from different religious or ethnic groups—any "forbidden" love.

The movie wisely never steps back to look at the larger picture, or deliver the "message." It is specifically the story of these men, this love. It stays in close-up. That's how Jack and Ennis see it. "You know I ain't queer," Ennis tells Jack after their first night together. "Me neither," says Jack.

Their story begins in Wyoming in 1963, when Ennis (Heath Ledger) and Jack (Jake Gyllenhaal) are about nineteen years old and get jobs tending sheep on a mountainside. Ennis is a boy of so few words he can barely open his mouth to release them; he learned to be guarded and fearful long before he knew what he feared. Jack, who has done some rodeo riding, is a little more outgoing. After some days have passed on the mountain and some whiskey has been drunk, they suddenly and almost violently have sex.

"This is a one-shot thing we got going on here," Ennis says the next day. Jack agrees. But it's not. When the summer is over, they part laconically: "I guess I'll see ya around, huh?" Their boss (Randy Quaid) tells Jack he doesn't want him back next summer: "You guys sure found a way to make the time pass up there. You weren't getting paid to let the dogs guard the sheep while you stemmed the rose."

Some years pass. Both men get married. Then Jack goes to visit Ennis and the undiminished urgency of their passion stuns them. Their lives settle down into a routine, punctuated less often than Jack would like by "fishing trips." Ennis's wife, who has seen them kissing, says nothing about it for a long time. But she notices there are never any fish.

The movie is based on a short story by E. Annie Proulx. The screenplay is by Larry McMurtry and Diana Ossana. Last summer I read McMurtry's *Lonesome Dove* books, and as I saw the movie I was reminded of Gus and Woodrow, the two cowboys who spend a lifetime together. They aren't gay; one of them is a womanizer, and the other spends his whole life regretting the loss of the one woman he loved. They're straight but just as crippled by a society that tells them how a man must behave and what he must feel.

Brokeback Mountain could tell its story and not necessarily be a great movie. It could be a melodrama. It *could* be a "gay cowboy movie." But the filmmakers have focused so intently and with such feeling on Jack and Ennis that the movie is as observant as work by Bergman. Strange but true: The more specific a film is, the more universal, because the more it understands individual characters, the more it applies to everyone. I can imagine someone weeping at this film, identifying with it because he always wanted to stay in the Marines, or be an artist or a cabinetmaker.

Jack is able to accept a little more willingly that he is inescapably gay. In frustration and need he goes to Mexico one night and finds a male prostitute. Prostitution is a calling with hazards, sadness, and tragedy, but it accepts human nature. It knows what some people need, and perhaps that is why every society has found a way to accommodate it.

Jack thinks he and Ennis might someday buy themselves a ranch and settle down. Ennis, who remembers what he saw as a boy: "This thing gets hold of us at the wrong time and wrong place and we're dead." Well, wasn't Matthew Shepard murdered in Wyoming in 1998? And Brandon Teena in Nebraska in 1993? Haven't brothers killed their sisters in the Muslim world to defend "family honor"?

There are gentle and nuanced portraits of Ennis's wife, Alma (Michelle Williams), and Jack's wife, Lureen (Anne Hathaway), who are important characters, seen as victims, too. Williams has a powerful scene where she finally calls Ennis on his "fishing trips," but she takes a long time to do that, because nothing in her background prepares her for what she has found out about her husband. In their own way, programs like *Jerry Springer* provide a service by focusing on people, however pathetic, who are prepared to defend what they feel. In 1963 there was nothing like that on TV. And in 2005, the situation has not entirely changed. One of the ads for *Brokeback Mountain*'s Oscar campaign shows Ledger and Williams together, although the movie's posters are certainly honest.

Ang Lee is a director whose films are set in many nations and many times. What they have in common is an instinctive sympathy for the characters. Born Chinese, he makes movies about Americans, British, Chinese, straights, gays; his sci-fi movie *Hulk* was about a misunderstood outsider. Here he respects the entire arc of his story, right down to the lonely conclusion.

A closing scene involving a visit by Ennis to Jack's parents is heartbreaking in what is said, and not said, about their world. A look around Jack's childhood bedroom suggests what he overcame to make room for his feelings. What we cannot be sure is this: In the flashback, are we witnessing what really happened to Jack, or how Ennis sees it in his imagination? Ennis, whose father "made sure me and my brother saw it."

Broken English ★ ★ ½

PG-13, 93 m., 2007

Parker Posey (Nora Wilder), Melvil Poupaud (Julien), Drea de Matteo (Audrey Andrews), Justin Theroux (Nick Gable), Gena Rowlands (Vivien Wilder-Mann), Peter Bogdanovich (Irving Mann), Tim Guinee (Mark Andrews), Josh Hamilton (Charlie Ross). Directed by Zoe Cassavetes and produced by Andrew Fierberg, Jason Kliot, and Joana Vicente. Screenplay by Cassavetes.

First shot, a close-up: Parker Posey. Next shots, mostly close-ups. She smokes, she regards her face in the mirror, she does her hair and gets ready to go to work. She captures perfectly that way women have of arming themselves against the merciless scrutiny of the world. Does any woman, looking in the mirror, think of herself as beautiful?

What Posey brings to this sequence is something I've often felt while watching her movies, even the incomprehensible ones like *Fay Grim*. She stands poised between serene beauty and throwing a shampoo bottle at the mirror. She always looks great, and she always seems dubious and insecure. She can make half her mouth curl into a reluctant smile. But when she fully smiles, she's radiant. She is well cast for *Broken English*, because her character, Nora Wilder, needs precisely that in-between quality.

In some seasons, she falls instantly in love. In others, she sinks into depression. The perfect man comes along and hurts her cruelly. The movie, written and directed by Zoe Cassavetes (daughter of director John Cassavetes and actress Gena Rowlands), is about a woman with a knack for trusting untrustworthy men. She dates an actor (Justin Theroux) and a nice normal guy (Josh Hamilton), and both times confides to her closest friend, Audrey (Drea de Matteo), that this guy might be the one, and both times she is crushingly wrong.

Then at a party she meets Julien (Melvil Poupaud), a French guy who seems too good to be true. Maybe that's where the story breaks down, if only because he *is* too good to be true. It's like he went to a feminist training academy to learn how to treat a woman with gentleness, warmth, and perfect sexual tact. He has to return to Paris. *Quel dommage.* She says she will join him there.

Meanwhile, there are subplots. Audrey is unhappy after five years of marriage. Nora's mother (Gena Rowlands) has wise but worried advice (most women "at your age," she tells Nora, have been snapped up). Nora, who works as the VIP concierge in a Manhattan boutique hotel, works all day to make others happy and then drinks and smokes and mourns about her life to Audrey.

Is Julien the answer? After all, she doesn't even speak French (unlikely, as the VIP concierge in a boutique hotel, but there you have it).

The question clearly becomes, Will she go to Paris and find Julien? If the answer is no, that's a rotten way to treat your audience. If it's yes, your movie is over. So I'm not giving away anything if I point out that, from the point of view of plot dynamics, she must first fail to find Julien and then succeed. As I've pointed out before, some movies give themselves away.

OK. She's in Paris. All she has to do is call Julien. How could there be a problem? Read no further if you can't guess . . . that she loses his number. And that after moping about Paris and meeting an extraordinary number of nice guys, she has a Meet Cute with Julien, but he is sullen and angry because she is on her way to the airport and has been in Paris and did not even call him. Obviously, a perfect Idiot Plot setup, because one word would solve everything. But he glowers between Metro stops, and when he finally discloses what bothers him, she says, "It's really complicated." Which it is not. All together now, as we telepathically chant the four words she needs to say.

So what happens is, *Broken English* establishes a sympathetic character, gets Parker Posey to make her real, and then grinds her in the gears of a plot we cannot believe. Surely these people are complex enough to have their futures settled by more than a Meet Cute and an Idiot Plot that can only hold out for two minutes? When the credits roll, we ask, along with Peggy Lee, "Is that all there is?" There is a very good movie named *Before Sunset* that begins more or less where this one ends. Which tells you something right there.

Broken Flowers ★ ★ ★ ★

R, 105 m., 2005

Bill Murray (Don Johnston), Jeffrey Wright (Winston), Sharon Stone (Laura), Frances Conroy (Dora), Jessica Lange (Carmen), Tilda Swinton (Penny), Julie Delpy (Sherry), Alexis Dziena (Lolita), Chloë Sevigny (Carmen's Assistant), Chris Bauer (Dan). Directed by Jim Jarmusch and produced by Jon Kilik and Stacey Smith. Screenplay by Jarmusch.

Broken Flowers stars Bill Murray as Don Johnston, a man who made his money in computers and now doesn't even own one. To sit at the keyboard would mean moving from his sofa, where he seems to be stuck. As the film opens, his latest girlfriend (Julie Delpy) is moving out. She doesn't want to spend any more time with "an over-the-hill Don Juan." After she leaves, he remains on the sofa, listening to music. He reaches out for a glass of wine, changes his mind, lets the hand drop.

This is a man whose life is set on idle. His neighbor Winston (Jeffrey Wright), on the other hand, is a go-getter from Ethiopia who supports a wife and five kids with three jobs and still has time to surf the Net as an amateur detective. One day, Don receives a letter suggesting that twenty years ago he fathered a son and that a nineteen-year-old boy may be searching for him at this very moment. Don is unmoved by this intelligence, but Winston is energized; he extracts from Don the names of all the women who could possibly be the mother, and he supplies Don with plane tickets and an itinerary so that he can visit the candidates and figure out which one might have sent the letter.

"The letter is on pink stationery," Winston says. "Give them pink flowers and watch their reaction." Don nods, barely, and embarks on his journey—not to discover if he has a child so much as to discover if he wants a child. At one point, he phones Winston from the road, complaining that he has been supplied with conventional rental cars. Why couldn't he have a Porsche? "I'm a stalker in a Taurus."

No actor is better than Murray at doing nothing at all and being fascinating while not doing it. Buster Keaton had the same gift for contemplating astonishing developments with absolute calm. Keaton surrounded himself with slapstick, and in *Broken Flowers,* Jim Jarmusch surrounds Murray with a parade of formidable women.

First stop, Laura (Sharon Stone). Her husband was a NASCAR champion but "died in a wall of flame." Her daughter (Alexis Dziena), who is named Lolita, offers Don her Popsicle and, unmistakably, herself. Neither daughter nor mother seems to know that the name Lolita has literary associations. Don does in fact spend the night with the mother, but we do not see precisely what goes on, and just as well: The sight of this passive and withdrawn man making love might be sad beyond calculation.

Second woman: Dora (Frances Conroy), who with her husband, Dan (Chris Bauer), is a Realtor, specializing in selling "quality prefabs" and currently living in a "wonderful example." Don's dinner with Dora and Dan grows unspeakably depressing after he asks the wrong question.

Third woman: Carmen (Jessica Lange), protected by her ambiguous assistant (Chloë Sevigny). Carmen is an "animal communicator," who talks to people's pets on their behalf. The movie doesn't take cheap shots at this occupation but suggests Carmen may be the real thing. "Is he saying something?" Don asks, as Carmen converses with her cat. Carmen: "He says you have a hidden agenda."

The fourth woman, Penny (Tilda Swinton), has a front yard full of motorcycles and lives in an atmosphere that makes Don feel threatened, not without reason. There was a fifth possible candidate, who has been eliminated from Don's list because, well, she's dead.

Were any of these women the mother of his child? I will leave that for you, and Don, to discover. After the film's premiere at Cannes, I observed: "Some actors give the kinds of performances where we want to get out of the room, stand on the lawn, and watch them through a window. Murray has the uncanny ability to invite us into his performance, into his stillness and sadness. I don't know how he does it. A Bill Murray imitation would be a pitiful sight: Passive immobility, small gestures of the eyes, enigmatic comments, yes, those would be easy, but how does he suggest the low tones of crashing chaotic uncertainty?"

Jarmusch first came into focus in 1983 with *Stranger than Paradise,* about a slick New Yorker who gets an unexpected visit from his Hungarian cousin, who is sexy and naive and soon leaves to visit her aunt in Cleveland. Then followed a series of films of various degrees of wonderfulness; I have admired them all except for *Dead Man* (1995); the critic Jonathan Rosenbaum regards me sadly every time this title is mentioned. Jarmusch makes films about outsiders, but they're not loners; they're soloists. Murray's character here is the ultimate Jarmusch soloist, in that he lacks even an instrument. His act is to walk onto the stage and not play.

How did Don fascinate these women in the first place? Why are most of them (relatively) happy to see him again? Perhaps they were simply curious. Perhaps they embodied nature, and he embodied a vacuum. At the end, there is an enigmatic scene that explains little or nothing. Still, it opens up the possibility that if Don ever did discover he had a son, he would try to do the right thing. That would mean he was doing something, and that would be a start.

Brooklyn Lobster ★ ★ ★

NO MPAA RATING, 90 m., 2006

Danny Aiello (Frank Giorgio), Jane Curtin (Maureen Giorgio), Daniel Sauli (Michael Giorgio), Marisa Ryan (Lauren Giorgio-Wallace), Ian Kahn (Justin Wallace), Heather Burns (Kerry Miller). Directed by Kevin Jordan and produced by Darren Jordan, Kevin Jordan, and Chris Valentino. Screenplay by Kevin Jordan.

Danny Aiello is an actor to depend on when you want a tough guy with a tender side, a sweet guy who can turn hard, and *Brooklyn Lobster* is a movie founded on his ability to show those two sides without seeming to shift gears. It's as if his nature is at war with itself. He loves his family with a genuine passion, and he runs a lobster house in Brooklyn that is his life's blood, and he's one of those guys, we all know a few, who thinks he expresses his love by the way he works so hard. It's a surprise to him, and it hurts, when his wife of many years tells him, "I've been alone throughout this entire marriage."

If you merge your family and your work, they are likely to go down together. It is Christmastime at Giorgio's Lobster Bar in Brooklyn, as you can tell by the large inflated Santa lobster balloon that floats above the restaurant. But inside not all is well, even before the lobsters die. Frank Giorgio (Aiello) is in trouble: "My bank forecloses, and the FDIC puts a gun to my head." His wife, Maureen (Jane Curtin), has moved out. His daughter, Lauren (Marisa Ryan), continues to run the bookkeeping side of the business, and knows better than anyone how desperate the situation is. Giorgio's has been in the family since 1938, but opening a restaurant on top of the basic lobster business was a mistake.

Frank's son, Michael (Daniel Sauli), might have been expected to take over as the third generation, but he got as far away as he could (Seattle) and is back now for the holidays with his fiancée, Kerry (Heather Burns). Her family has some money, and there's the possibility that they might want to invest, and the excellent possibility that it would be a mistake for everybody.

Meanwhile, Frank, facing a bank auction and forced by law to advertise it, puts a tiny ad in the Pets section of the classified ads. He figures lobsters are pets. As faithful readers will know from my review of *Aquamarine,* he is right. Lobsters make perfect pets. As the French poet Nerval observed, lobsters are "peaceful, serious creatures, who know the secrets of the sea, and don't bark." Amazing, isn't it, how that has come up twice in two recent reviews.

The movie, written and directed by Kevin Jordan, has a spontaneous, confident realism about it, and no wonder: It was inspired by his family's business, Jordan's Lobster Dock, in Brooklyn. I looked it up on the Web. It gets good reviews from CitySearch: prompt seating, good for groups, good for kids, but "Romantic? No." And, warning: "Stay away from the corn in the platters." Overcooked. The *Village Voice* says the whole steamed lobsters are "excellent, served with drawn butter" but says the illusion of a Maine lobster pound "is marred somewhat by the garish franchise restaurant next door."

The *Voice* will be happy to learn that in *Brooklyn Lobster,* the Aiello character is given the opportunity to sell out to a garish franchise restaurant, and responds with garish language of his own. Meanwhile, his son moves into the cramped quarters above the restaurant and bunks with his dad, the fiancée camps out in a motel, Frank's wife stays with her daughter, and there is every prospect that Christmas will be unhappy and New Year's miserable. But watch the quiet way Jordan and his actors pull redemption out of the gloom. There is a subtle way that the father and son begin to share unspoken conclusions. There is the feeling that a restaurant that has been in the family since 1938 is more than a restaurant, and its absence will leave less than a family.

I first encountered Jordan's work in 1999, when his *Goat on Fire and Smiling Fish* played at Toronto, charming audiences with its story of two brothers and their romantic and professional lives. It was picked up by distributors who insisted on renaming it. The new name: *Smiling Fish and Goat on Fire.*

Both *Fish* and *Lobster* have a strong feeling for family, and a way of allowing the action to grow out of the characters instead of being required by the script. People do goofy things in real life, including building a tent over their desk in the office or, in this film, taking out that ad in the Pets section. Watch Aiello try to remain self-righteous as he defends the placement of that ad. *Brooklyn Lobster* is a sweet and touching film, worth a visit. So, by the sound of it, is Jordan's Lobster Dock, which is at 3165 Harkness Ave. in Brooklyn, telephone (718) 934–6300.

Brothers ★ ★ ★ ½

R, 110 m., 2005

Connie Nielsen (Sarah), Ulrich Thomsen (Michael), Nikolaj Lie Kaas (Jannik), Bent Mejding (Henning), Solbjorg Hojfeldt (Else).

Directed by Susanne Bier and produced by Sisse Graum Olsen. Screenplay by Anders Thomas Jensen, based on the story by Bier.

Jannik has always been the embarrassment of the family, an aimless younger brother who, as *Brothers* opens, is being released from prison after committing a crime hardly worth his time and effort. Was he breaking the law simply to play his usual role in the family drama?

Michael is the good brother, a loving husband, a responsible father, a man who does his duty. When his Danish military unit is sent to Afghanistan, he goes without complaint, because he sees it as the right thing to do. Within a shockingly short time, his helicopter is shot down, and his wife, Sarah, is told he was killed.

Jannik, with no better choice, tries to do what he sees as his duty: to be kind to Sarah, to be a good uncle to the children, to help around the house. In subtle ways that are never underlined, he starts acting from a different script in his life; with Michael gone, a vacancy has been created in the family, and Jannik steps into it. Now he is the person you can trust.

It is not a spoiler to reveal that Michael was not killed in the helicopter crash, but captured by Afghan enemies. This is made clear very early; the movie is not about mysteries and suspense, but about behavior. As a prisoner he is treated badly, but his real punishment comes when his captors force an impossible choice upon him. If he wants to save his own life, he will have to take the life of a fellow prisoner, a man he likes, who is counting on him.

Strangely enough, this parallels Paul Schrader's *Dominion*, in which a priest is told that if he doesn't choose some villagers to be killed, the whole village will die. Michael's choice is more direct: Either he will die, or the other prisoner will. In theory, Michael should choose death. Not so clear is what the priest should have done; theology certainly teaches him to do no evil, but does theology account for a world where good has been eliminated as a choice?

Michael saves his own life; let the first stones be cast by those who would choose to die. Eventually he is freed and returns home to find things somehow different. He is no longer able to subtly condescend to his screwed-up little brother because Jannik has changed. And Michael has changed too. Sarah senses it immediately. There is a torment in him that we know is an expression of guilt.

It shows itself in strange ways: in his anger, for example, about the new kitchen cabinets that Jannik installed in his absence, and at the love the children have for their uncle. And in Michael's own relentlessly growing jealousy. "It's all right if you did," he tells his brother, "since you both thought I was dead. But I have to know: Did you make love?"

The answer to the question is simple (and perhaps not the one you expect). The meaning of the answer is very tricky, because Michael is a time bomb, waiting to explode. He has lost his view of himself in Afghanistan, and back at home in Denmark he cannot find it again, perhaps because the way is blocked by Jannik.

The movie was directed by Susanne Bier, who wrote a story that was turned into a screenplay by Anders Thomas Jensen. They worked together once before, on *Open Hearts* (2003), the story of a couple engaged to be married when the young man is paralyzed from the neck down in a senseless accident. Will she still love him? Will she stay with him? How does he feel about that? Bier and Jensen are drawn to situations in which every answer leads to a question.

The central performance in *Brothers* is by Connie Nielsen, as Sarah, who is strong, deep, and true. You may remember her from *The Devil's Advocate* and *Gladiator*. What is she doing in a Danish movie? She is Danish, although this is her first Danish film.

The brothers are Ulrich Thomsen as Michael and Nikolaj Lie Kaas as Jannik. Both have to undergo fundamental transformations, and both must be grateful to Bier and Jensen for not getting all psychological on them. *Brothers* treats the situation as a real-life dilemma in which the characters behave according to how they are made and what they are capable of doing.

Like *Open Hearts*, this is the kind of movie that doesn't solve everything at the end—that observes some situations are capable not of solution but only of accommodation. That's more true to life than the countless movies with neat endings—happy endings, and even sad ones. In the world, sometimes the problem comes and stays forever, and the question with the hardest answer is, well, okay, how are you going to live with it?

The Brothers Grimm ★ ★

PG-13, 118 m., 2005

Matt Damon (Wilhelm Grimm), Heath Ledger (Jacob Grimm), Peter Stormare (Cavaldi), Lena Headey (Angelika), Jonathan Pryce (General Delatombe), Monica Bellucci (Mirror Queen). Directed by Terry Gilliam and produced by Daniel Bobker and Charles Roven. Screenplay by Ehren Kruger.

Terry Gilliam's *The Brothers Grimm* is a work of limitless invention, but it is invention without pattern, chasing itself around the screen without finding a plot. Watching it is a little exhausting. If the images in the movie had been put to the service of a story we could care about, he might have had something. But the movie seems like a style in search of a purpose.

He begins with the Brothers Grimm, whose fairy tales enchant those lucky children whose parents still read to them. There is an eerie quality to the Grimm stories that's lacking in their Hollywood versions; no modern version of *Little Red Riding Hood* approaches the scariness of the original story, where the Big Bad Wolf was generated not by computers but by my quaking imagination.

Gilliam's intention is not to tell the fairy tales, however, although some of them have walk-ons in his movie; he makes the Brothers Grimm into con artists, circa 1796, who travel from village to village in Germany, staging phony magic and claiming it is real. Wilhelm Grimm (Matt Damon) is the hustler of the outfit, a mercenary cynic. His brother, Jacob (Heath Ledger), sort of believes in magic. It has been thus since "Jake" and "Will" were children, and Jacob sold the family cow for a handful of magic beans.

The con artists are unmasked by Delatombe (Jonathan Pryce), Napoleon's man in Germany. But instead of punishing them, he dispatches the lads to the village of Marbaden, where children are missing and it appears that in the haunted forest "the trees themselves set upon them." Delatombe's bizarre torturer, Cavaldi (Peter Stormare), is sent along to be sure the Grimms deliver the goods; they are apparently supposed to be eighteenth-century ghostbusters, or maybe the equivalents of the Amazing Randi, unmasking fraud.

The problem is, the forest really is enchanted. A local huntswoman named Angelika (Lena Headey) knows it is and tries to convince the boys, who become convinced only that they love her. There is another romantic complication when the evil five-hundred-year-old Mirror Queen (Monica Bellucci) casts a spell over events; when the Grimms attempt to enter her castle and break the spell, they're up against the real thing: A kiss from her can kill. Jacob is tempted. Considering that she is five hundred years old, I am reminded of Mark Twain's first words after being shown an ancient Egyptian mummy: "Is he, ah . . . is he dead?"

A great deal more happens in *The Brothers Grimm,* and none of it is as easy to follow as I have made it sound. The film is constructed of elements that probably seemed like a great idea in themselves but have not been assembled into a narrative we can follow and care about. There is also the problem of who exactly Gilliam thinks the Brothers Grimm are. At times they seem like romantic heroes, at times like clowns, at times like fake magicians, at times like real ones. Their own fairy tales had the virtue of being tightly focused and implacable in their sense of justice: Misbehavior was cruelly punished as often as virtue was rewarded. Their strict code is lacking in the movie, which is based on shifting moral sands. At times the Grimms are liars and charlatans, at times brave and true. Those times seem chosen at the convenience of the movie.

Gilliam has always been a director who fills the screen with rich visual spectacle. In *Brazil* and *12 Monkeys* and *The Adventures of Baron Munchausen,* in the past and in the future, his world is always hallucinatory in its richness of detail. Here the haunted forest is really very impressive, but to what end? In a movie like Tim Burton's *The Legend of Sleepy Hollow,* the night and shadows hold real menace. Here the trees seem more like an idea than a danger. And the movie, for all of its fantastic striving, stays on the screen and fails to engage our imagination.

Bubble ★ ★ ★ ★

R, 73 m., 2006

Debbie Doebereiner (Martha), Dustin James Ashley (Kyle), Misty Dawn Wilkins (Rose), Omar Cowan (Martha's Dad), Laurie Lee (Kyle's Mother), David Hubbard (Pastor), Kyle Smith (Jake), Decker Moody (Detective Don). Directed by Steven Soderbergh and produced by Gregory Jacobs. Screenplay by Coleman Hough.

Steven Soderbergh's *Bubble* approaches with awe and caution the rhythms of ordinary life itself. He tells the stories of three Ohio factory workers who have been cornered by life. They work two low-paying jobs, they dream of getting a few bucks ahead, they eat fast food without noticing it, two of them live with their parents, one of them has a car. Their speech is such a monotone of commonplaces that we have to guess about how they really feel, and sometimes, we suspect, so do they.

I haven't made the movie sound enthralling. But it is. The characters are so closely observed and played with such exacting accuracy and conviction that *Bubble* becomes quietly, inexorably hypnotic. Soderbergh never underlines, never points, never uses music to suggest emotion, never shows the characters thinking ahead, watches appalled as small shifts in orderly lives lead to a murder.

Everything about the film—its casting, its filming, its release—is daring and innovative. Soderbergh, the poster boy of the Sundance generation (for *sex, lies . . . and videotape* sixteen years ago), has moved confidently ever since between commercial projects *(Ocean's Eleven)* and cutting-edge experiments like *Bubble.* The movie was cast with local people who were not actors. They participated in the creation of their dialogue. Their own homes were used as sets. The film was shot quickly in high-definition video.

And when it opens in theaters, it will simultaneously play on HDNet cable and four days later be released on DVD. Here is an experiment to see if there is a way to bring a small art film to a larger audience; most films like this would play in a handful of big-city art houses, and you'd read this review and maybe reflect that it sounded interesting and then lose track of it. In a time when audiences are pounded into theaters with multimillion-dollar ad campaigns, here's a small film with a big idea behind it.

As the film opens, Martha (Debbie Doebereiner) awakens, brings breakfast to her elderly father, picks up Kyle (Dustin James Ashley) at his mobile home, stops at a bakery, and arrives at the doll factory where they both work. He operates machinery to create plastic body parts. She paints the faces and adds the eyelashes and hair. During their lunch hour in a room of Formica and fluorescence, they talk about nothing much. He doesn't have time to date. He'd like to get the money together to buy a car. He'd like a ride after work to his other job. Martha, who is fat and ten or fifteen years older than Kyle, watches him carefully, looking for clues in his shy and inward speech.

Rose (Misty Dawn Wilkins) begins work at the factory. She is introduced to the workforce and provides Kyle with a smile so small he may not even see it, but Martha does. How should we read this? In a conventional movie, Kyle would be attracted to Rose, and Martha would be jealous. But *Bubble* is more cautiously modulated. Martha, I believe, has never allowed herself to think Kyle would be attracted to her. What she wants from him is what she already has: a form of possession in the way he depends on her for rides and chats with her at lunch. Nor does Kyle seem prepared to go after Rose. He is shy, quiet, and withdrawn, smokes pot at home, keeps a low profile at work.

Rose at least represents change. She takes Martha along to a suburban house that she cleans, and Martha is shocked to find her taking a bubble bath. Rose explains that her apartment, which she shares with her two-year-old daughter, has only a shower. "I'm not too sure about her," Martha tells Kyle. "She scares me a little."

Rose asks Kyle out. In a bar, they share their reasons for dropping out of high school. Their date goes nowhere—not even when Rose gets herself asked into his bedroom—because Kyle is too passive to make a move, or maybe even to respond to one. He's too beaten down by life. "I'm very ready to get out of this area," says Rose, who observes that everybody is poor and there are no opportunities.

I am describing the events but not the fascination they create. The uncanny effect comes in large part from the actors. I learn that Debbie Doebereiner is the manager of a KFC. That Misty Dawn Wilkins is a hairdresser, and her own daughter plays her daughter in the movie. They are not playing themselves, but they are playing people they know from the inside out, and although Soderbergh must have worked closely with them, his most important work was in the casting: Not everybody could carry a feature film made of everyday life and make it work, but these three do. The movie feels so real a hush falls upon the audience, and we are made aware of how much artifice there is in conventional acting. You wouldn't want to spend the rest of your life watching movies like this, because artifice has its uses, but in this film, with these actors, something mysterious happens.

I said there was a murder. That's all I'll say about it. The local police inspector (Decker Moody) handles the case. He is played by an actual local police inspector. We have seen a hundred or a thousand movies where a cop visits the crime scene and later cross-examines people. There has never been one like this. In the flat, experienced, businesslike way he does his job, and in the way his instincts guide him past misleading evidence, the inspector depends not on crime-movie suspense but on implacable logic. *Bubble* ends not with the solution to a crime but with the revelation of the depths of a lonely heart.

Some theater owners are boycotting *Bubble* because they hate the idea of a simultaneous release on cable and DVD. I think it's the only hope for a movie like this. Let's face it. Even though I call the film a masterpiece (and I do), my plot description has not set you afire with desire to see the film. Unless you admire Soderbergh or can guess what I'm saying about the performances, you'll be there in line for *Annapolis* or *Nanny McPhee.* But maybe you're curious enough to check it out on cable, or rent it on DVD, or put it in your Netflix queue. That's how movies like this can have a chance. And how you can have a chance to see them.

The Bucket List ★

PG-13, 97 m., 2008

Jack Nicholson (Edward Cole), Morgan Freeman (Carter Chambers), Sean Hayes (Thomas), Rob Morrow (Dr. Hollins), Beverly Todd (Virginia Chambers). Directed by Rob Reiner and produced by Craig Zadan, Neil Meron, and Alan Greisman. Screenplay by Justin Zackham.

The Bucket List is a movie about two old codgers who are nothing like people, both suffering from cancer that is nothing like cancer, and setting off on adventures that are nothing like possible. I urgently advise hospitals: Do not make the DVD available to your patients; there may be an outbreak of bedpans thrown at TV screens.

The film opens with yet another voice-over narration by Morgan Freeman, extolling the saintly virtues of a white person who deserves our reverence. His voice takes on a sort of wonderment as he speaks of the man's greatness; it was a note that worked in *The Shawshank Redemption* and *Million Dollar Baby,* but not here, not when he is talking of a character played by Jack Nicholson, for whom lovability is not a strong suit.

Nicholson plays Edward, an enormously rich man of about seventy, who has been diagnosed with cancer, given a year to live, and is sharing a room with Carter (Freeman), about the same age, same prognosis. Why does a billionaire not have a private room? Why, because Edward owns the hospital, and he has a policy that all patients must double up, so it would look bad if he didn't.

This is only one among countless details the movie gets wrong. Doesn't Edward know that hospitals make lotsa profits by offering private rooms, "concierge service," etc.? The fact is, Edward and Carter must be roommates to set up their Meet Cute, during which they first rub each other the wrong way, and then have an orgy of male bonding. Turns out Carter has a "bucket list" of things he should do before he kicks the bucket. Edward embraces this idea, announces, "Hell, all I have is money," and treats Carter to an around-the-world trip in his private airplane, during which they will, let's see, I have the itinerary right here, visit the pyramids, the Taj Mahal, Hong Kong, the French Riviera, and the Himalayas.

Carter is faithfully married to his loving wife, Virginia (Beverly Todd), who is remarkably restrained about seeing her dying husband off on this madcap folly. She doesn't take it well, but I know wives who would call for the boys with butterfly nets. Edward, after four divorces, has no restraints, plenty of regrets, and uses his generosity to mask egotism, selfishness, and the imposition of his goofy whim on poor Carter. That his behavior is seen as somehow redemptive is perhaps the movie's weirdest fantasy. Meanwhile, the codgers have pseudo-profound conversations about the Meaning of It All, and Carter's superior humanity begins to soak in for the irascible Edward.

The movie, directed by Rob Reiner, is written by Justin Zackham, who must be very optimistic indeed if he doesn't know that there is nothing like a serious illness to bring you to the end of sitcom clichés. I've never had chemo, as Edward and Carter must endure, but I have had cancer, and believe me, during convalescence after surgery the *last* item on your bucket list is climbing a Himalaya. It's more likely to be topped by keeping down a full meal, having a triumphant bowel movement, keeping your energy up in the afternoon, letting your loved ones know you love them, and convincing the doc your reports of pain are real and not merely disguising your desire to become a drug addict. To be sure, the movie includes plenty of details about discomfort in the toilet, but they're put on hold once the trots are replaced by the globetrotting.

Edward and Carter fly off on their odyssey, during which the only realistic detail is the interior of Edward's private jet. Other locations are created, all too obviously, by special effects; the boys in front of the pyramids look about as convincing as Abbot and Costello wearing pith helmets in front of a painted backdrop. Meanwhile, we wait patiently for Edward to realize his inner humanity, reach out to his estranged daughter, and learn all the other life lessons Carter has to bestow. All Carter gets out of it is months away from his beloved family, and the opportunity to be a moral cheering section for Edward's conversion.

I'm thinking, just once, couldn't a movie open with the voice-over telling us what a great guy the Morgan Freeman character was? Nicholson could say, "I was a rich, unpleasant, selfish jerk, and this wise, nice man taught me to feel hope and love." Yeah, that would be nice. Because what's so great about Edward, anyway? He throws his money around like a pig and makes Carter come along for the ride. So what?

There are movies that find humor, albeit perhaps of a bitter, sardonic nature, in cancer. Some of them show incredible bravery, as in Mike Nichols's *Wit,* with its great performance by Emma Thompson. *The Bucket List* thinks dying of cancer is a laff riot, followed by a dime-store epiphany. The sole redeeming merit of the film is the steady work by Morgan Freeman, who has appeared in more than one embarrassing movie but never embarrassed himself. Maybe it's not Jack Nicholson's fault that his role cries out to be overplayed, but it's his fate, and ours.

Bug ★ ★ ★ ½

R, 110 m., 2007

Ashley Judd (Agnes White), Michael Shannon (Peter Evans), Harry Connick Jr. (Jerry Goss), Lynn Collins (R.C.), Brian F. O'Byrne (Dr. Sweet). Directed by William Friedkin and produced by Michael Ohoven, Holly Wiersma, Malcolm Petal, and Kimberly C. Anderson. Screenplay by Tracy Letts, based on his play.

William Friedkin's *Bug* begins as an ominous rumble of unease and builds to a shriek. The last twenty minutes are searingly intense: A paranoid personality finds its mate, and they race each other into madness. For Friedkin, director of *The Exorcist,* it's a work of headlong passion.

Its stars, Ashley Judd and Michael Shannon, achieve a kind of manic intensity that's frightening not just in itself but because you almost fear for the actors. They're working without a net.

The film is based on a play by Tracy Letts, an actor and playwright at Chicago's Steppenwolf Theatre, that was a hit in Chicago and New York. In the film, we meet Agnes (Judd), a waitress in a honky-tonk lesbian bar, living in a shabby motel. Her violent ex-husband (Harry Connick Jr.), just out on parole, walks back into her life, still violent. At about the same time her gay friend, R.C. (Lynn Collins), drags in a stray with haunted eyes. This is the polite stranger named Peter (Shannon), who says he doesn't want sex or anything else, is attentive and courteous, and is invited by Agnes to spend the night even though he seems (to us) like the embodiment of menace.

The story involves this man's obsession with bugs that he believes infect his cells and may have been implanted by the government during his treatment for obscure causes after military service in the Gulf. We think he's crazy. Agnes listens and nods and doesn't want him to leave; she feels safer around him. He begins to seem weirder. This doesn't bother her. With mounting urgency, she begins to share his obsession with bugs, and together they hurtle headlong into a paranoid fantasy that ties together in one perfect conspiracy all of the suspicions they've ever had about anything. There is a scene we're not prepared for, in which they're peering into a cheap microscope and seeing whatever they think they see.

Peter is mad, and Agnes's personality seems to need him to express its own madness. Ashley Judd's final monologue is a sustained cry of nonstop breathless panic, twisted logic, and sudden frantic insight that is a kind of behavior very rarely risked in or out of the movies. It may not be Shakespeare, but it's not any easier.

Shannon, a member of the Red Orchid Theatre in Chicago, delivers his own nonstop, rapid-fire monologue of madness; he has a frightening speech that scares the audience but makes perfect sense to Agnes. His focus and concentration compares in some ways to Peter Greene's work in Lodge Kerrigan's frightening *Clean, Shaven.*

The film is lean, direct, unrelenting. A lot of it takes place in the motel room, which by the end has been turned into an eerie cave lined with aluminum foil, a sort of psychic air raid shelter against government emissions or who knows what else? "They're watching us," Peter says.

The thing about *Bug* is that we're not scared for ourselves so much as for the characters in the movie. Judd and Shannon bravely cast all restraint aside and allow themselves to be seen as raw, terrified, and mad. The core of the film involves how quickly Judd's character falls into sympathy with Shannon's. She seems like a potential paranoid primed to be activated, and yet her transformation never seems hurried and is always convincing.

For Friedkin, the film is a return to form after some disappointments like *Jade.* It feels like a young man's picture, filled with edge and energy. Some reviews have criticized *Bug* for revealing its origins as a play, since most of it takes place on one set. But of course it does. There is nothing here to "open up" and every reason to create a claustrophobic feel. Paranoia shuts down into a desperate focus. It doesn't spread its wings and fly.

C

Caché ★ ★ ★ ★

R, 121 m., 2006

Daniel Auteuil (Georges Laurent), Juliette Binoche (Anne Laurent), Maurice Benichou (Majid), Annie Girardot (Georges' Mom), Bernard Le Coq (Georges' Editor), Daniel Duval (Pierre), Lester Makedonsky (Pierrot Laurent), Walid Afkir (Majid's Son). Directed by Michael Haneke and produced by Veit Heiduschka. Screenplay by Haneke.

The opening shot of Michael Haneke's *Caché* shows the facade of a townhouse on a side street in Paris. As the credits roll, ordinary events take place on the street. Then we discover that this footage is a video and that it is being watched by Anne and Georges Laurent (Juliette Binoche and Daniel Auteuil). It is their house. They have absolutely no idea who took the video, or why it was sent to them.

So opens a perplexing and disturbing film of great effect, showing how comfortable lives are disrupted by the simple fact that someone is watching. Georges is the host of a TV program about books; yes, in France they have shows where intellectuals argue about books and an audience that actually watches them. Georges and Anne live in their book-lined house with their son, Pierrot Laurent (Lester Makedonsky), a teenager who is sulky and distracted in the way that teenagers can be when they have little to complain about except their discontent.

Another video arrives, showing the farmhouse where Georges and his family lived when he was a child. All the videos they receive will have the same style: a camera at some distance, simply looking. Many of the shots in the film itself are set up and filmed in the same way, so that *Caché* could be watching itself just as the videos watch the Laurents. No comment is made in the videos through camera position, movement, editing—or perhaps there is the same comment all the time: Someone wants them to know that they are being watched.

Another video arrives, showing a journey down a suburban street and into a building. Georges is able to freeze a frame and make out a street name; going off alone, he follows the path of the video and finds himself in front of a door in an apartment building. The person inside is someone he knows, but this person (whom I will not describe) is unlikely to be the author of the alarming videos.

Georges conceals the results of his trip from his wife. Then another video arrives, showing him speaking with the occupant of the apartment. Now there is a fierce argument between Georges and Anne: She cannot trust him, she feels. He must tell her who the person is. He will not. In a way, he cannot. She feels threatened by the videos, and now threatened because her husband may be withholding information she needs to know. Binoche trembles with fury as the wife who feels betrayed by her husband; Auteuil, a master of detachment, folds into himself as a man who simply cannot talk about his deepest feelings.

Meanwhile, their lives continue. Georges does the TV show. Their son goes to school. There is a dinner party, at which a story about a dog will give you something to recycle with great effect at your own next dinner party. Georges goes to visit his mother. He asks about events that happened in 1961, when he was a boy. His mother asks him if something is wrong. He denies it. She simply regards him. She knows her son, and she knows something is wrong.

I have deliberately left out a great deal of information, because the experience of *Caché* builds as we experience the film. There are parallels, for example, between the TV news that is often on in the background, and some of the events in Georges' past. We expect that the mystery of the videos will be solved, explained, and make sense. But perhaps not. Here is a curious thing: In some of the videos, the camera seems to be in a position where anyone could see it, but no one ever does.

When *Caché* played at Cannes 2005 (where it won the prize for best direction), it had an English title, *Hidden*. That may be a better title than *Caché*, which can also be an English word, but more obscure. In the film, the camera is hidden. So are events in Georges' life. Some of what he knows is hidden from his wife. The son keeps secrets from his parents, and so on. The film seems to argue that life would have gone on well enough for the Laurents had it not been for the unsettling knowledge that they had become visible, that someone knew something about them, that someone was watching.

The last shot of the film, like many others, is taken from a camera that does not move. It regards events on the outside staircase of a building. There are a lot of people moving around. Closer to us than most of them is a figure with her back turned, placed just to the right of center; given basic rules of composition, this is where our eye will fall if all else in the shot is equal. Many viewers will not notice another element in the shot. Stop reading now if you plan to see the film, and save the review . . .

. . . and now observe that two people meet and talk on the upper left-hand side of the screen. They are two characters we recognize, and who should not know each other or have any way of meeting. Why do they know each other? What does it explain, that they do? Does it explain anything? Are there not still questions without answers? *Caché* is a film of bottomless intrigue. "The unexamined life is not worth living," said Socrates. An examined life may bring its own form of disquiet.

When *Caché* played at Cannes, some critics deplored its lack of a resolution. I think it works precisely because it leaves us hanging. It proposes not to solve the mystery of the videos but to portray the paranoia and distrust that they create. If the film merely revealed in its closing scenes who was sending the videos and why, it would belittle itself. We are left feeling as the characters feel, uneasy, violated, spied upon, surrounded by faceless observers. The nonexplanation supplied by the enigmatic last scene opens a new area of speculation that also lacks any solution or closure. And the secrets of Georges' past reach out their guilty tendrils to the next generation.

Canvas ★ ★ ★

PG-13, 100 m., 2007

Joe Pantoliano (John Marino), Marcia Gay Harden (Mary Marino), Devon Gearhart (Chris Marino), Sophia Bairley (Dawn). Directed by Joseph Greco and produced by Joe Pantoliano and Bill Erfurth. Screenplay by Greco.

Canvas is a serious film about mental illness and a sentimental heart-warmer, and it succeeds in both ways. It tells the story of a ten-year-old whose mother is schizophrenic and whose father is loyal and loving but stretched almost beyond his endurance. The portrayal of schizophrenia in the film has been praised by mental health experts as unusually accurate and sympathetic; the story of the boy and his dad is a portrait of love under enormous stress.

Writer-director Joseph Greco says the film, his first feature, was influenced by his own childhood with a schizophrenic mother. Even the father's determination to build a sailboat comes from Greco's own life. His film benefits from persuasive, moving performances from all three leads: Joe Pantoliano as John Marino, a construction worker; Marcia Gay Harden as Mary, his wife; and Devon Gearhart as their young son, Chris. There is also an affecting performance by Sophia Bairley as Dawn, a schoolmate who becomes Chris's friend and confidant.

As the film opens, Mary is just a little too demonstrative in her love for Chris, whom she possibly hasn't seen for a while. That night Chris is awakened by flashing blue lights through the window; his mother has had a panic attack, and his father and the police are bringing her back to the house. She is under medication, which doesn't seem to be working, and on another night, when she runs wild through a rainstorm, the police handcuff her "for her own safety," and she is committed to an asylum.

All of this is very hard on Chris, as cruel schoolmates taunt him about his crazy mother. When his father, desperate for distraction, begins to build a sailboat in the driveway, Chris begins to hear that his dad is crazy, too. He is a wise, solemn kid, but it all begins to get to him, especially when his mother inappropriately crashes his precious birthday party for a few friends in a local arcade.

The more movies I see, the more I wonder at what actors can do. Consider Joe Pantoliano. Famous for *The Sopranos,* established as a character actor playing gangster and comic types, known by everyone including himself as "Joey Pants," he has a role here that most people would never think of him for, and he brings it tenderness and depth. He still loves his wife and yearns for her return to health. He loves his son but isn't always perceptive enough of his needs. He spends money that he doesn't have on the boat. He has worked hard for twenty years and has a boss who isn't fair with him. Pantoliano brings to all of these dimensions a confidence and understanding that is a revelation; how many other actors are trapped by typecasting and have such unexplored regions within their talent?

Marcia Gay Harden finds a fine balance between madness and the temptations of overacting. Yes, she runs wild sometimes but always as a human being, not as a caricature. And as the son, Devon Gearhart, who is at the center of many of the crucial scenes, has an unaffected and natural sincerity that is effective and convincing. I have noticed recently several performances by children that have a simplicity and grace that adults can only envy.

The film's ending may be more upbeat than the characters could hope for in real life, but it doesn't cave in to neat solutions. One scene in particular looks like a manufactured happy ending until the camera pulls back and provides a context for it. *Canvas* is a heart-warmer, as I said, a touching story of these people for whom the only response to mental illness is love.

Cape of Good Hope ★ ★ ★

PG-13, 107 m., 2006

Debbie Brown (Kate), Eriq Ebouaney (Jean Claude), Nthati Moshesh (Lindiwe), Morne Visser (Morne), Quanita Adams (Sharifa), David Isaacs (Habib), Kamo Masilo (Thabo), Nick Boraine (Stephen van Heern). Directed by Mark Bamford and produced by Suzanne Kay Bamford and Genevieve Hofmeyr. Screenplay by Mark and Suzanne Kay Bamford.

In Cape Town, one of the most beautiful cities on Earth, we meet people who move uncertainly into their own futures. The iron curtain separating the races has lifted, and they are all (except one) citizens on equal footing, but Mark Bamford's *Cape of Good Hope* is a postapartheid film in which the characters are less concerned with politics than with matters of the heart. Of course, political and economic concerns drift in (they do regardless of whether we admit it), but the title is a good one, standing not only for that point at the bottom of Africa where the Indian and Atlantic oceans meet, but also for good hope itself, about love, choices, and the future.

The movie belongs to a genre that has been named "hyperlink cinema" by the critic Alissa Quart in *Film Comment*. She suggests the structure was invented by Robert Altman, and Altman certainly brought it into modern times and made it particularly useful for showing interlocking stories in a world where lives seem to crash into each other heedlessly. *Crash*, indeed, is an example of the genre, as are Altman's *The Player* and *Short Cuts*, and such films as *Traffic*, *Syriana*, *City of God*, *Amores Perros*, and *Nine Lives*.

Cape of Good Hope transports the hyperlink movie to South Africa, to show how lives previously divided by race and class now connect more unpredictably. Two women (one white, one Indian) work at an animal shelter with a refugee from the Congo. We meet an African maid and her mother and son, a white veterinarian, an older woman trying to fool herself into romance with a younger man, and others whose lives are more connected than they realize. Most of the hidden connections eventually have positive results; this is a movie with characters we care about, living ordinary lives with reasonable goals.

Kate (Debbie Brown) is the white woman who runs the animal shelter. She has never married, is having an affair with a married man. Her best friend is Sharifa (Quanita Adams), a Muslim woman who works with her at the shelter; Sharifa is married to Habib (David Isaacs), and they are a childless couple who argue over their inability to conceive a child. One day Kate meets young Thabo (Kamo Masilo), a boy who lives in a nearby African township. He has a clever dog named Tupac (when will the hyperlinks end?), and Kate hires him and his dog to entertain at the shelter's open house. Through Thabo we meet his mother, Lindiwe (Nthati Moshesh), the maid, and his grandmother, who is conspiring to marry Lindiwe to an elderly but affluent local minister. Oh, and Kate has dealings with a veterinarian named Morne (Morne Visser), who likes her, although she seems to prefer the detachment of an affair.

These characters are introduced briskly in their everyday lives against the backdrop of the Cape Town suburb of Hout Bay, one of those communities that are strung along the lower slopes of Table Mountain, which so benevolently looks down on rich and poor, happy and miserable.

For me, the most interesting character it overlooks is Jean Claude (Eriq Ebouaney, who played the title role in *Lumumba* and had a key role in Brian de Palma's *Femme Fatale*). He is a French-speaking refugee from the violence of the Congo who works at the animal shelter cleaning the cages. On Sundays, he volunteers at the Cape Town Observatory. As a volunteer, his official job is to sweep and clean, although he often engages young students in stories of the universe that leave them goggle-eyed. Jean Claude in fact has a Ph.D. in astronomy, but like the Beirut surgeon in *Yes* who works in London as a waiter, he cannot as a refugee find the employment he was trained for. There is a colossal irony when Jean Claude is fired by the head of the observatory because government policy dictates that such jobs should go to locals. "But I am not paid!" he points out. Nevertheless, he has to go.

Jean Claude meets Lindiwe and her son, Thabo, falls in love with her, is idolized by the boy, is an alternative to the loathed elderly minister. But if his application for Canadian citizenship comes through, will he have to leave her behind? Meanwhile, Kate continues to befriend Thabo, which leads her to an after-dark visit to a nearby African township where, as any city-smart person should know, she might not be entirely safe wandering the streets by herself. These stories are intercut, or hyperlinked, to reveal more and unexpected connections. Will Kate dump the married man and find room in her life for the veterinarian? Will Sharifa and her husband be able to conceive? Do Jean Claude and Lindiwe have a future? And what about the dog at the shelter who was trained to attack blacks? Will it learn to get along with all races in the new South Africa?

While we are absorbed in these stories, while some of the characters appeal enormously to us, we are at the same time being drawn subtly into the emerging South African multiracialism. What *Cape of Good Hope* argues, I think, is that we live in sad times if political issues define our lives. When politics do not create walls (as apartheid did), most people are primarily interested in their families, their romances, and their jobs. They hope to improve all three. The movie is about their hope.

The movie was directed by Mark Bamford; his wife, Suzanne Kay Bamford, cowrote and coproduced. At the Toronto festival, they told me they were Americans who were unable to interest Hollywood in the stories they wanted to tell. They moved to Cape Town "for one year" and are still there after four. Ironically, their screenplay for *Cape of Good Hope* attracted the interest of Hollywood, but the studios wanted to use an American cast to play the South Africans. That would have lost the particular local flavor that is one of the film's assets.

Capote ★ ★ ★ ★

R, 114 m., 2005

Philip Seymour Hoffman (Truman Capote), Catherine Keener (Nelle Harper Lee), Clifton Collins Jr. (Perry Smith), Chris Cooper (Alvin Dewey), Bruce Greenwood (Jack Dunphy), Bob Balaban (William Shawn), Amy Ryan (Marie Dewey), Mark Pellegrino (Dick Hickock). Directed by Bennett Miller and produced by Caroline Baron, William Vince, and Michael Ohoven. Screenplay by Dan Futterman, based on the book *Capote* by Gerald Clarke.

On November 15, 1959, Truman Capote noticed a news item about four members of a Kansas farm family who were shotgunned to death. He telephoned William Shawn, editor of the *New Yorker,* wondering if Shawn would be interested in an article about the murders. Later in his life Capote said that if he had known what would happen as a result of this impulse, he would not have stopped in Holcomb, Kansas, but would have kept right on going "like a bat out of hell."

At first Capote thought the story would be about how a rural community was dealing with the tragedy. "I don't care one way or the other if you catch who did this," he tells an agent from the Kansas Bureau of Investigation. Then two drifters, Perry Smith and Richard Hickock, are arrested and charged with the crime. As Capote gets to know them, he's consumed by a story that would make him rich and famous, and destroy him. His "nonfiction novel," *In Cold Blood,* became a best-seller and inspired a movie, but Capote was emotionally devastated by the experience and it hastened his death.

Bennett Miller's *Capote* is about that crucial

period of fewer than six years in Capote's life. As he talks to the killers, to law officers, and to the neighbors of the murdered Clutter family, Capote's project takes on depth and shape as the story of conflicting fates. But at the heart of his reporting is an irredeemable conflict: He wins the trust of the two convicted killers and essentially falls in love with Perry Smith, while needing them to die to supply an ending for his book. "If they win this appeal," he tells his friend Harper Lee, "I may have a complete nervous breakdown." After they are hanged on April 14, 1965, he tells Harper, "There wasn't anything I could have done to save them." She says: "Maybe, but the fact is you didn't want to."

Capote is a film of uncommon strength and insight, about a man whose great achievement requires the surrender of his self-respect. Philip Seymour Hoffman's precise, uncanny performance as Capote doesn't imitate the author so much as channel him, as a man whose peculiarities mask great intelligence and deep wounds.

As the story opens, Capote is a well-known writer (of *Breakfast at Tiffany's,* among others), a popular guest on talk shows, a man whose small stature, large ego, and affectations of speech and appearance make him an outsider wherever he goes. Trying to win the confidence of a young girl in Kansas, he tells her: "Ever since I was a child, folks have thought they had me pegged because of the way I am, the way I talk." But he was able to enter a world far removed from Manhattan and write a great book about ordinary Midwesterners and two pathetic, heartless killers. Could anyone be less like Truman Capote than Perry Smith? Yet they were both mistreated and passed around as children, had issues with distant and remote mothers, had secret fantasies. "It's like Perry and I grew up in the same house, and one day he went out the back door and I went out the front," he tells Harper Lee.

The film, written by Dan Futterman and based on the book *Capote* by Gerald Clarke, focuses on the way a writer works on a story and the story works on him. Capote wins the wary acceptance of Alvin Dewey (Chris Cooper), the agent assigned to the case. Over dinner in Alvin and Marie Dewey's kitchen, he entertains them with stories of John Huston and Humphrey Bogart. As he talks, he studies their house like an anthropologist. He convinces the local funeral director to let him view the mutilated bodies of the Clutters. Later, Perry Smith will tell him he liked the father, Herb Clutter: "I thought he was a very nice, gentle man. I thought so right up until I slit his throat."

On his trips to Kansas, Capote takes along a southern friend from childhood, Harper Lee (Catherine Keener). So long does it take him to finish his book that Lee in the meantime has time to publish her famous novel, *To Kill a Mockingbird,* sell it to the movies, and attend the world premiere with Gregory Peck. Harper Lee is a practical, grounded woman who clearly sees that Truman cares for Smith and yet will exploit him for his book. "Do you hold him in esteem, Truman?" she asks, and he is defensive: "Well, he's a gold mine."

Perry Smith and Dick Hickock are played by Clifton Collins Jr. and Mark Pellegrino. Hickock is not developed as deeply as in Richard Brooks's film *In Cold Blood* (1967), where he was played by Scott Wilson; the emphasis this time is on Smith, played in 1967 by Robert Blake and here by Collins as a haunted, repressed man in constant pain who chews aspirin by the handful and yet shelters a certain poetry; his drawings and journal move Capote, who sees him as a man who was born a victim and deserves not forgiveness but pity.

The other key characters are Capote's lover, Jack Dunphy (Bruce Greenwood), and his editor at the *New Yorker,* William Shawn (Bob Balaban). "Jack thinks I'm using Perry," Truman tells Harper. "He also thinks I fell in love with him in Kansas." Shawn thinks *In Cold Blood,* when it is finally written, is "going to change how people write." He prints the entire book in his magazine.

The movie *In Cold Blood* had no speaking role for Capote, who in a sense stood behind the camera with the director. If *Capote* had simply flipped the coin and told the story of the Clutter murders from Capote's point of view, it might have been a good movie, but what makes it so powerful is that it looks with merciless perception at Capote's moral disintegration.

"If I leave here without understanding you," Capote tells Perry Smith during one of many visits to his cell, "the world will see you as a monster. I don't want that." He is able to convince Smith and Hickock to tell him what happened on the night of the murders. He learns heartbreaking details, such as that they "put a different pillow under the boy's head just to shoot him." Capote tells them he will support their appeals and help them find another lawyer. He betrays them. Smith eventually understands that and accepts his fate. "Two weeks, and finito," he tells Capote as his execution draws near. Another good line for the book.

Cars ★ ★

G, 118 m., 2006

Voices of: Owen Wilson (Lightning McQueen), Paul Newman (Doc Hudson), Bonnie Hunt (Sally Carrera), Larry the Cable Guy (Mater), George Carlin (Fillmore), Paul Dooley (Sarge), Cheech Marin (Ramone), Jenifer Lewis (Flo), Tony Shalhoub (Luigi), Michael Wallis (The Sheriff), Richard Petty (The King), Michael Keaton (Chick Hicks), John Ratzenberger (Mack). Directed by John Lasseter and produced by Darla K. Anderson. Screenplay by Dan Fogelman, Lasseter, Kiel Murray, and Phil Lorin.

I wouldn't have thought that even in animation a 1951 Hudson Hornet could look simultaneously like itself and like Paul Newman, but you will witness that feat, and others, in *Cars.* This is the new animated feature by John Lasseter (*Toy Story, A Bug's Life*); it tells a bright and cheery story and then has a little something profound lurking around the edges. In this case, it's a sense of loss.

What have we lost? The movie's hero, a racing car named Lightning McQueen (voice by Owen Wilson), has just lost a big race, and then one day on the highway he goes astray and rolls into the forgotten hamlet of Radiator Springs, in Carburetor County. This was a happenin' town back when Route 66 was the way to get from Chicago to L.A., passing through Flagstaff, Arizona, and don't forget Winona. But now the interstates and time itself have passed it by, and the town slumbers on, a memory of an earlier America.

Lightning's dream is to win the Piston Cup, the grand prix of American racing. He's on his way to the race when he gets lost and then, more humiliating, impounded. Once released, he meets the population of Radiator Springs, led by Doc Hudson (Paul Newman), who may be an old-timer but probably knows something about Hudsons that Lightning doesn't: Because of their "step-down design," they had a lower center of gravity than the Big 3 models of their time and won stock car races by making tighter turns.

Other citizens include Mater (rhymes with *tow-mater*) the Tow Truck (Larry the Cable Guy), Sally the sexy Porsche (Bonnie Hunt), Fillmore the hippie VW bus (George Carlin), and Sarge the veteran Jeep (Paul Dooley). Tractors serve as the cows of Radiator Springs and even chew their cud, although what that cud consists of I'm not sure. Fan belts, maybe.

The message in *Cars* is simplicity itself: Life was better in the old days, when it revolved around small towns where everybody knew each other, and around small highways such as Route 66, where you made new friends, sometimes even between Flagstaff and Winona. This older America long has been much beloved by Hollywood, and apparently it survives in Radiator Springs as sort of a time capsule.

Doc Hudson, it turns out, was a famous race car in his day. That leads up to a race in which the vet and the kid face off, although how that race ends I would not dream of revealing. What I will reveal, with regret, is that the movie lacks a single Studebaker. The 1950s Studebakers are much beloved by all period movies, because they so clearly signal their period, from the classic Raymond Loewy–designed models to the Golden Hawk, which left Corvettes and T-Birds eating its dust. Maybe there's no Hawk in Radiator Springs because then Doc Hudson would lose his bragging rights.

The movie is great to look at and a lot of fun but somehow lacks the extra push of the other Pixar films. Maybe that's because there's less at stake here, and no child-surrogate to identify with. I wonder if the movie's primary audience, which skews young, will care much about the 1950s and its cars. Maybe they will. Of all decades, the 1950s seems to have the most staying power; like Archie and Jughead, the decade stays forever young, perhaps because that's when modern teenagers were invented.

Casanova ★ ★

R, 108 m., 2005

Heath Ledger (Casanova), Sienna Miller (Francesca Bruni), Oliver Platt (Paprizzio),

Jeremy Irons (Bishop Pucci), Lena Olin (Andrea Bruni), Charlie Cox (Giovanni), Natalie Dormer (Victoria). Directed by Lasse Hallstrom and produced by Betsy Beers, Mark Gordon, and Leslie Holleran. Screenplay by Jeffrey Hatcher and Kimberly Simi.

I have just been idly paging through volume three of *Casanova's Memoirs,* which covers the circa 1753 time frame of Lasse Hallstrom's new film. Casanova was a busy man. He found himself in Parma ("perplexities concerning my female traveling companion"), Bologna ("Henriette resumes the dress of her sex"), Geneva ("unpleasant adventure with an actress"), Venice ("adventure with the Marchetti girl"), Paris ("I practice cabalism for the duchess of Chartres"), Padua ("her father refuses and puts her in a convent"), and Vicenza ("my tragicomic scene at the inn"). That he also found the will and the way to undertake the adventures in this film is explained only because it is fictional.

Its most imaginary aspect might appear to be his love affair with a swashbuckling cross-dressing feminist named Francesca Bruni, but, as we have seen, he had already met a cross-dresser in 1753 and, for that matter, had been one. As for feminism as it existed at that time, all its beliefs seem to have included the implicit footnote "except for Casanova." What is accurate about the movie is that he was the quarry of the Inquisition and doomed to be locked up in the infamous dungeon reached from the Ducal Palace by the Bridge of Sighs, which even then had tourists lined up three deep on the nearby Ponte della Paglia, awaiting the invention of the Instamatic.

Casanova was such a genuinely fascinating person, so tireless, seductive, brilliant, revolutionary, and daring, that Hallstrom's *Casanova* hardly does him justice. He was a magician, an author, a lawyer, the secretary to a cardinal, a politician, and a violinist; invented the national lottery; was a spy and a diplomat; and has been played by Bela Lugosi, Donald Sutherland, Peter O'Toole, and now by Heath Ledger, whose other current film, *Brokeback Mountain,* has him playing a gay cowboy, a role that eluded Casanova only because cowboys hadn't been invented yet.

The film is no more implausible than Casanova's actual adventures. It shows him returning in Venice (he did), running across the rooftops (he did) while being chased by the Inquisition (he was) and protected by the ruler of Venice, the doge (also true). The doge orders him to get married. He selects the virginal Victoria (Natalie Dormer), only to find she is already affianced to Giovanni (Charlie Cox), whose sister Francesca (Sienna Miller) is a feminist who dons male garb and impersonates Giovanni after her brother (Giovanni, that is) challenges Casanova to a sword fight. She is the more skilled swordsperson, and Casanova, keen student of swordsmanship, transfers his lust to her, only to learn that she is engaged to Paprizzio (Oliver Platt), who is, according to my notes, "the lard king of Genoa."

It must be a wondrous thing to be the lard king of Genoa, and I would have wished Casanova time to quiz Paprizzio about his lofty estate, but the Inquisition is fed up with Casanova's flaunting of morality and appoints Pucci (Jeremy Irons) to apprehend and imprison him. By this time Casanova has grown somewhat weary, although when he resumes his real-life *Autobiography* it still has eight more volumes of tireless lubricity to go. As I watched the film, I kept having flash-forwards, or were they flash-sidewayses, to the forthcoming film *The Libertine,* in which Johnny Depp plays a Casanova wannabe who spends so much time sticking his nose into other people's business that it eventually falls off and has to be replaced by a silver one.

I also had flashbacks to *Dangerous Beauty* (1998), a film about romance and Venice that is so much better than *Casanova* that you might as well just go ahead and rent it. Catherine McCormick stars as a woman who is forced by circumstances to become a courtesan and so convincingly entertains King Henry of France that he saves Venice from the Turkish fleet.

I quote from my review:

"'What do you yearn for, King Henry?' asks Veronica. 'Your tears,' he says, pressing a knife to her throat. 'I don't think so,' she says, and a shadow of doubt crosses his face. 'Then what do I yearn for?' he asks. She graces him with a cold smile: 'Why don't we find out?' Cut to the next morning, as the doge and other nobles nervously await the king's reappearance. He emerges, settles himself somewhat painfully on a cushion, and says, 'You'll get your ships.'"

That the new *Casanova* lacks such wit is fatal. Ledger is a good actor, but Hallstrom's film is busy and unfocused, giving us the view of Casanova's ceaseless activity but not the excitement. It's a sitcom when what is wanted is comic opera.

The fictional character of Francesca Bruni is, oddly enough, not making her first appearance in a film about Casanova. In the 1954 comedy *Casanova's Big Night*, she is courted by Pippo Popolino (Bob Hope), a Casanova impersonator who puts on a mask and tries to seduce her.

"Take your mask off!" Francesca (Joan Fontaine) tells him.

"I couldn't do that," he says. "I haven't got anything on underneath it."

Cashback ★ ★ ½

R, 102 m., 2007

Sean Biggerstaff (Ben), Emilia Fox (Sharon), Shaun Evans (Sean), Michelle Ryan (Suzy), Stuart Goodwin (Jenkins), Michael Dixon (Barry). Directed and produced by Sean Ellis. Screenplay by Ellis.

You may have seen *Cashback* on cable. It was a nineteen-minute short subject from 2005 that was nominated for an Oscar, and maybe should have won, about a grocery store clerk who made time go faster by stopping it. All the other humans in the store froze in place, and the kid, an art student, was free to undress them for a life class right then and there (I think this is a federal offense).

The kid, named Ben, was played by Sean Biggerstaff, aka Oliver Wood, the Gryffindor Quidditch captain, in the first two Harry Potter films. The film was written and directed by Sean Ellis, a fashion photographer who was rumored to be making a feature about the same idea, and now has. With admirable thrift, he has included every minute of his original short; that was made possible because all the original actors were available.

What he has added is a lot of introspection for his hero, plus loneliness and self-analysis and so much soft-core nudity you'd think Russ Meyer was back in town. The MPAA's R rating cites "graphic nudity"; that means not only that they are nude, but that you can see that they are nude. The film itself is whimsical and gentle and actually a date movie, even if it's frank about the desire of a great many young people to see other young people as nature supplied them. No, really, they actually do feel that way, even if they are not old enough to get past the R rating, which may come as news to the MPAA.

As the film opens, Ben begins a voice-over narration that will last pretty much all the way through and, to begin with, replaces what his angry ex girlfriend Suzy (Michelle Ryan) said when they broke up. Whatever she was saying involves a lot of the upper front teeth overlapping the lower lip. Ben is morose at the loss of Suzy, can't sleep at night, and goes on the midnight shift at Sainsbury's (oh, the film is set in England). Then he begins to freeze time. To tell you the truth, I am not sure if he actually stops time or only fantasizes that he does; the second possibility is probably more likely.

There's a checkout clerk at the store named Sharon (Emilia Fox), who has one of those faces that looks at yours and makes friends. Ben begins to think less about Suzy. The heart of the movie involves his courtship with Sharon, which is mostly conducted by Sharon. He hangs out with a posse of male friends (the usual assorted geek, playboy, and loser types), who advise him in love, a subject which for them seems largely theoretical.

Ben and Sharon spend a lot of time talking, and Ben in his voice-over spends a lot of time talking about them talking, and that's a breakthrough right there, because so many teen romances in the movies operate on the premise of love at first sight and do not realize that while you should like someone in order to make out with them, getting beyond second base requires actual dialogue.

The movie is lightweight, as it should be. It doesn't get all supercharged. Ben and Sharon, despite setbacks, are delighted to be admired by such wonderful partners, and we are happy for them. And that's about it. Even though this movie stops time, it did not require a science adviser.

Casino Royale ★ ★ ★

PG-13, 144 m., 2006

Daniel Craig (James Bond), Eva Green (Vesper Lynd), Mads Mikkelsen (Le Chiffre), Judi Dench (M), Jeffrey Wright (Felix Leiter), Giancarlo

Giannini (Mathis). Directed by Martin Campbell and produced by Barbara Broccoli and Michael G. Wilson. Screenplay by Neal Purvis, Robert Wade, and Paul Haggis, based on the novel by Ian Fleming.

Casino Royale has the answers to all my complaints about the forty-five-year-old James Bond series, and some I hadn't even thought of. It's not that I didn't love some of the earlier films, like some, dislike others, and so on, as that I was becoming less convinced that I ever had to see another one.

This movie is *new* from the get-go. It could be your first Bond. In fact, it was the first Bond; it was Ian Fleming's first 007 novel, and he was still discovering who the character was. The longtime Saltzman-Broccoli producing team could never get their hands on the rights until now, despite earlier misadventures by others using the same title, and maybe it's just as well, because it provides a fresh starting place. And it returns to the family fold; with her father's passing, Barbara Broccoli is producer.

Yes, Daniel Craig makes a superb Bond: leaner, more taciturn, less sex-obsessed, able to be hurt in body and soul, not giving a damn if his martini is shaken or stirred. That doesn't make him the *best* Bond, because I've long since given up playing that pointless ranking game; Sean Connery was first to plant the flag, and that's that. But Daniel Craig is bloody damned great as Bond, in a movie that creates a new reality for the character.

Year after year, attending the new Bond was like observing a ritual. There was the opening stunt sequence that served little purpose except to lead into the titles; the title song; Miss Moneypenny; M with an assignment of great urgency to the Crown; Q with some new gadgets; an archvillain; a series of babes, some treacherous, some doomed, all frequently in stages of undress; the villain's master plan; Bond's certain death and a lot of chases. It could be terrific, it could be routine, but you always knew about where you were in the formula.

With *Casino Royale,* we get to the obligatory concluding lovey-dovey on the tropical sands, and then the movie pulls a screeching U-turn and starts up *again* with the most sensational scene I have ever seen set in Venice, or most other places. It's a movie that keeps on giving.

This time, no Moneypenny, no Q, and Judi Dench is unleashed as M, given a larger role, and allowed to seem hard-eyed and disapproving to the reckless Bond. This time, no dream of world domination, but just a bleeding-eyed rat who channels money to terrorists. This time a poker game that is interrupted by the weirdest trip to the parking lot I've ever seen. This time, no laser beam inching up on Bond's netherlands, but a nasty knotted rope actually whacking his hopes of heirs.

And this time, no Monte Carlo, but Montenegro, a fictional casino resort, where Bond checks into the Hotel Splendid, which is in fact, yes, the very same Grand Hotel Pupp in Karlovy Vary where Queen Latifah had her culinary vacation in *Last Holiday.* That gives me another opportunity to display my expertise on the Czech Republic by informing you that *Pupp* is pronounced *poop,* so no wonder it's the Splendid.

I never thought I would see a Bond movie where I cared, actually cared, about the people. But I care about Bond, and about Vesper Lynd (Eva Green), even though I know that (here it comes) a Martini Vesper is shaken, not stirred. Vesper Lynd, on the other hand, is definitely stirring, as she was in Bertolucci's wonderful *The Dreamers.* Sometimes shaken, too. Vesper and James have a shower scene that answers, at last, why nobody in a Bond movie ever seems to have any real emotions.

A review should not be a list. So I should not enumerate all the scenes I liked. But I learn from IMDb that the special credit for the "free running" scenes of Sebastien Foucan refers to the sensational opening Madagascar foot chase in which Foucan practices *parkour,* or the ability to run at walls and angles and bounce off them to climb or change direction; Jackie Chan could do similar feats.

Which brings up another thing. Most of the chases and stunts in *Casino Royale* take place in something vaguely approximating real space and time. Of course I know they use doubles and deceptive camera angles and edits to cover impossibilities, but the point is: They try to make it look real.

Recently, with the advent of portable cameras and computerized editing, action movies have substituted visual chaos for visual elegance. I think the public is getting tired of action sequences that are created in postproduction. I've been swamped with letters complaining about *The Bourne Ultimatum.* One guy said, "Why don't critics admit they're tired of it?" Actually, we're tired of writing about how tired of it we are.

The plot centers on a marathon high-stakes poker game, in which Bond will try to deprive Le Chiffre (Mads Mikkelsen) of ten million or more pounds that would go to finance terrorism. Le Chiffre (*The Cypher*) has problems on his own because he owes big-time money to the people who supply it to him. The director, Martin Campbell, builds suspense in the extended poker game by not being afraid to focus for long seconds on the eyes of the two main opponents, which is all the more effective because Le Chiffre's left eye has tears of blood, inspiring a classic Bond line. Bond's absences from the table are of more than ordinary interest.

This is Campbell's second Bond picture, after *GoldenEye* (1995), but he breaks with his own and everyone else's tradition. He's helped by Craig, who gives the sense of a hard man, wounded by life and his job, who nevertheless cares about people and right and wrong. To a certain degree, the earlier Bonds were lustful technicians. With this one, since he has a big scene involving a merchant's house in Venice, we can excuse ourselves for observing that if you prick him, he bleeds. ☞

Cassandra's Dream ★ ★

PG-13, 108 m., 2008

Ewan McGregor (Ian Blaine), Colin Farrell (Terry Blaine), Tom Wilkinson (Uncle Howard), Sally Hawkins (Kate), Hayley Atwell (Angela Stark). Directed by Woody Allen and produced by Letty Aronson, Stephen Tenenbaum, and Gareth Wiley. Screenplay by Allen.

Woody Allen's *Cassandra's Dream* is about two brothers, one single and modestly successful, one struggling but in a happy relationship, who are both desperate to raise money and agree to commit a crime together. The identical premise is used in Sidney Lumet's *Before the Devil Knows You're Dead,* which is like a master class in how Allen goes wrong.

The Lumet film uses actors (Ethan Hawke and Philip Seymour Hoffman) who don't look like brothers but feel like brothers. Allen's actors (Ewan McGregor and Colin Farrell) look like brothers but don't really feel related. Lumet's film involves family members in a crime that seems reasonable but goes spectacularly wrong. Allen has a family member propose a crime that seems spectacularly unreasonable and goes right, with, however, unforeseen consequences. One of the brothers in both movies is consumed with guilt. And so on.

Lumet seems comfortable with his milieu, middle-class affluence in a New York suburb. Allen's milieu is not and perhaps never will be the Cockney working class of London, and his actors seem as much tourists as he is. Nevertheless, they plug away, in a plot that is intrinsically absorbing at times even with so much going against it.

McGregor and Farrell play Ian and Terry Blaine, Ian a partner in his dad's restaurant, Terry a hard-drinking, chain-smoking garage mechanic. Terry at least seems comfortable with his life and his supportive girlfriend (Sally Hawkins), although he dreams of getting rich quick; he gambles unwisely at the dog tracks. Ian also wants cash, and not only for a fishy-sounding opportunity to invest in California hotels. While driving a classic Jaguar borrowed from the garage where his brother works, he meets a high-maintenance sexpot actress (Hayley Atwell) and presents himself as a "property speculator" far richer than he is.

The brothers share a dream to own a boat. Terry wins big at the track, enough to buy a rusty bilge bucket, fix it up, and have a great day sailing with their two girls. But then Terry loses big-time, owes ninety thousand pounds, and discovers that guys are after him to break his legs. That's when rich Uncle Howard (Tom Wilkinson) returns from China (or somewhere) to make a proposition. His business empire is built on fraud, a colleague is about to squeal, and Howard wants the boys to do him a favor and murder the man.

Wilkinson, always a cool persuader, couches this in terms of family loyalty. That convinces the boys not nearly as much as does their own desperation. What happens I will not detail. This stretch of the movie does work and involves us, but then the lads run smack into an ending that was, to me, completely possible but highly unsatisfactory. Its problem is its sheer blundering plausibility. Allen's great *Match Point* (2005), on the other hand, also about crime and social con games, had an ending that was completely implausible and sublimely satisfactory. Remember how that ring falls at the end? What is fiction for, if not to manipulate the possible?

Chaos no stars

NO MPAA RATING, 78 m., 2005

Kevin Gage (Chaos), Stephen Wozniak (Frankie), Kelly K. C. Quann (Sadie), Sage Stallone (Swan), Chantal Degroat (Emily), Maya Barovich (Angelica), Ken Medlock (Sheriff). Directed by David DeFalco and produced by Steven Jay Bernheim. Screenplay by DeFalco.

Chaos is ugly, nihilistic and cruel—a film I regret having seen. I urge you to avoid it. Don't make the mistake of thinking it's "only" a horror film, or a slasher film. It is an exercise in heartless cruelty and it ends with careless brutality. The movie denies not only the value of life but also the possibility of hope.

The movie premiered in late July at Flashback Weekend, a Chicago convention devoted to horror and exploitation films. As I write, it remains unreviewed in *Variety,* unlisted on Rotten Tomatoes. As an unabashed retread of *The Last House on the Left* (itself inspired by Ingmar Bergman's *The Virgin Spring*), it may develop a certain notoriety, but you don't judge a book by its cover or a remake by its inspiration. A few Web writers have seen it and try to deal with their feelings:

"What is inflicted upon these women is degrading, humiliating, and terrible on every level."

—Capone, Ain't It Cool News

"Disgusting, shocking, and laced with humiliation, nudity, profanity, and limit-shoving tastelessness."

—John Gray, Pitofhorror.com

"What's the point of this s—t anyway?"

—Ed Gonzalez, slantmagazine.com

But Capone finds the film "highly effective" if "painful and difficult to watch." And Gray looks on the bright side: David DeFalco "manages to shock and disturb as well as give fans a glimpse of hope that some people are still trying to make good, sleazy exploitation films." Gonzalez finds no redeeming features, adding, "DeFalco directs the whole thing with all the finesse of someone who has been hit on the head one too many times (is this a good time to say he was a wrestler?)."

I quote these reviews because I'm fascinated by their strategies for dealing with a film that transcends all barriers of decency. There are two scenes so gruesome I cannot describe them in a newspaper, no matter what words I use. Having seen it, I cannot ignore it, nor can I deny that it affected me strongly: I recoiled during some of the most cruel moments, and when the film was over I was filled with sadness and disquiet.

The plot: Angelica and Emily (Chantal Degroat and Maya Barovich) are UCLA students, visiting the country cabin of Emily's parents, an interracial couple. They hear about a rave in the woods, drive off to party, meet a lout named Swan (Sage Stallone), and ask him where they can find some Ecstasy. He leads them to a cabin occupied by Chaos (Kevin Gage), already wanted for serial killing, Frankie (Stephen Wozniak), and Sadie (Kelly K. C. Quann). They're a Manson family in microcosm. By the end of the film, they will have raped and murdered the girls, not always in that order. Nor does the bloodshed stop there. The violence is sadistic, graphic, savage, and heartless. Much of the action involves the girls weeping and pleading for their lives. When the film pauses for dialogue, it is often racist.

So that's it. DeFalco directs with a crude, efficient gusto, as a man with an ax makes short work of firewood. Gage makes Chaos repulsive and cruel, Quann is effective as a pathetic, dim-witted sex slave, and the young victims are played with relentless sincerity; to the degree that we are repelled by the killers and feel pity for the victims, the movie "works." It works, all right, but I'm with Gonzalez: Why do we need this s—t?

Charlie and the Chocolate Factory ★ ★ ★

PG, 115 m., 2005

Johnny Depp (Willy Wonka), Freddie Highmore (Charlie Bucket), David Kelly (Grandpa Joe),

Helena Bonham Carter (Mrs. Bucket), Noah Taylor (Mr. Bucket), Missi Pyle (Mrs. Beauregarde), James Fox (Mr. Salt), Deep Roy (Oompa Loompa), Christopher Lee (Dr. Wonka), Julia Winter (Veruca Salt), AnnaSophia Robb (Violet Beauregarde), Jordan Fry (Mike Teavee), Philip Wiegratz (Augustus Gloop). Directed by Tim Burton and produced by Brad Grey and Richard D. Zanuck. Screenplay by John August, based on the book by Roald Dahl.

Now this is strange. *Charlie and the Chocolate Factory* succeeds in spite of Johnny Depp's performance, which should have been the high point of the movie. Depp, an actor of considerable gifts, has never been afraid to take a chance, but this time he takes the wrong one. His Willy Wonka is an enigma in an otherwise mostly delightful movie from Tim Burton, where the visual invention is a wonderment.

The movie is correctly titled. Unlike *Willy Wonka and the Chocolate Factory* (1971), which depends on Gene Wilder's twinkling air of mystery, *Charlie and the Chocolate Factory* is mostly about—Charlie. Young Charlie Bucket (Freddie Highmore) is so plucky and likable, and comes from such an eccentric and marvelous household, that the wonders inside the chocolate factory are no more amusing than everyday life at the Bucket residence.

The Buckets live in a house that leans crazily in all directions and seems to have been designed by Dr. Caligari along the lines of his cabinet. The family is very poor. Charlie sleeps in a garret that is open to the weather, and his four grandparents all sleep (and live, apparently) in the same bed, two at one end, two at the other. His mother (Helena Bonham Carter) maintains the serenity of the home, while his father (Noah Taylor) seeks employment. Grandpa Joe (David Kelly) remembers the happy decades when he and everyone else in the neighborhood worked in the chocolate factory.

Alas, fifteen years before the story begins, Willy Wonka dismissed his employees and locked his factory gates. Yet the world still enjoys Wonka products; how does Willy produce them? One day, astonishingly, Wonka announces a contest: For the five lucky children who find golden tickets in their Wonka Bars, the long-locked factory gates will open, and Willy will personally escort them through the factory. A special surprise is promised for one of them. Of course Charlie wins one of the tickets, not without suspense.

This stretch of the film has a charm not unlike *Babe* or the undervalued *Babe: Pig in the City.* A metropolis is remade to the requirements of fantasy. Tim Burton is cheerfully inventive in imagining the city and the factory, and the film's production design, by Alex McDowell, is a wonder. David Kelly, as Grandpa Joe, is a lovable geezer who agrees to accompany Charlie to the factory; you may remember him racing off naked on a motorcycle in *Waking Ned Devine* (1998). And young Freddie Highmore, who was so good opposite Depp in *Finding Neverland,* is hopeful and brave and always convincing as Charlie.

The problem is that this time, he finds Neverland. Depp may deny that he had Michael Jackson in mind when he created the look and feel of Willy Wonka, but moviegoers trust their eyes, and when they see Willy opening the doors of the factory to welcome the five little winners, they will be relieved that the kids brought along adult guardians. Depp's Wonka—his dandy's clothes, his unnaturally pale face, his makeup and lipstick, his hat, his manner—reminds me inescapably of Jackson (and, oddly, in a certain use of the teeth, chin, and bobbed hairstyle, of Carol Burnett).

The problem is not simply that Willy Wonka looks like Michael Jackson; it's that in a creepy way we're not sure of his motives. The story of Willy and his factory has had disturbing undertones ever since it first appeared in Roald Dahl's 1964 novel (also named after Charlie, not Willy). Nasty and frightening things happen to the children inside the factory in the book and both movies; perhaps Willy is using the tour to punish the behavior of little brats, while rewarding the good, poor, and decent Charlie. (How does it happen that each of the other four winners illustrates a naughty childhood trait? Just Willy's good luck, I guess.)

We see the wondrous workings of the factory in the opening titles, a CGI assembly-line sequence that swoops like a roller coaster. When the five kids and their adult guardians finally get inside, their first sight is a marvel of imagination: a sugary landscape of chocolate rivers, gumdrop trees, and (no doubt) rock candy mountains. Behind his locked doors,

Willy has created this fantastical playground for—himself, apparently. As the tour continues, we learn the secret of his workforce: He uses Oompa Loompas, earnest and dedicated workers all looking exactly the same and all played, through a digital miracle, by the vaguely ominous Deep Roy. We're reminded of Santa's identical helpers in *Polar Express.*

It is essential to the story that the bad children be punished. Their sins are various: Veruca Salt (Julia Winter) is a spoiled brat; Violet Beauregarde (AnnaSophia Robb) is a competitive perfectionist; Mike Teavee (Jordan Fry) approaches the world with the skills and tastes he has learned through video games; and Augustus Gloop (Philip Wiegratz) likes to make a little pig out of himself.

All of these children meet fates appropriate to their misdemeanors. I might be tempted to wonder if smaller children will find the movie too scary, but I know from long experience with the first film that kids, for some reason, instinctively know this is a cautionary tale, and that even when a character is suctioned up by a chocolate conduit, all is not lost.

Charlie and his grandfather join wide-eyed in the tour, and there are subplots, especially involving Violet Beauregarde, before the happy ending. What is especially delightful are the musical numbers involving the Oompa Loompas, who seem to have spent a lot of time studying Hollywood musicals. The kids, their adventures and the song-and-dance numbers are so entertaining that Depp's strange Willy Wonka is not fatal to the movie, although it's at right angles to it.

What was he thinking of? In *Pirates of the Caribbean,* Depp was famously channeling Keith Richards, which may have primed us to look for possible inspirations for this performance. But leaving *Pirates* aside, can anyone look at Willy Wonka and not think of Michael Jackson? Consider the reclusive lifestyle, the fetishes of wardrobe and accessories, the elaborate playground built by an adult for the child inside. What's going on here?

But here is the important thing: Depp's miscalculated performance seems to exist almost outside the movie. It's fun despite his character. *Charlie and the Chocolate Factory* has its own life and energy, generated by Charlie and Grandpa Joe and their wacky household, by the other kids, by the special effects, and by the Oompa Loompas. While Willy pursues his mysterious concerns, the adventures go on without him.

Charlie Wilson's War ★ ★ ★

R, 97 m., 2007

Tom Hanks (Charlie Wilson), Julia Roberts (Joanne Herring), Philip Seymour Hoffman (Gust Avrakotos), Amy Adams (Bonnie Bach), Ned Beatty (Doc Long), Om Puri (President Zia). Directed by Mike Nichols and produced by Gary Goetzman. Screenplay by Aaron Sorkin, based on the book by George Crile.

Charlie Wilson's War is said to be based on fact, and I have no reason to doubt that. It stars Tom Hanks as Representative Charles Wilson, a swinging, hard-drinking, coke-using liberal Democrat from Texas who more or less single-handedly defeated the Russians in Afghanistan. Yes. The Soviets withdrew in 1989, the Berlin Wall fell, the Cold War was over, and Ronald Reagan got all the credit. How could Wilson's operation have taken place without anyone knowing? If Ollie North's activities could, why not these?

Here's how it all happened, told in a sharp-edged political comedy directed by Mike Nichols and written by Aaron (*The West Wing*) Sorkin. Charlie Wilson, whose personal life was, shall we say, untidy, was popular in the Second Congressional District of Texas because he never met a pork-barrel project he didn't like, especially if it meant federal funds for the Second Congressional District of Texas. Apart from that, nobody back home much cared that he was a good ol' boy who liked company in a hot tub and was rarely without a drink in his hand.

He had a soft spot for a right-wing Houston millionaire socialite named Joanne Herring (Julia Roberts), a sometime TV talk show hostess, who hated the commies and wanted them to stop killing the brave Afghans. She had some connections, since she was an honorary consul to Pakistan. She told Charlie the Afghans need weapons to shoot down Russian helicopters. Since he was on the Defense Appropriations Subcommittee, he was ideally placed to help them.

Problem was, the United States couldn't

afford to have American-made weapons found in Afghanistan. Herring's solution: The Israelis had lots of shoulder-mounted Soviet-made antiaircraft weapons, which they could supply to the Afghans through the back channel of Pakistan. *What?* asks Charlie. Pakistan and Israel working together?

Herring arranges for Wilson to meet her personal friend President Zia, the military dictator of Pakistan, who hates the Russians as much as she does. Zia sends him on a heart-breaking tour of Pakistan's refugee camps for displaced Afghans. Charlie finds the one man in the CIA who can actually help him: the pot-bellied, chain-smoking, hard-drinking outsider Gust Avrakotos (Philip Seymour Hoffman, with a squirrelly little mustache). Gust knows just the Israeli for them to talk to.

They will need money. The United States was then supplying the Afghan freedom fighters with a useless $5 million a year, but Charlie was a master at glad-handing, elbow-bending, and calling in favors, and that amount was quietly raised to $1 billion a year, all secret, because it was CIA funding, you see. With the use of some personal diplomacy and a Texas belly-dancer flown from Houston to Cairo, Charlie pulls off the deal.

All true, they say. Mrs. Herring, who was earlier Mrs. King and later Mrs. Davis, even agrees. Check out her Web site: joanneherring.com. She grew up in a house modeled on Mount Vernon and looks not totally unlike Julia Roberts. What is remarkable about the collaboration of Nichols and Sorkin is that they make this labyrinthine scheme not only comprehensible but wickedly funny, as Charlie Wilson uses his own flaws and those of others to do a noble deed. Well, it was noble at the time, although unfortunately, the "freedom fighters" later became the Taliban, and some of those weapons were no doubt used against American helicopters. As the man says, you can plan plans, but you can't plan results.

You might think Tom Hanks was miscast as the lovable sinner. Dennis Quaid, maybe, or Woody Harrelson. But Hanks brings something unique to the role: He plays a man spinning his wheels, bored with the girls and parties, looking for something to bring meaning to his slog through the federal bureaucracy. He and Gust (a perfect name) are well-matched. "Do you drink?" he asks the CIA man on their first meeting. "Oh, God, yes." Gust has been fighting for years to budge the CIA on Afghanistan, and now the right congressman falls into his hands.

Nichols fills the edges of the screen with unforced humor. There are "Charlie's Angels," his congressional staff of buxom young women, all of them smart. There's Charlie's special assistant, Bonnie, played by the lovable, fresh-faced Amy Adams (*Junebug, Enchanted*), who cleans up after him, gives him good advice, keeps his schedule, and adores him. And there is the presence of Hoffman himself, a smoldering volcano of frustration and unspent knowledge. It's hard to see how Charlie could have ended the Cold War without him, and impossible to see how Gust and Bonnie could have ended it without Charlie. The next time you hear about Reagan ending it, ask yourself if he ever heard of Charlie Wilson.

Cheaper by the Dozen 2 ★ ★ ★

PG, 94 m., 2005

Steve Martin (Tom "Dad" Baker), Bonnie Hunt (Kate "Mom" Baker), Eugene Levy (Jimmy Murtaugh), Piper Perabo (Nora Baker), Hilary Duff (Lorraine Baker), Alyson Stoner (Sarah Baker), Taylor Lautner (Eliot Murtaugh), Tom Welling (Charlie Baker), Jacob Smith (Jake Baker), Kevin Schmidt (Henry Baker), Carmen Electra (Sarina Murtaugh). Directed by Adam Shankman and produced by Shawn Levy and Ben Myron. Screenplay by Sam Harper, based on the novel by Frank B. Gilbreth Jr. and Ernestine Gilbreth Carey.

Cheaper by the Dozen 2 is the kind of title, like *The Other Side of the Mountain 2,* that starts you wondering why they didn't call it *This Side of the Mountain.* Or, more to the point, *Even Cheaper by Two Dozen.* All sequel titles tell you is that if you liked the doughnuts, why not buy another box. At which your mother would tell you to save some room for dinner, and I would suggest a new movie.

Still, as I watched this sequel, a certain good feeling began to make itself known. Yes, the movie is unnecessary. On the other hand, it is unnecessary at a higher level of warmth and humor than the recent remake *Yours, Mine and Ours.* And it has more plausible parents, even though neither one, so far as I know, is played by an actor who has any children.

Steve Martin, whose adamant loner in *Shopgirl* is possibly autobiographical (he wrote the original novel), uses his status as a non-accumulator of kids as a basis for Dad Baker here, who is affectionate but not soppy. And Bonnie Hunt, as Mom, is the kind of mother who understands she essentially has a job in management. I am not even a little surprised that Hunt has three brothers and three sisters and used to work as a nurse in the oncology ward at Northwestern Memorial Hospital in Chicago.

What I liked the most about the second *Dozen,* however, was another performance, the one by Alyson Stoner as their daughter Sarah. As a girl poised on the first scary steps of adolescence, she finds the kind of vulnerability and shy hope that Reese Witherspoon projected in *The Man in the Moon* (1991), which contains a first kiss so sweet you remember it fifteen years later.

In Sarah's case, romance finds her after her parents assemble the Fabulous Baker Boys and Girls for one last summer at a rented lake cottage. Kids are growing up fast. The daughters played by Hilary Duff and Piper Perabo have already flown the coop, college is looming for others, and the parents want to assemble the whole brood.

Since their earlier summer at the ramshackle beach rental on Lake Winnetka, Dad Baker's high school rival, Jimmy Murtaugh (Eugene Levy), has erected his own gargantuan family home, the Boulders, directly across the waters. He's made a lot more money than Tom Baker, whose job as a college football coach evaporates in some vague dialogue. The two fathers resume their lifelong rivalry, and Murtaugh shows off at a fancy Fourth of July clambake at the lake club, where the fireworks go off prematurely and destroy everything in sight. It is a rule of the cinema that all fireworks always go off prematurely except those used in sex scenes, and sometimes then, too.

Countering these predictabilities is the wonderful little subplot. For Sarah Baker and Eliot Murtaugh (Taylor Lautner), it's first love at first sight. This leads Sarah to experiment with makeup, because like all girls her age she is convinced she is an ugly duckling. God, thirteen can be horrible. I remember as a high school freshman, standing around at the Tigers' Den teenage hangout in Urbana, Illinois, cupping my hand to my mouth and checking to see if I had bad breath. At any given moment there would be half a dozen other kids also sniffing in dread and suspicion, all of us chewing Doublemint like crazy. If some girl had told us she didn't dance with boys who chewed gum, we would have gone home and wept ourselves to sleep.

Anyway, *Dozen 2* remembers that kind of suffering, and the way kids are supersensitive. Any teasing, however slight, however kind, however well-meaning, comes as a crushing blow. Mom Baker (Hunt) sees what's happening, calls Sarah "sweetheart," and sympathizes, but what's especially touching is when Sarah's older sister Lorraine (Hilary Duff) takes her upstairs and expertly applies the right style of makeup for a girl that age—which means, in effect, that when Sarah tremulously exposes herself to the family view, she looks absolutely lovely and you really can't notice much makeup at all. I personally couldn't see any, but then I hardly notice makeup unless we're talking Tommy Lee Jones as Two-Face in *Batman Forever.*

Speaking of makeup, Jimmy Murtaugh's new wife of six months' standing is Sarina, played by Carmen Electra, and the movie surprises us by making her nice. She's sexy, yes, but she really cares for her eight new stepkids, intervenes with her husband's monstrous ego, and passes the acid test, which is that Bonnie Hunt's character accepts her as (provisionally) human.

The movie is otherwise about what you'd expect. As family movies go, it skews younger than the better *Rumor Has It* and *The Family Stone.* It's a lot better than *Yours, Mine and Ours,* which has inexplicably grossed more than $45 million, all of which could have been more usefully dropped into Santa's little red bucket outside the theater.

Chicken Little ★ ★ ½

G, 82 m., 2005

With the voices of: Zach Braff (Chicken Little), Joan Cusack (Abby Mallard), Steve Zahn (Runt of the Litter), Amy Sedaris (Foxy Loxy), Mark Walton (Goosey Loosey), Garry Marshall (Buck Cluck), Don Knotts (Mayor Turkey Lurkey),

Patrick Stewart (Mr. Woolensworth), Wallace Shawn (Principal Fetchit), Fred Willard (Melvin [Alien Dad]), Catherine O'Hara (Tina [Alien Mom]). Directed by Mark Dindal and produced by Randy Fullmer. Screenplay by Steve Bencich and Ron J. Friedman.

As the hero of a story, Chicken Little is the poultry equivalent of the Boy Who Cried Wolf. Once you understand their mistakes, their stories are over and attention passes to the results of their errors. In Chicken Little's case, the sky was not falling. In the case of the Boy Who Cried Wolf, I cannot remember if he was eaten by one, but he was asking for it.

There is one way for Chicken Little to redeem himself, and that would be for the sky to actually fall. *Chicken Little,* a new animated cartoon from Disney, wisely takes this approach and even provides an explanation: Earth is being attacked from outer space. When Chicken Little claims he was hit on the head by a chunk of blue sky and the townspeople think it was only an acorn, the chicken is telling the truth.

The movie takes place in an all-purpose small town named Oakey Oaks, where chameleons change color while functioning as traffic signals. In a salute to the original British children's story, the film has a Turkey Lurkey (he's the mayor) and a Foxy Loxy (she's foxy, all right, but not very nice) and even a Goosey Loosey (Mark Walton, who will be cautious in adding this credit to his résumé). Chicken Little is voiced by Zach Braff; his father, Buck Cluck (Garry Marshall), obviously moved here from Brooklyn.

The plot: Chicken Little thinks the sky is falling, and he seems to be mistaken. He is ambushed and hounded by the press. There are no skies of mass destruction. He is shamed and humiliated. His friends loyally stand by him; they would be the goths, nerds, geeks, and outsiders in a human town: Abby (the Ugly Duckling) Mallard, voiced by Joan Cusack; Fish Out of Water, who wears a diver's helmet filled not with air but water and is not voiced because he doesn't talk, and you couldn't hear him anyway; and Runt of the Litter (Steve Zahn), who is so fat he can hardly see his stomach, let alone his feet.

Will Chicken Little ever be able to hold his head up again? In an attempt to redeem himself, he joins the town baseball team, but even though he plays in the big game, this sequence feels, frankly, as if the plot is killing time. That's because it is.

Then the heavy-duty plotting arrives, as the town is attacked by animated versions of the alien creatures, who remind us of Spielberg's *War of the Worlds* crossed with other alien-invasion pictures. Does Chicken Little save the day? Let's put it this way: Here is a movie where you don't have to wonder what a bear does in the woods.

The problem, I think, lies with the story. As a general rule, if a movie is not about baseball or aliens from outer space and you have to use them anyway, you should have started with a better premise. The best animated films are based on sturdy fables that deserve retelling *(Beauty and the Beast),* new stories involving archetypal emotions *(Finding Nemo),* or satire *(The Incredibles). Chicken Little* seems uncomfortably close to the Three Little Pigs and other not-ready-for-prime-time players. Yes, it's funny how they involve animal traits in the daily affairs of the town, and yes, the voice talent (especially Marshall and such verbal originals as Wallace Shawn, Fred Willard, and Don Knotts) is sometimes funny just because of the performers.

The movie did make me smile. It didn't make me laugh, and it didn't involve my emotions, or the higher regions of my intellect, for that matter. It's a perfectly acceptable feature cartoon for kids up to a certain age, but it doesn't have the universal appeal of some of the best recent animation.

The Children of Huang Shi ★ ★ ½

R, 125 m., 2008

Jonathan Rhys Meyers (George Hogg), Radha Mitchell (Lee Pearson), Chow Yun Fat (Jack Chen), Michelle Yeoh (Madame Wang), David Wenham (Barnes), Guang Li (Shi Kai). Directed by Roger Spottiswoode and produced by Arthur Cohn, Wieland Schulz-Keil, Peter Loehr, Jonathan Shteinman, and Martin Hagemann. Screenplay by James MacManus and Jane Hawksley.

George Hogg is a British journalist sent to China to cover the 1930s war involving Japanese invaders and communist and nationalist

Chinese. It's surprising he survived a day. Inexperienced and naive, he journeys into unfamiliar territory and spends way too much time standing in full view and taking photos. Some of the photos have real news value, such as a series involving a Japanese massacre of civilians, but, of course, the Japanese capture him and the photos.

This leads to the first of two moments when Hogg (Jonathan Rhys Meyers) is seconds from death; an executioner's sword seems already slicing down from the sky when he's rescued by a Chinese nationalist named Chen (Chow Yun Fat). Later he's rescued again, by a beautiful British woman named Lee Pearson (Radha Mitchell), a brave heroine who roams the countryside on horseback by herself, bringing food and medical help to the countless displaced people who need it.

She had a civilian occupation before necessity thrust this mission upon her. Soon Hogg finds the same thing happens to him: Lee takes him to an orphanage, puts him in charge of sixty children, and tells him he must feed and educate them, and tend to their health. How can he do that? Hogg has no training, but Lee gives him no choice. He teaches himself.

All of this seems impossible, but Roger Spottiswoode's film is based on fact; there was a real George Hogg. After he stars in an embarrassing public demonstration of the usefulness of flea powder, Hogg travels by mule to a nearby city where Madame Wang (Michelle Yeoh) runs a business dealing in seed, grains, and perhaps other things. He convinces her they are in business together: She gives him the seeds and shares in the harvest.

The scenes of Hogg making the orphanage into a functioning community transform the movie from an unlikely adventure into an absorbing life story. The filmmaking is careful but not original; one kid is a rebel, one kid is a quick learner, and so on, and there is a goat that bleats every time it is on the screen. Hogg and the children miraculously restore a rusty generator, coax crops from the stony soil, and hold English classes ("Table! Table! Chair! Chair!"), although I am not sure why twelve-year-old orphans in the middle of China in the late 1930s needed to learn English. Math, maybe?

Thrown out of their orphanage, Hogg and the orphans make an exhausting five-hundred-mile trek across snow-covered mountains to find refuge. When they finally reach their destination, they gaze in silence, and the goat gets one close-up when it doesn't bleat. During this stretch of film, Hogg has fallen in love with Lee, and we learn that Chen and Madame Wang have, as they say, a history. Other secrets are revealed, but they come a little too quickly after the film's leisurely middle passages.

The Children of Huang Shi tells an engrossing story of a remarkable man, but nevertheless it's underwhelming. Dramatic and romantic tensions never coil very tightly, as the film settles into a contented pace. The photography is awesome, especially scenes set in the Gobi desert, which yes, they travel across, although not the whole way, I'm sure. I'm pleased to have seen the film and it has a big heart, but that doesn't make it urgent viewing.

Note: The R rating is earned by some very mild, nonexplicit lovemaking, some violence, some drug content. Nothing so strong it would bother teenagers, who might enjoy this film more than I did.

Children of Men ★ ★ ★ ★

R, 109 m., 2007

Clive Owen (Theodore Faron), Julianne Moore (Julian Taylor), Michael Caine (Jasper Palmer), Chiwetel Ejiofor (Luke), Charlie Hunnam (Patric), Clare-Hope Ashitey (Kee), Peter Mullan (Syd), Pam Ferris (Miriam). Directed by Alfonso Cuaron and produced by Marc Abraham, Eric Newman, Hilary Shor, Iain Smith, and Tony Smith. Screenplay by Cuaron, Timothy J. Sexton, David Arata, Mark Fergus, and Hawk Ostby, based on the novel by P. D. James.

It is above all the look of *Children of Men* that stirs apprehension in the heart. Is this what we are all headed for? The film is set in 2027, when assorted natural disasters, wars, and terrorist acts have rendered most of the world ungovernable, uninhabitable, or anarchic. Britain stands as an island of relative order, held in line by a fearsome police state. It has been eighteen years since Earth has seen the birth of a human child.

We see today on the news the devastation of Baghdad, the latest city that has fallen through the safety net of civilization. We remember the war zones of Beirut, Algiers, Belfast, Vietnam. Surely it could not happen here? For a time after 9/11 it seemed anarchy might be unloosed upon our world, but now we have domestic calm, however transient.

Watching *Children of Men,* which creates a London in ruins, I realized after a point that the sets and art design were so well done that I took it as a real place. Often I fear it will all come to this, that the rule of law and the rights of men will be destroyed by sectarian mischief and nationalistic recklessness. Are we living in the last good times?

There is much to be said about the story of *Children of Men,* directed by Alfonso Cuaron and based on a lesser-known novel by P. D. James, who usually writes about a detective. But the story, like the stories of *Metropolis, Nosferatu,* or *Escape from New York,* is secondary to the visual world we are given to regard. Guerrilla fighters occupy abandoned warehouses. The homeless live in hovels. Immigrants are rounded up and penned in cages. The utilities cannot be depended upon. There are, most disturbing of all, no children. Only dogs and cats remain to be cared for and cherished.

As the film opens, the TV news reports that the world's youngest person has been stabbed to death in Buenos Aires because he declined to give an autograph. Theo Faron (Clive Owen), the film's hero, watches the news in a café and then leaves with his paper cup in his hand. Seconds later, a bomb destroys the café. This is essential: Faron is terrified. He crouches, and fear freezes his face. This will not be like conventional action pictures where the hero never seems to fear death.

Owen's character, indeed, seems to be central to the film's mood. He is tired, depressed, fearful, pessimistic. So is everyone else. They will all grow old and die, and then there won't be anybody else. We could imagine an aging society in which everyone lived in condos and the world was a vast retirement haven, but who would till the fields? Can you imagine a retirement home in which the decrepit fight over cans of peaches?

Britain, as the last functioning nation, has closed its borders, is deporting anyone who is not a citizen, and is engaged in a war between the establishment and a band of rebels who support immigrant rights. Faron is kidnapped by this group, headed by Julian Taylor (Julianne Moore), who was once his lover; they lost a child. Her associate, Luke (Chiwetel Ejiofor, in another unexpected character), backs her up with muscle and wisdom. Interestingly, there seems to be no racial prejudice in this Britain; they don't care what color you are, as long as you were on board before they pulled up the life rope. Julian's group wants Faron's influence to get travel papers for Kee (Clare-Hope Ashitey) so the young woman can be smuggled out of the country and to refuge in a rumored safe haven. Kee is a key to the future; the movie's advertising tells you why, but I will not.

The center of the film involves the journey toward the coast that Faron and Kee undertake with Julian, Luke, and Miriam (Pam Ferris), who is both watchdog and nurse. Along the way they are pursued by homeland security troops, and there is a chase scene with one of the most sudden and violent moments I have ever seen in a film. Not all of the chases in all of the *Bournes* equal this one, shot in a single take by one camera, for impact.

Their journey involves a rest stop at the country hideaway of an aging hippie (Michael Caine), who has known Faron for years; we are reminded again of how sweet Caine can seem in a character, how solicitous and concerned. It is a small but perfect performance. The journey continues toward the coast, and then there is a running gun battle (in the middle of an existing battle) down ruined streets of rubble and death. Many of the shots are, or seem, uninterrupted; there is the sense that this city is not a set but extends indefinitely in every direction, poisoned and lethal.

Here again, the action scenes seem rooted in sweat and desperation. Too many action scenes look like slick choreography, but Cuaron and Owen get the scent of fear and death, and nobody does anything that is particularly impossible. Small details: Even in the midst of a firefight, dogs scamper in the streets. Faron's hand reaches out to touch and reassure the nearest animal, and I was reminded of Jack London's belief that dogs (not cats so much) see us as their gods. Apparently sterility affects only humans on Earth; when we are gone, will the dogs still tirelessly search for us?

I have been using Hitchcock's term "MacGuffin" too much lately, but there are times when only it will do. The lack of children and the possibility of children are the MacGuffins in *Children of Men,* inspiring all the action, but the movie significantly never tells us why children stopped being born, or how they might become possible again. The children-as-MacGuffin is simply a dramatic device to avoid actual politics while showing how the world is slipping away from civility and coexistence. The film is not really about children; it is about men and women and civilization, and the way that fear can be used to justify a police state.

I admire that plot decision. I would have felt let down if the movie had a more decisive outcome; it is about the struggle, not the victor, and the climax in my opinion is open-ended. The performances are crucial because all of these characters have so completely internalized their world that they make it palpable, and themselves utterly convincing.

Alfonso Cuaron (born in 1961 in Mexico City) is not new to enormous sets and vast scopes. He was the director of *Harry Potter and the Prisoner of Azkaban* (2004), and I have long admired his overlooked *Great Expectations* (1998) and *A Little Princess* (1995), both of which created self-contained worlds of their own. They were in English; he returned to Spanish to make the worldwide hit *Y tu Mama Tambien* (2001).

Here he fulfills the promise of futuristic fiction; the characters do not wear strange costumes or visit the moon, and the cities are not plastic hallucinations but look just like today, except tired and shabby. Here is certainly a world ending not with a bang but a whimper, and the film serves as a warning. The only thing we will have to fear in the future, we learn, is the past itself. Our past. Ourselves.

The Chorus ★ ★ ½

PG-13, 95 m., 2005

Gerard Jugnot (Clement Mathieu), Jean-Baptiste Maunier (Pierre Morhange [young]), Jacques Perrin (Pierre Morhange [adult]), Francois Berleand (Rachin), Kad Merad (Chabert), Marie Bunel (Violette Morhange). Directed by Christophe Barratier and produced by Arthur Cohn, Nicolas Mauvernay, and Jacques Perrin. Screenplay by Barratier and Philippe Lopes-Curval.

This time the teacher is named Clement Mathieu. In earlier films it was Mr. Chips, Miss Jean Brodie, Mr. Holland, Mr. Crocker-Harris (in *The Browning Version*), John Keating (in *Dead Poets Society*), Joe Clark (in *Lean on Me*), Katherine Ann Watson (in *Mona Lisa Smile*), Jaime A. Escalante (in *Stand and Deliver*), and Roberta Guaspari (in *Music of the Heart*). In theaters right now, his name is Coach Carter. The actors have included Morgan Freeman, Meryl Streep, Edward James Olmos, Albert Finney, Robin Williams, Samuel L. Jackson, Julia Roberts, Maggie Smith, Richard Dreyfuss, and even, in one version of *Chips,* Peter O'Toole. They all have two things in common: Their influence will forever change the lives of their students, and we can see that coming from the opening frame.

I have nothing against the formula. Done well, it can be moving, as it was in *Mr. Holland's Opus.* But *The Chorus,* the film France selected as its Oscar candidate this year, does it by the numbers, so efficiently this feels more like a Hollywood wannabe than a French film. Where's the quirkiness, the nuance, the deeper levels?

The movie begins with a middle-aged man named Pierre (Jacques Perrin) being awakened from his slumber by the news of a death. That night he conducts an orchestra, and we learn that he is the world's greatest conductor. I would have been better pleased if he had merely been a really good conductor. Then Pierre makes a journey to the country to attend the funeral of the teacher who found him as a juvenile delinquent and instilled a love of music and learning in him.

All of this is quickly known, and more details are easy to come by because in the town, he meets his old classmate Pepinot, who produces the diary kept fifty years ago by Mr. Mathieu. It is the kind of helpful journal that seems to have been written as the treatment for a film.

But perhaps I am too cynical about a perfectly sincere sentimental exercise. We flash back to 1949 and the Fond de l'Etang boarding school; the name means (not its official title, I believe) something like the bottom of the pond. Here the students are considered pond scum, too impossible to reach in ordinary schools, and the headmaster maintains an iron discipline. Young Pierre (now played by young Jean-Baptiste Maunier) is a handful, sent to the school by a single mom who despairs for him.

Also new to the school this term is Clement Mathieu (Gerard Jugnot), a pudgy and somewhat unfocused middle-aged man who is hired as a teacher's assistant. He loves music, and one day when he hears the boys singing, a light glows in his eye and he decides to begin a boys' choir in the school. This, of course, is frowned upon by the headmaster, who disapproves of anything even remotely educational, as such headmasters always do, and hates even more the idea of students having fun. But Mr. Mathieu holds rehearsals anyway, secretly, in sort of a boarding school parallel of the Resistance.

We know without having to see the movie that there will be vignettes establishing how troubled the kids are, and scenes in which Mr. Mathieu loses all hope, and a scene where the kids surprise him, and a scene of triumph, and a glorious performance at the end. All done competently. What is disconcerting, however, is how well these boys sing. After a few months of secret lessons, they sing as well as—well, as well as Les Petits Chanteurs de Saint-Marc Choir, the professional boys' choir that does the actual singing. Every time those little rascals open their mouths, somebody seems to have slipped a CD into the stereo.

Wouldn't it work better for the movie if they were simply a really good choir? The choice of a real choir makes for a better sound track album, no doubt, but causes a disconnect in the film's reality. I guess we have to accept this, along with the cruel fate that inevitably awaits any teacher who dares to break the mold, defy the establishment, and challenge his students with the wonders of the world.

The Great Teacher Who Forever Changes Lives is not as rare as these movies would suggest.

As it happens, I have had several such teachers, none more lovably eccentric than Mrs. Seward of Urbana High School, who taught senior rhetoric by gazing out the window and rhapsodizing about the worms on her farm, who came up after heavy rains and glistened in their wormy perfection. She also taught us to write. I had been working for two years as a sportswriter on the local daily, but she disabused me of the notion that a sentence equaled a paragraph, and gently suggested that the day would come when I would no longer find Thomas Wolfe readable.

The Chorus is only a fair example of its genre. I would rank it below *Mr. Holland's Opus* and *Music of the Heart.* Am I wearied because I have seen too many movies telling similar stories? No, it is just that since I know the story and so does everybody else in the theater, it should have added something new and unexpected, and by that I do not mean hiring Les Petits Chanteurs de Saint-Marc.

Christmas in the Clouds ★ ★ ★

PG, 97 m., 2005

Tim Vahle (Ray Clouds on Fire), MariAna Tosca (Tina Pisati Little Hawk), Sam Vlahos (Joe Clouds on Fire), M. Emmet Walsh (Stu O'Malley), Graham Greene (Earl), Sheila Tousey (Mary), Rosalind Ayres (Mabel Winright), Jonathan Joss (Phil). Directed by Kate Montgomery and produced by Montgomery and Sarah Wasserman. Screenplay by Montgomery.

Christmas in the Clouds is part romantic comedy, part screwball comedy, and part historic breakthrough. The history is made because the movie is about affluent Native American yuppies. So many movies about American Indians deal in negative stereotypes that it's nice to find one that takes place at an upscale Indian-owned ski resort. The only alcoholic in the cast is a white undercover investigator for a guidebook.

The romance begins through a misunderstanding. Through an online dating service, Joe Clouds on Fire (Sam Vlahos) is paired off with Tina Pisati (MariAna Tosca). She's a chic New York professional woman whose name sounds Italian but whose family name is Little Hawk. He's a likable codger whose son, Ray Clouds on Fire (Tim Vahle), manages the resort. Joe has not been entirely honest about his age and is about thirty years older than Tina. Meanwhile, the resort is expecting a surprise visit from the critic of luxury hotels, and Mary the reservations manager (Sheila Tousey) keeps an eagle eye for anyone checking in who looks like he can spell Zagat.

This is the setup for an Idiot Plot, in which all misunderstandings could be cleared up with one or two lines of dialogue. Yes, but some Idiot Plots are charming, while most are merely dumb. This one I enjoyed, mostly because the actors have so much quiet fun with it. Of course Mary the manager thinks Tina Pisati is the critic. Of course Tina thinks that handsome young Ray is her pen pal, not crusty old Joe. And of course when Stu O'Malley checks in, no one fingers him as the critic, because he is grumpy, unkempt, and half loaded; it's M. Emmet Walsh, playing his usual role.

Tina is upgraded to a luxury corner suite. O'Malley gets shunted to a budget room, where he suffers from what passes for flu and may involve a large percentage of hangover. Tina has her eye on Ray. Ray thinks Tina is beautiful and sexy but refuses to cater to her because he is too ethical to kowtow to a critic. Old Joe knows the score but maintains a studious silence about his pen-pal correspondence, which no one at the resort knows about.

And then there is the matter of Earl (Graham Greene), the resort's chef, who has become a devout vegetarian and tries to discourage the customers from eating meat. He has a disconcerting way of referring to the animals on the menu by their first names and grows sorrowful when someone orders the turkey, which is a beloved pet.

Old Joe dreams of winning a Jeep Cherokee in an approaching bingo tournament. Grumpy old O'Malley hauls out of bed to play bingo. Eventually the two old-timers both end up in the Cherokee, stranded in a blizzard, while misunderstandings pile up back at the resort.

There is nothing here of earthshaking originality, but Kate Montgomery, the writer-director, has such affection for these characters that we can feel it through the screen. They're not simply pawns in the plot, we sense; they represent something she wants to say about the Native Americans she knows. And the actors, all with successful careers behind them, must be fed up with playing losers in social problem dramas; Greene, a natural comedian, expands magnificently as the vegetarian chef with an effortless line of patter about soy products, analog foods, and healthy nutrition. There may be a sitcom job for him lingering somewhere near this role.

As for Ray and Tina, well, in all versions of basic romantic comedy, we want them to kiss, they want to kiss, and the plot perversely frustrates all of us. But at the end of *Christmas in the Clouds,* after everything has worked out more or less as we hoped it would, I felt a surprising affection and warmth. There will be holiday pictures that are more high-tech than this one, more sensational, with bigger stars and higher budgets and indeed greater artistry. But there may not be many with such good cheer.

The Chronicles of Narnia: The Lion, the Witch and the Wardrobe ★ ★ ★

PG, 139 m., 2005

Tilda Swinton (White Witch), Georgie Henley (Lucy Pevensie), Skandar Keynes (Edmund Pevensie), William Moseley (Peter Pevensie), Anna Popplewell (Susan Pevensie), James McAvoy (Mr. Tumnus), Jim Broadbent (Professor Kirke); and the voices of: Liam Neeson (Aslan), Ray Winstone (Mr. Beaver), Dawn French (Mrs. Beaver), Rupert Everett (Fox). Directed by Andrew Adamson and produced by Mark Johnson and Philip Steuer. Screenplay by Ann Peacock, Adamson, Christopher Markus, and Stephen McFeely, based on the novel by C. S. Lewis.

C. S. Lewis, who wrote the Narnia books, and J. R. R. Tolkien, who wrote the Ring trilogy, were friends who taught at Oxford at the same time, were pipe-smokers, drank in the same pub, and took Christianity seriously, but although Lewis loved Tolkien's universe, the affection was not returned. Well, no wonder. When you've created your own universe, how do you feel when, in the words of a poem by E. E. cummings: "Listen: there's a hell / of a good universe next door; let's go."

Tolkien's universe was in unspecified Middle Earth, but Lewis's really was next door. In the opening scenes of *The Chronicles of Narnia: The Lion, the Witch and the Wardrobe,* two brothers and two sisters from the Pevensie family are evacuated from London and sent to live in a vast country house where they will be safe from the nightly Nazi air raids. Playing hide-and-seek, Lucy, the youngest, ventures into a wardrobe that opens directly onto a snowy landscape where before long Mr. Tumnus is explaining to her that he is a faun.

Fauns, like leprechauns, are creatures in the public domain, unlike Hobbits, who are under copyright. There are mythological creatures in Narnia, but most of the speaking roles go to humans such as the White Witch (if indeed she is human) and animals who would be right at home in the zoo (if indeed they are animals). The kids are from a tradition that requires that British children be polite and well-spoken, no doubt because Lewis preferred them that way. What is remarkable is that this bookish bachelor who did not marry until he was nearly sixty would create four children so filled with life and pluck.

That's the charm of the Narnia stories: They contain magic and myth, but their mysteries are resolved not by the kinds of rabbits Tolkien pulls out of his hat but by the determination and resolve of the Pevensie kids—who have a good deal of help, to be sure, from Aslan the Lion. For those who read the Lewis books as a Christian parable, Aslan fills the role of Christ because he is resurrected from the dead. I don't know if that makes the White Witch into Satan, but Tilda Swinton plays the role as if she has not ruled out the possibility.

The adventures that Lucy has in Narnia, at first by herself, then with her brother Edmund, and finally with the older Peter and Susan, are the sorts of things that might happen in any British forest, always assuming fauns, lions, and witches can be found there, as I am sure they can. Only toward the end of this film do the special effects ramp up into spectacular extravaganzas that might have caused Lewis to snap his pipe stem.

It is the witch who has kept Narnia in frigid cold for a century, no doubt because she is descended from Aberdeen landladies. Under the rules, Tumnus (James McAvoy) is supposed to deliver Lucy (Georgie Henley) to the witch forthwith, but fauns are not heavy hitters, and he takes mercy. Lucy returns to the country house and pops out of the wardrobe, where no time at all has passed and no one will believe her story. It is only after Edmund (Skandar Keynes) follows her into the wardrobe that evening that her breathless reports are taken seriously.

Edmund is gob-smacked by the White Witch, who proposes to make him a prince. Peter (William Moseley) and Susan (Anna Popplewell) believe Lucy and Edmund, and soon all four children are back in Narnia. They meet the first of the movie's CGI characters, Mr. and Mrs. Beaver (voices by Ray Winstone and Dawn French), who invite them into their home, which is delightfully cozy for being made of largish sticks. The Beavers explain the Narnian situation to them, just before an attack by computerized wolves whose dripping fangs reach hungrily through the twigs.

Edmund by now has gone off on his own and gotten himself taken hostage, and the Beavers hold out hope that perhaps the legendary Aslan (voice by Liam Neeson) can save him. This involves Aslan dying for Edmund's sins, much as Christ died for ours. Aslan's eventual resurrection leads into an apocalyptic climax that may be inspired by Revelations. Since there are six more books in the Narnia chronicles, however, we reach the end of the movie while still far from the Last Days.

These events, fantastical as they sound, take place on a more human, or at least more earthly, scale than those in *The Lord of the Rings.* The personalities and character traits of the children have something to do with the outcome, which is not being decided by wizards on another level of reality but will be duked out right there in Narnia. That the battle owes something to Lewis's thoughts about the first two world wars is likely, although nothing in Narnia is as horrible as the trench warfare of the first or the Nazis of the second.

The film was directed by Andrew Adamson, who directed both of the *Shrek* movies and supervised the special effects on both of Joel Schumacher's *Batman* movies. He knows his way around both comedy and action, and here combines them in a way that makes Narnia a charming place with fearsome interludes. We suspect that the Beavers are living on temporary reprieve and that wolves have dined on their relatives, but this is not the kind of movie where you bring up things like that.

Lewis famously said he never wanted the Narnia books to be filmed because he feared the animals would "turn into buffoonery or nightmare." But he said that in 1959, when he might have been thinking of a man wearing a lion suit, or puppets. The effects in this movie are so skillful that the animals look about as real as any of the other characters, and the critic Emanuel Levy explains the secret: "Aslan speaks in a natural, organic manner (which meant mapping the movement of his speech unto the whole musculature of the animal, not just his mouth)." Aslan is neither as frankly animated as the Lion King nor as real as the cheetah in *Duma,* but halfway in between, as if an animal were inhabited by an archbishop.

This is a film situated precisely on the dividing line between traditional family entertainment and the newer action-oriented family films. It is charming and scary in about equal measure, and confident for the first two acts that it can be wonderful without having to hammer us into enjoying it, or else. Then it starts hammering. Some of the scenes toward the end push the edge of the PG envelope, and like the Harry Potter series, the Narnia stories may eventually tilt over into R. But it's remarkable, isn't it, that the Brits have produced Narnia, the Ring, Hogwarts, Gormenghast, James Bond, Alice, and Pooh, and what have we produced for them in return? I was going to say the cuckoo clock, but for that you would require a three-way Google of Italy, Switzerland, and Harry Lime.

Cinderella Man ★ ★ ★ ½

PG-13, 144 m., 2005

Russell Crowe (Jim Braddock), Renée Zellweger (Mae Braddock), Paul Giamatti (Joe Gould), Craig Bierko (Max Baer), Bruce McGill (Jimmy Johnston), Paddy Considine (Mike Wilson), Ron Canada (Joe Jeanette), Connor Price (Jay Braddock). Directed by Ron Howard and produced by Brian Grazer, Howard, and Penny Marshall. Screenplay by Cliff Hollingsworth and Akiva Goldsman.

There is a moment early in *Cinderella Man* when we see Russell Crowe in the boxing ring, filled with cocky self-confidence, and I thought I knew what direction the story would take. I could not have been more mistaken. I walked in knowing nothing about Jim Braddock, "The Bulldog of Bergen," whose riches-to-rags-to-riches career inspired the movie. My friend Bill Nack of *Sports Illustrated,* who just won the A.J. Liebling Award, the highest honor a boxing writer can attain, could have told me all about Braddock, but I am just as happy to have gone in cold, so that I could be astonished by Crowe's performance.

I think of Crowe as a tough customer, known to get in the occasional brawl. Yes, he plays men who are inward and complex, as in *The Insider* and *A Beautiful Mind,* or men who are tempered and wise, as in *Master and Commander.* But neither he nor anyone else in a long time has played such a *nice* man as the boxer Jim Braddock. You'd have to go back to actors like James Stewart and Spencer Tracy to find such goodness and gentleness. Tom Hanks could handle the assignment, but do you see any one of them as a prize-fighter? Tracy, maybe.

As the film opens, Braddock is riding high with a series of victories that buy a comfortable, but not opulent, lifestyle for his wife, Mae (Renée Zellweger), and their children, Jay, Rosemarie, and Howard. Also doing okay is Braddock's loyal manager, Joe Gould (Paul Giamatti, in a third home run after *American Splendor* and *Sideways*). Then Braddock breaks his right hand, loses some matches so badly his license is taken away, and descends with his family to grim poverty in the early days of the Great Depression.

What is remarkable during both the highs and the lows is that Jim Braddock, as Crowe plays him, remains level-headed, sweet-tempered, and concerned about his family above all. Perhaps it takes a tough guy like Crowe to make Braddock's goodness believable. Mae is just the wife he deserves, filled with love and loyalty, and so terrified he will be hurt that she refuses to attend his fights and won't even listen on the radio.

Their poverty takes them from a nice family house to a cramped little apartment where there is no heat and hardly anything to eat. Braddock gets a job on the docks in Hoboken, slinging sacks of grain and coal, using his left arm because of his injured right hand, and although that job is a low point, it is also the secret to the left hook that will eventually get him named "Cinderella Man" by Damon Runyon.

The movie teams Crowe once again with director Ron Howard; they made *A Beautiful Mind* together, and the screenwriter of that film, Akiva Goldsman, cowrote this one with Cliff Hollingsworth. They find human ways to mirror the descent into despair; the Braddock family's poverty, for example, seems to weigh most heavily on the oldest son, Jay (Connor Price), who fears above all being sent away to live with "rich" relatives—rich here meaning those with something to eat. He steals a sausage from a butcher shop, is caught, and then, in a scene typical of Braddock's gentle wisdom, is not punished by his father, but talked to, softly and earnestly, because his father instinctively knows why his son stole the sausage, and that the kid's daring was almost noble.

Up to this point, there would not be a comeback, and no occasion for Damon Runyon nicknames. Jim Braddock gets one more chance at a fight, as Gould edges him past the doubts of promoter Jimmy Johnston (Bruce McGill). Without much time to train, he takes on a leading contender and to everyone's amazement wins the fight. One victory leads to another, and finally Gould is able to broker a title fight with the heavyweight champion Max Baer (Craig Bierko), who has killed two of his opponents and seems likely to kill the outweighed and outclassed Braddock.

What happens in the fight you will see. Ron Howard, Russell Crowe, Craig Bierko, the cinematographer Salvatore Totino, and the editors Daniel P. Hanley and Mike Hill step into a ring already populated by the ghosts of countless movie fights, most memorably those in *Raging Bull, Million Dollar Baby,* and the *Rocky* movies. They don't try to outfight those movies, but to outmaneuver them emotionally. The closest connection is with *Million Dollar Baby,* also a film about a fighter whose deepest motivation is the fear of poverty (at a press conference, Braddock says he fights in order to be able to buy milk for his family). The visual strategy of the big fight is direct and brutal, but depends not so much on the technical depiction of boxing as on the development of the emotional duel going on in the ring. When an underdog fights from the "heart" after his strength and skill are not enough, the result is almost always unconvincing—but not always.

Cinderella Man is a terrific boxing picture, but there's no great need for another one. The need it fills is for a full-length portrait of a good man. Most serious movies live in a world of cynicism and irony, and most good-hearted movie characters live in bad movies. Here is a movie where a good man prevails in a world where every day is an invitation to despair, where resentment would seem fully justified, where doing the right thing seems almost gratuitous, because nobody is looking and nobody cares. Jim Braddock is almost transparent in the simple goodness of his character; that must have made him almost impossible to play. Russell Crowe makes him fascinating, and it takes a moment or two of thought to appreciate how difficult that must have been.

Classe Tous Risques ★ ★ ★

NO MPAA RATING, 110 m., 1960 (rereleased 2006)

Lino Ventura (Abel Davos), Jean-Paul Belmondo (Eric Stark), Sandra Milo (Liliane), Marcel Dalio (Arthur Gibelin), Michel Ardan (Riton Vintran), Stan Krol (Raymond Naldi), Claude Cerval (Raoul Fargier), Simone France (Therese Davos), Michele Meritz (Sophie Fargier). Directed by Claude Sautet and produced by Jean Darvey. Screenplay by Sautet, Jose Giovanni, and Pascal Jardin, based on the novel by Jose Giovanni.

Abel is a convicted killer on the lam from the French who has lived in Italy long enough to acquire a wife and two sons. He loves his family more than crime. He thinks it is time to return to France. One last job should do it. If he went to more movies, he'd know that calling it your "last job" seems to put the jinx in.

Abel is played by Lino Ventura, with a sad, lived-in face. At the train station in Milan, he meets his wife, Therese (Simone France), their sons, and his partner, Raymond (Stan Krol). The details of the plan have been carefully prepared: They'll put the wife and kids on the train to a town just the other side of the French border, then stick up a bank messenger, make a getaway, switch cars, meet up again, and cross into France. Abel has pals in Paris he's sure will be happy to see him again. He did them a lot of favors.

The snatch-and-grab on a Milan street takes place, but the getaway is not as planned, and Abel and Raymond end up hiring a boat to get them to Nice. Here I will cloud certain details, moving ahead to a call Abel makes to Paris. He needs his old pals to drive down to Nice and meet him. This they are not eager to do. We see them hemming and hawing and explaining to each other how one needs to check in with his probation officer and another—anyway, what happens is, they recruit a kid none of them knows very well and hire him to drive down and look for the old man.

This kid is Eric Stark, played by Jean-Paul Belmondo at the dawn of his stardom. He makes the kind of entrance you notice, wearing a loud tweed overcoat that would be perfect for a stickup because witnesses would remember the coat instead of the guy inside. His entrance is an important moment in movie history. The French New Wave descended more or less directly from mainstream French crime films made in the 1950s, and if there is a missing link in that evolution, it might be this one. Claude Sautet's *Classe Tous Risques* was made in 1960, the same year Jean-Luc Godard's *Breathless* came out, and both starred Belmondo, who was the flavor of the year; he had appeared in ten other recent films and would have six more starring roles in 1960, usually playing a plug-ugly who was after the girl.

Breathless got all the publicity, and *Classe Tous Risques* hardly opened in America, although Sautet later would make many international successes *(Un Coeur en Hiver, Vincent, Francois, Paul . . . and the Others)*. It arrives now in a restored print with rewritten subtitles, a crisp, smart, cynical film about dishonor among thieves.

Sautet's film grows out of work like Jacques Becker's *Touchez Pas au Grisbi* (1954) and Jean-Pierre Melville's *Bob le Flambeur* (1955) and shares their affection for a middle-aged thief who would like to retire but finds that his old life reaches out and nails him. Jean Gabin gave one of his best performances in the Becker, and Melville's star, Roger Duchesne, made Bob the High Roller so likable that the movie inspired three *Ocean's Eleven* remakes. Ventura lacks Gabin's star power and Duchesne's silky, regretful heroism, but he has an implacable, lived-in face, and like them he embodies a code his world has abandoned.

By sending a kid for him, Abel's pals in Paris have insulted his ideas of loyalty and friendship. And who is this kid, anyway? Why did he take the job? Can he be trusted? Why is he fooling around with an actress (Sandra Milo) he just met, who is down on her luck when there isn't enough luck to go around? After the quick-moving opening episodes, the movie comes down to the relationship between the old guy and the kid—who has no reason at all to risk his life for Abel, except that he knows class when he sees it, understands the code the Parisians have forgotten, and wants to live by it.

The film doesn't make it a big point, but consider the meetings in Paris where Abel's pals recruit and hire Eric Stark. As moviegoers we are focusing on (a) Belmondo, so young, his career ahead of him, and (b) the evasions by which the pals hire a kid to do the job they are morally bound to do themselves. But in Sautet's mind, the scenes might equally have been (c) about the kid listening to them betraying a man who is counting on them. It's possible that before Eric ever sees Abel, he has already decided that Abel is the real thing, the kind of guy Eric could respect and trust.

Abel asks Eric more than once why he took the job. He doesn't get much of an answer, but then, men in such trades aren't big on discussing their philosophies. There is also the way Milo plays Liliane, the new girlfriend. She's in the tradition of women in gangster movies who sign on with a guy they like because he treats them right and isn't a rat. They're usually running away from a guy who treated them wrong and was a rat. Hard to believe this is the same actress who played Mastroianni's pouty, flamboyant mistress in Federico Fellini's *8½* (1963). Here she seems dialed down, wearier, just as she should.

Classe Tous Risques isn't a film in the same league with the titles by Becker, Melville, and Godard, but how many films are? It's more like one of those Humphrey Bogart films that isn't *The Big Sleep*, but you're glad you saw it anyway. Studying the Hollywood crime films of the 1930s and 1940s, the French gave them their name, "film noir," and embraced them with a particular Gallic offhandedness. Their French gangsters crossed hardness with cool and style. In *Touchez Pas au Grisbi, Bob le Flambeur,* and *Classe Tous Risques,* the heroes have not only loyalty but also a certain tenderness, a friendship that survives even when their friends act stupidly and get them all in trouble. In *Breathless,* the Belmondo hero acts stupidly himself and gets himself in trouble, and the modern age of crime films begins.

Ebert's essays on Breathless, Touchez Pas au Grisbi, *and* Bob le Flambeur *are in the Great Movies series at www.rogerebert.com.*

Clean ★ ★ ★ ½

R, 110 m., 2006

Maggie Cheung (Emily Wang), Nick Nolte (Albrecht Hauser), James Dennis (Jay), Beatrice Dalle (Elena), Jeanne Balibar (Irene Paolini), Don McKellar (Vernon), Martha Henry (Rosemary Hauser), James Johnston (Lee Hauser). Directed by Olivier Assayas and produced by Niv Fichman, Xavier Giannoli, Xavier Marchand, and Edouard Weil. Screenplay by Assayas.

Emily is always in motion, driven by disquiet, unhappy with herself and the decisions that got her here. Her mind seems elsewhere, focusing on what would bring her peace: heroin. She and her partner, Lee, are rock stars whose moment of fame has passed and stranded them in a Canadian motel. They fight, she drives off into the night, scores drugs, shoots up, and sleeps in the car. When she returns to the motel, Lee is dead of an overdose. She should quietly back away and leave town. Instead, she gets herself arrested and sentenced to six months for possession.

Maggie Cheung plays Emily with such intense desperation that she won the best actress award at Cannes 2004. Only a few actresses in the world could have handled this role from a technical point of view: Born in Hong Kong, a citizen of the movie world, she acts here mostly in English, with some French and Cantonese, and moves confidently through Vancouver, Paris, and London. She always looks as if she knows the rules, even when she has broken them; despite being broke and strung out, she retains enough personal authority to call in favors and ask old friends for jobs.

She and Lee (James Johnston) had a child named Jay (James Dennis), who is about six. She loves him, and maybe she tells herself she isn't raising him because it's better that way for Jay. The boy is living with Lee's parents, Albrecht and Rosemary Hauser (Nick Nolte and Martha Henry). When Emily goes to jail, of course she loses custody. She loses more than that, and observe how low her voice is, and how downcast her eyes, as she answers questions at an interrogation. She is defeated; she knows precisely how she destroyed her life and lost her boy.

Clean, written and directed by Cheung's former husband, Olivier Assayas, does a brisk, understated job of implying Emily's past by observing her present. In the eyes of her old friends, we understand what she used to be, and what they see now. She lives in the moment. Consider the steps in Paris by which she begins by asking for a job and ends up with a free room.

Cheung is on screen for most of *Clean*, but Nolte's smaller role is equally important. His wife is dying of cancer. They were in London when she fell ill, and now he and the boy live in a hotel and visit her in the hospital. His wife is bitter about Emily, but Albrecht is realistic: "Someday we won't be here. And she is the boy's mother." He talks with her soberly and with searching eyes, and she responds to his seriousness. She is a damaged person but not a bad one, wants her boy back again, and knows it will be some time before she can meet that responsibility.

Cheung is a considerable actress, famous in Asia for Hong Kong action pictures, respected in the West at film festivals. Incredibly, she has made about eighty movies; raised from the age of eight in England, she returned to Hong Kong as a model and got into movies at a time when the industry churned them out. I haven't seen most of her action films but have admired her in Wong Kar-Wai's *In the Mood for Love* (2000) and Wayne Wang's *Chinese Box* (1997), and was part of an audience at the Hawaii Film Festival that was fascinated by *The Soong Sisters* (1997), where she, Vivian Wu, and Michelle Yeoh played sisters who married three of the most powerful men of their time.

Those roles all, in one way or another, required her to be a great and grave beauty. It is astonishing how different the character in *Clean* is, with her restless style of smoking, walking, imploring, protesting. When her character grows anxious or angry, Cheung doesn't make the mistake of overacting; Emily is always closer to her bottoms than her tops. Watch her when her little boy tells her, "You killed my father." Her instincts as she handles that moment suggest she may make a good mother, after all.

I wonder what audiences will make of the

last shot of the movie. Is it too inconclusive, or too upbeat? You can read it either way, but I believe it is appropriate because what it says is, tomorrow we start again. Every tomorrow.

Click ★ ★

PG-13, 98 m., 2006

Adam Sandler (Michael Newman), Kate Beckinsale (Donna Newman), Christopher Walken (Morty), Henry Winkler (Ted Newman), David Hasselhoff (Mr. Ammer), Julie Kavner (Trudy Newman), Sean Astin (Bill Rando). Directed by Frank Coraci and produced by Steve Koren, Mark O'Keefe, Adam Sandler, Jack Giarraputo, and Neal H. Moritz. Screenplay by Koren and O'Keefe.

Scrooge was granted visions of Christmas Past and Christmas Future, and reformed his life. What happens to Adam Sandler in *Click* is like what happened to Scrooge, except with a lot more Christmases. He needs more than one lesson, and he gets more than one lesson. Way more.

In *Being There,* the hero, Chance, has spent all his life watching television. When he wanders out to freedom and is threatened on the street, he clicks a TV remote control to get another channel. In *Click,* Adam Sandler plays Michael, an architect who is given a universal remote that's truly universal. With it, he can take control of his life: freeze a scene, fast-forward, reverse, mute the sound, select the chapters of his choice, and even witness his parents at the moment of his conception (that's, of course, in the "Making of" documentary).

The movie is being sold as a comedy, but you know what? This isn't funny. Yes, there are some laughs, as when he finds he can turn the dog's barking up and down, or play around with the settings for hue and contrast, or when he discovers the picture-in-picture feature, which allows him to watch the ball game no matter what else is going on around him. But the movie essentially involves a workaholic who uses the universal remote to skip over all the bad stuff in his life and discovers in the process that he is missing life itself. Take away the gimmick of the universal remote and this is what a lot of us do, and it's sad.

It's not just sad, it's brutal. There's an undercurrent of cold, detached cruelty in the way Michael uses the magical device. He turns off the volume during an argument with his wife. He fast-forwards through a boring family dinner and, later, through foreplay. He skips ahead to avoid a bad cold. He jumps to the chapter where he gets a promotion. Eventually he realizes the family dog has died and been replaced by another, his kids have grown up, his wife is married to someone else, and he weighs four hundred pounds. It happened while he wasn't paying attention.

Like many another Sandler movie, this one lingers studiously over bodily functions. After losing enormous amounts of weight, for example, Michael plays with a big flap of loose skin around his stomach, plopping it up and down long after any possible audience curiosity has been satisfied. During an argument with his boss (David Hasselhoff), he freeze-frames the boss, jumps on his desk, and farts. When he puts his boss back on "play," the boss inexplicably decides his secretary has put feces in his salad. Anyone who can't tell poop from lettuce doesn't deserve to be a senior partner. They teach you that in business school.

Michael is surrounded by patient and saintly people. His wife, Donna (Kate Beckinsale), loves him but despairs of reaching him. She has that standard wifely role of complaining when he has to work late and can't be at the swimming meet/Fourth of July party, etc. Michael's parents (Henry Winkler and Julie Kavner) are sweet and loving but kvetch too much and talk too slowly, so Michael zaps right through the time he has remaining with them.

I am not sure if this story device could possibly have been made funny. It could have been elevated into a metaphysical adventure, as in *Eternal Sunshine of the Spotless Mind,* or made to generate a series of paradoxes, as in *Being John Malkovich,* but *Click* stays resolutely at level one—the tiresome explication of the basic premise. Once we get the idea, there are no more surprises, only variations on the first one.

The movie does have some wit about its product placement. The plot is set in motion when Michael goes out late at night to buy a universal remote, and only one store is open: Bed, Bath & Beyond. As a retail store name, this has always reminded me of the final subtitle in Kubrick's *2001,* which was "Jupiter and

Beyond the Infinite." *Beyond* the infinite. That's a fair piece. In the store Michael enters, Bed and Bath are easy to find, but Beyond is behind a mysterious door at the end of a very long corridor, where a man named Morty (Christopher Walken) makes him a gift of the universal remote. If they make *Click 2,* I want it to be about Morty.

Cloverfield ★ ★ ★

PG-13, 80 m., 2008

Michael Stahl-David (Rob Hawkins), Mike Vogel (Jason Hawkins), Odette Yustman (Beth McIntyre), Lizzy Caplan (Marlena Diamond), Jessica Lucas (Lily Ford), T. J. Miller (Hud). Directed by Matt Reeves and produced by J. J. Abrams and Bryan Burk. Screenplay by Drew Goddard.

Godzilla meets the "queasy-cam" in *Cloverfield,* a movie that crosses the Monster-Attacks-Manhattan formula with *The Blair Witch Project.* No, Godzilla doesn't appear in person, but the movie's monster looks like a close relative on the evolutionary tree, especially in one close-up. The close-up ends with what appears to be a POV shot of the guy with the video camera being eaten, but later he's still around. Too bad. If he had been eaten but left the camera's light on, I might have been reminded of the excellent video of my colonoscopy.

The movie, which has been in a vortex of rumors for months, is actually pretty scary at times. It's most frightening right after something very bad begins to happen in lower Manhattan and before we get a good look at the monster, which is scarier as a vaguely glimpsed enormity than as a big reptile. At least I think it's a reptile, although it sheds babies by the dozens, and they look more like spiders crossed with crabs. At birth they are already fully formed and functioning, able to scamper all over town, bite victims, grab them in subway tunnels, etc. I guess that makes the monster a female, although Godzilla, you will recall, had a baby, and the fanboys are still arguing over its gender. (Hold on! I just discovered online that those are not its babies at all, but giant parasitic lice, which drop off and go looking for dinner.)

The film, directed by Matt Reeves, is the baby of producer J. J. Abrams, creator of TV's *Lost.* It begins with home video–type footage and follows the fortunes of six twenty-something yuppies. The lead character is Rob (Michael Stahl-David), who is about to leave town for a job in Japan. At a farewell surprise party, Hud (T. J. Miller) takes over the camera and tapes friends wishing Rob well, including Jason (Mike Vogel) and the beautiful Lily (Jessica Lucas). Hud is especially attentive toward Marlena (Lizzy Caplan), who says she's just on her way to meet some friends. She never gets there. The building is jolted, the lights flicker, and everyone runs up to the roof to see all hell breaking loose.

The initial scenes of destruction are glimpsed at a distance. Then things heat up when the head of the Statue of Liberty rolls down the street. Several shots of billowing smoke clouds are unmistakable evocations of 9/11, and indeed, one of the movie's working titles was *1/18/08.* So the statute has run out on the theory that after 9/11 it would be in bad taste to show Manhattan being destroyed. So explicit are *Cloverfield's* 9/11 references that the monster is seen knocking over skyscrapers, and one high-rise is seen leaning against another.

The leaning high-rise contains Beth (Odette Yustman), whom Rob feels duty-bound to rescue from her forty-ninth-floor apartment near Central Park. The others all come along on this foolhardy mission (not explained: how, after walking all the way to Columbus Circle, they have the energy to climb forty-nine flights of stairs, Lily in her high heels). Part of their uptown journey is by subway, without the benefit of trains. They're informed by a helpful soldier that the last rescue helicopter leaving Central Park will "have wheels up at oh-six-hundred," prompting me to wonder how many helicopters it would take to rescue the population of Manhattan.

The origin of the monster goes unexplained, which is all right with me after the tiresome opening speeches in so many of the thirty or more Godzilla films. The characters speculate that it came from beneath the sea, or maybe from outer space, but incredibly not one of them ever pronounces the word "Godzilla," no doubt for trademark reasons.

The other incredible element is that the camcorder's battery apparently lasts, on the evidence of the footage we see, more than seven hours.

The entire film is shot in queasy-cam handheld style, mostly by Hud, who couldn't hold it steady or frame a shot if his life depended on it. After the sneak preview, I heard some fellow audience members complaining that they felt dizzy or had vertigo, but no one barfed, at least within my hearing. Mercifully, the movie is even shorter than its alleged ninety-minute running time; how much visual shakiness can we take? And yet, all in all, it is an effective film, deploying its special effects well and never breaking the illusion that it is all happening as we see it. One question, which you can answer for me after you see the film: Given the nature of the opening government announcement, how did the camera survive?

Coach Carter ★ ★ ★

PG-13, 140 m., 2005

Samuel L. Jackson (Coach Ken Carter), Robert Ri'chard (Damien Carter), Rob Brown (Kenyon Stone), Debbi Morgan (Tonya Carter), Ashanti (Kyra), Rick Gonzalez (Timo Cruz). Directed by Thomas Carter and produced by David Gale, Brian Robbins, and Michael Tollin. Screenplay by Mark Schwahn and John Gatins.

Samuel L. Jackson made news by refusing to costar with 50 Cent in a movie based on the rapper's life. He not only refused, but did it publicly, even though the film is to be directed by six-time Oscar nominee Jim Sheridan *(In America)*. A clue to Jackson's thinking may be found in his film, *Coach Carter,* based on the true story of a California high school basketball coach who placed grades ahead of sports. Like Bill Cosby, Jackson is arguing against the antiintellectual message that success for young black males is better sought in the worlds of rap and sports than in the classroom.

There is, however, another aspect to Jackson's refusal: He said he thought Sheridan wanted him to "lend legitimacy" to 50 Cent's acting debut. He might have something there. Jackson has an authority on the screen; he occupies a character with compelling force, commanding attention, and can bring class to a movie. He might, he said, be interested in working with 50 Cent after the rapper makes another five movies or so, and earns his chops.

This reasoning may not be fair. Consider the work that Ice Cube did in *Boyz N the Hood* (1991), his first movie and the beginning of a successful acting career. Or look at the promise that Tupac Shakur showed, especially in his last feature, *Gridlock'd* (1997), holding his own with the veteran Tim Roth. Maybe 50 Cent has the stuff to be an actor. Maybe not. Jackson's decision may have more to do with the underlying values of the rapper's life; he may not consider 50 Cent's career, so often involving violent episodes, to be much of a role model.

Role models are what *Coach Carter,* Jackson's film, is all about. He plays Ken Carter, who began as a sports star at Richmond (California) High School, setting records that still stand, and then had success in the military and as a small businessman. He's asked to take over as basketball coach, an unpaid volunteer position; the former coach tells him, "I can't get them to show up for school." Ken Carter thinks he can fix that.

The movie was directed by Thomas Carter *(Save the Last Dance),* no relation to the coach. It follows long-established genre patterns; it's not only a sports movie with the usual big games and important shots, but also a coach movie, with inspiring locker-room speeches and difficult moral decisions. There are certain parallels with *Friday Night Lights,* although there it's the movie itself, and not the coach, that underlines the futility of high school stars planning on pro sports as a career.

Certainly both movies give full weight to public opinion in the communities where they're set—places where the public's interest in secondary education seems entirely focused on sports, where coaches are more important than teachers, where scores are more important than grades.

Coach Carter wants to change all that. He walks into a gymnasium ruled by loud, arrogant, disrespectful student jocks, and commands attention with the fierceness of his attitude. He makes rules. He requires the students to sign a contract, promising to maintain a decent grade-point average as the price of being on the team. He deals with the usual personnel problems; a star player named Kenyon

Stone (Ron Brown) has a pregnant girlfriend named Kyra (Ashanti, in her, a-hem, first role), and she sees a threat to her future in Carter's determination to get his players into college.

Ken Carter's most dramatic decision, which got news coverage in 1999, was to lock the gymnasium, forfeit games, and endanger the team's title chances after some of his players refused to live up to the terms of the contract. The community, of course, is outraged that a coach would put grades above winning games; for them, the future for the student athletes lies in the NBA, not education. Given the odds against making it in the NBA (dramatically demonstrated in the great documentary *Hoop Dreams*), this reasoning is like considering the lottery a better bet than working for a living.

Jackson has the usual big speeches assigned to all coaches in all sports movies, and delivers on them, big time. His passion makes familiar scenes feel new. "I see a system that's designed for you to fail," he tells his players, pointing out that young black men are 80 percent more likely to go to prison than to go to college. The movie's closing credits indicate that six of the team members did go on to college, five with scholarships. Lives, not games, were won.

Colossal Sensation! ★ ★ ★

NO MPAA RATING, 97 m., 2005

Róbert Koltai (Naftalin), Sándor Gáspár (Dodo), Orsolya Tóth (Pipitér). Directed by Róbert Koltai and produced by Gábor P. Koltai. Screenplay by Péter Horváth and Róbert Koltai.

Colossal Sensation! sees the history of Hungary in the twentieth century through the eyes of twin circus clowns. For them, as for all Hungarians, it is a story of feast and famine, nostalgia and regret, suffering and triumph, although not all Hungarians had the misfortune (or was it the opportunity?) to destroy a wristwatch given to the Hungarian party leader by Stalin himself.

The year, 1903. Nonidentical twin boys are born into a circus family. One afternoon, they are jumping over an alligator, as circus kids will do, when the beast snaps at little Naftalin, leaving him with a lifelong limp. Dodo is taller, better-looking, and straighter-walking, and he becomes their leader. When he gets engaged, his fiancée is alarmed to find that Naftalin (Róbert Koltai) may come along on the honeymoon. Dodo (Sándor Gáspár) doesn't have the heart to leave him behind.

The movie begins in monochrome, switches to color in 1949, and fills the screen with brilliant reds for events in 1953, when the twins are employed by the Budapest Grand Circus. They do that trick where they pretend to smash a watch borrowed from the audience and then return it unharmed. Naftalin, alas, borrows the party leader's watch, and let us say the party leader is not amused by the results.

Dodo, who has spent his life looking out for his slightly smaller and younger brother, takes the rap and goes to prison. In 1956, during the Hungarian uprising, Naftalin and Dodo's girl, Pipitér (Orsolya Tóth), make friends with the clueless crew of a wandering Russian tank, leading to a series of events surreal enough for *Catch-22*.

The movie follows the grim reality of the Soviet occupation but is not itself grim; director Koltai, who wrote it with Péter Horváth, at one point has a character say, "We are very small dots in this, comrade." And indeed, instead of making his heroes the center of the world, he shows them making a living on the fringes; showbiz provides them with a home, but only limited success, and what little we see of their clown act seems routine and perfunctory. What they are good at is improvising a response to the emergencies of life.

Colossal Sensation! had its American premiere at the Wilmette Theater in suburban Chicago, where two years ago the Hungarian film *Gloomy Sunday* also played for the first time in the United States. The big art distributors won't risk their limited funds on sweet little comedies from Hungary (or on gloomy big tragedies). *Gloomy Sunday* was accomplished and ambitious in a way *Colossal Sensation!* doesn't really intend to be. But in its own modest way, the movie is a whimsical charmer.

The Constant Gardener ★ ★ ★ ★

R, 129 m., 2005

Ralph Fiennes (Justin Quayle), Rachel Weisz (Tessa Quayle), Danny Huston (Sandy Woodrow), Hubert Kounde (Arnold Bluhm), Bill Nighy (Sir Bernard Pellegrin), Pete

Postlethwaite (Marcus Lorbeer). Directed by Fernando Meirelles and produced by Simon Channing-Williams. Screenplay by Jeffrey Caine, based on the novel by John le Carre.

They meet as strangers who plunge at once into sudden sex. They catch their breath, marry, and begin to learn about each other. Justin is an official in the British government. Tessa is an activist. She goes to Africa with Justin, her motives unclear in his mind, and witnesses what she thinks is murder in an African hospital. Then she is murdered at a crossroads, along with her African driver. And a doctor named Arnold, whom she works with, is found dead, too. But why, Justin needs to know, did Tessa receive an e-mail asking her, "What were you and Arnold doing in the Nairobi Hilton Friday night? Does Justin know?"

The murder of Tessa takes place right at the start of *The Constant Gardener,* so it is not revealing too much to mention it. The movie is a progress back into her life, and a journey of discovery for Justin, who learns about a woman he never really knew. The flashback structure, told in remembered moments, passages of dialogue, scenes that are interrupted and completed later, is typical of John le Carre, whose novels resemble chess problems in which one solution is elegant and all of the others take too many moves. It is a style suited to the gifts of the Brazilian director Fernando Meirelles, whose great *City of God* (2003) told a story that was composed of countless tributaries that all flowed together into a mighty narrative stream.

The fragmented style is the best way to tell this story, for both the novel and the movie. *The Constant Gardener* is not a logical exercise beginning with mystery and ending at truth, but a circling around an elusive conspiracy. Understand who the players are and how they are willing to compromise themselves, and you can glimpse cruel outlines beneath the public relations facade. As the drug companies pour AIDS drugs into Africa, are they using their programs to mask the test of other drugs? "No drug company does something for nothing," le Carre has a character observe.

The Constant Gardener may be the angriest story le Carre has ever told. Certainly his elegant prose and the oblique shorthand of the dialogue show the writer forcing himself to turn fury into style. His novel involves drug companies that test their products on the poor of the Third World and are willing to accept the deaths that may occur because, after all, those people don't count. Why not? Because no one is there to count them.

Do drug companies really do this? Facts are the bones beneath the skin of a le Carre novel. Either he knows what he's talking about, or he is uncommonly persuasive in seeming to. *The Constant Gardener* at times plays like a movie that will result in indictments. What makes it extraordinary is that it also plays as a love story, and as an examination of the mysteries of the heart.

The performances need to be very good to carry us through sequences in which nobody, good or evil, seems very sure of the total picture. Ralph Fiennes plays Justin as a bureaucrat who seems detached from issues; he's the opposite of Tessa. As he tries to get to the bottom of her death, he sifts through his discoveries like an accountant unwilling to go home for the day until the books are balanced.

One way of looking at Tessa's death is that she was a hothead who had an affair with a handsome African man, went where she shouldn't have been, and got caught in one of those African border killings where toll-collecting soldiers with AK-47s enforce whatever they think is the law. Another way to look at it is to give her the benefit of the doubt. To wonder what was behind the embarrassing questions she asked at a press conference. To ask why statistics seem to be missing, if a drug study is designed to generate them.

As he probes through the wreckage of his wife's life, Justin encounters an array of characters who could have been airlifted in from Graham Greene—or from other le Carre novels, of course. Hubert Kounde plays Arnold Bluhm, the African who is not, in fact, Tessa's driver, but a doctor who is her colleague. Danny Huston, tall and courtly like his father, John, and like John often smiling at a private joke, plays Sandy Woodrow, the British high commissioner on the scene. Bill Nighy, that actor who often seems to be frowning through a migraine, is Sir Bernard Pellegrin, head of the Foreign Office and thus Justin and Sandy's boss. And Pete Postlethwaite, looking as if he has been left out too long in the weather, is

Lorbeer, a drug company man who works in the field—at what, it is dangerous to say.

The Constant Gardener begins with a strong, angry story and peoples it with actors who let it happen to them, instead of rushing ahead to check off the surprises. It seems solidly grounded in its Kenyan locations; like *City of God,* it feels organically rooted. Like many le Carre stories, it begins with grief and proceeds with sadness toward horror. Its closing scenes are as cynical about international politics and commerce as I can imagine. I would like to believe they are an exaggeration, but I fear they are not. This is one of the year's best films.

Constantine ★ ½

R, 120 m., 2005

Keanu Reeves (John Constantine), Rachel Weisz (Angela and Isabel Dodson), Shia LeBeouf (Chas), Djimon Hounsou (Midnite), Max Baker (Beeman), Pruitt Taylor Vince (Father Hennessy), Gavin Rossdale (Balthazar), Tilda Swinton (Gabriel), Peter Stormare (Satan). Directed by Francis Lawrence and produced by Lauren Shuler Donner, Benjamin Melniker, Michael E. Uslan, Erwin Stoff, Lorenzo di Bonaventura, and Akiva Goldsman. Screenplay by Kevin Brodbin and Frank Cappello, based on the comic book *Hellblazer* by Jamie Delano and Garth Ennis.

No, *Constantine* is not part of a trilogy including *Troy* and *Alexander.* It's not about the emperor at all, but about a man who can see the world behind the world, and is waging war against the scavengers of the damned. There was a nice documentary about emperor penguins, however, at Sundance. The males sit on the eggs all winter long in, like, 60 degrees below zero.

Keanu Reeves plays Constantine as a chain-smoking, depressed demon-hunter who lives above a bowling alley in Los Angeles. Since he was a child, he has been able to see that not all who walk among us are human. Some are penguins. Sorry about that. Some are half-angels and half-devils. Constantine knows he is doomed to hell because he once tried to kill himself, and is trying to rack up enough frames against the demons to earn his way into heaven.

There is a scene early in the movie where Constantine and his doctor look at his X-rays, never a good sign in a superhero movie. He has lung cancer. The angel Gabriel (Tilda Swinton) tells him, "You are going to die young because you've smoked thirty cigarettes a day since you were thirteen." Gabriel has made more interesting announcements. Constantine has already spent some time in hell, which looks like a postnuclear Los Angeles created by animators with a hangover. No doubt it is filled with carcinogens.

The half-angels and half-devils are earthly proxies in the war between God and Satan. You would think that God would be the New England Patriots of this contest, but apparently there is a chance that Satan could win. Constantine's lonely mission is to track down half-demons and cast them back to the fires below. Like Blade, the vampire-killer, he is surprisingly optimistic, considering he is one guy in one city dealing on a case-by-case basis, and the enemy is global.

Constantine has a technical adviser named Beeman (Max Baker), who lives in the ceiling of the bowling alley among the pin-spotting machines, and functions like Q in the James Bond movies. Here he is loading Constantine with the latest weaponry: "Bullet shavings from the assassination attempt on the pope, holy water from the river of Jordan, and, you'll love this, screech beetles." The screech beetles come in a little matchbox. "To the fallen," Beeman explains, "the sound is like nails on a blackboard." Later there is a scene where Constantine is inundated by the creatures of hell, and desperately tries to reach the matchbox and *get* those beetles to *screeching.*

Rachel Weisz plays Angela Dodson, an L.A. police detective whose twin sister, Isabel, has apparently committed suicide. Isabel reported seeing demons, so Angela consults Constantine, who nods wisely and wonders if Isabel jumped, or was metaphysically pushed. Later in the film, to show Angela that she also has the gift of seeing the world behind the world, Constantine holds her underwater in a bathtub until she passes out and sees the torments of hell. No bright white corridors and old friends and Yanni for her. You wonder what kind of an L.A. cop would allow herself to be experimentally drowned in a bathtub by a guy who lives over a bowling alley.

Together, they prowl the nighttime streets. At one point, Constantine needs to consult

Midnite (Djimon Hounsou), a former witch doctor who runs a private nightclub where half-angels and half-demons can get half-loaded and talk shop. There is a doorman. To gain admittance, you have to read his mind and tell him what's on the other side of the card he's holding up. "Two frogs on a bench," Constantine says. Could have been a lucky guess.

There is a priest in the film, the alcoholic Father Hennessy (Pruitt Taylor Vince), whose name, I guess, is product placement. Strange that there is a priest, since that opens the door to Catholicism and therefore to the news that Constantine is not doomed unless he wages a lifelong war against demons, but needs merely go to confession; three Our Fathers, three Hail Marys, and he's outta there. Strange that movies about Satan always require Catholics. You never see your Presbyterians or Episcopalians hurling down demons.

The forces of hell manifest themselves in many ways. One victim is eaten by flies. A young girl is possessed by a devil, and Constantine shouts, "I need a mirror! Now! At least three feet high!" He can capture the demon in the mirror and throw it out the window, see, although you wonder why supernatural beings would have such low-tech security holes.

Keanu Reeves has a deliberately morose energy level in the movie, as befits one who has seen hell, walks among half-demons, and is dying. He keeps on smoking. Eventually he confronts Satan (Peter Stormare), who wears a white suit. (Satan to tailor: "I want a suit just like God's.") Oh, and the plot also involves the Spear of Destiny, which is the spear that killed Christ, and which has been missing since World War II, which seems to open a window to the possibility of Nazi villains, but no.

Constantine's Sword ★ ★ ★

NO MPAA RATING, 95 m., 2008

Directed by Oren Jacoby and produced by Jacoby, James Carroll, Michael Solomon, and Betsy West. Screenplay by Carroll and Jacoby, based on the book by Carroll.

James Carroll speaks calmly and thoughtfully, and comes across as a reasonable man. He is our companion through *Constantine's Sword,* a film about the misalliance of church and state. In terms of screen presence, he is the opposite of one of his interview subjects, the Reverend Ted Haggard of Colorado Springs. To look upon Haggard's face is to wonder what he is really thinking because his mouth seems locked in an enormous smile ("Fiery-eyed and grinning maniacally, Mr. Haggard suggests a Paul Lynde caricature of a fire-and-brimstone preacher."—Stephen Holden, *New York Times*)

Carroll went to Colorado to interview Haggard and others about the alleged infiltration of the Air Force Academy by evangelical Christians. He also speaks with an academy graduate, Mikey Weinstein, who brought suit against the academy alleging that his cadet son, Casey, was the focus of officially sanctioned anti-Semitism. One academy chaplain, we learn, lectured new cadets on their duty to proselytize those who had not found Jesus.

For Haggard, that is the exercise of free speech. For Weinstein and Carroll, it is another chapter of the long-running history of Christianity's crusade against the Jews. Not long after, Carroll finds himself standing on the bridge in Rome where the Emperor Constantine is said to have had a vision of the cross of Jesus, with the words, "In this sign, you shall conquer." The linking of Christianity with the state began then and there, Carroll believes.

The film is a ninety-five-minute distillation of Carroll's best-seller *Constantine's Sword: The Church and the Jews* and is concerned with medieval anti-Semitism, the questionable record of Pius XII on Nazism, the Crusades, the wars in Vietnam and Iraq, and his own life as a former Catholic priest, the son of an Air Force general, an antiwar protestor, and still a practicing Catholic. That is too much ground to cover, but *Constantine's Sword* does an engrossing job of giving it a once-over. Perhaps it is the calm in Carroll's voice and the measured visual and editing style of the director, Oren Jacoby, that create an evocative journey out of what is really a hurtle through history.

Carroll has a lot of stories to tell us: Haggard and the explosion of evangelicalism ("a new megachurch of two-thousand-plus members comes into being every other day"); Constantine and the conversion of Rome from paganism; the Middle Ages and the crusaders who warmed up with the massacre of ancient Jewish cities in Germany; Edith Stein, a Jewish woman who became a Catholic nun and saint and a victim of Auschwitz; the Jewish family that has lived for centuries in the same district in Rome and supplied the popes with all their tableware for 150 years; and his own father, who was a strategist during the Cuban Missile Crisis.

Each topic is intrinsically interesting, even if the film sometimes seems short of visuals to illustrate it. There are too many shots of Carroll on the road, going places and looking at things. There isn't a lot new about his revisionist history of Christianity, but there is a lot that is not widely known, including the fact that the present pope has overturned the reforms of Vatican II and returned to the Mass a prayer for the conversion of the Jews. How much do we appreciate the Muslim prayers for *our* conversion? Or do they want us?

I've read over the years about the Air Force Academy controversy but didn't realize how deeply the academy's culture is embedded in evangelical zealotry. A similar controversy developed at the University of Colorado about an evangelical football coach's training sermons. Does religion belong in such contexts? In the academy's dining room, which seats thousands, every place setting for a week included a flyer promoting Mel Gibson's *The Passion of the Christ.* If those in charge of the academy did not understand instinctively why allowing that is an unacceptable crossing of the boundary between church and state, they should not have been allowed high office.

But I ramble. So does the movie, in an insidiously fascinating way. Perhaps it benefits by lacking a clear agenda and not following a rigid outline. Carroll is a man of limitless curiosity about his subjects, the kind of conversationalist you urge to keep on talking. As for Rev. Haggard, some months after his interview was filmed, he resigned as president of the National Association of Evangelicals, describing himself as a "liar and hypocrite" after his affair with a onetime male prostitute was revealed. I wonder how widely he was smiling then.

Control ★ ★ ★ ½

R, 121 m., 2007

Sam Riley (Ian Curtis), Samantha Morton (Debbie Curtis), Alexandra Maria Lara (Annik Honore), Joe Anderson (Hooky), James Anthony Pearson (Bernard Sumner), Toby Kebbell (Rob Gretton), Craig Parkinson (Tony Wilson), Harry Treadaway (Stephen Morris). Directed by Anton Corbijn and produced by Corbijn, Orian Williams, and Todd Eckert. Screenplay by Matt Greenhalgh, based on *Touching from a Distance* by Deborah Curtis.

Ian Curtis was one of those introverted teenagers who gaze sadly upon their own destiny. In his cramped bedroom in Macclesfield, England, his schoolboy's desk holds files labeled for poems, novels, and so on. The files are filled not so much with his work as with his dreams. He lies on his back on his narrow bed, smokes, ponders, listens to music. He would become the object of cult veneration as lead singer of the late-1970s band Joy Division, and he would commit suicide at twenty-three. There are times when we almost think that was his plan.

Control, one of the most perceptive of rock music biopics, has been made by two people who knew him very well. It is based on a memoir by his wife, Deborah (Samantha Morton), a teenager when they married, and directed by the photographer Anton Corbijn, whose early photos helped establish Curtis's image as young, handsome, and sorrowful. The title of Deborah's book, *Touching from a Distance,* could describe all his relationships.

There is irony in the band name Joy Division, because Ian seems to experience little joy and much inner division, as an almost passive participant in his own career. Listen to the two albums the band made, and you hear his lead vocals as relentless complaints against—what? The melancholy that prevents him from feeling the emotions expressed by his words?

The movie is quietly, superbly photographed and acted. It is in black and white and gray, of course, and we sense Ian was a man who dreamed in shadows, not colors. He is played by Sam Riley, who makes him seem always alone. There is a lot of performance footage, but Riley sees Ian not so much performing as functioning. His bandmates sometimes look at him with that inward expression people get when they wonder if they have enough gas to get to the next gas station.

Ian's marriage is, of course, a focus of the film, since his wife was not only its source but also a coproducer. He was clearly not ready for marriage. She was younger but more balanced and competent. Ian had an affair with Annik Honore (Alexandra Maria Lara), a Belgian, and the movie deals with that straight-on, not painting her as a home-wrecker but as another of the enablers Ian used. For him, I suspect, love meant not so much what he felt for a woman as what she felt for him.

Early in the film, Ian and Deborah attend a Sex Pistols concert, and Ian has his ideas altered about what a band is and what music is. His stage style with a microphone resembles a shy, introverted Johnny Rotten. We meet key players in the pivotal Manchester music scene of the period, including the entrepreneur Tony Wilson (Craig Parkinson), immortalized in Michael Winterbottom's *24 Hour Party People*, a film about the same time and place.

Ian Curtis suffered from epilepsy, a condition I'm not sure he fully understood. It seems to have come upon him around twenty, and sometimes during a stage performance we see him moving spasmodically and wonder if performing triggers episodes. Unlike epilepsy as experienced by, say, Prince Myshkin in Dostoyevsky's *The Idiot*, Ian's does not seem to involve a transition through an ecstatic state. He grows agitated, blanks out, regains consciousness, is confused and depressed. His body has betrayed him.

The extraordinary achievement of *Control* is that it works simultaneously as a musical biopic and the story of a life. There's no rags-to-riches cliché mongering because, for Ian, even the riches were sackcloth. And since his early death is so well-known, the movie consists of a progression, not a progress. The emotional monitor is always Deborah, patient, loyal, worried; Morton, who is thirty, is absolutely convincing as a plucky teenage bride. The shots with which Corbijn leads up to and out of Ian's suicide are meticulously modulated. They do not sensationalize or romanticize. They look on from a certain distance, as we do, as everyone did, while this life moved helplessly toward its close.

Was Ian Curtis bipolar? I'm not an expert, but the movie led me to feel that he was not and that lithium, say, would not have helped him. His discontent was not a disease but a malaise, not manic-depression but more like the state described in "The Anatomy of Melancholy" by Robert Burton:

> *All my joys to this are folly,*
> *Naught so sweet as melancholy.* ☞

Crash ★★★★

R, 100 m., 2005

Sandra Bullock (Jean), Don Cheadle (Graham), Matt Dillon (Officer Ryan), Jennifer Esposito (Ria), William Fichtner (Flanagan), Brendan Fraser (Rick), Terrence Dashon Howard (Cameron), Ludacris (Anthony), Thandie Newton (Christine), Ryan Phillippe (Officer Hansen), Larenz Tate (Peter), Shaun Toub (Farhad), Michael Pena (Daniel). Directed by Paul Haggis and produced by Haggis, Mark R. Harris, Robert Moresco, Cathy Schulman, and Tom Nunan. Screenplay by Haggis and Moresco.

Crash tells interlocking stories of whites, blacks, Latinos, Koreans, Iranians, cops and criminals, the rich and the poor, the powerful and powerless, all defined in one way or another by racism. All are victims of it, and all are guilty of it. Sometimes, yes, they rise above it, although it is never that simple. Their negative impulses may be instinctive, their positive impulses may be dangerous, and who knows what the other person is thinking?

The result is a movie of intense fascination; we understand quickly enough who the characters are and what their lives are like, but we have no idea how they will behave because so much depends on accident. Most movies enact rituals; we know the form and watch for variations. *Crash* is a movie with free will, and anything can happen. Because we care about the characters, the movie is uncanny in its ability to rope us in and get us involved.

Crash was directed by Paul Haggis, whose screenplay for *Million Dollar Baby* led to Academy Awards. It connects stories based on coincidence, serendipity, and luck, as the lives of the characters crash against each other like pinballs. The movie presumes that most people feel prejudice and resentment against members of other groups, and observes the consequences of those feelings.

One thing that happens, again and again, is that people's assumptions prevent them from seeing the actual person standing before them. An Iranian (Shaun Toub) is thought to be an Arab, although Iranians are Persian. Both the Iranian and the white wife of the district attorney (Sandra Bullock) believe a Mexican-American locksmith (Michael Pena) is a gang member and a crook, but he is a family man.

A black cop (Don Cheadle) is having an affair with his Latino partner (Jennifer Esposito) but never gets it straight which country she's from. A cop (Matt Dillon) thinks a light-skinned black woman (Thandie Newton) is white. When a white producer tells a black TV director (Terrence Dashon Howard) that a black character "doesn't sound black enough," it never occurs to him that the director doesn't "sound black," either. For that matter, neither do two young black men (Larenz Tate and Ludacris), who dress and act like college students but have a surprise for us.

You see how it goes. Along the way, these people say exactly what they are thinking, without the filters of political correctness. The district attorney's wife is so frightened by a street encounter that she has the locks changed, then assumes the locksmith will be back with his "homies" to attack them. The white cop can't get medical care for his dying father and accuses a black woman at his HMO of taking advantage of preferential racial treatment. The Iranian can't understand what the locksmith is trying to tell him, freaks out, and buys a gun to protect himself. The gun dealer and the Iranian get into a shouting match.

I make this sound almost like episodic TV, but Haggis writes with such directness and such a good ear for everyday speech that the characters seem real and plausible after only a few words. His cast is uniformly strong; the actors sidestep clichés and make their characters particular.

For me, the strongest performance is by Matt Dillon, as the racist cop in anguish over his father. He makes an unnecessary traffic stop when he thinks he sees the black TV director and his light-skinned wife doing something they really shouldn't be doing at the same time they're driving. True enough, but he wouldn't have stopped a black couple or a white couple. He humiliates the woman with an invasive body search, while her husband is forced to stand by powerless, because the cops have the guns—Dillon, and also an unseasoned rookie (Ryan Phillippe), who hates what he's seeing but has to back up his partner.

That traffic stop shows Dillon's cop as vile and hateful. But later we see him trying to care for his sick father, and we understand why he explodes at the HMO worker (whose race is only an excuse for his anger). He victimizes others by exercising his power, and is impotent when it comes to helping his father.

Then the plot turns ironically on itself, and both of the cops find themselves, in very different ways, saving the lives of the very same TV director and his wife. Is this just manipulative storytelling? It didn't feel that way to me because it serves a deeper purpose than mere irony: Haggis is telling parables, in which the characters learn the lessons they have earned by their behavior.

Other cross-cutting Los Angeles stories come to mind, especially Lawrence Kasdan's more optimistic *Grand Canyon* and Robert Altman's more humanistic *Short Cuts*. But *Crash* finds a way of its own. It shows the way we all leap to conclusions based on race—yes, all of us, of all races, and however fair-minded we may try to be—and we pay a price for that.

If there is hope in the story, it comes because as the characters crash into one another, they learn things, mostly about themselves. Almost all of them are still alive at the end and are better people because of what has happened to them. Not happier, not calmer, not even wiser, but better. Then there are those few who kill or get killed; racism has tragedy built in.

Not many films have the possibility of making their audiences better people. I don't expect *Crash* to work any miracles, but I believe anyone seeing it is likely to be moved to have a little more sympathy for people not like themselves. The movie contains hurt, coldness, and cruelty, but is it without hope? Not at all.

Stand back and consider. All of these people, superficially so different, share the city and learn that they share similar fears and hopes. Until several hundred years ago, most people everywhere on Earth never saw anybody who didn't look like them. They were not racist because, as far as they knew, there was only one race. You may have to look hard to see it, but *Crash* is a film about progress.

Cronicas ★ ★ ★

R, 98 m., 2005

John Leguizamo (Manolo Bonilla), Leonor Watling (Marisa Iturralde), Damián Alcázar (Vinicio Cepeda), Jóse María Yazpik (Iván Suárez), Alfred Molina (Victor Hugo Puente), Camilo Luzuriaga (Bolivar Rojas). Directed by Sebastian Cordero and produced by Alfonso Cuaron, Berta Navarro, Guillermo del Toro, Jorge Vergara, and Isabel Davalos. Screenplay by Cordero.

I don't know if John Leguizamo was thinking of Geraldo Rivera when he made *Cronicas,* but I was. Leguizamo plays the same kind of swashbuckling TV reporter who likes to be in the middle of breaking news stories, standing on camera in front of amazing events. Nothing wrong with that, unless you start thinking of yourself as the foreground and the story as the setting.

In *Cronicas,* Leguizamo plays Manolo Bonilla, a Miami-based star reporter for a Spanish-language network that blankets Latin America. He's in Ecuador covering the story of the Monster of Babahoyo, a serial killer who has murdered at least 150 young children. During a funeral for the latest victims, a man in a pickup truck grows confused and runs over a small boy. The funeral mob turns ugly, drags the man from his truck, beats him, dowses him with gasoline, and is prepared to set him afire.

Bonilla and his crew film the mob scene right up to the point the match is thrown. Then they're involved, along with Bolivar Rojas, a local policeman (Camilo Luzuriaga), in saving the man's life. But a lynching still seems likely, and the man, named Vinicio (Damian Alcazar), bargains with the reporter, telling him he has inside knowledge of the Monster and his methods.

At this point I am prepared to believe that Leguizamo can play just about anyone, and do it well. A list of his roles would take us from a drag queen *(To Wong Foo)* to Toulouse-Lautrec *(Moulin Rouge!)* to a dog whisperer *(The Honeymooners)* to a Shakespeare character *(Romeo + Juliet)* to a zombie hunter *(Land of the Dead).* Here he convincingly plays an experienced TV reporter, in a performance that knows the type and knows the job, and strikes a nice balance between how he covers the story and gets publicity for himself, two tasks he is equally suited for.

What's remarkable is that he plays the character while mostly speaking in Spanish. Yes, Leguizamo was born in Colombia, but his family soon moved to America, and he is not fluent in Spanish; the performance required him to learn the language and use a dialogue coach for line-by-line readings. That he could do that and stay in character as the persuasive, fast-talking media star Bonilla is remarkable.

Bonilla's conversations with Vinicio arouse in him, and in the audience, the suspicion that this man, who says he is a traveling Bible salesman, might actually be the Monster. He claims he gave the real Monster a lift one day, "and he needed someone to talk to." He claims that he can lead Bonilla to a grave that contains a body not discovered by the authorities —and Bonilla, hot for a scoop, deliberately keeps this secret from the cops and digs up the evidence himself.

He does his job with a two-person crew. Marisa Iturralde (Leonor Watling, from *Bad Education*) is his producer, and Ivan Suarez (Jose Maria Yazpik) is his cameraman; the movie knows, as not every movie does, that the cameraman is as instrumental in covering a story as the reporter, sometimes more. The dynamic is complicated because Marisa's husband, back in Miami, is Victor Hugo Puente (Alfred Molina), anchor of their sensationalistic newscast and a flamboyant ham with his own hunger for publicity.

The movie too quickly leads us to suspect Vinicio as the real Monster, I think, although the Law of Economy of Characters would probably lead us to suspect him no matter what. The question becomes: What will Bonilla do with the information he's gathering, how can he get the scoop without damaging the investigation, how can he keep Victor Hugo in Miami and away from the action, and how, for that matter, can the movie generate much suspense? Bonilla's private sleuthing is complicated, he complains to Marisa, because "we're stuck with the only honest cop in Latin America."

It goes without saying that Bonilla and Marisa are attracted to each other, but whether they do or don't betray Victor Hugo really has nothing to do with anything; it's just the obligatory romantic interlude. More interesting is whether Marisa betrays herself, since she has a journalistic conscience, and Bonilla seems to have mislaid his. Although I understand the strategy of keeping Victor Hugo in Miami, so that he's seen only on a TV monitor, Alfred Molina is such a gifted actor that I imagine his physical presence in Ecuador would have generated more dramatic interest than his absence.

As it is, the movie loses tension the moment we guess the essential truth behind the story, and the rest is all details. Mostly accurate details, however, in a rare movie that knows TV journalism inside-out; the director, Sebastian Cordero, an Ecuador-born UCLA graduate, gets the right feel for his news crew at work in the field, and Leguizamo and Watling bring a fascination to their characters that the story doesn't always deserve. There are also nice small moments, as when a great deal depends on knowing the Spanish word for *twin*. *Cronicas* is the kind of movie that grabs you while you're watching, even if later you wish it had grabbed a little harder.

Curious George ★ ★ ★

G, 86 m., 2006

With the voices of: Drew Barrymore (Maggie), Will Ferrell (Man in the Yellow Hat), Eugene Levy (Clovis), Joan Plowright (Miss Plushbottom), David Cross (Bloomsberry Jr.), Dick Van Dyke (Mr. Bloomsberry), Frank Welker (George). Directed by Matthew O'Callaghan and produced by Brian Grazer, Ron Howard, David Kirschner, Bonne Radford, and Jon Shapiro. Screenplay by Ken Kaufman, based on the books by Margret and H. A. Rey.

Definition of a good family movie: one that appeals to all members of the family. *Curious George* is not a family movie. It is a children's movie. There is nothing wrong with that, and a great deal that is admirable. For once, the younger children can watch a movie where they have a good chance of understanding everything that happens and everything that's said. The new generation of mainstream animation has so many in-jokes that even the editors of *People* magazine miss some of them. How many of the preschoolers watching *Shark Tale* realized that Sykes was named after a Charles Dickens character and looked like Martin Scorsese?

On the *Ebert & Roeper* TV show, Roeper and I technically disagreed about *Curious George*, even though our opinions of the movie were approximately the same. He voted thumbs down because it was aimed at children. I voted thumbs up because it was aimed at children. We agreed it was not going to be an ecstatic viewing experience for parents.

In theory, I should have voted against it. The critic must recommend what he or she enjoys, not what some hypothetical audience will enjoy. Critics who say, "This is sure to be enjoyed by teenagers," when they are not teenagers are dummies, and the audience is the ventriloquist. Some of my colleagues say their editors require them to recommend movies on the basis of the tastes of the readers. An editor who does that is instructing the critic in falsehood and incompetence.

Having said that, and since I am not a child, how can I ethically recommend *Curious George* as a movie for children? I will quote Walt Whitman: "Do I contradict myself? Very well, then I contradict myself. I am large, I contain multitudes." I have no idea what teenagers think, but I know what four-year-olds think because I was one, an expert one, and I believe that up to a certain age all children enjoy more or less the same things: bright colors, vivid drawings, encouraging music, a plot that is exciting but not too scary, and a character they can identify with. This character should have an older friend who guides him through neat adventures and keeps things from getting too scary. If that doesn't describe what you liked when you were three or four, then I blame your parents, Mr. and Mrs. Chainsaw.

George the monkey is easy for any kid to identify with. They have so much in common. George cannot make himself understood, he is driven here and there in mechanical vehicles without his consent, adults talk about things he does not understand, and sometimes it's just not fair how he's treated. Then he meets the Man in the Yellow Hat (the movie reveals that the man's name is Ted). Ted (voice by Will

Ferrell) makes friends with him, and because he is alone in the world, George stows away on Ted's ship and ends up in New York, where Ted is trying to save a museum. This undertaking requires Ted and George to fly above the city while holding on to a big bunch of balloons. Meanwhile, Ted has a girlfriend named Maggie (Drew Barrymore), but that's fine with George, because it means he gets another friend.

I am not sure Ted saves the museum in any meaningful way (it becomes a gallery of virtual-reality experiences), but George has a lot of fun and gets to paint lots of surfaces with bright primary colors, which passes the time pleasantly. There are songs sung by Jack Johnson, which are pleasant if kind of innocuous. The movie is faithful to the spirit and innocence of the books, and director Matthew O'Callaghan and his team create a visual look that is uncluttered, charming, and not so realistic that it undermines the fantasies on the screen.

Is this a movie for the whole family to attend? No, it is a movie for small children and their parents or adult guardians, who will take them because they love them very much. Even if they love them very much, they will have to be very, very patient, so maybe waiting for the DVD is a good idea, except then, of course, you will have to experience it over and over and over and over and over again.

D

Dan in Real Life ★ ★ ★

PG-13, 93 m., 2007

Steve Carell (Dan Burns), Juliette Binoche (Marie), Dane Cook (Mitch Burns), John Mahoney (Poppy Burns), Dianne Wiest (Nana), Emily Blunt (Ruthie Draper), Alison Pill (Jane Burns), Brittany Robertson (Cara Burns). Directed by Peter Hedges and produced by Jon Shestack and Brad Epstein. Screenplay by Pierce Gardner and Hedges.

Steve Carell of *The 40-Year-Old Virgin* has a personality, or maybe it is a lack of personality, that is growing on me. He is content to exist on the screen without sending wild semaphores of his intentions, his uniqueness, and how funny he is. He's an everyman like a very (very) low-key Jack Lemmon. That makes him right for a romantic comedy like *Dan in Real Life*, during which he isn't expected to go over the top, but be just romantic and funny enough, you see, to let the situation work on its own terms.

He plays Dan Burns, a newspaper advice columnist whose wife died four years before. He's raising three girls on his own, two teenagers and a preteen, and he must be doing a good job because they treat him like a slightly slow brother. At Thanksgiving, he takes them all to Rhode Island, where his parents (John Mahoney and Dianne Wiest) own a vast, rambling brown-shingled beach house you probably couldn't touch for $20 million. Since Mahoney's big job is wearing an apron in the kitchen, it's hard to see him as a guy owning that kind of real estate. Maybe he inherited. Also on hand is Dan's brother, Mitch (Dane Cook).

Dan goes into town in the afternoon and runs into Marie (Juliette Binoche) in a bookstore. They begin one of those conversations that threaten to continue for a lifetime. It's not love at first sight, but it's intrigue, approval, and yearning. She supplies her phone number. That evening, brother Mitch brings his girlfriend home to the brown castle and, yes, it's Marie.

That's the setup, and the movie deals with how to fit all those conflicting emotions into the house. Good thing it's big enough for lots of secret conversations on the move; the fact that social rules forbid them to declare their growing love makes Marie and Dan feel all the more like blurting it out, and Binoche is superb at looking upon her new man with the regret she'd feel for a puppy she can't adopt.

The movie's director and cowriter, Peter Hedges, made the overlooked little treasure *Pieces of April*, a 2003 Sundance hit, also about a Thanksgiving family reunion (which oddly enough, also involved a family named Burns). His plot this time is less fraught, maybe because enormous stakes are not involved; Mitch and Marie are not desperately in love, Dan and Marie hardly know each other, and social awkwardness is the most difficult hurdle between here and happiness. That's why the movie's so soothingly pleasant.

Yes, there are some loud moments and big laughs, some of them involving the three girls, who seem to be enduring simultaneous hormonal yearnings, but Mahoney and Wiest keep a steady hand on the tiller, and the fireplaces and arts and crafts furniture exert a calming influence. Juliette Binoche also has much to do with the film's charm. French but eloquent in English, she fills a place that Ingrid Bergman used to inhabit in the cinema: Able to be very serious, very sweet, and very beautiful, she has the gravitas to make this story seem more important than a mere game of switching partners.

If the film has a flaw, and I'm afraid it does, it's the Sondre Lerche songs on the sound track. They are too foregrounded and literal, either commenting on the action or expounding on associated topics. In such a laid-back movie, they're in our face. The songs are on the Web site, if you doubt me. But I got over the music and had a good enough time, although something tells me this is the kind of movie that will inspire countless queries from moviegoers asking me where that house is. I'll save the trouble: I tried to find out but couldn't. It looks real enough and not digital, but there's not a single exterior photo of it on the official Web site.

Darfur Now ★ ★ ★

PG, 99 m., 2007

Featuring Don Cheadle, George Clooney, Hejewa Adam, Pablo Recalde, Ahmed Mohammed Abakar, Luis Moreno-Ocampo, Adam Sterling. A documentary written and directed by Ted Braun and produced by Cathy Shulman, Don Cheadle, and Mark Jonathan Harris.

We all know, having absorbed it from the mediasphere, that genocide is taking place in Darfur, but we do not all know where Darfur is. Africa, yes, vaguely, we realize. Something to do with Sudan. But where or what is Sudan? If it accomplishes nothing else, *Darfur Now* locates Sudan on the map (tenth largest nation on Earth, just below Egypt—boy, are we dumb) and tells us Darfur is its western region, almost the size of France. The region is landlocked in central Africa, bordered by Libya, Chad, and the Central African Republic. More than that, the film provides faces for the people of the region.

One of them is Hejewa Adam, who wears an automatic rifle over her shoulder. She was a peaceful villager until government-backed Janjaweed (Arab fighters on horseback) killed her three-month-old son. Now she is a fighter who sees no other option. Another person on the ground is Ahmed Mohammed Abakar, a farmer forced off his land, who has become a refugee leader. And we meet Pablo Recalde, in charge of distributing food from the world to Darfur, where much of it is stolen by the Janjaweed.

It would appear that the function of the Janjaweed is to destroy the villages of Darfur, remove the people from their (subsistence level) agriculture, and starve them. That is because they are not the same as other Sudanese. It is instructive that Darfur and the Sudan were independent entities living in relative peace before they were arbitrarily cobbled together by the nineteenth-century British-dominated Egyptian government, one of many African "nations" created by European colonial powers with no regard to local history, languages, or tribal identity.

Outside Darfur a key player is Luis Moreno-Ocampo, a prosecutor for the International Criminal Court at The Hague, who seeks to prosecute the Sudan for genocidal crimes but finds opposition because many important nations, China included, value their oil trade with the Sudan and care little about impoverished Darfur. Meanwhile, a quarter of a million have starved and perhaps two or three million have lost their homes or lands.

Cut to California, where the admirable Don Cheadle, joined by George Clooney, leads a movement to inspire American and European intervention. Cheadle learned about genocide firsthand while making *Hotel Rwanda.* And we meet Adam Sterling, a student who begins a movement to divest California of its investments in the Sudan. It is successful, and Governor Arnold Schwarzenegger gladly signs such a bill into law, although its impact may be more symbolic than economic. Washington remains aloof from the issue, apart from the speeches of involved senators.

All of this you will learn and see in *Darfur Now.* It is not a compelling documentary (too much exposition, not enough on-the-spot reality), but it is instructive and disturbing. Darfurians like Hejewa Adam await the arrival of "the Americans" to save her land. Perhaps she should announce that she is building a nuclear program.

The Darjeeling Limited ★ ★ ★ ½

R, 91 m., 2007

Owen Wilson (Francis), Adrien Brody (Peter), Jason Schwartzman (Jack), Amara Karan (Rita), Camilla Rutherford (Alice), Wally Wolodarsky (Brendan), Waris Ahluwalia (The Chief Steward), Barbet Schroeder (The Mechanic), Irrfan Khan (The Father), Bill Murray (The Businessman), Anjelica Huston (Patricia), Natalie Portman (Girlfriend). Directed by Wes Anderson and produced by Anderson, Roman Coppola, Lydia Dean Pilcher, and Scott Rudin. Screenplay by Anderson, Coppola, and Jason Schwartzman.

Three brothers in crisis and desperation meet in India in *The Darjeeling Limited,* a movie that meanders so persuasively it gets us meandering right along. It's the new film by Wes Anderson, who after *Rushmore* and *The Royal*

Tenenbaums made *The Life Aquatic with Steve Zissou.* Of that peculiar film I wrote: "My rational mind informs me that this movie doesn't work. Yet I hear a subversive whisper: Since it does so many other things, does it have to work, too? Can't it just *exist*? 'Terminal whimsy,' I called it on the TV show. Yes, but isn't that better than no whimsy at all?" After a struggle with my inner whisper, I rated the movie at 2.5 stars, which means, "Not quite."

I quote myself so early in this review because I feel about the same way about *The Darjeeling Limited,* with the proviso that this is a better film, warmer, more engaging, funnier, and very surrounded by India, that nation of perplexing charm. The brothers, who have not been much in contact, have a reunion after one is almost killed in a motorcycle crash, and they take a journey on a train so wonderful I fear it does not really exist. (It is the fancy of the art director.)

The reunion is convened by Francis (Owen Wilson), whose head bandages make him look like an extra from *The Mummy.* Having nearly died (possibly intentionally), he now embraces life and wants to Really Get to Know his younger brothers. They are Peter (Adrien Brody), poised to divorce a wife he doesn't love when she announces she is pregnant; and Jack (Jason Schwartzman), who dials all the way home to eavesdrop on his former girlfriend's answering machine.

They travel with a mountain of Louis Vuitton luggage, which means the movie will no doubt play this year's Louis Vuitton Hawaii International Film Festival. Francis has an assistant, Brendan (Wally Wolodarsky), whose office is next to the luggage in the baggage car, from which he issues forth a daily itinerary from the computer and printer he has brought along. The document is encased in plastic by the laminating machine he has also brought along. Insisting on this schedule is typical of Francis; he expects without question that his brothers will comply.

Francis is the compulsive type, which is why his younger brothers find it hard to be in the same room with him. They got enough of that from their mother. He announces that their train journey of reconciliation will be enriched by visits to all the principal holy places along the way. They are also enriched by their careless purchase of obscure medications that contain little magical mystery tours of their own.

One of the film's attractions for me was its Indian context; Anderson and his actors made a trip through India while he was writing the screenplay. It avoids obvious temptations to exoticism by surprising us; the stewardess on the train, for example, speaks standard English and seems American. This is Rita (Amara Karan). She comes round offering them a sweet lime drink, which is Indian enough, but later, when Jack sticks his head out a train window, he sees her head sticking out, too, as she puffs on a cigarette. Soon they are in each other's arms, not very Indian of her.

Anderson uses India not in a touristy way but as a backdrop that is very, very there. Consider a lengthy scene where the three brothers share a table in the diner with an Indian man who is a stranger. Observe the performance of the stranger. As an Indian traveling in first class, he undoubtedly speaks English, but they do not exchange a word. He reads his paper. The brothers talk urgently and openly about intimacies and differences. He does not *react* in any obvious way. His unperturbed presence is a reaction in itself. There is a concealed level of performance: They probably know he can understand them, and he probably knows they know this. There he sits, a passive witness to their lives. It is impossible to imagine this role played any better. He raises the level of the scene to another dimension.

The casting of the three brothers is also a good fit. Their personalities jostle each other in a family sort of way; they're replaying old tapes. Then they have unplanned adventures as a result of the obscure medications and end up off the train and in the "real" India with all of that luggage. But Anderson doesn't have them discover each other, which would be a cliché; instead, they burrow more deeply inside their essential natures. Then Francis springs a surprise: Their journey will end with a meeting with their mother (Anjelica Huston), who for some years has been a nun in an Indian religious order. Her appearance and behavior is our catalyst for understanding the brothers.

I said the movie meanders. It will therefore

inspire reviews complaining that it doesn't fly straight as an arrow at its target. But it doesn't have a target, either. Why do we have to be the cops and enforce a narrow range of movie requirements? Anderson is like Dave Brubeck, whom I'm listening to right now. He knows every note of the original song, but the fun and genius come in the way he noodles around. And in his movie's cast, especially with Owen Wilson, Anderson takes advantage of champion noodlers.

Note: If you like this movie's whimsy and observant human comedy, there is a great Indian writer you must discover, and his name is R. K. Narayan. ☞

The Dark Knight ★ ★ ★ ★

PG-13, 152 m., 2008

Christian Bale (Bruce Wayne),Michael Caine (Alfred), Heath Ledger (Joker), Gary Oldman (James Gordon), Aaron Eckhart (Harvey Dent), Maggie Gyllenhaal (Rachel Dawes), Morgan Freeman (Lucius Fox). Directed by Christopher Nolan and produced by Nolan, Charles Roven, and Emma Thomas. Screenplay by Christopher Nolan and Jonathan Nolan.

Batman isn't a comic book anymore. Christopher Nolan's *The Dark Knight* is a haunted film that leaps beyond its origins and becomes an engrossing tragedy. It creates characters we come to care about. That's because of the performances, because of the direction, because of the writing, and because of the superlative technical quality of the entire production. This film, and to a lesser degree *Iron Man*, redefine the possibilities of the "comic book movie."

The Dark Knight is not a simplistic tale of good and evil. Batman is good, yes; the Joker is evil, yes. But Batman poses a more complex puzzle than usual: The citizens of Gotham City are in an uproar, calling him a vigilante and blaming him for the deaths of policemen and others. And the Joker is more than a villain. He's a Mephistopheles whose actions are fiendishly designed to pose moral dilemmas for his enemies.

The key performance in the movie is by the late Heath Ledger, as the Joker. Will he become the first posthumous Oscar winner since Peter Finch? His Joker draws power from the actual inspiration of the character in the silent classic *The Man Who Laughs* (1928). His clown's makeup more sloppy than before, his cackle betraying deep wounds, he seeks revenge, he claims, for the horrible punishment his father exacted on him when he was a child. In one diabolical scheme near the end of the film, he invites two ferry-loads of passengers to blow up the other before they are blown up themselves. Throughout the film, he devises ingenious situations that force Batman (Christian Bale), Commissioner Gordon (Gary Oldman), and District Attorney Harvey Dent (Aaron Eckhart) to make impossible ethical decisions. By the end of the film, the whole moral foundation of the Batman legend is threatened.

Because these actors and others are so powerful, and because the movie does not allow its spectacular special effects to upstage the humans, we're surprised how deeply the drama affects us. Eckhart does an especially good job on Harvey Dent, whose character is transformed by a horrible fate into a bitter monster. It is customary in a comic book movie to maintain a certain knowing distance from the action, to view everything through a sophisticated screen. *The Dark Knight* slips around those defenses and engages us.

Yes, the special effects are extraordinary. They focus on the expected explosions and catastrophes, and have some superb, elaborate chase scenes. The movie was shot on location in Chicago, but it avoids such familiar landmarks as Marina City, the Wrigley Building, or the skyline. Chicagoans will recognize many places, notably LaSalle Street and Lower Wacker Drive, but director Nolan is not making a travelogue. He presents the city as a wilderness of skyscrapers, and a key sequence is set in the still-uncompleted Trump Tower. Through these heights the Batman moves at the end of strong wires, or sometimes actually flies, using his cape as a parasail.

The plot involves nothing more or less than the Joker's attempts to humiliate the forces for good and expose Batman's secret identity, showing him to be a poseur and a fraud. He includes Gordon and Dent on his target list, and contrives cruel tricks to play with the fact that Bruce Wayne once loved, and Harvey Dent now loves, Assistant D.A. Rachel Dawes

(Maggie Gyllenhaal). The tricks are more cruel than he realizes, because the Joker doesn't know Batman's identity. Heath Ledger has a good deal of dialogue in the movie, and a lot of it isn't the usual jabs and jests we're familiar with: It's psychologically more complex, outlining the dilemmas he has constructed and explaining his reasons for them. The screenplay by Christopher Nolan and his brother Jonathan (who first worked together on *Memento*) has more depth and poetry than we might have expected.

Two of the supporting characters are crucial to the action and are played effortlessly by the great actors Morgan Freeman and Michael Caine. Freeman, as the scientific genius Lucius Fox, is in charge of Bruce Wayne's underground headquarters and makes an ethical objection to a method of eavesdropping on all of the citizens of Gotham City. His stand has current political implications. Caine is the faithful butler Alfred, who understands Wayne better than anybody and makes a decision about a crucial letter.

Nolan also directed the previous, and excellent, *Batman Begins* (2005), which went into greater detail than ever before about Bruce Wayne's origins and the reasons for his compulsions. Now it is the Joker's turn, although his past is handled entirely with dialogue, not flashbacks. There are no references to Batman's childhood, but we certainly remember it, and we realize that this conflict is between two adults who were twisted by childhood cruelty—one compensating by trying to do good, the other by trying to do evil. Perhaps they instinctively understand that themselves.

Something fundamental seems to be happening in the upper realms of the comic book movie. *Spider-Man II* (2004) may have defined the high point of the traditional film based on comic book heroes. A movie like the new *Hellboy II* allows its director free rein for his fantastical visions. But now *Iron Man* and even more *The Dark Knight* move the genre into deeper waters. They realize, as some comic book readers instinctively do, that these stories touch on deep fears, traumas, fantasies, and hopes. And the Batman legend, with its origins in film noir, is the most fruitful one for exploration. In his two Batman movies, Nolan has freed the character to be a canvas for a broader scope of human emotion. For Bruce Wayne is a deeply troubled man, let there be no doubt, and if ever in exile from his heroic role, it would not surprise me what he finds himself capable of doing.

Dark Water ★ ★ ★

PG-13, 120 m., 2005

Jennifer Connelly (Dahlia Williams), Ariel Gade (Cecilia Williams), Dougray Scott (Kyle), Pete Postlethwaite (Veeck), Tim Roth (Jeff Platzer), John C. Reilly (Mr. Murray), Perla Haney-Jardine (Natasha), Camryn Manheim (Mrs. Finkle). Directed by Walter Salles and produced by Doug Davison, Roy Lee, and Bill Mechanic. Screenplay by Rafael Yglesias, based on the film by Hideo Nakata.

Art Buchwald said the plot of *Last Tango in Paris* could be understood as the story of what people were willing to do to get an apartment in Paris. *Dark Water*, a new horror film starring Jennifer Connelly, suggests that in New York, people not only are willing to kill for an affordable apartment but may have to die, too. The movie is a remake of a 2002 thriller by the Japanese horror specialist Hideo Nakata, whose work also inspired the *Ring* pictures.

As *Dark Water* opens, Dahlia Williams (Connelly) is splitting up with her husband, Kyle (Dougray Scott), and needs to find a new home for herself and her daughter, Ceci (Ariel Gade). Her search takes her to Roosevelt Island, where a real estate agent named Murray (John C. Reilly) cheerfully shows them a flat that could be the New York pied-à-terre of the Amityville Horror.

The entrance hall is dark and dank. The superintendent (Pete Postlethwaite) lurks in his cubicle like a poisonous toad. The elevator seems programmed to devour little girls or their mothers. The rooms are dark and dank. Murray talks optimistically about a new coat of paint, and when he fails to find the second bedroom, he instantly redefines the living room as "dual-use." Little Ceci, who thinks the building is "yucky," is right on the money.

Still, the rent is right, and Dahlia is desperate. She takes the apartment, violating the ancient tradition that movie characters always live in apartments they could never afford in real life. She can afford this one. It's just that, well, that stain in the ceiling seems sort of malevolent and alive, as if it were eating up the apartment and will eat them, too. And a trip upstairs reveals unspeakable horrors.

What went on in this building? Who is the imaginary friend Ceci seems to have made? Her mother has fears of abandonment from her own childhood, and we wonder if she will allow her child to be endangered. Here is a world with few friendly faces: Reilly as the real estate agent would praise a death chamber for its square footage, Postlethwaite as the super seems to be harboring alien parasites in his eyebrows, and Dahlia's lawyer is played by Tim Roth, which is all you need to know.

Dark Water is the first film in English by Walter Salles (*Central Station, The Motorcycle Diaries)*, and he has a dark visual style that matches the building's pulsing gloominess. Like other recent horror directors, he is intrigued by the challenges of bathtubs and shower stalls, and the ways in which people can be trapped in them and drown, and the tendency of tap water to turn the color of blood, or Pennzoil. He is also aware of the possibilities in scenes where heedless children defy instructions and wander off on their own.

I have been criticized recently for giving a pass to films of moderate achievement because they accomplish what the audience expects, while penalizing more ambitious films for falling short of greater expectations. There may be some truth in such observations, but on the other hand, nobody in the real world goes to every movie with the same kind of anticipation. If I see a film by Ingmar Bergman, as I recently did, I expect it to be a masterpiece, and if it is not, Bergman has disappointed me. If I attend a horror film in which Connelly and her daughter are trapped in the evil web of a malevolent apartment building, I do not expect Bergman; if the movie does what it can do as well as it can be done, then it has achieved perfection within its own terms.

The Bergman film (*Saraband*) was a masterpiece. *Dark Water* achieves some, but not all, of what we might hope for. It is not *Rosemary's Baby.* The acting is effective, the supporting roles are performed with relish by the skilled technicians Postlethwaite, Reilly, and Roth, and the cinematographer, Affonso Beato, succeeds in making the stain on the ceiling look like an evil vastation and not just a leaky sink. The climax is certainly over the top, and we're never quite sure how all the parts of the mystery fit together, but, then, the movie is about the horror of the mystery, not about its solution. Most important, I cared about the Jennifer Connelly character; she is not a horror heroine, but an actress playing a mother faced with horror. There is a difference, and because of that difference, *Dark Water* works.

Dave Chappelle's Block Party ★ ★ ★

R, 100 m., 2006

Featuring Dave Chappelle, Mos Def, Erykah Badu, Lauryn Hill, Kanye West, Talib Kweli, Dead Prez, Jill Scott, the Roots, the Fugees, and Bilal. Directed by Michel Gondry and produced by Bob Yari, Dave Chappelle, and Gondry. Screenplay by Chappelle.

Dave Chappelle's Block Party is a fairly disorganized film about a fairly disorganized concert, redeemed by the good feeling that Chappelle sheds like a sunbeam on every scene. I came away from the movie with three observations: (1) I find a lot of rap nihilistic and negative, but the musicians featured here seemed accessible and positive. (2) Nevertheless, I was pathetically grateful when Lauryn Hill and the Fugees sang "Killing Me Softly with His Song" and when many of the others sang what used to be called songs. Thank God for melody. (3) Chappelle appears to be a nice man, in addition to being a funny one, and the buried message in this movie may be: "Can I sign a $50 million contract and still remain the person I am happy to be?"

The movie is a documentary about Chappelle's sudden inspiration to hold a rap and comedy concert at a free block party in Brooklyn. The location would be kept secret to avoid a mob scene, and the audience would include people from the block and others who were bused in. And by bused in, I mean from Dayton, Ohio, which is about twenty miles from Yellow Springs, where Chappelle lives. The film opens with him handing out tickets good for a bus ride, a hotel room, food, and admission to the concert. He offers them to the nice lady who runs the shop where he buys his cigarettes, and to a couple of young men on the street, and to a man who says he is too deaf to hear the music, and then, in an expansive mood, he invites the entire Central State College marching band. (The two young men from Ohio stand on a rooftop and say now they really feel they're in New York, because in the movies everybody is always standing on rooftops.)

That some of the lucky ticket winners are white and even middle-aged is part of the point: He wants them to come to a rap concert in Brooklyn, and he wants it to be a rap concert where everybody will feel at home. In this connection the musicians do not reflect a gangsta image, they use lyrics that are not particularly hostile or angry, and they employ the n-word, the f-word, and the mf-word only about every twenty words, instead of every fifth word.

On the stage is an all-star cast, including Mos Def, Erykah Badu, Kanye West, Talib Kweli, Dead Prez, Jill Scott, the Roots, Bilal, and Lauryn Hill with the reunited Fugees. If I told you I knew who all of them were, I'd be lying. The women (Badu, Scott, Hill) seem to please the crowd more than the men, maybe because their material leans more toward jazz and R&B. Mos Def is a surprise because a day earlier I'd seen him costarring with Bruce Willis in *16 Blocks,* a movie where his character talks incessantly in a high-pitched screech; on stage with Dave, he's got an entirely different personality, a different voice even, and seems cool, authoritative, likable. Kanye West you know about, and he wears his superstardom lightly.

There is an audience for rap and, let's face it, I am not a member of that audience. That's why I was surprised to enjoy so many of the performances in the film. Not that I am likely to become a convert. As I write this, I'm listening to the Dianne Reeves sound track album from *Good Night, and Good Luck,* and it is wonderful. Not that you are likely to become a convert. Maybe we can meet in the middle.

The concert doesn't exactly proceed like clockwork, and it doesn't help (or hurt much) that it rains. Chappelle is onstage most of the time, does a lot of spontaneous comedy, makes the crowd feel good. There is a lot of backstage footage of Chappelle talking about how the concert will go, how it is going, and how it went. He has a theory about musicians and comedians: All comedians wish they were musicians, and all musicians think they are funny. "I'm mediocre at both," he says, "but have managed to talk my way into a fortune."

It's that fortune that seems to be the problem. The concert was held on September 18, 2004. It was on August 3, 2004, that Chappelle signed his infamous $50 million contract with Comedy Central. In this movie, long before his "disappearance" and his confessional with Oprah, you can see those millions nagging at him. His block party seems like an apology or an amends for the $50 million, an effort to reach out to people, to protect his ability to walk down the street like an ordinary man.

Having watched Chappelle on his show, on Oprah, and now in this movie, filmed at the dawn of his life as the $50 Million Man, I get a sense of how he feels. There is something about a $50 million contract that feels wrong to him, that threatens to build a wall between his personality and the way he likes to use it. His Comedy Central show is (was?) so funny because he worked without a net. He was willing to try anything. He didn't obsess about whether it worked. Here he makes some ominous comments about executives and you intuit he's saying that the *Dave Chappelle Show* will never work if anyone other than Dave Chappelle has a license to provide input.

As for the movie, I've seen better comedy films and better concert films. It noodles around too much and gets distracted from the music. Michel Gondry, who directed, makes good fiction films (*Eternal Sunshine of the Spotless Mind*) but is not an instinctive documentarian and forgets that even a fly on the wall should occasionally find some peanut butter. As the record of a state of mind, however, the film is uncanny.

The Da Vinci Code ★ ★ ★

PG-13, 148 m., 2006

Tom Hanks (Robert Langdon), Audrey Tautou (Sophie Neveu), Ian McKellen (Sir Leigh Teabing), Alfred Molina (Manuel Aringarosa), Jean Reno (Bezu Fache), Paul Bettany (Silas), Jurgen Prochnow (Andre Vernet), Jean-Pierre Marielle (Jacques Sauniere). Directed by Ron Howard and produced by John Calley and Brian Grazer. Screenplay by Akiva Goldsman, based on the novel by Dan Brown.

They say *The Da Vinci Code* has sold more copies than any book since the Bible. Good thing it has a different ending. Dan Brown's novel is utterly preposterous; Ron Howard's movie is preposterously entertaining. Both contain accusations against the Catholic Church and its order of Opus Dei that would be scandalous, if anyone of sound mind could possibly entertain them. I know there are people who believe Brown's fantasies about the Holy Grail, the descendants of Jesus, the Knights Templar, Opus Dei, and the true story of Mary Magdalene. This has the advantage of distracting them from the theory that the Pentagon was not hit by an airplane.

Let us begin, then, by agreeing that *The Da Vinci Code* is a work of fiction. And that since everyone has read the novel, I need give away only one secret—that the movie follows the book religiously. Although the book is a potboiler written with little grace or style, it does supply an intriguing plot. Luckily Ron Howard is a better filmmaker than Dan Brown is a novelist, and he follows Brown's formula (exotic location, startling revelation, desperate chase scene, repeat as needed) and elevates it into a superior entertainment, with Tom Hanks as a theo-intellectual Indiana Jones.

Hanks stars as Robert Langdon, a Harvard semiotician in Paris for a lecture when Inspector Fache (Jean Reno) informs him of the murder of the museum curator Jacques Sauniere (Jean-Pierre Marielle). This poor man has been shot and killed late at night inside the Louvre; his wounds, although mortal, fortunately leave him time enough to conceal a safe-deposit key, strip himself, cover his body with symbols written in his own blood, arrange his body in a pose and within a design by Da Vinci, and write out, also in blood, an encrypted message, a scrambled numerical sequence, and a footnote to Sophie Neveu (Audrey Tautou), the pretty French policewoman he raised after the death of her parents. Most people are content with a dying word or two; Jacques leaves us with a film treatment.

Having read the novel, we know what happens then. Sophie warns Robert he is in danger from Fache, and they elude capture in the Louvre and set off on a quest that leads them to the vault of a private bank, to the French villa of Sir Leigh Teabing (Ian McKellen), to the Temple Church in London, to an isolated Templar church in the British countryside, to a hidden crypt, and then back to the Louvre again. The police, both French and British, are one step behind them all this time, but Sophie and Robert are facile, inventive, and daring. Also, perhaps, they have God on their side.

This series of chases, discoveries, and escapes is intercut with another story, involving an albino named Silas (Paul Bettany), who works under the command of The Teacher, a mysterious figure at the center of a conspiracy to conceal the location of the Holy Grail, and what it really is, and what that implies. The conspiracy involves members of Opus Dei, a society of Catholics who in real life (I learn from a recent issue of the *Spectator*) are rather conventionally devout and prayerful. Although the movie describes their practices as "maso-chastity," not all of them are chaste and hardly any practice self-flagellation. In the months ahead, I would advise Opus Dei to carefully scrutinize membership applications.

Opus Dei works within but not with the church, which also harbors a secret cell of cardinals who are in on the conspiracy (the pope and most other Catholics apparently don't have backstage passes). These men keep a secret that, if known, could destroy the church. That's why they keep it. If I were their adviser, I would point out that by preserving the secret they preserve the threat to the church, and the wisest strategy would have been to destroy the secret, say, a thousand years ago.

But one of the fascinations of the Catholic Church is that it is the oldest continuously surviving organization in the world, and that's why movies such as *The Da Vinci Code* are more fascinating than thrillers about religions founded, for example, by a science-fiction author in the 1950s. All the places in *The Da Vinci Code* really exist, although the last time I visited the Temple Church I was disappointed to find it closed for "repairs." A likely story.

Hanks, Tautou, and Reno do a good job of not overplaying their roles, and McKellen overplays his in just the right way, making Sir Leigh into a fanatic whose study just happens to contain all the materials for an audiovisual presentation that briefs his visitors on the secrets of Leonardo's *The Last Supper* and other matters. Apparently he keeps in close touch with other initiates. On the one hand, we have a conspiracy that lasts two thousand years and threatens the very foundations of Christianity, and on the other hand a network of rich dilettantes who resemble a theological branch of the Baker Street Irregulars.

Yes, the plot is absurd, but then most movie plots are absurd. That's what we pay to see. What Howard brings to the material is tone and style, and an aura of mystery that is undeniable. He begins right at the top; the Columbia Pictures logo falls into shadow as Hans Zimmer's music sounds simultaneously liturgical and ominous. The murder scene in the Louvre is creepy in a ritualistic way, and it's clever the way Robert Langdon is able to look at letters, numbers, and symbols and mentally rearrange them to yield their secrets. He's like the Flora Cross character in *Bee Season*, who used Kabbalistic magic to visualize spelling words floating before her in the air.

The movie works; it's involving, is intriguing, and constantly seems on the edge of startling revelations. After it's over and we're back on the street, we wonder why this crucial secret needed to be protected by the equivalent of a brain-twister puzzle crossed with a scavenger hunt. The trail that Robert and Sophie follow is so difficult and convoluted that it seems impossible that anyone, including them, could ever follow it. The secret needs to be protected up to a point; beyond that it is absolutely lost, and the whole point of protecting it is beside the point. Here's another question: Considering where the trail begins, isn't it sort of curious where it leads? Still, as T. S. Eliot wrote, "In my beginning is my end." Maybe he was onto something.

The Deal ★ ★ ½

R, 107 m., 2005

Christian Slater (Tom Hanson), Selma Blair (Abbey Gallagher), Robert Loggia (Jared Tolson), John Heard (Professor Roseman), Colm Feore (Hank Weiss), Angie Harmon (Anna), Kevin Tighe (John Cortland), Françoise Yip (Janice Long). Directed by Harvey Kahn and produced by Chris Dorr, Ruth Epstein, Kahn, and Robert Lee. Screenplay by Epstein.

The Deal is a thriller about Wall Street insiders, set during an oil crisis a few years in the future. The United States is at war with the "Confederation of Arab States," gas is $6 a gallon and getting more expensive, and there's enormous pressure to find new sources for oil.

More than most thrillers, this one seems to be based on expert insights; its author, Ruth Epstein, wrote the screenplay against a background of Wall Street experience, and its view of boardroom politics has a convincing level of detail. It's not in every thriller that you hear someone say, "Oil is a fungible commodity."

Christian Slater stars as Tom Hanson, an associate with an old-line Wall Street investment firm that has kept its reputation during a period of corporate scandals. That's why the firm is attractive to the giant Condor Corp. and its sleek president, Jared Tolson (Robert Loggia, never scarier than when he smiles).

Condor wants to merge with Black Star, a privately held Russian oil company that controls massive oil reserves. We know from the start that the deal is fishy because at the top of the film a lawyer tells Tolson he can't continue to work on the deal; a few hours later the lawyer is shot dead. Hanson, the Slater character, is brought in as his replacement. His assignment: Perform due diligence to be sure Black Star is sound and the merger is in the best interests of Condor's shareholders.

The movie surrounds this main story line with several other intersecting strands, of which the most interesting involves young Abbey Gallagher (Selma Blair), a graduate student and "tree hugger" from Harvard who is recruited by Hanson to join his firm on the grounds that she can get a better hearing for her environmental concerns from inside the establishment.

Blair does specific things with her character that are interesting; she makes Abbey not one of those Harvard superhumans but a sincere, sometimes naive young woman who could use some social polish. Soon she is working with Hanson, and although they are indeed attracted to each other, romance is not the focus of this movie.

The Deal appreciates how big institutions like Slater's have factions and infighting; when he lands the Condor account, there's jealousy from Hank Weiss (a leaner, meaner Colm Feore), who is supposed to be the firm's oil expert.

There is also a middle-aged woman in research who knows all sorts of things that nobody ever asks her about: for example, that there is no oil in the "oil fields" controlled by Black Star. What's going on? "Oil may have been shipped from there," Hanson is told by a cryptic insider, "but I can't tell you where it came out of the ground."

The movie is a little too laden with details for its own good, and it has more characters than it needs, but sometimes that complexity works; like the hero, we're feeling our way through a maze of motives and possibilities, and although it's fairly clear who cannot be trusted, it's not always clear who can be. "He's my only friend at the firm," Hanson says of one associate, "and he'd stab me in the back in a second."

The pressure to close the deal is enormous; Hanson's firm alone expects to bank $25 million in commissions. But would it be worth it if Black Star were phony and Condor's shareholders were buying a worthless company? More to the point, what if Black Star is the front for an oil-laundering scheme?

Plots like this once seemed paranoid, but no one who has seen the documentary *Enron: The Smartest Guys in the Room* will find the lies and deceit in this film surprising. It expresses a system of moral values that keeps running into the discovery that "in the real world," as they say, "things don't work that way." The last scenes of the movie are deeply cynical and yet, we have a sinking feeling, not a million miles from the way Wall Street and the federal government actually do business.

There is of course always the Ethics Task Force, set up by the SEC and the FBI to guard against Wall Street fraud. One of the movie's continuing puzzles involves the possibility that several characters may be working undercover for the task force or Black Star. Secret information has a way of getting around, and the seriousness of the people behind the deal is made fairly clear when Hanson finds a bleeding heart in his refrigerator. "Not a human heart," the cops quickly reassure him.

I admire the film's anger and intelligence, and the generally persuasive level of the performances; Robert Loggia really seems like a CEO, and Selma Blair really seems like an idealistic college graduate. Françoise Yip, for that matter, seems like the sort of best corporate friend who always seems to know more than she should, and to be trying to tell you more than she can say.

But the problem is, *The Deal,* like a lot of real-life Wall Street deals, is a labyrinth into which the plot tends to disappear. The ideas in the film are challenging, the level of expertise is high, the performances are convincing, and it's only at the level of story construction and dramatic clarity that the film doesn't succeed. One more rewrite might have been a good idea. I can't quite recommend it purely as a film, but as a double feature with *Enron: The Smartest Guys in the Room,* it's a slam dunk.

Dear Frankie ★ ★ ★ ½

PG-13, 102 m., 2005

Emily Mortimer (Lizzie Morrison), Gerard Butler (The Stranger), Sharon Small (Marie), Jack McElhone (Frankie Morrison), Mary Riggans (Nell Morrison). Directed by Shona Auerbach and produced by Caroline Wood. Screenplay by Andrea Gibb.

There is a shot toward the end of *Dear Frankie* when a man and a woman stand on either side of a doorway and look at each other, just simply look at each other. During this time they say nothing, and yet everything they need to say is communicated: their doubts, cautions, hopes. The woman is named Lizzie (Emily Mortimer), and the man, known in the movie only as "The Stranger," is played by Gerard Butler. Here is how they meet.

Lizzie has fled from her abusive husband and is raising her deaf son, Frankie (Jack McElhone), with the help of her mother (Mary Riggans). Instead of telling Frankie the truth about his father, Lizzie creates the fiction that he is away at sea—a crew member on a freighter named the *Accra.* Frankie writes to his dad, and his mother intercepts the letters and answers them herself. Frankie's letters are important to her "because it's the only way I can hear his voice."

The deception works until, one day, a ship named the *Accra* actually docks in Glasgow. Frankie assumes his father is on board, but a schoolmate bets his dad doesn't care enough to come and see him. After all, Frankie is nine and his father has never visited once.

Lizzie decides to find a man who will pretend,

for one day, to be Frankie's father. Her friend Marie (Sharon Small), who runs the fish and chips shop downstairs, says she can supply a man, and introduces The Stranger, whom Lizzie pays to pretend to be Frankie's dad for one day.

This sounds, I know, like the plot of a melodramatic tearjerker, but the filmmakers work close to the bone, finding emotional truth in hard, lonely lives. The missing father was brutal; Lizzie reveals to The Stranger, "Frankie wasn't born deaf. It was a gift from his dad." But Frankie has been shielded from this reality in his life and is a sunny, smart boy, who helps people deal with his deafness by acting in a gently funny way. When the kid at the next desk in school writes "Def Boy" on Frankie's desk, Frankie grins and corrects his spelling.

"Call me Davey," The Stranger says, since that is the name of Frankie's dad. So we will call him Davey, too. He is a man who reveals nothing about himself, who holds himself behind a wall of reserve, who makes the arrangement strictly business. We follow Frankie and his "dad" through a day that includes a soccer game, and the inevitable visit to an ice-cream shop. At the end of the day, Davey tells Lizzie and Frankie that his ship isn't sailing tomorrow after all—he'll be able to spend another day with his son. This wasn't part of the deal. But then Davey didn't guess how much he would grow to care about the boy, and his mother.

A movie like this is all in the details. The director, Shona Auerbach, and her writer, Andrea Gibb, see Lizzie, Frankie, and his grandmother not as archetypes in a formula, but as very particular, cautious, wounded people, living just a step above poverty, precariously shielding themselves from a violent past. The grandmother gives every sign of having grown up on the wrong side of town, a chain-smoker who moved in with her daughter "to make sure" she didn't go back to the husband.

Davey, or whatever his name is, comes into the picture as a man who wants to have his exit strategy nailed down. He insists money is his only motive. It is quietly impressive how the young actor Jack McElhone as Frankie understands the task of his character, which is to encourage this man to release his better nature. There is also the matter of how much Frankie knows, or intuits, about his father's long absence.

What eventually happens, while not entirely unpredictable, benefits from close observation, understated emotions, unspoken feelings, and the movie's tact; it doesn't require its characters to speak about their feelings simply so that we can hear them. That tact is embodied in the shot I started out by describing: Lizzie and The Stranger looking at each other.

"We shot several takes," Emily Mortimer told me after the film's premiere. "Shona knew it had to be long, but she didn't know how long, and she had to go into the edit and find out which length worked. She is a very brave director in that way, allowing space around the action."

Every once in a long while, a director and actors will discover, or rediscover, the dramatic power of silence and time. They are moving pictures, but that doesn't mean they always have to be moving. In Miranda July's *You and Me and Everyone We Know,* there is a scene where a man and a woman who don't really know each other walk down a sidewalk and engage in a kind of casual word play that leads to a defining moment in their lives. The scene is infinitely more effective than all the countless conventional ways of obtaining the same result. In the same way, the bold long shot near the end of *Dear Frankie* allows the film to move straight as an arrow toward its emotional truth, without a single word or plot manipulation to distract us. While they are looking at each other, we are looking at them, and for a breathless, true moment, we are all looking at exactly the same fact.

Dear Wendy ★ ½

NO MPAA RATING, 105 m., 2005

Jamie Bell (Dick), Bill Pullman (Krugsby), Mark Webber (Stevie), Alison Pill (Susan), Chris Owen (Huey), Michael Angarano (Freddie), Danso Gordon (Sebastian), Novella Nelson (Clarabelle). Directed by Thomas Vinterberg and produced by Sisse Graum Olsen. Screenplay by Lars von Trier.

Thomas Vinterberg's *Dear Wendy* is a tedious exercise in style, intended as a meditation on guns and violence in America but more of a meditation on itself, the kind of meditation that invites the mind to stray. Mine strayed to the fact that the screenplay is by Vinterberg's

Danish mentor, Lars von Trier, and the movie, although filmed on three-dimensional sets, feels as artificial and staged as his *Dogville* (2003). Once again a small group of people inhabits a small space, can all see each other out the window, and lives in each other's pockets.

The movie is set in Electric Park, a set in which two rows of buildings face each other and a third row supplies the end of the street. Towering overhead is the elevator for the mine shaft; the locals were mostly miners, but the mines are nearly played out. Dick (Jamie Bell), the orphaned son of a miner, lives with his protective black housekeeper, Clarabelle (Novella Nelson), and his life lacks purpose until he goes into a store to buy a toy gun.

The weapon, as it happens, is real. Dick is a pacifist but falls in love with the gun, which he names Wendy. Much of the movie consists of a letter he writes to Wendy, about how he loved her and lost her, and how everything went wrong. He descends into an abandoned mine for target practice, finds he has a psychic bond with Wendy (he can hit a bull's-eye blindfolded), and soon enlists other people his age into a secret society named the Dandies.

They meet in the mine, which they redecorate as the "Temple," and begin to dress in oddments of haberdashery, like fools or clowns. They have the obligatory unlimited supply of candles. They take a vow of nonviolence. Then Clarabelle's grandson Sebastian (Danso Gordon) appears on the scene, fresh from jail. The local sheriff (Bill Pullman) suggests that Dick "could be like Sebastian's friend, and keep an eye on him."

Sebastian is black because he is Clarabelle's grandson, of course, but also because as the only young black man in the film he is made into the catalyst for violence. This is the Vinterberg/von Trier version of insight into America, roughly as profound as the scene in *Dirty Love* where Carmen Electra holds a gun to a man's head simply because she likes to act black and thinks that will help. To call such reasoning racist is tempting, and yet I suspect in both movies the real reasons for it are stupidity and cluelessness.

Right away there is trouble. A romantic triangle forms, as Sebastian holds Wendy tenderly and Dick gets jealous. Sebastian helpfully supplies all of the Dandies with guns, and then a challenge emerges: Clarabelle visits her granddaughter at the end of the street every year and has become afraid to leave the house. The Dandies devise an ingenious scheme to protect her from danger during her one-block walk, despite the fact that the town seems to contain no danger. I am reminded of a guy I knew who said he carried a gun because he lived in a dangerous neighborhood, and another guy told him, "It would be a lot safer if you moved."

What happens during Clarabelle's progress down the street I will leave for you to experience if you are unwise enough to see the film. As the Dandies plan their operation, Dick draws a diagram of the town that looks uncannily like an aerial view of the chalk outlines on a soundstage floor that von Trier used to create Dogville. Odd, that the Dogma movement from Denmark, which originally seemed to call for the use of actual locations exactly as they were, has become more stylized and artificial than German Expressionism.

It is true that America has problems and that many of them are caused by a culture of guns and violence. It is also true that a movie like David Cronenberg's *A History of Violence* (or I could name countless others) is wiser and more useful on the subject than the dim conceit of *Dear Wendy.*

Apart from what the movie says, which is shallow and questionable, there is the problem of how it says it. The style is so labored and obvious that with all the goodwill in the world you cannot care what happens next. It is all just going through the motions, silly and pointless motions, with no depth, humor, edge, or timing. Vinterberg has made wonderful films, such as *The Celebration* (1998), filled with life and emotion. Here he seems drained of energy, plodding listlessly on the treadmill of style, racking up minutes on the clock but not getting anywhere.

Death at a Funeral ★ ★ ★

R, 90 m., 2007

Matthew Macfadyen (Daniel), Rupert Graves (Robert), Alan Tudyk (Simon), Daisy Donovan (Martha), Kris Marshall (Troy), Andy Nyman (Howard), Jane Asher (Sandra), Keeley Hawes (Jane), Peter Vaughan (Alfie), Ewen Bremner (Justin), Peter Dinklage (Peter), Peter Egan (Victor). Directed by Frank Oz and produced by

Sidney Kimmel, Share Stallings, Larry Makin, and Diana Phillips. Screenplay by Dean Craig.

When I was an altar boy, assisting at Requiem High Mass and planning how to spend my fifty-cent tip at the day-old pastry shop, funerals were sad affairs, with weeping and collapses and all that Latin. The only speaker was the priest, whose sermon reassured us that the Heavenly Father was reserving a space even now in the name of the faithful departed.

These days a lot of funerals have become vaudevillian, with readings, fond stories, laughter, favorite golden oldies, and everybody smiling about dear old Dad or whoever. If they don't send us off gently into that good night, neither do they rage, rage against the dying of the light (copyright Dylan Thomas, who raged plenty).

Frank Oz's *Death at a Funeral* finds its comedy in the peculiar human trait of being most tempted to laugh when we're absolutely not supposed to. Not that all of his characters are very amused. His story begins with the delivery of a casket to the British home of the mourning widow (Jane Asher) who lives with her son Daniel (Matthew Macfadyen) and his wife, Jane (Keeley Hawes), who hates living there so much she can hardly bear to remain even under the mournful circumstances. Not long after, a second casket is delivered, and we're off, and luckily we're all that's off.

Oz, working from a screenplay by Dean Craig, populates the funeral party with disasters waiting to happen. One of them involves Daniel's eulogy, which we see him rehearsing from three-by-five cards, which are a useful precaution if you forget your dad's name (priests always have a helpful memo tucked away in their breviary). Daniel is a prefailed novelist, which means he has not yet finished a novel in order to have it rejected. His despised brother, Robert (Rupert Graves), is a famed novelist living in Manhattan and is flying in just to make Daniel feel doubly miserable.

"Why do we only meet at funerals?" ask people who meet only at funerals. Simon (Alan Tudyk), engaged to a family cousin named Martha (Daisy Donovan), has been dragged along specifically to meet Martha's father (Peter Egan), who is sure to hate him. Simon doesn't improve his chances when, for reasons I will not reveal, he finds himself naked and doing unidentifiable animal impressions. Simon makes a perfect bookend for old Uncle Alfie (Peter Vaughan), who seems astonished to find himself clothed, not to mention invited anywhere.

Every funeral has an uninvited guest, often a mislaid spouse, angry creditor, police detective, or child not recorded in the family Bible. This funeral has Peter Dinklage, who is becoming my favorite go-to actor for any movie that needs someone to go to. Like Rosie Perez, Danny De Vito, Queen Latifah, or Christopher Walken, he has that ability to make you brighten up and take notice, because with such a person on the screen, *something* interesting is bound to happen. Dinklage can look handsome in that menacing way that suggests he's about to dine out on your fondest hopes and dreams.

The movie is part farce (unplanned entrances and exits), part slapstick (misbehavior of corpses), and part just plain wacky eccentricity. I think the ideal way to see it would be to gather your most dour and disapproving relatives and treat them to a night at the cinema. If they are over a certain age and you have ever seen Polident in their bathrooms, be sure to supply them with licorice ropes.

The Death of Mr. Lazarescu ★ ★ ★ ★

R, 154 m., 2006

Ion Fiscuteanu (Mr. Lazarescu), Luminita Gheorghiu (Mioara Avram), Gabriel Spahiu (Leo), Doru Ana (Sandu Sterian), Dana Dogaru (Miki Sterian), Florin Zamfirescu (Dr. Ardelean), Mimi Branescu (Dr. Mirica). Directed by Cristi Puiu and produced by Alexandru Munteanu. Screenplay by Puiu and Razvan Radulescu.

It must be like this with many people, and not just in Romania. A smelly old drunk calls for an ambulance after having a headache for four days. The ambulance service asks him so many questions, he doubts they believe him, and he asks his neighbors for help. They stretch him out on a sofa, ask him how he feels, and complain about the stink of his cats. They call the ambulance again.

The Death of Mr. Lazarescu will follow this dying man for most of the night, as he gradually slips away from the world and the world little notices. The movie is not heartless, but it is matter-of-fact and makes no attempt to heighten the drama. In its relentless gaze at exactly what happens, it reminds me of the Dardenne brothers (*The Son, The Child*), whose films see everything but do not intervene.

Mr. Lazarescu (Ion Fiscuteanu) has long lived in his cluttered Bucharest apartment. He has a sister in a nearby town and a child in Canada, neither much concerned with him. He gives such information to his neighbors, while slowly drifting out of contact with reality. Then the ambulance arrives, with the attendant Mioara (Luminita Gheorghiu) and the driver Leo (Gabriel Spahiu). In the course of this night, they will take him to four hospitals. It is a long night and a long film, but not a slow one because we are drawn so deeply into it.

At hospitals, the obviously incompetent Mr. Lazarescu is asked to fill out forms, sign consents, and answer questions he does not understand. Each hospital suggests sending him to another one. He is nevertheless given a scan that reveals a blood clot on his brain, and a problem with his liver that "nobody," a doctor observes, "is going to be able to do anything about." One of the CT scan technicians almost rejoices: "These neoplasms are Discovery Channel stuff!"

The film's focus is never on Mr. Lazarescu, who becomes disoriented and finally almost speechless, and who was probably not good company on his best days. It does not help that he wets himself during a CT scan, then soils his pants. We focus on the ambulance attendant, who is given one opportunity after another to dump her patient but stubbornly wants to be sure someone actually pays him attention. Her job is to take sick people to hospitals. If they are not admitted, her life is meaningless.

She is not portrayed as a heroine and indeed is passive in the face of sarcasm by a smart-ass resident who mocks her description of Mr. Lazarescu's problems. She knows that what he needs immediately is brain surgery to relieve the clot. One doctor who agrees with this diagnosis nevertheless insists on a signature of consent: "If I operate without his signature, I could go to jail." The doctor's solution is a perfect catch-22: "Drive him for a while until he's comatose and then bring him back."

At the fourth hospital, Mioara finds a doctor who is just ending her shift but wearily agrees to take the patient. And only then can Mioara leave—and disappear from the film because we follow the dying body of Mr. Lazarescu through the hands of all these strangers who have only an immediate role in his final day. Even in the first three hospitals, he has continued to wear his ratty stocking cap and threadbare knit sweater. Now at last he is undressed and bathed, the nurses sponging him and shaving his head with quiet professionalism.

The film, directed and cowritten by Cristi Puiu, has been described as a criticism of the health services in Romania. At least in Romania he is not asked for his insurance company, and he has a theoretical right to free medical care. On Cinematical.com, a doctor posted this message: "As a Romanian physician, I would say it's worse than shown. The misery of Romanian hospitals is not shown at all. By the way, this is based on a true story of a man turned down at five Bucharest hospitals in 1997 and eventually left in the street by the paramedics and found dead next morning (the paramedic got fired)."

There is no need to fire Mioara and her driver, although in the film's final shot we wonder whether Mr. Lazarescu is still alive. I have undergone various medical adventures in recent years and have been moved by the unfailing competence and care of the doctors and nurses I have come into contact with; I admire them even more because I sense this movie is accurate about many hospitals everywhere, in which everyone is overworked, there are more problems than solutions, and the smelly, incoherent Mr. Lazarescu seems doomed no matter what is done. He is not a candidate for triage.

I keep thinking about Mioara. She is insulted by young residents whose experience is far less than hers. She carries Mr. Lazarescu's X-rays around with her from one set of uncaring eyes to another. She could get angry, but she has been on the job too long for that. They all have. Here are no *E.R.*-style interns calling for transfusions or racing down corridors with gurneys. In *The Death of Mr. Lazarescu*, the patient is another detail in an endless series of impossible situations and exhausting overnight shifts. If you start thinking of Lazarescu, of all the Lazarescus, as people who deserve your full concern and attention, you could go mad. Yes, the doctors and nurses chat about getting an espresso or using each other's cell phones. Life goes on.

There is a rule about the movies: Never take an expert to a movie about his or her specialty. *The Death of Mr. Lazarescu* is an exception. I suspect medical professionals would see much they recognize in this movie. The credits include a long list of technical advisers, but it doesn't take an adviser to convince you the movie is authentic. Like *United 93* and the work of the Dardenne brothers, it lives entirely in the moment, seeing what happens as it happens, drawing no conclusions, making no speeches, creating no artificial dramatic conflicts, just showing people living one moment after another, as they must.

Note: The man's full name is Dante Remus Lazarescu. Dante wrote of the circles of hell. Remus was a cofounder of ancient Rome, killed by his twin. "Lazarescu" reminds us of Lazarus, who was lucky enough to find someone who could raise him from the dead.

D.E.B.S. ★ ½

PG-13, 91 m., 2005

Sara Foster (Amy), Meagan Good (Max), Jill Ritchie (Janet), Devon Aoki (Dominique), Jordana Brewster (Lucy), Jessica Cauffiel (Ninotchka), Michael Clarke Duncan (Academy President), Holland Taylor (Mrs. Peatree). Directed by Angela Robinson and produced by Jasmine Kosovic and Andrea Sperling. Screenplay by Robinson.

At some point during the pitch meetings for *D.E.B.S.* someone must certainly have used the words "Charlie's Lesbians." The formula is perfectly obvious: Four sexy young women work for a secret agency as a team that is gifted at lying, cheating, stealing, and killing. How do we know they have these gifts? Because of the movie's funniest moment, during the opening narration, when we learn that trick questions on SAT exams allow an agency to select high school graduates who can and will lie, cheat, steal, kill.

Amy (Sara Foster), the leader of the group, is a latent lesbian. Lucy Diamond (Jordana Brewster), a thief and master criminal, goes on a blind date with a semi-retired Russian assassin named Ninotchka (Jessica Cauffiel). When the D.E.B.S. monitor the date on a surveillance assignment, Amy is attracted to the smiling, seductive Lucy, which causes security complications. Pause for a moment to ask with me, would this movie be as interesting if the blind date had been with a guy? I submit it would not, because the lesbian material is all that separates *D.E.B.S.* from the standard teenage Insta-Flick.

The character traits of the "D.E.B.S." are only slightly more useful than the color-coded uniforms of the Teenage Mutant Ninja Turtles. In such movies, taxonomy is personality; once you've got the label straight, you know all you're ever going to know about the character. In addition to Amy, who is a lesbian, we meet Max (Meagan Good), who is black; Janet (Jill Ritchie), who is white; and Dominique (Devon Aoki), who corners the market on character attributes by being an Asian with a French accent who smokes all the time. I would not identify the characters by race, but the movie leaves us with no other way to differentiate them.

Dominique's smoking fascinates me. She never lights a cigarette, extinguishes one, or taps an ash. She simply exists with a freshly lit filter tip in her mouth, occasionally removing it to emit a perky little puff of uninhaled smoke. I wish I had stayed through the credits to see if there was a cigarette wrangler. Dominique's very presence on the screen inspires me to imagine an excited pitch meeting during which the writer-director, Angela Robinson, said with enthusiasm: "And Dominique, the Asian chick, smokes all the time!" At which the studio executives no doubt thanked the gods for blessing them with such richness and originality in character formation.

I have mentioned the pitch more than once because this movie is all pitch. It began as a popular short subject at Sundance, where audiences were reportedly amused by a send-up of the *Charlie's Angels* formula in which the angels were teenagers and one was a lesbian. The problem is, a short subject need only delight while a feature must deliver.

At one point in *D.E.B.S.* a team member uses the term "supervillain," not ironically but descriptively, leading to a new rule for *Ebert's Little Movie Glossary*: "Movies that refer to supervillains not ironically but descriptively reveal an insufficient disconnect between the pitch and the story." The rule has countless subsets, such as characters referring to themselves or others as heroes. Best friends who say, "I'm only comic relief" are given a provisional pass.

The Charlie figure in the movie is the president of the D.E.B.S. Academy, played by Michael Clarke Duncan, who looks spiffy in a tailored suit and rimless glasses. He gives them their orders, while never asking himself, I guess, how goes the homeland security when bimbos are minding the front lines. For that matter, Lucy Diamond, whose middle name I hope is Intheskywith, would rather make love than war, which leads to some PG-13 smooching.

Mrs. Peatree (Holland Taylor), headmistress of the D.E.B.S. Academy, asks Amy to turn the situation to her advantage by using herself as bait ("like Jodie did in that movie—you know the one, what was its name?"). I confess at this point I was less interested in Jodie's filmography than in the news that the D.E.B.S. Academy has a headmistress. I found myself wanting to know more about the academy's school song, lunchroom menu, student council, and parents' day. ("Janet has perfect scores in lying and cheating, but needs work on her stealing, and is flunking murder.") The uniform is cute little plaid skirts and white blouses, with matching plaid ties.

Other notes: I think I heard correctly, but may not have, that one character's "Freudian analysis" is that she suffers from a "dangerous Jungian symbiosis." Now there's a Freudian analysis you don't hear every day. I know I heard correctly when two of the girls share their dream: "Let's pretend we're in Barcelona, and you're at art school and I'm renting boats to tourists." The young people today, send them on junior year abroad, they go nuts. I note in passing that the movie quotes accurately from the famous shot in *Citizen Kane* where the camera moves straight up past the catwalks, drops, ropes, and pulleys above a stage. For me, that shot was like the toy in a box of Cracker-Jacks: not worth much, but you're glad they put it in there.

December Boys ★ ★

PG-13, 105 m., 2007

Daniel Radcliffe (Maps), Christian Byers (Spark), Lee Cormie (Misty), James Fraser (Spit), Sullivan Stapleton (Fearless), Victoria Hill (Teresa), Jack Thompson (Bandy McAnsh), Teresa Palmer (Lucy), Ralph Cotterill (Shellbank), Kris McQuade (Mrs. McAnsh), Frank Gallacher (Father Scully). Directed by Rod Hardy and produced by Richard Becker. Screenplay by Marc Rosenberg, based on the novel by Michael Noonan.

In Australia, the height of summer arrives, of course, in December, which is not how *December Boys* gets its name. The title comes because four boys at the height of adolescence all have December birthdays, and so the nuns at their orphanage have arranged a special treat: a holiday at the seaside. After that summer, nothing will ever be the same again, an observation the movie should use on its posters. Hang on; it is on the posters.

The lads go to stay with a salty old sea dog named Bandy McAnsh (Jack Thompson) and his sickly wife, Mrs. McAnsh (Kris McQuade). He has retired from the navy and they have settled here, their eyes to the sea, their backs to the barren landscape. This is in about 1960, years and years before anyone will think of soaking T-shirts in a soup of red dirt and selling them as Red Dirt Shirts.

The boys are Misty, the narrator (Lee Cormie), Spark (Christian Byers), Spit (James Fraser), and Maps (Daniel Radcliffe, in his first major post-Potter role). *Variety*, the showbiz bible, cuts to the chase in the opening words of its review: "Destined to be forever known as 'Harry Potter Gets Laid.'" As orphans, the boys (all except for Maps) are as eager to be adopted as puppies in an animal shelter. They meet a circus couple and decide they would make ideal parents. Fearless (Sullivan Stapleton) is a daredevil motorcycle rider, and his girlfriend, Teresa (Victoria Hill), is a French babe who has brought topless sunbathing to Australia years ahead of schedule.

The other three boys all wag their tails and try to seem adoptable. But Maps has his eye on another prize, a girl named Lucy (Teresa Palmer). As they have a flirtation and qualify the movie for *Variety*'s rewrite of the title, I was so forcibly reminded of another one that I wished I were seeing it instead. That would be *Flirting* (1991), where Thandie Newton and Noah Taylor play students at nearby Australian single-sex boarding schools and create the most tender and realistic love (not sex) scene I can remember. They set a high mark, which I'm afraid Maps and Lucy do not approach in a seduction that is by the numbers, only Lucy counts by twos.

She also gives Maps his first puff on a cigarette. The sight of Harry Potter smoking is a little like Mickey Mouse lighting up, but the period detail is accurate, and Radcliffe is convincing as the young man; he proves he can move beyond the Harry role, which I guess is the objective of this movie, but I am not sure that it proves he has star power—not yet, anyway, unless his costar, so to speak, is Harry Potter.

There are some elements in the film that baffle me, one of them being an underwater appearance by the Virgin Mary. I guess we might expect such a manifestation in some movies about Catholic orphans, but not in one so chockablock with mortal sins. To balance her, there is the earthy wisdom of Father Scully (Frank Gallacher), who escorts the lads on their holiday and gives them sales talks on being adopted, as if they were opposed to the idea. He knows the good Catholic couple, the McAnshes, and is their friend in need.

The movie is based on a novel by Michael Noonan, unread by me, which is described as "young adult fiction" by Amazon. Its young and adult elements fit together awkwardly, however, and it is hard to reconcile the storybook qualities of the first sequences with what the MPAA catalogues as PG-13-rated "sexual content, nudity, underage drinking, and smoking," and parents of younger Radcliffe fans will describe as "ohmigod." There seem to be two movies going on here at the same time, and *December Boys* would have been better off going all the way with one of them.

Dedication ★ ★

R, 93 m., 2007

Billy Crudup (Henry Roth), Mandy Moore (Lucy Reilley), Dianne Wiest (Carol), Bob Balaban (Arthur Planck), Bobby Cannavale (Don Meyers), Christine Taylor (Allison), Tom Wilkinson (Rudy Holt). Directed by Justin Theroux and produced by Daniela Taplin Lundberg, Galt Niederhoffer, and Celine Rattray. Screenplay by David Bromberg.

Henry Roth, the hero of *Dedication,* is a writer who does one thing correctly: He talks like he's taking dictation from himself. "Life is nothing but the occasional burst of laughter rising above the interminable wail of grief," he informs us, which may be true enough, but does little to set the mood for a romantic comedy.

Henry (Billy Crudup), possibly named after the author of *Call It Sleep,* threatens, like the real Roth, to become a one-book wonder. He writes children's books, which it is not in his nature to do because he hates children along with the rest of the human race. What kind of man goes out of his way to tell children that there is no Santa Claus?

He has written a best-seller, *Marty the Beaver,* with his collaborator, Rudy (Tom Wilkinson), an illustrator. Then Rudy dies, which is not a spoiler, but it might be a spoiler to reveal that he stays around for the rest of the movie in the form of a ghost. This strands Henry without his only friend. Henry, you understand, is a very odd man with a lot of problems, which seem less like a consistent syndrome than a collection of random neurotic tics.

For example, he is as attached to an old towel as Linus is to his security blanket. When he is having anxiety attacks, which are frequent, nothing will calm him but to put weights on his chest. And he manifests various forms of obsessive-compulsive behavior.

We meet his editor, Planck (Bob Balaban), who sits behind his desk looking mournful at the prospect of there being no further adventures of Marty the Beaver. He orders Henry to team up with another illustrator, Lucy (Mandy Moore), this despite Henry's inability to allow anyone into his life for purposes of collaboration on Marty the Beaver or anything else. And it's at about that point that *Dedication* jumps *onto* the rails and follows a familiar rom-com pathway: Will these two completely incompatible people work out their differences and eventually fall in love? What are the odds, considering they have the lead roles in the movie? Have we spent all that money only to see Mandy Moore's occasional laughter fading off into an interminable wail of grief? I think not.

The movie is a first-time directorial effort

by Justin Theroux, a splendid actor, son of the writer Phyllis, nephew of the novelist Paul. He might have done better to have adapted something by them. My candidate for a novel begging to be filmed: Paul's *Chicago Loop,* about a respectable businessman who leads a macabre secret life. Instead, he began with a first screenplay by David Bromberg, which plays like a serve-yourself buffet of bits and pieces cobbled from other movies.

Billy Crudup and Mandy Moore are immensely likable actors. We like them so much we regret having to see them in this story, even though occasionally they slip into a cranny of it and seem to create their own private outtakes. Consider, for example, Crudup's explanation of why any woman should be overjoyed to share life with such a basket case as he. True, such a life wouldn't be boring, but remember the ancient Chinese curse (are there no modern Chinese curses?), "May you live in interesting times."

Maybe I would like *Dedication* more if I had not seen its separate elements time and again. Once Henry and Lucy have been handcuffed together by the plot, for example, I know with a certainty that they will end up in love. But I also know the screenplay structure requires a false dawn before the real dawn. There must be an element that threatens their obligatory happiness. And there is, in the person of Jeremy (Martin Freeman), her former lover, now back in the picture. And there must be a private problem of her own to balance Henry's peculiarities. And there is, in the person of her mother (Dianne Wiest), who wants to evict her, raising the specter that she will move in with the Wrong Person.

In a movie of unlikelihoods, the most problematical is Balaban, as the publisher, offering Lucy $200,000 on the side as a bonus to do all she can to make Henry function again. If there was money like that in children's books, Marty the Beaver would have a lot of new little friends.

Delirious ★ ★ ★ ½

NO MPAA RATING, 107 m., 2007

Steve Buscemi (Les Galantine), Michael Pitt (Toby Grace), Alison Lohman (K'Harma Leeds), Gina Gershon (Dana), Elvis Costello (Himself).

Directed by Tom DiCillo and produced by Robert Salerno. Screenplay by DiCillo.

If he had not been an actor, Steve Buscemi could have been a paparazzo. But then, you can keep saying that about Buscemi. If he had not been an actor, he could have been an incompetent kidnapper (*Fargo*), or a cynical journalist (*Interview*), or a gangster (Tony Blundetto on *The Sopranos*), or a coffeehouse owner (*Art School Confidential*), or a fanatic record collector (*Ghost World*), or a drunk (*Trees Lounge*), or a director (which he was on *Trees Lounge, Interview,* and *Lonesome Jim*). Here's an actor who has 104 movie and TV roles listed on IMDB, and he could have been any of those characters.

There is a needy intensity about so many of his characters. As infants, before they could speak, they were already mentally saying, "I'm walkin' here! I'm walkin' here!" They insist on their space in a world that has never welcomed them, and that is a definition of paparazzi. "This is my spot!" they scream as they block off a foot of sidewalk to take one of countless millions of photographs of pitiful blond starlets emerging from limousines they screwed their way into.

Their dream is that one big picture. One like the shot that everybody has seen of Sophia Loren gazing in amusement at Jayne Mansfield's wayward neckline. More often, however, Buscemi's paparazzo in *Delirious* gets shots like Goldie Hawn having lunch or Elvis Costello not wearing his hat. For him, a big score is getting a photo of a star leaving the hospital after penile surgery. My advice: Take every shot you have of every actor leaving a hospital and say he just had penile surgery. How will it sound if he denies it?

Delirious, by writer-director Tom DiCillo, has a special quality because it does not make paparazzi a target but a subject. It *sees* Les, the name of the Buscemi character, whose name itself tells you what you need to know about him. It watches him work, it goes home with him, it listens while he espouses his paparazzi code to a new friend named Toby (Michael Pitt). Toby is a homeless street kid, sincere and maybe a little simple, but willing to work for free because he, perhaps alone among all the city's inhabitants, looks up to Les. But Toby is a handsome kid with a future, and his name tells his story, too: "to be." One of the first to figure that out is, appropriately, a casting director (Gina Gershon).

Les at first tells Toby to get lost. Then he takes mercy on him and allows him to be an unpaid assistant. He brings him home to his apartment, a cubby hole in a shabby building, and lets him sleep in the closet. And he teaches him the ropes, which is maybe the first time Les has actually articulated them for himself.

Their story centers on the starlet du jour, K'Harma Leeds (Alison Lohman), which, if you know what "karma" means, suggests she will sometimes be a lead, although not a speller. She's blond, pretty, clueless, thinks Toby is cute, and is a sitting duck for Les. She even invites Toby to a party. He asks if he can bring along a friend, and Les is such a bad strategist he actually starts taking pictures at the party instead of waiting to insinuate himself. He's like a fisherman so eager to reel in the line that he can't wait to hook a fish.

This is the best DiCillo movie I've seen, and he's made some good ones (*Box of Moonlight, The Real Blonde*). His second film was *Living in Oblivion* (1995), a generally well-reviewed story about the making of an indie film (with Buscemi playing the director), which DiCillo insists is *not* about the making of his first film, *Johnny Suede* (1991), starring the young Brad Pitt. He insists that over and over and over again.

What *Delirious* has is knowledge of overnight celebrities and those who feed on them, and insights into the self-contempt of the feeders. So much depends on Buscemi's performance here, and he has lived in the world of paparazzi targets. Just as in *Interview,* he was able to draw on the experience of doing countless publicity interviews. Buscemi plays Les not with disdain, as he might have, but with sympathy for a guy trying to get famous by taking photos of the famous; he is the flea on the flea. And Michael Pitt brings a touching innocence to his role as the flea on the flea on the flea. As for Alison Lohman, she just plain nails K'Harma, especially in a music video scene.

Note: The word "paparazzi" comes from the nickname "Paparazzo," for a celebrity photographer in Fellini's La Dolce Vita, *which didn't merely give us the name but almost invented the concept.*

Derailed ★ ★ ½

R, 100 m., 2005

Clive Owen (Charles Schine), Jennifer Aniston (Lucinda Harris), Melissa George (Deanna Schine), Vincent Cassel (Philippe LaRouche), RZA (Winston Boyko), Xzibit (Dexter). Directed by Mikael Hafstrom and produced by Lorenzo di Bonaventura. Screenplay by Stuart Beattie, based on the novel by James Siegel.

Derailed cannot be about what it seems to be about, not with a title like *Derailed,* but the story works if you're willing to meet it halfway. Critics of thrillers are hard on the new ones, applying logic with a merciless zeal, but they cave in when the thriller is from the 1940s. Imagine this movie with Barbara Stanwyck and Fred MacMurray, and it would work for you. Better still, just rent *Double Indemnity* and the hell with it.

The movie stars Clive Owen as Charles, a man with a lot of problems on his mind. His beloved daughter has diabetes, and her third kidney transplant has just failed. He has been fired from his big account at work. When we meet him, he realizes his wife borrowed money from his billfold and he can't pay the fare on his commuter train. Luckily, the movie is set in Chicago, which means that a smart and sexy brunette with sheer stockings and high heels offers to pay for his ticket. That is so typically Chicago.

Certain spoilers follow. Others do not. The brunette is Lucinda (Jennifer Aniston). He senses an attraction between them. He wants to meet her again, allegedly to repay the train fare, more likely to tempt himself with her appeal. She smiles back. They exchange business cards. They meet for lunch. Lunch becomes dinner. Dinner becomes a hotel. Sex becomes a necessity, and then a brutal man with a French accent (Vincent Cassel) breaks into the room, knocks Charles almost unconscious, and rapes Lucinda.

Charles tells his wife, Deanna (Melissa George), that he worked late at the office and then was mugged. Deanna buys this story, I guess. She is one of the more trusting wives in movie history. But the nightmare is not over. The mugger, named Philippe, has Charles's name and phone number. He guesses, correctly, that Charles and Lucinda did not call the police (she's married, too). He has blackmail in mind.

Charles luckily has an African-American friend at the ad agency where he works. This is Winston Boyko, played (and played well) by the rap artist RZA. As all white executives know (as, indeed, all executives of every race know), when you are in trouble and need to step outside the borders of the law, there's always a black guy in the mail room whom you can count on. This guy is always smarter and more experienced in the ways of the real world than any mere executive could ever hope to be. Winston knows how Philippe's mind works. He becomes Charles's adviser and dirty-work expert, charging only 10 percent of Philippe's extortion demand, which is kind of a finder's fee in reverse, for making sure Philippe gets lost.

More than that I will not reveal. Let me say that I was intrigued by the performances. Owen was my candidate for James Bond and can play hard and heartless rotters (see *Closer*), but here he is quiet and sad, with a sort of passivity. He lets his face relax into acceptance of his own bad fortune. Aniston does that interesting thing of not being a stereotyped sexpot but being irresistibly intriguing. That works with a man like Charles. Happily married, in debt, worried about his daughter and his job, he would be impervious to a sexy slut.

What gets him is that Lucinda has problems, too, and a sense of humor, and seems as reluctant as he is to have an affair. It's just that, well, they talk so easily together. She listens, she cares. How desperately this man needs someone to confide in, outside the world of his problems. By the time it gets around to sex, it isn't exactly sex anymore, it's more like a physical expression of the sympathy they have for each other. These are difficult notes to play, but Aniston and Owen form a little emotional duet that doesn't even need sheet music. Maybe you will approve of how the plot unfolds, or maybe not. Remember with *Unfaithful*, how you didn't know if you felt bad when Diane Lane cheated on Richard Gere, or were happy for her? Of course a lot depended on Gere not finding out.

I think probably in the last analysis, *Derailed* doesn't hold up. At the end we want more, or less, or different. But you didn't have a lousy vacation just because it rained for the last two days.

Derailed has a great setup, a good middle passage, and some convincing performances. Then it runs off the tracks. If you're an unforgiving logician, you'll be offended. If you like movies even when you know where they're going and you've been there before, *Derailed* may work for you. It depends on how willing you are to go along with it.

Deuce Bigalow: European Gigolo
no stars

R, 75 m., 2005

Rob Schneider (Deuce Bigalow), Eddie Griffin (T.J. Hicks), Til Schweiger (Heinz Hummer), Jeroen Krabbe (Gaspar Voorsboch), Hanna Verboom (Eva Voorsboch). Directed by Mike Bigelow and produced by Jack Giarraputo, Adam Sandler, and John Schneider. Screenplay by Rob Schneider, David Garrett, and Jason Ward.

Deuce Bigalow: European Gigolo makes a living cleaning fish tanks and occasionally prostituting himself. How much he charges, I'm not sure, but the price is worth it if it keeps him off the streets and out of another movie. *Deuce Bigalow* is aggressively bad, as if it wants to cause suffering to the audience. The best thing about it is that it runs for only seventy-five minutes.

Rob Schneider is back, playing a male prostitute (or, as the movie reminds us dozens of times, a "man-whore"). He is not a gay hustler but specializes in pleasuring women, although the movie's closest thing to a sex scene is when he wears diapers on orders from a giantess. Oh, and he goes to dinner with a woman with a laryngectomy who sprays wine on him through her neck vent.

The plot: Deuce visits his friend T.J. Hicks (Eddie Griffin) in Amsterdam, where T.J. is a pimp specializing in man-whores. Business is bad because a serial killer is murdering male prostitutes, and so Deuce acts as a decoy to entrap the killer. In his investigation, he encounters a woman with a penis for a nose. You don't want to know what happens when she sneezes.

Does this sound like a movie you want to

see? It sounds to me like a movie that Columbia Pictures and the film's producers (Jack Giarraputo, Adam Sandler, and John Schneider) should be discussing in long, sad conversations with their inner child.

The movie created a spot of controversy last February. According to a story by Larry Carroll of MTV News, Rob Schneider took offense when Patrick Goldstein of the *Los Angeles Times* listed this year's Best Picture nominees and wrote that they were "ignored, unloved, and turned down flat by most of the same studios that . . . bankroll hundreds of sequels, including a follow-up to *Deuce Bigalow: Male Gigolo,* a film that was sadly overlooked at Oscar time because apparently nobody had the foresight to invent a category for Best Running Penis Joke Delivered by a Third-Rate Comic."

Schneider retaliated by attacking Goldstein in full-page ads in *Daily Variety* and the *Hollywood Reporter.* In an open letter to Goldstein, Schneider wrote: "Well, Mr. Goldstein, I decided to do some research to find out what awards you have won. I went online and found that you have won nothing. Absolutely nothing. No journalistic awards of any kind. . . . Maybe you didn't win a Pulitzer Prize because they haven't invented a category for Best Third-Rate, Unfunny Pompous Reporter Who's Never Been Acknowledged by His Peers."

Reading this, I was about to observe that Schneider can dish it out, but he can't take it. Then I found he's not so good at dishing it out, either. I went online and found that Goldstein has won a National Headliner Award, a Los Angeles Press Club Award, a RockCritics.com award, and the Publicists' Guild award for lifetime achievement.

Schneider was nominated for a 2000 Razzie Award for Worst Supporting Actor but lost to Jar-Jar Binks. But Schneider is correct, and Goldstein has not yet won a Pulitzer Prize. Therefore, Goldstein is not qualified to complain that Columbia financed *Deuce Bigalow: European Gigolo* while passing on the opportunity to participate in *Million Dollar Baby, Ray, The Aviator, Sideways,* and *Finding Neverland.* As chance would have it, I *have* won the Pulitzer Prize, and so I am qualified. Speaking in my official capacity as a Pulitzer Prize winner, Mr. Schneider, your movie sucks.

The Devil and Daniel Johnston ★ ★ ★

PG-13, 110 m., 2006

Featuring Daniel Johnston, Louis Black, Bill Johnston, Mabel Johnston, Jeff Tartakov, Kathy McCarty, Gibby Haynes, and Jad Fair. A documentary written and directed by Jeff Feuerzeig and produced by Henry S. Rosenthal.

The Devil and Daniel Johnston opens with Johnston being introduced at a folk club in Austin, Texas, as "the greatest singer-songwriter alive today." This sort of statement is either true or really needs to be heard by the person being described. Daniel Johnston needs all the support he can find. He is a singer-songwriter and an artist whose underground tapes and gallery shows sell out, and he is a manic-depressive with other mental problems that have had him in and out of hospitals for years.

This documentary charts his life's journey through an apparently inexhaustible archive of video- and audiotapes. Jeff Feuerzeig, who won the best director award at Sundance 2005 for this film, has started with a subject who has filmed himself and been filmed by others for more than twenty years.

That allows us to see Daniel Johnston as a bright young kid who "lost all his confidence" in junior high school, who has had a romantic obsession with a classmate all his life, who was briefly a star on MTV, whose songs have been covered by Beck and Pearl Jam, whom Kurt Cobain called the "greatest living songwriter," whose friends included members of Sonic Youth and Half Japanese, and who still lives at home with his parents, who worry about what will happen to him when they are gone. His tapes are sold on the Web by an ex-manager, still a fan of his music, whom he fired and attacked with a pipe.

Despite the loyalty it inspires, Daniel Johnston's music does not seem to deserve quite the level of praise he has received. He made a crucial early decision to move away from the piano, which he could play, to the guitar, which he has not mastered. When the *Austin Chronicle* named him Austin's Folk Artist of the Year, its editor recalls, that created some unhappiness "in a town where a lot of people *can* play the guitar."

Johnston's life has often been highly medicated, and when he goes off meds for a week or two before a concert, he sometimes gets into trouble. After a happy trip to New York, he was returning home when he got off the bus in West Virginia and was involved in an incident that led to an elderly lady breaking her ankles jumping out a window. During a trip in his dad's private airplane, he caused a crash that could have killed them both. His artwork first got publicity when Cobain wore one of his T-shirts for weeks on end (whether it was always the same shirt, the movie neglects to say), and his drawings of devils, crucifixes, and eyeballs, especially eyeballs, have become famous in some circles.

Watching the movie, I was reminded of the documentary *Crumb* and its portrait of R. Crumb's brother, Charles, who almost never left his bedroom in his mother's home, and whose drawings and notebooks, Robert Crumb says, inspired him. There is a line that sometimes runs between genius and madness, sometimes encircles them. *The Devil and Daniel Johnston* shows us a life of accomplishment and achievement, ringed with sadness, dampened by drugs both prescribed and not (bad acid trips didn't help), and supported by parents whom the film characterizes as "fundamentalist," as if that led to Daniel's troubles. It looks to me more as if Johnston's parents are the luckiest thing that has ever happened to him, as they care for him on his good days and his impossible ones.

The Devil's Rejects ★ ★ ★

R, 101 m., 2005

Sid Haig (Captain Spaulding), Bill Moseley (Otis Firefly), Sheri Moon Zombie (Baby), William Forsythe (Sheriff Wydell), Ken Foree (Charlie Altamont), Matthew McGrory (Tiny), Leslie Easterbrook (Mother Firefly). Directed by Rob Zombie and produced by Mike Elliott, Andy Gould, Michael Ohoven, and Zombie. Screenplay by Zombie.

Here is a gaudy vomitorium of a movie, violent, nauseating, and really a pretty good example of its genre. If you are a hardened horror movie fan capable of appreciating skill and wit in the service of the deliberately disgusting, *The Devil's Rejects* may exercise a certain strange charm. If, on the other hand, you close your eyes if a scene gets icky, here is a movie to see with blinders on, because it starts at icky and descends relentlessly through depraved and nauseating to the embrace of roadkill.

How can I possibly give *The Devil's Rejects* a favorable review? A kind of heedless zeal transforms its horrors. The movie is not merely disgusting but also has an attitude and a subversive sense of humor. Its actors venture into camp satire but never seem to know it's funny; their sincerity gives the jokes a kind of solemn gallows cackle. Consider the fact that it's about a depraved family of mass murderers who name themselves after Groucho Marx characters (Otis P. Driftwood, Rufus Firefly, Captain Spaulding) and that the sheriff calls in a film critic to give him insights into their pathology. The critic is such a Groucho fan that he knows Groucho played God in Otto Preminger's *Skidoo* (1968), something I also knew, but I bet you didn't. The sheriff wants to bring in Groucho for questioning, but the critic knows he died in 1977. "Elvis died three days earlier and stole all the headlines," he moans, risking death at the hands of the sheriff's department's Elvis fans.

The Devil's Rejects movie has been written and directed by Rob Zombie (aka Robert Cummings and Robert Wolfgang Zombie), a composer and music video producer whose *House of 1,000 Corpses* (2003) was a *Texas Chainsaw Massacre* wannabe. Pause for a moment to meditate on the phrase "a *Texas Chainsaw Massacre* wannabe," and you will begin to form some idea of Zombie's artistic vision. Now give him credit, in this movie, not for transcending *Chainsaw Massacre* but for sidestepping its temptations and opening up a mordantly funny approach to the material. There is actually some good writing and acting going on here, if you can step back from the material enough to see it.

The film opens with a 1978 police assault on an isolated farmhouse where, we learn, seventy-five murders have taken place. Inside the house, the Firefly family armors itself with steel masks and vests, and shoots it out with the sheriff (William Forsythe). He is a hard-bitten, vengeful man who cheerfully informs a deputy to be cautious or he'll be "cold-slabbed, toe-tagged, and mailed to your mom in a plastic bag."

Mother Firefly (Leslie Easterbrook) is captured in the raid, but Otis Firefly (Bill Moseley) and his sister, Baby (Sheri Moon Zombie), escape through a storm sewer (odd, in the Texas desert) and meet up with their father, Captain Spaulding (Sid Haig). He is a man whose teeth are so bad they're more frightening than his clown makeup. He plays such a thoroughly disgusting person, indeed, that I was driven to www.sidhaig.com to discover that in real life Haig looks, well, presentable, and even played a judge in Tarantino's *Jackie Brown.* This was a relief to me, because anyone who really looked like Captain Spaulding would send shoppers screaming from the Wal-Mart.

The sheriff pursues the fugitive Fireflys, who kidnap innocent bystanders in the kind of motel no reasonable person would ever occupy, leading to the roadkill scene, which is, of its kind, one of the best I have seen. There is also a scene in which a staple gun is used to post the photos of murder victims in a particularly gruesome manner, and one where characters are nailed to chairs in a burning building and then rescued by a character who deals with the nails in a surprisingly forthright way.

I suppose you're getting the idea. There's a sense in which a movie like this can be endured only if you distance yourself from the material and appreciate its manipulation of the genre. It can be seen as dark (very dark) satire. Or you can just throw up. At the end, when we get mellow flashbacks to the characters sharing a laugh in happier days, we are reminded of all those movies that attempt to follow a sad ending with a happy one, and we have to admire the brutality with which Zombie skewers that particular cliché.

Okay now, listen up, people. I don't want to get any e-mail messages from readers complaining that I gave the movie three stars, and so they went to it expecting to have a good time, and it was the sickest and most disgusting movie they've ever seen. My review has accurately described the movie and explained why some of you might appreciate it and most of you will not, and if you decide to go, please don't claim you were uninformed.

The Devil Wears Prada ★ ½

PG-13, 106 m., 2006

Meryl Streep (Miranda Priestly), Anne Hathaway (Andy Sachs), Stanley Tucci (Nigel), Simon Baker (Christian), Emily Blunt (Emily), Adrian Grenier (Nate). Directed by David Frankel and produced by Wendy Finerman. Screenplay by Aline Brosh McKenna, based on the novel by Lauren Weisberger.

When I was young there was a series of books about boys and girls dreaming of the careers they'd have as grown-ups. I can't remember what the titles were, but let's say one was *Don Brown, Boy Announcer.* Don dreams of being a radio announcer, and one day, when an announcer falls ill at the scene of a big story, he grabs the mike and gets his chance: *The engineer nodded urgently to me and I began to describe the fire, remembering to speak clearly. I was nervous at first, but soon the words flowed smoothly.*

There were books about future coaches, nurses, doctors, pilots, senators, inventors, and so on. I also read the *Childhood of Famous Americans* series, but the "boy announcer" books were far superior, because they were about the childhood of me. *I took a deep breath and began. This was the chance I had been waiting for!*

The Devil Wears Prada is being positioned as a movie for grown-ups and others who know what, or who, or when, or where, Prada is. But while watching it I had the uncanny notion that, at last, one of those books from my childhood had been filmed. Call it *Andy Sachs, Girl Editor.* Anne Hathaway stars as a fresh-faced Midwesterner who comes to New York seeking her first job. "I just graduated from Northwestern," she explains. "I was editor of the *Daily Northwestern*!" Yes! *It had been a thrill to edit the student newspaper, but now, as I walked down Madison Avenue, I realized I was headed for the big time!*

Andy still dresses like an undergraduate, which offends Miranda Priestly (Meryl Streep), the powerful editor of *Runway,* the famous fashion magazine. Miranda, who is a cross between Anna Wintour, Graydon Carter, and a dominatrix, stands astride the world of fashion in very expensive boots. She throws things (her coat, her purse) at her assistants, rattles off tasks to be done immediately, and demands "the new Harry Potter" in "three hours." No, not the new book in the stores. The unpublished manuscript of the next book. Her twins want to read it. So get two copies.

Young Andy Sachs gets a job as the assistant to Miranda's assistant. That's Emily (Emily Blunt), who is terrified of Miranda. She is blunt to Andy: She'll need to get rid of that wardrobe, devote twenty-four hours a day to the job, and hope to God she remembers all of Miranda's commands. *I was impressed when I first saw the famous Miranda Priestly. She had the poise of Meryl Streep, the authority of Condoleezza Rice, and was better-dressed than anyone I'd ever met, except the Northwestern dean of women. And now she was calling my name! Gulp!*

Young Andy has a live-in boyfriend, which wasn't allowed in those old books. He is Nate (Adrian Grenier), who has a permanent three-day beard and loves her but wonders what has happened to "the old Andy I used to know." *I was heartbroken when I had to work late on Nate's birthday, but Miranda swamped me with last-minute demands.* Emily, the first assistant, lives for the day when she will travel to Paris with Miranda for Spring Fashion Week. But then Emily gets a cold or, as Miranda puts it, becomes "an incubus of viral plague." By this time Young Andy has impressed Miranda by getting the Harry Potter manuscript, and she's dressing better, too. *Nigel took me into the storage rooms, where I found myself surrounded by the latest and most luxurious fashion samples!* So Andy replaces Emily on the Paris trip.

"You are the one who has to tell Emily," Miranda kindly explains. *Ohmigod! I was dreaming! Paris, France! And as Miranda Priestly's assistant! But how would I break the news to Emily, who had dreamed of this day? And how could I tell Nate, whose own plans would have to be changed?* Actually, by this time Young Andy has a lot of things to discuss with Nate, including her friendship with Christian (Simon Baker), a famous writer for *New York* magazine. *Ohmigod! Christian said he would read my clippings!*

The Devil Wears Prada is based on the best-selling novel by Lauren Weisberger, which oddly enough captures the exact tone, language, and sophistication of the books of my childhood: *There was nowhere to wipe my sweaty palms except for the suede Gucci pants that hugged my thighs and hips so tightly they'd both begun to tingle within minutes of my securing the final button.* This novel was on the *New York Times* best-seller list for six months and has been published in twenty-seven countries. I hope some of the translators left the word "both" out of that sentence.

Streep is indeed poised and imperious as Miranda, and Hathaway is a great beauty (*Ella Enchanted, Brokeback Mountain*) who makes a convincing career girl. I liked Stanley Tucci, too, as Nigel, the magazine's fashion director, who is kind and observant despite being a careerist slave. But I thought the movie should have reversed the roles played by Grenier and Baker. Grenier comes across not like the old boyfriend but like the slick New York writer, and Baker seems the embodiment of Midwestern sincerity, which makes sense, because he is from Australia, the Midwest of the Southern Hemisphere.

Diary of a Mad Black Woman ★

PG-13, 116 m., 2005

Kimberly Elise (Helen McCarter), Shemar Moore (Orlando), Cicely Tyson (Myrtle), Steve Harris (Charles McCarter), Tyler Perry (Grandma Madea), Lisa Marcos (Brenda), Tamara Taylor (Debrah). Directed by Darren Grant and produced by Reuben Cannon and Tyler Perry. Screenplay by Perry, based on his play.

Diary of a Mad Black Woman begins as the drama of a wife of eighteen years, dumped by her cruel husband and forced to begin a new life. Then this touching story is invaded by the Grandma from Hell, who takes a chainsaw to the plot, the mood, everything. A real chainsaw, not a metaphorical one. The Grandma is not merely wrong for the movie, but fatal to it—a writing and casting disaster. And since the screenplay is by the man who plays Grandma in drag, all blame returns to Tyler Perry. What was he *thinking*?

There's a good movie buried beneath the bad one. Kimberly Elise stars as Helen, wife of Atlanta's attorney of the year. She lives with her husband, Charles (Steve Harris), in a house big enough to be the suburban headquarters of an insurance company. Their marriage seems ideal, but he cheats on her and assaults her with verbal brutality. When Helen comes home the next day, her clothes are being loaded into a U-Haul. That's how she finds out Charles is dumping her and moving in his mistress, Brenda (Lisa Marcos). Oh, and he has two children by Brenda.

Luckily for Helen, the U-Haul is driven by Orlando (Shemar Moore, from *The Young and the Restless*), who is handsome and kind and everything Charles is not. Helen weepingly flees to the house of her grandmother, and that's when everything goes spectacularly wrong.

Grandma Madea, who is built along the lines of a linebacker, is a tall, lantern-jawed, smooth-skinned, balloon-breasted gargoyle with a bad wig, who likes to wave a loaded gun and shoot test rounds into the ceiling. This person is not remotely plausible; her dialogue is so offensively vulgar that it's impossible to believe that the intelligent, sweet, soft-spoken Helen doesn't seem to notice. Madea at one point invades Charles's mansion, tells his mistress she is a ho (which is correct), and destroys all the furniture in his living room with a chainsaw she is able to find and employ within seconds. What's with this bizarre grandmother? She's like Moms Mabley at a church social. Did nobody realize that Grandma Madea comes from Planet X, would seem loud at the Johnson Family Picnic, is playing by different rules than anyone else in the cast, and fatally sabotages Kimberly Elise's valiant attempt to create a character we can care about?

The director is Darren Grant. Did he approve as Grandma took a chainsaw to his movie? Did he see Kimberly Elise in *Beloved* and *Woman, Thou Art Loosed* and realize what she was capable of in a Grandma-free movie? I can imagine this movie working perfectly well with Grandma played as a sympathetic human being, perhaps by Irma P. Hall.

For that matter, Helen has an aunt as well as a grandmother, and her aunt, Myrtle, is played with taste and sympathy by Cicely Tyson. It is impossible that Grandma the harridan could have given life to such gentle and civilized women as Myrtle and Helen. The math doesn't work, either. We learn that Myrtle was thirty-nine when Helen was born, and that makes Grandma about eighty-five, which is too old to operate a chainsaw.

Without the interruptions by Grandma Madea, the movie would be about Helen as a shattered woman who (1) tells the judge Charles can keep all his assets, because she doesn't want a penny; (2) goes to work as a waitress; and (3) is courted by the handsome Orlando, who is kind, understanding, sincere, and knows how to listen to women. No. 1 is impossible, because no judge is going to let a wife abandoned by an adulterer after eighteen years walk away without a penny, but never mind. Does Helen find happiness with Orlando?

Not so fast. The movie has a Christian agenda, which is fine with me, if only it had been applied in a believable way. After melodramatic events occur in the life of the evil Charles, Helen gets the opportunity to practice the virtues of forgiveness and redemption, at the apparent cost of her own happiness. We hate Charles so much that it's impossible to feel sorry for him, or believe in his miraculous recovery in body or reformation of character. It just doesn't play—especially while Helen keeps poor Orlando in the dark about her true feelings, for no better reason than to generate phony romantic suspense.

At the end of the film, Orlando makes a comeback that demonstrates he has carefully studied *An Officer and Gentleman*, but before then we have had one emotionally implausible scene after another involving Charles and Helen, interrupted by periodic raids by the Grandma Madea action figure, who brings the movie to a halt every time she appears. She seems like an invasion from another movie. A very bad another movie. I've been reviewing movies for a long time, and I can't think of one that more dramatically shoots itself in the foot.

Diminished Capacity ★★

NO MPAA RATING, 89 m., 2008

Matthew Broderick (Cooper), Alan Alda (Uncle Rollie), Virginia Madsen (Charlotte), Louis C.K. (Stan), Jimmy Bennett (Dillon), Dylan Baker (Mad Dog McClure), Bobby Cannavale (Lee Vivyan), Jim True-Frost (Donny Prine), Lois Smith (Belle). Directed by Terry Kinney and produced by Celine Rattray, Galt Niederhoffer, and Daniel Taplin Lundberg. Screenplay by Sherwood Kiraly, based on his novel.

Diminished Capacity is a mild pleasure from one end to the other, but not much more. Maybe that's enough, serving as a reminder that movie comedies can still be about ordinary people and do not necessarily have to feature vulgarity as their centerpiece. Yes, I'm still hurting from the *The Love Guru* nightmare.

Dim Cap, as Uncle Rollie shortens the phrase, is about Cooper, a Chicago political columnist (Matthew Broderick), and his Uncle Rollie (Alan Alda), who are both suffering from memory loss. With Cooper, who was banged against a wall in somebody else's bar fight, the impairment is temporary. With Uncle Rollie, it may be progressing; his sister, Belle (Lois Smith), who is Cooper's mother, asks Cooper to come home and help her talk Rollie into a mental health facility. It's easy for Cooper to get away since he's just been fired from his newspaper job (at the *Tribune,* as you can tell from countless hints, although the paper is mysteriously never mentioned).

Cooper drives to his small hometown to find his mother overseeing Rollie, who has a big new project: He has attached fishing lines to an old-fashioned typewriter, so that every time he gets a bite, a letter gets typed. He searches the resulting manuscripts for actual words and combines them into poetry. Well, if monkeys can do it, why not fish?

The plot deepens. Uncle Rollie treasures a baseball card given him by his grandfather. The card features Frank Schulte, who played right field for the 1908 Chicago Cubs, and I don't need to tell you what the Cubs did in 1908. It may be the only card of its kind in existence, and Cooper and his mom realize that if Rollie sold it, all of his unpaid bills would be behind him. Meanwhile, Cooper has run into his old girlfriend Charlotte (Virginia Madsen), who has split with her husband; they slowly rekindle their romance. And what with one thing and another Charlotte and her son drive with Cooper and Rollie back to Chicago for a big sports memorabilia convention. They're trailed by the fiendish, rifle-toting hometown drunk Donny Prine (Jim True-Frost), who wants to steal the card.

Matthew Broderick has two light comedies in release this summer; the other is *Finding Amanda,* where he goes to Vegas to try to rescue his niece from a life of sin. In both films he reminded me of his amiability and quietly meticulous comic timing. He and Madsen find the right note for two old lovers who are casually renewing their romance.

The convention provides the movie's big set piece, as our heroes meet a nice baseball card dealer named Mad Dog McClure (Dylan Baker) and a crooked one named Lee Vivyan (Bobby Cannavale). It is Mad Dog who levels Lee with a withering curse: "You're bad for the hobby!" Baker and Cannavale more or less walk away with the scenes at the sports convention.

There is, of course, a duel over the invaluable card, and a fight, and a highly improbable showdown on a catwalk far above the convention arena, and a bit part for Ernie Banks, and a big kiss between Cooper and Charlotte, and it's all very nice, but not a whole lot more. The film is a coproduction of Chicago's Steppenwolf Theater, directed by veteran actor Terry Kinney, and inspired by Sherwood Kiraly's novel. Kinney shows himself a capable director, but isn't the material a little lightweight for Steppenwolf?

Dirty Love no stars

R, 95 m., 2005

Jenny McCarthy (Rebecca), Carmen Electra (Michelle), Kam Heskin (Carrie), Eddie Kaye Thomas (John), Victor Webster (Richard). Directed by John Mallory Asher and produced by Trent Walford, Jenny McCarthy, Asher, Rod Hamilton, Kimberley Kates, B. J. Davis, and Michael Manasseri. Screenplay by McCarthy.

Dirty Love wasn't written and directed; it was committed. Here is a film so pitiful it doesn't rise to the level of badness. It is hopelessly incompetent. It stars and was scripted by Jenny McCarthy, the cheerfully sexy model who, judging by this film, is fearless, plucky, and completely lacking in common sense or any instinct for self-preservation.

Yes, it takes nerve to star in a scene where you plop down in a supermarket aisle surrounded by a lake of your own menstrual blood. But to expect an audience to find that funny verges on dementia. McCarthy follows it with a scene where the cops strip-search her and she's wearing a maxi pad that would be adequate for an elephant. She doesn't need to do this. It's painful to see a pretty girl who seems nice enough humiliating herself on the screen. I feel sorry for her.

The film basically consists of McCarthy and her half-dressed friends Carmen Electra and Kam Heskin grouped awkwardly on the screen like high school girls in that last heedless showoff stage before a designated driver straps them in and takes them home. At times they literally seem to be letting the camera roll while they try to think up something goofy to do. There is also a lot of crude four-letter dialogue, pronounced as if they know the words but not the music.

The plot: McCarthy plays Rebecca, who seems well dressed and with great wheels for someone with no apparent income. She is cheated on by her boyfriend, Richard (Victor Webster), aka Dick, who looks like the model on the cover of a drugstore romance novel about a girl who doesn't know that guys who look like that spend all of their time looking like that. When she discovers his treachery, Rebecca has a grotesque emotional spasm. She weeps, wails, staggers about Hollywood Boulevard flailing her arms and screaming, crawls on the pavement, and waves her butt at strangers while begging them to ravage her because she simultaneously is worthless and wants to teach Dick a lesson. Then, to teach Dick a lesson, she dates scummy losers.

These events are directed by McCarthy's former partner John Mallory Asher and photographed by Eric Wycoff so incompetently that Todd McCarthy, the esteemed film critic of *Variety*, should have won the Jean Hersholt Humanitarian Award for generosity after writing the "whole package has a cheesy look." This movie is an affront to cheese. Also to breasts. Jenny McCarthy has a technologically splendid bosom that should, in my opinion, be put to a better use than being vomited upon.

The Electra character, meanwhile, struts around like a ho in a bad music video, speaking black street talk as if she learned it phonetically, and pulling out a gun and holding it to a man's head because she thinks, obviously, that pulling guns on guys is expected of any authentic black woman. A scene like that would be insulting in any other movie; here it possibly distracts her from doing something even more debasing.

I would like to say more, but—no, I wouldn't. I would not like to say more. I would like to say less. On the basis of *Dirty Love*, I am not certain that anyone involved has ever seen a movie, or knows what one is. I would like to invite poor Jenny McCarthy up here to the Toronto Film Festival, where I am writing this review while wonderful films are playing all over town, and get her a pass, and require her to go to four movies a day until she gets the idea.

The Diving Bell and the Butterfly ★ ★ ★ ★

PG-13, 112 m., 2007

Mathieu Amalric (Jean-Dominique Bauby), Emmanuelle Seigner (Celine Desmoulins), Marie-Josee Croze (Henriette Durand), Anne Consigny (Claude), Patrick Chesnais (Dr. Lepage), Niels Arestrup (Roussin), Max von Sydow (Papinou). Directed by Julian Schnabel and produced by Kathleen Kennedy and Jon Kilik. Screenplay by Ronald Harwood

The Diving Bell and the Butterfly is a film about a man who experiences the catastrophe I most feared during my recent surgeries: "locked-in syndrome," where he is alive and conscious but unable to communicate with the world. My dread I think began when I was a boy first reading Edgar Allan Poe's "The Premature Burial" at an age much too young to contemplate such a possibility. At least the man in the film can see and hear; the hero of Dalton Trumbo's *Johnny Got His Gun* is completely locked inside his mind.

The film is based on a real man and the book he astonishingly succeeded in writing although he could blink only his left eye. The man was Jean-Dominique Bauby (Mathieu Amalric), who was the editor of *Elle,* the French fashion magazine, when he had his paralyzing stroke. A speech therapist (Marie-Josee Croze) suggests a system of communication: They will arrange the alphabet in the order of most frequently used letters, and he will choose a letter by blinking. By this method, word by word, blink by blink, he dictated his memoir, *The Diving Bell and the Butterfly,* published in 1997, shortly before he died.

It was a superhuman feat, but how could it be filmed? The director is the artist Julian Schnabel, who has made two previous films about artists creating in the face of determined obstacles: *Basquiat* (1996), about a New

York graffiti artist, and *Before Night Falls* (2000), about the persecuted Cuban poet Reinaldo Arenas. His solution, arrived at with screenwriter Ronald Harwood, is to show not merely the man in the bed, but to show what he sees and those around him and his memories and fantasies. This is not an easy way out because everything in the film is resolutely filtered through the consciousness of the locked-in man.

The result is not what you could call inspirational, because none of us would think to be in such a situation and needing inspiration. It is more than that. It is heroic. Here is the life force at its most insistent, lashing out against fate with stubborn resolve. And also with lust, hunger, humor, and all of the other notes that this man once played so easily. We see flashbacks to his children, to his mistress, to his fantasies. We see those around him now. And in a gravely significant scene, we see him meeting with his old father (Max von Sydow), who, Andrew Sarris notes, "gets off what may be the single most French line of all time," which is, "Having a mistress is no excuse for leaving the mother of your children; the world has lost its values."

Celine, the mother of his children and his former partner (played by Emmanuelle Seigner), remains loyal to him and even helps him communicate with another woman who also is a former lover (the male libido is indomitable). And all of the other women around him, including his nurse, his assistant, and a fantasy lover, are loving and patient and assure him that he is in some way the same vital man, filled with eagerness, lust, and brilliance. It is just that now it expresses itself one blink at a time.

The lead performance by Mathieu Amalric exists in two ways, as the unmoving man in bed and the vital man in his memories and fantasies. In that way it is fundamentally different from Daniel Day-Lewis's work in *My Left Foot*, about a man who could move only a toe. At least he could lurch and groan and cry. Both films find the inevitable solution to their challenge and the right actors to meet them.

Janusz Kaminski, the cinematographer, is in large part responsible for freeing the film from its own dangers of being locked in. From the cloudy opening POV shots of Jean-Dominique regaining consciousness, Kaminski fills the screen with life and beauty, so that it's not at all as depressing as it sounds. At the end we are left with the reflection that human consciousness is the great miracle of evolution, and all the rest (sight, sound, taste, hearing, smell, touch) are simply a toolbox that consciousness has supplied for itself. Maybe it would even be better to be Trumbo's Johnny than never to have been conscious at all.

Dolls ★ ★ ★

NO MPAA RATING, 113 m., 2005

Miho Kanno (Sawako), Hidetoshi Nishijima (Matsumoto), Tatsuya Mihashi (Hiro, the Boss), Chieko Matsubara (Woman in the Park), Kyoko Fukada (Haruna, the Pop Star), Tsutomu Takeshige (Nukui, the Fan). Directed by Takeshi Kitano and produced by Masayuki Mori and Takio Yoshida. Screenplay by Kitano.

Takeshi Kitano is known for directing pictures in which flashes of violence are punctuated by periods of waiting, reflection, and loneliness. Using the name of Beat Takeshi, he stars in them. He is a distinctive, original director; his *The Blind Swordsman: Zatoichi* (2004) took a durable Japanese series character and transformed him into a philosophical wanderer. In his film *Dolls,* he makes his longest journey from his action-film roots, into a land of three tragic relationships.

The title is taken from the Japanese tradition of Bunraku, or puppet plays. Elaborate dolls are moved about the stage, each one with two or three artists to manipulate their eyes, heads, arms. One artist is visible, the others hooded in black. A reader recites all of the dialogue, and there is music.

Kitano's film opens with a Bunraku performance, and then segues into the first of three live-action stories in which the characters seem moved about the stages of their own lives without wills of their own. We are reminded of Gloucester's line in *King Lear*: "As flies to wanton boys, are we to the gods; they kill us for their sport."

The first story involves Matsumoto (Hidetoshi Nishijima), who is engaged to Sawako (Miho Kanno). His parents insist he break off the engagement and marry his boss's daughter. Sawako attempts suicide, is brain-damaged, and is spirited out of a nursing home by Matsumoto, who devotes his life to being with her. They live in a hotel room, in a car, and finally in the wild; because she wanders away, he joins them with a length of rope, and as they walk through the countryside they become known as the Bound Beggars.

The second story involves a gangster boss named Hiro (Tatsuya Mihashi). As a young man he is in love with a woman (Chieko Matsubara), who meets him on a park bench every Saturday with two box lunches. One Saturday he breaks up with her; a woman would be a complication now that he has decided to become a yakuza. She says she will come every Saturday no matter what. Years later, old and disillusioned, he returns to the park to look for her.

The third story is about a pop idol named Haruna (Kyoko Fukada). A fan named Nukui (Tsutomu Takeshige) is obsessed with her. His job is to wave a warning light at a highway construction zone; Haruna is disfigured in a traffic accident that may have been caused (the movie is a little vague) by Nukui being distracted from his job by thoughts of her. After her injury she refuses to be seen by any of her fans; Nukui's determination to meet her leads to a gruesome decision.

Dolls moves with a deliberate pace. I have seen Bunraku performances in Japan, and found them long, slow, and stylized; the same can be said of the film. Kitano is not content to simply tell his stories, but wants to leave us time to contemplate them, to experience the passage of time for these characters and the way their choices will define them for the rest of their lives. The three active lovers in the film—Matsumoto, the woman, and the fan—willingly sacrifice their freedom and happiness in acts of romantic abnegation. Such gestures seem odd in the modern world, but not in classical tragedy, not in Bunraku, and not in the Japanese tradition of dramatic personal gestures.

The film has moments of great loveliness. Some of the landscapes, filled with autumn leaves of astonishing shades of red, are beautiful and lonely. The film is about three people who have unhappiness forced upon them, and three others who choose it. *Dolls* isn't a film for everybody, especially the impatient, but Kitano does succeed, I think, in drawing us into his tempo and his world, and slowing us down into the sadness of his characters.

Dominion: Prequel to the Exorcist ★ ★ ★

R, 111 m., 2005

Stellan Skarsgard (Father Merrin), Gabriel Mann (Father Francis), Clara Bellar (Rachel), Billy Crawford (Cheche), Antonie Kamerling (Lieutenant Kessel), Ralph Brown (Sergeant-Major), Julian Wadham (Major Granville), Eddie Osei (Emekwi). Directed by Paul Schrader and produced by James G. Robinson. Screenplay by Caleb Carr and William Wisher Jr.

Paul Schrader's *Dominion: Prequel to the Exorcist* does something risky and daring in this time of jaded horror movies: It takes evil seriously. There really are dark Satanic forces in the Schrader version, which takes a priest forever scarred by the Holocaust and asks if he can ever again believe in the grace of God. The movie is drenched in atmosphere and dread, as we'd expect from Schrader, but it also has spiritual weight and texture, boldly confronting the possibility that Satan may be active in the world. Instead of cheap thrills, Schrader gives us a frightening vision of a good priest who fears goodness may not be enough.

The film's hero, Merrin (Stellan Skarsgard), considers himself an ex-priest; during World War II he was forced by Nazis to choose some villagers for death in order that a whole village not be killed. This is seen by a Nazi officer as an efficient way to undermine Merrin's belief in his own goodness, and indeed forces the priest to commit evil to avoid greater evil. This is not theologically sound; the idea is to do no evil and leave it to God to sort out the consequences.

His trauma from this experience hurls Merrin out of the priesthood and into an archaeological dig in Africa, where he is helping to excavate a remarkably well-preserved church buried in the sand. Why this church, in this place? It doesn't fit in architectural, historical, or religious terms, and seems intended not so much to celebrate God as to trap something unspeakably evil that lies beneath it.

Schrader is famously a director of moral values crossed with dangerous choices; his own movies *(Hardcore, Light Sleeper, The*

Comfort of Strangers) and those he has written for Martin Scorsese *(Taxi Driver, Raging Bull)* deal with men obsessed with guilt and sin. His *Dominion* is not content to simply raise the curtain on William Friedkin's classic *The Exorcist* (1974), but is more ambitious: It wants to observe the ways Satan seduces man.

The film's battle between good and evil involves everyone on the dig, notably the young priest Father Francis (Gabriel Mann), who has been assigned by Rome to keep an eye on Merrin. Then there is the doctor Rachel (Clara Bellar), whose special concern is a deformed young man named Cheche (Billy Crawford). Curiously, Cheche seems to improve beyond all expectations of medicine, as if something supernatural were going on. Also on the site, in "British East Africa," is the Sergeant-Major (Ralph Brown), a racist who assigns the devil's doings to the local Africans.

In a lesser movie, there would be humid goings-on at the camp, and a spectacular showdown between the humans and special effects. Not in the Schrader version, which trusts evil to be intrinsically fascinating and not in need of f/x enhancement. His vision, however, was not the one the powers at Morgan Creek were looking for (although Schrader was filming a script by Caleb Carr and William Wisher Jr. that the producers presumably approved). After Schrader delivered his version, a scenario developed that is, I think, unprecedented in modern movie history. The studio, having spent millions on the Schrader version, hired the director Renny Harlin to spend more millions remaking it in a presumably more commercial fashion.

Harlin kept some of the actors, including Skarsgard, and substituted others (Gabriel Mann was replaced by James D'Arcy, Clara Bellar by Izabella Scorupco). The same cinematographer, the great Vittorio Storaro, filmed for both directors. After Harlin's version, *Exorcist: The Beginning,* did a break-even $82 million at the box office but drew negative reviews, Schrader succeeded in getting his version screened at a film festival in Brussels, where the positive reception inspired this theatrical release, a resurrection fully in keeping with the film's theme.

I've seen both versions and much prefer Schrader's, and yet it must be said that Harlin did not prostitute himself in his version. Indeed, oddly, it opens with more talk and less excitement than the Schrader version (Harlin dissipates the power of the Nazi sequence by fragmenting it into flashbacks).

What is fascinating from a movie buff's point of view is that the movie has been filmed twice in different ways by different directors. Maybe this is what Gus Van Sant was getting at when he inexplicably did his (almost) shot-by-shot remake of Hitchcock's *Psycho.* Film students are often given a series of shots and assigned to edit them to tell a story. They can fit together in countless ways, to greater or less effect. Here we have the experiment conducted with $80 million.

It's eerie, to see the same locations occupied by different actors speaking similar dialogue. Odd to see the young priest and the doctor occupying the same rooms but played by different people. Strange to see Skarsgard in both versions, some shots and dialogue exactly the same, others not. Curious how the subplot about the British shrinks in the Harlin version, while the horror is ramped up. I prefer the Schrader version, certainly, but you know what? Now that two versions exist and are available, each one makes the other more interesting.

Domino ★ ★ ★

R, 128 m., 2005

Keira Knightley (Domino Harvey), Mickey Rourke (Ed Mosbey), Edgar Ramirez (Choco), Rizwan Abbasi (Alf), Ian Ziering (Himself), Brian Austin Green (Himself), Christopher Walken (Mark Heiss), Mena Suvari (Kimmie), Jacqueline Bisset (Sophie Wynn), Lucy Liu (Taryn Miles), Delroy Lindo (Claremont Williams), Mo'Nique (Lateesha Rodriguez), Macy Gray (Lashandra Davis), Shondrella Avery (Lashindra Davis), Tom Waits (The Drifter). Directed by Tony Scott and produced by Samuel Hadida and Scott. Screenplay by Richard Kelly and Steve Barancik.

A character in Tony Scott's *Domino* is described as having "the attention span of a ferret on crystal meth," and that pretty much describes the movie. Not many movies have two narrations, one written, one spoken, and not many require them. But the damned thing has its qualities, and one of them is a headlong, twisting energy, a vitality that finds comedy in carnage. Here we have a man whose arm is shot off because it has a combination tattooed on it, and thieves disguised as four recent first ladies.

The movie was inspired by Domino Harvey, a friend of Scott's who was named Bounty Hunter of the Year in 2003 and died in June 2005, perhaps of an overdose, only thirty-five years old. Her life was not merely stranger than fiction but almost beyond invention: The daughter of the movie star Laurence Harvey and the fashion model Paulene Stone, she was sent, as they say, to all the best schools. She worked at day jobs before becoming a bounty hunter—a professional paid to track down and deliver dangerous prey. "My agenda is to kick ass," she famously said, and she must have been good at it to win that honor, although the awards ceremony is a paltry affair of folding chairs in a bare room.

The movie is inspired by her story but not based on it, and although famous people filled her life, the names are all changed here, and just as well, because there are times when Scott and his writers, Richard Kelly and Steve Barancik, spin free of reality and enter a parallel universe of pulp fiction. Consider again that man whose arm is shot off and tossed around like a Frisbee. Surely it would be easier to simply look at his arm and note the combination in a PDA, instant messaging being so much more efficient than the transfer of body parts.

The plot exists at the intersection of crime and show business, which has long needed traffic signals. Domino (Keira Knightley, who won an Oscar nomination for *Pride and Prejudice*) sees an ad for a bounty-hunting course run by a bail bondsman named Claremont Williams (Delroy Lindo) and his top hunters, Ed Mosbey (Mickey Rourke) and Choco (Edgar Ramirez). They just want to collect the tuition, but she insists on being taken seriously.

Mosbey might be expected to resist working with an unseasoned sexpot, but no: "Take a look at her," he tells Choco. "Come on, man, she ain't ugly. We walk down the street and people call us losers. We add her to the equation and people are going to think we're two of the coolest mothers who have ever lived." Domino, as it turns out, is the coolest mother of all. In a situation where a bad guy seems inclined to start shooting, she distracts him with a lap dance. The things a sweet young British actress has to do when she moves from Jane Austen to Hollywood.

Oh, it gets stranger. Mosbey's team also includes Alf (Rizwan Abbasi), an Afghan who knows a lot about blowing things up and whose existence on the streets of Los Angeles is a rebuke to the dream of homeland security. Choco is a tough guy from El Salvador who is offended that anyone would speak English in L.A. Rourke, who with this film and *Sin City* has rehabilitated his iconic status, is so hardened at times he seems to be channeling Warren Oates.

The movie has so many supporting characters it's a good thing it's edited at MTV velocity, or just introducing them would be feature-length. The funniest and most possibly true to life is Mark Heiss (Christopher Walken), a TV producer and ferret. He hires the bounty-hunting team for a reality TV show and then mixes in the (real) stars Ian Ziering and Brian Austin Green of *Beverly Hills 90210*, setting up a scene where they introduce themselves to some killers: "We're the celebrity hostages." There's also Claremont's lover, Lateesha (Mo'Nique), whose job at the Department of Motor Vehicles gives her access to a database of basically everybody. Her twin cousins, Lashandra (Macy Gray) and Lashindra (Shondrella Avery), exist in part, I suspect, so that they can be called Lashandra and Lashindra by Lateesha, although the movie gives them plenty else to do. Worth the price of admission is the Jerry Springer show where Lateesha produces a chart to explain her theory of new American racial groups, including Blacktinos and Hispanese.

All of this happens outside of any reasonable chronology. The story leaps around in time and logic, subtitles explain who characters are and then later have to correct themselves, and Domino's own narration is intercut with her cross-examination by an FBI agent (Lucy Liu). Domino is not entirely certain what she can testify about, in part because she is evasive, in part because of that time in the desert when her coffee was spiked with mescaline and a prophet (Tom Waits) appeared, or seemed to appear, or something.

Did I admire *Domino?* In a sneaky way, yes.

It's fractured and maddening, but it's alive. It begins with the materials of a perfectly conventional thriller. It heeds Godard's rule that "all you need for a movie is a girl and a gun." It gives us Knightley in a role all the more astonishing because I've just seen her in *Pride and Prejudice.* It not only stars Rourke and Walken but also uses them instead of just gawking at them. It blows up a Las Vegas casino, and it's a real one, not a fictional one. And it contains the line "I'll never tell you what it all meant," as if anyone could. Seeking guidance in understanding the movie's manic narrative, I poked around online and discovered in one review the explanation that the movie "totally challenges the bourgeois notion of the nuclear family." Oh.

Donkey Skin ★ ★ ★

NO MPAA RATING, 100 m., 1970 (rereleased 2005)

Catherine Deneuve (Queen/Daughter), Jean Marais (King), Jacques Perrin (Prince), Micheline Presle (Red Queen), Delphine Seyrig (Fairy Godmother), Fernand Ledoux (Red King), Henri Cremieux (Doctor), Sacha Pitoeff (Minister), Pierre Repp (Thibaud), Jean Servais (Narrator). Directed by Jacques Demy, and produced by Mag Bodard. Screenplay by Demy, based on a story by Charles Perrault.

Donkey Skin is told with the simplicity and beauty of a child's fairy tale, but with emotional undertones and a surrealistic style that adults are more likely to appreciate. A child and a parent seeing this movie would experience two different films. It was directed by the French New Wave legend Jacques Demy in 1970 and is based on a seventeenth-century tale by Charles Perrault; it's one of his original Mother Goose stories, which also include *Cinderella* and *Sleeping Beauty.*

In adapting it into a musical, Demy was probably thinking of Jean Cocteau's surrealistic masterpiece *The Beauty and the Beast* (1946), and Demy's own famous musicals, *The Umbrellas of Cherbourg* (1964) and *The Young Girls of Rochefort* (1967). His *Donkey Skin* makes the connection by costarring Jean Marais, who played three roles in *The Beauty and the Beast,* and Catherine Deneuve, who had the lead in both of the earlier Demy films.

The story involves two neighboring kingdoms. In the land ruled by Marais, the palace servants and even the horses are bright blue, like a medieval tryout for the Blue Man Group. In the land next door, ruled by Fernand Ledoux, everyone is red. Their maps must look like the Bush-Kerry election.

Sorrow in the blue kingdom. The queen (Deneuve) is dying. On her deathbed she orders the king, "Promise me you'll marry only when you find a wife more beautiful than me." This is not easily done. A search begins for such a woman, but as the king examines the portraits of the candidates, each is more ugly than the one before. Finally his advisers decide only one woman qualifies: the king's own daughter, who is played by Catherine Deneuve and, therefore, bears a striking resemblance to her mother.

The king decrees he will marry his daughter. You are beginning to understand why Disney filmed *Sleeping Beauty* and *Cinderella* but not this one. There is also the remarkable detail that the kingdom's riches depend upon a donkey who, instead of manure, produces coins and jewels.

"Is my love a sin?" asks the blue king. "All little girls, asked who they want to marry when they grow up, say, 'I want to marry Daddy.'" Not this little girl, who escapes by boat and consults her fairy godmother (Delphine Seyrig), who suggests she make a series of impossible demands, such as a dress the color of weather. What color is weather? We find out when Deneuve appears in one of several remarkable gowns that are elegant and showy beyond any normal dimension, all but burying the princess inside.

After the king orders additional dresses the color of the moon and the sun, his daughter runs out of demands and escapes into the forest cloaked in a donkey skin. There she is seen by the prince of the red kingdom (Jacques Perrin), who falls in love and demands that his servants determine the identity of the unknown girl, etc.

To this story Demy brings a particular sense of style. A great deal of the dialogue is sung by the actors, with music by Michel Legrand, although the film doesn't approach his wall-to-wall score for *The Umbrellas of Cherbourg.* There are also incongruous elements I doubt were found in the seventeenth-century original, including a helicopter, a woman who spits toads, doorways so low everyone must stoop to get through them, and a royal throne that looks like Hello, Kitty! At times, characters fade in and out of transparency.

Despite these visual marvels, the film somehow lacks variety. It is all more or less the same; the same tone, similar songs, a level emotional field, nothing too exciting or too depressing. It requires, I hate to say it, an arc. Lacking that, it nevertheless provides a visual feast and fanciful imaginations, and Deneuve was then, as she was before and since, a great beauty with the confidence such beauty requires.

Note: This is a review of a restored print with new digital sound. Ebert's review of the Cocteau version of The Beauty and the Beast *is a Great Movie at rogerebert.com.*

Don't Come Knocking ★ ★ ½

R, 122 m., 2006

Sam Shepard (Howard Spence), Jessica Lange (Doreen), Tim Roth (Sutter), Gabriel Mann (Earl), Sarah Polley (Sky), Fairuza Balk (Amber), Eva Marie Saint (Howard's Mother). Directed by Wim Wenders and produced by Peter Schwartzkopff. Screenplay by Sam Shepard.

Does every moment of a movie have to work for you? Or can you enjoy an imperfect one if it fills in places around the edges of your imagination? *Don't Come Knocking* is a curious film about a movie cowboy who walks off the set, goes seeking his past, and finds something that looks a lot more like a movie than the one he was making. There are scenes that don't even pretend to work. And others have a sweetness and visual beauty that stop time and simply invite you to share.

The opening shot is the key. On a black screen, we see two openings into the sky. From how they're placed, they could be the eyeholes in a ragged mask, maybe the Lone Ranger's. Then the shot reveals itself as a rock formation in Monument Valley; millions of years of evolution have left behind these two holes, joined by arches to the walls of a long-ago river canyon.

We are looking into the past, and at icons of the movie western; such rock formations were a backdrop in the classic films of John Ford. But the movie being filmed is far from *Stagecoach.* The mobile homes of the filmmakers are arranged in a circle, like wagons, but instead of a horse the assistant director rides a Segway. The western being made is so bad in a retro Johnny Mack Brown way that maybe it's a satire.

But, no. It's supposed to be a real western, starring Howard Spence (Sam Shepard), a once-great western star, now disappearing into cocaine and booze after a lifetime of scandal. *Don't Come Knocking* was written by Shepard and directed by Wim Wenders; they wrote and directed the great *Paris, Texas* (1984). What they should know is that once-great stars do not disappear into bargain-basement versions of their earlier work but move laterally into independent films that use their presence as an icon. That's what's happening here: Shepard may be playing a pathetic has-been, but what he really brings is an actor and playwright who embodies western myth in modern dress. I suppose I have seen all of Shepard's work on the screen and have never caught him being less than authentic.

That's true here, even at times when his Howard Spence is like a little boy who never grew up. Now he simply walks away from the set. He calls the mother he hasn't seen in thirty years (Eva Marie Saint) and goes to see her in Elko, Nevada. He arrives not as if decades have passed, but as if he's late coming home after school. As mothers will, she pages through the scrapbook she's kept of her famous son, and we see stories about drugs, divorces, brawls, and box-office disasters.

She tells him of a son he has in Butte, Montana. He goes to Butte in search of this unknown child and finds the boy's mother working as a waitress. She is Doreen (Jessica Lange), still attractive, amused that this joke should have walked back into her life. He follows her into a bar. "If you're looking for your son," she says, "that's him, right there in front of you."

The son is Earl (Gabriel Mann), very good as an uncertain and mannered young would-be folk singer with a lot of resentment toward his father. His girlfriend, Amber (Fairuza Balk), like a lot of young women who affect a ferocious Goth look, is timid and affectionate underneath. Howard realizes he is being followed by another young woman. This is Sky (Sarah Polley), his daughter by yet another woman, whose ashes she is carrying in an urn.

These people move in intersecting orbits through Butte, a city that seems to have essentially no traffic, and no residents not in the movie except for a few tavern extras and restaurant customers. Consider a scene where the enraged Earl throws all of his possessions out the window of his second-story apartment and into the street. His stuff remains there, undisturbed, for days. No complaints from the neighbors. No cops. Howard Spence spends a night on the sofa, sleeping, thinking, and smoking. It's a lovely scene. After Howard's meditative night, he comes to a peace of sorts with his son and daughter, and they with each other. As this process takes place, they all seem outlined against their own mental horizons, as archetypes who represent something: a cowboy's last hurrah, a rebellious son's acceptance of his father, a lost daughter's opportunity to fabricate a funeral for her mother by going in search of the mourners.

The characters stand for so much, it's all they can do to bear the weight. Tim Roth is more realistic, as a tracer for the insurance company that holds a bond on the movie. His job is to track down Howard Spence and bring him back alive. This he does with such dispatch that he hardly seems aware he is interrupting a family drama.

The cinematography by Franz Lustig looks wonderful from beginning to end, but no shot equals one where we see Howard Spence sitting in a lonely hotel room window overlooking a desolate city street. Surely when they framed this shot, Wenders, Lustig, and Shepard were thinking of Edward Hopper crossed with "Main Line on Main Street," the famous photograph by O. Winston Link. The cinematography evokes a romantic and elegiac mood, within which the peculiarities of the characters may seem sillier than was intended.

Don't Come Knocking finally doesn't work for me because instead of embodying its themes, it seems to be regarding them from outside, with awe, as if it is the high school production of itself. The supporting characters are all genuine enough, but the central role of Howard Spence is a problem. He needs to be more heroic or more pathetic—I'm not sure which. His life seems to be lived outside his experience, as if someone else made all those headlines in his mother's scrapbook. "Nothing that happened back then happened," he says, summing up his life with one line that puts its finger directly on the character's biggest problem.

Doom ★

R, 104 m., 2005

Karl Urban (John Grimm [Reaper]), Rosamund Pike (Samantha Grimm), Raz Adoti (Duke), The Rock (Sarge), Deobia Oparei (Destroyer), Ben Daniels (Goat), Richard Brake (Portman), Al Weaver (The Kid), Yao Chin (Mac), Robert Russell (Dr. Carmack). Directed by Andrzej Bartkowiak and produced by John Wells and Lorenzo di Bonaventura. Screenplay by David Callaham and Wesley Strick.

Doom has one great shot. It comes right at the beginning. It's the Universal logo. Instead of a spinning Earth with the letters U-N-I-V-E-R-S-A-L rising in the east and centering themselves over Lebanon, Kansas, we see the red planet, Mars. Then we fly closer to Mars until we see surface details and finally the Olduvai Research Station, helpfully described on the movie's Web site as "a remote scientific facility on Mars"—where, if you give it but a moment's thought, all of the scientific facilities are remote.

Anyway, that's the last we see of the surface of Mars. A lot of readers thought I was crazy for liking *Ghosts of Mars* (2001) and *Red Planet* (2000) and *Total Recall* (1990), but blast it all, at least in those movies *you get to see Mars.* I'm a science fiction fan from way back. I go to Mars, I expect to see it. Watching *Doom* is like visiting Vegas and never leaving your hotel room.

The movie has been "inspired by" the famous video game. No, I haven't played it, and I never will, but I know how it feels *not* to play it, because I've seen the movie. *Doom* is like some kid came over and is using your computer and won't let you play.

The movie involves a group of Marines named the Rapid Response Tactical Squad, which if they would take only the slightest trouble could be renamed the Rapid Action Tactical Squad, which would acronym into RATS. The year is 2046. In the middle of an American desert has been discovered a portal to an ancient city on Mars. The Olduvai facility has been established to study it, and now there is a "breech of level 5 security," and the RRTS is sent to Mars through the portal to take care of business. The leader is Sarge (The Rock), and their members include Reaper (Karl Urban), Destroyer (Deobia Oparei), Mac (Yao Chin), Goat (Ben Daniels), Duke (Raz Adoti), Portman (Richard Brake), and The Kid (Al Weaver). Now you know everything you need to know about them.

On Mars, we see terrified humans running from an unseen threat. Dr. Carmack (Robert Russell) closes an automatic steel door on a young woman whose arm is onscreen longer than she is, if you get my drift, and then he spends a lot of time huddled in the corner vibrating and whimpering. We meet Samantha Grimm (Rosamund Pike), sister of Reaper (aka John Grimm). She is an anthropologist at the station and has reconstructed a complete skeleton of a humanoid Martian woman huddled protectively over her child. If you know your anthropology, you gotta say those are bones that have survived a lot of geological activity.

The original Martians were not merely humanoid, Dr. Grimm speculates, but superhuman: They bioengineered a twenty-fourth chromosome. We have twenty-three. The extra chromosome made them super smart, super strong, super fast, and super quick to heal. But it turned some of them into monsters, which presumably is why the others built the portal to Earth, where—what? They became us but left the twenty-fourth chromosome behind? Is that the kind of intelligent design we want our kids studying?

Despite all of her chromosome counting, Dr. Grimm says at another point: "Ten percent of the human genome has not yet been mapped. Some say it's the soul." Whoa! The Human Genome Project was completed in 2003, something you would think a scientist like Dr. Grimm should know. I am reminded of the astronauts in *Stealth* reminding each other what a prime number is.

The monsters are still there on Mars. They are big mothers and must have awesome daily caloric requirements. How they survive, how they breathe Earth atmosphere in the station, and what, as carnivores, they eat and drink—I think we can all agree these are questions deserving serious scientific study. Meanwhile, their pastime is chasing humans, grabbing them, smashing them, eviscerating and disemboweling them, pulling them through grates, and in general doing anything that can take place obscurely in shadows and not require a lot of special effects.

Toward the end of the movie, there is a lengthy point-of-view shot looking forward over the barrel of a large weapon as it tracks the corridors of the research station. Monsters jump out from behind things and are blasted to death, in a sequence that abandons all attempts at character and dialogue and uncannily resembles a video game. Later, when the names of the actors appear on the screen, they are also blasted into little pieces. I forget whether the director, Andrzej Bartkowiak, had his name shot to smithereens, but for the DVD I recommend that a monster grab it and eat it.

Dot the I ★ ★ ★

R, 92 m., 2005

Gael Garcia Bernal (Kit), Natalia Verbeke (Carmen), James D'Arcy (Barnaby), Tom Hardy (Tom), Charlie Cox (Theo). Directed by Matthew Parkhill and produced by George Duffield and Meg Thomson. Screenplay by Parkhill.

There is an ancient French tradition that on the night before her marriage, the bride-to-be can choose a handsome stranger and share with him one last kiss. If you have never heard of this tradition, neither have I, because it, along with a great deal else, was invented for this movie. *Dot the I* is like one of those nests of Chinese boxes within boxes. The outer box is a love story. There are times when we despair of ever reaching the innermost box.

An opening scene is set in a French restaurant in London, where Carmen (Natalia Verbeke), a Spanish dancer, is having a dinner with her girlfriends on the eve of her wedding. The maitre d' explains the ancient tradition, Carmen believes him, looks around the restaurant, and her eyes settle on Kit (Gael Garcia Bernal). She kisses him. This is interesting: The kiss continues longer than we would expect. They seem to want it to go on forever. They have so much chemistry it threatens to trespass upon biology.

Kit is from Brazil, an out-of-work actor. Since Bernal is in fact from Mexico, he could perfectly well speak Spanish, which is why he is made Brazilian and would speak Portuguese, so that he and his Spanish friend will have to talk for our convenience in English. Sometimes it is jolly, this neocolonialism. As for the title, we are told that "a kiss dots the 'I' on the word 'love,'" but not in English, obviously, or Spanish or Portuguese, either (they both use "amor"). Maybe in German ("liebe"). Or maybe, we eventually realize, not in this movie.

Although Carmen and Kit are obviously made for each other, Carmen persists in her plan to marry the rich but odious Barnaby (James D'Arcy). As *Dot the I* moves along, it becomes clear that there is very little, however, that this Barnaby would not do.

The opening hour of the movie is a wonderfully complicated love story, during which Carmen goes ahead with her plans to marry Barnaby, and Kit fails in his attempt to emulate Benjamin in *The Graduate* and interrupt the ceremony with a wild goat cry of love. But Kit is not easily discouraged. He finds out Carmen's name from her friends in the restaurant, and contacts her to ask if they can meet: "Just once! Just one glass of water! In a brightly lit public place! We don't even have to speak!" She has mercy on him.

What happens next it would be unfair to reveal, and perhaps impossible. The movie not only scatters undotted I's and uncrossed T's in its wake, but unsquared circles, unfactored primes, unrisen soufflés, and unconsummated consummations. Matthew Parkhill, who wrote and directed it, is not a man to deny us the fruits of his boundless, some would say excessive, invention.

Watching the movie, I went through several stages. I liked the first half perfectly well as a love story involving sympathetic people. I hoped they would find happiness out from under the cloud of the snarfy Barnaby. Then—well, there was a surprise, and I rather liked the surprise, too, because it put things in a new light and made everyone just that much more interesting. And then another surprise, and another, until . . .

The last ten or fifteen minutes are going to require a great deal of patience with the filmmakers, as they riffle through the plot like a riverboat gambler with aces up his wazoo. I suppose that in a logical way it all makes sense—except that there is no logical way that it would happen in the first place. Having been tricked into accepting the characters as people we can trust in and care for, we now discover their world is but a stage, and they but players on it. Psychological realism and emotional continuity be damned!

Am I unhappy because the concluding scenes in the movie rob me of my feelings about the characters, or because the earlier scenes created those feelings? Certainly the film would not be better if the first hour had been given over to game-playing. The ingenuity of the film is admirable, I suppose, although we walk out of the theater with perplexing questions about motives, means, access, and techniques.

So let us observe that good work is performed here by all three of the leading actors—Bernal, who is so likable he had better play a villain soon just to add some Tabasco; Verbeke, who is so touchingly torn between love and loyalty, and then between loyalty and love; and D'Arcy, who creates a truly scary two-faced personality. To keep their emotional bearings in this plot is no small achievement. And let us concede that Matthew Parkhill has at least not taken the easy way out. Yes, we'd prefer a straightforward love triangle without the bells and whistles, but that might turn out boring, while *Dot the I* keeps our attention even while stomping on it.

Downfall ★ ★ ★ ★

R, 155 m., 2005

Bruno Ganz (Adolf Hitler), Alexandra Maria Lara (Traudl Junge), Juliane Kohler (Eva Braun), Corinna Harfouch (Magda Goebbels), Thomas Kretschmann (Hermann Fegelein), Ulrich Matthes (Joseph Goebbels), Heino Ferch (Albert Speer), Christian Berkel (Dr. Schenck), Ulrich Noethen (Heinrich Himmler). Directed by

Oliver Hirschbiegel and produced by Bernd Eichinger. Screenplay by Eichinger, based on the book *Inside Hitler's Bunker* by Joachim Fest and the book *Bis zur letzten Stunde* by Traudl Junge and Melissa Muller.

Downfall takes place almost entirely inside the bunker beneath Berlin where Adolf Hitler and his inner circle spent their final days, and died. It ventures outside only to show the collapse of the Nazi defense of Berlin, the misery of the civilian population, and the burning of the bodies of Hitler, Eva Braun, and Joseph and Magda Goebbels. For the rest, it occupies a labyrinth of concrete corridors, harshly lighted, with a constant passage back and forth of aides, servants, guards, family members, and Hitler's dog, Blondi. I was reminded, oddly, of the claustrophobic sets built for *Das Boot,* which took place mostly inside a Nazi submarine.

Our entry to this sealed world is Traudl Junge (Alexandra Maria Lara), hired by Hitler as a secretary in 1942 and eyewitness to Hitler's decay in body and mind. She wrote a memoir about her experiences, which is one of the sources of this film, and *Blind Spot* (2002) was a documentary about her memories. In a clip at the end of *Downfall,* filmed shortly before her death, she says she now feels she should have known more than she did about the crimes of the Nazis. But like many secretaries the world over, she was awed by the power of her employer and not included in the information loop. Yet she could see, as anyone could see, that Hitler was a lunatic. Sometimes kind, sometimes considerate, sometimes screaming in fits of rage, but certainly cut loose from reality.

Against the overarching facts of his personal magnetism and the blind loyalty of his lieutenants, the movie observes the workings of the world within the bunker. All power flowed from Hitler. He was evil, mad, ill, but long after Hitler's war was lost he continued to wage it in fantasy. Pounding on maps, screaming ultimatums, he moved troops that no longer existed, issued orders to commanders who were dead, counted on rescue from imaginary armies.

That he was unhinged did not much affect the decisions of acolytes like Joseph and Magda Goebbels, who decided to stay with him and commit suicide as he would. "I do not want to live in a world without National Socialism," says Frau Goebbels, and she doesn't want her six children to live in one, either. In a sad, sickening scene, she gives them all a sleeping potion and then, one by one, inserts a cyanide capsule in their mouths and forces their jaws closed with a soft but audible crunch. Her oldest daughter, Helga, senses there is something wrong; senses, possibly, she is being murdered. Then Magda sits down to a game of solitaire before she and Joseph kill themselves. (By contrast, Heinrich Himmler wonders aloud, "When I meet Eisenhower, should I give the Nazi salute, or shake his hand?")

Hitler is played by Bruno Ganz, the gentle soul of *Wings of Desire,* the sad-eyed romantic or weary idealist of many roles over thirty years. Here we do not recognize him at first, hunched over, shrunken, his injured left hand fluttering behind his back like a trapped bird. If it were not for the 1942 scenes in which he hires Frau Junge as a secretary, we would not be able to picture him standing upright. He uses his hands as claws that crawl over battlefield maps, as he assures his generals that this or that impossible event will save them. And if not, well: "If the war is lost, it is immaterial if the German people survive. I will shed not one tear for them." It was his war, and they had let him down, he screams: betrayed him, lied to him, turned traitor.

Frau Junge and two other secretaries bunk in a small concrete room, and sneak away to smoke cigarettes, which Hitler cannot abide. Acting as a hostess to the death watch, his mistress, Eva Braun (Juliane Kohler), presides over meals set with fine china and crystal. She hardly seems to engage Hitler except as a social companion. Although we have heard his rants and ravings about the Jews, the Russians, his own treacherous generals, and his paranoid delusions, Braun is actually able to confide to Junge, toward the end: "He only talks about dogs and vegetarian meals. He doesn't want anyone to see deep inside of him." Seeing inside of him is no trick at all: He is flayed bare by his own rage.

Downfall was one of 2005's Oscar nominees for Best Foreign Film. It has inspired much debate about the nature of the Hitler it presents. Is it a mistake to see him, after all, not as a monster standing outside the human race, but as just another human being?

David Denby, the *New Yorker*: "Considered as biography, the achievement (if that's the right word) of *Downfall* is to insist that the monster was not invariably monstrous—that he was kind to his cook and his young female secretaries, loved his German shepherd, Blondi, and was surrounded by loyal subordinates. We get the point: Hitler was not a supernatural being; he was common clay raised to power by the desire of his followers. But is this observation a sufficient response to what Hitler actually did?"

Stanley Kauffman, the *New Republic*: "Ever since World War II, it has been clear that a fiction film could deal with the finish of Hitler and his group in one of two ways: either as ravening beasts finally getting the fate they deserved or as consecrated idealists who believed in what they had done and were willing to pay with their lives for their actions. The historical evidence of the behavior in the bunker supports the latter view .... *Downfall*, apparently faithful to the facts, evokes—torments us with—a discomfiting species of sympathy or admiration."

Admiration I did not feel. Sympathy I felt in the sense that I would feel it for a rabid dog, while accepting that it must be destroyed. I do not feel the film provides "a sufficient response to what Hitler actually did," because I feel no film can, and no response would be sufficient. All we can learn from a film like this is that millions of people can be led, and millions more killed, by madness leashed to racism and the barbaric instincts of tribalism.

What I also felt, however, was the reality of the Nazi sickness, which has been distanced and diluted by so many movies with so many Nazi villains that it has become more like a plot device than a reality. As we regard this broken and pathetic Hitler, we realize that he did not alone create the Third Reich, but was the focus for a spontaneous uprising by many of the German people, fueled by racism, xenophobia, grandiosity, and fear. He was skilled in the ways he exploited that feeling, and surrounded himself with gifted strategists and propagandists, but he was not a great man, simply one armed by fate to unleash unimaginable evil. It is useful to reflect that racism, xenophobia, grandiosity, and fear are still with us, and the defeat of one of their manifestations does not inoculate us against others.

Down in the Valley ★ ★ ½

R, 125 m., 2006

Edward Norton (Harlan), Evan Rachel Wood (Tobe), David Morse (Wade), Bruce Dern (Charlie), Rory Culkin (Lonnie). Directed by David Jacobson and produced by Holly Wiersma, Edward Norton, and Adam Rosenfelt. Screenplay by Jacobson.

A carload of teenage girls on their way to the beach stop at a gas station, and one of them likes the look of the attendant, an older guy with bad-boy charm. She invites him along. He quits his job and jumps in the car. He says he's from South Dakota and has never seen the ocean. We don't know whether to believe that, or much of anything else he says, but she believes him, and so will her younger brother.

That's the setup for *Down in the Valley*, a movie that the actors and director take as far as they can until the story bogs down in questions too big to forgive. The first half is pitch-perfect, as Tobe (Evan Rachel Wood), who is eighteen, falls under the spell of Harlan (Edward Norton), who is thirtysomething but not quite grown up, or all there. He thinks of himself as a cowboy, loves that ten-gallon hat, takes her horseback riding, and gets into a dispute over whether the horse was stolen or only borrowed. He has a lot of misunderstandings like that.

Tobe lives in an ordinary house in the San Fernando Valley with her dad, Wade (David Morse), and thirteen-year-old brother, Lonnie (Rory Culkin). Wade works as a corrections officer but doesn't bring his work home with him: He is a careless parent who makes a big show of supervising his children but seems unaware that Harlan enters his daughter's bedroom at will. When Harlan meets him for the first time, he delivers one of those sincere, forthright speeches about wanting to treat the daughter with respect and earn the trust of the father, etc. Norton is such a nuanced actor that he simultaneously makes this speech sound like the absolute truth and a bald-faced lie.

Tobe is fascinated by Harlan, by his cowboy act, by his posturing, by his (or somebody's) horse, and by the sex. But she isn't dumb, and she grows disturbed about some of the things she senses. Her kid brother, Lonnie, on the other hand, is angry with his father and ready to fall for Harlan's line, and that leads to some closing scenes that plain don't work. Wade, having been absent or inattentive at crucial moments, becomes obsessed with hunting down Harlan after the "cowboy" gets into the big trouble that we've been expecting since the first scene. The chase actually leads to the movie set of a Western town, which is not merely symbolism, or even Symbolism, but SYMBOLISM!

The ending is a mess, but the film has qualities that make me happy to have seen it. I like the peculiar loneliness of Harlan's life; he lives in the Valley as if it were the old West, he haunts hillsides and wooded areas, he hides under culverts, he conceals from Tobe the fact that, apart from her, he has no resources at all. At the end, even if he's crazy, he's consistent.

And the performances can't be faulted. Norton finds that line dividing madness from plausibility and reminds me a little of how Treat Williams talks to Laura Dern in *Smooth Talk* (1985), permanently destroying her illusions. Wood, who starred in *Thirteen,* a similar story about teenagers out of control, is fascinating in the way she wills herself to believe what cannot be true. There's a little of *Kwik Stop* (2001) in Tobe's desire to escape from her life. And Culkin is convincing when he chooses the cowboy over his strict father, but the screenplay maintains his decision long after he should abandon it. Morse finds a difficult note, as a father who wants to love and protect his children but whose mind seems elsewhere and whose common sense is lacking.

All of these qualities are worthy. But when a movie begins to present one implausible or unwise decision after another, when its world plays too easily into the hands of its story, when the taste for symbolism creates impossible scenes, we grow restless. The movie has stopped being about its characters and has started being about its concept, stranding them in ideas instead of lives.

Dreamer ★ ★ ★

PG, 98 m., 2005

Kurt Russell (Ben Crane), Dakota Fanning (Cale Crane), Kris Kristofferson (Pop Crane), Elisabeth Shue (Lily Crane), Luis Guzman (Balon), Freddy Rodriguez (Manolin), David Morse (Palmer), Oded Fehr (Prince Sadir). Directed by John Gatins and produced by Hunt Lowry, Mike Tollin, and Brian Robbins. Screenplay by Gatins.

One of the most important stories in *Sports Illustrated*'s history was written by William Nack, the great writer, about horses and boxing. Nack grew up around racetracks and served in Vietnam, and when he returned noticed something new: A lot of horses were breaking down. In earlier years, it was rare for a horse to break a leg during a race. His investigation met a wall of silence, until one vet talked to him off the record, confirming his suspicions: Owners were using cortisone to deaden the pain of horses that should not be racing, and the broken bones were the result.

When a racehorse breaks a leg on the track, the horse is invariably put down. Nack's story "Breakdowns" told of the death of one such filly. I heard Nack read it once, at a signing for his book *My Turf,* and people in the audience were crying. The movie *Dreamer* is based on a true story of the unthinkable: a horse that broke a bone and came back to race again. She was Mariah's Storm, winner of the 1995 Turfway Breeder's Cup.

The movie is a well-made use of familiar materials, including the loyalty between a child and a horse that goes back to *National Velvet* (1944) and *The Black Stallion* (1979). It's aimed at an audience of teenagers that may never have heard of those films, and for them, *Dreamer* will be an exciting experience. It has a first-rate cast: Dakota Fanning as young Cale Crane, Kurt Russell as her father, Ben, and Kris Kristofferson as her grandfather, Pop.

Ben is a trainer for the rich and supercilious Palmer (David Morse). He likes the prospects of a filly named Sonador, which is Spanish for "dreamy"—close enough to Dreamer, especially since the title refers to Cale. She's at the track one day when her dad tells Palmer he doesn't think Sonador should run: "She doesn't want to race today." Palmer overrules him, the horse runs, and she breaks a leg.

Ben later admits, "If Cale hadn't have been with me that night, I'd have left that horse on the track." But Cale is there, and looking at her big sad eyes, her father has the leg splinted and wrapped, and brings the horse back to the stable. This inspires an argument with Palmer, who is forced to regard the results of his own bad judgment. Ben resigns, taking a payout—and the horse.

This is not something he can afford to do. Their farm, which is already "the only horse farm in Lexington, Kentucky, without any horses," is facing foreclosure. But Sonador mends, and Ben and Pop think maybe she can be bred. That's before Cale gives Sonador her head one day, and the two men watch Cale and the horse flying across the turf.

"We could see if she perks up in a real race," Ben says, almost to himself.

"Could be easy money," says Pop.

This is a long conversation for them, since they weren't on speaking terms, Pop living on his own in a cabin on the property. The saga of Sonador has broken the ice, and now they're talking together and daring to dream. As for Cale, she knows the horse can run and win. And Pop is right: There would be long odds on a horse making a comeback after an injury.

What happens next I will leave for you to discover, including the subplot involving the two Arab brothers who are rival horse owners. What is central is young Fanning's performance, as a mite of a girl who stands up to be counted. Fanning, it is said, appears in every third movie nowadays; she's busy, all right, but that's because she's good, and here she plays Cale as a girl who has watched horses and trainers and has grown up around the track, and who tempers her sentiment for Sonador with an instinct that the horse has more race left in her.

They say girls discover horses right before they discover boys. Whether that represents progress is a question every parent of a teenager must sometimes ponder, but certainly any girl in the target age group is going to make *Dreamer* one of her favorite films. For adults, the movie offers the appeal of solid, understated performances by Russell, Kristofferson, and Morse, whose villain doesn't gnash but simply calculates heartlessly. And then of course there is the horse racing. If your horse might win but might break the same leg again, you have so much riding on the race that the odds don't really come into it.

Duane Hopwood ★ ★ ★ ½

R, 83 m., 2005

David Schwimmer (Duane Hopwood), Janeane Garofalo (Linda), Judah Friedlander (Anthony), Susan Lynch (Gina), Dick Cavett (Fred), Steve Schirripa (Steve), Jerry Grayson (Carl), Bill Buell (Wally), John Krasinski (Bob Flynn). Directed by Matt Mulhern and produced by Melissa Marr, Lemore Syvan, and Marc Turtletaub. Screenplay by Mulhern.

Duane Hopwood is the portrait of a man who loves his wife, loves his children, knows how to be a good father, and is losing everything because of alcoholism. The movie is a wise and realistic portrait of the disease, showing the drunk not as a colorful or tragic character but simply as a sad man whose days occasionally contain moments of joy and hope. He is not without friends. People care for him. His wife is not heartless, but after he drives drunk with one of their daughters in the backseat, she goes into divorce court. She has given up hope about his drinking; she needs to protect her kids and cut her losses.

Duane is played by David Schwimmer in one of those performances that transform the way we think about an actor. *Friends* was a beloved show, but like all popular shows it fixes its actors in our minds; their TV characters are like ghosts standing beside every other role they play. No one stands beside Duane Hopwood, who is all by himself on those lonely winter mornings in Atlantic City, riding his bicycle home from his job as a pit boss in the casinos—a bicycle, because his license has been revoked.

The movie has so many things right. It understands that alcoholics reach a point where their friends are mostly other people on the same drinking schedule. They date out of bars because that is where they meet people. On Thanksgiving they cannot go home because they no longer have one but are invited to dinner at the homes of friends, where they feel even more spectacularly alone.

It knows this, too: that alcoholics don't think they're alcoholics. "I'm not a drunk," they say. Sure, they *get* drunk, but that's what they do, not what they are. What's a drunk, anyway? Some bum under a bridge with a pint in a brown paper bag? Duane has endangered a daughter he loves, lost a family he cherishes, been through traffic and divorce court, and yet cannot stop himself from going to a bar after work. Sometimes he drinks way too much. Sometimes he drinks too much. Sometimes he drinks almost too much. Sometimes he doesn't drink enough. Those are the only four "sometimes" for an alcoholic.

Duane Hopwood is not, however, a movie about drinking, and it lacks spectacular scenes of colorful alcoholism. It is more about waking up at the wrong time of day, working through a hangover, having times when your good essential nature shines through, and hating it that the woman who loves you now loves someone else because she must.

As Linda, his wife, Janeane Garofalo is precise and kind, caring for the man she married, not wanting to hurt him, but too wise to share his disease. There could be spectacular scenes of overacting and souped-up drama in their relationship, but unless the drunk is also violent, those rarely happen; it is more sadness and loss, with an occasional moment of acting out, as in the baseball bat scene, where the drunk is playing a confused role generated by his murky grief.

Duane has a few close friends. One is Carl (Jerry Grayson), his boss at the casino, who likes him and wants to help him. But Duane makes a stupid mistake on the job, and Carl has to deal with that. How he does this is more human (and probably more accurate) than what we expect from casino bosses in the movies. Another friend is Anthony (Judah Friedlander), a security guard who dreams of becoming a stand-up comic. He wants to become Duane's roommate because they can share rent and he will be closer to the casino and won't have to live with his mother anymore. One of the danger signals of alcoholism that Ann Landers never listed in her columns is when you get a roommate because he needs to save on rent and move out from his mother's house, and you are both over forty.

Then there are Fred and Wally (Dick Cavett and Bill Buell), the neighbors who invite Duane over for Thanksgiving. They are good souls, gay, I suppose, who in a quiet way see Duane in need and are kind to him. And there is Gina (Susan Lynch), the bartender Duane is dating. Like many alcoholics, even his dating is about himself, and he cannot help telling her, "I still love Linda." He doesn't want a lover; he wants a confessor.

Yes, he goes to one AA meeting, which is filled with people who look at him and know exactly who he is and what he's going through. He's there, he says, because "the judge thought it might be a good idea," even though "I don't really have a problem." Uh-huh. "In our experience," a guy tells him, "most of the people who come through that door have a problem."

Duane Hopwood, written and directed by Matt Mulhern, is a wise and touching film with a lot of love in it. I may have given the wrong impression: It's not entirely about drinking, but it's entirely about a drinker. He does other things. Shares joyful little moments with his girls. Wears a turkey suit when he is actually sober. Has a dead-on conversation with "Jogger Bob" (John Krasinski), his ex-wife's new boyfriend, who lectures the youngest daughter on how she is fat. Duane may be screwed up, but he knows that for Mommy's new boyfriend to tell a little girl she is fat is not a smart thing.

The quality of this movie is in its observation. The filmmaker Mulhern and Schwimmer, Garofalo, and the other actors have real lives and experiences in mind. *Duane Hopwood* shows ordinary days in ordinary lives. Its hero is a man who grieves for the loss of his happiness and does not know he should grieve for the loss of himself. Nobody has left him. He has gone away, into that place between himself and the next drink. That's where he lives. Everywhere else, he's only visiting. But he doesn't have a problem.

The Duchess of Langeais ★ ★ ★ ½

NO MPAA RATING, 138 m., 2008

Jeanne Balibar (Antoinette de Langeais), Guillaume Depardieu (Armand de Montriveau),

Bulle Ogier (Princesse de Blamont-Chauvry), Michel Piccoli (Vidame de Pamiers), Barbet Schroeder (Duc de Grandlieu), Anne Cantineau (Clara de Serizy). Directed by Jacques Rivette and produced by Martine Marignac and Maurice Tinchant. Screenplay by Pascal Bonitzer and Christine Laurent, based on the novel by Honore de Balzac.

The lovers in *The Duchess of Langeais* never consummate their love, but it consummates them. The film is about two elegant aristocrats whose stubborn compulsions eat them alive. They're bullheaded to the point of madness. Their story is told with a fair amount of passion, but it's interior passion, bottled up, carrying them to a point far beyond what either one expects or desires.

The director is Jacques Rivette, one of the founders of the French New Wave, here giving himself over to a deliberate style that intensifies the impact of his fairly simple story. He begins in the 1820s with Armand, the marquis of Montriveau (Guillaume Depardieu), a general whose battlefield exploits have made him a national hero. At a ball, Armand sees the celebrated Antoinette, the duchess of Langeais (Jeanne Balibar), and approaches her with unmistakable designs. She agrees to be visited by him. At his own door that evening, he exalts to himself: "The duchess of Langeais is my mistress!" That she is married never really figures in the story; her husband exists only as a throwaway line, and when she eventually locks herself up with a cloistered order of nuns, who knows if he was even consulted? (Now there's a conversation-stopper: Q: "How is your wife, Duke?" A: "Still cloistered with those nuns.")

The relationship between Armand and Antoinette takes place mostly at arm's length, on sofas in her rooms, which follow one after another, leading us more deeply into her chamber of secrets. Through these rooms and others, the characters walk on hardwood floors, their sharp footfalls creating a harsh counterpoint to their words of yearning and rejection. The marquis desires to possess the duchess. Such is only natural for a national hero. She does not intend to be touched, but refuses in such an alluring way that he is left with hope. Their conversations take months, during which the marquis gradually loses his temper, starts shouting at her, and one night even has her abducted and taken to his rooms, where he threatens to brand her with a red-hot iron.

If he were a rapist, all would be over, but he is not. What's her game, anyway? She invites him back again and again, makes it clear she will always be home to him after eight, and teases him by demanding more stories about his journey across the burning sands of the desert. After the end of each episode, she rises and goes to attend a ball. We see her at one of these affairs, where she could not be more remote and disdainful of the company if she were an automaton.

The story is eventually one of merciless teasing. The duchess has an aged relative, played by the great Michel Piccoli, who warns her: "Avoid, my dear duchess, getting too coquet with such a man." Armand is an eagle, he says, and will lose patience and snatch her away to his aerie. Still she leads Armand on. He asks to kiss the hem of her garment.

"I think so much of you," she says. "I will give you my hand."

He kisses it through the hem and asks, "Will you always think so much of me?"

"Yes, but we will leave it at that."

Adapted from a novel by Balzac, the movie makes much use of intertitles, one of which reads: "If the previous scene is the civil period of this sentimental war, the following is the religious one." I assume these are Balzac's words. The film opens with religion, as Armand recognizes her singing voice in the invisible choir of the cloistered convent on Majorca. It ends there, too, as one of his comrades unforgettably says (and read no further to avoid inescapable conclusions), "She was a woman. Now she is nothing. Let's tie a ball to each foot and throw her into the sea."

Will you like this film? The everyday moviegoer will find it as impenetrable as its heroine. But if you vibrate to nuances of style, if you enjoy tension gathering strength beneath terrible restraint, if you admire great acting, then you will. You might also notice Rivette's subtle design touches, with furniture, costumes, and candles.

Guillaume Depardieu, son of Gerard, plays the marquis as a tall, physically imposing figure who is gradually made the psychological captive of the duchess. And Jeanne Balibar, as Antoinette, makes the heroine into a real piece of work. Surely she knows she is driving this man mad and destroying herself. Why does she persist? Because she cannot help herself? Or because, sadistically, she knows that she can?

Duck Season ★ ★ ★

R, 85 m., 2006

Diego Catano (Moko), Daniel Miranda (Flama), Danny Perea (Rita), Enrique Arreola (Ulises). Directed by Fernando Eimbcke and produced by Christian Valdelievre. Screenplay by Eimbcke.

Not very much really happens in *Duck Season*, but in its rich details, it remembers how absorbing and endless every single day can seem when you're fourteen. It takes place mostly inside an apartment in a Mexican urban high-rise, where best friends Moko and Flama (Diego Catano and Daniel Miranda) are left alone one Sunday with a big bottle of Coke and a video game. The Coke they share with great care, and the game (Bush vs. bin Laden) they employ for counterfeit excitement. They're kids killing time.

Then the next act in their lives opens. Rita (Danny Perea) knocks on the door. She says she's sixteen but looks older. She wants to use their oven to cook herself a birthday cake. She claims her own stove doesn't work. Maybe, or maybe she wants company. She moves into the kitchen and then into their conversations. The younger teens imply more than they're ready to say, and the older one less than she means. In such a way does emotional information float across the river of time.

To describe the actions in the film would be a mistake, both because they should happen to you in your own time, and because the movie isn't about what happens but about how it happens and why, and you shouldn't look for really deep hows and whys. One of the things I enjoyed was the way no phony melodrama is cooked up; it's the meandering quality of the material that makes it feel real. The movie invests in these lives enough that when characters are simply sitting on the sofa and staring into space, we're not staring at them but with them.

Episodes. There's a little speculative flirtation. They order a pizza. There is an argument about whether it should be free because Ulises (Enrique Arreola), the delivery boy, misses the advertised deadline. You can make whatever you want from the symbolism of his name—not too much, I hope. Now there are four people in the apartment, and several dogs, which are present in spirit.

The two boys are best friends. The two older characters are both among strangers. None of these characters has any place better to go or anything better to do, and when magic ingredients appear in the brownies, it's no big deal; it simply enhances the ennui, making it Ennui!

I was reminded of another and better film, Hirokazu Kore-Eda's *Nobody Knows* (2004), the Japanese film about four siblings who are abandoned by their mother and shift for themselves in an apartment for several months. Both movies have perfect pitch when it comes to watching kids pass time: They don't kill it so much as toy with it. *Duck Season* is shot in black and white, which is a good choice, because color might enhance an experience that is intended to seem no more than it is.

Yes, some of the dialogue is funny. One or two developments are a surprise. But not real funny, and not a big surprise. When the dispute with the pizza man comes up, it's not so much about the money, more about their gratitude for something to argue about. The title of the movie comes from a painting hanging on the wall of the apartment, the kind of painting that nobody ever buys, but that walls seem to acquire. It shows ducks in flight. Perhaps the migration of the ducks foretells the lives of these four young people who are about to take flight. "Whither, midst falling dew,/While glow the heavens with the last steps of day,/Far, through their rosy depths, dost thou pursue/Thy solitary way?" Sister Rosanne promised us if we memorized a poem we would use it someday. It looks like she was right.

The Dukes of Hazzard ★

PG-13, 105 m., 2005

Seann William Scott (Bo Duke), Johnny Knoxville (Luke Duke), Jessica Simpson (Daisy

Duke), Burt Reynolds (Boss Hogg), Willie Nelson (Uncle Jesse), M. C. Gainey (Sheriff Coltrane), Lynda Carter (Pauline). Directed by Jay Chandrasekhar and produced by Bill Gerber. Screenplay by John O'Brien.

The Dukes of Hazzard is a comedy about two cousins who are closer'n brothers, and their car, which is smarter'n they are. It's a retread of a sitcom that ran from about 1979 to 1985, years during which I was able to find better ways to pass my time. Yes, it is still another TV program I have never, ever seen. As this list grows, it provides more and more clues about why I am so smart and cheerful.

The movie stars Johnny Knoxville, from *Jackass*, Seann William Scott, from *American Wedding*, and Jessica Simpson, from Mars. Judging by her recent conversation on TV with Dean Richards, Simpson is so remarkably uninformed that she should sue the public schools of Abilene, Texas, or maybe they should sue her. On the day he won his seventh Tour de France, not many people could say, as she did, that they had no idea who Lance Armstrong was.

Of course, you don't have to be smart to get into *The Dukes of Hazzard*. But people like Willie Nelson and Burt Reynolds should have been smart enough to stay out of it. Here is a lamebrained, outdated wheeze about a couple of good ol' boys who roar around the back roads of the South in the General Lee, their beloved 1969 Dodge Charger. As it happens, I also drove a 1969 Dodge Charger. You could have told them apart because mine did not have a Confederate flag painted on the roof.

Scott and Knoxville play Bo Duke and Luke Duke; the absence of a Puke Duke is a sadly missed opportunity. They deliver moonshine manufactured by their Uncle Jesse (Willie Nelson) and depend on the General to outrun the forces of Sheriff Roscoe P. Coltrane (M. C. Gainey). The movie even has one of those obligatory scenes where the car is racing along when there's a quick cut to a gigantic Mack truck, its horn blasting as it bears down on them. They steer out of the way at the last possible moment. That giant Mack truck keeps busy in the movies, turning up again and again during chase scenes and always just barely missing the car containing the heroes, but this is the first time I have seen it making 60 mph down a single-lane dirt track.

Jessica Simpson plays Daisy Duke, whose short shorts became so famous on TV that they were known as "Daisy Dukes." She models them to a certain effect in a few brief scenes but is missing from most of the movie. Maybe she isn't even smart enough to wear shorts. I learn from the Internet that Simpson has a dog named Daisy, but I have been unable to learn if she named it before or after being signed for the role, and whether the dog is named after the character, the shorts, the flower, or perhaps (a long shot) Daisy Duck.

The local ruler is Boss Jefferson Davis Hogg (Burt Reynolds), "the meanest man in Hazzard County," who issues orders to the sheriff and everybody else and who has a secret plan to strip-mine the county and turn it into a wasteland. I wonder if there were moments when Reynolds reflected that, karmawise, this movie was the second half of what *Smokey and the Bandit* was the first half of.

There are a lot of scenes in the movie where the General is racing down back roads at high speeds and becomes airborne, leaping across ditches, rivers, and suchlike, miraculously without breaking the moonshine bottles. Surely if you have seen, say, twelve scenes of a car flying through the air, you are not consumed by a need to see twelve more.

There is a NASCAR race in the film and some amusing dialogue about car sponsorship. You know the film is set in modern times because along with Castrol and Coke, one of the car sponsors is Yahoo! I noted one immortal passage of dialogue, about a charity that is raising money for "one of the bifidas." I was also amused by mention of *The Al Unser Jr. Story*, an "audiobook narrated by Laurence Fishburne."

The movie has one offensive scene, alas, that doesn't belong in a contemporary comedy. Bo and Luke are involved in a mishap that causes their faces to be blackened with soot, and then, wouldn't you know, they drive into an African-American neighborhood, where their car is surrounded by ominous young men who are not amused by blackface, or by the Confederate flag painted on the car. I was hoping maybe the boyz n the hood would carjack the General, which would provide a fresh twist to the story, but no, the scene sinks into the mire of its own despond.

Duma ★ ★ ★ ½

PG, 100 m., 2005

Alex Michaeletos (Xan), Eamonn Walker (Ripkuna), Campbell Scott (Peter), Hope Davis (Kristin). Directed by Carroll Ballard and produced by Stacy Cohen, E. K. Gaylord II, Kristin Harms, Hunt Lowry, and John Wells. Screenplay by Karen Janszen and Mark St. Germain, based on the book *How It Was with Dooms* by Carol Cawthra Hopcraft and Xan Hopcraft.

The twelve-year-old boy helped raise the cheetah after he and his father found it as a cub. The boy, named Xan, lives on a farm in South Africa, where he and Duma form a strong bond, but their friendship cannot last forever. An emergency forces the family to move to the city, and Xan realizes that Duma, now fully grown, should be returned to the wild.

There might be reasonable ways of doing that. Perhaps Xan (Alex Michaeletos) could call the animal welfare people. Instead, without telling his mother (Hope Davis), he decides to personally return Duma to the wilderness. There is a scene of the cheetah riding in the sidecar of an old motorcycle, which Xan drives into the desert. It could be a cute scene, maybe funny, in a different kind of movie, but *Duma* takes itself seriously and is not a cute children's story but a grand tale of adventure.

Xan has courage but not a lot of common sense. He is headed into the Kalahari Desert, where to get lost is, usually, to die. Of course the motorcycle runs out of gas. Then he meets another wanderer in the desert, named Ripkuna (Eamonn Walker), who once worked in the mines of Johannesburg but now prefers to work alone, perhaps for reasons we would rather not know. He warns Xan of the dangers ahead ("That is a place of many teeth, my friend; that is a place to die"). He has the knowledge to save the boy and the cheetah. But what is his agenda?

Duma is an astonishing film by Carroll Ballard, the director who is fascinated by the relationship between humans, animals, and the wilderness. He works infrequently, but unforgettably. Perhaps you have seen his *The Black Stallion* (1979), about a boy and a horse who are shipwrecked and begin a friendship that leads to a crucial horse race. Or his *Never Cry Wolf* (1983), based on the Farley Mowat book about a man who goes to live in the wild with wolves. Or the wonderful *Fly Away Home* (1996), about a thirteen-year-old girl who solos in an ultralight aircraft, leading a flock of pet geese south from Canada.

The wolf and geese stories were, incredibly, based on fact. So, perhaps even more incredibly, is *Duma*. There really were a boy and a cheetah, written about in the book *How It Was with Dooms* by Xan Hopcraft and his mother, Carol Cawthra Hopcraft. Even more to the point: This movie shows a real boy and a real cheetah (actually, four cheetahs were used). There are no special effects. The cheetah is not digitized. What we see on the screen is what is happening, and that lends the film an eerie intensity. Animals are fascinating when they are free to be themselves; when they are manipulated by CGI into cute little actors who behave on cue, what's the point?

How is this film possible? There are shots showing a desert empty to the horizon, except for the boy and the cheetah. No doubt handlers are right there out of camera range, ready to act in an emergency, but it is clear the filmmakers and the boy trust the animals they are working with.

True, cheetahs are a special kind of big cat; Wikipedia informs us, "Because cheetahs are far less aggressive than other big cats, cubs are sometimes sold as pets." Yes, but a pet that can, as Xan tells his dad (Campbell Scott), "outrun your Porsche." A pet that is a carnivore. It would seem that Duma can be trusted, but as W. G. Sebald once observed, "Men and animals regard each other across a gulf of mutual incomprehension."

And if Duma can be trusted, can the African man, Ripkuna? Where is he leading them? He must know that a reward has been posted for the missing boy and that a tame cheetah can be sold for a good amount of money. While these questions circle uneasily in our minds, *Duma* creates scenes of wonderful adventure. The stalled motorcycle is turned into a wind-driven land yacht. A raft trip on a river involves rapids and crocodiles. The cheetah itself plays a role in their survival. And the movie takes on an additional depth because Xan is not a cute one-dimensional "family movie" child, and Ripkuna is freed from the usual clichés about noble and helpful wanderers. These are characters free to hold surprises in the real world.

Watching this movie, absorbed by its storytelling, touched by its beauty, fascinated by the bond between the boy and the animal, I was also astonished by something else: The studio does not know if it is commercial! The most dismal stupidities can be inflicted on young audiences, but let a family movie come along that is ambitious and visionary, and distributors lose confidence. It's as if they fear some movies are better than the audience can handle.

Duma is an extraordinary film, and intelligent younger viewers in particular may be enthralled by it.

Dust to Glory ★ ★ ★

PG, 97 m., 2005

With appearances by Mario Andretti, Sal Fish, James Garner, Ricky Johnson, Chad McQueen, Steve McQueen, Jimmy N. Roberts, and Malcolm Smith. A documentary directed by Dana Brown and produced by Mike "Mouse" McCoy and Scott Waugh.

Let's be sure we have this right. The Baja 1000 is the world's longest nonstop point-to-point race. It has more than a dozen categories of vehicles, from $2 million racing cars to motorcycles to unmodified pre-1972 VW Beetles. The course changes every year. You can leave the course and take a shortcut, but that way you might miss one of the secret checkpoints. The race includes both dirt back roads and Mexican highways. The highways are not blocked to civilian traffic during the event, and the racers have to weave in and out of ordinary traffic. Oh, and they could get stopped by the highway police.

Dust to Glory tells the story of the 2003 running of this legendary race, which offers glory but not much money; they can't even sell tickets, since the fans essentially just walk over to the edge of the road and watch the cars go by. And yet the Baja 1000 attracts stars like Mario Andretti and Parnelli Jones, and in years past, celebrities like James Garner and Steve McQueen.

The documentary was directed by Dana Brown, son of Bruce *(The Endless Summer)* Brown, who uses some fifty cameras, including lightweight digital cameras mounted on cars and motorcycles. That's helpful because there is no one place to stand in order to get a good idea of the entire race, especially since each category of vehicle is dispatched separately—the fastest cars, trucks, and motorcycles first, the Beetles last. There is a ham radio operator who keeps in touch with the checkpoints, provides weather reports, reports accidents, and communicates with the drivers' support teams, but he looks less like Command Central than like a guy in a hut on a hill with some stuff from Radio Shack.

The record time for the race is sixteen hours. There is a winner in every category. You have to finish in thirty-two hours, and in this race, to finish at all is a victory. Most of the teams have two or three drivers, but the movie's star (maybe because he is also the coproducer) is Mike "Mouse" McCoy, a motorcycle racing legend who plans to drive solo, nonstop, for all 1,000 miles.

Since the race runs through the night and passes areas where fine silt makes a dust cloud that limits visibility, this is a dangerous thing to do, but then the Baja 1000 is dangerous anyway: not least for the spectators, who seem to stand awfully close to hairpin turns where vehicles can spin out. Miraculously, only one person was killed in 2003—a spectator hit by a motorcycle belonging not to a racer, but to another spectator, who was driving the wrong way on the course.

There is a kind of madness involved in a race like this, and that's apparently its appeal. Car companies like Porsche invest big money in their teams, despite the lack of a purse or even much TV coverage (how could ESPN spot cameras along all 1,000 miles, and how would it make sense of the countless categories?). The race is more like a private poker game held upstairs in somebody's suite during the World Series of Poker.

Does Mouse make it? I would not dream of telling you. I will, however, tell you that he has a camera on his motorcycle that records with a sickening thud an accident he has sixty miles from the finish line, during which he injures or breaks (he isn't sure) some ribs, a shoulder, and a finger.

The Dying Gaul ★ ★ ½

R, 105 m., 2005

Peter Sarsgaard (Robert), Campbell Scott (Jeffrey), Patricia Clarkson (Elaine), Robin Bartlett (Bella), Linda Emond (Dr. Foss), Ryan Miller (Max). Directed by Craig Lucas and produced by David Newman, Campbell Scott, George VanBuskirk, and Lisa Zimble. Screenplay by Lucas, based on a play by Lucas.

Woe to him who seeks to please rather than to appall.

Those words appear onscreen in the first shot of *The Dying Gaul.* Here is another quotation, from later in the film: "No one goes to the movies to have a bad time. Or to learn anything." The first quotation is from Herman Melville's *Moby Dick.* The second is by a Hollywood studio executive, about a screenplay he likes but thinks is not commercial. The screenplay is about a homosexual love affair. Make the lovers heterosexual, the executive tells the writer, and I'll cut you a check for one million dollars, here and now.

The executive is Jeffrey, played by Campbell Scott, who is becoming a master of characters with controlled but alarming emotions. The screenwriter is Robert, played by Peter Sarsgaard in a sincere and inward role a little unusual for him. His screenplay is about his former lover, who was also his agent.

"Americans hate gays," Jeffrey tells him flatly. Then he dangles temptation before Robert, who is broke and has child support to pay.

"Who do you think should direct this?"

"Gus Van Sant," says Robert, "since Truffaut is dead."

"Would you like me to show it to him?"

"Yes."

"That's good, because I already have."

This dialogue, by the writer-director Craig Lucas, depends on us to realize that Jeffrey has not shown the screenplay to Gus Van Sant and probably never will. The opening stages in a movie negotiation are like a romance, with the screenwriter as the blushing bride and the producer as the prince who strews riches at his feet. Just compromise this one time, Jeffrey tells Robert, and soon, like Spike Lee, you'll be making your own films in your own way.

The Dying Gaul grabs us immediately with this seduction by negotiation. It follows with scenes establishing another Hollywood convention: If you're doing business with someone, you are immediately "family." Robert is invited to Jeffrey's home and introduced to his wife, Elaine (Patricia Clarkson), and their children. Elaine likes his mind. On the other hand, Jeffrey likes Robert's body. "Let's hug," he tells Jeffrey at one point in their negotiations. Everybody hugs in Hollywood. It is a good way to look someone in the eye while stabbing them in the back. "You are very handsome," Jeffrey says in mid-hug. "And I'm getting a little turned on. Are you?"

Robert caves in and makes his story about heterosexuals at about the same time he and Jeffrey start having sex. It takes Robert less than ten seconds on the computer to find "Maurice" and replace it with "Maggie." Neither one of them observes that "Maurice" is the name of a novel about a gay man that E. M. Forster did not allow to be published until after his death. No doubt other rewriting will take out AIDS and substitute cancer. "It's going to be a beautiful movie," Jeffrey promises him.

At this point in *The Dying Gaul* I could see no way the movie could step wrong, but it does. The movie is based on Lucas's play and represents his directorial debut. His previous screenplays include *Longtime Companion* (1990), with its Oscar-nominated performance by Bruce Davison as the companion of a dying AIDS victim, and *The Secret Lives of Dentists* (2002), which also starred Campbell Scott and was about secrets and possessiveness in a marriage.

The Dying Gaul considers some of this same material but adds a dimension that is at first intriguing and then, I think, fatal. The troublesome device is an Internet chat room. Elaine, a former screenwriter who now has time and loneliness on her hands, likes Robert immediately. They gossip. He confesses that with his lover dead his sex life is conducted mostly online. Robert says the chat rooms are like "life after death," with disembodied voices floating in the ether. Elaine asks, "What's your favorite really dirty chat room?"

Before he answers, I should issue a spoiler warning. I will not reveal crucial details, but I will describe a few things you may prefer not to know. The movie proceeds with parallel affairs, one real, one virtual. Jeffrey and Robert become lovers, while Elaine creates a fictional identity in Robert's chat room and is soon one of Robert's regular correspondents. What she writes and what he thinks and what the result is, I will leave for you to discover. It is all done well enough. I object for two more fundamental reasons: (1) There is no reason to believe Robert particularly believes in the supernatural, and (2) Would it not occur to Robert that he had, after all, told Elaine about his favorite chat room? He has a bulb that needs to be changed, the one right above his head.

So there are implausibilities in the plot devices that lead the movie to its ultimate conclusion. And then the final developments themselves, I think, are wrong in both theory and practice. There is some ambiguity about why a final event takes place, and that's all right, but the way in which the movie reveals it is, I think, singularly ineffective. It leads to one of those endings where you sit there wishing they'd tried a little harder to think up something better.

It's all the more depressing because the performances are effective, especially the way Clarkson obliquely approaches the crisis in her marriage. And I liked the way Scott's character insists on being both gay and straight. There's a Hollywood producer for you: greedy.

E

Eastern Promises ★ ★ ★ ★

R, 96 m., 2007

Viggo Mortensen (Nikolai Luzhin), Naomi Watts (Anna Khitrova), Vincent Cassel (Kirill), Armin Mueller-Stahl (Semyon), Sinead Cusack (Helen), Jerzy Skolimowski (Stepan). Directed by David Cronenberg and produced by Robert Lantos and Paul Webster. Screenplay by Steve Knight.

David Cronenberg's *Eastern Promises* opens with a throat slashing and a young woman collapsing in blood in a drugstore and connects these events with a descent into an underground of Russians who have immigrated to London and brought their crime family with them. Like the Corleone family, but with a less wise and more fearsome patriarch, the Vory V Zakone family of the Russian Mafia operates in the shadows of legitimate business—in this case, a popular restaurant.

The slashing need not immediately concern us. The teenage girl who hemorrhages is raced to a hospital and dies in childbirth in the arms of a midwife named Anna Khitrova (Naomi Watts). Fiercely determined to protect the helpless surviving infant, she uses her Russian-born family (Sinead Cusack and Jerzy Skolimowski) to translate the dead girl's diary, and it leads her to a restaurant run by Semyon (Armin Mueller-Stahl), the head of the Mafia family. Her father begs her to go nowhere near that world.

Semyon has a vile son named Kirill (Vincent Cassel) and a violent but loyal driver and bodyguard, Nikolai (Viggo Mortensen). And the gears of the story shift into place when the diary, the midwife, and the crime family become interlocked.

Eastern Promises is no ordinary crime thriller, just as Cronenberg is no ordinary director. Beginning with low-rent horror films in the 1970s because he could get them financed, Cronenberg has moved film by film into the top rank of directors, and here he wisely reunites with Mortensen, star of their *History of Violence* (2005). No, Mortensen is not Russian, but don't even think about the problem of an accent; he digs so deeply into the role you may not recognize him at first.

Naomi Watts, playing an Anglicized second-generation immigrant, has no idea at first what she has gotten herself into and why the diary is of vital importance to these people. All she cares about is the baby, but she learns fast that the baby's life and her own are both at great risk. In fact, her entry into that world has driven a wedge into it that sets everybody at odds and challenges long-held assumptions.

The screenplay is by Steve Knight, author of the powerful film *Dirty Pretty Things* (2002), about a black market in body parts. It was set in London and had scarcely a native-born Londoner in it. He's fascinated by the worlds within the London world. Here, too. And his lines of morality are more murkily drawn here, as allegiances and loyalties shift, and old emotions turn out to be forgotten, but not dead.

Mortensen's Nikolai is the key player, trusted by Semyon. We are reminded of Don Corleone's trust in an outsider, Tom Hagen, over his own sons, Sonny and Fredo. Here Semyon depends on Nikolai more than Kirill, who has an ugly streak that sometimes interferes with the orderly conduct of business. Anna (Watts) senses she can trust Nikolai, too, even though it is established early that this tattooed warrior is capable of astonishing violence. At a time when movie "fight scenes" are as routine as the dances in musicals, Nikolai engages in a fight in this film that sets the same kind of standard that *The French Connection* set for chases. Years from now, it will be referred to as a benchmark.

Cronenberg has said he's not interested in crime stories as themselves. "I was watching *Miami Vice* the other night," he told Adam Nayman of Toronto's *Eye Weekly*, "and I realized I'm not interested in the mechanics of the mob but criminality and people who live in a state of perpetual transgression—that is interesting to me." And to me, as well. What the director and writer do here is not unfold a plot, but flay the skin from a hidden world. Their story puts their characters to a test: They can be true to their job descriptions within a hermetically sealed world where everyone shares the same values and expectations, and where outsiders are by definition the prey. But what happens when their cocoon is broached? Do they still possess fugitive feelings instilled by a long-forgotten babushka? And what if they do?

"Just don't give the plot away," Cronenberg begged in that interview. He is correct that it would be fatal, because this is not a movie of what or how, but of *why*. And for a long time, you don't see the why coming. It's that way with stories about plausible human beings, which is why I prefer them to stories about characters who are simply elements in fiction. There was a big surprise in *A History of Violence* that pretty much everybody entering the theater already knew. I have studied the trailer of *Eastern Promises*, and it doesn't give away a hint of its central business.

So let's leave it that way and simply regard the performances. I write little about casting directors because I can't know what really goes on, and of course directors make the final choice for key roles. But whatever Deirdre Bowen and Nina Gold had to do with the choices in this movie, including what might seem the unlikely choice of Mortensen, was pitch-perfect. The actors and the characters merge and form a reality above and apart from the story, and the result is a film that takes us beyond crime and London and the Russian Mafia and into the mystifying realms of human nature.

The Edge of Heaven ★ ★ ★ ★

NO MPAA RATING, 122 m., 2008

Baki Davrak (Nejat Aksu), Nursel Kose (Yeter Ozturk), Nurgul Yesilcay (Ayten Ozturk), Patrycia Ziolkowska (Lotte Staub), Hanna Schygulla (Susanne Staub), Tuncel Kurtiz (Ali Aksu). Directed by Fatih Akin and produced by Andreas Thiel, Klaus Maeck, and Akin. Screenplay by Akin.

The best approach is to begin with the characters, because the wonderful, sad, touching movie *The Edge of Heaven* is more about its characters than about its story. There is a reason for that: This is one of those films of interlocking narrative strands, called a hyperlink movie, but the strands never link. True, they link for us because we possess crucial information about the characters—but they never link for the characters because they lack that information. I liked it that way.

There is an old man named Ali (Tuncel Kurtiz) in Bremen, Germany. He is from Turkey. He has a smile that makes you like him. Think of Walter Matthau. One day (as is his habit, I suspect), he goes to visit a prostitute. This is a middle-aged Turkish woman named Yeter (Nursel Kose), who works from the doorway of a brothel. Yeter is heard speaking by a group of Turkish men, who assume she is Muslim and tell her they will kill her unless she quits the business. Ali makes her an offer: He will pay her to move in with him on a permanent basis. She accepts.

Spoiler warning, I suppose, although this segment of the film is titled "Yeter's Death." Ali gets drunk, he hits her, she falls, she's dead, he's in prison. She was heartbroken in life because her daughter, Ayten (Nurgul Yesilcay), had been long out of touch with her. Yeter's body is shipped back to Istanbul, where we meet Ali's son, Nejat (Baki Davrak). Nejat is a professor at a German university but makes it his business to track down Yeter's daughter and somehow make reparation. In this process he moves back to Istanbul and buys a German-language bookstore from a man who is homesick for Germany.

Back and forth, between Turkey and Germany, the strands tangle. We meet Yeter's daughter, who is a member of a militant group. Deeply in trouble with the authorities, she flees to Germany, where she is befriended and taken home by a young woman named Lotte (Patrycia Ziolkowska). The two fall quickly and passionately in love. For reasons we will leave to them, Ayten ends up in a Turkish prison, Lotte goes to Istanbul to try to help her, and . . . well, nevermind.

You must also meet Lotte's mother, Susanne, who is played by the magnificent Hanna Schygulla, the legendary German actress, best known for her Fassbinder films. She is not pleased with her daughter's romance but in the end goes to Istanbul so that she, too, can try to help Ayten. In Turkey she meets Nejat and ends up living in the same room that her daughter had rented from him.

One of the deepest pleasures of going to the movies for many years is that we can watch actors age and ripen and understand what is happening to ourselves. Hanna Schygulla was once a sexpot in Fassbinder's *The Bitter Tears of Petra von Kant* (1972), and was a commanding star in his great film *The Marriage of Maria Braun* (1979). She was Fassbinder's most important acting talent and his muse, and has appeared in eighty-two films or TV projects. She was a young vixen once, then a sultry romantic lead, and now she is a plumpish woman of sixty-five. My own age, it occurs to me. But *what* a woman of sixty-five! Not a second of plastic surgery. She wears every year as a badge of honor. And here she is so tactful, so warm, so quietly spoken, so glowing, that she all but possesses the film, and we love her for her years and her art.

All this time, while perhaps thinking such thoughts, we are waiting for the penny to drop. Surely some combination of these people will discover how they are connected? But they never do. Maybe that requires a spoiler warning, too, because we are so accustomed to all the stories converging at the end of a hyperlink film. Not this time. The characters are related in theme, but not in plot.

Fatih Akin, who wrote and directed, made the powerful *Head-On* (2004), which in a very different way was about being Turkish and feeling dispossessed or threatened. Here he gives us three parents, a son, and two daughters, all of whose lives are affected, even governed, by the fact that some are Turks, some German. Religion doesn't really enter into it so much, except in inspiring Yeter's retirement. Akin's purpose, I think, is a simple one: He wants us to meet these people, know them, sympathize with them. Even old Ali is not so very evil; he had no intention to murder Yeter, and who among us, drunk or sober, has never unwisely done shameful things? My hand is not raised.

What happened to me during *The Edge of Heaven* was that I did care about the characters. I found them fascinating. They were not overwritten and didn't spend too much time explaining or justifying themselves. They just got on with their lives, and their lives got on with them, all the time swimming in the seas of two different cultures, two different sets of possibilities. Even the authorities are not the villains in the film.

Now if five, or four, of the characters found out how they were connected, what difference would that make? We are all connected, if only we could stand tall enough, see widely enough, and understand adequately. Mere plot points are meaningless. Fatih Akin wants us to realize that, I believe, and he also wants us to understand his creatures, who are for the most part good people, have good intentions, make mistakes, suffer for their errors, and try to soldier on, as do we all.

Eight Below ★ ★ ★

PG, 120 m., 2006

Paul Walker (Jerry Shepard), Bruce Greenwood (Dr. Davis McLaren), Moon Bloodgood (Katie), Jason Biggs (Cooper), Gerard Plunkett (Dr. Andy Harrison), August Schellenberg (Mindo), Wendy Crewson (Eve McLaren), Belinda Metz (Rosemary), Panou Mowling (Howard). Directed by Frank Marshall and produced by Patrick Crowley, Doug Davison, and David Hoberman. Screenplay by David DiGilio, suggested by the film *Nankyoku Monogatari.*

You think penguins have it bad? At least they're adapted to survive in Antarctica. *Eight Below* tells the harrowing story of a dogsled team left chained outside a research station when the humans pull out in a hurry. The guide who used and loved them wants to return to rescue them but is voted down: Winter has set in, and all flights are canceled until spring. Will the dogs survive? Or will the film end in the spring, with the guide uttering a prayer over their eight dead bodies?

Remarkable how in a film where we *know* with an absolute certainty that all or most of the dogs must survive, *Eight Below* succeeds as an effective story. It works by focusing on the dogs. To be sure, the guide, Jerry (Paul Walker), never stops thinking about them, but there's not much he can do. He visits Dr. Davis McLaren (Bruce Greenwood), the scientist whose research financed the dogsled expedition, and he hangs out at his mobile home on a scenic Oregon coast, and he pursues a reawakening love affair with Katie (Moon Bloodgood), the pilot who ferried them to and from the station.

To give him credit, he's depressed, really depressed, by the thought of those dogs chained up in the frigid night, but what can he do?

Meanwhile, the subtitles keep count of how long the dogs have been on their own: 50 days . . . 133 days . . . 155 days . . .

If there is a slight logical problem with their fight for survival, it's that they have plenty of daylight to work with. Isn't there almost eternal night during the Antarctic winter, just as there's almost eternal day during the summer? I suppose we have to accept the unlikely daylight because otherwise the most dramatic scenes would take place in darkness.

The dog sequences reminded me of Jack London's dog novels, especially *White Fang* and *The Call of the Wild.* Do not make the mistake of thinking London's books are for children. They can be read by kids in grade school, yes, but they were written by an adult with serious things to say about the nature of dogs and the reality of arctic existence. There's a reason they're in the Library of America.

In *Eight Below,* as in Jack London, the dogs are not turned into cute cartoon pets but are respected for their basic animal natures.

To be sure, the sled dogs here do some mighty advanced thinking, as when one dog seems to explain a fairly complex plan to the other dogs by telepathy. I was also impressed by the selfless behavior of the dogs, as they bring birds to feed a member of the pack who has been crippled. I was under the impression that if a dog died in such circumstances, the others would eat it to avoid starvation, but apparently not. (You can't assume the idea didn't occur to Frank Marshall, the director, since he made *Alive,* the story of the Andes survivors.)

Could the dogs (six huskies and two malamutes) really have survived unsheltered for five months, scavenging for themselves through an Antarctic winter? I learn from *Variety* that *Eight Below* is inspired by a Japanese film, itself based on real events, but in the 1958 "true story," seven of nine dogs died. Still, the film doesn't claim to be a documentary, and the story, believable or not, is strong and involving. It's the stuff about the humans that gets thin: The film lacks a human villain, because the decision not to return for the dogs is wise and prudent, and not made by a mean man who hates dogs.

You might think, however, that when Jerry appeals to Dr. McLaren, the scientist would exert himself a little more to save the dogs, since they saved his life. (How he gets into trouble and what the dogs do to save him I will leave for you to experience; it provides the film's most compelling moments.)

Movies about animals always live with the temptation to give the animals human characteristics. Lassie, for example, could do everything but dial the telephone and drive the car. The brilliance of the English-language *March of the Penguins* involved dropping a French sound track in which the penguins expressed themselves in voice-over dialogue, and simply trusting to the reality of their situation. *Eight Below* is restrained, for the most part, in how it presents its dogs. When there are close-ups of a dog's face, absorbed in thought, anxiety, or yearning, we aren't asked to believe anything we don't already believe about dogs: They *do* think, worry, and yearn, and they love, too. Or if they don't, I don't want to know about it.

El Cantante ★ ★

R, 116 m., 2007

Marc Anthony (Hector Lavoe), Jennifer Lopez (Puchi), John Ortiz (Willie Colon), Manny Perez (Eddie). Directed by Leon Ichaso and produced by Julio Caro, Jennifer Lopez, Simon Fields, and David Maldonado. Screenplay by Ichaso, David Darmstaedter, and Todd Anthony Bello.

This bulletin just in: If you use cocaine or heroin, you are very likely to become addicted, and if you become addicted, there are usually two choices: (1) get clean, or (2) die. The math is clear and has been proven in countless biopics about addicted musicians. The presumption in many of the pictures is that artists somehow need drugs because they are so talented they just can't stand it, or because of the "pressure" they're under, or because they need to be high all the time and not just on the stage, or because people won't leave them alone, or because they feel insecure or unworthy.

All lies. They are addicted because they are addicted. They got addicted by starting to take the stuff in the first place. It's chemistry. At some point, they don't use to get high, but to stop feeling sick. It is a sad, degrading existence, interrupted by flashes of feeling "OK." George Carlin once asked, "How does cocaine make you feel?" And he answered: "It makes you feel like having some more cocaine."

El Cantante, the life and death story of Hector Lavoe (Marc Anthony), the godfather of salsa, retraces the same tired footsteps of many another movie druggie before him. He lies, cheats, disappoints those who love him, and finally dies, although even the movie loses patience with the dying process and cuts out before getting to his years with AIDS (from an infected needle). All along the way, he is enabled and berated in equal measure by his wife and sometime manager, Puchi (Jennifer Lopez), who is our guide to his story in black-and-white flashbacks.

The end of the movie is a foregone conclusion, and Hector's inexorable descent is depressing, although interrupted by many upbeat musical numbers. Indeed, there seem to be two films here: a musical, with Anthony doing a terrific job of covering Lavoe's music, and a drugalogue. The sound track would be worth having. But there is nothing special about Lavoe's progress toward the grave: just the same old same old.

Lavoe was a gifted musician in Puerto Rico who moved to New York, changed his name from Perez, partnered with the great trombonist Willie Colon (who could have borrowed the leftover Perez), and began to blend Latin genres, jazz, and a dash of rock into something that was known as salsa and became very big. We sense the excitement of the new music in Anthony's stage performances, where he is backed by orchestras full of gifted musicians (Colon is played by John Ortiz), and where his moves project the joy of the music.

But always in the wings, looking worried, is Puchi. She loves the guy and his music, but not his drugs, and they have ceaseless arguments about his drug use, sometimes punctuated by her own. These period sequences are intercut with a modern-day Puchi, looking not a day older, remembering her life with Hector and reciting the litany of his fall from life. Since Puchi lived until 2002, she must have learned something about drugs, if only to stop, but her memories mostly take the form of puzzled complaints: That was a great night, but then . . . he went out and scored, used, passed out, etc., etc. They have a child, who functions as an afterthought in a few scenes, but mostly they roast in their private hell.

If you're a fan of Lavoe and salsa, or Lopez and Anthony, you'll want to see the movie for what's good in it. Otherwise, you may be disappointed. The director (Leon Ichaso) and his cowriters haven't licked a crucial question: Why do we need to see this movie and not just listen to the music?

El Crimen Perfecto ★ ★

NO MPAA RATING, 105 m., 2005

Guillermo Toledo (Rafael), Monica Cervera (Lourdes), Luis Varela (Don Antonio), Fernando Tejero (Alonso), Enrique Villen (Inspector Campoy), Javier Gutierrez (Jaime), Kira Miro (Roxanne). Directed by Alex de la Iglesia and produced by Roberto Di Girolamo, Gustavo Ferrada, and de la Iglesia. Screenplay by Jorge Guerricaechevarria and de la Iglesia.

Rafael lives for two reasons: to make love to women, and to sell them clothes. He feels blessed by his job as the department manager of ladies' wear in YeYo's, the big Madrid department store where he claims to have been born and certainly seems to live. After hours, he treats salesgirls to champagne and caviar, a race down the aisles in a shopping cart, and a passionate denouement in a dressing room.

El Crimen Perfecto records Rafael's sudden and devastating loss of three things: his job, his happiness, and, worst of all, his bachelorhood. Alex de la Iglesia's comedy, which in many ways Jerry Lewis might have made, shows Rafael (Guillermo Toledo) as madcap and manic, a man who feels immune to ordinary laws: Witness his daily theft of a paper from a newsstand, and the way he steals kisses while walking down the street. When a security guard catches him having sex in a dressing room, Rafael bribes him and is warned he must stop—in three hours.

As the film opens, Rafael and his archenemy, Don Antonio (Luis Varela), manager of men's wear, are in a sales contest to determine who will become floor manager. Rafael seems to win, but then victory is snatched from his grasp, and in a ferocious struggle in a dressing room, Don Antonio is killed. In desperation Rafael tries to jam him into a basement incinerator that's too small for the body. Hints of Hitchcock begin to surface around here.

Rafael has been careful to hire only beautiful women as his employees, but one plain woman is on the staff. This is Lourdes (Monica Cervera), who desperately loves Rafael and is not above blackmailing him after she helps dispose of the body. Rafael would rather die than marry her, but what is he to do when he steps off the elevator one morning and is bushwhacked by a reality show on live TV? "Will you marry Lourdes?" the emcee screams. "Millions are waiting for your answer!"

El Crimen Perfecto has energy, color, spirit, and lively performances, but what it does not have are very many laughs. In a month that has seen *The 40-Year-Old Virgin,* a wonderful comedy about romance in retail, this one seems oddly old-fashioned; it has a 1950s feel. The humor is strong on sitcom complications and short on human nature, and Rafael is too likable to be as hateful as he ought to be, if he were really going to be funny.

I did like Cervera, as Lourdes, who comes on like a force of nature. Rafael is fond of lecturing to his troops that you can get anything you really set your heart on, but Lourdes is the only one who listens, believes, and puts his theories into practice. One of the movie's problems is that she's supposed to be unsympathetic, but we can't help admiring her; when the movie is cruel to her, which is often, it puts a damper on things. Better the good-hearted notes in *The 40-Year-Old Virgin,* which likes everybody in its cast, after their fashion.

The movie's third act moves beyond Jerry Lewis into desperation. Don Antonio's ghost turns up with a hatchet in his head and his hair still smoldering, to contribute cheerful suggestions; his presence is desperately not funny. A scene set on a Ferris wheel doesn't work in any of several possible ways, and a scene involving a fire sprinkler system suggests that the screenwriters' desperation was as great as the character who sounds the alarm. Watching a scene where bargain hunters storm the salesclerks seconds after the store opens, I was reminded of Harold Lloyd's *Safety Last,* which has an uncannily similar scene. Maybe de la Iglesia was paying homage. In that case, maybe the Ferris wheel scene was homage to the scene where Lloyd hangs from the hands of a clock. Or maybe not.

Elektra ★ ½

PG-13, 97 m., 2005

Jennifer Garner (Elektra), Goran Visnjic (Mark Miller), Will Yun Lee (Kirigi), Cary-Hiroyuki Tagawa (Roshi), Terence Stamp (Stick), Kirsten Prout (Abby Miller). Directed by Rob Bowman and produced by Arnon Milchan, Avi Arad, and Gary Foster. Screenplay by Zak Penn, Stuart Zicherman, and Raven Metzner.

Elektra plays like a collision between leftover bits and pieces of Marvel superhero stories. It can't decide what tone to strike. It goes for satire by giving its heroine an agent who suggests mutual funds for her murder-for-hire fees, and sends her a fruit basket before her next killing. And then it goes for melancholy, by making Elektra a lonely, unfulfilled overachiever who was bullied as a child and suffers from obsessive-compulsive disorder. It goes for cheap sentiment by having her bond with a thirteen-year-old girl, and then . . . but see for yourself. The movie's a muddle in search of a rationale.

Elektra, you may recall, first appeared on screen in *Daredevil* (2003), the Marvel saga starring Ben Affleck as a blind superhero. Jennifer Garner, she of the wonderful lips, returns in the role as a killer for hire, which seems kind of sad, considering that in the earlier movie she figured in the beautiful scene where he imagines her face by listening to raindrops falling on it.

Now someone has offered her $2 million for her next assassination, requiring only that she turn up two days early for the job—on Christmas Eve, as it works out. She arrives in a luxurious lakeside vacation home and soon meets the young girl named Abby (Kirsten Prout), who lives next door. Abby's father is played by Goran Visnjic with a three-day beard, which tells you all you need to know: Powerful sexual attraction will compel them to share two PG-13-rated kisses.

The back story, which makes absolutely no mention of Daredevil, involves Elektra's training under the stern blind martial arts master Stick (Terence Stamp), who can restore people to life and apparently materialize at will, yet is reduced to martial arts when he does battle. Her enemies are assassins hired by the Order of the Hand, which is a secret Japanese society that seeks the Treasure, and the Treasure is . . . well, see for yourself.

As for the troops of the Hand, they have contracted Movie Zombie's Syndrome, which means that they are fearsome and deadly until killed, at which point they dissolve into a cloud of yellow powder. I don't have a clue whether they're real or imaginary. Neither do they, I'll bet. Eagles and wolves and snakes can materialize out of their tattoos and attack people, but they, too, disappear in clouds. Maybe this is simply to save Elektra the inconvenience of stepping over her victims in the middle of a fight.

The Order of the Hand is not very well defined. Its office is a pagoda on top of a Tokyo skyscraper, which is promising, but inside all we get is the standard scene of a bunch of suits sitting around a conference table giving orders to paid killers. Their instructions: Kill Elektra, grab the Treasure, etc. Who are they and what is their master plan? Maybe you have to study up on the comic books.

As for Elektra, she's a case study. Flashbacks show her tortured youth, in which her father made her tread water in the family's luxury indoor pool until she was afraid she'd drown. (Her mother, on balcony overlooking pool: "She's only a girl!" Her father, at poolside: "Only using your legs! Not your hands!" Elektra: "Glub.")

Whether this caused her OCD or not, I cannot say. It manifests itself not as an extreme case, like poor Howard Hughes, but fairly mildly: She counts her steps in groups of five. This has absolutely nothing to do with anything else. A superheroine with a bad case of OCD could be interesting, perhaps; maybe she would be compelled to leap tall buildings with bound after bound after bound.

The movie's fight scenes suffer from another condition, attention deficit disorder. None of their shots are more than a few seconds long, saving the actors from doing much in the way of stunts and the director from having to worry overmuch about choreography. There's one showdown between Elektra and the head killer of the Hand that involves a lot of white sheets, but all they do is flap around; we're expecting maybe an elegant Zhang Yimou sequence, and it's more like they're fighting with the laundry.

Jennifer Garner is understandably unable to make a lot of sense out of this. We get a lot of close-ups in which we would identify with what she was thinking, if we had any clue what that might be. Does she wonder why she became a paid killer instead of a virtuous superheroine? Does she wonder why her agent is a bozo? Does she clearly understand that the Order of the Hand is the group trying to kill her? At the end of the movie, having reduced her enemies to yellow poofs, she tells Goran Visnjic to "take good care" of his daughter. Does she even know those guys in suits are still up there in the pagoda, sitting around the table?

Elevator to the Gallows ★ ★ ★ ½

NO MPAA RATING, 88 m., 1958 (rereleased 2005)

Jeanne Moreau (Florence Carala), Maurice Ronet (Julien Tavernier), Georges Poujouly (Louis), Yori Bertin (Veronique), Jean Wall (Simon Carala). Directed by Louis Malle and produced by Jean Thuillier. Screenplay by Noel Calef, Malle, and Roger Nimier.

She loves him. "Je t'aime, je t'aime," she repeats into the telephone, in the desperate close-up that opens Louis Malle's *Elevator to the Gallows* (1958). He needs to know this because he is going to commit a murder for them. The woman is Jeanne Moreau, in her first feature film role, looking bruised by the pain of love. She plays Florence, wife of the millionaire arms dealer Simon Carala (Jean Wall). Her lover, Julien Tavernier (Maurice Ronet), is a paratrooper who served in Indochina and Algeria, in wars that made Carala rich. Now he works for Carala and is going to kill him and take his wife.

Because Julien has access and a motive, he must make this a perfect crime. Malle, who apprenticed with the painstaking genius Robert Bresson, devotes loving care to the details of the murder. After office hours, Julien uses a rope and a hook to climb up one floor and enter a window of Simon's office. He shoots him, makes it look like a suicide, bolts the office from inside, leaves by the window. An elegant little locked-room mystery. Then he climbs back down and leaves to meet his mistress.

Stupidly, he has left behind evidence. It is

growing dark. Perhaps no one has noticed. He hurries back to the office and gets into an elevator, but then the power is shut off in the building for the night, and he is trapped between floors. Florence, meanwhile, waits and waits in the café where they planned their rendezvous. And then, in a series of shots that became famous, she walks the streets, visiting all their usual haunts, looking for the lover she is convinced has deserted her.

Moreau plays these scenes not with frantic anxiety but with a kind of masochistic despair, not really expecting to find Julien. It rains, and she wanders drenched in the night. Malle shot her scenes using a camera in a baby carriage pushed along beside her by the cinematographer Henri Decae, who worked with Jean-Pierre Melville on another great noir of the period, *Bob le Flambeur* (1955). Her face is often illuminated only by the lights of the cafés and shops that she passes; at a time when actresses were lit and photographed with care, these scenes had a shock value and influenced many films to come. We see that Florence is a little mad. An improvised jazz score by Miles Davis seems to belong to the night as much as she does.

Meanwhile, Julien struggles to free himself from the elevator. There is a parallel story. His parked car is stolen by a teenage couple—the braggart Louis (Georges Poujouly) and his girlfriend, Veronique (Yori Bertin). They get into a fender bender with a German tourist and his wife, and the tourists rather improbably invite them to party with them at a motel. This leads to murder, and the police of course suspect Julien because his car is found at the scene.

The more I see the great French crime films of the 1950s, the earlier seems the dawning of the New Wave. The work of Melville, Jacques Becker, and their contemporaries uses the same low-budget, unsprung, jumpy style that was adapted by Truffaut in *Jules and Jim* and Godard in *Breathless* (which owes a lot to the teenage couple in *Elevator*). Malle became a card-carrying New Waver, and *Elevator to the Gallows* could be called the first New Wave title, except then what was *Bob le Flambeur*?

These 1950s French noirs abandon the formality of traditional crime films, the almost ritualistic obedience to formula, and show crazy stuff happening to people who seem to be making up their lives as they go along. There is an irony that Julien, trapped in the elevator, has a perfect alibi for the murders he is suspected of but seems inescapably implicated in the one he might have gotten away with. And observe the way Moreau, wandering the streets, handles her arrest for prostitution. She is so depressed it hardly matters, and yet, is this the way the wife of a powerful man should be treated? Even one she hopes is dead?

Note: The movie played around the country in a beautifully restored 35 mm print that works as a reminder: Black and white doesn't subtract something from a film, but adds it.

The 11th Hour ★ ★

PG, 91 m., 2007

A documentary directed by Leila Conners Petersen and Nadia Conners and produced by Leonardo DiCaprio, Chuck Castleberry, Brian Gerber, and Petersen. Screenplay by Petersen, Conners, and DiCaprio.

I agree with every word in this tedious documentary. As you can guess from the title, *The 11th Hour* sounds a warning that we have pretty much depleted the woodpile of planet Earth and, to keep things running, have been reduced to throwing our furniture on the fire. It is a devastating message.

Once there was a time when Earth existed on current energy. This year's sunlight fell on this year's crops, feeding and warming this year's human beings. With the exploitation of coal and oil, however, we have set fire to millions of years of stored energy as fast as we can, and the result is poisonous pollution, global warming, and planetary imbalance. What lies at the end of this suicidal spending spree? Stephen Hawking paints a future in which Earth resembles Venus, with a temperature of 482 degrees Fahrenheit. There would still be rain, however, although unfortunately of sulfuric acid.

Earth is cartwheeling out of balance. Did you know, as I learned in the new issue of *Discover,* that while fish stocks disappear from the oceans, their place is being taken by an unimaginably huge explosion of jellyfish—literally brainless creatures with a lifestyle consisting of eating? Sounds like us.

The 11th Hour gathers a group of respected

experts to speak from their areas of knowledge about how we are despoiling our planet and what we might possibly do to turn things around. We don't have much time. The architects John Todd and Bruce Mau explain how we could build "green" buildings that would use solar energy, consume their own waste, and function much like a tree. There is no reason why every home (every newly built one, for sure) could not have solar panels on the roof to help heat, light, and cool itself. Well, one reason actually: The energy companies would resist any effort to redirect their own gargantuan subsidies toward eco-friendly homeowners.

We hear of the destruction of the forests, the death of the seas, the melting of the poles, the trapping of greenhouse gases. And in another forthcoming documentary, *In the Shadow of the Moon,* about the surviving astronauts who walked on the moon, we see their view of Earth from 250,000 miles away; it strikes us what an awfully large planet this is to be wrapped in such a thin and vulnerable atmosphere.

All of this is necessary to know. But are we too selfish to do anything about it? Why isn't everybody buying a hybrid car? They can get up to a third more fuel mileage. They are getting cheaper as gas grows more expensive. And here's the kicker: *They can go faster* because they have two engines. So you ask people if they're getting a hybrid, and they squirm and say, gee, they dunno, they'd rather stick to the old way of going slower, spending more on gas, and destroying the atmosphere. If booze companies advertise for responsible drinking and tobacco companies warn of health hazards, why don't gas companies ask you to buy a hybrid?

Some of these facts are in *The 11th Hour,* others are offered by me, and the point is: We more or less know all this stuff anyway. So does the movie motivate us to act on it? Not really. After I saw Al Gore's *An Inconvenient Truth,* my next car was a hybrid. After seeing *The 11th Hour,* I'd be thinking more about my next movie.

The film sidesteps one of the oldest laws of television news and documentaries: *Write to the picture!* When Gore's film tells you something, it shows you what it's talking about. Too much of the footage of *The 11th Hour* is just standard nature photography, as helicopter-cams swoop over hill and dale and birds look unhappy and ice melts.

This is intercut with fifty experts, more or less, who talk and talk and talk. The narrator and coproducer is Leonardo DiCaprio, who sounds like he's presenting a class project. Everyone is seen as talking heads, so we see them talk, then get some nature footage, then see them talk some more, until finally we're thinking, enough already; I get it. "A bore," Meyer the hairy economist once told the private eye Travis McGee, "is anyone who deprives you of solitude without providing you with companionship." This movie, for all its noble intentions, is a bore. Rent *An Inconvenient Truth* instead. Even if you've already seen it.

Elizabeth: The Golden Age ★ ★ ½

PG-13, 114 m., 2007

Cate Blanchett (Elizabeth I), Geoffrey Rush (Sir Francis Walsingham), Clive Owen (Sir Walter Raleigh), Samantha Morton (Mary, Queen of Scots), Abbie Cornish (Elizabeth Throckmorton), Jordi Molla (Philip II), Rhys Ifans (Robert Reston). Directed by Shekhar Kapur and produced by Tim Bevan, Eric Fellner, and Jonathan Cavendish. Screenplay by Michael Hirst and William Nicholson.

Elizabeth: The Golden Age is weighed down by its splendor. There are scenes where the costumes are so sumptuous, the sets so vast, the music so insistent, that we lose sight of the humans behind the dazzle of the production. Unlike *Elizabeth* (1998), by the same director, Shekhar Kapur, this film rides low in the water, its cargo of opulence too much to carry.

That's despite the return of the remarkable Cate Blanchett in the title role. Who else would be so tall, regal, assured, and convincing that these surroundings would not diminish her? We believe she is a queen. We simply cannot care enough about this queen. That Blanchett could appear in the same Toronto Film Festival playing Elizabeth and Bob Dylan, both splendidly, is a wonder of acting. But the film's screenplay, by Michael Hirst and William Nicholson, places her in the center of history that is baldly simplified, shamelessly altered, and pumped up with romance and action.

We see her kingdom threatened by two Catholics, Mary, Queen of Scots (Samantha Morton), who stood next in line to the throne, and Philip II of Spain (Jordi Molla), who was building a great armada to invade England. Elizabeth's treasury is depleted, her resources strained, her attention diverted by the arrival in her court of the dashing Sir Walter Raleigh (Clive Owen). He has just returned from the New Land with two gifts: the territory of Virginia, which he has named after her in honor of her virginity, and tobacco, which she smokes with great delight. Elizabeth was indeed by all accounts a virgin, but in 1585, when the story is set, she would have been over fifty and her virginity more or less settled. The film sidesteps the age issue by making her look young, sensuous, and fragrant, and yearning for a man such as Raleigh.

This Sir Walter, he is a paragon. He would have been thirty-two in 1585. Despite his shabby attire and rough-hewn manners, he uses brash confidence to rise in Elizabeth's esteem, and he becomes her trusted adviser and a mastermind of British military strategy. The film deals with the famous 1588 defeat of the armada with Raleigh at its center, commanding ships to be set afire and aimed to ram the Spanish vessels. He swings from ropes, brandishes his sword, saves himself by plunging into the sea, and in general proves himself a master swashbuckler, especially since history teaches us that the real Raleigh was ashore the whole time and played no role in the battles.

In the court, he is also a swordsman, seducing and impregnating Elizabeth's favorite lady-in-waiting, Elizabeth Throckmorton (Abbie Cornish). When Elizabeth hears this news, Blanchett rises to full fury in an awesome example of regal jealousy. She desired Raleigh for herself, of course, although there is no evidence that, in life, she had such feelings for him.

Some of the film's best scenes involve Mary, played by Samantha Morton as a heroic and devout woman who goes to the executioner's ax with dismay but royal composure. Elizabeth's own crisis of conscience over Mary's death is also well-played, but the film is far more interested by romantic intrigue and sea battles. I think it undervalues the ability of audiences to get involved in true historical drama instead of recycled action clichés.

Reviewing the earlier film, I suggested that Shekhar Kapur was perhaps influenced by the rich colors and tapestries of his native India. Here he seems carried away by them. There are scenes where the elaborate lace on Elizabeth's costume is so detailed and flawless that we don't think about the character, we wonder how long Blanchett must have had to stand there while holding the pose and not ruffling anything.

Can there be a third Elizabeth film? Of course there can. She lived until 1603, and some of her greatest glories were ahead of her. Shakespeare was active in London from the 1580s, although it was with Elizabeth's successor, James I, that his company enjoyed its great royal favor. No matter. With the same cavalier attitude to history as this second film, we could be talking about *Elizabeth and Shakespeare in Love.*

Elizabethtown ★ ★ ★

PG-13, 120 m., 2005

Orlando Bloom (Drew Baylor), Kirsten Dunst (Claire Colburn), Susan Sarandon (Hollie Baylor), Alec Baldwin (Phil DeVoss), Bruce McGill (Bill Banyon), Judy Greer (Heather Baylor), Jessica Biel (Ellen Kishmore), Paul Schneider (Jessie Baylor). Directed by Cameron Crowe and produced by Crowe, Tom Cruise, and Paula Wagner. Screenplay by Crowe.

I've seen Cameron Crowe's *Elizabethtown* twice, and remarkable is the difference between the two versions. Critics were warned before seeing the Toronto film festival version that it was not the final cut, and was it ever not. The new version is eighteen minutes shorter, and more than 18 percent better, and wisely eliminates the question of why anyone would want to wear a pair of shoes that whistled.

The final version centers the story where it belongs, on the most unrelenting Meet Cute in movie history. Orlando Bloom plays Drew Baylor, a shoe designer on a red-eye flight to Kentucky, where his father has died during a family visit. Kirsten Dunst plays Claire Colburn, who is the only flight attendant on the plane, just as

Drew is the only passenger. He just wants to be left alone. She insists he move up to first class, coddles him, makes bright and perky chat, and more or less insists on Meeting him, Cute or not.

Drew was contemplating suicide when the call came about his father's death. He's the designer of the Spasmodica shoe, a world-famous but flawed new product that his boss (Alec Baldwin) informs him will lose $972 million and is "a failure of mythic proportions, a folk tale that makes other people feel better because it didn't happen to them." Drew's suicide is put on hold for the visit to Elizabethtown, where his father was related to half the population and the best friend of the other half, and where Drew's mother, Hollie (Susan Sarandon), is still hated as the woman who kidnapped this beloved man and took him away to live in California. "But we live in Oregon," Drew, his mother, and his sister, Heather (Judy Greer), keep explaining, but no one is listening.

The movie crosses two familiar kinds of material: the city slicker who encounters the salt-of-the-earth small-town types, and the romance that blossoms even while the two participants keep agreeing it is over. Both of these areas are handled gently and with affection, as when Drew offers condolences to everybody about the death of his father, and a relative gently informs him that "condolences" is "an incoming phrase."

Claire the flight attendant seems destined to save Drew's life by drawing his thoughts away from suicide, placing his failure in perspective, and insisting that he fall in love with her. For someone with a full-time job, she seems to have a lot of time on her hands and materializes where needed (and where not needed). Their in-flight relationship continues with an all-night phone call that ends with them meeting at dawn and looking out over the sunrise and deciding, after the conversation runs out, that maybe they were better on the phone. So that's the end, right? No: "You are always trying to break up with me," she tells him, "and we're not even together." And later, in exasperation: "Just tell me you love me and get it over with."

Meanwhile, Drew makes discoveries about his father and his family that are mostly positive. His mother, Hollie, and sister, Heather, fly in, the mother in the middle of manic plans for the rest of her life: "I want to learn to cook. I want to learn to laugh. I want to learn to tap dance." There is much discussion over the desire of the "Californians" to have the father cremated, this despite the family plot waiting to embrace his remains.

This being a Cameron Crowe movie, there is a great deal of music in it, some supplied by a cousin named Jessie (Paul Schneider), who was once a drummer in a band that once actually played (very, very far down) on the same bill as his idols, Lynyrd Skynyrd. How his band has a reunion at the memorial service, and how this leads to the flight of a flaming bird, I will leave for you to discover.

It must be said that although Drew and Claire do seem to be falling in love, life with Claire might be maddening. She's the kind of person who would alphabetize alphabet soup. The climax of the movie is a cross-country road journey undertaken by Drew with copious maps, instructions, and CDs supplied by Claire, who instructs Drew on exactly where to go and what to see and who to meet and what to feel. All that redeems this exercise in compulsion is the fact that she is right.

This journey is charming, up to a point. In the first cut of the film, there was a great deal more of the journey, followed by a pointless epilogue in which the Spasmodica shoe turns out to be a hit after all, because with every step you take, it whistles. (Since much of the journey and all of the epilogue have been cut from the movie, this is not a spoiler unless the ban on spoilers has been extended to include deleted scenes on the DVD.)

The difference between the two versions is dramatic, even though they share most of the same footage. The longer version seemed to end, and end, and end. It was one of those situations where people in the audience were pulling on their sweaters, fishing under the seat for their empty popcorn boxes, and leaning forward ready to stand up, and *still* the movie wasn't over. The Spasmodica epilogue played like some kind of demented reluctance on Crowe's part to ever end the movie at all.

In its trimmed version, *Elizabethtown* is nowhere near one of Crowe's great films (like *Almost Famous*), but it is sweet and goodhearted and has some real laughs, and we can just about accept Claire's obsessive romantic behavior because if someone is going to insist that you have to fall in love, there are many possibilities more alarming than Claire.

Ellie Parker ★ ★ ★

NO MPAA RATING, 95 m., 2005

Naomi Watts (Ellie Parker), Rebecca Riggs (Sam), Scott Coffey (Chris), Mark Pellegrino (Justin), Blair Mastbaum (Smash), Chevy Chase (Dennis). Directed by Scott Coffey and produced by Coffey, Naomi Watts, Matt Chesse, and Blair Mastbaum. Screenplay by Coffey.

To be a movie star *and* a good actor *and* a happy person is so difficult that Meryl Streep may be the only living person who has achieved it. Maybe Paul Newman, later in life. Okay, Tilda Swinton, Catherine Keener, and Morgan Freeman. Maybe Frances McDormand.

I know such speculation is goofy, but it's how I feel after seeing *Ellie Parker,* a daring and truthful film by Scott Coffey, starring Naomi Watts as an actress who is trying to get a start in Los Angeles. It is one of the ironies of this film about a failing actress that it got made only because a successful actress (the star of *King Kong,* no less) agreed to appear in it. You'd think they could have given the job to someone who needed the job, but then they couldn't have lined up the financing, modest as it is.

This is the movie they should show in college acting classes instead of tapes of *Inside the Actors' Studio.* It is about auditioning for an idiotic Southern Gothic soap opera and then changing your makeup and accent in the car on your way to audition as a hooker in a softcore sex film. About trying to impress a group of "producers" who are so stoned they don't have a sober brain cell to pass from hand to hand around the room. About suspecting that the only thing worse than not getting the job would be to get it. About being broke. About depending on your friends, who are your friends because they depend on you. About lying to the folks back home. About going to clubs to be "seen" and getting so wasted you hope no one saw you, and about suspecting that while you were in a blackout your genitals may have been leading a life of their own. And it is about having to be smart, talented, beautiful, determined, and, yes, lucky, just to get to *this* point in your career.

Ellie Parker follows its heroine through about twenty-four hours of her life. Maybe more. I'm not sure and neither is she. The character is played by Naomi Watts with courage, fearless observation, and a gift for timing that is so uncanny it can make points all by itself. Watts, as Parker, is so familiar with her look, her face, her hair, her style, her makeup that she can transform herself from a belle to a slut in the rearview mirror while driving from one audition to another, and convince us that she really could do that, and has.

She deceives herself that she might meet a nice guy who would—what? Does she have *time* for a relationship if she's really serious about her career? Would a guy that nice settle for the life she has to lead? If he shared it, wouldn't that mean he was as desperate as she was? There's a scene here where a guy has sex with her and then confesses he fantasized that she was Johnny Depp. He should have told her this before they started so that she could have fantasized that she was Johnny Depp, too, and then both people in bed could have felt successful.

In between these harrowing adventures, she engages in acting exercises where she dredges up sense memories that are worn out from overuse, and goes to see her therapist, whose occupation, she realizes, can also be spelled "the rapist." She doesn't know where to go with this, and neither does her therapist. We understand why Hollywood is such a hotbed of self-improvement beliefs, disciplines, formulas, and cults. I walked into the Bodhi Tree psychic bookstore one day and saw a big star rummaging through the shelves. What was she looking for? Didn't she know those books were written to help people get to the point she was already at? Maybe the star was trying to reverse the process. Maybe self-help bookstores should have a section named "Uninstall."

Ellie Parker is a very good movie, fearless and true, observant and merciless. Watts was brave to make it and gifted to make it so well. Coffey shot it off and on, as he was able to raise funds. The truth in this movie has been earned and paid for. Young people considering acting as a career should study it carefully. If Ellie Parker's ordeal looks like it might be fun, you may have the right stuff.

Elsa & Fred ★ ★ ½

PG, 106 m., 2008

China Zorrilla (Elsa), Manuel Alexandre (Alfredo), Blanca Portillo (Cuca), Roberto Carnaghi (Gabriel), Jose Angel Egido (Paco), Gonzalo Urtizberea (Alejo). Directed by Marcos Carnevale and produced by Jose Antonio Felez. Screenplay by Carnevale, Lily Ann Martin, and Marcela Guerty.

Elsa and I have one big thing in common. We both love the famous scene in Fellini's *La Dolce Vita* when Anita Ekberg and Marcello Mastroianni wade in the waters of the Trevi Fountain in Rome at dawn. That shared love is almost but not quite enough to inspire a recommendation from me for *Elsa & Fred,* which is a sweet but inconsequential romantic comedy.

Alfredo (Manuel Alexandre) has been a widower for seven months. He has been moved into a new apartment in Madrid by his shrill daughter, Cuca (Blanca Portillo). What would make him happier would be if she would stop micromanaging his life. His dog, Bonaparte, is better company. Through a Meet Cute involving a fender bender, he meets Elsa (China Zorrilla), an Argentinean neighbor in the same building.

They are both lonely, both looking for companionship. Alfredo is seventy-eight. Elsa says she is seventy-seven. Can you believe everything she says? On her wall there is a photograph of Ekberg in the great Fellini scene. When she was young, Elsa tells Fred, she was a ringer for Ekberg—often mistaken for her. Now she is no longer young, but she begins to take on beauty in the eyes of her new admirer, and tentatively they begin a romance.

The structure of the film, directed by Marcos Carnevale of Argentina, is foreordained. They will flirt, grow closer, spat, make up, grow even closer, and then time will inexorably exact some sort of toll. All of those things happen right on schedule, although the two actors give them a bittersweet appeal. Subplots involving a business deal and old secrets from the past are fitfully interesting. More entertaining are such stunts as how they deal with the bill in an expensive restaurant.

Spoiler warning: But what I really loved was the film's last act, when Alfredo fulfills Elsa's lifelong dream. He flies her to Rome for the first visit of her life, and after seeing all the other sights, they do indeed wade in the Trevi Fountain at dawn, in a scene photographed to remind us vividly of the Fellini original. This scene held me spellbound. It is true that Elsa no longer resembles Ekberg, if she ever did. But in her mind she does, and old Alfredo looks like young Marcello, and none of us look as we wish we did, but all of us can dream.

Enchanted ★ ★ ★

PG, 108 m., 2007

Amy Adams (Giselle), Patrick Dempsey (Robert Phillip), James Marsden (Prince Edward), Timothy Spall (Nathaniel), Idina Menzel (Nancy Tremaine), Rachel Covey (Morgan Phillip), Susan Sarandon (Queen Narissa). Directed by Kevin Lima and produced by Barry Josephson and Barry Sonnenfield. Screenplay by Bill Kelly.

It's no surprise to me that Amy Adams is enchanting. She won my heart in *Junebug* (2005), where she told her clueless husband: "God loves you just the way you are, but he loves you too much to let you stay that way." You should have seen *Junebug* by now, which means you will not be surprised by how fresh and winning Amy Adams is in *Enchanted,* where her role absolutely depends on effortless lovability.

She's so lovable, in fact, she starts life as an animated princess in a Disney-style world. The birds, flowers, chipmunks, and cockroaches even love her and do her bidding. Listen, if you could employ the roaches of the world, you'd have a hell of a workforce. The princess is named Giselle, she has a beautiful singing voice, and although she resists singing "Someday, My Prince Will Come," I think she's always humming it to herself.

One day her prince does come. This is Prince Edward (James Marsden), and it is love at first sight, and there are wedding bells in the air before the wicked Queen Narissa (Susan Sarandon) puts the kibosh on romance by banishing Giselle to a place as far as possible from this magical kingdom. That would be

Times Square. It is so very far, indeed, that the movie switches from animation to real-life and stays there. But the animated prologue does a good job of setting the stage, so that we understand the ground rules of what will essentially be a live-action story playing by Disney animation rules.

What results is a heart-winning musical comedy that skips lightly and sprightly from the lily pads of hope to the manhole covers of actuality, if you see what I mean. I'm not sure I do. Anyway, Prince Edward follows her to New York, along with his manservant Nathaniel (Timothy Spall in full Jeeves sail) and her chipmunk. But do not rush to the conclusion that Giselle and Edward find love in Gotham, because there is the complication of Robert (Patrick Dempsey), the handsome single dad she meets. He's raising a daughter named Morgan (Rachel Covey), and Morgan of course likes her on the spot when she ends up living with them as a homeless waif from an unimaginable place.

Not so welcoming is Nancy (Idina Menzel), who already fills the girlfriend slot in Robert's life. She's nice enough, but can she hold her ground against a movie princess? Not in a PG-rated world. So the romance and the adventure play out in ways that would be familiar enough in an animated comedy, but seem daring in the real world. First we get animation based on reality (*Beowulf*), and now reality based on animation.

The movie has a sound background in Disney animation, starting with director Kevin Lima (*Tarzan, A Goofy Movie*) and including the music by Alan Menken and lyrics by Stephen Schwartz, who composed for *Pocahontas* and *The Hunchback of Notre Dame.* More important, it has a Disney willingness to allow fantasy into life, so New York seems to acquire a new playbook.

We know, for example, that there are bugs in Manhattan. Millions of them, in a city where the garbage left overnight on the sidewalk must seem like a never-ending buffet. But when Giselle recruits roaches to help her clean Robert's bathtub—well, I was going to say, you'll never think of roaches the same way again, but actually, you will. I am reminded of *Joe's Apartment* (1996), which used five thousand real roaches, and of which I wrote: "That depresses me, but not as much as the news that none of them were harmed during the production."

Anyway, the roach scene is soon over, and the scheming begins, much aided by Sarandon's evil queen, who fears the specter of her son Edward marrying the unworthy Giselle. I am not sure that Robert and Morgan fully understand from whence Giselle comes, but they respond to the magic in her, and so do we.

Encounters at the End of the World ★ ★ ★ ★

G, 99 m., 2008

Directed and narrated by Werner Herzog and produced by Henry Kaiser. Screenplay by Herzog.

Read the title of *Encounters at the End of the World* carefully, for it has two meanings. As he journeys to the South Pole, which is as far as you can get from everywhere, Werner Herzog also journeys to the prospect of man's oblivion. Far under the eternal ice, he visits a curious tunnel whose walls have been decorated by various mementos, including a frozen fish that is far away from its home waters. What might travelers from another planet think of these souvenirs, he wonders, if they visit long after all other signs of our civilization have vanished?

Herzog has come to live for a while at the McMurdo Research Station, the largest habitation on Antarctica. He was attracted by underwater films taken by his friend Henry Kaiser, which show scientists exploring the ocean floor. They open a hole in the ice with a blasting device, then plunge in, collecting specimens, taking films, nosing around. They investigate an undersea world of horrifying carnage, inhabited by creatures so ferocious we are relieved they are too small to be seen. And also by enormous seals who sing to one another. In order not to limit their range, Herzog observes, the divers do not use a tether line, so they must trust themselves to find the hole in the ice again. I am afraid to even think about that.

Herzog is a romantic wanderer, drawn to the extremes. He makes as many documentaries as fiction films, is prolific in the chronicles of his curiosity, and here moseys about McMurdo chatting with people who have chosen to live here in eternal day or night. They are a strange population. One woman likes to have herself zipped into luggage and performs this feat on the station's talent night. One man was once a banker and now drives an enormous bus. A pipe fitter matches the fingers of his hands together to show that the second and third are the same length—genetic evidence, he says, that he is descended from Aztec kings.

But I make the movie sound like a travelogue or an exhibit of eccentrics, and it is a poem of oddness and beauty. Herzog is like no other filmmaker, and to return to him is to be welcomed into a world vastly larger and more peculiar than the one around us. The underwater photography alone would make a film, but there is so much more.

Consider the men who study the active volcanoes of Antarctica and sometimes descend into volcanic flumes that open to the surface—although they must take care, Herzog observes in his wondering, precise narration, not to be doing so when the volcano erupts. It happens that there is another movie opening now that also has volcanic tubes (*Journey to the Center of the Earth*). Do not confuse the two. These men play with real volcanoes.

They also lead lives revolving around monster movies on video, a treasured ice-cream machine, and a string band concert from the top of a Quonset hut during the eternal day. And they have modern conveniences of which Herzog despairs, like an ATM machine, in a place where the machine, the money inside it, and the people who use it, must all be airlifted in. Herzog loves these people, it is clear, because like himself they have gone to such lengths to escape the mundane and test the limits of the extraordinary. But there is a difference between them and Timothy Treadwell, the hero of *Grizzly Man,* Herzog's documentary about a man who thought he could live with bears and not be eaten, and was mistaken. The difference is that Treadwell was a foolish romantic, and these men and women are in this godforsaken place to extend their knowledge of the planet and of the mysteries of life and death itself.

Herzog's method makes the movie seem like it is happening by chance, although chance has nothing to do with it. He narrates as if we're watching movies of his last vacation—informal, conversational, engaging. He talks about people he met, sights he saw, thoughts he had. And then a larger picture grows inexorably into view. McMurdo is perched on the frontier of the coming suicide of the planet. Mankind has grown too fast, spent too freely, consumed too much, and the ice is melting and we shall all perish. Herzog doesn't use such language, of course; he is too subtle and visionary. He is nudged toward his conclusions by what he sees. In a sense, his film journeys through time as well as space, and we see what little we may end up leaving behind us. Nor is he depressed by this prospect, but only philosophical. We came, we saw, we conquered, and we left behind a frozen fish.

His visit to Antarctica was not intended, he warns us at the outset, to take footage of "fluffy penguins." But there are some penguins in the film, and one of them embarks on a journey that haunts my memory to this moment, long after it must have ended.

Note: Herzog dedicated this film to me. I am deeply moved and honored. The letter I wrote to him from the 2007 Toronto Film Festival is in the Essays chapter.

Enron: The Smartest Guys in the Room ★ ★ ★ ½

NO MPAA RATING, 110 m., 2005

Narrated by Peter Coyote. Featuring Kenneth Lay, Jeff Skilling, Lou Pai, Mike Muckleroy, Sherron Watkins, Reverend James Nutter, Bethany McLean, Peter Elkind, and others. A documentary directed by Alex Gibney and produced by Gibney, Jason Kliot, and Susan Motamed, based on the book *The Smartest Guys in the Room: The Amazing Rise and Scandalous Fall of Enron* by Bethany McLean and Peter Elkind.

This is not a political documentary. It is a crime story. No matter what your politics, *Enron: The Smartest Guys in the Room* will make you mad. It tells the story of how Enron rose to become the seventh-largest corporation in America with what was essentially a Ponzi scheme, and in its last days looted the retirement funds of its employees to buy a little more time.

There is a general impression that Enron was a good corporation that went bad. The movie argues that it was a con game almost from the start. It was "the best energy company in the world," according to its top executives, Kenneth Lay and Jeffrey Skilling. At the time they made that claim, they must have known that the company was bankrupt, had been worthless for years, had inflated its profits and concealed its losses through bookkeeping practices so corrupt that the venerable Arthur Andersen accounting firm was destroyed in the aftermath.

The film shows how it happened. To keep its stock price climbing, Enron created good quarterly returns out of thin air. One accounting tactic was called "mark to market," which meant if Enron began a venture that might make $50 million ten years from now, it could claim the $50 million as current income. In an astonishing in-house video made for employees, Skilling stars in a skit that satirizes "HFV" accounting, which he explains stands for "Hypothetical Future Value."

Little did employees suspect that was more or less what the company was counting on.

Skilling and Lay were less than circumspect at times. When a New York market analyst questions Enron's profit-and-loss statements during a conference call, Skilling can't answer and calls him an "asshole"; that causes bad buzz on the street. During a Q&A session with employees, Lay actually reads this question from the floor: "Are you on crack? If you are, that might explain a lot of things. If you aren't, maybe you should be."

One Enron tactic was to create phony offshore corporate shells and move their losses to those companies, which were off the books. We're shown a schematic diagram tracing the movement of debt to such Enron entities. Two of the companies are named "M. Smart" and "M. Yass." These "companies" were named with a reckless hubris: One stood for "Maxwell Smart" and the other one . . . well, take out the period and put a space between "y" and "a."

What did Enron buy and sell, actually? Electricity? Natural gas? It was hard to say. The corporation basically created a market in energy, gambled in it, and manipulated it. It moved on into other futures markets, even seriously considering "trading weather." At one point, we learn, its gambling traders lost the entire company in bad trades, and covered their losses by hiding the news and producing phony profit reports that drove the share price even higher. In hindsight, Enron was a corporation devoted to maintaining a high share price at any cost. That was its real product.

The documentary is based on the best-selling book of the same title, cowritten by *Fortune* magazine's Bethany McLean and Peter Elkind. It is assembled out of a wealth of documentary and video footage, narrated by Peter Coyote, from testimony at congressional hearings, and from interviews with such figures as disillusioned Enron exec Mike Muckleroy and whistle-blower Sherron Watkins. It is best when it sticks to fact, shakier when it goes for visual effects and heavy irony.

It was McLean who started the house of cards tumbling down with an innocent question about Enron's quarterly statements, which did not ever seem to add up. The movie uses in-house video made by Enron itself to show Lay and Skilling optimistically addressing employees and shareholders at a time when Skilling in particular was coming apart at the seams. Toward the end, he sells $200 million in his own Enron stock while encouraging Enron employees to invest their 401(k) retirement plans in the company. Then he suddenly resigns, but not quickly enough to escape Enron's collapse not long after. Televised taking the perp walk in handcuffs, both he and Lay face criminal trials in Texas.

The most shocking material in the film involves the fact that Enron cynically and knowingly created the phony California energy crisis. There was never a shortage of power in California. Using tape recordings of Enron traders on the phone with California power plants, the film chillingly overhears them asking plant managers to "get a little creative" in shutting down plants for "repairs." Between 30 percent and 50 percent of California's energy industry was shut down by Enron a great deal of the time, and up to 76 percent at one point, as the company drove the price of electricity higher by nine times.

We hear Enron traders laughing about "Grandma Millie," a hypothetical victim of the rolling blackouts, and boasting about the millions they made for Enron. As the company goes belly-up, twenty thousand employees are fired. Their pensions are gone, their stock worthless. The usual widows and orphans are victimized. A power company lineman in Portland, who worked for the same utility all his life, observes that his retirement fund was worth $248,000 before Enron bought the utility and looted it, investing its retirement funds in Enron stock. Now, he says, his retirement fund is worth about $1,200.

Strange that there has not been more anger over the Enron scandals. The cost was incalculable, not only in lives lost during the power crisis, but in treasure: The state of California is suing for $6 billion in refunds for energy overcharges collected during the phony crisis. If the crisis had been created by al-Qaida, if terrorists had shut down half of California's power plants, consider how we would regard these same events. Yet the crisis, made possible because of legislation engineered by Enron's lobbyists, is still being blamed on "too much regulation." If there was ever a corporation that needed more regulation, that corporation was Enron.

Early in the film, there's a striking image. We see a vast, empty room, with rows of what look like abandoned lunchroom tables. Then we see the room when it was Enron's main trading floor, with countless computer monitors on the tables and hundreds of traders on the phones. Two vast staircases sweep up from either side of the trading floor to the aeries of Lay and Skilling, whose palatial offices overlook the traders. They look like the stairway to heaven in that old David Niven movie, but at the end they only led down, down, down.

Eros

R, 104 m., 2005

The Hand ★ ★ ★

Gong Li (Miss Hua), Chang Chen (Zhang). Directed by Wong Kar Wai and produced by Jacky Pang Yee Wah.

Equilibrium ★ ★ ★

Robert Downey Jr. (Nick Penrose), Alan Arkin (Dr. Pearl). Directed by Steven Soderbergh and produced by Jacques Bar, Raphael Berdugo, Gregory Jacobs, and Stephane Tchal Gadjieff.

The Dangerous Thread of Things ★

Christopher Buchholz (Christopher), Regina Nemni (Cloe), Luisa Ranieri (La Ragazza). Directed by Michelangelo Antonioni and produced by Marcantonio Borghese and Domenico Procacci. Screenplay by Antonioni and Tonino Guerra.

Are the three films in *Eros* intended to be (a) erotic, (b) about eroticism, or (c) both? The directors respond in three different ways. Wong Kar Wai chooses (c), Steven Soderbergh chooses (b), and Michelangelo Antonioni, alas, arrives at None of the Above.

Wong Kar Wai's film, named *The Hand,* stars Gong Li as Miss Hua, a prostitute who is at the top of her game the first time the shy tailor Zhang (Chang Chen) meets her. He has been sent by his boss to design her clothes, and as he waits in her living room he clearly hears the sounds of sex on the other side of the wall. Her client leaves, she summons him, and curtly interrogates him. He passes muster. To be sure he will think about her while designing her clothes, she says, she will supply him with an aid to his memory. This she does; the film's title is a clue.

Steven Soderbergh's film, *Equilibrium,* is a sketch starring Robert Downey Jr. as the neurotic client of Dr. Pearl (Alan Arkin), his psychiatrist. Downey goes through verbal riffs as only Downey can do, moping about a recurring dream. Because the doctor is not in his line of sight, he is unaware that Dr. Pearl, between cursory responses, has seen someone through the window and is eagerly trying to mime the suggestion that they meet later.

Michelangelo Antonioni's film, *The Dangerous Thread of Things,* takes place near a resort on a lake, out of season. A man named Christopher (Christopher Buchholz) and his wife, Cloe (Regina Nemni), stroll and talk and discuss their problems, and then he sees a sexy young woman (Luisa Ranieri), and his wife tells him where she lives.

He goes to visit her, in improbable quarters inside a crumbling medieval tower, and they have sex. She laughs a lot. After he leaves, she does the kind of dance on the beach that hippies used to perform at dawn in Chicago's Lincoln Park back when the world was young and dance standards were more relaxed.

The Wong Kar Wai film is erotic. At least I found it so, and in matters of eroticism one is always the only judge who matters. It has no nudity, no explicit sex, no lingering shots of Gong Li's beauty. It is about situation and personality. She sees him, understands him, creates his obsession with her almost casually. Later, when the tailor comes to measure her again, he uses his hands instead of a tape measure. She allows him. There is an extraordinary scene in his tailor shop where his hands and arms venture inside her dress as if she were wearing it. Time passes. There is a sad and poetic closure.

The Soderbergh film makes the point that few things are more boring than what arouses someone else—unless it also arouses you, of course, in which case you can forget the other person and just get on with it. Downey's dream is all he can think of, but the psychiatrist cannot force himself to listen, and neither can we; it's much more exciting to speculate on the (unseen) object of his hoped-for tryst.

The Antonioni film is an embarrassment. Regina Nemni acts all of her scenes wearing a perfectly transparent blouse for no other reason, I am afraid, than so we can see her breasts. Luisa Ranieri acts mostly in the nude. The result is soft-core porn of the most banal variety, and when the second woman begins to gambol on the beach one yearns for Russ Meyer to come to the rescue. When a woman gambols in the nude in a Meyer film, you stay gamboled with.

I return to Wong Kar Wai's *The Hand.* It stays with me. The characters expand in my memory and imagination. I feel empathy for both of them: Miss Hua, sadly accepting the fading of her beauty, the disappearance of her clients, the loss of her health, and Mr. Zhang, who will always be in her thrall. "I became a tailor because of you," he says. It is the greatest compliment it is within his power to give, and she knows it. Knows it, and is touched by it as none of the countless words of her countless clients have ever, could ever, touch her.

Evening ★ ½

PG-13, 117 m., 2007

Claire Danes (Young Ann), Toni Collette (Nina), Vanessa Redgrave (Ann Lord), Patrick Wilson (Harris), Hugh Dancy (Buddy), Natasha Richardson (Constance), Mamie Gummer (Lila), Eileen Atkins (Nurse), Meryl Streep (Older Lila), Glenn Close (Lila's mother). Directed by Lajos Koltai and produced by Jeffrey Sharp. Screenplay by Susan Minot and Michael Cunningham, based on a novel by Minot.

There are few things more depressing than a weeper that doesn't make you weep. *Evening* creeps through its dolorous paces as prudently as an undertaker. Upstairs, in the big Newport mansion, a woman is dying in a Martha Stewart bedroom. She takes a very long time to die, because the whole movie is flashbacks from her reveries. This gives us time to reflect on deep issues, such as, who is this woman?

Everybody in the film knows her, and eventually we figure out that she is Ann (Vanessa Redgrave), once the young sprite played in the flashbacks by Claire Danes. I know I must be abnormally obtuse to be confused on this question, but I persisted in thinking she might be the aged form of Lila, who as a young girl (Mamie Gummer) is getting married as the movie opens (it opens in a flashback, then flashes forward to the bed where it is flashing back from). How could I make such a stupid error? Because the mansion she is dying in looks like the same mansion Lila was married from, so I assumed old Lila was still living there. Maybe it's a different mansion. Real estate confuses me.

There are two grown daughters hanging around at the bedside: Constance (Natasha Richardson) and Nina (Toni Collette). But you can't figure out who they are from the flashbacks, because neither has been born yet. However, the flashbacks devote a great deal of time to examining how Lila has had a crush on Harris (Patrick Wilson), a young doctor and wedding guest whose mother was the family's housekeeper. Lila's brother Buddy (Hugh Dancy) has also had a lifelong crush on Harris, but his love dare not speak its name.

Ann is Lila's best friend and maid of honor, and she also falls in love with Harris.

Lila is scheduled to be married on the morrow to the kind of a bore who (I'm only guessing) would be happy as the corresponding secretary of his fraternity. She does not love him. She loves Harris. I already said that. But what makes this Harris so electrifying? Search me. If he is warm, witty, and wonderful on the inside, those qualities are well-concealed by his exterior, which resembles a good job of aluminum siding: It is unbending and resists the elements.

Oh, but I forgot: Harris has one ability defined in my *Little Movie Glossary.* He is a Seeing-Eye Man. Such men are gifted at pointing out things to women. Man sees, points, woman turns, and *now* she sees, too, and smiles gratefully.

Harris is a very highly evolved Seeing-Eye Man. Not once but twice he looks at the heavens and sees a twinkling star. "That's our star," he says, or words to that effect. "See it there?" He points. Young Ann looks up at the billions and billions of stars, sees their star, and nods gratefully. Director Lajos Koltai cuts to the sky, and we see it, too. Or one just like it.

In the upstairs bedroom, old Ann dies very slowly, remembering the events of the long-ago wedding night and the next morning. Out of consideration for us, her reveries are in chronological order, even including events at which she was not present, like before she arrived at the house. She is attended by a nurse with an Irish accent (Eileen Atkins), who sometimes prompts her: "Remember a happy time!" Dissolve to Ann's memory of a happy time. It is so mundane that if it qualifies as a high point in her life, it compares with Paris Hilton remembering a good stick of gum.

What horrors have I overlooked? Oh, the Plunge. Family tradition at weddings requires all male guests to plunge from a high rock into the sea. This inevitably leads to shots of the barren ocean, and cries of, "Buddy? Buddy?" But I'm not giving anything away because Buddy is good for no end of cries of "Buddy?" in this movie. At one point, he needs a doctor, and they remember that Harris is a doctor, and start shouting "Harris! Harris!" in the forest, having absolutely no reason to suppose Harris is within earshot.

Buddy inevitably is an alcoholic whose family members are forever moving the wine bottle out of his reach. He has to get drunk as an excuse to kiss Harris. This is pathetic. Buddy should grow up, bite the bullet, and learn that it takes no excuse to get drunk.

Later on, women in the flashbacks get pregnant and deliver the children who will puzzle us in the flash forwards, and there is one of those poignant chance encounters in Manhattan in the rain, where two old lovers meet after many years and have hardly anything to say. You know the kind of poignant encounter I'm thinking of. All too well, I imagine.

Everything Is Illuminated ★ ★ ★ ½

PG-13, 104 m., 2005

Elijah Wood (Jonathan), Eugene Hutz (Alex), Boris Leskin (Grandfather), Laryssa Lauret (Lista). Directed by Liev Schreiber and produced by Peter Saraf and Marc Turtletaub. Screenplay by Schreiber, based on the novel by Jonathan Safran Foer.

Liev Schreiber's *Everything Is Illuminated* begins in goofiness and ends in silence and memory. How it gets from one to the other is the subject of the film, a journey undertaken by three men and a dog into the secrets of the past. The movie is narrated by Alex (Eugene Hutz), a Ukrainian whose family specializes in "tours of dead Jews." Alex and his grandfather (also named Alex) drive American Jews in search of their roots to the places where many of their ancestors died.

The trip through a bewildering but beautiful Ukrainian countryside involves a Soviet-era car that may not exactly have air bags. The grandfather is the driver, although he claims to be blind and insists on going everywhere with his "seeing-eye bitch," whose name is Sammy Davis Junior Junior. Alex's English seems learned from a thesaurus that was one word off. He tortures words to force them into sentences from which they try to escape, and he keeps a journal with chapters like "Overture to the Commencement of a Very Rigid Search."

The movie's hero is Jonathan (Elijah Wood), a solemn, goggle-eyed American known as "The Collector" because he accumulates bits and pieces of his life and stores them in Ziploc bags, carefully labeled. He has come to Ukraine to find the woman who saved his grandfather's life. To this woman is due much gratitude, because Jonathan's grandmother passed along the belief that Ukraine treated Jews so badly that if the Nazis invaded, it might be an improvement.

The opening hour or so is a weirdly hilarious comedy, based on the intractable nature of the grandfather (Boris Leskin), his fierce love for Sammy Davis Junior Junior, and his truce with his grandson, who idolizes American popular culture, especially Michael Jackson. When Jonathan tells him Sammy Davis Jr. was Jewish, he is astonished: "What about Michael Jackson?" No, says Jonathan, definitely not Michael Jackson.

There is much perplexion (the kind of word the younger Alex savors) that Jonathan is a vegetarian, and in a hotel dining room he is told potatoes do not, cannot, have never come without meat. He is finally served one boiled potato, in a scene that develops as if Chaplin had been involved. Then he goes to his room, a narrow single bed in the midst of vast emptiness. Alex advises him to lock his door: "There are many dangerous people who would try to steal things from Americans and also kidnap them."

The journey continues. Sammy Davis Junior Junior begins to love Jonathan. Grandfather speaks like a crusty anti-Semite, Alex covers for him in his translation, and nobody seems to have heard of the hamlet of Trachimbrod, which they seek. Then abruptly the grandfather steers off the highway and into the middle of nowhere, and they find a beautiful white-haired old woman (Laryssa Lauret) living in a house in the middle of a field who simply says, "You are here. I am it."

The movie is based on a novel by Jonathan Safran Foer that reportedly includes many more scenes from the distant past, including some of magic realism in the eighteenth-century Ukrainian Jewish community. *Everything Is Illuminated* lives in the present, except for memories and enigmatic flashbacks to the Second World War. The gift that Schreiber brings to the material is his ability to move us from the broad satire of the early scenes to the solemnity of the final ones. The first third of the film could be inspired by Fellini's *Amarcord,* the last third by Bergman's darkest hours.

I described Jonathan as the hero of the film, but perhaps he is too passive to be a hero. He regards. He collects. Alex is the active character, cheerfully inventing English as he goes along, making the best of the journey's hardships, humoring his grandfather, telling the rich American what he wants to hear. Eugene Hutz, a singer in a punk gypsy band, brings notes of early John Turturro to the performance. Elijah Wood's performance is deliberately narrow and muted—pitch-perfect, although there is a distraction caused by his oversized eyeglasses, so thick they make his eyes huge. He visits, he witnesses, he puts things in Ziploc bags.

Then again, perhaps the real hero of the film is the grandfather, unless by default it is the old lady, who is a collector, too. For Grandfather, this is as much a journey of discovery as it is for Jonathan, and the changes that take place within him are all the more profound for never once being referred to in his dialogue. He never discusses his feelings or his memories, but in a way he is the purpose of the whole trip. The conclusion he draws from it is illustrated in an image that, in context, speaks more eloquently than words.

Everything Is Illuminated is a film that grows in reflection. The first time I saw it, I was hurtling down the tracks of a goofy ethnic comedy when suddenly we entered dark and dangerous territory. I admired the film but did not sufficiently appreciate its arc. I went to see it again at the Toronto Film Festival, feeling that I had missed some notes, had been distracted by Jonathan's eyeglasses and other relative irrelevancements (as Alex might say). The second time, I was more aware of the journey Schreiber was taking us on, and why it is necessary to begin where he begins to get where he's going.

Exiled ★ ★ ½

R, 100 m., 2007

Nick Cheung (Wo), Roy Cheung (Cat), Josie Ho (Jin), Lam Set (Fat), Francis Ng (Tai), Anthony Wong (Blaze), Simon Yam (Boss Fay). Directed and produced by Johnnie To. Screenplay by

Szeto Kam-yuen, Yip Tin-shing, and Milkyway Creative Team.

The opening scene in *Exiled* lacks only a score by Ennio Morricone to be a spaghetti Western. A fistful of knuckles raps on a door. No answer. Again. Again. The door opens. The man knocking asks for "Mr. Wo." A woman replies, "Not here. Wrong house." The routine is repeated again, for this is indeed the house of Mr. Wo (Nick Cheung), and the woman is his wife, Jin (Josie Ho).

The setting is the Chinese offshore island of Macao, in 1988, right before the Portuguese turned it over to the Chinese. Although all of the characters are Asian, the streets and buildings, mostly Portuguese architecture, look as Mexican as Chinese, and the plot and action look more spaghetti than noodles.

The two men who have turned up at Wo's house have been sent from Hong Kong to kill him. They are Blaze (Anthony Wong) and Fat (Lam Set). Then two more men turn up, and we discover they hope to protect him. They are Cat (Roy Cheung) and Tai (Francis Ng). A high-angle shot shows them staked out at perimeters of a sun-drenched square, smoking cigars. Nobody else is on the streets. Jin looks warily out a window sometimes.

All of this moves slowly ("suspensefully" would be stretching it), and then all hell breaks loose. Wo comes home and everyone starts shooting, and then, if there are survivors (draw your own conclusions), they all help Mrs. Wo set her house straight and sit down to a big meal, using chopsticks to extend their boarding-house reach. They were recently all shooting at each other, but they were childhood friends, and so after business comes pleasure.

Out of this meal comes a plot involving a ton of gold and the prospects of Boss Fay (Simon Yam), the Hong Kong godfather who wants Wo dead. A great deal more shooting goes on, and what we in the filmcrit biz are pleased to call "martial arts choreography." Well, it is choreography, damn it, when you move with agile and daring grace in ways the human body was not built for.

At this point I am tempted to begin a plot description, about who shoots who, and with what, and why. But we can only get a couple thousand words on a page, and if my editors are wise, they will allow me nowhere near that much, even if it would be enough. So let me simply say that enormous numbers of gangsters shoot enormous numbers of bullets at each other, and they're all lousy shots or they'd all soon be dead, while in fact, after a long time, only most of them are.

And don't you love that shot where a guy rolls on the floor from behind one thing to behind another thing, while shooting with both hands? Try it sometime. Both hands fully outstretched with firing guns, and you can roll fast enough to avoid being hit. No using your feet to push, because they never do. They just roll, like a carpet.

Johnnie To, the director, is highly respected in this genre, and I suppose he does it about as well as you'd want it to be done, unless you wanted acting and more coherence. He's compared to John Woo and Andrew Lau. So there you are. I have not made a study of the genre, which has many subtleties and conventions, but I admire *Exiled* for moving and building fluently. I have quoted Dr. Johnson so often that my editors have given up asking me, "What's his first name, and what is he a doctor of?" As faithful readers will know, it was Dr. Johnson who said, of a dog standing on its hind legs, "It is not done well, but one is surprised to find it done at all." So there you are again.

The Exorcism of Emily Rose ★ ★ ★

PG-13, 114 m., 2005

Laura Linney (Erin Bruner), Tom Wilkinson (Father Moore), Campbell Scott (Ethan Thomas), Shohreh Aghdashloo (Doctor), Jennifer Carpenter (Emily Rose), Colm Feore (Karl Gunderson), Mary Beth Hurt (Judge Brewster). Directed by Scott Derrickson and produced by Paul Harris Boardman, Beau Flynn, Gary Lucchesi, Tom Rosenberg, and Tripp Vinson. Screenplay by Boardman and Derrickson.

"Demons exist whether you believe in them or not," says the priest at the center of *The Exorcism of Emily Rose*. Yes, and you could also say that demons do not exist whether you believe in them or not, because belief by definition stands outside of proof. If you can prove it, you don't need to believe it.

Such truths are at the center of this intriguing and perplexing movie, which is based on the true story of a priest who was accused of murder after a teenage girl died during an exorcism. If the priest is correct and the girl was possessed by a demon, he is innocent. If the authorities called by the prosecution are correct, she died of psychotic epileptic disorder, and the priest created complications leading to her death. If, on the other hand, the exorcism theory is correct, drugs given to the girl to treat her "disorder" made her immune to exorcism and led to her death.

The movie is told through flashbacks from a courtroom, where Father Moore (Tom Wilkinson) is on trial. He has been offered a deal (plead guilty to reckless endangerment and do six months of a twelve-month sentence), but he refuses it: "I don't care about my reputation, and I'm not afraid of jail. All I care about is telling Emily Rose's story." His lawyer, Erin Bruner (Laura Linney), despairs and yet admires him for his conviction. She herself does not believe in demons. The prosecutor, Ethan Thomas (Campbell Scott), is a churchgoer and presumably does believe, but lawyers sometimes argue against what they believe to be true. That's their job.

And who is Emily Rose? As played by Jennifer Carpenter in a grueling performance, she is a college student who sees the faces of friends and strangers turn into demonic snarls. Her nightmares are haunting. She speaks in foreign languages. She loses an alarming amount of weight. She calls home for help, in tears. Her boyfriend can't reach her. The parish priest, Father Moore, is called in and determines that an exorcism is indicated.

He has authorization from the archdiocese, but after he is charged with murder, the church authorities order him to accept plea bargaining and create as little scandal for the church as possible. The Church is curiously ambivalent about exorcism. It believes that the devil and his agents can be active in the world, it has a rite of exorcism, and it has exorcists. On the other hand, it is reluctant to certify possessions and authorize exorcisms, and it avoids publicity on the issue. It's like those supporters of intelligent design who privately believe in a literal interpretation of Genesis but publicly distance themselves from it because that would undermine their plausibility in the wider world.

What is fascinating about *The Exorcism of Emily Rose* is that it asks a secular institution, the court, to decide a question that hinges on matters the court cannot have an opinion on. Either Emily was possessed by a demon and Father Moore did his best to save her, or she had a psychotic condition and he unwittingly did his best to kill her. The defense and the prosecution mount strong arguments and call persuasive witnesses, but in the end it all comes down to the personal beliefs of the jury. A juror who does not believe in demons must find Father Moore guilty, if perhaps sincere. A juror who does believe in demons must decide if Emily Rose was possessed or misdiagnosed. In a case like this, during the jury selection, are you qualified or disqualified by believing one way or the other?

The movie takes place in a small town surrounded by a Grant Wood landscape; houses and remote farms crouch in winter fields under a harsh sky. The key relationship is between the priest and his defense attorney. Erin Bruner does not believe in devils, but she believes in Father Moore, and she believes he believes in them. "There are dark forces surrounding this trial," he warns her, suggesting that she herself might be a target of demons. In this and other scenes the movie is studiously neutral on the subject of the priest: He would look, speak, and behave exactly the same if he were sane and sincere, or deluded and sincere.

Erin works for a powerful law firm that has been retained by the archdiocese. She wants to be named a partner, but she won't be if she agrees with Father Moore's wish to appear on the witness stand; the archdiocese wants to make a deal leading to a quick settlement, with no testimony from the priest, and the archdiocese, not the priest, is the client who is paying. Which way does Erin turn? The film is fascinating in the way it makes legal and ethical issues seem as suspenseful as possession and exorcism.

The movie was directed by Scott Derrickson and written by Paul Harris Boardman and Derrickson. The screenplay is intelligent and open to occasional refreshing wit, as when prosecutor Ethan Thomas makes an objection to one witness's speculations about demonology. "On what grounds?" asks the judge (Mary Beth Hurt). "Oh . . . silliness," he says.

Somehow the movie really never takes off into the riveting fascination we expect in the opening scenes. Maybe it cannot; maybe it is too faithful to the issues it raises to exploit them. A movie like *The Exorcist* is a better film because it's a more limited one that accepts demons and exorcists lock, stock, and barrel, as its starting point. Certainly they're good showbiz. A film that keeps an open mind must necessarily lack a slam-dunk conclusion. In the end, Emily Rose's story does get told, although no one can agree about what it means. You didn't ask, but in my opinion she had psychotic epileptic disorder, but it could have been successfully treated by the psychosomatic effect of exorcism if those drugs hadn't blocked the process.

F

Failure to Launch ★

PG-13, 97 m., 2006

Matthew McConaughey (Tripp), Sarah Jessica Parker (Paula), Zooey Deschanel (Kit), Justin Bartha (Ace), Bradley Cooper (Demo), Kathy Bates (Sue), Terry Bradshaw (Al). Directed by Tom Dey and produced by Scott Rudin and Scott Aversano. Screenplay by Tom J. Astle and Matt Ember.

During the course of *Failure to Launch,* characters are bitten by a chipmunk, a dolphin, a lizard, and a mockingbird. I am thinking my hardest why this is considered funny, and I confess defeat. Would the movie be twice as funny if the characters had also been bitten by a Chihuahua, a naked mole rat, and a donkey?

I was bitten by a donkey once. It was during a visit to Stanley Kubrick's farm outside London. I was the guest of the gracious Christiane Kubrick, who took me on a stroll and showed me the field where she cares for playground donkeys after their retirement. I rested my hand on the fence, and a donkey bit me. "Stop that!" I said, and the donkey did. If I had lost a finger, it would have been a great consolation to explain that it had been bitten off by one of Mrs. Stanley Kubrick's retired donkeys.

But I digress. *Failure to Launch* is about a thirty-five-year-old man named Tripp (Matthew McConaughey) who still lives at home with his parents. They dream of being empty nesters and hire a woman named Paula (Sarah Jessica Parker), who is a specialist at getting grown men to move out of their parents' homes. Her method is simple: You look nice, you find out what they like, and you pretend to like it, too. You encourage them to share a sad experience with you. And you ask them to teach you something. In this case, he likes paintball, her dog has to be put to sleep, and he teaches her to sail. Actually, it's not her dog and it's not really put to sleep, but never mind.

Sue and Al (Kathy Bates and Terry Bradshaw) are Tripp's parents. "I never sleep with my clients," Paula tells them. What she does is take hardened bachelors, force them to fall in love with her, and use that leverage to get them to move out of the parental home, after which she breaks up with them and they're fine. If this sounds to you like a cross between pathological cruelty and actionable fraud, I could not agree more. On the other hand, Tripp is no more benign. His strategy is to date a girl until she begins to like him and then take her home to bed, not telling her it is his parents' home. "The only reason he brings girls to dinner is because he's breaking up with them!" Sue warns Paula.

Oh, what stupid people these are. Stupid to do what they do, say what they say, think what they think, and get bitten by a chipmunk, a dolphin, a lizard, and a mockingbird. Actually, it's Tripp's friend Ace (Justin Bartha) who is bitten by the mockingbird. He is dating Paula's surly roommate, Kit (Zooey Deschanel). She hates the mockingbird because it keeps her awake at night. They hunt it with a BB gun, intending only to wound it, but alas the bird is peppered with BBs and seems to be dead, and . . . no, I'm not even going to go there. "You can't kill a mockingbird!" a gun salesman tells Kit. "Why not?" she asks. "You know!" he says. "That book, *To Kill a Mockingbird*!" No, she doesn't know. "I can't believe you don't know that," the guy says. Not know what? It's not titled *To Kill a Mockingbird Would Be Wrong.*

Ace gives the bird the kiss of life and they pump its furry little chest, and it recovers and bites Ace. Kit meanwhile has fallen in love with Ace. Which is my cue to tell you that Zooey Deschanel on this same weekend is opening in two movies; in this one she plays an airhead who saves the life of a mockingbird, and in the other one, *Winter Passing,* she plays an alcoholic actress who drowns her cat, which is dying from leukemia. It's an impressive stretch, like simultaneously playing Lady Macbeth and judging *American Idol.* Deschanel is actually very good in *Winter Passing* and fairly good in *Failure to Launch.* You know the joke about how polite Canadians are. If a movie is great they say it's "very good," and if a movie is terrible, they say it's "fairly good."

I cannot bring myself to describe how Tripp's friend Ace kidnaps him, locks him in a closet, and tricks Paula into being locked in the room with him so that they will be forced to confess their love to each other while Tripp remains tied to a chair and Ace uses hidden iSight cameras to telecast this event, live and with sound, for the entertainment of complete strangers in a restaurant, who watch it on a wall-sized video screen.

Now to get technical. The editing of the film is strangely fragmented. I first noticed this during a backyard conversation between the parents. There's unusually jerky cutting on lines of dialogue, back and forth, as if the film is unwilling to hold the characters in the same shot while they talk to one another. This turbulence continues throughout the film. Back and forth we go, as if the camera's watching a tennis match. I would question the editor, Steven Rosenblum, but he's the same man who edited *Braveheart, Glory,* and *The Last Samurai,* so I know this isn't his style. Did the director, Tom Dey, favor quick cutting for some reason? Perhaps because he couldn't stand to look at any one shot for very long? That's the way I felt.

The Fall ★ ★ ★ ★

R, 117 m., 2008

Catinca Untaru (Alexandria), Lee Pace (Roy Walker), Justine Waddell (Nurse Evelyn), Daniel Caltagirone (Governor Odious), Leo Bill (Charles Darwin), Sean Gilder (Walt Purdy), Julian Bleach (Indian Mystic), Marcus Wesley (Otta Benga), Robin Smith (Luigi). Directed and produced by Tarsem. Screenplay by Dan Gilroy, Nico Soultanakis, and Tarsem, based on the 1981 screenplay for *Yo Ho Ho,* by Valeri Petrov.

Tarsem's *The Fall* is a mad folly, an extravagant visual orgy, a free fall from reality into uncharted realms. Surely it is one of the wildest indulgences a director has ever granted himself. Tarsem, for two decades a leading director of music videos and TV commercials, spent millions of his own money to finance it, filmed it for four years in twenty-eight countries, and has made a movie that you might want to see for no other reason than because it exists. There will never be another like it.

The Fall is so audacious that when *Variety* calls it a "vanity project," you can only admire the man vain enough to make it. It tells a simple story with vast romantic images so stunning I had to check twice, three times, to be sure the film actually claims to have *absolutely no* computer-generated imagery. None? What about the Labyrinth of Despair, with no exit? The intersecting walls of zig-zagging staircases? The man who emerges from the burning tree? Perhaps the trick words are "computer-generated." Perhaps some of the images are created by more traditional kinds of special effects.

The story framework for the imagery is straightforward. In Los Angeles, circa 1915, a silent movie stuntman has his legs paralyzed while performing a reckless stunt. He convalesces in a half-deserted hospital, its corridors of cream and lime stretching from ward to ward of mostly empty beds, their pillows and sheets awaiting the harvest of World War I. The stuntman is Roy (Lee Pace), pleasant in appearance, confiding in speech, happy to make a new friend of a little girl named Alexandria (Catinca Untaru). She has broken her arm falling from a tree while picking oranges in a nearby grove; an elbow brace holds it sticking sideways from her body, and in that hand she carries an old cigar box everywhere, with her treasures.

Roy tells a story to Alexandria, involving adventurers who change appearance as quickly as a child's imagination can do its work. We see the process. He tells her of an "Indian" who has a wigwam and a squaw. She does not know these words and envisions an Indian from a land of palaces, turbans, and swamis. The verbal story is input from Roy; the visual story is output from Alexandria.

The story involves Roy (playing the Black Bandit) and his friends, a bomb-throwing Italian anarchist, an escaped African slave, an Indian (from India), and Charles Darwin and his pet monkey Otis. Their sworn enemy, Governor Odious, has stranded them on a desert island, but they come ashore (riding swimming elephants, of course) and wage war on him. One scene shows the governor's towering private carriage, pulled by hundreds of slaves, while others toil on its wheels like human hamsters. The governor is protected by leather-clad warriors with helmets shaped like coal scuttles.

Roy draws out the story for a personal motive; after Alexandria brings him some communion wafers from the hospital chapel, he persuades her to steal some morphine tablets from the dispensary. Paralyzed and having lost his great love (she is the princess in his story), he hopes to kill himself. There is a wonderful scene of the little girl trying to draw him back to life.

Either you are drawn into the world of this movie or you are not. It is preposterous, of course, but I vote with Werner Herzog, who says if we do not find new images, we will perish. Here a line of bowmen shoots hundreds of arrows into the air. So many of them fall into the back of the escaped slave that he falls backward and the weight of his body is supported by them, as on a bed of nails, dozens of foot-long arrows. There is a scene of the monkey Otis chasing a butterfly through impossible architecture. When the monkey is shot, I was touched by the death of the lovable little simian.

At this point in reviews of movies like *The Fall* (not that there are any), I usually announce that I have accomplished my work. I have described what the movie does, how it looks while it is doing it, and what the director has achieved. Well, what has he achieved? *The Fall* is beautiful for its own sake. And there is a sweet charm from the young Romanian actress Catinca Untaru, who may have been dubbed for all I know, but speaks with the innocence of childhood, working her way through tangles of words. She regards with equal wonder the reality she lives in and the fantasy she pretends to. It is her imagination that creates the images of Roy's story, and they have a purity and power beyond all calculation. Roy is her perfect storyteller, she is his perfect listener, and together they build a world.

Note: The R *rating should not dissuade bright teenagers from this celebration of the imagination.*

The Family Stone ★ ★ ★

PG-13, 102 m., 2005

Claire Danes (Julie Morton), Diane Keaton (Sybil Stone), Rachel McAdams (Amy Stone), Dermot Mulroney (Everett Stone), Craig T. Nelson (Kelly Stone), Sarah Jessica Parker (Meredith Morton), Luke Wilson (Ben Stone), Tyrone Giordano (Thad Stone), Brian White (Patrick Thomas). Directed by Thomas Bezucha and produced by Michael London. Screenplay by Bezucha.

I was poised to attack *The Family Stone* because its story of a family of misfits is no match for the brilliance of *Junebug*. I was all worked up to bemoan the way a holiday release with stars such as Claire Danes, Diane Keaton, Dermot Mulroney, and Luke Wilson gets a big advertising send-off, while a brilliant film like *Junebug*, ambitious and truthful, is shuffled off into "art film" purgatory. Then sanity returned: *Junebug* intends to be a great film, and is, and *The Family Stone* intends to be a screwball comedy, and is, and all they have in common is an outsider coming into a family circle. To punish *The Family Stone* because of *Junebug* would be like discovering that *The Producers* is not *The Sweet Smell of Success.*

So let's see what it is. As the movie opens, the Stones are preparing to celebrate Christmas. The oldest son, Everett (Dermot Mulroney), is bringing home his fiancée, Meredith (Sarah Jessica Parker), to meet the family. Meredith is not going to be an easy fit. She's aggressive, uptight, and hypersensitive, and dresses like someone who has never been undressed.

Waiting in the hometown are Everett's family: his mom, Sybil (Diane Keaton), his dad, Kelly (Craig T. Nelson), his brother Ben (Luke Wilson), his gay and deaf brother, Thad (Ty Giordano), and his kid sister, Amy (Rachel McAdams). We will also meet Thad's African-American partner, Patrick (Brian White), and their adopted son.

So, okay, if the Stones are okay with Patrick, they're strong on empathy and acceptance. Therefore, if they don't like Meredith, it is because she is not to be liked. And that does seem to be the case because (1) it is instantly obvious to the mother, Sybil, that this is the wrong woman for her son Everett, and (2) poor Meredith is one of those perfectionists who, in their rigid compulsion to do the right thing, always succeed in doing the wrong one.

Sir Michael Tippett, who wrote operas, said, "There is only one comic plot: the unexpected hindrances to an eventual marriage." While this definition does not encompass *A Night at the Opera* or *Babe: Pig in the City*, there is much truth in it. In Meredith's case, she is her own greatest hindrance to marriage, and the more she realizes that, the deeper the hole she digs.

The screenplay by director Thomas Bezucha establishes subplots around this central fact. We learn that Everett is drawn to Meredith partly because he believes that to be successful in business, he should be more like her and less like he really is. We learn that Ben, the Luke Wilson character, thinks of himself as a wild and crazy guy. We meet Meredith's sister Julie (Claire Danes), who flies in to rescue her sister and turns into a second fly in the same ointment. Julie is as relaxed and natural as Meredith is emotionally constipated. And then, in ways I will not reveal, it turns out there is another truth Sir Michael might have observed: Opposites attract.

The Family Stone is silly at times, leaning toward the screwball tradition of everyone racing around the house at the same time in a panic fueled by serial misunderstandings. There is also a thoughtful side, involving the long and loving marriage of Sybil and Kelly. Keaton and Nelson create touching characters in the middle of comic chaos. They have a scene together as true and intimate in its way as a scene involving a long-married couple can be. It doesn't involve a lot of dialogue, and doesn't need to, because it obviously draws on a lot of history.

There is an emerging genre of movies about family reunions at holiday time. It seems to be a truth universally acknowledged that most reunions at Christmas end happily, while most reunions at Thanksgiving end sadly. That's odd, because the way things shake out in the world of fragmented families, we tend to spend Thanksgiving with those we choose, and Christmas with those we must. If those two lists are identical in your life, your holidays must all be joyous, or all not.

What is always true is that the holiday itself imposes Aristotle's unities of time and place upon the plot. Most of the action takes place in the house or on the way to and from it, and whatever happens will have to happen before everybody heads back to the airport. That creates an artificial deadline that makes everything seem more urgent and requires that the truth be told or love declared right here and now, or not at all.

The Family Stone sorts out its characters admirably, depends on typecasting to help establish its characters more quickly, and finds a winding path between happy and sad secrets to that moment when we realize that the Family Stone will always think of this fateful Christmas with a smile, and a tear. What else do you want? If it's a lot, just rent *Junebug*.

Fantastic Four ★

PG-13, 123 m., 2005

Ioan Gruffudd (Reed Richards/Mr. Fantastic), Jessica Alba (Susan Storm/Invisible Woman), Michael Chiklis (Ben Grimm/Thing), Chris Evans (Johnny Storm/Human Torch), Kerry Washington (Alicia Masters), Julian McMahon (Victor Von Doom/Doctor Doom). Directed by Tim Story and produced by Avi Arad, Chris Columbus, Bernd Eichinger, and Ralph Winter. Screenplay by Michael France and Mark Frost, based on the comic book and characters by Jack Kirby and Stan Lee.

So you get in a spaceship and you venture into orbit to research a mysterious star storm hurtling toward Earth. There's a theory it may involve properties of use to man. The ship is equipped with a shield to protect its passengers from harmful effects, but the storm arrives ahead of schedule and saturates everybody on board with unexplained but powerful energy that creates radical molecular changes in their bodies.

They return safely to Earth, only to discover that Reed Richards (Ioan Gruffudd), the leader of the group, has a body that can take any form or stretch to unimaginable lengths. Call him Mr. Fantastic. Ben Grimm (Michael Chiklis) develops superhuman powers in a vast and bulky body that seems made of stone. Call him Thing. Susan Storm (Jessica Alba) can become invisible at will and generate force fields that can contain propane explosions, in case you have a propane explosion that needs containing but want the option of being invisible. Call her Invisible Woman. And her brother, Johnny Storm (Chris Evans), has a body that can burn at supernova temperatures. Call him the Human Torch. I almost forgot the villain, Victor Von Doom (Julian McMahon), who becomes Doctor Doom and wants to use the properties of the star storm and the powers of the Fantastic Four for his own purposes. He eventually becomes metallic.

By this point in the review, are you growing a little restless? What am I gonna do, list names and actors and superpowers and nicknames forever? That's how the movie feels. It's all setup and demonstration and naming and discussing and demonstrating, and it never digests the complications of the Fantastic Four and gets on to telling a compelling story. Sure, there's a nice sequence where Thing keeps a fire truck from falling off a bridge, but you see one fire truck saved from falling off a bridge, you've seen them all.

The Fantastic Four are, in short, underwhelming. The edges kind of blur between them and other superhero teams. That's understandable. How many people could pass a test right now on who the X-Men are and what *their* powers are? Or would want to? I was watching *Fantastic Four* not to study it but to be entertained by it, but how could I be amazed by a movie that makes its own characters so indifferent about themselves? The Human Torch, to repeat, *can burn at supernova temperatures!* He can become so hot, indeed, that he could *threaten the very existence of the earth itself!* This is absolutely, stupendously amazing, wouldn't you agree? If you could burn at supernova temperatures, would you be able to stop talking about it? I know people who won't shut up about winning fifty bucks in the lottery.

But after Johnny Storm finds out he has become the Human Torch, he takes it pretty much in stride, showing off a little by setting his thumb on fire. Later he saves the earth, while Invisible Woman simultaneously contains his supernova so he doesn't destroy it. That means Invisible Woman could maybe create a force field to contain the sun, which would be a big deal, but she's too distracted to explore the possibilities: She gets uptight because she will have to be naked to be invisible, because otherwise people could see her empty clothes; it is no consolation to her that invisible nudity is more of a metaphysical concept than a condition.

Are these people complete idiots? The entire nature of their existence has radically changed, and they're about as excited as if they got a makeover on *Oprah*. The exception is Ben Grimm, as Thing, who gets depressed when he looks in the mirror. Unlike the others, who look normal except when actually exhibiting superpowers, he looks like—well, he looks like his suits would fit the Hulk, just as the Human Torch looks like the Flash, and the Invisible Woman reminds me of Storm in *X-Men*. Is this the road company? Thing clomps around on his size 18 boulders and feels like an outcast until he meets a blind woman named Alicia (Kerry Washington) who loves him, in part because she can't see him. But Thing looks like Don Rickles crossed with Mount Rushmore; he has a body that feels like a driveway and a face with crevices you could hide a toothbrush in. Alicia tenderly feels his face with her fingers, like blind people often do while falling in love in the movies, and I guess she likes what she feels. Maybe she's extrapolating.

The story involves Dr. Doom's plot to . . . but perhaps we need not concern ourselves with the plot of the movie, since it is undermined at every moment by the unwieldy need to involve a screenful of characters who, despite the most astonishing powers, have not been made exciting, or even interesting. The X-Men are major league compared to them. And the really good superhero movies, such as *Superman*, *Spider-Man 2*, and *Batman Begins*, leave *Fantastic Four* so far behind that the movie should almost be ashamed to show itself in some of the same theaters.

The Fast and the Furious: Tokyo Drift ★ ★ ★

PG-13, 105 m., 2006

Lucas Black (Sean Boswell), Bow Wow (Twinkie), Nathalie Kelley (Neela), Brian Tee (D.K.), Sung Kang (Han), Leonardo Nam (Morimoto), Brian Goodman (Mr. Boswell), Sonny Chiba (Uncle Kamata). Directed by Justin Lin and produced by Neal H. Moritz. Screenplay by Chris Morgan.

After Sean wrecks a construction site during a car race, the judge offers him a choice: Juvenile Hall or go live with his father in Japan. So here he is in Tokyo, wearing his cute school uniform and replacing his shoes with slippers before entering a classroom where he does not read, write, or understand one word of Japanese. They say you can learn through total immersion. When he sees the beautiful Neela sitting in the front row, it's clear what he'll be immersed in.

The Fast and the Furious: Tokyo Drift is the third of the F&F movies; it delivers all the races and crashes you could possibly desire, and a little more. After only one day in school, Sean (Lucas Black) is offered a customized street speedster and is racing down the ramps of a parking garage against the malevolent D.K. (Brian Tee), who turns out to be Neela's boyfriend.

The racing strategy is called "drifting." It involves sliding sideways while braking and accelerating, and the races involve a lot of hairpin turns. The movie ends with a warning that professional stunt drivers were used and we shouldn't try this ourselves. Like the stunt in *Jackass* where the guy crawls on a rope over an alligator pit with a dead chicken hanging from his underwear, it is not the sort of thing likely to tempt me.

The movie observes two ancient Hollywood conventions. First, the actors play below their ages. Although the "students" are all said to be seventeen, Lucas Black is twenty-four, and his contemporaries in the movie range between nineteen and thirty-four. Maybe that's why the girls in the movie take their pom-poms home: They need to remind us how young they are.

They also are rich. After Sean wrecks the red racer that Han (Sung Kang) has loaned him, he has access to a steady supply of expensive customized machines, maybe because Han likes him, although the movie isn't heavy on dialogue. "I have money," Han tells Sean after the first crash. "It's trust I don't have." He lets Sean work off the cost of the car by walking into a bathhouse and trying to collect a debt from a sumo wrestler. Meanwhile, in the tiny but authentic Tokyo house occupied by his father (Brian Goodman), a U.S. military officer, Sean has to listen to a movie speech so familiar it should come on rubber stamps: "This isn't a game. If you're gonna live under my roof, you gotta live under my rules. Understood?"

Yeah, sure, Dad. Sean is scorned in Tokyo as a *gaijin*, or foreigner, and that gives him something in common with Neela (Nathalie Kelley), whose Australian mother was a "hostess" in a bar and whose father presumably was Japanese, making her half-gaijin. "Why can't you find a nice Japanese girl like all the other white guys?" Han asks him. Luckily, Neela speaks perfect English, as do Han and Twinkie (Bow Wow), another new friend, who can get you Air Jordans even before Nike puts them on the market.

The racing scenes in the movie are fast, and they are furious, and there's a scene where Sean and D.K. are going to race down a twisting mountain road, and Neela stands between the two cars and starts the race, and we wonder if anyone associated with this film possibly saw *Rebel Without a Cause.*

What's interesting is the way the director, Justin Lin, surrounds his gaijin with details of Japanese life, instead of simply using Tokyo as an exotic location. We meet the sumo wrestler, who will be an eye-opener for teenagers self-conscious about their weight. We see pachinko parlors, we see those little "motel rooms" the size of a large dog carrier, and we learn a little about the *yakuza* (the Japanese mafia) because D.K.'s uncle is the yakuza boss Kamata (Sonny Chiba). One nice touch happens during the race on the mountain road, which the kids are able to follow because of instant streaming video on their cell phones.

Lin, still only thirty-three, made an immediate impression with his 2002 Sundance hit, *Better Luck Tomorrow,* a satiric and coldly intelligent movie about rich Asian-American kids growing up in Orange County, California, and winning Ivy League scholarships while becoming successful criminals. That movie suggested Lin had the resources to be a great director, but since then he's chosen mainstream commercial projects. Maybe he wants to establish himself before returning to more personal work. His *Annapolis* (2006) was a sometimes incomprehensible series of off-the-shelf situations (why, during the war in Iraq, make a military academy movie about boxing?).

But in *The Fast and the Furious: Tokyo Drift* he takes an established franchise and makes it surprisingly fresh and intriguing. The movie is not exactly *Shogun* when it comes to the subject of an American in Japan (nor, on the other hand, is it *Lost in Translation*). But it's more observant than we expect and uses its Japanese locations to make the story about something more than fast cars. Lin is a skillful director, able to keep the story moving, although he needs one piece of advice. It was Chekhov, I believe, who said when you bring a gun onstage in the first act, it has to be fired in the third. Chekhov also might have agreed that when you bring Nathalie Kelley onstage in the first act, by the third act the hero at least should have been able to kiss her.

Fay Grim ★ ★

R, 118 m., 2007

Parker Posey (Fay Grim), Jeff Goldblum (Fulbright), James Urbaniak (Simon Grim), Saffron Burrows (Juliet), Liam Aiken (Ned Grim), Elina Lowensohn (Bebe), Leo Fitzpatrick (Carl Fogg), Chuck Montgomery (Angus James), Thomas Jay Ryan (Henry Fool). Directed by Hal Hartley and produced by Hartley, Michael S. Ryan, Martin Hagemann, Jason Kliot, and Joana Vicente. Screenplay by Hartley.

Hal Hartley's *Fay Grim* stars Parker Posey and Jeff Goldblum in a search for a mysterious terrorist named Henry Fool. This man, we learn, has been part of intrigues involving Chile, Iraq, Israel, France, Germany, Russia, England, China, and the Vatican (where the pope *threw a chair at him*). All in the last seven years.

Posey plays the title character, a mom from Queens whose son gets in trouble at school for showing around a hand-cranked toy movieola with pornographic images. Who mailed him the device? Could it have something to do with her brother Simon (James Urbaniak), a Nobel Prize–winning poet who has been jailed for helping Henry Fool escape the United States? Or with Henry Fool (Thomas Jay Ryan) himself? Enter Fulbright (Goldblum) and Fogg (Leo Fitzpatrick), CIA agents searching for Henry's missing confessions. Soon Fay is caught up in an international intrigue.

But a peculiar intrigue it is, because Hartley's style seems determined to dampen our interest in the plot. Working with a usually tilting camera, he photographs his characters taking part in lugubrious and maddening dialogue of bewildering complexity. And he minimizes the action, which mostly takes place offscreen.

When a man leaps from a hotel roof, for example, we don't see what happens, but we hear a crash. When a man is hit by a car, we don't see it happen, but Hartley cuts to a staged and unconvincing shot of him rolling off the car's hood. Shoot-outs are handled with montages of still images.

The result is that we feel deliberately distanced from the film. It is not so much an exercise in style as an exercise in search of a style. The story doesn't involve us because we can't follow it, and we doubt if the characters can either. But am I criticizing Hartley, a leading indie filmmaker, for not making a more conventional thriller, with more chases and action scenes? Not at all. I am criticizing him for failing to figure out what he wanted to do instead, and delivering a film that is tortured in its attempt at cleverness and plays endlessly.

Parker Posey and Jeff Goldblum labor at their characters, and are often fun to watch. But in the absence of a screenplay that engages them, they have to fall back on their familiar personalities and quirks. They bring more to the movie than it brings to them.

Fay Grim is the sequel to *Henry Fool*, Hartley's 1998 film, which won the screenwriting prize at Cannes. In that one, Henry first motivated Simon to become a poet and didn't seem involved in intrigues. He was an enigma with no purpose other than being enigmatic. Now we find out much more about Henry, but it all seems arbitrary and made up on the spot.

As for Hartley's tilted camera, tilt shots have traditionally been used to create a heightened sense of danger; the characters can hardly hold onto the screen. Here they're used for scenes of stultifying dialogue and seem more like a desperate attempt to add interest to flat material. I like it better when style seems to emerge from a story (as in *The Third Man*) than when it feels trucked in from the outside.

Note: Much is made of the fact that Henry's confessions may be encrypted. It is ironic, therefore, that the key encryption simply involves initials that are seen upside down and need to be turned over? But see if you can figure out how Fay finds the blind antiques dealer who can explain it all to her. Kind of a coincidence?

Fear and Trembling ★ ★ ★

NO MPAA RATING, 107 m., 2005

Sylvie Testud (Amelie), Kaori Tsuji (Fubuki), Taro Suwa (Monsieur Saito), Bison Katayama

(Monsieur Omochi), Yasunari Kondo (Monsieur Tenshi), Sokyu Fujita (Monsieur Haneda), Gen Shimaoka (Monsieur Unaji). Directed by Alain Corneau and produced by Alain Sarde and based on the novel by Amelie Nothomb.

The opening shot of *Fear and Trembling* shows the heroine at the age of five, sitting at the edge of the ancient rock garden at the Ryoanji Zen temple in Kyoto. This is an elegant arrangement of rocks on a surface of smooth pebbles. They are so placed that no matter where you sit, you can't see all of them at the same time. Some see the garden as a metaphor for Japanese society, intricately arranged so that it looks harmonious from every viewpoint, but is never all visible at once.

The heroine, whose name is Amelie, returns with her parents to her native Belgium. But she has fallen in love with Japan, and at the age of twenty, she returns to take a job with a vast corporation and "become a real Japanese." Now played by Sylvie Testud as a college graduate who speaks perfect Japanese, she is hired as a translator and assigned to work under the beautiful Fubuki (Kaori Tsuji). She idolizes this woman, so beautiful, so flawless, so tall—too tall, probably, to ever marry, Amelie reflects.

The story of her year at the Yumimoto Corp., based on a semiautobiographical novel by Amelie Nothomb, is the story of a westerner who speaks flawless Japanese but in another sense does not understand Japanese at all. In one way after another she commits social errors, misreads signals, violates taboos, and has her fellow workers wondering, she is told, "how the nice white geisha became a rude Yankee." That she is Belgian makes her no less a Yankee from the Japanese point of view; what is important is that she is not Japanese.

Consider her first blunder. She is ordered to serve coffee to visiting executives in a conference room. As she passes around the cups, she quietly says, "Enjoy your coffee." Soon after she leaves the room, the visitors walk out in anger, and Omochi (Bison Katayama), the boss of the boss of her boss, screams, "Who is this girl? Why does she speak Japanese?" But, she says, she was *hired* because she speaks Japanese. "How could they discuss secret matters in front of a foreigner who speaks Japanese?" the boss of her boss screams. "You no longer speak Japanese!"

She argues that it is impossible for her to forget how to speak Japanese, but this is taken as an example of her inability to understand Japan. She learns quickly that the corporate hierarchy is unbending: "You may only address your immediate superior, me," says Fubuki. Eager to find a role, Amelie begins to distribute the mail, only to find she is taking the job of the mailman. She assigns herself to updating every calendar in the office but is told to stop because it is a distraction. That's a shame, because she finds she enjoys her simple tasks. "How silly I was to get a college degree," she says in the narration, "when my mind was satisfied by mindless repetition. How nice it was to live without pride or brains!" Eventually she is assigned to clean the toilets.

This is indeed a woman who is lost in translation. But how accurate is this portrait of Japanese corporate life? I searched for a review from Japan but wasn't able to find one. My guess is that an actual Japanese corporation has been transformed here through a satirical filter into an exaggeration of basic truths: There is a hierarchy, there is suspicion of foreigners, no one who is not Japanese can ever possibly understand the Japanese, etc. Donald Richie has lived in Japan for most of the last fifty-six years and written invaluable books about its society and films; he was able to relax and adjust, he writes in his recently published journals, only when he realized that he would always be an invisible outsider, exempt from social laws because he was not expected to be able to understand them.

Fear and Trembling, directed by Alain Corneau, may be a sardonic view of Japanese corporate culture, but that's not all it is. The movie is also subtly sexual and erotic, despite the fact that almost every scene takes place in the office and there is not a single overt sexual act or word or gesture or reference. Sexuality in the movie's terms is transferred into the power of one person over another; Amelie begins by adoring Fubuki but eventually realizes that the other woman hates her and is jealous of her as a competitor. Fubuki finds her one demeaning task after another, and Amelie responds simply by—doing them. By submitting.

This response has a quietly stimulating result for Fubuki, who is aroused by the other woman's submission. The brilliance of the movie is to suppress all expression of this arousal; we have to sense it in small moments of body language, in almost imperceptible pauses or reactions, in the rhythm set up between command and obedience. Understanding Fubuki better than she understands herself, Amelie is eventually able to win the game by becoming so submissive, so much in fear of the taller, more powerful woman, that a kind of erotic release takes place. She exaggerates the "fear and trembling" that, it is said, one should exhibit when addressing the emperor.

The movie that comes to mind is *Secretary,* the 2002 film with James Spader as a lawyer whose new secretary, played by Maggie Gyllenhaal, gradually enters with him into an S&M relationship that she, as the submissive one, finds a source of power (and amusement). Much the same thing happens in *Fear and Trembling;* that it happens below the level of what is said and done and acknowledged makes it doubly erotic because it cannot be admitted or acknowledged. The film ends again in the Kyoto rock garden, whose message is perhaps: If you could see all the rocks at once, what would be the point of the garden?

Feast of Love ★ ★

R, 102 m., 2007

Morgan Freeman (Harry), Greg Kinnear (Bradley), Radha Mitchell (Diana), Jane Alexander (Esther), Alexa Davalos (Chloe), Toby Hemingway (Oscar), Selma Blair (Kathryn), Stana Katic (Jenny), Billy Burke (David), Fred Ward (Bat), Sherilyn Lawson (Doctor). Directed by Robert Benton and produced by Gary Lucchesi, Tom Rosenberg, and Richard S. Wright.

Morgan Freeman returns in *Feast of Love* as a wise counselor of the troubled and heartsick. Apart from his great films, of which there are many, this is almost his standard role, although he also seems to spend a lot of time playing God. Most of his insights seem not merely handed down the mountain, but arriving as a successful forward pass. At the beginning of the film, he gives us the ground rules: "They say that when the Greek gods were bored, they invented humans. Still bored, they invented love. That wasn't boring, so they tried it themselves. And then they invented laughter—so they could stand it."

The Greek gods had one thing going for them. They were immutable. Zeus was always Zeus and Hera was always Hera, and they were always in character, always Zeuslike and Heraesque. In *Feast of Love,* however, Freeman plays a professor named Harry who is forced to contend with confused lovers who don't know, or can't reveal, their own hearts.

He lives in Portland, Oregon, in a long and happy marriage with Esther (Jane Alexander). Spare hours are spent in Jitters coffee shop, where his coffee cup is an omnipresent prop and useful timing device; sips punctuate his wisdom. The shop is owned by Bradley (Greg Kinnear), who thinks he is in love with his wife, Kathryn (Selma Blair). But he is living in a fool's paradise, as Harry easily sees one evening when they all go to a bar after a women's softball game.

"I saw two women fall in love with one another tonight," he tells Esther when he gets home. Yes, he watched as Jenny (Stana Katic), a shortstop on the opposing team, put a quarter in the jukebox, a hand on Kathryn's leg, and whispered, "From now on, that will be our song." Harry is bemused: "Bradley was sitting right there, and he didn't see a thing."

Bradley has blindness when it comes to women. He brings home a dog for Kathryn's birthday present, although she has told him time and again that she hates and fears dogs. Maybe there is a clue to their incompatibility when, during a forced visit to the animal shelter, she named this particular dog "Bradley."

This Bradley, he's a pushover. Next he falls in love with a Realtor named Diana (Radha Mitchell), who walks into his shop on a rainy day. She smokes organic cigarettes. Those are the ones that kill you but don't support Big Tobacco. She's having a heartless, purely physical affair with the studly David (Billy Burke), whom she has not quite broken up with. Bradley doesn't see this.

Meanwhile, Oscar (Toby Hemingway), the counterman in the coffee shop, falls in love with a girl who walks in one day and makes her love for him clear. This is Chloe (Alexa Davalos), who is good and true, but Oscar has problems of his own. He lives with his father, Bat (Fred Ward), a drunk who staggers around so comically he looks like he thinks he's in a silent comedy and lurks in the bushes brandishing a knife. No movie can be very good that contains Fred Ward's worst performance (it's the fault of the character, to be sure).

Have I left out any combinations? Only the doctor (Sherilyn Lawson) who bandages Bradley's finger after he cuts himself as punishment for losing Diana. All of these scenarios unwind under the thoughtful gaze of Harry, who returns with his nightly reports to Esther. They have had a wounding personal loss—an esteemed son, dead of an overdose. But Esther seems content to sit at home alone until such intervals as Harry can free himself from his coffee shop, park bench, and other counseling stations.

There are some good things in the movie. Some scenes play well as self-contained episodes. The city of Portland is beautifully evoked. Jane Alexander and Morgan Freeman make a couple we love. Greg Kinnear raises fecklessness to an art. And there is a lot more nudity than you'd expect, if you like that sort of thing.

All of these stories are woven into a tapestry by director Robert Benton, working from a screenplay by Allison Burnett, which is based on the novel by Charles Baxter. Benton has made better movies about doomed marriages (*Kramer vs. Kramer*), but this one has no organic reality because it depends on three artifices: (1) the clockwork success and failure of relationships, (2) the need for Harry as a witness, (3) the lickety-split time span that compresses the action so much it loses emotional weight. Harry is always looking on as if he already knows how every story will turn out. We're looking on in exactly the same way.

Fever Pitch ★ ★ ★ ½

PG-13, 98 m., 2005

Drew Barrymore (Lindsey Meeks), Jimmy Fallon (Ben Wrightman). Directed by Bobby Farrelly and Peter Farrelly and produced by Drew Barrymore, Alan Greenspan, Nancy Juvonen, Gil Netter, Amanda Posey, and Bradley Thomas. Screenplay by Lowell Ganz and Babaloo Mandel, based on the book by Nick Hornby.

It must be Nick Hornby who understands men so well, and how they think about women, and how women think about them. His books have been the starting point for three wonderful movies about the truce of the sexes: *High Fidelity* (2000), *About a Boy* (2002), and now *Fever Pitch.* Their humor all begins in the same place, with truth and close observation. We know these people. We dated these people. We are these people.

Because *Fever Pitch* involves a Boston Red Sox fan and takes place during the miraculous 2004 season, do not make the mistake of thinking it is a baseball movie. It is a movie about how men and women, filled with love and motivated by the best will in the world, simply do not speak the same emotional language. She cannot understand why he would rather go to spring training camp in Florida than meet her parents. He cannot understand why this is even an issue.

Drew Barrymore and Jimmy Fallon star, as Lindsey and Ben, both around thirty. She thinks it may be time to get married. He already seems married, to the Red Sox. His love for the team, he confesses to her, "has been a problem with me . . . and women." She is a high-paid business executive. He is a high school teacher.

Should she date below her income level? She has a strategy meeting with her girlfriends. When men have these meetings, they talk about how a woman really understands them. Women talk about how a man doesn't really understand them. Men talk about how a woman looks. Women ask questions like: "Where has he been?" Ben is thirty and single. Lindsey at least *knows* why she's still single: She works all the time.

Their first date begins unpromisingly, with food poisoning and Lindsey hurling into a garbage can. But Ben is a nice guy and cleans up, puts her to bed, sleeps on the couch. In no time at all, they're in love. What she doesn't understand is, she's in love with Winter Guy.

Summer Guy is a Red Sox fan. She is from Venus; he is from Fenway Park. He has season tickets. The people in the nearby seats are his "summer family." When they talk Red Sox lore, it sounds like they know what they're talking about. When he considers selling his season tickets, they observe that "technically" he's supposed to return them to the team. His apartment looks like a sports memorabilia store. Even the telephone is made out of a baseball mitt. She looks at the T-shirts and warm-up jackets in his closet, and says, "This is not a man's closet."

Jimmy Fallon is perfectly cast in the role. *Saturday Night Live* veterans tend to disappear into the fourth dimension of "*SNL* comedies" that are usually pretty bad. Only occasionally does someone like Bill Murray find a wider range of roles. Fallon was recently in the awful *Taxi,* but here it must be said (as it could be said about John Cusack in *High Fidelity* and Hugh Grant in *About a Boy*) that you cannot imagine anyone else in the role. He achieves a kind of perfection in his high spirits, his boyish enthusiasm, his dependence on the Sox for a purpose in his life, and his bafflement about romance. He doesn't know that Freud's dying words were allegedly, "Women! What do they want?" But he would have understood them.

Drew Barrymore is also perfectly cast, in part because in real life, as in the movie, she's not only adorable but also a high-powered businesswoman (she is listed first among the film's producers). Her Lindsey likes Ben because he is a good and nice man, funny, considerate, and sexy. That's the Winter Guy. The Summer Guy is also all of those things, when his busy schedule as a Red Sox fan permits him. "All those things you feel for that team," she tells him in despair, "I feel them too, for you."

Well, come on. Think how the guy feels. The Sox are down 0-3 to the Yankees in the AL playoffs and behind in the fourth and apparently final game. He's at a party she wanted him to attend. He has a great time at the party, until he finds out *the Red Sox tied it up and won 6–4 in the 12th inning!* That will be a moment that he will always, always regret missing. Is he a fool? I would like to say that he is, but if I hadn't seen the final four minutes of the Illinois game against Arizona, *when they came from 15 behind to tie it up and win in overtime!* I would have been . . . discontented.

Yes, it's only a game. There's a bright little boy in the movie who says to Ben: "Let me just leave you with this thought. You love the Sox, but have they ever loved you back?" Lindsey loves him back. But one transgression follows another. Consider her thoughts as she watches the TV news, which shows her being hit by a foul ball and knocked out, while next to her Ben jumps up and down in excitement and hasn't noticed his girl is unconscious. Women remember things like that.

The movie has been directed by the Farrelly brothers, Peter and Bobby, who tend to make a different kind of movie *(Dumb and Dumber, Kingpin, There's Something About Mary, Stuck on You).* Here, they're sensitive and warmhearted, never push too hard, empathize with the characters, allow Lindsey and Ben to become people we care about. What's going on? first Danny *(Trainspotting)* Boyle makes *Millions,* and now this. Maybe the Farrellys were helped by the script by Lowell Ganz and Babaloo Mandel, who have nine children between them, and whose writing collaborations include *Parenthood, Forget Paris,* and *A League of Their Own,* which knew a lot about baseball.

What's really touching is the way Lindsey works and works to try to understand Ben. When he tries to tell her why he loves the Red Sox even though they always, always let him down, she says: "You have a lyrical soul. You can live under the best and worst conditions." What she doesn't understand is that the girlfriend of a Red Sox fan must also endure the best and the worst, and have a soul not only lyrical but forgiving. How does it feel when his Sox tickets are *always* more important than *anything* she suggests? "Here's a tip, Ben," she says. "When your girlfriend says let's go to Paris for the weekend—you go."

Final Destination 3 ★ ★

R, 92 m., 2006

Mary Elizabeth Winstead (Wendy Christensen), Ryan Merriman (Kevin Fischer), Texas Battle (Lewis Romero), Alexz Johnson (Erin), Sam Easton (Frankie), Kris Lemche (Ian McKinley), Gina Holden (Carrie Dreyer). Directed by James Wong and produced by Glen Morgan, Craig Perry, Wong, and Warren Zide. Screenplay by Morgan and Wong.

Final Destination 3 is in the relentless tradition of the original Dead Teenager Movies, which existed to kill all the teenagers in the movie except one, who was left alive to star in the sequel, explaining to fresh victims what happened at Camp Crystal Lake, or how we know what you did last summer. In *FD3*, the kids learn about their possible fates because one of them heard about the *FD1* case on the news. If the movie were self-aware, like the *Scream* pictures, he would have said, "This is just like that movie *Final Destination*."

The *FD1* opening formula is repeated. Some viewers may feel cheated by the It's Only a Dream Scene, but fans of the series will understand as a character has a premonition of disaster and watches in horror as her vision comes true. Wendy (Mary Elizabeth Winstead) is with a group of friends at a carnival and refuses to get on the roller coaster because she's convinced it will crash. It does, with many detailed scenes in which teenagers cling desperately to upside-down coaster cars, are beheaded, etc.

Wendy and her friend Kevin (Ryan Merriman) learn that the kids who didn't get on the doomed airplane in *FD1* died anyway, in the same order they were intended to board the plane. Is the same fate in store for the kids who didn't get on the roller coaster? Wendy, who was taking digital photos at the carnival, loads them into her computer and uses them to figure out what the likely order of victims will be; she and Kevin seem doomed along with the others, which is a reason right there not to spend the $79 to upgrade to iPhoto 6.

Do they all die? The point in these movies is not if they die, but how they die, and Fate must stay up nights devising ingenious executions. There is a crushing experience in the takeout lane at Fatburger, a crispy afternoon at a tanning salon, a beheading, a gruesome death by nail gun, an unfortunate fireworks accident, and at the end, everyone gets on a train when they should be checking into an emergency room just as a precaution.

Why are teenagers attracted to movies in which teenagers die? Maybe it's related to the basic appeal of all horror films: We sit in the audience and think, there but for the grace of God go we. There is also the reassurance that the movie will not contain a lot of long speeches or deep thought, and there will be few adults in the audience to tell you to get the hell off your cell phone because they paid for their tickets, etc.

There must be dozens of films in this genre. At Sundance 2006 there was at least a positive development in *Wristcutters*, when the characters discover that after you kill yourself, the world is pretty much the same as it was before, except grungy, poverty-stricken, and depressing. In *Wristcutters 2*, they should have a Third World suicide victim who finds the afterlife an improvement and thinks he is in heaven.

The problem with *FD3* is that since it is clear to everyone who must die and in what order, the drama is reduced to a formula in which ominous events accumulate while the teenagers remain oblivious. We see oil dripping, trucks rolling out of control, and hinges working loose, and we realize: The movie is obviously filmed from the POV of Fate itself. We see a nail gun, and we start calculating which character is next to be nailed.

Final Destination 3 is good looking and made with technical skill. The director is James Wong, who made *FD1* and was once a writer on *The X-Files* and *21 Jump Street*. He and the cinematographer, Robert McLachlan, do an especially good job of evoking a creepy sense of menace on a carnival midway. Has there ever been a carnival midway in a movie that *didn't* look like a sadomasochistic nightmare? The rides look fatal, the sideshows look like portals to hell, and you know that game where you slam down a big hammer to make the weight fly up and hit the bell? One kid pounds so hard the weight crashes through the bell and flies off into the air. I expected it to land on somebody's head, or maybe on the roller coaster tracks, and maybe it did and I missed it because there was a lot going on. But as nearly as I can figure, the weight is still up there somewhere.

Note: Ebert's review was cut short when a weight from a carnival game crashed through the window and wiped out his computer. Dann Gire, president of the Chicago Film Critics Association, has sent out warnings to the next six reviewers scheduled to write about the film.

Finding Amanda ★ ★ ½

R, 90 m., 2008

Matthew Broderick (Taylor Peters), Brittany Snow (Amanda), Steve Coogan (Jerry), Maura Tierney (Lorraine Mendon), Peter Facinelli (Greg). Directed by Peter Tolan and produced by Richard Heller and Wayne Allan Rice. Screenplay by Tolan.

A quietly perfect scene in *Finding Amanda* involves Taylor, the hero, arriving at a Las Vegas casino. Without overstating the case, the film makes it clear that Taylor is well-known here: The doorman, the bellboy, even the room maid greet him by name. That may be one of the danger signals of a gambling addiction. Another one may be taking a check from out of the middle of your wife's checkbook.

Taylor (Matthew Broderick) is indeed an addicted gambler. He claims to be recovering. Hasn't placed a bet since . . . earlier today. He is also, over a longer span of time, a recovering alcoholic and drug addict. He works as a well-paid writer for a TV sitcom that everybody seems to agree is terrible and lives in a comfortable home with his comely wife, Lorraine (Maura Tierney), who is fed up to here with his gambling and has called an attorney.

That sets the stage for the central drama of the film. Taylor's twenty-year-old niece, Amanda (Brittany Snow) has left home, gone to Vegas and become a "dancer," which, we learn, is a euphemism for "stripper," which is a euphemism for "hooker." The girl's mother is begging him to intervene. Taylor is happy to oblige, since it means a trip to Vegas, where even the room maid, etc.

And so commences a peculiar film that is really two films fighting to occupy the same space. The first film, the one of the "quietly perfect scene," is about Taylor, his addictions, his emotions, and Jerry (Steve Coogan), a host at the casino. The second film, which has no perfect scenes, is about his niece, her life, and her boyfriend, Greg (Peter Facinelli). If there were more of the first story line and less of the second, this would be a better film. If there were none of the second story line, it might really amount to something. But there we are.

Broderick is splendid as the gambler. He knows, as many addicts do, that the addictive personality is very inward, however much acting-out might take place. He plays Taylor as a man constantly taking inventory of himself: How does he feel? Could he feel better? Can he take a chance? Does he feel lucky? Will one little bet, or drink, really hurt? How about two? Taylor evolves as a sympathetic man, one to be pitied (as his wife knows, although she is running low on pity). He is likable, intelligent, decent, really does hope to help his niece, and has several monkeys scrambling for space on his back.

Brittany Snow (Amber Von Tussle in *Hairspray*) does what she can with the role of Amanda as written, but that's just the problem: how it's written. She has it all figured out how she can have a nice car, house, clothes, and boyfriend while hooking, which her old job at the International House of Pancakes did not make possible. Why she felt she had to move to Vegas to work at IHOP remains unexplained. Also unexplained, in my mind, is how she became a hooker (her "explanation" is harrowing and intended as heartbreaking, but sounds more like the story of someone looking for trouble). There is also the matter of the boyfriend, Greg. I know such men exist and someone has to date them, but why Amanda? This guy is such a scummy lowlife, he gives pimps a bad name. Why does she support him and endure his blatant cheating?

You will not find a convincing answer in this film. What you will find is a nicely modulated performance by Steve Coogan (*24-Hour Party People*) as Jerry, the casino's host, who knows Taylor from way back, extends him credit against his better judgment, knows an addictive gambler when he sees one and is looking at one. He makes Jerry not the heavy and not the comic foil, but an associate in a circular process of betting and losing and winning a little and betting and losing a lot, and so on. How Taylor's luck changes, and what happens, is for me entirely believable.

Finding Amanda will be followed closely in theaters by *Diminished Capacity,* a film starring Broderick as a newspaper columnist who goes to his hometown to help his uncle (Alan Alda). Broderick is just right in both films, acting his way under, over, around, and occasionally straight through the material. Now we need him in a better screenplay.

Finding Home ★

PG-13, 124 m., 2005

Lisa Brenner (Amanda), Genevieve Bujold (Katie), Louise Fletcher (Esther), Jeannetta Arnette (Grace), Misha Collins (Dave), Sherri Saum (Candace), Justin Henry (Prescott), Johnny Messner (Nick), Jason Miller (Lester), Andrew Lukich (C.J.). Directed by Lawrence D.

Foldes and produced by Victoria Paige Meyerink. Screenplay by Foldes and Grafton S. Harper.

The end credits for *Finding Home* thank no fewer than six experts on false memory. If only they had consulted even one expert on flashbacks involving false memories, or memories of any kind, or flashbacks of any kind. Here is a movie in which the present functions mostly as a launching pad for the past, which is a hotbed of half-remembered out-of-focus screams, knives, secrets, blood, and piano lessons.

As the story opens, Amanda (Lisa Brenner) is planning her first visit to her grandmother, Esther (Louise Fletcher), when she gets a message that Esther has died. Esther's death doesn't deprive Fletcher of screen time, however, since she's present in so many flashbacks that the time line could have just been flipped, with the story taking place in the past with flash-forwards. To be sure, the flashbacks are confused and fragmented, but the present-day scenes don't make any more sense, even though we can see and hear them, which you might think would be an advantage.

Amanda's grandmother owned and operated an inn on a Maine island. The inn is one of those New England clapboard jobs with a dock and cozy public rooms and two or three floors of guest rooms. Hold that thought. We'll need it. Because of whatever happened more than ten years ago, Amanda has been forbidden to ever mention the grandmother or the inn to her mother, Grace (Jeannetta Arnette). When Amanda is ferried to the island in a boat piloted by Dave (Misha Collins), she focuses on his knife with such intensity we're reminded of the zoom-lens eye belonging to Alastor "Mad-Eye" Moody in the latest Harry Potter picture. Admittedly, a character who toys with a knife all the time in a movie makes you think.

Dave is a nice young man, ostensibly, although he spends an alarming amount of time in his work shed, carving large blocks of wood into measurably smaller ones. "Who is that going to be?" Amanda asks him of one block that already looks so much like Amanda it might as well be wearing a name tag. "I don't know who is inside it yet," he says, a dead giveaway that he has read *The Agony and the Ecstasy* and knows that with Amanda he can safely steal anything Michelangelo ever said.

"You and Dave were inseparable," Amanda is told by Katie (Genevieve Bujold), her grandmother's best friend, who has managed the inn for years. Then what happened to make Amanda fear him so, and dislike him so, and stare so at his knife? I personally think Katie knows the whole story: "Something happened between your mother and grandmother that summer," she also tells Amanda. And, "Can you really believe what she tells you about that summer?"

Before we can answer these questions, Amanda's mother, Grace, herself arrives on the island, along with, let's see, thumbing through my notes here, the family lawyer (Jason Miller); Amanda's boss and boyfriend, Nick (Johnny Messner); Amanda's best friend, Candace (Sherri Saum), and *her* boyfriend, C. J. (Andrew Lukich); and the accountant Prescott (Justin Henry), who after all the trouble that nice Dustin Hoffman went to on his behalf in *Kramer vs. Kramer* has grown up to be a bad accountant. There is room for all these visitors because not a single guest is ever seen at the inn.

But hold on, how do I know Prescott is incompetent? Have you kept the inn fixed in your memory as I requested? The dock, the cozy public rooms, the clapboard siding, several acres of forested grounds? The hardwood floors, the pewter, the quilts, the Arts and Crafts furniture, the canned preserves? The smell of apple pies in the oven? Well, Amanda discovers that she has inherited the inn from her grandmother, who cut off Grace with a lousy brooch. Prescott the accountant then estimates that the inn could sell for, oh, about $400,000. It is unspeakably rude for a movie critic to talk aloud during a screening, but at the screening I attended, someone cried out, "I'll buy it!" Reader, that person was me.

Are Dave and Katie the caretaker depressed that Amanda might sell her grandmother's inn? Not as much as you might think. Does this have anything to do with the flashbacks, the screams, the blood, the knife, and the piano lessons? Not as much as you might think. Did Dave sexually assault Amanda ten years ago? Not as much as you might think. Why does another character choose this moment to announce she is pregnant? Who could the father be? Given the Law of Economy of Characters, it has to be someone on the island. Or maybe it was someone in one of the flashbacks who flash-forwarded in a savage act of phallic time travel and then slunk back to the past, the beast.

The solution to the mysteries, when it comes, is not so much anticlimactic as not climactic at all. I think it is wrong to bring a false memory on board only to discover that it is really false. After what this movie puts us through, the false memory at least should have a real false memory concealed beneath it. What were all those experts for?

Find Me Guilty ★ ★ ★

R, 125 m., 2006

Vin Diesel (Jackie DiNorscio), Peter Dinklage (Ben Klandis), Ron Silver (Judge Finestein), Linus Roache (Sean Kierney), Annabella Sciorra (Bella DiNorscio), Alex Rocco (Nick Calabrese). Directed by Sidney Lumet and produced by Bob Yari, Robert Greenhut, Bob DeBrino, T. J. Mancini, and George Vitetzakis. Screenplay by Mancini and Robert McCrea.

"When they f— with me," Jackie DiNorscio says, "they wake a sleeping giant." Actually, it's more like they bring his inner stand-up comedian to his feet. DiNorscio is the wild card in the longest trial in American history, a twenty-one-month extravaganza aimed at the Lucchese crime family of New Jersey. There are twenty defendants, and they all have defense attorneys except Jackie, who represents himself. His participation makes the trial curiously similar to *Mystery Science Theater 3000*, with dopey characters marching through with profundities while Jackie cracks jokes.

Jackie is played by Vin Diesel, something I didn't know going in. It took awhile to see through the makeup to Diesel, playing a paunchy goombah who is already serving a thirty-year sentence when the trial begins. He's offered a deal: testify against his fellow villains, and get a reduction in his sentence. "I don't rat on my friends," he says. That's for sure. He even forgives a cousin who pumps four bullets into him. "I love him," he says. "Live and let live." When the cops ask him to name the shooter, he intones, "My eyes were shut the whole time." Diesel is a good choice for this role, bringing it sincerity without nobility.

The movie was directed by a man who knows all about courtroom drama. Sidney Lumet directed *12 Angry Men,* which takes place almost entirely within a jury room, and there are vivid scenes of testimony in his *Serpico* and *The Verdict.* What's different this time is that the battle between good and evil is murky. Yes, the defendants are killers, thieves, extortionists, drug dealers, pimps, and otherwise ill-behaved. No one doubts they are guilty. But against their predations the movie sets Jackie DiNorscio, who says he is "not a gangster but a gagster," and pisses off the prosecution, the defense, the judge, and his fellow defendants. Only the jury likes him. "They say a laughing jury is not a hanging jury," says Ben Klandis (Peter Dinklage), the brains of the defense team. He sits next to Jackie in court and occasionally whispers advice.

Jackie didn't graduate grade school. He is loyal to mobsters who ordered him to be whacked. He spends less time defending himself than offering a running commentary on the judicial system. He cuts through the fog of testimony. "How did you *know* they were Italians?" he asks an FBI witness, who says he saw defendants paying homage to crime boss Nick Calabrese (Alex Rocco). The witness babbles about how they waved their hands and had black hair and sounded like they were talking Italian. Jackie cuts him to shreds, exposing at the same time the tendency of lawmen to describe what they saw as if they were objective observers without preconceptions. The FBI agent should have replied: "I knew they were Italians because I've been on this case for years and I knew every one of them by name."

Jackie's moral position is hard to define. He seems to value friendship and loyalty above all, and to disregard imperfections such as murder. He is loyal to Calabrese even after the mobster tells him, "If you mention my name in this courtroom one more time, I will cut your heart out." He loves the guy. Live and let live. The movie's title comes from his closing statement, in which he tells the jury he's already serving thirty years and has nothing to lose: "Find me guilty," he says, but let off his friends.

Are we cheering for him? Not precisely. But he is the underdog in a system that offends common sense with its ponderous slog through legal quicksand. A defense attorney who needs five days to summarize his argument doesn't have one. Subtitles remind us how many days the trial has lasted; they climb above five hundred. A defendant has a heart attack, is brought into court on a bed, falls out of the bed. A mother dies. The chief prosecutor, Sean Kierney (Linus Roache), doesn't like to be laughed at and retaliates by taking away the prized Barcalounger in Jackie's jail cell. The judge (Ron Silver) would cut Jackie loose from the case, except that might lead to a mistrial.

If the movie lacks a battle between good and evil, it also lacks drama. The outcome of the trial seems to be a foregone conclusion. *Find Me Guilty* exists in its moments. There is an electric conversation between Jackie and his former wife, Bella (Annabella Sciorra), that makes it perfectly clear why they drove each other crazy, and why they got married in the first place. The defense attorneys are presented in montages of gaseous idiocies, except for Klandis, the Dinklage character, who stands apart as a man concise, articulate, and professional. He is a dwarf. A court officer wheels forward a podium on a staircase, which he climbs to face the jury. Without one word being spoken, Klandis transforms this podium from a compensation for his height into an acknowledgment of his stature. He stands above the others with or without the stairs.

This movie by its nature is not thrilling, but it is genuinely interesting, and that is rare. It's not even really about a particular trial, but about a Kafkaesque system that can only work if there are no Jackies to point out its absurdities. We in the audience are left without cheering rights. Since the defendants (except for the cousin) are not actually seen doing anything evil, we don't yearn for their conviction. But surely they cannot be found innocent. The trial comes down to: Can Jackie get away with his act? And if he does, so what? He's still facing thirty years. Good and evil seem stuck on the same treadmill, and we are invited to focus on a contest between drones and a wise guy. You'd be surprised how entertaining that can be.

Firecracker ★ ★ ★ ½

NO MPAA RATING, 112 m., 2005

Karen Black (Eleanor/Sandra), Mike Patton (David/Frank), Susan Traylor (Ed), Kathleen Wilhoite (Jessica), Jak Kendall (Jimmy), Brooke Balderson (Pearl), Paul Sizemore (Officer Harry). Directed by Steve Balderson and produced by Clark Balderson. Screenplay by Steve Balderson.

Firecracker is a movie that was made outside the factory, beyond the rules, in a far place named Wamego, Kansas. We accustom ourselves to the weekly multiplex extrusions, and then something like this slips in, fresh from the wild. It's a black-and-white crime drama and a lurid color fantasy, a slice of life crossed with grotesque sideshow performers; it contains cruel family secrets, deadpan humor, horrifying mutilations, and possibly a visit from the Virgin Mary.

The movie is profoundly odd, which qualified it to open the Chicago Underground Film Festival. Imagine *In Cold Blood* crossed with *Freaks,* with the look of Alejandro Jodorowsky's *Santa Sangre.* It was written, directed, and filmed by Steve Balderson in his hometown of Wamego, inspired by a murder that happened there fifty years ago. The movie is so rooted in this small town that one of the locations is the house where the murder took place. So rooted that Balderson got permission to shoot in the house because his father's plumber lives there now.

The movie has one of the most immediately gripping opening scenes I can remember. In everyday black-and-white, the sleepy town is alarmed as two people, and then more, desperately run across lawns and down alleys. Mothers snatch their children out of the way. The runners converge on a backyard where digging is going on inside a tool shed. A female sheriff looks on. Another woman glances inside the shed and retches.

The rest of the movie is prelude. We meet a sad, wounded family: The mother, Eleanor (Karen Black), prays the rosary and tries to keep peace between her brutal older son, David (Mike Patton), and her sensitive younger son, Jimmy (Jak Kendall). There is a father, so withdrawn he is hardly visible.

David calls the shots, struts like a torturer, torments Jimmy for playing the piano: "Learn how to make a living, not sissy-boy piano recitals!"

It is the Fourth of July and the carnival is in town. Traveling carnivals often serve in horror movies as repositories of the bizarre in the wilderness of small-town boredom. Jimmy wants to go. David taunts him: "You want to see the girly show." Well, of course he does. In the world before *Playboy,* the carnival girly show was an erotic magnet; furtive men eyed the parade of strippers and followed them into the tent's smutty embrace. There was the same rumor every summer: "After the show, they do it with guys in the field behind the tent." Maybe it was true. Nobody I knew ever had the nerve to see.

The town is mostly in black and white, and the carnival is in saturated color: bold, dripping reds and yellows and dark brown shadows. The focus of attention is the "French singer" Sandra (also played by Karen Black). She is the captive, perhaps the slave, of the carnival owner, Frank (also played by Mike Patton, the rock singer). She hides herself in furs, feathers, hoods, scarves, and dresses that look shabby not because they have been worn so much but because they have been removed so often.

Jimmy wants to play for her. Maybe join the carnival and tour as her pianist. She remembers him from other summers, looking hungrily from the audience. She also remembers his brother, David, who got her pregnant last summer. The cruel Frank ended her pregnancy, but it is David she tells, "I'm not gonna let you hurt me again."

These characters and their sexual needs and fears are seen against an ominous background of sideshow people, played (as in *Freaks*) by themselves. The most striking is the Enigma, his skin entirely covered by an intricate jigsaw of blue tattoos that is beautiful or ugly, erotic or not, depending on your taste. There is also a giant, a lobster girl, and so on.

What happens between these people, I will leave for you to discover. The plot burrows more deeply, until the line between the black-and-white town and the color carnival seems to blur, and everything seems caught up in the same nightmare. The idea of having Karen Black and Mike Patton play dual roles is not a stunt but part of the strategy; no, the mother and the whore, the brother and the owner are not "the same person" but are connected at a deeper level, perhaps in Jimmy's mind, where they perform similar functions in opposite worlds. Black is uncanny in the way she creates two characters who are so opposite and convincing.

The film is visually jarring. Some shots by cinematographer Jonah Torreano look like lab experiments with the psychology of color. A shot, for example, of a woman in a red cape fleeing across a green field, the red so red, the green so green, that the impact is aggressive. There are inexplicable images, like bright blue bottles hanging from the stark branches of a tree next to a woman gowned in white, that work because they shift the whole movie away from reality into hallucination.

Then there are strange everyday details. There's a little girl put on a leash in the back yard by her mother. She sets off firecrackers. There is a sequence where a body is carried from a house to a shed while being concealed behind a big white sheet on a clothes line; the line is on rollers, so the sheet can be pulled along as a moving screen. There is the Hitchcockian scene where the mother asks at the cleaners for an "astringent" to remove the "shoe polish" on her carpet. A good enough story, but she has foolishly ripped up some of the carpet and brought it along, and anyone can see it's soaked with blood. And a scene where the color fades from the frame as life fades from a body.

Movie critics are criticized for preferring novelty because we are jaded by the ordinary. If only that were true of everybody; how much wasted time we could recapture. I praise *Firecracker* because it is original and peculiar, but also because it is haunted; there is an uneasy spirit living within this film that stirs uneasily and regards us with cold, unblinking eyes. The calm of small-town Kansas inspires the yearnings in those who do not fit there, who are drawn to the carnival, which doesn't fit anywhere.

First Descent ★ ½

PG-13, 110 m., 2005

Shawn Farmer (Himself), Terje Haakonsen (Himself), Nick Perata (Himself), Hannah Teter

(Herself), Shaun White (Himself). Directed by Kemp Curly and Kevin Harrison, and produced by Curly and Harrison. Screenplay by Harrison.

First Descent is boring, repetitive, and maddening about a subject you'd think would be fairly interesting: snowboarding down a mountain. And not just any mountain. This isn't about snowboarders at Aspen or Park City. It's about experts who are helicoptered to the tops of virgin peaks in Alaska, and snowboard down what look like almost vertical slopes.

I know nothing about snowboarding. A question occurs to me. If it occurs to me, it will occur to other viewers. The question is this: How do the snowboarders know where they are going? In shot after shot, they hurtle off snow ledges into thin air and then land dozens or hundreds of feet lower on another slope. Here's my question: As they approach the edge of the ledge, how can they know for sure what awaits them over the edge? Wouldn't they eventually be surprised, not to say dismayed, to learn that they were about to drop half a mile? Or land on rocks? Or fall into a chasm? Shouldn't the mountains of Alaska be littered with the broken bodies of extreme snowboarders?

I search the Internet and find that indeed snowboarders die not infrequently. "All I heard was Gore-Tex on ice," one survivor recalls after two of his companions disappeared. The movie vaguely talks about scouting a mountain from the air and picking out likely descent paths, but does the mountain look the same when you're descending it at 45 degrees and high speed? Can rocks be hidden just beneath the surface? Can crevasses be hidden from the eye?

The film features five famous names in the sport: veterans Shawn Farmer, Terje Haakonsen, and Nick Perata, and teenage superstars Hannah Teter and Shaun White. For at least twenty minutes at the top of the movie, they talk and talk about the "old days," the "new techniques," the "gradual acceptance" of snowboarding, the way ski resorts first banned snowboarders but now welcome them. "As the decade progressed, so did snowboarding," we learn at one point, leading me to reflect that as the decade progressed, so did time itself.

There are a lot of shots of snowboarders in the movie, mostly doing the same things again and again, often with the camera at such an angle that we cannot get a clear idea of the relationship between where they start and where they land. To be sure, if it's hard to ski down a virgin mountainside, it must be even harder to film someone doing it. (When I saw the IMAX documentary about climbing Everest, it occurred to me that a more interesting doc would have been about the people who carried the camera.) In this case, the action footage is repetitive and underwhelming, no match for the best docs about surfing, for example. The powerful surfing film *Riding Giants* (2004), directed by Stacy Perata, does everything right that *First Descent* does wrong.

The movie's fundamental problem, I think, is journalistic. It doesn't cover its real subject. The movie endlessly repeats how exciting, or thrilling, or awesome it is to snowboard down a mountain. I would have preferred more detail about how dangerous it is, and how one prepares to do it, and what precautions are taken, and how you can anticipate avalanches on virgin snow above where anybody has ever snowboarded before.

The kicker on the trailer says: "Unless you're fully prepared to be in a situation of life and death, you shouldn't be up here." So, okay, how can you possibly be fully prepared in a situation no one has been in before and that by definition can contain fatal surprises? Since the five stars of the movie are all still alive as I write this review, they must have answers for those questions. Maybe interesting ones. Maybe more interesting than what a thrill it is.

Flags of Our Fathers ★ ★ ★ ★

R, 132 m., 2006

Ryan Phillippe (John Bradley), Jesse Bradford (Rene Gagnon), Adam Beach (Ira Hayes), Barry Pepper (Mike Strank), John Benjamin Hickey (Keyes Beech), John Slattery (Bud Gerber), Paul Walker (Hank Hansen), Jamie Bell (Ralph Ignatowski). Directed by Clint Eastwood and produced by Eastwood, Steven Spielberg, and Robert Lorenz. Screenplay by William Broyles Jr. and Paul Haggis, based on the book by James Bradley and Ron Powers.

A veteran of the battle of Iwo Jima reflects in *Flags of Our Fathers* that the marines on the island were not fighting because of their flag or their country but for "the man in front of him and the man behind him." Clint Eastwood's film makes this argument in many ways; the men who survive the bloody carnage are often silent about it in later years, and one old man still has nightmares about a comrade lost on the battlefield.

Those who were hailed as the Iwo Jima heroes were indeed heroes (the battle resulted in twenty-nine Medals of Honor), but in the film they tend to be unresponsive to such praise; they cannot forget the dead friends left behind. The intensity of the battle can scarcely be imagined. The marines suffered one-third of all their World War II combat deaths on the tiny speck in the Pacific, and almost all the twenty-two thousand entrenched Japanese died, some by their own hands.

Eastwood's ambitious and enormously effective film has three aims: To re-create the hell of the Battle of Iwo Jima, to explore the truth and meaning of the famous photograph of the flag being raised over the island, and to record the aftermath in the lives of the survivors. He joined it with another film, *Letters from Iwo Jima,* about the Japanese experience; a garrison of defenders tunneled into the rock of the island to create fortified positions. It was clear to them that without air or sea support they would be defeated; their mission was to hold out as long as they could, and die.

The film opens with interlocking scenes from past and present, showing the battle under way and being remembered, with voice-overs from survivors. All the major themes are being introduced, although we will discover that only later. Then, after a tense prelude at sea, it focuses on the initial American landing, which was eerily quiet; no Japanese fire was encountered on the beach, and troops advanced inland easily, until being ambushed by concealed enemy positions. On that first day, two thousand lives were lost, almost all of them American.

The Japanese tactics, while ultimately doomed, were fearfully effective. Their positions were linked by tunnels in the solid rock, and their big gun positions were shielded by steel doors that swung shut after every firing. "How did they dig these things?" one marine asks. We learn in the second film that they did it mostly by hand. One of the baffling realities of the battle was that a machine-gun emplacement could be "cleaned out" by grenades or flame throwers, and then remanned by tunnel to become active again.

Eastwood focuses particularly on the soldiers who will be involved in the flag raisings on the island's Mount Suribachi. Yes, there were two, after the first flag was taken down and kept by a politician as a souvenir. The second flag raising was the one snapped by AP photographer Joe Rosenthal, whose photograph became arguably the most famous ever taken. And "snapped" is the correct word; he aimed his big Speed Graphic and clicked the shutter without framing or focusing, and obtained a perfectly composed, iconic picture. His good luck is underlined because the camera required a plate change after every shot.

The men who raised the flag were hailed as heroes, but who precisely were they? No faces were visible. Nor were those who raised the first flag credited because the official story was that there was only one event. The men themselves knew who they were and were not, but no one really wanted to know the truth; three of them were later killed, and three others were brought home to headline a national tour to sell U.S. bonds.

These were John "Doc" Bradley (Ryan Phillippe), Rene Gagnon (Jesse Bradford), and Ira Hayes (Adam Beach). Stateside, they are given a press agent to manage their tour and be sure they say the right things and project the right image to raise desperately needed money to fund the war. They raised some $26 million, not without personal conflict. Of the men, Bradley, a navy corpsman, is the spokesman, repeating in city after city, "The heroes are the men we left behind." Gagnon enjoys the fame and the attentions of a sexy girlfriend determined to become his wife. And Hayes, a Pima Indian, revolts against the idea of being cheered and wants only to return to action.

Their PR man is Keyes Beech (John Benjamin Hickey), who from the later 1940s through Vietnam would be the Pacific correspondent for the famed *Chicago Daily News* Foreign Service. Eastwood depicts him as focused on fantasy over substance and indifferent to news that there was an earlier flag raising, but in fact he is doing his job, which is to hold the three together, present an appropriate image, and help the war effort by raising money. The film told me something I did not know: Domestic enthusiasm for the war was becoming exhausted, funds were drying up, the government had run out of lenders. *Flags of Our Fathers* argues, not without reason, that the Rosenthal photograph electrified public opinion, and the money those men raised turned the financial tide.

Of the three, Bradley is the one whose life inspired the best-selling book by his son James, who worked with Ron Powers. But the most complex and tragic is the American Indian Hayes, whom America wanted to be a hero but not an American; he is routinely addressed as "chief," is refused service at a bar because he is not white, is condescended to by dignitaries. One fatuous public official memorizes some allegedly Pima words and addresses them to Hayes, who does not understand. "What's-a matter, chief? Don't know your own lingo?" Hayes responds coolly, "I guess I've been off the reservation for too long."

He is an alcoholic who is barely able to walk when the three men "scale" a papier-mâché model of Mount Suribachi at a fund drive in Chicago's Soldier Field. He weeps, recoils at praise, tries to blurt out the true story, and in the film's most moving scene he walks for miles in the western heat to tell the father of his dead friend the true story of that day in the Pacific. Adam Beach's performance is the most memorable in the film; the other actors, perhaps by design, tend to morph into young, crew-cut kids (many only eighteen or nineteen) who may be dead before they are even formed.

Eastwood's two-film project is one of the most visionary of all efforts to depict the reality and meaning of battle. The battle scenes, alternating between close-up combat and awesome aerial shots of the bombardment and landing, are lean, violent, horrifying. His cinematographer, Tom Stern, wisely bleeds his palette of bright colors and creates a dry, hot, desolate feeling; there should be nothing scenic about the film's look.

Much was made of the age of the director when he was making it, but I think that kind of praise only distracts from the accomplishment; filmmakers like Eastwood, Sidney Lumet, Robert Altman, Ingmar Bergman, and Akira Kurosawa do not fade but thrive and grow. There have been so many Eastwoods over the years, from the TV star, to the gunman of spaghetti Westerns, to the box-office king Dirty Harry, to the idiosyncratic director, to the jazz-loving filmmaker and composer, to the master of cinema and winner of two best-picture Oscars. What is the thread that draws him through his life? I think there are two threads: intelligence, and an instinct for the cinema that has compelled him toward ever more ambitious projects. He just gets better.

Flanders ★ ★ ★

NO MPAA RATING, 91 m., 2007

Adelaide Leroux (Barbe), Samuel Boidin (Demester), Henri Cretel (Blondel), Jean-Marie Bruveart (Briche), David Poulain (Leclercq), Patrice Venant (Mordac), David Legay (Lieutenant), Inge Decaesteker (France). Directed by Bruno Dumont and produced by Jean Brehat and Rachid Bouchareb. Screenplay by Dumont.

It was W. G. Sebold who said that animals and men gaze at each other across a gulf of mutual incomprehension. Here is a film that crouches on the screen like a great, sullen beast. It is impossible to embrace, impossible to dismiss. I do not know what it is thinking, how it perceives life. But the film is not about animals. It is about men and women, inarticulate to the point of silence, putting one weary foot ahead of another in a march toward sadness.

Flanders, by Bruno Dumont, won the Jury Prize at Cannes 2007. His *L'Humanite* won it in 1999. Both films require a special kind of viewer. I wrote of *L'Humanite* that it is "for those few moviegoers who approach a serious movie almost in the attitude of prayer." But we do not approach *Flanders* as if attending a religious service. We are its pastor, helpless to console it. It stands wet and lonely outside our church of the human race.

The movie takes place in a pale, cold season, February or March, in that rural area of Belgium that saw some of the most brutal fighting of World War I. It takes place in the present day, when the tractor's plow turns up with the earth some white, chalky stuff that might once have been bones. It is primarily about Barbe (Adelaide Leroux), a thin, unsmiling girl; Demester (Samuel Boidin), a passive farm worker; and Blondel (Henri Cretel), also a farm worker, so limited that he accepts Demester's blank silence as companionship.

Demester leans on a fence, staring at the fields. Barbe comes to stand next to him. "Did you get your letter?" she asks. He did, calling him to war. "You go on Monday?" He nods. "Shall we?" He nods. They walk across the fields, bed down in a hedgerow, and have sex with the efficiency of hedgehogs. It is not as good for her as it is for him because, we do not need to be told, it has never been good for either of them.

A group gathers in a rural tavern. They do not even get drunk. They drink their beer dutifully. Demester refuses to agree that he and Barbe are "a couple." She leaves the table and picks up Blondel. That will show him. But Demester does not much react, Blondel does not seem to have won anything, Barbe does not seem to think she has made much of a point.

Demester, Blondel, and other locals are trucked away to be sent to an unnamed war in an unnamed land. They commit atrocities and are themselves the victims of unspeakably horrible experiences. Demester, who survives, returns. Barbe, in the meantime, has had an abortion, spent time in a mental hospital, and is back on the farm. They have sex again. "I love you," Demester says. They are the saddest words in the movie.

This film has a few tangible pleasures, such as some somber shots of Demester walking far away in a field. Its achievement is theoretical. It wants to depict lives that are without curiosity, introspection, and hope. I watched with mournful restlessness. I admire it more today than yesterday when I saw it. I will never "like" it. I can imagine showing it to a film class and confronting the uncertain eyes of the students: What forlorn "masterpiece" had I forced upon them? How would I defend it?

I would say Dumont takes them about as far as they will ever want to go in the direction of human emptiness. Or maybe his film takes them nowhere, but simply occupies a place. It is *Waiting for Godot* without dialogue or the expectation of Godot. It is Bressonian, but demonstrates how Bresson is sublime and Dumont is implacably stolid. Consider Dumont's character of Barbe and then, if you have the chance, watch Bresson's miraculous *Mouchette.* You want to console Mouchette. You want to regard Barbe from across a room, wondering how her personality displaces so little karma.

The actors are all locals, unprofessional, but fully equal to Dumont's barren designs for them. I recall when Emmanuel Schotte, the star of Dumont's much more involving *L'Humanite,* won the best actor award at Cannes and all of my friends agreed that in his acceptance speech the actor seemed *exactly* the same as his character. Is that acting? Perhaps it is one goal of acting.

Gene Siskel sometimes said a film should be more interesting than a documentary of the same actors having lunch. I would be interested in seeing Adelaide Leroux and Samuel Boidin having lunch together, or even having sex together. It is unutterably depressing to reflect they might seem the same as here. If this is life, then death, I think, is no parenthesis.

Note: I give it three stars because I don't want to discourage anyone who finds this description intriguing. On my Web site is a place for readers to vote. Consult their rating carefully. My reviews of L'Humanite *and* Mouchette *are online.*

Flightplan ★ ★ ★ ½

PG-13, 97 m., 2005

Jodie Foster (Kyle Pratt), Peter Sarsgaard (Gene Carson), Sean Bean (Captain Rich), Erika Christensen (Fiona), Kate Beahan (Stephanie), Marlene Lawston (Julia Pratt). Directed by Robert Schwentke and produced by Brian Grazer. Screenplay by Peter A. Dowling and Billy Ray.

How can a little girl simply disappear from an airplane at 37,000 feet? By asking this question and not cheating on the answer, *Flightplan* delivers a frightening thriller with an airtight plot. It's like a classic Locked Room Murder, in which the killer could not possibly enter or leave, but the victim nevertheless is dead. Such mysteries always have solutions, and so does *Flightplan,* but not one you will easily anticipate. After the movie is over and you are on your way home, some questions may occur to you, but the film proceeds with implacable logic after establishing that the little girl does not seem to be on board.

The movie stars Jodie Foster in a story that bears similarities to her *Panic Room* (2002). In both films, a woman uses courage and intelligence to defend her child against enemies who hold all the cards. The problem she faces in *Flightplan* is more baffling: Who are her enemies? Why would they kidnap her daughter? How is it possible on an airplane?

For that matter, has it really happened? Foster plays Kyle Pratt, a jet propulsion engineer who has been employed in Germany on the design of the very airplane she is now using to cross the Atlantic. She is on a sad mission. Her husband, David, has died after falling—she insists he fell and did not jump—from a rooftop. The coffin is in the hold, and she is traveling with Julia (Marlene Lawston). She falls asleep, she wakes up, and Julia is gone.

Kyle methodically looks around the airplane, calm at first, then on the edge of panic. She tries to seem more rational than she feels so the crew won't dismiss her as a madwoman. Certainly they're tempted, because the passenger list lacks Julia's name, the departure gate at Munich says she did not get on the plane, and her boarding pass and backpack are nowhere to be found. The captain is Sean Bean, very effective as a man who knows what his job is and how to do it. Peter Sarsgaard plays the in-flight air marshal, under the captain's orders. They receive a message from Munich informing them that Julia was killed along with her father. Obviously, the traumatized mother is fantasizing.

And that's all you'll find out from me. There is no one else I want to mention, no other developments I want to discuss, no other questions I want to raise. If someone tries to tell you anything else about *Flightplan*, walk away.

The movie's excellence comes from Foster's performance as a resourceful and brave woman; from Bean, Sarsgaard, and the members of the cabin crew, all with varying degrees of doubt; from the screenplay by Peter A. Dowling and Billy Ray; and from the direction by Robert Schwentke, a German whose first two films were not much seen in North America. This one will be.

I want to get back to the notion of the airtight plot. Often in thrillers we think of obvious questions that the characters should ask, but do not, because then the problems would be solved and the movie would be over. In *Flightplan*, Jodie Foster's character asks all the right questions and plays the situation subtly and with cunning: She knows that once she crosses a line, she will no longer be able to help her daughter. There are times when she's ahead of the audience in her thinking, anticipating the next development, factoring it in.

As the situation develops, her response is flexible. Her tactics are improvised moment by moment, not out of some kind of frantic acting-out. Because she does what we would do, because she makes no obvious mistakes, because of the logic of everything the crew knows, she seems trapped. A passenger cannot disappear from an airplane, and Julia has disappeared, so either her mother is hallucinating, or something has happened that is apparently impossible.

Schwentke is limited, but not constrained, by the fact that most of his movie takes place on an airplane in midair. He uses every inch of the aircraft, and the plot depends on the mother's knowledge of its operation and construction. If she didn't know the plane better, really, than its pilots, her case would be hopeless. Even with her knowledge, she comes up against one bafflement after another. Should she doubt her sanity? Should we? We have, after all, seen Julia on the airplane. But for that matter, in two early scenes, we saw, and she saw, her husband, David, after he was dead. They spoke to each other. Didn't they?

The Foot Fist Way ★ ★

R, 87 m., 2008

Danny McBride (Fred Simmons), Mary Jane Bostic (Suzie Simmons), Ben Best (Chuck "The Truck" Wallace), Spencer Moreno (Julio Chavez), Carlos Lopez IV (Henry Harrison), Jody Hill (Mike McAlister). Directed by Jody Hill and produced by Erin Gates, Jody Hill, Robbie Hill, and Jennifer Chikes. Screenplay by Jody Hill, Danny McBride, and Ben Best.

The hero of *The Foot Fist Way* is loathsome and reprehensible and isn't a villain in any traditional sense. Five minutes spent in his company, and my jaw was dropping. Ten minutes, and I realized he existed outside any conventional notion of proper behavior. Children should not be allowed within a mile of this film, but it will appeal to *Jackass* fans and other devotees of the joyously ignorant.

The hero is named Fred Simmons. He's played by Danny McBride with a cool confidence in the character's ability to transgress all ordinary rules of behavior. Fred runs a Tae Kwan Do studio. He has the instincts of a fascist. His clients are drilled to obey him without question, to always call him "sir," to respect him above all others. Some of his clients are four years old. He uses profanity around them (and to them) with cheerful oblivion.

To a boy about nine years old, named Julio, he explains, "People are shit. The only person that you can trust is me, your Tae Kwan Do instructor." Julio needs consoling after he's disrespected by little Stevie, who is maybe a year younger. To teach Stevie respect, Fred beats him up. Yes. There are several times in the movie when Fred pounds on kids. He doesn't pull his punches. Most people in the audience will wince and recoil. I did. Others will deal with that material by reasoning that the fight stunts are faked and staged, their purpose is to underline Fred's insectoid personality, and "it's only a movie."

Which side of that fence you come down on will have a lot to do with your reaction. A zero-star rating for this movie could easily (in my case, even rapturously) be justified, and some fanboys will give it four. In all fairness it belongs in the middle. Certainly *The Foot Fist Way* doesn't like Fred; it regards him as a man who has absorbed the lingo of the martial arts but doesn't have a clue about its codes of behavior. He's as close to a martial arts practitioner as Father Guido Sarducci is to a Catholic priest. And the movie is often funny; I laughed in spite of myself.

Fred's offensiveness applies across a wide range of behavior. He is insulting to his wife's dinner guests, tries to kiss and maul students in his office, and asks one young woman who studies yoga: "Have you ever heard of it saving anyone from a gang-rape type of situation?" He has found very few friends. He introduces his students to his buddy from high school, Mike McAllister (Jody Hill, the director), who has a fifth-degree black belt and a penetrating stare that seems rehearsed in front of a mirror.

Fred and Mike worship above all others Chuck "The Truck" Wallace (Ben Best, the cowriter), a movie star whose credits include the intriguingly titled *7 Rings of Pain 2*. When Chuck appears at a nearby martial arts expo, Fred asks him to visit his studio's "testing day," and then invites him home and shows him the master bedroom ("the wife and I will bunk on the couch"). That he assumes a movie star will want to spend the night is surprising, although perhaps less so when The Truck gets a look at Fred's wife, Suzie (Mary Jane Bostic). Fred leaves the two of them together while he teaches a class and is appalled when he returns to find Suzie and The Truck bouncing on the couch. What does he expect? Suzie has photocopies of her boobs and butt in "work papers from the office," and excuses her behavior at a party by saying, "I got really drunk—Myrtle Beach drunk."

McBride's performance is appallingly convincing as Fred. Despite all I've written, Fred comes across as a person who might almost exist in these vulgar times. McBride never tries to put a spin on anything, never strains for laughs. He says outrageous things in a level, middle-American monotone. He seems convinced of his own greatness, has no idea of his effect on others, and seems oblivious to the manifest fact that he is very bad at Tae Kwan Do. He is a real piece of work.

I cannot recommend this movie, but I can describe it, and then it's up to you. If it sounds like a movie you would loathe, you are correct. If it doesn't, what can I tell you? What it does, it does well, even to its disgusting final scene.

Note: The title is a translation of Tae Kwan Do.

Forty Shades of Blue ★ ★ ★

NO MPAA RATING, 108 m., 2005

Rip Torn (Alan James), Dina Korzun (Laura), Darren Burrows (Michael), Paprika Steen (Lonni), Red West (Duigan). Directed by Ira Sachs and produced by Margot Bridger, Jawal Nga, and Donald Rosenfeld. Screenplay by Michael Rohatyn and Sachs.

Drunks can be such a royal pain in the ass. The falling-down ones tend to be comic or tragic or both, which keeps them from being boring. But how do you live with a maintenance drinker who has become laboriously convinced of his own great importance and who views the other people in his life as through a glass, darkly?

Consider Alan James (Rip Torn), the subject of Ira Sachs's *Forty Shades of Blue.* He is a legend in Memphis, where at a time remembered by him more vividly than by anyone else, he was instrumental in the interracial union of country, R&B, and the blues. This produced music less interesting than the pure forms of each but that could be sold to consumers who didn't know much about any. As the film opens, Alan is being honored at a banquet at which everyone except him seems to be attending as a duty. Extraordinary, how little interaction he has with any of the other guests, except for a tarty tramp he sneaks away with.

He came to the banquet with his girlfriend. This is Laura (Dina Korzun), whom he met when she was a translator for his group of English-speaking businessmen in Moscow. She has moved with him to Memphis, where they live in what she (and maybe he) thinks of as a luxury home, although it is furnished like a show home, circa 1970.

After the banquet is over, Laura lingers for a while, waiting in the bar, but Alan has disappeared. She has been left behind—not abandoned, which would be bad enough, but forgotten. She makes her way home. It is not the first time something like this has happened.

Laura has seen terrible things in her lifetime. We sense that. She puts up with almost anything from Alan because she has spent years putting up with worse. But how does Alan put up with himself? And how happy is he when Michael (Darren Burrows), his son from a previous marriage, turns up in town? We don't have to be told that Michael has seen his father at his worst, probably saw his own mother treated as Laura is now being treated, and, therefore, has none of the standard dislike for the new girlfriend. She's a victim, and they float around the house like victims of an emotional shipwreck.

There is a scene of some mastery, involving a party Alan throws in his own backyard—a big barbecue, with lots of booze and live music. His guests represent a cross section of the Memphis music communities, black and white, young and old, and they all have one thing in common: a vast indifference to Alan. Watch him move through this gathering like a ghost at a banquet. Listen to his speech, at which with a grandiose gesture he tries to make things up with Laura; he is so ignorant of healthy human emotion that he has no idea he is only insulting her again, publicly.

There is poignancy to his character, yes. He and Laura have a small son named Sam. He feels love for the boy, but it is generic love, marked down and not made of the finest ingredients. His heart is incapable of the manufacture of brand-name emotions. Every day for him is essentially a balancing act between his enormous regard for himself, his need to be drunk enough but not too drunk, and the sullen enjoyment of his possessions. His human relationships maintain his cover; he would prefer to devote his days to being pleasantly sloshed and acknowledging applause.

The story then essentially becomes Laura's, because she is the one who can feel and change. The question for her is, at what emotional cost is a comfortable life in Memphis overpriced? To be sure, Alan sometimes stirs himself to express warm sentiments and touch her gently, but she has grown beyond the point where these gestures work; he can touch, but she can't be touched, so they are working in different dimensions.

Forty Shades of Blue won the Grand Jury Prize at Sundance 2005. It might also have deserved acting awards for Torn and Korzun. I despised the character of Alan James so sincerely that I had to haul back at one point to remind myself that, hey, I've met Rip Torn and he's a nice guy and he's only acting. He's acting so well, he not only creates this character but makes him into an object lesson. Sometimes the worst drunks aren't the ones who pass out or go down in flames but the ones who just go on and on, relentlessly, staggering under the weight of their emptiness.

49 Up ★ ★ ★ ★

NO MPAA RATING, 135 m., 1996

Featuring Bruce Balden, Jacqueline Bassett, Symon Basterfield, Andrew Brackfield, John

Brisby, Suzanne Dewey, Charles Furneaux, Nicholas Hitchon, Neil Hughes, Lynn Johnson, Paul Kligerman, Susan Sullivan, and Tony Walker. Directed by Michael Apted and produced by Apted and Claire Lewis.

Tony has a vacation home in Spain now, with a veranda and a swimming pool. He's seen some hard times, but at forty-nine he is basking in contentment. We see him in the pool, tanned, splashing with his family.

When you live with Michael Apted's *Up* series of documentaries, there tends to be one character who most focuses your attention. For me, in *28 Up* through *42 Up*, it was Neil, the troubled loner. As a boy he wanted to be a tour bus guide, telling people what to look at. As an adult, he still has an impulse to lead and instruct, but it hasn't worked out, and he became a morose loner. In one film there was a shot of him standing next to a lake in Scotland, in front of his shabby mobile home, no one else in sight; I thought, "Neil will be dead by the next film." That didn't happen, and Neil provides the biggest surprise of *42 Up*.

But Tony's development in some ways may be just as fundamental a transition. What happens to him helps illustrate the importance, even the nobility, of this most extraordinary series of documentaries.

In 1963, Granada Television in Britain commissioned a film about a group of children born in 1956. Drawn mostly from the upper and lower ends of the British class system, they were asked about their plans and dreams. The idea was to revisit them every seven years and see how they were doing. As a plan, this was visionary, even foolhardy, but here we are at *49 Up*, and the children of the 1963 film have children and grandchildren of their own. Anyone who has followed the series develops a curious fascination with their lives, because they are lives. This is not reality TV with its contrivances and absurdities, but a meditation on lifetimes.

Consider Tony. At seven, he wanted to be a racing jockey. Brash, crew-cut, extroverted, he made it all seem clear. He did briefly become a jockey, even racing against the great Lester Piggott, but as an adult he was a London taxi driver.

Apted, the director who has been with the *Up* series from the beginning, was in 1963 a lad who wanted to be a movie director. He grew up to become one. In a sense, he is another of the film's subjects, growing older off-camera. There was a time when he was convinced Tony would eventually fall into a life of crime, and he asked some questions and shot some scenes in anticipation of that development.

Tony did not become a criminal, and Apted learned his lesson, he told me. He decided to never anticipate what might happen to his subjects—to simply revisit them and catch up with their lives. Similarly, he decided to bypass politics: Prime ministers and governments come and go during these films, but Apted doesn't see his subjects as political creatures; whatever their politics, he is concerned more with what is happening in their lives and how they feel about that.

I am not British, was born fourteen years before the subjects, and yet by now identify intensely with them, because some kinds of human experience—teenage, work, marriage, illness—are universal. You could make this series in any society. As its installments accumulate in my memory, they cause me to regard the arc of my own life—to ask if I, too, contained at seven the makings of who I would become.

Certainly between seven and fourteen my path was settled. I wrote for the grade-school newspaper and used a crude hektograph machine to write and publish the *Washington Street News*. I was always going to be a journalist, and very old friends who knew me at twelve say, "You haven't changed."

Neither has Tony. He has expanded in his ideas of what his life can provide him, but he is still the overconfident, driving, ebullient personality he was at seven. Bruce, who wanted to be a missionary at seven, got involved in inner-city schools that were a contrast to his upper-class background. Neil's life has contained enormous surprises, but he is always definitely Neil—worried, discontented, fretting that the world is not following his instructions.

You do not have to have seen any of the earlier films to understand this one. George Turner, Apted's cinematographer since *21* and editor since *28*, provides flashbacks to earlier days in each life. By now that is a daunting editing task, but he is able to do it and keep us up to speed.

The early films were shot in black-and-white. Then Apted went to color. Now he is using digital. The subtle visual alterations help to suggest the passage of time. So do gray hairs and potbellies. None of the original group has died; most have prospered and found happiness. And with the passing of every seven years, the more they look different than they were at seven, the more they are the same.

Michael Apted's *Up* series remains one of the great imaginative leaps in film. I came aboard early in the series and I, too, have grown older along with it. In Tony's eyes at seven, reflecting in his mind his triumphs as a jockey, I can see the same eyes at forty-nine, gazing upon his swimming pool in Spain. He ran the race, and he won.

The 40-Year-Old Virgin ★ ★ ★ ½

R, 116 m., 2005

Steve Carell (Andy Stitzer), Catherine Keener (Trish), Paul Rudd (David), Romany Malco (Jay), Seth Rogen (Cal), Elizabeth Banks (Beth), Leslie Mann (Nicky), Jane Lynch (Paula). Directed by Judd Apatow and produced by Apatow, Shauna Robertson, and Clayton Townsend. Screenplay by Apatow and Steve Carell.

Here's a movie that could have had the same title and been a crude sex comedy with contempt for its characters. Instead, *The 40-Year-Old Virgin* is surprisingly insightful, as buddy comedies go, and it has a good heart and a lovable hero. It's not merely that Andy Stitzer rides his bike to work, it's that he signals his turns.

Andy (Steve Carell) is indeed forty and a virgin, after early defeats in the gender wars turned him into a noncombatant. His strategy for dealing with life is to surround himself with obsessions, including action figures, video games, high-tech equipment, and "collectibles," a word that, like "drinkable," never sounds like a glowing endorsement.

Andy is one of those guys whose life is a work-around. What he doesn't understand, he avoids, finesses, or fakes. On the job at the electronics superstore where he works, his fellow employees spend a lot of time talking about women, and he nods as if he speaks the language. Then they rope him into a poker game, the conversation turns to sex, and they look at him strangely when he observes enthusiastically how women's breasts feel like bags of sand.

The buddies are wonderfully cast. David (Paul Rudd) is still hopelessly in love with a woman who has long since outgrown any possible interest in him; Jay (Romany Malco) is a ladies' man who considers himself an irresistible seducer; and Cal (Seth Rogen) is the guy with practical guidance, such as "date drunks" and "never actually say anything to a woman; just ask questions." All these guys have problems of their own and seem prepared to pass them on to Andy as advice; listen with particular care to the definition of "outercourse." Also at work is Paula (Jane Lynch), Andy's boss, a tall, striking woman who is definitely not a forty-year-old virgin; after asking him if he's ever heard of just being sex buddies, she promises him, "I'm discreet, and I'll haunt your dreams."

Andy would just as soon stay home and play with his action figures. But his friends consider it a sacred mission to end his forty-year drought. In a singles bar, under their coaching, he separates a tipsy babe from the crowd; his alarm should have gone off when she asks him to blow into the Breathalyzer so she can start her car. In a bookstore, he asks a cute salesclerk one question after another, which works charmingly until she finds out he has no answers. He goes to one of those dating round-robins where a buzzer goes off and you switch tables, giving the movie an opportunity to assemble a little anthology of pickup clichés.

And then there's Trish (Catherine Keener). She runs a store across the mall, where you can take in your stuff and she'll sell it on eBay. Andy knows right away that he really likes her, but he's paralyzed by shyness and fear, and the way she coaxes him into asking her out is written so well, it could be in a more serious movie. Or maybe it is; there's an insight and understanding under the surface of *The 40-Year-Old Virgin* that is subtle but sincere.

On the surface, the movie assembles a collection of ethnic types as varied as *Crash.* It has fun with them, but it likes them, and it's gentle fun that looks for humanity, not cheap laughs. Consider the character who unexpectedly performs a Guatemalan love song, or Andy's neighbors, who like to watch *Survivor* with him, although he has to bring the set. The movie approaches the subject of homosexuality without the usual gay-bashing, in a scene where the guys trade one-liners beginning "You're gay because . . ." and their reasons show more insight than prejudice.

But the best reason the movie works is that Carell and Keener have a rare kind of chemistry that is maybe better described as mutual sympathy. Keener is an actress at the top of her form, and to see her in *Lovely and Amazing* and *The Ballad of Jack and Rose* and then in *Virgin* is to watch an actress who starts every role with a complete understanding of the woman inside. Her task in the plot is to end Andy's virginity, but her challenge is to create a relationship we care about. We do. The character Trish is intuitively understanding, but more important, she actually likes this guy. Keener's inspiration is to have Trish see Andy not as a challenge but as an opportunity.

The movie was directed by Judd Apatow, who produced *Anchorman*, and written by Apatow and Carell, the *Daily Show* veteran who first developed the idea of a closeted virgin in a Second City skit. The screenplay is filled with small but perfect one-liners (as when Andy is advised to emulate David Caruso in *Jade*). At the end, for no good reason except that it strikes exactly the perfect (if completely unexpected) note, the cast performs a Bollywood version of *The Age of Aquarius*. By then, they could have done almost anything and I would have been smiling.

The Fountain ★ ★ ½

PG-13, 95 m., 2006

Hugh Jackman (Tomas/Tommy/Tom Creo), Rachel Weisz (Queen Isabel/Izzi Creo), Ellen Burstyn (Dr. Lillian Guzetti), Mark Margolis (Father Avila), Stephen McHattie (Grand Inquisitor Silecio), Fernando Hernandez (Lord of Xibalba), Cliff Curtis (Captain Ariel), Sean Patrick Thomas (Antonio). Directed by Darren Aronofsky and produced by Eric Watson, Arnon Milchan, and Iain Smith. Screenplay by Aronofsky.

As a believer that Darren Aronofsky is one of the rare originals among the recent class of new directors, I was eager to double back and view his *The Fountain* (2006), a movie about immortality that was released just about the time my own was being called into question.

Although as a doctoral candidate in English I was advised to be familiar with the existing criticism on a work before venturing to write my own, as a film critic I am usually writing before other reviews have even been published. But a year had passed. So after looking at the film, I checked out IMDb's "external reviews" section and discovered that, good lord, 221 reviews had been written on *The Fountain*. On other sites I discovered that its Metacritic rating was 51 (out of 100), and it scored exactly the same on the Tomatometer. Urgent to Aronofsky: Remember that when Terry Zwigoff was sleeping with that gun under his pillow, he still had *Crumb, Ghost World,* and *Bad Santa* ahead of him.

How bad could *The Fountain* be? I selected one review, *Variety*'s, because it was written from the premiere at Venice and was the first word on the film. I found that the "onetime wunderkind," who had been "overpraised for the then-hip, now-dated use of pseudo-science in *Pi*, and for the visual excess he deployed in the grungy *Requiem*," had now committed a film in which Hugh Jackman stars in "three stories in different time frames and switches throughout somewhat abruptly between them, although auds can parse which is going on when by paying attention to how much hair Jackman is sporting at any given time."

I was relieved to find that pseudo-science and visual excess are now behind us in the cinema. But let's talk about hair. In the first story, Jackman portrays a conquistador, in the second he is a modern scientist, and in the third he is bald and floating through space inside a magical bubble. Auds who cannot parse that must be plumb parsed out. And why trash Aronofsky's first two films just when I was trying to decide which I would write about as a Great Movie? He made *Pi* at twenty-nine (best director, Sundance), *Requiem for a Dream* at thirty-one (Oscar nom for Ellen Burstyn), and now, at thirty-seven, he was already a "onetime wunderkind." F. Scott Fitzgerald said

American lives didn't have *second* acts; he never said they don't have first ones.

Is the film a success? Not for most people, no. I imagine they don't realize, for one thing, that it all takes place in the present, and there is only one *real* Hugh Jackman character, Tommy. The conquistador named Tomas is the hero of the novel his wife, Izzi (Rachel Weisz), is writing, and the spaceman named Tom Creo is the hero of that novel's final chapter, which Tommy writes after his deathbed promise to his wife. *Creo* is Spanish for "I believe," Spanish is a language the conquistador would speak, and Tommy believes that a cure will be found for death. The tree sharing the space bubble with Tom is the Tree of Life that Tomas was seeking in the early chapters, and the movie explains that the bubble is en route to that nebula he and Izzi see in the sky, which (she would know and explain) was believed by the Mayans to be the origin of life.

I could go on like this, but having searched the 18,326 messages in my Gmail account, I find that one reader, Matt Withers of Brunswick, Maryland, has it all figured out in elegant detail. His explanation will be found at www.rogerebert.com.

Can a typical aud member be expected to do the heavy parsing that would figure all this out? I doubt it. Most movies, you like to have them all parsed before you buy the ticket. Did I have it figured out? It didn't take me long, and here was my thinking: Since there is not a single element in the film claiming that the same man is alive in all three time periods, he obviously is not.

There is a critical belief that you should not bring story elements to fiction that cannot be found there. The fictional identity of the first man is explained by Izzi's novel, in which she would obviously visualize her own lover as the hero. The fictional nature of the third man is explained because, hey, people don't go floating through the cosmos inside a bubble while levitating and eating bark, even in "the future." There are more things in heaven and Earth than are dreamed of in our philosophy, but not that. Stephen Hawking will back me up. The film's central section is unalloyed realism and generates the fantasy of the first and third. Since Izzi dies in it, magic isn't allowed. Fiction sets its rules.

That said, I will concede the film is not a great success. Too many screens of blinding lights. Too many transitions for their own sake. Abrupt changes of tone. And yet I believe we have not seen the real film. When a $75 million production goes into turnaround and is made for $35 million, elements get eliminated. When a film telling three stories and spanning thousands of years has a running time of ninety-five minutes, scenes must have been cut out. There will someday be a director's cut of this movie, and that's the cut I want to see.

Four Brothers ★ ★ ★

R, 102 m., 2005

Mark Wahlberg (Bobby Mercer), Tyrese Gibson (Angel Mercer), Andre Benjamin (Jeremiah Mercer), Garrett Hedlund (Jack Mercer), Terrence Howard (Lieutenant Green), Josh Charles (Detective Fowler), Sofia Vergara (Sofi), Taraji P. Henson (Camille), Chiwetel Ejiofor (Victor Sweet), Fionnula Flanagan (Evelyn Mercer). Directed by John Singleton and produced by Lorenzo di Bonaventura. Screenplay by David Elliot and Paul Lovett.

John Singleton's *Four Brothers* is an urban Western, or maybe it's an urban movie inspired by a Western; either way, it's intended to be more mythic than realistic. It connects with underlying moral currents in the way Westerns used to, back before greed, fear, anger, and "society" provided action movies with all the motivation they needed.

The movie opens with a sweet white-haired grandmother type who arrives at a Detroit convenience store late at night. Wrong store, wrong neighborhood, we're thinking. But Evelyn Mercer (Fionnula Flanagan) has a reason to be there: A frightened young kid has been caught shoplifting some candy, and she settles things with the store owner and puts the fear of God into the kid. Then two stickup guys walk into the store, and she is shot dead.

At the funeral, we meet her four adopted sons, two black, two white. She was a foster mother all of her life, and these were the only four she couldn't find homes for: Bobby (Mark Wahlberg), Angel (Tyrese Gibson), Jeremiah (Andre Benjamin), and Jack (Garrett

Hedlund). Bobby is the oldest, the natural leader, the one with a temper. Angel is the player with a hot babe (Sofia Vergara). Jeremiah is a success; he's married (to Taraji P. Henson), has a family, is involved in real estate deals. Jack is a rock-and-roller.

They all have the name Mercer, and they all consider Evelyn their mom, but they grew up on mean streets and have not spent a lot of time getting all sentimental about being "brothers." That begins to change at the funeral, when they wordlessly agree that their mother's death requires some kind of action. Jeremiah, the businessman, observes: "The people who did this are from the same streets we're from. Mom would have been the first to forgive them." True of Mom, not true of them.

This story is inspired by Henry Hathaway's *The Sons of Katie Elder* (1965), unseen by me but cited by my fellow critic Emanuel Levy. (I am awed by the number of films I have seen, and awed by the number I have not seen.) At first it looks like an open-and-shut case: Witnesses saw two gangbangers walk in and blast the store owner. Mom was a bystander, shot in cold blood. But as the brothers look at the tape from the security camera, they're struck by how ruthlessly she was murdered; they turn up evidence suggesting maybe there was something more to this killing. As long as we're talking about the influence of old movies, a crucial clue in *Four Brothers* involves when the lights are turned off on a basketball court; I was reminded of the almanac in John Ford's *Young Mr. Lincoln* (1939) that provides the phases of the moon.

I won't describe the rest of the plot, which unfolds like a police procedural, but I will note a nice touch involving the way Jeremiah looks guilty for a moment simply because he is successful and generous. And I'll mention the key supporting characters. Terrence Howard and Josh Charles play the two cops on the case, and Chiwetel Ejiofor *(Dirty Pretty Things)*, who is one of the nicest men alive, plays one of the meanest men in Detroit. He's a crime boss whose methods for humbling his underlings pass beyond mere cruelty into demented ingenuity.

For Singleton, the movie is a return to inner-city subjects after some fairly wide excursions *(Shaft, 2 Fast 2 Furious)*. In between those two he made the provocative *Baby Boy* (2001), which attacks some young black men who feel licensed to live at home with their mothers, thoughtlessly father children, avoid work, and perpetuate the cycle. That had the kind of critical insight into the kinds of realities that distinguish his first, and greatest, film, *Boyz n the Hood* (1991). (Singleton is also the producer of the drama *Hustle and Flow* [2005], a more ambitious and insightful urban film that also uses the talents of Howard and Henson.) *Four Brothers* basically wants to be an entertainment, although it deliberately makes the point that in an increasingly diverse society, people of different races may belong to the same family.

Four Brothers works as an urban thriller, if not precisely as a model of logic. There is, for example, a bloody and extended gun battle involving hundreds of rounds of machine-gun bullets and a stack of dead bodies, and afterward a cop observes, "It looks like self-defense." Yes, but since that cop cannot make the point after the smoke clears, why is there no investigation to tidy up the carnage? I guess I shouldn't ask questions like that in a Western, urban or otherwise; bad guys exist to get shot and good guys exist to shoot them, with a few key exceptions to keep things interesting. If you want to know how it all turned out, you need to get a transfer to the courtroom genre.

4 Months, 3 Weeks and 2 Days ★ ★ ★ ★

NO MPAA RATING, 113 m., 2008

Anamaria Marinca (Otilia), Laura Vasiliu (Gabita), Alex Potocean (Adi), Vlad Ivanov (Mr. Bebe). Directed by Cristian Mungiu. Produced by Mungiu and Oleg Mutu. Screenplay by Mungiu.

Gabita is perhaps the most clueless young woman to ever have the lead in a movie about her own pregnancy. Even if you think Juno was way too clever, two hours with Gabita will have you buying a ticket to Bucharest for Diablo Cody. This is a powerful film and a stark visual accomplishment, but no thanks to Gabita (Laura Vasiliu). The driving character is her roommate, Otilia (Anamaria Marinca), who does all the heavy lifting.

The time is the late 1980s. Romania still

cringes under the brainless rule of Ceausescu. In Cristian Mungiu's *4 Months, 3 Weeks and 2 Days,* Gabita desires an abortion, which was then illegal, not for moral reasons, but because Ceausescu wanted more subjects to rule. She turns in desperation to her roommate, Otilia, who agrees to help her and does. Helps her so much, indeed, she does everything but have the abortion herself. In a period of twenty-four hours, we follow the two friends in a journey of frustration, stupidity, duplicity, cruelty, and desperation, set against a background of a nation where if it weren't for the black market, there'd be no market at all.

For Gabita, the notion of taking responsibility for her own actions is completely unfamiliar. We wonder how she has survived to her current twentyish age in a society that obviously requires boldness, courage, and improvisation. For starters, she convinces Otilia to raise money for the operation. Then she asks her to go first to meet the abortionist. Then she neglects to make a reservation at the hotel the abortionist specifies. That almost sinks the arrangement: The abortionist has experience suggesting that hotel will be a safe venue and suspects he may be set up for a police trap. His name, by the way, is Mr. Bebe (Vlad Ivanov), and no, *bebe* is apparently not Romanian for "baby," but it looks suspicious to me.

The movie deliberately levels an unblinking gaze at its subjects. There are no fancy shots, no effects, no quick cuts, and Mungiu and his cinematographer, Oleg Mutu, adhere to a rule of one shot per scene. That makes camera placement and movement crucial, and suggests that every shot has been carefully prepared. Even shots where the ostensible subject of the action is half-visible, or not seen at all, serve a purpose, by insisting on the context and the frame. Visual is everything here; the film has no music, only words or silences.

Otilia is heroic in this context; she reminds me a little of the ambulance attendant in the 2005 Romanian film *The Death of Mr. Lazarescu,* who drove a dying man around all night insisting on a hospital for him. Otilia grows exasperated with her selfish and self-obsessed friend, but she keeps on trying to help, even though she has problems of her own.

One of them is her boyfriend, Adi (Alex Potocean), who is himself so self-oriented that we wonder if Otilia is attracted to the type. Even though she tries to explain that she and Gabita have urgent personal business, he insists on Otilia coming to his house to meet his family that night. He turns it into a test of her love. People who do that are incapable of understanding that to compromise would be a proof of their own love.

The dinner party she arrives at would be a horror show even in a Mike Leigh display of social embarrassment. She's jammed at a table with too many guests, too much smoking, too much drinking, and no one who pays her the slightest attention. As the unmoving camera watches her, we wait for her to put a fork in somebody's eye. When she gets away to make a phone call, Adi follows her and drags her into his room, and then Adi's mother bursts in on them and we see who Adi learned possessiveness from.

When the friends finally find themselves in a hotel room with the abortionist, the result is as unpleasant, heartless, and merciless as it could possibly be. I'll let you discover for yourself. And finally there is a closing scene where Otilia and Gabita agree to never refer to this night again. Some critics have found the scene anticlimactic. I think it is inevitable. If I were Otilia, I would never even see Gabita again. I'd send over Adi to collect my clothes.

Filmmakers in countries of the former Soviet bloc have been using their new freedom to tell at last the stories they couldn't tell then. *The Lives of Others,* for example, was about the East German secret police. And in Romania, the era has inspired a group of powerful films, including the aforementioned *Mr. Lazarescu, 12:08 East of Bucharest* (2006), and *4 Months,* which won the Palme d'Or at Cannes 2007, upsetting a lot of American critics who admired it but liked *No Country for Old Men* more.

The film has inspired many words about how it reflects Romanian society, but obtaining an illegal abortion was much the same in this country until some years ago, and also in Britain, as we saw in Leigh's *Vera Drake.* The fascination of the film comes not so much from the experiences the friends have, however unspeakable, but in who they are, and how they behave and relate. Anamaria

Marinca gives a masterful performance as Otilia, but don't let my description of Gabita blind you to the brilliance of Laura Vasiliu's acting. These are two of the more plausible characters I've seen in a while.

Fred Claus ★ ★

PG, 114 m., 2007

Vince Vaughn (Fred Claus), Paul Giamatti (Santa Claus), Miranda Richardson (Annette Claus), John Michael Higgins (Willie), Elizabeth Banks (Charlene), Rachel Weisz (Wanda), Kathy Bates (Mama Claus), Kevin Spacey (Clyde), Ludacris (DJ Donnie). Directed by David Dobkin and produced by Dobkin, Joel Silver, and Jessie Nelson. Screenplay by Dan Fogelman

Know how a character in one movie can be so terrific another movie is spun off just to take advantage? That happened with Ma and Pa Kettle, who had small roles in *The Egg and I,* which led to their very own series. But enough of today's seminar on the history of cinema. What I'm wondering is whether a *scene* can inspire a spin-off.

I'm thinking of the best scene in *Fred Claus,* which takes place at a twelve-step support group for brothers of famous people. Maybe it's called Recovering Siblings Anonymous. Fred Claus (Vince Vaughn), who has suffered all of his life in the shadow of his beloved younger brother, Santa Claus, sits in the circle and shares. Also at the meeting are Roger Clinton, Frank Stallone, and Stephen Baldwin, and I'm not spoiling a laugh, because it's what they say that is so funny.

I'm thinking, too bad Billy Carter didn't live to steal this movie. But there are plenty more brothers to go around. Neil Bush comes to mind. How about Clint Howard, although he's been doing well lately? Or Jeffrey Skilling of Enron, now serving twenty-four years while his brother Tom is the popular and respected Chicago weatherman? This could be a movie like the Fantastic Four, where the brothers form a team. Tom Skilling screws up the weather forecast at the North Pole after Clint Howard feeds him bad info from a garbled headset at Santa's Mission Control, and Neil Bush saves the day by arranging for an executive pardon.

If you at least chuckled during my pathetic attempt at humor, that's more than may happen during long stretches of *Fred Claus,* which has apparently studied *Elf* and figured out everything that could have gone wrong with its fish-out-of-water Christmas fable. The movie begins centuries ago in the Black Forest, when Mr. and Mrs. Claus and their first son, Fred, welcome a new bundle of joy: Nicholas Claus. Fred vows that he will be the bestest big brother little Nicky could ever hope for, but alas, Nicholas is such a paragon that you can't get over him, you can't get around him, and all Fred can do is go under him, in a bitter and undistinguished life. Think about it. What does Santa (Paul Giamatti) need with a brother? He's one-stop shopping.

It gets worse. Nicholas Claus becomes a saint. And it turns out, in a development previously unreported by theologians, that if you're a saint, that means both you and your family live forever. Yes! So Fred has to be St. Nick's brother forever and ever after. And this sad old planet would benefit, according to the Catholic count, by at least ten thousand immortal saints, although the Church reassures us with some confidence that they are all in heaven.

Flash forward to, yes, Chicago. Vince Vaughn should earn some kind of grace just for bringing this production to his hometown. He is in love with a meter maid (Rachel Weisz), who has moved here from London, which explains her accent if not her job choice. Fred stays pretty much out of touch with his famous kid brother, until he gets in a financial squeeze and has to call Santa for a $50,000 loan to open an off-track betting parlor across from the Chicago Mercantile Exchange—not a bad idea, actually.

The action moves to the North Pole and involves the flint-hearted Clyde Northcutt (Kevin Spacey), who is cracking down on cost overruns at the Pole, for whom, I'm not sure. That leads to turmoil among the elves, and Fred at last finds his role in life, but see for yourself.

The movie wants to be good-hearted but is somehow sort of grudging. It should have gone all the way. I think Fred Claus should have been meaner if he was going to be funnier, and Santa should have been up to something nefarious, instead of the jolly old ho-ho-ho routine. Maybe Northcutt could catch Santa undercutting his own elves by importing toxic toys from China, and Fred could save the lives of millions of kids by teaming up with Shafeek Nader.

Freedomland ★ ★

R, 113 m., 2006

Samuel L. Jackson (Lorenzo Council), Julianne Moore (Brenda Martin), Edie Falco (Karen Collucci), Ron Eldard (Danny Martin), William Forsythe (Boyle), Aunjanue Ellis (Felicia), Anthony Mackie (Billy Williams). Directed by Joe Roth and produced by Scott Rudin. Screenplay by Richard Price, based on his novel.

Freedomland assembles the elements for a superior thriller, but were the instructions lost when the box was opened? It begins with a compelling story about a woman whose car is hijacked with her four-year-old son inside. It adds racial tension and the bulldog detective work of a veteran police detective. And then it flies to pieces with unmotivated scenes, inexplicable dialogue, and sudden conclusions that may be correct but arrive from nowhere. The film seems edited none too wisely from a longer version that made more sense.

Julianne Moore appears in the opening scene, sobbing, her hands bleeding, staggering into a hospital with a story of her car being hijacked in a wooded area near a low-income housing development.

Samuel L. Jackson plays Lorenzo, the detective assigned to the case. He can't understand why her character, named Brenda, was driving through the isolated area at the time. She explains: She's a volunteer at a community children's center and took the wrong shortcut home. Lorenzo thinks she's hiding something, and she is: Her son was in the backseat of the car when it was taken.

When this story becomes public, it creates a furor. Cops from a nearby white district blanket the area, a black preacher complains that blacks are killed all the time in the district without this kind of police attention, and the woman's brother Danny (Ron Eldard) is a white cop who seems angry all the time—at his sister, at the black community, at Lorenzo.

Racial demonstrations are on the simmer, but the movie turns them on and off at will. Brenda, after all, is well-known and beloved in the area because of her volunteer work. Yet at one point a black woman tells her, "You stay away from my child!" Why would she say that? And why, for that matter, does Lorenzo announce a sudden about-face on the case when we haven't seen the evidence to support his conclusion? Why, for that matter, are untold resources used to search for the missing boy on the grounds and buildings of Freedomland, an abandoned orphanage, when there is every reason to believe he is not there?

And why, oh why, is Brenda apparently left in the personal custody of Lorenzo, who removes her from the hospital without formalities, drives her around, leaves her alone, has heart-to-heart talks with her, and ignores all police procedures for dealing with victims and/or witnesses? And what about that passionate discussion between Lorenzo and Brenda in which their body language and the close framing of the shots lead us to anticipate a development that never comes?

The scene ends weirdly with the two of them staring fiercely at each other, as if they were told to freeze while the writers came up with more dialogue.

This movie is filled with behavior that seems to exist only to provide things for the actors to do. There's an asthma attack early in the film that should pay off somehow but doesn't. Danny, the brother who is a cop, seems constantly poised to do something radical but never quite does. And why does his concern for his sister express itself in his decision essentially to ignore her and operate elsewhere in the plot? And does the angry preacher in the black neighborhood have a legitimate grievance, or is he just venting on command, to provide filler for the plot?

One scene works. It's a conversation between Brenda and Karen (Edie Falco), who is the leader of a group of mothers whose children have been kidnapped, molested, or killed. She gets Brenda alone for a fraught and crucial conversation (which is against all standard procedures, but never mind), and for the length of that conversation the movie is about something, and it works.

Freedomland is based on a novel by Richard

Price, whose *Clockers* made a better film. He adapts his story for director Joe Roth as if they know a lot of places in the neighborhood but don't remember how to get from one place to another. Individual scenes feel authentic, but the story tries to build bridges between loose ends.

Friends with Money ★ ★

R, 88 m., 2006

Jennifer Aniston (Olivia), Joan Cusack (Franny), Catherine Keener (Christine), Frances McDormand (Jane), Simon McBurney (Aaron), Jason Isaacs (David), Greg Germann (Matt), Scott Caan (Mike), Bob Stephenson (Marty). Directed by Nicole Holofcener and produced by Anthony Bregman. Screenplay by Holofcener.

Friends with Money resembles *Crash,* except that all the characters are white and the reason they keep running into one another is that the women have been friends since the dawn of time. Three of them are rich and married. The fourth is, and I quote, "single, a pothead, and a maid." That's Olivia (Jennifer Aniston), who used to teach at a fancy school in Santa Monica "but quit when the kids started giving her quarters."

The other friends are Jane (Frances McDormand), who screams at people who try to cut in line ahead of her; Christine (Catherine Keener), who writes screenplays with her husband; and Franny (Joan Cusack), whose biggest concern is that her husband spends too much money on their child's shoes. Jane's husband is Aaron (Simon McBurney). "He's so gay," says Olivia. Christine's husband is David (Jason Isaacs). They fight over what the characters should say in the screenplay they're writing, and then they simply fight: She tells him his breath stinks, and he tells her she's getting a lard butt. Not a demonstration of mutual support. Franny's husband is Matt (Greg Germann), whose problem, as far as this film is concerned, is that he has no problems.

The characters meet in various combinations and gossip about those not present, and all three couples spend a lot of time on the topic of Olivia, who they agree needs a husband, although their own marriages don't argue persuasively for wedded bliss. Olivia finally gets fixed up with a physical trainer named Mike (Scott Caan), who in some ways is the most intriguing character in the movie, and certainly the biggest louse. Consider how he asks to go along with her when she cleans houses, and what he asks her afterward, and the present he gives her, and the "friend from junior high school" he sees in a restaurant.

Meanwhile, the marriage of Jane and Aaron is melting down because of her anger. She's a famous dress designer who has decided not to wash her hair, which becomes so greasy her husband turns away from her in bed, although maybe he really is gay. Or probably not, and neither is his new friend, also named Aaron, although they do enjoy trying on sweaters together. Meanwhile, Christine and David are putting a second story on their house, which will give them a view, and we all know that if you're fighting, the best thing to do is remodel.

Friends with Money was written and directed by Nicole Holofcener, whose two previous features were wonderful studies of women and their relationships: *Walking and Talking* (1996) and *Lovely and Amazing* (2001). Both of them also starred Catherine Keener, who is expert at creating the kind of Holofcener character who speaks the truth with wit, especially when it is not required. Cusack can do that too, although she is underused here.

The movie lacks the warmth and edge of the two previous features. It seems to be more of an idea than a story. Yes, it's about how Olivia's friends all have money, and at one point Jane suggests they simply give her some to bring her up to their level. As it happens, characters do exactly that in novels I've read recently by Stendhal and Trollope, but in modern Los Angeles, it is unheard of. If you have millions and your friend is a maid, obviously what you do is tell her how much you envy her. Working for a living is a charming concept when kept at a reasonable distance.

The parts of the movie that really live are the ones involving Olivia and the two men in her life: first Mike, the fitness instructor, and then Marty (Bob Stephenson), a slob who lives alone, is very shy, and hires her to clean his house. When the rich friends go to a $1,000-a-plate benefit, they invite Olivia along and she brings Marty, and when she goes to pick him up, she suggests that maybe he should think about wearing a tie. This he is happy to do. At the dinner, he smooths down the tie with pride and satisfaction. Watch the way Aniston regards him while he does this. She is so happy for him. At last she is the friend with money. Not cash money, it's true, but a good line of credit in the bank of love.

Fugitive Pieces ★ ★ ★ ½

R, 108 m., 2008

Stephen Dillane (Jakob), Rade Sherbedgia (Athos), Rosamund Pike (Alex), Ayelet Zurer (Michaela), Robbie Kay (Young Jakob), Ed Stoppard (Ben), Rachelle Lefevre (Naomi). Directed by Jeremy Podeswa. Produced by Robert Lantos. Screenplay by Podeswa, based on the novel by Anne Michaels.

"To live with ghosts requires solitude."

So says the hero of *Fugitive Pieces,* a Canadian writer who as a child in Poland saw the Nazis murder his parents and drag away his sister. Rescued by a Greek archaeologist who was miraculously working on a dig near his hiding place, the boy is taken to safety on the man's home island in Greece, and eventually fate and a teaching position take them to Toronto. Having been gripped by the big silent eyes of the boy Jakob (Robbie Kay), we now meet him as an adult (Stephen Dillane). Both he and his savior, Athos (Rade Sherbedgia), are committed to recording the past so it will be saved from oblivion.

But it is his own past Jakob is most concerned about losing. He obsessively returns to his memories of his parents and sister, especially the tragic event he glimpsed from his hiding place behind some wallpaper. There are moments when he focuses on his lovely mother and we wonder if they ever happened; has desire augmented his memories? In the present, he is married to Alex (Rosamund Pike). He relentlessly tells her about the importance of not forgetting (one Holocaust survivor, he tells her, kept a photograph hidden under her tongue for three months; its discovery would have brought death). Alex encourages him to live sometimes in the present, but then she finds in his diary that he fears she is stealing that past away. "It makes your brain explode," she says, "his obsession with these details."

She walks out, and that triggers the thoughts about living in solitude. The line and all the poetic narration in the film come from the novel by Anne Michaels that inspired it. Jakob shares the original Toronto apartment he moved into with Athos, who grows older and, if such a thing is possible, kinder; such saints are rare. "You must try to be buried in ground that will remember you," he says, and that leads to Jakob's return to the Greek island, where he divides his year with Toronto.

There are neighbors in Toronto, Yiddish-speaking, whose son, Ben (Ed Stoppard), grows up and introduces the adult Jakob to another woman, a museum curator named Michaela (Ayelet Zurer). This woman is too good to be true, but then, for such a morose and fearful person, Jakob is blessed with wonderful people in his life. He takes her to Greece, he feels love, he begins to free himself from his ghosts.

Such a summary barely captures the qualities of *Fugitive Pieces,* written and directed by Jeremy Podeswa (*The Five Senses, Into the West*). He doesn't tell, he evokes, with the nostalgic images of his cinematographer, Gregory Middleton, the understated melancholy of the score by Nikos Kypourgos and the seamless time transitions of his editor, Wiebke von Carolsfeld. The film glides between the past and different periods in Jakob's later life, as it tries to show this man whose love for his family has essentially frozen him at the time he last saw them. He tortures himself: If he hadn't run away, would his sister have returned to their home? After being taken by the Nazis? Not likely.

There are other harrowing scenes, showing the Nazi occupation of the Greek island and the heroism of Athos in protecting Jakob and doing risky favors for neighbors. But the film is not about the Holocaust so much as it is about memory, how we use it, how we must treasure it, how we must not be enslaved by it. The lushly photographed earth tones of the Toronto scenes indeed almost evoke a storehouse for the past, and its shadows are finally burned away by the sunshine of Greece.

Since the film premiered in September 2007 at Toronto, more than one viewer has talked in wonder about its comforting qualities. For a film about the Holocaust, it is gentler than we might expect. A lot of that quality is caused by the face and presence of Rade Sherbedgia, an actor whose name you may not know although you have probably seen him many times. Some people have a quality of just smiling at you and making things heal. He does. And Stephen Dillane's worried, haunted face gives him the right person to work on, if only Athos, too, were not so absorbed in the past. If *Fugitive Pieces* has a message, it is that life can heal us, if we allow it.

Fun with Dick and Jane ★ ★ ½

PG-13, 90 m., 2005

Jim Carrey (Dick Harper), Téa Leoni (Jane Harper), Alec Baldwin (Jack McCallister), Richard Jenkins (Frank Bascome), Angie Harmon (Veronica), Jeff Garlin (Peter Scott). Directed by Dean Parisot and produced by Brian Grazer and Jim Carrey. Screenplay by Judd Apatow and Nicholas Stoller.

Fun with Dick and Jane recycles the 1977 comedy starring Jane Fonda and George Segal, right down to repeating the same mistakes. Those who do not learn from history are doomed to remake it. The movie stars Jim Carrey as Dick, an executive of a megacorp much like Enron who is promoted to vice president in charge of communications just in time to be its spokesman on live cable news as the corporation's stock melts down to pennies a share.

Téa Leoni plays his wife, Jane, who is a travel agent but has quit her job that very morning because of Dick's big promotion. They were looking forward to glorious affluence and now find they are broke, and the gardeners have come around to roll up the turf on their lawn and truck it away. They lose their retirement savings, their furniture, their light, their heat, and (the cruelest blow of all for their son) their flat-panel hi-def TV.

Dick goes out on job interviews, only to find that the jobs (a) do not exist, (b) have already been taken, or (c) are in the control of chortling sadists who know by heart the tape of his meltdown on TV. Soon Dick and Jane are reduced to theft, at first small-time and then on a larger scale, and that's when this film goes kablooie, just like the 1977 movie did.

There is a large but unexploited comic premise here: One of the largest corporations in America turned out to be worth less than zero and was built from a tissue of lies. Alec Baldwin and Richard Jenkins do a merciless job of playing characters that we may, for convenience, assume are inspired by Enron's fallen giants Kenneth Lay and Jeffrey Skilling.

We have seen the Enron documentaries and know what possibilities there are for ruthless dark comedy, as in the scenes where Enron executives deliberately and cold-bloodedly mastermind the California energy crisis, chuckling that a few grandmothers may have died of heat exhaustion but Enron has made millions. The California energy "shortage" fits any definition of terrorism except that it was engineered by Americans wearing lapel pins instead of Arabs wearing beards.

But the movie avoids the rich opportunities to plop Carrey and Leoni into the middle of a political lampoon and turns to tired slapstick, wigs, false beards, "funny" bank holdups, and so on. There is a late attempt at a comeback as the Baldwin character tries to get his loot out of the country, but by then it's all too neat and too late.

If you want to taste the opportunities that *Fun with Dick and Jane* bypassed, you might want to rent Michael Tolkin's *The New Age* (1994), which stars Peter Weller and Judy Davis in the story of an affluent Los Angeles couple who lose their jobs and descend gradually, in disbelief, from luxury to destitution. Dealing with financial demolition is more than a matter of waving a water pistol in a bank lobby, as a lot of people in Houston would be happy to assure us, if their phones were working.

G

G ★★

R, 96 m., 2005

Richard T. Jones (Summer G), Blair Underwood (Chip Hightower), Chenoa Maxwell (Sky Hightower), Andre Royo (Tre), Jillian Lindsey (Daizy Duke), Laz Alonzo (Craig Lewis), Sonja Sohn (Shelley James), Nicoye Banks (B. Mo Smoov), Lalanya Masters (Nicole Marshall). Directed by Christopher Scott Cherot and produced by Andrew Lauren and Judd Landon. Screenplay by Cherot and Charles E. Drew Jr., loosely based on a novel by F. Scott Fitzgerald.

G enters a world not much seen in the movies, the world of affluent African-Americans whose summer places are in the Hamptons. I wish it had approached this material with a clean slate and given us a story made from scratch. That it's fitfully based on F. Scott Fitzgerald's *The Great Gatsby* is only a distraction; noting how it followed the novel and how it didn't, I wondered why the clarity of Fitzgerald's story line was replaced by such a jumble of a plot.

The film is a fictional recycling of details from its immediate inspiration, Sean Combs, aka Diddy, although still called P Diddy when the movie was filmed in 2002. *G* is based not on his life but on his lifestyle: the Hamptons place, the elegant summer parties where everyone wears white, the crowds of stars and would-be stars. The movie is being described as a "hip-hop *Gatsby*," but there's not much more hip-hop in it than there is *Gatsby*.

Richard T. Jones stars as Summer G, a famous performer and producer who presides over his newly purchased Hamptons mansion and its population of constantly changing guests. This world is seen through the eyes of Tre (Andre Royo), a journalist sent to cover the world of black affluence. He stays with his cousin Sky (Chenoa Maxwell) and her husband, Chip (Blair Underwood), who is a rich stockbroker with a mean streak. If we're keeping count, we now have the equivalents of Jay Gatsby, Nick Carraway, and Daisy and Tom Buchanan.

G and Sky were in love once, long ago. Their lives separated. She married the rich guy. G became the even richer guy. At one of G's parties, he sees Sky and the earth moves. His heart still circles around her. Like Gatsby, he overcame obscurity and poverty, built an empire, and then bought his summer palace to attract her: "I built this world for you."

G is circled by hungry and ambitious performers and producers who know he holds the keys to their success. One hopeful couple is Craig (Laz Alonzo) and the girlfriend he is jealously possessive about, Nicole (Lalanya Masters). These characters do not work as an improvement on the Fitzgerald structure and contribute to an ending that entirely misses the point.

I know, I know, I'm always saying that a movie has to work as a movie and not be "faithful" to the book that inspired it. Filmmaking is not marriage, and adaptation is not adultery. But here we begin with a novel of legendary importance, where the ending is perfectly calculated to end the summer of parties on a note of futility, irony, and loss. *G* rearranges plot elements to make them into a soap opera, in which Summer G suffers the wrong loss in the wrong way for the wrong reasons.

No more about that. The movie is intrinsically interesting when it touches on class differences in the African-American community. Chip Hightower, for example, comes from old money and cringes when he regards hip-hop millionaires moving to the Hamptons. There goes the neighborhood. His opinion of Sky's friendship with Summer G: "I don't want my wife socializing with gangsters." At one point he actually conspires against G with the white head of the local homeowners' association.

Interesting, how much more of the discrimination in *G* is inspired by class and income than by race. Consider the conversation between a Humvee-load of rap stars and a car occupied by upper-middle-class Hamptons residents, both black and white. The Humvee people, heavy with bling, ask for directions. Notice how the tone changes when the car driver's white girlfriend realizes they're talking to celebrities. This movie, like *Crash* in its very different way, realizes that the old forms of prejudice in society are giving way to new ones.

The problem with *G* is not merely that the ending doesn't work and feels hopelessly contrived. It's also that the plot adds too many unnecessary characters and subplots, so that the main line gets misplaced. The question recycled through the movie (and its advertising) is, "Does hip-hop have heart?" Summer G certainly has one, and so does Sky, although she's not sure what it's telling her. In the classic form of the story, the narrator watches as the hero tries to regain the heart of his lost love, while her brutal husband mistreats her and his mistress. In *G* those functions are spread more widely among additional characters, so that A has a way of leading to C while B loses a place in line. The ending of *Gatsby* is inevitable. The ending of *G* is arbitrary and melodramatic.

If you haven't read *The Great Gatsby,* you may enjoy the movie more. On the other hand, maybe not; maybe it's too crowded and overloaded with subplots to really grab you. Either way, you can look forward to reading a great novel. The closing paragraphs contain some of the best prose ever written.

The Game of Their Lives ★ ½

PG, 95 m., 2005

Gerard Butler (Frank Borghi), Wes Bentley (Walter Bahr), Gavin Rossdale (Stanley Mortensen), Jay Rodan (Pee Wee), Zachery Bryan (Harry Keough), Jimmy Jean-Louis (Joe Gatjaens), Richard Jenik (Joe Maca), Craig Hawksley (Walter Giesler), John Rhys-Davis (Coach Bill Jeffrey). Directed by David Anspaugh and produced by Howard Baldwin, Karen Elise Baldwin, Peter Newman, and Ginger T. Perkins. Screenplay by Angelo Pizzo, based on the book by Geoffrey Douglas.

The Game of Their Lives tells the story of an astonishing soccer match in 1950, when an unsung team of Americans went to Brazil to compete in the World Cup, and defeated England, the best team in the world. So extraordinary was the upset, I learn on the Internet Movie Database, that "London bookmakers offered odds of 500-1 against such a preposterous event," and "The *New York Times* refused to run the score when it was first reported, deeming it a hoax."

So it was a hell of an upset. Pity about the movie. Obviously made with all of the best will in the world, its heart in the right place, this is a sluggish and dutiful film that plays more like a eulogy than an adventure. Strange, how it follows the form of a sports movie but has the feeling of an educational film. And all the stranger because the director, David Anspaugh, has made two exhilarating movies about underdogs in sports, *Hoosiers* (1986) and *Rudy* (1993).

In those films he knew how to crank up the suspense and dramatize the supporting characters. Here it feels more like a group of Calvin Klein models have gathered to pose as soccer players from St. Louis. Shouldn't there be at least one player not favored by nature with improbably good looks? And at least a couple who look like they're around twenty, instead of thirty-five? And a goalie who doesn't look exactly like Gerard Butler, who played *The Phantom of the Opera*? True, Frank Borghi, the goalie, is played by Gerard Butler, but that's no excuse: In *Dear Frankie,* Butler played a perfectly believable character who didn't look like he was posing for publicity photos.

The one personal subplot involves a player who thinks he can't go to Brazil because it conflicts with his wedding day. Instead of milking this for personal conflict, Anspaugh solves it all in one perfunctory scene: The coach talks to the future father-in-law, the father-in-law talks to his daughter, she agrees to move up the wedding, and so no problem-o.

This team is so lackluster, when they go out to get drunk, they don't get drunk. It's 1950, but there's only one cigarette and three cigars in the whole movie. The sound track could have used big band hits from the period, but William Ross's score is so inspirational it belongs on a commercial.

As the movie opens, we see a St. Louis soccer club from a mostly Italian-American neighborhood, and hear a narration that sounds uncannily like an audiobook. Word comes that soccer players from New York will travel to Missouri, an American team will be chosen, and they'll travel to Brazil. The players get this information from their coach, Bill Jeffrey (John Rhys-Davis), who is so uncoachlike that at no point during the entire movie does he give them one single word of advice about the game of soccer. Both Rhys-Davis and the general manager, Walter Giesler (Craig Hawksley), are perfectly convincing in their roles, but the screenplay gives them no dialogue to suggest their characters know much about soccer.

As for the big game itself, the game was allegedly shot on location in Brazil, but never do we get a sense that the fans in the long shots are actually watching the match. The tempo of the game is monotonous, coming down to one would-be British goal after another, all of them blocked by Borghi. This was obviously an amazing athletic feat, but you don't get that sense in the movie. You don't get the sense of soccer much at all; *Bend It Like Beckham* had better soccer—*lots* better soccer, and you could follow it and get involved.

At the end of the film, before a big modern soccer match, the surviving members of that 1950 team are called out onto the field and introduced. That should provide us with a big emotional boost, as we see the real men next to insets of their characters in the movie. But it doesn't, because we never got to know the characters in the movie. *The Game of Their Lives* covers its story like an assignment, not like a mission.

Game 6 ★ ★ ★ ½

R, 83 m., 2006

Michael Keaton (Nicky Rogan), Griffin Dunne (Elliot Litvak), Shalom Harlow (Paisley Porter), Bebe Neuwirth (Joanna Bourne), Catherine O'Hara (Lillian Rogan), Robert Downey Jr. (Steven Schwimmer), Ari Graynor (Laurel Rogan), Harris Yulin (Peter Redmond). Directed by Michael Hoffman and produced by Amy Robinson, Griffin Dunne, Leslie Urdang, and Christina Weiss Lurie. Screenplay by Don DeLillo.

Michael Keaton is a talker. His strength as an actor is in roles that position him on the scale between literate and glib; even in the wonderful lost film *Touch and Go* (1986), where he played a pro hockey player, he spoke like one who had a novel in him. In *Game 6*, he plays a playwright and talks like one, taking pleasure in choosing specific words to evoke exactly what he means. He is also a Boston Red Sox fan, and when the opening night of his new play coincides with the sixth game in the 1986 World Series, he has a lot to talk about: "I've been carrying this franchise on my back since I was six years old."

The original screenplay is by the novelist Don DeLillo, and it involves subjects (or obsessions?) he used in his novels *Underworld* (1997) and *Cosmopolis* (2003). From the first comes expertise on baseball, pitched somewhere between torch songs and Greek tragedy. From the second comes the Manhattan gridlock and the undercurrent of danger and violence in the streets. The playwright, named Nicky Rogan, abandons a cab after an exploding steam pipe sprays asbestos into the air, and retreats into a bar where he finds an old friend and fellow playwright, Elliot Litvak (Griffin Dunne). Because it is Nicky's opening night, they talk about a critic they both hate; Elliot believes this man destroyed his life and indeed seems to be entering madness.

This is DeLillo's first produced screenplay, but he has written for the stage, and perhaps his portrait of Steven Schwimmer (Robert Downey Jr.), the detested critic, is drawn from life. I can think of a candidate. Schwimmer has written such lethal reviews of plays that he lives in hiding, is forced to attend opening nights in disguise, and goes to the theater fully armed. Elliot speaks of him in wonder: "I opened a one-act play at 4 A.M. in the Fulton Fish Market. In the rain. For an audience of fish-handlers. Schwimmer was there."

In addition to his fears about opening night and his premonition that the Red Sox will once again destroy his dreams, Nicky is facing personal problems. While one of his cabs was stuck in traffic, he saw his daughter, Laurel (Ari Graynor), in another one; visits between cars stuck in traffic are also an *Underworld* theme. She informs him her mother is divorcing him: "She says Daddy's demons are so intense, he doesn't even know when he's lying." There is consolation in an affair he's having with an investor in his play (Bebe Neuwirth), but not much.

Writers find strange connections in their days and lives; they generate wormholes that connect people. How else to explain that one of the taxi drivers "used to be head of neurosurgery in the USSR," and the star of his new play (Harris Yulin) can't remember his dialogue because he has, the director says, "a parasite living in his brain." Yulin has a painful rehearsal where he fails again and again to remember the line that has just been repeated to him.

This material could be pitched at various levels. You can imagine it being incorporated into a sequel to *The Producers*, or being transformed into quasi-O'Neill. Keaton, DeLillo, and director Michael Hoffman make it into a celebration of spoken language; we're reminded that Hoffman directed *Restoration*

(1995) and the 1999 *A Midsummer Night's Dream.* After the Sundance opening of *Game 6,* I wrote, "DeLillo's dialogue allows for a complexity and richness of speech that is refreshing compared to the subject-verb-object recitation in many movies." Such dialogue requires an actor who sounds like he understands what he is saying, and Keaton goes one better and convinces us he is generating it. Life for him is a play, he is the actor, his speech is the dialogue, and he deepens and dramatizes his experience by the way he talks about it. Certainly what he says about the Red Sox has a weary grandeur.

Downey Jr., whose troubles of a few years ago were well documented, has come back with a vengeance; his career is ascendent, and since *Game 6* was finished in 2005, he has made ten other movies, ranging from *Good Night, and Good Luck* to *The Shaggy Dog,* and that's some range. Here he makes the critic Schwimmer into a study in affectation, a little Buddhist, a little loony, a little paranoid, a little fearless. Dunne, who also produced the movie with his filmmaking partner, Amy Robinson, plays the disintegrating playwright Elliot as a man halfway between barroom philosopher and Dumpster-diver. And for Nicky, everything comes down to which is more important: success for his play, or the Red Sox winning Game 6. Talk about backing yourself into a lose-lose situation.

Garfield: A Tail of Two Kitties ★ ★ ★

PG, 80 m., 2006

Bill Murray (Garfield [voice]), Breckin Meyer (Jon Arbuckle), Jennifer Love Hewitt (Liz Wilson), Billy Connolly (Lord Dargis), Ian Abercrombie (Smithee), Roger Rees (Mr. Hobbs), Lucy Davis (Abby Westminster), Tim Curry (Prince [voice]), Greg Ellis (Nigel [voice]), Bob Hoskins (Winston [voice]), Richard E. Grant (Preston [voice]), Jane Horrocks (Meenie [voice]), Rhys Ifans (McBunny [voice]). Directed by Tim Hill and produced by John Davis. Screenplay by Joel Cohen and Alec Sokolow, based on the comic strip by Jim Davis.

I don't watch a lot of television, because if you spend all your time on the couch you could become the cat equivalent of a couch potato, which would be one of those pillows with the crocheted message "If you can't say anything good about someone, sit right here with me." I have kneaded and nuzzled such pillows so many times I even know the author of the quotation: Alice Roosevelt Longworth, who on the basis of this pillow certainly must have been a cat lover.

But I confess I watched Ebert and Roeper on TV when they reviewed my first movie, *Garfield* (2004). I was eager to get my first review. Having spent years within the cramped panels of a newspaper comic strip, I gloried in the freedom of the cinema. It allowed me to show off my body language: My languorous stretches, my graceful pirouettes, my daring leaps and bounds, my shameless affection for my owner, Jon (Breckin Meyer).

There will be malcontents who will claim I am not the real author of this review, because how could a cat know that after you mention a character in a movie, you include the name of the actor in parentheses? Do these people believe a cat lives in a vacuum? I read all the movie reviews, especially those of Ebert, a graceful and witty prose stylist with profound erudition, whose reviews are worth reading just for themselves, whether or not I have any intention of viewing the movie. I need to read movie reviews because Jon watches DVDs all the time and likes to have me within petting distance, and I need advance warning about movies I will want to avoid, so I can slink off for a snooze under the sofa. Last night, for example, he watched *Cat People*—which, judging by the sound track, had no cats in it.

But I digress. Ebert, the smart and handsome one, gave thumbs up to my first movie, but Roeper, the other one, gave thumbs down and was particularly unkind. He went on forever, attacking Ebert for liking *Garfield.* This from a man with enough taste to praise *Duma.* How very disappointing. One of Roeper's complaints was that I was animated and all the other characters in the movie were "real." Do you have any idea how a statement like that hurts an actor who has worked all his life as a media cat? Yes, Richard Roeper, I was animated. Read my lips: I am a character in a comic strip. What Roeper should have done for perfect consistency is complain that Dennis was *not* animated in *Dennis the Menace.*

But forget his review of *Garfield.* No use

mewling over spilled milk. This week my new movie comes out, inspired (I am happy to report) by the gratifying box office success of the previous one. *Garfield: A Tail of Two Kitties* is my most ambitious work to date, starring me in a dual role as (ahem) Garfield and as a British cat named Prince. As in the first movie, I do Bill Murray's voice while playing myself. In my role as Prince, I do the voice of Tim Curry, an actor I have admired ever since Jon took me to a drive-in to see *Rocky Horror Picture Show* while he smoked human catnip.

I physically perform both roles, which, as any cat knows, is easier for a cat than a human, because we are always playing multiple roles, such as looking gratefully toward humans while shooting daggers at dogs. I love the scene where they use visual effects to show both cats at the same time, in a kind of mirror scene inspired by the Marx Brothers.

Garfield: A Tail of Two Kitties, is actually funnier and more charming than the first film. The plot contrives to get me to England in the suitcase of my master, who has flown over to propose to his girlfriend, Liz (Jennifer Love Hewitt), who is attending a conference on animals at Castle Carlyle, which Prince has just inherited from Lady Eleanor, a cat lover. With intelligent estate planning, I'm sure we'd see a gratifying rise in the numbers of homeowning cats.

Anyway, Prince is dumped in the river by the unspeakably vile Lord Dargis (Billy Connolly), Lady Eleanor's nephew, who will inherit the castle when Prince dies. Prince is washed through the sewer systems into London, where he gets his first taste of pub life; meanwhile, I arrive at Castle Carlyle and am mistaken for Prince by the barnyard animals. These are all real animals, and good actors, too; they do the voices of such actors as Bob Hoskins, Richard E. Grant, Jane Horrocks, and Rhys Ifans.

That all of these animals can talk goes without saying. No doubt some carpers in the chat rooms will observe that Jon's other pet, a dog, does not speak but only barks. I could give you the name of Jon's dog, but (yawn) frankly I can't be bothered. In this movie, Jon's dog may not be able to speak, but he apparently can read, which was as much of a surprise to me as to everyone else. Dogs, in my experience, have hyperactivity disorders that prevent them from concentrating on reading, because they are compelled to leap up in a frenzy and bark at every moving object. Some dogs do this to frighten, but most do it as a pathetic attempt to draw attention to themselves.

In any event, my career as a movie star now seems to be the real thing, and I am speaking with my agents about a third Garfield movie, in which I would like my character to be based on Casanova or Neil Armstrong, with a score by Josie and the Pussycats. Whether I get a thumbs up from Richard Roeper is a matter of profound indifference to me. Profound. (Yawn) Really, seriously, pro . . .

The Gates ★ ★ ★

NO MPAA RATING, 98 m., 2007

A documentary directed by Antonio Ferrera and Albert Maysles and produced by Ferrera, Maureen Ryan, and Vladimir Yavachev.

Many people missed the point of the Gates, those 7,500 frames flowing with orange curtains that were installed along the pathways of Central Park in 2005. The point was not to look at them, but to use them, to walk through them and under them. One New York park board member, opposed to the proposal by artists Christo and Jeanne-Claude, said the addition of the Gates to the park "would be like Picasso painting *Guernica* on top of *The Last Supper*," demonstrating that he did not grasp the difference between a painting and a frame. He might have saved himself embarrassment by consulting *A Pattern Language* by Christopher Alexander, the most important architect alive, who would have had something to say about gates, entrances, exits, doors, portals, and views.

Entrances have everything to do with what we feel about what we are entering. All buildings until the birth of modern architecture knew this, and you can see it in church doors, temple gates, city walls, shop entrances, and cottage doorsteps. Now the doors of a modern building are likely to be a continuation of the same hostile slab of glass or steel that makes the rest of the building sterile and aloof. There will be no place to rest for a moment, inside or out, and no shelf to rest a burden on, and no decorative details to declare, "This is not just any place you are entering, but this honorable place." I believe even criminals feel differently about the judges they encounter inside an old courthouse than inside a new one.

My wife and I walked under the Gates and beneath the curtains. Thousands of others were doing the same. Many of them no doubt made the same journey daily, scarcely thinking of it. Certainly our walk was enriched by trees, grass, shrubbery, ponds, views. But now the Gates, by framing those sights, gave them a new aspect and importance. Not "grass on a hill," but *this* view of a grassy hill. Not a pond, but *look* at the pond. A frame of any sort values what it encloses. And as we walked, we felt subtly ceremonial. We were not walking, but *walking through the gates.* People walked a little more slowly, and sometimes had little smiles, and talked less on their cell phones, and perhaps felt more *there.*

The Gates, a documentary by Antonio Ferrera and Albert Maysles, records the struggle starting in 1979 as Christo and Jeanne-Claude tried to get planning permission to install their gates (for only two weeks, but you'd think they were planning to leave them forever). This despite the fact that the artists were going to pay for it all themselves. One mayor after another, perhaps too timid to support duh artz, said no. Bloomberg said yes, instantly. So, I believe, would have Chicago's Mayor Daley, whose wrought-iron fences and islands of flowers and neoclassical columns and Millennium Park declare, "This is a city worthy of such pomp and formality, such beauty and pride." Those who say Daley has the mentality of a bungalow owner have no idea of the pride a bungalow owner can take in his home. Maybe they live in high-rises where committees buy hideously tortured iron and dump it in the lobby.

The documentary is pretty much what you'd expect: Two decades of ignorant contempt, followed by the city finding it was really surprisingly fond of the Gates. How far do you think our beloved Chicago sidewalk cows would have gotten among the philistines of fifty years ago? Why does London cling to manifestly impractical red pillar boxes for its postal system, pillars that look like bright red Victorian fire hydrants? Because they're fun, that's why.

Christo and Jeanne-Claude age during the film, their hair turning gray (or red, in her case), but they never stop campaigning. It must have seemed so simple to them: Hey, people, lighten up! Don't be afraid of fancy and imagination! They actually had to use two high-powered lawyers, Scott Hodes of Chicago and Theodore W. Kheel of New York, to argue the case in favor of their gift to the city. The one thing lacking is a good sit-down chat with Christopher Alexander, explaining why cities require more, not less, attention to human feelings that cannot be reasoned away. ☞

George A. Romero's Land of the Dead ★ ★ ★

R, 93 m., 2005

Simon Baker (Riley), John Leguizamo (Cholo), Asia Argento (Slack), Robert Joy (Charlie), Dennis Hopper (Kaufman), Eugene Clark (Big Daddy). Directed by George Romero and produced by Romero, Mark Canton, Bernie Goldmann, and Peter Grunwald. Screenplay by Romero.

In a world where the dead are returning to life, the word trouble *has lost its meaning.*
—Dennis Hopper in *Land of the Dead*

Now this is interesting. In the future world of *George A. Romero's Land of the Dead,* both zombies and their victims have started to evolve. The zombies don't simply shuffle around mindlessly, eating people. And the healthy humans don't simply shoot them. The zombies have learned to communicate on a rudimentary level, to make plans, however murky, and to learn from their tormenters. When the zombie named Big Daddy picks up a machine gun in this movie, that is an ominous sign.

The healthy humans, on the other hand, have evolved a class system. Those with money and clout live in Fiddler's Green, a luxury high-rise where all their needs are catered to under one roof—and just as well, because they are not eager to go outside. Other survivors cluster in the city at the foot of the tower, in a city barricaded against the zombie hordes outside. Mercenaries stage raids outside the safe zone in Dead Reckoning, a gigantic armored truck, and bring back canned food, gasoline, and booze.

The most intriguing single shot in *Land of*

the Dead is a commercial for Fiddler's Green, showing tanned and smiling residents, dressed in elegant leisure wear, living the good life. They look like the white-haired eternally youthful golfers in ads for retirement paradises. The shot is intriguing for two reasons: (1) Why does Fiddler's Green need to advertise, when it is full and people are literally dying to get in? And (2) What is going through the minds of its residents as they relax in luxury, sip drinks, shop in designer stores, and live the good life? Don't they know the world outside is one of unremitting conflict and misery?

Well, yes, they probably do, and one of the reasons George A. Romero's zombie movies have remained fresh is that he suggests such questions. The residents of Fiddler's Green and the zombies have much the same relationship as citizens of rich nations have with starving orphans and refugees. The lesson is clear: It's good to live in Fiddler's Green.

That's why Cholo (John Leguizamo) wants to move in. He's one of the best mercenaries in the hire of Kaufman (Dennis Hopper), who is the Donald Trump of Fiddler's Green. Kaufman sits in his penthouse, smokes good cigars, sips brandy, and gets rich, although the movie never explains how money works in this economy, where possessions are acquired by looting and retained by force. How, for that matter, do the residents of Fiddler's Green earn a living? Do they spend all day in their casual wear, flashing those white teeth as they perch on the arms of each other's lounge chairs? The thing that bothers me about ads for retirement communities is that the residents seem condemned to leisure.

Cholo works under Riley (Simon Baker), the leader of Kaufman's hired force and the movie's hero. Riley is responsible, calm, and sane. Cholo is not, and Leguizamo plays another one of his off-the-wall loose cannons. He has added an unreasonable amount of interest to any number of recent movies. Also important to the plot is Slack (Asia Argento), a sometime hooker who is beautiful and heroic and intended for better things, and is thrown into a pit of zombies to fend for herself. For that matter, zombies themselves are occasionally hung by the heels with bull's-eyes painted on them for target practice. And Romero finds still new and entertaining ways for unspeakably disgusting things to happen to the zombies and their victims.

The balance of power in this ordered little world is upset when Kaufman refuses Cholo's request to move into Fiddler's Green. There is a long waiting list, etc. Cholo steals Dead Reckoning, he is pursued, the zombies get (somewhat) organized, and Big Daddy (Eugene Clark) begins to develop a gleam of intelligence in his dead blue eyes.

The puzzle in all the zombie movies is why any zombies are still—I was about to write "alive," but I guess the word is "moving." Shooting them in the head or decapitating them seems simple enough, and dozens are mowed down with machine guns by the troops in Dead Reckoning. Guards at the city barriers kill countless more. Since they are obviously zombies and no diagnosis is necessary before execution on sight, why do they seem to be winning?

This and other questions may await Romero's next movie. It's good to see him back in the genre he invented with *Night of the Living Dead,* and still using zombies not simply for target practice but as a device for social satire. It's probably not practical from a box office point of view, but I would love to see a movie set entirely inside a thriving Fiddler's Green. There would be zombies outside but we'd never see them or deal with them. We would simply regard the Good Life as it is lived by those who have walled the zombies out. Do they relax? Have they peace of mind? Do the miseries of others weigh upon them? The parallels with the real world are tantalizing.

Get Rich or Die Tryin' ★ ★ ★

R, 134 m., 2005

Curtis "50 Cent" Jackson (Marcus), Terrence Howard (Bama), Joy Bryant (Charlene), Bill Duke (Levar), Adewale Akinnuoye-Agbaje (Majestic), Omar Benson Miller (Keryl), Tory Kittles (Justice), Ashley Walters (Antwan), Viola Davis (Grandma). Directed by Jim Sheridan and produced by Dr. Dre, Jimmy Iovine, Chris Lighty, Paul Rosenberg, and Sheridan. Screenplay by Terence Winter.

Get Rich or Die Tryin' offers a limited range of choices, but we'll probably never see a film titled *Get By and Don't Die.* The film is inspired by the haunting life story of Curtis "50 Cent" Jackson, who never knew his father, whose mother was a drug dealer killed when he was young, who sold drugs on the streets of New York City, and survived gunshot wounds to become one of the best-selling recording artists of modern times. It has been an amazing life, and he is only thirty.

Of course, the odds against a young drug dealer eventually selling 4 million copies of an album are so high that by comparison, getting into the NBA is a sure thing. A more accurate title might have been, *I Got Rich but Just About Everybody Else Died Tryin', and So Did I, Almost.* Given the harrowing conditions of his early life, Jackson's movie dwells on it with a strange affection; the movie is closer in tone to *Scarface* than to *Hustle and Flow,* the year's other rags-to-riches rap story.

Billboards for the movie have been protested by citizens' groups—not do-gooders or killjoys but people who have seen the bodies on the streets and attended the funerals and seen drugs taking a deadly tax on young manhood. *Hustle and Flow* is about a man (Terrence Howard) who wants to escape the drug world and become a musical artist. *Get Rich* is about a man who hangs on in the drug world as long as possible and becomes a musician because he is talented and very lucky. There is a difference between these two life strategies.

Still, I must review the movie, not offer counseling to Curtis Jackson. *Get Rich* is a film with a rich and convincing texture, a drama with power and anger. It shows its young hero taken in by grandparents who love him (Viola Davis and Sullivan Walker) after the death of his mother, and then being lured by the streets because, quite simply, he wants money for athletic shoes and, eventually, a car. There seem to be few other avenues of employment open to him, certainly none that he seeks, and although his mother tried to shield him from her business, he saw what happened and how it worked and he knows who the players are.

Early scenes in his career involve turf wars. The question of who stands on what corner to sell drugs is sometimes settled by death. Meanwhile, the customers, a great many of them whites from the suburbs, roll up in their cars and subsidize these deaths, one purchase at a time. Although the movies have accustomed us to associate drug dealers with briefcases filled with cash, the movie provides a more realistic job description: "All you get out there is long lonely nights." And "If you would add up all the time spent standing around, it was minimum wage. If you added prison time, it was below minimum wage." The lie in the movie's title is that you get rich. Someone gets rich, yes, but then someone wins the lottery every week.

The best thing that happens to Jackson is that he is sent to prison. This probably saves his life, and it's there that he's approached by Bama (Terrence Howard again), a guy he already knows from the neighborhood, who tells him, "You need a manager." This before he has a career. Jackson has always sung along with rap recordings, has started writing his own lyrics, and observes in the narration, "After Tupac, everybody wanted to be a gangster rapper." He has the timing a little off, though. It wasn't "after Tupac," but "after Tupac's death." I remember Tupac Shakur in *Gridlock'd* (1997), where opposite Tim Roth he showed that he was a gifted actor. Now he is dead. *Tupac Resurrection* (2003), the quasi-documentary based on his life and narrated by his own words, makes an instructive parallel to this film.

Jackson is a good actor, at least in this film, playing himself. The same can be said of Eminem after *8 Mile.* Whether he makes a career of acting is his choice. Joy Bryant is crucial in the film as Charlene, whom he has known since they were young, who loves him, who despairs of the danger he is in. There are smaller but significant roles for actors such as Bill Duke, playing a drug wholesaler who tries to run an orderly business but has too much turnover in the deadly front lines.

In an opening scene of the film, Jackson is shot and left to die. This scene might as well come early, since everyone in the audience will know this happened to the real 50 Cent. "I was about to die," he says in the narration. "I don't know why I was expecting my father to rescue me, been looking for him all my life." This theme, the search for the father, may have been one reason Jim Sheridan, an Irishman in his fifties, seemed like a good director for this assignment. He knows about fathers and prisons (see his *In the Name of the Father*) and he knows about poverty in New York (see his *In America*). Many of his visuals are brilliant; look at the way the bass on an automobile's sound system makes images in the rearview mirrors vibrate.

Sheridan has made a well-crafted film, but it contains more drugs and less music than many people will expect. I guess people don't attend movies about gangster rap looking for career guidance and inspiration, but *Hustle and Flow* has a lot more of each, and more music, too.

Get Smart ★ ★ ★ ½

PG-13, 110 m., 2008

Steve Carell (Maxwell Smart), Anne Hathaway (Agent 99), Dwayne Johnson (Agent 23), Alan Arkin (The Chief), Terence Stamp (Siegfried), James Caan (The President). Directed by Peter Segal and produced by Andrew Lazar, Charles Roven, Alex Gartner, and Michael Ewing. Screenplay by Tom J. Astle and Matt Ember.

The closing credits of *Get Smart* mention Mel Brooks and Buck Henry, creators of the original TV series, as "consultants." Their advice must have been: "If it works, don't fix it." There have been countless comic spoofs of the genre founded by James Bond, but *Get Smart* (both on TV and now in a movie) is one of the best. It's funny, exciting, preposterous, great to look at, and made with the same level of technical expertise we'd expect from a new Bond movie itself. And all of that is very nice, but nicer still is the perfect pitch of the casting.

Steve Carell makes an infectious Maxwell Smart, the bumbling but ambitious and unreasonably self-confident agent for CONTROL, a secret U.S. agency in rivalry with the CIA. His job is to decipher overheard conversations involving agents of KAOS, its Russian counterpart. At this he is excellent: What does it mean that KAOS agents discuss muffins? That they have a high level of anxiety, of course, because muffins are a comfort food. Brilliant, but he misses the significance of the bakery they're also discussing—a cookery for high-level uranium.

Smart is amazingly promoted to field agent by The Chief (Alan Arkin, calm and cool) and teamed with the beautiful Agent 99 (Anne Hathaway, who never tries too hard but dominates the screen effortlessly). They go to Russia, joining with Agent 23 (Dwayne Johnson, once known as The Rock). Their archenemy is waiting for them; he's Siegfried (Terence Stamp), a cool, clipped villain.

And that's about it, except for a series of special effects sequences and stunt work that would truly give envy to a James Bond producer. *Get Smart* is an A-level production, not a cheapo rip-off, and some of the chase sequences are among the most elaborate you can imagine—particularly a climactic number involving planes, trains, and automobiles. Maxwell Smart, of course, proves indestructible, often because of the intervention of Agent 99; he spends much of the center portion of the film in free fall without a parachute, and then later is towed behind an airplane.

The plot involves a KAOS scheme to nuke the Walt Disney concert hall in Los Angeles, during a concert being attended by the U.S. president. The nuclear device in question is concealed beneath the concert grand on the stage, which raises the question, since you're using the Bomb, does its location make much difference, give or take a few miles?

It raises another question, too, and here I will be the gloom-monger at the festivities. Remember right after 9/11, when we wondered if Hollywood would ever again be able to depict terrorist attacks as entertainment? How long ago that must have been, since now we are blowing up presidents and cities as a plot device for Maxwell Smart. I'm not objecting, just observing. Maybe humor has a way of helping us face our demons.

The props in the movie are neat, especially a Swiss Army–style knife that Maxwell never quite masters. The locations, many in Montreal, are awesome; I learned with amazement that Moscow was not one of them but must have been created on a computer. The action and chase sequences do not grow tedious because they are punctuated with humor. I am not given to quoting filmmakers in praise of their own work in press releases, but director Peter Segal does an excellent job of describing his method: "If we plan a fight sequence as a rhythmic series of punches, we would have a 'bump, bump, bam' or a 'bump, bump, smack.' We can slot in a punch line instead of a physical hit. The rhythm accentuates the joke and it becomes 'bump, bump, joke' with the verbal jab as the knockout or a joke, immediately followed by the last physical beat that essentially ends the conversation."

Yes. And the jokes actually have something to do with a developing story line involving Anne Hathaway's love life, the reason for her plastic surgery, and a love triangle that is right there staring us in the face. One of the gifts of Steve Carell is to deliver punch lines in the middle of punches and allow both to seem real enough, at least within the context of the movie. James Bond could do that, too. And in a summer with no new Bond picture, will I be considered a heretic by saying *Get Smart* will do just about as well?

Gilles' Wife ★ ★ ★

NO MPAA RATING, 103 m., 2005

Emmanuelle Devos (Elisa), Clovis Cornillac (Gilles), Laura Smet (Victorine), Alice and Chloe Verlinden (Twins), Colette Emmanuelle (Elisa's Mother), Gil Lagay (Elisa's Father). Directed by Frederic Fonteyne and produced by Patrick Quinet and Claude Waringo. Screenplay by Philippe Blasband and Fonteyne, based on the novel by Madeleine Bourdouxhe.

Let us assume you are a wife deeply contented with your husband, your children, your home, and your marriage. You discover that your husband is having an affair. You know the woman well enough to feel betrayed by her as well as by him. Also well enough to know this affair cannot endure. Do you explode with fury, throw out your husband, and end the marriage? Or do you wait out the affair? Do you offer emotional support to your husband, who you know is torn to pieces by what has happened to him?

You require more detail. I will provide it. This story takes place in a small French town in the 1930s. Your husband works in the factory, marches home every evening down the hill, helps tend your kitchen garden. You are pregnant with your third child. You are beautiful in the way that makes a man want to nuzzle you and be comforted, but not with a beauty that attracts attention. The other woman is glamorous, at least by the provincial standards of the village. Certainly the most glamorous woman who has ever looked seriously at him. She is your sister.

Now what do you do? You do not have a job, except the unending one of being a wife and mother. You wash, iron, teach, scold, cook, serve, clean up, mend, tend, treat, cure, bake, garden, repair, and turn warmly to your man in bed at night. You know him well enough to understand how the stupid goof would be powerless against a woman like *that* woman. You wish he were stronger, wiser, and more discerning, but he is not. He barely understands that his "lover" uses him only to supply sex and sneak away because she would not be able to stand him underfoot all day, and he would have nothing to talk to her about. He barely has anything to talk to you about. He barely has speech. John Prine wrote a song that could describe him:

How the hell can a man
Go off in the morning,
Come back in the evening,
And have nothing to say?

Now you know what you need to know about *Gilles' Wife,* the movie by Frederic Fonteyne, based on the novel by Madeleine Bourdouxhe—all except that I have not provided you with the subject of the film, which is the face of the actress Emmanuelle Devos. Of the face of her husband (Clovis Cornillac) and her sister, Victorine (Laura Smet), I need say little. He has the face of a man waiting in line for something more interesting men do not desire. She has the face of the trophy girl of a man who cannot afford a better trophy.

The film unfolds with little dialogue. On one level it could be a Bresson film of suffering and renunciation. A slightly different angle and it could be a story by Simenon, in which people have locked themselves into intolerable situations, thrown away the key, and now spend their days looking through their prison bars at the key, still there but just out of reach. It is a story not of passion (its passion is pathetic) but of patience.

Or perhaps it is the story of a woman who in another life would have been a social scientist but in this life is limited to one experiment, in which she tests her theory on her husband. Her theory is that no man can stand Victorine for long. Why should she lose husband, home, family, security, respectability, even the warmth they truly share, just because he wants to dart out at night and fool himself that he is a daring lover? From what we see of his sex life, he is like a motorcyclist who roars up a tricky ramp in order to leap a tiny chasm.

I do not approve of the way the movie ends,

and I think Fonteyne's elaborate camera move right before the end is just showing off and is not a word in the visual language he was using. It would have taken more courage and thought for the movie to have ended as it began. But I was fascinated by the face of Devos, and her face is specifically why I recommend the movie. There are some people who keep their thoughts to themselves because they don't have a one to spare. Others are filled with thoughts but keep them as companions. Devos, as Gilles' wife, is in the second category. She is too clever by half. What such people don't realize is that being too clever by half is only being too clever by half enough.

Glory Road ★ ★ ★

PG, 106 m., 2006

Josh Lucas (Coach Don Haskins), Derek Luke (Bobby Joe Hill), Damaine Radcliff (Willie "Scoops" Cager), Jon Voight (Coach Adolph Rupp). Directed by James Gartner and produced by Jerry Bruckheimer. Screenplay by Christopher Cleveland, Bettina Gilois, and Gregory Allen Howard.

Glory Road is like other sports movies, and different from all of them. It is the same in the way it shows a rookie coach with an underdog team; he finds resistance from his players at first, he imposes his system and is a merciless taskmaster, and do I have to ask you if they win the big game? This has been the formula for countless films, and *Glory Road* will not be the last.

But the movie is not really about underdogs and winning the big game. It's about racism in American sports and how Coach Don Haskins and his players on the 1965–66 basketball team from Texas Western University made a breakthrough comparable to that moment when Jackie Robinson was hired by the Brooklyn Dodgers. In Texas at that time, we learn, college basketball teams had been integrated, but there was an "informal rule" that you never played more than one black player at home, two on the road, or three if you were behind.

After Texas Western won the 1966 NCAA championship with an all-black team, defeating an all-white Kentucky team coached by the legendary Adolph Rupp, the rules were rewritten, and modern college and professional basketball began. Haskins and his team wrote the "emancipation proclamation of 1966," says Coach Pat Riley in an interview during the end credits. He starred on the defeated Kentucky team.

Glory Road tells its story not through personalities but in terms of the issues involved. It uses the basketball season as a backdrop to the story of how Haskins (Josh Lucas) inherited a weak, losing team at Texas Western and set out to recruit gifted black players from the schools and playgrounds of the North. The school's administration and some of the rich boosters were not very happy with him, until the team started to win. Strange how that works, isn't it?

An opening scene is brief but poignant: After Haskins coaches a girls' basketball team to victory, his players try to lift him up on their shoulders, but they aren't strong enough. Haskins is offered the head coaching position at Texas Western and jumps at it: This is his chance to coach a Division I team, no matter how weak. Haskins knows he has no chance of recruiting the best white players to come to Texas Western, so he and his assistant coach head north and find African-Americans who are happy to have scholarships and a chance to play. Chief among them are Bobby Joe Hill (Derek Luke) and Willie "Scoops" Cager (Damaine Radcliff).

They play a hotshot, Globetrotters-style basketball; Haskins thinks it is undisciplined and risky, and he drills them with his own man-on-man system. There are the predictable clashes between coach and players, but the movie doesn't linger on them. Instead, it shows Texas Western going on the road with a mostly black team in a South where the teams were mostly white. One player is beaten in a restroom. The team's motel rooms are trashed in east Texas. The white players begin to bond with their teammates who are the targets of such attacks. And then, when everything depends on the Big Game, Haskins announces that he plans to play only black athletes. He wants to make a point. By this time, the white players understand the point and agree with it.

Jon Voight plays Kentucky's Rupp, one of the most successful coaches in college history. Voight doesn't have a lot of screen time, but he uses it to create a character, not a stereotype. On the sidelines, we watch his face as he begins to realize what's happening. "This is a special team," he warns his players during a time-out. He is trying to tell them that ordinary sideline talks are irrelevant; if they cannot rise to this historic moment, they will lose.

Director James Gartner tells his story forcefully and makes a wise decision during the end titles to show black-and-white footage of many of the real people whose lives are depicted in the film. One of his decisions about the sound track is strange but perhaps effective: The play-by-play announcers somehow simultaneously seem to be the game announcers, so that loudspeakers in the gyms carry their commentary and opinions. That works for us, but how would it work with players and fans in real life?

Glory Road is an effective sports movie, yes, but as the portrait of a coach and team and the realities of administrations and booster clubs in a state obsessed with sports, it's a shadow of *Friday Night Lights* (2004). Where it succeeds is as the story of a chapter in history, the story of how one coach at one school arrived at an obvious conclusion and acted on it, and helped open up college sports in the South to generations of African-Americans. As the end credits tell us what happened in later life to the members of that 1966 Texas Western team, we realize that Haskins not only won an NCAA title but also made a contribution to the future that is still being realized.

Goal! The Dream Begins ★ ★ ★

PG, 117 m., 2006

Kuno Becker (Santiago Munez), Stephen Dillane (Glen Foy), Alessandro Nivola (Gavin Harris), Anna Friel (Roz Harmison), Tony Plana (Herman Munez), Sean Pertwee (Barry Rankin), Kiernan O'Brien (Hughie Magowen), Cassandra Bell (Christina), Marcel Iures (Erik Dornhelm), Miriam Colon (Mercedes). Directed by Danny Cannon and produced by Mark Huffam, Matt Barrelle, and Mike Jefferies. Screenplay by Dick Clement and Ian La Frenais.

Goal! The Dream Begins is a rags-to-riches sports saga containing all the usual elements, arranged in the usual ways, and yet it's surprisingly effective. We have the kid from Mexico who dreams of soccer stardom, his impoverished life in Los Angeles as an undocumented immigrant, his dad who scorns soccer, his grandmother who believes in him, the scout who gets him a tryout with a top British team, the superstar who befriends him, and even a pretty nurse. There is also a great deal of soccer, some of it looking real, some of it not.

The movie works because it is, above all, sincere. It's not sports by the numbers. The starring performance by Kuno Becker is convincing and dimensional, and we begin to care for him. He plays Santiago Munez, a busboy in an L.A. Chinese restaurant, who plays in an after-work soccer league so deprived that he wears cardboard shin protectors. Then he's spotted by a former soccer pro (Stephen Dillane), who tells him he has potential and arranges for him to get a tryout with Newcastle United.

That would, however, involve an air ticket to England. Santiago has some money saved, but his dad (Tony Plana) nicks it to buy a pickup truck and start his own landscaping business. This is cruel, but perhaps more practical than betting the money on a future in soccer. Santiago's grandmother (Miriam Colon) says she hasn't worked for a lifetime without having some savings, and pays for him to fly to London out of Mexico City—a wise precaution, since he has no American passport or identity.

In Newcastle, Santiago undergoes a rough initiation at the hands of the hardened soccer pros, gets his first experience of soccer in the mud, and almost loses his place on the team because of his asthma. What saves him is an accidental friendship with the team's superstar, Gavin Harris (Alessandro Nivola), a party animal. How the season turns out and how Santiago fares I will leave for you to discover, not only in this movie, but in *Goal! 2: Living the Dream,* which comes out in late 2006, and in *Goal! 3,* scheduled for 2007. The fact that *Goal! 4* is not in preproduction soon will, I am sure, be remedied.

Before *Goal!* began, I moaned to a colleague that I was dreading the screening. Any movie named *Goal!* that needs an exclamation mark seems to be protesting too much, and the words *The Dream Begins* suggest that the snores will follow shortly. I see an average of one sports movie a month in which an underdog (or underhorse or undergymnast) overcomes the odds to earn an exclamation mark. I know all about the grizzled coaches, the mean teammates, the dad who doesn't understand, and the girl who does.

I was surprised, then, to find myself enjoying

the movie almost from the beginning. It had some of the human reality of Gregory Nava's work in movies such as *Mi Familia* and the PBS series *American Family.* Not the depth or beauty, to be sure, but the feeling for a culture and family ties. And Becker, a Mexican star of films and TV and three English-language films little released in America, has not only star quality but also something more rare: likability. He makes us want his character to succeed.

Where possible, director Danny Cannon sidesteps some (not all) of the clichés. We suspect Santiago's father may be proud of his son after all but are unprepared for the way that plays out, and how Santiago's toughness is both the right and wrong choice. We know all about the understanding Irish nurse Roz (Anna Friel), except that she will have insight and understanding. We are relieved, in a way, to be spared an obligatory sex scene. And it is interesting that the boss of the Newcastle United team is not made into your standard Bob Hoskins or Colm Meany role but is written as a German and cast with a Romanian, Marcel Iures.

Goal! The Dream Begins is not a great sports film, and I can easily contain my impatience for *Goal! 2* and *Goal! 3* (which should, but will not, be titled *Goal! 3: The Dreamer Awakes*). But it is good and caring work, with more human detail than we expect. Specifically, it is more about Santiago's life as a young man than it is about who wins the big match. There's a subtext about immigrants in America that is timely right now, and a certain sadness in his father's conviction that some people are intended to be rich and others poor, and that the Munez family should be content and grateful to be poor. Santiago is not content, but he is driven not so much by ambition as by pure and absolute love of soccer, and that gives the movie a purity that shines through.

The Golden Compass ★ ★ ★ ★

PG-13, 114 m., 2007

Nicole Kidman (Mrs. Coulter), Dakota Blue Richards (Lyra), Daniel Craig (Lord Asriel), Sam Elliott (Lee Scoresby), Eva Green (Serafina Pekkala), Christopher Lee (First High Councilor), Tom Courtenay (Farder Coram), Derek Jacobi (Magisterial Emissary), Ben Walker (Roger), Simon McBurney (Fra Pavel), Ian McKellen (Iorek Byrnison), Ian McShane (Ragnar Sturlusson), Freddie Highmore (Pantalaimon), Kathy Bates (Hester), Kristin Scott Thomas (Stelmaria). Directed by Chris Weitz and produced by Bill Carraro and Deborah Forte. Screenplay by Weitz, based on the novel by Philip Pullman.

The Golden Compass is a darker, deeper fantasy epic than the *Lord of the Rings* trilogy, *The Chronicles of Narnia,* or the Potter films. It springs from the same British world of quasi-philosophical magic but creates more complex villains and poses more intriguing questions. As a visual experience, it is superb. As an escapist fantasy, it is challenging. Teenagers may be absorbed and younger children may be captivated; some kids in between may be a little conflicted, because its implications are murky.

They weren't murky in the original 1995 novel, part of the His Dark Materials trilogy by Philip Pullman, a best-seller in Britain, less so here. Pullman's evil force, called the Magisterium in the books, represents organized religion, and his series is about no less than the death of God, whom he depicts as an aged, spent force. This version by New Line Cinema and writer-director Chris Weitz (*About a Boy*) leaves aside religion and God, and presents the Magisterium as sort of a Soviet dictatorship, or Big Brother. The books have been attacked by American Christians over questions of religion; their popularity in the United Kingdom may represent more confident believers whose reaction to other beliefs is to respond, rather than suppress.

For most families, such questions will be beside the point. Attentive as I was, I was unable to find anything anti-religious in the movie, which works above all as an adventure. The film centers on a young girl named Lyra (Dakota Blue Richards), in an alternative universe vaguely like Victorian England. An orphan raised by the scholars of a university not unlike Oxford or Cambridge, she is the niece of Lord Asriel (Daniel Craig), who entrusts her with the last surviving Alethiometer, or Golden Compass, a device that quite simply tells the truth. The Magisterium has a horror of the truth because it represents an alternative to its thought control; the battle in the movie is about no less than man's preservation of free will.

Lyra's friend Roger (Ben Walker) disappears, one of many recently kidnapped children, and Lyra hears rumors that the Magisterium has taken them to an Arctic hideaway. At her college, she meets Mrs. Coulter (Nicole Kidman), who suspiciously offers her a trip to the North aboard one of those fantasy airships that look like they may be powered by steam. And the adventure proper begins.

I should explain that in this world, everyone has a spirit, or demon, which is visible, audible, and accompanies them everywhere. When they are with children, these spirits are shape shifters, but gradually they settle into a shape appropriate for the adult who matures. Lyra's is a chattering little creature who can be a ferret, mouse, fox, cat, even a moth. When two characters threaten each other, their demons lead the fight.

Turns out the Magisterium is experimenting on the captured children by removing their souls and using what's left as obedient servants without free will. Lyra challenges this practice, after taking the advice of the grizzled pilot Lee Scoresby (Sam Elliott) to find herself an armored bear. She enlists the magnificent bear Iorek, who must duel to the death with the top bear of the North. She also finds such friends as a flying witch named Serafina (Eva Green) and some pirate types named Gyptians, whose lifestyle resembles seafaring gypsies.

The struggle involves a mysterious cosmic substance named Dust, which embodies free will and other properties the Magisterium wants to remove from human possibility. By "mysterious," I mean that Dust appears throughout the movie as a cloud of dancing particles, from which emerge people, places, and possibilities, but I have no idea under which rules it operates. Possibly it represents our human inheritance if dogma did not interfere.

As Lyra, Dakota Blue Richards is a delightful find, a British-American schoolgirl who was twelve when she was discovered in an audition involving a total of ten thousand girls. She is pretty, plucky, forceful, self-possessed, charismatic, and just about plausible as the mistress of an armored bear and the protector of Dust. Nicole Kidman projects a severe beauty in keeping with the sinister Mrs. Coulter (had Pullman heard about our girl Ann when he wrote his book?), and Daniel Craig and Sam Elliott (with his famous moustache never more formidable) give her refined and rough surfaces to play against.

The cast is jammed with the usual roll call of stage and screen greats, some of them in person, some of them voice-over talent: Christopher Lee, Tom Courtenay, Derek Jacobi, Simon McBurney, Ian McKellen, Ian McShane, Kathy Bates, Kristin Scott Thomas. The British fantasy industry has become a bigger employer even than the old Hammer horror films. And why is it, by the way, that such tales seem to require British accents?

I realize this review itself may be murky because theological considerations confuse the flow. Let me just say that I think *The Golden Compass* is a wonderfully good-looking movie, with exciting passages and a captivating heroine in Lyra. That the controversy surrounding it obscures its function as a splendid entertainment. That for adults it will not be boring or too simplistic. And that I still don't understand how they know what the symbols on the Golden Compass represent, but it certainly seems articulate.

Gone Baby Gone ★ ★ ★ ½

R, 115 m., 2007

Casey Affleck (Patrick Kenzie), Michelle Monaghan (Angie Gennaro), Morgan Freeman (Jack Doyle), Ed Harris (Remy Bressant), John Ashton (Nick Poole), Amy Ryan (Helene McCready), Amy Madigan (Bea McCready), Titus Welliver (Lionel McCready). Directed by Ben Affleck and produced by Alan Ladd Jr., Sean Bailey, and Dan Rissner. Screenplay by Affleck and Aaron Stockard, based on the novel by Dennis Lehane.

Boston seems like the most forbidding city in crime movies. There are lots of movies about criminals in Los Angeles, Chicago, New York, and points between, but somehow in Boston the wounds cut deeper, the characters are angrier, their resentments bleed, their grudges never die, and they all know everybody else's business. The novelist Dennis Lehane captured that dour gloom in his books inspiring *Mystic River* and now *Gone Baby Gone.* What would it take to make his characters happy?

This is his fourth story involving Patrick Kenzie (Casey Affleck) and Angie Gennaro (Michelle Monaghan), lovers and business partners who are private investigators specializing in tracking down deadbeats. Approached by clients who have deadly matters on their minds, Patrick and Angie protest that they're just garden-variety PIs, don't carry guns, aren't looking for heavy lifting. Then somehow they end up with crucifixion murders, kidnapped babies, and, always, people who are not who or what they seem.

This could become a franchise, if we didn't start grinning at their claims to be basically amateurs. In *Gone Baby Gone,* Ben Affleck, in his debut as a director, assumes we haven't read the four novels, approaches Patrick and Angie head-on, and surrounds them with a gallery of very, very intriguing characters. He has his brother Casey and Monaghan play babes in a deep, dark woods, their youth and inexperience working for them as they wonder about what veteran cops don't question. The result is a superior police procedural and something more—a study in devious human nature.

I know, the title sounds like the movie should star Bill Haley and the Comets. But there is a rough authenticity from the first shots, especially when we meet a woman named Bea McCready (Amy Madigan) and her husband, Lionel (Titus Welliver), who don't think the cops are doing enough to track down her four-year-old niece. They think people who know the neighborhood and don't wear badges might find out more. They're right.

The police investigation is being led by Jack Doyle (Morgan Freeman) of the police Crimes Against Children task force, who, unlike a standard movie cop, doesn't resent these outsiders but suggests they work with his men Remy Bressant (Ed Harris) and Nick Poole (John Ashton). Not likely, but good for the story, as the trail begins in the wreckage of a life being lived by the little girl's single mother, Helene (Amy Ryan). She is deep into drugs, which she takes whenever she can sober up enough, and there seems to be a connection between her supplier and a recent heist of a pile of drug money.

Enough about the plot. What I like about the movie is the way Ben Affleck and his brother, both lifelong Bostonians, understand the rhythm of a society in which people not only live in each other's pockets, but are trying to slash their way out. This movie and *The Assassination of Jesse James . . .* announce Casey's maturation as an actor, and this movie also proves, after her film *The Heartbreak Kid,* that Michelle Monaghan should not be blamed for the sins of others.

And when you assemble Morgan Freeman, Ed Harris, Amy Madigan, and Amy Ryan as sidemen, the star soloists can go out for a cigarette and the show goes right on. One reason crime movies tend to be intrinsically interesting is that the supporting characters *have* to be riveting. How far would Jason Bourne get in a one-man show?

There are some secrets and concealed motives in *Gone Baby Gone,* but there always are in any crime movie without name tags saying "Good Guy" and "Bad Guy." What distinguishes the screenplay by Ben Affleck and Aaron Stockard, which departs from the novel in several ways, is (a) how well-concealed the secrets are, and (b) how much perfect sense they make when they're revealed. I am grateful when a movie springs something on me and I feel rewarded, not tricked.

I also like the way that certain clues are planted in plain view. We can see or hear them just fine. It's that we don't know they're clues. No glowering close-ups or characters skulking in a corner to give the game away. That's a tribute to the writing—and the acting, which doesn't telegraph anything. Actors talk about how well they like to get to know their characters. Sometimes it's better if they take them at face value and find out more about them along with the rest of us.

There are dark regions below the surface of the story. Was the child taken by a pedophile? There's a suspect, all right, but maybe he's too obvious. Certainly Helene, the mother, is no help. She's so battered by drugs and drink that she's hardly quite sure if a conversation is taking place. It's amazing the little girl made it to four; her aunt and uncle must have had a lot to do with that. The unspoken assumption is that somewhere a clock is ticking, and the longer the child remains missing, the more likely she will be found dead or never be found at all. And here are these two kids, skip tracers who have lives and destinies depending on them.

Gonzo: The Life and Work of Dr. Hunter S. Thompson ★ ★ ★ ½

R, 121 m., 2008

Johnny Depp (Narrator). Directed by Alex Gibney and produced by Gibney, Graydon Carter, Jason Kliot, Joana Vicente, Eva Orner, and Alison Ellwood. Screenplay by Gibney.

In all the memories gathered together in *Gonzo: The Life and Work of Dr. Hunter S. Thompson*, there was one subject I found conspicuously missing: the fact of the man's misery. Did he never have a hangover? The film finds extraordinary access to the people in his life, but not even from his two wives do we get a description I would dearly love to read, on what he was like in the first hour or two after he woke up. He was clearly deeply addicted to drugs and alcohol, and after a stupor-induced sleep he would have awakened in a state of withdrawal. He must have administered therapeutic doses of booze or pills or *something* to quiet the tremors and the dread. What did he say at those times? How did he behave? Are the words "fear and loathing" autobiographical?

Of course, perhaps Thompson was immune. One of the eyewitnesses to his life says in wonderment, "You saw the stuff go in, and there was no discernible effect." I don't think I believe that. If there was no discernible effect, how would you describe his behavior? If he had been sober all his life, would he have hunted wild pigs with a machine gun? Thompson was the most famous (or notorious) inebriate of his generation, but perhaps he really was one of those rare creatures who had no hangovers, despite the debaucheries of the day(s) before. How much did he consume? A daily bottle of bourbon, plus wine, beer, pills of every description.

The bottom line is, he got away with it, right up until his suicide, which he himself scripted and every one of his friends fully expected. As a journalist, he got away with murder. He reported that during a presidential primary Edward Muskie ingested Ibogaine, a psychoactive drug administered by a "mysterious Brazilian doctor," and this information, which was totally fabricated, was actually picked up and passed along as fact. Thompson's joke may have contributed to Muskie's angry tantrums during the 1972 Florida primary. No other reporter could have printed such a lie, but Thompson was shielded by his legend: He could print anything. "Of all the correspondents," says Frank Mankiewicz, George McGovern's 1972 campaign manager, "he was the least factual, but the most accurate."

He was an explosive, almost hypnotic, writer, with a savage glee in his prose. I remember eagerly opening a new issue of *Rolling Stone* in the 1970s and devouring his work. A great deal of it was untrue, but it dealt in a kind of exalted super-truth, as when he spoke of Richard Nixon the vampire roaming the night in Washington. Thompson had never heard of objectivity. In 1972 he backed George McGovern as the Democratic nominee, and no calumny was too vile for him to attribute to McGovern's opponents in both parties. I suppose readers were supposed to know that and factor it into the equation.

This documentary by Alex Gibney (*Taxi to the Dark Side, No End in Sight*) is remarkable, first of all, for reminding us how many pots Hunter dipped a spoon in. He rode with the Hells Angels for a year. Ran for sheriff of Pitkin County, home of Aspen, and lost, but only by 204 to 173. Covered the 1972 and 1976 presidential primaries in a way that made him a cocandidate (in the sense of codependent). Had a baffling dual personality, so that such as McGovern, Jimmy Buffett, Tom Wolfe, and his wives and son remember him fondly but say that he could also be "absolutely vicious."

He taught himself to write by typing Fitzgerald's *The Great Gatsby* again and again, we're told. How many times? we ask ourselves skeptically. Was that part of the fantastical legend? Nobody in the film was around while he was doing it. He became famous for writing about "the edge" in his Hells Angels book—that edge of speed going around a curve that you could approach, but never cross without wiping out and killing yourself. He did a lot of edge riding on his motorcycle and never wiped out. He said again and again that the way he chose to die was by his own hand, with a firearm, while he was still at the top. He died that way, using one of his twenty-two firearms, but "he was nowhere near the top," says Sondi Wright, his first wife.

He started to lose it after Africa, says Jann Wenner, who ran his stuff in *Rolling Stone.* He went to Zaire at great expense to cover the Rumble in the Jungle for the magazine, got hopelessly stoned, missed the fight (while reportedly in the hotel pool), and never filed a story. "After Africa," says Sondi, "he just couldn't write. He couldn't piece it together." He did some more writing, of course, such as a heartfelt piece after 9/11. But he had essentially disappeared into his legend, as the outlaw of Woody Creek, blasting away with his weapons, making outraged phone calls, getting impossibly high. Certainly he made an impression on his time like few other journalists ever do; the comparison would be with H. L. Mencken.

This film gathers interviews from a wide and sometimes surprising variety of people (Pat Buchanan, Jimmy Carter, Hells Angel Sonny Barger). It has home movies, old photos, TV footage, voice recordings, excerpts from files about Thompson. It is narrated by Johnny Depp, mostly through readings from Thompson's work. It is all you could wish for in a doc about the man. But it leaves you wondering, how was it that so many people liked this man who does not seem to have liked himself? And what about the hangovers?

Good Luck Chuck ★

R, 96 m., 2007

Dane Cook (Charlie Logan), Jessica Alba (Cam Wexler), Dan Fogler (Stu), Lonny Ross (Joe). Directed by Mark Helfrich and produced by Barry Katz and Mike Katz. Screenplay by Josh Stolberg.

Here is the dirty movie of the year, slimy and scummy, and among its casualties is poor Jessica Alba, who is a cutie and shouldn't have been let out to play with these boys. *Good Luck Chuck* layers a creaky plot device on top of countless excuses to show breasts, sometimes three at a time, and is potty-mouthed and brain-damaged.

It stars the potentially likable Dane Cook as the lovelorn Charlie Logan, leading me to wonder why, in the same week when Michael Douglas plays a flywheel named Charlie, that name seems to fit so well with characters who are two slices short of a pizza. Young Charlie, who is not called "Chuck" except in the title, is hexed by an eleven-year-old goth girl at a spin-the-bottle party. Because he fights off her enthusiastic assault, she issues this curse: Every woman he falls in love with will leave him and immediately find the man of her dreams.

Charlie grows up to become a dentist. His best friend is still the short, chubby, curly-haired Stu (Dan Fogler). The naming rule here is, Charlie for hero, Stu for best friend, and if there's a villain, he should be referred to only by his last name, which must have a Z or W in it, or a hissing sound. Stu, obsessed by breasts, has grown up to become a plastic surgeon, and so loves his craft that he has purchased Pam Anderson's former breast implants and keeps them in an oak display case, where they look surprisingly small, more like ice packs for insignificant wounds. One peculiarity of the dentist and the plastic surgeon is that they have adjacent offices with an adjoining door, so that Charlie can pop over to Stu's and offer a layman's opinion on his latest boob job.

Anyway, Charlie, who has been unlucky in love, meets Cam (Jessica Alba), who works at a seaquarium and loves penguins so much she might herself be willing to sit on one of their eggs all winter. Apart from being beautiful and friendly, her character trait is that she's a klutz, so physically dangerous she might even step on her own toes. Whatever she touches, she breaks, knocks over, turns on, or damages.

Although he's in love with Cam, Charlie is distracted by the seduction attempts of dozens of beautiful women because a rumor has spread all over town that if they sleep with him, they'll find the husband of their dreams. Stu does some follow-through research and finds out the rumor is true. Funny thing is, the women who crowd Charlie's waiting room all look as if they have come through the connecting door after enhancement by Stu. Charlie connects with so many of them that at one point the screen splits into sixteen separate copulation scenes, just to keep up.

You see Charlie's problem. Cam, a nice girl, doesn't want to date him because he's such a "sport." And Charlie realizes that if he ever sleeps with her, she'll immediately leave him for the man of her dreams. How will this paradox be resolved? By putting us through the agony of an automatic plot device, that's how.

The startling thing about the movie is how juvenile it is. Stu, in particular, is a creepy case of arrested development. Consider the whole scenario he stages with a fat woman who might break Charlie's hex. She's not only fat, she has pimples all over, and yes, we get a close-up of them. There is a word for this movie, and that word is ick.

Good Night, and Good Luck ★ ★ ★ ★

PG, 93 m., 2005

David Strathairn (Edward R. Murrow), Patricia Clarkson (Shirley Wershba), George Clooney (Fred Friendly), Jeff Daniels (Sig Mickelson), Robert Downey Jr. (Joe Wershba), Frank Langella (William Paley), Ray Wise (Don Hollenbeck), Dianne Reeves (Jazz Singer). Directed by George Clooney and produced by Grant Heslov. Screenplay by Clooney and Heslov.

Good Night, and Good Luck is a movie about a group of professional newsmen who with surgical precision remove a cancer from the body politic. They believe in the fundamental American freedoms, and in Senator Joseph McCarthy they see a man who would destroy those freedoms in the name of defending them. Because McCarthy is a liar and a bully, surrounded by yes-men, recklessly calling his opponents traitors, he commands great power for a time. He destroys others with lies and then himself is destroyed by the truth.

The instrument of his destruction is Edward R. Murrow, a television journalist above reproach, whose radio broadcasts from London led to a peacetime career as the most famous newsman in the new medium of television. Murrow is offended by McCarthy. He makes bold to say so, and why. He is backed by his producers and reporters and is supported by the leadership of his network, CBS, even though it loses sponsors, and even though McCarthy claims Murrow himself is a member of a subversive organization.

There are times when it is argued within CBS that Murrow has lost his objectivity, that he is not telling "both sides." He argues that he is reporting the facts, and if the facts are contrary to McCarthy's fantasies, they are nevertheless objective. In recent years, few reporters have dared take such a stand, but at the height of Hurricane Katrina, we saw many reporters in the field who knew by their own witness that the official line on hurricane relief was a fiction, and said so.

Murrow is played in *Good Night, and Good Luck* by David Strathairn, that actor of precise inward silence. He has mastered the Murrow mannerisms, the sidelong glance from beneath lowered eyebrows, the way of sitting perfectly still and listening and watching others, the ironic underplayed wit, the unbending will. He doesn't look much like Murrow, any more than Philip Seymour Hoffman looks much like Truman Capote, but both actors create their characters from the inside, concealing behind famous mannerisms the deliberate actions that impose their will. In that they are actually a little alike.

George Clooney costars as Fred Friendly, Murrow's producer, who remained active into the 1990s. Clooney also directed and cowrote the movie. Because his father was a newscaster, he knows what the early TV studios looked like, and it is startling to see how small was Murrow's performance space: He sits close to the camera, his famous cigarette usually in the shot, and Friendly sits beside the camera, so close that he can tap Murrow's leg to cue him. They are also close as professionals who share the same beliefs about McCarthy and are aware that they risk character assassination from the Wisconsin senator.

The other key character is McCarthy himself, and Clooney uses a masterstroke: He employs actual news footage of McCarthy, who therefore plays himself. It is frightening to see him in full rant, and pathetic to see him near meltdown during the Army-McCarthy hearings, when the Army counsel Joseph Welch famously asked him, "Have you no decency?" His wild attack on Murrow has an element of humor; he claims the broadcaster is a member of the Industrial Workers of the World, the anarchist "Wobblies," who by then were more a subject of nostalgic folk songs than a functioning organization.

The movie is entirely, almost claustrophobically, about politics and the news business. Even its single subplot underlines the atmosphere of the times. We meet Shirley and Joe Wershba (Patricia Clarkson and Robert Downey Jr.), who work for CBS News and keep their marriage a secret because company policy forbids the employment of married couples. Their clandestine meetings and subtle communications raise our own suspicions and demonstrate in a way how McCarthyism works.

Apart from the Wershbas, the movie is entirely about the inner life of CBS News. Every substantial scene is played in the CBS building, except for a banquet, a bar, a bedroom, and the newsreel footage. Murrow and Friendly circulate in three arenas: their production offices, the television studio, and the offices of their boss, William Paley (Frank Langella), who ran the network as a fiefdom but granted Murrow independence and freedom from advertiser pressure.

The movie is not really about the abuses of McCarthy but about the process by which Murrow and his team eventually brought about his downfall (some would say his self-destruction). It is like a morality play, from which we learn how journalists should behave. It shows Murrow as fearless but not flawless. Paley observes that when McCarthy said that Alger Hiss was convicted of "treason," Murrow knew Hiss was convicted not of treason but of perjury and yet did not correct McCarthy. Was he afraid of seeming to support a communist, Paley asks, perhaps guessing the answer. He has a point. Murrow's response indicates he might have been a great poker player.

There are small moments of humor. After one broadcast fraught with potential hazards, Murrow waits until he's off the air and then there is the smallest possible movement of his mouth: Could that have been almost a smile? David Strathairn is a stealth actor, revealing Murrow's feelings almost in code. Clooney by contrast makes Friendly an open, forthright kinduva guy, a reliable partner for Murrow's enigmatic reserve.

As a director, Clooney does interesting things. One of them is to shoot in black and white, which is the right choice for this material, lending it period authenticity and a matter-of-factness. In a way, black and white is inevitable, since both Murrow's broadcasts and the McCarthy footage would have been in black and white. Clooney shoots close, showing men (and a few women) in business dress, talking in anonymous rooms. Everybody smokes all of the time. When they screen footage, there is an echo of *Citizen Kane.* Episodes are separated by a jazz singer (Dianne Reeves), who is seen performing in a nearby studio; her songs don't parallel the action but evoke a time of piano lounges, martinis, and all those cigarettes.

Clooney's message is clear: Character assassination is wrong, McCarthy was a bully and a liar, and we must be vigilant when the emperor has no clothes and wraps himself in the flag. It was Dr. Johnson who said, "Patriotism is the last refuge of the scoundrel." That was more than two hundred years ago. The movie quotes a more recent authority, Dwight Eisenhower, who is seen on TV defending the basic American right of habeas corpus. How many Americans know what "habeas corpus" means, or why people are still talking about it on TV?

The Gospel ★ ★ ★

PG, 103 m., 2005

Boris Kodjoe (David Taylor), Idris Elba (Frank), Nona Gaye (Charlene), Clifton Powell (Pastor Fred Taylor), Aloma Wright (Ernestine), Donnie McClurkin (Terrance Hunter), Omar Gooding (Wesley), Tamyra Gray (Rain), Hezekiah Walker (Brother Gordon), Keshia Knight Pulliam (Maya), Dolores "Mom" Winans (Janet Perkins), Yolanda Adams (Herself), Fred Hammond (Himself), Martha Munizzi (Herself). Directed by Rob Hardy and produced by William Packer. Screenplay by Hardy.

The Gospel is the first mainstream movie I can remember that deals knowledgeably with the role of the church in African-American communities. It is not a particularly religious movie; the characters are believers, but the movie is not so much about faith and prayer as about the economic and social function of a church: how it operates as a stabilizing force, a stage for personalities, an arena for power struggles, and an enterprise that must make money or go out of business.

The counterpoint for all of this drama is

gospel music, a lot of it, performed by such well-known singers as Yolanda Adams, Fred Hammond, Martha Munizzi, *American Idol* finalist Tamyra Gray, and inspired gospel choirs in full praise mode. If the plot wanders through several predictable situations, and it does, the movie never lingers too long on those developments before cutting back to the best gospel music I've seen on film since *Say Amen, Somebody*. Like an Astaire and Rogers musical, this is a movie you don't go to for the dialogue.

As the story opens, Pastor Fred Taylor (Clifton Powell) presides over a thriving church in Atlanta. His son David and David's best friend, Frank, are both in the youth ministry. Flash forward fifteen years. David, now played by Boris Kodjoe, is a rising hip-hop star with a hit on the charts: "Let Me Undress You." Frank (Idris Elba) is an associate minister. The church is having financial problems and must close in thirty days unless funds can be found. At a meeting of a board of church overseers, Pastor Fred collapses. His son flies home to be at his bedside, gets the bad news, and is soon enough at his funeral.

Before his death, the old pastor turned the pulpit over to Frank. There was some jealousy among more veteran pastors, but that's nothing compared to the way David feels when he sees the big billboard out in front of his father's church, showing Frank with the motto: "A new church, a new man, a new vision!" It doesn't help that Frank has married Charlene (Nona Gaye), David's cousin.

Will David return to his concert tour? His friend and manager, Wesley (Omar Gooding), certainly hopes so: They've struggled a long time to get on the charts, to get the limousines and the hotel suites and the big crowds and such perks as the groupie David wakes up with the morning he gets the bad news about his father's health. Yes, David is a sinner, but he's not into drugs or booze, and it becomes clear, as his brief trip to Atlanta stretches to a week and then longer, that his spiritual life is calling to him. For Ernestine (Aloma Wright), his father's church secretary for many years, Frank is an interloper and David belongs in the pulpit.

The plot plays out in terms of David's and Frank's personal and professional rivalries, with the deadline for foreclosure looming always closer. None of these details, in themselves, are particularly new or interesting. What is new is the way the church is seen not in purely spiritual terms but as a social institution. Rob Hardy, who wrote and directed *The Gospel*, obviously knows a lot about black churches, their services, their music, their traditions, and the way the congregation interacts with the people at the altar. There are times here when call-and-response shades into put-up-or-shut-up.

I am not an expert on African-American church services, but I have attended some, at Bishop Arthur Brazier's Apostolic Church of God and at Rev. Michael Pfleger's St. Sabina's, and I appreciate the way the choir acts as a sound track for the service, softly coming up under the preacher's exhortation, taking over, backing down for more preaching, its body language expressing as much joy as the music, the congregation fully involved. It is accurate that you see some white faces in the congregations in this film: To recycle an old British advertising slogan, these services refresh parts the others do not reach.

Goya's Ghosts ★ ★ ★

R, 114 m., 2007

Javier Bardem (Brother Lorenzo), Natalie Portman (Ines/Alicia), Stellan Skarsgard (Francisco Goya), Randy Quaid (King Carlos IV), Jose Luis Gomez (Tomas Bilbatua). Directed by Milos Forman and produced by Saul Zaentz. Screenplay by Forman and Jean-Claude Carriere.

Milos Forman's *Goya's Ghosts* is an extraordinarily beautiful film that plays almost like an excuse to generate its images. Like the Goya prints being examined by the good fathers of the Inquisition in the opening scene, the images stand on their own, resisting the pull toward narrative, yet adding up to a portrait of grotesque people debased by their society. The priests lament Goya's negative portrait of Spain, which shows remarkable prescience on their part, since they're condemning in 1772 prints that were not created by the painter until 1799.

In fiction, fooling around with historical accuracy is allowed, and *Goya's Ghosts* indulges itself. Many of the characters did indeed exist, but I wonder if they really performed many of their actions in this film. The events concern not only the Spanish artist (Stellan Skarsgard) but Brother Lorenzo (Javier Bardem), one of the Inquisition's priests, and Ines Bilbatua (Natalie Portman), the beautiful young daughter of a local merchant.

Goya uses Ines as a model for the angels he paints for churches. He is also a court painter, engaged in a portrait of Queen Maria Luisa (Blanca Portillo) and a portrait commissioned by Lorenzo, who recognizes his genius. When Ines is spotted by Inquisition spies declining a dish of pork in a tavern, she is hauled in, accused of Judaism, and tortured until she confesses her "sin." Her father (Jose Luis Gomez) goes to Goya to ask him to intervene with Lorenzo, and all their lives are intertwined.

The Holy Office of the Inquisition referred to torture "as being put to the question." The theory was that God would give you strength to tell only the truth. Ines's father's theory is that people will confess to anything if they are tortured, an insight that has never gone out of style. The father persuasively argues this point with Lorenzo, in a scene that *Variety* unkindly compares to Monty Python. Fifteen years pass; Napoleon conquers Spain and abolishes the Inquisition; Lorenzo, having fled, signs on to the principles of the French Revolution and surfaces as a prosecutor for Napoleon. His job includes jailing the former Inquisitor General (Michael Lonsdale). Meanwhile, Ines is finally released from the dungeons, where she had a daughter, who . . .

Enough of this plot. It's filled with so much melodrama, coincidence, and people living their lives against the backdrop of history that Victor Hugo would feel overserved. There are so many dramatic incidents, indeed, that it's hard to figure out who the central figure is supposed to be. Lorenzo gets top billing, but they're all buffeted by the winds of fate. I didn't feel the strong identification with anyone that I had with Forman's *Amadeus,* but as consolation I was able to watch enraptured at a visual portrait of a time and place.

Consider an early scene. Footmen for King Carlos IV (Randy Quaid, and very good, too) throw an animal corpse in a field to attract vultures. Then the king shoots them, like pigeons. He also bags some rabbits, but Maria Luisa thinks she'd prefer the vultures for dinner. Other set pieces show the extraordinary cruelty of the dungeons, the obscene magnificence of the royal residences, the bawdiness of the taverns, the boldness of the bordellos, and streets teeming with life in the midst of death.

The actors invest their characters with surprising depth, considering how the plot has to keep so many story lines afloat. Skarsgard makes Goya into a man with a wonderful smile, an affable manner, and the confidence of an artist who stands outside the rules. Bardem, without making too much a point of it, shows an ambitious man, not enthusiastically evil but capable of the occasional vileness, who can convince himself he is both an Inquisitor for the church and a prosecutor for the emperor (the same job, really).

Natalie Portman, in a triple role, plays a beautiful young girl, a haggard torture victim, and a vulnerable prostitute, all with fearless conviction. And Randy Quaid has a smaller role as the king but is an inspired if unexpected casting choice, as in a scene where he performs on a violin and almost bashfully confesses he composed the piece himself.

Much of the depth of the film comes from the sound design of Leslie Shatz; we hear precision in the ways vast church doors open and close, we hear far-off bells and echoing interiors, and the sound of shoulders being dislocated is understated but persuasive. And the cinematography of Javier Aquirresarobe is, well, painterly—look at the compositions, the colors, and especially the shading.

Now I must tell you that *Goya's Ghosts* got cruel reviews when it opened late last fall in Europe. I don't make a habit of reviewing reviews, but the advance word on this picture was impossible to avoid ("Creaks along like an anemic snail" —Derek Malcolm; "Close to a disaster" —*Telegraph;* "Dull as dishwater" —Neil Smith). Sometimes I wonder if critics aren't reviewing the film they would have preferred rather than the one the director preferred.

I doubt that Forman and the legendary screenwriter Jean-Claude Carriere lacked the ability to tell a conventional story. I think the clue to their purpose is right there in the opening scene of the Goya drawings. Look carefully, and you may find something in the film to remind you of most of them. *Goya's Ghosts* is like the sketchbook Goya might have made with a camera.

Grace Is Gone ★ ★ ★

PG-13, 85 m., 2007

John Cusack (Stanley Phillips), Shelan O'Keefe (Heidi Phillips), Grace Bednarczyk (Dawn Phillips), Alessandro Nivola (John Phillips). Directed by James C. Strouse and produced by John Cusack, Grace Loh, Galt Niederhoffer, Daniela Taplin Lundberg, and Celine Rattray. Screenplay by Strouse.

John Cusack can project such tenderness and kindness. He doesn't often play roles that give him the chance, but when he does (*Say Anything, High Fidelity, Being John Malkovich*), he knows how to do it. His character, Stanley Phillips, in *Grace Is Gone* is one of his most vulnerable and is the key to the movie's success.

He is a suburban dad with two young daughters and a wife in the military. He supports the war in Iraq and would be there himself if he didn't have bad eyes. One day two Army officers come to his door, and he won't invite them in, as if reluctant to admit the news they've come to tell him. His wife has been killed in the war.

The girls are Heidi (Shelan O'Keefe), twelve years old, and Dawn (Grace Bednarczyk), who is eight. He sits them down in the living room to break the news and finds that he simply cannot. Instead, in a crazy evasion he improvises on the spur of the moment, he announces they will get in the car and drive to Enchanted Gardens, a Florida theme park they like. Heidi, who is very smart, thinks this sounds fishy: He's pulling them out of school to go on an unannounced holiday? Dawn doesn't ask any questions.

The trip involves the usual cookie-cutter roadside chain eateries and the usual interstate highway sameness, although it is punctuated by a stop to visit his brother (Alessandro Nivola), a layabout who rouses himself at the sight of Stanley to start attacking the war. Stanley won't be baited. He shares his secret, begs it be kept a secret, and loads the girls back in the car.

Enchanted Gardens, as it turns out, is not quite enchanted enough to be the right setting for breaking the bad news, which Heidi has more or less intuited on her own. But there does come a time on the beach when the truth must be told, and he does it gently and with love. That's what the movie is really about, anyway: not the war, but Stanley's love for his daughters.

There have been many scenes where mothers told children about the deaths of their fathers, but none where the roles are reversed, as in *Grace Is Gone*. The movie comes as a quiet revelation. Every time a news program features the faces and names of U.S. troops killed in Iraq, I feel a little shock when they show a woman. It doesn't seem right. Getting killed in the war doesn't seem right for anyone, of course, but you know what I mean.

Grace Is Gone is not a great movie, simply functional, but Cusack gives a great performance. The film somehow doesn't live up to his work. It wasn't shot on video (and for that matter, good video these days can look great), but the screen looks dingy and some life seems to be faded from it.

The story drags its feet a little, too, considering we know where they're going and what must happen when they get there. And a possible political confrontation between the two brothers is so adroitly sidestepped that the movie, although probably antiwar, never really declares itself. All we have is a father who has lost his wife, and two girls who have lost their mother. The way Cusack handles that, it's enough.

The Great Debaters ★ ★ ★ ★

PG-13, 127 m., 2007

Denzel Washington (Melvin B. Tolson), Forest Whitaker (James Farmer Sr.), Nate Parker (Henry Lowe), Jurnee Smollett (Samantha Booke), Denzel Whitaker (James Farmer Jr.), Jermaine Williams (Hamilton Burgess), Gina Ravera (Ruth Tolson), John Heard (Sheriff Dozier), Kimberly Elise (Pearl Farmer). Directed by Denzel Washington and produced by Todd Black, Joe Roth, Kate Forte, Washington, and Oprah Winfrey. Screenplay by Robert Eisele.

The Great Debaters is about an underdog debate team that wins a national championship, and some critics have complained that it follows the formula of all sports movies by leading up, through great adversity, to a victory at the end. So it does. How many sports movies, or movies about underdogs competing in any way, have you seen that end in defeat? It is human nature to seek inspiration in victory, and this is a film that is affirming and inspiring and re-creates the stories of a remarkable team and its coach.

The team is from little Wiley College in Marshall, Texas, an African-American institution in the heart of the Jim Crow South of the 1930s. The school's English professor, Melvin Tolson (Denzel Washington), is a taskmaster who demands the highest standards from his debate team, and they're rewarded with a national championship. That's what the "sports movie" is about, but the movie is about so much more, and in ways that do not follow formulas.

There are, for example, Tolson's secret lives. Dressed in overalls and work boots, he ventures out incognito as an organizer for a national sharecropper's union. He's a dangerous radical, the local whites believe, probably a communist. But he's organizing both poor whites and blacks, whose servitude is equal. He keeps his politics out of the classroom, however, where he conceals a different kind of secret: He is one of America's leading poets. Yes, although the movie barely touches on it, Tolson published long poems in such magazines as the *Atlantic Monthly,* and in 1947 was actually named poet laureate of Liberia. Ironic, that his role as a debate coach would win him greater fame today.

He holds grueling auditions and selects four team members: Henry Lowe (Nate Parker), who drinks and fools around but is formidably intelligent; Hamilton Burgess (Jermaine Williams), a superb debater; James Farmer Jr. (Denzel Whitaker), a precocious fourteen-year-old who is their researcher; and Samantha Booke (Jurnee Smollett), the substitute and only female debater they've heard of. Tolson drills them, disciplines them, counsels them, and leads them to a string of victories that results in a triumph over Harvard, the national champion.

We get a good sense of the nurturing black community that has produced these students, in particular James Farmer Sr. (Forest Whitaker), a preacher (young Denzel Whitaker, as his son, is no relation, and not named after Washington, for that matter). James Jr. would go on to found the Congress of Racial Equality (CORE). Tolson drives his team on long road trips to out-of-town debates, and one night traveling late, they have the defining emotional experience of the film: They happen upon a scene where a white mob has just lynched a black man and set his body afire. They barely escape with their own lives. And daily life for them is fraught with racist peril; especially for Tolson, who has been singled out by the local sheriff as a rabble-rouser. These experiences inform their debates as much as formal research.

The movie is not really about how this team defeats the national champions. It is more about how its members, its coach, its school and community believe that an education is their best way out of the morass of racism and discrimination. They would find it unthinkable that decades in the future, serious black students would be criticized by jealous contemporaries for "acting white." They are black, proud, single-minded, and focused, and it all expresses itself most dramatically in their debating.

The debates themselves have one peculiarity: The Wiley team always somehow draws the "good" side of every question. Since a debate team is supposed to defend whatever position it draws, it might have been intriguing to see them defend something they disbelieve, even despise. Still, I suppose I understand why that isn't done here; it would have interrupted the flow. And the flow becomes a mighty flood, in a powerful and impassioned story. This is one of the year's best films.

Note: In actual fact, the real Wiley team did beat the national champions, but from USC, not Harvard. Screenwriter Robert Eisele explains, "In that era, there was much at stake when a black college debated any white school, particularly one with the stature of Harvard. We used Harvard to demonstrate the heights they achieved."

The Greatest Game Ever Played ★ ★ ★

PG, 115 m., 2005

Shia LaBeouf (Francis Ouimet), Stephen Dillane (Harry Vardon), Josh Flitter (Eddie Lowery),

Peyton List (Sarah Wallis), Elias Koteas (Arthur Ouimet), Marnie McPhail (Mary Ouimet), Stephen Marcus (Ted Ray), Peter Firth (Lord Northcliffe), Michael Weaver (John McDermott). Directed by Bill Paxton and produced by David Blocker, Larry Brezner, Mark Frost, and David A. Steinberg. Screenplay by Frost.

The Greatest Game Ever Played was a game of golf, in case you thought your team might have been involved. In 1913, a working-class American amateur named Francis Ouimet defeated the great British player Harry Vardon to win the U.S. Open. Here is a movie that tells that story and exactly that story, devoting a considerable amount of its running time to the final games and playing like one superb sports telecast. Because some of the opening scenes seem borrowed from other underdog movies, I was surprised to realize, toward the end, how gripping the movie had become.

Shia LaBeouf stars as Francis Ouimet, a poor boy who lives with his family across from a golf course in Brookline, Massachusetts. From his windows and the front porch, Francis can see the golfers at play. So can his father, Arthur (Elias Koteas), an immigrant who steadfastly opposes his son's passion for golf: "A man should know his place." But Francis has a natural gift for the game and is encouraged by his mother (Marnie McPhail) and two players at the local club. As a teenager, he actually attends a demonstration by the great Harry Vardon.

As for Vardon, we find that he, too, is a working-class boy, born across from a golf course. Or, more precisely, born directly on one, since in the first scene of the movie we see his family's home on the Isle of Jersey being surveyed by men who plan to tear it down for the construction of a course. He asks one of the men what "golf" is. "A game for gentlemen," he is told.

Harry is not a gentleman, but he is a class act, and as played by Stephen Dillane he becomes a perfect foil in the great 1913 game. It would be too easy to make him a villain, but Harry and Francis both embody the tradition of generosity and good sportsmanship later practiced by Sam Snead. To Francis, Harry is an unspeakably grand man. But Harry sees himself in young Francis, and he knows that in the British class system he may be a great golfer but he will never be in the Establishment.

The villain of the piece is Lord Northcliffe (Peter Firth), then the proprietor of the powerful *Daily Mail* and *Daily Mirror*, and the underwriter of the British team. He expects nothing less than a championship from Harry, confiding: "The prime minister has promised me a seat in his cabinet if I bring back this title." That seems a little unlikely, since to command the *Mail* and the *Mirror* was much more grand than a cabinet seat, but the fact that he would say it tells you a lot about him.

The other central character in the story is a pudgy ten-year-old caddy named Eddie Lowery (Josh Flitter), who works for Francis for free and offers him sound advice with unshakable self-confidence. Eddie, who seems to be ten going on forty, is one of those kids who always did and always will know it all; it helps that he is sweet. The movie also involves a romance with the fragrant Sarah Wallis (Peyton List), a young woman who begins a friendship with Francis that looks promising until the movie essentially sidelines it in the excitement of the Greatest Game.

This is the second film directed by the actor Bill Paxton and could not possibly be more different from his first, *Frailty* (2001). In that one, he played a father who leads his two sons in a series of murders that were commanded, he believes, by an angel. *Frailty* was dark and brilliant and filled with fearful prospects; now this sunny film, which plays almost as if it's emotional rehab for Paxton.

I am not a golf fan but found *The Greatest Game Ever Played* absorbing all the same, partly because of the human element, partly because Paxton and his technicians have used every trick in the book to dramatize the flight and destination of the golf balls. We follow balls through the air, we watch them creep toward the green or stray into the rough, we get not only an eagle's-eye view but a club's-eye view and sometimes, I am convinced, a ball's-eye view.

The technique is at the service of a game in which everything is at risk and we like both players; our affection for them makes everything trickier, and certainly as the final rounds are played, the games themselves seem to have been scripted to create as much suspense as possible. I have no idea if the movie is based, stroke for stroke, on the actual competition at the 1913 U.S. Open. I guess I could find out, but I don't want to know. I like it this way.

The Great Raid ★ ★ ★

R, 132 m., 2005

Benjamin Bratt (Lieutenant Colonel Henry Mucci), James Franco (Captain Bob Prince), Connie Nielsen (Margaret Utinsky), Joseph Fiennes (Major Gibson), Marton Csokas (Captain Redding), Cesar Montano (Captain Juan Pajota). Directed by John Dahl and produced by Lawrence Bender and Marty Katz. Screenplay by Carlo Bernard and Douglas Miro, based on the books *The Great Raid on Cabanatuan* by William B. Breuer and *Ghost Soldiers* by Hampton Sides.

Here is a war movie that understands how wars are actually fought. After *Stealth* and its high-tech look-alikes, which make warfare look like a video game, *The Great Raid* shows the hard work and courage of troops whose reality is danger and death. The difference between *Stealth* and *The Great Raid* is the difference between the fantasies of the Pentagon architects of "shock and awe" and the reality of the Marines who were killed in Iraq.

The movie is based on the true story of a famous raid by U.S. Army Rangers and Philippine guerrillas, who attacked the Japanese POW camp at Cabanatuan and rescued more than five hundred Americans, with the loss of only two American and twenty-one Filipino lives. Nearly eight hundred Japanese died in the surprise attack. These numbers are so dramatic that the movie uses end credits to inform us they are factual.

The Great Raid has the look and feel of a good war movie you might see on cable late one night, perhaps starring Robert Mitchum, Robert Ryan, or Lee Marvin. It has been made with the confidence that the story itself is the point, not the flashy graphics. The raid is outlined for the troops (and for the audience) so that, knowing what the rescuers want to do, we understand how they're trying to do it. Like soldiers on a march, it puts one step in front of another, instead of flying apart into a blizzard of quick cuts and special effects. Like the jazzier but equally realistic *Black Hawk Down,* it shows a situation that has moved beyond policy and strategy, and amounts to soldiers in the field, hoping to hell they get home alive.

"You are the best-trained troops in the U.S. Army," their commander (Benjamin Bratt) tells the 6th Army Ranger Battalion. Perhaps that is close to the truth, but they have never been tested under fire; their first assignment involves penetrating Japanese-controlled territory, creeping in daylight across an open field toward the POW camp, hiding in a ditch until night, and then depending on surprise to rescue the prisoners, most of them starving, many of them sick, all of them survivors of the Bataan Death March.

Historical narration and footage provide the context: As the Japanese retreated, they killed their prisoners, and Americans in one camp were burned alive. In both this raid and a larger, more famous one at the nearby Los Banos camp, the challenge was to rescue the POWs before the Japanese believed the enemy was close enough to trigger the deaths of their prisoners.

Commanding the Rangers are the real-life war heroes Lieutenant Colonel Henry Mucci (Bratt) and Captain Bob Prince (James Franco), who plans the raid. In parallel stories, we meet the fictional Major Gibson (Joseph Fiennes), leader of the POWs, and a brave American nurse, also from real life, named Margaret Utinsky (Connie Nielsen). She works in the Manila underground, obtaining drugs on the black market that are smuggled into the camp. She and Gibson were once lovers (in what must be a fictional invention) but have not seen each other for years. Still, it is the idea of Margaret that sustains Gibson, whose strength is being drained by malaria.

The film is unique in giving full credit to the Filipino fighters who joined the Rangers and made the local logistics possible by enlisting the secret help of local farmers and villagers (their oxcarts were employed to carry prisoners too weak to walk). The Filipinos are led by Captain Juan Pajota (Cesar Montano), a forcible local actor who steps into the Hollywood cast and adds to its authenticity and sense of mission.

A brilliant strategic idea is to have a single American plane make several passes over the camp, lifting the eyes of the Japanese to the skies as rescuers were creeping toward them. The raid itself, when it comes, is at night, and would be hard for us to follow except that it follows so precisely the plans that were outlined earlier. One effective moment comes when an officer delays action to be absolutely sure that all is ready; with radio silence, he has to send a scout, and we grow almost as impatient as the waiting men.

The movie was directed by John Dahl, based on a screenplay by Carlo Bernard and Douglas Miro, and the books *The Great Raid on Cabanatuan* by William B. Breuer and *Ghost Soldiers* by Hampton Sides. Dahl is best known for two of the trickiest modern films noir, *Red Rock West* and *The Last Seduction.* Those films would seem to have nothing in common with a war movie, but in a way they do, because they avoid special effects and stay close to their characters while negotiating a risky and complicated plot.

The history of the movie is interesting. It was green-lighted by Harvey Weinstein of Miramax just a few days after 9/11; perhaps a story of a famous American victory seemed needed. It was completed by 2002 but, like a lot of Miramax inventory, sat on the shelf (Miramax won a "shelf award" at the Indie Spirits one year for the quality of its unreleased pictures). Now that Disney and Miramax are going separate ways, Miramax is releasing a lot of those films in the final months of its original management.

The Great Raid is perhaps more timely now than it would have been a few years ago, when "smart bombs" and a couple of weeks of warfare were supposed to solve the Iraq situation. Now that we are involved in a lengthy and bloody ground war there, it is good to have a film that is not about entertainment for action fans but about how wars are won with great difficulty, risk, and cost.

Great World of Sound ★ ★ ★
R, 106 m., 2007

Pat Healy (Martin), Kene Holliday (Clarence), Robert Longstreet (Layton), Rebecca Mader (Pam), John Baker (Shank), Tricia Paoluccio (Gloria). Directed by Craig Zobel and produced by David Gordon Green, Melissa Palmer, Richard A. Wright, and Zobel. Screenplay by George Smith and Zobel.

If you've ever wondered about how some of those would-be stars get on *American Idol,* here is a film about some who don't. *Great World of Sound* is a movie about an outfit that buys ads in the papers offering free auditions to new talent, and then tries to sell them a "professional recording session" that will produce a CD allegedly distributed to radio stations and record companies.

To some degree, this offer is real. To a very small degree. We actually even see one of the clients in the "professional" studio. But the real point is to get the hopefuls to show their "commitment" by "investing" $3,000 in their "futures." We follow two of the Great World salesmen on their odyssey through the cheap motels and fast-food grease pits of the South: Martin (Pat Healy), a neat, introverted worrywart, and Clarence (Kene Holliday), an ebullient African-American who, after spending three years on the streets of Houston, is happy to have this job or any job.

In a way, the movie resembles Albert and David Maysles's great documentary *Salesman* (1968), about door-to-door Bible salesmen. The salesmen in both films are led to expect much larger rewards than are possible. But *Great World* has another dimension: Although Martin and Clarence are fictional characters, many (but not all) of those who come to audition aren't in on the joke. They think it's a real audition: In that sense, they're as exploited in real life as in the story. (Director Craig Zobel says he got releases from everybody after the fact.)

Some of the performers make you wonder how they deluded themselves that they had talent. But one, a young African-American girl, sings her "New National Anthem," which is so good I think it should be recorded for real. Oddly enough, Martin likes it, too, and commits the con man's cardinal sin: investing in his own scam.

The movie resembles *Boiler Room* and *Glengarry Glen Ross* in how the recruiters of the salesmen tell expansive stories about how successful they have become. It's a little heartbreaking, however, how moderate the "riches" are that they promise their recruits. If they work hard and do good business, the salesmen are told, they can hope to clear $1,000 a month. Shank (John Baker), the head of the enterprise, adds a bit of stagecraft at one point, dialing his bank on a speaker phone and hearing his current balance read aloud. It was, as I recall, something like $13,000. Not millions.

The drama in the film arises as Martin has a crisis of conscience, while Clarence has a crisis of fear that he might be back on the streets soon. Watching them work the marks is fascinating, when one is dubious and the other desperate. *Great World of Sound,* a Sundance hit, is Zobel's first film, a confident, sure-handed exercise focusing on the American Dream turned nightmare.

Green Street Hooligans ★ ★ ★ ½

R, 106 m., 2005

Elijah Wood (Matt Buckner), Charlie Hunnam (Pete Dunham), Claire Forlani (Shannon Dunham), Marc Warren (Steve Dunham), Leo Gregory (Bovver), Geoff Bell (Tommy Hatcher), Kieran Bew (Ike), Henry Goodman (Carl Buckner). Directed by Lexi Alexander and produced by Gigi Pritzker, Deborah Del Prete, and Donald Zuckerman. Screenplay by Alexander, Dougie Brimson, and Josh Shelov.

"West Ham is mediocre. But their firm is first-rate." So a young American is told soon after arriving in London. West Ham is a London football team. "Firms" are the names for organized gangs of supporters who plan and provoke fights with the firms of opposing teams. The firms are quasi-military, the level of violence is brutal, and then the gang members return to their everyday lives as office workers, retail clerks, drivers, government servants, husbands, and fathers.

I first saw this world in Alan Clarke's *The Firm* (1988), one of Gary Oldman's early performances, which showed in disturbing detail how his character was drawn into what the press calls "football hooliganism." The fights can be crippling or deadly. They're all the more brutal because the gangs don't for the most part carry firearms, preferring to beat on one another with fists, bricks, iron bars, and whatever else they can pick up. Members of a firm have such fierce loyalty that they disregard risk. Unlike American street gangs, which are motivated by drug profits, British football firms are motivated by an addiction to violence.

Green Street Hooligans chooses an unexpected entry point into this world. Its hero is Matt Buckner (Elijah Wood), a bright Harvard student kicked out of school two months before graduating after his roommate forces him to take the fall for some cocaine found in their room. The Harvard business is not convincing but motivates Matt to visit his sister Shannon (Claire Forlani) in London. Her husband, Steve (Marc Warren), more or less forces his brother Pete (Charlie Hunnam) to take Matt to a football game.

Elijah Wood, who can seem harmless enough to be cast as Frodo in *The Lord of the Rings,* might appear to be the last person who'd be interested in the violent world of a firm. But the movie is about the way men who run in packs need to belong, and to prove themselves. In a series of gradual stages that are convincing because we see his early resistance wearing down, Matt tries to become accepted by the Green Street Elite. This involves fighting at their side, which he does with more recklessness than skill. When he is finally covered with blood, he belongs.

There's a lot of plot surrounding this progression. The GSE lives with memories of its glory days, when it was led by a legendary fighter known as the General. Its rivalry with Mill Hill is so vicious that matches between the two teams have not been scheduled since the General led a particularly nasty fight several years ago. Shannon, Matt's sister, is horrified that Matt has gotten involved with the GSE, and her husband tries to warn Matt.

But he has become addicted. He was a journalist at Harvard, an editor of the *Crimson,* and now he keeps a journal: "I'd never lived closer to danger—never felt more confident." Life in the firm makes his previous life seem insubstantial and unreal; what is real is bonding with other men and beating the crap out of opposing firms.

This seems to me insane. What pleasure can be found voluntarily seeking injury every weekend? Of course, the fuel of the firm is alcohol, its meeting place is a pub, and its war song is a boozy, defiant version of the last song you would think of: "I'm Forever Blowing Bubbles." There's an intriguing montage showing GSE members at home and at their daytime jobs; the 1988 Clarke film made clear that firm members are not outcasts but jobholders and family men who have violence as a hobby.

At first I thought the character of Matt was unnecessary. Why not simply dramatize the world of firms? Do we need a Hollywood star as an entry point for non-British audiences? If you must have one, Wood seems so *very* unlikely as a street fighter that I began a list of more plausible actors for the role. Then I realized that the movie's point is that someone like this nerdy Harvard boy might be transformed in a fairly short time into a bloodthirsty gang fighter. The message is that violence is hardwired into men, if only the connection is made. As someone who has never thrown a punch in his life, I find that alien to my own feelings, but I remember years ago, late on nights of drinking, when anger would come from somewhere and fill me. Certainly alcoholism is essential for firm membership: It is inconceivable that anyone would go into action sober.

The movie was directed by Lexi Alexander, a German woman who is herself a former kickboxing champion. It uses cinematography by Alexander Buono to capture the everyday reality of London streets and the kinetic energy unleashed in the fights. It also unfolds a tragic back story, as old secrets are revealed, leading up to the ultimate possibility of death. No, don't assume you know who will die. It isn't who you might think. Of the dead man, we are told: "His life taught me there's a time to stand your ground. His death taught me there's a time to walk away." I guess the time to walk away is before you get killed standing your ground, unless you have a very good reason for standing it. The most frightening thing about the members of the Green Street Elite is that they think they have such a reason, and it is loyalty to the mob.

Grindhouse ★ ★ ½

A double feature of:

Planet Terror ★ ★

Death Proof ★ ★ ★

R, 191 m., 2007

Rose McGowan (Cherry Darling/Pam), Kurt Russell (Stuntman Mike), Freddy Rodriguez (Wray), Rosario Dawson (Abernathy), Josh Brolin (Dr. William Block), Vanessa Ferlito (Arlene), Marley Shelton (Dakota Black), Jordan Ladd (Shanna), Jeff Fahey (JT), Sydney Tamiia Poitier (Jungle Julia), Michael Biehn (Sheriff Hague). Directed by Robert Rodriguez, Eli Roth, Quentin Tarantino, Edgar Wright, and Rob Zombie and produced by Elizabeth Avellan, Rodriguez, Eli Roth, Gabriel Roth, Erica Steinberg, and Tarantino. Screenplay by Rodriguez and Tarantino.

Quentin Tarantino's *Death Proof* and Robert Rodriguez's *Planet Terror* play as if *Night of the Living Dead* and *Faster, Pussycat! Kill! Kill!* were combined on a double bill under the parentage of the dark sperm of vengeance.

Together the two separate feature-length stories combine into *Grindhouse,* a deliberate attempt by the two directors to re-create the experience of a double feature in a sleazy B-house. Scratches and blemishes mar the prints, frames or even whole reels are purportedly missing, and the characters have the shallow simplicity of action figures entirely at the disposal of special effects. They are separated by a group of four trailers for still more B-minus pictures.

This evocation of a grindhouse may have existed somewhere, sometime, but my moviegoing reaches back to before either director was born, and I have never witnessed a double bill and supporting program much like the one they have created. No, not even in half-forgotten Chicago theaters like the McVickers, Roosevelt, Shangri-La, Monroe, Loop, or Parkway. Not even while trying specifically to find "Dog of the Week" candidates for Spot the Wonder Dog to bark at. And it must be said that when it comes to fabricating bad movies, Rodriguez and Tarantino have a failure of will. To paraphrase Manny Farber, you can catch them trying to shove art up into the crevices of dreck.

I can imagine the pitch meeting at which the two directors told Harvey and Bob Weinstein why they had to make this double-header. In that room were the most skilled conversational motormouths I've met, and I mean that as a compliment. If Tarantino tells you about the last time he ate an Italian beef sandwich, you want to film it in 70 mm. But let's face it. The fundamental reason young males went to schlock double features in the golden age was in the hope of seeing breasts or, lacking that, stuff blowed up real good. Now that the mainstream is showing lots of breasts and real big explosions, there is no longer a market for bad movies showing the same thing.

I recall a luncheon at Cannes thrown by the beloved schlockmeister Sam Arkoff of American International Pictures. "Sam!" said Rex

Reed, after seeing Arkoff's new film *Q*, about a Quetzalcoatl that swooped down on Wall Street to gobble up stockbrokers. "What a surprise! Right in the middle of all that schlock, a great Method performance by Michael Moriarty!" Arkoff blushed modestly. "The schlock was my idea," he said.

So, OK, *Grindhouse* is an attempt to re-create a double feature that never existed for an audience that no longer exists. What's the good news? Tarantino's *Death Proof*, which I liked better, splits into two halves involving quartets of women, most of them lesbians, who are targeted by Stuntman Mike (Kurt Russell), who uses his "death-proof" car as a murder weapon. The movie ends with a skillful scene involving a deadly highway game and a duel between two cars. That and another highway massacre are punctuated by long—too long—passages of barroom dialogue. The movie has two speeds—pause and overdrive.

Rodriguez's *Planet Terror* recycles the durable *Living Dead* formula: A band of the healthy fight off shuffling bands of zombies. I have written before about my weariness with zombies, who as characters are sadly limited. What distinguishes Rodriguez's picture is the extraordinary skill of the makeup, showing us oozing wounds, exploding organs, and biological horrors. The movie wants to be as repulsive and nauseating as possible. The plot, involving go-go dancers and an action-packed doctor, is a clothesline for gore, explosions, bodily mayhem, and juicy innards on parade.

Both directors are eager to work in as many references as possible, verbal and visual, to their favorite movies; Russ Meyer seems quoted a lot. The backgrounds are papered with more vintage movie posters than you'd expect to find in a Texas saloon, except maybe in Austin. There are also various cultural references. For example, deejay Jungle Julia's listeners recite lines from "Stopping by the Woods on a Snowy Evening," but you would be wrong to think that is a reference to a poem by Robert Frost. No, according to IMDb.com, it refers to Don Siegel's thriller *Telefon* (1977), where the words were "used as a posthypnotic signal to activate Russian sleeper agents."

Grindhouse is both impressive and disappointing. From a technical and craft point of view it is first-rate; from its standing in the canons of the two directors, it is minor. And I wonder what the point is when two of Tarantino's women are obsessed with *Vanishing Point* (1971), a movie Tarantino obviously treasures. It explains the appearance in the movie of a 1970 Dodge Challenger, but is an explanation really necessary? Hell, I had a '57 Studebaker Golden Hawk, and it spoke for itself. We feel like the dialogue is movie-buff jargon overheard in a Park City saloon.

My own field of expertise in this genre is the cinema of Russ Meyer, and I was happy to see QT's closing homage to the tough girls and the beaten stud in *Faster, Pussycat! Kill! Kill!* (1965), which John Waters has named as the greatest film of all time. One heroine even copies Tura Satana's leather gloves, boots, and ponytail. I may have spotted, indeed, the most obscure quotation from Meyer. In an opening montage of his *Beyond the Valley of the Dolls* (1970), there is a brief, inexplicable shot of a boot crushing an egg. Rodriguez uses the same composition to show a boot crushing a testicle. So the cinema marches on.

After failing in theaters as a double bill, *Grindhouse* was split by the Weinsteins into two shorter films. The Tarantino, then lengthened by the director, played at Cannes, where Harvey Weinstein admitted at a press conference that, for daring to release the combined films at a running time over three hours, he received a "public spanking." Now that might have made a movie.

Grizzly Man ★ ★ ★ ★

R, 103 m., 2005

As themselves: Timothy Treadwell, Amie Huguenard, Medical Examiner Franc G. Fallico, Jewel Palovak, Willy Fulton, Sam Egli. Directed by Werner Herzog and produced by Erik Nelson. Screenplay by Herzog.

"If I show weakness, I'm dead. They will take me out, they will decapitate me, they will chop me up into bits and pieces—I'm dead. So far, I persevere. I persevere."

So speaks Timothy Treadwell, balanced somewhere between the grandiose and the manic in Werner Herzog's *Grizzly Man*. He is talking about the wild bears he came to know and love during thirteen summers spent living among them in Alaska's Katmai National Park and Preserve. In the early autumn of 2003, one of the bears took him out, decapitated him, chopped him up into bits and pieces, and he was dead. The bear also killed his girlfriend.

In happier times, we see Treadwell as a guest on the David Letterman show. "Is it going to happen," Letterman asks him, "that we read a news item one day that you have been eaten by one of these bears?" Audience laughter. Later in the film, we listen to the helicopter pilot who retrieved Treadwell's bones a few days after he died: "He was treating them like people in bear costumes. He got what he deserved. The tragedy of it is, he took the girl with him."

Grizzly Man is unlike any nature documentary I've seen; it doesn't approve of Treadwell, and it isn't sentimental about animals. It was assembled by Herzog, the great German director, from some ninety hours of video that Treadwell shot in the wild, and from interviews with those who worked with him, including Jewel Palovak of Grizzly People, the organization Treadwell founded. She knew him as well as anybody.

Treadwell was a tanned, good-looking man in his thirties with a Prince Valiant haircut who could charm people and, for thirteen years, could charm bears. He was more complex than he seemed. In rambling, confessional speeches recorded while he was alone in the wilderness, he talks of being a recovering alcoholic, of his love for the bears and his fierce determination to "protect" them—although others point out that they were safe enough in a national park, and he was doing them no favor by making them familiar with humans. He had other peculiarities, including a fake Australian accent to go with his story that he was from down under and not from New York.

"I have seen this madness on a movie set before," says Herzog, who narrates his film. "I have seen human ecstasies and darkest human turmoil." Indeed, madness has been the subject of many of his films, fact and fiction, and watching Treadwell I was reminded of the ski-jumper Steiner in another Herzog doc, the man who could fly so far that he threatened to overshoot the landing area and crash in the parking lot. Or the hero of *Fitzcarraldo*, obsessed with hauling a ship across land from one river to another.

"My life is on the precipice of death," Treadwell tells the camera. Yet he sentimentalizes the bears and is moved to ecstasy by a large steaming pile of "Wendy's poop," which is still warm, he exults, and was "inside of her" just minutes earlier. He names all the bears and provides a play-by-play commentary as two of the big males fight for the right to court "Satin."

During his last two or three years in the wilderness, Treadwell was joined by his new girlfriend, Amie Huguenard. Herzog is able to find only one photograph of her, and when she appears in Treadwell's footage (rarely), her face is hard to see. Treadwell liked to give the impression that he was alone with his bears, but Herzog shows one shot that is obviously handheld—by Huguenard, presumably.

Ironically, Treadwell and Huguenard had left for home in the September that they died. Treadwell got into an argument with an Air Alaska employee, canceled his plans to fly home, returned to the "Grizzly Maze" area where most of the bears he knew were already hibernating, and was killed and eaten by an unfamiliar bear that, it appears, he photographed a few hours before his death.

The cap was on his video camera during the attack, but audio was recorded. Herzog listens to the tape in the presence of Palovak and then tells her: "You must never listen to this. You should not keep it. You should destroy it because it will be like the elephant in your room all your life." His decision not to play the audio in his film is a wise one, not only out of respect to the survivors of the victims, but because to watch him listening to it is, oddly, more effective than actually hearing it. We would hear, he tells us, Treadwell screaming for Huguenard to run for her life, and we would hear the sounds of her trying to fight off the bear by banging it with a frying pan.

The documentary is an uncommon meeting between Treadwell's loony idealism and Herzog's bleak worldview. Treadwell's footage is sometimes miraculous, as when we see his close bond with a fox that has been like his pet dog for ten years. Or when he grows angry with God because a drought has dried up the salmon run and his bears are starving. He *demands* that God make it rain and, what do you know, it does.

Against this is Herzog, on the sound track: "I believe the common character of the universe is not harmony, but hostility, chaos, and murder." And over footage of one of Treadwell's beloved bears: "This blank stare" shows not the wisdom

Treadwell read into it but "only the half-bored interest in food."

"I will protect these bears with my last breath," Treadwell says. After he and Huguenard become the first and only people to be killed by bears in the park, the bear that is guilty is shot dead. His watch, still ticking, is found on his severed arm. I have a certain admiration for his courage, recklessness, idealism, whatever you want to call it, but here is a man who managed to get himself and his girlfriend eaten, and you know what? He deserves Werner Herzog.

Guess Who? ★ ★ ★

PG-13, 105 m., 2005

Bernie Mac (Percy Jones), Ashton Kutcher (Simon Green), Zoe Saldana (Theresa Jones), Judith Scott (Marilyn Jones), Kellee Stewart (Keisha Jones). Directed by Kevin Rodney Sullivan and produced by Jason Goldberg, Erwin Stoff, and Jenno Topping. Screenplay by David Ronn, Jay Scherick, and Peter Tolan.

Thirty-eight years after Katharine Houghton brought Sidney Poitier home to meet her parents in *Guess Who's Coming to Dinner,* it's time for an African-American woman to bring her white fiancé home in *Guess Who.* Not much has changed over the years, or in the parents, who go through various forms of discomfort and disapproval before finally caving in when they realize the fiancé is, after all, a heck of a nice guy with a great future ahead of him.

Although racially mixed marriages are more frequent than they were in 1967, it is still probably true that no parents of any race have ever said to a child: "You're marrying someone of another race, and that's it!" When a child chooses a spouse from another group, it is usually because they have more things in common than the bits of DNA that separate them. Most parents—not all—eventually conclude that the happiness of their child is the most important factor of all.

Parents did not come quite so willingly to that conclusion in 1967, which is why Stanley Kramer's film, now often dismissed as liberal piety, took some courage to make. No doubt it worked better because the African-American who came to dinner was played by Sidney Poitier as a famous doctor who lived in Switzerland. And it was crucial that the parents were played not merely by white actors, but by the icons Spencer Tracy and Katharine Hepburn, whose screen presence carried great authority.

In *Guess Who,* the white fiancé is not quite the world-class catch that Poitier was. Named Simon and played by Ashton Kutcher, who must have had an interesting evening when he came home for dinner with Demi Moore, he is a Wall Street trader with a bright future, who has suddenly quit his job. He's in love with Theresa (Zoe Saldana), an artist. Her parents are Percy (Bernie Mac), a bank loan officer, and Marilyn (Judith Scott). Like Tracy and Hepburn, they live in an expensive home in an upscale suburb.

"You didn't tell me your parents were black!" Simon says when he meets them, in a lame attempt at humor. The fact is, Theresa didn't tell them he was white. Simon discovers this during the cab ride to the suburbs. "I didn't tell them because it doesn't matter," she says. The black cab driver (Mike Epps) looks in the rearview mirror and says, "It's gonna matter."

It does, and the movie is a little uneasy about how to deal with that fact. Percy has already run a credit check on Simon and discovered (a) that he has an impressive net worth, but (b) is newly unemployed. When he finds out Simon hasn't told Theresa about his joblessness, Percy decides that the young man is not to be trusted. He is also not to be trusted with Theresa's body, at least not under Percy's roof; her father insists that Simon sleep on the sofa-bed in the basement, and to be sure he stays there, Percy sleeps in the same bed with him. This leads to several scenes that are intended to be funny but sit there uncomfortably on the screen because the humor comes from a different place than the real center of the film.

Simon and Theresa are indeed in love, indeed seem compatible, indeed have us hoping things will work out for them. But Percy is smart and suspicious, with a way of setting traps for the unsuspecting younger man. One of the film's best scenes, because it reflects fundamental truths, comes at dinner, when Simon says he doesn't approve of the "ethnic jokes" that "some people" tell at work. Percy asks him to provide a sample. Simon refuses, but then he decides, in a fatal spasm of political correctness, that it "empowers" the joke if he *doesn't* tell it.

So he does. ("How do we know Adam and Eve weren't black? Ever try to get a rib away from a black man?") Not everyone around the table may think this is funny, but they all laugh—except Theresa, who senses the danger. Percy asks for another joke, and Simon obliges. And a third. Encouraged by Percy, Simon inevitably tells one joke too many—one that isn't funny, but racist. A terrible silence falls. Percy leaves the table. Simon is aghast. "I should never have told that joke," he says to Theresa. "You should never have started," she says. His mistake was to tell the first one. But she forgives him his mistake: "He dared you."

He did. And if the movie had spent more time walking that tightrope between the acceptable and the offensive, between what we have in common and what divides us, it would have been more daring. Instead, it uses sitcom and soap opera formulas that allow the characters easy ways out. (The scene where Percy finds Simon wearing Theresa's negligee is painfully awkward.) No one in the audience of any race is going to feel uncomfortable about much of anything on the screen.

That said, *Guess Who?* works efficiently on its chosen level. Bernie Mac, who often cheerfully goes over the top in his roles, here provides a focused and effective performance as a father who would subject a boyfriend of any race to merciless scrutiny. He has a moment of sudden intuition about Simon that is perfectly realized and timed. Ashton Kutcher is not the actor Sidney Poitier was, but the movie doesn't require him to be; his assignment is to be acceptable and sympathetic in a situation where he is coached through the hazards by his girlfriend.

The movie focuses primarily on the two men. If we heard a lot about strong black women after *Diary of a Mad Black Woman,* here we have a movie about a strong black man and about male bonding that has more to do with corporate than racial politics. Zoe Saldana, a true beauty, is lovable and charming as Theresa, but in her home she's upstaged by her father. As her mother, Marilyn, Judith Scott has a much smaller role than Katharine Hepburn had in the earlier movie, and although we meet Theresa's feisty sister, Keisha (Kellee Stewart), not much is done with the character.

Interracial relationships may be an area where the daily experience of many people is better informed and more comfortable than the movies are ready to admit. Certainly after the first few dates any relationship is based more on love, respect, and mutual care than it is on appearances. I think the couple in *Guess Who?* has figured that out, but if they haven't, I predict they'll have a wonderful starter marriage.

Gunner Palace ★ ★ ★ ½

PG-13, 85 m., 2005

A documentary directed by Michael Tucker and Petra Epperlein and produced by Epperlein.

Gunner Palace is a ground-level documentary, messy and immediate, about the daily life of a combat soldier in Iraq. It is not prowar or antiwar. It is about American soldiers, mostly young, who are strangers in a strange land, trying to do their jobs and stay alive.

It has become dangerous to be a news correspondent in Iraq. As I write this, the front-page story is about an Italian journalist who was freed from her kidnappers, only to be wounded by friendly fire while trying to cross to safety at an American checkpoint. The man who negotiated her freedom was killed. In recent months many news organizations have pulled out their reporters; even the supposedly safe Green Zone inside Baghdad has become dangerous.

That's why this film is so valuable. Not because it argues a position about the war and occupation, but because it simply goes and observes as soldiers work and play, talk and write letters home, and, on a daily basis, risk their lives in sudden bursts of violence. Sometimes they translate their experiences into songs. The African-American soldiers, in particular, use hip-hop as an outlet, and their lyrics are sometimes angry, more often lonely and poetic; all wars seem to create poets, and so has this one.

The movie was directed, produced, written, and edited by Michael Tucker and Petra Epperlein, a married American couple who live in Germany and visited Iraq twice, in late 2003 and 2004. They followed the 2/3 Field Artillery Division (the "gunners") of the army's 1st Armored Division. As it happens, a platoon from that division was also being followed by *Time* magazine, which picked "The American Soldier" as its 2003 Person of the Year. The woman on the cover, Specialist Billie Grimes, is the only woman seen in the film. Specialist Stuart

Wilf, much seen in the film, "is the centerfold" in *Time*, according to an online journal kept by Tucker, who notes that two *Time* reporters were wounded while reporting the article.

The cover story takes a large view: "About 40 percent of the troops are Southern, 60 percent are white, 22 percent are black, and a disproportionate number come from empty states like Montana and Wyoming. When they arrive at the recruiter's door, Defense Secretary Donald Rumsfeld told *Time*, 'They have purple hair and an earring, and they've never walked with another person in step in their life. And suddenly they get this training, in a matter of weeks, and they become part of a unit, a team.'"

Gunner Palace plays like the deleted scenes from the *Time* cover story. The self-proclaimed gunners of the title live in the half-destroyed ruins of a palace once occupied by Saddam's son Uday. What's left of the furnishings make it look like a cross between a bordello and a casino, and some rooms end abruptly with bomb craters, but there is still a functioning swimming pool, and the soldiers' own rock band blasts Smokey Robinson's *My Girl* from loudspeakers during their party time. We're reminded that songs by The Doors provided a sound track for *Apocalypse Now*, with the difference that the soldiers in that film were often stoned, and these young men (and one woman) seem more sober and serious.

Their job is impossible to define, which is one of their frustrations. At some times they are peacekeepers, at other times targets; they may be overseeing a community meeting, acting like paramedics as they handle a stoned street kid, breaking down doors during raids, engaging in firefights in the midnight streets. Eight of them were killed during this period of time; one of them, known as "Super Cop," was an Iraqi attached to their unit who was famous for capturing wanted fugitives. Another trusted Iraqi, an interpreter, was charged with passing intelligence to insurgents. "If it is true," Tucker writes in his journal, "he is responsible for at least four deaths."

The filmmakers go along with the gunners on their nighttime patrols, and the camera follows them into houses harboring suspected terrorists. Gunfire breaks out at unexpected moments. You don't see this on TV. Tucker, who photographed his own movie, was willing to take risks, and the gunners were willing to have him come along with them; you can sense by the way they relax in front of the camera and confide their thoughts that they were comfortable with him, accustomed to him. What's working here is the technique Frederick Wiseman uses in his documentaries: He hangs around for so long that he disappears into the scene, and his subjects forget that they're on camera.

That doesn't mean Tucker catches them off guard, or finds them cynical or disloyal. It's a truism of war that a combat soldier of any nation is motivated in action not by his flag, his country, his cause, or his leaders, but by his buddies. He has trained with them, fought with them, seen some of them die and others take risks for him, and he doesn't want to let them down. That's what we feel here, along with the constant awareness that death can come suddenly in the middle of a routine action. We hear about "IEDs," which are improvised explosive devices, easy to place, hard to spot, likely to be almost anywhere. A sequence involves the investigation of a carrier bag on a city street, a bag that turns out to contain—nothing.

It's clear the soldiers don't think their logistical support amounts to much. Long before Rumsfeld was asked the famous question about the lack of armor for military vehicles, we see these men improvising homemade armor for their trucks and joking about it. There is a serious side: The flimsy junkyard shields they add are as likely to create deadly shrapnel as to protect them.

I wondered during the movie whether a sound track album exists. Apparently not. There should be one, or perhaps the original lyrics could be covered by established artists. The lyrics composed by the soldiers provide a view of the war that is simply missing in the middle of all the political rhetoric and gaseous briefings.

On May 23, 2004, after he had finished his principal photography, director Tucker made a last entry in his online journal: "I've asked soldiers what they think about the war and their answers are surprisingly simple. After a year, the war isn't about WMDs, democracy, Donald Rumsfeld, or oil. It's about them. Simple. They just want to finish the job they were sent to do so they can go home."

H

Hairspray ★ ★ ★ ½

PG, 115 m., 2007

Nikki Blonsky (Tracy Turnblad), John Travolta (Edna Turnblad), Queen Latifah (Motormouth Maybelle), Michelle Pfeiffer (Velma Von Tussle), Christopher Walken (Wilbur Turnblad), Zac Efron (Link Larkin), Brittany Snow (Amber Von Tussle), Amanda Bynes (Penny Pingleton), James Marsden (Corny Collins), Elijah Kelley (Seaweed), Allison Janney (Prudy Pingleton). Directed by Adam Shankman and produced by Craig Zadan and Neil Meron. Screenplay by Leslie Dixon, based on the 1988 screenplay by John Waters and the 2002 musical stage play by Mark O'Donnell and Thomas Meehan.

Hairspray is just plain fun. Or maybe not so plain. There's a lot of craft and slyness lurking beneath the circa-1960 goofiness. The movie seems guileless and rambunctious, but it looks just right (like a Pat Boone musical) and sounds just right (like a golden oldies disc) and feels just right (like the first time you sang "We Shall Overcome" and until then it hadn't occurred to you that we should).

It bounces out of bed with Tracy Turnblad (Nikki Blonsky), a roly-poly bundle of joy, whose unwavering cheerfulness shines on the whole picture. "Good morning, Baltimore!" she sings, as she dances through a neighborhood where everyone seems to know and love her, even the garbagemen who let her ride on the roof of their back loader. She's like a freelance cheerleader.

At school she links up with best friend Penny Pingleton (Amanda Bynes), whose name is undoubtedly a tribute to Penny Singleton, who played Dagwood's Blondie. They live for the moment when the minute hand crawls with agonizing slowness to the end of the school day, and they can race home and dance along with *The Corny Collins Show*, the local teenage TV danceathon. In those days every local market had a show like that. Maybe Dick Clark plowed them under. I miss their freshness and naïveté.

Corny (James Marsden) is well named, as he presides over a posse of popular kids known as his Council. Tracy longs to be on the Council. The star of the show and head of the Council is Amber Von Tussle (Brittany Snow), whose mother, Velma (Michelle Pfeiffer), manages the station and enforces an all-white policy for the show, except for the monthly Negro Day organized by Maybelle (Queen Latifah), owner of a record shop.

All of this is recycled from the original 1988 John Waters film, which made Ricki Lake a star, and from the Broadway musical made from it, but it's still fresh the third time around. It's a little more innocent than Waters would have made it, but he does his part by turning up in a cameo role as a flasher (look quick and you see Ricki Lake and Pia Zadora, too). The plot involves Tracy's instinctive decency as she campaigns to integrate the program, endangering her campaign to get on the Council.

Tradition requires her mother, Edna, to be played by a man in drag: Divine in the film, Harvey Fierstein in the musical, and this time, John Travolta, who may be wearing a fat suit but still moves like the star of *Saturday Night Fever*. Tracy's father, Wilbur, is played by Christopher Walken, who has a hairpiece surely borrowed from his store, which is named "Hardy Har Har" and sells jokes and novelties. Oh, how I miss the Whoopee Cushion.

The plot wheels right along while repairing one outpost of Baltimore racism, and what's remarkable is that some fairly serious issues get discussed in song and dance. Tracy is sent to detention one day and learns a whole new style of dancing from the black students there and takes it to TV, reminding me of the days when TV preachers thought Elvis was the spawn of Satan. Now they look like him. Call in today for your "free" healing water.

The point, however, is not the plot but the energy. Without somebody like Nikki Blonsky at the heart of the picture, it might fall flat, but everybody works at her level of happiness, including her teen contemporaries Zac Efron, Taylor Parks, and Elijah Kelley (the last two Maybelle's children), and the usual curio-shop window full of peculiar adults (Jerry Stiller, Paul Dooley). You know the story, you've seen the movie and heard all about the musical, and you think you know what to expect. But the movie seems to be happening right now, or right then, and its only flaw as a period picture is that there aren't enough Studebakers in it.

Hamlet 2 ★ ★ ★

R, 92 m., 2008

Steve Coogan (Dana Marschz), Joseph Julian Soria (Octavio), Elisabeth Shue (Elisabeth Shue), Skylar Astin (Rand), Phoebe Strole (Epiphany), Marshall Bell (Mr. Rocker), Catherine Keener (Dana's Wife), David Arquette (Gary the Boarder), Amy Poehler (Cricket Feldstein), Shea Pepe (The Critic). Directed by Andrew Fleming and produced by Eric D. Eisner, Leonid Rozhetskin, and Aaron Ryder. Screenplay by Fleming and Pam Brady

The problem with a sequel to *Hamlet* is that everybody interesting is dead by the end. That doesn't discourage Dana Marschz, a Tucson high school drama teacher, from trying to save the school's theater program with a sequel named *Hamlet 2*. The shop class builds him a time machine, and he brings back the dead characters, plus Jesus, Einstein, and the very much alive Hillary Clinton. Music is by the Tucson Gay Men's Chorus.

Hamlet 2 stars the British comedian Steve Coogan, who with this film and *Tropic Thunder* may develop a fan base in America. He's sort of a gangling, flighty, manic Woody Allen type, but without the awareness of his neurosis. Oh, he knows he has problems. He's a recovering alcoholic, so broke he and his wife have to take in a boarder, and when his drama class is thrown out of the school lunchroom they have to meet in the gym during volleyball practice.

Anyone who has ever been involved in high school theatrical productions will recognize a few elements from *Hamlet 2*, here much exaggerated. There are the teacher's pets who usually play all the leads. The rebellious new student who's sort of an ethnic Brando. The pitiful costumes. The disapproving school board, which wants to discontinue the program. The community uproar over the shocking content (gay men singing "Rock Me, Sexy Jesus"?). The ACLU lawyer, named Cricket (Amy Poehler), who flies to the rescue but seems to have a tendency toward anti-Semitism. And above all the inspired, passionate, more than slightly mad drama teacher.

Mr. Marschz (to pronounce it, you have to sort of buzz at the end) has seen too many movies like *Dead Poets Society* and *Mr. Holland's Opus*, and tries to inspire his students with his bizarre behavior. This takes little effort, especially after he starts wearing caftans to school because his wife (Catherine Keener) thinks he's impotent because jockey shorts cut off his circulation. Principal Rocker (Marshall Bell) is his unremitting enemy, and Octavio (Joseph Julian Soria) is the brilliant but rebellious student (he comes across as street tough but is headed for Brown). Rand (Skylar Astin) and Epiphany (Phoebe Strole) are his special pets, now feeling left out.

And then there is Elisabeth Shue. Yes, the real Elisabeth Shue, Oscar nominee for *Leaving Las Vegas*. When Dana goes to the hospital for treatment of his broken f-you finger, he tells the nurse she looks like his favorite actress, Elisabeth Shue. "That's because I am Elisabeth Shue," she says, explaining that she got tired of all the BS in showbiz and decided to help people by becoming a nurse. She agrees to visit his class. You can imagine the questions she gets.

Chaotic rehearsals and legal maneuvers by Cricket succeed in getting the play staged—not in the school, but in an abandoned railroad shed. Some of the characters may have the same names as characters in *Hamlet*, but that's about as far as the resemblance goes. No danger of plagiarism charges. The Gay Men's Chorus is very good, Dana himself not so good in the role of Jesus, moon-walking on the water.

Much depends on the verdict of my favorite character in the movie, the critic of the high school paper (Shea Pepe), a freshman who is about five feet tall. Having eviscerated Dana's previous production, he helpfully gives him advice (he should stop remaking movies like *Erin Brockovich* and do something original). *Hamlet 2* is original, all right. But will the kid like it?

The movie is an ideal showcase for the talents of Coogan, whom you may remember from *A Cock and Bull Story* (2005), the film about a film of *Tristram Shandy*, where only one person involved in the production had ever read the book. He is a TV legend in the UK, but not so uber-Brit that he doesn't travel well. He seems somewhat at home in Tucson, which, let it be said, has got to be a nicer town than anybody in this movie thinks it is.

Hancock ★ ★ ★

PG-13, 92 m., 2008

Will Smith (John Hancock), Charlize Theron (Mary Embrey), Jason Bateman (Ray Embrey), Eddie Marsan (Red), Jae Head (Aaron Embrey), David Mattey (Man Mountain). Directed by Peter Berg and produced by Akiva Goldsman, Michael Mann, Will Smith, and James Lassiter. Screenplay by Vy Vincent Ngo and Vince Gilligan.

I have been waiting for this for years: a superhero movie where the actions of the superheroes have consequences in the real world. They always leave a wake of crashed cars, bursting fire hydrants, exploding gas stations, and toppling bridges behind them, and never go back to clean up. But John Hancock, the hero of *Hancock,* doesn't get away with anything. One recent heroic stunt ran up a price tag of seven million dollars, he's got hundreds of lawsuits pending, and when he saves a stranded whale by throwing it back into the sea, you can bet he gets billed for the yacht it lands on.

Hancock, the latest star showcase for Will Smith, has him playing a Skid Row drunk with superpowers and a super hangover. He does well, but there are always consequences, like when he saves a man whose car is about to be struck by a train, but causes a train wreck. What he needs is a good PR man. Luckily, the man whose life he saved is exactly that. He's Ray Embrey (Jason Bateman, the adopting father in *Juno*), and Ray has a brainstorm: He'll repay Hancock by giving him a complete image makeover. If this sounds like a slapstick comedy, strangely enough it isn't. The movie has a lot of laughs, but Smith avoids playing Hancock as a goofball and shapes him as serious, thoughtful, and depressed.

Embrey the PR whiz brings Hancock home to dinner to meet his wife, Mary (Charlize Theron), and son, Aaron (Jae Head). The first time she meets him, Mary gives Hancock an odd, penetrating look. Also the second time, and also the third time. OK, OK, already: We get it. One odd, penetrating look after another. They have some kind of a history, but Hancock doesn't know about it, and Mary's not talking.

She has a lot to keep quiet about, although thank goodness she eventually opens up, or the movie wouldn't have a second half. I will not reveal what she says, of course, because her surprise is part of the fun. I am willing to divulge some of the setup, with Ray coaching Hancock to start saying "thank you" and "you did a good job here," and stop flying down out of the sky and crushing $100,000 cars. Ray also gets him a makeover: Gone is the flophouse wardrobe, replaced by a slick gold and leather costume, and Hancock gets a shave, too. Does it himself, with his fingernails.

He appeared some eighty years ago in Miami, as far as he knows. He doesn't know very far. He has no idea where his powers came from, or why he never grows any older. He can fly at supersonic speeds, stop a speeding locomotive, toss cars around, and in general do everything Superman could do, but not cleanly, neatly, or politely. Part of his reform involves turning himself in to the law and serving a prison term, although the chief of police has to summon him from prison to help with a bank hostage crisis. (In prison, there's a guy named Man Mountain who must not read the papers, or he would never, ever try to make Hancock his victim.)

It's not long after the bank hostage business that Mary reveals her secret, Hancock starts asking deep questions about himself, and the movie takes an odd, penetrating turn. This is the part I won't get into, except to say that the origin stories of superheroes consistently underwhelm me, and Hancock's is one of the most arbitrary. Even Mary, who knows all about him, doesn't know all that much, and I have a shiny new dime here for any viewer of the movie who can explain exactly how Hancock came into being.

Not that it matters much anyway. I guess he had to come into being *somehow,* and this movie's explanation is as likely as most, which is to say, completely preposterous. Still, *Hancock* is a lot of fun, if perhaps a little top-heavy with stuff being destroyed. Will Smith makes the character more subtle than he has to be, more filled with self-doubt, more willing to learn. Jason Bateman is persuasive and helpful on the PR front, and it turns out Charlize Theron has a great deal to feel odd and penetrating about.

The Happening ★ ★ ★

R, 91 m., 2008

Mark Wahlberg (Elliot Moore), Zooey Deschanel (Alma Moore), John Leguizamo (Julian), Betty Buckley (Mrs. Jones), Ashlyn Sanchez (Jess), Spencer Breslin (Josh). Directed by M. Night Shyamalan and produced by Shyamalan, Sam Mercer, and Barry Mendel. Screenplay by Shyamalan.

If the bee disappears from the surface of the Earth, man would have no more than four years to live.

—Albert Einstein

An alarming prospect, and all the more so because there has been a recent decline in the honeybee population. Perhaps it is comforting to know that Einstein never said any such thing—less comforting, of course, for the bees. The quotation appears on a blackboard near the beginning of M. Night Shyamalan's *The Happening,* a movie that I found oddly touching. It is no doubt too thoughtful for the summer action season, but I appreciate the quietly realistic way Shyamalan finds to tell a story about the possible death of man.

One day in Central Park people start to lose their trains of thought. They begin walking backward. They start killing themselves. This behavior spreads through Manhattan, and then all of the northeastern states. Construction workers throw themselves from scaffolds. Policemen shoot themselves. The deaths are blamed on a "terrorist attack," but in fact no one has the slightest clue, and New York City is evacuated.

We meet Elliot Moore (Mark Wahlberg), a Philadelphia high school science teacher; the quote was on his blackboard. We meet his wife, Alma (Zooey Deschanel), his friend Julian (John Leguizamo), and Julian's daughter, Jess (Ashlyn Sanchez). They find themselves fleeing on a train to Harrisburg, Pennsylvania, although people learn from their cell phones that the plague, or whatever it is, may have jumped ahead of them.

Now consider how Shyamalan shows the exodus from Philadelphia. He avoids all the conventional scenes of riots in the train station, people killing one another for seats on the train, etc., and shows the population as quiet and apprehensive. If you don't know what you're fleeing, and it may be waiting for you ahead, how would you behave? Like this, I suspect.

Julian entrusts his daughter with Elliot and Alma, and goes in search of his wife. The train stops permanently at a small town. The three hitch a ride in a stranger's car and later meet others who are fleeing, from what or to what, they do not know. Elliot meets a man who talks about a way plants have of creating hormones to kill their enemies, and he develops a half-baked theory that man may have finally delivered too many insults to the grasses and the shrubs, the flowers and the trees, and their revenge is in the wind.

By now the three are trekking cross-country through Pennsylvania, joined by two young boys, whom they will eventually lose. They walk on, the wind moaning ominously behind them, and come to the isolated country home of Mrs. Jones (Betty Buckley), a very odd old lady. Here they eat and spend the night, and other events take place, and Elliot and Alma find an opportunity to discuss their love and reveal some secrets and speculate about what dread manifestation has overtaken the world.

Too uneventful for you? Not enough action? For me, Shyamalan's approach was more effective than smash-and-grab plot-mongering. His use of the landscape is disturbingly effective. The performances by Wahlberg and Deschanel bring a quiet dignity to their characters. The *strangeness* of starting a day in New York and ending it hiking across a country field is underlined. Most of the other people we meet, not all, are muted and introspective. Had they been half-expecting some such "event" as this, whatever its description?

I know I have. For some time the thought has been gathering at the back of my mind that we are in the final act. We have finally insulted the planet so much that it can no longer sustain us. It is exhausted. It never occurred to me that vegetation might exterminate us. In fact, the form of the planet's revenge remains undefined in my thoughts, although I have read of global deserts and starvation, rising sea levels and the ends of species.

What I admired about *The Happening* is that the pace and substance of its storytelling allowed me to examine such thoughts, and to ask how I might respond to a wake-up call from nature. Shyamalan allows his characters space and time as they look within themselves. Those they meet on the way are such as they might indeed plausibly meet. Even the television and radio news is done correctly, as convenient clichés about terrorism give way to bewilderment and apprehension.

I suspect I'll be in the minority in praising this film. It will be described as empty, uneventful, meandering. But for some it will weave a spell. It is a parable, yes, but it is also simply the story of these people and how their lives and existence have suddenly become problematic. We depend on such a superstructure to maintain us that one or two alterations could leave us stranded and wandering through a field, if we are that lucky.

Happily Ever After ★ ★

NO MPAA RATING, 100 m., 2005

Charlotte Gainsbourg (Gabrielle), Yvan Attal (Vincent), Alain Chabat (Georges), Emmanuelle Seigner (Nathalie), Alain Cohen (Fred), Angie David (The Mistress), Anouk Aimée (Vincent's Mother), Claude Berri (Vincent's Father), Aurore Clément (Mistress's Mother). Directed by Yvan Attal and produced by Claude Berri. Screenplay by Attal.

Happily Ever After is among other things a dirge for the death of the French style of adultery. These Parisian philanderers seem no more chic than your average cheating American. Recall the elegance of the adultery in a film such as Renoir's *The Rules of the Game,* and then regard a couple in this film having a food fight. Of course, in Renoir the elegance was all upstairs among the aristocrats, while the gamekeeper and the footman chased each other around the kitchen, fighting over the gamekeeper's wife. Has everyone in France moved into the kitchen?

The movie opens with a man making a crass pickup attempt at a bar. The woman who is his target efficiently dismisses and humiliates him, turns her attention to another man, and picks him up.

In no time at all they are plundering their netherlands in a parked car, and it is only when they get inside an apartment that we realize they are man and wife. It's a game to bring a little spice into their marriage.

That couple is Vincent, played by Yvan Attal, who also wrote and directed the movie, and Gabrielle (Charlotte Gainsbourg, his real-life wife). Another couple in the story are the miserable Georges (Alain Chabat) and his feminist wife, Nathalie (Emmanuelle Seigner), who finds fault with everything he does, including buying gender-appropriate toys for their children. What does a little boy need? A toy vacuum cleaner, obviously.

These two men join in an occasional poker game with Fred (Alain Cohen), a bachelor and obsessive ladies' man, and an Indian man who enjoys frequent and satisfying sex with his wife after twenty years. The plot, which is generous with its characters, also provides Vincent with a mistress (Angie David), who at one point is actually talking to him on her cell phone while sitting in a restaurant at the next table from Vincent's wife. We also meet Vincent's parents (Anouk Aimée and Claude Berri) and the mistress's mother (Aurore Clément), looking uncannily like a mistress herself.

If I spent a lot of time performing a census of the cast, it is because the movie seems to rotate among its characters as if taking inventory. Nothing happens in *Happily Ever After* that I cared much about.

There is a scene where Gabrielle is at a Virgin megastore, listening to an album on headphones, and Johnny Depp joins her at the same kiosk and listens to the same song. They smile enigmatically, about the album, I guess, and he walks away. Later, Gabrielle, who is a Realtor, discovers she is showing an apartment to a man who is—why, it's Johnny Depp. They get on the elevator and find themselves kissing, and the elevator goes up, and up, and up, no doubt being circled by the stairway to heaven.

Scenes like this cause me to become unreasonably restless.

Does Gabrielle know this man is Johnny Depp? Does the movie? Does Depp? Is the movie so cool everybody knows he's Johnny Depp but just doesn't say so? Is his appearance intended as an endorsement? Or is he not supposed to be Johnny Depp, in which case why was he cast?

If the movie had given Gabrielle and the man something to actually say or do, none of these questions would be anywhere near the surface of my mind. Depp would be playing a role, instead of making a cameo. The cuteness of his appearance is an emblem of the film's self-absorbed satisfaction with itself: It need not extend itself to involve or amuse us, because its characters are so content to circulate among each other's genitals.

There's nothing much wrong with the film; my complaint is that there's nothing much right about it. Why do I need to see it? What do I learn? Why should I smile? Does the movie approve of the feminist wife, disapprove, or consider her merely a collection of character traits? Why is so little made of the Indians, who after all have mastered the happiness the others seek? What does it say about a couple when a food fight escalates into an action scene? I don't know, and I don't care, and if they are all really going to live happily ever after it will not be in this movie or even, at their rate of growth, in its sequel.

Happy Endings ★ ★ ½

R, 128 m., 2005

Maggie Gyllenhaal (Jude), Tom Arnold (Frank), Jason Ritter (Otis), Laura Dern (Pam), Lisa Kudrow (Mamie), David Sutcliffe (Gil), Bobby Cannavale (Javier), Jesse Bradford (Nicky), Steve Coogan (Charley), Sarah Clarke (Diane). Directed by Don Roos and produced by Holly Wiersma and Michael Paseornek. Screenplay by Roos.

Maggie Gyllenhaal steals the show in *Happy Endings,* as a seductive gold digger who realizes that the fastest way to a rich dad is through his gay son. Her character, Jude, is a bold tease who first convinces Otis (Jason Ritter) that he's straight, then lets his dad, Frank (Tom Arnold), know that she prefers an older man. Her cynicism is part of her allure; her journey through their family leaves them in confusion and disarray, if momentarily happier.

Elsewhere in Don Roos's *Happy Endings* are characters not so engaging. The movie itself seems discouraged by its depressed characters and tries to cheer us up with written subtitles. After the opening scene, in which a woman running in the street is struck by a car, the first title slides onto the screen: "She's not dead."

We meet Mamie at seventeen; her mother, explains a subtitle, has just married a guy who owns a chain of restaurants. She has gained a sixteen-year-old stepbrother, Charley, "who will be a virgin for ten more minutes." Her seduction technique is concise: "You know, we're not really brother and sister." She becomes pregnant and goes to Phoenix to get an abortion.

The film leaps forward to the present. Charley, now played by Steve Coogan, has inherited his father's restaurants and runs the one that is still open. He's gay; his partner is Gil (David Sutcliffe). They're friends with a lesbian couple, Pam and Diane (Laura Dern and Sarah Clarke). Gil at one point donated sperm to help them have a baby, and indeed they have a baby, which is allegedly, however, not Gil's. Charley has deep suspicions; the kid looks a lot like Gil, and he thinks they're lying so they don't have to share the kid.

We meet Mamie again, now played by Lisa Kudrow as a counselor in an abortion clinic. She has a paid lover named Javier (Bobby Cannavale, from *The Station Agent*), who specializes in massages with "happy endings." *Spoiler warning:* She is visited one day by an alarming young man named Nicky (Jesse Bradford), who says he knows she didn't have an abortion in Phoenix and can provide the name and address of her son. There is a catch: Nicky wants to film their reunion for a documentary he thinks will win him a scholarship to the American Film Institute.

So, that's the setup and indeed at least half of the movie. All of these characters are connected in one way or another, even Jude and Mamie, when Jude needs counseling and Mamie seems singularly unhelpful. The film's problem is that we don't much like most of the characters, or care about them. Jude, who strictly speaking is the worst of the lot, at least has spirit and energy and tries to find happiness on her own terms.

The lesbian couple is singularly dour. The counselor needs counseling. Otis, the confused son, will be fine in a few years, but not now. The gay men, Gil and Charley, get involved in an intrigue about the baby that leads to a permanent break with Pam and Diane. Apart from the calculating Mamie, the only other sunshine in the movie comes from Arnold, as a true-blue dad who loves his son, Otis, whether he's gay or straight, and lusts for Mamie whether she's sincere or not. He probably knows she wants him for his money but is willing to overlook that because (a) he thinks he can handle himself, and (b) the one thing rich men believe more easily than poor men is that they are irresistible to sexy women half their age.

Happy Endings maintains a certain level of intrigue and occasionally bursts into life, especially when Gyllenhaal or Arnold are involved. I also like the way Mamie, the Kudrow character, becomes obsessed with Nicky's documentary; Final Cut Pro becomes as addictive for her as a video game. The movie's construction is clever and the dialogue well-heard, but the movie lacks the wicked magic of Roos's *The Opposite of Sex* (1998) and *Bounce* (2000). Both of those movies also had central roles for gay characters but saw them as warmer and more dimensional. In *Happy Endings* no one, gay or straight, seems much entertained by sex except when using it to manipulate, or be manipulated. For the father, and seductress and the masseur, cash seems to be crucial to sexual success; for the others, it seems to be a gloomy murkiness.

Hard Candy ★ ★ ★ ½

R, 103 m., 2006

Patrick Wilson (Jeff Kohver), Ellen Page (Hayley Stark), Sandra Oh (Judy Tokuda), Odessa Rae (Janelle Rogers), Gilbert John (Nighthawks Clerk). Directed by David Slade and produced by Michael Caldwell, David Higgins, Richard Hutton, and Jody Patton. Screenplay by Brian Nelson.

David Slade's *Hard Candy* is against pedophilia, but what does it think about sadomasochism? On one level it's a revenge picture about a fourteen-year-old girl who entraps a thirty-two-year-old pedophile on the Internet, gets herself invited to his home, and quickly has him strapped down and helpless. On another level, it plays into the classic porno scenario in which a dominating female torments her victim. That the female is a child makes it all the more disturbing. That the film is so well-made and effectively acted makes it even more challenging.

Let me put my questions to one side for a moment and simply consider the story. Jeff (Patrick Wilson) is a photographer who hangs out in Internet teen chat rooms and strikes up a predatory friendship with Hayley (Ellen Page). She agrees to meet him on neutral territory, a coffee shop, but soon suggests they go to his home. He offers her a drink. She laughs: "I know better than to accept a drink mixed by a strange man." So she mixes the drinks. And he passes out and wakes up securely tied to a table.

Now commences an extraordinary acting performance by both actors, especially Page. Although she plays fourteen, I understand she was seventeen when she made it; to involve a fourteen-year-old in this material would be wrong. As an actress, she makes Hayley into a calm, methodical, intelligent girl who announces she is going to castrate Jeff. She has medical textbooks, instructions from the Web, scalpels, and antiseptic, and he should look on the bright side: He'll have to go through this only once.

Before she carries out her threat, however, she plays mind games with him. She has followed him into other chat rooms, she says. She suspects he may have been implicated in the death of a young person. She explores his home and finds his stash of porno. He begs for mercy. She lets him beg.

How it all turns out, you will have to discover for yourself. There are a few other characters involved, including Sandra Oh as a curious neighbor, and some suspense of a conventional thriller type. But most of the movie simply involves Hayley and Jeff talking, and we're placed in the middle: We disapprove of what she's doing to him, but in a sense he was asking for it, because her evidence against him is persuasive, and he admits to a good deal of it.

If that were that, I would give the film an admiring review with special mention to the actors. But it isn't that simple. Isn't there a sense in which this film takes away with one hand and gives with the other? While it tells its horrifying parable about pedophilia, isn't it also dealing with sexually charged images that some audience members will find appealing? True, as far as I know, there is no tradition of pornography about men being tortured by young girls; usually the dominant female is adult, as she must be to feed into her victim's fantasies about authority figures. Still, what precisely is going on here, and is it anywhere near as clear as it seems? Is Hayley perhaps getting some pleasure of her own out of the situation she has created for Jeff? Are there two perverts in the room?

The film succeeds in telling its story with no nudity; the R rating comes "for disturbing violent and aberrant sexual content involving a teen, and for language." The young girl is not objectified but has free will throughout, lives in the moment, and improvises. There is undeniable fascination in the situation as it unfolds. It is an effective film. Although I may be concerned about how some audience members may react to it, I cannot penalize it on the basis of my speculations about their private feelings. Seen as a film, seen as acting and direction, seen as just exactly how it unfolds on the screen, *Hard Candy* is impressive and effective. As for what else it may be, each audience member will have to decide.

Harlan County, USA ★ ★ ★ ★

NO MPAA RATING, 103 m., 1976 (rereleased 2006)

A documentary directed and produced by Barbara Kopple.

At Sundance 2005, I went to a tribute screening for Barbara Kopple's great documentary *Harlan County, USA,* which won the Academy Award in 1976.

The film retains all of its power, in the story of a miners' strike in Kentucky where the company employed armed goons to escort scabs into the mines, and the most effective picketers were the miners' wives—articulate, indomitable, courageous. It contains a famous scene where guns are fired at the strikers in the darkness before dawn, and Kopple and her cameraman are knocked down and beaten.

"I found out later that they planned to kill us that day," Kopple said later, in a discussion I chaired at the Filmmakers' Lodge. "They wanted to knock us out because they didn't want a record of what was happening." But her cinematographer, Hart Perry, got an unforgettable shot of an armed company employee driving past in his pickup, and a warrant was issued for his arrest.

Kopple brought some friends along to the festival. Foremost among them was Hazel Dickens, a miner's wife and sister, now sixty-nine, who wrote songs for the movie and led the room in singing "Which Side Are You On?" Kopple also shared the stage with Utah miners who were on strike; although the national average pay for coal miners is fifteen to sixteen dollars an hour, these workers—who were striking for a union contract—are paid seven dollars for the backbreaking and dangerous work.

Using a translator, the Spanish-speaking miners told their story. One detail struck me with curious strength. A miner complained that his foreman demanded he give him a bottle of Gatorade every day as sort of a job tax. It is the small scale of the bribe that hit me, demonstrating how desperately poor these workers are. Work it out, and the Gatorade represents 10 percent of a daily wage.

Kopple and Perry spent eighteen months in Harlan County, filming what happened as it happened. Her editor, Nancy Baker, who was also onstage, took hundreds of hours of footage and brought it together with power and clarity. I asked Kopple what she thought about other styles of documentaries, such as Michael Moore's first-person adventures, or the Oscar-nominated *Story of the Weeping Camel,* which is scripted and has people who portray themselves but is not a direct record of their daily lives.

"I accept any and all kinds of documentaries," she said. "*Harlan County* came out of the tradition of Albert Maysles and Leacock and Pennebaker, documentarians who went somewhere and stayed there and watched and listened and made a record of what happened. That is one approach. There are others, just as valid. All that matters is making a good film."

Note: The conversation at Sundance between Kopple and Ebert is on the DVD.

Harry Potter and the Goblet of Fire ★ ★ ★ ½

PG-13, 157 m., 2005

Daniel Radcliffe (Harry Potter), Emma Watson (Hermione Granger), Rupert Grint (Ron Weasley), Brendan Gleeson (Alastor "Mad-Eye" Moody), Robert Pattinson (Cedric Diggory), Clemence Poesy (Fleur Delacour), Stanislav Ianevski (Viktor Krum), Ralph Fiennes (Lord Voldemort), Robbie Coltrane (Rubeus Hagrid), Katie Leung (Cho Chang), Frances de la Tour (Madame Maxime), Miranda Richardson (Rita Skeeter). Directed by Mike Newell and produced by David Heyman. Screenplay by Steven Kloves, based on the novel by J. K. Rowling.

Well into *Harry Potter and the Goblet of Fire,* Albus Dumbledore intones as only he can: "Dark and difficult times lie ahead." What does he think lay behind? In this adventure, Harry will do battle with the giant lizards, face the attack of the Death Eaters, and in perhaps the most difficult task of all for a fourteen-year-old, ask a girl to be his date at the Yule Ball. That Harry survives these challenges goes without saying, since in the world of print his next adventures have already been published, but *Goblet of Fire* provides trials that stretch his powers to the breaking point.

Harry (Daniel Radcliffe) was just turning thirteen in the previous movie, *Harry Potter and the Prisoner of Azkaban* (2004), and the Potter series turns PG-13 with this one. There is still at least a mail owl, and what looks like a mail raven (it may represent FedEx), but many of the twee touches of the earlier films have gone missing to make room for a brawnier, scarier plot. Is it fair to wonder if the series will continue to grow up with Harry, earning the R rating as he turns seventeen?

Certainly Lord Voldemort seems capable of limitless villainy. Although we glimpsed his face in *Sorcerer's Stone,* we see him full on the screen for the first time in *Goblet of Fire,* and he does not disappoint: Hairless, with the complexion of a slug, his nostrils snaky slits in his face, he's played by Ralph Fiennes as a vile creature who at last has been rejoined by his Death Eaters, who were disabled by Harry's magic earlier in the series. Hogwarts School and indeed the entire structure of Harry's world are threatened by Voldemort's return to something approaching his potential powers, and the film becomes a struggle between the civilized traditions of the school and the dark void of voldemortism.

The film is more violent, less cute than the others, but the action is not the mindless destruction of a video game; it has purpose, shape, and style, as in the Triwizard Tournament. Three finalists are chosen by the Goblet of Fire, and then the Goblet spits out an unprecedented fourth name: Harry Potter's. This is against the rules, since you have to be sixteen to compete in Triwizardry, and Harry is only fourteen, but Dumbledore's hands are tied: What the Goblet wants, the Goblet gets. The question is, who entered Harry's name, since Harry says he didn't?

The Triwizard Tournament begins near the start of the film, but after the Quidditch World Cup, which takes place within a stadium so vast it makes the Senate Chamber in *Star Wars* look like a dinner theater. The cup finals are interrupted by ominous portents; the Death Eaters attack, serving notice that Voldemort is back and means business. But the early skirmishers are repelled and the students return to Hogwarts, joined by exchange students from two overseas magic academies: From France come the Beauxbaton girls, who march on parade like Bemelman's maids all in a row, and from Durmstrang in central Europe come clean-cut Nordic lads who look like extras from *Triumph of the Will.*

Besides Harry, Cedric Diggory is the Triwizard contestant from Hogwarts, and the other finalists are Viktor Krum, a Quidditch master from Durmstrang who looks ready to go pro, and the lithe Fleur Delacour, a Beauxbaton siren. Together they face three challenges: They must conquer fire-breathing dragons, rescue captives in a dark lagoon, and enter a maze that, seen from the air, seems limitless. The maze contains a threat for Harry that I am not sure is anticipated by the Triwizard rules; within it waits Voldemort himself, who has been lurking offstage in the first three films and now emerges in malevolent fury.

Against these trials, which are enough to put you off your homework, Harry must also negotiate his fourth year at Hogwarts. As usual, there is a bizarre new teacher on the faculty. Alastor "Mad-Eye" Moody (Brendan Gleeson) is the new professor of Defense Against the Dark Arts and seems made of spare parts; he has an artificial limb, and a glass eye that incorporates a zoom lens and can swivel independently of his real eye.

There is also, finally, full-blown adolescence to contend with. I'd always thought Harry would end up in love with Hermione Granger (Emma Watson), even though their inseparable friend Ron Weasley (Rupert Grint) clearly has the same ambition. But for the Yule Ball, Harry works up the courage to ask Cho Chang (Katie Leung), who likes him a lot. Ron asks Hermione, but she already has a date, with the student most calculated to inspire Ron's jealousy. These scenes seem almost in the spirit of John Hughes's high school movies.

Most of the Potter series regulars are back, if only for brief scenes, and it is good to see the gamekeeper Hagrid (Robbie Coltrane) find love at last with Madame Maxime (Frances de la Tour), headmistress of Beauxbaton. Hagrid, you will recall, is a hairy giant. Frances is an even taller, but mercifully less hairy, giantess. One new character is the snoopy Rita Skeeter (Miranda Richardson), gossip columnist of the *Daily Prophet,* a paper that, like the portraits in earlier films, has pictures that talk.

With this fourth film, the Harry Potter saga demonstrates more than ever the resiliency of J. K. Rowling's original invention. Her novels have created a world that can be expanded indefinitely and produce new characters without limit. That there are schools like Hogwarts in other countries comes as news and offers many possibilities; the only barrier to the series lasting forever is Harry's inexorably advancing age. The thought of him returning to Hogwarts for old boy's day is too depressing to contemplate.

Harry Potter and the Goblet of Fire was directed by Mike Newell, the first British director in the series (he turned down the first Potter movie). Newell's credits range from the romantic *Four Weddings and a Funeral* to the devastating *Donnie Brasco* to the gentle *Enchanted April.* Such various notes serve him well in *Goblet of Fire,* which explores such a wide emotional range. Here he finds a delicate balance between whimsy and the ominous, on the uncertain middle ground where Harry lives, poised between fun at school, teenage romance, and the dark abyss.

Harry Potter and the Order of the Phoenix ★ ★ ½

PG-13, 138 m., 2007

Daniel Radcliffe (Harry Potter), Rupert Grint (Ron Weasley), Emma Watson (Hermione Granger), Helena Bonham Carter (Bellatrix Lestrange), Michael Gambon (Albus Dumbledore), Brendan Gleeson (Mad-Eye Moody), Gary Oldman (Sirius Black), Alan Rickman (Severus Snape), Maggie Smith (Minerva McGonagall), Imelda Staunton (Dolores Umbridge). Directed by David Yates and produced by David Barron and David Heyman. Screenplay by Michael Goldenberg, based on the novel by J. K. Rowling.

Whatever happened to the delight and, if you'll excuse the term, magic in the Harry Potter series? As the characters grow up, the stories grow, too, leaving the innocence behind and confusing us with plots so labyrinthine that it takes a Ph.D. from Hogwarts to figure them out. *Harry Potter and the Order of the Phoenix* still has much of the enchantment of the earlier films, but Harry no longer has as much joy. His face is lacking the gosh-wow-this-is-really-neat grin. He has internalized the secrets and delights of the world of wizards and is now instinctively using them to save his life.

An early scene illustrates this change. Harry and his cousin Dudley are attacked by dementors and in desperation he uses a secret spell to defeat them. But that earns the disapproval of his superiors at Hogwarts, and he is threatened with expulsion, because the spell is not to be used in public around Muggles. What is it, like a secret Masonic grip? When you're about to get your clock stopped by dementors and you know the spell, what are you expected to do? Fall over passively and get demented?

There comes a time, which I fear is approaching as we near the end of the series, that Harry and his friends will grow up and smell the coffee. They weren't trained as magicians for fun. And when they eventually arrive at some apocalyptic crossroads, as I fear they will, can the series continue to live in PG-13 land? The archvillain Voldemort is shaping up as the star of nightmares.

Harry (Daniel Radcliffe) has reason to fear that playtime is long behind. As a wizard chosen in childhood for his special powers, he has reason to believe Voldemort has returned and will have to be dealt with. The Ministry of Magic, like many a government agency, is hidebound in outdated convictions and considers Harry's warning to be heresy—and at Hogwarts, a fierce new professor of the dark arts, Dolores Umbridge (Imelda Staunton), has been installed to whip Harry into line.

Her enemies include Harry's protector, Dumbledore (Michael Gambon, looking as shabby as a homeless headmaster). Hermione (Emma Watson) and Ron (Rupert Grint) join

Harry in fomenting resistance to Umbridge (rhymes with "umbrage"), and soon they are mapping clandestine schemes to defend Dumbledore. Their plots, alas, seem more serious than the mischief Harry and friends would have thought up in earlier days. Yes, I know time passes, and the actors are seven years older than when they started filming. But if a kid starts watching Potter movies with this film, would he guess they used to be a little more whimsical?

By now, if we know anything at all about the Potter series, it's that nothing is as it seems, and the most unlikely characters have occult connections. Yes, but so many surprises have popped out of the hat that a veteran Potter watcher can almost, by a process of elimination, figure out who will surprise us next. For Harry, like many another leader before him, it is time to leave the nest and begin to work in the world. For the first time since we saw platform 9¾ at King's Cross, the city of London has a major role now, as Harry and sidekicks fly down the Thames and swoop past Big Ben.

That causes me to wonder, what is the practical connection between the world of magic and the world of Muggles? Will Harry, or should Harry, become a world leader? Can wands and spells be of use in today's geopolitical turmoil? Or are Hogwarts grads living in a dimension of their own? All will be told, I guess, in the final book in J. K. Rowling's series, and then the retail book industry will be back on its own again.

These things said, there is no denying that *Order of the Phoenix* is a well-crafted entry in the Potter series. The British have a way of keeping up production values in a series, even when the stories occasionally stumble. There have been lesser James Bond movies, but never a badly made one. And the necessary use of CGI here is justifiable because what does magic create, anyway, other than real-life CGI without the computers?

And as for the cast, the Potter series has turned into a work-release program for great British actors mired in respectable roles. Imelda Staunton is perfect here as the Teacher from Hell. Helena Bonham Carter looks like the double for all three of Macbeth's witches. And then take a roll call: Robbie Coltrane, Ralph Fiennes (in the wings as Voldemort), Michael Gambon, Brendan Gleeson, Richard Griffiths, Jason Isaacs, Gary Oldman, Alan Rickman, Fiona Shaw, David Thewlis, Emma Thompson, Warwick Davis, Julie Walters, and the incomparable Maggie Smith.

My hope, as we plow onward through Potters No. 6 and No. 7, is that the series will not grow darker still. Yet I suppose even at the beginning, with those cute little mail owls, we knew the whimsy was too good to last. Now that Harry has experienced his first kiss, with Cho Chang (Katie Leung), we can only imagine what new opportunities lie ahead. Agent 009.75?

Hate Crime ★ ★ ½

NO MPAA RATING, 104 m., 2006

Seth Peterson (Robbie Levinson), Bruce Davison (Pastor Boyd), Chad Donella (Chris Boyd), Cindy Pickett (Barbara McCoy), Susan Blakely (Martha Boyd), Lin Shaye (Kathleen Slansky), Giancarlo Esposito (Sergeant Esposito), Farah White (Detective Fisher), Brian J. Smith (Trey McCoy), Sean Hennigan (Jim McCoy). Directed by Tommy Stovall and produced by P. Dirk Higdon and Stovall. Screenplay by Stovall.

Hate Crime is set in motion with the murder of a gay man, but the title refers to more than one kind of hate and more than one kind of crime. At the end, we're left with good and evil in a bewildering tangle. The story is sometimes overwritten, often overwrought, includes an overheard conversation on the Nancy Drew level, and yet holds our attention and contains surprises right until the end.

The story begins with Robbie and Trey (Seth Peterson and Brian J. Smith), a long-established gay couple. A new neighbor moves in next door: Chris Boyd (Chad Donella). He makes it clear he hates homosexuals: "You're going to hell." A few nights later, while Trey is walking their dog in the park, he is beaten to death with a baseball bat.

Robbie is sure he knows who did it. The new neighbor, Chris, even has a previous hate crime on his record. A detective (Farah White) is assigned to the case, considers Chris a suspect, and then is joined by a senior detective (Giancarlo Esposito) who sees the case differently and has another suspect.

Meanwhile, we see the home life of Chris

Boyd. His father, Pastor Boyd (Bruce Davison), is the leader of a fundamentalist congregation much given to sermons that linger in loving detail on sinners in the hands of an angry God. His mother, Martha (Susan Blakely), is a sweet, worried woman who supports her husband primarily, it appears, because anything else might be a sin. Their family dinners are fraught with tension.

Also in the film, less crucial but well-drawn, are Cindy Pickett and Sean Hennigan as Trey's parents. Lin Shaye has a peculiar but vivid role as a neighbor who agrees with Pastor Boyd's religion in theory but considers Robbie and Trey "my family" and has reason to suspect the cops: "You can't trust anybody but yourself."

So now all the pieces are in place for a puzzle I will not reveal, since *Hate Crime* is actually more of a thriller than a social commentary. It provides a sympathetic and convincing portrait of its gay characters, but it has two weaknesses that undermine the power it might have developed.

One involves the melodramatic way the plot is resolved. The other involves Pastor Boyd, his wife, his son, and his church. Yes, plenty of fundamentalists believe homosexuals (and many others) are on the highway to hell. Yes, they are intolerant and extreme and do not do unto others as they would be done unto themselves. Yes, they talk a lot about Jesus but seem unable to practice his principles, especially those involving charity. Yes, Jesus in their theology is not a spiritual leader so much as their spokesmodel on reactionary social and political issues. To drive its point home, the movie counterpoints Pastor Boyd's hellfire and brimstone with the gentler Christianity of Robbie's church.

But there are other fundamentalists, a great many more, I believe, who are gentle and humane, positive and well-meaning, and although I may disagree with many of their beliefs, well, there are a lot of religious beliefs in the world and most people disagree with most of them. In a sense, Pastor Boyd and his team represent Islamic terrorists, and most fundamentalists are like most Muslims, religious but not extremist, valued members of the community, good citizens and neighbors.

I make this point because the portrait of the Boyds is painted by Tommy Stovall, the film's writer and director, with such broad and venomous strokes that if the gay characters had been portrayed in the same way, the film would rightly be seen as bigoted. The Boyds are such nutcases that the film is thrown out of balance; a moderated portrait of them might have made a more effective movie.

What does feel right is the tension between the two detectives, the younger woman played by White and the veteran played by Esposito. Both leap to instant conclusions about the crime, and although our sympathies are with the woman, both of their theories are inspired more by prejudice than police work.

Of the ending of the movie I will have nothing to say. I have been accused recently of "spoiling" endings by the simple act of suggesting there is something to be spoiled. Life for me was so much simpler before e-mails in which readers send bulletins: "By hinting that there is a twist, you spoiled the movie, because otherwise why would I expect a twist?" I would suggest to such readers that few movies proceed predictably on a preordained path to an obvious conclusion. If you want one that does, Lindsay Lohan's *Just My Luck* also opened the same day as *Hate Crime*. For the rest of us, the ending of *Hate Crime* raises complex moral issues that make the movie more thought-provoking than we possibly could have expected.

Head-On ★ ★ ★

NO MPAA RATING, 118 m., 2005

Birol Unel (Cahit), Sibel Kekilli (Sibel), Catrin Striebeck (Maren), Guven Kirac (Seref), Meltem Cumbul (Selma). Directed by Fatih Akin and produced by Ralph Schwingel and Stefan Schubert. Screenplay by Akin.

"Are you Turkish? Will you marry me?" This may not be the shortest marriage proposal in movie history, but it is certainly one of the most sincere. It comes early in *Head-On*, a film about two people who would deserve each other, except that no one deserves either one of them. Sibel is a Turkish woman of about twenty-two, living in Germany with her parents. Cahit, who is at least twenty years older, is also a Turk living in Germany, which is all Sibel needs to know, because what she needs is a Turkish husband (any Turkish husband will do) who can take her out of her home and the domination of her father and brother and the threat of being married off to a loathsome man of their choosing.

Not that Sibel is a prize. Her wrists are scarred after suicide attempts, and she meets Cahit in a mental institution, where he has been taken after driving his car into a wall at full speed. Not a promising couple. She explains the deal: She will cook and keep house for him, do his laundry and stay out of the way. He doesn't have to have sex with her, and she gets to have sex with anybody she wants. This sounds like a good enough deal to Cahit, who desperately needs a housecleaner (and a bath and a haircut) and is getting all the sex he needs from a buxom hairdresser who hangs out with him at the sleaziest saloon since *Barfly.*

Cahit (Birol Unel) and Sibel (Sibel Kekilli) are played with a deadpan self-destructiveness that sometimes tilts toward comedy, sometimes toward tragedy, sometimes simply toward grossing us out. Cahit picks up the empty bottles in a bar in return for free drinks, uses cocaine when he can get it, is morose about the unexplained loss of his first wife (maybe he misplaced her), and is a sight to behold when he is brought home by Sibel to meet her family. Her father, a bearded patriarch, looks on incredulously. Her brother whispers to the old man that at least Cahit will take her off their hands. To Cahit, he says: "Your Turkish sucks. What did you do with it?" Cahit: "I threw it away."

It is not that he hates Turkish or Turkey; it is that he hates himself. He prefers to speak German because that is the language of the society he moves in, one of garish bars and sudden fights and desperate bloody hangovers. Everyone in his world is a realist with no delusions. I treasured the scene where Cahit's new brother-in-law suggests they all make a trip to a brothel and is enraged when Cahit suggests that the man return home and sleep with his wife instead.

In a conventional movie, the formula would be: They put up with each other out of necessity, she starts to care for him, he begins to like her but she draws away, he grows angry and distant, she sees that he needs her, and they end by discovering that, what do you know, they actually love each other. *Head-On* goes through these stages in five minutes, on its way to much more desperate and harrowing adventures, which you will discover for yourself.

The film won the Berlin Film Festival and a lot of European Film Awards, and was praised partly, I imagine, because it provides a portrait (however dire) of Germany's large population of Turks and other immigrants—who, like undocumented Mexicans in America, are made to feel unwelcome while at the same time being essential to the functioning of the economy. The most memorable film I've seen about immigrants in Germany was *Ali—Fear Eats the Soul* (1974), by Rainer Werner Fassbinder, a director with an uncanny resemblance to Cahit, especially in the categories of personal hygiene, barbering, and drug abuse. In *Ali,* a middle-aged cleaning woman marries a much younger Moroccan man, and when she announces this fact to her family, a son (played by Fassbinder) stares at her for a second, stands up, and kicks out the screen of her television set.

Head-On not only includes a car crash, but also has the fascination of one. It is possible that no good can come to these characters, no matter what changes they make or what they can do for each other. Their marriage functions primarily to yank both parties out of their personal spirals of self-destruction and allow them to join in a double helix of personal misfortune.

From time to time, the movie cuts to a band performing on a stage of Turkish carpets on a bank of the Bosporus strait, with Istanbul in the background. These musical interludes suggest that we may be seeing a version of a ballad or folk legend, which has been processed through generations of urban grunge. What I can say for the film is what I could also say of *Barfly, Last Exit to Brooklyn,* and *Sid & Nancy,* which is that the characters in these movies are making their mistakes so we don't have to.

I can also observe that I watched with fascination. The movie is well and fearlessly acted, and the writer-director (Fatih Akin) is determined to follow the story to a logical and believable conclusion, rather than letting everyone off the hook with a conventional ending.

The Heartbreak Kid ★ ★

R, 108 m., 2007

Ben Stiller (Eddie Cantrow), Malin Akerman (Lila), Michelle Monaghan (Miranda), Jerry Stiller (Eddie's father), Rob Corddry (Mac), Carlos Mencia (Uncle Tito), Stephanie Courtney (Gayla), Ali Hillis (Jodi), Kathy

Lamkin (Lila's Mom). Directed by Bobby Farrelly and Peter Farrelly and produced by Ted Field and Bradley Thomas. Screenplay by Scott Armstrong and Leslie Dixon, based on the screenplay by Neil Simon and the short story *A Change of Plan* by Bruce Jay Friedman.

The premise of *The Heartbreak Kid* is that a man marries a woman who quickly becomes unbearable to him. The problem is that she just as quickly becomes unbearable to us. Perhaps it is a tribute to Malin Akerman, who plays the new bride, named Lila, that she gets the job done so well; after a point, we cringe when she appears on the screen.

Nor do we have much sympathy for her new husband, Eddie, played by Ben Stiller. Eddie is a shallow, desperate creature, driven by his hungers, always looking as if he'd like to gnash the flesh of those who oppose him. So here we have a marriage between two unpleasant people, and into these jaws of incompatibility is thrown the person of Miranda (Michelle Monaghan), a sweet girl who deserves better.

The movie is a remake of Elaine May's splendid 1972 comedy, written by Neil Simon, much revised by May. Her movie starred Charles Grodin as a passive-aggressive social climber, May's own daughter Jeannie Berlin as his alarming first wife, and Cybill Shepherd as the WASP goddess on a Florida beach whom he falls in love with on his honeymoon. That film was better in every way, not least because it did not require the Lila character to be revealed as a potty-mouthed sexual predator.

The plot outlines are the same. Man ends his prolonged bachelorhood with an unwise marriage, discovers on honeymoon (then to Florida, now to Mexico) that she has Big Problems. After she collapses with an ugly sunburn, he meets the real girl of his dreams on the beach, and they fall in love while he neglects to mention that he is married.

As Neil Simon and Elaine May knew, this is a good comic situation. As the Farrelly brothers do not know, there are certain kinds of scenes that are deal breakers, rupturing the fabric of comedy and becoming just simply, uncomfortably unpleasant. They have specialized in over-the-top transgressive comedy (*There's Something About Mary*), but always before with characters who could survive their sort of acid bath. Here the characters are made to do and say things that are outside their characters and maybe outside any characters.

Consider the question of the parents of the newlywed. Lila's mother (Kathy Lamkin) is revealed as a very overweight fatso, with the implication that Lila will eventually balloon to such a size. But what's so great about Eddie's father (Jerry Stiller), a vulgarian with an orange toupee, who sees women as throwaway commodities, advises his son to get all the sex he can, anywhere he can, and ends up in a Las Vegas hot tub with a blonde (Kayla Kleevage, yes, Kayla Kleevage) whose breasts are so big they bring the show to a halt the same way a three-legged woman might? There is also an example of a "Mexican Folklore Dance" that involves a donkey with unappetizing sexual equipment. The Farrellys' overkill breaks the fabric of their story.

There are small moments of real humor. The hair on the head of the first child of Eddie's best pal (Rob Corddry), for example. Lila's showdown between a deviated septum and a shrimp. The suspicions that Miranda's cousin (Danny McBride) has about Eddie. The way Eddie is vilified in the speeches after the wedding of a former girlfriend. More of that and less of peeing on poisonous jellyfish might have helped. But the film is a squirmy miscalculation of tone.

The Heart Is Deceitful Above All Things ★ ★

R, 98 m., 2006

Asia Argento (Sarah), Jimmy Bennett (Jeremiah [age seven]), Dylan and Cole Sprouse (Jeremiah [age eleven]), Peter Fonda (Grandfather), Ben Foster (Fleshy Boy), Ornella Muti (Grandmother), Kip Pardue (Luther), Michael Pitt (Buddy), Jeremy Renner (Emerson). Directed by Asia Argento and produced by Chris Hanley and Alain de la Mata. Screenplay by Argento and Alessandra Magania, based on short stories by J. T. LeRoy.

How should this movie be approached? As an exploitation of child abuse? As a fearless portrait of a childhood in hell? As an acting and filmmaking enterprise pushed to heroic extremes? *The Heart Is Deceitful Above All Things* is the unrelenting story of a little boy torn away from a loving foster home at the age of seven and subjected for years to a series of physical and psychological cruelties. There is no redemption, no surcease, and as the film ends, the barbarity continues. This film made me intensely uncomfortable, but that was its intention.

The material is drawn from short stories by J. T. LeRoy, whose work was widely considered to be autobiographical—the memories of an abused boy who grew up to become a prostitute and finally spilled out all his remembered pain in thinly disguised fiction. As it turns out, the fiction was more heavily disguised than its admirers realized: "J. T. LeRoy" now appears to be a forty-year-old woman named Laura Albert, and when "LeRoy" appeared in public he was played by Savannah Knoop, the half-sister of Albert's lover. With wigs, hats, and dark glasses, Knoop succeeded in playing a man by presenting LeRoy as a man willing to be seen as a woman. There is probably another movie here somewhere, maybe *Transamerica Meets James Frey.*

The stories were thought to be essentially truthful when Asia Argento adapted them and made this film, in which she stars as the boy's drug-abusing, mentally deranged mother. That they are fiction makes little difference to the film, since it would have been the same film either way, and we are relieved, not disappointed, that this childhood experience did not really exist. Such childhoods do exist, however, and we read from time to time of children taken from foster parents and returned to birth parents who mistreat or kill them.

The Heart Is Deceitful Above All Things opens with young Jeremiah (Jimmy Bennett), taken at seven from the home he loves and the people he considers his parents, and returned to the custody of his mother, Sarah (Argento). She shoves a toy rabbit in his face, promises him good times, throws a paper plate of SpaghettiOs in front of him, and tells him, "If my father had let me, you would have been flushed down some toilet."

Would social workers actually turn a child over to this mother? She dresses like a hooker because she is one. Jeremiah is sometimes in the same room as she services her tricks, and is introduced to a series of temporary daddies. Sarah "marries" one of them (Jeremy Renner), and when the newlyweds head to Atlantic City on their honeymoon, they lock the child in the house with instructions not to answer the phone. "There are cheese slices in the fridge," his mother says helpfully. The man returns alone ("She run out on me") and rapes the boy.

There are beatings all through the film, and more disturbing than any of them is a scene where the little boy thinks he has been bad and solemnly offers a belt to one of the men so that he can be beaten. There is a bizarre episode when he is collected from a shelter by his grandparents (Peter Fonda and Ornella Muti), who are sadistic fundamentalists. After a flash-forward, Jeremiah, now eleven and played by the twins Dylan and Cole Sprouse, is a sidewalk preacher in a little suit and tie. His mother finds him again and drags him back into her life, which for a time involves sharing the cab of a long-haul trucker. And on, and on, and on.

The cruelty of child abuse exists. It is a legitimate subject for a film. In this film, there is nothing else. The child is abused for ninety-eight minutes, and then the film is over. We know in theory that there are ways to edit around child actors so that they do not fully participate in scenes where they seem present, but what are we to make of a scene where the little boy is dressed and made up as a girl, and encouraged to approach one of Sarah's tricks? For young actors, there is not a clear distinction between performance and experience, and although I hope the child actors were not harmed in the making of the film, I feel no confidence that the experience left them untouched.

Objectively, looking at the film as an event and not as an experience, I feel admiration for Argento, who has not compromised the material or tried to force a happy ending, and is as merciless to Sarah as to Jeremiah. She is faithful to the horror in the original material. She does not exploit it in a way likely to please predators.

The Heart Is Deceitful evokes the reality of child abuse more closely than any other film I have seen. But, oh, what a sad and painful film this is, so despairing and merciless. If "J. T. LeRoy" had been real, we would wonder how he survived to write a book—to read and write at all. Yes, the human spirit is resilient, but this is not a film about resilience; it is a film about cruelty.

Many people, even adventurous filmgoers, will find the film unwatchable. Others may have the resources to place it in a context they can find useful. To be moved by pity and outrage is a given. To demand an upbeat ending or some kind of redemption or salvation is unrealistic; most lives like this end in early and cruel death. I cannot recommend the film, or dismiss it. My two-star rating represents a compromise between admiration and horror. You have read the review. You will decide to see the film, or turn away.

The Heart of the Game ★ ★ ★ ½

PG-13, 97 m., 2006

Featuring Bill Resler, Darnellia Russell, Devon Crosby Helms, Joyce Walker, April Russell, and Maude Lepley. Narrated by Chris "Ludacris" Bridges. A documentary directed by Ward Serrill and produced by Liz Manne and Serrill. Screenplay by Serrill.

How can she finish school, get basketball taken care of, and be a mommy?

—Talk-show caller

How can she not? *The Heart of the Game* tells the story of Darnellia Russell, a young woman who leads her Seattle high school basketball team to a state championship, graduates with honors, and is a mommy—despite the Washington Interscholastic Activities Association, which sues to prevent her from playing during her senior year. It is also the story of Bill Resler, a professor of tax law who looks like Santa Claus and coaches like a saint. "Have fun!" he says after every time-out.

The Heart of the Game, like *Hoop Dreams,* is a basketball documentary that began with no idea of where its story would lead. It begins in the classroom of Resler, a professor at the University of Washington, who hears that Roosevelt High School is looking for a new girls' basketball coach and applies for the job. A man in his fifties, he has three grown daughters and always followed their teams; now he gets to coach, although he keeps the day job and we get the impression that his coaching salary is little or nothing.

Resler's coaching philosophy is simple: "A full-court press the whole game. No offensive strategy, just run like hell." He runs his first team up and down the court until they drop, but he turns Roosevelt's Roughriders around and they start winning. "You can't defend against them," an opponent complains, "because even they don't know what they're going to do next."

Resler recruits Darnellia Russell, a middle-school star across town, for Roosevelt. It's a middle-class school with a majority of white students; her closest high school, Garfield, is mostly black. Russell's mother, April, thinks her child will "do better" at Roosevelt.

At first, she doesn't. She skips practices, and her grades are bad; the film's narrator (Ludacris) tells us she is "intimidated by how to be around so many white people." Resler works with her, encourages her studies, tells her he'll throw her off the team if she isn't at practice on time. "What I know," he says, "is that Darnellia is brilliant. The one issue she has to conquer is believing in how smart she is."

Resler names each of his Roughrider teams. We live through the seasons of the Pack of Wolves, the Tropical Storm, the Pride of Lions. He takes them to state finals during Russell's sophomore and junior years; then she gets pregnant by the boy she's been dating since ninth grade. She drops out to have the baby. Her mother and grandmother support her, and she applies to return for a senior year. That's when the WIAA steps in and sues to prevent her from playing again, threatening the Roughriders with forfeiting every game. The team votes to play anyway.

It's here that the film's politics become fascinating. The interscholastic association's bylaws allow exceptions in the cases of "hardships," but the WIAA says pregnancy is not a hardship: "She made her own choice." Callers to local talk shows argue against her; I quote one at the top of this review. But Seattle lawyer Kenyon E. Luce volunteers to represent Russell in court and wins. The WIAA appeals. His argument is that since male players are not punished when they're responsible for a pregnancy, it is discriminatory to penalize a pregnant woman.

Consider the WIAA argument: "She made her own choice." Yes, she did. She chose to have her baby. If she had chosen to have an abortion, she could have played next season, no questions asked. It is here that the values of the talk-show callers get confused. They apparently believe

Russell should have the baby but be penalized for having it. Yes, abstinence is also a choice, but tell that to a weeping teenage girl locked in the bathroom with a drugstore pregnancy test.

Russell's final season combines the legal court battle with a cross-town rivalry; its traditional archenemy, Garfield, is now coached by women's basketball legend Joyce Walker. Garfield has a tall team; Russell is 5-7, and Resler lists all of his starters as "guards." Director Ward Serrill, who has been following Resler since the day he took the job, is allowed into practice sessions and halftime locker rooms, but not into the "inner circle," a meeting of the team members themselves, with no one else present—including Resler.

"Look in their eyes!" Resler screams from the sidelines, a reminder that lions are the only animal that will return man's gaze. Is he obsessed with winning? There are more important things. Since the whole team voted to risk forfeiting their season, he decides that every single team member will play in the state championship game, no matter the score.

Sports movies have a purity of form. They always end with the big game, in triumph or heartbreak. So does *The Heart of the Game,* although the lawsuit still hangs over the team after the final free throw. By then we have come to have real respect for Russell's determination: Her grades improve so much she's on the honor roll, her baby is getting lots of mothering, fathering, grandmothering, and great-grandmothering, and she is voted player of the year.

Only later do questions occur. Resler casually mentions getting married in Alaska. It apparently is a second marriage, but we never meet his wife, and he never talks about her. When your husband is a university professor and takes on a second job that is arguably full time, does that cause problems? And although we see Russell's boyfriend several times, we never hear from him, nor does her mother talk directly about Russell's pregnancy. There are other stories stirring below the surface.

But perhaps by focusing on basketball itself, on the game and the legal and moral issue of Darnellia's pregnancy, the movie has enough to contend with. *The Heart of the Game* has the potential, like *Hoop Dreams,* to win a large audience. And Russell, like William Gates and Arthur Agee in that film, has the potential to use basketball as a way to graduate from college and have a better life.

Heights ★ ★ ★

R, 93 m., 2005

Glenn Close (Diana), Elizabeth Banks (Isabel), James Marsden (Jonathan), Jesse Bradford (Alec), Eric Bogosian (Henry), John Light (Peter), Andrew Howard (Ian), George Segal (Rabbi Mendel). Directed by Chris Terrio and produced by Ismail Merchant and Richard Hawley. Screenplay by Amy Fox, based on her stage play.

The most thankless task in Shakespeare may not be playing Lady Macbeth, but playing an actress who is playing Lady Macbeth. She can't even name the play she's in, referring instead to "the Scottish play," so that most people think they missed the first half of her sentence, while the rest of us reflect on what a long time has passed since we learned why she says that. In *Heights,* Glenn Close plays Diana, the actress who is playing Lady Macbeth and interrupts a rehearsal to declare, "We have forgotten passion." Yes, but in this movie they'll remember it soon enough.

The film is one of those interlocking dramas where all of the characters are involved in one another's lives, if only they knew it. We know, and one of our pleasures is waiting for the pennies to drop. Diana is the mother of Isabel (Elizabeth Banks), a photographer who is engaged to Jonathan (James Marsden). Meanwhile, Jonathan has been contacted by Peter (John Light), who is interviewing the subjects of a British photo exhibition in which a photograph of Jonathan suggests that Isabel should think twice, or three times, before marrying him.

At an audition, Diana meets Alec (Jesse Bradford), a young actor. He leaves his jacket behind. Diana discovers that Alex lives in the same building as Isabel and Jonathan, and gives the jacket to her daughter to return to the actor. The astonishing thing about this is that an unemployed actor could afford to live in the same building as two well-employed people who are sharing the rent.

Diana's husband is having an affair with a young actress, which Diana pretends to accept, while meanwhile she seems to audition young lovers everywhere she goes; she doesn't want to sleep with them so much as see if she's still famous enough that they think they have to sleep with her. Other characters include George Segal as a rabbi who is counseling the Jewish Jonathan and the Christian Isabel before their marriage; his experiment with flash cards is not successful.

That the threads of all of these lives intersect in about twenty-four hours is the movie's reality. That they are interesting is the movie's success. There is a sense in which this movie could simply play as a puzzle, but the acting is good enough to carry the contrivance. Glenn Close, hovering over the characters like a malevolent succubus, is wonderful here; her character must have had to dial down to play Lady Macbeth.

Much in the plot depends on the discovery of a secret that is not much of a secret to us at any point during the film. Oddly enough, that's not a problem, since the drama is based not on our surprise, but on the reaction of characters in the film. Suspecting, and then knowing, what they do not suspect and do not want to know allows us a kind of superiority that is one of the pleasures of being in the audience. After everything has been revealed, we do have a question, though: Why exactly did the character with a secret make the choices that are made? What would be proven? What would be accomplished? How would happiness come that way?

Apart from the movie's mysteries and revelations, its chief pleasure comes through simple voyeurism. It is entertaining to see the lives of complex people become brutally simple all of a sudden. They build elaborate facades of belief and image, they think they know who they are and what people think of them, and suddenly they're back at the beginning. That can be a disaster, or a relief. We start with nothing, we slowly construct this person we call ourselves, and eventually we live inside that person and it is too late to bring in another architect. Idea for a movie: A character takes a year's leave of absence from his life in order to go where he is unknown, and experience the adventure of starting from scratch.

But I digress. Let me just say that another of the movie's pleasures is the way it introduces characters for brief scenes in which it's suggested that another movie could be made by following them out of this one. One of those characters is Ian (Andrew Howard), a Welsh artist whom Isabel meets, and whose life takes a sudden turn. One of the other pleasures of narrative is when elaborate fictional scenes are built up, only to be smacked down.

Heights is not a great movie, and makes no great point, unless it is "To thine own self be true." But director Chris Terrio, working from a screenplay by Amy Fox (based on her play), sees the characters clearly and watches them with accuracy as they occupy their delusions, or lose them. The movie is one of the last produced by Ismail Merchant, who as always was attracted to stories and characters, not to genres, concepts, or marketing plans.

Hellboy II: The Golden Army ★ ★ ★ ½

PG-13, 120 m., 2008

Ron Perlman (Hellboy), Selma Blair (Liz Sherman), Doug Jones (Abe Sapien), Jeffrey Tambor (Tom Manning), Luke Gross (Prince Nuada), John Hurt (Trevor Bruttenholm), Seth McFarlane (Johann Kraus [voice]), Anna Walton (Princess Nuala). Directed by Guillermo del Toro and produced by Lawrence Gordon, Mike Richardson, and Lloyd Levin. Screenplay by del Toro, based on the comic book by Mike Mignola.

Imagine the forges of hell crossed with the extraterrestrial saloon on Tatooine and you have a notion of Guillermo del Toro's *Hellboy II: The Golden Army.* In every way the equal of his original *Hellboy* (2004), although perhaps a little noisier, it's another celebration of his love for bizarre fantasy and diabolical machines. The sequel bypasses the details of Hellboy's origin story but adds a legend read to him as a child by his adoptive father (John Hurt), in which we learn of an ancient warfare between humans and, well, everybody else: trolls, monsters, goblins, the Tooth Fairy, everybody.

There was a truce. The humans got the cities and the trolls got the forests. But humans have cheated on our end of the deal by building parking lots and shopping malls, and now Prince Nuada (Luke Gross) defies his father, the king, and hopes to start the conflict again. This would involve awakening the Golden Army: seventy times seventy slumbering mechanical warriors. Standing against this decision is his twin sister, Princess Nuala (Anna Walton).

And so on. I had best not get bogged down in plot description, except to add that Hellboy (Ron Perlman) and his sidekicks fight for the human side. His comrades include Abe Sapien (Doug Jones), sort of a fish-man, the fire-generating Liz Sherman (Selma Blair), a Teutonic adviser named Johann Kraus (Seth McFarlane), and of course Princess Nuala. Tom Manning (Jeffrey Tambor) from the secret center for extrasensory perception tags along but isn't much help except for adding irrelevancies and flippant asides.

Now that we have most of the characters onstage, let me describe the sights, which are almost all created by CGI of course, but how else? There's a climactic showdown between Hellboy and the prince, with the Golden Army standing dormant in what looks like the engine room of hell. Enormous interlocking gears grind against each other for no apparent purpose, except to chew up Hellboy or anything else that falls into them. Lucky they aren't perfectly calibrated.

There are also titanic battles in the streets of Manhattan, involving gigantic octo-creatures and so on, but you know what? Although they're well done, titanic battles in the streets of Manhattan are becoming commonplace in the movies these days. What was fascinating to me was what the octo-creature transformed itself into, which was unexpected and really lovely. You'll see.

The towering creatures fascinated me less, however, than some smaller ones. For example, swarms of tens of thousands of calcium-eaters, who devour humans both skin and bone and are the source of the Tooth Fairy legend. They pour out of the walls of an auction house and attack the heroes, and in my personal opinion Hellboy is wasting his time trying to shoot them one at a time.

I also admired the creativity that went into the Troll Market (it has a secret entry under the Brooklyn Bridge). Here I think del Toro actually was inspired by the Tatooine saloon in *Star Wars,* and brings together creatures of fantastical shapes and sizes, buying and selling goods of comparable shapes and sizes. It would be worth having the DVD just to study the market a frame at a time, discovering what secrets he may have hidden in there. The movies only rarely give us a genuinely new kind of place to look at; this will become a classic.

There are, come to think of it, other whispers of the *Star Wars* influence in *Hellboy II.* Princess Nuala doesn't have Princess Leia's rope of hair (just ordinary long blond tresses), but she's not a million miles distant from her. And Abe Sapien looks, moves, and sort of sounds so much like C3PO that you'd swear the robot became flesh and developed gills. I also noticed hints of John Williams's *Star Wars* score in the score by Danny Elfman, especially during the final battle. Not a plundering job, you understand, more of an evocation of mood.

What else? Two love stories, which I'll leave for you to find out about. And the duet performance of a song that is rather unexpected, to say the least. And once again a strong performance by Ron Perlman as Hellboy. Yes, he's CGI for the most part, but his face and voice and movements inhabit the screen figure, and make him one of the great comic heroes. Del Toro, who preceded *Hellboy II* with *Pan's Labyrinth* (2006) and the underrated *Blade II* (2002) is warming up now for *Doctor Strange* and *The Hobbit.* He has an endlessly inventive imagination and understands how legends work, why they entertain us, and that they sometimes stand for something. For love, for example.

Herbie: Fully Loaded ★ ★

G, 101 m., 2005

Lindsay Lohan (Maggie Peyton), Justin Long (Kevin), Breckin Meyer (Ray Peyton Jr.), Matt Dillon (Trip Murphy), Michael Keaton (Ray Peyton Sr.), Cheryl Hines (Sally). Directed by Angela Robinson and produced by Robert Simonds. Screenplay by Thomas Lennon, Ben Garant, Alfred Gough, and Miles Millar.

The question that haunted me during *Herbie: Fully Loaded* involved the degree of Herbie's intelligence. Is the car alive? Can it think? Does it have feelings? Can it really fall in love, or is its romance with that cute little yellow VW Bug just a cynical ploy to get publicity, since it has a new movie coming out?

To the dim degree that I recall the premise of the earlier *Herbie* movies, none of which I seem to have reviewed or indeed seen, Herbie was essentially just a car. A car with a personality, a car that feelings and emotions could be projected upon, a car that sometimes seemed to have a mind of its own, but nevertheless a car existing in the world as we know it. In *Herbie: Fully Loaded,* Herbie can blink his headlights and roll them from side to side, he can let his front bumper droop when he's depressed, and he can suddenly open his doors to cause trouble for people he doesn't like.

I see I have subconsciously stopped calling Herbie "it" and am now calling Herbie "he." Maybe I've answered my own question. If Herbie is alive, or able to seem alive, isn't this an astonishing breakthrough in the realm of artificial intelligence? That's if computer scientists, working secretly, programmed Herbie to act the way he does. On the other hand, if Herbie just sort of became Herbie on his own, then that would be the best argument yet for intelligent design.

Either way, a thinking car is a big story. It is an incredible, amazing thing. In *Herbie: Fully Loaded,* Herbie becomes the possession of a young woman named Maggie (Lindsay Lohan), who is the daughter of a famous racing family headed by her dad, Ray (Michael Keaton). The family dynasty falls on hard times after her brother Ray Jr. (Breckin Meyer) gets caught in a slump. She rescues Herbie from a junkyard, a friendly mechanic (Justin Long) rebuilds the car, and then Herbie offends the sensibilities of a hotshot racing champion (Matt Dillon). The champ challenges Herbie and Maggie, the Bug is entered in a NASCAR race, and I would not dream of telling you who wins.

The movie is pretty cornball. Little kids would probably enjoy it, but their older brothers and sisters will be rolling their eyes, and their parents will be using their iPods. The story is formula from beginning to end: the plucky girl and her plucky car, both disregarded by the dominant male culture, but gritting their teeth, or radiators, for a chance to prove themselves. The ineffectual dad. The teeth-gnashing villain. The racing footage. There is a moment when Herbie narrowly escapes being crushed into scrap metal in the junkyard, and his escape is sort of ingenious, but for the most part, this movie, like Herbie, seems to have been assembled from spare parts.

But let's rewind a little. *Herbie: Fully Loaded* opens with a montage of headlines and TV coverage from Herbie's original burst of fame, as chronicled in three earlier movies. That leads me to wonder (a) why Herbie ended up in a junkyard, when such a famous car should obviously be in a classic automobile museum in Las Vegas, and (b) why, when Maggie appears with the rebuilt and customized Herbie, no one in the racing media realizes this is the same car.

Never mind. The real story is Herbie's intelligence. The car seems to be self-aware, able to make decisions on its own, and able to communicate with Maggie on an emotional level, and sometimes with pantomime or example. Why then is everyone, including Lohan, so fixated on how fast the car can go? The car could be up on blocks and be just as astonishing.

It goes to show you how we in the press so often miss the big stories that are right under our noses. There is a famous journalistic legend about the time a young reporter covered the Johnstown flood of 1889. The kid wrote: "God sat on a hillside overlooking Johnstown today and looked at the destruction He had wrought." His editor cabled back: "Forget flood. Interview God."

Her Majesty ★ ★ ½

PG, 105 m., 2005

Sally Andrews (Elizabeth Wakefield), Vicky Haughton (Hira Mata), Liddy Holloway (Virginia Hobson), Mark Clare (John Wakefield), Craig Elliott (Stuart Wakefield), Alison Routledge (Victoria Wakefield), Anna Sheridan (Annabel Leach). Directed by Mark J. Gordon and produced by Walter Coblenz. Screenplay by Gordon.

Her Majesty has all the makings of a perfectly charming family picture, and then the plot runs off the rails. At some point during the writing process, a clearheaded realist should have stepped in and restored sanity. This hypothetical person would have realized (1) that the heroine's brother is not just a nasty young boy, but a psychopath, (2) that it is not necessary for the rhododendron lady to be having an affair with the mayor in order to be reprehensible, and (3) it is not very likely that Queen Elizabeth, on a state visit to New Zealand, would go out of her way to visit the village of Middleton and call on an old Maori lady in order to return a spear stolen from her grandfather.

I realize it is (3) where I'm asking for trouble. The notes for the movie say it is "inspired by real events." I learn that Queen Elizabeth did indeed visit New Zealand in 1953, and even the hamlet of Cambridge, which plays Middleton in the film. Now I will no doubt be informed that she also tracked down the old Maori woman on the porch of her humble shack and gave her the spear. In that case, the scene in question will not be inaccurate, but merely unbelievable.

Her Majesty is the kind of movie where you start out smiling, and then smile more broadly, and then really smile, and then realize with a sinking heart that the filmmakers are losing it. It stars a sunny-faced twelve-year-old named Sally Andrews as Elizabeth Wakefield, who is obsessed with the young Queen Elizabeth. A panning shot across her bedroom reveals enough QEII mementoes to bring a fortune on eBay. When she learns that the queen plans to visit her subjects in New Zealand, Elizabeth (the heroine, not the II) writes her more than fifty letters, suggesting Middleton as a destination. Apparently they work.

Elizabeth the Heroine has meanwhile made fast friends with Hira Mata (Vicky Haughton), the old Maori woman whose unpainted shack is an eyesore on the road into town. Hira takes Elizabeth the Heroine to a mountaintop and shows her that all she surveys—and land, the sea, and the sky—once belonged to the Maori, but now all that is left is her little patch of land. She reveals that Elizabeth II's ancestor once gave her grandfather a brace of dueling pistols in admiration of his bravery but that two weeks later her grandfather was murdered and the pistols and his spear were stolen.

The pistols turn up as a family heirloom of the loathsome Mrs. Hobson (Liddy Holloway), busybody and head of the Rhododendron Trust, who plans to present them to the queen during her inspection, of course, of the rhododendrons. This Hobson creature is a powdery-faced screecher whose sex life with the mayor involves unspeakable games based on beekeeping. She is insufferable, but consider Elizabeth the H's brother, Stuart (Craig Elliott), who, if he survives his adolescence, has a good chance of developing into New Zealand's most alarming criminal case study.

Stuart throws a brick through the Maori woman's window. He steals his sister's QEII collection and burns it. He gets fired for laziness and lies about it. He sneaks out to the Maori woman's house, douses it with gasoline, and prepares to burn it down, which is not a youthful prank but a crime for which I would throw the little bastard behind bars. And he locks up Elizabeth the H on the day when Elizabeth II is coming to town.

This is going too far. Stuart's depredations break through the veneer of small-town comedy and turn into some kind of sick weirdness. Elizabeth the H keeps smiling, preserves her pluck, and dutifully rehearses with the girls' drill team, and we would like to relax and smile with her and wish her the best, but we are distracted by the vile little desperado and his band of degenerate buddies.

I agree with the Maori woman that the land was her tribe's and was taken from them. I agree that treatment of the Maoris was a crime against humanity. I have seen *Rabbit-Proof Fence*, which is about the treatment of aboriginal orphans in Australia as recently as 1970. That a neighboring commonwealth nation engaged in such practices until 1970 argues that in 1953, Queen Elizabeth was not rummaging through the attic at Buckingham Palace looking for a Maori spear her relative might have stolen, so that she could return it to the friend of the nice young woman who has been writing her from Middleton. It's a feel-good scene for white viewers, but Maoris may view it a little more ironically.

There is a sense in which all of my logic is wasted. *Her Majesty*, directed by Mark J. Gordon, will work perfectly well for its intended audience of girls about Elizabeth the H's age, which is twelve; they will like her pluck and spirit, and won't ask themselves if her brother is a little over the top, since at that age they consider most brothers to be monsters. I do not want to discourage this audience, because entertaining family movies are hard enough to find, and maybe only a curmudgeon like me would ask the questions that distract me.

There's another movie from Down Under that is also about a small town and an important visit. That would be *The Dish* (2001), about a little Australian town where a radio telescope has been installed that will track man's first moon landing. The U.S. ambassador and the

Australian prime minister are scheduled to visit, and when things go very wrong, the way in which they are made to seem right is hilarious and inspired. I thought of *The Dish,* which found the perfect notes, and regretted that *Her Majesty,* which has all the right ingredients for its story, also has so many wrong ones.

Hide and Seek ★ ★

R, 100 m., 2005

Robert De Niro (Dr. David Callaway), Dakota Fanning (Emily Callaway), Famke Janssen (Dr. Katherine Carson), Elisabeth Shue (Elizabeth Young), Amy Irving (Alison Callaway), Dylan Baker (Sheriff Hafferty). Directed by John Polson and produced by Barry Josephson. Screenplay by Ari Schlossberg.

A small girl is haunted by fears after her mother's suicide. Her father, a psychiatrist, feels powerless to console her and thinks perhaps if they move out of the apartment where the death took place, that might help. Since John Polson's *Hide and Seek* is a thriller, he finds the ideal new home: a vast summer home, with lots of attics and basements and crannies and staircases, on a lakeside that must be jolly enough in the summertime but is deserted now, in the wintertime. All except for some friendly but peculiar neighbors.

This is a setup for a typical horror film, but for the first hour, at least, *Hide and Seek* feels more like M. Night Shyamalan and less like formula. Robert De Niro and Dakota Fanning, as Dr. David Callaway, the father, and Emily, his preadolescent daughter, create characters that seem, within the extremes of their situation, convincing and sympathetic. De Niro's Dr. David Callaway is a patient and reasonable man, who treats his daughter with kindness, but there's something else going on . . .

Consider, for example, the night when Callaway brings home a neighbor woman, Elizabeth (Elisabeth Shue), for dinner. "Did Daddy tell you that my mommy died?" little Emily asks, volunteering: "She killed herself in our bathtub. Slit her wrists with a razor." Callaway gently tells his daughter he doesn't think their guest needs to hear that right now, at dinner, but there is a way Emily has of staring out of her big round eyes and seeming to look into darker spheres than the rest of us can see.

Then there is the matter of her imaginary friend, Charlie. Dr. Callaway knows kids have imaginary friends and that troubled kids often invent confidants to share their fears. He consults a colleague (Famke Janssen), who specializes in children, meets Emily, and agrees. But then strange things begin to happen. Callaway is awakened in the middle of the night and finds a bloody message written on the bathroom walls. Something unpleasant happens to the family cat. Either Emily is acting out, or . . . well, perhaps Charlie is not imaginary at all.

This possibility is enhanced by the presence in the cast of Dylan Baker as the local sheriff, a nosy type who carries the keys to all the summer homes on a big ring on his belt. Baker is so reliable playing clean-cut but creepy types that once, when I saw him in a simply likable role, I was caught off guard. Here he hangs around way too much and always seems about to ask a question and then decides not to. There is also some oddness going on with the neighbors.

Up until about that point, the movie has played convincingly, within the terms of its premise. Dakota Fanning does an accomplished job of making us wonder what she knows and what she imagines. When she produces those scary drawings, for example, of people dying, are they prescient? Troubled? Or just a form of release?

To find out the answer to these and other more unexpected questions, you will have to see the movie. I found the third act to be a disappointment. There was a point in the movie when suddenly everything clicked, and the Law of Economy of Characters began to apply. That is the law that says no actor is in a movie unless his character is necessary. A corollary is that if a minor actor is set up as a suspect, he's a decoy. I began to suspect I knew the answer to Emily's nightmares and the nature of her imaginary friend, and I was right.

I would have been content, however, if the movie had found a way to make its solution more psychologically probable, or at least less contrived. In the best Shyamalan movies, everything fits, and you can go back and see them again and understand how all the parts worked. With *Hide and Seek,* directed by Polson from a screenplay by Ari Schlossberg, you don't get that satisfaction. It's not technically true to say the movie cheats, but let's say it abandons the truth and depth of its earlier scenes.

At Sundance, I saw Rebecca Miller's *The Ballad of Jack and Rose,* also a movie where the mother is killed. Also a movie where the father and daughter live together in isolation, on the far side of an island. Also a movie where the father brings home a woman for dinner, and the daughter resents her role in her father's life. But the Miller picture is interested in the dramatic developments in the situation—in character, and how it forms in one situation and tries to adapt to another.

Hide and Seek is not really interested in its situation, except as a way to get to the horror ending. I like horror films, but I don't like to feel jerked around by them. They're best when they play straight and don't spring arbitrary surprises. At the beginning of *Hide and Seek,* I thought I was going to be interested in the characters all the way to the end, but then the plot went on autopilot. In a movie like *The Ballad of Jack and Rose,* the characters keep on living and learning and hurting and hungering, and there's no surprise at the end to let them off the hook.

High Tension ★

R, 91 m., 2005

Cecile De France (Marie), Maiwenn Le Besco (Alex), Philippe Nahon (The Killer), Franck Khalfoun (Jimmy), Andrei Finti (Alex's Father), Oana Pellea (Alex's Mother). Directed by Alexandre Aja and produced by Alexandre Arcady and Robert Benmussa. Screenplay by Aja and Gregory Levasseur.

The philosopher Thomas Hobbes tells us life can be "poor, nasty, brutish and short." So is this movie. Alexandre Aja's *High Tension* is a slasher film about a madman prowling a rural area of France, chopping, slicing, and crunching his way through, let's see, a body count of five or six people, including a small child that the film does not neglect to show crumpled and dead in a cornfield. That's what it's about, anyway, until we discover it actually consists of something else altogether, something I think is not possible, given our current understanding of the laws of physics.

The movie premiered at Toronto 2003 in a version that would clearly have received an NC-17 rating. It has been edited down to an R, perhaps the hardest R for violence the MPAA has ever awarded, and into the bargain Lions Gate has dubbed great parts of it into English. Not all: There are inexplicable sections where the characters swear in French, which is helpfully subtitled.

I had forgotten how much I hate dubbing, especially when it's done as badly as in *High Tension.* It's lip-flap on parade. The movie was originally shot in French, but for purposes of dubbing, one of the characters, Alex (Maiwenn Le Besco), has been given an American accent. As she and her friend Marie (Cecile De France) arrive at the country home of Alex's family, Alex warns her: "Their French is even worse than mine." Since the parents hardly speak except to scream bilingually, this is not a problem.

The story: Alex and Marie are driving out to a country weekend with Alex's parents. Alex seems normal, but Marie is one of those goofy sorts who wanders into a cornfield for no better reason than for Alex to follow her, shouting "Marie! Marie!" while the wind sighs on the sound track—a track that beavers away with Ominous Noises throughout the movie; is there a technical term like Ominoise?

The girls are followed into the deep, dark woods by a large man in blood-soaked coveralls, who drives a battered old truck that must have been purchased used from a 1940s French crime movie. We know he's up to no good the first time we see him. We know this because he drops a woman's severed head out the window of his truck.

At the isolated country home, Marie gets the guest room in the attic and goes out into the Ominoise night to have a smoke. There is a swing hanging from a tree limb, and she sways back and forth on it while she smokes, so that later we can get the standard thriller shot of the swing seat still swinging, but now suddenly empty. This is not because Marie has been shortened by the decapitator, but because she has gone back into the house. Soon it's lights out, although there is enough in the way of moonglow and night lights for us to see Marie masturbate, perhaps so that we can see if it makes her lose her mind or anything.

The killer (Philippe Nahon) breaks into the house, stomps around heavily, and slaughters everyone except Alex, whom he takes prisoner, and Marie, who hides under the bed—yes, *hides under the bed.* The killer lifts up the mattress to check, but looks under the wrong end. Uh-huh. Marie should then remain still as a church mouse until the killer leaves, but no, she follows him downstairs and eventually ends up locked in the back of the truck with the kidnapped and chained Alex.

From the point when Marie crawls out from under the bed and follows the killer downstairs, she persists in making one wrong decision after another and ignoring obvious opportunities to escape. Perhaps she feels her presence is needed for the movie to continue, a likely possibility as the list of living characters shrinks steadily. She does have wit enough to pick up a big kitchen knife, so that we can enjoy the slasher movie cliché where such knives make the noise of steel-against-steel all by themselves, just by existing, and without having to scrape against anything.

After the truck leaves the deserted house and stops at a gas station, Marie has another opportunity to get help but blows it. Reader, take my advice and never hang up on a 911 operator just because you get mad at him because he's so stupid he wants to know where you're calling from, especially not if the slasher has picked up an ax.

The rest of the movie you will have to see for yourself—or not, which would be my recommendation. I am tempted at this point to issue a Spoiler Warning and engage in discussion of several crucial events in the movie that would seem to be physically, logically, and dramatically impossible, but clever viewers will be able to see for themselves that the movie's plot has a hole that is not only large enough to drive a truck through, but in fact does have a truck driven right through it.

Note: The film's British title is Switchblade Romance, *which, if you see the film, will seem curiouser and curiouser.*

The Hills Have Eyes ★ ½

R, 107 m., 2006

Aaron Stanford (Doug Bukowski), Kathleen Quinlan (Ethel Carter), Vinessa Shaw (Lynn Bukowski), Emilie de Ravin (Brenda Carter), Dan Byrd (Bobby Carter), Tom Bower (Gas Station Attendant), Ted Levine (Bob Carter). Directed by Alexandre Aja and produced by Wes Craven, Marianne Maddalena, and Peter Locke. Screenplay by Aja and Gregory Levasseur, based on the screenplay by Craven.

It always begins with the Wrong Gas Station. In real life, as I pointed out in my review of a previous Wrong Gas Station movie, most gas stations are clean, well-lighted places where you can buy not only gasoline but also groceries, clothes, electronic devices, Jeff Foxworthy CDs, and a full line of Harley merchandise. In horror movies, however, the only gas station in the world is located on a desolate road in a godforsaken backwater. It is staffed by a degenerate who shuffles out in his coveralls and runs through a disgusting repertory of scratchings, spittings, chewings, twitchings, and leerings, while thoughtfully shifting mucus up and down his throat.

The clean-cut heroes of the movie, be they a family on vacation, newlyweds, college students, or backpackers, all have one thing in common. They believe everything this man tells them, especially when he suggests they turn left on the unpaved road for a shortcut. Does it ever occur to them that in this desolate wasteland with only one main road, it *must* be the road to stay on if they ever again want to use their cell phones?

No. It does not. They take the fatal detour and find themselves the prey of demented mutant incestuous cannibalistic gnashing slobberers, who carry pickaxes the way other people carry umbrellas. They occupy junkyards, towns made entirely of wax, nuclear waste zones, and Motel Hell ("It takes all kinds of critters to make Farmer Vincent's fritters"). That is the destiny that befalls a vacationing family in *The Hills Have Eyes,* which is a very loose remake of the 1977 movie of the same name.

The Carter family is on vacation. Dad (Ted Levine) is a retired detective who plans to become a security guard. Mom is sane, lovable Kathleen Quinlan. A daughter and son-in-law (Vinessa Shaw and Aaron Stanford) have a newborn babe. There are also two other Carter children (Dan Byrd and Emilie de Ravin), and two dogs named Beauty and Beast. They have hitched up an Airstream and are on a jolly family vacation through the test zones where 331 atmospheric nuclear tests took place in the 1950s and 1960s.

After the Carters turn down the wrong road, they're fair game for the people who are the eyes of the hills. These are descendants of miners who refused to leave their homes when the government ordered them away from the testing grounds. They hid in mines, drank radioactive water, reproduced with their damaged DNA, and brought forth mutants who live by eating trapped tourists.

There is an old bomb crater filled with the abandoned cars and trucks of their countless victims. It is curiously touching, in the middle of this polluted wasteland, to see a car that was towing a boat that still has its outboard motor attached. No one has explained what the boat was seeking at that altitude.

The plot is easily guessed. Ominous events occur. The family makes the fatal mistake of splitting up; Dad walks back to the Wrong Gas Station, while the dogs bark like crazy and run away, and young Bobby chases them into the hills. Meanwhile, the mutants entertain themselves by passing in front of the camera so quickly you can't really see them, while we hear a loud sound, halfway between a *swatch* and a *swootch,* on the sound track. Just as a knife in a slasher movie can make a sharpening sound just because it exists, so do mutants make *swatches* and *swootches* when they run in front of cameras.

I received some appalled feedback when I praised Rob Zombie's *The Devil's Rejects* (2005), but I admired two things about it: (1) It desired to entertain and not merely to sicken, and (2) its depraved killers were individuals with personalities, histories, and motives. *The Hills Have Eyes* finds an intriguing setting in "typical" fake towns built by the government, populated by mannequins, and intended to be destroyed by nuclear blasts. But its mutants are simply engines of destruction. There is a misshapen creature who coordinates attacks with a walkie-talkie; I would have liked to know more about him, but no luck.

Nobody in this movie has ever seen a Dead Teenager Movie, so they don't know (1) you never go off alone, (2) you especially never go off alone at night, and (3) you never follow your dog when it races off barking insanely, because you have more sense than the dog. It is also possibly not a good idea to walk back to the Wrong Gas Station to get help from the degenerate who sent you on the detour in the first place.

It is not faulty logic that derails *The Hills Have Eyes,* however, but faulty drama. The movie is a one-trick pony. We have the eaters and the eatees, and they will follow their destinies until some kind of desperate denouement, possibly followed by a final shot showing that It's Not Really Over, and there will be a *The Hills Have Eyes II.* Of course, there was already a *The Hills Have Eyes Part II* (1985), but then again there was a *The Hills Have Eyes* (1977) and that didn't stop them. Maybe this will. Isn't it pretty to think so.

A History of Violence ★ ★ ★ ½

R, 96 m., 2005

Viggo Mortensen (Tom Stall), Maria Bello (Edie Stall), Ed Harris (Carl Fogarty), William Hurt (Richie Cusack), Ashton Holmes (Jack Stall), Stephen McHattie (Leland Jones), Greg Bryk (Billy Orser), Heidi Hayes (Sarah Stall). Directed by David Cronenberg and produced by Cronenberg, Chris Bender, and J. C. Spink. Screenplay by Josh Olson, based on a graphic novel by John Wagner and Vince Locke.

David Cronenberg says his title *A History of Violence* has three levels: It refers (1) to a suspect with a long history of violence, (2) to the historical use of violence as a means of settling disputes, and (3) to the innate violence of Darwinian evolution, in which better-adapted organisms replace those less able to cope. "I am a complete Darwinian," says Cronenberg, whose new film is in many ways about the survival of the fittest—at all costs.

The movie opens in a small Indiana town. Tom Stall (Viggo Mortensen) runs one of those friendly little diners that act as the village crossroads and clearinghouse. He's the kind of guy everybody likes, married to a lawyer named Edie (Maria Bello), father of the teenager Jack (Ashton Holmes) and young Sarah (Heidi Hayes). He has one of those middle American accents in which every word translates into "I'm just folks."

So persuasive are the Indiana scenes that, despite the movie's opening moments, we wonder if Cronenberg has abandoned his own history of violence and decided to make a small-town slice of life: a Capra picture, perhaps, with Viggo Mortensen as Jimmy Stewart. Then all hell breaks loose. Two tough guys enter the diner to try a stickup. They have guns, mean business, threaten the customers and a waitress. Moving so quickly he seems to have been practicing the scene as choreography, Tom Stall takes out the two guys and ends up on the local front pages as a hero.

He makes a shy hero. He doesn't want to give interviews or talk about what he has done, and there are strained moments in his household as his wife worries about a seismic shift in his mood, and his son can't understand an unstated change in their relationship. Read no farther if you want to preserve the reasons for these changes.

Tom Stall, as it turns out, has a secret he has been guarding for twenty years. He is named not Tom Stall but Joey, is not from Indiana but from Philadelphia, has tried to start a new life in a small town and failed because of this unexpected publicity. Soon more strangers arrive in town: Carl Fogarty (Ed Harris) turns up with two hard men in his employ. Something really bad has happened to Carl earlier in life, and we don't want to know how his face got that way.

Tom Stall has transformed himself so completely into a small-town family man that maybe there were years when he believed the story himself. The arrival of Fogarty makes that illusion impossible to sustain, and he must return to Philadelphia and to an extraordinary scene with a man named Richie Cusack (William Hurt), whose role in Tom's (or Joey's) life I will leave for you to discover. Let me say that Hurt has done a lot of good acting in a lot of intriguing roles, but during his brief screen time in *A History of Violence,* he sounds notes we have not heard before.

Another important element in the plot involves the Stall family, especially Edie, the wife, and Jack, the son. What do you do when you discover that your husband or father has concealed everything about his early life? Was he lying to you or protecting you? Did you love someone who did not really exist?

Cronenberg is a director with a wide range, usually played by the left hand. He has ventured into horror, the macabre, science fiction, satire, and the extremely peculiar. In his 2003 film *Spider,* he starred Ralph Fiennes as a mental patient in a halfway house whose reality balances between everyday details and haunting memories of his past. *Dead Ringers* (1988) has Jeremy Irons in a dual role as twins, one not so nice, the other not so nice either. *The Dead Zone* (1983) has Christopher Walken losing five years of his life and becoming a different kind of person. These shifts in personal reality seem fascinating to Cronenberg.

But what is Cronenberg saying about Tom, or Joey? Which life is the real one? The nature of Joey's early life was established by the world he was born into. His second life was created by conscious choice. Which is dominant, nature or nurture? Hyde or Jekyll? Are we kidding ourselves when we think we can live peacefully? Is our peace purchased at the price of violence done elsewhere? In *A History of Violence,* it all comes down to this: If Tom Stall had truly been the cheerful small-town guy he pretended to be, he would have died in that diner. It was Joey who saved him. And here is the crucial point: Because of Joey, the son, Jack, makes discoveries about himself that he might not have ever needed (or wanted) to make.

A History of Violence seems deceptively straightforward, coming from a director with Cronenberg's quirky complexity. But think again. This is a movie not about plot, but about character. It is about how people turn out the way they do, and about whether the world sometimes functions like a fool's paradise. I never give a moment's thought about finding water to drink. In New Orleans after Hurricane Katrina, would I have been willing to steal from stores or fight other people for drinkable water? Yes, if it meant life for myself and my family. But I would have made a pitiful thief and fighter, and probably would have failed.

Since I am wandering, let me wander farther: At the Toronto Film Festival I saw a screening of *Nanook of the North,* the great documentary about Eskimos surviving in the hostile Arctic wilderness. They live because they hunt and kill. Of the three levels *A History of Violence* refers to, I think Cronenberg is most interested in the third, in the survival of the fittest. Not the good, the moral, the nice, but the fittest. The movie is based on a graphic novel by John Wagner and Vince Locke. It could also be illuminated by *The Selfish Gene* by Richard Dawkins. I think that's why Cronenberg gives his hero a son: to show that Jack inherited what he did not ever suspect his father possessed.

Hitch ★ ★ ½

PG-13, 120 m., 2005

Will Smith (Hitch), Kevin James (Albert), Eva Mendes (Sara), Amber Valletta (Allegra), Michael Rapaport (Ben), Adam Arkin (Max). Directed by Andy Tennant and produced by James Lassiter, Will Smith, and Teddy Zee. Screenplay by Kevin Bisch.

"Ninety percent of what you're saying isn't coming out of your mouth."

So says the Date Doctor. You communicate with your body language, your posture, your mood, your attitude about yourself. Nothing a guy can say will impress a woman nearly as much as the nonverbal messages she receives. So stand up straight, Fat Albert, and stop slumping around as if your tummy can be hidden in the shadows.

Hitch is a romantic comedy, timed for Valentine's Day, starring Will Smith as Alex "Hitch" Hitchens, professional dating consultant. In the cutthroat world of New York romance, where fates are decided in an instant, your average Lonely Guy needs skilled counseling. Hitch is your man. He understands women: how to get their attention, how to seem heroic in their eyes, what to tell them, and what definitely not to tell them.

Some of his strategies would be right at home in a silent comedy, such as an opening Meet Cute in which a babe's beloved pet dog is apparently saved from instant death by a guy who wants to get to know her. Others are more subtle, involving inside intelligence so that you seem able to read her mind. Then there are the grand dramatic gestures.

For Hitch's client Albert (Kevin James), the romantic quarry seems forever beyond his reach. He is in love with the rich, powerful, and beautiful Allegra (Amber Valletta), and surely she would not date a shy and pudgy accountant—would she? But at a board meeting he is outraged by investment advice she is being given, and in a Grand Dramatic, etc., he resigns. That gets her attention. She's touched that the guy would care so much.

Yes, but how can Albert follow up? He's one of those guys whose shirts seem to come back from the laundry with the mustard already on them. Hitch works desperately to smooth him out, clean him up, and give him some class. Meanwhile, his own romantic life is in a shambles. He's fallen in love with a really hot babe who is also smart and cynical. This is Sara (Eva Mendes), who writes for a gossip column not a million miles apart from Page Six. None of his advice seems to work for Hitch, maybe because in the game of romantic chess, Sara can see more moves ahead, maybe because—can this be possible?—he is losing his cool by trying too hard.

Hitch, you will have perceived, is not a great cinematic breakthrough. It depends for its appeal on the performances, and gets a certain undeserved mileage because of the likability of Will Smith and Kevin James, who are both seen with sympathy. Allegra (Valletta) is a sweetheart, too, and not as unapproachable as she seems. But Sara is a real challenge, played by Eva Mendes as the kind of woman who seems more desirable the more she seems unattainable.

There is a purpose for a movie like *Hitch*, and that purpose is to supply a pleasant and undemanding romantic comedy that you can rent next Valentine's Day. It's not a first-run destination, especially with *Bride and Prejudice* and *The Wedding Date* playing in the same multiplex. It's not that I dislike it; it's that it just doesn't seem entirely necessary. The premise is intriguing, and for a time it seems that the Date Doctor may indeed know things about women that most men in the movies are not allowed to know, but the third act goes on autopilot just when the doctor should be in.

The Hitchhiker's Guide to the Galaxy ★ ★

PG, 110 m., 2005

Martin Freeman (Arthur Dent), Sam Rockwell (President Zaphod Beeblebrox), Mos Def (Ford Prefect), Zooey Deschanel (Trillian), Bill Nighy (Slartibartfast), Anna Chancellor (Questular Rontok), John Malkovich (Humma Kavula), Warwick Davis (Marvin the Paranoid Android), Alan Rickman (Marvin the Paranoid Android [voice]). Directed by Garth Jennings and produced by Gary Barber, Roger Birnbaum, Jonathan Glickman, Nick Goldsmith, and Jay Roach. Screenplay by Douglas Adams and Karey Kirkpatrick, based on the book by Adams.

It is possible that *The Hitchhiker's Guide to the Galaxy* should be reviewed by, and perhaps seen by, only people who are familiar with the original material to the point of obsession. My good friend Andy Ihnatko is such a person and considered the late Douglas Adams to be one of only three or four people worthy to be mentioned in the same breath as P. G. Wodehouse. Adams may in fact have been the only worthy person.

Such a Hitchhiker Master would be able to review this movie in terms of its in-jokes, its references to various generations of the Guide universe, its earlier manifestations as books, radio shows, a TV series, and the center of a matrix of Web sites. He would understand what the filmmakers have done with Adams's material, and how, and why, and whether the film is faithful to the spirit of the original.

I cannot address any of those issues, and I would rather plead ignorance than pretend to knowledge. If you're familiar with the Adams material, I suggest you stop reading right now before I disappoint or even anger you. All I can do is speak to others like myself, who will be arriving at the movie innocent of *Hitchhiker* knowledge. To such a person, two things are possible if you see the movie:

1. You will become intrigued by its whimsical and quirky sense of humor, understand that a familiarity with the books is necessary, read one or more of the *Hitchhiker* books, return to the movie, appreciate it more, and eventually be absorbed into the legion of Adams admirers.

2. You will find the movie tiresomely twee, and notice that it obviously thinks it is being funny at times when you do not have the slightest clue why that should be. You will sense a certain desperation as actors try to sustain a tone that belongs on the page and not on the screen. And you will hear dialogue that preserves the content of written humor at the cost of sounding as if the characters are holding a Douglas Adams reading.

I take the second choice. The movie does not inspire me to learn lots more about *The Hitchhiker's Guide to the Galaxy, The Ultimate Hitchhiker's Guide, The Salmon of Doubt,* and so on. Like *The Life Aquatic with Steve Zissou,* but with less visual charm, it is a conceit with little to be conceited about.

The story involves Arthur Dent (Martin Freeman), for whom one day there is bad news and good news. The bad news is that Earth is being destroyed to build an intergalactic freeway, which will run right through his house. The good news is that his best friend, Ford Prefect (Mos Def), is an alien temporarily visiting Earth to do research for a series of *Hitchhiker's Guides,* and can use his magic ring to beam both of them up to a vast spaceship operated by the Vogons, an alien race that looks like a cross between Jabba the Hutt and Harold Bloom. The Vogons are not a cruel race, apart from the fact that they insist on reading their poetry, which is so bad it has driven people to catatonia.

Once aboard this ship, Arthur and Ford are hitchhikers themselves, and quickly transfer to another ship named the *Heart of Gold,* commanded by the galaxy's president, Zaphod Beeblebrox (Sam Rockwell), who has a third arm that keeps emerging from his tunic like the concealed arm of a samurai warrior, with the proviso that a samurai conceals two arms at the most. Zaphod is two-faced in a most intriguing way. Also on the ship are Trillian (Zooey Deschanel), an earthling, and Marvin the Android (body by Warwick Davis, voice by Alan Rickman), who is a terminal kvetcher. There is also a role for John Malkovich, who has a human trunk and a lower body apparently made from spindly robotic cranes' legs; this makes him a wonder to behold, up to a point.

What these characters do is not as important as what they say, how they say it, and what it will mean to Douglas Adams fans. To me, it got old fairly quickly. The movie was more of a revue than a narrative, more about moments than an organizing purpose, and cute to the point that I yearned for some corrosive wit from its second cousin, the Monty Python universe. But of course I do not get the joke. I do not much want to get the joke, but maybe you will. It is not an evil movie. It wants only to be loved, but movies that want to be loved are like puppies in the pound: No matter how earnestly they wag their little tails, you can only adopt one at a time.

Hitman ★ ★ ★

R, 110 m., 2007

Timothy Olyphant (Agent 47), Dougray Scott (Mike Whittier), Olga Kurylenko (Nika), Robert Knepper (Yuri Marklov), Ulrich Thomsen (Mikhail Belicoff), Michael Offei (Jenkins). Directed by Xavier Gens and produced by

Pierre-Ange le Pogam, Charles Gordon, and Adrian Askarieh. Screenplay by Skip Woods.

This may only be my quirky way of thinking, but if you wanted to move through the world as an invisible hit man responsible for more than one hundred killings on six continents, would you shave your head to reveal the bar code tattooed on the back of your skull? Yeah, not me, either. But Agent 47 has great success with this disguise in *Hitman,* which is a better movie than I thought it might be.

Agent 47 (Timothy Olyphant) has no name because he was raised as an orphan from birth by a shadowy organization named the Agency, which is "known to all governments" and performs assassinations for hire. He was trained in all the killing skills and none of the human ones, which is why the young woman Nika (Olga Kurylenko) is such a challenge for him. A prostitute held in slavery by the drug-dealing brother of the Russian premier, she follows him, obeys him, offers herself to him, and although he remains distant, he cannot remain indifferent.

Agent 47 is in Russia on a job: assassinate Belicoff (Ulrich Thomsen), the premier. This he thinks he does. Yet Belicoff appears in public almost immediately after the hit, alive and speaking. How did this happen? An Interpol agent named Mike (Dougray Scott) is just as puzzled: "My man doesn't miss."

How it happens is not my business to tell you, but I will say that Agent 47 is betrayed by the Agency and finds himself being pursued by both Interpol and the Russian secret police. As he and Nika move from St. Petersburg to Moscow, there is one shoot-out after another, close escapes, daring leaps into the void, high-tech booby traps, and so on.

The movie, directed by Xavier Gens, was inspired by a best-selling video game and serves as an excellent illustration of my conviction that video games will never become an art form—never, at least, until they morph into something else or more.

What I found intriguing about the movie was the lonely self-sufficiency of Agent 47, his life without a boyhood, his lack of a proper name, his single-purpose training. When Nika comes into his life he is trained to guard against her, but he cannot because she is helpless, needy, depends on him, and is a victim like himself. So he takes her along with him (which only increases her danger) while not making love. You know what? I think he may be a virgin trained to make war, not love.

To the degree the movie explores their relationship, it is absorbing. There is also intrigue at the highest levels of Russian politics, as the moderate Belicoff is apparently targeted for death. All of that is well done. Other scenes involve Agent 47 striding down corridors, an automatic weapon in each hand, shooting down opponents who come dressed as Jedi troopers in black. These scenes are no doubt from the video game. The troopers spring into sight, pop up, and start shooting, and he has target practice. He also jumps out of windows without knowing where he's going to land, and that feels like he's cashing in a chip he won earlier in the game.

If you want to see what Agent 47 might have seemed like without the obligatory video game requirements, I urge you to rent Jean-Pierre Melville's *Le Samourai* (1967), which is about a lone-wolf assassin in Paris (Alain Delon). He, too, works alone, is a professional, cuts off his emotions, seems lonely and cold. But the movie is about him, not his killing score.

The key producer on *Hitman* was Adrian Askarieh, who told *Variety* he doesn't consult or collaborate with the makers of a video game he has purchased for filming, but instead focuses on the characters and situation. Wise. To the degree he doesn't try to reproduce the aim-and-shoot material, he has a movie here. To the degree Olyphant and Kurylenko can flesh out their characters, they do.

The movie is rated R, despite reports that the studio demanded edits to trim down the violence. It has a high body count, but very little blood and gore. I wish it had less. It's the people we care about in movies, not how many dead bodies they can stack up. *Hitman* stands right on the threshold between video game and art. On the wrong side of the threshold, but still, give it credit.

Honeydripper ★ ★ ★ ½

PG-13, 123 m., 2008

Danny Glover (Tyrone Purvis), Lisa Gay Hamilton (Delilah Purvis), Yaya DaCosta (China

Doll), Charles S. Dutton (Maceo Green), Gary Clark Jr. (Sonny Blake), Mable John (Bertha Mae Spivey), Vondie Curtis Hall (Slick), Stacy Keach (Sheriff Pugh). Directed by John Sayles and produced by Maggie Renzi. Screenplay by Sayles.

John Sayles's *Honeydripper* is set at the intersection of two movements that would change American life forever: the civil rights movement, and rhythm and blues. They may have more to do with each other than you might think, although that isn't his point. He's more concerned with spinning a ground-level human comedy than searching for pie in the sky. His movie is rich with characters and flowing with music.

The time, around 1950. The place, Harmony, Alabama. The chief location, the Honeydripper Lounge, which serves a good drink but is feeling the competition from a juke joint down the road. The proprietor, Pine Top Purvis (Danny Glover), is desperately in debt. The wife, Delilah (Lisa Gay Hamilton), is causing him some concern: Will she get religion and disapprove of his business? The best friend, Maceo (Charles S. Dutton), is a sounding board for his problems. The nightmare, the local sheriff (Stacy Keach), is a racist, but doesn't go overboard like most. Club characters: blues singer (Mable John) and her man (Vondie Curtis Hall).

Into Harmony one day comes a footloose young man named Sonny, played by Gary Clark Jr., in real life a rising guitar phenom. He drifts into the Honeydripper looking for a job or a meal and carrying something no one has ever seen before: a homemade electric guitar carved out of a solid block of wood. Pine Top has no work for him, and the youth is soon arrested by the sheriff (his crime: existing while unemployed) and put to work picking cotton for a crony.

Meanwhile, in desperation, Pine Top books the great Guitar Sam out of New Orleans and puts up posters all over town. Sure, he can't afford him, but the plan is, Guitar Sam will bring in enough business on one Saturday night to pay his own salary and also the lounge's worst bills. Pine Top finds out what real desperation is when Guitar Sam doesn't arrive on the train. He wonders if the kid with the funny guitar can play a little. After all, no one in Harmony knows what Guitar Sam really looks like.

Now all the pieces are in place for an unwinding of local race issues, personal issues, financial issues, and some very, very good music, poised just at that point when the blues were turning into rhythm and blues, which after all is what rock and roll is only an alias for. Because after all, yes, the kid can play a little. More than a little.

John Sayles has made nineteen films, and none of them is a two-character study. As the writer of his own work, he instinctively embraces the communities in which they take place. He's never met a man who was an island. Everyone connects, and when that includes black and white, rich and poor, young and old, there are lessons to be learned, and his generosity to his characters overflows into affection.

Danny Glover is well cast to stand at the center of this story. A tall, imposing, grave presence as Pine Top, he is not so much a music lover as a survivor. This is his last chance to save the Honeydripper and his means of making a living. And Gary Clark Jr. is the right man to be told: Tonight, you are Guitar Sam. He may be a prodigy, but he is broke, scared, young, and far from home. So this isn't one of those showbiz stories where a talent scout is in the audience, but a story where the audience looks at him with great suspicion until his music makes them smile.

As for the sheriff's role: As I suggested, lots of Alabama sheriffs were more racist than he is, which is not a character recommendation, but means that he isn't evil just to pass the time and would rather avoid trouble than work up a sweat. At that time, in that place, he was about the best you could hope for. Within a few more years, the Bull Connors would be run out of town, one man would have one vote, and the music of the African-American South would rule the world. That all had to start somewhere. It didn't start on Saturday night at the Honeydripper, but it didn't stop there, either.

The Honeymooners ★ ★ ★

PG-13, 85 m., 2005

Cedric the Entertainer (Ralph Kramden), Mike Epps (Ed Norton), Gabrielle Union (Alice

Kramden), Regina Hall (Trixie Norton), Eric Stoltz (William Davis), John Leguizamo (Dodge), Jon Polito (Kirby), Carol Woods (Alice's Mom), Anne Pitoniak (Miss Benvenuti). Directed by John Schultz and produced by Julie Durk, David T. Friendly, Eric Rhone, and Marc Turtletaub. Screenplay by Barry W. Blaustein, Danny Jacobson, Saladin K. Patterson, Don Rhymer, and David Sheffield.

The Honeymooners is a surprise and a delight, a movie that escapes the fate of weary TV retreads and creates characters that remember the originals, yes, but also stand on their own. Playing Ralph Kramden and Ed Norton, Cedric the Entertainer and Mike Epps don't even try to imitate Jackie Gleason and Art Carney; they borrow a few notes, just to show us they've seen the program, and build from there. And Gabrielle Union and Regina Hall, as Alice and Trixie, flower as the two long-suffering wives, who in this version get more story time and do not ever, even once, get offered a one-way ticket to the moon. Instead, Ralph even sweetly promises Alice he will "take her to the moon," although, to be sure, that's when he proposes marriage.

The externals of the movie resemble the broad outlines of the TV classic. The Kramdens live downstairs, the Nortons live upstairs, Ralph drives a bus, Ed is proud of his command of the sewer system's scenic routes. Ralph is a dreamer who falls for one get-rich-quick scheme after another, and the closet is filled with his failed dreams: the pet cactus, the Y2K survival kit. His wife, Alice, is the realist. All she wanted when she got married was to live in a home of their own. They're still renting.

Cedric the Entertainer is funny in the role, yes, but he's also sweet. He understands the underlying goodness and pathos of Ralph Kramden, who is all bluff. Mike Epps makes Norton into a sidekick like Sancho Panza, who realizes his friend is nutty, but can't bear to see him lose his illusions.

The plot: Alice and Trixie, who work as waitresses at a diner, meet a sweet little old lady (Anne Pitoniak) who wants to sell her duplex at a reasonable price. They're up against a wily real estate king (Eric Stoltz) who wants to turn the whole block into condos, but if they can come up with a $20,000 down payment, the house is theirs. That means $10,000 from the Kramdens, who have $5,000 in the bank; Alice thinks maybe she can borrow the rest from her mother (Carol Woods), a fearsome force of nature who served in Vietnam, was a Golden Gloves champ, and despises her son-in-law (her advice to Ralph on eating his dinner: "When you get to the plate, stop").

There is a problem with Alice's financial plan. The problem is that Ralph has spent all the money on a series of failed dreams. Desperate to raise cash, Ralph and Ed try hip-hop dancing in the park, at which they are very bad, and begging as blind men, at which they are worse. Then they find a greyhound dog in a trash bin, and decide to race it at the dog track.

Enter John Leguizamo as Dodge, a "trainer" recommended by the track's shady owner (Jon Polito). Leguizamo is optimistic ("I started with nothing and still have most of it left") and fancies himself a Dog Whisperer, but Izzy the dog doesn't seem to understand the principle behind racing, which is that he has to leave the gate and run around the track. Ralph, however, believes in the "homeless Dumpster dog," and in a big scene describes him as "a survivor . . . like Seabiscuit, Rocky, and Destiny's Child."

All of this is handled by the director John Schultz *(Like Mike)* with an easygoing confidence in the material. There's nothing frantic about the performances, nothing forced about the plot; the emphasis is on Ralph's underlying motive, which is to prove to Alice that he is not invariably a failure and can buy her a house one way or another. That was the secret of Gleason's *Honeymooners*—Ralph lost his temper and ranted and raved, but he had a good heart, and Alice knew it.

The supporting performances bring the movie one comic boost after another. Leguizamo's con-man dog trainer is an invention in flim-flammery, Polito's track owner is an opportunist, Stoltz finds just the right slick charm as the real estate sharpie, and Carol Woods is the mother-in-law Ralph Kramden deserves for his sins. Regina Hall and Gabrielle Union spend a lot of their scenes with each other, while the boys are out getting in trouble. They provide the engine that drives the movie's emotions: They want that house, they have a deadline to meet, and Ralph grows increasingly desperate because he doesn't want to let Alice down yet once again.

I was afraid Cedric the Entertainer and Mike Epps would try to imitate Gleason and Carney. Not at all. What they do is work a subtle tribute to the earlier actors into new inventions of their own. Cedric has that way of moving his neck around inside his collar that reminds us of Gleason, and the slow burn, and the wistful enthusiasm as he outlines plans that even he knows are doomed. Epps has the hat always hanging on at an angle, the pride in the sewer system, the willingness to go along with his goofy pal. And the movie's story actually does work as a story and not simply as a wheezy Hollywood formula. Sometimes you walk into a movie with quiet dread, and walk out with quiet delight.

Hoot ★ ½

PG, 105 m., 2006

Logan Lerman (Roy Eberhardt), Luke Wilson (Officer Delinko), Brie Larson (Beatrice Leep), Cody Linley (Mullet Fingers), Eric Phillips (Dana Matherson), Dean Collins (Garrett), Tim Blake Nelson (Curly Branitt). Directed by Wil Shriner and produced by Frank Marshall and Jimmy Buffett. Screenplay by Shriner, based on the novel by Carl Hiaasen.

Hoot has its heart in the right place, but I have been unable to locate its brain. Here is a movie about three kids who begin by disliking or fearing one another and end up as urban guerrillas, sabotaging the construction of a pancake house that will destroy a nesting ground for burrowing owls. Yes, there are such birds, who sublet burrows originally dug by squirrels and prairie dogs and such, or occasionally dig their own dream burrows. They seem wide-eyed with astonishment at their lifestyle, but actually that is just the way they look.

The hero of the movie is Roy Eberhardt (Logan Lerman), whom we meet on horseback in Montana, complaining that his family is moving again—this time to Florida. His dad has moved something like five times in eight years, which in the white-collar world means you are either incompetent or the CEO. In his new school, Roy is picked on by a bully and breaks the bully's nose, to create a subplot utterly unnecessary to the story.

His school career takes an upturn when he meets two extraordinary (not to mention unbelievable) students his own age. Beatrice the Bear (Brie Larson) is a soccer player with a fearsome reputation, which the movie halfheartedly establishes in a perfunctory manner before revealing her as a true-blue best pal who befriends Roy Eberhardt (he often is referred to by both names). Meanwhile, Roy Eberhardt is fascinated by a kid he sees running barefoot through the town. He tries to chase him, fails, finally catches up with him, is scared off by a sack of cottonmouth snakes, and eventually makes friends with him. This is Mullet Fingers (Cody Linley), a cross between Tarzan and Huckleberry Finn.

Mullet lives in hiding on a houseboat, doesn't go to school, and devotes his life to sabotaging the efforts by Curly (Tim Blake Nelson) to build the hated pancake house. He pulls up the surveying stakes, steals the seat from the bulldozer, and otherwise generates trouble for the local Keystone Kop, named Officer Delinko (Luke Wilson). Delinko is so incompetent that one night he stakes out the construction site and oversleeps because Mullet Fingers has painted all the windows of his prowler black.

The movie's climax involves one of those situations where everyone in the town arrives at the same time in the same place to hear incriminating evidence that forces the dastardly villains to abandon their plans. Oops, I gave away the ending, if you were expecting that the film would conclude with the death of the owls.

Hoot is based on a Newbery Honor novel by Carl Hiaasen, the Florida novelist. That gives it a provenance, but not a pedigree. (Having written the preceding sentence, I do not know what it means, but I like the way it reads.) I suspect the movie's target audience will think it plays suspiciously like an after-school special and lacks the punch and artistry of such superior family films as *Millions* and *Shiloh*. The villains are sitcom caricatures, the kids (especially Mullet Fingers) are likable but not remotely believable, and it is never quite explained why anyone would build a pancake house in a wilderness area that seems to be far from any major road.

Note: If you are a viewer of intelligence and

curiosity and live in a city where human beings still program some of the theaters, there is a much better movie right now about guerrillas fighting to protect an endangered species. It is Mountain Patrol: Kekexili. *You have a choice: an inane dead zone of sitcom clichés, or a stunning adventure shot on location in the high deserts of Asia.*

Hostage ★ ★ ★

R, 113 m., 2005

Bruce Willis (Jeff Talley), Kevin Pollak (Mr. Smith), Jonathan Tucker (Dennis Kelly), Ben Foster (Mars), Jimmy Bennett (Tommy Smith), Michelle Horn (Jennifer Smith), Jimmy "Jax" Pinchak (Sean Mack), Marshall Allman (Kevin Kelly), Serena Scott Thomas (Jane Talley). Directed by Florent Emilio Siri and produced by Mark Gordon, Arnold Rifkin, and Bob Yari. Screenplay by Doug Richardson, based on a novel by Robert Crais.

The opening titles of *Hostage* are shot in saturated blacks and reds with a raw, graphic feel, and the movie's color photography tilts toward dark high-contrast. That matches the mood, which is hard-boiled and gloomy. Bruce Willis, who feels like a resident of action thrillers, not a visitor, dials down here into a man of fierce focus and private motives; for the second half of the movie, no one except for (some of) the bad guys knows what really motivates him.

There's also an interesting use of the movie's three original villains, who are joined later by evildoers from an entirely different sphere. As the film opens, three gormless teenagers in a pickup truck follow a rich girl being driven "in her daddy's Escalade" to a mountaintop mansion with fearsome security safeguards. Their motive: Steal the Cadillac. These characters are Mars (Ben Foster), a mean customer with a record, and two brothers: Dennis and Kevin Kelly (Jonathan Tucker and Marshall Allman). Kevin is the kid brother along for the ride, appalled by the lawbreaking Mars leads his brother into.

Trapped inside the house when police respond to an alarm, they take hostages: Smith, the rich man (Kevin Pollak), his teenage daughter, Jennifer (Michelle Horn), and his young son, Tommy (Jimmy Bennett). Bruce Willis plays the police chief who leads the first response team, but after a bad hostage experience in Los Angeles, he has retired to Ventura County to avoid just such adventures, and hands over authority to the sheriff's department. Then, inexplicably, he returns and demands to take command again.

Moderate spoiler warning: What motivates him is that unknown kidnappers have captured Willis's own wife and child, and are holding them hostage. They want Willis to obtain a DVD in the Smith house, which (we gather) contains crucial information about illegal financial dealings. So we have a hostage crisis within a hostage crisis, and Willis is trying to free two sets of hostages, only one known to his fellow lawmen.

This is ingenious, and adds an intriguing complexity to what could have been a one-level story. Some other adornments, however, seem unlikely. Little Tommy is able to grab his sister's cell phone and move secretly throughout the house, using his secret knowledge of air ducts and obscure construction details. This development takes full advantage of the Air Duct Rule, which teaches us that all air ducts are large enough to crawl through, and lead directly to vantage points above crucial events in the action. Left unanswered is why the three hostage takers aren't concerned that the kid is missing for long periods of time.

Some elements exist entirely for the convenience of the plot. For example, the Kevin Pollak character functions long enough to establish his role and importance, then is conveniently unconscious when not needed, then is on the brink of death when Willis desperately wants to revive him, then miraculously recovers and is able to act with admirable timing at a crucial moment. I would love to examine his medical charts during these transitions.

But I am not much concerned about such logical flaws, because the main line of the movie is emotional, driven by the Bruce Willis character, who is able to project more intensity with less overacting than most of his rivals. He brings credibility to movies that can use some, and that will be invaluable in *Die Hard 4*. The mechanics of the final showdown are unexpected and yet show an undeniable logic, and are sold by the acting skills of Willis and Pollak.

The movie was directed by Florent Emilio Siri, creator of two Tom Clancy–written video games, which may explain why some of my colleagues were chortling when the Willis character uses his knowledge of Captain Woobah and Planet Xenon (persons and places unknown to me) to reassure Little Tommy. I say, if you know it, flaunt it. If he had been quoting Nietzsche, now that would have been a red flag.

What Siri brings to the show is an intimate visual style that keeps us claustrophobically close to the action, an ability to make action sequences clear enough to follow, and a dark sensibility that leads to at least two deaths we do not really expect. In scenes where a hero must outgun four or five armed opponents, however, *Hostage* does use the reliable action movie technique of cutting from one target to the next, so that we never see what the others are doing while the first ones are being shot. Waiting for their close-ups, I suppose.

Hot Rod ★ ★ ★

PG-13, 88 m., 2007

Andy Samberg (Rod Kimble), Isla Fisher (Denise), Jorma Taccone (Kevin Powell), Bill Hader (Dave), Danny R. McBride (Rico), Ian McShane (Frank Powell), Sissy Spacek (Marie Powell), Will Arnett (Jonathan), Chris Parnell (Barry Pasternak). Directed by Akiva Schaffer and produced by John Goldwyn and Lorne Michaels. Screenplay by Pam Brady.

Rod Kimble, the hero of *Hot Rod,* is Evel Knievel on a moped. He leads a life resembling an episode of *Jackass.* Not a day passes without him attempting a harebrained stunt, and failure doesn't discourage him because he knows in his heart that he is destined to become world famous.

Rod is played by Andy Samberg from *Saturday Night Live,* who on the basis of this film, I think, could become a very big star. With a trusting face, a gigantic smile, and an occasional Burt Reynolds mustache, he has the innocence of many great comedians, who always seem surprised at the way their schemes turn out; like Buster Keaton, he springs up after every disaster, ready for more, hoping to get rich, win the girl, be universally acclaimed, and so on.

Samberg is one of the first comedy stars spawned by the Internet. With his Berkeley buddies Jorma Taccone and Akiva Schaffer, he made short films that became enormously popular on the net and was signed by *SNL,* which also took Taccone and Schaffer aboard as writers. They're still together; Schaffer is the director of *Hot Rod,* and Taccone costars as Kevin, Rod's half brother and half-willing sidekick for his stunts.

Samberg is twenty-seven, but he looks about seventeen in the film and lives at home with his mom (Sissy Spacek) and stepdad (Ian McShane). He has been told of the daring heroism of his father, now deceased, and dreams of emulating him. But he can't even outmaneuver his stepfather, who routinely defeats him in fights. This does not involve abuse, but a ferocious rivalry between the two. When his mom breaks the news that his stepdad needs a heart transplant they can't afford, Rod is devastated. That means he loses any hope of defeating him in hand-to-hand combat.

Rod vows to raise the necessary $50,000 so that he can save his stepfather's life and then reduce him to a pulp. Some of his attempts at moneymaking are painful; hired as an entertainer at a children's party, he is hung upside-down and turned into a human piñata. His daredevil show involving the municipal swimming pool also turns out badly.

All his publicity efforts add up to an attempt to jump over fifteen buses (the real Evel Knievel once jumped fourteen buses, although close study of his career indicates he crashed about as often as Rod Kimble). To prepare for his jump, Rod begins a training regime, leading to a tumble down a hill that—well, see for yourself.

The movie is funny, I think, because it is sincere. It likes Rod. It doesn't portray him as a maniacal goofball, but as an ambitious kid who really thinks, every single time, that he will succeed. In creating this aura of sincerity, *Hot Rod* benefits from Sissy Spacek's performance: She plays the mom absolutely straight, without inflection, as if she were not in a comedy. That's the only right choice; supporting characters are needed to reinforce Rod, not compete with him.

Rod's would-be girlfriend Denise (Isla Fisher) is, of course, going with another guy, but Rod persists in the belief that his inevitable fame will win her over, as if girls are searching for guys with his job description (Knievel had to kidnap his own first wife, but, to be fair, he wasn't yet a daredevil). All of these characters and some of the conflicts are familiar from other movies, but *Hot Rod* puts a nice spin on them. It's funny pretty much all the way through, even in the final showdown between Rod and his stepdad. I have seen countless movie fights that stagger the imagination, but this one goes over the top and comes down on the other side. Just what Rod would like to do someday.

The Hottest State ★ ★

R, 117 m., 2007

Mark Webber (William Harding), Catalina Sandino Moreno (Sara Garcia), Ethan Hawke (Vince), Laura Linney (Jesse), Michelle Williams (Samantha), Sonia Braga (Mrs. Garcia), Jesse Harris (Dave Afton), Daniel Ross (Young Vince), Anne Clarke (Young Jesse). Directed by Ethan Hawke and produced by Yukie Kito and Alexis Alexanian. Screenplay by Hawke, based on his novel.

As a topic of fiction, the only things I have against young love are youth and romance. There has to be something more. Who would care about Romeo and Juliet if it hadn't been for their unfortunate misunderstanding? There has to be comedy, or tragedy, or suspense, or personality quirks, or *something* more than the fact that Young Person A loves Young Person B. This also applies to Old People A&B.

Ethan Hawke's *The Hottest State,* which he wrote, directed, and costars in, is based on his 1996 "semiautobiographical" novel, and therefore inspired in some way by his similarities to his hero: comes to New York from Texas, wants to be an actor, falls in love, etc. I would perhaps have enjoyed the movie more if it had been a "semibiographical" novel, based on *both* the boy and the girl. When his hero stands in the street reciting beneath her window from *Romeo and Juliet* (and he does), surely the point is not his gauche behavior but her failure to pour water on him.

The movie involves William (Mark Webber) and Sara Garcia (Catalina Sandino Moreno, from *Maria, Full of Grace*). She is a Latina from a wealthy background in Connecticut, cutting out any hope of culture clash, since Latinas will not have been unknown to him in Texas, although at least her background provides her with an interesting mother (Sonia Braga). William, we learn in flashbacks, is himself the product of young love that did not end well between a distant father (played by Hawke) and a mother (Laura Linney) whose realistic advice could be borrowed from Olympia Dukakis in *Moonstruck* (in place of sympathizing with William, she reminds him that in the long run he will be dead, and his heartbreak won't matter so much).

William and Sara meet in a bar, like each other, find out they're both in the arts, and play at boyfriend and girlfriend. Then they take a vacation to Mexico, seem to fall truly in love, finally have sex, and then when they meet next in New York she has decided she doesn't want him, or anyone, as a lover. Which breaks his heart and causes him to paste grieving messages on his windows, which she can see from hers. (Romantic tip: When a lover tells you they don't want to see you "or anyone," they already have someone else in mind.)

If the stakes were higher, all of this might matter more. But William and Sara have not interested us as themselves, and don't seem to interest each other as much as they like the romantic roles they're playing. Will the world be different, or their lives irrevocably changed, if they break up? I don't think so. Their tree falls in the forest, and nobody cares except the termites.

I admired Hawke's directorial debut, *Chelsea Walls* (2001), ever so much more than this movie because it was about more interesting people and more interesting love; it was set in the Chelsea Hotel, which, when people get beyond a certain threshold of "interesting," may be the only hotel in New York that will accept them. In *The Hottest State,* Hawke uses fairly standard childhood motivations for his unhappiness and reveals too little real interest in the Sara character. Why *did* she seem to fall in love and then announce she didn't want to see him anymore? From her point of view, I mean. In fact, the best angle on this whole story might be from her point of view.

House of D ★ ½

PG-13, 96 m., 2005

Anton Yelchin (Tommy), Tea Leoni (Mrs. Warshaw), David Duchovny (Tom Warshaw), Robin Williams (Pappass), Erykah Badu (Lady Bernadette), Magali Amadei (Coralie Warshaw), Harold Cartier (Odell Warshaw), Mark Margolis (Mr. Pappass), Zelda Williams (Melissa). Directed by David Duchovny and produced by Richard Barton Lewis, Jane Rosenthal, and Bob Yari. Screenplay by Duchovny.

Yes, I take notes during the movies. I can't always read them, but I persist in hoping that I can. During a movie like *House of D,* I jot down words I think might be useful in the review. Peering now at my three-by-five cards, I read *sappy, inane, cornball, shameless,* and, my favorite, *doofusoid.* I sigh. The film has not even inspired interesting adjectives, except for the one I made up myself. I have been reading Dr. Johnson's invaluable *Dictionary of the English Language,* and propose for the next edition:

doofusoid, adj. Possessing the qualities of a doofus; sappy, inane, cornball, shameless. "The plot is composed of doofusoid elements."

You know a movie is not working for you when you sit in the dark inventing new words. *House of D* is the kind of movie that particularly makes me cringe, because it has such a shameless desire to please; like Uriah Heep, it bows and scrapes and wipes its sweaty palm on its trouser-leg, and also like Uriah Heep it privately thinks it is superior.

I make free with a reference to Uriah Heep because I assume if you got past Dr. Johnson and did not turn back, Uriah Heep will be like an old friend. You may be asking yourself, however, why I am engaging in wordplay, and the answer is: I am trying to entertain myself before I must get down to the dreary business of this review. Think of me as switching off my iPod just before going into traffic court.

So. *House of D.* Written and directed by David Duchovny, who I am quite sure created it with all of the sincerity at his command, and believed in it so earnestly that it did not occur to him that no one else would believe in it at all. It opens in Paris with an artist (Duchovny) who feels he must return to the Greenwich Village of his youth, there to revisit the scenes and people who were responsible, I guess, for him becoming an artist in Paris, so maybe a thank-you card would have done.

But, no, we return to Greenwich Village in 1973, soon concluding Duchovny would more wisely have returned to the Greenwich Village of 1873, in which the clichés of Victorian fiction, while just as agonizing, would at least not have been dated. We meet the hero's younger self, Tommy (Anton Yelchin). Tommy lives with his mother, Mrs. Warshaw (Tea Leoni), who sits at the kitchen table smoking and agonizing and smoking and agonizing. (Spoiler warning!) She seems deeply depressed, and although Tommy carefully counts the remaining pills in her medicine cabinet to be sure his mother is still alive, she nevertheless takes an overdose and, so help me, goes into what the doctor tells Tommy is a "persistent vegetative state." How could Duchovny have guessed when he was writing his movie that such a line, of all lines, would get a laugh?

Tommy's best friend is Pappass, played by Robin Williams. Pappass is retarded. He is retarded in 1973, that is; when Tommy returns many years later, Pappass is proud to report that he has been upgraded to "challenged." In either case, he is one of those characters whose shortcomings do not prevent him from being clever like a fox as he (oops!) blurts out the truth, underlines sentiments, says things that are more significant than he realizes, is insightful in the guise of innocence, and always appears exactly when and where the plot requires.

Tommy has another confidant, named Lady Bernadette (Erykah Badu), who is an inmate in the Women's House of Detention. She is on an upper floor with a high window in her cell, but by using a mirror she can see Tommy below, and they have many conversations, in which their speaking voices easily carry through the Village traffic noise and can be heard across, oh, fifty yards. Lady Bernadette is a repository of ancient female wisdom, and advises Tommy on his career path and the feelings of Pappass, who "can't go where you're going"—no, even though he steals Tommy's bicycle.

The whole business of the bicycle being stolen and returned, and Pappass and Tommy trading responsibility for the theft, and the cross-examination by the headmaster of Tommy's private school (Frank Langella) is tendentious beyond all reason. (Tendentious, adj. Tending toward the dentious, as in having one's teeth drilled.) The bicycle is actually an innocent bystander, merely serving the purpose of creating an artificial crisis that can cause a misunderstanding, so that the crisis can be resolved and the misunderstanding healed. What a relief it is that Pappass and Tommy can hug at the end of the movie.

Damn! I didn't even get to the part about Tommy's girlfriend, and my case is being called.

House of Wax ★ ★

R, 113 m., 2005

Elisha Cuthbert (Carly Jones), Chad Michael Murray (Nick Jones), Brian Van Holt (Bo), Paris Hilton (Paige Edwards), Jared Padalecki (Wade), Jon Abrahams (Dalton), Robert Ri'chard (Blake). Directed by Jaume Collet-Sera and produced by Susan Levin, Joel Silver, and Robert Zemeckis. Screenplay by Chad Hayes and Carey Hayes.

The Dead Teenager Movie has grown up. The characters in *House of Wax* are in their twenties and yet still repeat the fatal errors of all the *Friday the 13th* kids who checked into Camp Crystal Lake and didn't check out. ("Since all the other campers have been beheaded, eviscerated, or skewered, Marcie, obviously there's only one thing for us to do: Go skinny-dipping at midnight in the haunted lake.")

In *House of Wax*, two carloads of college students leave Gainesville for a big football game in Baton Rouge and take an ominous detour along the way, leading them into what looks like the Texas Chainsaw Theme Park. "This town is not even on the GPS!" says one of the future Dead Post-Teenagers.

Some will complain that the movie begins slowly, despite a steamy sex scene involving Paris Hilton, and an ominous confrontation with a slack-jawed local man who drives a pickup truck, an innocent and utilitarian vehicle that in horror movies is invariably the choice of the depraved. I didn't mind the slow start, since it gave me time to contemplate the exemplary stupidity of these students, who surely represent the bottom of the academic barrel at the University of Florida.

Consider. They decide to camp overnight in a clearing in the dark, brooding woods. There is a terrible smell. The guy in the pickup truck drives up and shines his brights on them until Carly's ex-con brother, Nick (Chad Michael Murray), breaks one of the headlights. You do not get away with headlight-breaking in Chainsaw Country. The kids should flee immediately, but no: They settle down for the night.

In the morning, a fan belt is found to be mysteriously broken. An ominous sign: Fan belts do not often break in parked cars. Wade (Jared Padalecki) and girlfriend Carly (Elisha Cuthbert) unwisely take a ride into town for a replacement fan belt—from a guy they meet when they discover the source of the smell: a charnel pit of rotting roadkill. The guy is dumping a carcass into the pit at the time. Not the kind of person you want to ask for a lift. Is that a human hand sticking up from the middle of the pile? "This is weird," observes Paige. That night, when they are alone at the camp (not prudent), she treats her boyfriend, Blake (Robert Ri'chard), to a sexy dance that perhaps reminds him of a video he once saw on the Web.

The nearby town seems stuck in a time warp from the 1960s. The movie theater is playing *Whatever Happened to Baby Jane?* Yes, and for that matter, what happened to everybody else? No citizens prowl the streets, although some seem to be attending a funeral. Carly and Wade are attracted to a mysterious House of Wax that dominates the town, much as the Bates's home towered above *Psycho*. Wade scratches a wall of the house and says, "It *is* wax—literally!" This is either an omen, or the homeowners were victimized by siding salesmen. Had Wade and Carly only seen the 1953 Vincent Price thriller, they might have saved themselves, but no. They haven't even seen *Scream* and don't know they're in a horror movie.

The progress of the plot is predictable: One Post-Teenager after another becomes Dead, usually while making a stupid mistake like getting into a pickup or entering the House of Wax ("Hello? Anyone home?"). Knowing that at least one and preferably two of the Post-Teenagers will survive for the sequel, along with possibly one of the Local Depraved, we keep count: We know Paris Hilton is likely to die but are grateful that the producers first allow her to run in red underwear through an old shed filled with things you don't want to know about.

The early reviewers have been harsh with Miss Hilton ("so bad she steals the show," says the *Hollywood Reporter*), but actually she is no better or worse than the typical Dead Post-Teenager and does exactly what she is required to do in a movie like this, with all the skill, admittedly finite, that is required. *House of Wax* is not a good movie, but it is an efficient one and will deliver most of what anyone attending *House of Wax* could reasonably expect, assuming it would be unreasonable to expect very much.

Where the movie excels is in its special effects and set design. Graham "Grace" Walker masterminds a spectacular closing sequence in which the House of Wax literally melts down, and characters sink into stairs, fall through floors, and claw through walls. There is also an eerie sequence in which a living victim is sprayed with hot wax and ends up with a finish you'd have to pay an extra four bucks for at the car wash.

Howl's Moving Castle ★ ★ ½

PG, 120 m., 2005

With the voices of: Emily Mortimer (Young Sophie), Jean Simmons (Old Sophie), Christian Bale (Howl), Lauren Bacall (Witch of the Waste), Billy Crystal (Calcifer), Blythe Danner (Madame Suliman), Crispin Freeman (Prince Turnip), Josh Hutcherson (Markl). An animated film directed by Hayao Miyazaki and produced by Toshio Suzuki. Screenplay by Miyazaki, based on the novel by Diana Wynne Jones.

Almost the first sight we see in *Howl's Moving Castle* is the castle itself, which looks as if it were hammered together in shop class by wizards inspired by the lumbering, elephantine war machines in *The Empire Strikes Back*. The castle is an amazing visual invention, a vast collection of turrets and annexes, protuberances and afterthoughts, which makes its way across the landscape like a turtle in search of a rumble.

I settled back in my seat, confident that Japan's Hayao Miyazaki had once again created his particular kind of animated magic, and that the movie would deserve comparison with *Spirited Away, Princess Mononoke, My Neighbor Totoro, Kiki's Delivery Service,* and the other treasures of the most creative animator in the history of the art form.

But it was not to be. While the movie contains delights and inventions without pause and has undeniable charm, while it is always wonderful to watch, while it has the Miyazaki visual wonderment, it's a disappointment compared to his recent work. Adapted from a British novel by Diana Wynne Jones, it resides halfway between the Brothers Grimm and *The Wizard of Oz,* with shape-shifting that includes not merely beings but also objects and places.

Chief among the shape-shifters is the castle itself, which can swell with power and then shrivel in defeat. Inside the castle are spaces that can change on a whim, and a room with a door that opens to—well, wherever it needs to open. The castle roams the Waste Lands outside two warring kingdoms, which seem vaguely nineteenth-century European; it is controlled by Howl himself, a young wizard much in demand but bedeviled with personal issues.

The story opens with Sophie (voice by Emily Mortimer), a hatmaker who sits patiently at her workbench while smoke-belching trains roar past her window. When she ventures out, she's attacked by obnoxious soldiers but saved by Howl (voice by Christian Bale), who is himself being chased by inky globs of shapeless hostility. This event calls Sophie's existence to the attention of Howl's enemy, the Witch of the Waste (Lauren Bacall), who fancies Howl for herself and in a fit of jealousy turns Sophie into a wrinkled old woman, bent double and voiced now by Jean Simmons. For most of the rest of the movie, the heroine will be this ancient crone; we can remind ourselves that young Sophie is trapped inside, but the shape-switch slows things down, as if Grandmother were creeping through the woods to Red Riding Hood's house.

Sophie meets a scarecrow (Crispin Freeman) who bounces around on his single wooden leg and leads her to Howl's castle. Sophie names the scarecrow Turniphead, and we think perhaps a lion and a tin man will be turning up before long, but no. Nor is the castle run by a fraudulent wizard behind a curtain. Howl is the real thing, a shape-shifter who sometimes becomes a winged bird of prey. So is his key assistant, Calcifer (Billy Crystal), a fiery being whose job is to supply the castle's energy. Sophie also meets Markl (Josh Hutcherson), Howl's aide-de-camp, and sets about appointing herself the castle's housekeeper and maid of all work.

The plot deepens. Howl is summoned to serve both of the warring kingdoms, which presents him with a problem, complicated by the intervention of Madame Suliman, a sorceress voiced by Blythe Danner, who reminds us of Yubaba, the sorceress who ran the floating bathhouse in *Spirited Away.* These bloated old madame types seem to exert a fascination for Miyazaki scarcely less powerful than his fondness for young heroines. Howl cravenly sends old Sophie to represent him before King Sariman, and on her way there she gets into a race with the Witch of the Waste, who haunts the hinterlands where the castle roams. Sophie is obviously trapped in a web of schemes that's too old and too deep for her to penetrate, and there comes a moment when defeat seems certain and even Calcifer despairs.

All of this is presented, as only Miyazaki can, in animation of astonishing invention and detail. The castle itself threatens to upstage everything else that happens in the movie, and notice the way its protuberances move in time with its lumbering progress, not neglecting the sphincteresque gun turret at the rear. Sophie, old or young, never quite seems to understand and inhabit this world; unlike Kiki of the delivery service or Chihiro, the heroine of *Spirited Away,* she seems more witness than heroine. A parade of weird characters comes onstage to do their turns, but the underlying plot grows murky and, amazingly for a Miyazaki film, we grow impatient at spectacle without meaning.

I can't recommend the film, and yet I know if you admire Miyazaki as much I do you'll want to see it anyway. When his movies are working and on those rare occasions when they are not, Miyazaki nevertheless is a master who, frame by frame, creates animated compositions of wonderment. Pete Doctor (writer of *Toy Story*) and John Lasseter (director of *Toy Story*), his great American supporters, have supervised the English dubbing; online anime sites say, however, that the Japanese voices are more in character (we'll be able to compare on the DVD). In the meantime, the big screen is the only way to appreciate the remarkable detail of the castle, which becomes one of the great unique places in the movies.

Hustle and Flow ★ ★ ★ ½

R, 114 m., 2005

Terrence Howard (Djay), Taryn Manning (Nola), Paula Jai Parker (Lexus), Anthony Anderson (Key), DJ Qualls (Shelby), Taraji P. Henson (Shug), Isaac Hayes (Arnel), Elise Neal (Yevette), Ludacris (Skinny Black). Directed by Craig Brewer and produced by John Singleton and Stephanie Allain. Screenplay by Brewer.

Sometimes you never really see an actor until the right roles bring him into focus. Terrence Howard has made twenty-two movies and a lot of TV (starting with the *Cosby Show*), but now, in *Crash* and *Hustle and Flow,* he creates such clearly seen characters in such different worlds that his range and depth become unmistakable.

In *Crash* he was the successful Hollywood television director, humiliated when his wife was assaulted by a cop. In *Hustle and Flow,* he plays a Memphis pimp and drug dealer who yearns to make something of himself—to become a rap artist. His quest for success is seen so clearly and with such sympathy by writer-director Craig Brewer that the movie transcends the crime genre and becomes powerful drama.

The movie's first achievement is to immerse us in the daily world of Djay, Howard's character. He is not a "pimp" and a "drug dealer," as those occupations have been simplified and dramatized in pop culture. He is a focused young man, intelligent, who in another world with other opportunities might have, who knows, gone to college and run for Congress. He can improvise at length on philosophical subjects, as he proves in an opening scene about—well, about no less than the nature of man.

He has a childhood friend named Skinny Black (Ludacris), who has become a millionaire rap star. How close of a childhood friend is a good question; as nearly as I can tell, they went to different schools together. Skinny Black returns to the old neighborhood every Fourth of July for a sentimental reunion at the club where he got his start. The club owner (Isaac Hayes) is a friend of Djay's. The theory is, Djay will give his demo tape to Skinny Black, who will pull strings and make Djay a star.

But that's in the third act of the movie. The long second act, in some ways the heart of the film, involves Djay's attempts to meet his various business responsibilities while recording the demo. We get the ghetto version of renting the old barn and putting on a show. Djay picks up an ancient digital keyboard and enlists Key (Anthony Anderson), a family man and churchgoer, to work with him on the music. Key knows Shelby (DJ Qualls), a white kid with musical skills. They staple cardboard egg containers to the walls to soundproof a recording studio, enlist a hooker named Shug (Taraji P. Henson) to sing backup, and make the recording.

What Djay cannot be expected to understand is that Skinny Black gets countless demos pressed warmly into his hands every day. He does not have the power in the music industry that Djay imagines. Discovering a talented newcomer might be professional suicide. And beyond that is the whole worldview Skinny Black has bought into: his cars, his bodyguards, his image as a menacing rapper. Djay's first approach to him is miscalculated and all wrong. The way he uses his instincts to try again is smart, and brave.

But *Hustle and Flow* is not limited to Djay's rags-to-riches dream, because it is not a formula film. Much more interesting are his day-to-day relationships. Nola (Taryn Manning), the white woman who gets the benefit of his theory of human life, is his most profitable hooker, even though she tells Djay how much she hates getting into the cars of strange men. Shug, whom Djay gradually realizes he loves, is pregnant, probably not with Djay's child. Lexus (Paula Jai Parker) has an income as a stripper, which makes her more outspoken and independent.

Djay plays the pimp role and is effective enough, but his heart isn't in it. The dream of the demo record fills his mind—and obsesses Key and Shelby, to the dismay of Key's wife, who sees her churchgoing breadwinner spending his free time with a pimp ("What woman wouldn't be thrilled to have her man in a house full of whores?"). What happens is that Djay's horizon expands as his imagination is challenged. It isn't really the hope of stardom that keeps him going. It isn't the dubious connection with Skinny Black that inspires him. What we see in *Hustle and Flow* is rarely seen in the movies: the redemptive power of art. Djay is transformed when he finds something he loves doing and is getting better at. To create something out of your own mind and talent and see that it is good: That is a joy that makes the rest of his life seem shabby and transparent.

Terrence Howard modulates Djay with great love and consideration for the character. He never cheapens him, or condescends. He builds him inside out. He is a pimp and a dealer because he is smart and has ambition, and that is how, in his world, with his background, he can find success. The film accumulates many subtle moments to show how his feelings for Shug develop, how he begins by giving her the kind of "love" pimps use as a control mechanism, and slowly realizes that another kind of love is growing.

Shug is played by Taraji P. Henson as so wounded, so vulnerable, so loyal that we're astonished at the complex emotions developed by the story. Listen to her: "Letting me sing on the demo made me feel real. I know, moving up, you gonna get real good people, so I want you to know, it meant the world to me." What has transformed him has opened room for her transformation.

Hustle and Flow shows, among other things, what a shallow music-video approach many films take to the inner city, and then what complexities and gifts bloom there. Every good actor has a season when he comes into his own, and this is Howard's time.

I

I Am Legend ★ ★ ★

PG-13, 114 m., 2007

Will Smith (Robert Neville), Alice Braga (Anna), Dash Mihok (Alpha Male), Charlie Tahan (Ethan), Salli Richardson (Zoe), Willow Smith (Marley). Directed by Francis Lawrence and produced by Akiva Goldsman, James Lassiter, David Heyman, and Neal Moritz. Screenplay by Mark Protosevich and Goldsman, based on the novel by Richard Matheson.

The opening scenes of *I Am Legend* have special effects so good that they just about compensate for some later special effects that are dicey. We see Manhattan three years after a deadly virus has killed every healthy human on the island, except one. The streets are overgrown with weeds, cars are abandoned, the infrastructure is beginning to collapse. Down one street a sports car races, driven by Robert Neville (Will Smith), who is trying to get a good shot at one of the deer roaming the city. He has worse luck than a lioness who competes with him.

Neville has only his dog to keep him company. He lives barricaded inside a house in Greenwich Village, its doors and windows sealed every night by heavy steel shutters. That's because after dark the streets are ruled by bands of predatory zombies—hairless creatures who were once human but have changed into savage, speechless killers with fangs for teeth. In his basement, Neville has a laboratory where he is desperately seeking a vaccine against the virus, which mutated from a cure for cancer.

The story is adapted from a 1954 sci-fi novel by Richard Matheson, which has been filmed twice before, as *The Last Man on Earth* (1964), starring Vincent Price, and *The Omega Man* (1971), starring Charlton Heston. In the original novel, which Stephen King says influenced him more than any other, Neville cultivated garlic and used mirrors, crosses, and sharpened stakes against his enemies, who were like traditional vampires, not super-strong zombies. I am not sure it is an advance to make him a scientist, arm him, and change the nature of the creatures; Matheson developed a kind of low-key realism that was doubly effective.

In *I Am Legend,* the situation raises questions of logic. If Neville firmly believes he is the last healthy man alive, who is the vaccine for? Only himself, I guess. Fair enough, although he faces a future of despair, no matter how long his cans of Spam and Dinty Moore beef stew hold out; dogs don't live forever. And how, I always wonder, do human beings in all their infinite shapes and sizes, mutate into identical pale zombies with infinite speed and strength?

Never mind. Given its setup, *I Am Legend* is well-constructed to involve us with Dr. Neville and his campaign to survive. There is, however, an event that breaks his spirit, and he cracks up—driving out at night to try to mow down as many zombies with his car as he can before they kill him. He is saved with a bright light by a young woman named Anna (Alice Braga), who is traveling with a boy named Ethan (Charlie Tahan).

He takes them home and she explains they are trying to get to a colony of survivors in Vermont. Neville doubts that such a colony exists. I doubt that she and the boy would venture through Manhattan to get there. Yes, she has doubtless heard his nonstop taped voice on all AM frequencies, asking to be contacted by any other survivors. But we have seen every bridge into Manhattan blown up in a quarantine of the island, so how did they get there? Boat? Why go to the risk?

Never mind again because Anna and the boy import dramatic interest into the story when it needs it. And director Francis Lawrence generates suspense effectively, even though it largely comes down to the monster movie staple of creatures leaping out of the dark, gnashing their fangs, and hammering at things. The special effects generating the zombies are not nearly as effective as the other effects in the film; they all look like creatures created for the sole purpose of providing the film with menace, and have no logic other than serving that purpose.

I Am Legend does contain memorable scenes, as when the island is being evacuated, and when Neville says good-bye to his wife and daughter (Salli Richardson and Willow Smith), and when he confides in his dog (who is not computer-generated—most of the time, anyway). And if it is true that mankind has one hundred years to live before we destroy our planet, it provides an enlightening vision of how Manhattan will look when it lives on without us. The movie works well while it's running, although it raises questions that later only mutate in our minds. ☞

Ice Age: The Meltdown ★ ★ ½

PG, 90 m., 2006

With the voices of: John Leguizamo (Sid), Denis Leary (Diego), Ray Romano (Manny), Queen Latifah (Ellie), Seann William Scott (Crash), Josh Peck (Eddie), Jay Leno (Fast Tony), Chris Wedge (Scrat), Will Arnett (Lone Gunslinger), Jason Fricchione (Grandpa Molehog). Directed by Carlos Saldanha and produced by Lori Forte. Screenplay by Peter Gaulke, Gerry Swallow, and Jim Hecht.

Only Scrat, the ferocious little saber-toothed squirrel, retains his magic from the original *Ice Age* (2002). Most of the other characters are back in *Ice Age: The Meltdown,* but their story is more of a slog than a sprint. Remarkable that they're still around, although tens of thousands of years must have passed since the previous film. But if I am going to require logical continuity in an animated comedy, I might as well admit that Daffy Duck is not real, and that I refuse to do.

As *Ice Age: The Meltdown* opens, it is Scrat who observes the first danger signal of global change. He's engaged as usual in a perilous chase after an acorn, which is all the more desirable because where is the oak from which it fell? The squirrel climbs a vertical ice wall with his claws, almost falls, is saved when his tongue freezes to the ice, and then has to pull himself up by his own tongue, paw over paw. Don't you hate it when that happens? Then a jet of water springs from the ice face, and another, and another. The glacier is melting.

If kids have been indifferent to global warming up until now, this *Ice Age* sequel will change that forever. Giant chunks of icebergs and the polar ice cap fall off into the sea, the water levels rise, a temperate climate begins to emerge, and the animal family of the earlier film begins a long trek to save itself from drowning. There is said to be a hollow log at the end of the valley, in which they can float to safety.

The characters, as you will recall from the earlier film, have found a way to live together and not compete as species, although that leaves me a little vague about what the meat-eaters do at mealtimes. After Scrat (squeaks by Chris Wedge), we meet Manny the mammoth (voice by Ray Romano), who fears he is the last of his kind; Diego the tiger (Denis Leary); Sid the sloth (John Leguizamo); Fast Tony the turtle (Jay Leno); Lone Gunslinger the vulture (Will Arnett). And then, to the immeasurable delight of Manny, they encounter Ellie the female mammoth (Queen Latifah). Together, Manny and Ellie can save the mammoth race, if only Ellie can be convinced she is not a possum. Her delusion is encouraged by the possums Crash and Eddie (Seann William Scott and Josh Peck), who find having a mammoth as a sidekick is a great comfort.

Once the characters have been introduced and the ice shelf has started to melt, the movie essentially consists of a long trek, punctuated by adventures. Some of them are provided by the convenient thawing of two pre–ice age sea monsters, who are killing machines no doubt destined to evolve into sharks. There is also a perilous crossing of a melting ice bridge, which reminded me of the collapsing bridge in *The Lord of the Rings.*

The movie is nice to look at, the colors and details are elegant, the animals engaging, the action fast-moving, but I don't think older viewers will like it as much as the kids. The first *Ice Age* movie more or less exhausted these characters and their world, and the meltdown doesn't add much. Most of the conflict involves personalities: Can these species coexist? Well, of course they can, in a cartoon. And if global warming means simply that they don't have to freeze their butts off all the time and there are more acorns for Scrat, then what's the problem?

The Ice Harvest ★ ★ ★

R, 88 m., 2005

John Cusack (Charlie Arglist), Billy Bob Thornton (Vic), Connie Nielsen (Renata), Randy Quaid (Bill Guerrard), Oliver Platt

(Pete Van Heuten), Mike Starr (Roy Gelles). Directed by Harold Ramis and produced by Albert Berger and Ron Yerxa. Screenplay by Richard Russo and Robert Benton, based on the novel by Scott Phillips.

It's a busy Christmas Eve for Charlie Arglist, who visits his former in-laws, steers his drunken buddy out of trouble, buys toys for his kids, waives the stage rental for a stripper at his topless club, and cheats, lies, steals, and kills. Perhaps of all actors only John Cusack could play Charlie and still look relatively innocent by Christmas Day. He does look tired, however.

Charlie is a mob lawyer in Wichita, Kansas. He is, in fact, the best mob lawyer in all of Kansas. We know this because his friend Pete (Oliver Platt) announces it loudly almost everywhere they go. "I wish you wouldn't do that," Charlie says, but Pete is beyond discretion. Pete is married to Charlie's former wife and has inherited Charlie's former in-laws, a circumstance that inspires in Charlie not jealousy but sympathy. They are fascinated that the woman they have both married is the only adult they know who still sleeps in flannel jammies with sewn-on booties.

Charlie's holiday has begun promisingly. He and his associate Vic (Billy Bob Thornton) have stolen $2.2 million belonging to Bill Guerrard (Randy Quaid), the local mob boss. They think they can get away with this. They certainly hope so, anyway, because Roy Gelles (Mike Starr), a hit man for Guerrard, has been asking around town for Charlie, probably not to deliver his Christmas bonus. As Charlie tells Vic: "I sue people for a living. You sell pornography. Roy Gelles hurts people." Charlie also runs a topless bar and is attracted to its manager, Renata (Connie Nielsen), who has suggested that Charlie's Christmas stocking will be filled with more than apples and acorns if certain conditions are met.

It is all very complicated. There is the matter of the photograph showing a local councilman in a compromising position with Renata. The question of whether good old Vic can be trusted. And the continuing problem of what to do with Pete, who is very drunk and threatens a dinner party with a turkey leg, which in his condition is a more dangerous weapon than a handgun.

The Ice Harvest follows these developments with the humor of an Elmore Leonard project and the interlocking violence of a *Blood Simple.* The movie, directed by Harold Ramis, finds a balance between the goofy and the gruesome, as in a rather brilliant scene in which a mobster who is locked inside a trunk is nevertheless optimistic enough to shout out muffled death threats. For some reason there is always humor in those crime scenarios where tough guys find it's easy to conceive diabolical acts, exhausting to perform them. It's one thing to lock a man in a trunk, another to get the trunk into the backseat of a Mercedes, still another to push it down a dock and into a lake. If the job ended with locking the trunk, you'd have more people in trunks.

The key to the movie's humor is Cusack's calm patience in the face of catastrophe. He has always been curiously angelic—the last altar boy you'd suspect of having stolen the collection plate. In *The Ice Harvest* he is essentially a kind man. Consider his concern for Pete, a friend who has gotten very drunk on Christmas Eve because, as he confesses, he's not man enough to fill his chair at the family dinner table. That Charlie takes time to bail his friend out of tight spots and give him good advice speaks well of a man so heavily scheduled with stealing and killing.

Vic, the Thornton character, is one of those Billy Bob specials whose smile is charming but not reassuring. Consider the moment after he and Charlie obtain the briefcase filled with the loot and Vic drops Charlie off at home and Charlie reaches for the case and Vic reaches for it first and they realize they have not discussed who will keep the case for the time being, and Vic asks if this is going to be a problem, and you know that if Charlie takes the case it is definitely going to be a problem.

Nielsen has a bruised charm as the sexy Renata. She's sexy, but weary of being sexy. It is such a responsibility. The movie has a quiet in-joke when Charlie asks her, "Where are you from, anyway?" He doesn't think she sounds like she's from around here. Of Nielsen's last sixteen movies, all but one was American, and she has a flawless American accent, but in fact she is Danish. She never does answer Charlie's question. The obvious answer is: "A long way from Kansas."

I liked the movie for the quirky way it pursues humor through the drifts of greed, lust, booze, betrayal, and spectacularly complicated ways to die. I liked it for Charlie's essential kindness, as when he pauses during a getaway to help a friend who has run out of gas. And for the scene-stealing pathos of Platt's drunk, who like many drunks in the legal profession achieves a rhetorical grandiosity during the final approach to oblivion. And I especially liked the way Roy, the man in the trunk, keeps on thinking positively, even after Vic shoots the trunk and says, "That must have been the head end."

Ice Princess ★ ★ ★

G, 92 m., 2005

Joan Cusack (Mrs. Carlyle), Kim Cattrall (Tina Harwood), Michelle Trachtenberg (Casey Carlyle), Hayden Panettiere (Gen Harwood), Kirsten Olson (Nikki), Jocelyn Lai (Tiffany), Juliana Cannarozzo (Zoe). Directed by Tim Fywell and produced by Bridget Johnson. Screenplay by Hadley Davis.

The computer doesn't make the jumps. You do.
—Casey to Gen

Yes, *Ice Princess* is a formula movie. Yes, it makes all the stops and hits all the beats and, yes, it ends exactly as we expect it will. It even has the inevitable scene where the gifted young heroine is in the middle of her performance and she looks up into the audience—and there she is! Her mother! Who disapproves of figure skating but came to the semifinals without telling her, and now nods and smiles like dozens of other parents in dozens of other movies, recognizing at last that their child has the real stuff.

Yes, yes, and yes. And yet the movie works. I started by clicking off the obligatory scenes, and then somehow the film started to get to me, and I was surprised how entertained I was. Like *Shall We Dance* or *Saturday Night Fever,* it escapes its genre. That's partly because the screenplay avoids the usual rigid division of good and evil and gives us characters who actually change during the movie. Partly because the acting is so convincing. And partly because the actresses in the movie really can skate—or seem to. Well, no wonder, since two of them are figure skaters, but the surprise is that Michelle Trachtenberg seems able to skate too. That didn't look like a double on the ice, although *Variety,* the showbiz bible, reports, "Four different skaters sub for Trachtenberg in the more difficult performances."

Trachtenberg plays Casey Carlyle, a brilliant high school science student, who hopes to win a Harvard scholarship with a physics project. Her teacher advises her to find an original subject, and she gets a brainstorm: What if she films figure skaters, analyzes their movements on her computer, and comes up with a set of physics equations describing what they do and suggesting how they might improve?

Casey has always been a science nerd. She's pretty but doesn't know it, and so shy "I can't talk to anyone I haven't known since kindergarten." She goes to the ice rink in her Connecticut town run by Tina Harwood (Kim Cattrall), herself an Olympic figure skating contender until a disqualification at Saravejo. Now Tina coaches her daughter, Gen (Hayden Panettiere), toward championship status.

Casey's computer program works. She breaks down the moves, analyzes the physics, and advises Gen and other skaters on what they can change to improve their performance. Along the way, a funny thing happens; Casey has always enjoyed skating on the pond near her home, and now she grows fascinated by figure skating, and wants to start training.

This is horrifying news for her mom (Joan Cusack), a feminist and teacher who is pointing Casey toward Harvard and sniffs, "Figure skaters have no shelf life." Meanwhile, Gen confesses she envies Casey: "I hate to train all the time. I'd love to have a real life, like you." To her mom, Gen says, "I'm fed up with being a dunce in math class because I don't have time to do the homework."

The movie, written by Hadley Davis and directed by Tim Fywell, starts with a formula and then takes it to the next level. We have two obsessive stage mothers and two driven overachievers, and the girls want to trade places, to the despair of their moms (no dads are in sight, except for a proud Korean-American father). This leads to more substance than we're expecting, and more acting, too, since the central characters don't follow the well-worn routines supplied by the GCFDDPO formula (Gifted Child Follows Dream Despite Parental

Opposition). They strike out with opinions and surprises of their own.

I am informed that every actress in the movie does all of her own skating, but the movie's publicity is coy on the point, apart from pointing out that actresses Kirsten Olson (Nikki) and Juliana Cannarozzo (Zoe) are figure skaters making their first movie. All I know, as I said above, is that they look as if they do. What's important is not whether all the actors do their own skating, but that they play figure skaters so convincingly and bring a realistic dimension into their lives as high school students. Gen's first scene seems to set her up as the popular blond snob who's a fixture in all high school movies, but no: She makes a friend of Casey, and together the girls help each other figure out what they really want to do.

At one point, when a skater makes a really nice move on the ice, someone sniffs that it's because of Casey's computer. That's when she says the computer doesn't make the jumps. *Ice Princess* starts out with something like a computer formula too. But the formula doesn't make the moves. You can take it to another level, and that's what *Ice Princess* does. This movie is just about perfect for teenagers, and it's a surprise that even their parents are allowed to have minds of their own.

Illegal Tender ★ ★ ½

R, 105 m., 2007

Rick Gonzalez (Wilson Jr.), Wanda De Jesus (Millie DeLeon), Dania Ramirez (Ana), Jessica Pimentel (Young Millie), Manny Perez (Wilson DeLeon Sr.), Antonio Ortiz (Randy), Tego Calderon (Choco). Directed by Franc Reyes and produced by John Singleton. Screenplay by Reyes.

Even as the teenage girlfriend of a South Bronx drug dealer, Millie DeLeon is the investment adviser you'd want on your account. Without telling him, Millie invests his profits in Microsoft. This was in the late 1980s. "I only made one mistake," she tells her son years later. "I didn't buy enough."

What she bought, however, was enough to turn $2 million into a fortune, and as the story jumps forward twenty years, Millie (Wanda De Jesus) is living in an elegant suburban home, and one of her sons, Wilson DeLeon Jr. (Rick Gonzalez), is attending Danbury College, pulling down 4.0 grades, and is in love with a student named Ana (Dania Ramirez). He also dotes on his kid brother, Randy (Antonio Ortiz), who is by a different father, because Wilson DeLeon Sr. got gunned down in a Mob grudge on the day he was born.

They lead a life both comfortable and dangerous, as Millie realizes in the supermarket one day when she is spotted by a hit woman from her past. In a panic, she races home, tells the boys to start packing because they're moving again, and sets a revenge tragedy into motion.

Illegal Tender was written and directed by Franc Reyes, who is fascinated by the zero degrees of separation between low and high finance. Reyes's first film was *Empire* (2002), about another young South Bronx kingpin who is fascinated by the lifestyle of a flashy Wall Street wunderkind. His protagonist this time comes closer to making an escape, but the bad guys from her boyfriend's past have long memories and more reasons than we think for wanting her and her family dead.

My advice to her would be twofold: Move to a suburb a lot farther away from the Bronx than Connecticut, and do not give your son his father's name with a "junior" tacked on. How many Wilson DeLeon Jr.s can there be who are not the offspring of *the* Wilson DeLeon?

Never mind. This movie is based on drama, not logic. Otherwise, four or five hit men would not come calling in broad daylight and open fire at the outside of the DeLeon house. Hit men are supposed to be cleverer than that, no? And is it possible they could all, every last one, be wiped out by a fortyish housewife and her son whose entire gun experience consists of shooting three cans off a rock in only about eleven shots? And all before the cops arrive? A running gun battle in a rich suburb usually gets a pretty quick response.

We're not thinking a lot about things like that, however, because the dynamic of the picture circles Wanda De Jesus and her passionate performance as a mother who wants to protect her family. The other main strand is how Wilson Jr. evolves in a short time from Joe College to his father's son. This journey takes him back to Puerto Rico and a search for his father's past.

"How come you speak such good Spanish?" the kingpin asks him. "I'm Puerto Rican," he says. "Yeah," says the kingpin, "but most Puerto Ricans from New York speak lousy Spanish." I wanted Wilson Jr. to explain, "Plus, I got a four-point average in Spanish at school."

Like *Empire, Illegal Tender* has the potential to be a better film than it is. Franc Reyes obviously wants to make a rags-to-riches story about a Puerto Rican kid from the streets who climbs the American financial ladder, and almost equally obviously doesn't want to sell it to Hollywood as a guns-and-drugs picture. I urge him to just go ahead and do it. The film's producer, John Singleton, whose own life has taken him from South Central to the top in Hollywood, would probably support him. And if it's true that Reyes has his act so together that he shot this good-looking picture in only twenty-eight days, he could do it at the right price.

As it is, *Illegal Tender* works as a melodrama, and it benefits enormously from the performance of Wanda De Jesus. She isn't a big movie star, but is so good that she's cast by them and works with them in major roles; she costarred with Clint Eastwood in his *Blood Work,* has been cast in major roles by such as Michael Mann, Laurence Fishburne, and Joel Schumacher, is all over *CSI: Miami,* and has real screen presence. She sells us her character and her concerns, and with this screenplay, she has her work cut out for her.

Imaginary Heroes ★ ★ ★

R, 112 m., 2005

Sigourney Weaver (Sandy Travis), Emile Hirsch (Tim Travis), Jeff Daniels (Ben Travis), Michelle Williams (Penny Travis), Kip Pardue (Matt Travis), Deirdre O'Connell (Marge Dwyer), Ryan Donowho (Kyle Dwyer), Suzanne Santo (Steph Connors). Directed by Dan Harris and produced by Ilana Diamant, Moshe Diamant, Frank Hubner, Art Linson, Gina Resnick, and Denise Shaw. Screenplay by Harris.

Imaginary Heroes gives us yet one more troubled suburban family, with suicide and drugs and a chill at the dinner table. But it gives us something else: a heroine with a buried but real sense of humor, and an ability to look at life from the outside instead of only through her own needs. That this person is the mother in the family, and that the father is cold and distant, goes without saying; fathers in the movies, as a group, supply only a few more heroes than Nazis. But the mother is worth having, and makes the movie work despite its overcrowded plot.

Her name is Sandy Travis, and she is played by Sigourney Weaver as someone whose teenage years were spent in the 1970s, which means that in a sense she will always be younger, or at least more unpredictable, than her children. When she makes it clear in early scenes how much she hates Marge, her neighbor, we feel a certain self-satire under the anger. When she talks to her son, Tim (Emile Hirsch), she's the kind of adult kids need to talk to when they can't communicate with their parents. Unusual to find that in a parent.

The film is narrated by Tim, who tells us about his older brother, Matt (Kip Pardue). Matt is the best swimmer anyone has ever seen. He holds all the records and is headed for the Olympics. Then, only a minute or two into the film, he shoots himself in the head. Tim knows something about Matt that few people were allowed to find out: Matt hated swimming. Mostly he hated it because of the way he was driven by his father, Ben (Jeff Daniels), a cold perfectionist who made Matt's life a daily final exam.

That's all prologue. *Imaginary Heroes* starts with the family trying to recover emotionally. Ben insists that a plate be served for Matt at every meal, on the table in front of his empty chair. "That creeps me out," says Penny (Michelle Williams), the older sister home from college. Sandy says: "I won't be making all this food for every meal. It's a waste." That's what she does, speaking her mind in front of the family, coming across as the one who may not be beloved but at least sees clearly.

Tim is going through unsettled times at school. He is smaller than Matt was, has no athletic gifts, looks young for his age, is assumed at the funeral to be headed for high school when in fact he is already a senior. He seems to have no communication with his father, who takes a leave of absence at work and drifts off into shapeless days of sad park benches.

But Sandy sees him and senses his needs, and talks with him. They have one extraordinary conversation on the front porch swing in which she observes that they may be the only mother and son in town who can talk openly about masturbation. She tells Tim: "You may never know how really good I am for you until I die. I never loved my parents until they died."

Tim, who looks uncannily like Leonardo DiCaprio's younger brother, is dating a girl at school named Steph. She thinks they may be ready for sex.

"Steph told me she loves me," he tells his mother.

"Well, do you love her?" she asks.

"I don't know."

"Then you don't."

The relationship between Sandy and her son is the heart of the movie, and works, and Sandy's character on her own is an unfolding fascination. Who else could get busted for pot quite the way she does? And who else would say to her would-be drug dealer, "Your parents should be ashamed of you." It was a wise decision for Dan Harris, the writer-director, to avoid getting bogged down in the legal aftermath of the arrest; the point, for the story the movie wants to tell, is that she felt an urgent need to get high, and behaved more like a kid than like a prudent adult.

Dan Harris is a kid himself, only twenty-two when he sent this screenplay to Bryan Singer, director of *X-Men* and (more to the point) *Apt Pupil* and *The Usual Suspects.* Singer liked it, hired Harris to work on the screenplay for *X-2,* and then the new *Superman* movie Singer is directing, and after that *Logan's Run.* Then Harris came back at twenty-four to direct his own screenplay.

I can see what Singer saw in it: a sensitivity to characters, an instinct for the revealing, unpredictable gesture, and good dialogue. I think I see a little too much more besides. The film might have been stronger as simply the story of the family trying to heal itself after its tragedy, with the focus on Sandy and Tim. But Harris feels a need to explain everything in terms of melodramatic revelations and surprise developments, right up until the closing scenes. The emotional power of the last act is weakened by the flood of new information. The key revelation right at the end explains a lot, yes, but it comes so late that all it can do is explain. If it had come earlier, it would have had to be dealt with, and those scenes might have been considerable.

I haven't gone into detail about Marge (Deirdre O'Connell), the neighbor, or her son, Kyle Dwyer (Ryan Donowho), who is Tim's best friend. Marge never really worked for me except as a plot convenience, and Tim's friendship with Kyle, while it produces some risky and effective scenes, is best left for you to discover. What remains when the movie is over is the memory of Sandy and Tim talking, and of a mother who loves her son, understands him, and understands herself in a wry but realistic way. The characters deserve a better movie, but they get a pretty good one.

Imagine Me & You ★ ★

R, 93 m., 2006

Piper Perabo (Rachel), Lena Headey (Luce), Matthew Goode (Heck), Celia Imrie (Tessa), Anthony Head (Ned), Darren Boyd (Coop), Sharon Horgan (Beth). Directed by Ol Parker and produced by Sophie Balhetchet, Andro Steinborn, and Barnaby Thompson. Screenplay by Parker.

Romeo: *I'm straight, and really attracted to you.*
Juliet: *Good! I prefer men.*

Ever notice how in heterosexual romances the characters rarely talk about how they're heterosexual? There have been a few homosexual romances in which the sexuality of the characters goes without saying, but *Imagine Me & You* is not one of them. Here's a movie that begins with a tired romantic formula and tries to redeem it with lesbianism. And not merely lesbianism, but responsible lesbianism, in which the more experienced of the two women does everything she can to preserve the marriage of the woman she loves.

She loves Rachel (Piper Perabo). She is Luce (Lena Headey), and she first sees Rachel on Rachel's wedding day. Their eyes meet, and the screenplay elaborates on that for ninety minutes. Both women know at that moment, without a word being spoken, that they are destined for each other, but that doesn't prevent Rachel from going ahead with her marriage to Heck (Matthew Goode), although not without some alarming complications at the altar.

Much of the plot is devoted to explaining how Rachel and Luce (who runs a small but amazingly busy flower shop) can meet each other, go out on double dates with Heck and his pal Coop (Darren Boyd), and involve themselves in a romantic triangle; at one point Luce and Rachel are in the back room of the shop, snogging passionately among the petunias, when Heck walks in the front door. That generates one of those obligatory scenes in which the almost-discovered couple has to blush, breathe heavily, and make furtive adjustments to their clothes, while the unexpected visitor either notices nothing, or pretends to notice nothing. With Heck, there's a fine line between those two calibrations of noticing.

Luce does not want to break up Rachel's marriage. Unaware that as the more experienced lesbian she is required by tiresome clichés to be the predator, she nobly tries to suppress her feelings. But Rachel grows consumed by romantic obsession, and soon Heck senses that the honeymoon is over when technically it should still be humming right along.

The movie is set in London, which means that everyone can be more detached and civilized and unable to notice homosexuality than might be possible in, say, San Francisco. There are, however, no barriers between Rachel and Luce except for the fact of her marriage, which is easily disposed of once the plot gets down to work.

Most of the running time is devoted to sitcom devices involving family members, friends, double meanings, close escapes, and sincere heart-to-hearts, especially between Heck and Coop, who are awfully nice and terrifically sensitive. Rachel has a little sister named Beth (Sharon Horgan), who is so smart she says only things that are either accidentally or deliberately perceptive. And Rachel has parents (Celia Imrie and Anthony Head) who in the tradition of all British comedies are apparently insane right up to the point where they are required to demonstrate acceptance, insight, and unconditional love.

The sex in the movie is so mild that I assumed the R rating was generated primarily by the gay theme, until I learned the R is in fact because of too many f-words. That makes sense. If Rachel and Luce were of opposite genders, what they do together would be rated PG-13, and they'd have to hold on tight to keep from sliding into PG. There is a strange moment when Heck and Rachel decide to revive their marriage by making love outdoors on Hampstead Heath, and don't even get to the interruptus stage before two gay men emerge from the shrubbery and hold a conversation so innocuous they might have been taking a survey for the groundskeepers.

Perabo, as it happens, has made another movie about love between two women, the overlooked and underrated *Lost and Delirious* (2001), in which she costarred with Jessica Paré in a movie so infinitely superior (and sexier) that Perabo must have remembered it wistfully during the agonizingly belabored developments in this one.

I'm Not There ★ ★ ★ ½

R, 135 m., 2007

Christian Bale (Jack/Pastor John), Cate Blanchett (Jude), Marcus Carl Franklin (Woody), Richard Gere (Billy), Heath Ledger (Robbie), Ben Whishaw (Arthur), Charlotte Gainsbourg (Claire), David Cross (Allen Ginsberg), Bruce Greenwood (Keenan Jones), Julianne Moore (Alice Fabian), Michelle Williams (Coco Rivington). Directed by Todd Haynes and produced by James D. Stern, John Sloss, John Goldwyn, and Christian Vachon. Screenplay by Haynes and Oren Moverman.

I'm Not There is an attempt to consider the contradictions of Bob Dylan by building itself upon contradictions. Maybe that's the only way to do it. If you made a biopic with Dylan played by the same actor all the way through, it might become the portrait of a shape-shifting schizophrenic. Todd Haynes's approach is to create six or seven Dylans, depending on how you count, and use six actors to play them. This way each Dylan is consistent on his own terms, and the life as a whole need not hold together.

There are so many Bob Dylans that it is

difficult to sort out which ones you admire, and which you despise. I spent years disliking Dylan on the basis of the 1967 D. A. Pennebaker documentary *Don't Look Back,* and then underwent a conversion after seeing Martin Scorsese's 2005 doc *No Direction Home: Bob Dylan.* But what was either film but the portrait of a possible Dylan? No considerable artist since B. Traven has spent more effort concealing his tracks and covering his trail, and at the end of the day we are left with the music, which is all the artist really owes us.

If you are not much familiar with Dylan, this film is likely to confuse or baffle. If, like me, you know both of the documentaries well, have read some of the legends, have seen him in concert, and have been colonized by some of his songs, you are likely to respond with a wry admiration for the enormous risks Todd Haynes has taken here. As in his very different previous film, *Far from Heaven,* he is essentially remaking cinema to reveal what it is really trying and achieving. *Far from Heaven* exposed the gay subtext of 1950s Douglas Sirk melodramas, and *I'm Not There* shows how the other docs of Dylan have imposed consistency upon an elusive and mercurial person. What Haynes does is take away the reassuring segues that argue everything flows and makes sense, and show what's really chaos under the skin of the film.

He achieves that here by casting six actors in the role of Bob Dylan (real name Robert Allen Zimmerman, so the disguises begin before the movie). One of the actors is a young African-American boy (Marcus Carl Franklin) who claims to be Woody Guthrie; a second is Jack, a Greenwich Village folksinger (Christian Bale); a third is Robbie (Heath Ledger), appearing in a Hollywood film, who settles down, gets married, and has kids; a fourth is Jude (Cate Blanchett), a hero who alienated his fans by switching from acoustic to electric guitar and from folk to folk-rock; a fifth is an actor (Richard Gere) appearing in a Western about Billy the Kid; a sixth is a Dylan (Ben Whislaw) submitting to a contentious interview about his career, and then we double back to Christian Bale again, who plays either a seventh or a transformation of the first, Pastor John, a born-again Christian.

No effort is made to explain how these Dylans are connected, which is the point, I think. Dylanologists will recognize scenes inspired by specific moments in the singer's career and even specific shots on film; Blanchett is uncanny at embodying the Dylan of *Don't Look Back.* Bale is on target as the young Dylan who traveled from Minneapolis to Greenwich Village and reinvented himself as the heir to Woody Guthrie, but even then there may be deception; a 2000 documentary named *The Ballad of Ramblin' Jack* argues that Dylan was a copycat of Guthrie's original heir, Ramblin' Jack Elliott. Arlo Guthrie credits Ramblin' Jack with teaching him his father's music.

Dylan did appear in Sam Peckinpah's *Pat Garrett and Billy the Kid,* although not as Billy. He did convert to Christianity. Point by point, you can connect the Dylans in the film to chapters in the singer's life. And there is no difficulty in recognizing that a folksinger named Alice Fabian (Julianne Moore) represents Joan Baez, who felt betrayed by the young talent she had opened doors for. And that Claire (Charlotte Gainsbourg) represents Dylan's wife, Sara. And Allen Ginsberg (David Cross) is named Allen Ginsberg, so no problem there.

By creating this kaleidoscope of Dylans, Haynes makes a portrait not of the singer but of our perceptions. There is a parallel in Oliver Stone's *JFK,* which I think was intended not as a solution of the Kennedy assassination but as a record of our paranoia about it. And there is another work that seems relevant: Francois Girard's brilliant 1993 film *32 Short Films About Glenn Gould,* which uses actors to re-create a series of real and imagined scenes in the life of the reclusive Canadian pianist.

Coming away from *I'm Not There,* we have, first of all, heard some great music (Dylan surprisingly authorized use of his songs, both his own recordings and performed by others). We've seen six gifted actors challenged by playing facets of a complete man. We've seen a daring attempt at biography as collage. We've remained baffled by the Richard Gere cowboy sequence, which doesn't seem to know its purpose. And we have been left not one step closer to comprehending Bob Dylan, which is as it should be.

In Bruges ★ ★ ★ ★

R, 107 m., 2008

Colin Farrell (Ray), Brendan Gleeson (Ken), Ralph Fiennes (Harry), Clemence Poesy (Chloe), Jeremie Renier (Erik), Thekla Reuten (Marie), Jordan Prentice (Jimmy). Directed by Martin McDonagh and produced by Graham Broadbent and Pete Czernin. Screenplay by McDonagh.

You may know that Bruges, Belgium, is pronounced *broozh,* but I didn't, and the heroes of *In Bruges* certainly don't. They're Dublin hit men, sent there by their boss for two weeks after a hit goes very wrong. One is a young hothead who sees no reason to be anywhere but Dublin; the other, older, gentler, more curious, buys a guide book and announces: "Bruges is the best-preserved medieval city in Belgium!"

So it certainly seems. If the movie accomplished nothing else, it inspired in me an urgent desire to visit Bruges. But it accomplished a lot more than that. This film debut by the theater writer and director Martin McDonagh is an endlessly surprising, very dark human comedy, with a plot that cannot be foreseen but only relished. Every once in a while you find a film like this that seems to happen as it goes along, driven by the peculiarities of the characters.

Brendan Gleeson, with that noble shambles of a face and the heft of a boxer gone to seed, has the key role as Ken, one of two killers for hire. His traveling companion and unwilling roommate is Ray (Colin Farrell), who successfully whacked a priest in a Dublin confessional but tragically killed a little boy in the process. Before shooting the priest, he confessed to the sin he was about to commit. After accidentally killing the boy, he reads the notes the lad made for his own confession. You don't know whether to laugh or cry.

Ken and Ray work for Harry, apparently a Dublin crime lord, who for the first two-thirds of the movie we hear only over the phone, until he materializes in Bruges and turns out to be a worried-looking Ralph Fiennes. He had the men hiding out in London, but that wasn't far enough away. Who would look for them in Bruges? Who would even look for Bruges? Killing the priest was business, but "blowing a kid's head off just isn't done."

The movie does an interesting thing with Bruges. It shows us a breathtakingly beautiful city without ever seeming to be a travelogue. It uses the city as a way to develop the characters. When Ken wants to climb an old tower "for the view," Ray argues, "Why do I have to climb up there to see down here? I'm already down here." He is likewise unimpressed by glorious paintings, macabre sculptures, and picturesque canals, but is thrilled as a kid when he comes upon a film being shot.

There he meets two fascinating characters: First he sees the fetching young blonde Chloe (Clemence Poesy, who was Fleur Delacour in *Harry Potter and the Goblet of Fire*). Then he sees Jimmy (Jordan Prentice), a dwarf who figures in a dream sequence. He gets off on a bad footing with both, but eventually they're doing cocaine with a prostitute Jimmy picked up and have become friends, even though Ray keeps calling the dwarf a "midget" and having to be corrected.

Without dreaming of telling you what happens next, I will say it is not only ingenious but almost inevitable the way the screenplay brings all of these destinies together at one place and time. Along the way, there are times of great sadness and poignancy, times of abandon, times of goofiness, and that kind of humor that is *really funny* because it grows out of character and close observation. Colin Farrell in particular hasn't been this good in a few films, perhaps because this time he's allowed to relax and be Irish. As for Brendan Gleeson, if you remember him in *The General,* you know that nobody can play a more sympathetic bad guy.

Martin McDonagh is greatly respected in Ireland and England for his plays; his first film, a short named *Six Shooter* starring Gleeson, won a 2006 Oscar. In his feature debut, he has made a remarkable first film, as impressive in its own way as *House of Games,* the first film by David Mamet, whom McDonagh is sometimes compared with. Yes, it's a "thriller," but one where the ending seems determined by character and upbringing rather than plot requirements. Two of the final deaths are, in fact, ethical choices. And the irony inspiring the second one has an undeniable logic, showing that even professional murderers have their feelings.

An Inconvenient Truth ★ ★ ★ ★

PG, 100 m., 2006

Featuring Al Gore. A documentary directed by Davis Guggenheim and produced by Lawrence Bender, Scott Burns, and Laurie David.

I want to write this review so that every reader will begin it and finish it. I am a liberal, but I do not intend this as a review reflecting any kind of politics. It reflects the truth as I understand it, and it represents, I believe, agreement among the world's experts.

Global warming is real.

It is caused by human activity.

Mankind and governments must begin immediate action to halt and reverse it.

If we do nothing, in about ten years the planet may reach a "tipping point" and begin a slide toward destruction of our civilization and most of the other species on this planet.

After that point is reached, it would be too late for any action.

These facts are stated by Al Gore in the documentary *An Inconvenient Truth.* Forget that he ever ran for office. Consider him a concerned man speaking out on the approaching crisis. "There is no controversy about these facts," he says in the film. "Out of 925 recent articles in peer-review scientific journals about global warming, there was no disagreement. Zero."

He stands on a stage before a vast screen, in front of an audience. The documentary is based on a speech he has been developing for six years and is supported by dramatic visuals. He shows the famous photograph "Earthrise," taken from space by the first American astronauts. Then he shows a series of later space photographs, clearly indicating that glaciers and lakes are shrinking, snows are melting, shorelines are retreating.

He provides statistics: The ten warmest years in history were in the past fourteen years. Last year, South America experienced its first hurricane. Japan and the Pacific are setting new records for typhoons. Hurricane Katrina passed over Florida, doubled back over the Gulf, picked up strength from unusually warm Gulf waters, and went from Category 1 to Category 5. There are changes in the gulf stream and the jet stream. Cores of polar ice show that carbon dioxide is much, much higher than it has been in a quarter of a million years.

It once was thought that such things went in cycles. Gore stands in front of a graph showing the ups and downs of carbon dioxide over the centuries. Yes, there is a cyclical pattern. Then, in recent years, the graph turns up and keeps going up, higher and higher, off the chart.

The primary manmade cause of global warming is the burning of fossil fuels. We are taking energy stored over hundreds of millions of years in the form of coal, gas, and oil and releasing it suddenly. This causes global warming, and there is a pass-along effect. Since glaciers and snow reflect sunlight but seawater absorbs it, the more the ice melts, the more of the sun's energy is retained by the sea.

Gore says that although there is "100 percent agreement" among scientists, a database search of newspaper and magazine articles shows that 57 percent question the fact of global warming, while 43 percent support it. These figures are the result, he says, of a disinformation campaign started in the 1990s by the energy industries to "reposition global warming as a debate." It is the same strategy used for years by the defenders of tobacco. My father was a Luckys smoker who died of lung cancer in 1960, and twenty years later it still was "debatable" that smoking and lung cancer were linked. Now we are talking about the death of the future, starting in the lives of those now living.

"The world won't 'end' overnight in ten years," Gore says. "But a point will have been passed, and there will be an irreversible slide into destruction."

In England, Sir James Lovelock, the scientist who proposed the Gaia hypothesis (that the planet functions like a living organism), has published a new book saying that in one hundred years mankind will be reduced to "a few breeding couples at the poles." Gore thinks "that's too pessimistic. We can turn this around just as we reversed the hole in the ozone layer. But it takes action right now, and politicians in every nation must have the courage to do what is necessary. It is not a political issue. It is a moral issue."

When I said I was going to a press screening of *An Inconvenient Truth,* a friend said, "Al Gore talking about the environment! Bor . . . ing!" This is not a boring film. The director, Davis Guggenheim, uses words, images, and Gore's concise litany of facts to build a film that is fascinating and relentless. In thirty-nine years I have never written these words in a movie review, but here they are: You owe it to yourself to see this film. If you do not, and you have grandchildren, you should explain to them why you decided not to.

Am I acting as an advocate in this review? Yes, I am. I believe that to be "impartial" and "balanced" on global warming means one must take a position like Gore's. There is no other view that can be defended. Senator James Inhofe of Oklahoma, who chairs the Senate Environment Committee, has said, "Global warming is the greatest hoax ever perpetrated on the American people." I hope he takes his job seriously enough to see this film. I think he has a responsibility to do that.

What can we do? Switch to and encourage the development of alternative energy sources: solar, wind, tidal, and, yes, nuclear. Move quickly toward hybrid and electric cars. Pour money into public transit and subsidize the fares. Save energy in our houses. I did a funny thing when I came home after seeing *An Inconvenient Truth.* I went around the house turning off the lights.

The Incredible Hulk ★ ★ ½

PG-13, 114 m., 2008

Edward Norton (Bruce Banner), Liv Tyler (Betty Ross), Tim Roth (Emil Blonsky), Tim Blake Nelson (Samuel Sterns), Ty Burrell (Dr. Samson), William Hurt (General Ross), Lou Ferrigno (Voice of Hulk). Directed by Louis Leterrier and produced by Avi Arad, Kevin Feige, and Gale Anne Hurd. Screenplay by Zak Penn and Edward Norton, based on the Marvel comic books by Stan Lee and Jack Kirby.

The Incredible Hulk is no doubt an ideal version of the Hulk saga for those who found Ang Lee's *Hulk* (2003) too talky or, dare I say, too thoughtful. But not for me. It sidesteps the intriguing aspects of Hulkdom and spends way too much time in, dare I say, noisy and mindless action sequences. By the time the Incredible Hulk had completed his hulk-on-hulk showdown with the Incredible Blonsky, I had been using my Timex with the illuminated dial way too often.

Consider the dilemma of creating a story about the Hulk, who is one of the lesser creatures in the Marvel Comics stable. You're dealing with two different characters: mild-mannered scientist Dr. Bruce Banner and the rampaging, destructive Hulk, who goes into frenzies of aggression whenever he's annoyed, which is frequently, because the army is usually unloading automatic weapons into him. There is even the interesting question of whether Dr. Banner is really conscious inside the Hulk. In the Ang Lee version, he was, more or less, and confessed to Betty Ross: "When it happens, when it comes over me, when I totally lose control . . . I like it." In this 2008 version by Louis Leterrier, the best Banner can come up with is that being the Hulk is like a hyperthyroid acid trip, and all he can remember are fragments of moments.

It's obvious that the real story is the tragedy that Bruce Banner faces because of the Hulk-inducing substance in his blood. If Banner never turned into the Hulk, nobody would ever make a movie about him. And if the Hulk were never Banner, he would be like Godzilla, who tears things up real good but is otherwise, dare I say, one-dimensional.

The Ang Lee version was rather brilliant in the way it turned the Hulk story into matching sets of parent-child conflicts: Betty Ross (Jennifer Connelly) was appalled by her father the general (Sam Elliott), and Bruce Banner (Eric Bana) suffered at the hands of his father, a scientist who originally created the Hulk genes and passed them along to his child. (Nick Nolte had nice scenes as the elder Dr. Banner.)

In the new version, Betty (Liv Tyler) still has big problems with her father the general (William Hurt); she's appalled by his plans to harness the Hulk formula and create a race of super-soldiers. In both films, Banner (Ed Norton) and Ross are in love but don't act on it because the Hulk business complicates things way too much, although I admit there's a clever moment in *Hulk* 2008 when Bruce interrupts his big chance to make love with Betty because when he gets too excited, he turns into the Hulk, and Betty is a brave girl but not that good of a sport.

Consider for a moment General Ross's idea of turning out Hulk soldiers. They would be a drill sergeant's worst nightmare. When they weren't Hulks, why bother to train them? You'd only be using them in the fullness of their Hulkdom, and *then* how would you train them? Would you just drop thousands of Ed Nortons into enemy territory and count on them getting so excited by free fall that they became Hulks? (This transformation actually happens to Banner in *Hulk* 2008, by the way.)

So. What's to like in *The Incredible Hulk*? We have a sound performance by Ed Norton as a man who desperately does not want to become the Hulk and goes to Brazil to study under a master of breath control in order to curb his anger. And we have Liv Tyler in full, trembling sympathy mode. Banner's Brazilian sojourn begins with an astonishing shot: From an aerial viewpoint, we fly higher and higher above one of the hill cities of Rio, seeing hundreds, thousands, of tiny houses built on top of one another, all clawing for air. This is the *City of God* neighborhood, and as nearly as I could tell, we were looking at the real thing, not CGI. The director lets the shot run on longer than any reasonable requirement of the plot; my bet is, he was as astonished as I was, and let it run because it was so damned amazing.

The scenes involving Banner in Brazil are well conceived, although when he accidentally contaminates a bottled soft drink with his blood, the movie doesn't really deal with the consequences when the drink is consumed in the United States. The contamination provides General Ross with his clue to Banner's whereabouts, and army troops blast the hell out of the City of God; all through the movie, the general deploys his firepower so recklessly that you wonder if he has a superior, and if he ever has to account for the dozens, hundreds, thousands, who die while his guys are blasting at the Hulk with absolutely no effect.

Enter Emil Blonsky (Tim Roth), a marine General Ross recruits because he's meaner and deadlier than anyone else. Blonsky leads the chase in Rio. Later, Banner's research associate Dr. Samuel Sterns (Tim Blake Nelson) is forced to inject Blonsky with a little Hulkie juice, setting up a titanic rooftop battle in Harlem between Hulk and Blonsky. And this battle, as I have suggested, pounds away relentlessly, taking as its first victim our patience. *Iron Man*, the much better spiritual partner of this film, also ended with a showdown between an original and a copycat, but it involved two opponents who knew who they were and why they were fighting. When you get down to it, as a fictional creature, the Incredible Hulk is as limited as a bad drunk. He may be fun to be around when he's sober, but when he drinks too much, you just feel sorry for the guy.

Indiana Jones and the Kingdom of the Crystal Skull ★ ★ ★ ½

PG-13, 124 m., 2008

Harrison Ford (Indiana Jones), Cate Blanchett (Irina Spalko), Karen Allen (Marion Ravenwood), Ray Winstone (George "Mac" McHale), John Hurt (Professor Oxley), Jim Broadbent (Dean Stanforth), Shia LaBeouf (Mutt Williams). Directed by Steven Spielberg and produced by Frank Marshall. Screenplay by David Koepp.

Indiana Jones and the Kingdom of the Crystal Skull. Say it aloud. The very title causes the pulse to quicken, if you, like me, are a lover of pulp fiction. What I want is goofy action—lots of it. I want man-eating ants, swordfights between two people balanced on the backs of speeding jeeps, subterranean caverns of gold, vicious femme fatales, plunges down three waterfalls in a row, and the explanation for flying saucers. And throw in lots of monkeys.

The Indiana Jones movies were directed by Steven Spielberg and written by George Lucas and a small army of screenwriters, but they exist in a universe of their own. Hell, they created it. All you can do is compare one to the other three. And even then, what will it get you? If you eat four pounds of sausage, how do you choose which pound tasted the best? Well, the first one, of course, and then there's a steady drop-off of interest. That's why no Indy adventure can match *Raiders of the Lost*

Ark (1981). But if *Crystal Skull* (or *Temple of Doom* from 1984 or *Last Crusade* from 1989) had come first in the series, who knows how much fresher it might have seemed? True, *Raiders of the Lost Ark* stands alone as an action masterpiece, but after that the series is *compelled* to be, in the words of Indiana himself, "same old same old." Yes, but that's what I *want* it to be.

Crystal Skull even dusts off the Russians, so severely underexploited in recent years, as the bad guys. Up against them, Indiana Jones is once again played by Harrison Ford, who is now sixty-five but looks a lot like he did at fifty-five or forty-six, which is how old he was when he made *Last Crusade.* He has one of those Robert Mitchum faces that don't age; it only frowns more. He and his sidekick, Mac McHale (Ray Winstone), are taken by the cool, contemptuous Soviet uber-villainess Irina Spalko (Cate Blanchett) to a cavernous warehouse to seek out a crate he saw there years ago. The contents of the crate are hyper-magnetic (lord, I love this stuff) and betray themselves when Indy throws a handful of gunpowder into the air.

In ways too labyrinthine to describe, the crate leads Indy, Mac, Irina, and the Russians far up the Amazon. Along the way they've gathered Marion Ravenwood (Karen Allen), Indy's girlfriend from the first film, and a young biker named Mutt Williams (Shia LaBeouf), who is always combing his ducktail haircut. They also acquire Professor Oxley (John Hurt), elderly colleague from the University of Chicago, whose function is to read all the necessary languages, know all the necessary background, and explain everything.

What happens in South America is explained by the need to create (1) sensational chase sequences and (2) awe-inspiring spectacles. We get such sights as two dueling jeep-like vehicles racing down parallel roads. Not many of the audience members will be as logical as I am and wonder who went to the trouble of building *parallel* roads in a rain forest. Most of the major characters eventually find themselves at the wheels of both vehicles; they leap or are thrown from one to another, and the vehicles occasionally leap right over each other. And that Irina, she's something. Her Russian backups are mostly just atmosphere, useful for pointing their rifles at Indy, but she can fight, shoot, fence, drive, leap, and kick, and keep on all night.

All leads to the discovery of a subterranean chamber beneath an ancient pyramid, where they find an ancient city made of gold and containing . . . but wait, I forgot to tell you they found a crystal skull in a crypt. Well, sir, it's one of thirteen crystal skulls, and the other twelve are in that chamber. When the set is complete, amazing events take place. Professor Oxley carries the thirteenth skull for most of the time, and finds it repels man-eating ants. It also represents one-thirteenth of all knowledge about everything, leading Irina to utter the orgasmic words, "I want to *know*!" In appearance, the skull is a cross between the aliens of the special edition of Spielberg's *Close Encounters of the Third Kind* and the hood ornaments of 1950s Pontiacs.

What is the function of the chamber? "It's a portal—to another dimension!" Oxley says. Indy is sensible: "I don't think we wanna go that way." It is astonishing that the protagonists aren't all killed twenty or thirty times, although Irina will become The Woman Who Knew Too Much. At his advanced age, Professor Oxley tirelessly jumps between vehicles, survives fire and flood and falling from great heights, and would win on *American Gladiators.* Relationships between certain other characters are of interest, since (a) the odds against them finding themselves together are astronomical, and (b) the odds against them *not* finding themselves together in this film are incalculable.

Now what else can I tell you, apart from mentioning the blinking red digital countdown, and the moving red line tracing a journey on a map? I can say that if you liked the other Indiana Jones movies, you will like this one, and that if you did not, there is no talking to you. And I can also say that a critic trying to place it in a hierarchy with the others would probably keep a straight face while recommending the second pound of sausage.

In Good Company ★ ★ ★

PG-13, 131 m., 2005

Dennis Quaid (Dan Foreman), Topher Grace (Carter Duryea), Scarlett Johansson (Alex

Foreman), Marg Helgenberger (Ann Foreman), David Paymer (Morty), Philip Baker Hall (Eugene Kalb). Directed by Paul Weitz and produced by Chris Weitz and Paul Weitz. Screenplay by Paul Weitz.

Corporations have replaced Nazis as the politically correct villains of the age—and just in time, because it was getting increasingly difficult to produce Nazis who survived into the twenty-first century (*Hellboy* had to use a portal in time). *The Manchurian Candidate* used a corporation instead of the Chinese communists, and thrillers like *Resident Evil* give us corporations whose recklessness turns the population into zombies. *In Good Company* is a rare species: a feel-good movie about big business. It's about a corporate culture that tries to be evil and fails.

It doesn't start out that way. We meet Dan Foreman (Dennis Quaid), head of advertising sales at a sports magazine, who has the corner office and the big salary and is close to landing a big account from a dubious client (Philip Baker Hall). Then disaster strikes. The magazine is purchased by Teddy K (an unbilled Malcolm McDowell), a media conglomerator in the Murdoch mode, who takes sudden notice of a twenty-six-year-old hotshot named Carter Duryea (Topher Grace) and sends him in to replace Dan. Carter takes Dan's job and corner office but instinctively keeps Dan as his "assistant," perhaps sensing that someone in the department will have to know more than Carter knows.

Dan accepts the demotion. He needs his job to keep up the mortgage payments and support his family. But Carter, known as a "ninja assassin" for his firing practices, fires Morty (David Paymer), an old-timer at the magazine. As we learn more about Morty's home life, we realize this only confirms the suspicions of his wife, who thinks he's a loser.

Developments up to this point have followed the template of standard corporate ruthlessness, with lives made redundant by corporate theories that are essentially management versions of a pyramid scheme: Plundering victims and looting assets can be made to look, on the books, like growth.

Dan has a wife named Ann (Marg Helgenberger) and a pretty college-age daughter named Alex (Scarlett Johansson). He is concerned about Alex, especially after finding a pregnancy-testing kit in the garbage, but doesn't know how concerned he should be until he discovers that Carter, the rat, has not only demoted him but is dating his daughter.

In Good Company so far has been the usual corporate slasher movie, in which good people have bad things happen to them because of the evil and greedy system. Then it takes a curious turn, which I will suggest without describing, in which goodness prevails and unexpected humility surfaces. The movie was directed by Paul Weitz, who with his brother Chris made *American Pie* and the Hugh Grant charmer *About a Boy,* and with those upbeat works behind him I didn't expect *In Good Company* to attain the savagery of Neil LaBute's *In the Company of Men,* but I was surprised all the same when the sun came out.

Dennis Quaid has a comfort level in roles like this that makes him effortlessly convincing; as he tries to land the account from the big client, we see how Dan uses psychology and his own personality to sell the magazine. Young Carter is years away from that ease. Topher Grace plays him as a kid who doesn't know which Christmas present he wants to play with first; he has achieved success more quickly than the experience to deal with it. Like a pro sports rookie, he can think of no more imaginative way to celebrate his wealth than to buy a new Porsche; he finds that such joys do not last forever.

Scarlett Johansson continues to employ the gravitational pull of quiet fascination. As in *Lost in Translation* and *Girl with a Pearl Earring* (both much better films), she creates a zone of her own importance into which men are drawn not so much by lust as by the feeling that she knows something about life that they might be able to learn. That turns the Alex-Carter affair into something more interesting than the sub–*American Pie* adventure we might have expected.

David Paymer's character provides the movie with emotional ballast; he is not only out of work, but probably unemployable, at his age and salary level, and unsuited to survive at a lower level. His story is common enough. It is a corporate strategy to create narratives for employees to imagine, in which they begin as junior executives and ascend to the boardroom. Countless college graduates enter this dream world every year, without reflecting (a) that there are many fewer positions at the top than at the bottom, and (b) that therefore, if the corporations are still hiring at the bottom, it is because there are fatalities at the top. You can always get someone younger and cheaper to do the job of the older and more experienced.

There's one scene in the movie that works well even though it's less than convincing. The conglomerator Teddy K jets in for a meeting with the staff, at which he recites various corporate platitudes to an adoring audience (one of the keys to success in business is the ability to endure the gaseous inanities of Management-Speak as if they meant anything). Then Dan stands up and, with everything to lose, explains clearly and mercilessly just why Teddy K is full of it. Whenever anyone speaks the plain truth on such an occasion, there is a palpable shock; how can such enterprises survive realism? Consider the soldier who asked Donald Rumsfeld, please, sir, may we have some more armor?

I don't believe the real Dan would have made quite that speech, but then I don't believe the third act of *In Good Company.* I'd like to, but I just can't. I don't think corporate struggles turn out that way. Still, the movie is smart enough, the performances strong, and the subplots involving Johansson and Paymer have their moments. If nothing else, *In Good Company* shows that Paul Weitz has the stuff to tell a ruthless story—and he does, until he loses his nerve. Since most audiences no doubt will prefer his version to the one I imagine, who is to say he is wrong?

In Her Shoes ★ ★ ★ ½

PG-13, 129 m., 2005

Cameron Diaz (Maggie Feller), Toni Collette (Rose Feller), Shirley MacLaine (Ella Hirsch), Mark Feuerstein (Simon Stein), Francine Beers (Mrs. Lefkowitz), Ken Howard (Michael Feller), Candice Azzara (Sydelle), Norman Lloyd (The Professor). Directed by Curtis Hanson and produced by Ridley Scott, Carol Fenelon, Lisa Ellzey, and Hanson. Screenplay by Susannah Grant, based on the novel by Jennifer Weiner.

Curtis Hanson's *In Her Shoes* takes a good half-hour to make it clear it will not be a soppy chick flick, and for that matter, what is "chick flick" anyway but an insulting term for a movie that is about women instead of the usual testosterone carriers? The movie's setup would be right at home in a sitcom, but its next ninety-nine minutes do some rather unexpected things with characters who insist on breaking out of the stereotypes they started with. It's not every big-budget movie that gets its two biggest emotional payoffs with poems by Elizabeth Bishop and E. E. cummings.

Here are the opening stereotypes: Maggie Feller (Cameron Diaz) is a blond bimbo who gets drunk at her high school reunion, has sex in the toilet, and passes out. Her sister, Rose (Toni Collette), is a plain-Jane Philadelphia lawyer who is fifteen pounds on the wrong side of her Weight Watchers target goal. Their mother is dead, and their father, Michael (Ken Howard), lives with his new wife, Sydelle (Candice Azzara). Maggie still lives at home because the rent is free, but Sydelle kicks her out because she wants her room for her own daughter, invariably described as "my Marsha."

Maggie moves in with Rose. Some measure of her desperation is suggested when Rose tells her she might consider going back to school. Maggie: "You know how well that worked out." Rose: "I meant the literacy place." Maggie indeed flunks an MTV audition when she can't read the words on the teleprompter.

Meanwhile, she trashes Rose's apartment while stealing her clothes, her money, and a potential boyfriend. Rose throws her out. Maggie is desperate when she finds birthday cards mailed to the girls by a grandmother whose existence was concealed from them. This is Ella (Shirley MacLaine), and in desperation Maggie travels to Ella's retirement home in Florida and throws herself on the mercy of a total stranger.

It's around here that the movie slips out of the cute stuff and develops a bite. Ella is the kind of no-nonsense older woman MacLaine has been playing ever since the wonderful *Madame Sousatzka* (1988). She's not a sentimental "oldster" but a tough cookie who observes Maggie stealing from her and asks her, "How much money were you hoping to get from me?" She makes Maggie a deal: She'll match, penny for penny, whatever Maggie can make while working at the retirement home's assisted living center. And as Maggie begins to bond with people such as Mrs. Lefkowitz (Francine Beers) and the Professor (Norman Lloyd), she discovers, slowly and uncertainly, that she can be competent and responsible and maybe even respectable.

The movie's key scenes take place with Maggie among the old people, and the screenplay by Susannah Grant (based on the novel by Jennifer Weiner) establishes them as characters who have lived their lives well by accumulating experience and instinctively knowing how to deal with the likes of Maggie.

The Professor, who taught college English, is especially important to Maggie. He wants her to read to him, gently helps her understand the technique and purpose of reading, and guides her through possible dyslexia. He needs a reader because he is blind, and that is important, too, because Maggie has maybe been thinking a lot about what Rose told her: "You're not going to look like this forever, you know." She knows the Professor doesn't like her for her looks. She reads him "One Art," a poem by Elizabeth Bishop that is about "the art of losing," and as a woman who has made a lifestyle out of misplacing people, possessions, and responsibilities, Maggie finds it strangely comforting and does some offscreen reading on her own, setting up a powerful appearance later in the film of the E. E. cummings poem that begins:

i carry your heart with me (i carry it in
my heart) i am never without it (anywhere
i go you go, my dear . . .

There are various male characters in the movie, attached to various possibilities of hearts being, or not being, carried in other hearts. But the movie is really about the transformation of the women, of all three women. That's what's surprising: This isn't simply about Maggie being worked on by Ella and Rose but about how her growth nudges both of the other women into new directions.

In Her Shoes starts out with the materials of an ordinary movie and becomes a rather special one. The emotional payoff at the end is earned, not because we see it coming as the inevitable outcome of the plot but because it arrives out of the blue and yet, once we think about it, makes perfect sense. It tells us something fundamental and important about a character, it allows her to share that something with those she loves, and it does it in a way we could not possibly anticipate. Like a good poem, it blindsides us with the turn it takes right at the end.

This movie by Curtis Hanson comes after *L.A. Confidential* (1997), *Wonder Boys* (2000), and Eminem's *8 Mile* (2002). Three completely different movies, you'd think, and yet all bound by a common thread: the transformative power of the written word. The first is about gossip journalism, the second about writers on a campus, the third about a hip-hop poet. Now a life is changed by reading.

In My Country ★ ★ ½

R, 100 m., 2005

Samuel L. Jackson (Langston Whitfield), Juliette Binoche (Anna Malan), Brendan Gleeson (de Jager), Menzi Ngubane (Dumi Mkhalipi), Sam Ngakane (Anderson), Aletta Bezuidenhout (Elsa), Lionel Newton (Edward Morgan), Langley Kirkwood (Boetie). Directed by John Boorman and produced by Robert Chartoff, Mike Medavoy, Kieran Corrigan, and Lynn Hendee. Screenplay by Ann Peacock, based on a book by Antjie Krog.

In the final decades of apartheid in South Africa, few observers thought power would change hands in the country without a bloody war. But white rule gave way peacefully to the Nelson Mandela government, and Mandela and F. W. de Klerk, the departing prime minister, shared the Nobel Peace Prize.

That miracle nevertheless left a nation scarred by decades of violence—not only of whites against blacks, although that predominated. The Truth and Reconciliation Commission, the inspiration of Mandela, Archbishop Desmond Tutu, and other leaders in the new society, found a way to deal with those wounds without resorting to the endless cycle of bloody revenge seen in Northern Ireland, Bosnia, and elsewhere. The commission made a simple offer: Appear before a public tribunal, confess exactly what you did, convince us you were acting under orders, make an apology we can believe, and we will move on from there.

John Boorman's *In My Country* is set at the time of the commission's hearings and stars Samuel L. Jackson as Langston Whitfield, a *Washington Post* reporter covering the story, and Juliette Binoche as Anna Malan, a white Afrikaner, who is doing daily broadcasts for the South African Broadcasting Company. As the commission and its caravan of press and support staff travel rural areas, Whitfield and Malan find themselves in disagreement about the commission but strongly attracted to each other.

I confess I walked into the film with strong feelings. I've spent a good deal of time in South Africa, including a year at the University of Cape Town. I had the opportunity to discuss the commission with Archbishop Tutu. I believe the transitional period in South Africa is a model for an enlightened and humane reconciliation with past evils. *In My Country* shows the process at work and argues in its favor, and I tended to approve of it just on that basis.

Yet there is something not quite right about the film itself. The affair between Whitfield and Malan seems arbitrary, more like two writers having sex on the campaign trail than like two people involved in a romance that would be important to them. Both are married, and neither wants to leave his or her marriage, although perhaps in the grip of infatuation they waver. Although apartheid imposed criminal penalties for interracial sex under its "Immorality Act," that does not necessarily mean that interracial sex has to be in the foreground of a movie about Truth and Reconciliation—particularly if it's an affair involving a visiting foreigner. There seems something too calculated about the movie's pairing up of the political and the personal.

There is another unconvincing aspect: Whitfield, the *Washington Post* reporter, is not convinced that the commission hearings are useful or just. He thinks the wrongdoers are getting off too easy, and says so at press conferences, becoming an advocate and making no attempt to seem objective. It is up to Anna Malan (and the plot) to convince him otherwise. There is a certain poetic irony in an Afrikaner convincing an African-American that Mandela's new South Africa is on the right track, but isn't it more of a fictional device than a likely scenario?

A scene where Malan brings Whitfield home to her family farm seems contrived because we are not sure what Anna hopes to accomplish with it, and at the end of the scene, that is still unclear. True, during the visit we are able to see white unease about the transfer of power. ("They're not our police anymore. It's not our country anymore.") But the romance adds complications that are essentially a distraction from the main line of the story.

The movie, written by Ann Peacock, is based on a book by Antjie Krog, whose own radio and newspaper reports of the hearings inspired the character of Anna Malan. It has scenes of undeniable power. Many of them involve a character named de Jager (Brendan Gleeson), a South African cop with a zeal for torture and murder that go far beyond his job requirements. Whitfield's encounter with de Jager is tense and strongly played. There are also moments of real emotion during the testimony from a parade of whites (and one black) seeking forgiveness.

As it happens, I've seen another film on the same subject. That is *Red Dust*, a selection at Toronto 2004, starring Hilary Swank as a New York attorney who returns to her native South Africa to represent a political activist (Chiwetel Ejiofor) in the amnesty hearing for his torturer (Jamie Bartlett). Bartlett's character serves something of the same function as Gleeson's in the other film, but all of the characters and their stories are more complex and contradictory, reflecting their turbulent times.

Innocent Voices ★ ★ ★

R, 120 m., 2005

Leonor Varela (Kella), Carlos Padilla (Chava), Gustavo Munoz (Ancha), Jose Maria Yazpik (Uncle Beto), Ofelia Medina (Mama Toya), Daniel Gimenez Cacho (Priest), Jesus Ochoa (Bus Driver). Directed by Luis Mandoki and produced by Lawrence Bender, Mandoki, and Alejandro Soberon Kuri. Screenplay by Mandoki and Oscar Orlando Torres.

"When the war started, Dad left for the United States," the young narrator of *Innocent Voices* tells us. "Mom said now I was the man of the house." Chava is eleven years old, living in a barrio in El Salvador at the time of the civil war in the 1980s. Eleven is a dangerous age because when he turns twelve he will be drafted into the government army.

There have been several movies about civil wars in Latin America. In *Innocent Voices,* the government is being given American funds to fight the communist-led guerrillas. In Haskell Wexler's *Latino* (1985), the Contras are given American funds to fight the government. In Oliver Stone's *Salvador* (1986), a cynical journalist tries to cover both sides.

What sets *Innocent Voices* apart from these films is its resolute point of view through the eyes of Chava. He has no political opinions. His uncle is with the guerrillas, so he supports his uncle as he would a football team, and he fears the government because he does not want to be taken into the army. But he sees these choices as events in his own life and has no larger knowledge of their meaning.

In that way *Innocent Voices* resembles the best film about insurgencies in Latin America, which is *Men with Guns* (1997) by John Sayles, in which no country is named. It is, I wrote, "an allegory about all countries where men with guns control the daily lives of the people. Some of the men are with the government, some are guerrillas, some are thieves, some are armed to protect themselves, and to the ordinary people it hardly matters: The man with the gun does what he wants, and his reasons are irrelevant—unknown perhaps even to himself."

That is certainly the case in *Innocent Voices,* where politics seem meaningless at the local level, and it is simply a matter of armed men, some of them boys, who have machine guns and fire them recklessly, maybe because it is fun. Tactics and strategy seem lacking in this war; the armed teams on both sides travel the countryside, rarely encountering each other, intimidating the peasants, for whom the message from both camps is the same: Support us or we will kill you.

In this world, Chava (Carlos Padilla) lives a blessed life, as one of those streetwise kids like Pixote who knows everybody's business. His mother, Kella (Leonor Varela), scrambles to feed and protect her three children, and they retreat for a time to the more remote house of her mother, but Kella fears to move to a safer area because if her husband returns and they have moved, "he'll have no way to find us." Her mother sadly shakes her head: "Those who go north get swept away."

Chava makes a living, of sorts. He talks a bus driver into making him an unofficial conductor, shouting out the names of the stops. He goes to school, until the school is closed because of the war. He befriends Ancha (Gustavo Munoz), known as "fish brain" because he is retarded: "He is the only one not scared to have a birthday."

The most frightening scenes in the film are not necessarily the ones where men sweep the barrio with machine-gun fire and the residents cower behind their mattresses. They are the ones when the army comes to the school to take away the twelve-year-olds. On one of these sweeps, Chava improvises an inspired way for the boys to hide from the army; the secret is revealed in a single shot by director Luis Mandoki.

The frightening thing is that twelve-year-olds make good soldiers, up to a point. We see one kid transformed by a uniform and a weapon. He is too young to have a full appreciation of his own danger or the meaning of his actions, and it is great fun to have a real uniform and a real gun. That adults would use children in this way (and they do, all over the world) is a sin against the children and against the future.

The movie is effective without being overwhelming. It doesn't have the power of *City of God, Pixote, Salaam Bombay!* and other films about young boys living by their wits in the center of danger. Perhaps that is because Chava still has a safety net of sorts, in his home and his mother and in the help of the local priest (Daniel Gimenez Cacho), who takes a moral stand against violence but is given cruel thanks for his trouble. Chava is never entirely alone, and his personality ensures that he knows many people and is liked by them. His story is not one of a child in the urban wilderness but of a child who was on a steady course through school and life when the war interrupted him.

There is a link between *Innocent Voices* and another recent film, *Lord of War.* In that one,

Nicolas Cage plays an arms dealer who sells weapons to whoever has the money. His chief competitor will sell only to the side he believes to be right. The Cage character has no such reluctance, pointing out that guns and money attract each other, and he might as well profit as anyone else. That brings us full circle to *Men with Guns.* Wars had more meaning and were fought less lightly when men had to kill each other with their hands, at close quarters. Guns make it so easy, even a child can do it.

Inside Deep Throat ★ ★ ★

NC-17, 90 m., 2005

A documentary directed by Fenton Bailey and Randy Barbato and produced by Brian Grazer, Bailey, and Barbato. Screenplay by Bailey and Barbato.

In the beginning, Gerard Damiano was a hairdresser. Listening to his clients talk about sex, which in his salon was apparently all they talked about, he realized that pornography had cross-over appeal. All you had to do was advertise a movie in such a way that couples would come, instead of only the raincoat brigade. With a budget of $25,000 and an actress named Linda Lovelace, he made *Deep Throat* (1972), which inspired a national censorship battle, did indeed attract couples, and allegedly grossed $600 million, making it the most profitable movie of all time.

Deep Throat was made on the far fringes of the movie industry; Damiano later complained that most of the profits went to people he prudently refused to name as the mob. Since the mob owned most of the porn theaters in the prevideo days and inflated box office receipts as a way of laundering income from drugs and prostitution, it is likely, in fact, that *Deep Throat* did not really gross $600 million, although that might have been the box office tally.

Inside Deep Throat, a documentary that premiered at Sundance and is now going into national release, was made not on the fringes but by the very establishment itself. The studio is Universal, a producer is Brian Grazer *(A Beautiful Mind, How the Grinch Stole Christmas)* and the directors are Fenton Bailey and Randy Barbato *(Party Monster, The Eyes of Tammy Faye).* The rating, of course, is NC-17. It is a commentary on the limitations of the rating system that Universal would release a documentary about an NC-17 film, but would be reluctant to make one.

The movie uses new and old interviews and newsreel footage to remember a time when porn was brand-new. In my 1973 review of *Deep Throat,* written three days after a police raid on the Chicago theater showing it, I wrote: "The movie became 'pornographic chic' in New York before it was busted. Mike Nichols told Truman Capote he shouldn't miss it, and then the word just sort of got around: This is the first stag film to see with a date."

A year or two earlier, porn audiences darted furtively into shabby little theaters on the wrong side of town; now they lined up for *Deep Throat* and talked cheerfully to news cameras about wanting to see it because, well, everybody else seemed to be going. The movie was not very good (even its director, Gerard Damiano, would tell you that), but it was explicit in a way that was acceptable to its audiences, and it leavened the sex with humor. Not very funny humor, to be sure, but it worked in the giddy, forbidden atmosphere of a mixed-gender porn theater.

The modern era of skin flicks began in 1960 with Russ Meyer's *The Immoral Mr. Teas,* which inspired Meyer and others to make a decade of films featuring nudity but no explicit sex. Then a Supreme Court ruling seemed to permit the hard-core stuff, and *Deep Throat* was the first film to take it to a mass audience. (Meyer himself never made hard-core, explaining (1) he didn't like to share his profits with the mob, and (2) he didn't think what went on below the waist was nearly as visually interesting as the bosoms of his supervixens.) The movie was raided in city after city, it was prosecuted for obscenity, it was seized and banned, and the publicity only made it more popular. There were predictions that explicit sex would migrate into mainstream films, even rumors that Stanley Kubrick wanted to make a porn film.

But by 1974 the boomlet was pretty much over, and the genre had gone back into the hands of the raincoat rangers. When I interviewed Damiano that year, he said porn would soon be a thing of the past: "The only thing that's kept it going this long is the FBI and the Nixon administration. Without censorship to encourage people's curiosity, the whole thing would have been over six months ago." And that was pretty much the story until home video came onto the market, creating a new and much larger audience, but destroying what shreds of artistic ambition lurked in the styles of the film-based pornographers (see *Boogie Nights* for the story of that transition).

Inside Deep Throat has some headlines that go against popular wisdom:

—While everybody remembers that Linda Lovelace later said she had virtually been raped on screen, the movie suggests that her troubles were the doing of her sadistic lover at the time, not Damiano. By the time she was fifty, she was posing for *Leg Show* magazine and saying she thought she looked pretty good for her age.

—While everyone remembers the report of a presidential commission that found pornography to be harmful, not many people remember that was the *second* commission to report on the subject, not the first. The 1970 commission, headed by former Illinois Governor Otto Kerner, found that pornography was not particularly linked to antisocial behavior, and that indeed sex criminals as a group tended to have less exposure to pornography than nonsex criminals. This report, based on scientific research and findings, was deemed unacceptable by the Reagan White House, which created a 1986 commission headed by Attorney General Edwin Meese, which did no research, relied on anecdotal testimony from the witnesses it called, and found pornography harmful.

—Charles Keating Jr. and his Citizens for Decent Literature got a lot of publicity for leading the charge against *Deep Throat* and Larry Flynt. Keating got less publicity when he was charged with racketeering in the Lincoln Savings and Loan scandal, and eventually served four years in prison.

As for *Inside Deep Throat,* it remembers a time before pornography was boring, and a climate in which nonpornographic films might consider bolder sexual content. It has some colorful characters, including a retired Florida exhibitor whose wife provides a running commentary on everything he says. And it tells us where they are now: Damiano is comfortably retired, Linda Lovelace died in a traffic accident, and her costar, Harry Reems, is a recovering substance abuser who now works as a Realtor in Park City, Utah, home of the Sundance Film Festival.

Inside Man ★ ★ ½

R, 128 m., 2006

Denzel Washington (Detective Keith Frazier), Clive Owen (Dalton Russell), Jodie Foster (Madeline White), Willem Dafoe (Captain Darius), Chiwetel Ejiofor (Detective Bill Mitchell), Christopher Plummer (Arthur Case), Kim Director (Stevie). Directed by Spike Lee and produced by Brian Grazer. Screenplay by Russell Gewirtz.

Spike Lee's *Inside Man* has a detective tell a bank robber: "You saw *Dog Day Afternoon.* You're stalling." The problem is, we've seen *Dog Day Afternoon,* and Lee is stalling. Here is a thriller that's curiously reluctant to get to the payoff, and when it does, we see why: We can't accept the motive and method of the bank robbery, we can't believe in one character and can't understand another, and if a man was old enough in the early 1940s to play an important wartime role, how old would he be now? Ninety-five? He might still be chairman of the bank he founded, but would he look like Christopher Plummer?

To give the movie its due, many of these same questions occur to the hero, Detective Keith Frazier. Denzel Washington plays him as a cross between a street cop and one of those armchair sleuths who sees through a crime and patiently explains it to his inferiors. Frazier is early on the scene after four armed robbers invade a Wall Street bank, take hostages, and start issuing demands. As the crisis drags on, Frazier realizes the guys inside don't *want* their demands to be met; they're stalling. But why?

The robbers are led by Clive Owen, who spends most of the movie wearing a mask. Since we see him in the first shot of the film, talking about the crime in the past tense, we know he won't be killed. What we wonder is where he studied the craft of bank robbery. His gang walks in, bolts the door, has everyone lie flat on the floor, and does all the usual stuff such as leaping over teller partitions and intimidating weeping customers. They also throw around completely unnecessary smoke bombs, and the smoke drifts out to the street, alerting a beat cop that something is wrong. Did they *want* to be trapped inside the bank?

I'm not going to go into any detail about how the crisis plays out. And I'm going to conceal the purpose of the robbery. What I must point out is that Plummer, as the bank president, doesn't look to be in his nineties. Giving him a mustache, a walking stick, and some wrinkles doesn't do it. Yet we have to believe that in mid–World War II he was old enough to have risen high enough to do something important enough that after the bank is surrounded, he calls in a woman who seems to have mysterious links to powerful people.

This is Madeline White (Jodie Foster). She knows everybody. She can walk into the mayor's office without an appointment. The mayor orders the cops to "extend her every courtesy." Who or what is Madeline White? I've seen the movie, and I don't know. She is never convincingly explained, and what she does is not well-defined. She's one of those characters who is all buildup and no delivery.

I once knew a man named Jean-Jacques de Mesterton, whose biography described him as "a professional adventurer, political adviser, and international facilitator." You can Google him. I asked him what, exactly, he did. "If you have a problem," he said, "first, you call the police. Then you call the FBI. If you still have a problem, you call me." I guess Madeline White is supposed to be the Jean-Jacques of New York, but although she purses her lips, frowns, and won't take any nonsense, she's basically a red herring.

The whole plot smells fishy. It's not that the movie is hiding something but that when it's revealed, it's been left sitting too long at room temperature. *Inside Man* goes to much difficulty to arrive at too little. It starts with the taut action of a superior caper movie, but then it meanders; eventually the narration slows to the pace of a Garrison Keillor story on *A Prairie Home Companion*, which is nice if you are a prairie, but if not, not.

The screenplay by Russell Gewirtz needs a few more runs through rewrite. Because the film was directed by Spike Lee, it is not without interest; Lee finds so many interesting details that don't involve the plot that we're reluctant when he gets back to business. A cameo involving a little boy and his video game is a self-contained editorial. A Sikh is accused of being an Arab terrorist, and you want to say, "People! Listen up! Guy with a turban! Sikh! Not Arab!" There's a nutty sequence in which the hostage-takers use a foreign language that has to be translated by a bystander's ex-wife.

The performances, for that matter, are first rate; Washington is convincing even when he has little to be convincing about, and Foster is smart and tough as she decisively does more or less nothing. Well, to be fair, a little more more than less.

The Interpreter ★ ★ ★

PG-13, 128 m., 2005

Nicole Kidman (Silvia Broome), Sean Penn (Tobin Keller), Catherine Keener (Dot Woods), Jesper Christensen (Nils Lud), Yvan Attal (Philippe), Earl Cameron (Zuwanie). Directed by Sydney Pollack and produced by Tim Bevan, Eric Fellner, and Kevin Misher. Screenplay by Charles Randolph, Scott Frank, and Steven Zaillian.

Sydney Pollack's *The Interpreter* is a taut and intelligent thriller, centering on Nicole Kidman as an interpreter at the United Nations and Sean Penn as a Secret Service agent. And, no, they don't have romantic chemistry: For once, the players in a dangerous game are too busy for sex—too busy staying alive and preventing murder. They do, however, develop an intriguing closeness, based on shared loss and a sympathy for the other person as a human being. There's a moment when she rests her head on his shoulder, and he puts a protective arm around her, and we admire the movie for being open to those feelings.

The story was filmed largely on location in and around the United Nations, including the General Assembly Room; it's the first film given permission to do that. I mention the location because it adds an unstated level of authenticity to everything that happens. There's a scene where a security detail sweeps the building, and it feels like a documentary. Like when Drew Barrymore runs onto the field at Fenway Park in *Fever Pitch*, the U.N. scenes provide what Werner Herzog calls "the voodoo of location"—the feeling of the real thing instead of the artifice of sets and special effects.

The movie has a realism of tone, too. This isn't a pumped-up techno-thriller, but a procedural, in which Secret Service agents Keller (Penn) and Woods (Catherine Keener) are assigned to the U.N. after an interpreter named Silvia Broome (Kidman) overhears a death threat. The threat is against an African dictator named Zuwanie (Earl Cameron), once respected, now accused of genocide. He announces that he will address the General Assembly to defend his policies. The head of the Secret Service (played by Pollack himself) says the last thing the United States needs, at this point in history, is the assassination of a foreign leader on American soil.

Zuwanie is clearly intended to represent Robert Mugabe of Zimbabwe, also once hailed as a liberator, now using starvation as a political tool. Silvia, we learn, grew up in Zuwanie's country, was a supporter of Zuwanie, saw her parents killed, became disillusioned. She speaks many languages, including Ku, the tongue of the (fictional) country of Matobo, and five years ago became a U.N. interpreter.

After she reports the death threat, she expects to be believed. But Keller draws an instant conclusion: "She's lying." A polygraph indicates "she's under stress, but not lying." Is she, or isn't she? We meet a gallery of suspects, including Zuwanie's white security chief and two of his political opponents. Keller looks into Silvia's background, convinced she has reasons for wanting Zuwanie dead, although she says she joined the U.N. because she supports peaceful change.

"Vengeance is a lazy form of grief," she tells the agent, who has some grief and vengeance issues of his own. She also tells him of a custom from Matobo: When a man kills a member of your family and is captured, he is tied up and thrown into the river, and it is up to your family to save him or let him drown. If he drowns, you will have vengeance, but you will grieve all of your days. If you save him, you will be released from your lament. This is not a practice I was familiar with, and seems even to have escaped the attention of the Discovery Channel; I'd like to see a family debating whether to save the killer or drown him. Maybe a family like the Sopranos.

What I admire most about the film is the way it enters the terms of this world—of international politics, security procedures, shifting motives—and observes the details of all-night stakeouts, shop talk, and interlocking motives and strategies. More than one person wants Zuwanie dead, and more than one person wants an assassination attempt, which is not precisely the same thing.

Nicole Kidman is a star who consistently finds dramatic challenges and takes chances. Consider her in *Birth, The Human Stain, Dogville, The Hours, The Others,* and *Moulin Rouge.* Here, with a vaguely South African accent and a little-girl fear peering out from behind her big-girl occupation, she sidesteps her glamour and is convincing as a person of strong convictions. Sean Penn matches her with a weary professionalism, a way of sitting there and just looking at her, as if she will finally break down and tell him what he thinks she knows. It's intriguing the way his character keeps several possibilities in his mind at once, instead of just signing on with the theory that has the most sympathy from the audience.

The final scene is perhaps not necessary; it has "obligatory closure" written all over it. But at least we are spared romantic clichés, and I was reminded of Robert Forster and Pam Grier in Tarantino's *Jackie Brown,* playing two adults with so much emotional baggage that for them romance is like a custom in another country.

Note: I don't want to get Politically Correct; I know there are many white Africans, and I admire Kidman's performance. But I couldn't help wondering why her character had to be white. I imagined someone like Angela Bassett in the role and wondered how that would have played. If you see the movie, run that through your mind.

Interview ★ ★ ★

R, 86 m., 2007

Steve Buscemi (Pierre Peders), Sienna Miller (Katya), Michael Buscemi (Robert Peders), Tara Elders (Maggie), Molly Griffith (Waitress). Directed by Steve Buscemi and produced by Gijs van de Westelaken and Bruce Weiss. Screenplay by Buscemi and David Schechter.

The Washington correspondent for a newsweekly is assigned to interview a celebrity sex icon, to his disgust and eventually to hers. Pierre (Steve Buscemi) has never seen a performance by Katya (Sienna Miller) and has done so little homework he hardly knows anything about her except that he loathes the very idea of such a woman. Katya has processed so many interviews that she's sick of them, turns up an hour late, and is not so much surprised that Pierre knows nothing about her as astonished that he has the nerve to try to fake the interview.

Such things happen. I once went to talk to Burt Lancaster about a movie named *Castle Keep*. The interview lasted four minutes. "You didn't like the picture, did you?" he asked. No, I said. "Then we have nothing to talk about, do we?" He walked out. Years later, I had a perfectly pleasant interview with Lancaster; stars just get ground down by the publicity process.

Interview was directed and cowritten by Buscemi, who plays the impatient newsman so well you can almost sense his toes curling in his shoes. Katya is apparently intended to be a Paris Hilton type. She plays the dumb sex kitten to perfection but has hidden levels of intelligence, insight, and game-playing. I've found over the years that most famous "dumb starlets" are smart. If they were really dumb, they would be unknown.

The Pierre character makes the mistake of condescending to Katya, insulting her, and making it clear he'd rather be in Washington covering a breaking story. The interview crashes, they walk out, and then paparazzi stalking Katya push Pierre into traffic, he gets a cut on his head, and she insists on taking him to her nearby apartment.

That's act one. Act two turns into a two-hander with them talking, drinking, smoking, doing some cocaine, flirting, dueling, insulting, and playing nasty head games. This formula is familiar enough; think of Neve Campbell and Dominic Chianese in James Toback's *When Will I Be Loved* (2004) and Ethan Hawke and Uma Thurman in Richard Linklater's *Tape* (2001), not to mention the Burtons in Mike Nichols's *Who's Afraid of Virginia Woolf?* (1966).

Why did it need to be done again? The original director on this project was Theo van Gogh, a Dutch director murdered in the street by an Islamic assassin who disapproved of one of his films. Van Gogh had planned to remake it in English with Miller and Buscemi, so the film went ahead. Buscemi handles it skillfully, using van Gogh's method of filming with three simultaneous video cameras. He and Miller are especially good at making plausible shifts in emotional speed. Will they sleep together or strangle each other? Are they really sharing their darkest, most shameful secrets? Which is the better actor? Which, for that matter, is the better interviewer?

A subtext of the film is that both actors most certainly know the types they're playing and are fed up with them, enough to put a cutting edge on their characters. Miller has known vacuous bimbos and can occasionally play one on TV, perhaps for her own amusement because celebrity journalists are so pathetically hungry for bimbo sound bites. Buscemi has doubtless encountered countless interviewers from hell.

If I have a problem with the movie, it's the too-neat O. Henry ending. I would have rather plunged deeper into the fearful waters they tread. A perfectly realistic movie on such a situation would have been fascinating, but here it has been adjusted, alas, to the requirements of the audience. Why do people get so angry at movies that end in mystery and unresolved wounds, like *Lost in Translation?* Why do they like it when a movie, however fascinating, goes on autopilot to wrap things up at the end?

What would really happen in this situation? The two characters would pass out, wake up with fearful hangovers, retain a blurred memory of the night before, not be sure if they slept together, hope to never see each other again, or shudder in shame if they did. Buscemi caught that dynamic in his perceptive debut film about alcoholism, *Trees Lounge* (1996), and look at how perfectly Joey Lauren Adams's *Come Early Morning* (2006) portrays it with Ashley Judd. The problem with most stories about drinking all night and burrowing to the truth, however, is that if you can drink that much, you can't burrow, or if you can, it's not worth a damn.

Still, I found *Interview* kind of fascinating, especially in the ways Buscemi and Miller make their performances into commentaries on the types of characters they play. When actors are really turned loose to play actors, they can achieve merciless accuracy; see Naomi Watts portray a day in the life of an actress in Scott Coffey's *Ellie Parker* (2005). If all the world's a stage for the rest of us, for them it's a backstage.

In the Shadow of the Moon ★ ★ ★ ★

PG, 100 m., 2007

With Buzz Aldrin, Alan Bean, Eugene Cernan, Michael Collins, Jim Lovell, John Young, Charlie Duke, Edgar D. Mitchell, Harrison Schmitt, and Dave Scott. A documentary directed by David Sington and produced by Duncan Copp.

We think of the *Apollo* voyages to the moon more in terms of the achievement than the ordeal. On the night of July 20, 1969, we looked up at the sky and realized that men, who had been gazing at the moon since they were boys, had somehow managed to venture there and were walking on its surface.

Yes, but consider the journey. Three men were packed like sardines in a tiny space capsule ("Spam in a can," the Gemini astronauts called themselves) and sent on a 480,000-mile round trip in a vessel whose electrical wiring was so questionable it had already burned three of them alive on a test pad. The capsule sat atop a rocket that had a way of blowing up. They had no way of knowing where, on the moon, they would land, if they got there. Compared to them, Evel Knievel was a Sunday driver.

Yes, but they took their chances, and they made it. Six of the seven *Apollo* missions landed on the moon, and the saga of *Apollo 13* was a masterpiece of ingenuity in the face of catastrophe. Now here is a spellbinding documentary interviewing many of the surviving astronauts, older men now, about their memories of the adventure. One who is prominently missing is Neil Armstrong, first man on the moon, who says he was first only by chance, and gets too much attention. Gene Siskel sat next to him on an airplane once and thought to himself, "Here is a man who is very weary of being asked what it was like to walk on the moon." So they talked about other things.

Of the others, every one is still sharp and lively and youthful in mind, even often in body. I attended the Conference on World Affairs in Boulder, Colorado, several times with Rusty Schweickart and noticed that he tended to be on panels that were about everything but space exploration. Yet here, in front of the cameras, they open up in a heartfelt way. The most stunning moment reveals how desperately they wanted to be part of the missions: Gus Grissom, one of the three astronauts killed in the launch-pad fire, earlier told John Young he doubted the safety of the wiring in the 100 percent oxygen atmosphere of the capsule but didn't dare complain because he might be booted out of the program for a negative attitude.

When you were on the moon, they remember, you could blank out Earth by holding up your thumb in front of your face. Yet they were struck by how large the planet was, and how thin and fragile its atmosphere, floating in an infinite void and preserving this extraordinary thing, life. And below, we were poisoning it as fast as we could.

The interviews with the astronauts are intercut with footage that is new, in great part, and looks better than it has any right to do. A researcher for this production spent years screening NASA footage that was still, in many cases, in its original film cans and had never been seen. The film was cleaned up and restored, the color refreshed, and the result is beautiful and moving. The *Apollo* missions were, after all, the most momentous steps ever taken by mankind; our species, like all living things, has evolved to live and endure on the planet of its origin. Random life spores may have traveled from world to world by chance, but this was the first time any living thing looked up and said, "I'm going there." These astronauts are still alive, but as long as mankind survives, their journeys will be seen as the turning point—to what, it is still to be seen.

In the Valley of Elah ★ ★ ★ ★

R, 120 m., 2007

Tommy Lee Jones (Hank Deerfield), Charlize Theron (Detective Emily Sanders), Susan Sarandon (Joan Deerfield), James Franco (Sergeant Dan Carnelli), Jonathan Tucker (Mike Deerfield), Frances Fisher (Evie), Jason Patric

(Lieutenant Kirklander), Josh Brolin (Chief Buchwald). Directed by Paul Haggis and produced by Patrick Wachsberger, Steven Samuels, Darlene Caamano Loquet, Haggis, and Larry Becsey. Screenplay by Haggis.

I don't know Tommy Lee Jones at all. Let's get that clear. I've interviewed him, and at Cannes we had one of those discussions at the American Pavilion. He didn't enjoy doing it, but he felt duty-bound to promote his great film *The Three Burials of Melquiades Estrada.* During my questions he twisted his hands like a kid in the principal's office. He remains a mystery to me, which is why I feel free to share some feelings about him. I'm trying to understand why he is such a superb actor.

Look at the lines around his eyes. He looks concerned, under pressure from himself, a man who has felt pain. Look at his face. It seems to conceal hurtful emotion. He doesn't smile a lot, but when he does, it's like clouds are lifting. Listen to his voice, filled with authority and hard experience. Notice when he speaks that he passes out words as if they were money he can't afford. Whether these characteristics are true of the private man, I have no way of knowing.

Paul Haggis's *In the Valley of Elah* is built on Tommy Lee Jones's persona, and that is why it works so well. The same material could have been banal or routine with an actor trying to be "earnest" and "sincere." Jones isn't trying to be anything at all. His character is simply compelled to do what he does and has a lot of experience doing it. He plays a Vietnam veteran named Hank Deerfield, now hauling gravel in Tennessee. He gets a call from the Army that his son Mike, just returned from a tour in Iraq, is AWOL from his squad at Fort Rudd. That sounds wrong. He tells his wife, Joan (Susan Sarandon), that he's going to drive down there and take a look into things. "It's a two-day drive," she says. He says, "Not the way I'll drive it."

He checks into a cheap motel. His investigations in the area of Fort Rudd take him into topless bars, chicken shacks, the local police station, the base military police operation, and a morgue where he's shown something cut into pieces and burned, and he IDs the remains as his son. Looking through his son's effects, he asks as a distraction if he can have his Bible while he's pocketing his son's cell phone. It's been nearly destroyed by heat, but a friendly technician salvages some video from it, filled with junk artifacts but still retaining glimpses of what it recorded on video: glimpses of hell.

To describe the many avenues of his investigation would be pointless and diminish the film's gathering tension. I'd rather talk about what Haggis, also the writer and coproducer, does with the performance. Imagine the first violinist playing a note to lead the orchestra into tune. Haggis, as director, draws that note from Jones, and the other actors tune to it. They include Charlize Theron as a city homicide detective, Jason Patric as a military policeman, Sarandon as Deerfield's wife, and various other police and military officers and members of Mike's unit in Iraq.

None of these characters are heightened. None of them behave in any way as if they're in a thriller. Other directors might have pumped them up, made them colorful or distinctive in some distracting way. Theron could (easily) be sexy. Patric could (easily) be a bureaucratic paper pusher. Sarandon could (easily) be a hysterical worrier, or an alcoholic, or push it any way you want to. You know how movies make supporting actors more colorful than they need to be, and how happily a lot of actors go along with that process.

Not here. Theron, who is actually the costar, so carefully modulates her performance that she even ignores most of the sexism aimed at her at the police station. Nor is there any hint of sexual attraction between her and anybody else, nor does she sympathize with Hank Deerfield and work on his behalf. Nor, for that matter, does she compete with him. She simply does her job and raises her young son.

I don't think there's a scene in the movie that could be criticized as "acting," with quotation marks. When Sarandon, who has already lost one son to the Army, now finds she has lost both, what she says to Jones over the telephone is filled with bitter emotion but not given a hint of emotional spin. She says it the way a woman would if she had held the same conversation with this man for a lifetime. The movie is about determination, doggedness, duty, and the ways a war changes a man. There is no release or climax at the end, just closure. Even the final dramatic gesture only says exactly what Deerfield explained earlier that it says, and nothing else.

That tone follows through to the movie's consideration of the war itself. Those who call *In the Valley of Elah* anti-Iraq-war will not have been paying attention. It doesn't give a damn where the war is being fought. Hank Deerfield isn't politically opposed to the war. He just wants to find out how his son came all the way home from Iraq and ended up in charred pieces in a field. Because his experience in Vietnam apparently had a lot to do with crime investigation, he's able to use intelligence as well as instinct. And observe how Theron, as the detective, observes him, takes what she can use, and adds what she draws from her own experience.

Paul Haggis is making good films these days. He directed *Crash* and wrote *Million Dollar Baby,* both Oscar winners, and was nominated as cowriter of *Letters from Iwo Jima.* He and his casting directors assembled an ideal ensemble for this film, which doesn't sensationalize but just digs and digs into our apprehensions. I have been trying to think who else could have carried this picture except Tommy Lee Jones, and I just can't do it. Who else could tell Theron's young son the story of David and Goliath (which took place in the Valley of Elah) and make it sound like instruction in the tactics of being brave?

Into the Blue ★ ★ ★

PG-13, 110 m., 2005

Paul Walker (Jared), Jessica Alba (Sam), Scott Caan (Bryce), Ashley Scott (Amanda), Josh Brolin (Bates), James Frain (Reyes), Tyson Beckford (Primo), Dwayne Adway (Roy). Directed by John Stockwell and produced by David A. Zelon. Screenplay by Matt Johnson.

Into the Blue is, of all things, an adventure story. Not a high-powered thriller with goofy special effects, but a story about people and hazards and treasure and love, in which every single thing that everybody does is physically possible for people to really do (except that they can apparently hold their breath indefinitely). The movie is written, acted, and directed as a story, not as an exercise in mindless kinetic energy.

Paul Walker and Jessica Alba star as Jared and Sam, lovers who live on a leaky boat in the Bahamas and search for buried treasure. They haven't found much, but they have their love to keep them warm. Tied up at a nearby dock is the larger and more powerful boat of Bates (Josh Brolin), who has money and success and wants to hire Jared, but there's something creepy about him.

Jared's friend Bryce (Scott Caan) flies in from the mainland with a girlfriend named Amanda (Ashley Scott) he says he picked up the night before. They all go diving together and find two kinds of treasure in more or less the same place: one ancient, one right up-to-date. They could become very rich. But Bryce is greedy and wants to push them in a direction that Jared and Sam are ethically opposed to.

But my description sounds dry and abstract, and the movie is juicy with fun. I'm trying not to tell you too much about what happens, because one of the pleasures of *Into the Blue* is that it develops as a narrative, not as a series of action scenes, and the characters don't mindlessly hurry from one impossible stunt to another but weigh their options, advocate opposing strategies, and improvise when they get in danger.

A lot of the movie takes place underwater, and director John Stockwell and cinematographers Shane Hurlbut and Peter Zuccarini do a good job of keeping us oriented under the sea. We know more or less where everything is, and what it means, and how it can be involved in the story; when there's an underwater emergency that almost kills Bryce, it is handled as if the characters (or the writers) have some practical information about scuba diving. There is also the surprise of having something very bad happen to a character we had every reason to expect would be around until the end of the movie.

The opening scenes are deceptive. The Alba character seems to have wandered over from the *Sports Illustrated* Swimsuit Issue, or maybe she thinks she's in the video. Then the plot kicks in and she gets a lot to do while *still* looking fine in a swimsuit. She also looks surprisingly sweet, after the stripper she played in *Sin City.* Caan, like his old man, does a good job of playing a persuasive jerk, and Walker is intriguing in the way he has his standards but can be talked out of them. People actually change their minds during this movie; in most action films, they're issued with an identity in their first scene and are limited by that identity for the rest of the movie.

Into the Blue offers modest pleasures. It is not an essential film, but if you go to see it, it will not insult your intelligence, and there's genuine suspense toward the end. It is a well-made example in a genre that has been cheapened and made routine. There's evidence the filmmakers spent more time talking about the characters and story than about how special effects would allow them to cheat on the narrative logic. And at the end of the film, there are some small surprises about who has survived and who has not. Usually you can predict the final head count at the end of the first act.

Into the Wild ★ ★ ★ ★

R, 150 m., 2007

Emile Hirsch (Christopher McCandless), Marcia Gay Harden (Billie McCandless), William Hurt (Walt McCandless), Jena Malone (Carine McCandless), Catherine Keener (Jan Burres), Brian Dieker (Rainey), Vince Vaughn (Wayne Westerberg), Zach Galifianakis (Kevin), Kristen Stewart (Tracy), Hal Holbrook (Ron Franz). Directed by Sean Penn and produced by Penn, Art Linson, and Bill Pohlad. Screenplay by Penn, based on the book by Jon Krakauer.

For those who have read Thoreau's *Walden*, there comes a time, maybe lasting only a few hours or a day, when the notion of living alone in a tiny cabin beside a pond and planting some beans seems strangely seductive. Certain young men, of which I was one, lecture patient girlfriends about how such a life of purity and denial makes perfect sense. Christopher McCandless did not outgrow this phase.

Jon Krakauer's *Into the Wild*, which I read with a fascinated dread, tells the story of a twenty-two-year-old college graduate who cashes in his law school fund and, in the words of Mark Twain, lights out for the territory. He drives west until he can drive no farther, and then north into the Alaskan wilderness. He has a handful of books about survival and edible wild plants, and his model seems to be Jack London, although he should have devoted more attention to that author's *To Build a Fire*.

Sean Penn's spellbinding film adaptation of this book stays close to the source. We meet Christopher (Emile Hirsch), an idealistic dreamer in reaction against his proud parents (William Hurt and Marcia Gay Harden) and his bewildered sister (Jena Malone). He had good grades at Emory; his future in law school was right there in his grasp. Why did he disappear from their lives, why was his car found abandoned, where was he, and why, why, why?

He keeps journals in which he sees himself in the third person as a heroic loner, renouncing civilization, returning to the embrace of nature. In centuries past such men might have been saints, retreating to a cave or hidden hermitage, denying themselves all pleasures except subsistence. He sees himself not as homeless, but as a man freed from homes.

In the book, Krakauer traces his movements through the memories of people he encounters on his journey. It was an impressive reporting achievement to track them down, and Penn's film affectionately embodies them in strong performances. These are people who take in the odd youth, feed him, shelter him, give him clothes, share their lives, mentor him—and worry as he leaves to continue his quest, which seems to them, correctly, as doomed.

By now McCandless has renamed himself Alexander Supertramp. He is validated by his lifestyle choice. He meets people such as Rainey and Jan (Brian Dieker and Catherine Keener), leftover hippies still happily rejecting society, and Wayne (Vince Vaughn), a hard-drinking, friendly farmer. The most touching contact he makes is with Ron (Hal Holbrook), an older man who sees him clearly and with apprehension, and begins to think of him as a wayward grandson. Christopher lectures this man, who has seen it all, on what he is missing, and asks him to follow him up a steep hillside to see the next horizon. Ron tries, before he admits he is no longer in condition.

And then McCandless disappears from the maps of memory, into unforgiving Alaska.

Yes, it looks beautiful. It is all he dreamed of. He finds an abandoned bus where no bus should be and makes it his home. He tries hunting, not very successfully. He lives off the land, but the land is a zero-tolerance system. From his journals and other evidence, Penn reconstructs his final weeks. Emile Hirsch plays him in a hypnotic performance, turning skeletal, his eyes sinking into his skull while they still burn with zeal. It is great acting, and more than acting.

This is a reflective, regretful, serious film about a young man swept away by his uncompromising choices. Two of the more truthful statements in recent culture is that we need a little help from our friends, and that sometimes we must depend on the kindness of strangers. If you don't know those two things and accept them, you will end up eventually in a bus of one kind or another. Sean Penn himself, fiercely idealistic, uncompromising, a little less angry now, must have read the book and reflected that there, but for the grace of God, went he. The movie is so good partly because it means so much, I think, to its writer-director. It is a testament like the words that Christopher carved into planks in the wilderness.

I grew up in Urbana, Illinois, three houses down from the Sanderson family—Milton and Virginia and their boys, Steve and Joe. My close friend was Joe. His bedroom was filled with aquariums, terrariums, snakes, hamsters, spiders, and butterfly and beetle collections. I envied him like crazy. After college he hit the road. He never made a break from his parents, but they rarely knew where he was. Sometimes he came home, and his mother would have to sew $100 bills into the seams of his blue jeans. He disappeared in Nicaragua. His body was later identified as a dead Sandinista freedom fighter. From a nice little house surrounded by evergreens at the other end of Washington Street, he left to look for something he needed to find. I believe in Sean Penn's Christopher McCandless. I grew up with him.

The Invasion ★ ★

PG-13, 95 m., 2007

Nicole Kidman (Carol), Daniel Craig (Ben), Jeremy Northam (Tucker), Jackson Bond (Oliver), Jeffrey Wright (Dr. Galeano). Directed by Oliver Hirschbiegel and produced by Joel Silver. Screenplay by David Kajganich, based on the novel *The Body Snatchers* by Jack Finney.

The Invasion is the fourth, and the least, of the movies made from Jack Finney's classic science-fiction novel *The Body Snatchers.* Here is a great story born to be creepy, and the movie churns through it like a road company production. If the first three movies served as parables for their times, this one keeps shooting off parable rockets that fizzle out. How many references in the same movie can you have to the war in Iraq and not say anything about it?

Don Siegel's classic *Invasion of the Body Snatchers* (1956) was about alien pods that arrived on Earth, sucked up the essence of human hosts, and became duplicates of them—exact copies, except for what made them human. It was widely decoded as an attack on McCarthyism. Phil Kaufman's *Invasion of the Body Snatchers* (1978), inexplicably described by Pauline Kael as "the American movie of the year," was said to have something to do with Watergate and keeping tabs on those who are not like you. Abel Ferrara's *Body Snatchers* (1994), by far the best of the films, might have been about the spread of AIDS.

And *The Invasion*? One of the alien beings argues persuasively that if everyone were like them, there'd be no war in Iraq, no genocide in Darfur—no conflict in general, I guess, although they don't seem to have much of a position on global warming. I don't have a clue what the movie thinks, if anything, about Iraq, which is mentioned so frequently, but it may be a veiled attack on cults that require unswerving conformity from their members. Which cults? I dunno.

In all four movies, alien spores arrive on Earth from space. In the early films they take the form of pods, which look like very large brown snow peas. Some viewers complained after Kaufman's movie that they couldn't believe aliens could truck those pods all over San Francisco, to which the obvious reply is: Do you expect a movie titled *Invasion of the Body Snatchers* to be plausible?

In Oliver Hirschbiegel's new version, the spores piggy-back on a returning space shuttle that crashes and scatters debris from Dallas to Washington. Anyone who touches the debris gets the infection, which is then spread by touch and the exchange of vomit (in more ways than you might imagine). In Washington, a psychiatrist named Carol (Nicole Kidman) has a patient who complains, "My husband just . . . isn't my husband anymore." Versions of this line do duty in all four films. The pod people look like the people they occupy and have the same memories ("Remember Colorado?"), but they walk like mannequins with arthritis, except when they're running like zombies.

Carol's estranged husband, Tucker (Jeremy Northam), is a disease control expert who becomes infected and after four years suddenly wants to start spending time with their child, Oliver (Jackson Bond). Little Oliver texts his mom that his dad isdifferent. Carol's current good friend is a doctor named Ben (Daniel Craig), who is one of many to notice a new "flu virus" that is spreading through the land.

His colleague, a researcher named Dr. Galeano (Jeffrey Wright), gets a sample of the virus, and in a performance that would be the envy of every scientist since Newton, gazes at it through a microscope and almost immediately explains what it is, how it reproduces, how it takes over when we fall asleep, and (apparently only a day or two later) how to defeat it with an antibody that can seemingly be manufactured so quickly and in such quantities that it can be sprayed from crop dusters. By this point the movie has lost all coherence, not to mention flaunting a scene where a helicopter lands atop a towering skyscraper in Washington, where federal law decrees no building can be taller than the Capitol.

This may not be entirely Hirschbiegel's fault. Warner Bros. didn't approve of his original version and brought in the Wachowskis to rewrite it and James McTeigue (*V for Vendetta*) to direct their revisions. All three served time on the *Matrix* movies: just the team you'd want to add a little incomprehensible chaos.

The genius of the Ferrara version was to make his very sympathetic heroine a young girl on an Army base who can't get anyone to listen to her. You know how adults can be when kids claim they've seen aliens. The problem with this new version is that it caves in and goes for your basic car chase scenes (spinning tires, multiple crashes, car in flames, dozens of pod people hanging onto it, etc). If aliens are among us, we will not be saved by stunt driving.

Nicole Kidman, Daniel Craig, Jeremy Northam, little Jackson Bond, Jeffrey Wright, and other cast members do what they can with dialogue that can hardly be spoken, and a plot that we concede must be implausible but does not necessarily have to upstage the *Mad* magazine version. And the aliens themselves are a flop. Just like zombies, they're pushovers: easy to spot, slow-moving, not too bright, can be shot dead or otherwise disposed of. OK. Now we've had *Invasion of the Body Snatchers* twice, *Body Snatchers,* once and *Invasion* once. Somebody should register the title *Of The.*

Iron Man ★ ★ ★ ★

PG-13, 126 m., 2008

Robert Downey Jr. (Tony Stark/Iron Man,) Terrence Howard (Colonel Rhodes), Jeff Bridges (Obadiah Stane/Iron Monger), Gwyneth Paltrow (Pepper Potts). Directed by Jon Favreau and produced by Ari Arad. Screenplay by Mark Fegus and Hank Ostby.

When I caught up with *Iron Man,* a broken hip had delayed me and the movie had already been playing for three weeks. What I heard during that time was that a lot of people loved it, that they were surprised to love it so much, and that Robert Downey Jr.'s performance was special. Apart from that, all I knew was that the movie was about a big iron man. I didn't even know that a human occupied it and halfway thought that the Downey character's brain had been transplanted into a robot, or a fate equally weird.

Yes, I knew I was looking at sets and special effects—but I'm referring to the reality of the illusion, if that makes any sense. With many superhero movies, all you get is the surface of the illusion. With *Iron Man,* you get a glimpse into the depths. You get the feeling, for example, of a functioning corporation. Consider the characters of Pepper Potts (Gwyneth Paltrow), Stark's loyal aide, and Obadiah Stane (Jeff Bridges), Stark's business partner. They don't feel drummed up for the occasion. They seem to have worked together for a while.

Much of that feeling is created by the chemistry involving Downey, Paltrow, and Bridges. They have relationships that seem fully formed and resilient enough to last through the whole movie, even if plot mechanics were not about to take them to another level. Between the two men, there are echoes of the relationship between Howard Hughes and Noah Dietrich in Scorsese's *The Aviator* (2004). Obadiah Stane doesn't come onscreen waving flags and winking at the camera to announce he is the villain; he seems adequately explained simply as the voice of reason at Stark's press conference. (Why did "Stark," during that scene, make me think of "raving mad"?) Between Stark and Pepper, there's that classic screen tension between "friends" who know they can potentially become lovers.

Downey's performance is intriguing and unexpected. He doesn't behave like most superheroes: He lacks the psychic weight and gravitas. Tony Stark is created from the persona Downey has fashioned through many movies: irreverent, quirky, self-deprecating, wisecracking. The fact that Downey is allowed to think and talk the way he does while wearing all that hardware represents a bold decision by the director, Jon Favreau. If he hadn't desired that, he probably wouldn't have hired Downey. So comfortable is Downey with Tony Stark's dialogue, so familiar does it sound coming from him, that the screenplay seems almost to have been dictated by Downey's persona.

There are some things that some actors can safely say onscreen, and other things they can't. The Robert Downey Jr. persona would find it difficult to get away with weighty, profound statements (in an "entertainment movie," anyway—a more serious film like *Zodiac* is another matter). Some superheroes speak in a kind of heightened, semiformal prose, as if dictating to *Bartlett's Familiar Quotations*. Not Tony Stark. He could talk that way and be Juno's uncle. *Iron Man* doesn't seem to know how seriously most superhero movies take themselves. If there is wit in the dialogue, the superhero is often supposed to be unaware of it. If there is broad humor, it usually belongs to the villain. What happens in *Iron Man*, however, is that sometimes we wonder how seriously even Stark takes it. He's flippant in the face of disaster, casual on the brink of ruin.

It's prudent, I think, that Favreau positions the rest of the characters in a more serious vein. The supporting cast wisely does not try to one-up him. Gwyneth Paltrow plays Pepper Potts as a woman who is seriously concerned that this goofball will kill himself. Jeff Bridges makes Obadiah Stane one of the great superhero villains by seeming plausibly concerned about the stock price. Terrence Howard, as Colonel Rhodes, is at every moment a conventional straight arrow. What a horror show it would have been if they were all tuned to Tony Stark's sardonic wavelength. We'd be back in the world of *Swingers* (1996), which was written by Favreau.

Another of the film's novelties is that the enemy is not a conspiracy or spy organization. It is instead the reality in our own world today: Armaments are escalating beyond the ability to control them. In most movies in this genre, the goal would be to create bigger and better weapons. How unique that Tony Stark wants to disarm. It makes him a superhero who can think, reason, and draw moral conclusions, instead of one who recites platitudes.

The movie is largely founded on its special effects. When somebody isn't talking, something is banging, clanging, or laying rubber. The armored robotic suits utilized by Tony and Obadiah would upstage lesser actors than Downey and Bridges; it's surprising how much those two giant iron men seem to reflect the personalities of the men inside them. Everything they do is preposterous, of course, but they seem to be doing it, not the suits. Some of their moments have real grandeur—as when Tony tests his suit to see how high it will fly, and it finally falls back toward Earth in a sequence that reminded me of a similar challenge in *The Right Stuff*.

The art direction is inspired by the original Marvel artists. The movie doesn't reproduce the drawings of Jack Kirby and others, but it reproduces their feeling, a vision of out-scaled enormity, seamless sleekness, secret laboratories made not of nuts and bolts but of . . . vistas. A lot of big budget f/x epics seem to abandon their stories with half an hour to go and just throw effects at the audience. This one has a plot so ingenious it continues to function no matter how loud the impacts, how enormous the explosions. It's an inspiration to provide Tony with that heart-saving device; he's vulnerable not simply because Obadiah might destroy him, but because he might simply run out of juice.

That leaves us, however, with a fundamental question at the bottom of the story: Why must the ultimate weapon be humanoid in appearance? Why must it have two arms and two legs, and why does it matter if its face is scowling? In the real-world competitions between fighting machines, all the elements of design are based entirely on questions of how well they allow the machines to attack, defend, recover, stay upright, and overturn their enemies. It is irrelevant whether they have conventional eyes, or whether those eyes narrow. Nor does it matter whether they have noses, because their oxygen supply is obviously not obtained by breathing. The solution to such dilemmas is that the armored suits look the way they do for entirely cinematic reasons. The bad iron man should look like a mean machine. The good iron man should utilize the racing colors of Tony Stark's favorite sports cars. It wouldn't be nearly as much fun to see a fight scene between two refrigerators crossed with the leftovers from a boiler room.

At the end of the day it's Robert Downey Jr. who powers the liftoff separating this from most other superhero movies. You hire an actor for his strengths, and Downey would not be strong as a one-dimensional mightyman. He is strong because he is smart, quick, and funny, and because we sense his public persona masks deep private wounds. By building on that, Favreau found his movie, and it's a good one.

The Island ★ ★ ★

PG-13, 127 m., 2005

Ewan McGregor (Lincoln Six Echo), Scarlett Johansson (Jordan Two Delta), Djimon Hounsou (Albert Laurent), Sean Bean (Merrick), Michael Clarke Duncan (Starkweather), Steve Buscemi (McCord). Directed by Michael Bay and produced by Bay, Ian Bryce, Laurie MacDonald, and Walter F. Parkes. Screenplay by Caspian Tredwell-Owen, Alex Kurtzman, and Roberto Orci.

The Island runs 127 minutes, but that's not long for a double feature. The first half of Michael Bay's new film is a spare, creepy science-fiction parable, and then it shifts into a high-tech action picture. Both halves work. Whether they work together is a good question. The more you like one, the less you may like the other. I liked them both, up to a point, but the movie seemed a little too much like surf 'n' turf.

The first half takes place in a sterile futuristic environment where the inhabitants wear identical uniforms (white for the citizens, black for their supervisors). Big-screen TVs broadcast slogans and instructions, and about twice a day everybody gathers before them for the lottery. This sealed world, its citizens believe, has been created to protect them from pollution that has poisoned the earth. There is, however, one remaining "pathogen-free zone," which looks a lot like a TV commercial for *The Beach*. Winners of the lottery get to go there.

Yeah, sure, we're thinking. But the citizens in the white suits don't think very deeply; "they're educated to the level of fifteen-year-olds," we're told. There was a time when that would have made them smarter than most of the people who ever lived, but in this future world, education has continued to degrade, and we see adults reading aloud from *Fun with Dick and Jane*, a book that on first reading I found redundant and lacking in irony.

The true nature of this sealed world is not terrifically hard to guess; even those who failed to see through *The Village* may decode its secret. But the inhabitants are childlike and blissful, all except for a few troublesome characters like Lincoln Six Echo (Ewan McGregor), who wants bacon for breakfast but is given oatmeal. This inspires him to develop what all closed systems fear, a curiosity. "Why is Tuesday night always tofu night?" he asks his supervisor. "What is tofu? Why can't I have bacon? Why is everything white?" Then one day he sees a flying bug where no bug should be, or fly.

Sidestepping some intervening spoilers, I can move on to the second half of the movie, in which Lincoln Six Echo and the equally naive Jordan Two Delta (Scarlett Johansson) escape from the sealed world and are chased by train, plane, automobile, helicopter, and hovercycle in a series of special effects sequences that develop a breathless urgency. How the heroes manage to discover the underlying truth about their world while moving at such a velocity suggests they are quicker studies than we thought.

The movie never satisfactorily comes full circle, and although the climax satisfies the requirements of the second half of the story, it leaves a few questions unanswered. We wonder, for example, why a manufacturing enterprise so mammoth could have been undertaken in secret. Were government funds involved? We don't need to know the answers to these questions, it's true, but they would have allowed Bay (*Armageddon*) to do what the best science fiction does, and use the future as a way to critique the present. Does stem cell research ring a bell?

The Island has certain special effects, not its largest or most sensational, that reminded me of the creativity in a film like Spielberg's *Minority Report*. For example, little ladybug-like robots that crawl up your face and into your eye sockets, and transmit information from your brain before working their way through your plumbing and being expelled like kidney stones. I hate it when that happens. And consider the effective way CGI is used to show the actors interacting with themselves.

McGregor and Johansson do a good job of playing characters raised to be docile, obedient, and not very bright. The way they have knowledge gradually thrust upon them is carefully modulated by Bay, so that we can see them losing their illusions almost in spite of themselves. Michael Clarke Duncan has only three or four scenes, but they're of central importance, and he brings true horror to them. Sean Bean has the Sean Bean role, as a smug corporate monster. And the beloved Steve Buscemi plays an important character who has brought all of his bad habits into the sterile future world.

Buscemi is an engineer, or maybe a janitor, and lives in what must be the boiler room. All closed systems, no matter how spotless and pristine, always have an area filled with rusty machinery, cigarette butts, oily rags, and a guy who reads dirty magazines and knows how everything really works. Even in *Downfall*, the harrowing drama about Hitler's last days, there was a boiler room in the bunker where Eva Braun and her buddies could sneak away for a smoke. The Buscemi character turns out to be surprisingly well-informed and helpful, but then again, if the plot had to depend on characters educated only to the level of fifteen-year-olds, we might still be in the theater.

Note (spoiler warning): It was a little eerie watching The Island *only a month after reading Kazuo Ishiguro's new novel,* Never Let Me Go. *Both deal with the same subject: raising human clones as a source for replacement parts. The creepy thing about the Ishiguro novel is that the characters understand and even accept their roles as "donors," while only gradually coming to understand their genetic origins. They aren't locked up but are free to move around; some of them drive cars. Why do they agree to the bargain society has made for them? The answer to that question, I think, suggests Ishiguro's message: The real world raises many of its citizens as spare parts; they are used as migratory workers, minimum-wage retail slaves, even suicide bombers.* The Island *doesn't go there, but, then, did you expect it would?*

Isn't This a Time! ★ ★ ★ ½

NO MPAA RATING, 90 m., 2006

A documentary directed by Jim Brown and produced by Brown, Michael Cohl, and William Eigen. With Pete Seeger, Ronnie Gilbert, Fred Hellerman, Erik Darling, Eric Weissberg, Leon Bibb, Theodore Bikel, Arlo Guthrie, and Peter, Paul, and Mary.

In September 2004 at the Toronto Film Festival, the Weavers sang together for possibly the last time. The event had great meaning for those who knew the Weavers and remembered their songs; in progressive circles they supplied the sound track for a good part of the 1950s and 1960s—the Weavers, and those who followed in their footsteps, such as Arlo Guthrie, Peter, Paul, and Mary, and Leon Bibb. If feelings stir within you when you hear "Goodnight, Irene" and "Wimoweh" and "This Land Is Your Land" and "If I Had a Hammer" and "Midnight Special" and "Rock Island Line," then the Weavers are a part of you.

The Weavers were Pete Seeger, Ronnie

Gilbert, Lee Hays, and Fred Hellerman. In 1982 they held what then was billed as their farewell concert, at Carnegie Hall, and it was documented in *The Weavers: Wasn't That a Time!* I thought it was one of the best and most moving musical documentaries ever made. More than twenty years later, in 2003, the Weavers gathered to sing in Carnegie one more time, in honor of Harold Leventhal, who was celebrating fifty years as an impresario. It was Leventhal who booked them in the good years and the bad, after they fell victim to the McCarthy-era blacklist and were barred from the mainstream after spending the late 1940s at the top of the charts.

The gathering at Toronto marked the premiere of *Isn't This a Time!*, the doc about the 2003 concert. After it, the Weavers sang one last time. Jim Brown, who directed the 1982 doc, returned to film the 2003 concert. If the sequel is slightly less compelling than the 1982 film, that's because time has taken a toll; Lee Hays has died, Seeger, the grand old man of American folk music, was eighty-four in 2003, and Gilbert and Hellerman were almost eighty. They were joined by Erik Darling and Eric Weissberg, and it was an evening of tears and joy. No longer are the famous voices quite as they were, but the spirit is undimmed and the emotion is, if anything, more powerful.

The power of *Isn't This a Time!* comes partly from the songs themselves, including those listed above and many more, such as "On Top of Old Smoky" and "Kumbaya" and "When the Saints Go Marching In" and "Brother, Can You Spare a Dime?" and of course "So Long, It's Been Good to Know You." It comes from the contributions of Leon Bibb, Peter, Paul, and Mary, Theo Bikel, and Arlo Guthrie, who organized the concert. It comes too from history: It was Arlo's father, Woody Guthrie, who invented the kind of music that Seeger and the Weavers performed, and Seeger and Woody Guthrie sang in the original Almanac Singers, a group identified with the 1930s labor movement.

The Weavers of 2003 did not sing as well as they did in 1982, or 1952, but if anything they had more heart, because of more memories. Backstage before the 2004 Toronto reunion, Seeger expressed concerns about his voice, but that night he sang with a renewed strength, and in *Isn't This a Time!* the music is accompanied not merely by guitars and Seeger's recorder but also by conviction and a defiance of time. They were all older, but they were survivors, and they sang in tribute to Leventhal (who died in October 2005).

Leventhal, they said, was much more than an impresario; he was a man willing to risk his career to stand up against the blacklist and the notion that artists should be prevented from working because of their political beliefs. As the film unfolds, the 2003 concert is intercut with older footage of the Weavers, with bits of their history, with memories of their lives and songs.

The night of the premiere in Toronto, I introduced the Weavers, having earlier amused Seeger backstage by reciting all of the Almanacs' "Talking Union," which he frankly doubted I really knew.

"There's a kind of eerie moment in the movie," I said to Seeger, "when Arlo Guthrie observes that he has now performed with you twice as long as his father did."

"Time," said Seeger. "Time, time. A beautiful mystery."

Hellerman smiled. "At least it keeps everything from happening at once," he said.

It's All Gone Pete Tong ★ ★ ★

R, 90 m., 2005

Paul Kaye (Frankie Wilde), Mike Wilmot (Max Haggar), Beatriz Batarda (Penelope), Kate Magowan (Sonja), Pete Tong (Himself). Directed by Michael Dowse and produced by Allan Niblo and James Richardson. Screenplay by Dowse.

Frankie Wilde is the king of the club scene in Ibiza, a Mediterranean island where jumbo jets ferry in party animals on package tours. He stands like a colossus above the dance floor, vibrating in sympathy with his audience. Lately he's even started to produce a few records. He has a big house, a beautiful wife, and a manager who worships him. What could go wrong?

Frankie goes deaf. Maybe it was the decibel level in his earphones, night after night. Maybe it's a side effect from his nonprescription drugs; given enough cocaine, he makes Al Pacino's Scarface look laid-back. Frankie

(Paul Kaye) tries to fake it, but his sets become exercises in incompatible noise.

He and his manager, Max (Mike Wilmot), share a painful truth: "Generally, the field of music, other than the obvious example, has been dominated by people who can hear." (When I hear a line like that, I am divided between admiration for the writing and concern for audience members who will be asking each other who the obvious example is.) Frankie goes berserk one night and is carried out of his club and out of his world.

It's All Gone Pete Tong presents Frankie's story in mockumentary form. Like Werner Herzog and Zak Penn's *Incident at Loch Ness*, it goes to some effort to blur the line between fact and fiction. It insists Frankie Wilde was an actual disc jockey and interviews "real" witnesses to his rise and fall; there are fake Web sites discussing his legend, but the movie is fiction. There really is a Pete Tong, however; he's a British disc jockey who is seen interviewing Frankie in a doc-within-the-mock.

The title is real, too. *It's All Gone Pete Tong* is Cockney rhyming slang for "It's all gone wrong," and that's what it's gone, all right, for Frankie Wilde. His wife and her son bail out, his manager despairs, and Frankie descends into a slough of despond, drink, and cocaine. Occasionally he is attacked by a large, hallucinatory stuffed bear, reminding me of the bats that attacked Hunter S. Thompson on the road to Vegas. There is a time when he has sticks of dynamite strapped like a crown to his head, but the movie was a little manic just at that moment and I am not completely sure if the dynamite was real or a fantasy. Real, I think.

The downward arc of the first two acts of the movie is made harrowing and yet perversely amusing by the performance of Paul Kaye, a British comedian who sees Frankie as a clown who overacts even in despair. Then comes salvation in the form of a speech therapist named Penelope (Beatriz Batarda), who begins by teaching Frankie to lip-read and ends by saving his life and restoring him to happiness. Much of the solution involves Frankie's discovery that he can feel the vibes of the music through the soles of his feet; the discovery comes because, as he claims at one point, he is "the Imelda Marcos of flip-flops."

The movie works because of its heedless comic intensity; Kaye and his writer-director, a first-timer named Michael Dowse, chronicle the rise and fall of Frankie Wilde as other directors have dealt with emperors and kings. Frankie may not be living the most significant life of our times, but tell that to Frankie. There is a kind of desperation in any club scene (as *24-Hour Party People* memorably demonstrated); it can be exhausting, having a good time, and the relentless pursuit of happiness becomes an effort to recapture remembered bliss from the past.

Note: For me, a bonus was the island of Ibiza itself. It became famous in America in the early 1970s as the home of an author named Clifford Irving, who forged the memoirs of Howard Hughes and almost got away with it. In his defense, let it be said that Irving probably did a better job on the book than Hughes would have and that he gave to the world his mistress, Nina Van Pallandt, who starred in Robert Altman's The Long Goodbye *(1973) as a woman one would gladly forge for, and with.*

I Want Someone to Eat Cheese With ★ ★ ★

NO MPAA RATING, 80 m., 2007

Jeff Garlin (James), Bonnie Hunt (Stella Lewis), Sarah Silverman (Beth), Amy Sedaris (Ms. Clark), Joey Slotnick (Larry), Gina Gershon (Mrs. Pilletti), David Pasquesi (Luca), Paul Mazursky (Charlie), Mina Kolb (Mrs. Aaron), Richard Kind (Herb Hope), Dan Castellaneta (Dick), Tim Kazurinsky (Bill Bjango), Steve Dahl (Father). Directed by Jeff Garlin and produced by Garlin, Erin O'Malley, and Steve Pink. Screenplay by Garlin.

Every fifteen or twenty times out of the gate, a Second City sketch will end not on a punch line, but on a moment of quiet insight and sympathy. *I Want Someone to Eat Cheese With*, a virtual reunion of Second City actors, is a comedy made from such moments. It is a minor movie, but a big-time minor movie, if you see what I mean. It celebrates its modesty, it becomes our friend, and we're surprisingly touched by it even though it doesn't rock us. If there is such a thing as a must-see three-star movie, here it is.

The film is the love child of Jeff Garlin, who plays Larry David's sidekick on *Curb Your Enthusiasm.* Garlin coproduces, writes, directs, and stars, surrounding himself with other Second City veterans going back even to the Golden Age, such as Mina Kolb and Paul Mazursky. He plays James, a thirty-nine-year-old actor in the current Second City troupe, living at home with his mother (Kolb) and spending long, lonely late hours stretched out on the hood of his car in the shadow of Wrigley Field, eating junk food from an all-night store. He has not had sex in five years, and confides this in a voice that suggests he wishes it had been six or seven.

Second City actors typically live in the city, not in an insular showbiz ghetto. They swim with the others in the underpaid but always busy Chicago theater scene. They have friends like Larry (Joey Slotnick), the clerk at the all-night store, who tries to prevent James from buying pudding and pound cake at midnight. And like Stella (Bonnie Hunt), a schoolteacher, who never exactly becomes his girlfriend, and whose students are informed on Career Day that, in Willy Wonka terms, "You are the chocolate river of your life." And like his mom, who is smart and loving and channels Kolb herself, rather than collapsing into stereotypes.

James obsesses with being cast for the title role of a new production of *Marty.* Yes, he'd be perfect for it. I wouldn't dream of telling you who gets the role, but Marty's mother is played by Gina Gershon. Yes, Gina Gershon. Meanwhile, James's manager, Herb Hope (Richard Kind), looks at him with that Richard Kind kind of pity and fires him, explaining he's doing him a favor.

James mopes about Chicago, mostly along the Old Town–Wrigley Field axis. He has empty hours to fill before, and especially after, his Second City gig. Leaving early from an Overeaters Anonymous meeting, he flees to an ice cream parlor, and behind the counter is Beth (Sarah Silverman). She is the one who wants someone to eat cheese with. Beth all but assaults James with her bold provocations, even taking him along to buy brassieres. Is this what he was really missing?

Like *Curb Your Enthusiasm,* which Garlin has directed on occasion, *I Want Someone to Eat Cheese With* has a conversational tone. Unlike too many movies made and populated by comedians, it has no striving for effect, no anxiety that we won't get the joke. It is a movie made by friends about friends, and we get to feel curiously as if they are our friends.

Sometimes they are. Tim Kazurinsky plays Bill Bjango, whose name alone stirs trains of thought, and there is a cameo role for talk jock Steve Dahl, who may not be a Second City alum but certainly provides air time for the troupe. Others such as Amy Sedaris and David Pasquesi have vivid supporting roles, funny, but in character. The movie feels like episodic television, not trying to score all its points at once because it knows these lives will go on and on, advancing, retreating, mixing, regretting, living. What do you want to do tonight, Marty? I dunno. What do you want to do?

J

The Jacket ★ ★

R, 102 m., 2005

Adrien Brody (Jack Starks), Keira Knightley (Jackie), Kris Kristofferson (Dr. Becker), Jennifer Jason Leigh (Dr. Lorenson), Daniel Craig (Mackenzie), Kelly Lynch (Jean), Brad Renfro (Stranger). Directed by John Maybury and produced by George Clooney, Peter Guber, and Steven Soderbergh. Screenplay by Massy Tadjedin.

In Iraq in 1991, an American soldier momentarily trusts a small boy, who has a gun and shoots him in the head. "That was the first time I died," says Jack Starks, the soldier, played by Adrien Brody as if he's not quite sure he didn't. That's not a criticism, but a description: The metaphysical and real horrors undergone by Jack in this movie include dying, not dying, feeling like he's dead, wishing he were dead, and being locked alive for long periods in a morgue drawer. No way to treat a returning hero.

Adrien Brody is an ideal actor for such a role, since his face can reflect such dread and suffering. He also has a cocky, upbeat speed (see *Bread and Roses*), but since *The Pianist* directors have used him for mournfulness. He has a lot to mourn this time.

After he is declared dead in Iraq, it's discovered he's alive after all, and Jack is returned to the States and treated for amnesia. Out on his own, he's hitching through Vermont when he comes upon a spaced-out mother (Kelly Lynch) and her worried young daughter; their car has broken down. After helping them, he gets a lift with a passing motorist, who soon enough kills a cop. Jack passes out and wakes up to find himself a convicted cop killer, sent to a mental asylum. If only he could find that woman and daughter, he could establish an alibi. But the woman was zoned out, and the daughter was only a child.

The asylum is not one of your modern and enlightened asylums. Edgar Allan Poe would raise his eyebrows. It's run by Dr. Becker (Kris Kristofferson), whose theories are a cover for his sadism, or maybe it's the other way around. He believes that locking cold, wet patients in morgue drawers for long hours will help them—I dunno, get in touch with their feelings, or remember why they're there. Who knows.

The movie now begins to play with time. In a gas station, Jack, forlorn and homeless, is befriended by a woman named Jackie (Keira Knightley, from *Bend It Like Beckham*). She takes him home, cares for him, and here's where we have to get crafty to preserve plot points. To make a long plot short, when he is in the morgue drawer, Jack's brain, traumatized by a head wound, amnesia, and shock treatments, is able to time travel. Or maybe Jack himself physically time travels; the people who meet him on his journeys certainly think he's really there.

It's up to Jackie to believe this story and act on it, so that Jack can use his knowledge of the future to make important decisions in the present. Or maybe it's in the future that he makes the decisions, and in the past that he carried them out. Take notes. Able to assist him, if she believes his story, is Dr. Lorenson (Jennifer Jason Leigh) and even the evil, retired Dr. Becker himself. Lorenson always looked askance at Becker's barbaric methods. Try it yourself sometime, looking askance. Can be fun.

Meanwhile, the movie, taking its cue from Jack's deep weariness and depression, trudges through its paces as if it were deep and meaningful, which I am afraid it is not. It involves two or three time-paradox tricks too many to take seriously as anything other than a plot crafted to jump through all the temporal hoops. I was reminded of *Jacob's Ladder* (1990), also about a traumatized vet who descends into the abyss between the real and the imagined. I admired it at the time but have been meaning to view it again after Father Andrew Greeley told me he thinks it's one of the most spiritual films of our time.

The Jacket will probably not make Andy's list. It has some touching moments between Jack and Jackie, whose curious willingness to trust him is explained in reasonable terms. But Dr. Becker comes intact from an old Hammer horror film, and would be right at home in *Scream and Scream Again* (1969), which involves a character who keeps waking up to find his inventory of body parts is shrinking. Becker's torturous "treatments" of Jack are so bizarre that the gentler and more philosophical possibilities in the story go astray.

The director, John Maybury, made *Love Is the Devil* (1998), a film about the British artist Francis Bacon, whose portraits of his subjects often seemed to catch them in their post–*Scream and Scream Again* periods. It was a perceptive, good film. In *The Jacket* you can sense an impulse toward a better film, and Adrien Brody and Keira Knightley certainly take it seriously, but the time-travel whiplash effect sets in, and it becomes, as so many time-travel movies do, an exercise in early entrances, late exits, futile regrets. If there is anything worse than time creeping at its petty pace from day to day, it would be if time jumped around. Better to die at the end, don't you think, than randomly, from time to time?

The Jane Austen Book Club ★ ★ ★ ½

PG-13, 105 m., 2007

Kathy Baker (Bernadette), Maria Bello (Jocelyn), Emily Blunt (Prudie), Amy Brenneman (Sylvia), Hugh Dancy (Grigg), Maggie Grace (Allegra), Lynn Redgrave (Sky), Jimmy Smits (Daniel), Marc Blucas (Dean). Directed by Robin Swicord and produced by John Calley, Julie Lynn, and Diana Napper. Written by Swicord, based on the book by Karen Joy Fowler.

Jane Austen wrote six novels, which are pillars of English literature in spite of being delightful, wise, warm, and beloved. Robin Swicord's *The Jane Austen Book Club* centers on its six members, who meet over six months to discuss the novels, which seem to have an uncanny relevance to events in their own lives, just as the newspaper horoscope always seems to be about you. No, it is not necessary to have read the novels or seen all the Jane Austen movie adaptations, but that would add another dimension to this film.

What you need to know is that Austen is usually concerned about her heroine's struggle to find the right romantic partner for *her*, despite her rivals, class prejudice, her own diffidence, the blindness of her loved one, the obstinacy of her family, and economic necessities. You could say that Austen created "chick lit" and therefore "chick flicks." You could, but I would not, because I despise those terms as sexist and ignorant. As a man, I would hate to have my tastes condescended to as the opposite of chick lit, which, according to Gloria Steinem, is "prick lit." I read Jane Austen for a simple reason, not gender-related: I cannot put her down and often return to her in times of trouble.

Remarkable, that a woman who died at forty-one in 1817 should still be so popular, all her books in print in countless editions, inspiring movies that routinely win Oscars, the subject of Karen Joy Fowler's best-selling *The Jane Austen Book Club*, and her life the subject of another 2007 movie, *Becoming Jane*. One edition of her *Pride and Prejudice* ranks above two thousand on Amazon's best-selling fiction list, which is surprising if you reflect that there are at least nine other current editions of the same novel on sale. ("See all 8,882 search findings," Amazon offered, but I didn't have the nerve.)

The movie is a celebration of reading, and oddly enough that works, even though there is nothing cinematic about a shot of a woman (or the club's one male member) reading a book. Such shots are used as punctuation in the film, where they work like Ozu's "pillow shots," quiet respites from the action. The only drawback to them from my point of view was that all the characters seem to be reading standard editions—not a Folio Society subscriber among them.

The club is founded by Bernadette (Kathy Baker), a woman of (naturally) about sixty, who has been divorced (of course) six times. She thinks it will help console her friend Jocelyn (Maria Bello), who as the film opens is attending a funeral for her beloved Rhodesian ridgeback. Any woman who has an expensive service for her dog needs a man in her life. Or maybe not. Maybe she's got it figured out.

The club membership grows by adding other emotionally needy members. Prudie (Emily Blunt) is a miserable high school French teacher who was planning her first trip to France only to have her younger and distant husband (Marc Blucas) call it off for unspecified "business reasons." Sylvia (Amy Brenneman) is being divorced by Daniel (Jimmy Smits), despite her illusion that theirs is a happy marriage. Sylvia's lesbian daughter, Allegra (Maggie Grace), also has a romantic crisis going and is closeted from her mother, though not from us. Circling in Prudie's life is her mother (Lynn Redgrave), an ex-hippie pothead who is not a bit like Austen's formidable dowagers, except that she meddles.

And there is a male member of the club, Grigg (Hugh Dancy), whom Jocelyn wants to pair off with Sylvia, although he would like to pair off with Jocelyn, something she does not see because like many an Austen heroine she is blind! blind! to true love that is staring her right in the eyes. Grigg is not, shall we say, a born reader of Jane Austen; he prefers science fiction, although his tastes are admirable and he is forever promoting Ursula K. Le Guin.

These six meet at one another's houses, their discussions intercut with developments in their private lives, which they share, sometimes obliquely, at the meetings. In this process they demonstrate how great books can illuminate and counsel us all. The person who does not read is often under the impression that they're being picked on by fate. A reader knows it's necessary because of the story line.

Some will quibble and cavil that the movie is too contrived: six books, six members, six sets of problems, six, six, six (and sex, of course). Contrivance is actually part of the appeal. One of the reasons we return to Austen, Dickens, Trollope, and the estimable Mrs. Gaskell is that their novels are contrived. The structure and ultimate destination are easily foreseeable, but what's fascinating are their characters, how they think and talk, how colorful and urgent they are, and how blind! blind! they are to what they should surely do if only we could advise them.

I settled down with this movie as with a comfortable book. I expected no earth-shaking revelations and got none, and everything turned out about right in a clockwork ending that reminded me of the precision the Victorians always used to tidy up their loose ends. It is crucial, I think, that writer-director Swicord (author of the screenplays for *Little Women, Memoirs of a Geisha,* and *The Perez Family*) has created characters who really do seem to have read the books and talk like they have. And she has created a book club that, like all book clubs, is really about its members. Chick flick indeed! Guys, take your best buddy to see this movie. Tell him, "It's really cool, dude, even though there aren't any eviscerations."

Jarhead ★ ★ ★ ½

R, 122 m., 2005

Jake Gyllenhaal (Tony Swofford), Peter Sarsgaard (Allen Troy), Lucas Black (Chris Kruger), Chris Cooper (Lieutenant Colonel Kazinski), Jamie Foxx (Staff Sergeant Sykes). Directed by Sam Mendes and produced by Lucy Fisher and Douglas Wick. Screenplay by William Broyles Jr. based on the book by Anthony Swofford.

Jarhead is a war movie that rises above the war and tells a soldier's story. It tells it with the urgency and pointlessness that all men's stories have, because if something has happened to us, then it is important to us no matter how indifferent the world may be. "Four days, four hours, one minute. That was my war," the Marine sniper Tony Swofford tells us. "I never shot my rifle."

The movie is uncanny in its effect. It contains no heroism, little action, no easy laughs. It is about men who are exhausted, bored, lonely, trained to the point of obsession, and given no opportunity to use their training. The most dramatic scene in the movie comes when Swofford has an enemy officer in the crosshairs of his gun sight and is forbidden to fire because his shot may give advance warning of an air strike.

His spotter, Troy, goes berserk: "Let him take the shot!" Let him, that is, kill one enemy as his payback for the hell of basic training, the limbo of the desert, the sand and heat, the torture of months of waiting, the sight of a highway traffic jam made of burned vehicles and crisp, charred corpses. Let him take the shot to erase for a second the cloud of oil droplets he lives in, the absence of the sun, the horizon lined with the plumes of burning oil wells. Let him take the goddamn shot.

The movie is based on the best-selling 2003 memoir *Jarhead,* by Tony Swofford, who served in the first Gulf War. It is unlike most war movies in that it focuses entirely on the personal experience of a young man caught up in the military process. At one point, Swofford (Jake Gyllenhaal) is being interviewed by a network newswoman who asks him why he serves. He has already given two or three routine answers. She persists, and finally he looks in the camera and says: "I'm twenty years old, and I was dumb enough to sign a contract."

His best friend is his spotter, Troy (Peter Sarsgaard). Their small unit of scout-snipers has been led through training by Staff Sergeant Sykes (Jamie Foxx), who knows why he serves: He loves his job. Others in the group include borderline psychos and screwups, but mostly just average young Americans who have decided the only thing worse than fighting a war is waiting to fight one—in the desert, when the temperature is 112 and it would be great for the TV cameras if they played a football game while wearing their anti-gas suits.

Jarhead is a story like Robert Graves's *Goodbye to All That,* in the way it sees the big picture entirely in terms of the small details. Sykes briefs them about Hussein's invasion of the Kuwait oil fields but says their immediate task is to guard the oil of "our friends, the Saudis." This they do by killing time. The narration includes one passage that sounds lifted straight from the book, in which Swofford lists the ways they get through the days: They train, they sleep, they watch TV and videos, they get in pointless fights, they read letters from home and write letters to home, and mostly they masturbate.

These are not the colorful dogfaces of World War II movies with their poker games, or the druggies in *Apocalypse Now.* They have no wisecracks, we see no drugs, they get drunk when they can, and there is a Wall of Shame plastered with the photos of the girls back home who have dumped them. They go on patrols in the desert, looking for nothing in the middle of nowhere, and their moment of greatest tension comes when they meet eight Arabs with five camels. They sense a trap. Their fingers are on their triggers. They are in formation for action. Swofford and one of the Arabs meet on neutral ground. He comes back with his report: "Somebody shot three of their camels."

In a war like this, the ground soldier has been made obsolete by air power. Territory that took three months to occupy in World War I and three weeks in Vietnam now takes ten minutes. Sykes warns them to expect seventy thousand casualties in the first days of the war, but as we recall, the Iraqis caved in and the war was over. Now we are involved in a war that does require soldiers on the ground, against an enemy that no longer helpfully wears uniforms. Yet many of its frustrations are the same, and I am reminded of the documentary *Gunner Palace,* about an Army field artillery division that is headquartered in the ruins of a palace once occupied by Saddam's son Uday. They are brave, they are skilled, and death comes unexpectedly from invisible foes in the midst of routine.

Jarhead was directed by Sam Mendes *(American Beauty),* and it is the other side of the coin of David O. Russell's *Three Kings,* also about the Gulf War. If Russell had *Catch-22* as his guide, it is instructive that the book Swofford is reading is *The Stranger,* by Camus. The movie captures the tone of Camus' narrator, who knows what has happened, but not why, nor what it means to him, nor why it happens to him. Against this existential void the men of the sniper unit shore up friendships and rituals. Their sergeant is a hard-ass, not because he is pathological but because he wants to prepare them to save their lives. They are ready. They have been trained into a frenzy of readiness, and all they find on every side, beautifully visualized by the film, is a vastness—first sand, then sand covered with a black rain, then skies red with unchanging flames twenty-four hours a day.

It is not often that a movie catches exactly what it was like to be this person in this place at this time, but *Jarhead* does. They say a story can be defined by how its characters change. For the rest of his life, Swofford tells us, whether he holds it or not, his rifle will always be a part of his body. It wasn't like that when the story began.

Jellyfish ★ ★ ★

NO MPAA RATING, 78 m., 2008

Sarah Adler (Batya), Nikol Leidman (Little Girl), Gera Sandler (Michael), Noa Knoller (Keren), Ma-nenita De Latorre (Joy), Zharira Charifai

(Malka). Directed by Etgar Keret and Shira Geffen and produced by Amir Harel, Ayelet Kait, Yael Fogiel, and Laetitia Gonzalez. Screenplay by Geffen.

Jellyfish tells the stories of three young women whose lives, for a change, do not interlock so much as coexist. It never quite explains why these three were chosen and not three others. I found that refreshing because with some films based on entwined lives, you spend more time untangling the plot than caring about it.

In *Jellyfish,* one character is a waitress for a wedding catering firm, another is a new bride, and the third is a home care worker for elderly women. To be sure, there is a mystical vision (or memory) at the end of the film, but I'm not sure I understand the logic behind it, and I don't think I require one. It inexplicably spans a generation but works just as it is.

The film is set in Tel Aviv, but it's not an "Israeli film." That's where it was made, but it's not about anything particularly Israeli. It could take place in countless cities, and it's not "about" anything at all, in the way of a message, a theme, or a revelation. What it offers is a portrait of some time in these lives, created with attentive performances and an intriguing way of allowing them to emerge a little at a time.

The film also gives us sharply defined supporting characters. The most enigmatic, sufficient to be the center of a movie of her own, is an angelic little girl who wanders up to Batya (Sarah Adler) at the beach. She has an inner tube around her middle, which she refuses to be parted from. There are no parents in sight. Batya takes the girl to the police, who aren't much interested. They advise her to care for her over the weekend, while they wait to see if a missing-persons report comes in.

That seems a strange police decision (are there no social agencies in Israel?), but it allows a scene where Batya takes the child to her catering job, and the little girl gets her fired, and in the process she meets a woman who is a freelance wedding photographer, and so on. The photographer is fired, too, and the women end up smoking on a loading dock, discussing turns of fate. Batya has problems, and water is one of their common themes: (a) the little girl seemingly emerged from the sea, and (b) the leak in her apartment ceiling has covered the floor with about four inches of water. A tenuous link, but there you have it.

Another lead character is Keren (Noa Knoller), who breaks her ankle in a particularly ignominious way at her own wedding: She's locked into a toilet cubicle and tries to climb over the door. She and her husband have to cancel their plans for a cruise, end up in a hotel room they hate, and what's worse, the elevator goes out, and at one point it seems that her husband might have bodily carried her up twelve flights of stairs. Maybe only six. Try that sometime. The husband meets a mysterious woman from the top-floor suite, and they spend way too much time together because they're both smokers. The woman says she is a writer, but there's more to it than that.

The most realistic, down-to-earth woman in the film is Joy (Ma-nenita De Latorre), from the Philippines, who works as a minder. Her latest client, dumped on her by the woman's actress daughter, is a short-tempered case study who shouts at her to speak Hebrew or German. The girl does speak English, which is enough in many situations around the world, is learning Hebrew as fast as she can, isn't being paid much, and has a good heart. She convinces the old woman to see her daughter as Ophelia in a decidedly peculiar *Hamlet* (it seems to be written not in iambic pentameter, but in chanted repetition).

These stories have as their justification the fact that they are intrinsically interesting. I think that's enough. *Jellyfish* won the Camera d'Or at Cannes 2007 for best first feature. Given all the temptations that lure gifted first-time filmmakers with three stories to tell, each story with its own story within it, I think director Etgar Keret and his codirector and writer, Shira Geffen, are commendable, since they bring it in at seventy-eight minutes. You can easily see how it could have overstayed its welcome, especially if it ever got around to explaining that little girl, and if she's who she seems to be in the dream or vision or hallucination or whatever. Rather than an explanation in a case like that, I prefer the vision to appear, make its impact, and leave unexplained.

Jiminy Glick in La La Wood ★ ½

R, 90 m., 2005

Martin Short (Jiminy Glick/David Lynch), Jan Hooks (Dixie Glick), Elizabeth Perkins (Miranda Coolidge), Linda Cardellini (Natalie Coolidge), Janeane Garofalo (Dee Dee), Corey Pearson (Ben DiCarlo), Carlos Jacott (Barry King), John Michael Higgins (Andre Divine). Directed by Vadim Jean and produced by Bernie Brillstein, Paul Brooks, Peter Safran, and Martin Short. Screenplay by Martin Short, Paul Flaherty, and Michael Short.

The problem with Jiminy Glick is that he doesn't know who he is. Or, more precisely, Martin Short doesn't know who he is. Jiminy is allegedly a chubby TV news entertainment reporter from Butte, Montana, who alternates between fawning over celebrities, insulting them, and not quite knowing who they are. I can sympathize. When I ran into Jiminy at the Toronto Film Festival, I didn't know he was Martin Short; the makeup job was masterful, and I hadn't seen the character in his earlier TV manifestations. One of the side effects of seeing five hundred movies a year is that you miss a lot of TV.

Martin Short himself is one of the funniest men alive, or can be, and has been. But Jiminy Glick needs definition if he's to work as a character. We have to sense a consistent comic personality, and we don't; Short changes gears and redefines the character whenever he needs a laugh. That means Jiminy is sometimes clueless, sometimes uses knowledgeable in-jokes, sometimes is a closeted gay, sometimes merely neuter, sometimes an inane talk show host, and at other times essentially just Martin Short having fun with his celebrity friends.

Jiminy Glick in La La Wood takes the character to the Toronto Film Festival, where he confronts celebrities in situations that are sometimes spontaneous, sometimes scripted. He stays in a hotel from hell with his wife, Dixie (Jan Hooks), and their twin sons, Matthew and Modine. He is obsessed with getting an interview with the reclusive Ben DiCarlo (Corey Pearson), director of *Growing Up Gandhi,* in which the young Mahatma is seen as a prizefighter. He is also entranced by the presence of the legendary star Miranda Coolidge (Elizabeth Perkins).

The movie combines two story lines: Jiminy interviewing celebs, and Jiminy trapped in a nightmarish murder scenario narrated by David Lynch (played by Short himself, uncannily well). Lynch lights his already-lit cigarette and intones ominous insights about the lonely highway of doom, and Miranda's blood-drenched handkerchief turns up in Jiminy's possession; perhaps he did not merely dream that he murdered her.

The murder plot is a nonstarter (not funny, not necessary), and although Short does a good David Lynch, he stops at imitation and doesn't go for satire. He's at his best in a couple of sit-down interviews with cooperative movie stars (Kurt Russell and Steve Martin), in what feel like improvised Q&A sessions; he asks Martin, for example, if it's true that the commies still run Hollywood, and Martin refuses to name names—except for Meg Ryan and Tom Hanks. There is also an intriguing discussion of Martin's theory of tabletops and testicles, which put me in mind of his famous magic trick where eggs and lit cigarettes emerge from his fly.

A comedy could be made about inane celebrity interviewers, yes, but it would have to be more reality-oriented. When a real person like Joe Franklin exists, how can Jiminy Glick outflank him? A comedy could be made about the Toronto Film Festival, but it would need to know more about festivals; interviewers from Butte, Montana, do not ordinarily have a private festival publicity person to knock on the hotel room every morning with a list of the day's interviews, and Glick (or Short) misses a chance to skewer publicists, junkets, and the hissy fits of critics afraid they'll miss a big movie.

Some stand-alone moments are funny. Jiminy thinks Whoopi Goldberg is Oprah Winfrey ("Remember, my name is spelled O-p-e-r-a," she advises him). Rappers in a hotel corridor try to teach an African how to sound like an American hip-hopper, but try as he will, "Y'allknowhaimean" comes out as "Yao Ming." And Jiminy and Kurt Russell begin a discussion about Elvis Presley, whom Russell starred with as a child actor and later, as an adult, played in a movie. Where this discussion eventually leads is hard to believe and impossible to describe. And when David Lynch says, "My name is David Lynch. I'm a director," I like Jiminy's reply: "Well, who isn't, dear?"

Jimmy Carter Man from Plains ★ ★ ★

PG, 126 m., 2007

A documentary written and directed by Jonathan Demme and produced by Demme and Neda Armian.

Jimmy Carter could be sitting in the shade watching his peanuts grow, but at eighty-three he maintains a ceaseless schedule of travel, speeches, talk show appearances, and meetings, most devoted to his obsession with peace in the Middle East. Jonathan Demme's new documentary, *Jimmy Carter Man from Plains*, shows a man whose beliefs, both political and religious, seem to reinvigorate him; he even carries his own luggage in airports and hotels.

Demme, a skilled documentarian as well as a considerable feature director (*The Silence of the Lambs, Philadelphia*), follows Carter in late 2006 on a tour to promote his newest book, *Palestine: Peace Not Apartheid.* The former president, who brokered the famous Camp David handshake between Israeli prime minister Menachem Begin and Egyptian president Anwar Sadat, believes there will never be peace in the region if the two sides do not talk and eventually agree, and throughout the tour he is picketed and challenged by pro-Israel demonstrators, who especially dislike his use of the word "apartheid." We get the feeling he might have chosen another word if he'd realized how that one would upstage rational discussion about his book.

The impression we get is that Carter is a man at peace with himself. He rarely raises his voice, doesn't get impatient with aides, is stern but not angry with interviewers who have not read his book. He and Rosalynn, his wife since 1946, read a verse from the Bible every night before bedtime, and sometimes he takes the pulpit at his local church; his brand of Christianity teaches him that he is his brother's keeper, and we see him building housing for the poor in the aftermath of Katrina. If he has differences with the current occupant of the White House, and he does, we have to sense them between the lines; he doesn't seize the opportunity of an omnipresent camera to make partisan speeches.

Watching the film, I recalled Demme's 1992 documentary *Cousin Bobby*, about his cousin Robert Castle, a white Episcopalian priest who had served an inner-city church in Harlem for many years. There are ways in which the cousin and President Carter are similar, including their sleeves-up, rigorous style of putting their faith into action. They don't want to build enormous architectural monuments to themselves, but help ordinary folks get on with their lives. Neither one will have any trouble squeezing through the eye of the needle.

The fact is that Jimmy Carter is an immensely good man, as far as I can tell from Demme's film and everything else I know about him. One reason to see this film might be to learn more about his views on the Middle East, but a better reason might be to observe how he attends to the privilege and responsibility of doing what he believes is the right thing. It cannot be a pleasure, the never-ending round of airports, buses, taxis, hotel rooms, and interviews. He doesn't make things easy on himself by accepting the use of private jets, and he waits in line along with everyone else. He doesn't accept fees for speeches. I think he flies first class more because of the Secret Service than his own insistence. I don't see any ego-gratification going on. He seems to believe he is doing his duty, and if I am ever eighty-three, or seventy-three, I hope I can find the same energy and dedication in my own little sphere.

I saw this film for the first time at the 2007 Toronto Film Festival. On the same day, I read a news story about the book *Dead Certain* by Robert Draper in which President George W. Bush confided some of his plans for retirement. Bush told Draper: "I'll give some speeches, to replenish the ol' coffers—I don't know what my dad gets—it's more than fifty to seventy-five thousand per speech. . . . Clinton's making a lot of money." In another interview, he noted Clinton's recent work with the United Nations and said that after he retired, "You won't catch me hanging around the U.N."

I wrote about that in my report from Toronto, closing with the reflection that everyone should choose the retirement plan that is right for them.

Journey to the Center of the Earth ★ ★

PG, 92 m., 2008

Brendan Fraser (Trevor Anderson), Josh Hutcherson (Sean), Anita Briem (Hannah). Directed by Eric Brevig and produced by Charlotte Huggins, Beau Flynn, and Cary Granat. Screenplay by Michael Weiss, Jennifer Flackett, and Mark Levin, inspired by the novel by Jules Verne.

There is a part of me that will always have affection for a movie like *Journey to the Center of the Earth.* It is a small part and steadily shrinking, but once I put on the 3-D glasses and settled into my seat, it started perking up. This is a fairly bad movie, and yet at the same time maybe about as good as it could be. There may not be an eight-year-old alive who would not love it. If I had seen it when I was eight, I would have remembered it with deep affection for all these years, until I saw it again and realized how little I really knew at that age.

You are already familiar with the premise, that there is another land inside of our globe. You are familiar because the Jules Verne novel has inspired more than a dozen movies and countless TV productions, including a series, and has been ripped off by such as Edgar Rice Burroughs, who called it Pellucidar and imagined that the earth was hollow and there was another world on the inside surface. (You didn't ask, but yes, I own a copy of *Tarzan at the Earth's Core* with the original dust jacket.)

In this version, Brendan Fraser stars as a geologist named Trevor, who defends the memory of his late brother, Max, who believed the center of the earth could be reached through "volcanic tubes." Max disappeared on a mysterious expedition, which, if it involved volcanic tubes, should have been no surprise to him. Now Trevor has been asked to spend some time with his nephew, Max's son, who is named Sean (Josh Hutcherson). What with one thing and another, wouldn't you know they find themselves in Iceland, and peering down a volcanic tube. They are joined in this enterprise by Hannah (Anita Briem), whom they find living in Max's former research headquarters near the volcano he was investigating.

Now begins a series of adventures, in which the operative principle is: No matter how frequently or how far they fall, they will land without injury. They fall very frequently and very far. The first drop lands them at the bottom of a deep cave, from which they cannot possibly climb, but they remain remarkably optimistic: "There must be a way out of here!" Sure enough, they find an abandoned mine shaft and climb aboard three cars of its miniature railway for a scene that will make you swear the filmmakers must have seen *Indiana Jones and the Temple of Doom.* Just like in that movie, they hurtle down the tracks at breakneck speeds; they're in three cars, on three more or less parallel tracks, leading you to wonder why three parallel tracks were constructed at great expense and bother, but just when such questions are forming, they have to (1) leap a chasm, (2) jump from one car to another, and (3) crash. It's a funny thing about that little railway: After all these years, it still has lamps hanging over the rails, and the electricity is still on.

The problem of lighting an unlit world is solved in the next cave they enter, which is inhabited by cute little birds that glow in the dark. One of them makes friends with Sean and leads them on to the big attraction—a world bounded by a great interior sea. This world must be a terrible place to inhabit; it has man-eating and man-strangling plants, its waters harbor giant-fanged fish and fearsome sea snakes that eat them, and on the farther shore is a Tyrannosaurus rex.

So do the characters despair? Would you despair if you were trapped miles below the surface in a cave and being chased by its hungry inhabitants? Of course not. There isn't a moment in the movie when anyone seems frightened, not even during a fall straight down for thousands of feet, during which they link hands like skydivers and carry on a conversation. Trevor gets the ball rolling: "We're still falling!"

I mentioned 3-D glasses earlier in the review. Yes, the movie is available in 3-D in "selected theaters." Select those theaters to avoid. With a few exceptions (such as the authentic

IMAX process), 3-D remains underwhelming to me—a distraction, a disappointment, and more often than not offering a dingy picture. I guess setting your story inside the earth is one way to explain why it always seems to need more lighting.

The movie is being shown in 2-D in a majority of theaters, and that's how I wish I had seen it. Since there's that part of me with a certain weakness for movies like this, it's possible I would have liked it more. It would have looked brighter and clearer, and the photography wouldn't have been cluttered up with all the leaping and gnashing of teeth. Then I could have appreciated the work of the plucky actors, who do a lot of things right in this movie, of which the most heroic is keeping a straight face.

Joyeux Noel ★ ★ ★

PG-13, 110 m., 2006

Diane Kruger (Anna Sorensen), Benno Furmann (Nikolaus Sprink), Guillaume Canet (Lieutenant Audebert), Dany Boon (Ponchel), Bernard Le Coq (General Audebert), Gary Lewis (Father Palmer), Daniel Bruhl (Horstmayer), Alex Ferns (Gordon), Steven Robertson (Jonathan), Robin Laing (William). Directed by Christian Carion and produced by Christophe Rossignon. Screenplay by Carion.

On Christmas Eve 1914, a remarkable event took place in the trenches where the Germans faced the British and the French. There was a spontaneous cease-fire, as the troops on both sides laid down their weapons and observed the birth of the savior in whose name they were killing one another. The irony of this gesture is made clear in the opening scenes of *Joyeux Noel,* in which schoolchildren of the three nations sing with angelic fervor, each in their own language, about the necessity of wiping the enemy from the face of the earth.

The Christmas Eve truce actually happened, although not on quite the scale Christian Carion suggests in his film. He is accurate, however, in depicting the aftermath: Officers and troops were punished for fraternizing with the enemy in wartime. A priest who celebrated Mass in No Man's Land is savagely criticized by his bishop, who believes the patriotic task of the clergy is to urge the troops into battle and reconcile them to death.

The trench warfare of World War I was a species of hell unlike the agonies of any other war, before or after. Enemies were dug in within earshot of each other, and troops were periodically ordered over the top so that most of them could be mowed down by machine-gun fire. They were being ordered to stand up, run forward, and be shot to death. And they did it. An additional novelty was the introduction of poison gas.

Artillery bombardments blew up the trenches so often that when they were dug out again, pieces of ordnance, bits of uniforms, shattered wooden supports, and human bones interlaced the new walls. A generation lost its leaders. European history might have been different if so many of the best and brightest had not been annihilated. Those who survived were the second team. *Goodbye to All That* by Robert Graves is the best book I have read about the experience.

Carion's film, a 2006 Oscar nominee, is a trilingual portrait of a short stretch of the front lines, a small enough microcosm of the war that we're able to follow most of the key players. We meet some of them as they volunteer for service. There is a German tenor named Sprink (Benno Furmann), who leaves the opera to serve in uniform. Two Scottish brothers sign up, Jonathan and William (Steven Robertson and Robin Laing), who agree, "At last, something's happening in our lives!" They are joined by their parish priest, Father Palmer (Gary Lewis), who follows them into uniform as a stretcher bearer. The French are led by Lieutenant Audebert (Guillaume Canet), whose father (Bernard Le Coq) is the general in charge of these lines. Audebert throws up before leading his men into battle, but that's to be expected.

On Christmas Eve, the Danish singer Anna Sorensen (Diane Kruger) is brought to a support area to sing for German officers and the crown prince, but she insists on being taken to the front lines. She says she wants to sing for the ordinary troops, but her real hope is to see Sprink, her lover. Reaching the lines, she is surprised to find that thousands of little Christmas trees have been supplied by Berlin and form a decoration on top of the German trenches.

The Scots and the French are equally surprised by the trees, and by the sound of singing as Sprink and Sorenson sing "Silent Night" and "Adeste Fidelis." Slowly, tentatively, soldiers begin to poke their heads up over the ramparts, and eventually they lay down their arms and join in the cratered No Man's Land to listen to the singing, and then to the bagpipes of the Scots, and then to celebrate Mass. The next morning, Christmas Day, there is even a soccer game. Precious bits of chocolate are shared. And they bury their dead, whose bodies have been rotting between the lines.

These men have much in common with one another. They come from the same kinds of homes, went to the same kinds of schools, and worship the same kinds of gods. They are required to fight, and most of them are required to die. In a remarkable moment of common interest, they share information about plans for artillery attacks, and all gather in one trench while the other is shelled, then switch trenches for the response. This is treason, I suppose.

Joyeux Noel has its share of bloodshed, especially in a deadly early charge, but the movie is about a respite from carnage, and it lacks the brutal details of films like *Paths of Glory, A Very Long Engagement,* and, from later wars, *Saving Private Ryan* and *Platoon.* Its sentimentality is muted by the thought that this moment of peace actually did take place, among men who were punished for it and who mostly died soon enough afterward. But on one Christmas they were able to express what has been called, perhaps too optimistically, the brotherhood of man.

Junebug ★ ★ ★ ★

R, 107 m., 2005

Alessandro Nivola (George), Amy Adams (Ashley), Embeth Davidtz (Madeleine), Scott Wilson (Eugene), Benjamin McKenzie (Johnny), Frank Hoyt Taylor (David Wark), Celia Weston (Peg). Directed by Phil Morrison and produced by Mike Ryan and Mindy Goldberg. Screenplay by Angus MacLachlan.

Junebug is a movie that understands, profoundly and with love and sadness, the world of small towns; it captures ways of talking and living I remember from my childhood with the complexity and precision of great fiction. It observes small details that are important *because* they are small. It has sympathy for every character in the story and avoids two temptations: It doesn't portray the small-town characters as provincial hicks, and it doesn't portray the city slickers as shallow materialists. Phil Morrison, who directed this movie, and Angus MacLachlan, who wrote it, understand how people everywhere have good intentions, and how life can assign them roles where they can't realize them.

Tone is everything in this movie; it's not so much what people say, as how they say it, and why. Consider this dialogue:

> Peg: *You comin' to bed?*
>
> Eugene: *Not now. I'm looking for something. My Phillips-head.*

That much is exactly right. A certain kind of person (my father was one) finds a Phillips-head screwdriver easier to lose than almost everything else. So now wait until it's later at night, and observe Eugene in the kitchen. He looks in the refrigerator and then he says: "Now where would I be if I was a screwdriver?"

If you get that right, you get everything else right, too. And here is other dialogue that rings with clarity and truth:

> Ashley to Johnny: *God loves you just the way you are, but he loves you too much to let you stay that way.*
>
> Peg, under her breath at a baby shower, after her son's new wife from the city has given her other daughter-in-law a silver spoon: *That won't go in the dishwasher.*

Who are these people? The story begins in Chicago, where an art dealer named Madeleine (Embeth Davidtz) is holding a benefit for Jesse Jackson Jr. At the event, she meets George (Alessandro Nivola), and they fall in love and get married. His family from North Carolina is invited but doesn't attend. Six months later, she learns of a folk artist named David Wark (Frank Hoyt Taylor), who lives near George's family in the Winston-Salem area. They decide to kill two birds with one stone: She'll sign up the artist and meet the family.

Here is the family she meets. Peg (Celia Weston) is the matriarch who criticizes everyone, second-guesses every decision, and is never wrong, according to her. Eugene (Scott Wilson) is her husband, who has withdrawn into a deep silence and a shadowy presence, and spends many hours in his basement wood-carving corner. Johnny (Benjamin McKenzie) is George's younger brother, newly married to his high school sweetheart, Ashley (Amy Adams). She is pregnant.

As George and Madeleine arrive, Ashley is about to give birth. Johnny is responding to this, as he does to everything, by withdrawing, not talking to anybody, working under his car in the garage. Ashley, on the other hand, is always chatty: She's a good soul, cheerful, optimistic, supportive. The four people in this household are so locked into their roles that the arrival of the Chicagoans is like a bomb dropping.

Madeleine, the outsider, smiles all the time. If she feels that this family is strange and disturbing, she doesn't say so. George behaves as he knows he should but remains enigmatic: We don't find out what he really thinks about his family until the movie's last line, if then.

The artist, David Wark, is a profound eccentric with an accent and values that seem to have been imported from the eighteenth century. His folk art incorporates imperfectly controlled images from a half-understood world. "I like all the dog heads and computers," Madeleine tells him, "and the scrotums." This is not intended as a funny line. Wark has just finished an allegorical painting about the freeing of the slaves. He explains that he can't paint a face unless it belongs to somebody he knows, and he doesn't know any black people, which is why all the slaves have white faces.

There is tension between George and Johnny, between Ashley and Johnny, between the world and Johnny. He spends long hours away from everyone, but watch him in the family room when a documentary about meerkats comes on TV. He knows his wife "loves meerkats." He races around desperately to find a blank video so he can tape the show. It would mean so much to him to give her this video. He fails. Ashley explains about the tab that keeps you from recording over something, but he responds with anger and, of course, takes it out on her.

Two events happen at once. Madeleine believes she can win David Wark away from a New York gallery, and Ashley goes into labor. George thinks Madeleine's place is with the family, at the hospital. She doesn't agree: "I'll be over as soon as I do this. You know how important this is to me."

Now here is the question: How important is Ashley and Johnny's baby to George? (Johnny, of course, is nowhere to be found, certainly not at the hospital.) If he were in Chicago, George certainly would not fly down to be at the hospital. But when he moves into his family's house, he follows its rules. This leads to a scene of incredible power between Ashley and her brother-in-law, in which we see that Ashley truly is good, and brave, and sweeter than peaches. Small wonder that Amy Adams won the Sundance acting award.

Junebug is a great film because it is a true film. It humbles other films that claim to be about family secrets and eccentricities. It understands that families are complicated and their problems are not solved during a short visit, just in time for the film to end. Families and their problems go on and on, and they aren't solved; they're dealt with.

Consider a guarded moment between Madeleine and Eugene, her father-in-law. She observes cautiously of his wife, "She's a very strong personality." This is putting it mildly. Eugene replies quietly, "That's just her way. She hides herself. She's not like that inside." And then he adds two more words: "Like most." Thank God for actors like Wilson, who know how those two words must be said. They carry the whole burden of the movie.

Juno ★ ★ ★ ★

PG-13, 92 m., 2007

Ellen Page (Juno MacGuff), Michael Cera (Paulie Bleeker), Jennifer Garner (Vanessa Loring), Jason Bateman (Mark Loring), Allison Janney (Bren MacGuff), J. K. Simmons (Mac MacGuff), Olivia Thirby (Leah). Directed by Jason Reitman and produced by Lianne Halfon, John Malkovich, Mason Novick, and Russell Smith. Screenplay by Diablo Cody.

Jason Reitman's *Juno* is just about the best movie of the year. It is very smart, very funny, and very touching; it begins with the pacing of a screwball comedy and ends as a portrait of characters we have come to love. Strange, how during Juno's hip dialogue and cocky bravado, we begin to understand the young woman inside, and we want to hug her.

Has there been a better performance this year than Ellen Page's creation of Juno? I don't think so. If most actors agree that comedy is harder than drama, then harder still is comedy depending on a quick mind, utter self-confidence, and an ability to stop just short of going too far. Page's presence and timing are extraordinary. I have seen her in only two films, she is only twenty, and I think she will be one of the great actors of her time.

But don't let my praise get in the way of sharing how much fun this movie is. It is so very rare to sit with an audience that leans forward with delight and is in step with every turn and surprise of an uncommonly intelligent screenplay. It is so rare to hear laughter that is surprised, unexpected, and delighted. So rare to hear it coming during moments of recognition, when characters reflect exactly what we'd be thinking, just a moment before we get around to thinking it. So rare to feel the audience joined into one warm shared enjoyment. So rare to hear a movie applauded.

Ellen Page plays Juno MacGuff, a sixteen-year-old girl who decides it is time for her to experience sex, and enlists her best friend, Paulie (Michael Cera), in an experiment he is not too eager to join. Of course she gets pregnant, and after a trip to an abortion clinic that leaves her cold, she decides to have the child. But what to do with it? She believes she's too young to raise it herself. Her best girlfriend, Leah (Olivia Thirby), suggests looking at the ads for adoptive parents in the *Penny Saver:* "They have 'Desperately Seeking Spawn,' right next to the pet ads."

Juno informs her parents, in a scene that decisively establishes how original this film is going to be. It does that by giving us almost the only lovable parents in the history of teen comedies: Bren (Allison Janney) and Mac (J. K. Simmons). They're older and wiser than most teen parents are ever allowed to be, and warmer and with better instincts and quicker senses of humor. Informed that the sheepish Paulie is the father, Mac turns to his wife and shares an aside that brings down the house. Later, Bren tells him, "You know, of course, it wasn't his idea." How infinitely more human and civilized their response is than all the sad routine "humor" about parents who are enraged at boyfriends.

Mac goes with Juno to meet the would-be adoptive parents, Vanessa and Mark Loring (Jennifer Garner and Jason Bateman). They live in one of those houses that look like Martha Stewart finished a second before they arrived. Vanessa is consumed with her desire for a child, and Mark is almost a child himself, showing Juno "my room," where he keeps the residue of his ambition to be a rock star. What he does now, at around forty, is write jingles for commercials.

We follow Juno through all nine months of her pregnancy, which she pretends to treat as mostly an inconvenience. It is uncanny how Page shows us, without seeming to show us, the deeper feelings beneath Juno's wisecracking exterior. The screenplay by first-timer Diablo Cody is a subtle masterpiece of construction, as buried themes slowly emerge, hidden feelings become clear, and we are led, but not too far, into wondering if Mark and Juno might possibly develop unwise feelings about one another.

There are moments of instinctive, lightning comedy: Bren's response to a nurse's attitude during Juno's sonar scan, and her theory about doctors when Juno wants a painkiller during childbirth. Moments that blindside us with truth, as when Mac and Juno talk about the possibility of true and lasting love. Moments that reveal Paulie as more than he seems. What he says when Juno says he's cool and doesn't even need to try. And the breathtaking scene when Juno and Vanessa run into each other in the mall, and the future of everyone is essentially decided. Jennifer Garner glows in that scene.

After three viewings I feel like I know some scenes by heart, but I don't want to spoil your experience by quoting one-liners and revealing surprises. The film's surprises, in any event, involve not merely the plot but insights into the characters, including feelings that coil along just beneath the surface so that they seem inevitable when they're revealed.

The film has no wrong scenes and no extra scenes, and flows like running water. There are two repeating motifs: the enchanting songs, so simple and true, by Kimya Dawson, and the seasonal appearances of Paulie's high school cross-country team, running past us with dogged consistency, Paulie often bringing up the rear, until his last run ends with Paulie, sweaty in running shorts, racing to Juno's room after her delivery. ☞

Just Friends ★

PG-13, 94 m., 2005

Ryan Reynolds (Chris Brander), Amy Smart (Jamie Palamino), Anna Faris (Samantha James), Chris Klein (Dusty), Christopher Marquette (Mike). Directed by Roger Kumble and produced by Chris Bender, William J. Johnson, Michael Ohoven, J. C. Spink, and William Vince. Screenplay by Adam "Tex" Davis.

The best scenes in *Just Friends* take place offscreen. If they were in the movie, they would involve the makeover of Chris, the hero. As the film opens he is a fat, unpopular nerd in high school. Flash forward ten years, and he is thin, fit, rich, handsome, and working in the music industry. Obviously, during the missing decade he hired Oprah's trainer and studied the self-help tapes sold by that guy on late-night TV—you know, the guy who will make you into a person willing to accept success. You have to *be willing*, that's the trick. The guy's methods are proven because he is a success himself, having been willing to make millions by selling his tapes.

But already we're off the subject of the film. This will be a hard subject to stay on. I am going to the kitchen right now to set the timer on the stove to go off every sixty seconds as a reminder to stay on the subject. Now I'm back from the kitchen. You know that late-night TV guy? Basically, he's offering an updated version of the old classified ad that said, "Send twenty-five cents to learn how to get hundreds of quarters through the mail." *Ding!*

In *Just Friends,* Ryan Reynolds plays Chris, who looks like he gets his fat suits from Jiminy Glick's tailor. He wants to hook up with a sexy babe named Jamie, played by Amy Smart. Jamie likes Chris a whole lot, but only as a friend. When a girl says she likes you as a friend, what she means is: "Rather than have sex with you, I would prefer to lose you as a friend."

Chris is crushed. In adventures that will no doubt be included in the deleted scenes on the DVD, he apparently moves to L.A., loses 150 pounds, becomes a hockey star, opens an account at SuperCuts, and turns into a babe magnet. His boss wants him to sign up an overnight pop superstar named Samantha, who is called Samantha because screenwriters love women named Samantha because when you call them "Sam" it sounds like you know them, when in fact their entire backstory may be limited to the fact that their nickname is "Sam." *Ding!*

Sam is supposed to make us think of Brittany or Britney or Britannia or whatever her name is. Now I remember: Her name is Paris Hilton. The other night at dinner I met a Motorola executive who told me Paris Hilton is their best customer for cell phones because she has gone through seventy of them. As Oscar Wilde once said, "To lose one cell phone may be regarded as a misfortune; to go through seventy looks like carelessness."

Sam is played by Anna Faris, who in *The Hot Chick* played the best friend of Rachel McAdams, whose character is magically transported into the body of Rob Schneider, causing the audience to urgently desire that he had been transported into her body instead, because then he would look like her. Actually, they do trade bodies, but the plot follows the Rob Schneider body, which is like taking the Gatorland exit on your way to Disney World. The assignment of Anna Faris is to relate to Rob Schneider's body as if it contained Rachel McAdams, a challenge I doubt even Dame Judi Dench would be equal to. *Ding!*

Sam and Chris are on a private jet to Paris Hilton when it makes an emergency landing in Chris's hometown in New Jersey, where he meets up with Jamie again on Christmas Eve. There is not a spark of chemistry between Chris and Jamie, although the plot clearly requires them to fall in love. There is so much chemistry involved with the Anna Faris character, however, that she can set off multiple chain reactions with herself, if you see what I mean. The problem with Chris is that although he's a cool dude in L.A., the moment he finds himself with Jamie again, he reverts to hapless dweebdom.

On the *Just Friends* message board at the Internet Movie Database, "ecbell-1" writes: "I live about a block away from where they filmed this movie." It was François Truffaut who said it was impossible to pay attention to a movie filmed in a house where you once lived because you would constantly be distracted by how it looked different and they had changed the wallpaper, etc. Did "ecbell-1" experience this phenomenon? "It was pretty cool," he writes, "because I watched some of it being filmed, and even got to meet some of the actors." Nothing about the Truffaut theory. The New Jersey house, by the way, is in "ecbell-1's" hometown of Regina, Saskatchewan. *Ding! Ding! Awopbopaloobop, Alopbamboom!*

Just Like Heaven ★ ★ ★

PG-13, 101 m., 2005

Mark Ruffalo (David Abbott), Reese Witherspoon (Elizabeth Masterson), Donal Logue (Jack Houriskey), Jon Heder (Darryl), Dina Spybey (Abby Brody), Ben Shenkman (Brett Rushton), Ivana Milicevic (Katrina), Rosalind Chao (Fran). Directed by Mark Waters and produced by Laurie MacDonald and Walter F. Parkes. Screenplay by Peter Tolan and Leslie Dixon, based on the novel *If Only It Were True* by Marc Levy.

In *Just Like Heaven,* a man falls in love with a woman only he can see. She's not a ghost, because she's not dead, but a spirit. Why is she visible only to him? Perhaps because he has moved into her apartment. In a movie like this there is no logical reason for such matters. They simply are, and you accept them.

The woman is Elizabeth, played by Reese Witherspoon. The man is David, played by Mark Ruffalo. These are two of the sweetest actors in the movies, and sweetness is what they give their characters in *Just Like Heaven.* There is not a mean bone in their bodies, and not a dark moment in the movie, unless, of course, you take the plot seriously, in which case it is deeply tragic.

Elizabeth is a young doctor at a San Francisco hospital. She is still single in her late twenties, and pulls twenty-six-hour shifts in the emergency room. A friend despairs of her unmarried status and wants to fix her up. "I'm perfectly capable of meeting men on my own," she says. The friend: "I know you are. I just want you to meet one that's not bleeding."

David was a landscape gardener until two years ago, when his first wife, Laura, died suddenly. Now he drinks too much and pays a lot of attention to the sofa he is sitting on at the moment. He's astonished when Elizabeth suddenly appears in the apartment and orders him to stop making a mess of things.

Although a good long talk would clear up everything at any point during the movie, the talk is postponed because the movie must move toward happiness with agonizing reluctance. David, manifestly confronted with a supernatural presence, consults Darryl (Jon Heder), the clerk in a psychic bookstore. He brings in a priest for a painfully overacted exorcism. He employs Asian ghostbusters. Elizabeth taunts him about "Father Flanagan and the Joy Luck Club." But she lacks crucial knowledge about what has happened to her.

We meet her sister, her nieces, her coworkers, and the creepy doctor who took over her job when she became a spirit. Can Elizabeth and David, who are now in love, take steps to return her to a corporal existence that will make their relationship immeasurably more satisfactory? Can David's best buddy, Jack (Donal Logue), help him with a little body-snatching? Can one movie support these many coincidences and close calls and misunderstandings?

Yes. The movie works, and so we accept everything, even the preposterous scene where a man is unconscious on the floor and Elizabeth tells David the man's lung is leaking air into his chest cavity, or whatever, and he must open a hole with a paring knife and keep it open with the plastic pour spout of a vodka bottle. As the chest is vented and the victim breathes again, I was poignantly reminded of the heart valve that gave Ignatius Reilly so much concern in *A Confederacy of Dunces,* that funniest of all novels from sad New Orleans.

I also liked the dialogue, by Peter Tolan and

Leslie Dixon, as when it turns out that Elizabeth's little niece can also see her: "My fate is in the hands of a four-year-old who has seven other imaginary friends." And when she finally persuades David to take her case: "You have two realities to choose from. The first is that a woman has come into your life in a very unconventional way and she needs your assistance. The second is that you're a crazy person, talking to himself on a park bench."

The Idiot Plot is a term devised for bad movies where the problems could be cleared up with a few words, if everyone in the plot were not an idiot. When the movie is good, it is kept afloat by the very frustration that sinks an Idiot Plot. There is a contest between what we want and what the characters do, and we get involved in spite of ourselves. Elizabeth explains perfectly clearly how her sister Abby (Dina Spybey) could be made to believe he is in touch with her spirit: She could tell David family secrets only Elizabeth would know. Wonderful, brilliant, and yet instead they mope about on hilltops with bittersweet regret. This woman could have been saved with days to spare, and there they are with fifteen minutes on the clock.

Just My Luck ★ ★

PG-13, 108 m., 2006

Lindsay Lohan (Ashley Albright), Chris Pine (Jake Hardin), Faizon Love (Damon Phillips), Missi Pyle (Peggy Braden), Samaire Armstrong (Maggie), Bree Turner (Dana). Directed by Donald Petrie and produced by Arnon Milchan, Arnold Rifkin, and Petrie. Screenplay by I. Marlene King and Amy B. Harris.

Some movies make me feel like I'm someone else. Other movies make me wish I were. Watching *Just My Luck,* I wished I were a teenage girl, not for any perverse reason, but because then I might have enjoyed it a lot more. I don't think it's for grown-ups, and I don't much think it's for teenage boys. But a teenage girl (even better, a preteen) might enjoy a romantic fantasy in which the heroine is old enough to get a top job at a marketing firm and wear Sarah Jessica Parker's clothes, and innocent enough that she has an entire romance based entirely on kissing. It's not only the romance that's kiss-based; so is the plot.

Lindsay Lohan is the star, and I have liked her ever since *The Parent Trap* (1998) and I like her here, too, but like many another former child star, it's time for her to move on to more challenging roles. I am lucky enough to have seen her in Robert Altman's forthcoming *A Prairie Home Companion,* so I know what we have to look forward to. Just our luck that we'll have *Just My Luck* to look back on.

Lohan plays Ashley, a young Manhattan career woman with extraordinarily good luck. It stops raining when she steps outside. Paper money sticks to her shoes. She can always get a cab. One day Damon Phillips (Faizon Love), a powerful record mogul, turns up at her office while her boss, Peggy Braden (Missi Pyle), is stuck in the elevator. Ashley has taken notes at previous meetings, knows the pitch, and delivers it to keep the mogul from walking out. She wins the contract, gets a new title, a raise, and an office, and finds herself producing an extravagant masquerade ball as a promotion.

In a parallel story, we meet Jake (Chris Pine). His luck is always bad. It starts raining when he walks outside. He finds a $5 bill, but it's covered with dog poop. His pants split. He works as a janitor at a bar and bowling alley, where he also runs the sound board and manages a band of young Brits who apparently want to look and sound as much as possible like the Beatles, circa 1964. The movie uses a real band, McFly: "Unlike most boy bands today," the press notes inform us, "McFly write their own songs and play their own instruments." The alternatives are too depressing to contemplate.

The entire plot hinges on a single kiss. At the masked ball, Ashley is kissed by Jake, and somehow her good luck leaps from her lips to his, and he is blessed while now it rains on her and she can't get a cab. Many other dire events occur before Ashley realizes what must have happened. Since the person who kissed her was one of the professional dancers at the party, Ashley tracks down all twenty of them and kisses them—but no luck, because Jake was only pretending to be one of the dancers, see, and was really a gate-crasher trying to get McFly's demo CD into the hands of Damon

Phillips. If you're one of those people who think I have a great job, imagine me watching Ashley work her way down the kiss list.

Eventually everything is sorted out, not before many misunderstandings and a lot of complex luck-trading that involves spit-swapping. McFly sings several songs, one of them a production number looking like a road company version of *A Hard Day's Night,* and Ashley's friends (Bree Turner and Samaire Armstrong) take her in after her apartment floods and tirelessly support her, advise her, cheer her, and help dress her. When Sarah Jessica Parker's dry cleaning is mistakenly delivered to Ashley's apartment, that's good luck. What happens later is bad luck for Ashley, and especially for Sarah Jessica Parker.

Just My Luck is perfectly efficient in its own way, delivering exactly what anyone would expect in a Lindsay Lohan movie with this premise. I wish it delivered more. It's safe, competent, and bland. I had a fairly monotonous time. You may like it more. For your sake, I hope so.

K

Keane ★ ★ ★ ½

R, 100 m., 2005

Damian Lewis (William Keane), Abigail Breslin (Kira Bedik), Amy Ryan (Lynn Bedik), Liza Colon-Zayas (1st Ticket Agent), John Tormey (2nd Ticket Agent), Brenda Denmark (Commuter), Ed Wheeler (Bus Driver), Christopher Evan Welch (Motel Clerk). Directed by Lodge H. Kerrigan and produced by Andrew Fierberg and Steven Soderbergh. Screenplay by Kerrigan.

Lodge Kerrigan's *Keane* opens with a man ranging the Port Authority Bus Terminal, looking for his lost daughter. He has a newspaper clipping he shows to people, who hurry on, sensing madness. The girl has been missing for weeks or months. It's not clear. This search has been part of the daily life of the man, named William Keane, who then retreats into a rough street world: a bottle of beer at one gulp, vodka, cocaine, prostitutes, reckless sex.

Keane, like Peter Winter, the subject of Kerrigan's *Clean, Shaven* (1994), is a schizophrenic on a quest for his daughter. But Winter has a daughter. Did Keane have a daughter, did she disappear, did she even exist? There is an enormous difference between the two films, generated by the urgency of Keane's desire to function in the world. He reminds himself he must look presentable to go on his search. He buys clothes for the missing girl. His episodes of abandon and confusion alternate with moments when he is quiet and tries to calm himself and focus.

Keane is played by Damian Lewis, a British actor recently seen in *An Unfinished Life* as the abusive boyfriend of Jennifer Lopez. Here he inhabits an edge of madness that Kerrigan understands with a fierce sympathy. There is no reason for us to believe that Keane (or his daughter) would be better off if he found her. The camera regards him mercilessly, and his performance involves us because he portrays not hopeless madness but his drive to escape his demons.

In a cheap flophouse, he meets Lynn (Amy Ryan) and her seven-year-old daughter, Kira (Abigail Breslin). They're down and out. Her husband has abandoned them, maybe to seek work, maybe to escape. Keane receives disability checks and gives Lynn money, which she needs badly enough to accept, especially since he is in a sweet, calm phase and doesn't want anything for it, or at least not anything she might not be willing to provide.

Lynn can't pick up Kira after school. Will Keane meet her, bring her home, and keep an eye on her from 4 to 7? He will. He does. They go to McDonald's. They go ice skating. This Keane might have made a good father. Which Keane is it? The mother goes seeking her husband and entrusts Kira to Keane overnight. What will happen? The suspense grows not out of the child's danger, if she is in any, but out of Keane's fears about himself. He has been going through a calm period. He is terrified of the responsibility he has suddenly been given. Does he confuse Kira with his lost daughter?

Kerrigan's films create worlds of personal obsession. After *Clean, Shaven,* he made *Claire Dolan* (1998), the story of an Irish prostitute (Katrin Cartlidge, 1961–2002, her early death from a sudden infection a sad loss after great performances). She works in Manhattan, wants to leave the life, must escape a dangerous pimp. In all three films, characters on the margins seek children they think will bring them happiness.

Some movies shed light on others. Regarding *Keane,* I think of *Flightplan,* the Jodie Foster thriller that opened a week earlier. Both films are excellent in their own way, seeking their own intentions, aimed at different audiences. Both begin with a lost daughter. The characters played by Foster and Lewis realize that if they are perceived as mad, all hope is lost for their search. Both try to function in a way that will allow them to continue.

There are some critics who will honor *Keane* and scorn *Flightplan,* and others who will praise *Flightplan* and never see, or even hear of, *Keane.* One is a commercial thriller, the other made by a transgressive independent. They both appeal to the same feelings in the audience. The parent has lost a daughter. The world presents a danger to the parent's search. *Keane* adds the grave complication of Kira.

The suspense in both films comes from our desire to see the parents survive and prevail.

The complete filmgoer is open to the movie on the screen and asks it to work in its own ways for its own purposes. He does not fault one for not being the other but is grateful for both if they are successful. Anyone seeking an understanding of the ways movies work might want to see both of these films and think about the ways they are different, and the ways they are not.

Keeping Up with the Steins ★ ★ ★

PG-13, 99 m., 2006

Jeremy Piven (Adam Fiedler), Larry Miller (Arnie Stein), Jami Gertz (Joanne Fiedler), Daryl Hannah (Sandy Sacred Feather), Garry Marshall (Irwin Fiedler), Daryl Sabara (Benjamin Fiedler), Doris Roberts (Rose Fiedler), Cheryl Hines (Casey Nudelman), Carter Jenkins (Zachary Stein). Directed by Scott Marshall and produced by A. D. Oppenheim, David Scharf, and Mark Zakarin. Screenplay by Zakarin.

I never tire of quoting Godard, who said, "The way to criticize a movie is to make another movie." Now comes more proof. A few weeks after *When Do We Eat?* a dreary comedy about a dysfunctional Jewish family at Passover, here is *Keeping Up with the Steins,* a fresh and lovable comedy about a dysfunctional Jewish family planning their son's bar mitzvah.

The family is headed by Adam Fiedler (Jeremy Piven), a Hollywood agent who is envious when his archrival, Arnie Stein (Larry Miller), throws a bar mitzvah for his own thirteen-year-old that includes an ocean cruise, a giant model of the *Titanic,* and a trained porpoise wearing a yarmulke. "I'm king of the world," the younger Stein cries, his arms outstretched as the *Titanic* sails into a ballroom and Adam Fiedler grows morose.

Adam consults with his wife, Joanne (Jami Gertz), about a bar mitzvah to shame the Steins. It may involve booking Dodger Stadium and having his son, Benjamin (Daryl Sabara of *Spy Kids*), arrive from the sky. Money is no object. Hiring a singer? How about Neil Diamond?

The problem with this grandiose scheme is that young Benjamin has no heart for it. Because he narrates the movie, we learn from his point of view that he feels embarrassed by all the attention, overwhelmed by the scope of the ceremony, and terrified by his inability to master Hebrew in time to read it aloud during the religious prelude to the conspicuous consumption. He is also sad that his grandfather Irwin (Garry Marshall) has not been invited; Irwin and Adam have not been on speaking terms for years.

Benjamin appeals to his mother to downsize the bar mitzvah plans and secretly invites Grandfather Irwin to the ceremony. We discover that Irwin now enjoys a delightful new lifestyle on an Indian reservation with his young girlfriend, Sacred Feather (Daryl Hannah). When Irwin and Sacred Feather arrive at the Fiedlers' for dinner, Sacred Feather turns out to have dietary restrictions that make Jewish customs seem positively permissive. Marshall and Hannah have small roles, but they're perfectly realized.

Another key character is Benjamin's grandmother and Irwin's first wife, Rose (Doris Roberts). How will the once-married couple get along, and will Sacred Feather get caught in the middle? The movie could handle these questions with overacting, screaming matches, and overwrought drama, as *When Do We Eat?* does, but no. The screenplay by Mark Zakarin (a writer for *The L Word* on TV) uses its share of exaggeration and hyperbole, but the characters behave according to their natures and needs, as we all do.

The movie was directed by Scott Marshall, son of Garry, nephew of Penny, and, therefore, born with comic timing in his genes. His plot is not astonishingly original; it bears some similarity to the competition over holiday decorations in the awful *Christmas with the Kranks* (2004) and cheerfully goes for one-liners and sight gags. But it is always about something, and if a bar mitzvah marks a boy's entry into manhood, Benjamin's shows him becoming his own man.

I was grateful to Piven and Gertz for making the parents into people who act more like parents than like movie characters. To be sure, any Hollywood agent has a tendency toward the grandiose and the cocky, but Joanne is a steadying influence on Adam, who after all loves his son more than he loves outspending his rival.

At one point in the film, Adam looks at home movies of his own bar mitzvah, a humble backyard affair. His wife has never seen them before. They are a reminder of the underlying purpose of the ceremony, which is not to outspend the neighbors but to wish a young man godspeed in his life. Because the movie never really forgets this, *Keeping Up with the Steins* never loses its footing.

Kicking and Screaming ★ ★ ★

PG, 95 m., 2005

Will Ferrell (Phil Weston), Robert Duvall (Buck Weston), Kate Walsh (Barbara Weston), Mike Ditka (Himself), Dylan McLaughlin (Sam Weston), Josh Hutcherson (Bucky Weston), Musette Vander (Janice Weston), Elliott Cho (Byong Sun). Directed by Jesse Dylan and produced by Jimmy Miller. Screenplay by Leo Benvenuti and Steve Rudnick.

The problem with team sports involving kids is that the coaches are parents. The parents become too competitive and demanding, and put an unwholesome emphasis on winning. One simple reform would enormously improve childhood sports: The coaches should be kids, too. Parents could be around in supervisory roles, sort of like the major league commissioner, but kids should run their own teams. Sure, they'd make mistakes and the level of play would suffer and, in fact, the whole activity would look a lot more like a Game and less like a Sporting Event. Kids become so coopted by the adult obsession with winning that they can't just mess around and have fun.

This insight came to me midway through *Kicking and Screaming,* which illustrates my theory by giving us a father-and-son coaching team who will haunt the nightmares of their players for decades to come. The movie is actually sweet and pretty funny, so don't get scared away: It's just that when a kid hears an adult say, "I eat quitters for breakfast and I spit out their bones," that kid is not going to rest easier tonight.

Will Ferrell stars as Phil Weston, an adult who still feels like a kid when his dad, Buck (Robert Duvall), is around. Buck is a version of Bull Meechum, the character Duvall played in *The Great Santini* (1979), where he was trying to run his family like a Marine unit. Buck coaches in the local kids' soccer league, and as the movie opens, he trades his grandson—*his own grandson*—because the kid is no good. That makes Phil mad: He was always told he was a loser, and now his own kid is getting the same treatment from Buck.

So Phil decides to become a coach himself. But he's just as obsessed with winning as his dad. He makes three key recruits. Two of them are the kids of the local Italian butcher; they're great players. The third is Mike Ditka, as himself; he's Buck's neighbor, the two men hate each other, and Ditka agrees to become Phil's assistant coach.

Phil's basic coaching strategy is simple: Get the ball to the Italians. The movie could have taken better advantage of Ditka by really focusing on his personality, but that would have shouldered aside the father-son rivalry, and so I guess they have it about right, with Ditka supplying advice and one-liners from the sidelines. He makes one crucial contribution to the plot: He introduces Phil to coffee. Phil has never been a coffee drinker, but from the first sip he finds it addictive, and then maddening. "What is that fascinating aroma?" he asks, before going on a caffeine binge that actually leads to him being barred for life from a coffee shop.

With Ferrell in the movie, we might expect a raucous comedy like *Old School,* or maybe *Dodgeball,* a movie I have to keep reminding myself Ferrell was not in. But no, *Kicking and Screaming* is more like *The Bad News Bears* or *The Mighty Ducks,* with the underdogs coming from the bottom of the league standings to eventually—but I dare not reveal the ending, even though it will be obvious to every sentient being in the theater.

Will Ferrell is now a major movie star. I learn of his status from the industry analyst David Poland, who has crunched the numbers and come up with the "real" list of box-office heavyweights. He says the top ten stars in terms of actual ticket sales are, in order: Will Smith, Tom Cruise, Adam Sandler, Jim Carrey, Russell Crowe, Tom Hanks, Eddie Murphy, Ben Stiller, Will Ferrell, and Denzel Washington. The highest-ranking woman on the list is Reese Witherspoon, at No. 12.

The list is fascinating because it sets Ferrell apart from several other recent *Saturday*

Night Live alums cycling through hapless comedies; he has broken loose from the *SNL* curse that, for example, haunts Martin Short in *Jiminy Glick.* Ferrell plays actual characters, as he did in *Elf,* rather than recycled *SNL* skit creatures. In *Kicking and Screaming,* he understands that the role requires a certain vulnerability and poignancy, and although he goes berserk with all the coffee, it is kept within character. His soccer coach has an emotional arc and is not simply a cartoon. Duvall, of course, is superb. No one has a meaner laugh. He even begins to smile and you wish you were armed. He goes head-to-head with Ditka and you wait for them to spit out the bones.

The movie is pure formula from beginning to end, and it doesn't pay as much attention to the individual kids as it might have—especially to Byong Sun (Elliott Cho), the smallest member of the team, who seems to have something really going on down there among the knees of his opponents. There is also the usual thankless role of the hero's wife, played here by Kate Walsh; her job is to talk sense to Phil, which is never much fun. Buck's wife is a sexy bombshell played by Musette Vander, but she turns out to be sensible and sane, which is a disappointment. Still, *Kicking and Screaming* is an entertaining family movie, and may serve a useful purpose if it inspires kids to overthrow their coaches and take over their own sports.

The Kid and I ★ ★ ★

PG-13, 93 m., 2005

Tom Arnold (Bill Williams), Eric Gores (Aaron Roman), Richard Edson (Guy Prince), Joe Mantegna (Davis Roman), Henry Winkler (Johnny Bernstein), Shannon Elizabeth (Shelby Roman), Linda Hamilton (Susan Mandeville), Arielle Kebbel (Arielle). Directed by Penelope Spheeris and produced by Tom Arnold, Spheeris, and Brad Wyman. Screenplay by Arnold.

There is something I don't know about *The Kid and I.* Although I could easily find it out, I have decided to write the review without knowing it. The movie is about a kid with cerebral palsy, whose favorite movie is *True Lies* with Arnold Schwarzenegger, and whose dream is to star in an action movie of his own. He wants to jump out of airplanes, beat up bad people, and kiss a girl, and because his father is a millionaire, he gets his chance.

Here is what I don't know: Is Eric Gores, who plays the kid, really disabled, or is he an actor? I ask because the answer involves how we respond to the difference between documentary and fiction. The performance by Gores is so convincing that if he's an actor, it's an impressive achievement. If he's not an actor, then it's impressive in a different way, because he overcomes disabilities to create a character we believe and care about.

Ten seconds on the Internet, and I would know. But the answer would skew my review. If Gores is an actor, we are looking at fiction. If he is disabled, then we are looking at a documentary in which a professional cast and crew interact with him. Or are we? Should it matter? That's where it gets tricky. Isn't a disabled actor as capable of playing a role in a movie as anyone else? Didn't the Italian neorealists teach us that everyone has one role he can play perfectly, and that role is himself?

I think the most honest strategy, having put my cards on the table, is to review the film on its own terms. *The Kid and I,* written by Tom Arnold and directed by Penelope Spheeris, doesn't sentimentalize the material, that's for sure. It begins as a dark comedy, with Bill Williams (Arnold) playing a has-been onetime movie star who is out of work and out of hope. He prepares a press release on his suicide and various other suicide notes, then leaves his house to give away his clothes to a bum named Guy (Richard Edson). The bum follows him home and sabotages the suicide plans. Now Bill is still alive and has no money *and* no clothes, and the trade papers are reporting his death. This could be the setup for a Preston Sturges story.

A millionaire named David Roman (Joe Mantegna) contacts him. He wants to hire Bill to write and act in an action movie like *True Lies,* which would star Roman's son Aaron. The real Tom Arnold did star in the original *True Lies,* and in this and many other details, the movie incorporates facts and names from real life. Bill is incredulous. When he meets Aaron, he is not instantly won over by the kid's courage, charm, personality, etc., and states flatly that the film cannot be done. But Aaron has a way of ignoring or deflecting negativity. He just keeps right on making his plans: "In the movie," he explains, "I want a girlfriend. I want to kiss a girl." He even specifies the girl he wants to kiss: Arielle Kebbel, whom he has studied in the pages of *Maxim*.

The rich David Roman has a new spouse named Shelby (Shannon Elizabeth), who may quality as a "trophy wife" but is not a bad person, and helps convince Bill to take on the project. The details of the movie they make I will leave for you to discover. "We can get Penelope Spheeris to direct," Bill says at one point, adding that she won't cost a lot of money.

Spheeris plays herself in the film, is seen on camera, and her approach to both the outer and inner films is the same: She depends on realism, up to a certain point, and then it becomes "a movie." We see how stunts are handled, how effects are obtained, how shots are cheated to make it appear that the star does things he is not really doing. We see, in fact, more or less what might really happen if a disabled kid with a rich dad made this movie. Or if an actor played a disabled kid, etc.

And the result is—well, what is it? Heartwarming? In a technical sense, yes, but the movie doesn't pander and there aren't a lot of violins playing (or any, as I recall). The overall tone reflects the sardonic comedy Arnold might really make, right down to his suggestion that the kid's girlfriend could be Rosie O'Donnell. I wonder why he didn't suggest Roseanne Barr.

One tricky scene is handled especially well. That's the one they leave until the last day of the shooting, the hot-tub scene involving Kebbel. When Kebbel turns up on the set, she turns out to be not an alarmingly erotic menace from *Maxim* but a sweet girl who treats Aaron well, doesn't condescend to the situation, and is, let it be said, a charming hot-tub companion.

In this and other dicey moments, the movie finds a way to avoid being creepy on the one hand and corny on the other: It works by being forthright and businesslike about the movie-within-the-movie. And this is accurate: Movies cost a lot of money and involve skilled and impatient professionals; just because the kid's dad is rich changes nothing. Executive producers are always rich. That's how they get to be executive producers.

The Kid and I is not a great film, but you know what? It achieves what it sets out to achieve, and it isn't boring, and it kept me intrigued and involved. As an actor, Gores creates an engaging and convincing character that I liked and cared about—and believed.

I make it a practice to avoid watching trailers and reading Internet speculation on forthcoming movies, and in this case I'm relieved that I knew nothing about the movie going in. When you come out, check the Internet, which is what I'm about to do, and then ask yourself if your thinking about the movie is affected, knowing what you know now. The answer to that question cuts to the heart of the mystery about how we relate to movies.

Kids in America ★ ★ ★

PG-13, 91 m., 2005

Gregory Smith (Holden Donovan), Stephanie Sherrin (Charlotte Pratt), Nicole Richie (Kelly Stepford), Malik Yoba (Will Drucker), Julie Bowen (Principal Weller), Caitlin Wachs (Katie Carmichael), Emy Coligado (Emily Chua), Crystal Celeste Grant (Walanda Jenkins), Chris Morris (Chuck McGinn), Alex Anfanger (Lawrence Reitzer), Adam Arkin (Ed Mumsford), George Wendt (Coach Thompson), Andrew Shaifer (Chip Stratton), Rosanna Arquette (Abby Pratt), Elizabeth Perkins (Sondra Carmichael). Directed by Josh Stolberg and produced by Andrew Shaifer. Screenplay by Shaifer and Stolberg.

Once in a blue moon, a movie escapes the shackles of its genre and does what it really wants to do. *Kids in America* is a movie like that. It breaks out of Hollywood jail. You know all those "brainless high school comedies"? Here's what one would look like if it had brains. It's a movie for every kid who was different, every kid with a political thought, every kid who ever got suspended for exercising the freedom of speech, every kid who had an article censored in the school paper, or did something shocking in a talent show, or actually believed what the idealistic teachers told him.

Yes, all of that, but I'm making it sound too serious. This is also a comedy that bites, and a romance during which a boy and a girl fall in love while they are engaged in an experiment to reproduce movie kisses. They start with the greatest movie kiss of all time, which he thinks is the one between John Cusack and Ione Skye in *Say Anything,* the kiss in the rain that lasts about three seconds and you almost miss it. When Holden (Gregory Smith of *Everwood*) describes it to Charlotte (Stephanie Sherrin), she simply says "show me" and walks out into the rain. They eventually get around to the longest kiss in movie history, which I always thought was the one between Cary Grant and Ingrid Bergman in *Notorious,* but no, it was between Jane Wyman and Regis Toomey in *You're in the Army Now,* and it clocked in at 185 seconds. Of course, only a kid who works in a video store would know that.

There is nobody stupid in this movie. Not even Kelly (Nicole Richie of *The Simple Life*), the head of the cheerleader squad. Not even Principal Weller (Julie Bowen), who enforces medieval policies but is scary, she's so articulate. Not even the football coach (George Wendt). Not even the drama coach (Andrew Shaifer), who once staged a reading of Oliver Stone's *Platoon* with all the expletives removed, and what's more, he has Harvey Fierstein's autograph. The stupid people are all offscreen, like the anatomy teacher described by Holden: "He lives with his mom and has never seen a naked body, including his own."

The characters talk about real things in real words. Amazing. Consider the girl who runs the school's Celibacy Club but gets suspended for wearing a "Safe Sex or No Sex" button and sticking condoms to her blouse. The school policy is: no sex. But what about girls who do have sex, she wants to know, and get pregnant or have abortions? Principal Weller's policy is celibacy or else. Consider the crisis involving the school's Minority Club, which has "traditionally" been for African-Americans only. "You can kiss my Chinese ass," says an Asian student. Another kid wants in because he's fat. And what about Lawrence (Alex Anfanger)? The head of the club concedes: "You're so gay, Cher dresses like you."

The school reaches the crisis point during the annual Holiday Hoopla talent show, when Holden does a reading from Shakespeare. He gets as far as "to be or not to be" and decides "I choose not to be," attacking school policies and ending up with a real showstopper.

Principal Weller tries to contain the uprising; she's running for superintendent of schools and is worried about her image. But the students outmaneuver her and her flunkies, leading up to a hijacked pep rally where Holden commandeers the audiovisual hookup and shows a montage of heterosexual kissing in the corridors, leading up to a protest about the expulsion of the gay student. This leads to a development that will certainly add to the list of famous movie kisses.

Kids in America was directed by Josh Stolberg; he and Shaifer coproduced and wrote the screenplay. They say it was inspired by actual news stories, including one about a girl thrown out of school after her journal was seized and read without her permission. Another girl got expelled for wearing a "Barbie is a lesbian" T-shirt. The movie is properly angry at the repression and discrimination that masquerades as school policy, but the surprising thing is how funny and entertaining they make it. High school students are so consistently depicted as substance-abusing, sex-crazed airheads, you'd think Hollywood was trying to teach them they're as dumb as the movies about them. *Kids in America* is a call to the barricades, and a lot of fun.

The King ★ ★ ★ ½

R, 105 m., 2006

Gael Garcia Bernal (Elvis Valderez), William Hurt (David Sandow), Pell James (Malerie Sandow), Paul Dano (Paul Sandow), Laura Harring (Twyla Sandow). Directed by James Marsh and produced by Milo Addica and James Wilson. Screenplay by Addica and Marsh.

He is straight out of the Navy. He travels to Corpus Christi, Texas, takes a motel room, and attends church. After the service, he asks the pastor for a hug. The pastor hugs him and says, "I don't believe I know you." The young man says his name is Elvis: "My mother told me about you. Her name was Yolanda. She told me your name." This is not the sort of thing an evangelical minister wants to hear when his wife's name is not Yolanda.

Going to church was not quite the first thing Elvis (Gael Garcia Bernal) did in Corpus Christi. First he met the preacher's sixteen-year-old daughter, Malerie (Pell James). Now he moves on both fronts, seducing the daughter while playing a devout churchgoer for the father. Minister David Sandow is played by William Hurt as a man who once was a sinner but, as he tells Elvis, "That was before I became a Christian. Before I met my wife."

William Hurt can be so subterranean, we don't know where he's tunneling. Here he seems to be one thing while becoming its opposite. The last thing he wants in his life is a child from an early affair. On the other hand, Elvis makes a good impression. The pastor's son, Paul (Paul Dano), sings with his band at church services and at school is the leader of a campaign to introduce intelligent design into the curriculum. But we sense, and maybe the pastor does, that the energy Paul is channeling into Christian activism could turn against the church in a flash. Paul and his band perform a song one Sunday that enrages the pastor. Not long after, the son goes missing. The pastor, his family, and the congregation pray for his safe return, but the Lord is not in a position to answer their prayers.

At some point during this setup, we realize *The King* will *not* be a movie about the hypocrisy of the pastor. Pastor David is about as good a man as is possible under the circumstances, although there is room for improvement. And Elvis is not a blameless victim.

I have slipped over crucial sections of the movie because things occur that should come as a complete surprise to you. One thing that will not astonish anyone is Elvis's ability to sneak into Malerie's bedroom almost at will. We know from *Down in the Valley* and countless other movies that the bedrooms of teenage girls are sadly lacking in security and that their parents sleep the sleep of the dead. Malerie falls in love with Elvis, but his feelings for her are a good question: He knows, and she doesn't, that they have the same father.

The King descends so deeply and steadily into evil that it generates a dread fascination. After Paul disappears, the preacher reaches out to Elvis, acknowledging him in front of the congregation, treating him as a son, inviting him into his house. Because at any moment we possess more information than anyone except Elvis (and more insight into Elvis than he ever will have about himself), we see mistakes being made for perfectly reasonable motives. The preacher's decision comes under the heading of forgiveness and charity, but no good can come of it.

What has Elvis been planning in the years since David and Yolanda sinned? Certainly some of his actions in the movie are unpremeditated, but the way he responds to them shows a frightening degree of calculation. That Garcia Bernal's character looks open-faced and trustworthy is a great advantage; that he is utterly amoral helps him, too, because he can look straight in your eye and lie pleasingly and with conviction.

The movie was directed by James Marsh, a British documentarian, from a screenplay by Milo Addica (*Monster's Ball*). It's the kind of work where characters develop on their own, without consulting the book of clichés. We have so many preconceived notions about the types in this movie (hellfire preacher, sexpot daughter, dutiful son, black sheep) that it's surprising to see them behaving as individuals; they make decisions based on what they know and when they know it, and that's always too little and too late. The character who sees clearly, or intuits accurately, is the preacher's wife, Twyla (Laura Harring). At the service when David welcomes Elvis to the church, she walks out the door and straight down the middle of the street. But even that isn't the close of anything.

What the movie leaves us with are theological questions. Are the sins of the father visited on the son? Are we justified in protecting ourselves when fate threatens us? Are some people just plain bad? Should you think twice before doing the right thing? Are you sure you know what it is? Underneath all these is a fundamental question: Why does God allow bad things to happen to good people? I was startled the other day when the pope visited Auschwitz and asked God the same question. The party line, in the pope's church and in Pastor David's, is that the Lord works in mysterious ways, his wonders to unfold. Some wonders we can do without.

Kingdom of Heaven ★ ★ ★ ½

R, 145 m., 2005

Orlando Bloom (Balian of Ibelin), Eva Green (Sibylla), Liam Neeson (Godfrey of Ibelin), David Thewlis (Hospitaler), Marton Csokas (Guy de Lusignan), Brendan Gleeson (Reynald),

Jeremy Irons (Tiberias), Ghassan Massoud (Saladin), Edward Norton (King Baldwin). Directed by Ridley Scott and produced by Scott. Screenplay by William Monahan.

The first thing to be said for Ridley Scott's *Kingdom of Heaven* is that Scott knows how to direct a historical epic. I might have been kinder to his *Gladiator* had I known that *Troy* and *Alexander* were in my future, but *Kingdom of Heaven* is better than *Gladiator*—deeper, more thoughtful, more about human motivation, and less about action.

The second thing is that Scott is a brave man to release a movie at this time about the wars between Christians and Muslims for control of Jerusalem. Few people will be capable of looking at *Kingdom of Heaven* objectively. I have been invited by both Muslims and Christians to view the movie with them so they can point out its shortcomings. When you've made both sides angry, you may have done something right.

The Muslim scholar Hamid Dabashi, however, after being asked to consult on the movie, writes in the new issue of *Sight & Sound:* "It was neither pro- nor anti-Islamic, neither pro- nor anti-Christian. It was, in fact, not even about the Crusades. And yet I consider the film to be a profound act of faith." It is an act of faith, he thinks, because for its hero, Balian (Orlando Bloom), who is a nonbeliever, "All religious affiliations fade in the light of his melancholic quest to find a noble purpose in life."

That's an insight that helps me understand my own initial question about the film, which was: Why don't they talk more about religion? Weren't the Crusades seen by Christians as a holy war to gain control of Jerusalem from the Muslims? I wondered if perhaps Scott was evading the issue. But not really: He shows characters more concerned with personal power and advancement than with theological issues.

Balian, a village blacksmith in France, discovers he is the illegitimate son of Sir Godfrey (Liam Neeson). Godfrey is a knight returning from the Middle East, who paints Jerusalem not in terms of a holy war but in terms of its opportunities for an ambitious young man; it has a healthy economy at a time when medieval Europe is stagnant. "A man who in France has not a house is in the Holy Land the master of a city," Godfrey promises. "There at the end of the world you are not what you were born, but what you have it in yourself to be." He makes Jerusalem sound like a medieval Atlanta, a city too busy to hate.

For the one hundred years leading up to the action, both Christians and Muslims were content to see each other worship in the Holy City. It was only when Christian zealots determined to control the Holy Land more rigidly that things went wrong. The movie takes place circa 1184, as the city is ruled by the young King Baldwin (Edward Norton), who has leprosy and conceals his disfigured face behind a silver mask. Balian takes control of the city after the death of its young king. Then the Knights Templar, well known from *The Da Vinci Code,* wage war on the Muslims. Saladin (Ghassan Massoud) leads a Muslim army against them, and Balian eventually surrenders the city to him. Much bloodshed and battle are avoided.

What Scott seems to be suggesting, I think, is that most Christians and Muslims might be able to coexist peacefully if it were not for the extremists on both sides. This may explain why the movie has displeased the very sorts of Muslims and Christians who will take moderation as an affront. Most ordinary moviegoers, I suspect, will not care much about the movie's reasonable politics, and will be absorbed in those staples of all historical epics, battle and romance.

The romance here is between Balian and Sibylla (Eva Green), sister of King Baldwin. You might wonder how a blacksmith could woo a princess, but reflect that Sir Godfrey was correct, and there are indeed opportunities for an ambitious young man in Jerusalem, especially after his newly discovered father makes him a knight and Tiberias (Jeremy Irons) enlists him as an aide to Baldwin.

One spectacular battle scene involves the attack of Saladin's forces on Christian-controlled Jerusalem, and it's one of those spectacular set-pieces with giant balls of flame that hurtle through the air and land close, but not too close, to the key characters. There is a certain scale that's inevitable in films of this sort, and Scott does it better than anybody.

Even so, I enjoyed the dialogue and plot more than the action. I've seen one or two vast desert cities too many. Nor do thousands of charging horses look brand-new to me, and the hand-to-hand combat looks uncannily like all other hand-to-hand combat. Godfrey gives Balian a lesson in swordsmanship (chop from above), but apparently the important thing to remember is that if you're an anonymous enemy, you die, and if you're a hero, you live unless a glorious death is required. You'd think people would be killed almost by accident in the middle of a thousand sword-swinging madmen, but every encounter is broken down into a confrontation between a victor and a vanquished. It's well done, but it's been done.

What's more interesting is Ridley Scott's visual style, assisted by John Mathieson's cinematography and the production design of Arthur Max. A vast set of ancient Jerusalem was constructed to provide realistic foregrounds and locations, which were then enhanced by CGI backgrounds, additional horses and troops, and so on. There is also exhilarating footage as young Balian makes his way to Jerusalem, using the twelfth-century equivalent of a GPS: "Go to where they speak Italian, and then keep going."

The movie is above all about the personal codes of its heroes, both Christian and Muslim. They are men of honor: Gentlemen, we would say, if they were only a little gentle. They've seen enough bloodshed and lost enough comrades to look with a jaundiced eye at the zealots who urge them into battle. There is a scene where Baldwin and Saladin meet on a vast plain between their massed troops, and agree, man-to-man, to end the battle right then and there. Later, one of Balian's prebattle speeches to his troops sounds strangely regretful: "We fight over an offense we did not give, against those who were not alive to be offended." Time for a Truth and Reconciliation Commission?

King Kong ★ ★ ★ ★

PG-13, 187 m., 2005

Naomi Watts (Ann Darrow), Jack Black (Carl Denham), Adrien Brody (Jack Driscoll), Andy Serkis (Kong/Lumpy), Thomas Kretschmann (Captain Englehorn), Colin Hanks (Preston), Kyle Chandler (Bruce Baxter). Directed by Peter Jackson and produced by Jan Blenkin, Carolynne Cunningham, Fran Walsh, and Jackson. Screenplay by Walsh, Philippa Boyens, and Jackson, based on a story by Merian C. Cooper and Edgar Wallace.

It was beauty killed the beast.

There are astonishments to behold in Peter Jackson's new *King Kong*, but one sequence, relatively subdued, holds the key to the movie's success. Kong has captured Ann Darrow and carried her to his perch high on the mountain. He puts her down, not roughly, and then begins to roar, bare his teeth, and pound his chest. Ann, an unemployed vaudeville acrobat, somehow instinctively knows that the gorilla is not threatening her but trying to impress her by behaving as an alpha male—the king of the jungle. She doesn't know how Queen Kong would respond, but she does what she can: She goes into her stage routine, doing backflips, dancing like Chaplin, juggling three stones.

Her instincts and empathy serve her well. Kong's eyes widen in curiosity, wonder, and finally what may pass for delight. From then on, he thinks of himself as the girl's possessor and protector. She is like a tiny, beautiful toy that he has been given for his very own, and before long they are regarding the sunset together, both of them silenced by its majesty.

The scene is crucial because it removes the element of creepiness in the gorilla/girl relationship in the two earlier Kongs (1933 and 1976), creating a wordless bond that allows her to trust him. When Jack Driscoll climbs the mountain to rescue her, he finds her comfortably nestled in Kong's big palm. Ann and Kong in this movie will be threatened by dinosaurs, man-eating worms, giant bats, loathsome insects, spiders, machine guns, and the Army Air Corps, and could fall to their death into chasms on Skull Island or from the Empire State Building. But Ann will be as safe as Kong can make her, and he will protect her even from her own species.

The movie more or less faithfully follows the outlines of the original film, but this fundamental adjustment in the relationship between the beauty and the beast gives it heart, a quality the earlier film was lacking. Yes, Kong in 1933 cares for his captive, but she doesn't care so much for him. Kong was always misunderstood, but in the 2005 film there is someone who knows it. As

Kong ascends the skyscraper, Ann screams not because of the gorilla but because of the attacks on the gorilla by a society that assumes he must be destroyed. The movie makes the same kind of shift involving a giant gorilla that Spielberg's *Close Encounters of the Third Kind* did when he replaced 1950s attacks on alien visitors with a very 1970s attempt to communicate with them (by 2005, Spielberg was back to attacking them in *War of the Worlds*).

King Kong is a magnificent entertainment. It is like the flowering of all the possibilities in the original classic film. Computers are used not merely to create special effects but to create style and beauty, to find a look for the film that fits its story. And the characters are not cardboard heroes or villains seen in stark outline but quirky individuals with personalities.

Consider the difference between Robert Armstrong (1933) and Jack Black (2005) as Carl Denham, the movie director who lands an unsuspecting crew on Skull Island. A Hollywood stereotype based on C. B. DeMille has been replaced by one who reminds us more of Orson Welles. And in the starring role of Ann Darrow, Naomi Watts expresses a range of emotion that Fay Wray, bless her heart, was never allowed in 1933. Never have damsels been in more distress, but Fay Wray mostly had to scream, while Watts looks into the gorilla's eyes and sees something beautiful there.

There was a stir when Jackson informed the home office that his movie would run 187 minutes. The executives had something around 140 minutes in mind, so they could turn over the audience more quickly (despite the greedy twenty minutes of paid commercials audiences now have inflicted upon them). After they saw the movie, their objections were stilled. Yes, the movie is a tad too long, and we could do without a few of the monsters and overturned elevated trains. But it is so well done that we are complaining, really, only about too much of a good thing. This is one of the great modern epics.

Jackson, fresh from his *Lord of the Rings* trilogy, wisely doesn't show the gorilla or the other creatures until more than an hour into the movie. In this he follows Spielberg, who fought off producers who wanted the shark in *Jaws* to appear virtually in the opening titles. There is an hour of anticipation, of low, ominous music, of subtle rumblings, of uneasy squints into the fog and mutinous rumblings from the crew, before the tramp steamer arrives at Skull Island—or, more accurately, is thrown against its jagged rocks in the first of many scary action sequences.

During that time we see Depression-era bread lines and soup kitchens, and meet the unemployed heroes of the film: Ann Darrow (Watts), whose vaudeville theater has closed, and who is faced with debasing herself in burlesque; Carl Denham (Black), whose work for a new movie is so unconvincing the backers want to sell it off as background footage; and Jack Driscoll (Adrien Brody), a playwright whose dreams lie off-Broadway and who thrusts fifteen pages of a first-draft screenplay at Denham and tries to disappear.

They all find themselves aboard the tramp steamer of Captain Englehorn (Thomas Kretschmann), who is persuaded to cast off just as Denham's creditors arrive on the docks in police cars. They set course for the South Seas, where Denham believes an uncharted island may hold the secret of a box-office blockbuster. On board, Ann and Jack grow close, but not *too* close, because the movie's real love story is between the girl and the gorilla.

Once they reach Skull Island, the second act of the movie is mostly a series of hair-curling special effects, as overgrown prehistoric creatures endlessly pursue the humans, occasionally killing or eating a supporting character. The bridges and logs over chasms, so important in 1933, are even better used here, especially when an assortment of humans and creatures falls in stages from a great height, resuming their deadly struggle whenever they can grab a convenient vine, rock, or tree. Two story lines are intercut: Ann and the ape, and everybody else and the other creatures.

The third act returns to Manhattan, which looks uncannily evocative and atmospheric. It isn't precisely realistic, but more of a dreamed city in which key elements swim in and out of view. There's a poetic scene where Kong and the girl find a frozen pond in Central Park, and the gorilla is lost in delight as it slides on the ice. It's in scenes like this that Andy Serkis is most useful as the actor who doesn't so much play Kong as embody him for the f/x team. He adds the body language. Some of the

Manhattan effects are not completely convincing (and earlier, on Skull Island, it's strange how the fleeing humans seem to run beneath the pounding feet of the T-rexes without quite occupying the same space). But special effects do not need to be convincing if they are effective, and Jackson trades a little realism for a lot of impact and momentum. The final ascent of the Empire State Building is magnificent, and for once the gorilla seems the same size in every shot.

Although Watts makes a splendid heroine, there have been complaints that Black and Brody are not precisely hero material. Nor should they be, in my opinion. They are a director and a writer. They do not require big muscles and square jaws. What they require are strong personalities that can be transformed under stress. Denham the director clings desperately to his camera no matter what happens to him, and Driscoll the writer beats a strategic retreat before essentially rewriting his personal role in his own mind. Bruce Baxter (Kyle Chandler) is an actor who plays the movie's hero and now has to decide if he can play his role for real. And Preston (Colin Hanks) is a production assistant who, as is often the case, would be a hero if anybody would give him a chance.

The result is a surprisingly involving and rather beautiful movie—one that will appeal strongly to the primary action audience and cross over to people who have no plans to see *King Kong* but will change their minds the more they hear. I think the film even has a message, and it isn't that beauty killed the beast. It's that we feel threatened by beauty, especially when it overwhelms us, and we pay a terrible price when we try to deny its essential nature and turn it into a product, or a target. This is one of the year's best films.

Ebert's Great Movie review of the 1933 King Kong *is online at rogerebert.com.*

King of California ★ ★ ★

PG-13, 93 m., 2007

Michael Douglas (Charlie), Evan Rachel Wood (Miranda), Willis Burks II (Pepper). Directed by Michael Cahill and produced by Alexander Payne, Michael London, Avi Lerner, and Randall Emmett. Screenplay by Cahill.

In *King of California,* Michael Douglas looks like Whiskers McCrazy. Why do people who look like this resent being treated as if they look like this? Security guards are attracted to him like bears to honey. Did it occur to anyone that the movie might have been funnier if he'd been groomed like the tycoons he's played in all those corporate roles, his hair slicked back like Pat Riley's?

To be sure, it would be hard to explain how his character, Charlie, got the wardrobe and the grooming in the institution he has just been discharged from, but that could be part of the fun: "I cut my hair in a mirror with a nail-clipper, and didn't you ever see one of those prison-break movies where they make Nazi uniforms out of old blankets?" He would be explaining that to his sixteen-year-old daughter, Miranda (Evan Rachel Wood), who has been living parentless at home for the last two years; her mother walked out some time ago, and she keeps child welfare off her back by convincing each set of authorities that she is actually with the other parent. That's a confusing sentence, but then it's an explanation intended to confuse.

Meanwhile, she works overtime at McDonald's, still somehow affords the cost of living in their increasingly run-down house, and acts like she is level-headed and competent, even if she's scared. She's unsettled that her strange father has reappeared, and it's obvious he is less prepared to make survival decisions than she is. He's manic-depressive, is my guess, and has been busy studying ancient documents that convince him a treasure in gold was buried by early Spanish conquistadors somewhere near where they are now, in Santa Clarita. He obtains a metal detector and enlists poor Miranda in an obsessive search that takes them through parking lots and down the sides of highways.

Their search is at first fruitless, but Charlie remains undaunted, and Miranda gamely goes along. There is something quietly hypnotic about his quest that begins to win her over into the delusion that he just possibly might be right. Of course, he could be wrong, too, but at least their mission gives them a purpose. Using the metal detector and surveying instruments, he convinces himself he has found the gold, which is now buried under the aisle of a Costco. Have you ever seen a guy like this using a metal detector in a Costco? I actually think I may have. Just field-testing it, maybe. Exploiting his daughter's talent as a minimum-wage employee, Charlie convinces her to get a job at the Costco and steal a key. And then, one dark night . . .

Well, yes, the plot of *King of California* is absurd. Maybe not so absurd to Charlie, however, whose quest is positioned as an assault on the bland conformity of society. What kind of a man, in possession of certain information that a fortune is buried under Costco, would be such a wimp that he wouldn't go after it? Douglas does an interesting thing with the role. He starts with our assumption that he is unbalanced, which of course he is, and then doesn't overact the looniness but simply focuses on the obsession. His unspoken assumption that Miranda shares his goal removes the need for him to convince her—at least in his mind.

The film, in its own off-center way, is worth seeing, if only because of the zealotry of the Douglas performance and the pluck of Evan Rachel Wood, nineteen when she made it, who since *Thirteen* (2003) has become a young star with a future. The first-time writer-director Michael Cahill doesn't exactly convince me that this film cried out to be his debut, as he follows into the strange places Charlie leads him. But at least he wants to work off the map and not turn out another standard study of angst, violence, or terminal hipness. We have not seen these characters before, which is a rare gift from a movie.

Charlie and Miranda make observations along the way about how things have changed, even in her young life. Some of them involve the family's old neighborhood, which they used to have to themselves before all those other home owners moved in and turned it into a suburb. "We used to be surrounded by nothing," he says. Her reply is that they still are, but now nothing has a population. I know how he feels every time I pass the yuppie restaurants on the stretch of Clark Street formerly dominated by the Last Stop Before Expressway Liquor Store.

There is a belief in this movie that a flywheel like Charlie is actually saner than the boring people around him. At least he embraces life and goes for the gold. But there is a name for his condition, and he quite possibly may have been discharged prematurely. No matter how his quest concludes, it will not be, for a mental health professional, a happy ending. But we are not professionals, and we enjoy him instead of diagnosing him. When you stand back a step from the movie, you admire Douglas and Wood for starting with potentially unplayable characters and playing them so well we actually care about a quest that, in a way, seems more designed for Abbott and Costello.

The King of Kong: A Fistful of Quarters ★ ★ ★

PG-13, 90 m., 2007

Featuring Steve Wiebe, Billy Mitchell, Walter Day, Nicole Wiebe, Todd Rogers, Steve Sanders, Doris Self. A documentary directed by Seth Gordon and produced by Ed Cunningham. Screenplay by Gordon.

Remember Donkey Kong? This would have been in the early 1980s, and you would have been standing in a video arcade, bar, truck stop, or bowling alley, trying to save the damsel in distress from the gorilla. It was voted the third best coin-operated arcade video game of all time (after Pac-Man and Galaga). Yes, and now it is 2007, and grown men still chase each other across the country in pursuit of the world-record Donkey Kong score.

The King of Kong: A Fistful of Quarters, a documentary that is beyond strange, follows two archenemies in their grim, long-term rivalry, which involves way more time than any human should devote to Donkey Kong. I am reminded of the butler's line in *A New Leaf* to Walter Matthau: "You are carrying on in your own lifetime, sir, a way of life that was extinct before you were born."

In this corner, the man in black, wearing a goatee and looking like a snake oil pitchman, is Billy Mitchell of Hollywood, Florida, in real life a hot sauce tycoon (Rickey's World Famous Sauces), who says he is the man who first retailed chicken wings in their modern culinary form in Florida. That was not enough for one lifetime. He also achieved the first perfect game in the history of Pac-Man, his high score on Donkey Kong stood unchallenged for twenty-five years, and in 1999 he was named Video Game Player of the Century. In 2004, Mitchell began a series of special commemorative labels on hot sauce bottles to honor major gaming events and their champions.

In the other corner, looking like your average neighbor, Steve Wiebe of Seattle, who got laid off at Boeing the very day he and his wife bought a new house. He has kids, he's likable, and he plays Donkey Kong on a machine in his garage, where we gather he spends hours and hours and hours. He's now working as a high school science teacher.

The referee: Walter Day, halfway between them in Iowa, who runs a Web site named Twin Galaxies, and is the chief scorekeeper of competitive gaming. Day's serenity was severely challenged when Wiebe mailed in a home videotape showing himself breaking Mitchell's famous record. In the world of Donkey Kong, this was as monumental as Barry Bonds beating Hank Aaron's record, except that Wiebe is the Hank Aaron of these two, if you see what I mean.

Mitchell fires back. He questions the record, the machine, the video, and Wiebe's character. Wiebe dips into his meager savings to go to Florida and challenge Mitchell head-on. Mitchell won't show. Or he does show at a few conventions and is easy to spot with his satanic wardrobe and pneumatic wife, but never quite turns up to play. He's glimpsed sometimes passing ominously in the background.

This isn't fun for these men. It's deadly serious. A world championship is at stake, and only gradually do we realize how very few people give a damn. Unlike recent docs about spelling bees, Scrabble, and crossword puzzles, there aren't large audiences in this film. Game players may turn up by the thousands at conventions, but apparently only a handful care much about Donkey Kong; it's like a big auto show vs. a parade of Model T's.

The documentary stares incredulously at the Machiavellian Mitchell, who seems to play the same role in the world of Donkey Kong as masked marauders do in pro wrestling. We hate this guy. Why won't he play Wiebe? What's with that tape he sends in that seems to show him beating Wiebe's record, but has some curious technical difficulties? Is this little world too heavily invested in Mitchell as its superstar? How long can Wiebe's wife remain patient and supportive of his lonely quest? Will Walter Day burn out and retire?

All questions to which you will find answers, sort of, in the film. I would never dream of giving away the ending. But I can give away what happened after the ending. This film premiered at the Tribeca Film Festival on May 5, 2007. Today I went to www.TwinGalaxies.com and discovered that on July 13, 2007, the twenty-fifth anniversary of his original record, "in front of an audience of hundreds," Billy Mitchell topped his own record by scoring 1,050,200 points. I have a sinking feeling that Steve Wiebe is out in the garage right now.

King of the Corner ★ ★ ★ ½

R, 93 m., 2005

Peter Riegert (Leo Spivak), Eli Wallach (Sol Spivak), Isabella Rossellini (Rachel Spivak), Eric Bogosian (Rabbi Evelyn Fink), Beverly D'Angelo (Betsy Ingraham), Jake Hoffman (Ed Shifman), Rita Moreno (Inez), Harris Yulin (Pete Hargrove), Ashley Johnson (Elena Spivak). Directed by Peter Riegert and produced by Lemore Syvan. Screenplay by Riegert and Gerald Shapiro.

Leo Spivak is trapped in the Bermuda Triangle of middle age: He hates his job, his father is dying, his teenage daughter is rebelling. He'd rather be the father, the child, or the boss—anything but Leo, the man in the middle, well paid and with a corner office, but devoting his days to market research. When he subjects instant stew to a blind taste-testing and the consumers say it tastes like dog food, they know how he feels most of the time.

King of the Corner is Peter Riegert's movie. He directed it, he cowrote it, and he stars as Leo. It's a well-chosen project for one of his particular talents, which is to play intelligent, sardonic losers. One of Leo's problems is that he knows his goals are worthless: If his market-research firm makes its money testing lousy products on dim-witted consumers, why would he even want to be the vice president?

One reason might be that Ed Shifman also

wants the job. Ed (Jake Hoffman) is Leo's young protégé, or "management trainee," and scores points by stealing Leo's ideas and taking them directly to the boss (Harris Yulin). Ed will work for half the money, and won't be borderline depressive all the time. Together, they test products such as the Flaxman Voice-Altering Telephone, which answers the phones of timid widows with sturdy male voices, including Gregory Peck's.

At home, Leo is worried about his daughter, Elena (Ashley Johnson), who is staying out too late with an elusive lout named Todd who would rather honk for her than come to the door. He's worried, but not as worried as his despairing wife, Rachel (Isabella Rossellini), who seems borderline hysterical. Leo tries one of those excruciating conversations where he simultaneously advises Elena against sex and in favor of precautions. "Dad," she whines, "we're not doing anything." Uh-huh.

Every other weekend Leo flies out to Arizona, where his father, Sol (Eli Wallach), is in a retirement home. Sol was a salesman like Leo, always on the road, dragging his samples around like Willy Loman. When his wife died he moved to Arizona, found a girlfriend (Rita Moreno), and did a lot of fox-trotting before age caught up with him. Now he wants to die: "Why is it so hard for me to die? Other people do it every day." Leo has had an uneasy relationship with his father, but Leo, we begin to understand, is a good man who desperately wants to be seen as a good man: by his wife, his daughter, his father, even by Ed.

King of the Corner is not plot-driven. It's like life: just one damn thing after another. It's based on a collection of short stories named *Bad Jews and Other Stories* by Gerald Shapiro, who cowrote the screenplay with Riegert. Leo and his father were both bad Jews in the sense that they were not believers, although to a certain degree they were observant, if only because of family tradition. What it means to be a good Jew, or a good son or a good man, is discovered by Leo only after his father dies.

The whole movie has been leading up to this moment, and I don't want to describe it in detail because it needs to happen to you, to unfold as the logical answer to the question of why the movie exists and where it thinks it is going. I will say a brief word about a freelance rabbi named Evelyn Fink (Eric Bogosian), who begins every conversation by specifying there be no jokes about his names.

Other rabbis from his class have nice jobs with good congregations, but Rabbi Fink is still picking up a living from funeral homes that need a rabbi in a hurry. He begins to question Leo about his father at the funeral home, but when sobbing from the next room becomes a nuisance, he suggests they go somewhere else to talk. Where they go tells you a lot about the freelance rabbi.

Bogosian's role is brief, but perfectly realized. His eulogy at the funeral does what no eulogy should dare; it tells the truth. And then Leo discovers what he thinks about his father, his life, and himself. It is a scene that brings the whole movie into a poignant focus. In the "kaddish," the prayer for the dead, he becomes a good Jew at last.

A movie like this depends on the close observation of behavior. It is not so much about what the characters do as who they are, who they fear they are, and who they want to be. Leo, as played by Riegert, has reached an accommodation with life by keeping a certain dry distance from it. That's why a midmovie meeting seems so odd. He accidentally runs into the girl he lusted after in high school (Beverly D'Angelo), and that sets into motion a peculiar chain of events.

I am not sure I believe them, especially when he visits her home and meets her husband, but observe Riegert's body language. There are times, here and in his boss's office, when he does things that are completely inexplicable. He falls to his knees, or invites a fight, or behaves with sudden recklessness. Why does he do these things? Is he crazy? No, not at all; he is reminding himself he is alive by stepping right outside the ordained limits of his life. At times like these he reminds me of the line in the Stevie Smith poem about the swimmer who is "not waving, but drowning."

Kings and Queen ★ ★ ★

NO MPAA RATING, 150 m., 2005

Emmanuelle Devos (Nora Cotterelle), Mathieu Amalric (Ismael Vuillard), Maurice Garrel (Louis Jenssens), Catherine Deneuve (Mme. Vasset), Magalie Woch (Arielle), Elsa Wolliaston (Dr.

Devereux), Nathalie Boutefeu (Chloe Jenssens), Jean-Paul Roussillon (Abel Vuillard). Directed by Arnaud Desplechin and produced by Pascal Caucheteux. Screenplay by Roger Bohbot and Desplechin.

When you ask someone for the truth about themselves, you may get the truth, or part of the truth, or none of the truth, but you will certainly get what they would like you to think is the truth. This is a useful principle to keep in mind during *Kings and Queen,* a film that unfolds like a court case in which all of the testimony sounds like the simple truth, and none of it agrees.

We begin with a character named Nora (Emmanuelle Devos), smart, chic, an art gallery owner who buys a rare illustrated edition of *Leda and the Swan* as a present for her father, a famous author. We learn she has been divorced twice, will soon marry a very rich man, and has an eleven-year-old son named Elias. She visits her father, Louis (Maurice Garrel), who is in great pain; it is revealed he's dying of stomach cancer. What does he think about his daughter, and she of him? We think we know.

We meet another character, a violinist named Ismael (Mathieu Amalric). He was Nora's most recent lover. He is functional enough in a strange way, but behaves so unwisely that he finds himself in a mental institution. We sit in on his consultations with the hospital administrator (Catherine Deneuve), who is onscreen just about long enough for him to tell her, "You're very beautiful," and for her to reply, "I've been told." There is also his French-African psychiatrist (Elsa Wolliaston). Neither is much charmed by his theory that women lack souls. Ismael makes a friend at the hospital, a young woman named Arielle (Magalie Woch), who is so fond of attempting suicide that it would be a shame if she should succeed and thus bring her pastime to an end.

Nora has seemed like a decent enough woman, but what kind of a mother would not want to raise her own child? The boy's father is out of the picture (in more ways than one), and she strikes on the notion that Ismael, the former lover, is just the person to adopt Elias. Ismael loves the little boy, who loves him, and if this were a different sort of a movie such an arrangement might work.

Kings and Queen is, however, a *very* different sort of movie, in which it will not work for reasons that are explained by Ismael in a way both insightful and peculiar. Nora's father meanwhile leaves a journal entry that completely redefines everything we thought we knew about their relationship, and Ismael has an encounter with the leader of the string quartet where he thinks he is a valued member, but is mistaken. Sometimes you don't really want to know what people really think about you.

I have revealed nothing crucial, except that there are crucial revelations. The point of the movie is to call into question our personal versions of our own lives, and the emphasis on *Leda and the Swan* may be a nudge to suggest we construct myths to give a shape and meaning to lives we have lived with untidy carelessness.

The movie, directed by Arnaud Desplechin and written by him with Roger Bohbot, begins as such a straightforward portrait of ordinary life that it's unsettling to find layer after layer of reality peeled away. It opens with what seems like a conventional array of emotions, and then shows that they're like the bandages on Arielle's wrists, concealing deep desperation. The feelings of the dying father are particularly painful because of the way he has chosen to reveal them.

By the end of the film, we're a little stunned; everything seemed to be going so nicely, to be sure with the ordinary setbacks and tragedies of life, but nothing approaching mythic, tragic, chaotic, emotional decay. You think you know someone, you think they know themselves, and suddenly you're both dealing with a complete stranger. Meanwhile, "Moon River" is playing on the sound track, but is far from a comfort.

Kinky Boots ★ ★ ★

PG-13, 94 m., 2006

Joel Edgerton (Charlie Price), Chiwetel Ejiofor (Lola/Simon), Sarah-Jane Potts (Lauren), Nick Frost (Don), Ewan Hooper (George), Linda Basset (Melanie), Jemima Rooper (Nicola). Directed by Julian Jarrold and produced by Nicholas Barton, Suzanne Mackie, and Pater Ettedgui. Screenplay by Geoff Deane and Tim Firth.

One of the gifts of movies is the way they introduce us to new actors, turning them this way and that in the light of the screen, allowing us to see the fullness of their gifts. Consider Chiwetel Ejiofor, whose first leading role was in *Dirty Pretty Things* (2002), as a Nigerian doctor reduced in London to working in a mortuary. Then came a romantic role in *Love Actually* (2003), a South African activist in *Red Dust* (2004), a space opera villain in *Serenity* (2005), and a New York detective in Spike Lee's *Inside Man* (2006). Along the way he has worked for Steven Spielberg, Woody Allen, and John Singleton (as a vicious mobster in *Four Brothers* in 2005) and has done Shakespeare and *The Canterbury Tales* for TV. Born in London in 1974, he works easily with British, American, and Nigerian accents.

Now he plays a drag queen in *Kinky Boots*. It is a performance all the more striking because he doesn't play any kind of drag queen I've ever seen in the movies. He plays the role not as a man pretending to be a woman, and not as a woman trapped in a man's body, and not as a parody of a woman, and not as a gay man, but as a *drag queen*, period: Lola, a tall, athletic performer in thigh-high red boots who rules the stage of a drag club as if she were born there, and who is a pretty good singer, too. In preparing for the role, Ejiofor must have decided not to simper, not to preen, not to mince, but to belt out songs with great good humor that dares the audience to take exception. If "simper," "preen," and "mince" are stereotypical words, well, then most drag queens, including Lola's backup dancers, are stereotypical performers. Not Lola.

With *Kinky Boots* we find ourselves watching another one of those British comedies in which unconventional sex is surrounded by a conventional story. The film's other hero is Charlie Price (Joel Edgerton), whose father dies and leaves him a Northampton shoe factory that is nearly bankrupt because men aren't buying traditional dress shoes. Through a coincidence we must accept, Charlie meets Lola, who complains that women's shoes don't stand up to the weight of a full-sized man in drag. Charlie thinks maybe his factory could supply a proper pair of boots with stiletto heels for Lola, and he lovingly crafts the boots himself, only to hear Lola respond: "Please, God, tell me I have not inspired something burgundy." What does he prefer? "Red! Red!"

Lola comes to Northampton to design a line of footwear, receiving a chilly reception from some of the union men in the factory, especially the gay-hating Don (Nick Frost). Don is the reigning arm-wrestling champion in a local pub, and of course it is only a matter of time until Don and Lola are elbow to elbow in a showdown. Meanwhile, Charlie's snotty fiancée, Nicola (Jemima Rooper), is a real estate agent hoping to recycle his factory into condos, while the plucky shoe worker Lauren (Sarah-Jane Potts) believes in Charlie, Lola, and the factory.

Drag queens are more mainstream in British entertainment than they are in America, even if we exclude Dame Edna Everage, who seems to be in drag not as a man, not as a woman, but as a self-contained gender. The movie is in the naughty-but-nice British tradition in which characters walk on the wild side but never seem to do anything else there. If Lola, whose birth name is Simon, has sex of any kind in *Kinky Boots*, it is offscreen. I was reminded of the wholesome kinkiness of *Personal Services* (1987), Terry Jones's comedy about Cynthia Payne, the "luncheon voucher madam" who treated retired gents to naughty noontime lingerie shows, heavy on whips, boots, and corsets. Some of them paid with the luncheon vouchers they received as old-age pensioners. A recent example of this innocent genre is *Mrs. Henderson Presents*, in which Dame Judi Dench runs the most wholesome strip club in Soho.

Kinky Boots has few surprises, unless you seriously expect the factory to go bankrupt. The climax comes at the annual shoe show in Milan, where last-minute developments unfold right on schedule; having provided us with Lola, the movie is conventional in all other departments. But Ejiofor's performance as Lola shows an actor doing what not every actor can do: taking a character bundled with stereotypes, clearing them out of the way, and finding a direct line to who the character really is. Just in the way she walks in those kinky red boots, Lola makes an argument that no words could possibly improve upon.

Note: It's pronounced Chew-i-tell Edge-o-for.

Kinky Boots *is based on a true story. Check it out at www.divine.co.uk.*

Kiss Kiss, Bang Bang ★ ★ ½

R, 103 m., 2005

Robert Downey Jr. (Harry Lockhart), Val Kilmer (Gay Perry), Michelle Monaghan (Harmony Faith Lane), Corbin Bernsen (Harlan Dexter). Directed by Shane Black and produced by Joel Silver. Screenplay by Black.

"All you need to make a movie is a girl and a gun," as I so tirelessly quote Jean-Luc Godard. Pauline Kael refined that insight after seeing a movie poster in Italy that translated as "Kiss Kiss Bang Bang." These four words, she wrote, "are perhaps the briefest statement imaginable of the basic appeal of the movies. The appeal is what attracts us and ultimately makes us despair when we begin to understand how seldom movies are more than this."

Shane Black has dealt with lots of girls and guns in his screenplays, including the *Lethal Weapon* pictures, *The Long Kiss Goodnight,* and *Last Action Hero.* Now comes his directorial debut, *Kiss Kiss, Bang Bang,* to which he adds a comma and a lot more. After Tony Scott's *Domino,* which has a narrator who says, "I'll never tell you what it all meant," here's another narrator who chats with the audience. His parting words: "Don't worry. I saw *Lord of the Rings;* I'm not gonna have the movie end twenty times."

Both of these movies may be action retreads of Charlie Kaufman's screenplay for *Adaptation,* in which the process of writing the screenplay becomes part of the story. *Domino* makes next to no sense but is shot in a style that makes sense irrelevant. *Kiss Kiss, Bang Bang* is slowed down and straightened out just enough so that we can see it makes no sense. Does that matter? Two answers: (1) No, when what is happening on the screen works as itself, without regard for the plot, and (2) Yes, when we can see that the movie is plainly spinning its wheels.

The movie is narrated by Harry Lockhart (Robert Downey Jr.), a would-be actor from New York who moves to Los Angeles and finds himself taking private-eye lessons from Gay Perry (Val Kilmer), a gay detective. We could play a version of the Kevin Bacon game with this movie, because Downey also starred in the movie version of *The Singing Detective* (2003), also about a detective who narrates his own story.

Kiss Kiss, Bang Bang is made for a fairly specific audience; it helps if you are familiar with the private-eye genre in general and the works of Raymond Chandler in particular (the movie has five chapter headings, all taken from Chandler's titles). But do the titles come from Harry Lockhart, or do they exist outside his mind and suggest that Black's screenplay has another level of comment on top? That would be roughly like the subtitles in *Domino,* which have a different point of view than the narration.

But now the review is spinning its wheels. *Kiss Kiss, Bang Bang* contains a lot of comedy and invention but doesn't much benefit from its clever style. The characters and plot are so promising that maybe Black should have backed off and told the story deadpan, instead of mugging so shamelessly for laughs. It could still be a comedy, but it wouldn't always be digging its elbow into our ribs. I kept wanting to add my own subtitles: "I get it! I get it!"

The film begins with Harry's stage debut as a child magician who saws a girl in half as she screams, "I'm going to be an actress!" Flash forward to years later in Los Angeles, where he meets Gay Perry (get it?), who agrees to tutor him in private-eyeing and sends him to a Hollywood party where he meets that very same girl, Harmony Faith Lane (Michelle Monaghan). Maybe it's inevitable she turns up here; Harry's narration observes of the women in Los Angeles: "It's like someone took America by the East Coast and shook it, and all the normal girls managed to hang on."

Then ensue events so complex that Harry loses a finger not once but twice, which is bad, because fingers have fingerprints, although the danger of being fingerprinted is greatly reduced by the manner of his losing the finger for the second time. This is in the process of investigating a series of murders, which he does primarily to impress Harmony Faith Lane.

The movie might reward deep textual study; consider that in the chapter named after Chandler's *The Lady in the Lake,* a gun is thrown into the lake, giving us the girl-and-the-gun formula in a form so subtle that right now you are wondering why I don't simply cave in and tell you if the movie is any good or not.

Well, yes and no. See above. I've seen the movie twice, foolishly thinking I might understand it better the second time. Understanding it is not the point. The dialogue exists not to explain anything or advance the story. It exists entirely in order to be dialogue. When the characters speak, it is an example of their verbal style, which is half film noir and half smart-ass. The dialogue, and just about everything else in the movie, is there for its own sake. Like a smorgasbord, it makes no attempt at coherence. Put a little of everything on your plate and you'll be stuffed by the end, but what did you eat?

I dunno. I liked Downey's pose that he was writing the movie as he was living it, and Kilmer's gay detective, who functions as a parody of gay parodies. But did I need to see it twice? Not really. Do you need to see it once? Not exactly.

The Kite Runner ★ ★ ★ ★

PG-13, 120 m., 2007

Khalid Abdalla (Amir), Homayoun Ershadi (Baba), Shaun Toub (Rahim Khan), Atossa Leoni (Soraya), Said Taghmaoui (Farid), Zekiria Ebrahimi (Young Amir), Ali Danesh Bakhtyari (Sohrab), Ahmad Khan Mahmoodzada (Young Hassan), Nabi Tanha (Ali), Elham Ehsas (Young Assef). Directed by Marc Forster and produced by William Hornberg, Walter F. Parkes, Rebecca Yeldham, and E. Bennett Walsh. Screenplay by David Benioff, based on the novel by Khaled Hosseini.

How long has it been since you saw a movie that succeeds as pure story? That doesn't depend on stars, effects, or genres, but simply fascinates you with how it will turn out? Marc Forster's *The Kite Runner,* based on a much-loved novel, is a movie like that. It superimposes human faces and a historical context on the tragic images of war from Afghanistan.

The story begins with boys flying kites. It is the city of Kabul in 1978, before the Russians, the Taliban, the Americans, and the anarchy. Amir (Zekiria Ebrahimi) joins with countless other boys in filling the sky with kites; sometimes they dance on the rooftops while dueling, trying to cut other kite strings with their own. Amir's friend is Hassan (Ahmad Khan Mahmoodzada), the son of the family's longtime servant. He is the best kite runner in the neighborhood, correctly predicting when a kite will return to Earth and waiting there to retrieve it.

The boys live in a healthy, vibrant city, not yet touched by war. Amir's father, called Baba (Homayoun Ershadi), is an intellectual and secularist who has no use for the mullahs. His servant, Ali (Nabi Tanha), has been with the family for years, has become like family himself. And Baba, whose kindly eyes are benevolent, loves both boys.

There is a neighborhood bully named Assef (Elham Ehsas), jealous of Amir's kite, his skills, and his kite runner. And on a day that will shape the course of many lives, he and his gang track down Hassan, attack him, and rape him. Amir arrives to see the assault taking place and, to his shame, sneaks away. And then a curious chemistry takes place. Amir feels so guilty about Hassan that his feelings transform into anger, and he tries insulting his friend, even throwing ripe fruit at him, but Hassan is impassive. Then Amir tries to plant evidence to make Hassan seem to be a thief, but even after Hassan (untruthfully and masochistically) confesses, Baba forgives him. It is Hassan's father who insists he and his son must leave the home, over Baba's protests.

The film has opened with the modern-day Amir, now living in Los Angeles, receiving a telephone call from his father's friend Rahim Khan: "You should come home. There is a way to be good again." And then commences a remarkable series of old memories and new realities, of the present trying to heal the wounds of the past, of an adult trying to repair the damage he set in motion as a boy. For if he had not lied about Hassan, they would all be together in Los Angeles and the telephone call would not have been necessary.

Working from Khaled Hosseini's bestseller, Forster and his screenwriter, David Benioff, have made a film that sidesteps the emotional disconnects we often feel when a story moves between past and present. This is all the same story, interlaced with the fabric of these lives. There is also a touching sequence as Amir and his father, now older and ill, meet a once-powerful Afghan general and his daughter, Soraya (Atossa Leoni). For Amir and Soraya, it is instant love, but protocol must be observed, and one of the warmest scenes in the movie involves the two old men discussing the future of their children. I want to mention once again the eyes, indeed the whole face, of the actor Homayoun Ershadi, as Amir's father; here is a face so deeply good it is difficult to imagine it reflecting unworthy feelings.

What happens back in Afghanistan (and Pakistan) in the year 2000 need not be revealed here, but the scenes combine great suspense with deep emotion. One emblematic moment: a soccer game where the audience, all men and all oddly silent, are watched by guards with rifles. The film works so deeply on us because we have been so absorbed by its story, by its destinies, by the way these individuals become so important that we are forced to stop thinking of "Afghans" as simply a category in body counts on the news.

The movie is acted largely in English, although many (subtitled) scenes are in Dari, which I learn is an Afghan dialect of Farsi, or Persian. The performances by the actors playing Amir and Hassan as children are natural, convincing, and powerful; recently I have seen several such child performances, which adults would envy for their conviction and strength. Ahmad Khan Mahmoodzada, as Hassan, is particularly striking, with his serious, sometimes almost mournful face. (The boys in the film, who feared Afghan reprisals for appearing in the rape scene, were moved by Paramount to safety in the United Arab Emirates.)

One of the areas in which the movie succeeds is in its depiction of kite flying. Yes, it uses special effects, but they function to represent what freedom and exhilaration the kites represent to their owners. I remember my own fierce identification with my own kites as a child. I was up there; I was *represented.* Yet there is a fundamental difference between the kite flyer (Amir) and the kite runner (Hassan). Perhaps that sad wisdom in Hassan's eyes comes from his certainty that all must fall to Earth, sooner or later.

This is a magnificent film by Marc Forster, who since *Monster's Ball* (2001) has made *Finding Neverland* (2004), *Stay* (2005), and *Stranger Than Fiction* (2006). All fine work, but *The Kite Runner* equals *Monster's Ball* in its emotional impact. Like *House of Sand and Fog* and *Man Push Cart,* it helps us to understand that the newcomers among us come from somewhere and are somebody.

Kit Kittredge: An American Girl ★ ★ ★ ½

G, 100 m., 2008

Abigail Breslin (Kit), Julia Ormond (Mrs. Kittredge), Chris O'Donnell (Mr. Kittredge), Max Thieriot (Will), Zach Mills (Stirling Howard), Joan Cusack (Miss Bond), Stanley Tucci (Jefferson J. Berk), Willow Smith (Countee), Madison Davenport (Ruthie Smithens), Jane Krakowski (Miss Dooley), Glenne Headley (Mrs. Howard), Wallace Shawn (Mr. Gibson). Directed by Patricia Rozema and produced by Elaine Goldsmith-Thomas, Lisa Gillan, Ellen L. Brothers, and Julie Goldstein. Screenplay by Ann Peacock, based on the stories by Valerie Tripp.

Considering that it is inspired by one of the dolls in the American Girl product line, *Kit Kittredge: An American Girl* is some kind of a miracle: an actually good movie. I expected so much less. I was waiting for some kind of banal product placement, I suppose, and here is a movie that is just about perfect for its target audience and more than that. It has a great look, engaging performances, real substance, and even a few whispers of political ideas, all surrounding the freshness and charm of Abigail Breslin, who was eleven when it was filmed.

The movie is set in Cincinnati at the dawn of the Great Depression; perfectly timed, it would appear, as we head into another one. Kit pounds furiously on the typewriter in her tree house, determined to become a girl reporter, while a big story is happening right downstairs in her family house: Its mortgage is about to be foreclosed. Her dad (Chris O'Donnell) has lost his car dealership and gone to Chicago seeking work, her mom (Julia Ormond) is taking in boarders, and there's local hysteria about muggings and robberies allegedly committed by hoboes.

Kit meets a couple of hoboes. Will (Max Thieriot) is about her age, and his sidekick Countee (Willow Smith) is a little younger. They live in the hobo camp down by the river, along with as nice a group of hoboes as you'd ever want to meet, and Kit tries selling their story and photos to the editor of the local paper (snarling Wallace Shawn). No luck. But other adventures ensue: She adopts a dog, her mom acquires chickens, Kit sells the eggs, and the new boarders are a colorfully assorted lot. And she sees such unthinkable sights as neighbors' furniture being moved to the sidewalk by deputies. Will that happen at her address?

The boarders include a magician (Stanley Tucci), a nurse (Jane Krakowski), the erratic driver (Joan Cusack) of a mobile library truck, and assorted others, eventually including even a monkey. Kit's mom hides her treasures in a lock box, but it is stolen, and unmistakable clues point to the hoboes. A footprint found under a window, for example, has a star imprint that exactly matches the boots found in Will's tent, and the sheriff names him the prime suspect. But hold on! Kit and her best friends, Stirling and Ruthie (Zach Mills and Madison Davenport), develop another theory, which would clear Will and implicate someone (dramatically lowered voice) a lot closer to home.

All of this (the missing loot, Kit's ambitions, Important Clues) is, of course, the very lifeblood of the Nancy Drew and Hardy Boys books, and *Kit Kittredge* not only understands that genre but breathes life into it. This movie, intelligently and sincerely directed by Patricia Rozema (*Mansfield Park*) does not condescend. It does not cheapen or go for easy laughs. It is as serious about Kit as she is about herself and doesn't treat her like some (indignant exclamation) dumb girl.

If you have or know or can borrow a girl (or a boy) who collects the American Girl dolls, grab onto that child as your excuse to see this movie. You may enjoy it as much as the kids do—maybe more, with its period costumes, settings, and music. The kids may be astonished that banks actually foreclosed on people's homes in the old days (hollow laugh). And there may be a message lurking somewhere in the movie's tolerance of hoboes. The American Girl dolls have already inspired TV movies about Molly, Felicity, and Samantha. What's for sure is that if *Kit Kittredge* sets the tone for more upcoming American Girl movies, we can anticipate some wonderful family films.

Kontroll ★ ★ ★ ½

R, 105 m., 2005

Sandor Csanyi (Bulcsu), Zoltan Mucsi (Professor), Csaba Pindroch (Muki), Sandor Badar (Lecso), Zsolt Nagy (Tibi), Bence Matyassy (Bootsie), Gyozo Szabo (Shadow), Eszter Balla (Szofi). Directed by Nimrod Antal and produced by Tamas Hutlassa. Screenplay by Jim Adler and Antal.

On the London underground you sometimes realize the train has roared through an abandoned station, past a ghost platform illuminated only from the train windows; you get a murky glimpse of advertising posters from decades ago. In *Kontroll*, which takes place entirely within the Budapest subway system, such a subterranean world has a permanent population.

The trains are run on an honor system, and inspectors with red-and-black armbands prowl the underground, asking riders to show their tickets. The passengers descend from the sunshine to be accosted by kontrollers who are slovenly, unkempt, sallow-faced, with a certain madness in their eyes. Many riders consider the trains to be free and treat the inspectors like vagrants asking for a handout.

It is strange to work entirely under the ground in noisy, hostile, rat-infested caverns, and even stranger for those like the kontroller Bulcsu (Sandor Csanyi), who never ever returns to the surface. Once he was an architect who dreamed of buildings that would reach to the sky, but now he has retreated to a waking grave, sleeps on benches, eats the indescribable food vended in the system, and heads a crew of three other inspectors as haunted as he is.

Theirs is a miserable job, made more unbearable by the periodic visits of their boss, who descends from light and comfort to urge greater vigilance. The kontrollers don't really care if people are riding free; what they care about is meeting a daily quota of deadbeats in a duel of wills. They risk their lives, they engage in reckless chases and fights, not because they care about the fares, but because it is the price they pay to continue their melancholy existence.

There is a killer in the system, a hooded figure who emerges from the shadows to push passengers in front of trains. He seems to know the underground as well as the kontrollers, and, like the Phantom of the Opera, to occupy his own hidden world. The security cameras see only his hood. Bulcsu and his crew are faced with daily train delays because of jumpers, and while they can't blame those who were pushed, they wonder why suicides don't have the decency to kill themselves with less inconvenience to others.

Kontroll is the first feature by Nimrod Antal, born of Hungarian parents, raised in Los Angeles, returning to Budapest for this haunting film shot during the five hours every night when the subway shuts down. His film opens with a statement read by a self-conscious spokesman for the subway system, explaining that Antal was granted permission to film with some reluctance, and with the hope that audiences will realize the film is only symbolic. Is this spokesman real or fictional? Certainly the symbolism is more Kafkaesque than political, as the kontrollers apply logic (you must have a ticket) to an illogical situation (riders know they will rarely be asked to show one). We feel we've entered one of those postnuclear science-fiction societies where the surface has become uninhabitable, and a few survivors cling to subterranean life.

Bulcsu's colleagues include a new recruit named Tibi (Zsolt Nagy), who is trying to learn a job he has not yet realized is his doom. There is the Professor (Zoltan Mucsi), who seems to consider kontrolling a holy vocation, and Muki (Csaba Pindroch), who is a narcoleptic, a dangerous condition when you work next to subway tracks.

One day a bear wanders into the system. This is a young woman named Szofi (Eszter Balla), who always wears a bear suit, perhaps because she is employed as a bear, or more likely because it is her fashion choice. She keeps an eye out for her father, an alcoholic train driver who possibly thinks he sees bears and is occasionally comforted to find out he is correct. Bulcsu begins to have feelings for the bear.

In a world denied respect by society, the inhabitants seek it from each other. Bulcsu's crew stages competitions with other crews, most dangerously at the end of the day, when they challenge each other to foot races down the tracks between stations, just before the last train of the day. The point is not so much to win as to survive. That is also perhaps the point of the film.

Kontroll is the first work by a director who is clearly gifted and who has found a way to make a full-bore action movie on a limited budget; there are no special effects in the movie, all of the trains are real, and I gather that at one point when we see Bulcsu barely crawling onto a platform ahead of a moving train, he is really doing exactly that.

Nimrod Antal has a feeling for action, but what distinguishes *Kontroll* is his control of characters and mood. He could have given us a standard group of misfits, but his characters are all peculiar in inward, secretive ways, suggesting needs they would rather not reveal. His visuals create a haunted house where the lights are off in most of the rooms, and there may indeed be a monster in the closet.

Kung Fu Hustle ★ ★ ★

R, 99 m., 2005

Stephen Chow (Sing), Yuen Wah (Landlord), Yuen Qiu (Landlady), Leung Siu Lung (The Beast), Huang Sheng Yi (Fong), Chan Kwok Kwan (Brother Sum), Lam Tze Chung (Sing's Sidekick), Dong Zhi Hua (Doughnut), Chiu Chi Ling (Tailor). Directed by Stephen Chow and produced by Chow, Po Chu Chui, and Jeffrey Lau. Screenplay by Tsang Kan Cheong, Chow, Lola Huo, and Chan Man Keung.

There is an opinion in some quarters that martial arts movies are violent. Many are, to be sure, but the best ones have the same relationship to violence that Astaire and Rogers have to romance: Nobody believes they take it seriously, but it gives them an excuse for some wonderful choreography.

Lurking beneath the surface of most good martial arts movies is a comedy. Sometimes it bubbles up to the top, as in Stephen Chow's *Kung Fu Hustle.* The joke is based not so much on humor as on delight: The characters have overcome the laws of gravity and physics. To be able to leap into the air, spin in a circle, and kick six, seven, eight, nine enemies before landing in a graceful crouch is enormously gratifying.

Realists grumble that such things are impossible. Well, of course they are. The thing about Astaire and Rogers is that they were really doing it, in long unbroken takes, and we could see that they were. Stephen Chow uses concealed wires, special effects, trick camera angles, trampolines, and anything else he can think of. We know it, and he knows we know it. But the trickery doesn't diminish his skill, because despite all the wires and effects in the world, a martial arts actor must be a superb athlete. Hang your average movie star on the end of a wire and he'll look like he's just been reeled in by the Pequod.

Kung Fu Hustle is Chow's seventh film as a director and sixty-first job as an actor, counting TV. He is forty-two years old and has been busy. His only other film seen by me is *Shaolin Soccer* (2002), the top-grossing action comedy in Hong Kong history. Purchased by Miramax, it was held off the market for two years, cut by thirty minutes, and undubbed: Yes, Harvey Weinstein replaced the English sound track with subtitles. The movie opened a year ago, inspiring a review in which I gave my most rational defense of the relativity theory of star ratings.

Now comes *Kung Fu Hustle.* This is the kind of movie where you laugh occasionally and have a silly grin most of the rest of the time. It must have taken Chow a superhuman effort to avoid singing a subtitled version of "Let Me Entertain You"—or, no, I've got a better example—of "Make 'Em Laugh," the Donald O'Connor number in *Singin' in the Rain.* In that one, O'Connor crashed into boards and bricks, wrestled with a dummy, ran up one wall and through another one, and sang the whole time. Stephen Chow doesn't sing, but he's channeling the same spirit.

The movie is centered in a Shanghai slum named Pig Sty Alley. It's ruled by a dumpy landlady (Yuen Qiu) who marches around in slippers and has one of those cartoon cigarettes that always stays in her mouth no matter what happens. Shanghai is terrorized by the Axe Gang, which mostly leaves Pig Sty Alley alone because the pickings are too slim. But when counterfeit gang members are confronted by neighborhood kung fu fighters, the real gang moves in to take revenge. The Axe Gang doesn't exactly blend in: They all wear black suits and top hats, and carry axes. That'll make you stand out. I am reminded of Jack Lemmon's story about the time he saw Klaus Kinski buying a hatchet at Ace Hardware.

The war between the Pig Stygians and the Axe Gang is an excuse for a series of sequences in which the stylized violence reaches a kind of ecstasy. Of course nothing we see is possible, but the movie doesn't even pretend it's possible: Maybe everyone is having matching hallucinations. One of the jokes is that completely unlikely characters, including the landlady and local middle-aged tradesmen, turn out to be better warriors than the professionals.

Chow not only stars and directs, but cowrote and coproduced. We get the sense that his comedies are generated in the Buster Keaton spirit, with gags being worked out on the spot and everybody in orbit around the star, who is physically skilled, courageous, and funny. Chow plays Sing, also the name of his character in *Shaolin Soccer* and at least six other movies. This time he's an impostor, pretending to be an Axe Gang member in order to run a shakedown racket in Pig Sty Alley. Imagine how inconvenient it is when the real Axe Gang shows up and he's in trouble with everyone. By the end of the movie, he's going one-on-one with The Beast (Leung Siu Lung) in a kung fu extravaganza. The joke is that most of what Sing knows about kung fu he learned by reading a useless booklet sold to him by a con man when he was a child.

It's possible you don't like martial arts movies, whether funny or not. Then why have you read this far? Or you prefer the elegant and poetic epics like *Crouching Tiger, Hidden Dragon* or *House of Flying Daggers.* Those are not qualities you will find in *Kung Fu Hustle.* When I saw it at Sundance, I wrote that it was "like Jackie Chan and Buster Keaton meet Quentin Tarantino and Bugs Bunny." You see how worked up you can get, watching a movie like this.

Kung Fu Panda ★ ★ ★

PG, 91 m., 2008

With the voices of: Jack Black (Po), Dustin Hoffman (Master Shifu), Angelina Jolie

(Tigress), Ian McShane (Tai Lung), Jackie Chan (Monkey), Seth Rogen (Mantis), Lucy Liu (Viper), David Cross (Crane), Randall Duk Kim (Oogway), James Hong (Mr. Ping), Michael Clarke Duncan (Commander Vachir), Dan Fogler (Zeng). Directed by John Stevenson and Mark Osborne and produced by Melissa Cobb. Written by Jonathan Aibel and Glenn Berger.

Kung Fu Panda is a story that almost tells itself in its title. It is so hard to imagine a big, fuzzy panda performing martial arts encounters that you intuit (and you will be right) that the panda stars in an against-all-odds formula, which dooms him to succeed. For the panda's target audience, children and younger teens, that will be just fine, and the film presents his adventures in wonderfully drawn Cinemascope animation. It was also shown in some IMAX venues.

The film stars a panda named Po (voice by Jack Black), who is so fat he can barely get out of bed. He works for his father, Mr. Ping (James Hong), in a noodle shop, which features Ping's legendary Secret Ingredient. How Ping, apparently a stork or other billed member of the avian family, fathered a panda is a mystery, not least to Po, but then the movie is filled with a wide variety of creatures who don't much seem to notice their differences.

They live in the beautiful Valley of Peace with an ancient temple towering overhead, up zillions of steps, which the pudgy Po can barely climb. But climb them he does, dragging a noodle wagon, because all the people of the valley have gathered up there to witness the choosing of the Dragon Warrior who will engage the dreaded Tai Lung (Ian McShane) in kung fu combat. Five contenders have been selected, the "Furious Five": Monkey (Jackie Chan), Tigress (Angelina Jolie), Mantis (Seth Rogen), Viper (Lucy Liu), and Crane (David Cross).

Tigress looks like she might be able to do some serious damage, but the others are less than impressive. Mantis in particular seems to weigh about an ounce, tops. All five have been trained (for nearly forever, I gather) by the wise Shifu, who with Dustin Hoffman's voice is one of the more dimensional characters in a story that doesn't give the others a lot of depth. Anyway, it's up to the temple master, Oogway (Randall Duk Kim), an ancient turtle, to make the final selection, and he chooses—yes, he chooses the hapless and pudgy Po.

The story then becomes essentially a series of action sequences, somewhat undermined by the fact that the combatants seem unable to be hurt, even if they fall from dizzying heights and crack stones open with their heads. There's an extended combat with Tai Lung on a disintegrating suspension bridge (haven't we seen that before?), hand-to-hand-to-tail combat with Po and Tai Lung, and, upstaging everything, an energetic competition over a single dumpling.

Kung Fu Panda is not one of the great recent animated films. The story is way too predictable and, truth to tell, Po himself didn't overwhelm me with his charisma. But it's elegantly drawn, the action sequences are packed with energy, and it's short enough that older viewers will be forgiving. For the kids, of course, all this stuff is much of a muchness, and here they go again.

L

Ladies in Lavender ★ ★

PG-13, 103 m., 2005

Judi Dench (Ursula Widdington), Maggie Smith (Janet Widdington), Daniel Bruhl (Andrea Marowski), Miriam Margolyes (Dorcas), Natascha McElhone (Olga Danilof), David Warner (Dr. Francis Mead). Directed by Charles Dance and produced by Nicolas Brown, Elizabeth Karlsen, and Nik Powell. Screenplay by Dance.

Ladies in Lavender assembles those two great dames, Judi Dench and Maggie Smith, and sends them off to play sisters sharing a cozy little cottage on the Cornwall coast. That is an inspiration. What they do there is a disappointment. Their days are spent gardening and having tea, their evenings with knitting and the wireless, until one dark and stormy night a strange young man is washed up on their shore.

This is Andrea Marowski (Daniel Bruhl). He is handsome, sweet, and speaks hardly a word of English. But Janet Widdington (Smith) discovers he has some German, and unearths her ancient textbook. Soon she and her sister, Ursula (Dench), discover that Andrea is Polish, a violinist, and a gifted one at that. What they do not discover is how he happened to be in the sea on that stormy night, which is the very thing we want to know. There is no word of a shipwreck. Perhaps he is a magical creature, left over from *The Tempest.*

The sisters have lived in calm and contentment for many years. Janet is a widow; Ursula has never married, and probably never had sex, although from the way she regards Andrea she may be thinking it's never too late to start. Ursula becomes possessive of the handsome young man; Janet observes this, doesn't like it, and mostly but not entirely keeps her thoughts to herself.

Andrea is visited by good Dr. Mead (David Warner), who advises bed rest, although perhaps not as much as Andrea chooses to enjoy; it is pleasant, watching the sun stream in through the window and being served tea by the sisters' crusty maid, Dorcas (Miriam Margolyes), who was born to play Doll Tearsheet. Eventually, however, Andrea ventures outside and catches the eye of Olga Danilof (Natascha McElhone), a landscape painter; she is not a very good painter, but she is a beautiful young woman, speaks German, and is soon spending time with Andrea while Ursula goes into a quiet and tactful form of anguish. Of course, coincidentally, Olga happens to possess the key to Andrea's fate as a violinist.

There is a moment's suspense when Dr. Mead, who also fancies Olga, ventures the suggestion that Olga and Andrea, chattering away in German, might be spies observing coastal activities; in which case, apparently, he thinks an appropriate punishment would be for Andrea to go to prison and Olga to fall in love with the doctor. It is 1936, and Europe seems on the brink of war, although for the Widdington sisters that's not much of a concern. The local police chief drops by for a chat, is satisfied, and leaves. He is so polite that if they had been spies, I wonder if he would have wanted to spoil such a nice day by mentioning it.

Ladies in Lavender, directed by the actor Charles Dance, is perfectly sweet and civilized, and ends with one of those dependable scenes where—gasp!—look who's in the audience at the concert! It's a pleasure to watch Smith and Dench together; their acting is so natural it could be breathing. But Daniel Bruhl is tiresome as Andrea; he has no dark side, no anger, no fierceness, and although we eventually discover why he left Poland, we do not know if it was from passion or convenience. He is an ideal dinner guest; the kind of person you are happy enough to have at the table but could not endure on a three-day train journey.

I am reminded of Lindsay Anderson's *The Whales of August* (1987), also about two elderly sisters in a house on a coast. That one starred Bette Davis and Lillian Gish, who engaged in subtle verbal gamesmanship, both as characters and as actors. It is probably true that we should not attend a movie about old ladies in a big old house expecting much in the way of great drama (although *Whatever Happened to Baby Jane?* has its moments), but *The Whales of August* had a fire that the relaxed *Ladies in Lavender* is entirely lacking.

In the category of movies about older women

risking a last chance on love, you could hardly improve on *A Month by the Lake* (1995), with Vanessa Redgrave falling for, and being dropped by, Edward Fox. We want her to win her man, and the problem with *Ladies in Lavender* is that although Ursula can kid herself, we can't.

Lady Chatterley ★ ★

NO MPAA RATING, 168 m., 2007

Marina Hands (Lady Connie Chatterley), Jean-Louis Coulloc'h (Parkin), Hippolyte Girardot (Sir Clifford), Helene Alexandridis (Mrs. Bolton), Helene Fillieres (Hilda). Directed by Pascale Ferran and produced by Gilles Sandoz. Screenplay by Roger Bohbot, Ferran, and Pierre Trividic, based on the novel *John Thomas and Lady Jane* by D. H. Lawrence.

Lady Chatterley is a kinder, gentler version of the story most people know as *Lady Chatterley's Lover.* It's based on an earlier version of D. H. Lawrence's once-scandalous novel that had the too-perfect title *John Thomas and Lady Jane.* While involving Lawrence's approval of transcendent lust, the film also has a great deal of time for flowers, running water, close-ups of hands, and long shots of trees. Also, of course, for the class struggle, lustful sex, and close attention to the genitals.

Let's begin with the genitals, or, as Groucho Marx called them, the netherlands. The story involves the young and fragrant Lady Connie Chatterley (Marina Hands) and her husband, Sir Clifford (Hippolyte Girardot), a wealthy mine owner who was paralyzed from the waist down in World War I. The movie's opening shot shows Connie waving good-bye from their country house as Clifford walks to his car and drives away, so we must assume they were married before the war. But Connie remains childless, and there is no heir to their estate.

Which leads us to questions involving the netherlands. Wandering the grounds lonely as a cloud, Connie comes upon the gamekeeper, Parkin (Jean-Louis Coulloc'h). He is sponging himself bare-chested, which inspires her (and us) to inspect her own naked body in a mirror. Life creeps along quietly at the country house, where Sir Clifford seems to observe a daily word limit, and the housekeeper, Mrs. Bolton (Helene Alexandridis), says little, wrings her hands, and has a look fraught with worry about, at a guess, everything.

But back to the netherlands. Connie and Parkin begin a love affair. Day after day she goes flower collecting in the woods, and they meet in his hut to make love on the floor. One day, as he is undressing, she says, "Turn around," and she (and we) gets a close-up of the netherlands flagpole. Later, after sex, she views him again and observes, "It's so funny, how now it's only a little bud." Which leads to the conclusion that her sex education with Sir Clifford must have been sadly limited, even before the war.

That may help explain why Clifford is satisfied to do without her all day every day and be content when she returns late with a handful of daffodils. She is a kind and dutiful wife, to be sure, and they spend quiet time reading, apparently always the same books. In other versions of the story, Clifford is enraged that Connie has been bagged by the gamekeeper, but here he seems almost willfully determined not to know. He would even understand if Connie were to become pregnant by another man (an Englishman, of "decent stock") to provide him with an heir, and she goes off with her sister for a month at the seaside, presumably to arrange this, although at the time she is already two months pregnant. Maybe three. Since Parkin is a strong, muscular man, Sir Clifford is about to be presented with the world's largest short-term baby.

All of this is shown with admittedly gorgeous photography, lyrical montages, and sylvan melodies. The film is spoken in French, directed by Pascale Ferran, although we are to understand that the characters are English. It won six Cesar awards, the French Oscars, including best film, best actress, most-promising actress, and best screenplay, and was nominated for four more. But not for best actor! Since Jean-Louis Coulloc'h takes the thankless role of Parkin and distinguishes it, that seems unfair.

I must also report that on www.rotten-tomatoes.com, the film is scoring an astonishing 100 percent favorable rating on the Tomatometer from those major critics the site deems "cream of the crop." Alas, my vote will spoil the perfect game, unless I am demoted to skim. Why do they love it so? They admire the way sex grows into true love, the gentleness and sweetness of the relationship, and that the film does not rush into sex but moseys there, in 168 minutes heavy with pastoral lyricism, and that Connie and Parkin learn to see, really see, the other person across the class divide.

So I am almost alone in my lack of enchantment, and yet even I feel some affection. Jean-Louis Coulloc'h is a fascinating Parkin. He's not a rough-hewn macho man, but a man who prefers to be left alone, a man whose mother said he was as much girl as boy, a tender lover, a brave partner, a tactful friend. And he seems real, not like a male model ready for underwear ads. He "looks a bit like Oliver Stone with a sleeker nose," writes my friend Lisa Nesselson, *Variety*'s Paris correspondent. Marina Hands is quiet, serene, daring, and beautiful, although David Noh, a good critic banished from the cream of the crop, not unfairly observes "one barely believes a single thought ever clouds Hands' porcelain brow."

All of the qualities its admirers see in the film are indeed there and visible, but I was not much moved. Lawrence wrote much better novels that inspired much better movies (*Sons and Lovers, Women in Love, The Rainbow, The Fox*). Most of them include some version of the full monty, which in a Lawrence film is like the toy in a box of Cracker Jack. Watching this film, I reflected that there are only so many boxes of Cracker Jack you can eat before you decide to hell with the toy. ☞

The Lake House ★ ★ ★ ½

PG, 105 m., 2006

Keanu Reeves (Alex Wyler), Sandra Bullock (Kate Forster), Christopher Plummer (Simon Wyler), Ebon Moss-Bachrach (Henry Wyler), Dylan Walsh (Morgan), Shohreh Aghdashloo (Anna). Directed by Alejandro Agresti and produced by Doug Davison and Roy Lee. Screenplay by David Auburn.

The Lake House tells the story of a romance that spans years but involves only a few kisses. It succeeds despite being based on two paradoxes: time travel, and the ability of two people to have conversations that are, under the terms established by the film, impossible. Neither of these problems bothered me in the slightest. Take time travel: I used to get distracted by its logical flaws and contradictory time lines. Now, in my wisdom, I have decided to simply accept it as a premise, no questions asked. A time-travel story works on emotional, not temporal, logic.

In *The Lake House,* it works like this: A woman (Sandra Bullock) lives in a glass house built on stilts over a lake north of Chicago. She is moving out and leaves a note for the next tenant (Keanu Reeves). He reads the note and sends a strange response to the address she supplies: He thinks she has the wrong house because, "No one has lived in this house for years." She writes back to disagree. It develops that he thinks it is 2004 and she thinks it is 2006, and perhaps she moved in after he left, instead of moving out before he arrived, although that wouldn't fit with—but never mind.

This correspondence continues. They both leave their letters in the mailbox beside the sidewalk that leads to the bridge that leads to the glass house. The mailbox eventually gets into the act by raising and lowering its own little red flag. The two people come to love each other, and this process involves the movie's second impossibility. We hear them having voice-over conversations that are ostensibly based on the words in their letters, but unless these letters are one sentence long and are exchanged instantaneously (which would mean crossing time travel with chat rooms), they could not possibly be conversational.

Never mind. They also have the same dog. Never mind, I tell you, never mind! I think, actually, that I have the answer to how the same dog could belong to two people separated by two years, but if I told you, I would have to shoot the dog. The key element in *The Lake House* that gives it more than a rueful sense of loss is that although Alex's letters originate in 2004 and Kate's in 2006, *he is, after all, still alive in 2006,* and what is more, *she, after all, was alive in 2004.* Is there a way for them to send letters across the gap that will allow them to meet where she was in 2004, or where he will be in 2006, or vice versa? There is, although it involves many paradoxes, including the one that in 2004 all of this is ahead of both of them, and in 2006 Alex knows everything but Kate either knows nothing or knows it too late to act on it. None of this prevents her letter of romantic anguish: *That was you that I met!*

Enough of the plot and its paradoxes. What I respond to in the movie, directed by Alejandro Agresti and written by the Pulitzer and Tony winner David Auburn (*Proof*), is its fundamental romantic impulse. It makes us hope these two people somehow will meet. All during the movie, we're trying to do the math: It should be possible, given enough ingenuity, for them to eventually spend 2007 together, especially since he theoretically can keep the letters he received from her in 2004 and ask her out on a date and show them to her, although by then she'd know she wrote them—or would she? They do arrange one date, which involves them in some kind of time-loop misunderstanding, I think. She later understands what happened, but I don't think I do. I mean, I understand the *event* she refers to, but not whether it is a necessary event or can be prevented.

A great deal depends on the personalities involved. Bullock is an enormously likable actor in the right role, and so is Reeves, although here they're both required to be marginally depressed because of events in their current (but not simultaneous) lives. Many of his problems circle around his father, Simon Wyler (Christopher Plummer), a famous Chicago architect. The old man is an egocentric genius who designed the lake house, which his son dislikes because, like Louis himself, it lives in isolation; there aren't even any stairs to get down to the water.

Alex is an architect himself, currently debasing himself with suburban condos, and Kate is a doctor whose confidante is an older mentor at the hospital (Shoreh Aghdashloo). Alex has a confidant too, his brother Henry (Ebon Moss-Bachrach). A plot like this makes confidants more or less obligatory, since the protagonists have so little opportunity to confide in each other, except for their mysterious ability to transform written correspondence into a conversation. Now about that dog: Dogs live outside of time, don't you think?

Lake of Fire ★ ★ ★ ½

NO MPAA RATING, 152 m., 2007

With Noam Chomsky, Alan M. Dershowitz, Nat Hentoff, Dallas Blanchard, Norma McCorvey, Peter Singer, Randall Terry, Frederick Clarkson, Bill Baird, Frances Kissling, Michael Griffin, and Paul Hill. A documentary written, directed, and produced by Tony Kaye.

Readers often complain about documentaries that don't tell "both sides." Those who care deeply about the issue of abortion in America, no matter which side they are on, may complain that this film tells the other side. This is a brave, unflinching, sometimes virtually unwatchable documentary that makes such an effective case for both pro-choice and pro-life that it is impossible to determine which side the filmmaker, Tony Kaye, stands on. All you can conclude at the end is that both sides have effective advocates, but the pro-lifers also have some alarming people on their team.

One of them is an earnest young man named Paul Hill, neat haircut, aviator glasses, who says we should execute all abortionists. He doesn't stop there. We should also execute all blasphemers. What is a blasphemer? he's asked. Well, he says, like people who say "God damn it." Anyone who says "God damn it" should be executed? "Yes," he says firmly. Later, he murders a Florida doctor who performed abortions. It's one of two murders in the film, which result in the death penalty, which pro-life advocates generally support.

Other pro-lifers buy property next to abortion clinics and build platforms so their supporters can climb onto them and shout over fences at young women entering the clinic. They consider abortion to be murder, plain and simple, and they are also against birth control and sex education, which have proven in recent years to reduce unplanned pregnancies and therefore abortions.

On behalf of their argument, Hill shows graphic footage of abortions and their consequences. The scene that shook me most deeply has a doctor sorting through a pan of blood, fluid, and body parts to be sure he has removed an entire fetus. Tiny hands and feet can clearly be seen. There is also a shot of what look like full-term babies stacked in a freezer, but something about the shot, and the method of storage, leads me to disbelieve it. Nevertheless, throughout the film we see more than enough to convince us that what is being aborted is often recognizably human.

The sanest voice of reason on the pro-life side is Nat Hentoff, the veteran left-wing writer for the *Village Voice*, described as a civil libertarian and an atheist. He argues from a logical, not religious, point of view that when a sperm and an egg unite, a human being is in the process of formation, and the process should not be interrupted. His dispassionate remarks, whether or not you agree with them, are a calm center in the middle of a strident storm.

Another key witness in the film is Norma McCorvey, who was the anonymous "Jane Roe" in the 1973 Supreme Court decision Roe v. Wade. She was a pro-choice activist for years, had her home and car shot at, felt a virtual prisoner in her house, and then there was an unanticipated development. The property next door was purchased by antiabortionists, she started to visit them, she found their office so calm and friendly that she was converted, and she now speaks at pro-life events. We also meet, anonymously, some of the young women who apply at abortion clinics and hear their stories. And we hear grim statistics: If abortion is made illegal again in America, the abortion rate will remain about the same as it was before Roe v. Wade, but the fatality rate will start climbing. Before the Supreme Court decision, the leading cause of death among young women, we're told, was not cancer, not heart disease, not accidents, but side effects of illegal abortions.

The film has been a life's work for Kaye, a British citizen, now fifty-five, who has been filming it on and off for seventeen years. He shoots in 35 mm widescreen, using black-and-white (color would be unbearable). His film is long at 152 minutes but doesn't seem long because at every moment something absorbing, disturbing, depressing, or infuriating is happening. True, he comes down on neither side of the debate. But what he shows inadvertently is how the tradition of freely exchanged ideas in America has been replaced by entrenched true believers who drown out voices of moderation.

Alan M. Dershowitz, the Harvard law professor, tells a parable in the film that seems to apply. A rabbi is asked to settle a dispute between a husband and wife. He hears the husband's view. "You're right," he tells him. He hears the wife's view. "You're right," he tells her. One of his students protests: "Rabbi, they both can't be right." The rabbi nods. "You're right," he says.

La Mujer de mi Hermano (My Brother's Wife) ★

R, 89 m., 2006

Barbara Mori (Zoe Edwards), Christian Meier (Ignacio Edwards), Manolo Cardona (Gonzalo Edwards), Gabriela Espino (Laura), Angelica Aragon (Cristina), Beto Cuevas (Padre Santiago), Bruno Bichir (Boris). Directed by Ricardo de Montreuil and produced by Stan Jakubowicz. Screenplay by Jaime Bayly.

I do not, alas, remember every detail of those steamy Isabel Sarli melodramas from Argentina that used to play on Times Square and provide such a diversion from the New York Film Festival. Having now seen the new Argentinean-Mexican-Peruvian-American film *La Mujer de mi Hermano* (*My Brother's Wife*), I suspect I know the reason: There were no details.

Sarli, a former Miss Argentina, was married to her director, Armando Bo, who cast her in films never to be forgotten, such as *Thunder Among the Leaves, Positions of Love, The Hot Days, Naked Temptation, Tropical Ecstasy, Fuego,* and *Fever*. In these films the plot was entirely disposable, except as a device to propel Sarli on an insatiable quest not so much for sex as for admiration. She clearly thought she was the sexiest woman alive, and that itself made her erotic, even in a scene where she attempted suicide by jumping off some rocks and into a pride of sea lions.

I have not thought about Isabel Sarli in years, not since reviewing Theo Angelopoulos's *Ulysses' Gaze* in 1997. It starred Harvey Keitel as a movie director who returns to his roots in Greece and makes love to lots of women. I quote from my review: "I was reminded of Armando Bo's anguished 1960s Argentinean soft-core sex films, which starred his wife, Isabel Sarli, whose agony was terrible to behold and could only be slaked in the arms of a man. (Keitel) and the women make love in this movie as if trying to apply unguent inside each other's clothes."

The Sarli role in *La Mujer de mi Hermano* is filled (and that is the word) by Barbara Mori, a TV Azteca and Telemundo star who provides persuasive reasons why there are ever so many more plunging necklines on the Spanish-language channels than on their chaste Anglo equivalents. If Oprah were on Telemundo, Tom Cruise would have stayed on the couch.

The movie's title translates as *My Brother's Wife*, although it would be more accurate to call it *My Husband's Brother*, since it is told entirely from the point of view of Zoe (Mori). She has been married for ten years to Ignacio (Christian Meier), who is a "businessman." In these movies, "businessman" translates as "doesn't satisfy his wife." Zoe complains to a friend that Ignacio likes to have sex only on Saturdays. We find this hard to believe until a scene where a symbolic unguent application is interrupted by Ignacio: "Remember that today's not Saturday." When she cannot believe her ears (or any other organ), he whines, "Honey, that's the way I am."

What a contrast with his brother Gonzalo (Manolo Cardona), an artist with the kind of 5 o'clock shadow where the whiskers seem forced out through his skin by testosterone. Zoe attends one of Gonzalo's gallery openings and purchases a painting, which Ignacio throws into the pool of his multimillion-dollar house, an example of modern domestic architecture that looks as if Frank Lloyd Wright's Fallingwater had conceived a child with Donald Trump.

Ignacio begins to suspect something, although not nearly enough and none too quickly, as Zoe and Gonzalo star in *Never on Saturday*. The two brothers, they love each other, and yet dark secrets from their past beg to be revealed. Indeed, by this point secrets from anybody's past would be welcome. The movie is astonishingly simpleminded, depicting characters who obediently perform their assigned roles as adulterers, cuckolds, etc. At least with Isabel Sarli you had the impression she was not only having a good time while she made her movies, but enjoyed hours and hours just looking at them.

Lars and the Real Girl ★ ★ ★ ½

PG-13, 106 m., 2007

Ryan Gosling (Lars), Emily Mortimer (Karin), Paul Schneider (Gus), Kelli Garner (Margo), Patricia Clarkson (Dr. Dagmar), Nancy Beatty (Mrs. Gruner). Directed by Craig Gillespie and produced by John Cameron, Sarah Aubrey, and Sidney Kimmel. Screenplay by Nancy Oliver.

How do you make a film about a life-size love doll ordered through the Internet into a life-affirming statement of hope? In *Lars and the Real Girl* you do it with faith in human nature and with a performance by Ryan Gosling that says things that cannot be said. And you surround him with actors who express the instinctive kindness we show to those we love.

Gosling, who has played neo-Nazis and district attorneys, now plays Lars Lindstrom, a painfully shy young man who can barely stand the touch of another human being. He functions in the world and has an office job, but in the evening he sits alone in a cabin in the backyard of his family home. His mother died years ago, his depressive father more recently. Now the big house is occupied by his brother Gus (Paul Schneider) and pregnant sister-in-law, Karin (Emily Mortimer). She makes it her business to invite him to dinner, to share their lives, but he begs off with one lame excuse after another and sits alone in the dark.

One day a coworker at the office, surfing Internet porn, shows Lars a life-size vinyl love doll that you can order customized to your specifications. A few weeks later a packing crate is delivered to Lars, and soon his brother and sister-in-law are introduced to the doll. She is, they learn, named Bianca. She is a paraplegic missionary of Brazilian and Danish blood, and Lars takes her everywhere in a wheelchair. He has an explanation for everything, including why she doesn't talk or eat.

The movie somehow implies without quite saying that, although the doll comes advertised with "orifices," Lars does not use Bianca for sex. No, she is an ideal companion, not least because she can never touch him. With a serenity bordering on the surreal, Lars takes her everywhere, even to church. She is as real as anyone in his life can possibly be at this point in the development of his social abilities.

Gus is mortified. Karin is more accepting; she believes that, for Lars, any change is progress. They arrange for Lars and Bianca to start seeing Dagmar (Patricia Clarkson), a therapist, who advises them to allow Lars to live with his fantasy. Dagmar "treats" Bianca and confides in Lars. Nothing is said in so many words, but we sense that she thinks Bianca functions the way pets do with some closed-in people: The doll provides unconditional love, no criticism, no questions.

The miracle in the plot is that the people of Lars's community arrive at an unspoken agreement to treat Bianca with the same courtesy that Lars does. This is partly because they have long and sadly watched Lars closing into himself and are moved by his attempt to break free. The film, directed by Craig Gillespie and written by Nancy Oliver (*Six Feet Under*), wisely never goes for even one moment that could be interpreted as smutty or mocking. There are, to be sure, some moments of humor; you can't take a love doll everywhere without inspiring double takes. And Gus sometimes blurts out the real-world truths we are also thinking.

There are so many ways *Lars and the Real Girl* could have gone wrong that one of the film's fascinations is how adroitly it sidesteps them. Its weapon is absolute sincerity. It is about who Lars is and how he relates to this substitute for human friendship, and that is all it's about. It has a kind of purity to it. Yes, it's rated PG-13, and that's the correct rating, I believe. It could inspire conversations between children and their parents about masturbation, loneliness, acceptance of unusual people, empathy.

We all know a few people who walk into a socially dangerous situation, size it up, and instantly know what to say and how to set people at ease. My Aunt Martha could do that. She was a truth teller, and all some situations need is for someone to tell the truth instead of pussyfooting around embarrassments. Consider, in this film, the neighbor named Mrs. Gruner (Nancy Beatty). She rises to the occasion in a way both tactful and heroic. While Gus is worried about what people will think, Mrs. Gruner (and Karin and Dagmar) are more concerned with what Lars is thinking.

As we watch this process, we glimpse Lars's inner world, one of hurt but also hidden hope. Nine actors out of ten would have (rightly) turned down this role, suspecting it to be a minefield of bad laughs. Ryan Gosling's work here is a study in control of tone. He isn't too morose, too strange, too opaque, too earnest. The word for his behavior, so strange to the world, is serene. He loves his new friend, treats her courteously, and expects everyone else to give her the respect he does.

How this all finally works out is deeply satisfying. Only after the movie is over do you realize what a balancing act it was, what risks it took, what rewards it contains. A character says at one point that she has grown to like Bianca. So, heaven help us, have we. If we can feel that way about a new car, why not about a lonely man's way to escape from sitting alone in the dark? ☞

Last Days ★ ★ ★

R, 97 m., 2005

Michael Pitt (Blake), Lukas Haas (Luke), Asia Argento (Asia), Scott Patrick Green (Scott), Nicole Vicius (Nicole), Ricky Jay (Detective), Thadeus A. Thomas (Salesman). Directed by Gus Van Sant and produced by Van Sant and Dany Wolf. Screenplay by Van Sant.

Gus Van Sant has made three movies in which the camera follows young men as they wander toward their deaths. All three films resolutely refuse to find a message in the deaths. No famous death can take place in our society without being endlessly analyzed by experts, who find trends, insights, motives, and morals with alarming facility. It's brave of Van Sant to allow his characters to simply wander off, in John Webster's words, "to study a long silence."

In *Gerry* (2002), death is accidental, caused by carelessness. Two friends fecklessly wander into a desert, get lost, and don't get found. In *Elephant* (2003), death is preceded by murder and is deliberate but pointless. Two friends carry out a plan to kill students and teachers at their high school, and then they too are shot. Now in *Last Days,* death is a condition that overtakes a character as he mumbles and stumbles into the final stage of drug addiction.

These deaths are not heroic or meaningful, and although they may be tragic, they lack the stature of classical tragedy. They are stupid and careless, and in *Elephant* they are monstrous, because innocent lives are also taken. If Van Sant is saying anything (I am not sure he is), it's that society has created young men who do not live as if they value life.

Last Days is dedicated to the suicide of Kurt Cobain, who led the band Nirvana, influential in the creation of grunge rock. Grunge as a style is a deliberate way of presenting the self as disposable. In a disclaimer that distances itself from Cobain with cruel precision, the movie says its characters are "in part, fictional."

The movie concerns a singer named Blake

(Michael Pitt), who wanders about a big stone house in a wet, gloomy forest area. The first scenes show him throwing up, stumbling down a hillside to a stream, bathing himself, drying his clothes at a campfire, and, in the middle of the night, singing "Home on the Range." The movie seems unwilling to look at his face very clearly; it is concealed by lanky hair and a hooded coat, and the camera prefers long shots to close-ups. We notice that he is wearing the sort of wrist tag you get in a hospital. Blake walks aimlessly through the house, prepares meals (Cocoa Puffs, macaroni and cheese), and listens without comment as people talk to him in person and on the phone.

They're worried about him. Kim Gordon of Sonic Youth plays a woman who asks him, "Do you talk to your daughter? Do you say I'm sorry that I'm a rock and roll cliché?" No answer. "I have a car waiting, and I want you to come with me." No answer. A detective (Ricky Jay) turns up, cannot find Blake (who hides in the woods), and relates an anecdote about a magician who could catch a bullet in his teeth (most of the time). A musician turns up and wants Blake's help with a song he is writing about a girl he left behind in Japan. A (real) Yellow Pages salesman (Thadeus A. Thomas) turns up and tries to sell Blake an ad. Harmony Korine turns up (all the characters have the same names as the actors) and talks about playing Dungeons & Dragons with Jerry Garcia.

None of this interests Blake. One night he wanders into a nearby town, into a bar, and out of the bar again. No doubt some of the people in the bar know he is a famous rock star, but his detachment is so complete it forms a wall around him; you look at him, and you know nothing is happening there.

There is a moment at the house when some friends are about to leave, and one man pauses and looks for a long time as Blake, seen indistinctly through the windows of a potting shed, moves aimlessly. That is where his body will be found in the morning. In a curious coda to such a minimalist film, Van Sant shows Blake's ghostly image leaving his body and ascending, not by floating up to heaven, but by climbing—using the frames of a window as a ladder.

Last Days is a definitive record of death by gradual drug exhaustion. After the chills and thrills of *Sid & Nancy* and *The Doors*, here is a movie that sees how addicts usually die, not with a bang but with a whimper. If the dead had it to do again, they might wish that, this time, they'd at least be conscious enough to realize what was happening.

Last Holiday ★ ★ ★

PG-13, 112 m., 2006

Queen Latifah (Georgia Byrd), LL Cool J (Sean Matthews), Timothy Hutton (Matthew Kragen), Gerard Depardieu (Chef Didier), Alicia Witt (Ms. Burns), Giancarlo Esposito (Senator Dillings), Michael Nouri (Representative Stewart). Directed by Wayne Wang and produced by Laurence Mark and Jack Rapke. Screenplay by Jeffrey Price, Peter S. Seaman, and J. B. Priestly.

Last Holiday is a movie that takes advantage of the great good nature and warmth of Queen Latifah, and uses it to transform a creaky old formula into a comedy that is just plain lovable. To describe the plot is to miss the point, because this plot could have been made into countless movies not as funny and charming as this one.

Latifah plays a salesclerk named Georgia Byrd who works in a big chain store in antediluvian New Orleans, giving cooking demonstrations. At home alone in the evenings, she prepares elaborate gourmet dishes, watching TV cooking shows and training herself to be a great chef. Then, more often than not, she eats a lonely Lean Cuisine, because she's on a diet.

The need for dieting comes to a sudden halt when she receives bad news: She has three or four weeks to live. Her HMO won't cover the expensive treatment, which might not work anyway, and so Georgia throws caution to the wind, cashes in her 401(k), and buys a ticket to Karlovy Vary in the Czech Republic. That's where her hero, Chef Didier (Gerard Depardieu), rules the kitchen, and she decides to go out in style, eating everything on the menu and treating herself to all the services of the spa and the ski slopes.

Karlovy Vary is a jewel box of a spa town ninety minutes outside of Prague. Its hotels are high and wide but not deep because steep mountain walls rise close behind them. A stream runs down the center of the town, and at the top of the little valley is the Grandhotel

Pupp, where Georgia checks in. My wife and I were in Karlovy Vary four years ago for a film festival, and, like Georgia, we did a double take when we discovered that the correct pronunciation of the hotel rhymes with "poop." Yes, but it is a magnificent edifice, and soon Georgia is walking eagerly into the dining room to order—well, everything on the menu.

Visiting this hotel is another party, consisting of a retail tycoon named Matthew Kragen (Timothy Hutton), who owns the chain of giant stores, including the one Georgia resigned from in New Orleans. At his table are his mistress (Alicia Witt), a senator (Giancarlo Esposito), and a congressman (Michael Nouri). They are startled when Chef Didier pays more attention to the woman dining by herself than to their self-important table. They don't know that Georgia has already invaded the chef's kitchen and impressed him with her cooking skills—both disciplined and improvised.

Who is this woman? Kragen's table becomes consumed with curiosity, especially since Georgia Byrd is obviously very wealthy. There's a montage that reminds us of *Pretty Woman,* as she raids a high-fashion dress shop (while "If I Were a Rich Girl" plays on the sound track) and subjects herself to being beaten with birch leaves at the spa ("I Feel Pretty"). A spa in Karlovy Vary is not quite as spartan as one in America and does not count so many calories; after your treatments, you are free to recover with roast duck and dumplings, followed by apple strudel.

By making no claims, putting on no airs, telling no lies, and acting as if she has nothing to lose, Georgia transforms the hotel. The important guests are in awe of her. The staff is in love with her. The chef adores her. And there is even romance in the air because of her unmistakable chemistry with Sean Matthews (LL Cool J), a New Orleans coworker who is shy but—I will not reveal more.

All of these things may be true and yet not inspire you to see this movie. I am the first to admit that the plot is not blindingly original, although transporting the action to Karlovy Vary at least adds an intriguing location. The movie is a remake of a 1950 film that starred Alec Guinness in the Queen Latifah role, and the story was not precisely original even then.

All depends on the Queen, who has been known to go over the top on occasion but in this film finds all the right notes and dances to them delightfully. It is good to attend to important cinema like *Syriana* and *Munich,* but on occasion we must be open to movies that have more modest ambitions: They want only to amuse us, warm us, and make us feel good. *Last Holiday* plays like a hug.

When a movie can do that, a strange transformation takes place. Scenes that in a lesser movie would be contrived and cornball are, in a better movie, redeemed by the characters. There is a moment here when Georgia and another hotel guest find themselves on a ledge on the roof of the Hotel Pupp. A crowd gathers below. Such a scene could be creaky and artificial. Not here. It works.

And what, you ask, about the Idiot Plot? The whole story depends on a series of elaborate misunderstandings. One word would set everybody straight. Yes, true, and yet the movie smiles and winks at its own contrivances, and we enjoy them. The point of this story is not to discover the truth about Queen Latifah's past life, but to enjoy the unfolding of her future life (if, of course, she has one).

The movie was directed by Wayne Wang, whose *Joy Luck Club* and *Maid in Manhattan* showed a sure feel for romantic comedy with a human dimension. The key thing he does with Queen Latifah is to accept her. She is not elbowed into an unlikely comic posture or remade into a cliché but accepted for who she is. Or perhaps not for who she really is (for which of us knows the mystery of another?) but for whom she can play so comfortably and warmly on the screen. One of the movie's best scenes comes when she gives advice to the tycoon's mistress—who is conventionally sexy but senses that Georgia is sexy in a transcendent way because of who she is. The mistress is sexy to look at. Georgia is sexy when you *see* her. The men at the other table can't take their eyes off her.

The Last Mistress ★ ★ ★ ½

NO MPAA RATING, 114 m., 2008

Asia Argento (Vellini), Fu'ad Ait Aattou (Ryno de Marigny), Roxane Mesquida (Hermangarde), Claude Sarraute (Marquise de Flers), Yolande Moreau (Comtesse d'Artelles),

Michael Lonsdale (Vicomte de Prony). Directed by Catherine Breillat and produced by Jean-Francois Lepetit. Screenplay by Breillat, based on the novel by Jules Barbey d'Aurevilly.

In *The Last Mistress,* a passionate and explicit film about sexual obsession, everything pauses for a scene depicting a wedding. It is 1835, in a church in Paris. Vows are exchanged between Ryno de Marigny, a notorious young libertine, and the high-born Hermangarde, whose wealth will be a great comfort to the penniless Ryno. The film opens with two gossipy old friends wondering why the Marquise de Flers would sacrifice her beloved granddaughter to this rake.

I wondered why time was devoted to the ceremony, in a film where Hermangarde speaks scarcely one hundred words and the great passion is between Ryno and his mistress of ten years, the disreputable Vellini. Then I realized it was an excuse to work in the Biblical readings ("requested by the bride and groom"—surely a modern touch?). The Gospel contains God's strictures about man and wife, divorce and adultery, letting no man put asunder, etc. The epistle is Paul to the Corinthians, venting his admonishments to women, who must always take second place, cover their heads in the sight of the Lord, obey their masters, and so on.

These readings enter the film precisely to be contradicted by Vellini (Asia Argento) in every atom of her being. Born out of wedlock to an Italian princess and a Spanish matador, she is technically wed to an English aristocrat but in fact is the most impetuous courtesan in Paris. When she overhears young Ryno (Fu'ad Ait Aattou) describe her as a "mutt," she permits herself the smallest smile before taking another lick of her ice cream (shaped like what we now call a torpedo).

Their relationship begins with her hatred, or what she convinces Ryno is her hatred; it inspires his uncontrollable desire and leads to a duel with her husband during which Ryno is nearly killed with a bullet near his heart. As he lingers near death, so inflamed is Vellini that she bursts into his bedchamber and licks the blood from his wound. The doctor growls about "infection," but never mind: She has been inspired by his sacrifice. Any man who would suffer that much for her love would surely suffer more.

The Last Mistress is the latest film from the French director Catherine Breillat, famous for the explicit eroticism of such films as *Fat Girl* and *Romance.* Here she makes an elegant period piece, with all the costumes, carriages, servants, chateaus, and mannered behavior we would expect, and then explodes its decorum with a fiery performance by Argento. Does she love her young prize, with his lips full as a woman's? Does he love her, with her two front teeth tilted inward like a vampire's? Love has nothing to do with it. They are in the grip of erotomania.

That in itself could be fairly routine, if it were not for the way Breillat frames her story. Understand that Ryno sincerely loves Hermangarde (Roxane Mesquida). Two days before the marriage, he says his formal farewell to Vellini, which is followed by helpless sex. Later the same night, he pays a courtesy call on the old Marquise de Flers (Claude Sarraute), who arranged the marriage and considers it her "masterpiece," so sure is she about Ryno.

Alas, she has been informed of his affair with Vellini and now asks for a confession. This he supplies in tender and earnest terms. Then she asks for details. These he supplies in lurid flashbacks. The marquise prides herself on being a liberated woman of the previous century. "Damn this herb tea!" she says. "A little port will warm us up." Soon she is stretched out full length in her chair, her feet propped on a divan, drinking in the details of his story.

It is Claude Sarraute's performance that I loved most of all in the film. I can easily imagine spending the night in the salon of this old lady and telling her everything she wants to hear. Her face is so intelligent, her manner so direct that my only fear would be to disappoint her. Astonished, I discover from *Variety* that Sarraute is a "distinguished journalist and commentator who last dabbled in acting more than fifty years ago." She gives dimension and meaning to Ryno's long story of powerless surrender.

Argento's performance is also remarkable. Dressed to flaunt her immorality (in one costume, she is the devil), she puffs on cigars, draws blood, follows the newlyweds to their remote coastal hideaway. Ryno hates himself for being unable to resist her. In one shot, Breillat fills the screen with naked flesh and two items of jewelry: his wedding ring and Vellini's bracelet in the shape of a serpent.

One of the old gossips is played by the immortal Michael Lonsdale, who predicted that Ryno would never be able to stay away from Vellini and takes some satisfaction in being proven right, but not as much as he takes in a properly roasted chicken. Of all the vices, he observes, gluttony lasts the longest and never disappoints. As for debauchery, poor Ryno is desperately overserved, and it is hard for us, even as he surrenders to devouring need, not to feel sorry for him.

La Vie En Rose ★ ★ ★ ★

PG-13, 140 m., 2007

Marion Cotillard (Edith Piaf), Sylvie Testud (Momone), Pascal Greggory (Louis Barrier), Emmanuelle Seigner (Titine), Jean-Paul Rouve (Louis Gassion), Clotilde Courau (Anetta Gassion), Jean-Pierre Martins (Marcel Cerdan), Gerard Depardieu (Louis Leplee). Directed by Olivier Dahan and produced by Alain Goldman. Screenplay by Dahan and Isabelle Sobelman.

She was the daughter of a street singer and a circus acrobat. Her mother dumped her with her father, who dumped her with his mother, who ran a brothel. In childhood, diseases rendered her temporarily blind and deaf. She claimed she was cured by St. Therese, whose shrine the prostitutes took her to. One of the prostitutes adopted her until her father returned, snatched her away, and put her to work in his act. From her mother and the prostitute she heard many songs, and one day when his sidewalk act was doing badly, her father commanded her, "Do something." She sang "La Marseilles." And Edith Piaf was born.

Piaf. The French word for "sparrow." She was named by her first impresario, Louis Leplee. He was found shot dead not long after—possibly by a pimp who considered her his property. She stood four feet, eight inches tall, and so became "The Little Sparrow." She was the most famous and beloved French singer of her time—of the century, in fact—and her lovers included Yves Montand (whom she discovered) and the middleweight champion Marcel Cerdan. She drank too much, all the time. She became addicted to morphine and required ten injections a day. She grew old and stooped before her time and died at forty-seven.

Olivier Dahan's *La Vie en Rose,* one of the best biopics I've seen, tells Piaf's life story through the extraordinary performance of Marion Cotillard, who looks like the singer. The title, which translates loosely as "life through rose-colored glasses," is from one of Piaf's most famous songs, which she wrote herself. She is known for countless other songs, perhaps most poignantly for "Non, Je ne Regrette Rien" ("No, I Regret Nothing"), which is seen in the film as her final song; if it wasn't, it should have been.

How do you tell a life story so chaotic, jumbled, and open to chance as Piaf's? Her life did not have an arc but a trajectory. Joy and tragedy seemed simultaneous. Her loves were heartfelt but doomed; after she begged the boxer Cerdan to fly to her in New York, he was killed in the crash of his flight from Paris. Her stage triumphs alternated with her stage collapses. If her life resembled in some ways Judy Garland's, there is this difference: Garland lived for the adulation of the audience, and Piaf lived to do her duty as a singer. From her earliest days, from the prostitutes, her father, and her managers, she learned that when you're paid, you perform.

Oh, but what a performer she was. Her voice was loud and clear, reflecting her early years as a street singer. Such a big voice for such a little woman. At first she sang mechanically but was tutored to improve her diction and to express the meaning of her words. She did that so well that if you know what the words *Non, je ne regrette rien* mean, you can essentially feel the meaning of every other word in the song.

Dahan and his cowriter, Isabelle Sobelman, move freely through the pages of Piaf's life. A chronology would have missed the point. She didn't start here and go there; she was always, at every age, even before she had the name, the little sparrow. The action moves back and forth from childhood to final illness, from applause to desperation, from joy to heartbreak (particularly in the handling of Cerdan's last visit to her). This mosaic storytelling style has been criticized in some quarters as obscuring facts (quick: How many times was she married?). But think of it this way: Since there are, in fact, no wedding scenes in the movie, isn't it more accurate to see husbands, lovers, friends, admirers, employees, and everyone else as whirling around her small, still center? Nothing in her early life taught her to count on permanence or loyalty. What she counted on was singing, champagne, infatuation, and morphine.

Many biopics break down in depicting their subjects in old age, and Piaf, at forty-seven, looked old. Gene Siskel once referred to an actor's old-age makeup as making him look like a turtle. In *La Vie en Rose* there is never a moment's doubt. Even the hair is right; her frizzled, dyed, thinning hair in the final scenes matches the real Piaf in the videos I cite below. The only detail I can question is her resiliency after all-night drinking sessions. I once knew an alcoholic who said, "If I wasn't a drinker and I woke up with one of these hangovers, I'd check myself into the emergency room."

Then there are the songs, a lot of them. I gather from the credits that some are dubbed by other singers, some are sung by Piaf herself, and some, in parts at least, by Cotillard. In the video clips you can see how Piaf choreographed her hands and fingers, and Cotillard has that right, too. A singer who has been dead fifty years and sang in another language must have been pretty great to make it onto so many saloon jukeboxes, which is how I first heard her. Now, of course, she's on my iPod, and I'm listening to her right now. *Pour moi toute seule.*

Note: Free video clips of Piaf singing are at www.youtube.com/watch?v=rbsl5_203Ms.

Layer Cake ★ ★ ★ ½

R, 105 m., 2005

Daniel Craig (XXXX), Colm Meaney (Gene), Sienna Miller (Tammy), Michael Gambon (Eddie Temple), Kenneth Cranham (Jimmy Price), George Harris (Morty), Jamie Foreman (Duke). Directed by Matthew Vaughn and produced by Adam Bohling, David Reid, and Vaughn. Screenplay by J. J. Connolly, based on his novel.

Like Scorsese's *Casino* and *GoodFellas,* the British crime movie *Layer Cake* opens with a narration describing a criminal world made in heaven. Also like *Casino* and *GoodFellas,* it is about an inexorable decline toward the torments of hell. The voice explaining everything to us belongs to Daniel Craig, who plays the competent and conservative middleman in a well-run London cocaine operation. Nobody ever calls him by name during the movie, and in the closing credits he's referred to as "XXXX," which may be one-upmanship on "XXX," or probably not.

Craig's credo, spelled out as if he's lecturing at a management seminar, involves knowing your suppliers, knowing your customers, paying your bills, and never getting too greedy. His front is real estate. His exit plan is retirement in the near future. All of that changes when he is summoned to a private club for a luncheon meeting with his immediate superior, Jimmy Price (Kenneth Cranham), a hard man with cold eyes and a menacing Cockney charm. Jimmy wants him to sort out an Ecstasy deal that went bad, and as a sort of twofer, also find the missing daughter of *his* boss, Eddie Temple (Michael Gambon), the kind of man whose soul has warts on its scars.

XXXX does not much like either assignment. They involve cleaning up the kinds of messes he has scrupulously avoided in his own dealings. What's the use of playing it safe if you work for people who want you to take their chances for them? The Ecstasy deal is especially dicey: One of Jimmy's cronies named Duke (Jamie Foreman) stole Ecstasy pills allegedly worth a million pounds. The Serbs he stole them from want them back. Jimmy's ideal scenario, never stated in so many words, would involve XXXX grabbing the pills for Jimmy while Duke is thrown to the Serbs.

XXXX has some hard men who work for him and might be able to get this job done. More complicated is the matter of the girl, especially when another girl named Tammy (Sienna Miller) enters the picture. There are key supporting roles for such actors as the indispensable Colm Meaney, who looks as if he should be found guilty and sent down for life just for the way he has of listening to you.

The movie was directed by Matthew Vaughn, who produced *Lock, Stock and Two*

Smoking Barrels and *Snatch,* and this one works better than those films because it doesn't try so hard to be clever and tries harder to be menacing. It's difficult to take danger seriously when it's packaged in fancy camera work, although Guy Ritchie's *Lock, Stock* did have a carefree visual genius. *Layer Cake* is more in the Scorsese vein, in which a smart and ambitious young man has it all figured out and then gradually loses control to old-fashioned hoods who don't have the patience for prudence when it's easier to just eliminate anyone who gets in their way. The problem is that every dead enemy tends to leave a more dangerous living enemy standing next in line.

There is a kind of scene that both American and British crime movies do very well, in which low-lifes enjoy high life. They've had success in their business of crime, but their preparation for life has not equipped them with interesting ways to stay amused. They almost always lack imagination about what constitutes fun, and dutifully spend their money on cars, cigars, women, champagne, and memberships in private clubs, none of which finally seem to be worth the trouble. We are reminded of the last days of Scarface, a young man who desperately needed something constructive to do with his spare time.

XXXX's dilemma is that he has the resources to enjoy himself but works for people who speak a different language. He is really in the wrong line of work. He could steal more money with the kinds of high finance that distinguished Enron, and run a smaller risk of finding his head in a bucket of ice and his body elsewhere. As his life begins to heat up and events unfold more quickly than he can follow them, we're reminded of Ray Liotta in *GoodFellas,* whose life spun out of control.

Daniel Craig was said to be the front-runner for the next James Bond, until it began to be said that Pierce Brosnan might return for a farewell lap. My own money is on Clive Owen, but who would wish James Bond on anyone? Craig is fascinating here as a criminal who is very smart, and finds that is not an advantage because while you might be able to figure out what another smart person is about to do, dumbos like the men he works for are likely to do anything.

Le Doulos ★ ★ ★ ½

NO MPAA RATING, 108 m., 1962 (rereleased 2008)

Jean-Paul Belmondo (Silien), Serge Reggiani (Maurice), Jean Dessailly (Inspector Clain), Fabienne Dali (Fabienne), Michel Piccoli (Nuttheccio), Monique Hennessy (Therese). Directed by Jean-Pierre Melville and produced by Georges de Beauregard and Carlo Ponti. Screenplay by Melville, based on the novel by Pierre Lesou.

Near the end of *Le Doulos,* Jean-Paul Belmondo reinterprets everything that has gone before, his words illustrated by flashbacks to the film we have seen. That is essentially a wink by the writer-director, Jean-Pierre Melville, suggesting that he was misleading us all along. This goes with his territory: "I take care never to be realistic," he said in a 1963 interview. Does it matter that what we're seeing is not necessarily what we're getting? Not at all. The movie is entirely about how it looks and feels.

I am an admirer of Melville; his *Bob le Flambeur* and *Le Samourai* are in my Great Movies collection. He helped introduce film noir to the New Wave generation and was such a lover of all things American that he renamed himself after Herman Melville. His heroes tend to drive Detroit cars that look huge on the streets of Paris; when one character in this film parks three spaces down from the car of another, how can he *not* notice the twenty-footer and be tipped off the other guy is already there? Melville was also a fetishist of American men's clothing styles, he said, and you will scarcely see a beret in his films. Indeed, *le doulos,* which means "the finger man" in Parisian criminal slang, is the name for the small-brimmed fedora that most of the men wear.

The film is made of elements Melville said he came to love in the black-and-white American crime movies of the 1930s: shadows, night, trench coats, guns, tough guys, cigarettes, slinky dames, cocktail bars, crooked cops, betrayal, loot, and a plot shutting out the world and confining the characters within their own lives and space. It looks gorgeous in the newly restored 35 mm print by Rialto Pictures, which will no doubt issue it as a DVD.

The film opens with a newly released prisoner (Serge Reggiani) calling on a man who set up a diamond heist for him. He later has good reason to believe the Belmondo character fingered him, in a plot that leads through nightclubs, whisky bars (no wine for Melville), dark underpasses, and deserted suburban wastelands. There are three lovely lady friends, including Therese (Monique Hennessy), who is attached to Nuttheccio (Michel Piccoli), a shady nightclub owner. Belmondo ties her up and gags her, which is perhaps what she deserves, depending on what we choose to believe. (The movie drew some criticism for its treatment of women, leading Melville to defend himself: He did not mistreat the women; his characters did.)

To see both Belmondo and Piccoli in 1962 is to be reminded how early they embodied their distinctive screen presences: Piccoli, the balding, saturnine slickster with the five o'clock shadow, and Belmondo, the oily outlaw punk. One trick that Melville plays is to dress them, and others, in essentially identical trench coats and hats, and then shoot them in shadows or from behind, so that we are misled for a while about who we're watching. This, coupled with a habit that some of them have of straightening their hats before a mirror, perhaps suggests they are interchangeable, playing different games by the same rules. See, too, how meticulously Alain Delon treats his hat in *Le Samourai,* about a hit man who lives with a code as rigid as a samurai's. The Belmondo character here has a code, too, but he keeps it so concealed it doesn't do him much good.

The plot is, as I've suggested, baffling. I'll give a shiny new dime to anyone who understands Belmondo's illustrated lecture at the end. It is designed to explain that he is *not* the finger man everyone (and the film until then) thinks he is—but can he be believed? It really matters not, as we enjoy plunging into an underworld of deadly confusion.

The Legend of Zorro ★ ½

PG, 129 m., 2005

Antonio Banderas (Zorro), Catherine Zeta-Jones (Elena), Adrian Alonso (Joaquin), Rufus Sewell (Armand), Rick Chinlund (McGivens), Raul Mendez (Ferroq). Directed by Martin Campbell and produced by Laurie MacDonald, Walter F. Parkes, and Lloyd Phillips. Screenplay by Alex Kurtzman and Roberto Orci.

The Legend of Zorro commits a lot of movie sins, but one is mortal: It turns the magnificent Elena into a nag. You will recall *The Mask of Zorro* (1998), which first united Antonio Banderas and Catherine Zeta-Jones as Zorro and Elena, in a resurrection of the character first played by Douglas Fairbanks Sr. and subsequently by Tyrone Power, John Carroll, Guy Williams and—here's a team for you—George Hamilton and Anthony Hopkins.

Hopkins played the elder Zorro in the 1998 film, and Banderas played a street urchin who grew up to be a bandit but was taken under old Zorro's wing and taught the tricks of the trade, such as swordsmanship, horsemanship, and charm. That was a grand movie, filled with swashes and buckles. Banderas and Zeta-Jones rose to the occasion with performances of joy and unbounded energy, and it was probably the best Zorro movie ever made, although having not seen them all I can only speculate.

Now come Banderas and Zeta-Jones again, with the same director, Martin Campbell, and of all the possible ideas about how to handle the Elena character, this movie has assembled the worst ones. The sublime adventuress has turned into the kind of wife who wants her husband to quit Zorroing because "you do not know your own son," and besides, Zorro comes home late, she never knows where he is, etc. We are inflicted with such dialogue as:

"People still need Zorro!"

"No—you still need Zorro!"

"You're overreacting!"

Saints preserve us from Mr. and Mrs. Zorro as the Bickersons. And what are we to make of their son, Joaquin (a good little actor named Adrian Alonso)? He dresses like Little Lord Fauntleroy but has developed, apparently by osmosis, all of the skills of his father, such as shadowing bad guys, eavesdropping on plots, improvising in emergencies, and exposing a dastardly scheme to overthrow the government.

He's a bright kid, but not bright enough to recognize that Zorro is his own father. To be sure, Zorro wears a mask, but let me pose a hypothetical exercise for my readers. Imagine your own father. That's it. Now place him in a typical setting: pushing back from the dinner table, cutting off some jerk in an intersection, or scratching his dandruff. Now imagine your dad wearing black leather pants, a black linen shirt, a black cloak, a flat black hat, and a black mask that covers his eyes. Got that? Now imagine him pushing back from the table. Still your dad, right? You can almost hear your mom: "Now don't you go getting any ideas about that whip."

To be sure, Zorro's work keeps him away from home a lot, which is one of the things Elena is complaining about. Maybe the son has never seen his father. In that case, Elena has a point. Meanwhile, the villains have a plot to use a superweapon in order to bring about the collapse of the union and protect us from "inferior races," by which they mean Zorro and all of his kind. Strange, how movie characters who hate "inferior races" somehow themselves never look like breeding stock. If they reproduced, they would found a line of dog whisperers and undersecretaries of defense.

The circumstances under which Zorro and the villain fight a duel with polo mallets is unprecedented in the annals of chivalry, but never mind: What's with this secret society named the Knights of Aragon, who have secretly controlled the world for centuries? When you belong to an ancient order that runs the world and you're reduced to dueling with polo mallets, it's like you're running the Scientology office in Thule.

There is a neat scene here where Zorro and his horse race a train, and then the horse leaps from a trestle and lands on top of the train. That Zorro thinks a horse would do this shows that Zorro does not know as much about horses as he should. For that matter, the horse itself is surprisingly uninformed. It must have had the mumps the week the other horses studied about never jumping blind from a high place onto something that, assuming it is there, will be going 40 mph.

I am searching for the correct word to describe the scene where Zorro is served with divorce papers. Ah, I've found it! Shame I can't use it. Four letters. This is a family newspaper. Starts with "s." Then Zorro has to attend a fancy dress ball where Elena turns up as the escort of Armand (Rufus Sewell), a wealthy French vineyard owner. This is like Supergirl dating Jughead. For maximum poignancy, we need a scene where little Joaquin approaches Armand and says, "Father?"

L'Enfant ★ ★ ★ ★

R, 100 m., 2006

Jeremie Renier (Bruno), Deborah Francois (Sonia), Jeremie Segard (Steve), Fabrizio Rongione (Young Thug), Olivier Gourmet (Plainclothes Officer), Stephane Bissot (Receiver), Mireille Bailly (Bruno's Mother). Directed by Jean-Pierre and Luc Dardenne and produced by Jean-Pierre and Luc Dardenne and Denis Freyd. Screenplay by Jean-Pierre and Luc Dardenne.

We talk about the "point of view" of a film. *L'Enfant* sees with the eye of God. The film has granted free will to its central character, Bruno, and now it watches, intense but detached, to see how he will use it. Bruno is so amoral he doesn't register the meaning of his actions. At first his behavior is evil. He attempts repairs. Whether he is redeemed is a good question. At the end he is weeping, but he cannot weep forever, and he has a limited idea of how to survive and make a living.

But let me just bluntly tell you what happens in the film, while observing that *L'Enfant*, more than almost any film I can think of, is not about plot development but about putting one foot in front of the other. We meet Sonia and Bruno. She has just borne his child. The baby in her arms, she finds Bruno begging from cars at a traffic light, while serving as a lookout for a burglary in progress. She shows him their child. He is as interested as if she had shown him her new phone card.

Sonia (Deborah Francois) looks in her late teens. Bruno (Jeremie Renier) looks older, yet in no way seems an adult, and indeed his criminal pals are all kids of around fourteen. He lives entirely in the moment. While Sonia was in the hospital, he sublet her apartment. When he divides loot from a robbery, he spends his share immediately. He buys a used perambulator because Sonia wants one. He rents an expensive convertible because he wants one. There will always be more money. Working? Working is for losers.

In a cafe, he meets a woman he does business

with. He mentions the baby. She tells him, "People pay to adopt." Promising Sonia to watch the baby for an afternoon, he arranges to sell the child. Bruno lives in a grim world of unfriendly streets; he and Sonia have spent nights huddled on a river bank. But no place in the movie is bleaker than the empty building where the sale of the child takes place. He never sees the buyers. They never see him. The child is left in a room, is taken, the money left behind. He returns to Sonia and proudly shows her the money ("This is ours!"). When she despairingly asks about the baby, he says, "We can have another one." She faints dead away and is taken to the hospital. This is a surprise to him.

L'Enfant, which won the Golden Palm at Cannes 2005, is the new film by the Dardenne brothers, Jean-Pierre and Luc, whose *The Son* (2002) made such an impact, audiences were moved in a deep, rare way. The Dardennes do not make morality tales. Their character Bruno is not aware that what he does is good or bad. He is unformed. There is a scene where he and Sonia tussle playfully in a car and then romp outside in a park like a couple of kids. Does he love her? Love is outside his emotional range. He takes money, spends it, doesn't even cultivate the persona of a hustler. He is that most terrifying kind of human being, the one who doesn't feel ordinary emotions or even understand that other people do.

The Dardennes achieve their effects through an intense visual focus. They follow their characters as if their camera can look nowhere else. In *L'Enfant,* their gaze is upon Bruno. They deliberately do not establish the newborn child as a character. Unlike the (equally powerful) *Tsotsi,* their film doesn't show Bruno caring for the child. The child is simply something he carries, like loot or a video game. The movie also avoids the opportunity to develop Sonia, except as her behavior responds to Bruno's. When she lets out a cry of grief and faints, this is not so much what she does as what Bruno sees her do.

Observe particularly the camera strategy in the last half of the film. Often when a handheld camera follows a character, it feels subjective; we are invited to identify, as if the camera is a point of view we share with the character. In the passages after Sonia faints in *L'Enfant,* the camera focuses so intensely on Bruno that everything else seems peripheral vision. But it doesn't "identify" with him, and it doesn't represent his point of view. It watches to see what he will do.

There is a theological belief that God gives us free will and waits to see how we will use it. If he were to interfere, it would not be free will at all. If we choose well, we will spend eternity in the sight of God; if badly, banished from his presence. If God were to issue instructions, what would be the point of his creation? If we are not free to choose evil, where is the virtue in choosing good?

It's with that in mind that the visual strategy of the Dardennes reflects the eye of God. Having made a universe that has set this creature Bruno into motion, God (and we) look to see what he will do. Bruno has little intellectual capital and a limited imagination. He has been so damaged that he lacks ordinary feelings; when he visits his mother to arrange for an alibi, we get some insights into his childhood. After Sonia faints, he sets about trying to get the baby back. Does he do this because he knows that selling the baby was wrong? Or because Sonia is a companion and convenience for him, and he must try to restore her to working order?

The greatness of the Dardennes is that they allow us to realize that these are questions, and leave us free to try to answer them. What happens at the end of the film perhaps suggests grief and a desire to repent. I hope it does. But *L'Enfant* is not so simple as to believe that for Bruno there can be a happy ending. Here is a film where God does not intervene, and the directors do not mistake themselves for God. It makes the solutions at the ends of other pictures seem like child's play.

The Libertine ★ ★ ★

R, 114 m., 2006

Johnny Depp (Rochester), Samantha Morton (Elizabeth Barry), John Malkovich (King Charles II), Rosamund Pike (Elizabeth Malet), Tom Hollander (Sir George Etherege), Johnny Vegas (Charles Sackville). Directed by Laurence Dunmore and produced by Lianne Halfon, John Malkovich, and Russell Smith. Screenplay by Stephen Jeffreys.

"You will not like me," the Earl of Rochester assures us, staring fiercely out of darkness. "You will not like me now, and you will like me a good deal less as we go on." These are the opening words of Stephen Jeffreys's play *The Libertine,* where in Scene 2 we find Rochester in conversation with the actress Elizabeth Barry: "In my experience, those who do not like you fall into two categories: the stupid, and the envious. The stupid will like you in five years' time, the envious never."

So there's our choice: stupid, or envious. I think I would choose stupid. To be envious of John Wilmot, the second earl of Rochester (1647–1680), would be difficult; he died at thirty-three of venereal diseases that ate away his nose, so that he attended Parliament wearing a silver replacement. One of those who did like Rochester was his king, Charles II, restored to the throne after the death of Cromwell. One of Charles's first acts was to allow women back on the English stage, which is why Elizabeth Barry can be an actress in the first place, although one gathers that if her role had been played by a boy, the second earl might have been no less interested.

The Libertine, a film by Laurence Dunmore, is based on Jeffreys's play, which opened in 1994 at the Royal Court in London and was brought to Chicago's Steppenwolf Theater with John Malkovich as Rochester. Here Malkovich plays Charles, and Johnny Depp plays Rochester as the kind of decaying rogue and licentious voluptuary who reaches such an alarming state that it is not a matter of liking or disliking him, but hoping not to catch something from him. Depp has an affection for outrageous roles, and Rochester is not as far removed as you might imagine from Jack Sparrow, the hero of *The Pirates of the Caribbean,* especially in personal hygiene and dental care. Rochester was in youth a hero of British naval engagements, a gifted and mercurial man whose father had helped protect young Charles during his exile. Now Charles has returned and is amused by Rochester's audacity and impudence: The earl composes poetry of startling obscenity, writes reckless satires, is not afraid to lampoon the king to his face. Sometimes Charles banishes Rochester to the country, but then he relents and invites him back to London, because for all his sins the earl is one of the smartest and most entertaining men of his time: good value for the money. All Charles asks is that Rochester keep the lid on, cool it a little. Alas, discretion does not come easily to Rochester.

The film doesn't follow the earl's rise and fall so much as his fall and fall. As a sex addict, he equals Casanova in willingness: "Now, ladies, an announcement," Depp's character says in his opening monologue. "I am up for it. All the time." He is up for gentlemen as well, although the movie is not as interested in that side of his activities. We see him offering Elizabeth Barry (Samantha Morton) lessons on acting, then falling in love with her; she is the smartest woman he has ever met, although that must be tempered with the observation that a smart woman would stay away from him. He welcomes his good wife, Elizabeth Malet (Rosamund Pike), when she comes up from the country, yet does not curtail his visits to the fleshpots and bordellos. She has a touching scene observing that when he returns after an evening with the harlots, she might not mind so much if he were happy—but no, he is sad, and will complain to her, and wish that he had been with her. These sentiments are not as consoling as he imagines.

Rochester crawls in and out of countless embraces, engages in an orgy of remarkable ingenuity, and writes, produces, and performs in a play that Charles commissions for the entertainment of the French king. This play is so outrageous that the Kings Are Not Amused, as we say in capital letters. The movie is pretty much downhill after that, but of course it is. There is no way the story can end happily, as Rochester descends into wine, women, and the pox. There comes a time when a comely wench no longer makes his eye sparkle, and the second earl is no longer up for it all the time. Watching the earl conquer one erotic target after another, I was reminded of a lecture I once attended by the authors of *The 60-Minute Orgasm.* An attentive older woman in the front row asked, "Do you have anything at around five minutes?"

I admire Depp's performance, which plays fair with his opening comment and contains nothing that would inspire us to like him. I was engaged by the patience of Charles II, played by Malkovich as a man smart enough to prefer amusement to flattery; when he cautions Rochester to dial down, it isn't that he's personally offended but that it's a bad idea for the king to be seen giving license to offense. Morton's character bewitches Rochester by out-thinking him, which he finds more intriguing than any sexual favor. And Pike, as Rochester's wife, is touching as a woman who will put up with almost anything but not, finally, with everything.

Libertines are not built for third acts. No self-respecting libertine lives that long. Depp finds sadness in the earl's descent, and a desire to be loved even as he makes himself unlovable. What a brave actor Depp is, to take on a role like this. Still, at the screenplay stage, *The Libertine* might have seemed a safer bet than *The Pirates of the Caribbean,* a movie studio executives reportedly thought was unreleasable. In both cases, Depp accepts the character and all of its baggage, and works without a net. He is capable of subtle nuances, but the pirate and the earl are not, and Depp gamely follows them into wretched excess. You will not like the second earl of Rochester. But you will not be able to take your eyes from him. Having made his bed, he does not hesitate to sleep in it.

Lights in the Dusk ★ ★ ★ ½

NO MPAA RATING, 78 m., 2008

Janne Hyytiainen (Koistinen), Maria Jarvenhelmi (Mirja), Ilkka Koivula (Lindholm). Directed and produced by Aki Kaurismaki. Screenplay by Kaurismaki.

More and more I am learning to love the films of Aki Kaurismaki, that Finnish master of the stories of sad and lonely losers. Like very few directors (such as Tati, Fassbinder, Keaton, Fellini), he has created a world all his own, and you can recognize it from almost every shot. His characters are dour, speak little, expect the worst, smoke too much, are ill-treated by life, are passive in the face of tragedy. Yes, and they are funny.

It is a deadpan humor. Kaurismaki never signals us to laugh, and at festivals there is rarely a roar of laughter, more often the exhalation people make when they are subduing a roar of laughter. His characters are lovable, but nobody seems to know that. *Lights in the Dusk* is the third film in his "loser trilogy," preceded by *Drifting Clouds,* the story of an unemployed couple hopelessly in debt, and *The Man Without a Past,* the story of a homeless man who has no idea who he is. How can I convince you these stories are deeply amusing? I can't. Take my word for it.

In *Lights in the Dusk,* everybody on the screen smokes more than ever, perhaps because it is the highlight of their day. We meet Koistinen (Janne Hyytiainen), a night watchman who says "I have no friends" because it is true: He has no friends. Well, there is the woman who runs the late-night hot dog stand. She is nice to him, but he is cold to her.

Koistinen is shunned at work by his fellow security guards. After three years, the manager cannot remember his name. People stare at him in restaurants. One night he is approached at his solitary table in a cafe by an attractive blonde who asks, "Is this seat taken?" He asks her why she sat there when the café is empty. "Because you looked like you needed company."

They date, if that is the word. They sit rigidly through a movie, almost silently through a dinner, and he stands in the corner at a disco. He invites her to dinner in his basement flat, which has large pipes running through it. He offers her a fresh bagel: "The roast is in the oven." She says, "Koistinen, I have to make a trip. My mother is ill." He asks, "When?" She says, "Right now," and stands up and leaves.

He protests to three bruisers that their dog has been tied outside a bar for days, without water. They take him offscreen and he returns beaten. Most of Kaurismaki's beatings are offscreen, mercifully. There is a plot behind all of his misfortune, which leads to jail time and then a cot in a homeless shelter. He disastrously tries to take action against those who have used him. The hot-dog girl seeks him out. The dog finds a new owner. There is a happy ending, lasting about thirty seconds.

It isn't what happens, it's how it happens. You'll have a hard time finding Kaurismaki in a theater in most cities (and states), but he's waiting for you on DVD. Put a Kaurismaki in your Netflix queue. Most any film will do. You will start watching it and feel strangely disoriented because none of the usual audience cues are supplied. You're on your own. You will watch it engrossed and fascinated right up until the very end, which will not feel much like an ending. You will for some reason feel curious to see another Kaurismaki film. If by any chance you dislike the film and turn it off, let it wait a day, and start it again. You were wrong.

Lions for Lambs ★ ★ ½

R, 88 m., 2007

Robert Redford (Dr. Stephen Malley), Meryl Streep (Janine Roth), Tom Cruise (Senator Jasper Irving), Michael Pena (Ernest Rodriguez), Derek Luke (Arian Finch), Andrew Garfield (Todd Hayes), Peter Berg (Lieutenant Colonel Falco). Directed by Robert Redford and produced by Redford, Matthew Michael Carnahan, Tracy Falco, and Andrew Hauptman. Screenplay by Carnahan.

Useful new things to be said about the debacle in Iraq are in very short supply. I'm not sure that's what *Lions for Lambs* intends to demonstrate, but it does, exhaustingly. Essentially, if I have this right, we should never have invaded Iraq, but now that we're there, (1) we can't very well leave, and (2) we can't very well stay, so (3) the answer is, stay while in the process of leaving.

The movie is a talkathon with a certain amount of military action. It could be presented about as well as a radio play. Directed by Robert Redford, it uses an all-star cast, which focuses attention away from the dialogue and toward the performances. Since I doubt that's what Redford intended, it doesn't speak well for the screenplay by Matthew Michael Carnahan. When a third of a movie involves a verbal duel between Tom Cruise and Meryl Streep, what are we supposed to do, not notice who's talking?

The movie follows three story lines, plus a flashback linking all of them. In Washington, a veteran journalist (Streep) sits down for an exclusive interview with a Republican senator (Cruise) who has presidential ambitions. In Los Angeles, a political science professor (Redford) sits down to discuss the purposes of life with a brilliant but disappointing student (Andrew Garfield). And in Afghanistan, two of the professor's former pupils (Michael Pena and Derek Luke) are involved in a firefight on a snowy mountain peak.

As it happens, they are involved in the very military strategy that the senator is touting to the journalist. It involves seizing the high ground in Afghanistan earlier in the season than the Taliban can get there, to control mountain passes and therefore prevent Taliban troop movements. The Cruise character presents this as a strategic breakthrough on a level with, I dunno, Nelson's rout of Napoleon. It's actually supposed to convince Streep the war can be won.

In Los Angeles, the promising student has just stopped caring, and the talk with his professor is designed to reignite his passion. He should get involved in his nation's politics—take an interest, take a stand. The flashback shows the two soldiers winning a classroom debate by calling the other side's bluff: They have enlisted in the military.

The movie is anti–Bush's war, I guess. The journalist makes better points than the senator, anyway. What the professor and his student think is hard to say, although they are very articulate in muddying the waters. As for the two enlistees, it is safe to assume that at the end of the film they are wondering whether their debate strategy was the right one.

There is a long stretch toward the beginning of the film when we're interested, under the delusion that it's going somewhere. When we begin to suspect it's going in circles, our interest flags, and at the end, while rousing music plays, I would have preferred the Peggy Lee version of "Is That All There Is?"

Lipstick & Dynamite, Piss & Vinegar: The First Ladies of Wrestling ★ ★ ½

NO MPAA RATING, 83 m., 2005

Featuring Ella Waldek, Gladys "Killem" Gillem, Ida May Martinez, Johnnie "The Great" Mae Young, Lillian "The Fabulous Moolah" Ellison, Penny Banner, and Diamond Lil. A documentary directed by Ruth Leitman and produced by Anne Hubbell, James Jernigan, Leitman, and Debbie Nightingale.

Lipstick & Dynamite, Piss & Vinegar: The First Ladies of Wrestling tells us just enough about the early days of professional women wrestlers to suggest there must be a great deal more to tell. The documentary visits elderly women who, then and now, can best be described as tough broads, and listens as they describe the early days of women's wrestling. What they say is not as revealing as how they say it; as they talk we envision not a colorful chapter in showbiz history, but a hardscrabble world in which they were mistreated, swindled, lied to, injured, sometimes raped or beaten—and tried, it must be said, to give as good as they got.

The documentary, by Ruth Leitman, does an extraordinary job of assembling the survivors from the early days of a disreputable sport, beginning with Gladys "Killem" Gillem, whose sideshow act began as a change of pace from the strippers. Footage from the late 1930s and 1940s includes a sideshow barker describing the unimaginable erotic pleasures to be found inside the All-Girl Revue. I remember such sideshows at the Champaign County Fair, where you worked your way past the Octopus and the Tilt-a-Whirl to the girlie tent, always at the bottom of the midway, where dancers in ratty spangled gowns paraded before we horny teenagers, and then the barker said, "All right, girls, back inside the tent!" We followed them in, slamming down the exact change; if a murder had taken place during the show, there would have been no witnesses, because there was absolutely no eye contact between the sinners.

But I digress. The appeal of women's wrestling, then and, I suspect, even now, had a lot to do with the possibility of a Janet Jackson moment. But the sideshow wrestlers gave way to a sport that toured the same venues as men's professional wrestling; sometimes the women were the curtain-raisers, although, as they tell it, the men were terrified that the women would become a bigger draw. We meet such legends of the sport as The Fabulous Moolah (Lillian Ellison), who was the biggest star of the sport and had the most longevity, surviving even into the heyday of the WWF and finding a new generation of fans.

Moolah, now in her eighties, still works as a wrestling promoter. We get a glimpse of her home life; she lives with The Great Mae Young and Diamond Lil, a dwarf wrestler, in a household that would give pause to John Waters. Although Moolah and Young are apparently a couple, the role of Diamond Lil becomes harder to define the more Moolah praises her skills as an invaluable maid of all work. Among the film's other unforgettable characters are Penny Banner, "the blond bombshell," and Ella Waldek, who sounds as if she has chain-smoked Camels from birth and later went into the detective business.

Men seem to have come into the lives of these women primarily as exploiters, rapists, and occasional transient husbands. The promoter Billy Wolfe, a key figure in the early days, is remembered without affection for taking half of what he said were their earnings, and sleeping with as many of them as he could. When the women describe their sexual experiences, their voices reflect more hardened realism than indignation. They were often abandoned when young, made their way on their own, paid their dues.

Magicians have a credo: "The trick is told when the trick is sold." They don't give away their secrets for free. Neither, I suspect, do women wrestlers. Glimpsed on every face in this movie, echoing in every voice, are hints of the things they've seen and the stories they could tell if they didn't have a lifelong aversion to leveling with the rubes. What we get is essentially the press-book version of their careers, which is harrowing enough; Ruth Leitman is said to be working on a fictional screenplay based on her material, and I have a suspicion it may be bloodcurdling. At the end of the film, at the Gulf Coast Wrestlers' Reunion, there is not a lot of sentiment, and no visible tears. One woman after another seems to have attended in order to say, "I'm still here," as if being alive after what they've been through is a form of defiance.

The Lives of Others ★ ★ ★ ★

R, 137 m., 2006

Martina Gedeck (Christa-Maria Sieland), Ulrich Muehe (Captain Gerd Wiesler), Sebastian Koch (Georg Dreyman), Ulrich Tukur (Lieutenant Colonel Anton Grubitz), Thomas Thieme (Minister Bruno Hempf), Hans-Uwe Bauer (Paul Hauser), Volkmar Kleinert (Albert Jerska), Mattias Brenner (Karl Wallner). Directed by Florian Henckel von Donnersmarck and produced by Quirin Berg and Max Wiedemann. Screenplay by von Donnersmarck.

He sits like a man taking a hearing test, big headphones clamped over his ears, his body and face frozen, listening for a faraway sound. His name is Gerd Wiesler, and he is a captain in the Stasi, the notorious secret police of East Germany. The year is, appropriately, 1984, and he is Big Brother, watching. He sits in an attic day after day, night after night, spying on the people in the flat below.

The flat is occupied by a playwright named Dreyman (Sebastian Koch) and his mistress, the actress Christa-Maria Sieland (Martina Gedeck). Wiesler (Ulrich Muehe) first saw Dreyman at the opening of one of his plays, where he was informed by a colleague that Dreyman was a valuable man: "One of our only writers who is read in the West and is loyal to our government." How can that be? Wiesler wonders. Dreyman is good-looking, successful, with a beautiful lover; he must be getting away with something. Driven by suspicion, or perhaps by envy or simple curiosity, Wiesler has Dreyman's flat wired and begins an official eavesdropping.

He doesn't find a shred of evidence that Dreyman is disloyal. Not even in whispers. Not even in guarded allusions. Not even during pillow talk. The man obviously believes in the East German version of socialism, and the implication is that not even the Stasi can believe that. They are looking for dissent and subversion because, in a way, they think a man like Dreyman *should* be guilty of them. Perhaps they do not believe in East Germany themselves but have simply chosen to play for the winning team.

Wiesler is a fascinating character. His face is a mask, trained by his life to reflect no emotion. Sometimes not even his eyes move. As played in Muehe's performance of infinite subtlety, he watches Dreyman as a cat awaits a mouse. And he begins to internalize their lives—easy, because he has no life of his own, no lover, no hobby, no distraction from his single-minded job.

Although the movie won the Academy Award for the best foreign-language film of 2006, you may not have seen it, so I will repress certain developments. I will say that Wiesler arrives at a choice, when his piggish superior officer, the government minister Bruno Hempf (Thomas Thieme), develops a lust for Christa-Maria and orders Wiesler to pin something, anything, on Dreyman so that his rival will be eliminated. But there is nothing to pin on him. A loyal spy must be true to his trade, and now Wiesler is asked to be false to prove his loyalty.

The thing is, Wiesler has no one he can really talk to. He lives in a world of such paranoia that the slightest slip can be disastrous. Consider a scene in the Stasi cafeteria when a young officer unwisely cracks an antigovernment joke; Wiesler goes through the motions of laughter and then coldly asks for the man's name. The same could happen to Wiesler. So as he proceeds through his crisis, he has no one to confide in, and there is no interior monologue to inform us of his thoughts. There is only that blank face, and the smallest indications of what he might be thinking. And then instinctive decisions that choose his course for him.

The Berlin Wall falls in 1989 (the event is seen here), and the story continues for a few more years to an ironic and surprisingly satisfactory conclusion. But the movie is relevant today, as our own government ignores habeas corpus, practices secret torture, and asks for the right to wiretap and eavesdrop on its citizens. Such tactics did not save East Germany; they destroyed it by making it a country its most loyal citizens could no longer believe in. Driven by the specter of aggression from without, it countered with aggression from within, as sort of an antitoxin. Fearing that its citizens were disloyal, it inspired them to be. True, its enemies were real. But the West never dropped the bomb, and East Germany and the other USSR republics imploded after essentially bombing themselves.

The Lives of Others is a powerful but quiet film, constructed of hidden thoughts and secret desires. It begins with Wiesler teaching a class in the theory and practice of interrogation; one chilling detail is that suspects are forced to sit on their hands so that the chair cushion can be saved for possible use by bloodhounds. It shows how the Wall finally fell, not with a bang, but because of whispers.

Note: In the movie, one lover is a government informer. In real life, the actor Muehe discovered that his own wife was a Stasi informant. ☞

Loggerheads ★ ★ ★

NO MPAA RATING, 93 m., 2005

Tess Harper (Elizabeth), Bonnie Hunt (Grace), Michael Kelly (George), Michael Learned

(Sheridan), Kip Pardue (Mark), Ann Owens Pierce (Ruth), Chris Sarandon (Robert), Valerie Watkins (Lola), Robin Weigert (Rachel). Directed by Tim Kirkman and produced by Gill Holland. Screenplay by Kirkman.

All of the characters in Tim Kirkman's *Loggerheads* are good people, by their own lights. The lights of some people allow them to be content, while the lights of others fill them with sadness and regret. Sometimes you can move from one group to another. Not always.

The story involves the years 1990 and 1991 and three areas of North Carolina: Asheville, Eden, and Kure Beach. The characters are dealing in one way or another with homosexuality and adoption. One of the characters provides a connecting link involving the others. That makes it sound like things are all figured out, but *Loggerheads* is not a movie where the emotions are tidy and the messages are clear. It is about people trying to deal with the situations they have landed in.

We meet a woman named Grace (Bonnie Hunt) who works behind a rental-car counter and has moved back to Asheville to live with her mother, Sheridan (Michael Learned). In Eden, we meet a pastor named Robert (Chris Sarandon) and his wife, Elizabeth (Tess Harper). On Kure Beach, George (Michael Kelly) runs a shabby motel, and Mark (Kip Pardue) sleeps on the beach and observes the nocturnal behavior of loggerhead turtles. Loggerheads always return to the place where they were born, and that is something not everyone in the movie finds it easy to do.

I want to go slow in describing the plot because its developments unfold according to the needs of the characters. The movie is not about springing surprises on us but about showing these people in a process of discovery. The performances are not pitched toward melodrama; the actors all find the right notes and rhythms for scenes in which life goes on and everything need not be solved in three lines of dialogue.

George and Mark, for example, sense easily that they are both gay but become more friends than lovers. The pastor and his wife had a son they have not seen since he was seventeen, and they observe that among their friends and neighbors, "nobody ever asks about him." Grace gave up a child for adoption when she was seventeen and now wants to find that child, but in North Carolina an "anonymous" adoption cannot be undone.

These characters are not extreme examples of their type. The pastor is not a religious extremist but has ordinary conservative values. Here's how that works: When a new family moves in across the street, Robert suggests to Elizabeth that she ask them to come to church on Sunday. Then she informs him, "There is no woman in that house," and she thinks they're a gay couple. "Should I invite them to church?" she asks. Her husband says, "Let's just wait and see if they come on their own."

Elizabeth is much distracted by her longtime neighbor Ruth (Ann Pierce), who has placed an anatomically complete reproduction of Michelangelo's *David* on her front lawn. "If it were the *Venus de Milo,*" Ruth says, "you wouldn't hear a peep out of anybody." Elizabeth suggests she put the statue in the backyard, so the neighbors won't have to look at it. "That's your solution to everything," Ruth says. "Move it to the backyard."

On Kure Beach, George gives Mark a room to stay in, and Mark thinks this may involve a "barter arrangement," but no, George is just doing him a favor. Unlike many gay men in movies, these two characters are not as concerned with sex as with their life choices; in different ways, both choose to live on the beach and are content to be far from the action. They talk about matters of life and death, George often seated comfortably, Mark usually standing or pacing, smoking.

In Asheville, Grace and Sheridan have issues going back to the day the mother insisted that her pregnant daughter give the baby up for adoption. "I was just trying to do what was best for everyone involved," she says in her defense. "I know you were," says Grace, and she does, however much she wanted to keep the baby and however empty the rest of her life has become.

Events now happen to these people that I will not describe. They bring some happiness, some sadness, some closure. It is Elizabeth, the pastor's wife, who moves most decisively to put her life in line with her feelings. Curiously, we are by no means sure that her husband, Robert, will not someday follow her in that direction.

These people are not robots programmed by

the requirements of the plot. They want to be happy, and they want to feel they are doing the right thing. One of the characters, in my opinion, does the wrong thing but thinks it's the right thing. Sad, but there you are. *Loggerheads* offers these hopes: that our understanding of happiness can encompass more possibilities as we grow older, and that to find that happiness, we will have to do what we decide is the right thing, and not what someone else has decided for us.

London ★

R, 92 m., 2006

Chris Evans (Syd), Jessica Biel (London), Jason Statham (Bateman), Joy Bryant (Mallory), Kelli Garner (Maya), Isla Fisher (Becca). Directed by Hunter Richards and produced by Paul Davis-Miller, Ash R. Shah, and Bonnie Timmermann. Screenplay by Richards.

At one point in *London,* a Japanese experiment is described. Scientists place containers of white rice in two rooms. One container is praised. Nice rice. Beautiful rice. The other container is insulted. Ugly rice. Bad rice. At the end of a month, the rice in the first container is fresh and fragrant. The rice in the other room is decayed and moldy. If there is any validity to this experiment, I expect *London* to start decaying any day now. Bad movie. Ugly movie.

Another experiment is described. Baby bunnies. They are removed from their mother. Every time one is killed, the mother's vital signs show a sudden spike. *London* was given birth by the writer and director Hunter Richards, and if there is anything to the bunny theory, he's going to get jumpy when the reviews of his movie appear. There may be perspiration and trembling. Maybe anxiety attacks.

The rice and bunny experiments are two of many topics discussed by Syd (Chris Evans) and Bateman (Jason Statham) as they pace the floor of an upstairs bathroom at a Manhattan party, inhaling untold amounts of cocaine. Syd also guzzles tequila from a bottle. He met Bateman in a bar and insisted the older man, a Brit, accompany him to the party. He needed someone along for moral support because it was a going-away party for his girlfriend, London (Jessica Biel), and Syd wasn't invited. After I got to know Syd, I was not surprised that he wasn't invited, and I was not surprised that she was going away.

Let's track back a little. When first we see Syd, he has just treated himself to cocaine and the remains of a beer, and passed out in his apartment. The phone rings, he learns about the party, uses the f-word for the first of, oh, several hundred times, and smashes up the place, including a big aquarium. Curious that when the aquarium shatters, there are no shots of desperate fish gasping on the floor. Maybe Nemo has already led them to freedom.

At the party, Syd and Bateman get relentlessly stoned while discussing the kinds of tiresome subjects that seem important in the middle of the night in a bar when two drunks are analyzing the meaning of it all. Bartenders have been known to drink in order to endure these conversations. They usually consist of the two drunks exchanging monologues. During the parts when sober people would be listening, drunks are waiting until they get to talk again. Syd and Bateman are powerless over dialogue and their scenarios have become unmanageable.

There are personal confessions. Syd relates his unhappy romance with London, and we get flashbacks of them fighting, loving, talking, weeping, and running through all the other exercises in Acting 101. Bateman was married once, but it didn't work out. What a surprise. Now he pays good money to have S&M mistresses humiliate him. He describes their procedures in clinical detail, and we get flashbacks of those, too. Ugly. Bad. Syd is amazed that Bateman pays two hundred dollars to be treated in such a way, although I am not sure if he is amazed that it is so much, or so little.

Occasionally one of the women from downstairs drifts into the bathroom. We meet Mallory (Joy Bryant) and Maya (Kelli Garner). Beautiful. Nice. They could do better. One of them says she heard Syd tried to commit suicide. That's a lie, says Syd, explaining a misunderstanding that occurred involving the drugs his dog takes for epilepsy. There is also a great deal of talk about God and faith, and whether Syd or Bateman feels the most pain. This discussion is theoretical, since neither one is feeling anything. "With all the drugs on the market, you'd think they'd have a pill to take the edge off of leaving a chick," Syd observes. Of course, he didn't leave her; she left him. But the treatment would probably be the same.

Evans and Statham have verbal facility and energy, which enables them to propel this dreck from one end of ninety-two minutes to the other, and the women in the movie are all perfectly adequate at playing bimbo cokeheads. I have seen all of these actors on better days in better movies, and I may have a novena said for them.

Two things mystify me. (1) How can you use that much cocaine and drink that much booze and remain standing and keep speaking, especially in the case of Syd, who was already stoned when he started? (2) Where is the camera? At least half of the movie is shot in the bathroom, which has a mirror along one wall. The mirror should be reflecting a camera, but I didn't see one. Well, of course, it's the job of the professionals to keep the camera hidden, and maybe cinematographer Jo Willems was trying to hide it in another movie.

Lonesome Jim ★ ★ ★

R, 91 m., 2006

Casey Affleck (Jim), Liv Tyler (Anika), Mary Kay Place (Sally), Seymour Cassel (Don), Kevin Corrigan (Tim), Jack Rovello (Ben), Mark Boone Junior (Evil), Rachel Strouse (Rachel), Sarah Strouse (Sarah). Directed by Steve Buscemi and produced by Jake Abraham, Buscemi, Galt Niederhoffer, Celine Rattray, and Gary Winick. Screenplay by James C. Strouse.

God loves you just the way you are, but he loves you too much to let you stay that way.

—Ashley to her husband in *Junebug*

There was a time when young men in fiction went to big cities, seeking victory. Now they return to small towns, escaping defeat. *Lonesome Jim* follows, for example, *Winter Passing, Elizabethtown,* and *Garden State.* These movies tell us the big city will crush you but your hometown is a center of depression, weirdness, and parents near to madness. It's risky even when you only visit, as in *Junebug.*

These movies are not bad; they range from good to great. But they dramatize a disintegration of native American optimism. You can't make it there, and you can't make it anywhere. Consider Lonesome Jim. He went to New York City to be a great writer, although his choice of role models sends up an ominous signal; the photos on the wall of his childhood bedroom, he explains, show victims of alcohol, drugs, or suicide, sometimes all three. He ought to have an alternative wall for modern writers who are successful and yet sane, such as Don DeLillo, Paul Theroux, Dave Eggers, Rohinton Mistry, and Eudora Welty.

But never mind. Jim returns home to Indiana, portrayed here as a sinkhole of failed dreams and nutty losers. This is unfair to Indiana; look what a cherished home the state made for the hero of *A History of Violence.* Perhaps Jim would find any state depressing, particularly in a film directed by Steve Buscemi, who is one of the best actors alive and a director of movies such as *Trees Lounge* and this one, in which the heroes are sad sacks. The sad sack Buscemi plays in *Trees Lounge* at least is fueled by resentment and anger and flashes of romantic optimism; Lonesome Jim is mired in the slough of despond. Played by Casey Affleck, he's in the same hole as his brother Tim (Kevin Corrigan), who never left home. One brother tells the other: "You're divorced, with a s— job in a lumberyard, and live with mom and dad. I'm a f—up, but you're a damn tragedy." Apart from the divorce, this could be either brother describing the other.

Jim moves in with Tim and their mom and dad (Mary Kay Place and Seymour Cassel). Dad is sour and jaundiced. Mom is implacably cheerful, which may be worse. She runs the lumber and ladder works, which her brother, called Evil (Mark Boone Junior), uses as a depot for drug deals. Tim and Jim discuss suicide. Tim runs his car into a tree, and although he survives, Jim has to take over his duties as the coach of a girls' basketball team that has not scored a single point in fourteen games. Not even Gene Hackman, in *Hoosiers,* could coach this team to victory. Luckily, Jim's brother's nurse is the sympathetic single mother Anika (Liv Tyler). It happens that Anika and Jim already know each other from a night of sudden sex.

In sad-sack movies there is often a helpful woman around to help the despairing heroes. In *Garden State* it was Natalie Portman, in *Elizabethtown,* Kirsten Dunst. Both were salvation angels, but Tyler has a gentle approach to this kind of role that is perfect for the tone of *Lonesome Jim.* Watch her eyes when he tells her, "There are so many fun and cheery people in the world. Don't you think you'd be better off with one of them?" She's a born nurse. Affleck finds a nice gradation in the way he allows his need for her to struggle with his fear for her.

Meanwhile, things go from worse to much worse for the family. Evil's schemes manage to get his sister arrested as a drug dealer, but look how optimistic she is when Jim visits her in prison. She enjoys talking to the other inmates, she says; arguably they're more entertaining than her family. God help her, the character played by Mary Kay Place could be Ashley from *Junebug,* grown up and with a family of her own.

The hero Buscemi played in *Trees Lounge* had even more desperate problems than Jim, but he at least dredged from his alcoholism the desire to survive. Lonesome Jim seems to embrace defeat. Having mastered the part about great writers being depressed and suicidal, he seems ready to retire without bothering to do the actual writing.

The movie is based on a screenplay by the Indiana writer James C. (Jim) Strouse. He has written a forlorn and poetic story, and Buscemi has made it into a movie about taking a deep breath and deciding to stop being a mope. The question is, can Jim accept the love of a woman like Anika? Can he allow himself to be happy? It's a close call for Jim, but it's his choice to make. You can actually be ecstatic living right there in Indiana. I know lots of people who are.

The Longest Yard ★ ★ ★

PG-13, 113 m., 2005

Adam Sandler (Paul "Wrecking" Crewe), Chris Rock (Caretaker), Burt Reynolds (Coach Nate Scarborough), James Cromwell (Warden Hazen), Walter Williamson (Errol Dandridge), Michael Irvin (Deacon Moss), Nelly (Earl Megget), Edward Bunker (Skitchy Rivers). Directed by Peter Segal and produced by Jack Giarraputo. Screenplay by Sheldon Turner, based on the story by Albert S. Ruddy and the screenplay by Tracy Keenan Wynn.

Before I left for the Cannes Film Festival, I saw *The Longest Yard,* and I did an advance taping of an episode of *Ebert & Roeper* on which I gave a muted thumbs-up to Roeper's scornful thumbs-down. I kinda liked it, in its goofy way. There was a dogged ridiculousness to the film that amused me, especially in the way Adam Sandler was cast as a star quarterback. Once you accept Sandler as a quarterback, you've opened up the backfield to the entire membership of the Screen Actors Guild.

Now I have seen twenty-five films at Cannes, most of them attempts at greatness, and I sit here staring at the computer screen and realizing with dread that the time has come for me to write a review justifying that vertical thumb, which is already on video and will go out to millions of TV viewers seeking guidance in their moviegoing.

I do not say that I was wrong about the film. I said what I sincerely believed at the time. I believed it as one might believe in a good cup of coffee; welcome while you are drinking it, even completely absorbing, but not much discussed three weeks later. Indeed, after my immersion in the films of Cannes, I can hardly bring myself to return to *The Longest Yard* at all, since it represents such a limited idea of what a movie can be and what movies are for.

Yet there are those whose entire lives as moviegoers are spent within the reassuring confines of such entertainments. In many cities and some states, there are few ways for them to get their eyes on movies that can feed their souls. They will have to be content with a movie in which Adam Sandler plays an alcoholic has-been football hero who gets drunk, drives dangerously, is thrown into jail, and becomes the pawn in a football game pitting a team of fellow prisoners against a team made up of prison guards. As I sit here, so help me God, I can't remember who got the idea for this game or why. I could look it up, but it's fascinating to watch myself trying to reconstruct a movie that was not intended to be remembered as long as it takes to get to the parking lot. This is how you learn. Through experience.

I recall that for some reason the big game is broadcast live on a sports network, maybe because the Sandler character was once a football hero and went down in flames over the drunk-driving scandal, and so there is a possibility of good ratings. His mentor is a former prisoner, played by Burt Reynolds, who starred in Robert Aldrich's original *The Longest Yard* (1974) and whose character this time is described in my notes as the Heisman Trophy winner of 1955. Assuming my notes are correct, he was about twenty-one when he won the trophy and now Reynolds is about seventy-one, although now that I have done the math I don't know where to go with it. Certainly he is older than Sandler and younger than God.

James Cromwell plays the warden. I have met him on industry occasions. He is a militant Screen Actors Guild spokesman and a fiercely intelligent man who takes roles like this for the same reason I review them, because we are professionals and this is what we do. He would rather be in better movies and I would rather review them, but we have both seen a lot worse than this. There is a sense in which attacking this movie is like kicking a dog for not being better at calculus.

You think you know where I am headed. I am going to admit that I was wrong. I am going to withdraw that upturned thumb even as its ghostly video image beams out across the nation. I will compare it to the shimmering authority of a hologram of Obi-Wan Kenobi, expressing wisdom that was true enough when the hologram was recorded, but may not be helpful by the time it is seen.

But no, I am not going to do that at all. When the show was recorded I said what I believed, and for my sins I am appending three stars to the top of this review. I often practice a generic approach to film criticism, in which the starting point for a review is the question of what a movie sets out to achieve. *The Longest Yard* more or less achieves what most of the people attending it will expect. Most of its audiences will be satisfied enough when they leave the theater, although few will feel compelled to rent it on video to share with their friends. So, yes, it's a fair example of what it is.

I would, however, be filled with remorse if I did not urge you to consider the underlying melancholy of this review and seek out a movie you could have an interesting conversation about. After twelve days at Cannes, I was reminded that movies can enrich our lives, instead of just helping us get through them.

It may be that your local multiplex is not showing any films that have, or will, or would qualify for Cannes. There is a studied unwillingness among the major distributors to rise very frequently above the lowest common denominator, except during Oscar season. But there are actually some very worthy films in national release. If *Kontroll* is playing in your town, for example, that would be an idea. Or *Brothers*, or *Dominion: Prequel to the Exorcist*, or *Layer Cake*, or *Unleashed*. These are not great films, you understand, but they exist in a world that knows what greatness is, and they urge themselves toward it. If you can get to *Crash*, that is the movie you must see, and you should immediately drop any thought of seeing anything else instead.

Note: I attended a press conference of the Cannes jury. Its president, Emir Kusturica, said at one point that Cannes "kills uniformity." Its films are made one at a time. "To be global," he said, "to make a film that plays everywhere, you have to be slightly stupid." How do you like that; the bastard went and spoiled The Longest Yard *for me.*

Look at Me ★ ★ ★ ½

PG-13, 100 m., 2005

Marilou Berry (Lolita Cassard), Jean-Pierre Bacri (Etienne Cassard), Agnes Jaoui (Sylvia Miller), Laurent Grevill (Pierre Miller), Virginie Desarnauts (Karine Cassard), Keine Bouhiza (Sebastien), Gregoire Oestermann (Vincent), Serge Riaboukine (Felix), Michele Moretti (Edith). Directed by Agnes Jaoui and produced by Jean-Philippe Andraca and Christian Berard. Screenplay by Jean-Pierre Bacri and Jaoui.

Here is a difference, small but not insignificant, between Hollywood and French films. Consider the inevitable scene where the child is performing onstage, and the theater door opens, and there is the parent who has denied the child's talent, but now nods and smiles and sees that the child is truly gifted after all.

Now turn to *Look at Me*, the unforgiving new French film about a chubby classical singer and her egotistical father. She rehearses stubbornly and has a beautiful voice. He is a famous writer and a snob, absorbed in the appreciation of himself. She gives a recital in an old church in the country, and the audience admires her singing. Does the father arrive late, his eyes filled with tears as he acknowledges her gifts? No, the father arrives on time but sneaks out to smoke and make cell calls.

People can be cruel out of ignorance or carelessness, but it takes a knack to be cruel as a strategy. Etienne Cassard (Jean-Pierre Bacri), the father, is a man full of himself. He has written great books, or at least people assure him they are great, and he is a publisher. People are wary of him and suck up to him.

Etienne has a gift for ignoring his twenty-year-old daughter, Lolita (Marilou Berry), perhaps because he doesn't think it helps his image to have her plumpness in view. He has a sleek, younger trophy wife named Karine (Virginie Desarnauts), whom he is happy to display, but he ignores her, puts her down, ridicules her, gently corrects her, doesn't listen to her.

Given this situation, you'd think you could anticipate the drift of the film, but no: It doesn't pity its characters just because they are badly treated. Lolita, for example, is suspicious and defensive. She has felt unpopular for so long that she's developed a paranoia that prevents her from trusting others. No, not even Sebastien (Keine Bouhiza), the boy who cares for her, attends to her, would like her if she were not so sure no one could possibly like her.

There is also the matter of Lolita's music teacher, Sylvia, played by Agnes Jaoui, who cowrote the movie with Bacri and directs it. Sylvia's teaching helps support her husband, Pierre (Laurent Grevill), a novelist who is stuck in obscurity. Does Sylvia's attitude toward Lolita change when she learns that the girl's father is a famous writer and publisher? A man who could help her Pierre? Lolita thinks it does, and is probably right. So Lolita uses her father as leverage with her teacher, and soon Etienne has seen to the publication of Pierre's book.

Now watch closely. Pierre's book is an enormous success. This (a) reflects well upon Etienne because he discovered Pierre and sponsored him, but (b) underlines the inconvenience that Etienne himself has published nothing much in recent years. Pierre meanwhile follows Etienne like a fawning dog, ignoring his wife because he's blinded by the famous people at Etienne's parties. Lolita observes all of this and detests it, and carefully nurtures her misery.

There are scenes in this movie of social cruelty beyond all compare. Etienne is capable of making his daughter think he is calling her attractive, and then correcting her: He was talking to the woman next to her. Whomever he's talking to on his cell phone is always more important than whomever he's talking to in person. At dinner, when the attention strays from him for long, Etienne's eyes narrow and his conversational knives are thrown.

This performance comes from an actor who was so vulnerable in the previous movie he made with Jaoui. That was *The Taste of Others* (2000), where he plays an unremarkable man who falls in love with an amateur actress and her circle in a local theater company. In that movie, he was essentially playing the Pierre character—the adoring dog. He goes from meekness to arrogance so convincingly he even seems to have a different face in the two films. Marilou Berry's performance is remarkable, too, in the defiant way she faces the world, and in the way she uses a miraculous voice that is not miracle enough for her.

The most sympathetic character is the one who would be the heavy in the Hollywood version: Karine, the young stepmother. She reaches out to Lolita even after being rejected. She wants to be the girl's friend. She puts up with the boorish behavior of her husband, and she tries to repair the wounds he causes to their friends. In some sense, the overbearing father and the resentful daughter have created each other; the stepmother is the innocent bystander. The thing about a movie like this is, the characters may be French, but they're more like people I know than they could ever be in the Hollywood remake.

Look Both Ways ★ ★ ★ ½

PG-13, 100 m., 2006

William McInnes (Nick), Justine Clarke (Meryl), Anthony Hayes (Andy), Lisa Flanagan (Anna), Andrew S. Gilbert (Phil), Daniella Farinacci (Julia), Sacha Horler (Linda), Maggie Dence (Joan), Edwin Hodgeman (Jim), Andreas Sobik (Train Driver). Directed by Sarah Watt and produced by Bridget Ikin. Screenplay by Watt.

Death is for the living, and not for the dead so much.

—Errol Morris's *Gates of Heaven*

It doesn't really matter if you look both ways. The piano may be falling from the sky. If we gave much thought to the possibility that we could die at any moment, we could hardly endure life. Sarah Watt's *Look Both Ways* tells the stories of several people who come close to death and deal with that experience. What choice do they have? The movie is not cheerful, nor is it morbid; it leaves us not encouraged but resolute.

Watt weaves together their stories, like *Crash* or perhaps even more like *Magnolia.* In Adelaide, Australia, a man is struck and killed by a train, and that event attracts a photographer named Nick (William McInnes), a reporter named Andy (Anthony Hayes), their editor Phil (Andrew S. Gilbert), and the victim's wife, Julia (Daniella Farinacci). Andy has a theory that many "accidents" are in fact suicides, and his examination of the death scene inspires an article speculating that the victim deliberately stepped in front of the train. Andy even stands on the tracks himself, as an experiment.

Nick takes a photograph of the wife, Julia, in anguish as she learns of her husband's death. Phil the editor runs the photo across half the front page, and Andy's speculations inside. These are not the acts of an editor much concerned with the feelings of the widow.

All the men have things on their minds. Nick has just learned that testicular cancer has spread throughout his body. Andy has learned that his girlfriend, Anna (Lisa Flanagan), is pregnant.

And then there is Meryl (Justine Clarke), a witness to the man's death. She is a painter of seascapes for sympathy cards, and she meets the photographer Nick on the scene. Their first meeting is casual, the next less so, and then to their surprise they are making love. The next day, Nick says he "isn't ready" for a relationship. "I meet you on the first day, we sleep together on the second, and on the third you're not ready," Meryl says. "That's a pretty tight schedule." They fight, they separate, and then they meet again and he tells her the truth.

With Andy and Anna, the pregnancy is a surprise. They hadn't seen each other in a month. "I've been incredibly busy," he says. Uh-huh. He doesn't want a kid. She points out that she didn't intend to get pregnant, and for that matter, "You were there, too." Will she get an abortion? On the other hand, will she stop smoking?

As the film considers these questions, the live action is interrupted from time to time by Meryl's violent fantasies in which a train roars off a bridge and crushes her, a monster attacks from the woods, and so on. To these animated visuals, which are abrupt and violent, the movie adds montages from the pasts of the characters, especially Nick; when he learns of his cancer, his life flashes before his eyes, somewhat prematurely.

This kind of description, of course, could apply to a bad movie as well as a good one. What distinguishes Sarah Watt's writing and direction is that she doesn't allow her characters to stand for anything other than themselves. They are confused, uncertain, imperfect, yearning, lonely, scared. They bumble in the direction of survival. And the movie enriches their lives with memories; Nick, for example, recalls his own father's death, which he sees much differently after he learns of his cancer. He is also very mildly impatient by the way people react to his news. When he uses the word "cancer," two of them say exactly the same thing: "*Cancer* cancer?" Is there any other kind?

It's pretty brutal, the way the newspaper treats the dead man's widow to all that coverage the next morning. But she receives a heartwarming visit from the engineer of the train. It's harsh the way a pregnancy forces Andy and Anna to decide what, exactly, is the reality of their relationship. There is cosmic irony involved in Nick and Meryl falling in love just when they have absolutely no future. After they kiss and make up, notice especially a montage of images used by Sarah Watt. In that montage are love and death and the whole damn thing.

I watched the movie in a kind of fascination. It is poetic and unforgiving, romantic and stark. Death is the subject we edge around. If it is on the sidewalk, we step into the street. If it is on the telephone, we hang up. We don't open its letters. To know that we will die is such a final and unanswerable rebuke. And yet without death we'd all be bored out of our minds, if indeed we had even developed minds in the first place. Sometimes I think the whole process of evolution leads up to our ability to comprehend the words: *Gather ye rosebuds while ye may.*

Looking for Comedy in the Muslim World ★ ★ ★
PG-13, 98 m., 2006

Albert Brooks (Albert Brooks), John Carroll Lynch (Stewart), Sheetal Sheth (Maya), Jon Tenney (Mark), Fred Dalton Thompson (Committee Chair). Directed by Albert Brooks and produced by Steve Bing, Herb Nanas, and Tabrez Noorani. Screenplay by Brooks.

Q: *Why is there no Halloween in India?*
A: *They took away the Gandhi.*

Ho, ho. Of course, if there is no Halloween in India, then they wouldn't know they didn't have one, so the joke would not be funny. In a country that does have Halloween, such as the United States, anyone young enough to find the joke funny (under eight, say) wouldn't know who Gandhi was.

So you see we're in a minefield here. Who knows what makes people laugh? In an opening scene of *Looking for Comedy in the Muslim World,* Albert Brooks is summoned to a secret State Department meeting. It's chaired by Fred Dalton Thompson, who was an actor before he was a senator, and now plays one in the movies. The president is concerned about reaching the world's Muslims, Thompson explains. He's tried wars and spying, the usual stuff, and now he thinks he might try humor. Brooks's assignment: Spend a month in India and Pakistan and write a five hundred–page report on what makes Muslims laugh.

That's the premise for a movie that might inspire a sequel titled *Searching for Comedy in the Albert Brooks World.* I mean that as a compliment. Brooks's movie has a lot of humor in it, but it's buried, oblique, throwaway, inside, apologetic, coded, and underplayed. Midway through the movie he does a free stand-up comedy show in New Delhi, and nobody laughs at anything. Rodney Dangerfield attacked sullen audiences aggressively: "Folks! Folks! There's a guy up here onstage, telling jokes!" Brooks is incapable of bluntness. He sidles up to his material and slinks away from it.

I recall that Brooks did once perform the material from his New Delhi concert on TV (references are made to the *Tonight* show and Ed Sullivan). It was funny then: the "improv" set where he changes all of the audience suggestions, and the skit about the incompetent ventriloquist. But everything he does bombs in Delhi. It would also bomb in America, because he performs as if it's not funny.

His concert is an experiment: see what the audience does and doesn't laugh at, and put it in his report. Of course, he has no idea how many people in the audience are Muslims; India has lots of them, but a lot more Hindus. And when he tries to go to Pakistan, it involves an illegal border crossing and a stand-up session before a bunch of would-be stand-up comics sitting around a campfire.

Brooks is aided in his survey by a local woman, Maya (Sheetal Sheth), who types 125 words a minute, is terrifically encouraging, and has a jealous Iranian boyfriend. He has a couple of minders from the State Department, the *Fine Woodworking* subscriber Stuart (John Carroll Lynch) and his partner, Mark (Jon Tenney), always carrying on a simultaneous conversation on a cell phone. They try the man-on-the-street approach, asking people what makes them laugh with about as much success as Jay Leno has asking people how many states there are.

The laughs tend to be hidden in the crevices. Brooks walks by offices every day, for example, filled with people who are answering the phone for big American corporations. There are two bigger laughs in the movie, one involving his dressing room for the stand-up show, the other involving his meeting with executives of the Al-jazeera network. And some medium laughs. And a lot of chuckles. And a stubborn unwillingness to force the laughs. Brooks has a persona that apologizes for everything, including being a persona. No matter how much you laugh, you get the feeling he wanted you to laugh less.

Because I have seen all of Brooks's movies, liked most of them, and loved some, I was in training for *Looking for Comedy in the Muslim World.* Veteran Brooks watchers will be able to hear the secret melodies and appreciate the way he throws away even the throwaways. It's also interesting how he *doesn't* take cheap shots at India or Pakistan. When a Muslim woman asks him, "Are you a Jew?" he's set up for a slam dunk, but he walks away from it. He acts not like a comic wiseguy but like a clueless citizen sent on a baffling State Department mission. Well, that's what he's playing.

I liked the movie. I smiled a lot. It maintained its tone in the face of bountiful temptations to get easy laughs. It never identifies a Muslim (or Hindu) sense of humor, but then again, Brooks never does anything funny, so maybe that's why. Of course they have a sense of humor in India, because the best-selling English-language novelist in the country is P G. Wodehouse. If you don't know who Wodehouse was, that's all right; you didn't know who Gandhi was, either. If you know who Gandhi was but still don't get the Halloween joke, that may have been because you were pronouncing "Gandhi" correctly.

Lord of War ★ ★ ★ ½

R, 122 m., 2005

Nicolas Cage (Yuri Orlov), Ethan Hawke (Jack Valentine), Jared Leto (Vitaly Orlov), Bridget Moynahan (Ava Fontaine), Ian Holm (Simeon Weisz), Sammi Rotibi (Baptiste Junior), Eamonn Walker (Baptiste Senior). Directed by Andrew Niccol and produced by Niccol, Philippe Rousselet, and Norman Golightly. Screenplay by Niccol.

Yuri Orlov argues that his products kill fewer people than tobacco and alcohol. He has a point, but it's more fun and takes longer to die that way. There are few pleasures to be had from an AK-47 bullet to the brain, and no time to enjoy them. Yuri is an international arms dealer who has "done business with every army but the Salvation Army." He cheerfully tours the world's flashpoints, a war-to-war salesman in a dark suit and tie.

Lord of War is a bleak comedy, funny in a *Catch-22* sort of way, and at the same time an angry outcry against the gun traffic that turns twelve-year-olds into killers and cheapens human life to the point where might makes not only right but everything else as well. Yuri is played by Nicolas Cage in another of those performances you cannot easily imagine anyone else doing; he plays an immigrant from Ukraine who has the cocky self-assurance, the snaky surface charm, the breezy intellectual justification for the most indefensible acts. He will sell to anyone, anytime, he tells us during his narration, which confides the secrets of his trade: He never sold to Osama bin Laden because, "He was always bouncing checks."

Yuri's world is a small one. He has few competitors and a short but frequently updated list of clients. The world's leading arms dealer when Yuri goes into business is Simeon Weisz (Ian Holm), who prefers not to do business with people he thinks are evil, although his definition of evil is extremely flexible. Yuri asks Simeon to let him team up, an offer Simeon rejects; he'll eventually lose a lot of business by that decision.

The clients come from all over. There is a moment in the film when Yuri gets some bad news: Peace talks have started in a particularly promising market. He shifts his focus to the Bosnian arena. When they say they're having a war, "they keep their word."

He also finds two good customers in Africa: the Liberian dictator Baptiste Senior (Eamonn Walker) and his son, Baptiste Junior (Sammi Rotibi). Senior is capable of shooting people dead without notice just in a fit of pique. During a meeting with Yuri, he kills an inattentive aide and seems ready to shoot Yuri next, but Yuri grabs the gun back and says, "Now you'll *have* to buy it because it's a used gun." It's the kind of joke that appeals to Senior. Yuri's life and even his fortune are saved.

Yuri lives in Manhattan luxury with the former model Ava Fontaine (Bridget Moynahan), who believes him, or pretends to believe him, when he says he's in the international shipping business. That business takes a turn for the better with the collapse of the Soviet Union and the sudden appearance on the black market of enormous caches of weapons. Luckily, Yuri is related to a now-retired general in Ukraine, and they do business.

The movie, written and directed by Andrew Niccol (*The Truman Show, Gattaca*), has some of the same stylistic aggressiveness as David O. Russell's *Three Kings*. Consider a brilliant early montage that takes a bullet's-eye view as it moves from ore to the assembly line to finishing, packaging, distribution, sale, and eventual use; the montage ends with the bullet passing through the brain of a young man. It makes the point that at every step along the way, arms manufacturers are producing death as their end product.

That doesn't much bother Yuri, who believes

that wars will be fought regardless of whether he sells arms. In that he is correct. There is the disagreement, however, of a stubborn Interpol agent named Valentine (Ethan Hawke), who thinks he could save some lives by putting Yuri out of business. Some of their encounters resemble the "Spy vs. Spy" feature in *Mad* magazine, as when Valentine chases a ship filled with arms, and Yuri is able to repaint its name and disguise it before the law gets close enough.

Helping Yuri at first, and then a distinct problem for him, is his younger brother Vitaly (Jared Leto). When they're desperately disguising the ship and need a Dutch flag they do not have, it is Vitaly's lateral thinking that suggests a French flag flown sideways looks like a Dutch flag.

After movies like *Hotel Rwanda, Before the Rain,* and *Welcome to Saravejo,* the cold cynicism of *Lord of War* plays like a deadly footnote. People are killed because guns are available; wars lower the average age of soldiers until in some places they are fought by children with no idea of their original cause. It's hypnotic, like the gaze of a poisonous snake, how Yuri stares into the face of this horror and counts his profits. Will fate and justice eventually catch up with him? Maybe, unless money is the answer. In Yuri's experience, it usually is.

Lords of Dogtown ★ ★

PG-13, 107 m., 2005

Emile Hirsch (Jay Adams), Victor Rasuk (Tony Alva), John Robinson (Stacy Peralta), Michael Angarano (Sid), Nikki Reed (Kathy Alva), Heath Ledger (Skip Engblom), Rebecca De Mornay (Philaine), Johnny Knoxville (Topper Burks). Directed by Catherine Hardwicke and produced by John Linson. Screenplay by Stacy Peralta.

In the summer of 1975, modern skateboarding was invented in the Santa Monica and Venice Beach areas of California. The young members of the Zephyr Team, sponsored by a permanently stoned surfboard store owner, revolutionized the sport, performing acrobatics and crazy stunts on skateboards that had until then been seen as fancy scooters. They became famous, they made a lot of money, they grew up, and one of them, Stacy Peralta, made a 2002 documentary about them named *Dogtown and Z-Boys.*

It was a good documentary. As I wrote at the time: "It answers a question I have long been curious about: How and why was the first skateboarder inspired to go aerial, to break contact with any surface and do acrobatics in midair? Consider that the pioneer was doing this for the very first time over a vertical drop of perhaps fifteen feet to a concrete surface. It's not the sort of thing you try out of idle curiosity."

Now we have *Lords of Dogtown,* a fiction film based on the very same material, and indeed, written by Peralta. Not only is there no need for this movie, but its weaknesses underline the strength of the doc. How and why Peralta found so much old footage of skateboarding in 1975 is a mystery, but he was able to give us a good sense of those kids at that time. Although Catherine Hardwicke, the director of *Lords of Dogtown,* has a good feeling for the period and does what she can with her actors, we've seen the originals, and these aren't the originals. Nobody in the fiction film pulls off stunts as spectacular as we see for real in the documentary.

The story line remains the same. The kids live in what was then one of the remaining beachfront slums, down the coast from the expensive Malibu area. The beach was ruled by surfers, but in the afternoon, when the waves died down, some of the surfers, or their younger brothers, fooled around on skateboards. One day, Skip Engblom, the shop owner, comes up with a key breakthrough, polyurethane wheels: "They grip." With the additional traction, the Z-Boys try skating the sides of the big open drainage canal that runs through the area. Then comes a brainstorm: Because of a drought, the area's swimming pools were drained. They started "borrowing" pools when the owners weren't home, to skate the curved sides.

Emile Hirsch stars as Jay Adams, Victor Rasuk is Tony Alva, and John Robinson, with long blond hair that gets him photographed a lot in the emerging skateboarding magazines, plays Stacy Peralta. They all seem like pale imitations of the originals, as indeed they must be. Heath Ledger plays Skip, their mentor, who sponsors the Zephyr Team, gives them their first priceless T-shirts, and eventually, stoned and drunk, ends up making surfboards in somebody else's back room. But he was the catalyst.

In the documentary, there was a Z-Girl along with the Z-Boys, but here all we get is Nikki Reed as Kathy, Tony's sister. We also meet Rebecca De Mornay, as Jay's mother, who, like all mothers in Southern California films, looks like she oughta be in pictures. Both the surfing and skateboarding sequences are fun to watch, within reason, but after seeing *Dogtown and Z-Boys* and the haunting surfing documentary *Riding Giants* (2004), we know the real thing is more awesome. The best surfing scenes take place when surfers ride waves dangerously close to the Pacific Island Pier and the rocks at its base; the pier mysteriously burns down that summer. "They wanted it gone," Skip mourns.

Skateboarding is a sport combining grace, courage, and skill, and here we see it being born. What we do not quite understand is how long one can be a skateboarder before you feel like you've been there and done that. Stacy Peralta obviously feels great nostalgia for that period in his life, which was the foundation for fame and fortune, but at this point it is time for him to either (a) move on to films about something else, or (b) deal with the dark aftermath of those golden days.

There were a lot of drugs around; although we see Skip here as a survivor, he's more of a victim. And like the earlier movie, this one doesn't really deal with injuries or accidents. In a sport where you can free fall to concrete, were there deaths? Was anyone paralyzed? There's a touching scene here where the kids take a friend in a wheelchair into one of the empty swimming pools and let him ride the sides a little, but he's in the chair because of cancer, not skateboarding.

The Lost City ★ ★ ★

R, 143 m., 2006

Andy Garcia (Fico Fellove), Bill Murray (The Writer), Ines Sastre (Aurora Fellove), Lorena Feijoo (Leonela), Tomas Milian (Don Federico Fellove), Elizabeth Pena (Miliciana Munoz), Dustin Hoffman (Meyer Lansky), Millie Perkins (Dona Cecilia Fellove), Enrique Murciano (Ricardo Fellove), Nestor Carbonell (Luis Fellove), Richard Bradford (Don Donoso Fellove). Directed by Andy Garcia and produced by Frank Mancuso Jr. and Garcia. Screenplay by Guillermo Cabrera Infante.

Andy Garcia's *The Lost City* feels like the distillation of countless conversations and family legends, rehearsed from time immemorial by Cubans who fled their homeland and sought to re-create it in their memories. In every family such stories, repeated endlessly, can become tedious, but there is another sense in which they are a treasured ritual. There was a Cuba, remembered firsthand only by those who are growing older now, that was a beloved place and stopped existing when Castro came to power in 1959.

Garcia's family lived in that older Cuba, and so did Guillermo Cabera Infante, the Cuban writer and film critic who wrote this screenplay. (The project, long discussed, was not easy for Garcia to finance; Infante died in February 2005.) Infante and Garcia do not deceive themselves that the old Cuba was a paradise: It is seen as corrupt, controlled in key areas by the Mafia, and built on a class system in which many were poor so that a few could be rich. The problem is that Castro did not cure the ills so much as distribute them more evenly, so that more could be miserable. Garcia and Infante are against the old and the new, against both the rotten Batista regime and the disappointment of Castro and Che Guevara. There is a moment in the film when a senator agrees that Batista must be overthrown but argues wistfully that it must be done "constitutionally." Fat chance.

Garcia stars in the film as Fico Fellove, a suave operator who owns and runs a Havana nightclub named El Tropico. Showgirls perform a Vegas-style revue, the customers are elegant and intriguing, and at the door their big, sleek American cars glisten in the neon lights. Fico wants this life to continue forever, and like Rick in *Casablanca*, he is not particularly political. At a time when Batista's grip seems to be weakening, when reports from the mountains magnify Castro's popularity, he receives a visitor: the gangster Meyer Lansky (Dustin Hoffman), who wants to become Fico's partner in turning El Tropico into a casino. It is the kind of offer Fico can refuse, although that might not be prudent.

Fico's brothers have a different orientation in

the dying days of the old regime. Luis (Nestor Carbonell) embraces the revolutionary cause, and Ricardo (Enrique Murciano) journeys into the mountains to fight with the rebels. The rest of the family deplores their decisions; Fico comforts Aurora (Ines Sastre), Luis's wife, who complains that her husband is away so much he must be cheating. He is not cheating but rebelling, but never mind: Fico ends by falling in love with her himself.

Commenting on all of these events is an enigmatic character named The Writer, played by Bill Murray as a jester who speaks in jokes that contain the truth. His running commentary on Meyer Lansky is bold to the point of recklessness. It is never quite explained who The Writer is, although some articles on the film claim he represents the screenwriter, Infante.

If so, he gives Infante an opening into the story that he can use to speak directly, if obliquely, of the absurdity of the times. Indeed, Infante himself played such a role under both Batista and Castro, saying what he believed in such a way that no one could be quite certain he had gone too far. Batista nevertheless jailed him, and Castro uneasily made him a cultural attaché in Belgium, not then a key posting. A lifelong communist, Infante felt Castro betrayed the party's principles, and he eventually chose exile. His *Twentieth Century Job,* a collection of his movie reviews, has some of the same wry, dubious philosophy expressed by The Writer in the film.

I enjoyed Murray and his scenes, but the character doesn't fit with the rest of the film. Fico Fellove is not a particularly witty or sunny character and does not suffer fools gladly. Why does he make an exception for The Writer? There are scenes where we almost wonder if The Writer is intended to be physically present at all; for all that Fico takes notice of him, perhaps he is a ghost visible only to us.

The main line of *The Lost City* involves the fall of Batista, Castro's entry into Havana, the divisions that open up in the family, and the quick disillusionment with the new regime, which is as arbitrary as the old, and more dogmatic. A musicians' union dispute at the nightclub symbolizes the way power is misused by those who have only just possessed it. Fico's loss is magnified by the heartbreak of the old musician who choreographed the shows and danced as a counterpoint to the girls; he has lost his whole world.

The movie evokes that long-ago world carefully and with a certain poetry; it was shot in the Dominican Republic. There is a lot of music, much of it from the period and performed by the same musicians or their successors. The costumes and the interiors set off the way the characters carry themselves, with grace and confidence.

At 143 minutes, the movie is too long, but it has a lot to cover and a lot to say, and I imagine Garcia has a reason why every scene is necessary. There is romance and some action, but it is not a romance or an adventure film; it is a personal version of what happened in Cuba and what it felt like at the time. Communicating that effectively, it lacks a larger view; newsreel footage covers historical events that another film might have tried to stage, and the implication is that for characters like Fico, the revolution took place more in the news than in his own life, and he was not quite prepared for such an upheaval. At the end he and a great many others leave Cuba for Miami or New York, where, for Fico, Meyer Lansky awaits.

A Lot Like Love ★

PG-13, 95 m., 2005

Ashton Kutcher (Oliver), Amanda Peet (Emily), Kathryn Hahn (Michelle), Kal Penn (Jeeter), Ali Larter (Gina), Taryn Manning (Ellen), Gabriel Mann (Peter), Jeremy Sisto (Ben). Directed by Nigel Cole and produced by Armyan Bernstein and Kevin J. Messick. Screenplay by Colin Patrick Lynch.

A Lot Like Love is a romance between two of the dimmer bulbs of their generation. Judging by their dialogue, Oliver and Emily have never read a book or a newspaper, seen a movie, watched TV, had an idea, carried on an interesting conversation, or ever thought much about anything. The movie thinks they are cute and funny, which is embarrassing, like your uncle who won't stop with the golf jokes. This is not the fault of the stars, Ashton Kutcher and Amanda Peet, who are actors forced to walk around in Stupid Suits.

When I was at Boulder for a conference at the University of Colorado, I found myself walking across campus with a kid who confessed he was studying philosophy.

"What do you plan to do with it?" I asked.

He said he wasn't sure. All of his friends were on career tracks, but "I dunno. I just find this stuff interesting."

Yes! I said. Yes! Don't treat education as if it's only a trade school. Take some electives just because they're interesting. You have long years to get through, and you must guard against the possibility of becoming a bore to yourself.

A Lot Like Love, written by Colin Patrick Lynch and directed by Nigel Cole, is about two people who have arrived at adulthood unequipped for the struggle. The lives of Oliver and Emily are Idiot Plots, in which every misunderstanding could be solved by a single word they are vigilant never to utter. They Meet Cute, over and over again. They keep finding themselves alone because their lovers keep walking out on them. Well, no wonder. "I'm going," one of her lovers says, and goes. Any more of an explanation and she might have had to take notes.

He has an Internet start-up selling diapers over the Web. She's dumped by a rock musician in the opening scene, where she seems to be a tough Goth chick, but that's just the costume. Later Ollie gives her a camera and she becomes a photographer, and even has a gallery exhibit of her works, which look like photos taken on vacation with cell phone cameras and e-mailed to you by the children of friends.

The movie is ninety-five minutes long, and neither character says a single memorable thing. You've heard of being too clever by half? Ollie and Emily are not clever enough by three-quarters. During a dinner date they start spitting water at each other. Then she crawls under the table, not for what you're thinking, but so they can trade sides and spit in the opposite direction. Then it seems like she's choking on her food, but he refuses to give her the Heimlich maneuver, and even tells the waitress not to bother. So take a guess: Is she really choking, or not? If she's playing a trick, she's a doofus, and if she isn't, he's a doofus. They shouldn't be allowed to leave the house without a parent or adult guardian.

They continue to Meet Cute over many long years, which are spelled out in titles: "Three Years Later," "Six Months Later," and so on. I was reminded of the little blue thermometers telling you the software will finish downloading in nineteen hours. Their first Meet Cute is a doozy: On a flight to New York, she enlists him in the Mile-High Club before they even know each other's names. But that's Strike One against him, she says, because she had to make the first move. Yeah, like a guy on an airplane should push into the rest room for sex with a woman he doesn't know. That's how you get to wear the little plastic cuffs.

Later they Meet Cute again, walk into a bar, drink four shots of Jack Daniels in one minute, and order a pitcher of beer. No, they're not alcoholics. This is just Movie Behavior; for example, at first she smokes and then she stops and then she starts again. That supplies her with a Personality Characteristic. Still later, they sing together, surprisingly badly. The movie is filled with a lot of other pop music. These songs tend toward plaintive dirges complaining, "My life can be described by this stupid song." At one point he flies to New York to pitch his dot-com diapers to some venture capitalists and is so inarticulate and clueless he could be a character in this movie. To call the movie dead in the water is an insult to water.

The Love Guru ★

PG-13, 87 m., 2008

Mike Myers (Guru Pitka), Jessica Alba (Jane Bullard), Justin Timberlake (Jacques Grande), Romany Malco (Darren Roanoke), Meagan Good (Prudence), Omid Djalili (Guru Satchabigknoba), Ben Kingsley (Guru Tugginmypuddha), Verne Troyer (Cherkov). Directed by Marco Schnabel and produced by Michael De Luca and Mike Myers. Screenplay by Myers and Graham Gordy.

What is it with Mike Myers and penis jokes? Having created a classic funny scene with his not-quite-visible penis sketch in the first Austin Powers movie, he now assembles, in *The Love Guru,* as many more penis jokes as he can think of, none of them funny except for one based on an off-screen *thump.* He supplements this subject with countless other awful moments involving defecation and the deafening passing of gas. Oh, and elephant sex.

The plot involves an American child who is raised in an Indian ashram (never mind why) and becomes the childhood friend of Deepak Chopra. Both come to America, where Chopra becomes a celebrity, but Guru Pitka (Myers) seems doomed to anonymity. That's until Jane Bullard (Jessica Alba), owner of the Toronto Maple Leafs, hires him to reconcile her star player, Darren Roanoke (Romany Malco), with his estranged wife, Prudence (Meagan Good). Just at the time of the Stanley Cup play-offs, Prudence has left her husband for the arms and other attributes of star Los Angeles player Jacques "Le Coq" Grande (Justin Timberlake), said to have the largest whatjamacallit in existence.

And what *don't* they call it in *The Love Guru*? The movie not only violates the Law of Funny Names (usually not funny), but rips it from the Little Movie Glossary and tramples it into the ice. Yes, many scenes are filmed at the Stanley Cup finals, where we see much of the Maple Leafs' dwarf coach (Verne Troyer), also the butt of size jokes (you will remember him as Mini-Me in the Powers films). There is also a running gag involving the play-by-play commentators and occasional flashbacks to the guru's childhood in India, where he studied under Guru Tugginmypuddha (Ben Kingsley). One of the guru's martial arts involves fencing with urine-soaked mops. Uh-huh.

Myers, a Canadian, incorporates some Canadian in-jokes; the team owner's name, Bullard, evokes the Ballard family of Maple Leaf fame. At the center of all of this is Guru Pitka, desperately trying to get himself on *Oprah* and finding acronyms in some of the most unlikely words. He has a strange manner of delivering punch lines directly into the camera and then laughing at them—usually, I must report, alone.

Myers is a nice man and has made some funny movies, but this film could have been written on toilet walls by callow adolescents. Every reference to a human sex organ or process of defecation is not automatically funny simply because it is naughty, but Myers seems to labor under that delusion. He acts as if he's getting away with something, but in fact all he's getting away with is selling tickets to a dreary experience. There's a moment of invention near the beginning of the film (his flying cushion has a back-up beeper), and then it's all into the Dumpster. Even his fellow actors seem to realize no one is laughing. That's impossible because they can't hear the audience, but it looks uncannily like they can, and do.

Love in the Time of Cholera ★ ½

R, 138 m., 2007

Javier Bardem (Florentino Ariza), Giovanna Mezzogiorno (Fermina Daza), Benjamin Bratt (Dr. Juvenal Urbino), Catalina Sandino Moreno (Hildebranda Sanchez), Hector Elizondo (Don Leo), Liev Schreiber (Lotario Thurgot), Fernanda Montenegro (Transito Ariza), Laura Harring (Sara Noriega), John Leguizamo (Lorenzo Daza). Directed by Mike Newell and produced by Scott Steindorff. Screenplay by Ronald Harwood, based on the novel by Gabriel García Márquez.

Small wonder that *One Hundred Years of Solitude,* Gabriel García Márquez's best novel, has never been filmed. Watching *Love in the Time of Cholera,* based on another of his great works, made me wonder if he is even translatable into cinema. Gabo's work may really live only there on the page, with his lighthearted badinage between the erotic and the absurd, the tragic and the magical. If you extract the story without the language, you are left with dust and bones but no beating heart.

Consider the story of *Love in the Time of Cholera.* A young man named Florentino (Javier Bardem) is struck by the thunderbolt of love when he first regards Fermina (Giovanna Mezzogiorno). Guarded by her fiercely watchful father (John Leguizamo), she finds ways to accept Florentino's love letters and his love, but when her father discovers what is going on, he ships her far away. Young love cannot survive forever at a distance, and Fermina, half-convinced by her father's ferocity that Florentino is beneath her, marries a successful man, a doctor named Juvenal Urbino (Benjamin Bratt). He is not a bad man, this doctor, and their marriage is not unhappy, and if Juvenal has a wandering eye, well, so did many men in South America of 150 years ago.

Florentino remains faithful to his first love, in spirit, if not in flesh. He makes love with many women, but he never loves them. That part of his heart is reserved forever for Fermina. Fifty years pass, the doctor dies, Florentino reappears to announce that his love is strong as ever, she wallops him, then she accepts him, and the decades are erased in their eyes, although not from their faces.

This is, perhaps, not a profound or classic story. Is it tragedy or soap opera? Ah, that's where Gabriel García Márquez has us. It is both, at the same time, and sad and funny, and there is foolishness in it, and drollery, and his prose dances over the contradictions. The British scandal rag *News of the World* (fondly known as *Screws of the World*) used to have a motto, "All human life is here," but it better applies to Gabo. He is said to have popularized the uniquely South American style of magic realism, but when I read him I feel no realism, only magic.

Now his delicate fantasy has been made concrete in this film. Characters who live in our imaginations have been assigned to actors, and places that exist in dreams have been assigned to locations. Yes, I know that's what all movies do with all stories, and most of the time it works. But not this time. I don't know when, watching a movie, I have been more constantly aware of the actors who were playing the roles. That's not a criticism but an observation.

Take, for example, Javier Bardem, because he is such a good actor. In *No Country for Old Men,* I completely lost sight of him in the character of the murderous Anton Chigurh. Now Chigurh is an absurd monstrosity, not really believable in any sense, but he *works* in the movie. Florentino Ariza is supposed to be believable, and in the book we care for him, but in the movie, why, that's Javier Bardem! And when he is an old man, why, that's Javier Bardem with all that makeup! Gene Siskel used to describe old-age makeup as making young actors look like turtles. The problem is not with bad old-age makeup, but with the impossibility of old-age makeup. Twenty or thirty years, yes, and then you're pushing it. Better take the solution of *The Notebook* and have two characters played by Rachel McAdams and Ryan Gosling when young, Gena Rowlands and James Garner when old. That way everyone can relax.

There is another problem with the movie, and it has to do with Mike Newell's direction. He is too bread-and-butter here. The story requires light footwork, a kind of dancing over the ice before it cracks, and Newell strides steadily onward. It does not matter much that the events all unfold right on time; they should seem to unfold themselves and be surprised that they have. Nothing should seem preordained, not even when Gabo uses leaps back and forth through time to let you know perfectly well what is coming. Good lord, you should think, it came to pass exactly as he said it would! Instead, you think, now her husband is going to die, and Florentino will reappear, and . . .

I'm wondering, as I started by saying, if what makes García Márquez so great a writer is his work's insistence on being read, not seen. The last internationally released film adaptation of his work, Arturo Ripstein's *No One Writes to the Colonel* (1999), played at Sundance and folded; the only country where it opened theatrically was Spain. Ruy Guerra's *Erendira* (1983) also barely opened. For an author whose *Solitude* has sold more than sixty million copies, that's not much of a record; some short stories have also been filmed, to little notice. I am told by the critic Jeff Schwager that Gabo himself has written the stories and screenplays for many Spanish-language films (IMDb lists thirty-eight!), but as none of them have leaped the language barrier with much ease, I wonder how successful they were.

Is there another great modern writer so hard to translate successfully into cinema? Saul Bellow? Again, it's all in the language. The only thing Saul and Gabo have in common is the Nobel Prize. Now that's interesting.

A Love Song for Bobby Long ★ ★ ★

R, 119 m., 2005

John Travolta (Bobby Long), Scarlett Johansson (Pursy Will), Gabriel Macht (Lawson Pines), Deborah Kara Unger (Georgianna), Dane Rhodes (Cecil), David Jensen (Junior), Clayne Crawford (Lee), Sonny Shroyer (Earl). Directed by Shainee Gabel and produced by Gabel, David Lancaster, R. Paul Miller, and Bob Yari. Screenplay by Gabel, based on the novel *Off Magazine Street* by Ronald Everett Capps.

There is a lazy, seductive appeal to the lives of the two boozers in *A Love Song for Bobby Long.* The notion of moving to New Orleans and drinking yourself to death is the sort of escape plan only an alcoholic could come up with, involving the principle of surrender to the enemy. If you are a writer and a failed English professor like Bobby Long, you can even wrap yourself in the legend of other literary drunks. It's all wonderfully romantic, especially in the movies, where a little groaning in the morning replaces nausea, headaches, killer hangovers, and panic attacks. A realistic portrait of suicidal drinking would contain more terror and confusion, but never mind. *Leaving Las Vegas* did that, and this is a different movie.

Bobby Long is played by John Travolta like a living demonstration of one of those artist's conceptions of what Elvis would look like at seventy. White-haired, unshaven, probably smelly, he lives on Magazine Street in the Quarter with a former student named Lawson Pines (Gabriel Macht), who thinks he is a genius. Years ago, Bobby was a legend on campus, Lawson's charismatic mentor. Then something happened, which we are pretty sure we will find out about, and here he is without wife or family, living on the sofa surrounded by piles of books.

He and Lawson spend a lot of time quoting literature to each other. Ben Franklin, Charles Dickens, the usual twentieth-century gods. This is entertaining all by itself, apart from the good it does for the characters. It reminded me of Alan Bennett's play, *The History Boys,* in which memorizing literary quotations is recommended as a means of fertilizing the mind. Bobby and Lawson are well fertilized but too disorganized to plant anything; an unfinished novel and a would-be memoir languish in the shadows. In *Sideways,* when Miles (Paul Giamatti) says he can't commit suicide because he has a responsibility to his unpublished novel, his buddy Jack (Thomas Haden Church) helpfully points out that the New Orleans legend John Kennedy Toole killed himself before *A Confederacy of Dunces* was published. So there is a precedent.

Bobby and Lawson seem prepared to keep on drinking and quoting and smoking forever, when a sudden change occurs in their lives. Their housemate, a jazz singer named Lorraine, has died. Now her daughter, Pursy (Scarlett Johansson), materializes, too late for the funeral. Pursy is a discontented and suspicious eighteen-year-old, who will soon prove to be the most mature member of the household. The boys tell Pursy her mother left her a third of the house, which is sort of true; actually, her mother left Pursy all of the house, but information like that could only confuse Pursy about the right of Bobby and Lawson to continue living there forever.

Pursy moves in, creating a form of family in which she is both the child and the adult, and Bobby and Lawson drift in between. At one point Lawson's halfway girlfriend Georgianna (Deborah Kara Unger) asks, "They know you're not going to school?" Pursy: "Yeah, it ranks right up there with being out of vodka and cigarettes."

The revelations in *A Love Song for Bobby Long* are not too hard to spot coming. There are only a few fictional developments that seem possible, and it turns out that they are. The movie is not about plot anyway, but about characters and a way of living. Pursy acts as a catalyst to create moments of truth and revelation, and those in turn help Bobby find a limited kind of peace with his past, and Lawson to find a tentative hope in his own possible future.

What can be said is that the three actors inhabit this material with ease and gratitude: It is good to act on a simmer sometimes, instead of at a fast boil. It's unusual to find an American movie that takes its time. It's remarkable to listen to dialogue that assumes the audience is well read. It is refreshing to hear literate conversation.

These are modest pleasures, but real enough. The movie tries for tragedy and reaches only pathos, but then Bobby lost his chance to be a tragic hero by living this long in the first place. Travolta has an innate likability quotient that works with characters like this; you can sense why a student would follow him to New Orleans and join him in foggy melancholy. There doesn't have to be a scene explaining that. You can also sense how Pursy would change things, just by acting as a witness. Alcoholics get uncomfortable when they're surrounded by people with insights. They like to control the times and conditions of their performances, and don't want an audience to wander backstage. Just by seeing them, Pursy forces them to see themselves. Once they do that, something has to give.

Lucky Number Slevin ★ ★

R, 109 m., 2006

Josh Hartnett (Slevin), Morgan Freeman (The Boss), Ben Kingsley (The Rabbi), Lucy Liu (Lindsey), Stanley Tucci (Brikowski), Bruce Willis (Mr. Goodkat). Directed by Paul McGuigan and produced by Christopher Eberts, Andreas Grosch, Kia Jam, Robert Kravis, Tyler Mitchell, Anthony Rhulen, and Chris Roberts. Screenplay by Jason Smilovic.

Lucky Number Slevin is too clever by half. It's the worst kind of con: It tells us it's a con, so we don't even have the consolation of being led down the garden path. The rug of reality is jerked out from under us in the opening scenes, and before long the floor is being dismantled. Crouched in the dark, I am resentful. Since the plot is irrelevant and the dialogue too mannered to be taken seriously, all I'm left with are the performances and the production design.

The performances, to be sure, are juicy. A team of A-list actors do their specialty numbers, and it's fun to see pros at work. The movie begins with a man in a wheelchair (Bruce Willis) telling an inexplicable story to a stranger in an airport lounge—an empty lounge, which immediately labels the scene as dubious at best, fantasy at worst. The story involves a fixed horse race, and there is mention of the Kansas City Shuffle. It is not clear exactly what the Kansas City Shuffle is, but Willis observes that you can't have one without a body. This is not what you want to hear from a stranger in an empty airport lobby.

Cut to Josh Hartnett, playing Slevin, arriving at the New York apartment of his friend Nick and being mistaken for Nick by hired goons working for The Boss (Morgan Freeman). The Boss, played by Freeman with his usual suave charm, tells Slevin (or Nick) he owes a lot of money but the debt can be forgotten if he will kill the son of The Boss's rival crime kingpin, The Rabbi (Ben Kingsley). In no time at all, Slevin/Nick is hauled by an alternative set of goons before The Rabbi, who makes him an alternative offer he can't refuse.

The Rabbi and The Boss occupy Manhattan penthouses that face each other, and at times they stalk their terraces, fiercely glaring across the street. I was reminded of *The Singing Kid* (1936), in which Al Jolson and Cab Calloway occupy facing penthouses and perform a duet from their balconies. Even in a crime movie as peculiar as *Lucky Number Slevin,* a duet between Freeman and Kingsley would be too much to hope for.

Willis meanwhile resurfaces as Mr. Goodkat, a gun for hire who, as nearly as we can tell, is not currently hired. There's also the cop Brikowski (Stanley Tucci), who seems about to do something at any moment. Much more intriguing is Lindsey (Lucy Liu), who introduces herself to Slevin as his friend Nick's neighbor and moves into his life. She works in the coroner's office, which may mean she will be seeing a lot more of Slevin.

Mannered put-ons like this raise the hairs on the back of my neck. They think they're more clever than I am, and they may be right, but that doesn't make me like them. One of the redeeming graces of *Brick,* which opened the same weekend, is that although it stars modern teenagers who talk and act as if they're in a 1940s film noir, it plays it straight: As far as the movie is concerned, they really do talk and act that way, and the plot is treated as sincerely as if Bogart were starring in it.

Lucky Number Slevin, on the other hand, goes to some pains to make it clear it is only an exercise in style. Here we are, looking at a crime mystery involving warring hoodlums and beautiful neighbors and a confused guy from out of town and a gunman and a cop, and the movie knows we're deluded and they're all just conceits. It's smarter than we are. Well, it must be, because it got us to watch it.

Do I rule out all trickery in movies? Of course not. I was happy to be fooled by *The Sixth Sense,* but that's because I *was* fooled. I had problems with *The Usual Suspects,* but at least I didn't see the last scene coming. When a movie makes it clear that its characters are going through a charade for the amusement of the director (and when the characters themselves make it clear they all but know they are actors in a movie), I get restless: They're having such a good time with each other, why do they need me? Then when there's a level of trickery even beyond the apparent foolery—reader, I feel like they're yanking my chain.

Lust, Caution ★ ★ ★

NC-17, 158 m., 2007

Tony Leung (Mr. Yee), Joan Chen (Mrs. Yee), Tang Wei (Wong Chia Chi [Mrs. Mak]), Chu Tsz-ying (Lai), Wang Leehom (Kuang Yu Min), Anupam Kher (Indian Jeweler). Directed by Ang Lee and produced by William Kong and Lee. Screenplay by James Schamus and Wang Hiu Ling.

Ang Lee's *Lust, Caution* is first languid, then passionate, as it tells the story of a young woman who joins a political murder plot and then becomes emotionally involved with her enemy. It begins at a 1942 mah-jongg game in Hong Kong, when erotic undertones become clearly audible to us, and then flashes back to Shanghai, 1938, during the Japanese occupation of China. One of the rich ladies at the game table is revealed to have been a college student and not really the wife of a wealthy (but unseen) tycoon.

The underlying plot gradually reveals itself. Too gradually, some will believe, unless the languor is necessary to create the hothouse atmosphere that survives in the midst of war. The mah-jongg game is taking place in the home of Mr. Yee (Tony Leung), whose wife (Joan Chen) is the hostess. Since coming from Shanghai, he has moved up in the collaborationist government, handles interrogations and tortures, and is repaid by status and access to such restricted items as nylon stockings, cigarettes, even diamonds. When Mr. Yee comes home in the middle of the game, he exchanges a significant look with Mrs. Mak (Tang Wei), who first joined the circle in Shanghai.

It's clear to us there's something secret and intimate between them. But who is this wealthy Mrs. Mak, who travels in a chauffeured car but whose husband is always away on business? The flashback reveals her as Wong Chia Chi, a young student who on summer vacation falls in with a group of radical Chinese patriots and takes a key role in their hope of assassinating one of the Chinese who are working with the Japanese. Her assignment: become Mr. Yee's lover.

This she did in Shanghai, but the war separated them before she was able to bring about an opportunity for Yee's murder (she is not expected to do it herself). A natural actress, she took easily to the roles of lover and rich woman. But she had some difficulty in sacrificing her virginity, which was necessary for her to convincingly play a married woman.

We do not see Mr. Yee at work, torturing his countrymen, but Leung is able to project the man's capability for menace and begins to do that in bed with her. Then commence the scenes that earned the film its NC-17 rating. They are not specifically hard-core in detail, but involve so many arcane and athletic sexual positions that the MPAA's injunction against the depiction of "thrusting" is left with their clothes on the floor.

When their sex drifts steadily into S&M, the nature of their relationship shifts. It is impossible to say that Wong Chia Chi/Mrs. Mak *likes* his tastes in pain and bondage, but they create a fearful intimacy that, for both of them, transcends their lives apart. And it is that tension, between private fascination and public danger, that gives the movie its purpose.

Failing to find the connecting link between such Ang Lee films as *Sense and Sensibility, Brokeback Mountain,* and *The Hulk,* I was quickly corrected by readers who said, obviously, all his films are about people trying to realize their essential natures despite the constraints of society. Readers, you were right. Here we have a woman who hates her lover enough to help kill him and yet is mesmerized by him. And a man whose official position would be destroyed by the exposure of this affair (especially if it were discovered whom Mrs. Mak really is). Yet the heart, as Pascal said, has its reasons. Mr. Yee and Mrs. Mak are just as transgressive as the *Brokeback* lovers, just as entranced by a form of sex that is frowned on by their societies.

There is not a frame of the film that is not beautiful, but there may be too many frames. Why does Ang Lee go into such depth and detail to establish this world, and why does he delay the film's crucial scenes? I don't know, but of course seeing the film the first time I didn't know that was what he was doing, and

I grew restless before I grew involved. Asked to edit the sex scenes to avoid the dreaded NC-17 rating, Lee quite properly refused and was backed all the way by James Schamus, his cowriter and, significantly, head of Focus Features, which released the film.

The nature of the sex is Lee's subject, and he is too honest to suppress that. His moments of full frontal nudity avoid the awkwardness of most movie sex scenes in which the lovers, although alone, carefully mask their naughty bits. The scenes are not edited for erotic effect, it must be observed, but are treated in terms of their psychological meaning.

Film by film, Ang Lee, from Taipei out of the University of Illinois, has become one of the world's leading directors. This film was his second Golden Lion winner in three years at the Venice Film Festival. But it is not among his best films. It lacks the focus and fire that his characters finally find. Less sense, more sensibility. ☞

M

Madagascar ★ ★ ½

PG, 80 m., 2005

With the voices of: Ben Stiller (Alex the Lion), Chris Rock (Marty the Zebra), David Schwimmer (Melman the Giraffe), Jada Pinkett Smith (Gloria the Hippo), Sacha Baron Cohen (Julian), Cedric the Entertainer (Maurice). Directed by Eric Darnell and Tom McGrath and produced by Teresa Cheng and Mireille Soria. Screenplay by Mark Burton and Billy Frolick.

One of the fundamental philosophical questions of our time is why Goofy is a person and Pluto is a dog. From their earliest days when Mickey Mouse was still in black and white, cartoons have created a divide between animals who are animals and animals who are human—or, if not human in the sense that Paris Hilton is human, then at least human in the sense that they speak, sing, have personalities, and are voiced by actors like Ben Stiller, Chris Rock, David Schwimmer, and Jada Pinkett Smith.

Now comes *Madagascar,* an inessential but passably amusing animated comedy that has something very tricky going on. What happens if the human side of a cartoon animal is only, as they say, a veneer of civilization? Consider Alex the Lion. In the Central Park Zoo, he's a star, singing "New York, New York" and looking forward to school field trips because he likes to show off for his audiences.

Alex (voice by Ben Stiller) lives the good life in the zoo, dining on prime steaks every day provided by his keepers. His friends include Marty the Zebra (Chris Rock), Melman the Giraffe (David Schwimmer), and Gloria the Hippo (Jada Pinkett Smith). If Alex likes it in the zoo, Marty has wanderlust. He wants to break out and live free. One night he escapes from the zoo, and his three friends catch up with him just as he's about to board a train for Connecticut, acting on bad advice from the giraffe, who has informed him that is where "the wild" can be found.

The animals are captured, crated up, and shipped off aboard a cargo ship to a wild animal refuge in Africa. On the way, a mutiny by rebellious penguins leads to them being swept off the deck and washed ashore in Madagascar. They're back in the wild, all right, but without survival training. The local population, primarily a colony of lemurs, is ruled by King Julian (Sacha Baron Cohen) and his right-paw man Maurice (Cedric the Entertainer).

Some of the locals think maybe the New Yorkers are obnoxious tourists, even though Alex stages his zoo act, much in the same sense captured prisoners of war entertain the commandant. Then the intriguing problem of the human/animal divide comes into play. Alex misses his daily stacks of sirloin and porterhouse. He is a meat-eater. He eats steak. "Which is you," Marty the Zebra is warned. At one point, driven wild by hunger, Alex even tries to take a bite out of Marty's butt.

This is the kind of chaos that always lingers under the surface of animal cartoons. How would Goofy feel if Pluto wanted to marry one of his daughters? There is a moment at which *Madagascar* seems poised on the brink of anarchy, as the law of the wild breaks down the detente of the zoo, and the animals revert to their underlying natures. Now that could have been interesting, although one imagines children being led weeping from the theater while Alex basks on a zebra-skin rug, employing a toothpick.

The movie is much too safe to follow its paradoxes to their logical conclusions, and that's probably just as well. The problem, though, is that once it gets the characters to the wild it doesn't figure out what to do with them there, and the plot seems to stall. *Madagascar* is funny, especially at the beginning, and good-looking in a retro cartoon way, but in a world where the stakes have been raised by *Finding Nemo, Shrek,* and *The Incredibles,* it's a throwback to a more conventional kind of animated entertainment. It'll be fun for the smaller kids, but there's not much crossover appeal for their parents.

Madison ★ ★ ★

PG, 94 m., 2005

James Caviezel (Jim McCormick), Jake Lloyd (Mike McCormick), Mary McCormack (Bonnie McCormick), Bruce Dern (Harry Volpi), Brent Briscoe (Tony Steinhart), Paul Dooley (Mayor Vaughn). Directed by William Bindley and produced by Bindley and Martin Wiley. Screenplay by William Bindley and Scott Bindley.

What is it about Indiana that inspires movies about small-town dreamers who come from behind to win? William Bindley's *Madison,* the story of a town that races its own hydroplane on the Ohio River, joins *Breaking Away* (a bicycle race), *Hoosiers* (high school basketball), and *Rudy* (local boy is too small to play football for Notre Dame, but that doesn't stop him). All four stories are inspired by fact; maybe that has something to do with it. A story about Bobby Knight would of course have to be based on fiction.

As *Madison* opens in 1971, times are hard for the town, which was once the busiest port above New Orleans and one of the richest cities in the state. Factories are closing, people are moving to big cities to find work, and although Madison is the only town to enter its own boat in the Gold Cup, things look grim for this year's race.

The boat is *Miss Madison,* an unlimited hydroplane (I think that means anything goes with engines and speed). The Gold Cup has been held since 1950; local businessman Jim McCormick (James Caviezel) used to pilot the boat but retired after an injury ten years earlier. Now he is suddenly needed again, by the town and the boat, and comes out of retirement to the pride of his son, Mike (Jake Lloyd), and the concern of his wife, Bonnie (Mary McCormack), who like so many movie wives frets that her spouse is either (a) going to get killed, or (b) not be home for dinner.

Miss Madison's engine has exploded during a time trial and the boat itself is seriously damaged. It looks as if the town will not have an entry in the very year it hosts the famous annual race, but then Mike and his crew go to work. They need a new engine and can't afford one, so under cover of darkness they slip off to a nearby town and steal the engine from an airplane displayed in the courthouse square. Without being a mechanic, I am fairly sure such an engine, if it were indeed still in the plane, would be filled with dead leaves and hornets' nests and would need more than a trip through Jiffy Lube, but never mind: It purrs right along on race day.

For the town, meanwhile, the race is heaven-sent. It provides a boost for civic morale, keeps a few more citizens from moving away, attracts tourist dollars and television publicity, and gives everyone a chance to sit on the river banks in their lawn chairs with their picnic baskets. Much of this is made possible by Mayor Don Vaughn (Paul Dooley, who played the father in *Breaking Away*). He shifts some city funds, probably illegally, to find the money to back *Miss Madison.*

As sporting events go, hydroplane racing is pretty straightforward. The powerful boats race around a river course, making lots of waves and noise. Some of the boats have commercial sponsors, and one of the unique elements in *Madison* is negative product placement. One of the boats has "Budweiser" written all over it, and much is made about the rich and high-powered brewery team, but they're the bad guys and we want to see Bud lose to *Miss Madison.*

The cast is stalwart. Jim Caviezel, who made this movie in his pre-*Passion* days, is a salt-of-the-earth small-town dad who shares a secret with his son: a hidden cave that's "one of the special things about where we live." Mary McCormack, as wife and mother, is stuck with the obligatory speech, "You have a choice to make—me or the boat." But after she pays her dues with that tired line, she perks up and brings some sunshine into the movie. There is also sadness, which I will not reveal, except to say that driving one of these boats might be a good way to compete for the Darwin Award.

Who else? Oh: Bruce Dern. He's the expert mechanic who can turn around a stolen antique airplane engine in twenty-four hours. I saw him not long ago while revisiting *After Dark, My Sweet* (1993) and was happy to see him again. He has a way of chewing his dialogue as if he wants to savor it first before sharing it with us.

Mad Money ★ ½

PG-13, 104 m., 2008

Diane Keaton (Bridget Cardigan), Queen Latifah (Nina Brewster), Katie Holmes (Jackie Truman), Ted Danson (Don Cardigan), Adam Rothenberg (Bob Truman). Directed by Callie Khouri and produced by James Acheson, Jay Cohen, and Frank DeMartini. Screenplay by Glenn Gers and John Mister.

There is something called "found poetry." The term refers to anything that was not written as poetry but reads as if it was. I would like to suggest a new category: found reviews. These are not really reviews but serve the same function. I found one just now, and after a struggle with myself, I have decided to share it with you. It is about *Mad Money*, a movie in which Diane Keaton, Queen Latifah, and Katie Holmes are lowly workers who team up to rob a Federal Reserve Bank.

I was noodling around Rotten Tomatoes, trying to determine who played the bank's security chief, and noticed the movie had not yet been reviewed by anybody. Hold on! In the "Forum" section for this movie, "islandhome" wrote at 7:58 a.m. January 8: "review of this movie . . . tonight i'll post." At 11:19 a.m. January 10, "islandhome" was finally back with the promised review. It is written without capital letters, flush-left like a poem, and I quote it spelling and all:

hello sorry i slept when i got back
well it was kinda fun
it could never happen in the way it was portraid
but what ever its a movie
for the girls most will like it
and the men will not mind it much
i thought it was going to be kinda like how tobeat the high cost of living
kinda the same them but not as much fun
ill give it a 4 Out of 10

I read this twice, three times. I had been testing out various first sentences for my own review, but somehow the purity and directness of islandhome's review undercut me. It is so final. "for the girls most will like it / and the men will not mind it much." How can you improve on that? It's worthy of Charles Bukowski.

Anyway, here's how I was going to start out:

Mad Money is astonishingly casual for a movie about three service workers who steal millions from a Federal Reserve Bank. There is little suspense, no true danger, their plan is simple, the complications are few, and they don't get excited much beyond some high-fives and hugs and giggles. If there was ever a movie where Diane Keaton would be justified in bringing back "la-di-da," this is that movie.

Keaton costars with Queen Latifah and Katie Holmes. She's set up as a rich wife whose husband (Ted Danson) gets downsized. They owe a mountain of debt, their house is being repossessed, and she thinks she might as well (gulp) get a job. The best she can do is emptying the garbage at the Federal Reserve.

That's when she spots a loophole in the bank's famous security system. She figures out a way to steal used bills on the way to the shredder and smuggle them out of the building stuffed into her bra and panties, and those of her partners in crime, Katie and the Queen. This system works. And the beauty is, the money isn't missed because it has supposedly already been destroyed. All they're doing is spending it one more time on its way to the shredder. A victimless crime, unless it brings down the economy, of course.

I would have gone on to observe that the movie makes it all look so easy and painless that it's a good thing it opens with a flash-forward showing them in a panic mode, so we know that sooner or later something exciting will happen. In the meantime, we get more scenes starring Ted Danson, with a hairstyle that makes him look alarmingly like a cross between David Cronenberg and Frankenstein's monster. And there's of course a chief of security who is constantly being outwitted. And so on.

Mad Money is actually a remake of a 2001 TV movie, I discovered on IMDb. Britain's Granada made it about a team of cleaners who pull the same scam on the Bank of England. Two character first names are the same (Bridget and Jackie), but the last name of the Keaton and Danson characters is changed from Watmore to Cardigan. Go figure. Or don't. The bottom line is, some girls will like it, the men not so much, and I give it 1½ stars out of 4.

Mamma Mia! ★ ★

PG-13, 98 m., 2008

Meryl Streep (Donna), Pierce Brosnan (Sam), Colin Firth (Harry), Stellan Skarsgard (Bill), Julie Walters (Rosie), Dominic Cooper (Sky), Amanda Seyfried (Sophie), Christine Baranski (Tanya). Directed by Phyllida Lloyd and produced by Judy Craymer and Gary Goetzman. Screenplay by Catherine Johnson, based on the stage musical.

I saw the stage version of *Mamma Mia!* in London, where for all I know it is now entering the second century of its run, and I was underwhelmed. The film version has the advantage of possessing Meryl Streep, Pierce Brosnan, Amanda Seyfried, Colin Firth, and Julie Walters—but they are assets stretched fairly thin. And there are the wall-to-wall songs by ABBA, if you like that sort of thing. I don't, not much, with a few exceptions.

But here's the fact of the matter. This movie wasn't made for me. It was made for the people who will love it, of which there may be a multitude. The stage musical has sold thirty million tickets, and I feel like the grouch at the party. So let me make that clear and proceed with my minority opinion.

The action is set on a Greek isle, where the characters are made to slide down rooftops, dangle from ladders, enter and exit by trapdoors, and frolic among the colorful local folk. The choreography at times resembles calisthenics, particularly in a scene where the young male population, all wearing scuba flippers, dance on the pier to "Dancing Queen" (one of the ABBA songs I do like).

It would be charity to call the plot contrived. Meryl Streep plays Donna, who runs a tourist villa on the island, where she has raised her daughter, Sophie (Seyfried), to the age of twenty. Sophie, engaged to Sky (Dominic Cooper), has never known who her father is. But now she's found an old diary and invited the three possible candidates to her forthcoming wedding. She'll know the right one at first sight, she's convinced. They are Sam (Pierce Brosnan), Bill (Stellan Skarsgard), and Harry (Colin Firth), and if you know the first thing about camera angles, shot choice, and screen time, you will quickly be able to pick out the likely candidate—if not for sperm source, then for the one most likely to succeed in one way or another.

Meryl Streep's character of course knows nothing of her daughter's invitations, but even so, it must be said she takes a long time to figure out why these particular men were invited. Wouldn't it be, like, obvious? She has earnest conversations with all three, two of whom seem to have been one-night stands; for them to drop everything and fly to Greece for her after twenty years speaks highly of her charms.

The plot is a clothesline on which to hang the songs; the movie doesn't much sparkle when nobody is singing or dancing, but that's rarely. The stars all seem to be singing their own songs, aided by an off-screen chorus of, oh, several dozen, plus full orchestration. Meryl Streep might seem to be an unlikely choice to play Donna, but you know what? She can play anybody. And she can survive even the singing of a song like "Money, Money, Money." She has such a merry smile, and seems to be actually having a good time.

Her two best friends have flown in for the occasion: Tanya (Christine Baranski, an often-married plastic surgery subject) and Rosie (Julie Walters, plainer and pluckier). With three hunks their age like Brosnan, Firth, and Skarsgard on hand, do they divvy up? Not exactly. But a lot of big romantic decisions do take place in just a few days.

The island is beautiful. Moviegoers will no doubt be booking vacations there. The energy is unflagging. The local color feels a little overlooked in the background; nobody seems to speak much Greek. And then there are the songs. You know them. You may feel you know them too well. Or maybe you can never get enough of them. Streep's sunshine carries a lot of charm, although I will never be able to understand her final decision in the movie—not coming from such a sensible woman. Never mind. Love has its way.

The Man ★ ½

PG-13, 79 m., 2005

Samuel L. Jackson (Agent Derrick Vann), Eugene Levy (Andy Fidler), Miguel Ferrer (Agent Peters), Luke Goss (Joey Trent), Anthony Mackie (Booty), Susie Essman (Lieutenant Rita Carbone), Horatio Sanz (Diaz). Directed by Les Mayfield and produced by Robert N. Fried. Screenplay by Jim Piddock, Margaret Oberman, and Stephen Carpenter.

The Man is another one of those movies, like *Lethal Weapon 2*, where the outsider finds himself in the dangerous world of cops and robbers. The cop this time is Derrick Vann, a hard-boiled Detroit ATF agent played by Samuel L. Jackson, and the outsider is Andy Fidler (Eugene Levy), a dental supplies salesman from Wisconsin. Fidler loves his product so much he chats up strangers about the glories of flossing.

The plot: Agent Vann's partner, who is on the take, has died in connection with a heist of guns from the ATF lock-room. A crook named Booty (Anthony Mackie) may be the key to the killing. Vann, an honest agent, mistakes Fidler for an underworld contact working with Booty. When he finds out how very wrong he is, he still needs Fidler to pretend to be a black-market arms dealer if the sting is going to work.

Whether the sting and the movie work are two different questions. Jackson and Levy are in full sail as their most familiar character types: Jackson hard as nails, Levy oblivious to the world outside his own blissfully limited existence. They could play these characters in their sleep. Their differences provide the setup for the whole movie: these two guys linked together in an unlikely partnership during which their personalities (and Fidler's problems with intestinal gas) will make it difficult for them to share the front seat of Vann's customized Caddy.

The Man is very minor. The running time of seventy-nine minutes indicates (a) thin material, and (b) mercy toward the audience by not stretching it any further than what is already the breaking point. You know a movie like this is stalling for time when it supplies Agent Vann with a family so that his wife can call him in the middle of the action: "Your daughter wants to know if you'll be at her recital tonight." Yes, it's the ancient and sometimes reliable Dad Too Busy for Child's Big Moment formula. Does Vann wrap up the case in time to walk into the room just as the recital is beginning? Do he and his daughter exchange a quiet little nod to show family does, after all, come first? I would not dream of giving away such a plot detail.

Levy has funny moments as the fussy dental supplies fetishist but never goes into full obnoxious mode as Joe Pesci did in *Lethal Weapon 2*. He plays the character like a conventioneer trying to be nice to an alarming taxi driver. Jackson plays the cop like a man who has found a bug in the front seat of his car. What's interesting, however, is that they don't get locked into a lot of black-white shtick; their differences are defined through occupation, not race, except for the odd ethnic in-joke involving hot sauce.

The inescapable fact about *The Man* is that this movie is completely unnecessary. Nobody needed to make it, nobody needs to see it, Jackson and Levy are too successful to waste time with it. It plays less like a film than like a deal.

At Telluride I was talking to James Mangold, the director of *Walk the Line* and other ambitious pictures, and he said an interesting thing: Hollywood executives are reluctant to greenlight a project that depends on the filmmakers being able to pull it off. They want familiar formulas in safe packages. An original movie idea involves faith that the script will work, the director knows what he's doing, and the actors are right for the story. Too risky. Better to make a movie where when you hear the pitch you can already envision the TV commercial, because the movie will essentially be the long form of the thirty-second spot.

Go online, look at the trailer for *The Man*, and you will know everything you could possibly need to know about this movie except how it would feel if the trailer were eighty minutes long.

Manderlay ★ ★ ★

NO MPAA RATING, 139 m., 2006

Bryce Dallas Howard (Grace), Isaach De Bankole (Timothy), Danny Glover (Wilhelm), Willem Dafoe (Grace's Father), Lauren Bacall (Mam), Zeljko Ivanek (Gambler). Directed by Lars von Trier and produced by Vibeke Windelov. Screenplay by von Trier.

Alabama, 1933. A caravan of black limousines carries gangsters from a gold-mining town in Colorado to a rural Alabama area where slavery still survives as an institution. Alabama looks uncannily like Colorado, as it must: The story that began in Lars von Trier's *Dogville* (2004) continues here, with the same visual strategy of placing all the action on a sound stage, with chalk lines indicating the outlines of locations. A few rudimentary props flesh out the action, including doors, windows, and machine guns.

The movie is the second in a trilogy by von Trier, who has never visited the United States but has set several movies here, all of them generated by his ideas about American greed, racism, and the misuse of power. To say his America is not recognizable to any American is beside the point; neither is the America in most Hollywood entertainments. Presenting imaginary worlds as if they were real is how movies work.

Von Trier's purpose is fiercely polemical. The

Danish iconoclast holds strong ideas about our society and expresses them in satiric allegories of such audacity that we cast loose from realism and simply float with his conceits. The crucial difference between *Manderlay* and the almost unbearable *Dogville* is not that his politics have changed but that his sense of mercy for the audience has been awakened. The movie is thirty-eight minutes shorter than *Dogville* (although none too fleeting at 139 minutes), and the story is more clearly and strongly told.

He begins with a plantation in Alabama where slavery has never been abolished: Mam (Lauren Bacall) rules with an iron hand, assisted by her foreman, Wilhelm (Danny Glover), a slave who believes his people are not ready for the responsibilities of freedom. Driving up to the gates of the imaginary plantation, Grace (Bryce Dallas Howard) and her gangster father (Willem Dafoe) are surprised to find slavery still flourishing. Grace declares this cannot be, that the plantation must be informed of such historical events as the Civil War and the Emancipation Proclamation.

Grace's father has crimes to commit and wants to keep moving: "This is a local matter," he tells his daughter, echoing the argument used for generations. She thinks not and persuades him to leave behind a lawyer and four thugs with machine guns. Using brute force if necessary, she will impose democracy on this backwater. Von Trier's parallels with Iraq are not impossible to find; this Alabama is no more fictional than the prewar Iraq depicted by the neocon advocates of war.

Mam dies soon after Grace frees the slaves, and Grace herself steps into the power vacuum, establishing a benevolent transitional authority. She will teach the slaves to vote, and then hold elections. Soon, but not yet, they will govern themselves. Doubts are expressed by the slave Wilhelm, who cites the insights in a book hidden under Mam's mattress—a volume categorizing the various kinds of slaves and their abilities. The slaves, he says, have grown accustomed to the plantation routine; dinner under Mam was always at seven, but what time will it be if the matter is open for discussion? And who will plant the crops and plan the harvest? Jobs don't get done by themselves.

Grace has her gangsters wear blackface and serve dinner to the slaves, who find the exercise offensive. She orders crops planted and rejoices at the harvest, although gamblers arrive to cheat the slaves, and company stores recycle the wages right back into the pockets of those who pay them. Again, there are contemporary parallels: One of the purposes of every colonial exercise is to open up markets for the occupying power.

I wouldn't go so far as to claim *Manderlay* is fun to watch. Von Trier, who can make compulsively watchable films *(Breaking the Waves)*, has found a style that will alienate most audiences. Maybe it's necessary. On his bargain budgets, he certainly couldn't afford to shoot on a real plantation, with period detail. His actors work for peanuts (and even so, Nicole Kidman and James Caan bailed out after *Dogville*). The stark artificiality of his sets makes it clear he's dealing with parable and excuses his story from any requirement of reality. The real action generated by his story begins after the film ends. If audiences still exist for movies like this and debate them afterward—if, that is, not every single moviegoer in America is lost to mindless narcissistic self-indulgence—the arguments afterward will be the real show. Many moviegoers are likely to like the film less than the discussions it drags them into.

The film has a closing montage of photographs showing the history of African-Americans in America, from slavery through decades of poverty and discrimination to the civil rights movement, both its victories and defeats. Von Trier no doubt intends this montage to be an indictment of America, but I view it more positively: From a legacy of evil, our democracy has stumbled uncertainly in a moral direction and within our lifetimes has significantly reduced racism.

No doubt if everyone in America had always been Danish, we could have avoided some of our sins, but there you have it.

Note: Just in time to be tacked on to the end of this review, von Trier has issued a statement of revitality to Variety. *Ray Pride of* Movie City News *quotes him in part: ". . . I intend to reschedule my professional activities in order to rediscover my original enthusiasm for film. Over the last few years I have felt increasingly burdened by barren habits and expectations (my own and other people's) and I feel the urge to tidy up. In regards to product development this will mean more time on freer terms; i.e., projects will be allowed to undergo true development and not merely be required to meet preconceived demands. This is partly to liberate me from routine, and in particular from scriptural structures inherited from film to film. . . ."*

The most delightful element of this statement is his assumption that his films are "required to meet preconceived demands."

Man in the Chair ★ ½

PG-13, 107 m., 2007

Christopher Plummer (Flash Madden), Michael Angarano (Cameron Kincaid), M. Emmet Walsh (Mickey Hopkins), Robert Wagner (Taylor Moss), Tracey Walter (Mr. Klein), Mitch Pileggi (Floyd), Joshua Boyd (Murphy White). Directed by Michael Schroeder and produced by Schroeder, Randy Turrow, and Sarah Schroeder. Screenplay by Michael Schroeder.

Man in the Chair is a movie about a high school student who enlists two movie industry veterans from old-folks' homes to help him with his project. And I mean old folks. Flash Madden (Christopher Plummer) claims to have been given his nickname by Orson Welles on the set of *Citizen Kane,* which means, if he was twenty-five at the time, he is ninety-one now. And Mickey Hopkins (M. Emmet Walsh), a writer, claims to have written *Queen Christina,* which, if he was twenty-five at the time, would make him ninety-nine.

Of course we know Mickey didn't write *Queen Christina* (or *Gone with the Wind,* another one of his "credits"), and the odds are against Flash's story, too. The chances are they are both lying, but the kid, Cameron (Michael Angarano) doesn't think of that, and neither does the writer-director, Michael Schroeder, although it might have made this a better movie.

What it is, instead, is a half-baked idea for a movie with way too many characters and subplots. Do we really need another lovable cheering section of characters (and character actors) who live at the Motion Picture Home and have individual headlined character traits? Do we need animal haters who catch and kill dogs as a business? Do we need the kid to have a mean father? Do we need him to have a competitor who bullies him at school? Do we need for old Flash to be such an alcoholic that to still be drinking like that at ninety-one must mean he only started at ninety?

The movie works so hard at juggling its clichés that it fails to generate interest in its story—which turns out to be not the skateboarding drama the kid had in mind, but a docudrama Flash sells him on about the mistreatment of old folks like Mickey. Then the animal subplot takes over as the old folks and the kid attack the cruel dog pound, uh-huh. And there is a stunt involving gasoline that is way too far over the top.

Christopher Plummer is a superb actor. I applauded him off-Broadway as the best Iago I have ever seen. No doubt there were aspects of the *idea* of this character that appealed to him, but did he measure its probability? And as for Mickey, M. Emmet Walsh, also a great character actor, has made a living looking moth-eaten and ramshackle, but good Lord, what they do to Mickey in this picture, it's a mercy his poor mother isn't alive to see it (if she were 25 when she had Mickey, she'd be 124 now).

I know an old writer. His name is William Froug, he lives in Florida, and if you look him up on Amazon you will see he is still writing brilliant and useful books about screenwriting and teleplays. He is not merely as sharp as a tack, he is the standard by which they *sharpen* tacks. If he had been advising the kid, the kid would have made a better movie, and if he had been advising the director of *Man in the Chair,* we would have been spared the current experience. Just because you're old doesn't mean you have to be a decrepit caricature. One thing that keeps Froug young is that, unlike Flash Madden, he almost certainly does not sit on an expressway overpass guzzling Jack Daniel's from a pint bottle.

Note: If flashbacks are meant to recall reality, it is unlikely that the slate on Citizen Kane *would have misspelled the name of Orson Welles.*

Man Push Cart ★ ★ ★

NO MPAA RATING, 87 m., 2006

Ahmad Razvi (Ahmad), Leticia Dolera (Noemi). Directed by Ramin Bahrani and produced by

Bahrani, Pradip Ghosh, and Bedford T. Bentley III. Screenplay by Bahrani.

Man Push Cart was filmed in Manhattan by an American born in Iran and an American born in Pakistan, and embodies the very soul of Italian neorealism. Free of contrived melodrama and phony suspense, it ennobles the hard work by which its hero earns his daily bread. He owns a stainless-steel bagel wagon, which he pushes through the lonely predawn streets. He sells bagels and sweet rolls and juice and coffee, and many customers call him by his first name, although they would never think to ask his last one.

The character, named Ahmad (Ahmad Razvi), has had a life before this, but the pushcart now defines the parameters of his existence. He was a Pakistani rock star, although how that career ended and he came to New York to push a cart (which would be a subject of a more conventional film) is barely suggested. Ahmad's wife is dead, his in-laws will not allow him to see his son, and maybe he originally came to America to seek the child. Now he sells bagels.

We see the world he inhabits outside the cart. He knows the other nearby vendors, including a Hispanic woman at a magazine stand. Romance would be a possibility, except that romance is not a possibility in Ahmad's life. It is too filled with the making of a living. Like so many Americans who work low-wage jobs, sometimes two or even three of them, his work essentially subsidizes his ability to keep on working.

Ramin Bahrani, the writer-director, shot his film on a shoestring, in less than three weeks. He often used a concealed camera, shooting what was really happening. There's a scene of unforced spontaneity when Ahmad offers to sell some bootleg videos. The two guys he pitches say they know where to they can get bootlegs, two for eight bucks, in Brooklyn. Those two guys did not know they were in a movie.

Ahmad's cart is stolen, and therefore his livelihood. We get a glimpse backstage of how the vending cart economy operates. What can he do without a cart and a way to replace it? He will, we understand, keep pushing, if not the cart, then something. *Man Push Cart* as a title encapsulates human survival at a most fundamental economic level.

Bahrani's film was accepted by Sundance 2006. The festival offered an opportunity for his low-budget effort to find audiences, and I immediately invited it to my Overlooked Film Festival last April. A central Illinois audience reacted, if anything, more favorably than the Sundance crowd. The film's story is simple, moving, and inescapable.

In a film like this, it is pointless to describe *screenplay, acting,* or *direction.* The film is resolutely utilitarian. No effort is made to create a visual look; the camera simply, impassively regards. Razvi's acting never strains for effect; it embodies the bleakness and exhaustion of his character. Bahrani, as director, not only stays out of the way of the simplicity of his story, but relies on it; less is more, and with restraint he finds a grimy eloquence.

Bahrani was inspired by *The Myth of Sisyphus,* by Albert Camus, the story of a man who spends his life pushing a rock up a hill, only to see it roll down again, and only to push it back up again. Well, what else can he do? *Man Push Cart* is not an indictment of the American economy or some kind of political allegory. It is about what it is about. I think the message may be that it is better, after all, to push the cart than to face a life without hope at the bottom of the hill.

March of the Penguins ★ ★ ★ ½

G, 80 m., 2005

Morgan Freeman (Narrator). A documentary directed by Luc Jacquet and produced by Yves Darondeau, Christophe Lioud, and Emmanuel Priou. Screenplay by Jordan Roberts.

After a long summer of feasting, their bodies stately and plump, the emperor penguins of Antarctica begin to feel, toward autumn, a need to march inland to the breeding grounds "where each and every one of them was born." They are all of a mind about this and walk in single file, thousands of them, in a column miles long. They all know where they are going, even those making the march for the first time, and when they get there these countless creatures, who all look more or less the same to us, begin to look more or less desirable to one another. Carefully, they choose their mates.

This is not a casual commitment. After the female delivers one large egg, the male gathers it into a fold of his abdomen, plants his feet to protect it from the ice below, and then stands there all winter with no food or water, in howling gales, at temperatures far below zero, in total darkness, huddled together with the other fathers for warmth. The females meanwhile march all the way back to the sea, now even more distant, to forage for food. When the females return to the mass of countless males, they find their mates without error and recognize the cries of chicks they have never seen. As they nurse the chicks, the males crawl back to the sea for food.

March of the Penguins is simply, and astonishingly, the story of this annual cycle. It was filmed under unimaginable conditions by the French director Luc Jacquet and his team, including cinematographers Laurent Chalet and Jerome Maison. There is not much to choose from in setting up their shots: On the coldest, driest, and (in winter) darkest continent on Earth, there is snow, and there is ice, and there are penguins. There is also an ethereal beauty.

Although the compulsion to reproduce is central to all forms of life, the penguins could be forgiven if they'd said the hell with it and evolved in the direction of being able to swim to Patagonia. The film's narrator, Morgan Freeman, tells us that Antarctica was once a warm land with rich forests that teemed with creatures. But as the climate grew colder over long centuries, one life form after another bailed out, until the penguins were left in a land that, as far as they can see, is inhabited pretty much by other penguins, and edged by seas filled with delicious fish. Even their predators, such as the leopard seal, give them a pass during the dark, long, cold winter.

"This is a love story," Freeman's narration assures us, reminding me for some reason of Tina Turner singing "What's Love Got to Do with It?" I think it is more accurately described as the story of an evolutionary success. The penguins instinctively know, because they have been hardwired by evolutionary trial and error, that it is necessary to march so far inland because in spring the ice shelf will start to melt toward them, and they need to stand where the ice will remain thick enough to support them. As a species, they learned this because the penguins who paused too soon on their treks had eggs that fell into the sea. Those who walked farther produced another generation, and eventually every penguin was descended from a long line of ancestors who were willing to walk the extra mile.

Why do penguins behave in this manner? Because it works for them, and their environment gives them little alternative. They are Darwinism embodied. But their life history is so strange that until this century it was not even guessed at. The first Antarctic explorers found penguins aplenty but had little idea where they came from, where they went to, and indeed whether they were birds or mammals.

The answers to those questions were discovered by a man named Apsley Cherry-Garrard, as described in one of the most remarkable books ever written, *The Worst Journey in the World* (1922). He was writing not about the journey of the penguins but about his own trek with two others through the bitter night to their mating grounds. Members of Robert F. Scott's 1910–1912 expedition to the South Pole, they set out in the autumn to follow the march of the penguins, and walked through hell until they found them, watched them, and returned with one of their eggs. Cherry-Garrard retired to England, where he lived until 1959; his friends felt the dreadful march, and the earlier experience of finding the frozen bodies of Scott and two others, contributed to his depression for the rest of his life.

For Jacquet and his crew, the experience was more bearable. They had transport, warmth, food, and communication with the greater world. Still, it could not have been pleasant, sticking it out and making this documentary, when others were filming a month spent eating at McDonald's. The narration is a little fanciful for my taste, and some of the shots seem funny to us, but not to the penguins. When they fall over, they do it with a remarkable lack of style. And for all the walking they do, they're ungainly waddlers. Yet they are perfect in their way, with sleek coats, grace in the water and heroic determination. It's poignant to watch the chicks in their youth, fed by their parents, playing with their chums, the sun climbing higher every day, little suspecting what they're in for.

Margot at the Wedding ★ ★ ★

R, 93 m., 2007

Nicole Kidman (Margot), Jennifer Jason Leigh (Pauline), Zane Pais (Claude), Jack Black (Malcolm), John Turturro (Jim), Flora Cross (Ingrid), Ciaran Hinds (Dick), Halley Feiffer (Maisy). Directed by Noah Baumbach and produced by Scott Rudin. Screenplay by Baumbach.

I wonder if his family knew Noah Baumbach was taking notes? First in *The Squid and the Whale* and now with *Margot at the Wedding,* he puts an intelligent but alarming family under the microscope and finds creepy-squirmy things crawling around. Of course, there is no reason to be certain the family in either movie is inspired by his own. But given the degree of familiarity, there's no reason not to, either. Besides, the character Margot in this one is accused of storing up every family pain, humiliation, and embarrassment for recycling in her short stories. Isn't there a rule that if you bring a literary crime onstage in the first act, you have to commit it in the third?

The movie opens as Margot (Nicole Kidman) and her son, Claude (Zane Pais), are traveling by train to the wedding of Pauline (Jennifer Jason Leigh), the sister she is not on speaking terms with. Pauline still lives in the big family house up east. With a child of her own, the precocious Ingrid (Flora Cross), and another on the way, Pauline's planning to marry Malcolm (Jack Black), who can spend up to a week writing a letter to the editor and is growing a mustache that he hopes will look funny.

Margot, the writer, has deliberately not brought along her husband, Jim (John Turturro), because she has plans to meet Dick (Ciaran Hinds), her former and perhaps future lover, at a local book signing. Dick has a daughter, Maisy (Halley Feiffer), who is just at that age when she has power but not wisdom about sexuality. Maisy and Ingrid will bond and no doubt start a first draft of *Ingrid and/or Maisy at the Wedding.*

All of these characters gather with some apprehension for an outdoor wedding that may not have been planned out of the pages of *American Bride.* And Margot is brutal with Pauline, advising her that Malcolm is not worthy to be her husband. We're not sure. He seems extremely inward and eccentric, and possibly unemployable, but maybe he's just what a high-powered ball of nerves like Pauline needs, if not as a husband, then as a letter writer. He is certainly the only person on the horizon without a neurotic agenda.

It is never explained why the two sisters haven't been speaking, but I understand why. They are such equals that neither one has ever been able to gain the upper hand. All of their lifestyle choices seem intended as rebukes to each other. They've spent a lifetime both trying to stand on the same place and push the other away. There's no great painful event in the past, just the mutual feeling that each is complete without a sister. Notice the scene when Pauline challenges Margot to climb a tree.

On the other hand, they're able to be brutally truthful with each other, especially in conversations about their sexual desirability. What does it do to a woman when she spends years pushing off men who want to sleep with her and gradually finds there's no one to push? Where are male chauvinist pigs when you need them? Many of their conversations take place in front of the kids, who look like they are in training to become the next generation of dysfunctionality.

Writing about this movie from the Toronto festival, Jim Emerson had a great observation: "It's like a Neil LaBute picture cowritten by Jules Feiffer." Yes, and Elaine May might have done one of her ghost rewrites, so to speak. The characters are into emotional laceration for fun. They are verbal, articulate, self-absorbed, selfish, egotistical, cold, and fascinating. They've never felt an emotion they couldn't laugh at.

Which brings us full circle. *Margot at the Wedding* may not be based on Noah Baumbach's own family, but it demonstrates a way of looking at families that he must have learned somewhere. Both of his parents were writers and, to one degree or another, film critics; I remember Gene Siskel telling a friend at dinner that film critics eventually became critical of everything: "For example, your tie is hideous." In revenge, the friend went to Marshall Field's and asked to buy their ugliest tie. Two salesclerks helped him in a spirited debate to select the tie that qualified. My friend wore it the next time they met. Siskel identified the brand of the tie correctly and said: "If you like that tie, it shows you have better taste than 99 percent of men." So it goes with the family in this movie. All of its members are engaged in a mutual process of shooting each other down. Watching *Margot at the Wedding* is like slowing for a gaper's block.

Marie Antoinette ★ ★ ★ ★

PG-13, 123 m., 2006

Kirsten Dunst (Marie Antoinette), Jason Schwartzman (King Louis XVI), Rip Torn (King Louis XV), Judy Davis (Comtesse de Noailles), Asia Argento (Madame Du Barry), Marianne Faithfull (Empress Maria Teresa), Danny Huston (Joseph). Directed by Sofia Coppola and produced by Coppola and Ross Katz. Screenplay by Coppola, based on the book by Antonia Fraser.

Ten things that occurred to me while watching *Marie Antoinette:*

1. This is Sofia Coppola's third film centering on the loneliness of being female and surrounded by a world that knows how to use you but not how to value and understand you. It shows Coppola once again able to draw notes from actresses who are rarely required to sound them.

2. Kirsten Dunst is pitch-perfect in the title role, as a fourteen-year-old Austrian princess who is essentially purchased and imported to the French court to join with the clueless Louis XVI (Jason Schwartzman) to produce an heir. She has self-possession, poise, and high spirits, and they are contained within a world that gives her no way to usefully express them. So she frolics and indulges herself, within a cocoon of rigid court protocol.

3. No, the picture is not informative and detailed about the actual politics of the period. That is because we are entirely within Marie's world. And it is contained within Versailles, which shuts out all external reality. It is a self-governing architectural island, like Kane's Xanadu, that shuts out politics, reality, poverty, and society.

4. Schwartzman, like Bill Murray's character in *Lost in Translation,* plays a sexually passive sad sack who would rather commiserate than take an active role. Danny Huston is priceless as Marie's older brother, brought in from Austria to give the young king a few helpful suggestions about the birds and the bees. The old king, randy Louis XV (Rip Torn) would certainly need no inspiration to perform, as his mistress, Madame du Barry (Asia Argento), immediately observes.

5. All three of Coppola's films, and this one most of all, use locations to define the lives of the characters. Allowed complete access to Versailles, she shows a society as single-mindedly devoted to the care and feeding of Marie Antoinette as a beehive centers on its queen.

6. On the border for the official handover, Marie is stopped, stripped, and searched to ascertain, brutally, if she is indeed a virgin and, for that matter, a female. In a deal like this, it pays to kick the tires. I was reminded of the scene in von Sternberg's *Scarlett Empress* where Catherine arrives at the court of the czar and the royal physician immediately crawls under her skirt to check her royal plumbing. Every detail is covered by the French authorities; they even confiscate her beloved dogs, but tell her, "You can have as many French dogs as you like."

7. Coppola has been criticized in some circles for her use of a contemporary pop overlay—hit songs, incongruous dialogue, jarring intrusions of the Now upon the Then. But no one ever lives as Then; it is always Now. Many characters in historical films seem somehow aware that they are living in the past. Marie seems to think she is a teenager living in the present, which of course she is—and the contemporary pop references invite the audience to share her present with ours. Forman's *Amadeus* had a little of that, with its purple wigs.

8. Everyone in the audience knows Marie Antoinette was beheaded, and I fear we anticipate her beheading with an unwholesome curiosity. Coppola brilliantly sidesteps a beheading and avoids bloated mob scenes by employing light, sound, and a balcony to use Marie's death as a curtain call. Hired, essentially, to play a princess, she is a good trouper and faithful to her role. It is impossible to avoid thoughts of Diana, Princess of Wales.

9. Every criticism I have read of this film would alter its fragile magic and reduce its

romantic and tragic poignancy to the level of an instructional film.

10. It is not necessary to know anything about Marie Antoinette to enjoy this film. Some of what we think we know is mistaken. According to the Coppola version, she never said, "Let them eat cake." "I would never say that," she says indignantly. What she says is, "Let them eat custard." But, paradoxically, the more you know about her, the more you may learn, because Coppola's oblique and anachronistic point of view shifts the balance away from realism and into an act of empathy for a girl swept up by events that leave her without personal choices. Before she was a queen, before she was a pawn, Marie was a fourteen-year-old girl taken from her home, stripped bare, and examined like so much horseflesh. It is astonishing with what indifference for her feelings the court aristocracy uses her for its pleasure, and in killing her disposes of its guilt. ☞

Marilyn Hotchkiss' Ballroom Dancing and Charm School ★ ★

PG-13, 103 m., 2006

Robert Carlyle (Frank Keane), Marisa Tomei (Meredith Morrison), Mary Steenburgen (Marienne Hotchkiss), Sean Astin (Joe Buco), Donnie Wahlberg (Randall Ipswitch), Danny DeVito (Booth), John Goodman (Steve Mills), David Paymer (Rafael Horowitz), Camryn Manheim (Lisa Gobar), Adam Arkin (Gabe DiFranco), Sonia Braga (Tina). Directed by Randall Miller and produced by Eileen Craft, Miller, Morris Ruskin, and Jody Savin. Screenplay by Miller and Savin.

When he was twelve years old, Steve promised Lisa that they would meet again on the fifth day of the fifth month of the fifth year of the new millennium, at a reunion of their class at Marilyn Hotchkiss' Ballroom Dancing and Charm School. Now Steve is forty-eight, it is May 5, 2005, and he's piloting his station wagon down a lonely highway to make that rendezvous. If you're still reading, I'm as surprised as I am that I'm still writing.

Think about this. You liked a schoolmate when you were twelve and for almost forty years have focused on this reunion. Are you crazy? When I was twelve, I did not even take ballroom dancing classes, for which I thank the nuns of St. Mary's Grade School. It was all we could do to practice for the rhythm band. A rhythm band, as you rich kids may not know, is a band consisting entirely of cheap rhythm instruments. Sister Marie Donald would put a record on the Victrola and we would accompany it by ringing our triangles, rubbing our ratchet sticks together, and pounding on tambourines. If a kid was left over, he would bang a desk lid up and down. The school had a piano, but it was in the auditorium.

Anyway, while racing to his rendezvous with Lisa, Steve (John Goodman) is in a car crash. The crash is witnessed by Frank (Robert Carlyle), who is driving a bakery truck. Frank calls 911, encourages Steve to hang in there, and accompanies him in the ambulance to the hospital. Steve keeps blubbering about Lisa: "I made this appointment almost forty years ago! I promised Lisa I'd be there!"

"Keep him talking!" a paramedic advises Frank. This is not a problem. Steve talks on and off during the entire movie, telling the story of his relationship with Lisa and the dynamics of their class at the Marilyn Hotchkiss school. Occasionally his heartbeat falters, and we hear the ominously level tone of a heart monitor flatlining. But then Frank asks him another question, and thank God! The monitor starts beeping again, as Steve shares another memory from his past. He talks so much, the HMO must be shipping him to a hospital in another state.

Frank himself is grieving; his wife has committed suicide, for unexplained reasons. He promises Steve he will go to the Marilyn Hotchkiss reunion and look for Lisa, and this he does. He is painfully shy as he asks one woman after another if she is Lisa, but Lisa does not seem to have taken the appointment as seriously as Steve. Meanwhile, Frank has a run-in with Randall Ipswitch (Donnie Wahlberg), who warns him to keep his hands off his half-sister Meredith Morrison (Marisa Tomei). Randall is so angry, he even gives Frank's bakery truck four flat tires.

Was there ever a place in this or any reasonably adjacent universe where *Marilyn Hotchkiss' Ballroom Dancing and Charm School* could be considered a plausible story? I doubt it. It matches nothing in my experience. I have written before about the Thelma Leah Rose Ballroom Dancing Academy, which was above the Princess Theater on Main Street in Urbana, Illinois, and where I learned the fox-trot, the waltz, the mambo, the canasta, the pinochle, and many other dances—all of them, my wife confides, very badly.

We were younger than today's twelve-year-olds have ever been. I can assure you that the little Steves and Lisas in our class did not make appointments for forty years hence. We looked at each other with fear and loathing. The only reason I took the dance class in the first place was that I was in training for the St. Mary's Seventh- and Eighth-Grade Prom, at the Urbana-Lincoln Hotel. Sister Nathan and Sister Rosanne laid down the ground rules: They wanted to see daylight between the dancers. As far as I was concerned, they could have seen Indiana.

The adults at the Hotchkiss reunion are played by an assortment of splendid actors. Mary Steenburgen is the heir to the Hotchkiss legacy, and the students include Sean Astin, David Paymer, Adam Arkin, and Sonia Braga. Tomei is adorable as the bighearted Meredith, who despite her attack-dog half-brother sees that Frank has a wounded heart, and she attempts to mend it. I hope she gets the flour out of her hair. All I can say about Lisa is, when we finally meet her, she's smoking. As a far better critic than I once wrote, there wasn't a wet eye in the house.

Married Life ★ ★ ★

PG -13, 90 m., 2008

Pierce Brosnan (Richard Langley), Chris Cooper (Harry Allen), Patricia Clarkson (Pat Allen), Rachel McAdams (Kay Nesbitt). Directed by Ira Sachs and produced by Steve Golin, Sachs, Sidney Kimmel, and Jawal Nga. Screenplay by Sachs and Oren Moverman, based on the novel *Five Roundabouts to Heaven* by John Bingham.

Remember the time businessmen were expected to drink martinis at lunch, and the time they were expected not to? Ira Sachs's *Married Life* begins with Harry taking Richard into his confidence at a martinis-and-cigarettes lunch that confirms the movie is set in 1949. Harry (Chris Cooper) is a buttoned-down, closed-in respectable type. Richard (Pierce Brosnan) is more easygoing. You can tell by the way they smoke. Harry is painfully earnest as he tells his friend that he plans to leave his wife for a much younger woman. The younger woman truly and deeply loves him. All his wife wants is sex.

Why does Harry share this information? I think he wants understanding and forgiveness from a man he respects. He has arranged for the young woman to join them at lunch. Here she comes now. She is Kay (Rachel McAdams). She has the bottle-blond hair and the bright red lipstick, the Monroe look. But don't get the wrong idea. She's a sweet kid, and she really does love Harry. The movie has a voice-over narration by Richard, but we don't need it to tell from the look in his eyes that Richard desires Kay, and that from the moment he sees her he wants to take her away from the dutiful Harry.

How dutiful is Harry? So devoted to his wife that he can't stand the thought of telling her he wants a divorce. He decides to take pity on her, spare her that pain, and murder her instead. Sort of a mercy killing. He's serious about this. He knows how devoted his wife is to him and how this news would shatter her, and he doubts she could stand it.

This story, which crosses film noir with the look and feel of a Douglas Sirk film, balances between its crime element and its social commentary: Everything Harry does is within the terms of a circa-1950 middle-class suburban marriage, with what we have been taught are all of its horrors. Marriage is always bad in these dark movies. I personally think it was better than in 1950s comedies, but then that's just me. We have the same problems, but we smoke less and use more jargon. And no generation thinks its fashions look funny, although Gene Siskel used to amuse himself by watching people walking down the street and thinking to himself, "When they left home this morning, they thought they looked good in that."

But enough. What about Harry's wife? She is Pat, played by Patricia Clarkson, who is so expert at portraying paragons of patient domestic virtue: so trusting, oblivious, or preoccupied that she never thinks to question Harry's absences when he's seeing Kay. Richard observes all of this in a low-key, factual way; it's as if he's telling us the story over martinis. He even addresses us directly at times.

Will Harry really try to kill his wife? Many men have killed their wives for less, shall we call them, considerate motives. Sachs and his cowriter, Oren Moverman, have based their screenplay on the pulp novel *Five Roundabouts to Heaven* by John Bingham, who, I learn from the critic Keith Uhlich, was a British intelligence agent and the original for John Le Carre's character George Smiley. Smiley, however, would be the Richard character here, not the Harry. The story has been ported from the land of roundabouts to the land of four-way stops, all except for Richard, who is British and urbane, which with Harry possibly passes for trustworthy.

Pierce Brosnan is becoming a whole new actor in my eyes, after this film, *The Matador, Evelyn,* and *The Tailor of Panama.* It's the kiss of death to play James Bond, but at least it gives you a chance to reinvent yourself. Chris Cooper reinvents himself in every film; can this be the same actor from *Adaptation*? Here he seems so respectable. Rachel McAdams does a nice job of always seeming honest and sincere, even when she makes U-turns, but Patricia Clarkson, as always, has a few surprises behind that face that can be so bland, or scornful, or in between. Still housewives run deep.

There is so much passion in this story that it's a wonder how damped down it is. Nobody shouts. And we discover that Harry is not the only person in the story who can surprise us. The lesson, I think, is that the French have the right idea, and adultery is no reason to destroy a perfectly functioning marriage. But is the movie about marriage, or sex, or murder, or the murder plot, or what? I'm not sure. It deals all those cards, and fate shuffles them. You may not like it if you insist on counting the deck after the game and coming up with fifty-two. But if you get fifty-one and are amused by how the missing card was made to vanish, this may be a movie to your liking.

Martian Child ★ ★

PG, 106 m., 2007

John Cusack (David), Joan Cusack (Liz), Bobby Coleman (Dennis), Amanda Peet (Harlee), Sophie Okonedo (Sophie), Oliver Platt (Jeff), Richard Schiff (Lefkowitz). Directed by Menno Meyjes and produced by David Kirschner, Ed Elbert, and Corey Sienega. Screenplay by Seth Bass and Jonathan Tolins, based on a novel by David Gerrold.

"I'm not human," little Dennis says at one point in *Martian Child.* So he believes. The lonely orphan has convinced himself that he was not abandoned by his parents but arrived here from Mars. To protect himself against the sun, he walks around inside a cardboard box with a slit cut for his eyes and wears a weight belt around his waist to keep himself from drifting up into the sky. At no point during the film does anyone take mercy on the kid and explain that the sun is much more pitiless on Mars and the gravity much lower.

Still, this isn't a film about planetary science but about love. Dennis attracts the attention of a lonely science fiction writer named David (John Cusack), a widower who can't get the cardboard box out of his mind and goes back to the orphanage one day with some suntan cream. Eventually, almost against his own will, he asks Dennis to come home with him for a test run and decides to adopt him. The movie is the sentimental, very sentimental, story of how that goes.

Few actors in the right role can be sweeter or more lovable than John Cusack, and he is those things almost to a fault in *Martian Child,* which is so bland and safe that it might appeal more directly to children than adults. Cusack plays another widower in his much more affecting movie *Grace Is Gone,* and you wonder why he took two fairly similar roles so closely together.

This is not to say *Martian Child* lacks good qualities. Young Bobby Coleman plays Dennis as consistent, stubborn, and suspicious, and Amanda Peet has a warm if predictable role as the woman in David's life who starts out as best friend and ends up where female best friends often do, in his arms. But it is Joan Cusack, John's real-life sister playing his movie sister, whose contribution is most welcome, because she brings a little sassiness and cynicism to a film that threatens to drown in lachrymosity.

The movie leaves no heartstring untugged. It even has a beloved old dog, and you know what happens to beloved old dogs in movies like this. Or if you don't, I don't have the heart to tell you. And there is the standard board of supervisors in control of adoptions, which without exception in this genre adopts a policy against adoptive parents who are loving and loved, or who exhibit the slightest sign of being creative or unorthodox in any way. I suspect they would rather have a kid adopted by a mercenary than a science fiction writer, especially one who hasn't already ripped off Dennis's gravity belt and left him to float up into the sky, where it is very cold and even lonelier than inside a cardboard box. ☞

Masculine, Feminine ★ ★ ★

NO MPAA RATING, 103 m., 1966 (rereleased 2005)

Jean-Pierre Leaud (Paul), Chantal Goya (Madeleine), Marlene Jobert (Elisabeth), Michel Debord (Robert), Catherine-Isabelle Duport (Catherine-Isabelle). Directed by Jean-Luc Godard and produced by Anatole Dauman. Screenplay by Godard, based on *La Femme de Paul* and *Le Signe* by Guy de Maupassant.

"We went seeking greatness in movies, and were most often disappointed. We waited for a movie like the one we wanted to make, and secretly wanted to live."

That's the line I remember best from Godard's *Masculine, Feminine*, and not the more famous "We are the children of Marx and Coca-Cola." When we found a movie like the one we secretly wanted to live, we did not even seek greatness; greatness could take care of itself. The joke at the center of *Masculine, Feminine* (1966) is that its young French characters were fascinated by America, and its young American audiences were fascinated by them. When the movie came out, we all focused on "Marx and Coca-Cola," but now I see that the operative word is "children."

I was barely older than the characters when I wrote my review of the film. I affected a certain detachment ("the French New Wave is coming full circle and recording what has happened to those influenced by it"). I didn't own up to what I really liked about the movie: the way its young hero moves casually through a world of cafés and bistros and the bedrooms of beautiful young girls, including a pop star who is maddeningly indifferent to him.

I wanted to be Paul, the character played by Jean-Pierre Leaud, or at least be Leaud, and appear in movies by Truffaut and Godard, or at least live in Paris and walk down the same streets. All of the rest—the radical politics, the sex talk, the antiwar graffiti Paul sprayed on the car of the American ambassador—was simply his performance art. By acting in that way, he could meet girls like the pop singer Madeleine (Chantal Goya) and her sexy roommates. If you didn't have the money to live in the world of a girl like that, it was a useful strategy to convince her of the purity of your poverty.

I call them "girls" deliberately, and Leaud's character is a boy. Pauline Kael, who loved the film, was even more heartless in her description, calling them "this new breed between teenagers and people." She is alert to the way they boldly discuss birth control but don't in fact have the pill or know much about sex. Yes, the French are said to be great sophisticates, but the birth control method promised to Madeleine by Paul is one with many a slip 'twixt the method and the control.

The movie has been restored in a new 35mm print. You can appreciate Godard's vigorous early visual style; long before the Dogma movement, he shoots with natural sound and light, he inserts his characters into real times and places, and he practices his own form of withdrawal by separating the movie into fifteen chapters, each one with a title. There is an extended sequence where Leaud's character "interviews" a beauty contest winner, and the entire conversation is completely understood by both of them to be a pick-up attempt.

In a buried sense, everything Leaud does in the film is single-mindedly designed to get him into bed with girls who are not very interested (or interesting). He says he is a communist. He supports the workers. He paints slogans. He makes radical political comments. He is at the barricades in the sense that barricades are found in the streets, and when he hangs out in cafés the streets are right outside. In the movie's first shot, we see him trying to flip a cigarette into his mouth in one smooth movement, Belmondo style, as in Godard's first film, *Breathless.* He never gets it right. From the way he smokes we suspect that smoking is not the point: Smoking like Belmondo is the point.

The movie was inspired by two short stories by Guy de Maupassant. I have just read one of them, *The Signal,* which is about a married woman who observes a prostitute attracting men with the most subtle of signs. The woman is fascinated, practices in the mirror, discovers she is better than the prostitute at attracting men, and then finds one at her door and doesn't know what to do about him. If you search for this story in *Masculine, Feminine,* you will not find it, despite some talk of prostitution. Then you realize that the signal has been changed but the device is still there: Leaud's character went to the movies, saw Belmondo attracting women, and is trying to master the same art. Like the heroine of de Maupassant's story, he seems caught off guard when he makes a catch.

The actress Chantal Goya was interviewed about her experience on the movie. She remembers the first day: "Jean-Pierre Leaud, whom I didn't know from Adam, or Eve, came over to me and, looking me straight in the eye, asked me point blank, 'Will you marry me?' I told him, 'We'll see later. I'm in a hurry. Bye.' I went home at noon." I'll have to see the film again to be sure, but I have the strangest feeling that moment is in the movie. The appeal of *Masculine, Feminine* may be that it's not a movie like the one they wanted to make and secretly wanted to live, but the movie they did make, and were living.

The Matador ★ ★ ★ ½

R, 96 m., 2006

Pierce Brosnan (Julian Noble), Greg Kinnear (Danny Wright), Hope Davis (Bean), Philip Baker Hall (Mr. Randy), Adam Scott (Phil Garrison), Dylan Baker (Lovell). Directed by Richard Shepard and produced by Pierce Brosnan, Bryan Furst, Sean Furst, and Beau St. Clair. Screenplay by Shepard.

I walked into *The Matador* expecting one film, and saw another. On paper, this sounds like a formula thriller, and the casting seems to confirm that: Pierce Brosnan as a hit man, and Greg Kinnear as a businessman who meets him in a hotel bar. But Brosnan redefines "hit man" in the best performance of his career ("I facilitate fatalities"), and Kinnear plays with, and against, his image as a regular kinda guy. By the time Hope Davis, Kinnear's wife, meets this killer her husband has told her so much about, she has her first question ready: "Did you bring your gun?"

The movie has a plot in which I suppose it matters who gets whacked, and why, but it's essentially a character study, in which Brosnan, Kinnear, and Davis are invited to riff on the kinds of characters they often play—maybe even get even with them. Every actor who has ever played James Bond spends years reading about how his latest role helps him to "shed the Bond image," but Brosnan appears in *Matador* with his character of Julian Noble so firmly in place that no shedding, molting, or other divestment is necessary.

Julian and Danny Wright (Kinnear) meet in the middle of the night in the hypermodern bar of a Mexico City hotel so sterile it makes the facilities in *Lost in Translation* look funky. During a moment of alcoholic truth, Mr. Wright shares with Mr. Noble the story of the death of his infant son. Julian counters with a dirty joke. Danny is insulted and walks out. But the next day they begin again after Danny demands, and receives, an apology.

Julian Noble's awkward joke is a defining moment in the movie, establishing him as a man cut off from all others, a man who confesses, "I don't live anywhere," a man wandering lost through booze and hookers, a man afraid of losing the skills that make him a useful hit man. He has lost the ability to carry on an appropriate conversation, and when Danny Wright is willing to listen to him, simply listen, he becomes grateful and they become friends.

If Julian needs a confidant, Danny needs a distraction from financial desperation. He has lost not only his child but also his job, and he is in Mexico City trying to cobble together some kind of improbable business deal. Julian offers to take him to a bullfight, and in a wonderfully written scene the conversation turns to the mechanics of hired killing. Julian picks out a man from the crowd, a man obviously with bodyguards, and walks Danny through a dress rehearsal of how he would kill the guy and get away safely.

Months pass. Back in Denver, we meet Carolyn (Hope Davis), Danny's wife. She is known as Bean. Yes, Bean. Bean and Danny are still in love; there's a sweet scene where she remembers how in high school he told her how pretty she was. The doorbell rings and it's Julian, desperate, falling to pieces, telling Danny something that we suspect may be true: "You are my only friend in the world."

Julian moves in, fascinating Bean, Danny, and their young son. Ironically, Julian is equally fascinated by Bean and Danny's love for each other: He's made his way through life, he says, "running from any emotion."

Other characters become involved. There is talk of Julian's panic attacks and a meltdown in the Philippines. His employer, Mr. Randy (Philip Baker Hall), has lost patience; he's like an investor who loved a stock but knows it's time to dump it. Julian's life may be in danger. At a crucial moment he walks through a hotel lobby carrying a gun and wearing only boots and Speedos, and although there is a reason for this, the real reason is to show Julian reduced to despair and public humiliation and meeting it with jaunty indifference.

Brosnan is so intriguing to watch in the movie. Unshaven, trembling, hung over, fearful, charming, confiding, paranoid, trusting, he clings to Danny and Bean like a lost child at the zoo. Where did he get those shirts he wears? They look like they were bought six at a time out of the back of a van at a truck stop. The richness of his comic performance depends on the way he savors and treasures this character; at no point does Brosnan apologize for Julian, or stand outside of him, or seem to invite our laughter. He is like the charming stranger you meet in a bar, who you know could become your best friend if he were not so obviously a time bomb.

Against Brosnan, Kinnear and Davis are perfect foils, enjoying his character as much as he does. The three actors do something that is essential to this kind of comedy: They refuse to be in on the joke. It's not funny for them. They never wink. The movie's writer-director, Richard Shepard, balances the macabre and the sentimental, and he understands that although his film contains questions like, "Don't successful people always live with blood on their hands?" its real subject is friendship.

Match Point ★ ★ ★ ★

R, 124 m., 2006

Jonathan Rhys-Meyers (Chris Wilton), Scarlett Johansson (Nola Rice), Emily Mortimer (Chloe Hewett Wilton), Matthew Goode (Tom Hewett), Brian Cox (Alec Hewett), Penelope Wilton (Eleanor Hewett). Directed by Woody Allen and produced by Letty Aronson, Lucy Darwin, Stephen Tenenbaum, and Gareth Wiley. Screenplay by Allen.

One reason for the fascination of Woody Allen's *Match Point* is that each and every character is rotten. This is a thriller not about good vs. evil but about various species of evil engaged in a struggle for survival of the fittest—or, as the movie makes clear, the luckiest. "I'd rather be lucky than good," Chris, the tennis pro from Ireland, tells us as the movie opens, and we see a tennis ball striking the net; it is pure luck which side it falls on. Chris's own good fortune depends on just such a lucky toss of a coin.

The movie, Allen's best since *Crimes and Misdemeanors* (1989), involves a rich British family and two outsiders who hope to enter it by using their sex appeal. They are the two sexiest people in the movie—their bad luck, since they are more attracted to each other than to their targets in the family. Still, as someone once said (Robert Heinlein, if you must know), money is a powerful aphrodisiac. He added, however, "Flowers work almost as well." Not in this movie, they don't.

The movie stars Jonathan Rhys-Meyers as Chris, a poor boy from Ireland who was on the tennis tour and now works in London as a club pro. He meets rich young Tom (Matthew Goode), who takes a lesson, likes him, and invites him to attend the opera with his family. During the opera, Tom's sister Chloe (Emily Mortimer) looks at Chris once with interest and the second time with desire. Chris does not need to have anything explained to him.

Tom's own girlfriend is Nola (Scarlett Johansson), an American who hopes to become an actress or Tom's wife, not in that order. Tom and Chloe are the children of Alec and Eleanor Hewett (Brian Cox and Penelope Wilton), who have serious money, as symbolized by the country house where the crowd assembles for the weekend. It's big enough to welcome two Merchant-Ivory productions at the same time.

Chloe likes Chris. She wants Chris. Her parents want Chloe to have what she wants. Alec offers Chris a job in "one of my companies"—always a nice touch, that. Tom likes Nola, but to what degree, and do his parents approve? All is decided in the fullness of time, and now I am going to become maddeningly vague in order not to spoil the movie's twists and turns, which are ingenious and difficult to anticipate.

Let us talk instead in terms of the underlying philosophical issues. To what degree are we prepared to set aside our moral qualms in order to indulge in greed and selfishness? I have just finished rereading *The Wings of the Dove* by Henry James, in which a young man struggles heroically with just such a question. He is in love with a young woman he cannot afford to marry, and a rich young heiress is under the impression he is in love with her. The heiress is dying. Everyone advises him he would do her a great favor by marrying her; then after her death, inheriting her wealth, he could afford to marry the woman he loves. But isn't this unethical? No one has such moral qualms in Allen's film, not even sweet Chloe, who essentially has her daddy buy Chris for her. The key question facing the major players is: greed or lust? How tiresome to have to choose.

Without saying why, let me say that fear also enters into the equation. In a moral universe, it would be joined by guilt, but not here. The fear is that in trying to satisfy both greed and lust, a character may have to lose both, which would be a great inconvenience. At one point this character sees a ghost, but this is not Hamlet's father, crying for revenge; this ghost drops by to discuss loopholes in a "perfect crime."

When *Match Point* premiered at Cannes 2005, the critics agreed it was "not a typical Woody Allen film." This assumes there is such a thing. Allen has worked in a broad range of genres and struck a lot of different notes, although often he uses a Woody Figure (preferably played by himself) as the hero. *Match Point* contains no one anything like Woody Allen, is his first film set in London, is constructed with a devious clockwork plot that would distinguish a film noir, and causes us to identify with some bad people. In an early scene, a character is reading *Crime and Punishment,* and during the movie, as during the novel, we are inside the character's thoughts.

The movie is more about plot and moral vacancy than about characters, and so Allen uses typecasting to quickly establish the characters and set them to their tasks of seduction, deception, lying, and worse. Rhys-Meyers has a face that can express crafty desire, which is not pure lust but more like lust transformed by quick strategic calculations. Goode, as his rich friend, is clueless almost as an occupation. Mortimer plays a character incapable of questioning her own happiness, no matter how miserable it should make her. Johansson's visiting American has been around the block a few times, but like all those poor American girls in Henry James, she is helpless when the Brits go to work on her. She has some good dialogue in the process.

"Men think I may be something special," she tells Chris.

"Are you?"

"No one's ever asked for their money back."

Match Point, which deserves to be ranked with Allen's *Annie Hall, Hannah and Her Sisters, Manhattan, Everyone Says I Love You,* and *Crimes and Misdemeanors,* has a terrible fascination that lasts all the way through. We can see a little way ahead, we can anticipate some of the mistakes and hazards, but the movie is too clever for us, too cynical. We expect the kinds of compromises and patented endings that most thrillers provide, and this one goes right to the wall. There are cops hanging around trying to figure out what, if anything, anyone in the movie might have been up to, but they're too smart and logical to figure this one out. Bad luck.

Me and You and Everyone We Know ★ ★ ★ ★

R, 95 m., 2005

John Hawkes (Richard), Miranda July (Christine), Miles Thompson (Peter), Brandon Ratcliff (Robby), Carlie Westerman (Sylvie), Hector Elias (Michael), Brad Henke (Andrew), Natasha Slayton (Heather), Najarra Townsend (Rebecca), Tracy Wright (Nancy). Directed by Miranda July and produced by Gina Kwon. Screenplay by July.

Miranda July's *Me and You and Everyone We Know* is a film that with quiet confidence creates a fragile magic. It's a comedy about falling in love when, for you, love requires someone who speaks your rare emotional language. Yours is a language of whimsy and daring, of playful mind games and bold challenges. Hardly anybody speaks that language, the movie suggests—only me and you and everyone we know, because otherwise we wouldn't bother knowing them.

As a description of a movie, I suppose that sounds maddening. An example. A young woman walks into a department store, and in the shoe department she sees a young man who fascinates her. His hand is bandaged. She approaches him and essentially offers the gift of herself. He is not interested; he's going through a divorce and is afraid of losing his children. She asks him how he hurt his hand. "I was trying to save my life," he says. We've already seen how it happened: He covered his hand with lighter fluid and set it on fire to delight his two sons. He didn't think lighter fluid really burns you when you do that. He was wrong. He was thinking of rubbing alcohol.

Now imagine these two characters, named Christine (Miranda July) and Richard (John Hawkes), as they walk down the street. She suggests that the block they are walking down is their lives. And so now they are halfway down the street and halfway through their lives, and before long they will be at the end. It is impossible to suggest how poetic this scene is; when it's over, you think, that was a perfect scene, and no other scene can ever be like it.

Richard and Christine are at the center of the film, but through Richard's sons we meet other characters. His seven-year-old is named Robby and is played by Brandon Ratcliff, who read my review from Sundance and wrote me a polite and helpful letter in which he assured me he's as smart as an eleven-year-old. In the movie, he visits an online sex chat room even though he knows nothing about sex. He knows enough about computers to sound like he does, however, by cutting and pasting words, and using open-ended questions. Asked what turns him on, he writes "poop," not because it does, but possibly because it is the only word he can spell that he thinks has something to do with the subject.

His fourteen-year-old brother, Peter (Miles Thompson), is being persecuted by two girls in his class named Heather (Natasha Slayton) and Rebecca (Najarra Townsend). They are intensely interested in oral sex but unsure about its theory and technique. They decide to practice on Peter. I know this sounds perverse and explicit, and yet the fact is, these scenes play with an innocence and tact that is beyond all explaining. They are about what an embarrassment and curiosity sex is when you're old enough to know it exists but too young to know how it's done and what it's for. They are much intrigued by a neighbor who is a dirty old man in theory but not in practice.

Other characters have other plans for perfect lifetimes. Young Peter, once he shakes off the relentless Heather and Rebecca, is fascinated by Sylvie (Carlie Westerman), a ten-year-old neighbor who does comparison shopping to get the best price on kitchen appliances. Peter catches her ironing some towels. They are going straight into her hope chest, she explains. She is preparing her own dowry. Her future husband, when she grows up and finds him, had better be ready to be good and married.

There is also an art curator (Tracy Wright) who has a strange way of evaluating art, as if she's afraid it may violate rules she's afraid she doesn't know. She has a sexual hunger that proves particularly hard to deal with. She is, however, able to project her longings into the uncomprehending world; the strategy she uses, and the result it brings, is a scene of such inevitability and perfection that we laugh at least partly out of admiration.

Miranda July is a performance artist; this is her first feature film (it won the Special Jury Prize at Sundance, and at Cannes won the Camera d'Or as best first film, and the Critics' Week grand prize). Performance art sometimes deals with the peculiarities of how we express ourselves, with how odd and wonderful it is to be alive. So does this film. As Richard slowly emerges from sadness and understands that Christine values him, and he must value her, for reasons only the two of them will ever understand, the movie holds its breath, waiting to see if their delicate connection will hold.

Me and You and Everyone We Know is a balancing act, as July ventures into areas that are risky and transgressive, but uses a freshness that disarms them, a directness that accepts human nature and likes to watch it at work. The MPAA gave it an R rating "for disturbing sexual content involving children," but the one thing it isn't is disturbing. When the movie was over at Sundance, I let out my breath and looked across the aisle at another critic. I wanted to see if she felt how I did. "What did you think?" she said. "I think it's the best film at the festival," I said. "Me too," she said.

Melinda and Melinda ★ ★ ★ ½

PG-13, 99 m., 2005

Radha Mitchell (Melinda), Chloe Sevigny (Laurel), Jonny Lee Miller (Lee), Will Ferrell (Hobie), Amanda Peet (Susan), Chiwetel Ejiofor (Ellis), Wallace Shawn (Sy), Larry Pine (Max). Directed by Woody Allen and produced by Letty Aronson. Screenplay by Allen.

Woody Allen's *Melinda and Melinda* begins with friends having dinner in a Chinese restaurant. One of the friends is played by Wallace Shawn, who (Allen's audiences will know) has had a famous restaurant meal or two. Shawn is a playwright, debating another playwright (Larry Pine) about whether the world is essentially tragic or comic. They devise two versions of a story, which changes in detail and tone according to whether it is comedy or tragedy, and the film cuts between those possibilities.

The exercise involves two couples, both disrupted by the unexpected entrance of a character named Melinda (played by Radha Mitchell). For Susan the independent filmmaker (Amanda Peet) and her husband, Hobie (Will Ferrell), an out-of-work actor, she is the downstairs neighbor. For the rich woman Laurel (Chloe Sevigny) and her husband, Lee (Jonny Lee Miller), an alcoholic actor, she is Laurel's old college friend.

In both cases, Melinda is the catalyst for adultery, which does not play out the same way in the two stories. Indeed, almost all the characters except Melinda are different in the two stories because you would cast a comedy differently than a tragedy. Unexpected characters like Ellis Moonsong (Chiwetel Ejiofor), a composer, turn up to supply the third point in two romantic triangles at once.

From time to time, Allen reminds us that all of these characters are being imagined by people at dinner, and all of their feelings are being created out of thin air. The film's last shot, a bold masterstroke, leaves this perfectly clear, and strands us looking at the closing credits, which as always are played over some good traditional jazz. Why won't Woody choose one of these stories or the other? Why won't he either cheer or sadden us? When he abandoned comedy for neo-Bergman exercises like *Interiors,* at least they were Bergmanesque all the way through, with no excursions into romantic comedy. Why can't he make up his mind?

But you see, he has. Allen has made up his mind to pull the rug out from under us as we stand at the cocktail party of life, chattering about how we got there, when we plan to leave, and how we'll get back home. He has shown that the rug, the party, and all of the guests are shadows flickering on the walls. *Melinda and Melinda* is a movie about the symbiosis of the filmmaker and the audience, who are required to conspire in the creation of an imaginary world. He shows us how he does it and how we do it. In its complexity and wit, this is one of his best films.

That creates a particular challenge for the actors, who are expected to act as if they are in either a comedy or a tragedy and do not know about the other half of the movie. Radha Mitchell, who is the crossover character, rises to the challenge and is impudent in the comedy and touching in the tragedy; she must have had to compartmentalize her emotions, but then that's what actors do.

The two stories are a little sketchy because neither one is required to have a beginning, middle, and end—to deliver in traditional terms. They're works in progress. That may sound frustrating, but it's sort of exciting, as if Allen is allowing us to read his early drafts. Perhaps in Woody Allen's mind a dinner party is held nightly at which his optimistic and pessimistic selves argue about his next project. *Melinda and Melinda* may be a dramatization of his creative process.

Before the movie opened, A. O. Scott wrote a provocative article in the *New York Times,* concluding: "Instead of making the movies we expect him to, (Allen) stubbornly makes the movies he wants to make, gathering his A-list casts for minor exercises in whimsy and bile that tend not to be appreciated when they arrive in theaters. How could they be? Mr. Allen will never again be his younger self, and his audience, as long as we refuse to acknowledge that fact, will never grow up, guaranteeing our further disappointment. Maybe what we have on our hands is a dead shark."

That's a reference to *Annie Hall,* which won the Oscar and was the high point of America's relationship with Woody Allen ("A relationship is like a shark. It has to constantly move forward or it dies"). With Scott's words I have some sympathy. Woody Allen made members of my generation laugh when we were young, and now he doesn't make us feel young anymore. Scott argues that by refusing to repeat himself, Allen has left himself open to the charge of repeating himself: There he goes again, doing something different. I cannot escape the suspicion that if Woody had never made a previous film, if each new one was Woody's Sundance debut, it would get a better reception. His reputation is not a dead shark but an albatross, which, with admirable economy, Allen has arranged for the critics to carry around their own necks.

Melinda fails the standards of most audiences because it doesn't deliver a direct emotional charge. It doesn't leave us happy or sad for the characters, or even knowing which characters we were supposed to care about. That, however, is not Allen's failure, but his purpose. More than any other film that comes to mind, *Melinda and Melinda* says, clearly and without compromise, that movies are only movies. They're made up of thin air, the characters are not real, they could turn out however the director wants them to. We get all worked up about what Frankie does in *Million Dollar Baby,* and would get just as worked up if he did the opposite, both times talking about Frankie as if he were real and had actually done something. At the end of *Melinda and Melinda,* we realize that neither Melinda nor Melinda is real, but Woody Allen certainly is.

Memoirs of a Geisha ★ ★ ½

PG-13, 137 m., 2005

Ziyi Zhang (Sayuri), Ken Watanabe (The Chairman), Michelle Yeoh (Mameha), Gong Li (Hatsumomo), Koji Yakusho (Nobu), Youki Kudoh (Pumpkin), Kaori Momoi (Mother), Suzuka Ohgo (Chiyo). Directed by Rob Marshall and produced by Douglas Wick, Lucy Fisher, and Steven Spielberg. Screenplay by Robin Swicord and Doug Wright, based on the book by Arthur Golden.

I suspect that the more you know about Japan and movies, the less you will enjoy *Memoirs of a Geisha.* Much of what I know about Japan I have learned from Japanese movies, and on that basis I know this is not a movie about actual geishas but depends on the romanticism of female subjection. The heroines here look so very beautiful and their world is so visually enchanting as they live trapped in sexual slavery.

I know, a geisha is not technically a prostitute. Here is a useful rule: Anyone who is "not technically a prostitute" is a prostitute. As dear old Henry Togna, proprietor of the Eyrie Mansion in London, used to cackle while describing to me his friend the Duchess of Duke Street, "Sex for cash, m'dear. That's my definition."

Is the transaction elevated if there is very little sex, a lot of cash, and the prostitute gets hardly any of either? Hard to say. Certainly the traditions of the geisha house are culturally fascinating in their own right. But if this movie had been set in the West, it would be perceived as about children sold into prostitution, and that is not nearly as wonderful as "being raised as a geisha."

Still, I object to the movie not on sociological grounds but because I suspect a real geisha house floated on currents deeper and more subtle than the broad melodrama on display here. I could list some Japanese films illustrating this, but the last thing the audience for *Memoirs of a Geisha* wants to see is a more truthful film with less gorgeous women and shabbier production values.

This is one of the best-looking movies in some time, deserving comparison with *Raise the Red Lantern* (in more ways than one). On the level of voluptuous visual beauty, it works if you simply regard it. The women are beauties, their world swims in silks and tapestries, smoke and mirrors, and the mysteries of hair when it is up vs. hair when it is down.

I am not disturbed in the least that the three leading Japanese characters in the film are played by women of Chinese descent. This casting has been attacked as ethnically incorrect, but consider that the film was made by a Japanese-owned company; the intent was not to discriminate against Japanese, but in favor of the box office. The movie was cast partly on the basis of star power: Ziyi Zhang, Gong Li, and Michelle Yeoh are not only great beauties and gifted actresses but box-office dynamite. Even in Japan, Zhang and Li outgross any Japanese actress.

They do wonders with their characters, who are trapped in a formula fiction but suggest possibilities they cannot explore. There isn't the faintest suggestion of free will, but then free will has never played much of a role in the world of a geisha. That's made clear at the outset, circa 1929, when a widowed fisherman sells his daughters on the human market in Kyoto. The older girl, although hardly old enough for sex, is sold directly into prostitution, while the nine-year-old Chiyo (Suzuka Ohgo) is sold to a geisha house where she will be an unpaid servant until it is determined if she is elegant enough for the house's clientele.

The house is run by Mother (Kaori Momoi), and its ruling geisha is Hatsumomo (Li). Chiyo quickly becomes best friends with Pumpkin (Youki Kudoh), a girl about her age, and they are raised by the house under a strict discipline that trains them for a lifetime of flattering wealthy men. They learn that love has no role in this world (although Hatsumomo sets a bad example). Geisha lore hints that they do fall in love with clients, but the operative word is "client" and the love is not free. Nobody wants it to be—not the geisha, who is earning her living, or the client, who is using money to control a woman while maintaining his independence and, for that matter, to observe a distinction between his geisha and his wife.

The key male in the story is the Chairman (Ken Watanabe), who first encounters Chiyo when she is a child and suggests her to Mother. As Chiyo and her beauty grow, it becomes clear she may represent a threat to the dominance of Hatsumomo. The story resumes when she is in her mid-teens and is purchased from Mother by Mameha (Yeoh), Hatsumomo's rival, whose master plan is to use her control of the younger girl to win control of Mother's house away from Hatsumomo, who expects to inherit the reins. Hatsumomo in response acquires Pumpkin as her own proxy in the battle. It is amazing that a client stepping through their doors is not killed in the crossfire.

Chiyo is renamed Sayuri and is now played by Zhang. The movie, almost like a tourist, prowls the geisha quarter of Kyoto, visits a sumo wrestling match, and attends a dance performance where Sayuri stars. Then World War II intervenes (that is the best word for its role in the film), and in peacetime the Chairman now desperately needs Sayuri, who has always loved and still does love him, perhaps because he steered her as a child into the best geisha house. It suits him for Sayuri to become the friend of his colleague Nobu (Koji Yakusho), and there is great intrigue surrounding the auctioning of Sayuri's virginity. This takes place, if my math is sound, at her fairly advanced age of about twenty-six, which reminds me that Oscar Levant claimed: "I've been in Hollywood so long, I knew Doris Day before she was a virgin."

I realize that my doubts and footnotes are completely irrelevant to the primary audience for this movie, which wants to see beauty, sex, tradition, and exoticism all choreographed into a dance of strategy and desire. *Memoirs of a Geisha* (directed by Rob Marshall of *Chicago*) supplies what is required elegantly and with skill. The actresses create geishas as they imagine them to have been, which is probably wiser than showing them as they were. There is a sense in which I enjoyed every frame of this movie, and another sense in which my enjoyment made me uneasy. I felt some of the same feelings during *Pretty Baby*, the 1978 film in which Brooke Shields, playing a girl of twelve, has her virginity auctioned away in New Orleans. The difference is that *Pretty Baby* doesn't evoke nostalgia or regret the passing of the world it depicts.

Memories of Tomorrow ★ ★ ★ ½

NO MPAA RATING, 122 m., 2007

Ken Watanabe (Masayuki Saeki), Kanako Higuchi (Emiko Saeki), Kenji Sakaguchi (Naoya Ito), Kazue Fukiishi (Rie Saeki), Asami Mizukawa (Keiko Ikuno), Noritake Kinashi (Shigejuki Kizaki). Directed by Yukihiko Tsutsumi and produced by Sunao Sakagami and Tatsuo Kawamura. Screenplay by Uiko

Miura and Hakaru Sunamoto, based on the novel by Hiroshi Ogiwara.

At first it's a matter of a missed word, a forgotten name. Then he forgets how to drive a familiar route. The advertising executive keeps his worries to himself, but he can't hide his problems, and eventually a doctor delivers a dread prognosis: early onset Alzheimer's. He is only forty-nine.

Memories of Tomorrow is the first movie I've seen about the disease that is told from the sick person's point of view, not that of family members. The director, Yukihiko Tsutsumi, often uses a subjective camera to show the commonplace world melting into bewildering patterns and meanings. The subject of the film, Saeki, is a high-octane ad executive with a young and eager team, and as a perfectionist, it depresses him to discover his own imperfections mounting. He forgets dates, times, business meetings. In one breathtaking scene, he gets lost in Tokyo's urban maze and takes instructions from a secretary over his cell phone while literally running back to his office.

The character is played by Ken Watanabe (*Batman, Memoirs of a Geisha, Letters from Iwo Jima*), and there is a personal element in his brave and painful performance. Watanabe is now forty-eight, and since he was thirty, I learn from the *Japan Times*, he has been fighting leukemia. His Saeki is just as determined to fight Alzheimer's and is much aided by his patient and courageous wife, Emiko (Kanako Higuchi), who writes notes naming everything in their house, prepares his daily schedule, and keeps up a brave front.

He holds on as long as he can, even accepting a lesser position and a smaller pension to stay with his company, but finally he must retire and return to a home where now it is his wife who goes out every morning to earn a salary. He has better days and worse days, and a day fraught with fear when he must make a speech at his daughter's wedding. He loses the text of his speech. "Just say anything," his wife whispers. "I'm here for you." She takes his hand.

She has the patience of a saint, but one day he physically hurts her. The director handles this painful moment with great visual tact, not showing it but instead cutting to the sudden darting of fish in an aquarium. And then his wife snaps, telling him with cold anger what a distant husband he has been, how flawed, how cruel.

The movie isn't structured like a melodrama but reflects a slow fading of the light. There are moments of almost unbearable sadness, as in what he reveals to a nurse at the end of a tour of a nursing home. And we observe the indifference of the company where he has been a salaryman all his life: Yes, thanks for your contribution; now go quietly, please, and don't let the clients know. Some films on Alzheimer's attempt to show an upside. I don't think there is an upside. At least with cancer you get to be yourself until you die.

The Memory of a Killer ★ ★ ★ ½

R, 120 m., 2005

Koen De Bouw (Eric Vincke), Jan Decleir (Angelo Ledda), Werner De Smedt (Freddy Verstuyft), Hilde De Baerdemaeker (Linda De Leenheer), Jo De Meyere (Baron De Haeck), Geert Van Rampelberg (Tom Coemans). Directed by Erik Van Looy and produced by Hilde De Laere and Erwin Provoost. Screenplay by Carl Joos and Van Looy, based on a novel by Jef Geeraerts.

The Memory of a Killer contains the elements of a typical police procedural, transcended and brought to a sad perfection by the performance of a veteran Belgian actor named Jan Decleir. In his appearance Decleir reminds me of Anthony Quinn, and in his behavior of Jean Gabin—the Gabin of the late gangster films, playing men who are weary of crime and yet live by an underworld code.

Decleir plays Angelo Ledda, a professional hit man. He is assigned to go to Antwerp in Belgium and kill a man. He protests that he is too old—he's retired. "Men like us never retire," his boss says. Angelo tells the waitress to bring fries with his steak, and she reminds him that he's already ordered them. Here is the first hint: He is in the early stages of Alzheimer's. In Belgium, he visits his senile older brother in an institution. An orderly describes the onset of his brother's symptoms. "I know how it begins," Angelo says firmly.

He is a contract killer who knows he is losing his mind. Like the hero of *Memento,* he writes notes to himself on his arm. But *The Memory of a Killer* is not another version of *Memento;* it is a full-bore traditional "policier," beginning with a plainclothes cop busting a man who is selling his eleven-year-old daughter, and continuing with a series of killings, as powerful men try to conceal their connection to child prostitution. The first man Angelo kills is a prosecutor who will not drop the investigation. His second assignment . . .

I'll leave that for you to discover. It is an assignment he will not accept. "No one will," he tells the man who wants him to do the job. Angelo is a killer, but he is also a man unwilling to cross a certain line. In her review of this movie, Manohla Dargis has a lovely observation: "Here is a thriller that asks, Are men essentially good or do they just sometimes forget to be bad?" Angelo is forgetting to be anything.

The police/criminal side of the plot could be from a novel by Ed McBain or Nicholas Freeling; the psychological side could be from Georges Simenon. The movie is based on the novel *The Alzheimer Case* by the Belgian writer Jef Geeraerts, which unthreads a plot involving buried perversion and aristocratic hauteur, contrasting it with the declining years of this hardworking professional man, the contract killer.

Koen De Bouw plays Eric Vincke, the fortyish cop assigned to the original child prostitution case; he follows the thread as it leads to powerful people and stays on the case in defiance of his superiors. Along the way, he comes to realize that Angelo Ledda is on both sides of the moral equation: as a murderer to begin with, and then as a man working against the same perverts Vincke is after. His first challenge is to figure out who Ledda really is; the old man may be declining, but he is experienced and canny, and he uses a masterstroke to throw the police off his scent.

There are crime stories, and then there are stories about people involved in crime. *The Memory of a Killer* is in the second category. It follows a rich European fictional tradition, which in addition to the authors I've mentioned also includes Michael Dibdin, Henning Mankell, and Maj Sjowall and Per Wahloo. In their work, crime is used as a quick entry into the secrets of the heart, and guilt is not assigned so easily. When Gabin plays a crook in a movie like *Touchez pas au Grisbi,* he somehow becomes the hero.

As the plot of *The Memory of a Killer* leads into a labyrinth of decadence and obscurity, one murder connects to another, and desperate men take risky measures. Old Angelo is the wild card, sought by both sides, working in the shadows, hiding out in places remembered from his childhood in Antwerp. He knows his way around. He realizes that, one way or another, he is on his last job. And that makes him doubly dangerous, because he has nothing to lose but his life, which is slipping away anyway.

Watch Decleir's performance. He never goes for the easy effect, never pushes too hard, is a rock-solid occupant of his character. Everything he has to say about Angelo is embodied, not expressed. By the end we care so much for him that the real suspense involves not the solution of the crimes but simply his well-being. Talks are already under way for a Hollywood remake of *The Memory of a Killer,* and the names of many actors have been proposed; the *Hollywood Reporter* lists DeNiro, Caan, Hopper, Hopkins. But this performance will not be easily equaled. Gene Hackman, maybe. Morgan Freeman. Robert Mitchum, if he were alive. Decleir is the real thing.

The Merchant of Venice ★ ★ ★ ½

R, 138 m., 2005

Al Pacino (Shylock), Jeremy Irons (Antonio), Joseph Fiennes (Bassanio), Lynn Collins (Portia), Zuleikha Robinson (Jessica), Kris Marshall (Gratiano), Charlie Cox (Lorenzo). Directed by Michael Radford and produced by Cary Brokaw, Michael Cowan, Barry Navidi, and Jason Piette. Screenplay by Radford, based on the play by William Shakespeare.

Thinking to read *The Merchant of Venice* one more time, I took down the volume of Shakespeare's tragedies, only to be reminded that this dark and troubling play is classified with his comedies. Its two natures come from different spheres; sunny scenes of romance alternate with sadness, desperation, and guile. When Jessica, Shylock's daughter, steals his fortune and leaves his home to marry Lorenzo, it's as if she's escaping from one half of the play to the other.

Michael Radford's new production is, incredibly, the first theatrical film of the play in the sound era. There were several silent versions, and it has been done for television, but among the most important titles in Shakespeare's canon, this is the play that has been sidestepped by not only Hollywood but every film industry in the world. The reason is plain to see: Shylock, the moneylender who demands repayment with a pound of flesh, is an anti-Semitic caricature; filmmakers turned away and chose more palatable plays.

Yet Shylock is an intense, passionate character in a great play, and Radford's film does him justice. Although Shylock embodies anti-Semitic stereotypes widely held in Shakespeare's time, he is not a one-dimensional creature like Marlowe's *The Jew of Malta,* but embodies, like all of Shakespeare's great creations, a humanity that transcends the sport of his making. Radford's Shylock, played with a rasping intensity by Al Pacino, is not softened or apologized for—that would deny the reality of the play—but he is *seen* as a man not without his reasons.

The film opens by visualizing an event referred to only in dialogue in the original: We see the merchant Antonio (Jeremy Irons) spit at Shylock on the Rialto bridge, as part of a demonstration against the Jews who are both needed and hated in Venice—needed, because without moneylenders the city's economy cannot function, and hated, because Christians must therefore do business with the same people they have long executed a blood libel against.

That Antonio spits at Shylock, asks him for a loan of 3,000 ducats, and boldly tells him he would spit at him again is, in modern terms, asking for it. That Shylock loans him the money against the guarantee of a pound of flesh is not simply a cruelty, but has a certain reason; Shakespeare's dialogue makes it clear that Shylock proudly declines to accept any monetary interest from Antonio and has every reason to think Antonio can repay the loan, which means that Shylock will have borrowed the money at cost to himself and loaned it to Antonio for free.

That Antonio comes within a whisper of losing his flesh and his life is, after all, the result of a bargain he quickly agreed to, because he also thought he would escape without paying interest. Shakespeare's great courtroom scene, in which the Doge must decide between the claims of Shylock and the life of Antonio, is undercut by the farce of the cross-dressing Portia's last-second appeal; on the merits of the case, Shylock should win.

But I have written as if you know who Shylock and Antonio and Portia are, and you may not; *The Merchant of Venice* is studiously avoided in those courses that seek to introduce Shakespeare to students, who can tell you all about Romeo and Juliet. One of the strengths of the film is its clarity. A written prologue informs us of the conditions of Jewish life in Venice in 1586; Jews were forced to live in a confined area that gave the word "ghetto" to the world, were forbidden to move through the city after dark (although they seem to do a lot of that in the film), and were tolerated because Christians were forbidden to lend money at interest, and somebody had to.

The plot is driven from the comic side by the desire of Bassanio (Joseph Fiennes) to wed the fair Portia (Lynn Collins). She has been left by her father's will in the position of a game show prize; her suitors are shown chests of gold, silver, and lead, and made to choose one; inside the lucky chest is the token of their prize. Elementary gamesmanship cries out "Lead! Choose the lead!" but one royal hopeful after another goes for the glitter, and the impoverished Bassanio still has a chance.

He will need money to finance his courtship, and turns to his friend Antonio. The play famously opens with Antonio's melancholy ("I know not why I am so sad"), but the casting of Jeremy Irons makes that opening speech unnecessary; he is an actor to whom sadness comes without effort, and a dark gloom envelops him throughout the play. The reason for this is implied by Shakespeare and made clear by Radford: Antonio is in love with Bassanio, and in effect is being asked for a loan to finance his own romantic disappointment. Whether he and Bassanio were actually lovers is a good question. How genuinely Bassanio can love Portia the lottery prize is another. That these two questions exist in the same place is a demonstration of the way in which Shakespeare boldly juxtaposes inner torment and screwball comedy.

Shylock is a cruel caricature, but isn't he also one of the first Jews allowed to speak for himself in gentile European literature, to argue his case, to reveal his humanity? It's possible that Shakespeare never actually met a Jew (to be a Catholic was a hanging offense in his England), but then he never visited Venice, either—or France, Denmark, or the seacoast of Bohemia. His Shylock begins as a lift from literary sources, like so many of his characters, and is transformed by his genius into a man of feelings and deep wounds. There is a kind of mad incongruity in the play's intersecting stories, one ending in sunshine, marriage, and happiness, the other in Shylock's loss of everything—daughter, fortune, home, and respect. And Shylock's great speech, beginning "Hath not a Jew eyes?" is a cry against anti-Semitism that rings down through the centuries. It is wrong to say that *The Merchant of Venice* is not "really" anti-Semitic—of course it is—but its venom is undercut by Shakespeare's inability to objectify any of his important characters. He always sees the man inside.

Pacino is a fascinating actor. As he has grown older he has grown more fierce. He is charged sometimes with overacting, but never with bad acting; he follows the emotions of his characters fearlessly, not protecting himself, and here he lays bare Shylock's lacerated soul. He has a way of attacking and caressing Shakespeare's language at the same time. He loves it. It allows him reach and depth. His performance here is incandescent.

Of the others, Irons finds the perfect note for the treacherous role of Antonio; making his love for Bassanio obvious is the way to make his behavior explicable, and so Antonio for once is poignant, instead of merely a mope. The young people, Bassanio and Portia, resolutely inhabit their comedy, unaware of the suffering their romance is causing for others. Only Jessica (Zuleikha Robinson) still seems inexplicable; how can she do what she does to her father, Shylock, with such vacuous contentment?

The film is wonderful to look at, saturated in Renaissance colors and shadows, filmed in Venice, which is the only location that is also a set. It has greatness in moments, and is denied greatness overall only because it is such a peculiar construction; watching it is like channel-surfing between a teen romance and a dark abysm of loss and grief. Shylock and Antonio, if they were not made strangers by hatred, would make good companions for long, sad conversations punctuated by wounded silences.

Michael Clayton ★ ★ ★ ★

R, 119 m., 2007

George Clooney (Michael Clayton), Sean Cullen (Gene Clayton), Tom Wilkinson (Arthur Edens), Tilda Swinton (Karen Crowder), Sydney Pollack (Marty Bach), Michael O'Keefe (Barry Grissom), Ken Howard (Don Jefferies), Denis O'Hare (Mr. Greer). Directed by Tony Gilroy and produced by Jennifer Fox, Kerry Orent, Sydney Pollack, and Steve Samuels. Screenplay by Gilroy.

George Clooney brings a slick, ruthless force to the title role of *Michael Clayton*, playing a fixer for a powerful law firm. He works in the shadows, cleaning up messes, and he is a realist. He tells clients what they don't want to hear. He shoots down their fantasies of "options." One client complains bitterly that he was told Clayton was a miracle worker. "I'm not a miracle worker," Clayton replies. "I'm a janitor."

Clooney looks as if he stepped into the role from the cover of *GQ*. It's the right look. Conservative suit, tasteful tie, clean shaven, every hair in place. Drives a leased Mercedes. Divorced, drives his son to school, has him on Saturdays. Has a hidden side to his life. Looks prosperous but lost his shirt on a failed restaurant and needs $75,000 or bad things might happen. Would certainly have $75,000 if he didn't frequent a high-stakes poker game in a back room in Chinatown. Not much of a personal life.

Clayton works directly with Marty Bach (Sydney Pollack), the head of the law firm; it's one of those Pollack performances that embody authority, masculinity, intelligence, and knowing the score. But one of Bach's top partners has just gone berserk, stripping naked in Milwaukee during a deposition hearing and running through a parking lot in the snow. This is Arthur Edens (Tom Wilkinson), who opens the film with a desperate voice-over justifying himself to Michael.

The video of the deposition is not a pretty sight. One of the people watching it in horror is Karen Crowder, the chief legal executive for one of Marty Bach's most important clients, a corporation being sued for poisonous pollution. Crowder is played by Tilda Swinton, who has been working a lot lately because of her sheer excellence; she has the same sleek grooming as Clayton, the power wardrobe, every hair in place. Thinking of Clooney, Pollack, Wilkinson, and Swinton, you realize how much this film benefits from its casting. Switch out those four and the energy and tension might evaporate.

The central reality of the story is that the corporation is guilty, it is being sued for billions, the law firm knows it is guilty, it is being paid millions to run the defense, and now Arthur Edens holds the smoking gun, and it's not quite all he's holding when he runs naked through the parking lot.

Enough of the plot. Naming the film after Michael Clayton is an indication that the story centers on his life, his loyalties, his being just about fed up. Arthur Edens is a treasured friend of his, a bipolar victim who has stopped taking his pills and now glows with reckless zeal and conviction. We meet Clayton's family, we get a sense of the corporate culture he inhabits, and we sense how controlling the risks of other people sends him to the poker tables to create and confront his own risks—sort of an antidote.

The legal-business-thriller genre has matured in the last twenty years, led by authors like John Grisham and actors like Michael Douglas. It involves high stakes, hidden guilt, desperation to contain information, and mighty executives blindsided by *gotcha!* moments. We're invited to be seduced by the designer offices, the clubs, the cars, the clothes, the drinks, the perfect corporate worlds in which sometimes only the restroom provides a safe haven.

I don't know what vast significance *Michael Clayton* has (it involves deadly pollution but isn't a message movie). But I know it is just about perfect as an exercise in the genre. I've seen it twice, and the second time, knowing everything that would happen, I found it just as fascinating because of how well it was all shown happening. It's not about the destination but the journey, and when the stakes become so high that lives and corporations are on the table, it's spellbinding to watch the Clooney and Swinton characters eye to eye, raising each other, both convinced the other is bluffing.

The movie was written and directed by Tony Gilroy, son of the director Frank D. Gilroy (*The Subject Was Roses*). It's the directing debut for Gilroy, who is a star screenwriter (all three *Bourne* pictures, *Extreme Measures, The Devil's Advocate, Proof of Life*). As a first-time director, his taste runs toward the classical style and not toward the Bourne shaky cam.

Working with the great cinematographer Robert Elswit (*Syriana; Good Night, and Good Luck; Magnolia*), he uses stable, brooding establishing shots, measured editing that underlines the tension in conversations, and lighting that separates the fluorescent sterility of Clayton's business world from the warmth of family homes and the eerie quiet of a field at dawn.

When he shows us Arthur Edens's loft, it has the same sort of chain-link enclosure that Gene Hackman's character had in *The Conversation*, and they are the same kinds of characters: paranoid, in possession of damaging evidence, not as well protected as they think. The thing about Michael Clayton is, he's better at knowing how well protected they are and what they think. ☞

A Mighty Heart ★ ★ ★ ½

R, 100 m., 2007

Angelina Jolie (Mariane Pearl), Dan Futterman (Daniel Pearl), Archie Panjabi (Asra Nomani), Irrfan Khan (Captain), Will Patton (Randall Bennett), Denis O'Hare (John Bussey), Aly Khan (Omar Saeed Sheikh). Directed by Michael Winterbottom and produced by Brad Pitt, Dede Gardner, and Andrew Eaton. Screenplay by John Orloff, based on the memoir by Mariane Pearl.

A Mighty Heart begins with shots of the teeming streets of Karachi, Pakistan, a city with a population that seems jammed in shoulder-to-shoulder. Terrorists will emerge from this sea of humanity, kidnap the American journalist Daniel Pearl, and disappear. The film is about the desperate search for Pearl (Dan Futterman) before the release of the appalling video showing him being beheaded. It is told largely through the eyes of, and based on a memoir by, his widow, Mariane.

We know how the story is going to end. The real drama is played out with the natures of the people looking for him. They include his pregnant wife, a French radio journalist who conceals her grief behind a cool and calculating facade to help her husband's chances; their friend Asra (Archie Panjabi), whose apartment becomes a nerve center; a Pakistan security official (Irrfan Khan), whose uncertain position reflects the way his country accepts American money and harbors terrorists; an American agent (Will Patton), whose skills are better adapted to American cities; and one of Pearl's bosses at the *Wall Street Journal* (Denis O'Hare), who offers encouragement without much reason.

Standing at the center of the story is Mariane Pearl, played by Angelina Jolie in a performance that is both physically and emotionally convincing. A few obvious makeup changes make her resemble the woman we saw so often on TV (curly hair, darker skin, the swelling belly), but Jolie's performance depends above all on inner conviction; she reminds us, as we saw in some of her earlier films like *Girl, Interrupted* (1999), that she is a skilled actress and not merely (however entertainingly) a tomb raider.

The movie, directed by the versatile British filmmaker Michael Winterbottom (*24 Hour Party People, The Road to Guantanamo*), is notable for what it leaves out. Although we do meet the possible suspect Omar Saeed Sheikh (Aly Khan), there are not any detailed scenes of Pearl with his kidnappers, no portrayals of their personalities or motivations, and we do not see the beheading and its video. That last is not just because of Winterbottom's tact and taste, but because (I think) he wants to portray the way Pearl has almost disappeared into another dimension. His kidnappers have transported him outside the zone of human values and common sense. We reflect that the majority of Muslims do not approve of the behavior of Islamic terrorists, just as the majority of Americans disapprove of the war in Iraq.

Many thrillers depend on action, conflict, triumph, and defeat. This one depends on impotence and frustration. The kidnappers cannot do more than snatch one unarmed man after he gets out of a taxi, and Pearl's friends are lost in a maze of clues, lies, gossip, and dead ends. The movie has been described as a "police procedural," but I saw it more as a stalemate.

Mariane Pearl reminds us in her book, and the movie reminds us, too, that some 230 other journalists have lost their lives since Pearl's kidnapping, most of them during the conflict in Iraq. That means they proportionately had a higher death rate than combat soldiers. That's partly because they are ill-prepared for the risks they take, and partly because they're targets. The Americans who complain about "negative" news are the ideological cousins of those who shoot at CNN crews. The news is the news, good or bad, and those who resent being informed of it are pitiful. More Americans are well informed about current sports and auto-racing statistics, I sometimes think, than anything else.

What is most fascinating about Mariane Pearl, in life and in this movie, is that she is not a stereotyped hysterical wife, weeping on camera, but a cool, courageous woman who behaves in a way best calculated to save her husband's life. Listen to her speak and sense how her mind works. While you experience the fear and tension that Winterbottom records, see also how she tries to use it and not merely be its victim.

What is best about *A Mighty Heart* is that it doesn't reduce the Daniel Pearl story to a plot, but elevates it to a tragedy. A tragedy that illuminates and grieves for the hatred that runs loose in our world, hatred as a mad dog that attacks everyone. Attacks them for what seems, to the dog, the best of reasons.

Millions ★ ★ ★ ★

PG, 97 m., 2005

James Nesbitt (Ronnie Cunningham), Daisy Donovan (Dorothy), Lewis McGibbon (Anthony Cunningham), Alex Etel (Damian Cunningham), Christopher Fulford (The Man). Directed by Danny Boyle and produced by Graham Broadbent, Andrew Hauptman, and Damian Jones. Screenplay by Frank Cottrell Boyce.

"It isn't the money's fault it got stolen."

That is the reasoning of Anthony Cunningham, who at nine is more of a realist than his seven-year-old brother, Damian. Therefore, it isn't their fault that a bag containing 265,000 British pounds bounced off a train and into Damian's playhouse and is currently stuffed under their bed.

Danny Boyle's *Millions,* a family film of limitless imagination and surprising joy, follows the two brothers as they deal with their windfall. They begin by giving some of it away, taking homeless men to Pizza Hut. Damian wants to continue their charity work, but Anthony leans toward investing in property. They have a deadline: In one week the U.K. will say goodbye to the pound and switch over to the euro; maybe, thinks Anthony, currency speculation would be the way to go.

Here is a film that exists in that enchanted realm where everything goes right—not for the characters, for the filmmakers. They take an enormous risk with a film of sophistication and whimsy, about children, money, criminals, and saints. Damian collects the saints—"like baseball cards," says Richard Roeper. He knows all their statistics. He can see them clear as day, and have conversations with them. His favorite is St. Francis of Assisi, but he knows them all: When a group of Africans materializes wearing halos, Damian is ecstatic: "The Ugandan martyrs of 1881!"

The boys' mother has died, and Damian asks his saints if they have encountered a Saint Maureen. No luck, but then heaven is limitless. Their dad, Ronnie (James Nesbitt), has recently moved them into a newly built suburb outside Liverpool, where the kids at school are hostile at first. Anthony finds it cost-efficient to bribe them with money and neat stuff. Damian, under advice from St. Francis, wants to continue giving money to the poor. Anthony warns him urgently that throwing around too much money will draw attention to them, but Damian drops 10,000 pounds into a charity collection basket. When the boys find out the money was stolen, Damian thinks maybe they should give it back, which is when Anthony comes up with the excellent reasoning I began with.

Perhaps by focusing on the money and the saints I have missed the real story of *Millions,* which involves the lives of the boys, their father, and the woman (Daisy Donovan) who works at the charity that finds the fortune in its basket. The boys are dealing with the death of their mother, and the money is a distraction. Their father is even lonelier; maybe too lonely to ever marry again, maybe too distracted to protect his boys against the bad guy (Christopher Fulford), who dreamed up the perfect train robbery and is now skulking about the neighborhood looking for his missing bag of loot.

By now you may have glanced back to the top of the review to see if I really said *Millions* was directed by Danny Boyle, who made *Shallow Grave, Trainspotting,* and the zombie movie *28 Days Later.* Yes, *the* Danny Boyle. And the original screenplay and novel are by Frank Cottrell Boyce, who wrote *Hilary and Jackie* and *24 Hour Party People.* What are these two doing making a sunny film about kids?

I don't require an answer for that, because their delight in the film is so manifest. But they are serious filmmakers who do not know how to talk down to an audience, and although *Millions* uses special effects and materializing saints, it's a film about real ideas, real issues, and real kids. It's not sanitized, brainless eye candy. Like all great family films, it plays equally well for adults—maybe better, since we know how unusual it is.

One of its secrets is casting. In Alex Etel and Lewis McGibbon the film has found two of the most appealing child actors I've ever seen. Alex is like the young Macaulay Culkin *(Home Alone)* except that he has no idea he is cute, and like the young Haley Joel Osment *(The Sixth Sense)* in that he finds it perfectly reasonable to speak with dead people. There is no overt cuteness, no affected lovability, not a false note in their performances, and the movie allows them to be very smart, as in Anthony's theory about turning the pounds into dollars and buying back into euros after the new currency falls from its opening-day bounce.

Of course, that involves the difficulty of two boys ages seven and nine trying to convert 265,000 pounds into anything. They can't just walk into a bank with a note from their dad. The movie handles this and other problems with droll ingenuity, while also portraying a new suburban community in the making. An opening shot by Boyle, maybe a sly dig at Lars von Trier's *Dogville,* shows the boys visiting the site of their new neighborhood when it consists only of chalk outlines on the ground. After the new homeowners move in, a helpful policeman cheerfully advises a community meeting that they should expect to be burgled, and he tells them which forms to ask for at the police station.

Boyce, a screenwriter who often works with Michael Winterbottom, is so unpredictable and original in his work that he could be called the British Charlie Kaufman, if they were not both completely distinctive. He got the inspiration for *Millions*, he says, from an interview in which Martin Scorsese said he was reading the lives of the saints.

The idea of characters getting a sudden cash windfall is not new, indeed has been a movie staple for a century. What's original about the movie is the way it uses the money as a device for the young brothers to find out more about how the world really works, and what is really important to them. The closing sequence is a bit of a stretcher, I will be the first to admit, but why not go for broke? One of the tests of sainthood is the performance of a miracle, and since Damian is clearly on the road to sainthood, that is permitted him. For that matter, Boyce and Boyle have performed a miracle with their movie. This is one of the best films of the year.

Millions (A Lottery Story) ★ ★ ★ ½

No MPAA Rating, 101 m., 2008

With Phylis Breth, Barb and Dwain Nelson, Donna Lange, Curtis Sharp, Susan and Donny Breth, and Lou Eisenberg. A documentary directed by Paul La Blanc and produced by La Blanc and Jordon Katon.

Millions (A Lottery Story) is not so much about six lottery winners as about six people whom I watched with growing fascination and affection. What did I expect when the movie began? Former millionaires now on Skid Row, I suppose, contrasted with misers counting their compound interest and intercut with bizarre misadventures. What I found were people who, if I may say so, are utterly unfazed by their sudden wealth, and who have developed strategies for coping not with wealth or poverty, but with life. They all seem happy, and it has nothing to do with the lottery.

The movie follows four kitchen workers from a Minnesota high school and two New Yorkers who were once famous because they were the first to win $5 million at the dawn of the lottery and became the stars of television ads. The Minnesotans, sixteen altogether, split up $95,450,000 on a shared Powerball ticket, which works out to $5,965,625 apiece, a figure none of them ever once mentions.

They're from Holdingford, Minnesota, a town that Garrison Keillor himself once called "the Lake Wobegonest town in Minnesota." The town is so typical of his monologues that not only are the high schoolers' grades above average, but the interstate highway makes a four-mile detour just to avoid it. Of the four women we meet, all come from large families (I'm talking like eleven or sixteen kids), all worked hard on family dairy farms, many still keep dairy cattle as a second job, and none of them quit their jobs in the high school kitchen.

Phylis Breth is most eloquent about staying on the job. "These are my best friends, and I love my work." She is a dishwasher, and uses a little laugh to end many sentences. "I've got bad knees, I've had four surgeries, and this job keeps you going. On days when they serve mashed potatoes or cheese, it gets pretty hectic." Like some of the others, she bought a new house, not a mansion, just comfy, and she finally has what she long dreamed of, a refrigerator with an ice-cube maker. She still hits all the garage sales, pouncing on a two-dollar ice cream scoop.

Of the New Yorkers, who won in the early 1970s, Lou Eisenberg lives in retirement in West Palm Beach, in a very basic condo. All of his winnings are gone, and he gets by on Social Security and a small pension. But he has a girlfriend, knows people everywhere he goes, bets at the dog track daily. He spent every lottery check almost as it came in. Why didn't he invest for the future? "I never thought I would live to be seventy-six."

The other, Curtis Sharp, has also run through his winnings. Some of them went to invest in a company claiming to make an electric automobile that could run forever without ever being recharged. At one point the company was valued at "billions," he assures us, before the government came in and charged the organizer with selling fraudulent stock. Curtis still believes the guy was on the level: "Someday that investment is going to pay off." Having been a "drinker and fornicator," he moved to Nashville to buy a beer joint. Then he saw the light, found Jesus, and is a preacher.

The two of them became famous for their New York Lotto commercials. "A Jew and a black man," Lou says. "A good fit." Curtis was known for his bowler hats and collected one hundred. Before winning, Lou had owned a beauty shop, but something came over him one day, he developed panic attacks, and found he could not speak or look people in the eye. He got a job at $240 a week, screwing in lightbulbs. The Lotto saved him: "It was like a shot in the arm." It sure was. We see clips of him gabbing away on TV with Johnny Carson, Regis Philbin, Ted Koppel, Sammy Davis Jr.

There are times in this documentary that I was reminded of work by Errol Morris. The director, Paul La Blanc, has the same ear for the American vernacular and the same eye for obsessions. Take Phylis Breth, for example. Many women clean house for days before letting a camera crew into their homes, but let's say her housekeeping is not Wobegonian. But then we meet her daughter, Susan, the opposite. As she provides a tour of her orderly pantry shelves, ticking off "1994 pickles . . . last year's tomato juice," she proudly shows us that most of her preserves are in jars that originally held the retail version of the same substances. Her homemade salsa is in a salsa jar, for example, with the original label still on.

If there is one thing the Holdingford ladies are sure of, it's that their winnings will send their children through college. Apart from that, they carry on as before. Susan's husband, Donny, is known as the "wood man," because if you have a fallen tree, he comes around and cuts it into firewood. With pride he shows a shed jammed with logs. They heat their home all winter with wood, in a climate that goes to thirty below. "I've burned wood all my life, and I will keep on burning wood as long as the good Lord lets me," he says.

Getting to know these people, I realized I knew others exactly like them. The women could come from my downstate Illinois family. Giving me a recipe once, my Aunt Mary said, "One tater for everybody, one for the pot, and one for fear of company." For fear. Perfect. I wrote it down as part of the recipe.

Mindhunters ★ ★ ½

R, 106 m., 2005

Val Kilmer (Jake Harris), Christian Slater (J. D. Reston), LL Cool J (Gabe Jensen), Jonny Lee Miller (Lucas Harper), Kathryn Morris (Sara Moore), Clifton Collins Jr. (Vince Sherman), Will Kemp (Rafe Perry), Patricia Velasquez (Nicole Willis), Eion Bailey (Bobby Whitman). Directed by Renny Harlin and produced by Cary Brokaw, Akiva Goldsman, Robert F. Newmyer, Jeffrey Silver, and Rebecca Spikings. Screenplay by Wayne Kramer and Kevin Brodbin.

One of Those Among Us Is a Killer, and We Cannot Leave This (a) Isolated Country Estate, (b) Besieged Police Station, (c) Antarctic Research Outpost, (d) Haunted House, (e) Space Station, (f) Rogue Planet, or (g) Summer Camp Until We Find Out Who It Is—or Until We All Die. It is a most ancient and dependable formula, invariably surprising us with the identity of the killer, because the evidence is carefully rigged to point first to one suspect and then another, until they persuasively clear their names by getting murdered.

In *Mindhunters,* a thriller directed by Renny Harlin, the suspects and/or victims are assembled on an isolated island that has been rigged up by the FBI as a training facility. It looks like a real town but is equipped with video cameras and hidden technology so supervisors can see how well trainees handle real-life problems, not that getting your head shattered into supercooled fragments is a challenge they'll be facing every day on the job.

The formula was used early and well by Agatha Christie, whose influence on *Mindhunters* has been cited by such authorities as the *Hollywood Reporter* and *Film Threat.* In the London play *The Mousetrap,* which is now in the second century of its run, she assembled a group of characters in a snowbound country house; one of them died, and the others tried to solve the murder during long conversations in the sitting room involving much malt whiskey, considerable tobacco, unwise "looks around the house," and the revelation that some of the people are not really strangers to one another. It was possibly this play that gave us the phrase, "Where were you when the lights went out?"

To the Agatha Christie formula, *Mindhunters*

adds another literary inspiration: George Orwell's *Decline of the English Murder,* a brilliant essay in which he celebrated the golden age of British poisoning and other ingenious methods of disposal. The victims were usually married to their killer, who tended to be a meek accountant who had fallen into a trap set by a floozy: "In the last analysis," Orwell writes, "he (commits) murder because this seems to him less disgraceful, and less damaging to his career, than being detected in adultery."

But by 1946, when Orwell was writing, British standards had fallen off fearfully, and in the famous case of the Cleft Chin Murder, "The background was not domesticity, but the anonymous life of the dance-halls and the false values of the American film." So there we go again, vulgar Americans with our wicked influence on the Brits, who in murder as elsewhere maintained elegant traditions until we spoiled the game by just having people kill each other.

Orwell might have been cheered by *Mindhunters,* although Christie would have wanted a more ingenious solution. They both might have thought that the killer in the movie goes to a dubious deal of difficulty to create elaborate murder situations that depend on perfect timing, skillful mechanics, a deep knowledge of the characters, and a single-minded focus on providing the movie with *gotcha!* scenes. Does the killer in any one of these movies ever have a moment of weariness and depression? ("What the hell, instead of rigging the liquid nitrogen and rewiring the town, I think I'll just shoot somebody.")

Not in *Mindhunters.* The people who arrive on the island are there for an exercise in the profiling of a mass killer. Can they construct a psychological profile to narrow the search to the likely suspects? Val Kilmer plays their instructor, as the kind of expert you suspect has studied *The Dummy's Guide to Profiling.* The others include LL Cool J as Gabe Jensen, a Philadelphia cop who is along as an observer; the brainy Sara Moore (Kathryn Morris); the sexy Nicole Willis (Patricia Velasquez); Vince Sherman (Clifton Collins Jr.), who uses a wheelchair; J. D. Reston (Christian Slater), a cocky showboat; and so on.

They all have a single character trait, announced with such frequency that apparently, when they packed for the island, they were allowed to bring along only one. There is the character who likes to smoke. The character who will not go anywhere without a gun. Perhaps not amazingly, each victim dies because of the weakness revealed by his trait. The ingenuity of their deaths is impressive. Murder traps are rigged all over the island; you may think they are unbelievably complicated, but I say they're nothing a rogue agent couldn't accomplish if he were assisted by an army of key grips, carpenters, best boys, electricians, set designers, art directors, special effects wizards, makeup experts, and half a dozen honey wagons.

Is the film worth seeing? Well, yes and no. Yes, because it is exactly what it is, and no, for the same reason. What always amuses me in Closed World Murders is how the survivors keep right on talking, scheming, suspecting, and accusing: They persist while bodies are piling up like cordwood. At some point, even if you were FBI material, wouldn't you run around screaming and looking for a boat so you could row the hell off that island?

The mystery, when it is solved, is both arbitrary and explained at great length. The killer gives a speech justifying his actions, which is scant comfort for those already dead. As a courtesy, why not post a notice at the beginning: "The author of a series of murders that will begin this evening would like his victims to know in advance that he has good reasons, which follow." Of course, expert profilers might be able to read the note and figure out his identity, although not, I suspect, in this case.

I will leave you with only one clue. In *House of Wax,* the movie theater is playing *Whatever Happened to Baby Jane?* In this movie, the theater marquee advertises *The Third Man.* No, the male characters are not numbered in order, so you can't figure it out that way, nor is the killer necessarily a woman. So think real hard. What else do you know about *The Third Man*? If you have never seen *The Third Man,* I urge you to rent it immediately, as a preparation (or substitute) for *Mindhunters.*

MirrorMask ★ ★

PG, 101 m., 2005

Stephanie Leonidas (Helena), Gina McKee (Joanne), Jason Barry (Valentine), Rob Brydon (Helena's Father), Dora Bryan (Nan), Robert Llewellyn (Gryphon), Andy Hamilton (Small

Hairy), Nik Robson (Pingo). Directed by Dave McKean and produced by Simon Moorhead. Screenplay by Neil Gaiman and McKean.

MirrorMask must have been a labor of love to make. Watching it is also a labor of love. The movie is a triumph of visual invention, but it gets mired in its artistry and finally becomes just a whole lot of great stuff to look at while the plot puts the heroine through a few basic moves over and over again.

The story involves Helena (Stephanie Leonidas), who is fed up with working for the Campbell Family Circus. "It's your father's dream," says her mother, Joanne (Gina McKee). Yes, but it's not Helena's dream, and she resents her parents for denying her an ordinary girlhood. "I hope you die," she tells her mom, which is an unwise move for any character who even vaguely suspects she might be in a fantasy movie. Her mom promptly collapses and is hospitalized with an unspecified but alarming illness.

Helena's fantasy life is lived through drawings of an imaginary city that looks as if Ralph Steadman were the mayor. Through a process best described by that reliable shortcut "magical," she enters this world, a fantastical universe where fish swim through the air and the people from her real world appear transformed by bizarre masks and costumes. It is a world of light and dark; the Queen of Light (also played by Gina McKee) is in a trancelike state, and apparently it's up to Helena to venture into the Dark Lands and return with the means to restore goodness and awaken the queen.

The movie's fantasy world has an eerie beauty. This beauty enchanted me for several minutes, and then it began to wear on me, and finally it was a visual slog. Sorry. The story resembles what happens in Bernard Rose's *Paperhouse* (1988), in which a girl draws a house in another world, falls ill, enters that world, and finds herself responsible for saving the lonely little boy who lives in the house. In Rose's film, the images are stark and clear, with the directness of a child's drawings. In *MirrorMask*, with artist Dave McKean as director and production designer, the images are fuzzy and foggy, and Helena encounters one weird scenario after another in a world where the nonsense logic seems cloned from Wonderland.

Helena's more hazardous adventures occur after she crosses over to the dark side and is mistaken for her mirror image, a dark and sinister girl who apparently embodies all the sinister aspects of her subconscious. The Queen of Shadows (McKee again) mistakes good Helena for bad Helena, placing good Helena in some danger but also giving her access to information that may save the day—always assuming that real Helena (who seems to have a separate existence) doesn't bring everything to a sudden end by ripping her drawings from the walls.

Jason Barry has an important role as Valentine, a juggler who becomes Helena's counselor in this alternative universe, and there are countless very strange creatures, some with shoes for heads, others weirder than that, who seem to be by Hieronymus Bosch on an acid trip. One by one, frame by frame, these inventions are remarkable; stills from the film will give you an idea of the imagination that went into it.

But there's no narrative engine to pull us past the visual scenery. Landscapes recede vaguely into dissolving grotesqueries as Helena wanders endlessly past one damn thing after another, and since everything that happens in this world is absolutely arbitrary, there's no way to judge whether any action is helpful. It's a world where no matter what Helena does, an unanticipated development will undo her effort and require her to do something else. Watching *MirrorMask*, I suspected the filmmakers began with a lot of ideas about how the movie should look, but without a clue about pacing, plotting, or destination.

Miss Congeniality 2: Armed and Fabulous ★ ½

PG-13, 115 m., 2005

Sandra Bullock (Gracie Hart), Regina King (Sam Fuller), William Shatner (Stan Fields), Heather Burns (Cheryl), Ernie Hudson (McDonald), Diedrich Bader (Joel), Enrique Murciano (Jeff Foreman), Treat Williams (Collins). Directed by John Pasquin and produced by Sandra Bullock and Marc Lawrence. Screenplay by Lawrence.

Having made the unnecessary *Miss Congeniality*, Sandra Bullock now returns with the doubly unnecessary *Miss Congeniality 2: Armed and Fabulous*. Perhaps it is not entirely unnecessary in the eyes of the producers, since the first film had a worldwide gross of $212 million, not counting home video, but it's unnecessary in the sense that there is no good reason to go and actually see it.

That despite the presence of Sandra Bullock, who remains a most agreeable actress and brings what charm she can to a character who never seems plausible enough to be funny. Does a character in a comedy need to be plausible? I think it helps. It is not enough for a character to "act funny." A lot of humor comes from tension between who the character is and what the character does, or is made to do. Since Miss Congeniality is never other than a ditz, that she acts like one is not hilarious.

You will recall that Gracie Hart (Bullock) is an FBI agent who in the first film impersonated a beauty pageant contestant in order to infiltrate—but enough about that plot, since all you need to know is that the publicity from the pageant has made her so famous that *MC2* opens with a bank robber recognizing her and aborting an FBI sting. Gracie is obviously too famous to function as an ordinary agent, so the FBI director makes her a public relations creature—the new "face of the bureau."

Since the Michael Caine character in the first film successfully groomed her into a beauty pageant finalist, you'd think Gracie had learned something about seemly behavior, but no, she's still a klutz. The bureau supplies her with Joel (Diedrich Bader), a Queer Guy for the Straight Agent, who gives her tips on deportment (no snorting as a form of laughter), manners (chew with your mouth closed), and fashion (dress like a Barbie doll). She is also assigned a new partner: Sam Fuller (Regina King), a tough agent with anger management issues, who likes to throw people around and is allegedly Gracie's bodyguard, assuming she doesn't kill her.

As Gracie is rolled out as the FBI's new face, there's a funny TV chat scene with Regis Philbin (Regis: "You don't look like J. Edgar Hoover." Gracie: "Really? Because this is his dress"). Then comes an emergency: Miss United States (Heather Burns), Gracie's buddy from the beauty pageant, is kidnapped in Las Vegas, along with the pageant manager (William Shatner).

Gracie and Sam fly to Vegas and humiliate the bureau by tackling the real Dolly Parton under the impression she is an impostor. Then they find themselves doing Tina Turner impersonations in a drag club. They also reenact the usual clichés of two partners who hate each other until they learn to love each other. And they impersonate Nancy Drew in their investigation, which leads to the thrilling rescue of Miss United States from the least likely place in the world where any kidnapper would think of hiding her.

Now a word about the name of Regina King's character, Sam Fuller. This is, of course, the same name as the famous movie director Sam Fuller *(The Big Red One, Shock Corridor, The Naked Kiss)*. Fuller (1912–1997) was an icon among other directors, who gave him countless cameo roles in their movies just because his presence was like a blessing; he appeared in films by Amos Gitai, Aki Kaurismaki and his brother Mika Kaurismaki, Larry Cohen, Claude Chabrol, Steven Spielberg, Alexandre Rockwell (twice), Wim Wenders (three times), and Jean-Luc Godard, the first to use him, in *Pierrot le Fou*, where he stood against a wall, puffed a cigar, and told the camera, "Film is like a battleground."

It may seem that I have strayed from the topic, but be honest: You are happier to learn these factoids about Sam Fuller than to find out which Las Vegas landmark the kidnappers use to imprison Miss United States and William Shatner. The only hint I will provide is that they almost drown, and Sandra Bullock almost drowns, too, as she did most famously in *Speed 2*, a movie about a runaway ocean liner. I traditionally end my reviews of the *Miss Congeniality* movies by noting that I was the only critic in the world who liked *Speed 2*, and I see no reason to abandon that tradition, especially since if there is a *Miss Congeniality 3* and it doesn't have Sam Fuller in it, I may be at a loss for words.

Mission: Impossible III ★ ★ ½

PG-13, 126 m., 2006

Tom Cruise (Ethan Hunt), Philip Seymour Hoffman (Owen Davian), Ving Rhames (Luther Stickell), Billy Crudup (John Musgrave), Michelle Monaghan (Julia), Jonathan Rhys Meyers (Declan), Keri Russell (Lindsey), Maggie Q (Zhen), Laurence Fishburne (Theodore Brassel). Directed by J. J. Abrams and produced by Tom Cruise and Paula Wagner. Screenplay by Alex Kurtzman, Roberto Orci, and Abrams, based on the TV series created by Bruce Geller.

Ethan Hunt is in some respects the least inquisitive man in action movie history. In *Mission: Impossible* (1996), he risked his life to (I quote from my original review) "prevent the theft of a computer file containing the code names and real identities of all of America's double agents." But Ethan (Tom Cruise) must prevent this theft *after* it happens because first he must "photograph the enemy in the act of stealing the information and then follow him until he passes it along." The plot also involves crucial uses for latex masks and helicopters, one of which flies through the Chunnel from England to France, which is difficult considering helicopter blades are wider than the Chunnel.

In *Mission: Impossible 2* (2000), Ethan has to stop a villain with a deadly virus: Twenty-four hours after exposure, you die. The heroine (Thandie Newton) does, however, survive at the end of the movie, leaving her available for the sequel, although by *Mission: Impossible III,* Ethan Hunt is engaged to a sweet nurse named Julia (Michelle Monaghan), who thinks he is a highway traffic control engineer. Helicopters are again involved, and Ethan falls for the old latex mask trick again and even uses a latex mask himself, so that others can be fooled and he doesn't have to feel so bad. In a nice visual pun, the helicopters encounter giant energy-generating windmills in deserts near Berlin that uncannily resemble deserts near Palm Springs. It's kind of neat when one propeller slices off another, wouldn't you agree? Observing the curious landscape outside Berlin, I was reminded that Citizen Kane built his Xanadu "on the desert coasts of Florida."

Ethan Hunt's assignment in *M:I3* is to battle the villain Owen Davian (Philip Seymour Hoffman) for control of the Rabbit's Foot. In Ethan's final words in the movie, after countless people have been blown up, shot, crushed, and otherwise inconvenienced, he asks his boss, Brassel (Laurence Fishburne), "What is the Rabbit's Foot?" Ethan should know by now it is a MacGuffin, just like the virus and the computer file.

Why does Ethan risk his life and the lives of those he loves to pursue objectives he does not understand? The answer, of course, is that the real objective of all the *M:I* movies is to provide a clothesline for sensational action scenes. Nothing else matters, and explanatory dialogue would only slow things down. This formula worked satisfactorily in *M:I,* directed by Brian De Palma, and *M:I2,* directed by John Woo, and I suppose it works up to a point in *M:I3,* directed by J. J. Abrams, if what you want is nonstop high-tech action. Even the deadlines are speeded up this time; instead of a twenty-four-hour virus, we have an explosive capsule that detonates five minutes after it zips up your nose.

The action takes us to Berlin, the Vatican City, Shanghai, and the Chesapeake Bay Bridge, although there seems to be no real reason to visit any of those cities except to stage CGI stunts involving their landmarks. I did smile at a scene where Ethan parachutes from a building and ends up hanging upside down in his harness in front of a speeding truck. I liked a moment when he jabs a needle of adrenaline into a woman's heart to bring her out of her drugged stupor; Quentin Tarantino should send him a bill. And there is the intriguing speech by an agency techie about the Anti-God Compound, a deadly by-product of technological overachievement, which might simply destroy everything. If there is an *M:I4,* I recommend the Anti-God Compound as the MacGuffin.

I didn't expect a coherent story from *Mission: Impossible III,* and so I was sort of surprised that the plot hangs together more than in the other two films. I was puzzled, however, by the nature of Ethan's relationship with Julia, his sweet fiancée. If he belongs to a secret organization that controls his life and can order him around, doesn't she deserve to know that? Or, if not, is it right for him to marry her? And when she meets his coworkers from the office, do they all talk like he does, about how if you hit the brakes, it can cause a chain reaction, slowing down traffic for hundreds of miles?

Such questions are beside the point. Either you want to see mindless action and CGI sequences executed with breakneck speed and technical precision, or you do not. I am getting to the point where I don't much care. There is a theory that action is exciting and dialogue is boring. My theory is that variety is exciting and sameness is boring. Modern high-tech action sequences are just the same damn thing over and over again: high-speed chases, desperate gun battles, all possible modes of transportation, falls from high places, deadly deadlines, exotic locations, and characters who hardly ever say anything interesting. I saw *M:I* and *M:I2* and gave them three-star ratings because they delivered precisely what they promised. But now I've been there, done that, and my hope for *M:I4*, if there is one, is that it self-destructs while mishandling the Anti-God Compound.

The Mist ★ ★

R, 125 m., 2007

Thomas Jane (David Drayton), Marcia Gay Harden (Mrs. Carmody), Laurie Holden (Amanda Dumfries), Andre Braugher (Brent Norton), Toby Jones (Ollie), William Sadler (Jim Grondin), Jeffrey DeMunn (Dan Miller), Frances Sternhagen (Irene), Alexa Davalos (Sally), Nathan Gamble (Billy Drayton). Directed by Frank Darabont and produced by Darabont and Liz Glotzer. Screenplay by Darabont, based on the story by Stephen King.

Combine (1) a mysterious threat that attacks a town and (2) a group of townspeople who take refuge together, and you have a formula apparently able to generate any number of horror movies, from *Night of the Living Dead* to *30 Days of Night*. All you have to do is choose a new threat and a new place of refuge, and use typecasting and personality traits so we can tell the characters apart.

In *The Mist*, based on a Stephen King story, a violent storm blows in a heavy mist that envelops that favorite King locale, a village in Maine. When the electric power goes out, David Drayton (Thomas Jane) and his young son, Billy (Nathan Gamble), drive slowly into town to buy emergency supplies at the supermarket. They leave Mom behind, which may turn out to be a mistake. Inside the store, we meet a mixed bag of locals and weekenders, including Brent Norton (Andre Braugher), the Draytons' litigious neighbor; Mrs. Carmody (Marcia Gay Harden), a would-be messianic leader; and the store assistant, Ollie (Toby Jones), who, like all movie characters named Ollie, is below average height and a nerd.

You may not be astonished if I tell you that there is Something Out There in the mist. It hammers on windows and doors and is mostly invisible until a shock cut that shows an insect the size of a cat, smacking into the store window. Then there are other things, too. Something with tentacles ("What do you think those tentacles are attached to?" asks David). Other things that look like a cross between a praying mantis and a dinosaur. Creatures that devour half a man in a single bite.

David and Mrs. Carmody become de facto leaders of two factions in the store: (1) the sane people, who try to work out plans to protect themselves, and (2) the doomsday apocalypse mongers, who see these events as payback for the sinful ways of mankind. Mrs. Carmody's agenda is a little shaky, but I think she wants lots of followers, and I wouldn't put the idea of human sacrifice beyond her. David advises everybody to stay inside, although of course there are hotheads who find themselves compelled to go out into the mist for one reason or another. If you were in a store and man-eating bugs were patrolling the parking lot, would you need a lot of convincing to stay inside?

David proves a little inconsistent, however, when he leads a group of volunteers to the drugstore in the same shopping center to get drugs to help a burned man. There is a moral here, and I am happy to supply it: Never shop in a supermarket that does not have its own prescription department. There is another moral, and that is that since special effects are so expensive, it is handy to have a mist so all you need is an insect here, a tentacle there, instead of the cost of entire bug-eyed monsters doing a conga line.

The movie was written and directed by Frank Darabont, whose *The Shawshank Redemption* is currently number two on IMDb's all-time best movies list, and who also made *The Green Mile*. Both were based on Stephen King's work, but I think he picked the wrong story this time. What helps, however, is that the budget is adequate to supply the cardboard characters with capable actors and to cobble together some gruesome and slimy special effects.

Everyone labors away to bring energy to the clichés, including Toby Jones, who proves that a movie Ollie may have unsuspected resources. Thomas Jane is energetic in the thankless role of the sane leader, but Marcia Gay Harden—well, give her a break; it's not a plausible or playable role. I also grew tired of Andre Braugher's neighbor, who takes so much umbrage at imagined slights that he begins to look ominously like a plot device.

If you have seen ads or trailers suggesting that horrible things pounce on people, and they make you think you want to see this movie, you will be correct. It is a competently made Horrible Things Pouncing on People movie. If you think Frank Darabont has equaled the *Shawshank* and *Green Mile* track record, you will be sadly mistaken. If you want an explanation for the insect monsters (and this is not really giving anything away), there is speculation that they arrived through a rift in the space-time continuum. Rifts in space-time continuums are one of the handiest inventions of science fiction, so now you've got your complete formula: threat to town, group of townspeople, and rift. Be my guest. ☞

Mister Lonely ★ ★

NO MPAA RATING, 112 m., 2008

Diego Luna (Michael Jackson), Samantha Morton (Marilyn Monroe), Denis Lavant (Charlie Chaplin), Anita Pallenberg (The Queen), James Fox (The Pope), Esme Creed-Miles (Shirley Temple), Richard Strange (Abraham Lincoln), Werner Herzog (Father Umbrillo). Directed by Harmony Korine and produced by Nadja Romain. Screenplay by Harmony Korine and Avi Korine.

I wish there were a way to write a positive two-star review. Harmony Korine's *Mister Lonely* is an odd, desperate film, lost in its own audacity, and yet there are passages of surreal beauty and preposterous invention that I have to admire. The film doesn't work, and indeed seems to have no clear idea of what its job is, and yet (sigh) there is the temptation to forgive its trespasses simply because it is utterly, if pointlessly, original.

All of the characters except for a priest played by Werner Herzog and some nuns live as celebrity impersonators. We can accept this from the Michael Jackson clone (Diego Luna), and we can even understand why when, in Paris, he meets a Marilyn Monroe impersonator (Samantha Morton), they would want to have a drink together in a sidewalk café. It's when she takes him home with her that the puzzlements begin.

She lives in a house with the pretensions of a castle in the Highlands of Scotland. It is inhabited by an extended family of celebrity impersonators, and they portray, to get this part out of the way, Charlie Chaplin (Denis Lavant), the Pope (James Fox), the Queen (Anita Pallenberg), Shirley Temple (Esme Creed-Miles), Abraham Lincoln (Richard Strange), Buckwheat, Sammy Davis Jr., and, of course, the Three Stooges. Now consider. How much of a market is there in the remote Highlands for one, let alone a houseful, of celebrity impersonators? How many pounds and pence can the inhabitants of the small nearby village be expected to toss into their hats? How would it feel to walk down the high street and be greeted by such a receiving line? What are the living expenses?

But such are logical questions, and you can check credibility at the door. This family is not only extended but dysfunctional, starting with Marilyn and Charlie, who are a couple, although she says she thinks of Hitler when she looks at him, and he leaves her out in the sun to burn. Lincoln is foul-mouthed and critical of everyone, Buckwheat thinks of himself as foster parent of a chicken, and the Pope proposes a toast: They should all get drunk in honor of the deaths of their sheep.

Perhaps that's how they support themselves: raising sheep. However, there seem scarcely two dozen sheep, which have to be destroyed after an outbreak of one of those diseases sheep are always being destroyed for. They're shotgunned by the Three Stooges. Or maybe there are chickens around somewhere that we don't see. The chickens would probably be in the movie in homage to Werner Herzog, who famously hates chickens.

Now you are remembering that I mentioned Herzog and some nuns. No, they do not live on the estate. They apparently live in South America, where they drop sacks of rice on hungry villages from an altitude of about two thousand feet. Rinse well. When one of the nuns survives a fall from their airplane, she calls on all of the nuns to jump, to prove their faith in God. I would not dream of telling you if they do.

Herzog feels a bond with Korine, who was

still a teenager when he wrote the screenplay for Larry Clark's great *Kids* (1995). Korine is visionary and surrealistic enough to generate admiration from Herzog, who also starred in his *Julien Donkey-Boy* (he plays a schizophrenic's father, who listens to bluegrass while wearing a gas mask). In addition to the chickens, *Mister Lonely* has another homage to Herzog, a shot of an airplane taking off, which you would have to be very, very familiar with the director's work to footnote.

Various melodramatic scenarios burrow to the surface. Marilyn is fraught with everything a girl can be fraught with. Lincoln has anger-management problems. The Pope insists he is not dead. Everyone works on the construction of a theater, in which they will present their show, expecting to—what? Stand in a spotlight and do tiny bits evoking their celebrities? Then fulsome music swells, and the underlying tragedy of human existence is evoked, and the movie is more fascinating than it has any right to be, especially considering how fascinating it is that it was made at all.

Mondovino ★ ★ ★

PG-13, 135 m., 2005

Featuring Michael Broadbent, Hubert de Montille, Aime Guibert, Jonathan Nossiter, Robert Parker, Michel Rolland, and Neal Rosenthal. A documentary directed by Jonathan Nossiter and produced by Emmanuel Giraud and Nossiter. Screenplay by Nossiter.

Mondovino applies to the world of wine the same dreary verdict that has already been returned about the worlds of movies, books, fashion, politics, and indeed modern life: Individuality is being crushed, marketing is the new imperialism, people will like what they are told to like, and sales are the only measurement of good. Briefly (although his movie is not brief), the wine lover Jonathan Nossiter argues that modern tastes in wine are being policed by an unholy alliance involving the most powerful wine producer, the most ubiquitous wine adviser, and the most influential wine critic. Together, they are enforcing a bland, mass-produced taste on a world of wine drinkers who fancy themselves connoisseurs, but basically like what they are told to like.

This does not surprise me, since I have long suspected that "oenophile" is a polite word for a trainee alcoholic who has money and knows how to pronounce the names of several wines that have worked for him in the past. I thought *Sideways* was particularly observant as it watched Miles, the oenophile played by Paul Giamatti, advance during the course of a day from elaborate sniffing, chewing, and tasting rituals to pouring the bucket of slops over his head. I treasure the Mike Royko column in which he advised the insecure on how to deal with a snotty sommelier: He will present you with the cork. Salt it lightly and eat it. This will clear your palate.

There are people who know good wine from bad, and some of them are in this movie, although you will have to take their word for it, all the time remembering that every wine drinker thinks he knows good wine from bad, even at the level where Paisano is judged superior to Mogen David, as indeed some believe. *Mondovino* says distinctive wines are being punished because they do not taste familiar; the unique local taste of great wines is being leveled by "microoxygenization," a mysterious process recommended by the wine consultant Michel Rolland that produces wines that are approved by the wine critic Robert Parker, and therefore becomes the standard for mass producers like Robert Mondavi. As Mondavi and other giants march through Europe buying up ancient vineyards, Rolland and Parker are right behind him to standardize the product.

Rolland is described in the movie as "always laughing; you have to like him." Indeed, the man seems bubbling over with private humor as he speeds in his chauffeured car from one vineyard to another, dispensing valued advice one step ahead of the serious, even self-effacing Parker, whose opinion can make or break a vineyard. That Parker is so powerful is proof that countless wine drinkers do not have taste of their own, because by definition there can be no such thing as a wine that everyone values equally; a great wine should be a wine that you think is great, and if you think it's great because Parker does, then you don't know what you like and simply require a prelubrication benediction.

This much I know from common sense. How many of the rest of Nossiter's charges are true, I cannot know, but he is persuasive. He is fluent in the language of every country he visits, talks with the powerful vintners and the little local growers, visits veteran retailers, and consults with a wine expert from Christie's who wonders "to what extent individuality has flown out the window" and concludes it has taken wing to a very great extent indeed.

Much is made of *terroir,* a French word meaning "soil" but also meaning a region, a specific place, a magical quality that a particular area imparts to the grapes it produces. Every great wine should be specifically from its own time and place, in theory, but in practice that would mean that some wines were great and most wines were not, and that's no way to run a global industry. The new goal, Nossiter believes, is to produce pretty good wine and train consumers to consider it great because they're told it is and can find the real thing only with some difficulty. Nossiter thinks some French vineyards are holding out, but that the Italians have more or less caved in to Mondavism.

He makes this argument in a film that is too long and needlessly mannered. There is no particular reason for a restless handheld camera in a documentary about wine. If we are watching a documentary about cock-fighting or the flight of the bumblebee, we can see the logic of a jumpy camera, but vineyards don't move around much and are easy to keep in frame. I am more permissive about Nossiter's other camera strategy, which is to interrupt a shot whenever a dog comes into view, in order to focus on the dog. This I understand. Whenever a dog appears at a social occasion, I immediately interrupt my conversation to greet the dog and often find myself turning back to its owner with regret.

Despite its visual restlessness and its dogs, *Mondovino* is a fascinating film, not because Nossiter turns red-faced with indignation, but because he allows his argument to make itself. There comes a point when we learn all we are likely to learn about modern wine, and the movie continues cheerfully for another thirty or forty minutes, just because Nossiter is having so much fun. Although modern wines may have lost their magic, traveling from one vineyard to another has not, and just when we think Nossiter is about to wrap it up, off he goes to Argentina. It was certainly only by an effort of will that he prevented himself from visiting our excellent Michigan vineyards. They have some magnificent dogs.

Mongol ★ ★ ★ ½

R, 126 m., 2008

Tadanobu Asano (Temudgin), Honglei Sun (Jamukha), Khulan Chuluun (Borte), Odnyam Odsuren (Young Temudgin), Amarbold Tuvshinbayar (Young Jamukha), Bayartsetseg Erdenabat (Young Borte), Amadu Mamadakov (Targutai). Directed by Sergei Bodrov and produced by Sergey Selyanov. Screenplay by Arif Aliyev and Bodrov.

Mongols need laws. I will make them obey—even if I have to kill half of them.

—Genghis Khan

Sergei Bodrov's *Mongol* is a ferocious film, blood-soaked, pausing occasionally for passionate romance and more frequently for torture. As a visual spectacle, it is all but overwhelming, putting to shame some of the recent historical epics from Hollywood. If it has a flaw, and it does, it is expressed succinctly by the wife of its hero: "All Mongols do is kill and steal."

She must have seen the movie. That's about all they do in *Mongol.* They do not sing, dance, chant, hold summit meetings, have courts, hunt, or (with one exception) even cook or eat. They have no culture except for a series of sayings: "A Mongol does, or does not . . ." a long list of things, although many a Mongol seems never to have been issued the list, and does (or does not) do them anyway. As a result, the film consists of one bloody scene of carnage after another, illustrated by hordes of warriors eviscerating one another while bright patches of blood burst upon the screen.

At the center of the killing is invariably the khan, or leader, named Temudgin (Tadanobu Asano), who is not yet Genghis Kahn, but be patient: This film is the first of a trilogy.

The film opens with Temudgin (Odnyam Odsuren) at the age of nine, taken by his father to choose a bride from the Merkit clan. This will settle an old score. But along the way they happen upon a smaller clan, and there Temudgin first sets eyes on ten-year-old Borte (Bayartsetseg Erdenabat), who informs him he should choose her as his bride. He agrees, and thus is forged a partnership that will save his life more than once.

Years pass, the two are married, and Borte (played as an adult by Khulan Chuluun) makes a perfect bride but one hard to keep possession of. She is kidnapped by another clan, bears the first of two children claimed by Temudgin despite reasons to doubt, and follows her man into a series of battles that stain the soil of Mongolia with gallons of blood.

It happens that I have seen another movie about Mongols that suggests they do more than steal and kill. This is the famous nine-hour, three-part documentary *Taiga* (1995) by Ulrike Ottinger, who lived with today's yurt dwellers, witnessed one of their trance-evoking religious ceremonies, observed their customs and traditions, and learned in great detail how they procure and prepare food. There is also a wrestling match that is a good deal more cheerful than the contests in *Mongol.* But you do not have the time for a nine-hour documentary on this subject, I suppose, nor does *Mongol.* The nuances of an ancient and ingeniously developed culture are passed over, and it cannot be denied that *Mongol* is relentlessly entertaining as an action picture.

It left me, however, with some questions. Many involve the survival of the young Temudgin. Having inherited all his father's enemies, he is captured more than once, and we actually see him being fed so he can grow tall enough to kill ("Mongols do not kill children"). His neck and hands are imprisoned in a heavy wooden yoke, and when he escapes, he has the energy to run for miles across the steppe. On another occasion, he falls through the ice of a lake, and the movie simply ignores the question of how he is saved, unless it is by Tengri, God of the Blue Sky. Yes, I think it was Tengri, who also appears as a wolf and saves him more than once. If you want to be Genghis Khan, it helps to have a god in your corner.

Finally Temudgin is imprisoned in a cell surrounded by a moat populated by savage dogs. No such arrangement can hold him, of course, and he leads his clan into yet another series of battles, as gradually it occurs to him that this is no way to live, and the Mongols need to be united under a strong leader who will enforce less anarchistic battle practices. It's at about that point the movie ends, and we reflect that Temudgin has to survive two more such films to become Genghis Khan. And we think our election campaigns run on too long.

Monster-in-Law ★

PG-13, 100 m., 2005

Jennifer Lopez (Charlie Cantilini), Jane Fonda (Viola Fields), Michael Vartan (Kevin Fields), Wanda Sykes (Ruby), Adam Scott (Remy), Annie Parisse (Morgan), Monet Mazur (Fiona), Will Arnett (Kit). Directed by Robert Luketic and produced by Paula Weinstein, Chris Bender, and J. C. Spink. Screenplay by Anya Kochoff and Richard La Gravenese.

Faithful readers will know I'm an admirer of Jennifer Lopez, and older readers will recall my admiration for Jane Fonda, whom I first met on the set of *Barbarella* (1968), so it has been all uphill ever since. Watching *Monster-in-Law,* I tried to transfer into Fan Mode, enjoying their presence while ignoring the movie. I did not succeed. My reveries were interrupted by bulletins from my conscious mind, which hated the movie.

I hated it above all because it wasted an opportunity. You do not keep Jane Fonda offscreen for fifteen years only to bring her back as a specimen of rabid Momism. You write a role for her. It makes sense. It fits her. You like her in it. It gives her a relationship with Jennifer Lopez that could plausibly exist in our time and space. It gives her a son who has not wandered over after the *E.R.* auditions. And it doesn't supply a supporting character who undercuts every scene she's in by being more on-topic than any of the leads.

No, you don't get rid of the supporting character, whose name is Ruby and who is played by Wanda Sykes. What you do is lift the whole plot up on rollers and use heavy equipment to relocate it in Ruby's universe, which is a lot more promising than the rabbit hole this movie falls into. *Monster-in-Law* fails the Gene Siskel Test: "Is this film more interesting than a documentary of the same actors having lunch?"

The movie opens by establishing Charlotte "Charlie" Cantilini (Lopez) as an awfully nice person. She walks dogs, she works as a temp, she likes to cook, she's friendly and loyal, she roughs it on Venice Beach in an apartment that can't cost more than $2,950 a month, she has a gay neighbor who's her best bud. I enjoyed these scenes, right up until the Meet Cute with Young Dr. Kevin Fields (Michael Vartan), a surgeon who falls in love with her. She can't believe a guy like that would really like a girl like her, which is unlikely, since anyone who looks like Jennifer Lopez and walks dogs on the boardwalk has already been hit on by every dot-com entrepreneur and boy band dropout in Santa Monica, and Donald Trump and Charlie Sheen.

Dr. Kevin's mother, Viola, played by Fonda, is not so much a clone of Barbara Walters as a rubbing. You get the outlines, but there's a lot of missing detail. In a flashback, we see that she was a famous television personality, fired under circumstances no one associated with this movie could possibly have thought were realistic—and then allowed to telecast one more program, when in fact security guards would be helping her carry cardboard boxes out to her car. Her last show goes badly when she attempts to kill her guest.

When we meet her, she's "fresh off the funny farm," guzzling booze, taking pills, and getting wake-up calls from Ruby, who is played by Sykes as if she thinks the movie needs an adult chaperone. Viola is seen as a possessive, egotistical, imperious monster who is, and I quote, "on the verge of a psychotic break." The far verge, I would say. When she learns that Dr. Kevin is engaged to marry Charlie, she begins a campaign to sabotage their romance, moaning, "My son the brilliant surgeon is going to marry a temp."

The movie's most peculiar scenes involve Charlie being steadfastly and heroically nice while Viola hurls rudeness and abuse at her. There is a sequence where Viola throws a "reception" for her prospective daughter-in-law and invites the most famous people in the world so the little temp will be humiliated; Charlie is so serene in her self-confidence that even though she's dressed more for volleyball than diplomacy, she keeps her composure.

All during her monster act, we don't for a second believe Fonda's character because if she really were such a monster, she would fire Ruby, who insults her with a zeal approaching joy. Anyone who keeps Ruby on the payroll has her feet on the ground. Another problem is that Dr. Kevin is a world-class wimp, who actually proposes marriage to Charlie while his mother is standing right there. No doubt Dr. Phil will provide counsel in their wedding bed.

Eventually we realize that Fonda's character consists entirely of a scene waiting to happen: the scene where her heart melts, she realizes Charlie is terrific, and she accepts her. Everything else Viola does is an exercise in postponing that moment. The longer we wait, the more we wonder why (a) Charlie doesn't belt her, and (b) Charlie doesn't jump Dr. Kevin—actually, I meant to write "dump," but either will do. By the time the happy ending arrives, it's too late, because by then we don't want Charlie to marry Dr. Kevin. We want her to go back to walking the dogs. She was happier, we were happier, the dogs were happier.

Mountain Patrol: Kekexili ★ ★ ★ ½

NO MPAA RATING, 90 m., 2006

Duobuji (Ri Tai), Lei Zhang (Ga Yu), Liang Qi (Liu Dong), Xueying Zhao (Leng Xue). Directed by Chuan Lu and produced by Wan Zhongjun. Screenplay by Chuan.

You are away from home for two or three years at a stretch. You belong to a band of armed men who patrol the desolate Kekexili region of Tibet in mud-covered jeeps and military vehicles. Your existence is sanctioned by the government, but you are not "officially employed." You have not been paid in a year. Your leader observes, "We are short of men, short of money, short of guns." You are four miles above sea level, the air is thin, the sun pitiless, you cannot see a living thing on the horizon, and there are others out there, better equipped, ready to kill you.

This is the life of the characters in *Mountain Patrol: Kekexili*, and what is their mission? To save the endangered Tibetan antelope, whose pelts were so prized by silly women that their population was reduced in the 1990s from millions to thousands. Why do you dedicate your life and endure this misery for such a cause? The movie contains no idealistic speeches, and the patrol members are not tree huggers.

A journalist from Beijing (Lei Zhang) ventures to this far country to spend some time living with the mountain patrol. He meets their legendary leader, Ri Tai (Duobuji). They roar off into the desolation, a band of hardened men, hunting their dinner, roasting it over fires, cutting it with knives that are also weapons. Ri Tai is a man of few words, a man consumed by his mission, and he and his men remind me of the desperadoes in Cormac McCarthy's *Blood Meridian.* They are hunting poachers instead of Native Americans, but their focus is as intense. They consider themselves the hand of justice.

What is remarkable is that this film is based on a true story and filmed on the actual locations. These are hard, violent men, risking their lives to save an animal species. In appearance and behavior, they could be commandos, insurgents, terrorists. The poachers are no less desperate, and the film opens with the murder of a patrolman. In a strange way, the patrol and the poachers feel a bond; they are the only humans on this high plateau, both drawn there by a fascination with the antelope, and they share an existence no one else knows.

It is conventional to speak of the beauty of a vast, unspoiled wilderness, but the Kekexili is not where you would choose to live for three years. It is very dry. Color has been bleached from the land, which is sand and ochre and stark shadows. The desert offers no relief, and the mountains offer ambush. There is a particularly horrifying scene where a man steps into dry quicksand. He struggles, and then he simply stops moving and becomes utterly passive as inch by inch he sinks to his death, and then there is nothing to show he was there.

The journalist makes some discoveries. Ri Tai, the patrol leader, tells him that when they capture antelope pelts from the poachers, they sometimes sell them, because it is the only way to finance their operation. He explains that technically they lack the power to arrest the poachers, although in this country where anyone can disappear without a question, the measures they take are not closely scrutinized. When after long intervals they return to their wives and families, the women seem to accept their mission, although some wives, even in Tibet, might reasonably ask why their husband must leave his family unprovided for while roaming around in search of poachers.

Mountain Patrol is a Chinese film, which raises questions that are hard to answer. Is it designed to paint a positive picture of China's occupation of Tibet? Or can it be read as a parable: Protecting the antelope from poachers is the same as protecting Tibet from Chinese poaching? Because there are no ideological speeches, because the motives of the patrolmen are expressed in actions instead of words, we cannot be sure.

One of the American distributors of the film is National Geographic, and in its landscapes and ethnographic insights this looks at times like a documentary. But it plays like a Western involving foes who are equally hard and unsparing. The movie leaves us with the encouraging news that the Chinese government has taken over patrol duties, that the poaching has been reduced, and that the antelope herds are starting to grow again, that rich women no longer have the nerve or the heart to wear shawls made of shahtoosh, the wonderful fabric made from the pelts of four murdered Tibetan antelope. We are also left with wonder about what drew these desperate men to this desolate place for their thankless struggle.

Mr. and Mrs. Smith ★ ★ ★

PG-13, 119 m., 2005

Brad Pitt (John Smith), Angelina Jolie (Jane Smith), Adam Brody (Benjamin), Kerry Washington (Jasmine), Vince Vaughn (Eddie). Directed by Doug Liman and produced by Lucas Foster, Akiva Goldsman, Eric McLeod, Arnon Milchan, and Patrick Wachsberger. Screenplay by Simon Kinberg.

There is a kind of movie that consists of watching two people together on the screen. The plot is immaterial. What matters is the "chemistry," a term that once referred to a science but now refers to the heat we sense, or think we sense, between two movie stars. Brad Pitt and Angelina Jolie have it, or I think they have it, in *Mr. and Mrs. Smith,* and because they do, the movie works. If they did not, there'd be nothing to work with.

The screenplay is a device to revive their marriage by placing them in mortal danger, while at the same time providing an excuse for elaborate gunfights and chase scenes. I learn from *Variety* that it was written by Simon Kinberg as his master's thesis at Columbia. If he had been studying chemistry instead of the cinema, he might have blown up the lab, but it wouldn't have been boring.

Pitt and Jolie play John and Jane Smith, almost certainly not their real names, who met in Bogota "five or six" years ago, got married, and settled down to a comfortable suburban lifestyle while not revealing to each other that they are both skilled assassins. John keeps his guns and money in a pit beneath the tool shed. Jane keeps her knives and other weapons in trays that slide out from under the oven.

As the movie opens, they're in marriage counseling; the spark has gone out of their relationship. On a typical day, they set off separately to their jobs: he to kill three or four guys, she to pose as a dominatrix while snapping a guy's neck. Can you imagine Rock Hudson and Doris Day in this story? Gable and Lombard and Hepburn and Tracy have also been invoked, but given the violence in their lives, the casting I recommend is The Rock and Vin Diesel. In the opening scene, they could fight over who has to play Mrs. Smith.

Sorry. Lost my train of thought. Anyway, John and Jane individually receive instructions to travel to a remote desert location in the Southwest and take out a mysterious target. They travel there separately, only to discover that their targets are themselves. It's one of those situations where they could tell each other, but then they'd have to kill each other. "If you two stay together, you're dead," says Eddie (Vince Vaughn), another tough guy, who lives at home with his mother because it's convenient and she cooks good and on and on.

The question becomes: Do John and Jane kill each other like the professionals they are, or do they team up to save their lives? The solution to this dilemma requires them to have a fight that reminded me of the showdown between Uma Thurman and Daryl Hannah in *Kill Bill 2*. After physical violence that should theoretically have broken every bone in both their beautiful bodies, they get so excited that, yes, they have sex, which in their case seems to involve both the martial and marital arts.

There is a chase scene. The movie was directed by Doug Liman *(The Bourne Identity)*, who is good at chase scenes, and here he gets a laugh by having Jolie drive a van while being pursued by three muscle cars. Liman is able to find a lot of possibilities in the fact that it's one of those vans with two sliding doors in the rear.

The movie pauses from time to time for more sessions with the marriage counselor, during which it appears that professional killing is good for their relationship. After we get our money's worth of action, their problems are resolved, more or less. Although many lives have been lost, the marriage is saved.

None of this matters at all. What makes the movie work is that Pitt and Jolie have fun together on the screen, and they're able to find a rhythm that allows them to be understated and amused even during the most alarming developments. There are many ways that John and Jane Smith could have been played awkwardly, or out of sync, but the actors understand the material and hold themselves at just the right distance from it; we understand this is not really an action picture, but a movie star romance in which the action picture serves as a location.

I've noticed a new trend in the questions I'm asked by strangers. For years it was, "Seen any good movies lately?" Now I am asked for my insights into Brad and Angelina, Tom and Katie, and other couples created by celebrity gossip. I reply that I know nothing about their private lives except what I read in the supermarket tabloids, which also know nothing about their private lives. I can see this comes as a disappointment. So I think I'll start speculating about threesomes enlisting The Rock, Vin Diesel, and Vince Vaughn, selected at random. This may be an idea for the sequel.

Mr. Magorium's Wonder Emporium ★ ★ ★

G, 93 m., 2007

Dustin Hoffman (Mr. Edward Magorium), Natalie Portman (Molly Mahoney), Jason Bateman (Henry Weston), Zach Mills (Eric Applebaum), Ted Ludzik (Bellini the Bookbuilder). Directed by Zach Helm and produced by James Garavente and Richard N. Gladstein. Screenplay by Helm.

Mr. Magorium is 243 years old, he informs us. He has possibly survived so long by being incapable of boredom. Life for him is a daily adventure, which he shares with the children who pack into his magical toy store. And let's talk about the toy store first. If the movies consist of millions and millions of rooms, some of them indoors, some outdoors, some only in our minds, Mr. Magorium's Wonder Emporium is one of the most delightful. It is jammed to the ceilings and bursting the walls with toys that, in some cases, seem to be alive, and in most cases seem to be real *toys*, and not the extrusions of market research.

The emporium, a quaint old store squeezed in between two modern monoliths, has been run since time immemorial by Edward Magorium, who is played by Dustin Hoffman as a daffy old luv with a slight overbite, a hint of a lisp, a twinkle of the eyes, and boundless optimism. He is so optimistic he is looking forward to his next great experience, which will be death. And he dearly hopes that after he departs, the emporium will be taken over by young Molly Mahoney (Natalie Portman), who is his only employee, except for Bellini the Bookbuilder (Ted Ludzik), who does not seem quite real and possibly just operates in the basement as a freelancer.

Molly is not sure she is ready to shoulder such a responsibility, and her lack of self-confidence provides the conflict without which the movie would be left in search of a plot. She was once a prodigy at the piano, but her failure of nerve on the stage has spread into other areas of her life, and it is Edward's mission to correct that. Looking on (and narrating) is Eric (Zach Mills), a young boy who seems to live at the store as unofficial monitor of all activities.

One dark day an accountant shows up. This is Henry Weston (Jason Bateman), who has been assigned by ominous shadowy parties to look into the emporium's books, which seem to have fallen behind by roughly two centuries. The emporium is threatened with financial ruin, and even if it survives, will Molly care to take over? Because no one else but Molly will do, you see. She contains the same kind of magical spark that has allowed Edward to keep things humming along.

All of this perhaps sounds like a wonderful family movie, and to a degree it is, although the story arcs involving Molly and the accountant and the threats to the store are all recycled from countless other films. The plot is forever being upstaged by the emporium. We want to stop worrying about Molly's self-esteem and just play with more neat stuff. And is there ever any real doubt that there will be a happy ending? None. It's just that everybody has to pretend there is.

Hoffman has countless characters inside of him, and this is one of his nicest. Edward Magorium is very matter-of-fact about his great age, his astonishing store, and his decision that it is time to move on to the next life. He takes it all for granted. Portman, as Molly, doesn't think it's that simple, and she has the thankless task of holding out against the old man's certainty. The suspense, such as it is, will possibly enthrall kids up to a certain age, but their parents, once they get over the visual delights of the emporium, will be grateful the proceedings last only ninety-three minutes. That's about as long as this notion will carry us, or a little longer.

The first-time direction and screenplay are by Zach Helm, who wrote Marc Forster's metaphysical comedy *Stranger Than Fiction* (2006), with Will Ferrell as a tax man who starts hearing a voice in his head describing what he does all day, a little before he does it. Dustin Hoffman was in that movie, too, as an English professor who determines that the hero's life is being written by a novelist and uses his skills to figure out who it is. Helm has the kind of imagination that makes you want to see what he'll do next. And he has the taste or luck to have assembled production designer Therese DePrez, art director Brandt Gordon, and set decorator Clive Thomasson, without all of whom the emporium would not live up to its billing. This isn't quite the over-the-top fantasy you'd like it to be, but it's a charming enough little movie, and probably the younger you are, the more charming.

Mrs. Henderson Presents ★ ★ ★

R, 103 m., 2006

Judi Dench (Laura Henderson), Bob Hoskins (Vivian Van Damm), Kelly Reilly (Maureen), Christopher Guest (Lord Cromer), Will Young (Bertie), Thelma Barlow (Lady Conway). Directed by Stephen Frears and produced by

Laurie Borg and Norma Heyman. Screenplay by Martin Sherman.

All the way across the Atlantic, on a flight that took twenty-four hours and involved refueling in Newfoundland and Iceland, I studied Arthur Frommer's *Europe on $5 a Day.* You will guess from the title this was some time ago. Following Frommer's instructions, I took the tube to Russell Square, checked into a hotel that would give me bed and breakfast for $2.50, took the tube to Westminster, and gazed upon Big Ben.

Then the throbbing magnetic pull of Soho attracted me, as it has so many young men, and soon I stood regarding the facade of the Windmill Theater. WE NEVER CLOSE, said the neon sign. That meant they were open and that I would soon be over my daily budget.

Yes, it was just like you see it in this movie, but a little shabbier. There were comics and song-and-dance acts, and above all there were dancing girls, and then the lighting shifted and you could see nude models, posed without moving, in "artistic tableaux." I gazed in bliss and wonder. The lighting shifted again, and they disappeared, because how long, really, could a girl be expected to pose like that on a clamshell? All very well for Venus, but hard work six times a day for a variety artiste.

The Windmill Theater introduced nudity to the British stage through the brilliant expedient of convincing the Lord Chamberlain (who censored the shows) that a nude, *if she did not move,* was not "theater" but "art" and fell under the same exemption that permitted nudes in the National Gallery. Oh, how I agreed. Faithful readers will have followed the controversy over whether video games can be an art form. If I argue that they cannot, how then can I claim that a nude model at the Windmill could be art? Anyone who can ask such a question has been spending too much time in the basement with a joystick.

I visited the Windmill in the summer of 1961. Within a few years the barriers fell. Strip clubs opened all over Soho and the Windmill was yesterday's news, one of the casualties of the sexual revolution. Philip Larkin, who would have become poet laureate had he not declined the honor, did what a poet laureate is supposed to do and wrote a poem to mark the changing climate:

Sexual intercourse began
In nineteen sixty-three
(which was rather late for me)
Between the end of the Chatterley ban
And the Beatles' first LP.

Mrs. Henderson Presents is a fond showbiz tale directed by Stephen Frears, who is one year older than I am and, therefore, would also remember the Windmill as it used to be. That he attended it in his youth I have not the slightest doubt. So would have the Beatles, and Denis Thatcher and Stephen Hawking.

The film tells the story of the theater's founding by Laura Henderson (Judi Dench), whose husband left her a widow in the 1930s. She came home from India with some money and nothing to do. "I'm bored with widowhood," she told a friend. "I have to smile at people. In India there was always someone to look down on." One day she saw the abandoned theater on Great Windmill Street and decided to buy the old barn and put on a show.

As her impresario she hired Vivian Van Damm (Bob Hoskins). They presented a variety programme. Her inspiration was a "nonstop revue" all day and evening. The theater was a hit until it was widely copied and began to lose money, and then she had an inspiration. "Let's have naked girls—don't you think?" she asked Vivian.

Their decision to include nudity saved the theater, and when war came Mrs. Henderson refused to close her doors, because (a) the theater was below street level and, therefore, somewhat safe, and (b) it was important for troop morale. When her son died in the first war, she told people, she found a French postcard among his possessions and thought it likely he had never seen a real nude woman. She was determined to spare the new generation of British heroes this depressing fate.

"We never close" became the war cry of the Windmill. All during the blitz, theaters, restaurants, and pubs closed, but never the Windmill. Frears, working from a screenplay by Martin Sherman, tells this story through the relationship of Mrs. Henderson and Van Damm, both high-spirited and stubborn. Van Damm may have been running a nude show, but his discipline was strict and his standards high—higher, I suspect, in this movie than in life. Although they became fast friends, the owner and her manager maintained a British reserve, and it is some years before Mrs. Henderson learns there was a Mrs. Van Damm.

Other key roles in the story are played by Maureen (Kelly Reilly), a Windmill girl whom Mrs. Henderson approves of for her "British nipples," and Lord Cromer (Christopher Guest), the Lord Chamberlain, who one suspects approves of them, too. Mrs. Henderson has a droll luncheon audience with Cromer where they debate exactly what she proposes to reveal in her revue. "Will you show the foliage?" he asks. "Try the brie," she suggests. He tries the cheese, finds it agreeable, and returns to "the somewhat sordid topic of the pudendum." Why are men always so concerned, Mrs. Henderson wonders, about "the Midlands"? She promises that her lighting will be subtle, but by the time I attended the Windmill the illumination of geography encompassed the Lake District all the way to Land's End.

Dench and Hoskins bring ineffable personal styles to roles that could have been potted showbiz. One touch is just right: Van Damm is always natty in dress and grooming. Impresarios in that era glowed with prosperity, no matter how shaky their finances. Mrs. Henderson is in the tradition of British ladies whose age, bearing, and accent set the stage for the occasional shocking word; watch the Lord Chamberlain as she suggests a synonym for pudendum.

Mrs. Henderson Presents is not great cinema, and neither was the Windmill great theater, but they both put on a good show. As I recall those days, the nudes fade and what I am nostalgic for are the desperately jolly song-and-dance numbers and the earnest young magicians pulling pigeons from their pants. A few years ago my wife and I were among sixteen people in a tiny theater on Jermyn Street for a one-man show named "Is It Magic, or Is It Manilow?" It was neither. But it would have worked at the Windmill, if enriched by the occasional artistic tableau.

Mrs. Palfrey at the Claremont ★ ★ ★

NO MPAA RATING, 108 m., 2006

Joan Plowright (Mrs. Palfrey), Rupert Friend (Ludovic Meyer), Zoe Tapper (Gwendolyn), Anna Massey (Mrs. Arbuthnot), Robert Lang (Mr. Osborne), Marcia Warren (Mrs. Post), Georgina Hale (Mrs. Burton), Millicent Martin (Mrs. De Salis). Directed by Dan Ireland and produced by Lee Caplin, Carl Colpaert, and Zachary Matz. Screenplay by Ruth Sacks, based on the novel by Elizabeth Taylor.

You may think there is no hotel in London like the Claremont, where Mrs. Palfrey becomes a lodger. No hotel where respectable gentlefolk can live by the month and have their breakfasts and dinners served to them in a dining room where good manners prevail. No hotel where the bellman is an aged ruin who nevertheless barks commands at the desk clerk. No hotel where the elevator is a brass cage that rises and falls majestically and discharges its passengers from behind ornate sliding doors.

But here and there such relics survive. A very few of my readers will have stayed at the Eyrie Mansion on Jermyn Street when it was run by Henry and Doddy Togna, and they will nod in recognition, although the Mansion, to be sure, had no dining room. They will remember Bob the hall porter, who drove Henry crazy by getting drunk every eighth day ("If Bob got drunk every seventh day, on a regular schedule like, we could plan for it").

Mrs. Palfrey (Joan Plowright) books into the Claremont almost blindly. She is in flight from life with her grown daughter in Scotland and wants to be independent. She is a stoic. Shown her room (twin beds of different heights, a desk, a mirror, a straight chair, and an armchair), she says, "Oh, dear!" Learning from the aged ruin that the bathroom is down the hall and the early bird gets the hot water, she cannot even manage an "Oh, dear!"

In the dining room, she meets the regulars, particularly the brisk Mrs. Arbuthnot (Anna Massey), who tells the others to shut up when they require such coaching. There is also dear Mr. Osborne (Robert Lang), who asks her to a "do" at the Masons' Hall. Mrs. Palfrey hopes to spend time with her grandson Desmond, who works in the city, but he is an ingrate who never returns her calls. Then one day, while returning from the branch library with a copy of *Lady Chatterley's Lover* for Mrs. Arbuthnot, she stumbles on the sidewalk and is rescued by a nice young man named Ludovic (Rupert Friend). He invites her into the borrowed basement flat where he lives, serves her tea, rubs disinfectant on her bruise, and explains he is a writer who supports himself as a street musician.

Ludovic is too good to be true, really. Too kind, too gentle, too patient with a lady sixty years his senior. But *Mrs. Palfrey at the Claremont* is the kind of movie where nice people turn up, and soon Ludovic is doing Mrs. Palfrey a favor. She is embarrassed that everyone in the dining room wonders why her grandson has never appeared at dinner, so she asks Ludovic to pretend to be Desmond, and he agrees.

Just as teenagers enjoy escapist movies, so do the elderly. They simply prefer a gentler pace. What is touching about *Mrs. Palfrey* is that she is allowed to be elderly and not turned into a hip-hop granny. This movie is based on a novel by Elizabeth Taylor (the novelist, not the actress) and a screenplay by Ruth Sacks, herself in her eighties. Incredibly, it represents the biggest screen role that the great Joan Plowright (herself seventy-seven) has ever had, and it's little surprise she has won the AARP award as actress of the year.

Among the regulars in the Claremont dining room, there is that minute scrutiny inmates of such establishments always carry out because of boredom, jealousy, or simple curiosity. All I really miss are complaints about the food. I recall my aunt Mary O'Neill sadly surveying her dinner at a retirement home and complaining: "How am I expected to eat this, Rog? Sliced chicken, mashed potatoes, and cauliflower. It's all white, honey! It needs carrots."

Mrs. Palfrey at the Claremont has a parabola that is not startling. Mrs. Palfrey will undergo some disappointments and surprises, and Ludovic will learn a life lesson or two, and we accept all that because it comes with the territory. The movie is a delight, in ways both expected and rare. The scenes between Plowright and Lang, as the old gentleman, are classic—both the Masonic "do" and his proposal of marriage, which is argued on admirably practical grounds but inspires more than one "Oh, dear!"

Mr. Woodcock ★ ★ ★

PG-13, 87 m., 2007

Billy Bob Thornton (Mr. Woodcock), Seann William Scott (John Farley), Susan Sarandon (Beverly Farley), Amy Poehler (Maggie Hoffman), Ethan Suplee (Nedderman). Directed by Craig Gillespie and produced by Bob Cooper. Screenplay by Michael Carnes and Josh Gilbert.

Billy Bob Thornton is in full *Bad Santa* mode in *Mr. Woodcock,* an uneasy comedy about an adult who returns home to discover his mother is planning to marry the gym teacher who made his high school days a living hell. The thing about Thornton is, he makes no compromises and takes no prisoners when he plays guys like Woodcock. He's a hateful jerk, and he means it. That makes the movie better, actually, than if we sensed a heart of gold under the crust, but it doesn't exactly make it funnier.

Woodcock uses his position in authority to pick on the weak and helpless in his gym classes, including the overweight, the stuttering, and those who are simply no good at physical education. He slams them with basketballs thrown at wounding velocity, he runs them around the gym for looking funny, he finds their weaknesses and mocks them. "It'll make men out of them," he explains. No, it won't. It'll make Woodcocks out of them.

Seann William Scott plays John Farley, the hometown boy who has gone out into the world and written a best-selling self-help book that, like most self-help books, tells you the same things your mother and Norman Vincent Peale told you, and charges for the privilege. Anyone read *The Secret* lately? Give me a break. Anyway, from what we learn about it, Farley's book recycles the usual slogans and meaningless platitudes and has made him a celebrity.

But all his adult wealth and fame turns to ashes when he discovers his mom, Beverly (Susan Sarandon), is dating Mr. Woodcock, and all his old fears come back. Give Thornton and the director, Craig Gillespie, full points for playing Woodcock as an uncompromising, insulting, tactless, hurtful, sadistic buttwipe. When Farley finally challenges him to a fight, his reply is: "You must like getting spanked, Farley. I guess it runs in the family." Ouch. That's even in the trailer.

I can imagine this as a softball comedy, but it's perversely more interesting as hardball. Take the Sarandon character. She's been alone for years, Woodcock is nice to her, she craves company and attention, and the guy apparently really does like her. Her son is making a rare visit home, but her life will go on, and she has to be free to make the best of it. That's better than making her an innocent victim.

I'm not sure, but I suspect that Woodcock's treatment of kids borders on the illegal, yet he's named Educator of the Year and doesn't seem to give a flying flatulency in a windstorm if everybody hates him. Will he be cruel to Beverly Farley? Hard to say, but that's what her son fears.

To laugh at parts of this film would indicate one has a streak of Woodcockism in oneself. But to gaze in stupefied fascination is perfectly understandable. That's what makes Thornton such a complex actor. He can play a tough coach like the one in *Friday Night Lights* as a three-dimensional human being and then make Mr. Woodcock into a monster. And hey, why, after all these years, hasn't Woodcock ever been promoted to a coaching position? Maybe because he likes to be a bully, and the football players might beat him bloody.

Anyway, all is resolved, one way or another, in a rather contrived ending that might have something to do with the film's three weeks of reshoots, as reported by Patrick Goldstein in the *LA Times* and documented on IMDb. I would have been happier if young John Farley had torn his positive thinking book to shreds, slammed Mr. Woodcock in the gut with a medicine ball, and told him to drop and give him fifty quick ones or he'd do it again.

Munich ★ ★ ★ ★

R, 164 m., 2005

Eric Bana (Avner), Daniel Craig (Steve), Geoffrey Rush (Ephraim), Mathieu Kassovitz (Robert), Ciaran Hinds (Carl), Hanns Zischler (Hans), Michael Lonsdale (Papa), Mathieu Amalric (Louis), Lynn Cohen (Golda Meir). Directed by Steven Spielberg and produced by Barry Mendel, Kathleen Kennedy, Spielberg, and Colin Wilson. Screenplay by Tony Kushner, based on the book *Vengeance* by George Jonas.

Steven Spielberg's *Munich* is an act of courage and conscience. The director of *Schindler's List,* the founder of the Shoah Foundation, the most successful and visible Jew in the world of film, has placed himself between Israel and the Palestinians, looked at decades of terrorism and reprisal, and had one of his characters conclude, "There is no peace at the end of this." Spielberg's film has been called an attack on the Palestinians and he has been rebuked as "no friend of Israel." By not taking sides, he has taken both sides.

The film has deep love for Israel and contains a heartfelt moment when a mother reminds her son why the state had to be founded: "We had to take it because no one would ever give it to us. Whatever it took, whatever it takes, we have a place on Earth at last." With this statement, I believe, Spielberg agrees to the bottom of his soul. Yet his film questions Israel's policy of swift and full retribution for every attack.

Munich opens with a heart-stopping reenactment of the kidnapping and deaths of Israeli athletes at the 1972 Munich Olympics. It then shows Prime Minister Golda Meir (Lynn Cohen) with her cabinet, stating firmly, "Forget peace for now." It shows the formation of a secret Israeli revenge squad to kill those responsible. It concludes that although nine of the eleven eventually were eliminated, they were replaced and replaced again by men even more dangerous, while the terrorists responded with even more deaths. What was accomplished?

The movie is based upon a book by George Jonas, a 1956 Hungarian freedom fighter, now a conservative Toronto political writer, who has been an acquaintance for twenty-five years. I thought to ask him what he thought of Spielberg's view of his material, but I didn't. I wanted to review the movie as an interested but not expert outsider, sharing (with most of the film's audience) not a great deal more knowledge than the film supplies. Those who know more, who know everything, are often the wrong ones to consult about a film based on fact. The task of the director is to transmute fact into emotions and beliefs—and beliefs, we need to be reminded, are beliefs precisely because they are not facts.

Munich takes the form of a thriller matched with a procedural. Eric Bana stars as Avner, a former bodyguard to Meir, who is made leader of the secret revenge squadron. He and his men are paid off the books, have no official existence, and are handled by a go-between named Ephraim (Geoffrey Rush). Why it is necessary to deny their existence is not quite explained by the film, since they are clearly carrying out Israeli policy and Israel wants that known; they even use bombs instead of bullets to generate more dramatic publicity.

Avner is assigned only four teammates: Robert (Mathieu Kassovitz), a toymaker, expert at disarming bombs, now asked to build them; Carl (Ciaran Hinds), who removes the evidence after every action; Steve (Daniel Craig), the trigger man; and Hans (Hanns Zischler), who can forge letters and documents. They travel with assumed names and false passports, and discover the whereabouts of many of their targets by paying bounties to a shadowy Frenchman named Louis (Mathieu Amalric).

Eventually Avner meets Louis' "Papa" (Michael Lonsdale), who has been selling information for years. Papa fought in the French Resistance and is now disillusioned: "We paid this price so Nazi scum could be replaced by Gaullist scum. We don't deal with governments." The family, he believes, is the only unit worth fighting for. His speech is moving, but does he really believe Avner and his money do not come from a government?

The film's most exciting moments are in the details of assassination. Plastic bombs are planted, booby traps are baited, there is a moment of Hitchcockian suspense when the team waits for a little girl to leave for school before calling her father's telephone; they have failed to see her reenter the house and are astonished when she answers the phone. As the team tries to prevent the explosion, we reflect how it is always more thrilling in a movie, when someone needs to run desperately, for it to be an awkward older man.

The teammates move among world capitals. One night, in a comic screwup with deadly possibilities, Avner's men and a PLO team are booked into the same "safe house." As the operation proceeds, it takes a psychic toll on Avner, who moves his family to Brooklyn, who grows paranoid, who questions the ethical basis of the operation he heads: "Jews don't do wrong because our enemies do wrong," he argues, and "if these people committed crimes we should have arrested them." To which he is told, "Every civilization finds it necessary to negotiate compromises with its own values."

The same debate is going on right now in America. If it is true that civilizations must sometimes compromise their values, the questions remain: What is the cost, and what is the benefit? Spielberg clearly asks if Israel has risked more than it has gained. The stalemate in the Middle East will continue indefinitely, his film argues, unless brave men on both sides decide to break with the pattern of the past. Certainly in Israel itself it is significant that old enemies Ariel Sharon, from the right, and Shimon Peres, from the left, are now astonishingly both in the same new party and seeking a new path to peace. For the Palestinians, it may be crucial that the PLO's corrupt Arafat no longer has a personal stake in the status quo and a new generation of leaders has moved into place.

Spielberg's film is well-timed in view of these unexpected political developments, which he could not have foreseen (Sharon left his Likud Party on November 21, 2005, and Peres left his Labour Party a week later). Far from being "no friend of Israel," he may be an invaluable friend, and for that very reason a friend of the Palestinians as well. Spielberg is using the effective form of a thriller to argue that loops of mutual reprisal have led to endless violence in the Middle East, Ireland, India and Pakistan, the former Yugoslavia, the former Soviet Union, Africa, and on and on. Miraculous that the pariah nation of South Africa was the one place where irreconcilable enemies found a way to peacefully share the same land together.

At crucial times in a nation's history, its best friends may be its critics. Spielberg did not have to make *Munich,* but he needed to. With this film he has dramatically opened a wider dialogue, helping to make the inarguable into the debatable. As a thriller, *Munich* is efficient, absorbing, effective. As an ethical argument, it is haunting. And its questions are not only for Israel but for any nation that believes it must compromise its values to defend them.

Murderball ★ ★ ★ ★

R, 85 m., 2005

Featuring Mark Zupan, Joe Soares, Keith Cavill, Andy Cohn, Scott Hogsett, and Bob Lujano. A documentary directed by Henry Alex Rubin and

Dana Adam Shapiro and produced by Jeffrey Mandel and Shapiro.

"How do you eat your pizza with your elbows?"

It's a natural question for a little boy to ask a quadruple amputee, and Bob Lujano is happy to answer it. He and the other stars of the documentary *Murderball* wish more people would ask more questions, instead of becoming inhibited around people in wheelchairs. After this movie, maybe they will. You don't have to feel shy around quadriplegics who play wheelchair rugby.

This is one of those rare docs, like *Hoop Dreams,* where life provides a better ending than the filmmakers could have hoped for. Also like *Hoop Dreams,* it's not really a sports film; it's a film that uses sport as a way to see into lives, hopes, and fears. These tough all-Americans compete in international championships. Once they were shattered young men waking up in hospital beds and being told they would never walk again.

Consider Mark Zupan, probably the best player in the sport today. He was paralyzed when he was eighteen. He fell asleep in the bed of a pickup driven by his friend Christopher Igoe, who drove away not realizing Mark was aboard. The truck crashed, and Mark was thrown into a canal and wasn't found for thirteen hours. It took them a long time, but he and Igoe are friendly again.

During a discussion after a festival screening of the movie, he was asked, "If you could, would you turn back the clock on that day?" You could have heard a pin drop as he answered: "No, I don't think so. My injury has led me to opportunities and experiences and friendships I would never have had before. And it has taught me about myself." He paused. "In some ways, it's the best thing that ever happened to me."

This is hard to believe, but from him, I believe it. The movie follows Zupan and his teammates on Team USA during a couple of seasons where the off-court drama is fraught with tension. We meet Joe Soares, an all-American for many years, who with advancing age is dropped from the American team, is angry, and gets revenge by joining the Canadians. Under Soares, Canada beats the United States for the first time in twelve years. There is no love between Soares and Zupan ("If he were on fire, I wouldn't piss on him to put it out").

Wheelchair rugby is a full-contact sport. Chairs are reinforced to take the hammering. One strategy is to knock over your opponent's chair and land him on the floor; that's not a foul, although the referees helpfully put the players back on their wheels. Has anybody been injured *again* while playing the game? So far, no.

Many people think quadriplegics have no control over their four limbs, like Christopher Reeve, but most of them retain some degree of movement. Their level of disability is rated on a scale from 0.5 to 3.5, and a team can have a total of 8 points on the court at once. This leads to an ironic paradox: The athletes spend their lives overcoming and diminishing their disabilities, then hope for higher handicaps.

Although the sports scenes are filled with passion and harrowing wheelchair duels, the heart of the movie is off the court. We follow a young man named Keith Cavill, who has been wounded in a motocross accident and is painfully undergoing the slow process of rehabilitation. Encouragement from wheelchair athletes is crucial to his state of mind. Later, Team USA visits Walter Reed Army Medical Center, where newly arrived casualties from Iraq are facing the new reality of their lives. War injuries such as Cavill's are becoming more common; explosions cause more casualties than gunfire in Iraq, and *Harper's* magazine reports that improved body armor has created a large number of wounded soldiers whose body trunks are unblemished but whose arms and legs are devastated.

If Zupan is the hero of the movie, Soares is its enigma. He had a tough childhood. After losing the use of his legs from polio, he dragged himself around for years before his poor Portuguese-American family provided him with a chair. He fought for respect in school, fought for an education, was a fierce competitor on the court, and seems ferocious as he leads Team Canada against his former teammates.

At home, he wants his son Robert to be a jock like Dad. But Robert prefers to play the viola and observes wistfully that one of the household tasks he doesn't like involves "dusting Dad's trophy wall." Then an unexpected development (miraculously caught on camera) causes Soares to take a deep breath and reevaluate his life and his relationship with his son. Rehabilitation is not limited to the body.

As the players talk frankly about their lives, we learn everything we always wanted to know about quadriplegic sex but were afraid to ask. One player says the chair works like a babe magnet: Women are dying to ask him if he can perform sexually. The answer, according to a documentary quoted in the film, is often "yes," and little animated figures show us some of the moves. We also learn that people in chairs have long since gotten over any self-consciousness in talking about their situation, and they hate it when people avoid looking at them or interacting with them. "I'm a guy in a chair," Zupan says. "I'm just like you, except I'm sitting down."

Murderball, directed by Henry Alex Rubin and Dana Adam Shapiro, produced by Jeffrey Mandel and Shapiro, and photographed by Rubin, works like many great documentaries to transcend its subject and consider the human condition. We may not be in chairs and may not be athletes, but we all have disabilities, sometimes of the spirit. To consider the bleak months and sleepless nights when these men first confronted the reality of their injuries, and now to see them in the full force of athletic exuberance, is to learn something valuable about the human will. Remember Bob Lujano, whom the kid asked about eating pizza? He has a motto: "No arms, no legs, no problem."

Music Within ★ ★ ½

R, 93 m., 2007

Ron Livingston (Richard Pimentel), Melissa George (Christine), Michael Sheen (Art Honneyman), Yul Vazquez (Mike Stoltz), Rebecca De Mornay (Richard's Mother), Hector Elizondo (Dr. Ben Padrow). Directed by Steven Sawalich and produced by Sawalich and Brett Donowho. Screenplay by Bret McKinney, Mark Andrew Olsen, and Kelly Kennemer.

I have good things to write about *Music Within,* but I have some troubles with it, too. First, the good stuff: This is an entertaining, sometimes inspiring film about a man named Richard Pimentel (Ron Livingston), who serves in Vietnam and is almost completely deafened when a shell lands near him in battle. Returning to America, he receives not exactly expert treatment for his disability and is cast out into the world to find himself all but unemployable. Among the friends he makes in the disabled community is Art Honneyman (Michael Sheen), who has cerebral palsy but is a powerhouse of intelligence and wit.

The two of them experience firsthand the discrimination, sometimes unconscious, that the world inflicts on those who look, sound, or act differently. In one of the movie's most infuriating scenes, they are asked to leave a restaurant "because you're disturbing the other customers." How are they disturbing them? By being there. By existing. By Honneyman being twisted and in a wheelchair and talking awkwardly.

Pimentel's own experiences and what he sees happening to his friends inspire him to become a disability-rights activist, and although the movie doesn't quite say so, he must have been the driving force behind the Americans with Disabilities Act (1990) because no one else is mentioned. Taken just on these terms, the movie works, it's effective, and I believe audiences will respond to it.

My own feelings are a little more complex. They began forming in early childhood. Growing up in Urbana, Illinois, I was unknowingly at the center of a rehabilitation movement that formed after the Second World War. Thousands of returning vets were in wheelchairs. Unlike Pimentel, who is told in the film he doesn't qualify for veteran's college funds because he is deaf, many of them attended universities on the G.I. Bill.

The University of Illinois sits on a landscape flat as a pancake. Ideal for wheelchairs. The Urbana-Champaign community, starting in 1946, began to build ramps into buildings, adapt elevators and washrooms, make curb cuts, and equip buses with chair lifts. This was not done overnight, but the town became known as wheelchair-friendly. Our local TV sportscaster, Tom Jones, was in a wheelchair. Our wheelchair athletes, organized in a program by Dr. Tim Nugent, helped launch wheelchair sports. During Vietnam, the loudest antiwar protester on campus was an SDS member named Rudy Frank who walked with so many braces he looked like Robocop. There was Ken Viste, my photo chief at the *Daily Illini.* He was in a chair, but that didn't keep him off the sidelines while shooting sports events. Disabled people were no big deal.

Things like that were happening all over the country, and I learned a little about them in 1962 when I went along as an aide on a tour of Southern Africa with eighteen wheelchair athletes, who demonstrated that life did not end with forms of paralysis. All of this was before Pimentel went to Vietnam.

The national disability-rights movement had many parents. Such men as Robert Burgdorf, Justin Whitlock Dart Jr., and Senator Bob Dole were instrumental. Remember Ron Kovic, who was born on the Fourth of July? Here in Chicago, my friend Marca Bristo founded Access Living to support the disabled who wanted to live independently. She lobbied relentlessly in city hall and Springfield. She was appointed chair of the National Council on Disability. No, she didn't create the Americans with Disabilities Act. But Google both her and Pimentel and decide for yourself who played a larger role in the movement.

What bothers me is that *Music Within* takes an individual story, an inspiring one, yes, and then thinks that's all there is to be told. It wasn't one guy who got mad. It was decades of struggle, decades of rejection, decades of streets that couldn't be crossed, stairs that couldn't be climbed, houses that couldn't be lived in, and customers who couldn't be bothered. Richard Pimentel was more a beneficiary of the disability rights movement than a pioneer. So why do I give the movie two and a half stars? Because what it does, it does sincerely and fairly well. Just remember that its hero stands for countless others.

Must Love Dogs ★ ★

PG-13, 98 m., 2005

Diane Lane (Sarah), John Cusack (Jake), Elizabeth Perkins (Carol), Christopher Plummer (Bill), Dermot Mulroney (Bob), Stockard Channing (Dolly), Ali Hillis (Christine), Brad William Henke (Leo). Directed by Gary David Goldberg and produced by Goldberg, Jennifer Todd, and Suzanne Todd. Screenplay by Goldberg, based on the novel by Claire Cook.

Must Love Dogs is like a puppy with big brown eyes and a wagging tail who weeps with eagerness to lick your hand, but you take a look around the pound and decide to adopt the sad-eyed beagle who looks as if she has seen a thing or two. In dogs, as in love stories, it is better to choose wisdom over infatuation.

The movie stars two of the most likable actors in the movies, Diane Lane and John Cusack. There is a sense in which you can simply sit there in the theater and regard them with satisfaction.

Cusack in particular has a gift of intelligent speech that no doubt inspires discerning women to let him know, one way or another, that he can have his way with them if he will just keep talking. Here he plays a man named Jake who builds racing boats by hand, out of wood.

"They may not win," he observes, "but they lose beautifully." His divorce recently became final.

Diane Lane is a fortyish kindergarten teacher named Sarah who is also divorced; her family despairs because it seems she will never remarry. She belongs to one of those families that functions like the supporting cast of *Cheers*, offering one-liner insights and unwanted advice. Her sister Carol (Elizabeth Perkins) posts a phony singles ad about her on the Internet. This leads to an obligatory scene in which she has one date apiece with a series of spectacularly unlikely candidates, including one who bursts into tears almost continuously.

Fate and a helpful prod from the plot eventually bring Sarah and Jake together, although it is not love at first sight, or if it is, they deny it to themselves. Meanwhile, there is another man in the picture; Dermot Mulroney plays the separated father of the cutest of her little preschool toddlers and seems like a plenty nice guy. What she should know, as the screenplay certainly does, is that "separated" is not the same thing as "divorced." A wise woman of my acquaintance advises her single female friends, "Married men are for married women"—a rule that is more complex than at first it seems.

It is a pleasure to regard Cusack and Lane, or Jake and Sarah, as they Meet Cute and go through the usual romantic calisthenics of the love story. They must each doubt their own feelings, and each doubt the other's feelings, and miss a connection through a misunderstanding, and become convinced the other person is dating someone else, and clear all of the other hurdles placed with clockwork precision before the inevitable finish line. The movie is pleasant, sedate, subdued, and sweet, but there is not a moment of suspense in it.

It is melancholy to reflect that Cusack played a teenager in his first romantic comedies, the masterpieces *The Sure Thing* (1985) and *Say Anything* (1989), and now he plays an adult in a screenplay not anywhere near as risky, truthful, or moving. Consider the depth and truth of the girl's father in that film, played by John Mahoney, and then consider Diane Lane's father in this movie, played by Christopher Plummer.

Plummer is a great actor; he played the best Iago I have ever seen on the stage. But here his character is created from off-the-shelf sitcom templates. He was allegedly happily married for forty-five years, but after his wife dies he plunges into the Internet dating game so avidly that one of his blind dates turns out to be—his own daughter. He offers kindly wisdom, twinkling eyes, a wee hint of a brogue, and the audacity to keep two or three middle-aged ladies on the string at the same time, just so they won't grow overconfident.

Stockard Channing, who plays one of them, handles his heartlessness with such wisdom that I'd like to see her in a whole film about a woman in such a predicament.

Lane and Cusack, meanwhile, take one step forward (they both say *Dr. Zhivago* is their favorite movie!) and two steps back (she sleeps with Mulroney but hates herself in the morning). Given the fact that his occupation is building boats by hand, what do you think the odds are that she will sooner or later commandeer a racing crew to help her pursue her dream? All too good?

The movie toys with heartbreak because it knows, and we know, no hearts will be broken. If one should get dropped by accident, well, the Cusack character thinks that when your heart breaks, "it grows back bigger." So maybe it's a good thing for it to be broken? Or what? These actors with their gifts deserve characters that the movie takes more seriously and puts at more risk. The Channing character is like a visitor from a parallel universe in which such movies are made.

My Best Friend ★ ★ ★

PG 13, 95 m., 2007

Daniel Auteuil (Francois), Dany Boon (Bruno), Julie Gayet (Catherine), Julie Durand (Louise). Directed by Patrice Leconte and produced by Olivier Delbosc and Marc Missonnier. Screenplay by Leconte and Jerome Tonnerre.

My Best Friend tells the story of Francois, a man who has no friends at all. Who tells him that? All of his friends, at his birthday party. Once they get started on the subject, they bluntly confess they don't like him. No, not even his business partner. Don't like him and never have. Francois is stunned; obviously he never really knew what friendship was. He confused it with acquaintanceship, maybe, or partnership, or people he spent a lot of time with.

Francois is played by the sad-eyed Daniel Auteuil, one of the most familiar faces in French films (recently he starred in *Cache,* that intriguing film about the man who received anonymous videos of himself and his family). As an actor he is so flexible he can move from playing the sad-sack antiques dealer in this picture to playing Napoleon in the next film he made.

Here he is a man so alone and lonely that when he finds he has no friends, he is compelled at an auction to pay a small fortune he can't afford for a Greek vase whose owner commissioned it in memory of *his* best friend "and filled it with my tears." I am reminded of Daniel Curley's novel *A Stone Man, Yes,* with a title inspired by a man eternally chasing his love around a Greek vase; good enough for a stone man, yes, but not for one of flesh and blood.

Francois's partner, Catherine (Julie Gayet), doubts Francois's claims that he does indeed have a best friend. Appalled by how much he has put their company in debt, she makes him a bet. Unless he can produce a true and convincing best friend in ten days, he will have to give her the vase. Fair enough. But the search goes badly; his best friend at school, tracked down after many years, turns out always to have hated him.

One day Francois gets into the taxi of Bruno (Dany Boon), who has an opinion on everything. Francois is put off by the man's assurance and nonstop chattering, but when they meet again and again (coincidences are invaluable in movies), the driver begins to intrigue him, and eventually he hires Bruno as a tutor to teach him how to make friends. Of course the driver takes the job; there is nothing about human nature that the French do not think they know. The lessons are the stuff sitcoms are made of, and *My Best Friend* seems destined to be remade by Hollywood.

The film unfolds easily, with affection for the man no one likes, and at ninety-five minutes, it doesn't overstay its welcome. It was directed by Patrice Leconte, who makes intelligent films combining sympathy for his characters with a quick wit, a dark undertow, and a love of human peculiarity. He told me that on his tombstone he wanted the words: "This man loved to make movies." And he said: "I believe a filmmaker is like a chemist. You mix elements that have nothing to do with each other, and you see what will happen. Sometimes it blows up in your face."

Let me interrupt the flow of this review to mention some of his titles I think are extraordinarily good and the way they combine opposites: *Monsieur Hire* (shy bachelor and bold sex object), *The Hairdresser's Husband* (man obsessed with hairdressers and a hairdresser), *Ridicule* (a landowner and the king), *The Girl on the Bridge* (suicidal girl and circus knife thrower), *The Widow of Saint-Pierre* (condemned man and governor's wife), *The Man on the Train* (criminal and quiet loner), and *Intimate Strangers* (psychiatrist mistakes accidental visitor for client). Three of those titles have been on my annual Best Ten lists.

Certainly Francois and Bruno have nothing to do with each other. Or perhaps they do, but Francois with his blinders wouldn't notice it. As for Bruno, his lifelong obsession with facts and figures and dates is interesting; by knowing enough about the surface of the world to appear on a quiz show, he can avoid the depths.

These two men need each other. We know that. Patrice Leconte knows that. But do they know that? Thinking about the casting, if there's a Hollywood remake, I'm thinking Robert Downey Jr. as Francois and Adam Sandler as Bruno.

My Kid Could Paint That ★ ★ ★

PG-13, 83 m., 2007

With Marla Olmstead, Mark Olmstead, Laura Olmstead, Amir Bar-Lev, Anthony Brunelli, Elizabeth Cohen, and Michael Kimmelman. A documentary produced and directed by Amir Bar-Lev.

The truth lurking beneath *My Kid Could Paint That* is that your kid *couldn't* paint that. The documentary considers the perplexing case of Marla Olmstead, a four-year-old girl from Binghamton, New York, who got a lot of publicity because at her age she was producing abstract paintings that sold for hundreds and then thousands of dollars, were awarded gallery shows, generated a firestorm in the art community, and were the subject of a controversial segment on *60 Minutes.*

The paintings are pretty good. They are as good as some, not most, abstract paintings. They play into the hands of those who dismiss abstract art as the process of applying paint to canvas with a technique that looks random and unconsidered. Some, not all, abstract art gains its importance not because of its intrinsic quality but because of its price. At $25, it looks like dribbles. At $25 million, it looks like a masterpiece.

The story as told by Mark, Marla's dad, an amateur painter himself, is that one day little Marla was on the kitchen table while he was painting, and she grabbed a brush and started painting, too. The child showed an instinctive feeling for color, pattern, composition, and texture, and because of her age and the abstract-art-debunking angle, she started to get worldwide publicity.

The problem was, no one had actually seen Marla creating a whole work from start to finish except, presumably, her parents. *60 Minutes* came to do a piece on the girl, put their equipment all over the house, and installed a secret camera in the basement ceiling. Through it, they were able to see Marla beginning a painting with urgent whispered instructions from her father. We never see him touch a brush to the painting, but on the other hand, the finished painting doesn't look like a "Marla," but like something any child could paint.

Is the little girl the star of a hoax by her family? Amir Bar-Lev, the maker of this film, says he doesn't know, and the film has an open ending. He grew quite close to the Olmsteads and at times worried that he was betraying their confidence. My own verdict as an outsider is, no, Marla didn't paint those works, although she may have applied some of the paint.

But it's more complicated than that. As I said, some of the paintings are pretty good. People might pay hundreds if they were by a kid, but would they pay thousands unless they actually liked them? The irony may be that Mark Olmstead is a gifted painter who could never break into the closed circle of abstract art without a gimmick like Marla.

My favorite modern painter is Gillian Ayres, OBE. Ayres (born 1930) is a well-known British abstract expressionist whose huge canvases, often measuring several feet in their dimensions, look like finger painting because they are. With untrammeled exuberance, she paints in bright colors with a thick impasto. Chaz and I had not heard of her when we saw one of her paintings in a warehouse and simultaneously agreed we loved it. No, a kid couldn't paint that.

In the last analysis, I guess it all reduces to taste and instinct. Some paintings are good, says me, or says you, and some are bad. Some paintings could be painted by a child, some couldn't be.

Mysterious Skin ★ ★ ★ ½

NO MPAA RATING, 99 m., 2005

Joseph Gordon-Levitt (Neil McCormick), Brady Corbet (Brian Lackey), Michelle Trachtenberg (Wendy Peterson), Jeffrey Licon (Eric Peterson), Bill Sage (Coach Heider), Mary Lynn Rajskub (Avalyn Friesen), Elisabeth Shue (Ellen McCormick), George Webster (Young Brian), Chase Ellison (Young Neil). Directed by Gregg Araki and produced by Araki, Jeffrey Levy-Hinte, and Mary Jane Skalski. Screenplay by Araki, based on a novel by Scott Heim.

"The summer I was eight years old," a character says at the beginning of *Mysterious Skin,* "five hours disappeared from my life." He remembers being at a Little League game, and then the next thing he remembers is being found hiding in his basement at home, with blood from a nosebleed all over his shirt. What happened during those five hours? And why does he continue to have blackouts, nosebleeds, and nightmares for the next ten years?

This character's name is Brian, and he is played as a child by George Webster, wearing glasses too large for his face. As a teenager, played by Brady Corbet, he has grown into the glasses but remains a shy and inward boy. He sees a TV show about a girl named Avalyn in a nearby Kansas town who believes she was abducted by aliens. He meets her, solemnly regards the scar on her leg where a "tracking device" was implanted, and when he talks about his nosebleeds she nods knowingly: "The old nose trick, so the scar can't be seen."

Although Brian's narration opens *Mysterious Skin,* he isn't the film's central character. That would be Neil, played by Chase Ellison as an eight-year-old and by Joseph Gordon-Levitt as a young man. He remembers Little League very well. He idolized his coach (Bill Sage), went home with him, was seduced with video games and sexually molested. The molestation continued that whole summer, as Neil identified with the coach as a father figure, valued his importance in the coach's life, and developed a compulsion to please older men. That leads him in adolescence to become a prostitute, not so much for the money as because he has been programmed that way.

Mysterious Skin, written and directed by Gregg Araki and based on a novel by Scott Heim, is at once the most harrowing and, strangely, the most touching film I have seen about child abuse. It is unflinching in its tough realism; although there is no graphic sex on the screen, what is suggested, and the violence sometimes surrounding it, is painful and unsentimental. There is little sense that Neil enjoys sex, or that he is "gay" in the way, for example, that his friend Eric is—Eric, who likes flamboyant hairstyles and black lipstick but never seems to have sex. Then there's Neil's soul mate, Wendy (Michelle Trachtenberg). "If I hadn't been queer, we would have gotten married and had kids and all of that," Neil tells us. She accepts Neil's nature, warns him of its risks, and at one point objectively observes, "Where normal people have a heart, Neil McCormick has a bottomless black hole."

The film's scenes set in childhood are filled with the kinds of mysteries childhood contains, including Neil's feelings about the endless string of boyfriends brought home by his mother (Elisabeth Shue), and Brian's conviction that a UFO hovered one night over his house. In their later teen years, the two boys have no contact. Neil turns tricks at the public park, while Brian hangs out at the library and keeps a notebook of his nightmares about aliens. His friendship with Avalyn (Mary Lynn Rajskub) is based on memories of balloon-headed aliens performing weird sex probes, until Avalyn tries a weird probe of her own, which Brian is completely unable to deal with.

Neil's experiences are sad and harsh, and sometimes comic, as when he has sex while stoned, and simultaneously provides the public address commentary on a local baseball game. He follows Wendy to New York, and in the early 1990s learns some things about AIDS that cause him to leave hustling for a while and test opportunities in the fast food industry. His encounter with a dying AIDS victim is sad and tender ("This is going to be the safest encounter you've ever had. If you could just rub my back. I really need to be touched"). And then there is a brutal encounter that sends him fleeing home to Kansas on Christmas Eve, and to a crucial encounter with Brian, who thinks maybe since they were on the same Little League team, Neil might remember something helpful. He does.

Mysterious Skin begins in the confusion of childhood experiences too big to be processed, and then watches with care and attention as its characters grow in the direction that childhood pointed them. It is not a message picture, doesn't push its agenda, is about discovery, not accusation. Above all it shows how young people interpret experiences in the terms they have available to them, so that for Neil the memory of the coach remains a treasured one, until he digs more deeply into what really happened, and for Brian the possibility of alien abduction seems so obvious as to be beyond debate. The film begins with their separate myths about what happened to them when they were eight, and then leads them to a moment when their realities join. How that happens, and what is revealed, is astonishing in its truthfulness.

There is accomplished acting in this film, and there needs to be. This is not an easy story. Joseph Gordon-Levitt evokes a kind of detached realism that holds him apart from the sordid details of his life, while Brady Corbet's character seems frozen in uncertain childhood, afraid to grow up. Both are lucky to have friends of tact and kindness: Michelle Trachtenberg's Wendy knows there is something deeply wounded about Neil, but accepts it and worries about him. And Jeffrey Licon, as Eric, becomes Brian's closest friend without ever seeming to require a sexual component; he watches, he is curious about human nature, he cares.

Mysterious Skin is a complex and challenging emotional experience. It's not simplistic. It hates child abuse, but it doesn't stop with hate; it follows the lives of its characters as they grow through the aftermath. The movie clearly believes Neil was born gay; his encounter with the coach didn't "make" him gay, but was a powerful influence that aimed his sexuality in a dangerous direction. Brian on the other hand was unable to process what happened to him, has internalized great doubts and terrors, and may grow up neither gay nor straight, but forever peering out of those great big glasses at a world he will never quite bring into focus.

My Summer of Love ★ ★ ★

R, 85 m., 2005

Natalie Press (Mona), Emily Blunt (Tamsin), Paddy Considine (Phil), Dean Andrews (Ricky), Paul Antony-Barger (Tamsin's Father), Lynette Edwards (Tamsin's Mother), Kathryn Sumner (Sadie). Directed by Pawel Pawlikovsky and produced by Chris Collins and Tanya Seghatchian. Screenplay by Pawlikovksy and Michael Wynne, based on the novel by Helen Cross.

Her brother has gone bonkers. He's pouring all the booze down the drain and announcing he's turning the pub into a worship center for Jesus people. Mona and Phil inherited the pub from their parents and live upstairs; Phil (Paddy Considine) has come to Jesus belatedly, after a spell in prison. Mona (Natalie Press) gets on her moped, which has no engine but nevertheless functions as a symbol of escape, and wheels it into the country outside their small Yorkshire town. That's the day she meets Tamsin.

The title of *My Summer of Love* gives away two games at once: that she will fall in love, and that autumn will come. Mona is a tousled blonde, sixteen years old, dressed in whatever came to hand when she got up in the morning, bored by her town, her brother, and her life. Her boyfriend has just broken up with her in a particularly brutal way. Tamsin (Emily Blunt) is a rich girl, about the same age, sleek and brunette, on horseback the first time Mona sees her. She's spending the summer at her family's country house. "You're invited," she tells Mona. "I'm always here."

Tamsin's mother is absent. Her father is present but seems absent. The first time Mona visits, Tamsin shows her the room of her dead sister: "It's been kept as a shrine." The sister died, Tamsin says, of anorexia. The country girl and the city girl become friends almost by default; there seems to be no one else in the town they would want to talk to—certainly not the members of Phil's worship group.

That their summer leads to love is not quite the same thing as that it leads to a lesbian relationship. It's more like a teenage crush, composed in equal parts of hormones and boredom. But Tamsin and Mona promise to love each other forever, and as they swim in forest pools and ride around the countryside, they form their own secret society.

Phil, in the meantime, is engaged in the construction of a giant cross, made of iron and wood, which he wants to place on the top of a hill overlooking the town. Mona passes through the pub on her way upstairs, avoiding the prayer groups; left unexplained is how the brother and sister are supporting themselves. For Phil, religion seems less a matter of spiritual conviction than emotional hunger; he has been bad, now is good, and requires forgiveness and affirmation. Nothing wrong with that, unless he begins to impose his new lifestyle on Mona.

The movie is sweet and languid when the girls are together, edgier when Mona is around Phil. The question of Tamsin's father is complicated by the presence of his "personal assistant." The big summer house is empty and lonely, lacking a mother and haunted by the ghost of the dead sister. Pawel Pawlikovsky, the director and cowriter (with Michael Wynne), wisely allows the time to seem to flow, instead of pushing it. That's why, when Phil visits Tamsin's house looking for Mona, how Tamsin behaves and what happens is such a cruel surprise. She is, we realize, a convincing actress. When more revelations come in a closing scene, they are not exactly a surprise, not exactly a tragedy, not exactly very nice. We begin to sense the buried irony in the title.

Emily Blunt is well cast as Tamsin, a rich girl, product of the best schools, who cultivates decadence as her way of standing apart from what's expected of her. Natalie Press as Mona, on the other hand, is straight from the shoulder: She's without illusions about life, has given up on her brother, looks forward to marriage and family as a dreary prospect. Without quite saying so, she knows she'll never find a husband in her Yorkshire valley who is up to her speed. Will she, after this summer, identify as a lesbian? Doubtful. The summer stands by itself.

I'm not sure if the movie has a point. I'm not sure it needs one. I learn from *Variety* that the screenplay is inspired by a novel by Helen Cross that also involves a miners' strike and some murders. All of that is missing here, and what's left is a lazy summer of sweaty, uncertain romance; this isn't a coming-of-age movie so much as a movie about being of an age. At the end, when Tamsin tries to explain herself to Mona, we understand how completely different these two teenage girls are; how one deals in irony and deception, and with the other, what you see is what you get, whether you want it or not.

My Winnipeg ★ ★ ★ ★

NO MPAA RATING, 80 m., 2008

Darcy Fehr (Guy Maddin), Ann Savage (Mother), Amy Stewart (Janet Maddin), Louis Negin (Mayor Cornish), Brendan Cade (Cameron Maddin), Wesley Cade (Ross Maddin), Fred Dunsmore (Himself). Directed by Guy Maddin and produced by Jody Shapiro and Phyllis Laing. Screenplay by Maddin.

If you love movies in the very sinews of your imagination, you should experience the work of Guy Maddin. If you have never heard of him, I am not surprised. Now you have. A new

Maddin movie doesn't play in every multiplex or city or state. If you hear of one opening, seize the day. Or search where obscure films can be found. You will be plunged into the mind of a man who thinks in the images of old silent films, disreputable documentaries, movies that never were, from eras beyond comprehension. His imagination frees the lurid possibilities of the banal. He rewrites history; when that fails, he creates it.

First, a paragraph of dry fact. Maddin makes films that use the dated editing devices of old movies: Iris shots, breathless titles, shock cutting, staged poses, melodramatic acting, recycled footage, camera angles not merely dramatic but startling. He uses these devices to tell stories that begin with the improbable and march boldly into the inconceivable. My paragraph is ending now, and you have seen how difficult it is to describe his work. I will end with two more statements: (1) Shot for shot, Maddin can be as surprising and delightful as any filmmaker has ever been, and (2) he is an acquired taste, but please, sir, may I have some more?

Consider his film *My Winnipeg*. The city fathers commissioned it as a documentary, to be made by "the mad poet of Manitoba," as a Canadian magazine termed him. Maddin has never left his hometown, although, judging by this film, it has left him. It has abandoned its retail landmarks, its sports traditions, and even the daily local soap opera, *Ledge Man*, which ran for fifty years and starred Maddin's mother. As every episode opened, a man was found standing on a ledge and threatening to jump, and Maddin's mother talked him out of it.

Is that true? It's as true as anything else in the film. My friend Tony Scott of the *New York Times* thought he should check out some of the facts in *My Winnipeg* but decided not to. Why should he doubt the film? I certainly believe that after a stable fire at the racetrack, terrified horses stampeded into a freezing river and were frozen into place—their heads rising from the ice for the rest of the winter, for skaters to picnic on. I believe there are two taxi companies, one serving streets, and the other back lanes shown on no map. I believe Guy Maddin himself was born in the Winnipeg Arena during a game, nursed in the women's dressing room, and brought back a few days later for his first hockey match.

I also believe this because it is shown in the film: After Manitoba joined the hated (American-controlled) National Hockey League, the arena was enlarged to hold larger crowds. When the tragic decision was made to destroy the beloved arena by demolition, only the new parts collapsed, leaving the bones of the old arena still standing. "Demolition is one of our few growth industries," he says, acting as his own narrator.

Maddin was raised in this city, which he says has "ten times the sleepwalking rate" of any other. His childhood occurred in a house built as three white squares, one for his mother's beauty parlor, one for his aunt's family, one for his own. The scents of the parlor drifted up into his bedroom, and "every word of conversation swirled up out of that gynocracy." He attended a convent school named the Academy of the Super Vixens, ruled by "ever-opiating nuns."

Many of these facts are glimpsed through the windows of a train that seems headed out of town but never gets there. The narration is hallucinatory: "Old dreamy addresses, addresses, addresses, dreamy river forks. We see maps of the rivers fading into the fork of a woman's loin and back again." We are told that shadow-rivers flow beneath the visible ones. That the local madams were highly respected and streets were named after them and their brothels. That white-bearded Mayor Cornish (Louis Negin) personally judged the city's annual Golden Boy pageant, measuring biceps and thighs before scandal forced him out: too many Golden Boys on the city payroll!

I try to evoke, but I have failed! Failed! Disaster! I have tried to evoke the opiations of Guy Maddin, only to discover that the mother in the film is played by Ann Savage, star of *Detour*. Yes! A film in the Great Movies Collection of my Web site! Detour! Rocky road ahead! Savage! Maddin's father lies in state under a rug in the living room! Dead—not forgotten. Savage stepping around him! Watch your step. Savage! See this film!

N

Nacho Libre ★ ½

PG, 91 m., 2006

Jack Black (Ignacio/Nacho), Hector Jimenez (Esqueleto), Richard Montoya (Guillermo), Ana de la Reguera (Sister Encarnacion). Directed by Jared Hess and produced by Jack Black, David Klawans, Julia Pistor, and Mike White. Screenplay by Jared Hess, Jerusha Hess, and White.

Jack Black is not very funny in *Nacho Libre,* and that requires some meditation. Jack Black is essentially, intrinsically, and instinctively a funny actor. He has that Christopher Walken thing going where you smile when he appears in a movie. It takes some doing to make a Jack Black comedy that doesn't work. But *Nacho Libre* does it.

The premise of the movie is just fine in theory and must have sounded great at the pitch meeting: Black plays Brother Ignacio, a monk who lives in a backwater of Mexico, cooks slop for orphans, and lusts after the beautiful Sister Encarnacion (Ana de la Reguera). Because he wants to be famous and make money and buy better food to cook for the orphans, he begins a secret career as a masked wrestler.

The sport he attempts to infiltrate actually exists in Mexico and the American Southwest. It is called *lucha libre,* and I learn from Wikipedia that it's freestyle wrestling with more freedom and less strategy than the American variety. A lucha libre wrestler is known as a *luchador.* The sport is depicted with affection in the movie. If the luchadors (especially the giant Ramses, with his golden mask) seem a little ridiculous, well, all professional wrestlers seem a little ridiculous, don't they? What can you say about a sport whose heroes include Haystacks Calhoun?

The problem with *Nacho Libre* is not its content but its style. It is curiously disjointed. Episodes meander on and off the screen without much conviction. While in training, Brother Ignacio climbs a rocky cliff to eat the yolk of an eagle's egg, and what's the payoff? He eats it and dives back into the water. Jokes do not build to climaxes, confrontations are misplaced, the professional wrestling itself is not especially well-staged, and Black's tag-team partner, Esqueleto (Hector Jimenez), is not well-defined; it's funny that he answers all of Ignacio's theories by saying he "believes in science," but what's the punch line? He tags along all too literally because the writers haven't carved out a role for him to play.

As for Sister Encarnacion, she is neither sexy enough nor pious enough to be funny as one or the other. She seems like an innocent not sure what she thinks about Brother Ignacio or anybody else. Nor is Brother Ignacio especially lecherous; his seduction technique is to ask her to "join me in my quarters for some toast." Again, funny, but freestanding and leading nowhere.

One of the writers on the film is Mike White (*Chuck & Buck, The School of Rock, The Good Girl, Orange County*), who usually can do no wrong. The director is Jared Hess, whose *Napoleon Dynamite* (2004) is much beloved by many moviegoers. I have been assured so often that I missed the boat on *Napoleon* that I plan to go back and have another look at it; but now here is *Nacho Libre,* which has the same incomplete and fitful comic timing I thought I found in the earlier film.

I suppose there will be those who find *Nacho Libre* offensive in one way or another, but with comedy, a little political incorrectness comes with the territory. Yes, Mexico in the movie seems to be a country where English is the language and Spanish is a hobby. Yes, Brother Ignacio is mugged by a wild child for a bag of nacho chips. And yes, Brother Ignacio's cooking is so bad that this may be the first orphanage in the history of fiction where an urchin approaches the cook and asks, "Please, sir, may I have less food?" (This doesn't actually happen in the movie, but it should have.)

I dunno. I sat there and watched scenes flex their muscles and run off in the direction of comedy and trip over something. I saw the great Jack Black occasionally at wit's end. I saw wrestling matches that were neither painful nor funny, and not well enough choreographed to make much sense. The film begins with a certain air of dejection, as if it already suspects what we're about to find out.

The Namesake ★ ★ ★ ½

PG-13, 122 m., 2006

Kal Penn (Gogol Ganguli), Tabu (Ashima Ganguli), Irrfan Khan (Ashoke Ganguli), Sahira Nair (Sonia Ganguli), Jacinda Barrett (Maxine Ratliff), Zuleikha Robinson (Moushimi Mazumdar). Directed by Mira Nair and produced by Lydia Dean Pilcher and Nair. Screenplay by Sooni Taraporevala, based on the novel by Jhumpa Lahiri.

The Namesake is Mira Nair's ninth feature, and I suspect the one closest to her heart. It tells the story of a young couple who have an arranged marriage in Calcutta and move to New York, where they discover each other and their new country, and have two children. Then the story shifts to center on their son, while keeping them in the picture. Nair, born in India, educated at Harvard, married to a Ugandan, must have felt a resonance on every page of her source, the beloved novel by Jhumpa Lahiri.

The first meeting of the young woman, Ashima (Tabu), and her proposed husband, Ashoke (Irrfan Khan), is filmed with subtle charm. Her prospective mother-in-law warns her that life will be hard in New York, far from home, friends, family, all she knows. "Won't he be there?" she asks shyly, and the solemn Ashoke smiles, and their future is sealed. Her new husband is an aspiring architect, earning enough at first to afford only a low-rent flat in a marginal neighborhood, but America has its consolations: "In this country, the gas is on twenty-four hours a day!" he tells her.

Nair tenderly handles their first days of warily walking and talking around each other, and tentatively making love. It goes easier than it might have because this is a marriage that was arranged between the right two people, and their respect and regard (and eventually deep love) only grow.

Along comes a son, Gogol (Kal Penn), and a daughter, Sonia (Sahira Nair, the director's niece). Much is made of how Gogol got his name, which is not Indian or American but inspired by his father's favorite author; as an adolescent the boy comes to hate it and changes his name to Nikolai (or "Nicky"), the author Gogol's own first name. But there is a reason for "Gogol," and it has much importance for his father, who often mentions Gogol's short story "The Overcoat." In that story, interestingly, the hero has a laughable name, which Gogol explains "happened quite as a case of necessity . . . it was utterly impossible to give him any other name." How the American boy got his name becomes the stuff of family legend.

The movie concerns itself largely with being Indian and American at the same time. With making close ties with other Indian immigrants, sprinkling curry powder on the Rice Krispies, moving to a split-level suburban house, sending the children to college. Gogol, or Nicky, acquires a white girlfriend named Maxine (Jacinda Barrett), who apparently truly loves him but says the wrong things during a period of family mourning, so that Gogol shuts her out. Then he marries a Bengali girl named Moushimi (Zuleikha Robinson), who has grown much more sophisticated since he first met her years ago during negotiations between their parents. His sister marries a nice white boy named Ben. "Times are changing," Ashima philosophizes.

The culture gap is demonstrated when Gogol brings Maxine home to meet his parents and warns her: "No kissing. No touching." He has never even seen his own parents touch. But Maxine impulsively kisses his parents on their cheeks, and the earth does not move. They would prefer him to marry "a nice Bengali girl who makes samosas every Thursday," as Moushimi describes herself, but the film reveals that the children of the second generation do not always follow the scripts of their parents.

The movie covers some twenty-five or thirty years, so it is episodic by nature. What holds it together are the subtle, loving performances by Tabu and Khan, both Bollywood stars. They never overplay, never spell out what can be said in a glance or a shrug, communicate great passion very quietly. As Gogol, Kal Penn is not a million miles removed from the character he played in *Harold and Kumar Go to White Castle,* although he is a lot smarter. He is an angel until about thirteen, and then his parents, heaven help them, find they have given birth to an American teenager.

The Namesake tells a story that is the story

of all immigrant groups in America: parents of great daring arriving with dreams, children growing up in a way that makes them almost strangers, the old culture merging with the new. It has been said that all modern Russian literature came out of Gogol's "Overcoat." In the same way, all of us came out of the overcoat of this same immigrant experience.

Note: Read "The Overcoat" at www.geocities.com/short_stories_page/gogolovercoat.html.

Nanny McPhee ★ ★ ★

PG, 97 m., 2006

Emma Thompson (Nanny McPhee), Colin Firth (Cedric Brown), Angela Lansbury (Great Aunt Adelaide), Kelly Macdonald (Evangeline), Celia Imrie (Selma Quickly), Imelda Staunton (Mrs. Blatherwick), Thomas Sangster (Simon Brown). Directed by Kirk Jones and produced by Tim Bevan, Lindsay Doran, Eric Fellner, and Debra Hayward. Screenplay by Emma Thompson, based on the Nurse Matilda books by Christianna Brand.

There is a darkness in a lot of British children's fiction, from Roald Dahl to Harry Potter, and it provides both scariness and relief: The happy endings are arrived at via many close calls. Consider *Nanny McPhee*, named for a governess who seems closer to Mrs. Doubtfire than Mary Poppins. Garbed in a black dress that looks stuffed with flour sacks, she has warts on her face, fire in her eyes, and a walking stick that sends off sparks when she slams it on the cobblestones, which is a lot.

Nanny McPhee (Emma Thompson) is the eighteenth governess employed in the Brown household after the death of his wife left Cedric Brown (Colin Firth) to raise seven children on his own. These children, who seem to have been born within about eight years of each other, are a lawless tribe dedicated to driving away nannies, and we see several of them fleeing the house, one of them screaming, "They've eaten the baby!"

Cedric starts getting mysterious messages: "The person you need is Nanny McPhee." They are followed by Nanny herself, a formidable and foreboding presence who seems to command magical powers and quickly whips the children into shape. She has a set of rules for them to learn and a frown that terrifies them, and soon all is peaceful (or perhaps apprehensive), even at bedtime in the dormitory room the kids all share.

The Browns inhabit a big old country house with countless architectural grotesqueries and lots of gardens and staircases; only in fiction could this be the residence of a man facing financial ruin. Cedric Brown is the local funeral director, in debt and counting on an inheritance from his rich Great Aunt Adelaide (Angela Lansbury), who has made one stipulation: He must marry within thirty days.

There is an obvious candidate for his heart: Evangeline (Kelly Macdonald), the scullery maid, who is beloved by the children and by Cedric, although he's such a doofus he doesn't realize it. Instead, Cedric seems doomed to marry Mrs. Quickly (Celia Imrie), who is well named, since like Shakespeare's Mistress Quickly she seems to be one step removed from a tart, possibly in the wrong direction.

As plans for the marriage advance, Nanny McPhee admirably improves the behavior of the Brown children, and here's a funny thing: Every time she succeeds in getting one of her rules enforced, a wart disappears from her face. She also seems to be slimming. By the end of the movie she will look like the Emma Thompson we know and love, and not a moment too soon.

Will Cedric marry Mrs. Quickly? Or will he realize Evangeline is his true love? Will the children turn into model kids? Will it snow in August? All of these questions are answered in due time, in a movie that embraces eccentricity as a social value.

Watching the movie, I reflected that the difference between American and British children in the movies is that the American kids tend to run their families, and the British kids (Harry Potter excepted) tend to require, and deserve, many hard lessons in life. It is also refreshing that British kids do not succeed because they find out they are good at sports (Quidditch excepted). In American movies the kids end in triumph, pumping their fists into the air and chanting "yes!" In British movies, they end as well-behaved miniature adults who have come to see the truth of all the wisdom bestowed upon them.

All of this is connected somehow with the decision that Cedric Brown makes to admit Nanny McPhee into his house in the first place. If a formidable and terrifying female, dressed in black and banging a lethal walking stick, should arrive at an American door all covered with warts, the residents would push the panic button on their security systems. Only in this world (based on the Nurse Matilda books by Christianna Brand) would such a creature be welcomed.

Will kids like the movie? I suspect they will. Kids like to see other kids learning the rules even if they don't much want to learn them themselves. Here is the Brown family, teetering on the brink of poverty and yet living in a house rich American kids could only envy. Lots of staircases, lots of hiding places, lots of gardens, and even a big old kitchen ruled by a red-faced cook, Mrs. Blatherwick (Imelda Staunton), who throws things at them but always seems to have a few chickens in a pot in case anyone should want sandwiches.

National Treasure: Book of Secrets ★ ★

PG, 104 m., 2007

Nicolas Cage (Ben Gates), Jon Voight (Patrick Gates), Harvey Keitel (Sadusky), Ed Harris (Jeb Wilkinson), Diane Kruger (Abigail Chase), Justin Bartha (Riley Poole), Bruce Greenwood (U.S. President), Helen Mirren (Emily Appleton). Directed by Jon Turteltaub and produced by Jerry Bruckheimer and Turteltaub. Screenplay by Cormac Wibberley and Marianne Wibberley.

National Treasure: Book of Secrets has without a doubt the most absurd and fevered plot since, oh, say, *National Treasure* (2004). What do I mean by fevered? What would you say if I told you that Mount Rushmore was carved only in order to erase landmarks pointing to a fabled City of Gold built inside the mountain? That the holders of this information involved John Wilkes Booth and a Confederate secret society named the Knights of the Golden Circle? And that *almost exactly the same people* who tracked down the buried treasure in the first movie are involved in this one?

Yes, even the same FBI agent and the same national archivist and Benjamin Franklin Gates (Nicolas Cage) and his father, Patrick Henry Gates (Jon Voight). They're famous now (one has written a best-seller), but they *never* discuss the coincidence that they are involved in an uncannily similar adventure. Yes, once again they are all trapped within the earth and dangling over a terrifying drop. And their search once again involves a secret document and a hidden treasure. No, this time it's not written in invisible ink on the back of the Declaration of Independence. It involves a missing page from Booth's diary, a coded message, an extinct language, and a book that each U.S. president hands over to his successor, which contains the truth about Area 51, the so-called moon landings, Nixon's missing eighteen minutes, the JFK assassination, and, let's see . . . oh, yeah, the current president would like to know what's on page 47, although if he is the only man allowed to look at the book, how does he know that he doesn't know what's on page 47?

I have only scratched the surface. The heroes of this tale have what can only be described as extraordinary good luck. Benjamin once again is an intuitive code breaker, who has only to look at a baffling conundrum to solve it. And what about their good fortune when they are on top of Mount Rushmore, looking for hidden signs, and Benjamin interprets an ancient mention of "rain from a cloudless sky" and passes out half-liter bottles of drinking water for everyone to sprinkle on the rock so the old marking will show up? It's not a real big mountain, but it's way too big for six people to sprinkle with Crystal Geyser. But, hey! After less than a minute of sprinkling, here's the mark of the spread eagle!

Compared to that, the necessity of kidnapping the president from his own birthday party and leading him into a tunnel beneath Mount Vernon is a piece of cake, even though it is never quite made clear how Benjamin knows about the tunnel. Oh, yeah: He has George Washington's original blueprints. For that matter, it's never explained why so many people over so many generations have spent so much time and money guarding the City of Gold. And why leave clues if they are designed never to be interpreted, and for that matter you don't want anyone to interpret them? And although lots of gold has been mined in South Dakota, how much would it take to build a *city*? Remember, all the gold in Fort Knox is only enough to fill Fort Knox, which is about as big as City Hall in the underground city.

Yes, I know, all of this is beside the point. That person who attends *National Treasure: Book of Secrets* expecting logic and plausibility is on a fool's mission. This is a Mouth Agape Movie, during which your mouth hangs open in astonishment at one preposterous event after another. This movie's plot plays tennis not only without a net, but also without a ball or a racket. It spins in its own blowback. And, no, I don't know what that means, but this is the kind of movie that makes you think of writing it.

I gotta say, the movie has terrific if completely unbelievable special effects. The actors had fun, I guess. You might, too, if you like goofiness like this. Look at the cast: Cage and Voight and Helen Mirren and Ed Harris and Diane Kruger and Harvey Keitel and Justin Bartha and Bruce Greenwood. You could start with a cast like that and make one of the greatest movies of all time, which is not what happened here.

The New World ★ ★ ★ ★

PG-13, 130 m., 2006

Colin Farrell (Captain John Smith), Q'Orianka Kilcher (Pocahontas), Christopher Plummer (Captain Newport), Christian Bale (John Rolfe), August Schellenberg (Powhatan), Wes Studi (Opechancanough), David Thewlis (Captain Wingfield). Directed by Terrence Malick and produced by Sarah Green. Screenplay by Malick.

Terrence Malick's *The New World* strips away all the fancy and lore from the story of Pocahontas and her tribe and the English settlers at Jamestown, and imagines how new and strange these people must have seemed to one another. If the Indians stared in disbelief at the English ships, the English were no less awed by the somber beauty of the new land and its people. They called the Indians "the naturals," little understanding how well the term applied.

Malick strives throughout his film to imagine how the two civilizations met and began to speak when they were utterly unknown to each other. We know with four centuries of hindsight all the sad aftermath, but it is crucial to *The New World* that it does not know what history holds. These people regard one another in complete novelty, and at times with a certain humility imposed by nature. The Indians live because they submit to the realities of their land, and the English nearly die because they are ignorant and arrogant.

Like his films *Days of Heaven* and *The Thin Red Line*, Malick's *The New World* places nature in the foreground, instead of using it as a picturesque backdrop as other stories might. He uses voice-over narration by the principal characters to tell the story from their individual points of view. We hear Captain John Smith describe Pocahontas: "She exceeded the others not only in beauty and proportion, but in wit and spirit, too." And later the settler John Rolfe recalls his first meeting: "When first I saw her, she was regarded as someone broken, lost."

The New World is Pocahontas's story, although the movie deliberately never calls her by any name. She is the bridge between the two peoples. Played by a fourteen-year-old actress named Q'Orianka Kilcher as a tall, grave, inquisitive young woman, she does not "fall in love" with John Smith, as the children's books tell it, but saves his life—throwing herself on his body when he is about to be killed on the order of the chief, her father—for far more complex reasons. The movie implies, rather than says, that she is driven by curiosity about these strange visitors, and empathy with their plight as strangers, and with admiration for Smith's reckless and intrepid courage. If love later plays a role, it is not modern romantic love so much as a pure, instinctive version.

And what of Smith (Colin Farrell)? To see him is to know he knows the fleshpots of London and has been raised without regard for women. He is a troublemaker, under sentence of death by the expedition leader, Captain Newport (Christopher Plummer), for mutinous grumblings. Yet when he first sees Pocahontas, she teaches him new feelings by her dignity and strangeness. There is a scene where Pocahontas and Smith teach each other simple words in their own languages, words for sky, eyes, and lips, and the scene could seem contrived, but it doesn't because they play it with such a tender feeling of discovery.

Smith is not fair with Pocahontas. Perhaps you know the story, but if you don't, I'll let the movie fill in the details. She later encounters the settler John Rolfe (Christian Bale) and from him finds loyalty and honesty. Her father, the old chief Powhatan (August Schellenberg), would have her killed for her transgressions, but "I cannot give you up to die. I am too old for it." Abandoned by her tribe, she is forced to live with the English. Rolfe returns with her to England, where she meets the king and is a London sensation, although that story, too, is well-known.

There is a meeting that she has in England, however, that Malick handles with almost trembling tact, in which she deals with a truth hidden from her, and addresses it with unwavering honesty. What Malick focuses on is her feelings as a person who might as well have been transported to another planet. Wearing strange clothes, speaking a strange language, she can depend only on those few she trusts, and on her idea of herself.

There are two new worlds in this film, the one the English discover, and the one Pocahontas discovers. Both discoveries center on the word "new," and what distinguishes Malick's film is how firmly he refuses to know more than he should in Virginia in 1607 or London a few years later. The events in his film, including the tragic battles between the Indians and the settlers, seem to be happening for the first time. No one here has read a history book from the future.

There are the familiar stories of the Indians helping the English survive the first winter, of how they teach the lore of planting corn and laying up stores for the winter. We are surprised to see how makeshift and vulnerable the English forts are, how evolved the Indian culture is, how these two civilizations could have built something new together—but could not, because what both societies knew at that time did not permit it. Pocahontas could have brought them together. In a small way, she did. She was given the gift of sensing the whole picture, and that is what Malick founds his film on, not tawdry stories of love and adventure. He is a visionary, and this story requires one.

Note: This review is based on a viewing of the re-edited version of The New World, *which runs about 130 minutes; I also saw the original 150-minute version and noticed no startling changes.*

Night Watch ★ ★

R, 114 m., 2006

Konstantin Khabensky (Anton Gorodetsky), Vladimir Menshov (Boris Geser), Valery Zolotukhin (Kostya's Father), Mariya Poroshina (Svetlana), Galina Tyunina (Olga), Viktor Verzhbitsky (Zavulon), Dmitry Martynov (Yegor). Directed by Timur Bekmambetov and produced by Konstantin Ernst and Anatoli Maksimov. Screenplay by Bekmambetov and Sergei Lukyanenko.

I confess to a flagging interest in the struggle between the forces of Light and Darkness. It's like Super Sunday in a sport I do not follow, like tetherball. We're told the future of the world hangs in the balance, and then everything comes down to a handful of hungover and desperate characters surrounded by dubious special effects. I want to hear Gabriel blow that horn.

Movies about apocalyptic showdowns always begin with an origin story; the rules for the struggle were established long ago, but now a recent crisis has altered the balance. That's the case with Timur Bekmambetov's *Night Watch,* the first in a fantasy trilogy from Russia. We learn that in the year 1342, the Warriors of Light and the Warriors of Darkness met in battle on a bridge, and so bloody was their carnage that it appeared both teams of Others (so called, I think, because they are not Sames) would lose all of their warriors, which might have been a good thing for Earth in the long run. But it was not to be; Geser and Zavulon, the leaders of Light and Darkness, establish a truce, which holds until Moscow 1992, when a new Other is born whose existence may reopen the ancient struggle.

We learn that during all the centuries in between, the truce was enforced; the Warriors of Light ran a Night Watch, and the Warriors of Darkness ran a Day Watch, to keep tabs on each other. Sometimes, when they were shorthanded, they hired a freelancer from the other side, which is like trusting mercenaries because now they're working for you. But now a young boy has been born who senses the Call and is drawn toward vampires—but hold on, how did they get in here? It appears that Others and Vampires are either interchangeable or operate in sync with each other, and the vampire hero Anton (Konstantin Khabensky), working for Light, attempts to rescue young Yegor (Dmitry Martynov) from the vampires of Darkness. Whichever team gets Yegor holds the edge. This is like Quidditch in hell.

You will sense that my understanding of the

plot is not crystal clear. Do not depend upon me for a rational synopsis. In the meantime, a vortex is heading for Moscow, as symbolized by ground-level shots of special-effects birds whirling about the roof of a tall building. Severe turbulence seizes an airplane, and the power plant in Moscow blows up, throwing everything into darkness. Then Anton is savagely attacked and brought into the office of the president of the light company, who sweeps everything off his desk and turns it into an operating theater to save him by plunging his fist into the chest of the victim, just like those magic healers we used to hear about in the Philippines. The Others are hardy; one warrior removes his own spine and uses it as a bludgeon. I wondered how he remained standing and had movement in his limbs, but it didn't seem to bother him.

Let us return to the endangered airplane. The passengers scream; the plane plunges wildly through the air and at one point is actually seen so close to the ground that it passes power cables. Then it's left to bounce about forgotten by the plot, until a perfunctory shot shows it aloft again and cruising smoothly. That's after the lights go back on in Moscow, which is odd, since how can the power plant function after it has exploded into smithereens? The movie is so plot-heavy it scurries between developments like a puppy surrounded by pigeons. I cringe in anticipation of the e-mails explaining all of this to me; those who understand the plot of *Night Watch* should forget about the movies and get right to work on string theory.

One interesting quality of the film is its use of characters who seem as if they might actually live in Moscow. They have a careworn look. Most Light vs. Darkness movies involve elaborate wardrobes, as if, between Apocalypsi, the warriors refit at a custom leather shop. But the Others look scruffy, drink vodka and blood more or less interchangeably, and speed around the city not in a customized Vampire-mobile but in a truck of the sort used to transport refrigerated meat. While indoors, they spend a lot of time in rooms that remind me of Oscar Wilde's dying words: "Either this wallpaper goes, or I do."

The subtitles for the movie rise to the occasion, literally. They do not simply materialize at the bottom of the screen but rather unspool dynamically, dance across the picture, evaporate, explode, quiver, and seem possessed. Not since a modern benshi version of the Mexican silent classic *The Grey Automobile* (1919) have I seen such subtitles. Benshis, of course, were the Japanese performers who stood next to the screen during silent films and explained the plot to the audience. If ever a benshi were needed in a modern movie, *Night Watch* is that film.

Nine Lives ★ ★ ★ ½

R, 115 m., 2005

Kathy Baker (Camille), Amy Brenneman (Lorna), Elpidia Carrillo (Sandra), Glenn Close (Maggie), Stephen Dillane (Martin), Dakota Fanning (Maria), William Fichtner (Andrew), Lisa Gay Hamilton (Holly), Holly Hunter (Sonia), Jason Isaacs (Damian), Joe Mantegna (Richard), Ian McShane (Larry), Molly Parker (Lisa), Mary Kay Place (Alma), Sydney Tamiia Poitier (Vanessa), Aidan Quinn (Henry), Miguel Sandoval (Ron), Amanda Seyfried (Samantha), Sissy Spacek (Ruth), Robin Wright Penn (Diana). Directed by Rodrigo Garcia and produced by Julie Lynn. Screenplay by Garcia.

They meet by accident in the supermarket. It's been—how many years? They were in love once. They were a couple. They were "Damian and Diana" to everyone who knew them. Now they're both married to others. She's pregnant. They smile and exchange meaningless commonplaces. They separate. Each of their carts is filled with items for the use of a person the other will never meet.

In another aisle, they meet again. Not by accident. There is more to be said, but not very much that can be safely said without an enormous upheaval in their lives. It is clear to us, perhaps to them, that they never should have broken up. No matter what has happened, no matter whom they married, he says, "we're Damian and Diana." That will never change.

Thank God *Nine Lives* is an episodic film, so everything they have to say or do has to be contained in about twelve minutes. To know why they broke up or to see them get back together would involve us in a full-length love story of the sort we are familiar with.

It might be a good one. But here, in this meeting that is seen in one unbroken shot in a supermarket, we see the crucial heart of their relationship. It is based on the truth that their lives have moved on. Perhaps they should have stayed together. But they didn't. It's not important to know whether they start seeing each other again. But it is important for them to know that they want to, because to live without that knowledge is to dishonor their real feelings. This little story, starring Robin Wright Penn and Jason Isaacs, is told in *Nine Lives*, a collection of nine vignettes written and directed by Rodrigo Garcia. Each one contains a moment of truth, each one is about the same length, each one is told in a single shot, although the camera work isn't showy.

Sometimes the episodes seem obvious at first. Kathy Baker plays a woman who will undergo breast surgery in a few hours. In her hospital bed, she is frightened and angry; she's short-tempered with the nurses and hard on her husband (Joe Mantegna). A nurse adds a sedative to her IV drip, and she grows calmer and then—well, happy. She sees the good in things. The sedative has done its work.

But the episode is about so much more than that. It is about the indignity of surgeons inserting knives into your unconscious body, and about the fear of loss, and the impersonality of hospitals but the humanity of nurses, and the patience and love of her husband. Was she acting bitchy? When you're about to get a breast removed, you're not going for a good grade in deportment. Sometimes we behave badly for the best reasons in the world, and this movie knows that.

Other scenes. There is a prisoner (Elpidia Carrillo) who gets crazy because this is visitors' day and her daughter is on the other side of the glass, and the telephone doesn't work. An angry daughter (Lisa Gay Hamilton) who returns after a long absence to the home where she was raised and abused; this woman, so wounded, so borderline, is the same woman who, we discover in the hospital scene, is the nurse who is gentle and cares. Sissy Spacek plays a despairing mother in a dysfunctional household in one segment, and turns up in another prepared, perhaps, to have a forbidden night in a motel with Aidan Quinn. Glenn Close and Dakota Fanning visit a cemetery together in the last story, where the final shot will blindside you.

There is notoriously not a market for short films. You can't book them or advertise them, it's impossible to try to review them (and besides, where can the readers see them?). But short films are a form with purpose, just as short stories are. Some stories need only introduce us to a character or two and spend enough time with them for us to discover something about their natures, and perhaps our natures. The greatest short-story writers, such as William Trevor and Alice Munro, can awe us; their stories are short but not small.

Here Garcia does the same thing. The son of the novelist Gabriel Garcia Marquez, he has the same love for his characters, and although his stories are all (except for one) realistic, he shares his father's appreciation for the ways lives interweave and we touch each other even if we are strangers. A movie like this, with the appearance of new characters and situations, focuses us; we watch more intently, because it is important what happens. These characters aren't going to get bailed out with 110 minutes of plot. Their lives have reached a turning point here and now, and what they do must be done here and now, or forever go unknown.

9 Songs ★ ★

NO MPAA RATING, 71 m., 2005

Kieran O'Brien (Matt), Margo Stilley (Lisa). Directed by Michael Winterbottom and produced by Andrew Eaton and Winterbottom. Screenplay by Winterbottom.

Show rock concert, show sex, show icy wastes of Antarctica. Repeat eight times. That's essentially the structure of Michael Winterbottom's *9 Songs*, a movie that marks an important director's attempt to deal with explicit sex. As an idea, the film is fascinating, but as an experience it grows tedious; the concerts lack close-ups, the sex lacks context, and Antarctica could use a few penguins.

To begin with the sex: The story involves a British scientist named Matt (Kieran O'Brien) and an American named Lisa (Margo Stilley) who is visiting London for obscure reasons; she mentions jobs and studying. They meet at a rock concert in Brixton, go back to his place, and have sex. It is real sex. Real, in the sense that the actors are actually doing what they seem to be doing, and real, in the sense that instead of the counterfeit moaning and panting of pornography, there is the silence of concentration and the occasional music of delight.

All together, they go to nine concerts and hear nine songs, but this is not a concert film and the performers mostly are seen in long shot, over the heads of the crowd, which is indeed the way most of us see rock concerts. That works for realism, but it does the musicians no favors.

The nine sex scenes are filmed with the detachment of someone who has no preconceived notion of what the characters will be doing, or why. They lack the choreography of pornography, and they act as a silent rebuke to the hard-core image of sex. Winterbottom seems deliberately reluctant to turn up the visual heat; he accepts shadows and obscurities and creates a certain confusion (in the words of the limerick) about who is doing what and with which and to whom. The occasional shots of genital areas are not underlined but simply occur in the normal course of events.

There is also some dialogue. No attempt is made to see Matt and Lisa as characters in a conventional plot. They talk as two people might talk, who have fallen into an absorbing sexual relationship but are not necessarily planning a lifetime together. Matt likes her more than she likes him. There's a revelation late in the film, concerning the flat where she lives, that is kind of a stunner. What Winterbottom is charting is the progress of sex in the absence of fascination; if two people are not excited by who they are outside of sex, there's a law of diminishing returns in bed. Yes, they try to inspire themselves with blindfolds and bondage, but the more you're playing games, the less you're playing with each other. Their first few sexual encounters have the intricacy and mystery of great tabletop magic; by the end, they're making elephants disappear but they know it's just a trick.

The Antarctic footage is mostly of limitless icy wastes. Matt's narration observes that a sub-zero research station causes simultaneous claustrophobia and agoraphobia—"like a couple in bed." Yes. They're afraid to be trapped, and afraid to leave. There is some truth here.

The sex scenes betray the phoniness of commercial pornography; when the Adult Film Awards give a prize for best acting, they're ridiculed, but after seeing this film you'll have to admit the hard-core performers are acting, all right; *9 Songs* observes the way real people play and touch and try things out, and make little comments and have surprised reactions.

That said, *9 Songs* is more interesting to write about than to see. Its minimalism is admirable as an experiment but monotonous as an experience. To the degree that O'Brien and Stilley exchange dialogue on-screen and inhabit characters, they suggest that a full-blown movie about these characters might be intriguing. What Winterbottom does in part I'd like to see him do in whole: show a relationship in which two reasonably intelligent and sensitive adults pick each other up for sex, enjoy it, repeat it, and then have to decide if they want to take the relationship to the next level.

In many movies, the first sexual encounter is earthshaking, and then the lucky couple is magically in love forever—or at least until the story declares otherwise. In real life, sex is easy but love is hard. Sex is possible with someone you don't know. Love is not. In a way, *9 Songs* is about the gradual realization by Lisa and, more reluctantly, by Matt, that there is not going to be any love and that the sex is, therefore, going to become kind of sad.

Nobody Knows ★ ★ ★ ½

PG-13, 141 m., 2005

Yuya Yagira (Akira), Ayu Kitaura (Kyoko), Hiei Kimura (Shigeru), Momoko Shimizu (Yuki), Hanae Kan (Saki), You (Keiko). Directed and produced by Hirokazu Kore-eda. Screenplay by Kore-eda.

As *Nobody Knows* opens, we watch a mother and two kids moving into a new apartment. They wrestle some heavy suitcases up the stairs. When the movers have left, they open the suitcases and release two younger children, who are a secret from the landlord. "Remember the new rules," the mother says. "No going outside. Not even on the veranda—except for Kyoko, to do the laundry."

Kyoko is the second oldest, about ten. The oldest, a boy named Akira, is about twelve. He regards his mother with guarded eyes. So do we. There is something too happy about her, as she acts like one of the kids. It is not the forced happiness of a person trying to keep up a brave front, or the artificial happiness of someone who is high, but the crazy happiness of a person who is using laughter to mask the reality of her behavior. It fools the little kids, Shigeru and Yuki, who are perhaps seven and four.

The mother, named Keiko, played by a pop star named You, leaves Akira some money and goes away. She returns very late at night, still cheerful, as if it is the most natural thing in the world to leave her children alone, let them prepare their own dinners, and save some for her. "She stinks of booze," Akira says quietly to Kyoko.

Keiko confides in Akira that she has met a new guy, who seems "sincere" and might marry her. "Again?" he says. He is very quiet around her. She goes away again, for a much longer time, until the money she left runs out, and then she returns with gifts, including a backpack for Kyoko—ironic, since Kyoko is forbidden to leave the building. Keiko gives Akira more money, leaves again, and days and weeks pass; when Kyoko asks if she will return, Akira says she will not.

This story, written and filmed by Hirokazu Kore-eda, is based on a true story from Tokyo, where four children were abandoned by their mother and lived in an apartment for months, unmissed and undetected. He tells the story not as a melodrama about kids in danger, but as a record of long, lonely days, of the younger children playing their games and watching TV, of Akira going out into the city to buy food and find money. He gets some from a man in a pachinko parlor, who tells him not to ask again: "You know, Yuki isn't my kid." All four of the children have different fathers. Now they have no mother, but they have each other. Akira could contact the authorities, but "that happened before," he tells a friend, "and it was a real mess."

Akira is played by Yuya Yagira, who filmed the role over eighteen months, during which he grew a little and his voice broke. It is not just a cute kid performance, but real acting, because Kore-eda doesn't give him dialogue and actions to make his thoughts clear, but prefers to observe him observing, coping, and deciding. Yagira won the best actor award at Cannes.

What is most poignant is the sight of these kids wasting their lives. Kyoko asks her mother if she can go to school, but her mother laughs and says she will be happier at home. Akira was in school at one point and studies his books at night, until finally his only subject is arithmetic—figuring how much longer their money will last. There's a wistful shot of him looking at kids in a schoolyard, and one idyllic moment when he is asked to join a baseball game, and given a shirt and cap to wear.

He meets a girl his age named Saki (Hanae Kan), who prefers the streets to her home. They are too young for sex, but too old to be children. She picks up a guy, goes into a bar with him, comes out, and gives Akira some money. He tries to push it away, but she says, "All I did was sing karaoke with him." This time.

Kore-eda is the most gifted of the young Japanese directors. His *Maborosi* (1995), about a widow who remarries and takes her child to live in a small village, and *After Life* (1998), about a waiting room in heaven, are masterful. Here he is more matter-of-fact, more realistic, in suggesting the slow progress of time, the cold winter followed by the hot summer days, the desperation growing behind Akira's cautious expression. The fact that he doesn't crank up the energy with manufactured emergencies makes the impending danger more dramatic: This cannot go on, and it is going to end badly.

But don't the adults in the building, or anywhere else, know what is happening in the apartment? Hard to say. The landlady comes at one point to collect the rent but then seems to let the subject drop. The gas, lights, and water are turned off, but that doesn't ring an alarm bell. Yuki's possible father knows Keiko has been away but doesn't follow up to see if she's returned; perhaps he'd rather not know.

There are moments in Yuya Yagira's performance that will break your heart. One comes when he takes a few precious coins to a pay telephone to call a number where he might find his mother, or news of her. He's put on hold, and drops in one coin after another until they are all gone and he is disconnected, and bends his head forward against the telephone.

Kore-eda creates a sense of intimacy within the apartment. He shoots close to the kids (there's no room to get farther away), and underlines their claustrophobic imprisonment. They like each other, they have some toys, they get more or less enough to eat, usually less. One day Akira even takes their shoes out of a closet and lets them put them on, and takes them outside for a walk in the great, free, wide-open world that is so indifferent to them.

No Country for Old Men ★ ★ ★ ★

R, 123 m., 2007

Tommy Lee Jones (Sheriff Ed Tom Bell), Javier Bardem (Anton Chigurh), Josh Brolin (Llewelyn Moss), Woody Harrelson (Carson Wells), Kelly Macdonald (Carla Jean Moss), Garret Dillahunt (Deputy Wendell), Tess Harper (Loretta Bell). Direced by Ethan Coen and Joel Coen and produced by Coen, Coen, and Scott Rudin. Screenplay by Coen and Coen, based on the novel by Cormac McCarthy.

The movie opens with the flat, confiding voice of Tommy Lee Jones. He describes a teenage killer he once sent to the chair. The boy had killed his fourteen-year-old girlfriend. The papers described it as a crime of passion, "but he tolt me there weren't nothin' passionate about it. Said he'd been fixin' to kill someone for as long as he could remember. Said if I let him out of there he'd kill somebody again. Said he was goin' to hell. Reckoned he'd be there in about fifteen minutes."

These words sounded verbatim to me from *No Country for Old Men,* the novel by Cormac McCarthy, but I find they are not quite. And their impact has been improved upon in the delivery. When I get the DVD of this film, I will listen to that stretch of narration several times; Jones delivers it with a vocal precision and contained emotion that is extraordinary, and it sets up the entire film, which regards a completely evil man with wonderment, as if astonished that that such a merciless creature could exist.

The man is named Anton Chigurh. No, I don't know how his last name is pronounced. Like many of the words McCarthy uses, particularly in his masterpiece *Suttree,* I think it is employed like an architectural detail: The point is not how it sounds or what it means, but the brushstroke it adds to the sentence. Chigurh (Javier Bardem) is a tall, slouching man with lank black hair and a terrifying smile, who travels through Texas carrying a tank of compressed air and killing people with a cattle stun gun. It propels a cylinder into their heads and whips it back again.

Chigurh is one strand in the twisted plot. Ed Tom Bell, the sheriff played by Jones, is another. The third major player is Llewelyn Moss (Josh Brolin), a poor man who lives with his wife in a house trailer and one day, while hunting, comes across a drug deal gone wrong in the desert. Vehicles range in a circle like an old wagon train. Almost everyone on the scene is dead. They even shot the dog. In the back of one pickup are neatly stacked bags of drugs. Llewelyn realizes one thing is missing: the money. He finds it in a briefcase next to a man who made it as far as a shade tree before dying.

The plot will involve Moss attempting to make this $2 million his own, Chigurh trying to take it away from him, and Sheriff Bell trying to interrupt Chigurh's ruthless murder trail. We will also meet Moss's childlike wife, Carla Jean (Kelly Macdonald), a cocky bounty hunter named Carson Wells (Woody Harrelson), the businessman (Stephen Root) who hires Carson to track the money after investing in the drug deal, and a series of hotel and store clerks who are unlucky enough to meet Chigurh.

No Country for Old Men is as good a film as the Coen brothers, Joel and Ethan, have ever made, and they made *Fargo.* It involves elements of the thriller and the chase but is essentially a character study, an examination of how its people meet and deal with a man so bad, cruel, and unfeeling that there is simply no comprehending him. Chigurh is so evil he is almost funny sometimes; "He has his principles," says the bounty hunter, who has knowledge of him.

Consider another scene in which the dialogue is as good as any you will hear this year. Chigurh enters a rundown gas station in the middle of wilderness and begins to play a word game with the old man (Gene Jones) behind the cash register, who becomes very nervous. It is clear they are talking about whether Chigurh will kill him. Chigurh has by no means made up his mind. Without explaining why, he asks the man to call the flip of a coin. Listen to what they say, how they say it, how they imply the stakes. Listen to their timing. You want to applaud the writing, which comes from the Coen brothers, out of McCarthy.

The $2 million turns out to be easier to obtain than to keep. Moss tries hiding in obscure hotels. Scenes are meticulously constructed in which each man knows the other is nearby. Moss can run, but he can't hide. Chigurh always tracks him down. There seems to be a hole in the plot around here somewhere. Skip the next paragraph to avoid a spoiler.

Yes, the money briefcase has a transponder in it, but why does Chigurh have the corresponding tracker? If the men in the drug deal all killed each other and the man who unknowingly carried the transponder died under the tree, how did Chigurh come into the picture? I think it's because he set up the deal and planned to buy the drugs with the "invested" $2 million, end up with the drugs, and get the money back. That the actual dealers all killed each other in the desert and the money ended in the hands of a stranger was not his plan. That theory makes sense, or it would, if Chigurh were not so peculiar that it is hard to imagine him negotiating such a deal. "Do you have any idea," Carson Wells asks him, "how crazy you really are?"

Read safely again. This movie is a masterful evocation of time, place, character, moral choices, immoral certainties, human nature, and fate. It is also, in the photography by Roger Deakins, the editing by the Coens, and the music by Carter Burwell, startlingly beautiful, stark, and lonely. As McCarthy does with the Judge, the hairless exterminator in his *Blood Meridian* (Ridley Scott's next film), and as in his *Suttree*, especially in the scene where the river bank caves in, the movie demonstrates how pitiful ordinary human feelings are in the face of implacable injustice. The movie also loves some of its characters and pities them, and has an ear for dialogue not as it is spoken but as it is dreamed.

Many of the scenes in *No Country for Old Man* are so flawlessly constructed that you want them to simply continue, and yet they create an emotional suction, drawing you to the next scene. Another movie that made me feel that way was *Fargo*. To make one such film is a miracle. Here is another. ☞

No Direction Home: Bob Dylan ★ ★ ★ ★

NO MPAA RATING, 225 m., 2005

Featuring Bob Dylan, Joan Baez, Liam Clancy, Peter Yarrow, Dave Van Ronk, Allen Ginsberg, Maria Muldaur, and others. Directed by Martin Scorsese and produced by Margaret Bodde, Susan Lacy, Jeff Rosen, Scorsese, Nigel Sinclair, and Anthony Wall.

It has taken me all this time to accept Bob Dylan as the extraordinary artist he clearly is, but because of a new documentary by Martin Scorsese, I can finally see him freed from my disenchantment. I am Dylan's age, and his albums were the sound track of my college years. I never got involved in the war his fans fought over his acoustic and electric styles: I liked them all, every one.

Then in 1968 I saw *Don't Look Back*, D. A. Pennebaker's documentary about Dylan's 1965 tour of Great Britain. In my review I called the movie "a fascinating exercise in self-revelation" and added, "The portrait that emerges is not a pretty one." Dylan is seen not as a "lone, ethical figure standing up against the phonies," I wrote, but is "immature, petty, vindictive, lacking a sense of humor, overly impressed with his own importance, and not very bright."

I felt betrayed. In the film, he mercilessly puts down a student journalist and is rude to journalists, hotel managers, fans. Although Joan Baez was the first to call him on her stage when he was unknown, after she joins the tour, he does not ask her to sing with him. Eventually she bails out and goes home.

The film fixed my ideas about Dylan for years. Now Scorsese's *No Direction Home: Bob Dylan*, a 225-minute documentary that played in two parts on PBS, creates a portrait that is deep, sympathetic, perceptive, and yet finally leaves Dylan shrouded in mystery, which is where he properly lives.

The movie uses revealing interviews made recently by Dylan, but its subject matter is essentially the years between 1960, when he first came into view, and 1966, when after the British tour and a motorcycle accident he didn't tour for eight years. He was born in 1941, and the career that made him an icon essentially happened between his twentieth and twenty-fifth years. He was a very young man from a little Minnesota town who had the mantle of a generation placed, against his will, upon his shoulders. He wasn't there at Woodstock; Arlo Guthrie was.

Early footage of his childhood is typical of many Midwestern childhoods: the small town of Hibbing, Minnesota, the homecoming parade, bands playing at dances, the kid listening to the radio and records. The early sounds he loved ran all the way from Hank Williams and Webb Pierce to Muddy Waters, the Carter Family, and even Bobby Vee, a rock star so minor that young Robert Zimmerman for a time claimed to be Bobby Vee.

He hitched a ride to New York (or maybe he didn't hitch; his early biography is filled with romantic claims, such as that he grew up in Gallup, New Mexico). In Greenwich Village he found the folk scene, and it found him. He sang songs by Woody Guthrie, Pete Seeger, others, then was writing his own. He caught the eye of Baez, and she mentored and promoted him. Within a year he was—Dylan.

The movie has a wealth of interviews with people who knew him at the time: Baez, Pete Seeger, Mike Seeger, Liam Clancy, Dave Von Ronk, Maria Muldaur, Peter Yarrow, and promoters such as Harold Leventhal. There is significantly no mention of Ramblin' Jack Elliott. The 2000 documentary *The Ballad of Ramblin' Jack* says it was Elliott who introduced Dylan to Woody Guthrie, suggested the harmonica holder around his neck, and essentially defined his stage persona; "There wouldn't be no Bob Dylan without Ramblin' Jack," says Arlo Guthrie, who also is not in the Scorsese film.

Dylan's new friends in music all admired the art but were ambivalent about the artist. Van Ronk smiles now about the way Dylan "borrowed" his "House in New Orleans." The Beat generation, especially Jack Kerouac's *On the Road*, influenced Dylan, and there are many observations by the Beat poet Allen Ginsberg, who says he came back from India, heard a Dylan album, and wept, because he knew the torch had been passed to a new generation.

It is Ginsberg who says the single most perceptive thing in the film: For him, Dylan stood atop a column of air. His songs and his ideas rose up from within him and emerged uncluttered and pure, as if his mind, soul, body, and talent all were one.

Dylan was embraced by the left-wing musical community of the day. His "Blowin' in the Wind" became an anthem of the civil rights movement. His "Only a Pawn in Their Game" saw the killer of Medgar Evers as an insignificant cog in the machine of racism. Baez, Pete Seeger, the Staple Singers, Odetta, and Peter, Paul, and Mary—all sang his songs and considered him a fellow warrior.

But he would not be pushed or enlisted, and the crucial passages in this film show him drawing away from any attempt to define him. At the moment when he was being called the voice of his generation, he drew away from "movement" songs. A song like "Mr. Tambourine Man" was a slap in the face to his admirers, because it moved outside ideology.

Baez, interviewed before a fireplace in the kitchen of her home, still with the same beautiful face and voice, is the one who felt most betrayed: Dylan broke her heart. His change is charted through the Newport Folk Festival: early triumph, the summit in 1964 when Johnny Cash gave him his guitar, the beginning of the end with the electric set in 1965. He was backed by Mike Bloomfield and the Butterfield Blues Band in a folk-rock-blues hybrid that his fans hated. When he took the new sound on tour, audiences wanted the "protest songs" and shouted "Judas!" and "What happened to Woody Guthrie?" when he came onstage. Night after night, he opened with an acoustic set that was applauded and then came back with the Butterfield Blues Band and was booed.

"Dylan made it pretty clear he didn't want to do all that other stuff," Baez says, talking of political songs, "but I did." It was the beginning of the Vietnam era, and Dylan had withdrawn. When he didn't ask Baez onstage to sing with him on the British tour, she says quietly, "It hurt."

But what was happening inside Dylan? Was he the jerk portrayed in *Don't Look Back*? Scorsese looks more deeply. He shows countless news conferences where Dylan is assigned leadership of his generation and assaulted with inane questions about his role, message, and philosophy. A photographer asks him, "Suck your glasses" for a picture. He is asked how many protest singers he thinks there are: "There are 136."

At the 1965 Newport festival, Pete Seeger recalls: "The band was so loud, you couldn't understand one word. I kept shouting, 'Get that distortion out!' If I had an ax I'd chop the mike cable right now!" For Seeger, it was always about the words and the message. For Dylan, it was about the words, and then it became about the words and the music, and it was never particularly about the message.

Were drugs involved in these years? The movie makes not the slightest mention of them, except obliquely in a scene where Dylan and Cash do a private duet of "I'm So Lonesome I Could Cry," and it's clear they're both stoned. There is sad footage near the end of the British tour, when Dylan says he is so exhausted, "I shouldn't be singing tonight."

The archival footage comes from many sources, including documentaries by Pennebaker and Murray Lerner *(Festival)*. Many of the interviews were conducted by Michael Borofsky, and Jeff Rosen was a key contributor. But Scorsese provides the master vision, and his factual footage unfolds with the narrative power of fiction.

What it comes down to, I think, is that Robert Zimmerman from Hibbing, Minnesota, who mentions his father only because he bought the house where Bobby found a guitar, and mentions no other member of his family at all, who felt he was from nowhere, became the focus for a time of fundamental change in music and politics. His songs led that change but they transcended it. His audience was uneasy with transcendence. It kept trying to draw him back down into categories. He sang and sang, and finally, still a very young man, found himself a hero who was booed. "Isn't it something, how they still buy up all the tickets?" he asks, about a sold-out audience that hated his new music.

What I feel for Dylan now and did not feel before is empathy. His music stands and it will survive. Because it embodied our feelings, we wanted him to embody them, too. He had his own feelings. He did not want to embody. We found it hard to forgive him for that. He had the choice of caving in or dropping out. The blues band music, however good it really was, functioned also to announce the end of his days as a standard-bearer. Then after his motorcycle crash in 1966, he stopped touring for eight years and went away into a personal space where he remains.

Watching him singing in *No Direction Home*, we see no glimpse of humor, no attempt to entertain. He uses a flat, merciless delivery, more relentless cadence than melody, almost preaching. But sometimes at the press conferences we see moments of a shy, funny, playful kid inside. And just once, in his recent interviews, seen in profile against a background of black, we see the ghost of a smile.

No End in Sight ★ ★ ★ ★

NO MPAA RATING, 122 m., 2007

A documentary directed by Charles Ferguson and produced by Ferguson, Jenny Amias, Audrey Marrs, and Jessie Vogelson. Screenplay by Ferguson.

Remember the scene in *A Clockwork Orange* where Alex has his eyes clamped open and is forced to watch a movie? I imagine a similar experience for the architects of our catastrophe in Iraq. I would like them to see *No End in Sight*, the story of how we were led into that war and more than three thousand American lives and hundreds of thousands of other lives were destroyed.

They might find the film of particular interest because they would know so many of the people appearing in it. This is not a documentary filled with antiwar activists or sitting ducks for Michael Moore. Most of the people in the film were important to the Bush administration. They had top government or military jobs, they had responsibility in Iraq or Washington, they implemented policy, they filed reports, they labored faithfully in the service of U.S. foreign policy, and then they left the government. Some jumped, some were pushed. They all feel disillusioned about the war and the way the White House refused to listen to them about it.

The subjects in this film now feel that American policy in Iraq was flawed from the start, that obvious measures were not taken, that sane advice was disregarded, that lies were told and believed, and that advice from people on the ground was overruled by a cabal of neocon goofballs who seemed to form a wall around the president.

The president and his inner circle *knew*, just *knew*, for example, that Saddam had or would have weapons of mass destruction, that he was in league with al-Qaeda and bin Laden, and that in some way it was all hooked up with 9/11. Not all of the advice in the world could penetrate their obsession, and they fired the bearers of bad news.

It is significant, for example, that a Defense Intelligence Agency team received *orders* to find links between al-Qaeda and Saddam. That there were none was ignored. Key adviser Paul Wolfowitz's immediate reaction to 9/11 was "war on Iraq." Anarchy in that land was all but ensured when the Iraqi army was disbanded against the urgent advice of General Jay Garner, the American administrator, who was replaced by the neocon favorite Paul Bremer. That meant that a huge number of competent military men, most of them no lovers of Saddam, were rendered unemployed—and still armed. How was this disastrous decision arrived at? People directly involved said it came as an order from administration officials who had never been to Iraq.

Did Bush know and agree? They had no indication. Perhaps not. A national intelligence report commissioned in 2004 advised against the war. Bush, who apparently did not read it, dismissed it as guesswork—a word that seems like an ideal description of his own policies.

Who is Charles Ferguson, director of this film? Onetime senior fellow of the Brookings Institution, software millionaire, originally a supporter of the war, visiting professor at MIT and Berkeley, he was trustworthy enough to inspire confidence from former top officials. They mostly felt that orders came from the precincts of Vice President Cheney, that Cheney's group disregarded advice from veteran American officials, and in at least one case channeled a decision to avoid Bush's scrutiny. The president signed, but didn't read, and you can see the quizzical, betrayed looks in the eyes of the men and women in the film, who found that the more they knew about Iraq, the less they were heeded.

Although Bush and the war continue to sink in the polls, I know from some readers that they still support both. That is their right. And if they are so sure they are right, let more young men and women die or be maimed. I doubt they will be willing to see this film, which further documents an administration playing its private war games. No, I am distinctly not comparing anyone to Hitler, but I cannot help be reminded of the stories of him in his Berlin bunker, moving nonexistent troops on a map and issuing orders to dead generals. ☞

No Reservations ★ ★

PG, 104 m., 2007

Catherine Zeta-Jones (Kate Armstrong), Aaron Eckhart (Nick Palmer), Abigail Breslin (Zoe), Patricia Clarkson (Paula), Bob Balaban (Therapist). Directed by Scott Hicks and produced by Sergio Aguero and Kerry Heysen. Screenplay by Carol Fuchs.

Here is a love story that ends "and they cooked happily ever after." It's the story of Kate, a master chef who rules her kitchen like a warden, and Nick, perhaps equally gifted, who comes to work for her and is seen as a rival. Since Kate is played by the beautiful Catherine Zeta-Jones and Nick by the handsome Aaron Eckhart, is there any doubt they will end up stirring the same pots and sampling the same gravies?

No Reservations also has something to do with how a woman "should" behave. Kate's restaurant is owned by Paula (Patricia Clarkson), who hauls Kate out front to meet her "fans" but wants her to stay in the kitchen when a customer complains. This is contrary to Kate's nature. She doesn't want to waste time glad-handing, but if anyone dares to complain about her pâté or her definition of "rare," she storms out of the kitchen, and soon the customer storms out of the restaurant. We've heard about male chefs throwing tantrums (I think it's required), but for Kate to behave in an unladylike manner threatens her job.

There's a subplot. Kate finds herself caring for round-eyed little Zoe (Abigail Breslin), the orphaned child of her sister. Kate has long since vowed never to marry or have children, so this is an awkward fit. But Zoe gets along fine with Nick, who lets her chop basil in the kitchen and tempts her with spaghetti, and soon she's playing matchmaker between the two grown-ups. From meeting in the refrigerator room for shouting matches, they progress to thawing the crab legs.

The movie is focused on two kinds of chemistry: of the kitchen and of the heart. The kitchen works better, with shots of luscious-looking food, arranged like organic still lifes. But chemistry among Nick, Kate, and Zoe is curiously lacking, except when we sense some fondness—not really love—between Zoe and her potential new dad.

Kate and Nick are required by the terms of the formula to be drawn irresistibly together, despite their professional rivalry. But I didn't feel the heat. There was no apparent passion; their courtship is so laid-back it seems almost like a theoretical exercise. For that matter, Kate treats little Zoe like more of a scheduling problem than a new adoptive daughter. The actors dutifully perform the rituals of the plot requirements but don't involve us (or themselves) in an emotional bond.

The movie is a remake of *Mostly Martha* (2002), a German film very much liked by many, unseen by me. Watching its trailer, I can't decide anything about the quality of the original film, but I do recognize many of the same scenes and even similar locations. *No Reservations* doesn't seem to reinvent it so much as recycle it.

There are some nice things in the film. Zeta-Jones is convincing as a short-tempered chef, if not as a replacement mom and potential lover. Clarkson balances on the tight wire a restaurant owner must walk. Bob Balaban, as Kate's psychiatrist, has a reserve that's comically maddening. Aaron Eckhart struggles manfully with an unconvincing character (is he really afraid to run his own kitchen?). We feel Abigail Breslin has the stuff to emerge as a three-dimensional kid if she weren't employed so resolutely as a pawn.

But *No Reservations*, directed by the usually superior Scott Hicks (*Shine, Hearts in Atlantis, Snow Falling on Cedars*), has too many reservations. It goes through the motions, but the characters seem to feel more passion for food than for one another.

North Country ★ ★ ★ ★

R, 123 m., 2005

Charlize Theron (Josey Aimes), Frances McDormand (Glory), Sean Bean (Kyle), Richard Jenkins (Hank Aimes), Jeremy Renner (Bobby Sharp), Michelle Monaghan (Sherry), Woody Harrelson (Bill White), Sissy Spacek (Alice Aimes). Directed by Niki Caro and produced by Nick Wechsler. Screenplay by Michael Seitzman, based on the book *Class Action* by Clara Bingham and Laura Leedy Gansler.

After Josey Aimes takes her kids and walks out on the boyfriend who beats her, she doesn't find a lot of sympathy back at home. "He caught you with another man? That's why he laid hands on you?" asks her father. "You can actually ask me that question?" she says. He can. In that place, at that time, whatever happened was the woman's fault. Josey has returned to her hometown in northern Minnesota, where her father works in the strip mines of the Mesabi Iron Range.

She gets a job as a hairdresser. It doesn't pay much. She can make six times more as a miner. She applies for a job and gets one, even though her new boss is not happy: "It involves lifting, driving, and all sorts of other things a woman shouldn't be doing, if you ask me. But the Supreme Court doesn't agree." Out of every thirty miners, twenty-nine are men. Josey, who is good-looking and has an attitude, becomes a target for lust and hate, which here amount to the same thing.

North Country, which tells her story, is inspired by the life of a real person, Lois Jenson, who filed the first class-action lawsuit for sexual harassment in American history. That the suit was settled as recently as 1991 came as a surprise to me; I would have guessed the 1970s, but no, that's when the original court decision came down. Like the court's decisions on civil rights, it didn't change everything overnight.

The filmmakers say Josey Aimes is a character inspired by Jenson's lawsuit but otherwise is fictional; the real Jenson is not an Erin Brockovich–style firebrand and keeps a low profile. What Charlize Theron does with the character is bring compelling human detail. We believe she looks this way, sounds this way, thinks this way. After *Monster*, here is another extraordinary role from an actress who has the beauty of a fashion model but has found resources within herself for these powerful roles about unglamorous women in the world of men.

The difference is that her Aileen Wuornos, in *Monster*, was a murderer, no matter what society first did to her. All Josey Aimes wants is a house of her own, good meals and clothes for her kids, and enough money to buy her son hockey skates once in a while. Reasonable enough, it would seem, but even her father, Hank (Richard Jenkins), is opposed to women working in the mines, because it's not "women's work," and because she is taking the job away from a man "who needs it to support his family." Josey replies, "So do I." But even the women in the community believe there's something wrong if she can't find a man to take care of her.

North Country is the first movie by Niki Caro since the wonderful *Whale Rider.* That was the film about a twelve-year-old Maori girl in New Zealand who is next in an ancestral line to be chief of her people but is kept from the position because she is female. Now here is another woman told what she can't do because she is a woman. *Whale Rider* won an Oscar nomination for young Keisha Castle-Hughes, who lost to Charlize Theron. Now Theron and Caro have gone to the Academy Awards again.

Caro sees the story in terms of two worlds. The first is the world of the women in the community, exemplified by a miner named Glory (Frances McDormand), who is the only female on the union negotiating committee and has a no-nonsense, folksy approach that disarms the men. She finds a way to get what she wants without confrontation. The other female miners are hardworking survivors who put up with obscenity and worse, and keep their heads down because they need their jobs more than they need to make a point. Josey has two problems: She is picked on more than the others, and one of her persecutors is a supervisor named Bobby Sharp (Jeremy Renner), who shares a secret with her that goes back to high school and has left him filled with guilt and hostility.

In the male world, picking on women is all in a day's work. It's what a man does. A woman operates a piece of heavy machinery unaware that a sign painted on the cab advertises sex for sale. The women find obscenities written in excrement on the walls of their locker room. When McDormand convinces the union to ask for portable toilets for the women, "who can't hold it as long as you fellas," one of the first women to use one has it toppled over while she's inside.

There is also all sorts of touching and fondling, but if a woman is going to insist on having breasts, how can a guy be blamed for copping a feel? After Bobby Sharp assaults Josey, his wife screams at her in public: "Stay away from Bobby Sharp!" It is assumed and widely reported that Josey is a tramp, and she is advised to "spend less time stirring up your female coworkers and less time in the beds of your male coworkers."

She appeals to a local lawyer (Woody Harrelson), who takes the case partly because it will establish new law. It does. The courtroom protocol in the closing scenes is not exactly conventional, but this isn't a documentary about legal procedure; it's a drama about a woman's struggle in a community where even the good people are afraid to support her. The court scenes work magnificently on that level.

North Country is one of those movies that stir you up and make you mad because it dramatizes practices you've heard about but never really visualized. We remember that McDormand played a female police officer in this same area in *Fargo,* and we value that memory because it provides a foundation for Josey Aimes. McDormand's role in this movie is different and much sadder but brings the same pluck and common sense to the screen. Put these two women together (as actors and characters) and they can accomplish just about anything. Watching them do it is a great movie experience.

The Notorious Bettie Page ★ ★ ★ ½

R, 100 m., 2006

Gretchen Mol (Bettie Page), Chris Bauer (Irving Klaw), Jared Harris (John Willie), Sarah Paulson (Bunny Yeager), Cara Seymour (Maxie), David Strathairn (Estes Kefauver), Lili Taylor (Paula Klaw), Jonathan M. Woodward (Marvin). Directed by Mary Harron and produced by Christine Vachon, Pamela Koffler, and Katie Roumel. Screenplay by Harron and Guinevere Turner.

In the 1950s a pretty girl from Nashville named Bettie Page became the most famous model of her time—in certain circles. Marilyn Monroe followed a nude calendar photo into Hollywood stardom, but Bettie Page's fame was within the specialist market of pinups and bondage photography. She was tied, trussed, handcuffed, chained, and restrained while wearing high heels, nylons, garter belts, corsets, and pointy brassieres, or nothing much at all, and yet her posing was so unaffected and her attitude so cheerful that she was like sunshine in the dark world of porn.

These things I know in a secondhand way because Page has been a cult figure for years, the subject of quasi-scholarly books and grainy videos. My friend Russ Meyer described her once as "the nicest girl you'd ever want to meet." Now she is the subject of a curiously moving biopic, *The Notorious Bettie Page,* which is not very sexy or scandalous, nor is Bettie Page (Gretchen Mol) very notorious. "Celebrated" might have been a better word.

You might expect such a film would aim for scandal. Not at all. Nor is it an attack on censorship or prudery; it doesn't defend Bettie and the pornographers she worked with, but presents them as mundane laborers in the world of sex, finding a market and supplying it. Most of Bettie's bondage photos were taken by Irving Klaw (Chris Bauer), an unremarkable New Yorker who worked with his sister, Paula (Lili Taylor). "Boots and shoes, shoes and boots," Paula muses to Bettie. "They can't get enough of them. Why? I guess it takes all kinds to make a world."

Klaw became one of the targets of 1955 Senate hearings into pornography, and Klaw retired from the business. Bettie moved south to Miami and worked with cheesecake photographer Bunny Yeager. Then she drifted out of modeling as casually as she drifted in, becoming a born-again Christian but never apologizing for her work, because if God created the female form, why would he be offended by its display?

I have here a three-DVD set called *The Bettie Page Collection,* in which Bettie says the bondage work was pleasant because "we were always tied up by Paula, who was gentle and didn't make the knots too tight." Except for that time she was suspended from two trees. Bunny Yeager recalls that her most popular photos featured Bettie with two cheetahs, and we see both women posing with the animals, Bettie wearing a cheetah bikini. Yeager then provides a tour of her one hundred most famous models, remembering something about every single woman, including one who sewed her own posing costumes.

I looked through Bettie Page's photos and films hoping to find the same kinds of clues that must have inspired Mary Harron, who directed *The Notorious Bettie Page,* and Guinevere Turner, who wrote it with her. What I see is a pretty young woman with a spontaneous smile, who seems completely at home in whatever degree of nudity or distress. As Yeager famously said, "When she's nude, she doesn't seem naked." The material doesn't even come close to later notions of hard core, and if there were men anywhere, I missed them on fast-forward. The bondage and spanking sessions are between playful women, in short loops with titles involving sorority initiations and bad girls. Sometimes you can clearly see that the spanking is pretend, with no actual contact.

So that is the real Bettie Page. Who is this woman created by Mol, Harron, and Turner? It was Harron who starred Taylor in *I Shot Andy Warhol* (1996), another film about the underside of fame. Here she sees Bettie Page as a young woman not so much naive as simply incapable of depravity; she glides through the porno scene as a grateful visitor having a good time. The film suggests that after being abused as a child and gang-raped as a teenager, Bettie found a friendly refuge in the smut mills of the Klaws; on her first visit to Irving's studio she's immediately offered a sandwich.

The tone of the movie is subdued and reflective. It does not defend pornography but regards it (in its 1950s incarnation) with quiet nostalgia for a more innocent time. There is a kind of sadness in the movie as we reflect that most of these women and the men they inflamed are now dead; their lust is like an old forgotten song. Bettie Page is still alive in her eighties and corresponds with some of her faithful fans, also in their eighties.

In the Senate hearings held by Senator Estes Kefauver (David Strathairn), a father testifies that his son died while attempting something he may have learned from one of Klaw's films. In the movies, the witnesses at such hearings are routinely mocked as puritanical hypocrites, but Harron's film feels sympathy for the father, and so do we. We also feel, on the other hand, that Irving and Paula Klaw are not so very evil, and the clients of their "photography studio" (usually professional men) are so awed by the opportunity to photograph naked women that they treat the models as goddesses.

Mol is finally the key to the mysterious appeal of the film, to its sweetness and sadness. She plays a woman who for whatever reason does not consider her body an occasion for sin but a reason for celebration. In a haunting scene in an acting class (taught by Austin Pendleton), she is assigned to "do nothing" on the stage and responds by absentmindedly beginning to remove her clothes. The way I read the scene, she was undressing *in order* to do nothing, because for Bettie Page, to be dressed was to be doing something.

November ★ ★ ★

R, 73 m., 2005

Courteney Cox (Sophie), James Le Gros (Hugh), Michael Ealy (Jesse), Nora Dunn (Dr. Fayn), Anne Archer (Sophie's Mother), Nick Offerman (Officer Roberts). Directed by Greg Harrison and produced by Jake Abraham, Danielle Renfrew, and Gary Winick. Screenplay by Benjamin Brand.

November opens in a perfectly conventional way, as the story of an ordinary evening that goes wrong. Sophie and Hugh (Courteney Cox and James Le Gros) are driving home when she gets a snack attack and pulls the car to the curb by an all-night convenience store. He goes in to buy her something. A young man enters to rob the store. He starts shooting. Hugh is killed.

The film has developed this episode as if it will be about its aftermath. We anticipate a story in which Sophie deals with the death of someone she loves, and indeed the movie continues in that vein, as she visits a psychiatrist (Nora Dunn), complains of headaches, confesses to being unfaithful to Hugh, and in general seems to be gearing up for some heavy-duty soul-searching.

But then a strange thing happens. A lot of strange things happen. To tell you all of them would be unfair to the film, but I can tell you the first, I think. Sophie is a photographer. She met Hugh by taking his portrait. She teaches a photography class. Students present slide shows of their work for discussion and criticism. Sophie is clicking her way through one student's work when the last photo is revealed as . . .

She looks at the screen, stunned. The photo shows the convenience store on the night of the death. There's her car, parked at the curb. An indistinct figure inside may be Hugh. Who took this picture? How did it end up in the carousel of the slide projector? What does it mean?

The police send around a cop named Roberts (Nick Offerman), who is not particularly helpful. Although Sophie has been routinely questioned in connection with the death, there is no suspicion that she was involved with it. Was the taker of the photograph involved? How could the photograph have been taken by someone who then crossed the street, committed the crime, and was not seen by Sophie? Or was the photo taken as a coincidence?

Sophie tells the cop how to do his job. He should go to the photo store that developed the slide and get a list of everyone who was a customer the day the slide was developed. Officer Roberts follows her advice. Funny thing: It turns out it's Sophie's photo, paid for with her credit card.

And now I will say no more about the plot, except to observe that the movie cycles two more times through the events of that night, providing us with additional but not necessarily helpful versions of what happened.

As audience members, we can choose two responses: (1) intrigue with the method of the film, as it explores the nature of parallel realities, or (2) impatience with the film because it seems to be toying with us. I found myself poised between the two responses, experiencing a conflict that I rather enjoyed. It's intriguing when a film is about tension, and its method is about tension, and the two seem to be pulling against each other.

Cox, well-known from TV, rarely gets an opportunity to revise her famous image, but here she is serious, inward, coiled. She carries the film; the other characters circulate through her consciousness as possibilities and hypotheses. The opening scenes are dark, with blue-green lighting, and then later the film seems to break into red and black; I was reminded of the mother of this technique, the moment in Ingmar Bergman's *Persona* when the film breaks and must repair itself.

The one thing the film does not provide is an explanation. At seventy-three minutes, it barely has time to pose its questions, let alone answer them. But answers would be beside the point. When reality seems to splinter, there is only one answer, and it is: "Reality has seemed to splinter." Any other explanation, for example a speech by the psychiatrist or the cop explaining exactly what has really happened, would be contrivance. Better to allow *November* to descend into confusion and despair.

Ah, but the final segment of the film is subtitled "Acceptance," and we are reminded that acceptance is the fifth of Elisabeth Kübler-Ross's five stages of dying. The others are denial, anger, bargaining, and depression. It is useful to note that Kübler-Ross does not define "acceptance" as a "happy" stage. It is simply an end of resistance to death.

A movie that explained Hugh's murder, or whatever really happened in the convenience store, would be ending at the "bargaining" stage. It would not deny death. It would be beyond anger. It would have decided that to understand what happened would be the "answer." Most movies are satisfied to arrive at that point. Most audiences think that's what movies should aim for. But *November* does not bargain and does not explain. Take note of what happens at the end, consider that the final section is titled "Acceptance," and you may have the key to the mystery.

O

Ocean's Thirteen ★ ★ ½

PG-13, 122 m., 2007

George Clooney (Danny Ocean), Brad Pitt (Rusty Ryan), Matt Damon (Linus Caldwell), Andy Garcia (Terry Benedict), Don Cheadle (Basher Tarr), Bernie Mac (Frank Catton), Ellen Barkin (Abigail Spoonder), Al Pacino (Willie Banks), Elliott Gould (Reuben Tishkoff). Directed by Steven Soderbergh and produced by Jerry Weintraub. Screenplay by Brian Koppelman and David Levien.

The genius of the past decays remorselessly into the routine of the present, and one example is the downfall of the caper picture.

The classic caper genre had rules set in stone. It began (1) with an impregnable fortress (vault, casino, museum, or even Fort Knox). Then we met (2) a group of men who hoped to impregnate it. There was (3) a setup about the defenses of the fortress, and (4) a chalk talk in which the mastermind told the others what they were going to do and how they were going to do it. This had the advantage of also briefing the audience, so that the actual caper could proceed in suspenseful silence while we understood what they were doing and why.

The modern caper movie, such as Steven Soderbergh's *Ocean's Thirteen,* dispenses with such tiresome exposition and contains mostly action and movie star behavior. Only the characters know what the plan is, and we are expected to watch in gratitude and amazement as they disclose it out of their offscreen planning and plotting. Fair enough, if it's done with energy and style. If, however, their plan involves elements that are preposterously impossible, I feel as if I'm watching one of Scrooge McDuck's schemes.

All of the *Ocean's* movies, including the long-ago Sinatra version (1960), are remade or inspired by a great French caper movie, Jean-Pierre Melville's *Bob le Flambeur* (*Bob the Gambler*, 1956), in which Bob actually laid down chalk lines in an open field to walk his accomplices through a raid on a casino. The movie is on DVD in the Criterion Collection; see what you're missing now that the formula has been adapted for ADD sufferers.

Ocean's Thirteen begins as aging and beloved casino legend Reuben Tishkoff (Elliott Gould) plans to open his latest and greatest Vegas casino. Alas, he has taken for a partner the devious double-crosser Willie Banks (Al Pacino, very good), who swindles him out of the casino and lands him in the emergency room with shock and grief. Then Reuben's loyal friends (played by George Clooney, Brad Pitt, Don Cheadle, Bernie Mac, Matt Damon, etc.) gather at his bedside and vow to sabotage the opening of the new casino.

I don't know what kind of resources these rootless but glamorous men have, except that they are apparently unlimited. They manufacture trick card shufflers, sabotage the roulette wheels, and even give the man they think is the guru of casino ratings (David Paymer) something resembling the heartbreak of psoriasis. These plans are not explained; they are simply pulled out of the heroes' hats, or thin air.

To be sure, Soderbergh is a gifted director and (under a pseudonym) cinematographer, and he has a first-rate cast. Most of the audience will probably feel they got their money's worth, and that's the bottom line. But I grew impatient with the lickety-split pacing. This material is interesting enough that it needs care and attention, not the relentlessness of a slide show.

I know full well I'm expected to Suspend My Disbelief. Unfortunately, my disbelief is very heavy, and during *Ocean's Thirteen* the suspension cable snapped. I think that was when they decided to manufacture a fake earthquake to scare all the high-rollers on opening night. How did they plan to do this? Why, by digging under the casino with one of the giant tunnel-boring machines used to dig the Eurotunnel between France and England.

Yes, you can buy your own. There were originally eleven. One sold on eBay for around $7 million. A boring machine, I find, weighs about six hundred tons. How easy do you think it would be for a handful of Vegas slicksters to buy such a machine, transport it to America, move it cross-country, and use it to drill a tunnel under the Strip (which never sleeps), all the while removing untold tons of earth, rock, and sand without being noticed? And without causing earthquakes in all the other casinos they bored under?

I am reminded of that IMAX documentary about climbing Mount Everest. All I could think of was, if it's hard for the climbers, think about how hard it is for the guys carrying the big IMAX camera up the mountain. I wanted to see a doc about them. Now if you had a movie about smuggling a six-hundred-ton tunnel-boring machine under Vegas, *that* would be a caper.

Ocean's Thirteen proceeds with insouciant dialogue, studied casualness, and a lotta stuff happening, none of which I cared much about because the movie doesn't pause to develop the characters, who are forced to make do with their movie star personas. Take Don Cheadle, for example. After the magnificence of his performance in *Hotel Rwanda* and the subtle, funny, sad power of his leading role in Kasi Lemmons's upcoming *Talk to Me,* we get him hanging around in this picture looking like they needed him to get to thirteen. I guess he has to make movies like this to pay the mortgage. My advice? Rent. You have no idea the headaches of home ownership. ☞

Off the Map ★ ★ ★ ½

PG-13, 108 m., 2005

Joan Allen (Arlene Groden), Valentina de Angelis (Bo Groden), Sam Elliott (Charley Groden), J. K. Simmons (George), Jim True-Frost (William Gibbs), Amy Brenneman (Adult Bo). Directed by Campbell Scott and produced by Scott and George Van Buskirk. Screenplay by Joan Ackermann.

Somewhere in the back of nowhere, in an adobe house with no lights or running water, a family lives in what could be called freedom or could be called poverty. We're not sure if they got there because they were 1960s hippies making a lifestyle experiment, or were simply deposited there by indifference to conventional life. They grow vegetables and plunder the city dump and get $320 a month in veteran's benefits, but they are not in need and are apparently content with their lot.

Now there is a problem. "That was the summer of my father's depression," the narrator tells us. She is Bo Groden, played in the movie by Valentina de Angelis at about age twelve, and heard on the sound track as an adult (Amy Brenneman). "I'm a damn crying machine," says her dad, Charley (Sam Elliott). He sits at the kitchen table, staring at nothing, and his wife and daughter have learned to live their lives around him.

His wife is Arlene, played by Joan Allen in a performance of astonishing complexity. Here is a woman whose life includes acceptance of what she cannot change, sufficiency within her own skin, and such simple pleasures as gardening in the nude. She is a good wife and a good mother, but not obviously; it takes us the whole movie to fully appreciate how profoundly she observes her husband and daughter, and provides what they need in ways that are below their radar.

Charley has a friend named George (J. K. Simmons), who sort of idolizes him. Sometimes they fish, sometimes they talk. Arlene wants George to impersonate Charley, visit a psychiatrist, and get some antidepressants. George would rather fish. One day a stranger arrives at their home, which is far from any road. He carries a briefcase, says he is from the IRS, and is there to audit them, since the Groden family has reported an annual income of less than $5,000 for several years.

This man is William Gibbs (Jim True-Frost). He is stung by a bee, takes to the sofa, confesses his dissatisfaction with tax-collecting, and, what with one thing and another, never leaves. Eventually he lives in an old school bus on the property. He falls in love with Arlene, in a nondemonstrative way, and is good company for Charley. "Ever been depressed?" Charley asks him. "I've never not been," William says.

These characters in this setting could become caricatures or grotesques. But the director, Campbell Scott, and the writer, Joan Ackermann, refuse to underline them or draw arrows pointing to their absurdities. They accept them. Their movie is freed from a story that must hurry things along; life unfolds from day to day. Will Charley recover from his depression? Will William leave? Will Bo, who is being home-schooled, get to go to a real school? The movie suggests no urgency to get these questions answered.

Instead, in a stealthy and touching way, it

shows how people can work on one another. Charley may be depressed because of a chemical imbalance, or he may be stuck because his life offers him no opening for heroism. Arlene keeps herself entertained by surprising herself with her oddities; she handles financial emergencies by observing with detachment that sooner or later they will probably have to deal with them. Bo keeps busy writing letters to food corporations, complaining about insect parts found in their products, and composing personal questions for the "Ask Beth" newspaper column. William Gibbs starts to paint, and completes a watercolor, three feet high by forty-one long, showing the earth meeting the sky.

It is not clear if William has joined them to heal, to escape, or to die. But his presence in the family, which is accepted without comment, budges the emotional ground under Charley just enough so that he slides toward the edge of his depression. Perhaps it is William's undemonstrative love for Arlene, never acted on, that reawakens Charley's desire for this magnificent beast, his wife.

Campbell Scott is an actor, and as a director he is able to trust his actors entirely. If they are doing their jobs, we will watch, no matter whether the story centers on a man sitting at a table and everyone else essentially waiting for him to get up. The life force bubbling inside young Bo, suggested by Valentina de Angelis in a performance of unstudied grace, lets us know things will change, if only because she continues to push at life. *Off the Map* is visually beautiful, as a portrait of lives in the middle of emptiness, but it's not about the New Mexico scenery. It's about feelings that shift among people who are good enough, curious enough, or just maybe tired enough to let that happen.

Variety, the showbiz bible, always assesses a movie's commercial prospects in its reviews. Its chief critic, the dependable Todd McCarthy, loves this film but does his duty to the biz by noting: "Pic's unmelodramatic nature and unmomentous subject matter will make this a tough sell even on the review-driven specialized circuit." True, and by now you have sensed whether you would like it or not. If you think you would not, be patient, for sooner or later you will find yourself compelled to get up from the table.

Oldboy ★ ★ ★ ★

R, 120 m., 2005

Min-sik Choi (Dae-su Oh), Ji-tae Yoo (Woo-jin Lee), Hye-jung Gang (Mido). Directed by Chan-wook Park and produced by Dong-joo Kim. Screenplay by Jo-yun Hwang, Joon-hyung Lim, and Park.

A man gets violently drunk and is chained to the wall in a police station. His friend comes and bails him out. While the friend is making a telephone call, the man disappears from an empty city street in the middle of the night. The man regains consciousness in what looks like a shabby hotel room. A bed, a desk, a TV, a bathroom cubicle. There is a steel door with a slot near the floor for his food tray. Occasionally a little tune plays, the room fills with gas, and when he regains consciousness the room has been cleaned, his clothes have been changed, and he has received a haircut.

This routine continues for fifteen years. He is never told who has imprisoned him, or why. He watches TV until it becomes his world. He fills one journal after another with his writings. He pounds the wall until his fists grow bloody, and then hardened. He screams. He learns from TV that his blood and fingerprints were found at the scene of his wife's murder. That his daughter has been adopted in Sweden. That if he were to escape, he would be a wanted man.

Oldboy, by the Korean director Chan-wook Park, watches him objectively, asking no sympathy, standing outside his plight. When, later, he does talk with the man who has imprisoned him, the man says: "I'm sort of a scholar, and what I study is you."

In its sexuality and violence, this is the kind of movie that can no longer easily be made in the United States; the standards of a puritanical minority, imposed on broadcasting and threatened even for cable, make studios unwilling to produce films that might face uncertain distribution. But content does not make a movie good or bad—it is merely what it is about. *Oldboy* is a powerful film not because of what it depicts, but because of the depths of the human heart it strips bare.

The man, named Dae-su Oh (Min-sik Choi), is a wretch when we first meet him, a drunk who has missed his little daughter's birthday and now sits forlornly in the police station, ridiculously wearing the angel's wings he bought her as a present. He is not a bad man, but alcohol has rendered him useless.

When he suddenly finds himself freed from his bizarre captivity fifteen years later, he is a different person, focused on revenge, ridiculously responsive to kindness. Wandering into a restaurant, he meets a young woman who, he knows from the TV, is Korea's "Chef of the Year." This is Mido (Hye-jung Gang). Sensing that he has suffered, feeling an instinctive sympathy, she takes him home with her, hears his story, cares for him, comes to love him. Meanwhile, he sets out on a methodical search to find the secret of his captivity. He was fed pot stickers day after day, until their taste was burned into his memory, and he travels the city's restaurants until he finds the one that supplied his meals. That is the key to tracking down his captors.

It is also, really, the beginning of the movie, the point at which it stops being a mystery and becomes a tragedy in the classical sense. I will not reveal the several secrets that lie ahead for Dae-su, except to say that they come not as shabby plot devices, but as one turn after another of the screws of mental and physical anguish and poetic justice. I can mention a virtuoso sequence in which Dae-su fights with several of his former jailers, his rage so great that he is scarcely slowed by the knife sticking in his back. This is a man consumed by the need for revenge, who eventually discovers he was imprisoned by another man whose need was no less consuming, and infinitely more diabolical.

I am not an expert on the Korean cinema, which is considered in critical circles as one of the most creative in the world (*Oldboy* won the Grand Jury Prize at Cannes 2004). I can say that of the Korean films I've seen, only one *(The YMCA Baseball Team)* did not contain extraordinary sadomasochism. *Oldboy* contains a tooth-pulling scene that makes Laurence Olivier's Nazi dentist in *Marathon Man* look like a healer. And there is a scene during which an octopus is definitely harmed during the making of the movie.

These scenes do not play for shock value but are part of the whole. Dae-su has been locked up for fifteen years without once seeing another living person. For him the close presence of anyone is like a blow to all of his senses. When he says in a restaurant, "I want to eat something that is alive," we understand (a) that living seafood is indeed consumed as a delicacy in Asia, and (b) he wants to eat the life, not the food, because he has been buried in death for fifteen years.

Why would Mido, young, pretty, and talented, take this wretched man into her life? Perhaps because he is so manifestly helpless. Perhaps because she believes his story, and even the reason why he cannot reclaim his real name or identity. Perhaps because in fifteen years he has been transformed into a man she senses is strong and good, when he was once weak and despicable. From his point of view, love is joined with salvation, acceptance, forgiveness, and the possibility of redemption.

All of this is in place during the several scenes of revelation that follow, providing a context and giving them a deeper meaning. Yes, the ending is improbable in its complexity, but it is not impossible, and it is not unmotivated. *Oldboy* ventures to emotional extremes, but not without reason. We are so accustomed to "thrillers" that exist only as machines for creating diversion that it's a shock to find a movie in which the action, however violent, makes a statement and has a purpose.

Oliver Twist ★ ★ ★ ½

PG-13, 130 m., 2005

Ben Kingsley (Fagin), Barney Clark (Oliver Twist), Jamie Foreman (Bill Sykes), Harry Eden (Artful Dodger), Leanne Rowe (Nancy), Edward Hardwicke (Mr. Brownlow), Mark Strong (Toby Crackit), Liz Smith (Old Woman). Directed by Roman Polanski and produced by Robert Benmussa, Polanski, and Alain Sarde. Screenplay by Ronald Harwood, based on the novel by Charles Dickens.

Roman Polanski's *Oliver Twist* and his previous film, *The Pianist*, seem to be completely unlike, but I believe they have a deep emotional connection. *Oliver Twist* tells the story of an orphan in a dangerous city, whose survival sometimes depends upon the very people who would use him badly. *The Pianist* is about a Jew who hides himself in Warsaw during the Holocaust and at a crucial moment is spared by a German soldier. Both Oliver and the pianist do benefit from the kindness of strangers, but the intervention of their captors is crucial.

Oliver is about ten when he is taken into the world of Fagin and his young pickpockets, and Polanski was ten in 1943, when his parents were removed by the Nazis from the Krakow Ghetto and he was left on his own, moving from one temporary haven to another in the city and the countryside. In the black market economy of wartime Poland, he would have met or seen people like Fagin, Bill Sykes, Nancy, and the Artful Dodger, resorting to thievery and prostitution to survive. In that sense, *Oliver Twist* more directly reflects his own experience than *The Pianist.*

Now rotate the story another turn, and we find that Charles Dickens himself spent a similar childhood. With his father in debtor's prison, he was sent at twelve to work in a boot-blacking factory not unlike the workhouse where Oliver briefly lands; he asks in his memoirs "how I could have been so easily cast away at such an age." That Oliver, Dickens, and Polanski all survived to find prosperity and success could not erase the early pain, and in *Oliver Twist* Polanski approaches the material not as another one of those EngLit adaptations but with a painful and particular focus.

The story, like many of Dickens's stories, centers on a young person who is thrown into a stormy sea of vividly seen adult characters and who is often entirely in the dark about his own history and prospects. David Copperfield asks at the beginning of his story "whether I shall turn out to be the hero of my own life, or whether that station will be held by anybody else." He is writing, of course, after its events have all taken place, and he still does not know the answer.

Because the adult characters possess the power and make the decisions, it's particularly interesting to see what Polanski does with the key character in *Oliver Twist,* who is Fagin (Ben Kingsley), the grotesque old man who rules a household of pickpockets. Fagin is a Jew in the Dickens novel, an anti-Semitic caricature (although to be sure the Christians in the novel are also named by religion and are seen for the most part as hypocrites, sadists, and fools). Polanski's version never identifies Fagin as Jewish and does not depict him as the usual evil exploiter of young boys. Exploiter, yes, but evil, no: It is likely, as Fagin observes, that he has saved his charges from far worse fates awaiting them in the cruel streets of London and taught them the skills and cunning to survive.

That is why the next-to-final scene of the movie is so intriguing. Oliver has been rescued by his benefactor, the kind bookseller Mr. Brownlow (Edward Hardwicke), and has become a young gentleman. Fagin has been condemned to death. Oliver asks to see Fagin, and Brownlow takes him to the old man's cell, where they find a pathetic, self-pitying ruin. In the novel, Oliver asks Fagin to pray with him and says, "Oh! God forgive this wretched man!" In the movie, he says that, and something more: "You were kind to me."

For so Fagin was, after his fashion. It was Bill Sykes, the cruelest of all Dickens's villains, who meant him harm. In a movie that is generally faithful to Dickens, despite some smoothing out of the labyrinthine plot, Polanski's key change is to observe that Fagin does not simply exploit the boys; the old man and his pickpockets are struggling together to survive, according to the hard law that society has taught Fagin and he is teaching the boys. Fagin in his way is kinder than the workhouses and the courts of respectable society. The line "You were kind to me" is not a sentimental addition intended to soften the ending, but proceeds, I believe, directly from Polanski's heart and is a clue to why he wanted to make the movie. He must have met a Fagin or two, who were not good people yet not as bad as they might have been.

In Dickens there is always the contrast between horror and comedy; his biographer Peter Ackroyd observes that the novelist sometimes referred to his plots as "streaked bacon," made of fat, meat, and gristle. There is the sunny benevolence of Mr. Brownlow, who trusts the accused pickpocket with money and books. The pure goodness of the old country woman (Liz Smith), who pities and dotes on the child. The heroism of Nancy (Leanne Rowe), who risks her own life to save Oliver's. And even the mixed feelings of the Dodger (Harry Eden), who betrays Nancy to Bill and then has second thoughts and regrets.

True evil in the film is seen in Bill Sykes, who comes to such a ghoulish and appropriate end, and in the society that surrounds and permits all of the characters. Dickens grew up in a world of workhouses for children, child prostitution, "charity" institutions run with cruelty and greed, schools that taught nothing and were run for profit, and people who preyed on children, starved and mistreated them, and praised themselves for their benevolence. Those who haven't read Dickens since school, or never, may confuse him with the kindly storyteller of popular image; his works are filled with such fury that he must create a Mr. Brownlow from time to time simply to return calm to the story.

Polanski's film is visually exact and detailed without being too picturesque. This is not Ye Olde London, but Ye Harrowing London, teeming with life and dispute. The performances are more vivid and edgy than we might suspect; Kingsley's Fagin is infinitely more complex than in the usual versions. Jamie Foreman's Bill Sykes has a piggish, merciless self-regard. Rowe, as Nancy, becomes not a device of the plot but a resourceful young woman whose devotion to Bill is outlasted by her essential goodness. And Barney Clark, who was eleven when the film was made, is the right Oliver, a child more acted against than acting. *Oliver Twist* was Dickens's first proper novel, after the episodic *Pickwick Papers*. In it he found his voice by listening to the memories of the child he had been. Polanski, I think, is listening to such memories as well.

The Omen ★ ★ ★

R, 110 m., 2006

Julia Stiles (Katherine Thorn), Liev Schreiber (Robert Thorn), Mia Farrow (Mrs. Baylock), David Thewlis (Jennings), Pete Postlethwaite (Father Brennan), Michael Gambon (Bugenhagen), Seamus Davey-Fitzpatrick (Damien). Directed by John Moore and produced by Moore and Glenn Williamson. Screenplay by David Seltzer.

The Omen is a faithful remake of the 1976 film, and that's a relief; it depends on characters and situations and doesn't go berserk with visuals. In an age of effects run wild, what would a "contemporary" remake look like? No doubt lightning would zap from little Damien's ears, and his mother would not merely topple from a balcony but spin down to the bowels of the earth.

The story outline is as before: Worried astro-theologians in Vatican City ponder the meaning of comets in the heavens and upheavals on Earth, and an American diplomat and his wife have a baby boy in a Rome hospital. The husband is told the child has died, and he is urged by a sinister doctor to substitute a baby born the same day to an unwed mother. He agrees, keeps this a secret from his wife, and together they raise Damien, of whom it can be said that if he were made of snips and snails and puppy-dog tails, it would be an improvement.

The parents are Robert and Katherine Thorn (Liev Schreiber and Julia Stiles). After his boss's tragic death, the way becomes clear for Robert to become the American ambassador to Great Britain. Since he is the president's godson, it is all too clear that Damien's path ahead is preordained: He could become president and hasten Armageddon. I suppose there also will be remakes of *Damien: Omen II* (1978) and *Omen III: The Final Conflict* (1981), although after *The Final Conflict, Omen IV: The Awakening* (1991) did not seem urgently required.

The most shocking scene in the 1976 movie was set at Damien's garden party, when his nanny cried out to him from the roof of the ambassador's mansion, jumped off with a rope around her neck, and hanged herself. When the replacement nanny turns up, a chuckle runs through the audience: She is Mrs. Baylock, played by Mia Farrow, who as Rosemary also had a baby not destined to become a Gerber model.

Enough of the plot. Let us consider instead the genre of theological sensationalism. I've observed before that when it comes to dealing with demons and suchlike, Roman Catholics have the market cornered. Preachers of other faiths can foam and foment all they want about Satanic cults, but when it comes to knowing the ground rules and reading ominous signs, what you want at the bedside is a priest who knows his way around an exorcism.

The Omen begins in the Vatican observatory, where the heavens are seen to fulfill prophecy by placing a star above Rome on the night of Damien's birth, just as there was a star above Bethlehem when Jesus was born. That the Antichrist gets his own star makes you wonder who's running the heavens, but never mind. The pope is informed, and his advisers add up the signs: The Jews have returned to the land of Zion, there are tumults of the earth and sea, and in a parallel I think needs a lot of looking into, the common market is an ominous portent. The film opens with a montage of such preapocalyptic events as the collapsing World Trade Center, Hurricane Katrina, and the 2004 tsunami; perhaps the haste with which *The Omen* incorporates real-life tragedy into a horror movie is also a sign that the end is near.

Father Brennan (Pete Postlethwaite) is the point man for the Catholics, breathlessly bursting into Robert's office to warn him, "The child must die!" What child? "Your son, Mr. Thorn! The son of the devil!" Father Brennan must have skipped class at the seminary during the sessions on pastoral counseling techniques. He does not make an impressive appearance, looking less like a messenger of truth and more like he has a problem with the sacramental wine.

Other events conspire to convince Robert that Damien is a peculiar child, something his wife has suspected from the first, and especially after the kid uses his scooter to knock her off a balcony and smiles as she falls to the marble floor far below. There is also the matter of the paparazzo (David Thewlis) whose photographs turn up so many hidden images we could possibly reconstruct *Blow-Up* from them.

The two men visit a remote monastery that can be reached only by rowboat (here, with the lonely lake covered in mist, we are getting some visual effects, but lovely ones). There they meet an old priest so close to death that the Grim Reaper would be livelier, and the trail leads on to a demonologist (Michael Gambon, in full wretched decadence mode). Before long they're opening graves and making you wonder what the standards are for coroners in the area.

All of this is done with mood and style by director John Moore (*Behind Enemy Lines*), who knows that the story itself is engrossing enough that we don't need X-Men stuff in the visuals. Schreiber is, I think, a good choice for Ambassador Thorn; he is readier to fear the worst than Gregory Peck, who played the role in 1976. Farrow is never creepier than when she's at her most sweetly reassuring. Stiles has a difficult role; how can a mother want her own child dead, even if he is the Antichrist? I guess that's a question that answers itself.

The British character actors (Thewlis, Gambon, Postlethwaite) bring so much creepy atmosphere onto the screen that they could have walked right over from the matinee performance of *Nosferatu.* It was George Orwell who said, "At fifty, everyone has the face he deserves." We can only marvel at what they must have done to deserve theirs.

On a Clear Day ★ ★

PG-13, 99 m., 2006

Peter Mullan (Frank Redmond), Brenda Blethyn (Joan Redmond), Jamie Sives (Rob), Billy Boyd (Danny Campbell), Sean McGinley (Eddie Fraser), Ron Cook (Norman), Jodhi May (Angela), Benedict Wong (Chan). Directed by Gaby Dellal and produced by Sarah Curtis and Dorothy Berwin. Screenplay by Alex Rose.

Do you know who Peter Mullan is? A lot of people don't, but since 1990 he has moved quietly but firmly into the first rank of British film actors. A Scot, he had small roles in pictures such as *Riff-Raff, Shallow Grave, Braveheart,* and *Trainspotting,* and then in 1998 he starred in Ken Loach's *My Name Is Joe,* playing a recovering alcoholic just at that stage when he begins to believe that he might be able to trust himself. The performance came out of nowhere to win the Best Actor award at Cannes.

Since then, one powerful performance after another. In Mike Figgis's *Miss Julie* (1999), he was the servant who has an affair with a countess in a film based on the Strindberg play. In Michael Winterbottom's *The Claim,* a Thomas Hardy story moved to the Sierra Nevada, he runs a frontier town with an iron hand. He directed *The Magdalene Sisters* (2002), an angry exposé of the practice in Ireland of condemning sexually curious girls to a lifetime of unpaid servitude in church laundries. In *Young Adam* (2003), he was the barge captain whose wife is stolen away by a young man they hire as crew.

I mention these titles to call attention to an extraordinary talent, and as a way of backing into my review of *On a Clear Day,* which is a conventional film for an unconventional actor. When you start out working with Ken Loach, Danny Boyle, and Michael Winterbottom, it shows recognition of sorts, I suppose, but not necessarily progress to qualify as the lead in a Baked Potato People movie (see note). Mullan is at about the same stage in his career as Al Pacino was when he made *Bobby Deerfield.* Actors sometimes make the mistake of thinking that because they can play anyone, they should.

Mullan plays Frank Redmond, who has just been laid off his job after half a lifetime spent working as a shipbuilder in Glasgow. He is a man with inner torments (he blames himself for the drowning of a small son), and with time on his hands he sinks into depression and is hospitalized with a panic attack. Not to fear: The movie offers those varieties of depression and panic that function not as real problems but as plot conveniences, setting the other characters astir.

His wife, Joan (Brenda Blethyn), decides the time has come at last to take the test and become a bus driver. His other buddies turn into natural-born male bonders and turn up as a kind of chorus, led in wisdom by Chan (Benedict Wong), owner of the local takeaway shop, who advises them, "A gem cannot be polished without friction, or a man perfected without trials." Or maybe that's just in one of his fortune cookies. No matter; Frank's crisis has served to budge them all out of their ruts, and his friends listen to Chan's proverb, confess they didn't know he spoke English, and enlist him on the buddy team.

Frank starts to swim. One day, impulsively, he swims the Clyde. Eventually a plan takes shape: He will swim the English Channel. This will budge him out of depression, and he can prove to himself that he is still to be reckoned with, despite his unemployment. Joan meanwhile is afraid to tell him of her bus-driving plans.

The movie leads up, as it must, to his Channel swim. Whether Frank succeeds I will leave for you to discover. It's a safe bet this is not the kind of movie where he is going to drown. But nothing in *On a Clear Day* is especially compelling. The movie doesn't dig deep enough. And after the Channel attempt—what then? Attempt to better his record? Get a job at the takeaway? Joan, the wife, seems altogether more sensible and goal-oriented, and although we are happy for Frank as he attempts to realize his dream, we are not so happy that we make offerings to the gods of cinema for allowing us to see this movie. I would, however, be prepared to sacrifice this movie as an offering toward Peter Mullan's future career.

Note: Baked Potato People movies are named in honor of my friend Billy "Silver Dollar" Baxter, who liked to announce: "I've been tubbed, I've been rubbed, I've been scrubbed. I'm huggable, lovable, and eatable." He said he found those words on a little paper flag stuck into a baked potato.

Once ★ ★ ★ ★

R, 85 m., 2007

Glen Hansard (Guy), Marketa Irglova (Girl), Hugh Walsh (Drummer), Gerry Hendrick (Guitarist), Alastair Foley (Bassist), Geoff Minogue (Eamon). Directed by John Carney and produced by Martina Niland. Screenplay by Carney.

I'm not at all surprised that my esteemed colleague Michael Phillips of the *Chicago Tribune* selected John Carney's *Once* as the best film of 2007. I gave it my Special Jury Prize, which is sort of an equal first; no movie was going to budge *Juno* off the top of my list. *Once* was shot for next to nothing in seventeen days, doesn't even give names to its characters, is mostly music with not a lot of dialogue, and is magical from beginning to end. It's one of those films where you hold your breath, hoping it knows how good it is and doesn't take a wrong turn. It doesn't. Even the ending is the right ending, the more you think about it.

The film is set in Dublin, where we see a street musician singing for donations. This is the Guy (Glen Hansard). He attracts an audience of the Girl (Marketa Irglova). She loves his music. She's a pianist herself. He wants to hear her play. She doesn't have a piano. He takes her to a music store where he knows the owner, and they use a display piano. She plays some Mendelssohn. We are in love with this movie. He is falling in love with her. He just sits there and listens. She is falling in love with him. She just sits there and plays. There is an unusual delay before we get the obligatory reaction shot of the store owner, because all the movie wants to do is sit there and listen, too.

This is working partly because of the deeply good natures we sense these two people have. They aren't "picking each other up." They aren't flirting—or, well, technically they are, but in that way that means "I'm not interested unless you're too good to be true." They love music, and they're not faking it. We sense to a rare degree the real feelings of the two of them; there's no overlay of technique, effect, or style. They are just purely and simply themselves.

Hansard is a professional musician, well known in Ireland as leader of a band named the Frames. Irglova is an immigrant from the Czech Republic, only seventeen years old, who had not acted before. She has the kind of smile that makes a man want to be a better person so he can deserve being smiled at.

The film develops their story largely in terms of song. In between, they confide their stories. His heart was broken because his girlfriend left him and moved to London. She takes him home to meet her mother, who speaks hardly any English, and to join three neighbors who file in every night to watch their TV. And he meets her child, which comes as a surprise. Then he finds out she's married. Another surprise, and we sense that in his mind he had already dumped the girl in London and was making romantic plans. He's wounded, but brave. He takes her home to meet his dad, a vacuum cleaner repairman. She has a Hoover that needs fixing. It's kismet.

He wants to record a demo record, take it to London, and play it for music promoters. She helps him, and not just by playing piano. When it comes down to it, she turns out to be levelheaded, decisive, take-charge. An ideal producer. They recruit other street musicians for a session band, and she negotiates a rock-bottom price for a recording studio. And so on. All with music. And all with their love, and our love for their love, only growing. At one point he asks if she loves him, and she answers in Czech, and the movie doesn't subtitle her answer because if she'd wanted subtitles, she would have answered in English, which she speaks perfectly well.

Once is the kind of film I've been pestered about ever since I started reviewing again. People couldn't quite describe it, but they said I had to see it. I *had* to. Well, I did. They were right.

Ong-Bak: The Thai Warrior ★ ★ ★

R, 107 m., 2005

Tony Jaa (Ting), Petchthai Wongkamlao (George), Pumwaree Yodkamol (Muay Lek), Rungrawee Borrijindakul (Ngek), Chetwut Wacharakun (Peng), Sukhaaw Phongwilai (Khom Tuan). Directed by Prachya Pinkaew and produced by Pinkaew and Sukanya Vongsthapat. Screenplay by Suphachai Sithiamphan.

"No stunt doubles.
"No computer graphics.
"No strings attached."

These nine words represent the most astonishing element of *Ong-Bak: The Thai Warrior*, the first Thai film to break through in the martial arts market. Having seen documentaries showing how stunt men are "flown" from wires that are eliminated in postproduction, having seen entire action sequences made on computers, I sat through the movie impressed at how real the action sequences seemed. Then I went to the Web site and discovered that they *were* real.

Yes, they do a lot with camera angles and editing tricks. With the right lens and angle and slow-motion you can make it look like an actor is defying gravity, when in fact he is simply making a big jump from a trampoline. But some of the shots cannot easily be faked.

In *Red Trousers* (2004), a documentary about Hong Kong stuntmen, we find that they perform a lot of falls simply by—falling. *Ong-Bak* opens with a tree-climbing contest in which the competitors try to capture a red flag at the top of a tree, while kicking and shoving their opponents off the limbs. Say all you want about wide-angle lenses that exaggerate distance, but we see the tree in an undistorted shot that establishes its height, and these guys are falling a long way and they are landing hard.

The movie stars Tony Jaa, a young actor who is already an accomplished stuntman and expert in Muay Thai boxing, a sentence I have typed just as if I had the slightest idea what Muay Thai boxing is. Thank you, Web site. Jaa, who plays the hero, Ting, is an acrobat and stuntman in the league of Jackie Chan or Buster Keaton, and there's an early chase through city streets where he does things just for the hell of it, like jumping through a large coil of barbed wire, jumping over two intersecting bicycles, and sliding under a moving truck.

This chase, and the tree-climbing scene, set the pace for the movie. It is 107 minutes long, and approximately seven minutes are devoted to the plot, which involves the theft of an ancient Buddhist statue from the hero's village. He has been trained by Buddhist monks and will not fight for reasons of vengeance, money, or personal gain, but he agrees to go to Bangkok and retrieve the sacred statue, and for a monk with a vow of pacifism he certainly relaxes his rule against fighting. One bloody sequence has him taking on three opponents in an illegal boxing club where enormous sums are wagered by Khom Tuan (Sukhaaw Phongwilai), the local crime lord.

I arrived at the movie prepared to take notes on my beloved Levenger Pocket Briefcase, which I lost at Sundance and then miraculously had restored to me. But I found when the movie was over that I had written down its title, and nothing else. That's because there's really nothing to be done with this movie except watch it. My notes, had I taken them, would have read something like this:

"Falls from tall tree.

"Chase through streets.

"Runs on tops of heads of people.

"Runs across the tops of market stalls, cars, and buses.

"Barbed wire!

"Fruit Cart Scene!!! Persimmons everywhere!

"Illegal boxing club. Breakaway chairs and tables pounded over heads.

"Chase scene with three-wheeled scooter-taxis, dozens of them.

"Ting catches fire, attacks opponents with blazing legs."

And so on, and on. The movie is based on the assumption, common to almost all martial arts movies, that the world of the hero has been choreographed and cast to supply him with one prop, location, and set of opponents after another. Ting needs a couple dozen three-wheelers for a chase scene? They materialize, and all other forms of transportation disappear. He fights twenty opponents at once? Good, but no one is ever able to whack him from behind; they obediently attack him one at a time, and are smashed into defeat.

The plot includes a pretty girl (Pumwaree Yodkamol), who I think is the girlfriend of George (Petchthai Wongkamlao), a friend of Ting's from the village who has become corrupted by Bangkok and betrays him. I was paying pretty close attention, I think, but I can't remember for sure if Ting and the girl ever get anything going, maybe because any romance at all would drag the action to a halt for gooey dialogue. I think they look at each other like they'll get together after the movie.

Did I enjoy *Ong-Bak*? As brainless but skillful action choreography, yes. And I would have enjoyed it even more if I'd known going in that the stunts were being performed in the old-fashioned, precomputer way. *Ong-Bak* even uses that old Bruce Lee strategy of repeating shots of each stunt from two or three angles, which wreaks havoc with the theory that time flows ceaselessly from the past into the future, but sure does give us a good look when he clears the barbed wire.

The Orphanage ★ ★ ★ ½

R, 106 m., 2007

Belen Rueda (Laura), Fernando Cayo (Carlos), Roger Princep (Simon), Geraldine Chaplin (Aurora), Mabel Rivera (Pilar), Montserrat Carulla (Benigna). Directed by Juan Antonio Bayona and produced by Guillermo del Toro, Alvaro Augustin, Joaquin Padro, and Mar Targarona. Screenplay by Sergio G. Sanchez.

Now here is an excellent example of why it is more frightening to await something than to experience it. *The Orphanage* has every opportunity to descend into routine shock and horror, or even into the pits with the slasher pictures, but it pulls the trigger only a couple of times. The rest is all waiting, anticipating, dreading. We need the genuine jolt that comes about midway to let us see what the movie is capable of. The rest is fear.

Hitchcock was very wise about this. In his book-length conversation with Truffaut, he used a famous example to explain the difference between surprise and suspense. If people are seated at a table and a bomb explodes, that is surprise. If they are seated at a table and you know there's a bomb under the table attached to a ticking clock, but they continue to play cards, that's suspense. There's a bomb under *The Orphanage* for excruciating stretches of time.

That makes the film into a superior ghost story, if indeed there are ghosts in it. I am not sure: They may instead be the experience or illusion of ghosts in the mind of the heroine, and since we see through her eyes, we see what she sees and are no more capable than she is of being certain. That means when she walks down a dark staircase, or into an unlit corridor or a gloomy room, we're tense and fearful, whether we're experiencing a haunted house or a haunted mind. And when she follows her son into a pitch-black cave, her flashlight shows only a thread of light through unlimited menace.

The movie centers on Laura (Belen Rueda), who as a young girl was raised in the orphanage before being taken away one day and adopted. Now in her thirties, she has returned with her husband, Carlos (Fernando Cayo), and their young son, Simon (Roger Princep), to buy the orphanage and run it as a home for sick or disabled children. She has memories here, most of them happy, she believes, but as images begin to swim into her mind and even her vision, she has horrifying notions about what might have happened to the playmates she left behind on that summer day thirty years ago.

Simon, too, seems disturbed, and since no other children have arrived, he creates imaginary playmates. One of them, a boy with a sack over his head, he shows in a drawing to his mother, who is startled because this very image exists in her own mind. Does that mean—well, what could it mean? Telepathy? Or the possibility that Simon, too, is the product of her imagination? The line between reality and fantasy is so blurred in the film that it may even be, however unlikely, that Simon exists and is imagining her.

It matters not for us because we are inside Laura's mind no matter what. And when a decidedly sinister "social worker" (Montserrat Carulla) turns up, he learns because of her that he is adopted and dying. He apparently runs away, even though he needs daily medication. His parents spend months searching for him, putting posters everywhere, convinced he is not dead. But many children may have died at the orphanage. The parents consult a psychic (Geraldine Chaplin), who possibly provides what people claim they want from a psychic (but really don't): the truth.

The film, a Spanish production directed by Juan Antonio Bayona and produced by Guillermo del Toro (*The Devil's Backbone, Pan's Labyrinth*), is deliberately aimed at viewers with developed attention spans. It lingers to create atmosphere, a sense of place, a sympathy with the characters, instead of rushing into cheap thrills. Photographed by Oscar Faura, it has an uncanny way of re-creating that feeling we get when we're in a familiar building at an unfamiliar time, and we're not quite sure what to say if we're found there, and we might have just heard something, and why did the lights go out? You may be capable of walking into any basement on Earth, but if you go down the stairs into the darkened basement of the house you grew up in, do you still . . . feel something?

Oscar Nominated Shorts 2005 ★ ★ ★ ★

NO MPAA RATING, 120 m., 2005

The 2005 short subject Oscar nominees. Animated: *Birthday Boy,* directed by Sejong Park; *Ryan,* directed by Chris Landreth; and *Gopher Broke,* directed by Jeff Fowler. Live action: *Two Cars, One Night,* directed by Taika Waititi and Ainsley Gardiner; *7:35 in the Morning,* directed by Nacho Vigalondo; *Wasp,* directed by Andrea Arnold; and *Little Terrorist,* directed by Ashvin Kumar.

Seven of 2005's Oscar-nominated short subjects and the 2004 Oscar-winning student animated film have been gathered into a two-hour package going into release around the country. Every year readers ask me where and how they can see the shorts nominated for Oscars, and every year until now I've had to reply that, well, they can't. The distribution of short subjects is a notoriously difficult challenge, but a package like this, timed for release at Oscar time, is the perfect solution.

Only one of the animated films and none of the live-action shorts are by American directors. The finalists come from Australia, Canada, New Zealand, Spain, India, and Britain. (The student Oscar winner saves the day; it's from filmmakers at the New York University film school.)

Also a trend: One of the animated nominees and three of the four live-action films are about children who are neglected or in danger.

And the nominees are:

Live-Action Short Subjects

—*Wasp,* from the United Kingdom, directed

by Andrea Arnold, is a heartbreaking and angering twenty-three-minute drama about a single mother and her four children, one a baby. She fears having the children taken away from her, and with good reason: During a long day and night, she chats up a former boyfriend, claims she is only baby-sitting the children, takes them home, and finds only white sugar from a bag to feed them. Then she brings them along to the pub where she's meeting the boyfriend, parking them outside and rushing out to give them potato chips and a Coke, "to share around." Hour follows hour as she plays pool and is sweet-talked by her date, while the kids wait outside, sad and hungry. The film is notable above all for not underlining its points, but simply making them: This woman should not be a mother, and these children should not have these lives. The movie won the 2005 Oscar.

—*7:35 in the Morning,* from Spain, directed by Nacho Vigalondo, is an odd and haunting eight-minute film that begins with a woman entering a café and sitting down with coffee and a pastry. She notices two musicians standing by the back wall. "What's with that?" she asks the owner, who does not answer. The customers all seem stiff, frightened, uncertain. A man appears and begins to sing a song about the woman, her coffee and pastry, and his thoughts about her. The customers and employees have already been rehearsed, and sing parts of the song from lyrics cupped in their hands. Then there is a scene where, frightened and awkward, they dance. The reason for their behavior eventually becomes clear, and terrifying.

—*Little Terrorist,* from India, directed by Ashvin Kumar, takes place along the border between India and Pakistan. A young boy crawls beneath a barbed-wire fence and enters a minefield in order to retrieve a cricket ball. Guards, who cannot see how young he is, fire warning shots and he runs in fear—to the other side of the field. Now he is in another country. A village schoolmaster and his wife give him shelter and a quick alibi during a house-to-house search, but now he must get back home. In fifteen minutes, the film builds genuine and poignant drama.

—*Two Cars, One Night,* from New Zealand, directed by Taika Waititi and Ainsley Gardiner, begins with two cars parked in the lot of a hotel with a bar and restaurant. There are two boys, one nine, one younger, in one car, and a twelve-year-old girl in the other. The adults who brought them are in the bar for the evening. The kids make faces and then they make friends, sharing without even mentioning it the loneliness of sitting in the cars at night and waiting for who knows how long.

Animated Short Subjects

—*Ryan,* from Canada, the 2005 Oscar winner by Chris Landreth, is an animated fourteen-minute documentary that cuts deeply into the truth of a human life. The subject is Ryan Larkin, who circa 1970 made animated films considered among the best and most influential in Canadian history, and then went astray into drug addiction and alcoholism. The film takes place largely in a vast room filled with long, empty tables, where Landreth talks with Larkin about his life; there are cutaways to important figures from his past.

The animation technique is dramatic, striking, and wholly original. Apparently beginning with live-action footage, Landreth converts the figures into grotesque cutaways of skull and sinew, eyes and hair, partial faces surrounded by emptiness or marred by bright visual scars representing angst. The effect is hard to describe, impossible to forget; the animation takes the documentary content to another emotional level.

—*Birthday Boy,* from Australia, by Sejong Park, is set in Korea in 1951 and shows a young boy all alone in a deserted wartime village. He plays, he wanders, he talks to himself, he sees tanks passing on rail cars, he sees planes flying overhead, he misses his mother. Like *Grave of the Fireflies,* it shows war providing a landscape in which childhood is exposed and vulnerable.

—*Gopher Broke,* from the USA, directed by Jeff Fowler, is in the tradition of Hollywood animated cartoons; it follows a gopher who digs a hole in a dirt road so that produce trucks will bounce fruit and vegetables into the road. All fine, except for the squirrels, crows, and other varmints who are faster than the gopher. Then there is a problem with a cow.

—*Rex Steele: Nazi Smasher* is the bonus film, winner of the 2004 student animation Oscar. Directed by Alexander Woo, it's Indiana Jones crossed with Sky Captain, as a superhero enters a Nazi citadel atop a South American volcano and faces dire peril. High-spirited and kinetic.

Not included in the program, presumably because their makers chose not to participate, are the animated shorts *Guard Dog,* by Bill Plympton, and *Lorenzo,* by Mike Gabriel and Baker Bloodworth of Disney, and the live-action short *Everything in This Country Must,* by Gary McKendry.

Oscar Nominated Shorts 2006

The complete programs ran in Chicago, New York, Los Angeles, San Francisco, Detroit, Berkeley, Atlanta, Seattle, and Denver. I saw them all; here are capsule reviews:

Animated Shorts

—*The Moon and the Son: An Imagined Conversation,* from the USA, directed by John Canemaker and Peggy Stern. Re-creation of a painful relationship between a son and his angry father, who does prison time for arson. Photographs dissolve into animation that uses bold symbols and childlike drawings to create powerful emotions. The father and son (voiced by Eli Wallach and John Turturro) have an afterlife conversation where much is explained, nothing is resolved, and the pain continues: "I'm damned sure it's not the film you hoped for," the son says, "but it's the conversation we could never have."

—*9,* from the USA, directed by Shane Acker. In a futuristic world of ominous machinery and scraps of technology, humanoid creatures with camera lenses for eyes defend themselves against a fearsome mechanical ant. The sound track by David Steinwedel creates an atmosphere of creeping, crashing menace. The warfare is elaborated as a game of hide-and-seek, beautifully animated and intriguingly unwholesome.

—*Badgered,* from Great Britain, directed by Sharon Colman, is a fable involving a badger, two crows, and an underground missile silo. The badger's problems begin when he tries to silence the crows, scratches through the floor of his den, and lands on the control panel of the missile launcher.

—*One Man Band,* from the USA, directed by Andrew Jimenez and Mark Andrews, is from Pixar. In a town square in Europe, two one-man bands compete for the golden coin of a hard-to-please little girl. They one-up each other with virtuosity and amazing musical tricks, but it's a buyer's market. (This film played commercially before Pixar's *Cars.*)

—*The Mysterious Geographic Explorations of Jasper Morello,* from Australia, directed by Anthony Lucas. A short that plays like an epic collaboration between H. G. Wells and Tim Burton. An extraordinary airship voyage in the steam age, through storms and shipwreck to an uncharted land where strange blood-eating creatures seem to offer the cure for a plague. The animation style is haunting and evocative, and the narration establishes the mood of eerie unknown.

Documentary Shorts

—*The Death of Kevin Carter: Casualty of the Bang Bang Club,* directed by Dan Krauss. The Bang Bang Club comprised the white South African photographers who covered the violence of apartheid. Kevin Carter won the 1994 Pulitzer Prize for a famous picture of a starving girl in the Sudan being tracked by a vulture. He was criticized for not helping the girl. Carter increased his drug use, lost eighteen crucial rolls of film, sank into depression, and killed himself. A friend regrets that he didn't live to see the new South Africa; his daughter wonders if he died at the right time; the subtext is that drug addiction was the real problem.

—*God Sleeps in Rwanda,* by Kimberlee Acquaro and Stacy Sherman. The 1994 massacre of a million Tutsi by the Hutu tribe left the country 70 percent female. We follow the lives of five women in the next decade. They tell of being raped and tortured; some become pregnant, many die of AIDS (drugs for the disease cost as much as a typical salary). A former Hutu government minister is charged, and the trial is the first to define rape as a war crime. One survivor studies law, another works as a tailor; the female majority is both a burden and an opportunity, as the nightmare of genocide still haunts the land.

—*The Mushroom Club,* directed by Steven Okazaki. In Hiroshima sixty years after the bomb, some remember, some forget. Vandals set fire to paper cranes children have left at the war memorial. Loud-speaker trucks prowl the streets, chanting militaristic slogans. Jet Skis and rock music mar the quiet of the Peace Park.

We meet bomb survivor Keiji Nakazawa, whose anime film *Barefoot Gen* remembers the attack. And an old woman who was fifteen when the bomb fell and needed twenty-seven operations to repair her face and her fused fingers. Another old woman combs the river banks for bits of fused steel and glass. And we meet a woman whose parents were told it was their fault, and not the radiation, that caused their child to be born disabled. An annual ceremony remembers the tragedy, but many young people seem to have forgotten.

—*A Note of Triumph: The Golden Age of Norman Corwin,* by Corinne Marrinan and Eric Simonson. Corwin, who still teaches at USC, was the producer of *On a Note of Triumph,* a historic 1945 radio broadcast on V-E Day. He appears along with others who remember the broadcast: Walter Cronkite, Robert Altman, Norman Lear, Studs Terkel. The night of the broadcast, "there was hope for the world," Terkel says. "I can still recite most of it," Altman says. Corwin was a poet who used radio as his medium. He recalls early days as a newspaperman, and how he created experimental radio simply because he didn't know what couldn't be done. The film stands as a rebuke to modern formula broadcasting.

Live-Action Shorts

—*Our Time Is Up,* from the USA, by Rob Pearlstein and Pia Clemente. Kevin Pollack stars as a cold, detached psychiatrist who listens impassively as his clients complain of obsessive fondling, fear of the dark, fear of germs, bad relationships, and fear of turtles. Developments in his life inspire him to begin telling them the truth. They improve and are grateful. A simplistic fable, competently made but hardly of Oscar caliber.

—*The Last Farm,* from Iceland, directed by Runar Runarsson and Thor S. Sigurjonsson. Spare, deeply moving: An old farmer and his wife are scheduled to enter a retirement home. It is their last few days on the farm. Using his skill as a farmer and ingenuity in his use of materials, he carries out one final task. The bleak photography complements the impassive performance by Jon Sigurbjornsson as the farmer.

—*Cashback,* from Great Britain, directed by Sean Ellis and Lene Bausager. Sean Bigerstaff plays an art student who works overnight at a supermarket. Time passes exceedingly slowly, and his boss is an oaf. Fellow employees hold scooter races and play dodgeball with milk cartons. He imagines he can freeze time, move unobserved among the staff and customers, and undress the women to sketch them for his art classes. Workday comedy edges into imagination and eroticism.

—*The Runaway (Ausreisser),* from Germany, directed by Ulrike Grote. Walter (Peter Jordan) is an architect confronted by a small boy (Maximilian Werner) who wants to be taken to school. He has no idea who the boy is, but the boy follows him and calls him "Father," and it develops that he may be Walter's child by a former girlfriend. Walter tries to shake the kid but can't. Where is the boy's mother? Takes an unexpected turn that may please some but left me underwhelmed.

—*Six Shooter,* from Ireland, directed by Martin Mcdonagh. Brendan Gleeson is touching as a man whose wife dies in a hospital. On the train ride home across Ireland, he sits across from an obnoxious young man of heartless cruelty who learns that the couple across the aisle have lost their baby. The kid is loud, obscene, and cruel; how long can the others put up with him? The film ends in macabre developments, but what is remembered is Gleeson's quiet suffering and the boy's extraordinary inhumanity.

OSS 117: Cairo, Nest of Spies ★ ★ ★

NO MPAA RATING, 99 m., 2008

Jean Dujardin (Hubert Bonisseur de la Bath), Berenice Bejo (Larmina El Akmar Betouche), Aure Atika (Princess Al Tarouk), Philippe Lefebvre (Jack Jefferson), Constantin Alexandrov (Setine). Directed by Michel Hazanavicius and produced by Eric Altmayer and Nicolas Altmayer. Screenplay by Jean-Francois Halim, based on the novels by Jean Bruce.

Well, to begin with, *OSS 117: Cairo, Nest of Spies* is a terrific title. Better than the film, but there you are. Watching it, I began to shape a review about how its hero, French agent 117, was influenced by James Bond out of Inspector Clouseau and Austin Powers (try not to picture that). But then I discovered from *Variety* that the character Agent 117 actually appeared in a novel in 1949; its author, Jean Bruce, wrote no less than 265 novels about him, qualifying for second place, I guess, behind Georges Simenon's Inspector Maigret. And the agent appeared in seven earlier movies.

The books and movies, I gather (not having read or seen any of them), were more or less straightforward action, so although Ian Fleming may have created 007 with a debt to 117, what he brought new to the table was the idea of comedy. And if the Bond movies are themselves quasi-serious on some level, Mike Myers went completely over the top with Austin Powers, inspiring the makers of this new film to try to make *him* seem laid-back. Their agent is now the subject of a parody so far over the top that, well, it's not every day you see two spies fighting by throwing dead chickens at each other.

The movie stars Jean Dujardin as Agent 117 (real name: Hubert Bonisseur de la Bath), whom in 1955 is sent by the French secret service to Egypt to deflect the impending Suez crisis, bring peace among the Americans, Russians, and Egyptians, and settle the problems of the Arab world. No problem-o. Jean Dujardin, who looks more than a little like the young Sean Connery, is in a Bondian film that begins with an extreme action sequence, has titles based on the view through a roving gun sight, and cuts directly to Rome and 117 in a tuxedo, making out with a beauty garbed in satin, who tries to stab him in the back.

The movie travels familiar ground, with a nod as well to *Top Secret, Airplane!* and that whole genre. Even compared to them, it pushes things just a little—not too far, but toward the loony. For example, Agent 117's cover role in Cairo is as the owner of a wholesale chicken business. When he discovers that the chickens cluck and the roosters crow when the lights are on, but not when they're off, he has no end of fun playing with the light switch. This is a guy who's short some bulbs.

How stupid is he? Leaving Rome for Cairo, he meets his local contact, a lithesome beauty named Larmina El Akmar Betouche (Berenice Bejo) and on the trip from the airport complains about how much dust there is in the desert. Shown the Suez Canal, he congratulates the Egyptians for having the foresight to dig it four thousand years ago. He assures her that Arabic is a ridiculous language, and she is dreaming if she thinks millions of people speak it. And his sleep is interrupted one morning by a call to prayer from a muezzin in the tower of a nearby mosque. "Shut the **** up!" he bellows out the window, and then climbs the tower and silences the troublemaker.

The movie relishes its 1955 look, not just in the costumes and locations, but in such details as special effects and fight scenes. Remember hand-to-hand combat pre–Bruce Lee? No end of tables and chairs get trashed, while the distinctly Bondian musical score pounds away relentlessly. One nice 1950s touch: "Cigarette?" he's asked. "I'm trying to start," he replies.

For a parody, the movie is surprisingly competent in some of the action scenes, when the dim-witted hero turns out to have lightning improvisational skills. And there is an escape scene that develops in unforeseen ways. Dujardin is somehow able to play his clueless hero as a few degrees above the doofus level, mixing in a little suave seductiveness and then effortlessly drifting into charmingly crafted comments that are bold insults, if only he understood that.

My only problem is, there's a little too much of *117*. Only ninety-nine minutes long, it nevertheless seems to go on more than necessary. There is a limit to how long such a manic pitch can be maintained. It's the kind of film that might seem funnier if you kept running across twenty minutes of it on cable. Yet I suppose that is not a fatal fault, and I have developed the same kind of affection for 117 that I have for Austin Powers. Who else would tell that lithesome beauty, "You're not a Lebanese reporter posted to Rome! You're actually the niece of Egypt's King Farouk!" It was the "Egypt's King Farouk" part that got me. Like she didn't know who he was. And like he didn't know Farouk had been deposed by Nasser. Well, that I can believe.

Outsourced ★ ★ ★

PG-13, 102 m., 2007

Josh Hamilton (Todd Anderson), Ayesha Dharker (Asha), Asif Basra (Purohit N. Virajnarianan), Matt Smith (Dave), Larry Pine (Veteran Tourist). Directed by John Jeffcoat and produced by Tom Gorai. Screenplay by George Wing and Jeffcoat.

There is nothing in India more mysterious than the lovely land itself. The riot of colors, the careless jumble of the cities, the frequent friendliness and good humor of a people who are so different from us except that, often, they speak the same language. More or less.

Outsourced begins with an American sent to India to train the low-paid employees of a new call center for his company, American Novelty Products. It sells, he explains, "kitsch to redneck schmucks." His Indian assistant asks him, "Excuse me. What is 'redneck'? What is 'kitsch'? What is 'schmuck'?" And what are these products? American eagle sculptures. Wisconsin cheesehead hats. Branding irons for your hamburgers.

The American is named Todd (Josh Hamilton), although everyone hears it wrong and calls him "Mr. Toad." His assistant has a much more sensible name, Purohit N. Virajnarianan (Asif Basra). Although wages are low in India, Purohit will make 500,000 rupees as the new manager. That comes out to about $11,000, enough for him to realize a long-delayed marriage to his betrothed.

Todd is a stranger in a very strange land. Some of his experience reminded me of my own at the Calcutta and Hyderabad film festivals. He wildly overtips a beggar woman at the airport. He finds himself riding in one of those three-wheeled open-air taxis. He makes the mistake of eating street food. He encounters new definitions of the acceptable (on a crowded bus, a young boy politely stands up to offer Todd his seat, then sits back down on his lap). He is constantly bombarded by offers to go here, go there, buy this, see that. Sometimes these offers are worth listening to, as when they lead him to a charming rooming house.

And what about the call center itself? It looks like a concrete-block storage hut, still under construction. Inside, Purohit oversees twelve or fifteen employees struggling with customer complaints.

Question: "I'm ordering my American eagle from India?" Answer: "It is not made here, sir. It is made in China."

Average length of a call: over twelve minutes. Todd's instructions: Get it down to six. Impossible. He starts with pep talks and lessons in pronunciation: "Say you are in Chicago. Pronounce it sha-CAW-ga." They obediently repeat, "Shy-CALL-go." But one employee seems ahead of the curve. This is the beautiful, helpful Asha (Ayesha Dharker), whom you may have seen in the title role of *The Terrorist* and the quite different role of Queen Jamillia in *Star Wars: Episode II—Attack of the Clones.*

She questions Todd during his classes, tells him he needs to know more about India, has a smile that dismisses his doubts. She becomes his teacher on such mysteries as Kali, the goddess of destruction. ("Sometimes it is good to destroy. Then things can start again.") And of course they fall in love, although it is not to be because she was promised in an arranged marriage at the age of four. "Then why are we here?" he asks her on a business trip, as they debate a position they find in a book at the Kama Sutra Hotel. "This is like a trip to Goa," she says, referring to the idyllic southern province of India, formerly Portuguese. In her mind, before a lifelong arranged marriage, one trip to Goa is permitted.

Outsourced is not a great movie, and maybe couldn't be this charming if it was. It is a film bursting with affection for its characters and for India. It never pushes things too far, never stoops to cheap plotting, is about people learning to really see one another. There is a fundamental sweetness and innocence to it. Josh Hamilton, a veteran of more than forty movies, finds a defining role here, as an immensely amiable man. To look upon Ayesha Dharker is to like her. And in a time when the word "chemistry" is lightly bandied about, what they generate is the real thing. As in all Indian movies, there is no sex, but because this is a U.S. production, there is some kissing, and wow, it beats anything in the *Kama Sutra.*

Over Her Dead Body ★ ★

PG-13, 95 m., 2008

Eva Longoria Parker (Kate), Paul Rudd (Henry), Lake Bell (Ashley), Lindsay Sloane (Chloe), Stephen Root (Sculptor), Jason Biggs (Dan), William Morgan Sheppard (Father Marks). Directed by Jeff Lowell and produced by Paul Brooks, Scott Niemeyer, Peter Safran, and Norm Waitt. Screenplay by Lowell.

Why is nobody utterly in awe of ghosts in *Over Her Dead Body* and so many other ghost-coms? Here is a supernatural manifestation from another realm, and everybody treats it as a plot device. The movie even drags in a Catholic priest, who seems bewilderingly ignorant of his church's beliefs about ghosts (they don't exist) and treats the situation as an opportunity for counseling.

The setup: It's the wedding day of Henry and Kate (Paul Rudd and Eva Longoria). She's a Type A perfectionist who races manically around the reception venue, straightening place settings, adjusting decorations, and flying into a rage at the ice sculptor (Stephen Root) who has delivered an ice angel—without wings! She orders him to take it back and bring her one with wings, which, as everybody knows, all angels possess. He argues reasonably that you can't just stick wings on an ice sculpture. In a tragic accident involving the sculpture, Kate is killed.

Flash forward a decent amount of time and Henry, still in mourning, is informed by his sister, Chloe (Lindsay Sloane), that it's time for his life to begin again. He should start dating. He won't hear of it. He's still in love with Kate. She persuades him to visit Ashley (Lake Bell), a psychic she knows. He does so. Is she a real psychic? Sometimes. She begins to get vibes. So does he. Neither one needs to be psychic to realize they are falling in love with each other.

I guess it's all right for psychics (as opposed to psychiatrists) to date their clients, but Ashley seeks advice. She gets it from Dan (Jason Biggs), her partner in a catering business. Also from Father Marks (William Morgan Sheppard), who also doesn't know that his church doesn't believe in psychics. (Was he ordained by mail order? The Church teaches that consulting a psychic is a sin, although it doesn't totally rule out info from the other side, suggesting it could be disinformation from Satan.) Anyway, meanwhile . . . eek! The ghost of Kate appears, none too pleased that another woman has designs on her man. She intends to sabotage their romance.

What happens then? Kate looks completely real, although she has no material presence and can walk through walls, etc. I always wonder why walls are meaningless to such beings, but they never fall through floors. Do elevators go up without them? Never mind. The plot plays out as you would expect it to, as the amazing presence of a ghost is effortlessly absorbed into the formula plot. If it were me and a ghost, I'd put my personal agenda on hold and ask all sorts of questions about the afterlife. Wouldn't you?

Heaven, in this movie, is represented in the standard way: Everything is blindingly white, and everyone is garbed in white, even an angel (Kali Rocha) who has, by the way, no wings. Well, of course it doesn't. Being a pure spirit, it has no need to fly. Kate switches back to a conventional wardrobe for her sojourns here below. How would I depict heaven? As a featureless void with speaking voices. I haven't decided about subtitles.

Even in a movie with a ghost, the hardest thing to believe is a revelation that Dan makes to Ashley. They have worked together five years, and yet she is astonished. I will leave the revelation for you to discover, only adding that I believe it would be impossible for Dan to work five years in the catering industry without his secret being obvious to everyone.

Consider for a moment how this movie might play if it took itself seriously. Would it be better than as a comedy? I suspect so. Does the premise "her ghost turns up and fights the new romance" make you chuckle? Me neither. It's the kind of angle that could seem funny only at a pitch meeting. Not only have we been there, done that, we didn't want to go there, do that in the first place.

Overlord ★ ★ ★ ★

NO MPAA RATING, 88 m., 1975 (rereleased 2006)

Brian Stirner (Tom), Davyd Harries (Jack), Nicholas Ball (Arthur), Julie Neesam (The Girl), Sam Sewell (Trained Soldier), John Franklyn-Robbins (Dad), Stella Tanner (Mum). Directed by Stuart Cooper and produced by James Quinn. Screenplay by Christopher Hudson and Cooper.

I wrote from the 2004 Telluride Film Festival:

"The most remarkable discovery at this year's Telluride is *Overlord*, an elegiac 1975 film that follows the journey of one young British soldier to the beaches of Normandy. The film, directed by Stuart Cooper, won the Silver Bear at Berlin—but sank quickly from view after a limited release and was all but forgotten until this Telluride revival.

"Unlike *Saving Private Ryan* and other dramatizations based on D-Day, *Overlord* is an intimate film, one that focuses closely on Tom Beddoes (Brian Stirner), who enters the British army, goes through basic training, and is one of the first ashore on D-Day. Beddoes is not a macho hero but a quiet, nice boy, who worries about his cocker spaniel and takes along *David Copperfield* when he goes off to war.

"The movie tells his story through a remarkable combination of new and archival footage. It was produced by the Imperial War Museum in London, where Cooper spent three years looking at documentary and newsreel footage from World War II. About 27 percent of the film is archival, and awesomely real—for example, a scene where soldiers and their landing boat are thrown against rocks by furious waves.

"There are sights I had never seen before, including monstrous mechanical wheels that propel themselves across the beach to explode land mines and flatten barbed wire. One of these machines is driven by a ring of rockets around its rim, and as it rolls forward, belching fire and smoke, it looks like a creature of hell.

"*Overlord,* whose title comes from the code word for one of the invasion plans, uses archival footage to show the devastation of bombing raids, from above and below. Cooper's cinematographer, the Kubrick favorite John Alcott, used lenses and film stock that matched the texture of this footage, so the black-and-white film seems all of a piece. Tom's story is not extraordinary; he says goodbye to his parents, survives some hazing during basic training, makes a few close friends, and becomes convinced he will die in the landing. This prospect does not terrify him, and he writes a letter to his parents, consoling them in advance.

"He meets a local girl (Julie Neesam) at a dance, in a club filled with soldiers on leave. All of the clichés of such scenes are abandoned. She is a nice girl, he is a nice boy, they are kind to each other, tender and polite, and agree to meet again on Monday. But on Monday he is part of the early stages of the invasion, which seems, he writes his parents, like an entity that is growing to unimaginable proportions while he becomes a smaller and smaller speck of it. He has a fantasy in which he meets the girl again; to describe it would reveal too much about this film, which is a rare rediscovery."

I reprint this earlier report because I'm writing this from Cannes and was not able to see the film again before deadline. *Overlord* remains firmly and clearly in my memory as a different kind of war film, one that sees through the eyes of one soldier and follows his story not through exciting adventures but through the routine steps designed to deliver an efficient and useful warrior to a place where he is needed.

The poignancy in the film comes because he knows, and his parents know, and the girl he meets knows, that his future is on hold. He may return home, he may have a future with the girl, and then again, maybe not, and this is the reality they all acknowledge in one sense or another.

The movie has been restored in a new 35mm print and combines its newsreel and fictional footage so effectively that it has a greater impact than all fiction, or all documentary, could have achieved. I still remember the rocket-driven mechanical wheel I wrote about from Telluride. I do not recall ever having seen such a machine depicted in a movie; that it is real is awesome.

Over the Hedge ★ ★ ★

PG, 87 m., 2006

Voices of: Bruce Willis (RJ the Raccoon), Garry Shandling (Verne the Turtle), William Shatner (Ozzie the Possum), Steve Carell (Hammy the Squirrel), Wanda Sykes (Stella the Skunk), Nick Nolte (Vincent the Bear), Thomas Haden Church (Dwayne the Verminator), Allison Janney (Gladys), Avril Lavigne (Heather the Possum), Eugene Levy (Lou the Porcupine), Catherine O'Hara (Penny the Porcupine). Directed by Tim Johnson and Karey Kirkpatrick and produced by Bonnie Arnold. Screenplay by Len Blum, Lorne Cameron, David Hoselton, and Kirkpatrick.

Over the Hedge is one of the few comic strips in which you will find debates about the Theory of Relativity, population control, and global warming. None of those issues are much discussed in the new animated feature inspired by the strip, but there is a great deal about suburban sprawl, junk food, and the popularity of the SUV. ("How many people does it hold?" "Usually one.")

The movie opens with the coming of spring and the emergence from hibernation of many forest animals, including some that do not actually hibernate, but never mind. Vincent the bear (voice by Nick Nolte) awakens to find that his entire stash of stolen food has been—stolen! He apprehends the master thief RJ the raccoon (Bruce Willis) and gives him a deadline to return the food or else. RJ cleverly mobilizes the entire population of the forest to help him in this task (during which he does not quite explain the bear and the deadline). And together they confront an amazing development: During the winter, half of their forest has been replaced by a suburb, and they are separated from it by a gigantic hedge.

That's the setup for a feature cartoon that is not at the level of *Finding Nemo* or *Shrek* but is a lot of fun, awfully nice to look at, and filled with energy and smiles. It's not a movie adults would probably want to attend on their own, but those taking the kids are likely to be amused, and the kids, I think, will like it just fine.

Once again we get an animal population where all the species work together instead of eating each other, and there is even the possibility of interspecies sex, when a human's housecat falls in love with Stella the skunk (Wanda Sykes). There is also the usual speciesism: Mammals and reptiles are first-class citizens, but when a dragonfly gets fried by an insect zapper, not a tear is shed.

These animals once ate leaves and roots and things, but all that has changed since Hammy the golfing squirrel (Steve Carell) discovered nacho chips. The animals find these so delicious they are the forest equivalent of manna, and RJ is happy to lead them to the promised land of nachos and other junk food in the garbage cans and kitchens of humans.

Like all humans who like to live with a view of beautiful forests, the humans in *Over the Hedge* are offended that they are occupied by animals. Gladys (Allison Janney), the head of the homeowners' association, is personally affronted that RJ and his cronies might violate her garbage can, and she brings in Dwayne (Thomas Haden Church), a pest control expert known ominously as the Verminator.

"I want them exterminated as inhumanely as possible," she tells him. She's all heart.

The encroachment of the animals and the efforts of the Verminator don't approach the wit and genius of a similar situation in the Oscar-winning *Wallace & Gromit: The Curse of the Were-Rabbit* (2005), but, then, how could they? This movie is pitched at a different level. But the action scenes are fun, the characters are well-drawn and -voiced, and I thought the film's visual look was sort of lovely. If the animals lack the lofty thinking of their originals on the comics page, they are nevertheless a notch or two above the IQ levels of many an animated creature. They have to be. It's a hard life for a forager these days, when you're caught between an angry bear on one side of the hedge and a street hockey game on the other.

P

The Pacifier ★ ★

PG, 90 m., 2005

Vin Diesel (Shane Wolfe), Lauren Graham (Claire Fletcher), Faith Ford (Julie Plummer), Carol Kane (Helga), Brad Garrett (Vice Principal Murney), Brittany Snow (Zoe Plummer), Max Thieriot (Seth Plummer), Morgan York (Lulu Plummer). Directed by Adam Shankman and produced by Gary Barber, Roger Birnbaum, and Jonathan Glickman. Screenplay by Thomas Lennon and Ben Garant.

In *The Pacifier,* Vin Diesel follows in the footsteps of those Arnold Schwarzenegger comedies where the muscular hero becomes a girly-man. Diesel doesn't go to the lengths of Schwarzenegger in *Junior,* where Arnold was actually pregnant, but he does become a baby-sitter, going where no Navy SEAL has gone before.

Diesel plays Shane Wolfe, hard-edged commando ("We are SEALs—and this is what we do"). In the pretitle sequence, he and three other scuba-diving SEALs shoot down a helicopter, wipe out four gunmen on Jet Skis, bomb a boat, and rescue Plummer, an American scientist kidnapped by Serbians. They want "Ghost," the scientist's foolproof encryption key. That the scientist uses the names of his children as the password for his locked briefcase suggests that the Serbians could have saved themselves a lot of trouble by just finding the geek who hacked Paris Hilton's cell phone and aiming him at Plummer's hard drive.

Anyway. One thing leads to another, and soon Wolfe has a new assignment, which is to baby-sit and protect Plummer's five children while his wife and a Navy intelligence officer go to Geneva to open his safety deposit box. They're supposed to be gone only a couple of days, but one week follows another as they unsuccessfully try to, yes, guess the password.

From time to time the movie cuts to a Swiss bank, where two executives wait patiently while the wife and the Navy guy try one word after another. That two Swiss bank officials are willing to sit in a room day after day and listen to people guessing a password is yet one more example of why the Swiss banking system has such an exemplary reputation.

That leaves Wolfe in charge of an unhappy teenage boy, a boyfriend-crazy teenage girl, and three noisy moppets. Because he is not good at names, he tags them the Red Team, and calls them "Red One," "Red Two," and so on. They do not much take to this, and make his life a living hell.

This premise is promising, but somehow the movie never really takes off. We know that Diesel will begin as gravel-voiced and growly, and that he'll soften up and get to love the kids. We know that in two weeks all of the kids' personal problems will be solved, their behavior will improve, and they'll start cleaning up around the house. We're not much surprised when the Plummer nanny, a curious creature created by Carol Kane with an impenetrable accent, stalks out. Using the Law of Economy of Characters, we know that any neighbors who seem unnecessary yet are given dialogue will be more than merely neighbors.

There's one subplot that seems to offer more opportunities for comedy than it does. Seth (Max Thieriot), the older Plummer boy, wants to be an actor, despite the kidding he gets at high school. He's appearing in a production of *The Sound of Music,* where, unfortunately, he keeps dropping members of the Trapp family. The play's director, who seems to have been imported from *Waiting for Guffman,* walks off the job, and Shane Wolfe takes over the direction. Uh-huh. And he has a tender heart-to-heart with the kid about following his dream and being an actor if that's what will make him happy.

Meanwhile, Wolfe is also supposed to be guarding the kids against, I dunno, more Serbian kidnappers, maybe, although North Koreans also come into the mix. He has an uncanny ability to follow events on supermarket security monitors, which are not usually positioned where customers can see them, and so protects the Plummer girls when their Firefly Girls cookie stand is attacked by rival scouts. He is also challenged to a wrestling match with a coach who is more than strange (Brad Garrett), and deals with an anal-retentive school principal by showing that Navy SEALs have better split-second timing than clock-watching bureaucrats.

All very nice, sometimes we smile, but nothing compelling. The director is Adam

Shankman, whose previous film, *Bringing Down the House,* starred Queen Latifah as a convict who moves in on Steve Martin's middle-class life. Shankman begins with situations that should work, but he doesn't quite boost them over the top into laugh-out-loud. Maybe he's counting too much on the funny casting. Casting is funny only when the cast is given something funny to do, a truth that should be engraved above the portals of every film school.

Palindromes ★ ★ ★ ½

NO MPAA RATING, 100 m., 2005

Ellen Barkin (Joyce Victor), Stephen Adly Guirgis (Joe/Earl/Bob), Jennifer Jason Leigh (Aviva), Emani Sledge (Aviva), Will Denton (Aviva), Hannah Freiman (Aviva), Shayna Levine (Aviva), Valerie Shusterov (Aviva), Sharon Wilkins (Aviva), Rachel Corr (Aviva/Henrietta), Richard Masur (Steve Victor), Debra Monk (Mama Sunshine), Matthew Faber (Mark Wiener), Robert Agri/John Gemberling (Judah), Stephen Singer (Dr. Fleischer), Alexander Brickel (Peter Paul), Walter Bobbie (Bo Sunshine), Richard Riehle (Dr. Dan). Directed by Todd Solondz and produced by Mike S. Ryan and Derrick Tseng. Screenplay by Solondz.

Todd Solondz's *Palindromes* is a brave and challenging film for which there may not be much of an audience. That is not a fault of the film, which does not want to be liked and only casually hopes to be understood. What it wants is to provoke. You do not emerge untouched from a Solondz film. You may hate it, but you have seen it, and in a strange way it has seen you.

Palindromes contains characters in favor of abortion and characters opposed to it, and finds fault with all of them. The film has no heroes without flaws and no villains without virtues, and that is true no matter who you think the heroes and villains are. To ambiguity it adds perplexity by providing us with a central character named Aviva, a girl of about thirteen played by eight actors, two of them adults, one a boy, one a six-year-old girl. She is not always called Aviva.

The point, I think, is to begin with the fact of a girl becoming pregnant at a too-early age and then to show us how that situation might play out in different kinds of families with different kinds of girls.

The method by which Aviva becomes pregnant is illegal in all cases, since she is underage, but there is a vast difference between a scenario in which Aviva persuades a reluctant young son of a family friend to experiment with sex, and another where she runs away from home and meets a truck driver.

Perhaps Solondz is suggesting that our response to Aviva's pregnancy depends on the circumstances. He doesn't take an obvious position on anything in the movie, but simply presents it and leaves us to sort it out. We probably can't. *Palindromes* is like life: We know what we consider to be good and bad, but we can't always be sure how to apply our beliefs in the messy real world.

Consider an early scene in the film where one of the Avivas gets pregnant and wants to have the child. Her mother (Ellen Barkin) argues that this will destroy her life; an abortion will allow her to continue her education and grow up to be a normal adolescent, rather than being a mother at thirteen. The mother goes on to make a long list of possible birth defects that might occur in an underage pregnancy.

Later in the film, we meet the "Sunshine Family," a household full of adopted children with birth defects: one with Down syndrome, one born without arms, and so on. It occurs to us that these are the hypothetical children Barkin did not want her daughter to bear. The children are happy and seem pleased to be alive. Yes, but does Solondz consider the adoptive parents of the Sunshine Family to be good and moral people? Not precisely, not after we find Father Sunshine conspiring to bring about a murder.

The plot circles relentlessly, setting up moral situations and then pulling the moral ground out from under them. The movie is almost reckless in the way it refuses to provide us with a place to stand. It is all made of paradoxes. Pregnancy is pregnancy, rape is rape, abortion is abortion, murder is murder, and yet in the world of *Palindromes* the facts and categories shift under the pressure of human motives—some good, some bad, some misguided, some well-intentioned but disastrous.

We look for a clue in the movie's title. A "palindrome" is a word that is spelled the same way forward and backward: Aviva, for example, or madam or racecar. Is Solondz saying that it doesn't matter which side of the issue we enter from, it's all the same and we'll wind up where we started?

While following the news during the Terri Schiavo case, I was struck by how absolutely sure of their opinions everyone was, on both sides. Could the reporters have found a few people willing to say that after giving the matter a lot of thought, they'd decided it was a tragedy no matter which way you looked at it? Solondz is perhaps arguing for moral relativism, for the idea that what is good in a situation is defined by the situation itself, not by absolute abstractions imposed from outside.

Todd Solondz has made a career out of challenging us to figure out what side of any issue he's on. You can't walk out of one of his movies *(Welcome to the Dollhouse, Happiness, Storytelling)* and make a list of the characters you like and the ones you don't. There's something to be said for and against everybody. Most movies, like most people, are so certain, and we like movies we can agree with. He makes movies where, like a member of the debate team, you sometimes feel as if you're defending a position just because that's the side you were assigned.

If the movie is a moral labyrinth, it is paradoxically straightforward and powerful in the moment; each individual story has an authenticity and impact of its own. Consider the pathos brought to Aviva by the actress Sharon Wilkins, who is a plus-size adult black woman playing a little girl, and who creates perhaps the most convincing little girl of them all. Or Jennifer Jason Leigh, three times as old as Aviva but barely seeming her age. These individual segments are so effective that at the end of each one we know how we feel, and why. It's just that the next segment invalidates our conclusions.

I look at a movie like this, and I consider what courage it took to make it. Solondz from the beginning has made a career out of refusing to cater to broad, safe tastes. He shows us transgressive or evil characters, invites us to identify with their pathos, then shows us that despite our sympathy, they're rotten anyway. You walk out of one of his films feeling like you've just failed a class in ethics, and wondering if in this baffling world anyone ever passes.

Pan's Labyrinth ★ ★ ★ ★

R, 120 m., 2006

Ivana Baquero (Ofelia), Maribel Verdu (Mercedes), Sergi Lopez (Vidal), Ariadna Gil (Carmen), Alex Angulo (Doctor), Doug Jones (Pan/Pale Man). Written, directed, and produced by Guillermo del Toro.

Pan's Labyrinth is one of the greatest of all fantasy films, even though it is anchored so firmly in the reality of war. On first viewing, it is challenging to comprehend a movie that on the one hand provides fauns and fairies, and on the other hand creates an inhuman sadist in the uniform of Franco's fascists. The fauns and fantasies are seen only by the eleven-year-old heroine, but that does *not* mean she's "only dreaming"; they are as real as the fascist captain who murders on the flimsiest excuse. The coexistence of these two worlds is one of the scariest elements of the film; they both impose sets of rules that can get an eleven-year-old killed.

Pan's Labyrinth took shape in the imagination of Guillermo del Toro as long ago as 1993, when he began to sketch ideas and images in the notebooks he always carries. The Mexican director responded strongly to the horror lurking under the surface of classic fairy tales and had no interest in making a children's film, but instead a film that looked horror straight in the eye. He also rejected all the hackneyed ideas for the creatures of movie fantasy and created (with his Oscar-winning cinematographer, art director, and makeup people) a faun, a frog, and a horrible Pale Man whose skin hangs in folds from his unwholesome body.

The time is 1944 in Spain. Bands of anti-Franco fighters hide in the forest, encouraged by news of the Normandy landings and other setbacks for Franco's friends Hitler and Mussolini. A troop of Franco's soldiers is sent to the remote district to hunt down the rebels and is led by Capitan Vidal (Sergi Lopez), a sadist under cover as a rigid military man.

Commandeering a gloomy old mill as his headquarters, he moves in his new wife, Carmen (Ariadna Gil), who is very pregnant, and her daughter from her first marriage, Ofelia (Ivana Baquero). The girl hates her stepfather, who indeed values Carmen only for breeding purposes. Soon after arriving, Vidal shoots dead two farmers whose rifles, they claim, are only for hunting rabbits. After they die, Vidal finds rabbits in their pouches. "Next time, search these assholes before wasting my time with them," he tells an underling. He orders Mercedes (Maribel Verdu), his chief servant, to cook the rabbits for dinner: "Maybe a stew." What a vile man.

Ofelia encounters a strange insect looking like a praying mantis. It shudders in and out of frame, and we're reminded of del Toro's affection for odd little creatures (as in *Cronos,* with its deep-biting immortality bug). The insect, friendly and insistent, seems to her like a fairy, and when she says so, the bug becomes a vibrating little man who leads her into a labyrinth and thus to her first fearsome meeting with the faun (Doug Jones, who specializes in acting inside bizarre costumes). Some viewers have confused the faun with Pan, but there is no Pan in the picture and the international title translates as *Labyrinth of the Faun.*

The faun seems to be both good and evil; what are we to make of a huge pile of used shoes, especially worrisome in the time of the Holocaust? But what he actually offers is not good or evil, but the choice between them, and del Toro says in a commentary that Ofelia is "a girl who needs to disobey anything except her own soul." The whole movie, he says, is about choices.

The faun fits neatly into Ofelia's worries about her pregnant mother; he gives her a mandrake root to hide under the mother's bed and feed with two drops of blood daily. The mandrake root is said to resemble a penis, but this one, in special effects that are beyond creepy, looks like a half-baby made from wood, leaves, and earth. Ofelia discovers that Carmen is aiding the rebels but keeps her secret because she doesn't want to be responsible for hurting anyone, a trait that will benefit her.

The film is visually stunning. The creatures do not look like movie creations but like nightmares (especially the Pale Man, with eyes in the palms of his hands). The baroque organic look of the faun's lair is unlike any place I have seen in the movies. When the giant frog delivers up a crucial key in its stomach, it does so by regurgitating its entire body, leaving an empty frog skin behind. Meanwhile, Vidal plays records on his phonograph, smokes, drinks, shaves as if tempting himself to slash his throat, speaks harshly to his wife, threatens the doctor, and shoots people.

Del Toro moves between many of these scenes with a moving foreground wipe—an area of darkness, or a wall or a tree that wipes out the military and wipes in the labyrinth, or vice versa. This technique insists that his two worlds are not intercut, but live in edges of the same frame. He portrays most of the mill interiors in a cold blue-gray slate but introduces life tones into the faces of characters we favor, and into the fantasy world. It is no coincidence that the bombs of the rebels introduce red and yellow explosions into the monotone world they attack.

Guillermo del Toro (born 1964) is the most challenging of directors in the fantasy field because he invents from scratch or adapts into his own vision. He has made six features since his debut at twenty-nine with *Cronos* (1993), and I have admired, even loved, all of them, even those like *Hellboy, Mimic,* and *Blade II* that did not receive the universal acclaim of *Cronos* and *The Devil's Backbone* (a ghost story also set in Franco's Spain). He is above all a visually oriented director, and when he says "films are made of looks," I think he is referring not only to the gazes of his actors but to his own.

Born in Mexico, he has worked there and overseas, like his gifted friends and contemporaries Alfonso Cuaron (born 1961) and Alejandro Gonzalez Inarritu (born 1963). Isn't it time to start talking about a New Mexican Cinema, not always filmed in Mexico but always informed by the imagination and spirit of the nation? Think of del Toro's remarkable films, and then consider too Cuaron's *Children of Men, Harry Potter and the Prisoner Of Azkaban* (the best-looking Potter film), *Great Expectations* (an overlooked masterpiece), and *Y Tu Mama Tambien.* Or Inarritu's *Amores Perros, 21 Grams,* and *Babel.*

Some of these are in one way or another genre films, but there is so much impact and intensity, and such a richness of visual imagination, that they flatter their genres instead of depending on them. The three directors trade actors and technicians, support one another, make new rules, are successful without compromise. Cuaron's 1998 *Great Expectations,* set in a Spanish-moss-dripping modern Florida and starring Ethan Hawke, Gwyneth Paltrow, and Anne Bancroft (in guess which roles), is a stunning reworking of Dickens and illustrates how all three of these directors can put hands on a project and make it their own.

What makes del Toro's *Pan's Labyrinth* so powerful, I think, is that it brings together two kinds of material, obviously not compatible, and insists on playing true to both, right to the end. Because there is no compromise, there is no escape route, and the dangers in each world are always present in the other. Del Toro talks of the "rule of three" in fables (three doors, three rules, three fairies, three thrones). I am not sure three viewings of this film would be enough, however. ☞

Paper Clips ★ ★ ★

G, 82 m., 2005

Featuring Linda Hooper, Sandra Roberts, Dagmar Schroeder-Hildebrand, Peter Schroeder, David Smith. A documentary directed by Elliot Berlin and Joe Fab and produced by Fab, Robert M. Johnson, and Ari Daniel Pinchot. Screenplay by Fab.

In 1998, three middle-school teachers in Whitwell, Tennessee (population 1,500), came up with a project for the eighth-grade class: Learn about intolerance by studying the Holocaust. The students read *The Diary of Anne Frank* and did Internet research, discovering that during World War II, the Norwegians wore paper clips in their lapels as a silent gesture of solidarity and sympathy with Hitler's victims.

A student, no one seems to remember which one, said it was impossible to imagine six million of anything, let alone Jews who died in the Holocaust. That led somehow to the notion of gathering six million paper clips in one place at one time, as a tribute to the victims. The project started slowly, with a clip here and a clip there, and fifty thousand from one donor, and then the *Washington Post* and Tom Brokaw got on the story, and by the time Whitwell's third group of eighth-graders was running the project, they had twenty-nine million paper clips.

That could be a story like the one about the kid who was dying and wanted to collect business cards, and got millions and millions as his desperate parents announced he had recovered and no longer wanted more cards. But the Whitwell story goes to another level, a touching one, as the students make new friends through their project. Two of them are Peter and Dagmar Schroeder, White House correspondents from Germany, who visit the town and write about it. Many more were Holocaust survivors, who as a group visited Whitwell for a potluck dinner at the Methodist church, classes at the school, and a community reception.

And then there was the train car. The Schroeders found one of the actual rail cars used to transport Jews to the death camps, and arranged for it to be shipped to Whitwell. Local carpenters repaired the leaky roof and rotting floor, and the car was placed outside the high school as a Holocaust memorial. Inside were eleven million paper clips, representing six million Jews and five million gypsies, homosexuals, Jehovah's Witnesses, and others who were murdered by the Nazis. Also a suitcase that German children had filled with notes to Anne Frank.

Paper Clips, which tells this story, is not a sophisticated or very challenging film, nor should it be. It is straightforward, heartfelt, and genuine. It plays more like a local news report, and we get the sense that the documentary, like the paper clip project, grows directly out of the good intentions of the people involved. Whitwell at the time had no Jews, five African-Americans, and one Hispanic, we learn; there weren't even any Catholics. By the time the project was completed, the horizons of the population had widened considerably.

David Smith, one of the teachers involved, says he knows he is stereotyped as a southerner and admits that he stereotypes northerners. In changing their perceptions about minorities, the students of Whitwell also changed perceptions others may have held about them. That America has been divided by pundits into blue states and red states does not mean there are not good-hearted people living everywhere; in a time of divisiveness, there is something innocently naive about the paper clip project, which transforms a silly mountain of paper clips into a small town's touching gesture.

Paradise Now ★ ★ ★

PG-13, 90 m., 2005

Kais Nashef (Said), Ali Suliman (Khaled), Lubna Azabal (Suha), Amer Hlehel (Jamal), Hiam Abbass (Said's Mother), Ashraf Barhom (Abu-Karem), Mohammad Bustami (Abu-Salim). Directed by Hany Abu-Assad and produced by Bero Beyer. Screenplay by Abu-Assad, Beyer, and Pierre Hodgson.

What I am waiting for is a movie about a suicide bomber who is an atheist, who expects oblivion after his death and pulls the trigger after having reasoned that the deaths of his victims will advance a cause so important that he, and they, must die. When religion enters into the picture, it clouds the meaning of the act: How selfless is your sacrifice if you believe you will be instantly rewarded for eternity?

"What happens afterward?" asks one of the two suicide bombers in *Paradise Now.*

"Two angels will pick you up."

"Are you sure?"

"Absolutely."

The movie involves two days in the lives of Said (Kais Nashef) and Khaled (Ali Suliman), two Palestinians, garage mechanics, best friends, who are recruited to cross into Israel and blow themselves up. They are not shown as fanatics. They prepare for their task as one would prepare for any difficult assignment. The organization that supports them provides training, encouragement, praise, shaves and haircuts, suits and ties, a ceremonial dinner, and a chance to make videos that will be shown on television.

On his video, Said articulates the Palestinian position, expressing anger that the Israelis have stolen the status of victims he believes belongs by right to his own people. Does this speech make the film propaganda, or does it function simply as a record of what such a man would say on such an occasion? I'm not sure it matters. If we are interested in a film that takes us into the lives of suicide bombers, we must be prepared to regard what we find there. Certainly what Said says will not come as a surprise to any Israeli. It's simply that they disagree.

We may disagree, too, and yet watch the film with a fearsome fascination. The director and cowriter, Hany Abu-Assad, uses the interesting device of undercutting the heroism of his martyrs with everyday details. During one taping of a farewell message, the camera malfunctions. During another, one of the bombers interrupts his political sermon with a personal shopping reminder for his mother. When the leader of the terrorist group personally visits the two men, he seems less like a charismatic leader than a bureaucrat a little bored by this obligatory task.

Then there is the matter of the woman Suha (Lubna Azabal); she and Said are beginning to love each other. A Palestinian born in France and raised in Morocco, she has great status in the Palestinian community because she is the daughter of Abu Assam, a revered leader. But she is not an advocate of suicide bombs. Influenced no doubt by the skepticism of the West, she questions terrorist acts on both theological and practical grounds: Islam forbids suicide, and she wonders if one qualifies as a martyr if one has martyred oneself. She believes the effect of the bombings is to create innocent victims and inspire retaliation in a never-ending cycle of violence.

The director, Abu-Assad, is himself a Palestinian, born in Israel; his crew included Palestinians, Israelis, and Westerners, and during the filming was reportedly threatened by both sides in the conflict. It hardly matters, in a way, which side his protagonists are on; the film is dangerous because of its objectivity, its dispassionate attention to the actual practical process by which volunteers are trained and prepared for the act of destruction.

Paradise Now, like another 2005 film, *The War Within,* and the 1999 Indian film *The Terrorist,* humanizes suicide bombers. But in my mind, at least, that creates not sympathy but pity; what a waste, to spend your life and all your future on behalf of those who send you but do not go themselves. These movies by necessity tell us versions of the same story: A true believer prepares for death, and we watch to see if death will come.

That is why I await the movie about the atheist who blows himself up. He will need to convince himself objectively of the wisdom of his decision. When religion is involved, it sidesteps the issue, since religion provides an absolute rationale. The problem is that all religions provide this service—yours, mine, theirs. When higher powers are invoked to justify death on both sides of a dispute, does heaven send four angels?

The Passenger ★ ★ ★ ½

PG-13, 119 m., 1975 (rereleased 2005)

Jack Nicholson (David Locke), Maria Schneider (Girl), Jenny Runacre (Rachel Locke), Ian Hendry (Martin Knight), Steven Berkoff (Stephen), Ambroise Bia (Achebe), Jose Maria Caffarel (Hotel Keeper), James Campbell (Witch Doctor). Directed by Michelangelo Antonioni and produced by Carlo Ponti. Screenplay by Peter Wollen, Antonioni, and Mark Peploe.

There is an emptiness in the films of Michelangelo Antonioni that the director seems to love more than the people who intrude upon it. His films are never crowded. Even *Blow-Up*, set in London, and *La Notte*, in Milan, seem barely inhabited; he is drawn to spaces empty of people, save a few characters who wander irresolutely through in search of—well, of nothing. They want not to find but to seek.

The Passenger (1975) begins with a man in a North African village surrounded by desert. He hires a boy to lead him out into the wilderness, and then a man appears to lead him farther still and abandon him. Emptiness surrounds him. The man returns to the town alone. He is David Locke (Jack Nicholson), a journalist who was seeking an interview with guerrillas rumored to be somewhere in the desert hills.

His hotel lacks the usual comings and goings. There is a clerk, and one other resident, a man named Robertson (Charles Mulvehill). They have had a conversation about nothing much. Locke enters Robertson's room and finds him dead. Without premeditation, he exchanges identities with the corpse. He swaps their passports, switches their clothes, tells the clerk there of the dead man, and in London it is thought that David Locke is dead. His wife (Jenny Runacre) and associate (Ian Hendry) begin to edit the footage he took in the desert.

They are looking in the footage for David Locke himself, just as the photographer in *Blow-Up* seeks a corpse he thinks he sees on the grass of a park. The more intensely these characters look, the less they see. The new Robertson meanwhile decides to meet certain appointments that the old Robertson had made; this takes him to Munich and a meeting with representatives of the guerrillas. He finds he is a gun dealer.

Locke (we will call him that) meets a young woman (Maria Schneider), whose name is never given; in the credits she is the Girl. She joins him on his travels. He has no plans—neither his own nor Robertson's. "What are you running away from?" she asks him as they drive in a big American convertible. "Turn your back to the front seat." She does, sees the road receding behind her, and laughs.

He is not running away, or toward. He is simply in motion. Many of the shots suggest people with time on their hands in empty cities. The girl wants to invest his movements with importance, wants him to be someone and want something. He has revealed his secret, and at one point she says: "But Robertson made these appointments. He believes in something. That's what you wanted, isn't it?" In other words, he became Robertson because he had no plans or desires and Robertson did?

Not really. Locke does desire not to be found by his wife or associate, and the one moment of urgency in the film comes as he is almost recognized, and flees with the girl. There is a brief scene indicating that they have made love, but the movie is not about love or sex. He wants to leave the girl behind because she will get into trouble—his trouble, or Robertson's. She follows.

All leads up to a final shot of great beauty and complexity, in which he falls back exhausted on a hotel bed. The camera moves with infinite slowness toward a window with iron bars, and then somehow through the window into the piazza outside. A car appears and disappears. Another car appears. It contains people looking for him. The girl appears in the square, walking at a distance, observing, not implicated. The camera, still in the same unbroken shot, reenters the hotel and the room.

I have limited myself to describing the action because the film resolutely exists through its action, to which it declines to give meaning. At the outset Locke wanted to interview the rebels and Robertson wanted to sell them guns. By taking Robertson's place, Locke has abandoned his own plan without taking up Robertson's. Nicholson plays him as a man with no purpose; the appearance of the girl provides him with a companion and a witness, but not with a plan or a future.

What of the girl? Schneider gives a performance of breathtaking spontaneity. She is without calculation, manner, or affect. She reacts cleanly and without complication to events, she is concerned about the man and loyal to him, she understands nothing, and at the end she understands less. She is the only witness to his adventure. Without her, it would scarcely have happened. What did it mean? This is not a question to ask in a film by Antonioni. In *L'Avventura,* a character disappears on an island and never appears again. Her friends search for her and then abandon the search, which for a time gave them purpose. In *Blow-Up* a photographer shoots an event in a park and in studying his photographs thinks he may have photographed a murder. But there is no body, and the photographs yield less the more he studies them. In *The Passenger,* one man becomes another and then both evaporate. The girl is left in the empty piazza.

I did not admire the film in 1975. In a negative review, I observed that Antonioni had changed its title from *The Reporter* to *The Passenger,* apparently deciding it was about the girl, not Locke. Maybe it is simply about passengers who travel in someone else's life: Locke in Robertson's, the girl in Locke's. I admire the movie more thirty years later. I am more in sympathy with it.

When a film so resolutely refuses to deliver on the level of plot, what we are left with is tone. *The Passenger* is about being in a place where nobody knows you or wants to know you, and you are struck by your insignificance. There was a world where it was important that Robertson was Robertson and Locke was Locke. In the desert among strangers, it is not even important that Robertson be Robertson and Locke be Locke. The little white car that crisscrosses the square in the final shot belongs to a driving school. To its driver, it is important to pass the course and get a driver's license. Robertson and Locke disappear, and this is first gear, this is second, here is the clutch, here is the brake.

Peaceful Warrior ★ ★ ½

PG-13, 121 m., 2006

Nick Nolte (Socrates), Scott Mechlowicz (Dan Millman), Amy Smart (Joy), Ashton Holmes (Tommy Warner), Paul Wesley (Trevor Scott), Agnes Bruckner (Susie), Tim DeKay (Coach Garrick). Directed by Victor Salva and produced by Mark Amin, Cami Winikoff, Robin Schorr, and David Welch. Screenplay by Kevin Bernhardt, based on the book *Way of the Peaceful Warrior* by Dan Millman.

If *Peaceful Warrior* were not based on a true story, I might have an easier time believing it. It's the kind of parable that is perfectly acceptable as the saga of Mr. Miyagi, but when the movie opens with the words "inspired by true events," I get edgy. I keep wondering what "inspired" means. Did Dan Millman, the author of the book that inspired the movie, really meet a man who could levitate?

What I do believe is that Nick Nolte can play a man who can levitate. Nolte sounds a note of weary clarity in the film; when he utters self-help clichés ("Stop gathering information from outside yourself and start gathering information from inside"), he underplays it so well and looks so serious that we think maybe he knows this firsthand.

Nolte plays the only attendant at an all-night Texaco station that looks so old-fashioned it could be the Fatal Gas Station in a horror movie: you know, where the sinister old scarecrow in overalls tells the kids to turn left and go down the old dirt road into the swamp. This station, however, seems well-lighted and orderly, and Nolte's character is always busy under the hood of a car. "This is a service station," he says at one point. "We offer service. There's no higher purpose."

He has such conversations with Dan Millman (Scott Mechlowicz), a character based on the author of the 1980 self-help best-seller that inspired the movie. Dan is a gymnast on the Berkeley team, a hotshot who's always trying out risky stuff in the gym. After a nasty fall his coach tells him, "Nobody on this planet can do what you're trying to do."

Dan is out jogging the first night he meets the Nolte character, whom he eventually thinks of as Socrates. As he's leaving, he turns back and finds that Socrates is now standing on the roof of the station, fifteen feet or more above the ground. How did he do that? Later, Dan also wants to know how Socrates appears in his bedroom during sex, and on top of a beam in the gymnasium. Quizzed on such puzzles, Socrates has helpful answers such as pointing to his forehead while saying, "Take out the trash, Dan."

Dan's motorcycle hits a car and he breaks his femur in seventeen places. This is inspired by the real Dan's accident in which he broke his leg in twenty-one places. Told he will never compete in gymnastics again, he contemplates suicide but eventually finds himself back at the service station, where Socrates shares such wisdom as "The journey is what brings us happiness, not the destination." I was happy to hear this, because it explains what Godard meant when he said, "The cinema is not the station; the cinema is the train."

The story arc of *Peaceful Warrior* is so familiar that in addition to being inspired by fact, it is inspired by at least two-thirds of all the sports movies ever made. To quote myself (this situation has come up before): I can't give away the ending because it gives itself away. Oddly enough, it's not the plausible stuff like the gymnastics that fascinates me in the story, but the mystery of Socrates. Does Socrates even exist? Is his gas station really there? If Dan bought himself a Baby Ruth from the candy machine, could he eat it? Of course these questions betray me as hopelessly focused on realism.

Sometimes in an imperfect movie there is consolation simply in regarding the actors. You possibly have the impression that Nolte has been in a lot of commercial hits and is, or was until recently, an action star. But run his name through IMDb.com and you'll discover that he is, and essentially always has been, an art film actor. Yes, he had some big hits, but *48 Hours* was a breakthrough at the time, and when he does a superhero epic, it's the inventive *Hulk* by Ang Lee.

Nolte has been through some hard times and posed for at least one mug shot that went around the world. He has picked himself up and patched himself back together, and is convincing as a wise survivor. A movie based on his life might have the same parabola as Millman's, if you substituted drinking for gymnastics. There is a sense in which the role of Socrates speaks to him more loudly than to Dan, and that sense makes the performance sort of fascinating.

All the rest is formula: the coach, the team, the training, the accident, the comeback. The fact that doubles and visual effects are used for some of the gymnastics stunts is obvious but not objectionable, because of course they are. But it's funny, isn't it, how the most amazing stunt in the movie is performed off-screen. How *did* he get up there?

The Perfect Holiday ★ ★ ½

PG, 96 m., 2007

Gabrielle Union (Nancy), Morris Chestnut (Benjamin), Charlie Murphy (J-Jizzy), Katt Williams (Delicious), Faizon Love (Jamal), Queen Latifah (Narrator), Terrence Howard (Mr. Bah-Humbug), Malik Hammond (John-John), Khail Bryant (Emily), Jeremy Gumbs (Mikey), Jill Marie Jones (Robin), Rachel True (Brenda). Directed by Lance Rivera and produced by Shakim Compere, Leifur B. Dagfinnsson, Mike Elliott, Joseph P. Genier, Queen Latifah, and Marvin Peart. Screenplay by Rivera, Marc Calixte, Nat Mauldin, and Jeff Stein.

The Perfect Holiday is a big-hearted romantic comedy based on Meet Cutes, mistaken identities, rebounding fibs, a Santa Claus operating under false pretenses, a nasty rapper, a three-hundred-pound elf, three cute kids, and Gabrielle Union, whose only Christmas wish is that a nice man would pay her a compliment. The movie's biggest suspension of disbelief involves Gabrielle Union having that problem.

She's Nancy, the beautiful mother of the three kids, divorced from a famous rapper named J-Jizzy (Charlie Murphy, Eddie's older brother). He's a Scrooge with no time for his kids, even though the oldest boy (Malik Hammond) keeps trying to bring his parents back together. When Nancy's daughter, Emily (Khail Bryant), overhears her mother's wish, she passes it on to a department store Santa, who is the aspiring songwriter Benjamin (Morris Chestnut). He sees Nancy and Emily together, knows just what to say to Nancy when they meet, and soon the two are deeply in love.

Only problems are, he doesn't know she's the rapper's ex-wife, and she doesn't know he was Santa, doesn't really sell office supplies, and has a song contract with her ex-husband. Benjamin's lucky break is to write a lovely Christmas ballad, which J-Jizzy records after his manager (Katt Williams) explains that the song "I Love the Ho-Ho-Hos" just doesn't sound right. How this all works out involves the usual "rom-com" twists and turns, mistakes and misunderstandings, and despair before delight.

The movie has odd notions of record production. Although it clearly begins deep into Christmas season, there's time for J-Jizzy to record a holiday album, for his manager to disparage it, for them to discover Benjamin's song and record it, and for the album to be in stores before December 25. I suppose if the plot requires that, we have to go along.

One device that seems a little strange is the materialization throughout the movie of an odd couple made up of the Narrator (Queen Latifah) and Mr. Bah-Humbug (Terrence Howard). They observe the action, she tries to help out, he tries to spoil things, she gets all the best moments, and he hardly seems to know what his assignment is in the plot. They're supernatural, somehow. The presence of the Queen is a reminder of her movie *The Last Holiday,* a real charmer, and although she's a coproducer of *The Perfect Holiday,* those expecting a sequel to her best performance will be disappointed.

What isn't disappointing is the energy level throughout the picture, including appealing performances by Malik Hammond and Khail Bryant, the kids who essentially drive the plot. I also liked Faizon Love as Santa's elf and Benjamin's sidekick, and Jill Marie Jones and Rachel True have fun as Nancy's long-suffering girlfriends. There's not much that's original about the film, but it's played with high spirits and good cheer, there are lots of musical interludes, and it's pitched straight at families.

The Perfect Man ★

PG, 96 m., 2005

Hilary Duff (Holly Hamilton), Heather Locklear (Jean Hamilton), Chris Noth (Ben Cooper), Mike O'Malley (Lenny Horton), Ben Feldman (Adam Forrest), Aria Wallace (Zoe Hamilton), Vanessa Lengies (Amy). Directed by Mark Rosman and produced by Susan Duff, Marc E. Platt, and Dawn Wolfrom. Screenplay by Gina Wendkos.

Is there no one to step forward and simply say that Heather Locklear's character in *The Perfect Man* is mad? I will volunteer. Locklear plays Jean Hamilton, a woman whose obsessive search for the "perfect man" inspires sudden and impulsive moves from one end of the country to another, always with her teenage daughter, Holly (Hilary Duff), and Holly's seven-year-old sister, Zoe (Aria Wallace). Apparently, there can only be one Perfect Man candidate per state.

As the movie opens, Holly is preparing to attend a prom in Wichita when her mother announces, "It's moving time!" Her latest boyfriend has broken up with her, so they all have to pile into the car and head for New York, where Mom providentially has a job lined up at a bakery—a job that pays well enough for them to move into an apartment that would rent for, oh, $4,000 a month.

Holly keeps an online blog named GirlOnTheMove.com, where she chronicles her mom's craziness for all the world. "Post me on Match.com," her mom tells Holly after they arrive in New York, but Holly thinks maybe it might be fun to see if her mom just—you know, *meets* someone. Jean's way of meeting someone is certainly direct: She attends a PTA meeting at Holly's new school and suggests special PTA meetings for single parents and teachers. In desperation, Holly creates an imaginary online friend for her mom, who says all the things a woman wants to hear.

How does Holly know this is true? Because she's made a new friend at school (she's always making new friends, because she's always moving to new schools). This friend, named Amy (Vanessa Lengies) has an Uncle Ben (Chris Noth) who runs a bistro and is a bottomless well of information about what women want to hear, and what a Perfect Man consists of. Holly names the imaginary friend Ben, sends her mom Uncle Ben's photo, and recycles what he tells her into the e-mail. Example of his wisdom: "When a woman gets an orchid, she feels like she's floating on a cloud of infinite possibility." If I met a woman who felt like she was floating on a cloud of infinite possibility after receiving an orchid, I would be afraid to give her anything else until she'd had a good physical.

The Perfect Man takes its idiotic plot and uses it as the excuse for scenes of awesome stupidity. For example, when Jean walks into Uncle Ben's restaurant and there is a danger they might meet, Holly sets off the sprinkler system. And when Holly thinks Ben is marrying another woman, she interrupts the wedding—while even we know, because of the tortured camera angles that strive not to reveal this, that Ben is only the best man.

Meanwhile, Jean has another prospect, a baker named Lenny (Mike O'Malley), who is a real nice guy but kind of homely, and invites her to a concert by a Styx tribute band. This involves driving to the concert in Lenny's pride and joy, a 1980 Pontiac Trans-Am two-door hardtop; Jean has to take off her shoes before entering the sacred precincts of this car. My personal opinion is that Lenny would be less boring after six months than the cloud of infinite possibilities guy.

The Perfect Man crawls hand over bloody hand up the stony face of this plot, while we in the audience do not laugh because it is not nice to laugh at those less fortunate than ourselves, and the people in this movie are less fortunate than the people in just about any other movie I can think of, simply because they are in it.

Perfume: The Story of a Murderer ★ ★ ★ ★

R, 145 m., 2007

Ben Whishaw (Jean-Baptiste Grenouille), Dustin Hoffman (Giuseppe Baldini), Alan Rickman (Antoine Richis), Rachel Hurd-Wood (Laura Richis), John Hurt (Narrator). Directed by Tom Tykwer and produced by Bernd Eichinger. Screenplay by Andrew Birkin, Eichinger, and Tykwer, based on the novel by Patrick Suskind.

Not only does *Perfume* seem impossible to film, it must have been almost impossible for Patrick Suskind to write. How do you describe the ineffable enigma of a scent in words? The audiobook, read by Sean Barrett, is the best audio performance I have ever heard; he snuffles and sniffles his way to greatness, and you almost believe he is inhaling bliss or the essence of a stone. I once almost destroyed a dinner party by putting it on for "five minutes," after which nobody wanted to stop listening.

Patrick Suskind's famous novel involves a twisted little foundling whose fishwife mother casually births him while chopping off cod heads. He falls neglected into the stinking charnel house that was Paris three hundred years ago, and is nearly thrown out with the refuse. But Grenouille grows into a grim, taciturn survivor (Ben Whishaw) who possesses two extraordinary qualities: He has the most acute sense of smell in the world and has absolutely no scent of his own.

This last attribute is ascribed by legend to the spawn of the devil, but the movie *Perfume: The Story of a Murderer* makes no mention of this possibility, wisely limiting itself to vile if unnamed evil. Grenouille grows up as a tanner, voluptuously inhaling the world's smells, and eventually talks himself into an apprenticeship with Baldini (Dustin Hoffman), a master perfumer, now past his prime, whose shop is on an overcrowded medieval bridge on the Seine.

Mention of the bridge brings to mind the genius with which director Tom Tykwer (*Run, Lola, Run*) evokes a medieval world of gross vices, all-pervading stinks, and crude appetites. In this world, perfume is like the passage of an angel—some people think, literally. Grenouille effortlessly invents perfect perfumes, but his ambition runs deeper; he wants to distill the essence of copper, stone, and beauty itself. In pursuit of this last ideal he becomes a gruesome murderer.

Baldini tells him the world center of the perfume art is in Grasse, in southern France, and so he walks there. I was there once myself, during the Cannes festival, and at Sandra Schulberg's villa met *les nez de* Grasse, "the noses of Grasse," the men whose tastes enforce the standards of a global industry. They sat dressed in neat business suits around a table bearing a cheese, which they regarded with an interest I could only imagine. On the lawn, young folk frolicked on bedsheets strewn with rose petals. You really must try it sometime.

It is in the nature of creatures like Grenouille (I suppose) that they have no friends. Indeed he has few conversations, and they are rudimentary. His life, as it must be, is almost entirely interior, so Tykwer provides a narrator (John Hurt) to establish certain events and facts. Even then, the film is essentially visual, not spoken, and does a remarkable job of establishing Grenouille and his world. We can never really understand him, but we cannot tear our eyes away.

Perfume begins in the stink of the gutter and remains dark and brooding. To rob a person of his scent is cruel enough, but the way it is done in this story is truly macabre. Still it can be said that Grenouille is driven by the conditions of his life and the nature of his spirit. Also, of course, that he may indeed be the devil's spawn.

This is a dark, dark, dark film, focused on an obsession so complete and lonely it shuts out all other human experience. You may not savor it, but you will not stop watching it, in horror and fascination. Ben Whishaw succeeds in giving us no hint of his character save a deep, savage need. And Dustin Hoffman produces a quirky old master whose life is also governed by perfume, if more positively.

Hoffman reminds us here again, as in *Stranger Than Fiction,* what a detailed and fascinating character actor he is—able to bring to the story of Grenouille precisely what humor and humanity it needs, and then tactfully leaving it at that. Even his exit is nicely timed.

Why I love this story, I do not know. Why I have read the book twice and given away a dozen copies of the audiobook, I cannot explain. There is nothing fun about the story, except the way it ventures so fearlessly down one limited, terrifying, seductive dead end and finds there a solution both sublime and horrifying. It took imagination to tell it, courage to film it, thought to act it, and from the audience it requires a brave curiosity about the peculiarity of obsession.

Persepolis ★ ★ ★ ★

PG-13, 95 m., 2008

Chiara Mastroianni (Marjane), Catherine Deneuve (Tadji [Mother]), Danielle Darrieux (Grandmother), Simon Abkarian (Ebi [Father]), Francois Jerosme (Uncle Anouche), Gabrielle Lopes (Young Marjane). Directed by Marjane Satrapi and Vincent Paronnaud and produced by Marc-Antoine Robert and Xavier Rigault. Screenplay by Satrapi and Paronnaud, based on Satrapi's graphic novels.

I attended the Teheran film festival in 1972 and was invited to the home of my guide and translator to meet her parents and family. Over tea and elegant pastries, they explained proudly that Iran was a "modern" country, that they were devout Muslims but did not embrace the extremes of other Islamic nations, that their nation represented a new way. Whenever I read another story about the clerical rule that now grips Iran, I think of those people and millions of other Iranians like them, who do not agree with the rigid restrictions they live under—particularly the women. Iranians are no more monolithic than we are, a truth not grasped by our own zealous leader. Remember, on 9/11 there was a huge candlelight vigil in Teheran, in sympathy with us.

That was the Iran that Marjane Satrapi was born into in 1969, and it was the Iran that ended in the late 1970s with the fall and exile of the shah. Yes, his rule was dictatorial; yes, his secret police were everywhere and his opponents subjected to torture. But that was the norm in the Middle East and in an arc stretching up to the Soviet Union. At least most Iranians were left more or less free to lead the lives they chose. Ironically, many of them believed the fall of the shah would bring more, not less, democracy.

Satrapi remembers the first nine or ten years of her life as a wonderful time. Surrounded by a loving, independently minded family, living in a comfortable time, she resembled teenagers everywhere in her love for pop music, her interest in fashion, her Nikes. Then it all changed. She and her mother and her feisty grandmother had to shroud their faces from the view of men. Makeup and other forms of western decadence were forbidden. At her age she didn't drink or smoke, but God save any woman who did.

Satrapi, now living in Paris, told her life story in two graphic novels, which became best-sellers and have now been made into this wondrous animated film. The animation is mostly in black and white, with infinite shades of gray and a few guest appearances, here and there, by colors. The style is deliberately two-dimensional, avoiding the illusion of depth in current animation. This approach may sound spartan, but it is surprisingly involving, wrapping us in this autobiography that distills an epoch into a young woman's life. Not surprisingly, the books have been embraced by smart teenage girls all over the world, who find much they identify with. Adolescence is fueled by universal desires and emotions, having little to do with government decrees.

Marjane, voiced as a child by Gabrielle Lopes and as a teenager and adult by Chiara Mastroianni, is a sprightly kid, encouraged in her rambunctiousness by her parents (voiced by Catherine Deneuve and Simon Abkarian), and applauded by her outspoken grandmother (Danielle Darrieux). She dotes on the stories of her spellbinding Uncle Anouche (Francois Jerosme), who has been in prison and sometimes in hiding but gives her a vision of the greater world.

In her teens, with the Ayatollah Khomeini under full steam, Iran turns into a hostile place for the spirits of those such as Marjane. The society she thought she lived in has disappeared, and with it much of her freedom as a woman to define herself outside of marriage and the fearful restrictions of men. Sometimes she fast-talks herself out of tight corners, as when she is almost arrested for wearing makeup, but it is clear to her parents that Marjane will eventually attract trouble. They send her to live with friends in Vienna.

Austria provides her with a radically different society, but one she eventually finds impossible to live in. She was raised with values that do not fit with the casual sex and drug use she finds among her contemporaries there, and after going a little wild with rock and roll and acting out, she doesn't like herself, is homesick, and returns to Iran. But it is even more inhospitable than she remembers. She is homesick for a nation that no longer exists.

In real life, Marjane Satrapi eventually found a congenial home in France. I imagine Paris offered no less decadence than Vienna, but her experiences had made her into a woman more sure of herself and her values, and she grows into—well, the author of books and this film, which dramatize so meaningfully what her life has been like. For she is no heroine, no flag-waving idealist, no rebel, not always wise, sometimes reckless, but with strong family standards.

It might seem that her story is too large for one ninety-eight-minute film, but *Persepolis* tells it carefully, lovingly, and with great style. It is infinitely more interesting than the witless coming-of-age western girls we meet in animated films; in spirit, in gumption, in heart, Marjane resembles someone like the heroine in *Juno*—not that she is pregnant at sixteen, of course. While so many films about coming of age involve manufactured dilemmas, here is one about a woman who indeed does come of age, and magnificently.

Note: Persepolis *shared the jury prize at Cannes 2007 and has been selected by France as its official Oscar entry in the foreign-language category, a rare honor for any animated film.*

Pete Seeger: The Power of Song ★ ★ ★ ★

NO MPAA RATING, 93 m., 2007

Featuring Pete Seeger, Toshi Seeger, Bob Dylan, Natalie Maines, Tom Paxton, Bruce Springsteen, David Dunaway, Bess Lomax Hawes, Joan Baez, Ronnie Gilbert, Jerry Silverman, Henry Foner, Eric Weissberg, Arlo Guthrie, Peter Yarrow, Mary Travers, Julian Bond, Tommy Smothers, and Bonnie Raitt. A documentary directed by Jim Brown and produced by Michael Cohl and William Eigen.

I don't know if Pete Seeger believes in saints, but I believe he is one. He's the one in the front as they go marching in. *Pete Seeger: The Power of Song* is a tribute to the legendary singer and composer who thought music could be a force for good, and proved it by writing songs that have actually helped shape our times ("If I Had a Hammer," "Turn, Turn, Turn") and popularizing "We Shall Overcome" and Woody Guthrie's unofficial national anthem, "This Land Is Your Land." During his long career (he is eighty-eight) he has toured tirelessly with song and stories, never happier than when he gets everyone in the audience to sing along.

This documentary, directed by Jim Brown, is a sequel of sorts to Brown's wonderful *The Weavers: Wasn't That a Time* (1982), which centered on the farewell Carnegie Hall concert of the singing group Seeger was long associated with. The Weavers had many big hits circa 1950 ("Goodnight Irene," "Kisses Sweeter Than Wine") before being blacklisted during the McCarthy years; called before the House Un-American Activities Committee and asked to name members of the Communist Party, Seeger invoked not the Fifth, but the First Amendment. The Weavers immediately disappeared from the playlists of most radio stations, and Seeger did not appear on television for seventeen years, until the Smothers Brothers broke the boycott.

But he kept singing, invented a new kind of banjo, did more for the rebirth of that instrument than anyone else, cofounded two folksong magazines, and with Toshi, his wife of sixty-two years, did more and sooner than most to live a "green" lifestyle, just because it was his nature. On rural land in upstate New York, they lived for years in a log cabin he built himself, and we see him still chopping firewood and working on the land. "I like to say I'm more conservative than Goldwater," Wikipedia quotes him. "He just wanted to turn the clock back to when there was no income tax. I want to turn the clock back to when people lived in small villages and took care of each other."

With access to remarkable archival footage, old TV shows, home movies, and the family photo album, Brown weaves together the story of the Seegers with testimony by admirers who represent his influence and legacy: Bruce Springsteen, Bob Dylan, Natalie Maines of the Dixie Chicks, Tom Paxton, Joan Baez, Arlo Guthrie, Peter Yarrow, Mary Travers, Julian Bond, and Bonnie Raitt. There is also coverage of the whole Seeger family musical tradition, including brother Mike and sister Peggy.

This isn't simply an assembly of historical materials and talking heads (however eloquent), but a vibrant musical film as well, and Brown has remastered the music so that we feel the real excitement of Seeger walking into a room and starting a sing-along. Unique among musicians, he doesn't covet the spotlight but actually insists on the audience joining in; he seems more choir director than soloist.

You could see that in 2004 at the Toronto Film Festival, in the "final" farewell performance of the Weavers, as he was joined onstage by original group members Ronnie Gilbert and Fred Hellerman, who go back fifty-seven years together, and more recent members Erik Darling and Eric Weissberg. Missing from the original group was the late Lee Hays, who cowrote "If I Had a Hammer."

The occasion was the showing of an interim Brown doc, *Isn't This a Time,* a documentary about a Carnegie Hall "farewell concert" in honor of Harold Leventhal's fiftieth anniversary as an impresario. It was Leventhal who booked them into Carnegie Hall the first time in the late 1940s, and Leventhal who brought them back to the hall when the group's left-wing politics had made them victims of the show business blacklist. Although Seeger has sung more rarely in recent years, claiming his voice is "gone," he was in fine form that night in Toronto, his head as always held high and thrown back, as if focused in the future.

Sadly, for many people, Seeger is still associated in memory with the Communist Party USA. Although never a "card-carrying member," he was and is adamantly left-wing; he broke with the party in 1950, disillusioned with Stalinism, and as recently as this year, according to Wikipedia, apologized to a historian: "I think you're right. I should have asked to see the gulags when I was in the U.S.S.R."

What I feel from Seeger and his music is a deep-seated, instinctive decency, a sense of fair play, a democratic impulse reflected by singing along as a metaphor. I get the same feeling from Toshi, who coproduced this film and has coproduced her husband's life. How many women would sign on with a folksinger who planned to build them a cabin to live in? The portrait of their long marriage, their children and grandchildren, is one of the most inspiring elements in the film. They actually live as if this land was made for you and me.

Pierrepoint, the Last Hangman ★ ★ ★ ½

R, 98 m., 2006

Timothy Spall (Albert Pierrepoint), Juliet Stevenson (Anne Fletcher), Eddie Marsan (Tish Corbitt), Cavan Clerkin (George Cooper), Christopher Fulford (Charlie Sykes), Ian Shaw (Percy). Directed by Adrian Shergold and produced by Christine Langan. Screenplay by Jeff Pope and Bob Mills.

Timothy Spall has been graced by nature with a face at once morose and discontented, although when he smiles it is like the first day of spring. In *Pierrepoint, the Last Hangman,* he plays Albert Pierrepoint, the last official chief hangman for the United Kingdom, credited with at least

435 executions. He kept a meticulous journal, with neatly ruled columns for name, date, place, length of rope, and total time required. He was an exemplary civil servant, the best at his trade, and when the right man was required to hang more than two hundred Nazi war criminals, Field Marshal Montgomery personally asked him to perform the task.

By the nature of his job, a hangman remains anonymous, and Pierrepoint preferred it that way. His everyday job was delivering provisions for a grocery wholesaler, and when an execution came along he traveled to the prison by train, spent the night, and was given his expenses and a hot meal in addition to his fee of about eight dollars. Pierrepoint was the third member of his family to work as a hangman and took pride in his system of calculating the exact length of rope to use on each condemned prisoner. By measuring their height and weight, and estimating their neck muscles by their occupations, he aimed to kill them instantly by breaking the spine between the second and third vertebrae. He was thus spared the embarrassment of a client still alive and strangling, or a dead one with his head snapped off.

Adrian Shergold's film of Pierrepoint's life paints a portrait of respectable, working-class mediocrity with a secret at its center; Mike Leigh's *Vera Drake* (2004) was a similar, if more nuanced, portrait of a quiet housewife who was an abortionist. While still a grocery drayman, Pierrepoint, already past thirty, shyly proposes marriage to possibly the first girl to go out with him to the cinema. Annie (Juliet Stevenson) continues to work in a tobacconist's and keeps a comfy little home for him, all teapots and footrests, china Scotty dogs, evenings around the wireless, and, for dinner, "your favorite—pork chop." Does she know about his other job? Yes, but doesn't say so until he tells her himself. She guards their extra money in a pipe tobacco tin, planning for the day when they can buy the local pub.

The movie is unflinching in watching Pierrepoint at work. He always follows the same routine, designed as a time-and-motion study to escort the prisoner from his cell to his doom with no time to realize what is happening. He handcuffs the client, says, "Follow me, sir," leads the way across the corridor, and leaves the prisoner standing on the trap without quite realizing it. A white hood is whipped from Pierrepoint's jacket pocket, put over the client's head, followed by the noose, and a lever is pulled. Albert's father's average was 13.5 seconds per execution. Albert dispatches one client in less than eight.

He is a man of principle. He believes the condemned have been judged, sentenced to pay their debt, and, when they are dead, have paid it. He bathes and prepares their corpses with care and respect and is outraged when a prison comes up one coffin short. His man has paid his dues and deserves proper handling, he shouts, as angry as we see him. Often after work he'll stop at the pub (which eventually becomes his) and join his pal Tish (Eddie Marsan) in a vaudeville song. One night Tish proudly turns up with a hot date, falls in love with her, is jilted, and performs a quavering solo of "Jealous Love."

Spoiler warning: After an especially hard day, Albert comes home and the solicitous Annie suggests he have a drink with his mates. "I don't have any mates," he says. It is true. He hardly knows anyone at the pub, and doesn't even know Tish's real name, which is why it is a shock when he discovers he is expected to hang him. One review of the film calls this development "a contrived subplot," but Wikipedia reports that Tish really did strangle his unfaithful lover on an evening when he and Albert sang "Danny Boy" at the pub, and Albert really did hang Tish. All that seems contrived is that the hangman would not have heard about the murder and anticipated the result.

Pierrepoint boasted of sleeping soundly after each execution. His tunnel vision permitted no doubt; his was a difficult job, but necessary, and worth doing correctly, with full respect for each client. Only after he arrived in Germany and had to dispatch thirteen Nazis on his first day did he begin to weaken. It was too much like an assembly line. And when he returned home, the national tabloids outed him and he was cheered in the streets as a hero, then later targeted by opponents of the death penalty. "It isn't right," he said to Annie, who was a little tickled to have photographers on her doorstep.

He eventually retired, moved to the seaside with Annie, continued as a celebrity, and wrote his memoirs, in which, Wiki says, he concluded: "Executions solve nothing, and are only an antiquated relic of a primitive desire for revenge which takes the easy way and hands over the responsibility for revenge to other people. The trouble with the death penalty has always been that nobody wanted it for everybody, but everybody differed about who should get off." This realization came a little late for his 435 or more clients, but at least he gave them the very best service.

The key to the film is in the performances by Spall and Stevenson—and by Eddie Marsan, who looks a little like Pee Wee Herman, and who you may recall as the painfully bashful suitor of Vera Drake's daughter. Others just pass through, so to speak, including the murderess Ruth Ellis, subject of the 1985 film *Dance with a Stranger.* The utter averageness of the characters, their lack of insight, their normality, contrasts with the subject matter in an unsettling way. What is most intriguing about the film is that while it is not in favor of capital punishment, it doesn't make Pierrepoint into an evil or deranged man, just a dutiful workman. Every year dozens of civil servants are honored on the Queen's List, but Pierrepoint, whose service to the Crown was more essential than many door holders and pen pushers, labored on year after year in the shadows, insisting on his hot meal.

Pierrot le Fou ★ ★ ½

NO MPAA RATING, 110 m., 1965 (rereleased 2007)

Jean-Paul Belmondo (Ferdinand), Anna Karina (Marianne). Directed by Jean-Luc Godard and produced by Georges de Beauregard. Screenplay by Godard, based on the novel *Obsession* by Lionel White.

Godard's *Pierrot le Fou* (1965) is the same film I liked so much when it opened here in 1968 and assigned a three-and-a-half-star rating. In fact, it is probably a better film, because it is being shown in a new 35 mm print. But while I once wrote of it as "Godard's most virtuoso display of his mastery of Hollywood genres," I now see it more as the story of silly characters who have seen too many Hollywood movies.

There was a point when it was revolutionary to show young lovers flaunting society, committing crimes thoughtlessly, and running hand in hand over hill and dale, beach and field. And then there was a point where it was postrevolutionary. Or maybe, to take a more optimistic view of the progress of cinema, prerevolutionary.

The film stars Jean-Paul Belmondo, then thirty-two, and Anna Karina, then twenty-five, as Ferdinand and Marianne, Ferdinand's baby-sitter and onetime girlfriend, who run away together from a party and from their spouses. First stop, Marianne's flat, when Ferdinand goes into the next room, sees a dead body, and returns to the living room. Later, she passes the body, which Godard shows us only by filming Belmondo's eyes watching her. Nice touch. And she sings a song. Then they hit the road in a series of stolen cars, supporting themselves by stickups.

It is so very boring when infatuation and sex have to take the place of a genuine interest in the other person, which Ferdinand discovers more quickly than Marianne, perhaps because that delightful and beautiful woman is mad. There are times when she wishes he were crazier and calls him "Pierrot," the name of a character from Italian stage comedy and opera who is a clown and a fool. "My name is Ferdinand," he tirelessly corrects her.

At the party they run away from there is a famous scene in which an older man with a cigar is seen standing against a wall. This is Samuel Fuller, the American director, playing himself and explaining, "My name is Samuel Fuller. I'm an American film director in Paris making an action picture." He is filmed in color; the rest of the party is filmed in bold tints. What does that mean? It means that we notice it and wonder what it means, which can be said for a lot of Godard's shots.

Barreling through the countryside, the couple make use of old movies. During a dicey moment, Marianne remembers a Laurel and Hardy trick. She faces the guy with the gun, she looks up, he looks up, and she punches him in the stomach. There is also an auto robbery, involving a car on a turntable in a grease pit, that Keaton might have invented, less violently to be sure.

I was in full flood of admiration for Jean-Luc Godard in the 1960s. Seemed like everyone was. One year, they showed three of his films at the New York Film Festival. The thing was, he made shots that knew they were shots, and you watched them knowing they were shots, and they knew you were watching, and you were all in on it together.

There was a barnyard scene in *Weekend* (1968) where the camera rotated in a circle once, twice, and then rotated back the other way just a little, *to show that it knew, and you knew, that it was rotating.* How cool. And a tracking shot of an unbelievably long traffic jam, which remains one of the great shots, but great about what? I wrote in my review of that film: "At some point, we realize that the subject of the shot is not the traffic jam but the fact that the shot is so extended. 'Politics is a traveling shot,' Godard told us a few years ago, and now we know what he meant." Uh-huh.

Godard's early black-and-white films were masterpieces. Later, he needed to dial down. Still later, he disappeared into long and (for many) pointless stylistic video exercises that remained widely unseen. He still retained the ability to make much-debated films, like *Hail Mary* (1986), but he wasn't drawn that way. *Pierrot le Fou* stood at the tipping point between the great early films like *My Life to Live* and later films that were essentially about themselves, or adult children at play.

I closed my earlier review of *Pierrot le Fou* by writing: "Godard, a former film critic, once said that the only valid way to criticize a movie was to make one of your own. That is true of his own work, at least." To which I now add: But perhaps not entirely in the way he intended.

The Pink Panther ★ ½

PG, 92 m., 2006

Steve Martin (Inspector Jacques Clouseau), Kevin Kline (Chief Inspector Dreyfus), Beyonce Knowles (Xania), Jean Reno (Gendarme Ponton), Emily Mortimer (Nicole), Henry Czerny (Yuri), Kristin Chenoweth (Cherie). Directed by Shawn Levy and produced by Robert Simonds. Screenplay by Len Blum and Steve Martin.

What is the moviegoer with a good memory to do when confronted with *The Pink Panther,* directed by Shawn Levy and starring Steve Martin? Is it possible to forget Blake Edwards and Peter Sellers? It is not. Their best Pink Panther movies did wonderfully what could not be done so well by anyone else, and not even, at the end, by them. (There was the sad *Trail of the Pink Panther* in 1982, cobbled together from outtakes after Sellers died in 1980.) Inspector Clouseau has been played by other actors before Martin (Alan Arkin and Roger Moore), but what's the point? The character isn't bigger than the actor, as Batman and maybe James Bond are. The character is the actor, and I would rather not see Steve Martin, who is himself inimitable, imitating Sellers.

Clouseau is wrong, and so is Kevin Kline as Inspector Dreyfus, the role Herbert Lom made into a smoldering slow burn. Kline and Martin both wear the costumes and try the bad French accents, but it's like the high school production of something you saw at Steppenwolf, with the most gifted students in drama class playing the John Malkovich and Joan Allen roles. Within thirty seconds of Kline's appearing on the screen, I was remembering the Kevin Kline Rule from my "Little Movie Glossary," which observes that whenever Kline wears a mustache in a movie, he also has a foreign accent. Please do not write in with exceptions.

The movie credits Edwards as one of the sources of the story, which is fair enough, since the movie's ambition is to be precisely in the tradition of the Pink Panther movies. It's a prequel, taking place before *The Pink Panther* (1963) and showing Clouseau plucked from obscurity for his first big case. The French soccer coach has been murdered on the field in view of countless cheering fans, and the Pink Panther diamond has been stolen at the same time. The pressure is on Dreyfus to solve the case. His inspiration: Find the most incompetent inspector in France, announce his appointment, and use him as a decoy while the real investigation secretly goes on.

Clouseau, of course, qualifies as spectacularly incompetent, and his first meeting with Dreyfus begins unpromisingly when he succeeds in piercing the chief inspector's flesh with the pin on his badge. Clouseau is assigned Ponton (Jean Reno), an experienced gendarme, as his minder. Reno survives the movie by dialing down.

Clouseau, as before, has the ability to begin with a small mistake and build it into a catastrophe. Consider a scene where he drops a Viagra pill, and in trying to retrieve it, short-circuits the electricity in a hotel, sets it on fire, and falls through a floor. The mounting scale of each disaster is like a slapstick version of the death scenes in *Final Destination 3*, where a perfectly ordinary day in the stock room can end with a death by nail gun.

The Panther movies always featured beautiful women or, in the case of Capucine, a woman rumored to have been born a man, although I'll bet John Wayne hadn't heard that when they costarred in *North to Alaska*. The beauties this time are Beyonce Knowles, Emily Mortimer, and Kristin Chenoweth, and their task is essentially to regard Clouseau as if they have never seen such a phenomenon before in their lives.

Ponton, in the meantime, is subjected to the same kinds of attacks that Sellers used to unleash on Cato (Burt Kwouk), but I dunno: Even in purely physical scenes, something is missing. I think maybe the problem is that Steve Martin is sane and cannot lose himself entirely to idiocy. Sellers, who liked to say he had no personality, threw himself into a role as if desperate to grab all the behavior he could and run away with it and hide it under the bed.

There are moments that are funny in a mechanical way, as when Clouseau causes a giant globe to roll out of an office and into the street, and it turns up much later to crash into a bicycle racer. But at every moment in the movie, I was aware that Sellers was Clouseau, and Martin was not. I hadn't realized how thoroughly Sellers and Edwards had colonized my memory. Despite Sean Connery, I was able to accept the other James Bonds, just as I understand that different actors might play Hamlet. But there is only one Clouseau, and zat ees zat.

Poseidon ★ ★

PG-13, 99 m., 2006

Kurt Russell (Robert Ramsey), Josh Lucas (Dylan Johns), Richard Dreyfuss (Richard Nelson), Jacinda Barrett (Maggie James), Emmy Rossum (Jennifer Ramsey), Mike Vogel (Christian), Mia Maestro (Elena), Jimmy Bennett (Conor James), Andre Braugher (Captain Bradford), Freddy Rodriguez (Valentin), Kevin Dillon (Lucky Larry), Stacy Ferguson (Gloria). Directed by Wolfgang Petersen and produced by Petersen, Duncan Henderson, Mike Fleiss, and Akiva Goldsman. Screenplay by Mark Protosevich, based on the novel by Paul Gallico.

An odd and unexpected word kept nudging its way into my mind as I sat watching *Poseidon*. That word was "perfunctory." I hoped that other words would replace it. I knew I was not enjoying the movie, but I hoped it would improve or, lacking that, discover an interesting way to fail. But no. It was perfunctory, by which I mean, according to the dictionary that came with my computer: cursory, desultory, hurried, rapid, fleeting, token, casual, superficial, careless, halfhearted, sketchy, mechanical, automatic, routine, and offhand.

Yes. And if you want to see the opposite of those qualities, consider some of the other films by the director Wolfgang Petersen, most notably *Das Boot* (1981), but also *In the Line of Fire* (1993) and *The Perfect Storm* (2000). It may have been the latter movie that won him the assignment to remake *The Poseidon Adventure* (1972). In *The Perfect Storm*, he shows a fishing boat trying to climb an overwhelming wall of water, and failing. It is one of the best adventure movies of recent years, with vivid characters, convincing special effects, and a tangible feel for the relentless sea.

Having made such considerable movies, Petersen does not seem to have been inspired by the opportunity to remake a movie that was not all that good to begin with. Everyone in his audience already knows the story, and much of the suspense depends on who gets the Shelley Winters role and has to hold his or her breath for a long time under water. *Poseidon* follows, as it must, the formula for a disaster movie, which involves (1) a container holding a lot of characters; (2) cameos to establish them in broad, simplistic strokes; (3) a catastrophe; (4) the struggle of the survivors; and (5) the loss of at least one character we hate and one character we like, and the survival of the others, while thousands of extras die unmourned. It might be interesting to add (6) deadly snakes on the loose, but they've all been signed up for the forthcoming *Snakes on a Plane*.

The container can be an ocean liner, an airplane, a skyscraper, a Super Bowl stadium, whatever. Doesn't matter. This time it is an ocean liner, overturned by a "rogue wave" that leaves it floating upside down. The ship's captain (Andre Braugher) assures the passengers, who were just celebrating New Year's Eve, that they will be safe in the giant ballroom. A few daring souls think otherwise. They decide to save themselves by, essentially, escaping up the down staircase.

These characters include the heroic Dylan Johns (Josh Lucas), the equally heroic Robert Ramsey (Kurt Russell), his daughter Jennifer (Emmy Rossum), the obnoxious Lucky Larry (Kevin Dillon), the suicidal Richard Nelson (Richard Dreyfuss), the mother (Jacinda Barrett) and her son, Conor (Jimmy Bennett), and a stowaway (Mia Maestro). All of their human stories will play out against the drama of the endangered ship. As they say.

What do I mean by "perfunctory"? I mean that Petersen's heart isn't in it. He is too wise a director to think this is first-rate material, and too good a director to turn it into enjoyable trash. We realize with a sinking heart that we will have to experience various stock situations, including (1) a perilous traverse over a dizzying drop; (2) escape from seemingly locked rooms; (3) repeated threats of drowning and electrocution; (4) crucial decisions in which the right button will save them and the wrong one will doom them; and (5) ingenious reasoning by people who know nothing about ships but are expert at finding the charts, maps, and diagrams they can instantly decode. ("This is the ballast tank!" "The bulkheads are activated by water pressure!" "This is the way out!")

During all this time, exterior CGI shots will show the ship being rocked by enormous explosions, although curiously the lights come on from time to time when they are convenient, and the characters have all the flashlights they need to allow us to see the action. The characters will also all find time to sort out all the romantic complications, family differences, personal hangups, and character flaws that have been carefully introduced for this purpose.

There is nothing wrong with the performances. All of the actors are professionals, although none have as much fun as Shelley Winters, who is the actor everyone remembers from the 1972 movie. They are wet a lot, desperate a lot, endangered a lot, and surrounded by a lot of special effects. Then some of them survive and others die. You don't know a thing at the end of the movie you didn't know at the beginning. In the proper hands, this could have been a sequel to *Airplane!* named *Ocean Liner!* in which once the characters battle their way to the top (i.e., bottom) of the overturned ship, a second wave flips it again, and they have to retrace their steps.

A Prairie Home Companion ★ ★ ★ ★

PG-13, 105 m., 2006

Woody Harrelson (Dusty), Tommy Lee Jones (Axeman), Garrison Keillor (G.K.), Kevin Kline (Guy Noir), Lindsay Lohan (Lola Johnson), Virginia Madsen (Dangerous Woman), John C. Reilly (Lefty), Maya Rudolph (Molly), Meryl Streep (Yolanda Johnson), Lily Tomlin (Rhonda Johnson), L. Q. Jones (Chuck Akers), Tim Russell (Stage Manager), Sue Scott (Makeup Lady), Tom Keith (Effects Man). Directed by Robert Altman and produced by Altman, Wren Arthur, Joshua Astrachan, Tony Judge, and David Levy. Screenplay by Garrison Keillor.

What a lovely film this is, so gentle and whimsical, so simple and profound. Robert Altman's *A Prairie Home Companion* is faithful to the spirit of the radio program, a spirit both robust and fragile, and yet achieves something more than simply reproducing a performance of the show. It is nothing less than an elegy, a memorial to memories of times gone by, to dreams that died but left the dreamers dreaming, to appreciating what you've had instead of insisting on more.

This elegiac strain is explained by the premise that we are watching the last performance of the weekly show. After a final singing of "Red River Valley" (the saddest of all songs), the paradise of the Fitzgerald Theater will be torn down so they can put up a parking lot. After thirty years, the show will be no more.

The show is hosted by a man referred to as G.K., played by Garrison Keillor as a version of himself, which is about right, because he always seems to be a version of himself. Keillor, whose verbal and storytelling genius has spun a whole world out of thin air, always seems a step removed from what he does, as if bemused to find himself doing it. Here his character refuses to get all sentimental about the last program and has a dialogue with Lola (Lindsay Lohan), a young poet who likes suicide as a subject. It seems to her G.K. should offer up a eulogy; there is sufficient cause, not only because of the death of the program but also because a veteran of the show actually dies during the broadcast.

"I'm of an age when if I started to do eulogies, I'd be doing nothing else," he says.

"You don't want to be remembered?"

"I don't want them to be *told* to remember me."

So the last show is treated like any other. In the dressing room, incredibly cluttered with bric-a-brac and old photos, we meet Lola's mother and her aunt, Yolanda and Rhonda Johnson (Meryl Streep and Lily Tomlin). They are the two survivors from a four-sister singing act: "The Carter Family was like us, only famous." Their onstage duets are hilarious, depending on a timing that rises above the brilliant to the transcendent; they were doing this double act on the Academy Awards telecast in March 2006.

We also meet Chuck Akers (L. Q. Jones), an old-time C&W singer, and Dusty and Lefty (Woody Harrelson and John C. Reilly), two cowboy singers who threaten to make the last program endless as they improvise one corny joke after another. We also meet the people who make the show work: the stage manager, Molly (Maya Rudolph), and, borrowed from the show itself, the makeup lady (Sue Scott), Al the backstage guy (Tim Russell), the sound effects man (Tom Keith), the bandleader (Rich Dworsky), and the P.H.C. house band. Molly is surely so pregnant she should stay calm, but she is driven to distraction by G.K.'s habit of never planning anything and moseying up to the microphone at the last conceivable moment.

Adding another level is the materialization in the real world of Guy Noir, Private Eye (Kevin Kline). Listeners of the program will know that Keillor and his stock company perform adventures from the life of Noir as a salute to old-time radio drama. In Altman's movie, Noir is a real person, a broken-down gumshoe who handles security for the show (he lights his cigarettes with wooden kitchen matches, just like Philip Marlowe in Altman's *The Long Goodbye*). Guy is visited by a character described as the Dangerous Woman (Virginia Madsen), who may perhaps be an angelic one.

The final visitor to the Fitzgerald Theater is Axeman (Tommy Lee Jones), who represents the investors who have bought the lovely theater and will tear it down. He doesn't recognize the bust of a man in the theater's private box, but we do: It is F. Scott Fitzgerald, that native son of St. Paul in whose honor the theater is named. A little later, Ed Lachman's camera helps Altman observe that Fitzgerald and Guy Noir have profiles so similar as to make no difference.

Like the show that inspired it, *A Prairie Home Companion* is not about anything in particular. Perhaps it is about everything in general: about remembering, and treasuring the past, and loving performers not because they are new but because they have lasted. About smiling and being amused, but not laughing out loud, because in Minnesota loud laughter is seen as a vice practiced on the coasts. About how all things pass away, but if you live your life well, everything was fun while it lasted. There is so much of the ghost of Scott Fitzgerald hovering in the shadows of this movie that at the end I quoted to myself the closing words of *The Great Gatsby*. I'm sure you remember them, so let's say them together: "And so we beat on, boats against the current, borne back ceaselessly into the past."

The Prestige ★ ★ ★

PG-13, 135 m., 2006

Hugh Jackman (Robert Angier), Christian Bale (Alfred Borden), Scarlett Johansson (Olivia), Michael Caine (Cutter), Rebecca Hall (Sarah Borden), Andy Serkis (Mr. Alley), Piper Perabo (Julia Angier), David Bowie (Nikola Tesla). Directed by Christopher Nolan and produced by Emma Thomas and Aaron Ryder. Screenplay by Jonathan Nolan and Christopher Nolan, based on the novel by Christopher Priest.

Christopher Nolan's *The Prestige* has just about everything I require in a movie about magicians, except . . . the Prestige. We are instructed at the outset, in a briefing by Michael Caine, that every magic trick consists of three acts: (1) the Pledge, in which a seemingly real situation is set up; (2) the Turn, in which the initial reality is challenged; and (3) the Prestige, where all is set right again. An example, one not used in the film, would be (1) a woman, and it's always a woman except with Penn and Teller, is placed into a box; (2) the box is sawed in half and the halves separated;

and (3) magically, the "victim" is restored in one piece.

The Pledge of Nolan's *The Prestige* is that the film, having been metaphorically sawed into two, will be restored; it fails when it cheats, as for example if the whole woman produced on the stage were not the same one so unfortunately cut into two. Other than that fundamental flaw, which leads to some impenetrable revelations toward the end, it's quite a movie—atmospheric, obsessive, almost satanic.

It takes place in Victorian London, at a time and place where seances and black magic were believed in by the credulous. Somerset Maugham's novel *The Magician* captures that period perfectly in its fictional portrait of Aleister Crowley, "the most evil man in the world," who created the illusion that he *really was* an occult practitioner of dark forces. He had a gift for persuading women to materialize in his bed. These days, when most of us are less superstitious, it is the technical craft of a David Copperfield that impresses us. We see the trick done but do not for a moment believe it is really happening.

Houdini, the great transitional figure between "magical" acts and ingenious tricks, was at pains to explain that everything he did was a trick; he offered rewards, never collected, for any "supernatural" act he could not explain. The Amazing Randi carries on in the same tradition, bending spoons as easily as Uri Geller. And yet in Houdini's time there were those who insisted he was doing real magic; how else could his effects be achieved?

Daniel Mark Epstein wrote about the Houdini believers in a 1986 issue of the *New Criterion,* which I read as I read everything I can get my hands on about Houdini. The thing was, Houdini really did free himself from those fetters and chains and sealed trunks dropped into the river, and survived the Chinese water torture (an effect used prominently in *The Prestige* night after night). But there were those who argued his tricks were physically impossible, and thus must be supernatural.

Houdini would have been active at the time of *The Prestige,* but his insights would have been fatal to the movie's plot, which is the problem with the plot. We meet two apprentice magicians, Robert Angier (Hugh Jackman) and Alfred Borden (Christian Bale), who work as fake "volunteers" from the audience for Milton the Magician (the invaluable Ricky Jay). They assist in tying up a helpless damsel, in reality Robert's wife, Julia (Piper Perabo), and lowering her into the Chinese water torture box. Concealed by curtains, she somehow escapes, as Houdini always did, but one night Alfred ties her knots too tightly, she cannot escape, and by the time a manager (Michael Caine) rushes onstage with an ax, it is too late to save her from drowning.

This sets off a lifelong hatred between Robert and Alfred, during which Robert (now in love with his new assistant, Olivia, played by Scarlett Johansson) rises to the top of the profession. The frigid and ominous Alfred falls to the bottom, is reduced to performing in fleapits, and yet presents an illusion named the Transported Man in which he walks into a door on one side of the stage and instantly emerges from a door at the other. How is that physically possible? It's the sort of thing that made his fans claim Houdini was supernormal. Robert becomes obsessed with finding the secret of the trick.

But magicians do not explain their illusions, not even to their peers, unless money changes hands. ("The trick is told when the trick is sold.") The Transported Man begins, you will agree, with a terrific Pledge. Now how will Robert ever discover the secret of the Prestige? He treks into the snows of Colorado to visit the hidden laboratory of the (real-life) Nikola Tesla (David Bowie), who is believed to have manufactured the trick for Albert. Tesla, the discoverer/inventor of alternating current, was believed at the time to be capable of all manner of wonders with the genie of electricity, but how could AC, or even DC, explain the Transported Man?

You will not learn here. What you will learn in the movie is, I believe, a disappointment—nothing but a trick about a trick. With a sinking heart, I realized that *The Prestige* had jumped the rails, and that rules we thought were in place no longer applied.

I have been in love with magic all my life. I'm no good at it, even though I bored my friends for years with cheesy illusions and even today can make a dime disappear from your forehead. These days I am most impressed with the skills required for close-up magic. Teddy Nava, the son of the writer/directors Gregory Nava and Anna Thomas, can make cards change *while I am holding them in my hands.* Now how does he do that? Not through divine intervention, I am fairly sure. But I was *holding* them! The trick is told when the trick is sold. Yes, but what if it takes months of practice after you're told the trick? Nikola Tesla isn't going to help me then, by running alternating current down Teddy's arm and up mine.

Pretty Persuasion ★ ★

R, 104 m., 2005

Evan Rachel Wood (Kimberly Joyce), Ron Livingston (Percy Anderson), James Woods (Hank Joyce), Jane Krakowski (Emily Klein), Elisabeth Harnois (Brittany Wells), Selma Blair (Grace Anderson), Adi Schnall (Randa Azzouni), Stark Sands (Troy), Danny Comden (Roger Nicholl), Jaime King (Kathy Joyce). Directed by Marcos Siega and produced by Todd Dagres, Carl Levin, and Matt Weaver. Screenplay by Skander Halim.

Pretty Persuasion is the kind of teenage movie where James Woods can play the heroine's dad and not be the worst person in the story. He comes close, but then everyone comes close, except for the innocent bystanders. The movie stars Evan Rachel Wood, who is amazingly good playing a spiteful, cruel high school student. There are so many movies where the heroine is persecuted by the popular bombshell and her posse that it's almost a genre, but never has the bombshell been this evil.

Wood plays Kimberly Joyce, the product of a Bel Air home where malice is served at every meal. Her millionaire father, Hank (James Woods), is aggressively hateful, a fast-talker who mows down the opposition in every conversation and amuses himself by telling racist jokes to his daughter and her new stepmother, Kathy (Jaime King). What Kimberly learns at home, she improves on at school. Her sidekicks are Brittany (Elisabeth Harnois) and Randa (Adi Schnall), an Arab girl who gets to listen to Kim's ranking of the races (Arabs come last, but Kim is gentle when she tells Randa). What Randa thinks is hard to say, since she rarely speaks, is intimidated and dominated by Kimberly, and has been chosen as a mascot, not a friend.

Kimberly dislikes her English teacher, Percy Anderson (Ron Livingston), partly because of his classroom matter, partly because she dislikes all teachers, and partly because she suspects (correctly) that he harbors lustful thoughts for them. The thoughts don't bother Kimberly, a sexual predator, but they give her an idea: Why don't the three girls accuse Mr. Anderson of sexually molesting them? It could be good publicity for the acting career Kimberly dreams about. The two friends go along, carefully schooled by Kimberly.

The movie, directed by Marcos Siega and written by Skander Halim, exists uneasily somewhere between comedy and satire. When Mr. Anderson gives his wife (Selma Blair) a skirt like the students wear and asks her to read an essay while he "grades" her, it might be funny if the movie itself were not so much more lethal.

What the movie gets right is that sexual molestation, especially against attractive, articulate students in rich neighborhoods, is a publicity magnet. The story attracts predatory TV reporter Emily Klein (Jane Krakowski), who turns it into a running commentary on the virus of social depravity, without realizing she's a carrier. Mr. Anderson loses his job, the case is taken to trial, and the rest you will learn.

I admired the willingness of the screenplay to venture into deep waters. Like *Lolita,* this is a movie about young girls, but not for them. It makes some hard-edged observations about the current popularity, if that is the word, of suits charging sexual harassment (I refer not to the crime itself, which is evil, but to the way it is sometimes exploited to destroy innocent reputations). It is also dead right about the way some TV news outlets cover such "news" stories with a fervor entirely lacking as they regard more important topics. Coverage of molestation easily shades into voyeurism.

I also admire Wood, who in a few movies has emerged as a young actress who can bring an eerie conviction even to tricky and complex scenes. In *Thirteen* (2003), she played a good girl who makes the mistake of friendship with a girl her age who introduces her to drugs, sex, and lying. Here she essentially takes the other role and is just as convincing: She finds a coldness and heartlessness in Kimberly that moves beyond the high-school hellion category and into malevolence.

So the movie is daring and well acted. Yet it isn't very satisfying because the serious content keeps breaking through the soggy plot intended to contain it. The material in *Pretty Persuasion* needed to be handled as heavy drama or played completely for comedy, and by trying to have it both ways, the movie has it neither way. The audience gets emotional whiplash, its laughter interrupted by scenes where lives are destroyed.

I am also uneasy about the racism in the dialogue. I understand its purpose, I guess: to expose the way it works as a sickness, passed from generation to generation. But is the movie using its pose of exposing racism as a cover to slip in offensive jokes about Jews and Arabs that are, strictly speaking, not necessary to tell this story? It would have been interesting to see the movie with its opening-night audience and see if anyone laughed at those jokes. I have a feeling they might have, and for them, the point of the movie will be lost. It is, I admit, rather easily lost.

Pride & Prejudice ★ ★ ★ ★

PG, 127 m., 2005

Keira Knightley (Elizabeth Bennet), Matthew Macfadyen (Darcy), Brenda Blethyn (Mrs. Bennet), Donald Sutherland (Mr. Bennet), Simon Woods (Charles Bingley), Rupert Friend (Lieutenant Wickham), Tom Hollander (William Collins), Rosamund Pike (Jane Bennet), Jena Malone (Lydia Bennet), Judi Dench (Lady Catherine), Carey Mulligan (Kitty Bennet), Talulah Riley (Mary Bennet). Directed by Joe Wright and produced by Tim Bevan, Eric Fellner, and Paul Webster. Screenplay by Deborah Moggach, based on the novel by Jane Austen.

It is a truth universally acknowledged, that a single man in possession of a good fortune, must be in want of a wife.

Everybody knows the first sentence of Jane Austen's *Pride and Prejudice.* But the chapter ends with a truth equally acknowledged about Mrs. Bennet, who has five daughters in want of husbands: "The business of her life was to get her daughters married." Romance seems so urgent and delightful in Austen because marriage is a business, and her characters cannot help treating it as a pleasure. *Pride and Prejudice* is the best of her novels because its romance involves two people who were born to be in love, and who care not about business, pleasure, or each other. It is frustrating enough when one person refuses to fall in love, but when both refuse, we cannot rest until they kiss.

Of course all depends on who the people are. When Dorothea marries the Reverend Casaubon in Eliot's *Middlemarch,* it is a tragedy. She marries out of consideration and respect, which is all wrong; she should have married for money, always remembering that where money is, love often follows, since there is so much time for it. The crucial information about Mr. Bingley, the new neighbor of the Bennet family, is that he "has" an income of four or five thousand pounds a year. One never earns an income in these stories, one has it, and Mrs. Bennet (Brenda Blethyn) has her sights on it.

Her candidate for Mr. Bingley's hand is her eldest daughter, Jane; it is orderly to marry the girls off in sequence, avoiding the impression that an older one has been passed over. There is a dance, to which Bingley brings his friend Darcy. Jane and Bingley immediately fall in love, to get them out of the way of Darcy and Elizabeth, who is the second Bennet daughter. These two immediately dislike each other. Darcy is overheard telling his friend Bingley that Elizabeth is "tolerable, but not handsome enough to tempt *me.*" The person who overhears him is Elizabeth, who decides she will "loathe him for all eternity." She is advised within the family circle to count her blessings: "If he liked you, you'd have to talk to him."

These are the opening moves in Joe Wright's new film *Pride & Prejudice,* one of the most delightful and heartwarming adaptations made from Austen or anybody else. Much of the delight and most of the heart comes from Keira Knightley, who plays Elizabeth as a girl glowing in the first light of perfection. She is beautiful, she has opinions, she is kind but can be unforgiving. "They are all silly and ignorant like other girls," says her father in the novel, "but Lizzie has something more of quickness than her sisters."

Knightley's performance is so light and yet fierce that she makes the story almost realistic; this is not a well-mannered *Masterpiece*

Theatre but a film where strong-willed young people enter life with their minds at war with their hearts. The movie is more robust than most period romances. It is set earlier than most versions of the story, in the late 1700s, when Austen wrote the first draft; that was a period more down to earth than 1813, when she revised and published it. The young ladies don't look quite so much like illustrations for *Vanity Fair,* and there is mud around their hems when they come back from a walk. It is a time of rural realities: When Mrs. Bennet sends a daughter to visit Netherfield Park, the country residence of Mr. Bingley, she sends her on horseback, knowing it will rain and she will have to spend the night.

The plot by this point has grown complicated. It is a truth universally acknowledged by novelists that before two people can fall in love with each other, they must first seem determined to make the wrong marriage with someone else. It goes without saying that Lizzie fell in love with young Darcy (Matthew Macfadyen) the moment she saw him, but her pride has been wounded. She tells Jane: "I might more easily forgive his vanity had he not wounded mine."

The stakes grow higher. She is told by the dashing officer Wickham (Rupert Friend) that Darcy, his childhood friend, cheated him of a living that he deserved. And she believes that Darcy is responsible for having spirited Bingley off to London to keep him out of the hands of her sister Jane. Lizzie even begins to think she may be in love with Wickham. Certainly she is not in love with the Reverend Collins (Tom Hollander), who has a handsome living and would be Mrs. Bennet's choice for a match. When Collins proposes, the mother is in ecstasy, but Lizzie declines and is supported by her father (Donald Sutherland), a man whose love for his girls outweighs his wife's financial planning.

All of these characters meet and circle one another at a ball in the village Assembly Hall, and the camera circles them. The sequence involves one unbroken shot and has the same elegance as Visconti's long single take as he follows the count through the ballrooms in *The Leopard.* We see the characters interacting, we see Lizzie avoiding Collins and enticing Darcy, we understand the politics of these romances, and we are swept up in the intoxication of the dance. In a later scene, as Lizzie and Darcy dance together, everyone else somehow vanishes (in their eyes, certainly) and they are left alone within the love they feel.

But a lot must happen before the happy ending, and I particularly admired a scene in the rain where Darcy and Lizzie have an angry argument. This argument serves two purposes: It clears up misunderstandings, and it allows both characters to see each other as the true and brave people they really are. It is not enough for them to love each other; they must also love the goodness in each other, and that is where the story's true emotion lies.

The movie is well cast from top to bottom; like many British films, it benefits from the genius of its supporting players. Judi Dench brings merciless truth-telling to her role as a society arbiter; Sutherland is deeply amusing as a man who lives surrounded by women and considers it a blessing and a fate; and as his wife, Blethyn finds a balance between her character's mercenary and loving sides. She may seem unforgivably obsessed with money, but better be obsessed with money now than with poverty hereafter.

When Lizzie and Darcy finally accept each other in *Pride & Prejudice,* I felt an almost unreasonable happiness. Why was that? I am impervious to romance in most films, seeing it as a manifestation of box office requirements. Here it is different, because Darcy and Elizabeth are good and decent people who would rather do the right thing than convenience themselves. Anyone who will sacrifice their own happiness for higher considerations deserves to be happy. When they realize that about each other their hearts leap and, reader, so did mine.

Prime ★ ★ ★

PG-13, 105 m., 2005

Meryl Streep (Lisa Metzger), Uma Thurman (Rafi Gardet), Bryan Greenberg (David Bloomberg), Jon Abrahams (Morris), Madhur Jaffrey (Rita). Directed by Ben Younger and produced by Jennifer Todd and Suzanne Todd. Screenplay by Younger.

Flawed is a word movie critics use more often than jewelers. They have looked into the heart of a sparkling gem and found an imperfection. Every movie should be perfect, and on such grounds, *Prime* is flawed. Its flaw is that it employs an Idiot Plot in a story that is too serious to support it. I can forgive and even embrace an Idiot Plot in its proper place (consider Astaire and Rogers in *Top Hat*). But when the characters have depth and their decisions have consequences, I grow restless when their misunderstandings could be ended by words that the screenplay refuses to allow them to utter.

Prime is such a movie, yet I must recommend it because in its comedy of errors are actors who bring truth at least to their dialogue. Meryl Streep and Uma Thurman have line readings that work as delicate and precise adjustments of dangerous situations. They're dealing with issues that are real enough, even if they've been brought about by contrivance. And Streep has that ability to cut through the solemnity of a scene with a zinger that reveals how all human effort is, after all, comic at some level: How amusing, to think we can control fate!

The movie crosses two dependable story structures: (1) the romance between lovers widely separated in age, and (2) a mistaken identity that leads to complications. The trouble begins when Rafi Gardet (Uma Thurman) and David Bloomberg (Bryan Greenberg) fall in love. They know there is an age difference, but because they both lie a little, they don't realize how big it is: Rafi is thirty-seven and David is twenty-three.

Rafi discusses her concerns with her psychiatrist, Lisa Metzger (Streep), who argues tolerantly that if the relationship is otherwise sound and healthy, then age alone is not a reason to terminate it. In this matter Lisa is counseled by her own psychiatrist, Rita (Madhur Jaffrey). Now comes a spoiler warning for anyone who has not seen a commercial or trailer for the movie, where Universal eagerly reveals the plot secret. It is: David is Lisa's son. Since they have different last names and his age has been lied about, she has no reason to guess this. On one hand you have a hypothetical case of a man about twenty-seven dating a woman about thirty-four, and on the other you have the real case of a Jewish son of twenty-three dating a thirty-seven-year-old divorced Gentile. This disconnect creates some interesting moments for the Streep character, who is not narrow-minded but whose feelings as a mother are not hypothetical, while her opinions as an analyst certainly are.

Prime gets too much mileage by persisting in the device of the mistaken identity. But it does lead to interesting moments. After Lisa discovers to her horror that the man in Rafi's life is her son, she flees to her own psychiatrist for advice and is told she has a responsibility to her client. In my opinion, that responsibility is to declare a conflict of interest, but then I'm not a shrink and besides, then we wouldn't have a movie. So Lisa continues the sessions, and perhaps only Streep could produce such gradations of facial expressions as her client describes her son's lovemaking, his opinion of his mother, and admirable details of his physique.

As the movie develops, we're asked to take sides: Should this romance continue? I am in favor of love but do not believe it conquers all. Rafi's clock is ticking. David has no eagerness to be a father. Rafi is a babe who looks much younger than her years, but the day will come when someone assumes she is David's mother, and they had better be prepared for that day. There is also the religious difference, but here Lisa the psychiatrist strikes a reasonable note that I will leave for her to explain.

The movie works through the performances. The director, Ben Younger *(Boiler Room)*, does some nice things with scenes such as the family dinner where everyone makes nice and ignores the elephant in the room. There are some one-liners that zing not only with humor but also truth. On the whole I was satisfied. The Idiot Plot was necessary up to a point. I thought that point was too long delayed. It is also a problem that this is a comedy about matters that are not, in most people's lives, very funny. There is a final shot in which Rafi and David regard each other with affection and nostalgia, and I wondered if the characters were expressing something else, as well: the wish that they could meet in another movie and start over.

Private Property ★ ★ ★ ½

NO MPAA RATING, 95 m., 2007

Isabelle Huppert (Pascale), Yannick Renier (Francois), Jeremie Renier (Thierry), Kris Cuppens (Jan), Raphaelle Lubansu (Anne), Patrick Descamps (Luc). Directed by Joachim Lafosse and produced by Joseph Rouschop. Screenplay by Lafosse and Francois Pirot.

I met her near the beginning, at Cannes, sitting on the lawn of a villa sloping down toward the sea. It was 1977, the year Isabelle Huppert made

The Lacemaker. She was twenty-four, had already made more than a dozen features, starting at seventeen. She told me how that happened: "I walked up to the studio door in Paris, knocked, and said, 'I am here.'" She was. She has a quiet confidence that is almost terrifying.

At fifty-four, but looking no age at all in particular, she has made eighty-nine film and television projects. She works all the time. Everybody wants her. She told me: "When I need to escape, I get on a plane and fly to Chicago. It is my secret city. I go where I want, do what I want, nobody recognizes me, nobody can find me."

Now here she is in Joachim Lafosse's *Private Property.* She plays the divorced mother of twin sons, who treat her badly, which she allows. They live in a big country house outside a Belgian town, bought for them by her ex-husband when he left. The husband has remarried and has a child. She has started to date a man, and they talk about running a B&B somewhere. It is time for her to live her own life. Her sons don't think so.

They are Francois and Thierry, played by Yannick and Jeremie Renier, real-life brothers but not twins. Francois does odd jobs around the house and postpones his future; Thierry goes to school. The boys play games, they laze about, they are waited on hand and foot by their mother. Why should they leave? They have it good. They hate the new boyfriend and the fact that their mother is dating.

The film opens with Huppert, as Pascale, stripping and looking at herself intently in a mirror. Only Huppert could do this in quite the way she does. She is not presenting her nudity for examination; she is presenting her examination itself. One of the boys is watching her. If she realizes that (I think she does), it is a matter of indifference, as again later when she showers while another son is in the bathroom.

I don't think this is intended to signal incestuous feelings. I think it signals that too many barriers have fallen between them, and she cannot reconstruct the walls that all parents need to put up sometimes. The architect Christopher Alexander believes every house that has enough room should have a "couple's domain," an area off-limits for the children. Good fences make good families. Meals, we assure ourselves, "are the one time the family can get together." In this family, they work as war. Pascale cooks, sets the table, serves the meal, and then sits down to hostility from Thierry and silent, withdrawn embarrassment from Francois.

She wants to keep peace. She does it by suppressing her own feelings. She knows what she wants, her freedom, but she can't take it. Will the boys still be there when they are thirty? They're stuck on Mom. We remember Huppert's great performance in Michael Hancke's *The Piano Teacher* (2001), which won her the best actress prize at Cannes ("unanimously," the jury specified). She played a fortyish woman who was still living with her mother, sleeping in the same bed, masochistically mutilating herself, then taking retribution in the sadistic manipulation of young men she had studied carefully. Both films draw on some of the same compulsions and inhibitions.

What draws us into *Private Property* is how so many things happen under the surface, never commented upon. At any given moment, we cannot say for sure what the characters fully feel, since they often act at right angles to their emotions. Lafosse said at film festival interviews that he was not even sure if the film was primarily about the mother. Is she simply carried along on the tide of her family? Are they drifting out to sea?

The story's ending is brought about by actions involving the house. I will not be more specific. But it is hard to see how those actions could provoke all that happens. Sometimes the pressure in a family builds so that something relatively inconsequential pulls everything apart. We are accustomed to films in which the characters have fairly specific motivations. Huppert is inspired in the way she withdraws from confrontations and expresses her wishes enough to provoke others, but never enough to realize them. An emotional balancing act showing such weakness takes a strong actress to pull it off.

The Prize Winner of Defiance, Ohio ★ ★ ★ ½

PG-13, 99 m., 2005

Julianne Moore (Evelyn Ryan), Woody Harrelson (Kelly Ryan), Laura Dern (Dortha Schaefer), Trevor Morgan (Bruce Ryan at 16),

Ellary Porterfield (Tuff Ryan at 13–18), Simon Reynolds (Ray the Milkman), Frank Chiesurin (Freddy Canon). Directed by Jane Anderson and produced by Jack Rapke, Steve Starkey, and Robert Zemeckis. Screenplay by Anderson, based on the book by Terry Ryan.

The Prize Winner of Defiance, Ohio, said to tell a true story, subtitles itself: "How my mother raised ten kids on twenty-five words or less." And she does; in an era when companies gave valuable prizes for jingles and slogans, Evelyn Ryan is the best "contester" in America. She wins cash prizes, a deep freezer, trips, cars, and lots and lots of the sponsors' products. When her entry is chosen over 250,000 others in a big Dr Pepper contest, she proudly tells a daughter: "And it wasn't even my best one!"

Evelyn, played by Julianne Moore, is like the small-town cousin of Cathy, the Connecticut housewife she played in *Far From Heaven* (2002). Cathy was trapped in a sterile marriage and a world where men made all the decisions and women were locked in supporting roles. Judging by the body count around her dinner table in Ohio, Evelyn Ryan's marriage is not sterile, but it is a trap.

Her husband, Kelly (Woody Harrelson), puts back a six-pack and a pint of whiskey every night, drinking up his paycheck. He's a nice guy when he's sober but undergoes such terrifying personality changes that the family is afraid to enter the kitchen when he's listening to a baseball game. He never actually beats Evelyn, although she is sometimes injured as a side effect of his rages and suffers emotional anguish when he pounds on the brand-new freezer with a frying pan. When the cops are called, they stand around with him in the kitchen, discussing those Red Sox.

Evelyn handles her domestic situation with an eerie detachment and a relentless cheerfulness. She smiles, she looks on the bright side, she charms, she showers her children with attention and praise, and she lives tensely through her husband's rages. She doesn't scream at him but makes quiet comments about his drinking, and sad little asides he doesn't always understand. "You know what your problem is?" he says at one point. "You're too damn happy." A little later in the film, she tells him: "I don't need you to make me happy. I just need you to leave me alone when I am."

The power in the film comes from the disconnect between the anger and emotional violence in the marriage, and the way Evelyn keeps her dignity, protects her children, fights to put food on the table, and deals with a husband she always calls "Father." She is "Mother," of course. She has never been outside of Ohio, never had a spare dollar in the bank, never been able to express her creativity except through the contests. Moore plays this woman as a victim whose defenses are dignity and optimism. It's a performance of a performance, actually: Evelyn Ryan plays a role that conceals the despair in her heart.

The word "alcoholic" is never used in the household, although Kelly Ryan is a classic alcoholic. When the parish priest comes to offer advice, it is to advise Evelyn to submit and pray and support her husband; when he leaves, one of the kids observes that the priest's breath "smells just like Dad's."

There is a running battle with the milkman over the weekly bill. They are hours from being homeless when a contest prize allows them to put a down payment on a house. Homework goes on around the dining room table while Kelly, in the kitchen, swings between bitterness and tears; he feels shame because his wife supports the family with her contests, and it comes out either weepy or angry. Of course, if he would stop drinking and go to AA, he could hold up his end of the marriage, but that does not occur to him as a possibility.

"So far, three of my chicks have found their nests, and I am so very proud of them," Evelyn tells us in narration at one point. "That's where my prayers went. That's where they all went." It's the repetition, the use of the word "all," that carries the message. She did not pray for herself, or for her husband. She does have one ambition: to travel to Goshen, Indiana, for a meeting of a "Contester Club" convened by a fellow contestant (Laura Dern) who is a pen pal.

The movie is based on a memoir by Terry ("Tuff") Ryan, one of two children who became authors. The other kids all turned out well, too. The film ends with one of those moments that blindsides you with an unexpected surge of emotion. But for the most part *Prize Winner,* written and directed by Jane Anderson, avoids obvious sentiment and predictable emotion, and shows this woman somehow holding it together year after year, entering goofy contests that for her family mean life and death.

This is Anderson's feature film debut as a director, after work on television. As a writer, she was responsible for *The Positively True Adventures of the Alleged Texas Cheerleader-Murdering Mom* (1993), starring Holly Hunter in one of the lost treasures among recent films. She is fascinated by mothers driven to extremes by the problem of having all of the responsibility and none of the power.

The Producers ★ ★ ★

PG-13, 120 m., 2005

Nathan Lane (Max Bialystock), Matthew Broderick (Leo Bloom), Uma Thurman (Ulla), Will Ferrell (Franz Liebkind), Roger Bart (Carmen Ghia), Gary Beach (Roger De Bris), Jon Lovitz (Mr. Marks). Directed by Susan Stroman and produced by Mel Brooks and Jonathan Sanger. Screenplay by Brooks and Thomas Meehan.

I know the 1968 movie *The Producers* virtually by heart, and it's one of the funniest movies I've ever seen. That makes it tricky for me to review this 2005 musical version—both because it's different and because so often it is the same. There are stretches in Susan Stroman's opening scenes that follow Mel Brooks's 1968 version so closely it's as if Gus Van Sant, having finished his shot-by-shot remake of *Psycho*, advanced directly to this assignment.

The new movie is a success, that I know. How much of a success, I cannot be sure. Someone who has seen the original once or twice, or never, would be a better judge. It is unfair to observe of Nathan Lane and Matthew Broderick that they are not Zero Mostel and Gene Wilder, but there you have it: They're not.

There is poetic justice here. When Broderick and Lane left the Broadway and London productions and were replaced by other actors, their replacements were sniffed at in some quarters as "the road company." Now comes the movie, and in following Mostel and Wilder, *they* become the road company. Each and every actor in the 1968 movie, including Kenneth Mars, Christopher Hewett, Andreas Voutsinas, Lee Meredith, Dick Shawn, William Hickey, and Renée Taylor, was so perfectly cast that a kind of inevitability befell them.

Now I look at Uma Thurman as the sexpot Ulla and Will Ferrell as the Nazi playwright Franz, and I think they're really good, they bring both new and old things to their roles, but—well, it's just not fair to them for me to remember the older movie, but I cannot help myself. When they sing and dance, I like them the most, because they're not reminding me of anything from 1968. When Thurman refers to herself in the third person as "Ulla" and describes the high standards of her low conduct, she achieves a kind of joy of performance that deserves to be seen without Meredith standing just offstage tapping her toe.

The story itself is a great construction. Brooks wrote an original screenplay whose characters are driven by greed, need, neurosis, cheerfully shameful sexual behavior, and a deep cynicism about show business. It is a tribute to his work that it could be transferred virtually intact to the musical stage thirty-five years later and effortlessly become a historic hit.

The new songs written by Brooks embodied the original film's spirit, and Stroman added a few inspired touches, such as little old ladies choreographed with their walkers; they were transgressive in the same outrageous Brooks tradition. The only flaw was one of excess; in a scene set in prison toward the end, he has Lane recap virtually the entire movie as a one-man repertory troupe, and if it goes on too long, well, of course it does. Moderation is not a quality possessed by anyone associated with a movie that advises us, "If you've got it, baby—flaunt it!"

It is a tribute to this film that it worked for me despite my personal history. It was fun, it was funny, it was alive, although the color palette seemed to have darker colors and I remember the original as a movie made from golds and yellows and browns. There is a moment when Max Bialystock, the con-man producer, promises wealth and triumph to Leo Bloom, the nervous accountant who has cooked up their crooked financing, and a fountain erupts on cue behind him. In 1968 it was the fountain at Lincoln Center; now it's one in Central Park. I am absolutely incapable of judging the impact of this scene because I was startled and delighted in 1968, but watching this film I could hardly focus on the dialogue, I was so intent on waiting for the eruption.

So I had better end these meditations with a

simple observation: If I had fun, most other viewers are likely to have more fun, because they won't have my baggage. I've painted myself into a corner. I cannot do better than to end with my favorite Mel Brooks story. Mel and I were in an elevator in New York at the time of the original film, and a lady got on, looked at him, and said, "Sir, I have seen your film and it is vulgar!" Brooks replied: "Madame, my film rises below vulgarity."

The Promise ★ ½

PG-13, 103 m., 2006

Cecilia Cheung (Princess Qingcheng), Dong-Kun Jang (Kunlun), Hiroyuki Sanada (General Guangming), Nicolas Tse (Wuhuan), Liu Ye (Snow Wolf), Hong Chen (Manshen). Directed by Chen Kaige and produced by Chen Hong, Han Sanping, and Ernst "Etchie" Stroh. Screenplay by Chen Kaige and Zhang Tan.

The Promise is pretty much a mess of a movie; the acting is overwrought, the plot is too tangled to play like anything *but* a plot, and although I know you can create terrific special effects at home in the basement on your computer, the CGI work in this movie looks like it was done with a dial-up connection. What a disappointment from Chen Kaige, who has made great movies (*Farewell, My Concubine*) and no doubt will make them again.

The plot involves a touch of the crucial romantic misunderstanding in *Vertigo.* Princess Qingcheng (Cecilia Cheung) thinks she is in love with the great General Guangming (Hiroyuki Sanada), who has saved her life after she offended the king (Cheng Qian). But actually she is in love with the slave Kunlan (Dong-Kun Jang), who is impersonating the general. Kunlan has been assigned to protect the king from an outlander assassin named Wuhuan (Nicolas Tse) and another assassin named Snow Wolf (Liu Ye). This is all going to be on the final.

Qingcheng's love for the general (or Kunlan) is doomed whether or not she discovers that the former slave is impersonating his master. That is because in the early scenes of the movie, we saw Qingcheng as a child, being told by the Goddess Manshen (Chen Hong) that although she will have beauty and power and be a princess, she will lose every man she ever loves. This has possibilities. Since she loves Kunlan (thinking he is the general), what would happen if Kunlan were lost as per the prophecy, and she ended up with the real general? Would she then think she loved him and live happily ever after, not realizing he is not really the man she loves? Would her mistake grant him immunity? At some point I wanted James Stewart to appear and herd everybody up into a bell tower.

One of Kunlan's gifts is the ability to run really, really fast. I'm thinking of the Flash here. The problem with attaining that velocity is that Kunlan obviously must abandon the world of gravity and physical reality, and become a computer-generated graphic, and you know, it's a funny thing, CGI running may be faster than real running, but it never seems like anybody is really working at it. We're watching an effect instead of an achievement.

The CGI work in the movie is cheesy. One problem with CGI is that it inspires greed in directors. Chen Kaige reportedly had one thousand real extras for one of his battle scenes, and considering that Orson Welles put on a great battle in *Falstaff* with close-ups of about nine actors, that should have been plenty. But no. He uses CGI to multiply those soldiers until they take on all the reality of the hordes of *Troy,* who were so numerous that in one shot it was obvious they would all fit inside their city only by standing on each other's shoulders. Enough is enough.

Another difficulty is that the story is never organized clearly enough to generate much concern in our minds. The characters are not people but collections of attributes, and isn't it generally true that the more sensational an action scene, the less we care about the people in it? It's as if the scene signals us that it's about itself, and the characters are spectators just as we are.

I spent a fair amount of time puzzling over my notes and rummaging on the Web for hints about the details of the plot, and in the process discovered a new Movie Law. You are familiar with the Law of Symbolism: If you have to ask what something symbolized, it didn't. Now here is the Law of Plots: If you can't describe it with clarity, there wasn't one. I know someone will throw up *Syriana* as an objection, but there is a difference between a plot that is about confusion and a plot that is merely confused.

The Promotion ★ ★

R, 85 m., 2008

Seann William Scott (Doug), John C. Reilly (Richard), Jenna Fischer (Jen), Lili Taylor (Laurie), Fred Armisen (Scott), Gil Bellows (Board Exec), Bobby Cannavale (Dr. Timm), Rick Gonzalez (Ernesto). Directed by Steve Conrad and produced by Steven A. Jones and Jessika Borsiczky Goyer. Screenplay by Conrad.

The Promotion is a human comedy about two supermarket employees who are always ill at ease. It's their state of being. I felt a little ill at ease watching it because I was never quite sure whether I was supposed to be laughing at them or feeling sorry for them. It's one of those off-balance movies that seems to be searching for the right tone.

The setting: a Chicago supermarket. The central characters: Doug (Seann William Scott), thirty-three, a loyal employee, and Richard (John C. Reilly), mid-thirties, a Canadian who has immigrated to America with his Scottish wife, Laurie (Lili Taylor), and their daughter. Doug is recently married to Jen (Jenna Fischer). When their supermarket chain decides to open a new store, the two men are in line for a promotion to store manager.

They both desperately desire and need this job. Doug has convinced his wife he's a "shoo-in," and they invest all of their savings in a nonrefundable deposit on a house. Richard is a recovering alcoholic and drug addict, now in AA, trying to prove he is a trustworthy husband and father. The two men fight for the job not in a slapstick way but in an understated, underhanded way that Doug feels bad about, Richard not so much. ("We're all just out here to get some food," Richard philosophizes. "Sometimes we bump into each other.")

The movie is unusually quiet and introspective for a comedy. Doug provides a narration, and Richard gets one of his own in the form of a self-help tape he obsessively listens to. Doug decides Richard is a "nice guy" and observes, "all Canadians are nice." That's before Richard fakes an injury to lodge a dreaded "in-store complaint" that could cost Doug his job.

Richard himself is on a self-destruct mission. Consider an episode when Doug hits a young black man who has thrown a bottle of Yoo-Hoo at him in the parking lot. Doug apologizes to a "community forum," backed up by a panel including Richard and the store's board of directors. He says something about a "few bad apples." Apology accepted. Afterward, however, when they're all standing around relieved, Richard tells one of the community leaders, "You are not a black apple to me." Explaining this digs him in deeper, until he's reduced to speechlessness. He has a gift for saying the wrong things at the wrong times.

Richard actually is nice at times, however. As a member of a motorcycle gang, he once watched his fellow members roar through a toll gate without paying, and then sheepishly told the collector, "I'll pay for them all." Doug empathizes with Richard, even to the point of defending him to the board, but he feels rotten inside: Having lied to his wife that he has the job, he finds a present of long-sleeve shirts they can't afford. He's afraid he's stuck in the ranks of the short-sleeve guys.

I was interested in the fates of these two men, but mildly. I was expected to laugh, but I only smiled. Some of the race-based situations made me feel uncomfortable. All of the characters, especially the straight-arrow chairman of the board (Gil Bellows), needed to be pushed further into the realms of comedy. More could have been done with the store's other employees. At the end of *The Promotion,* I wondered what the atmosphere was like on the set every day. How does it feel to make a movie where the characters don't seem sure who they are?

Proof ★ ★ ★ ★

PG-13, 99 m., 2005

Gwyneth Paltrow (Catherine), Anthony Hopkins (Robert), Hope Davis (Claire), Jake Gyllenhaal (Hal). Directed by John Madden and produced by John Hart, Robert Kessel, Alison Owen, and Jeff Sharp. Screenplay by David Auburn and Rebecca Miller, based on the play by David Auburn.

John Madden's *Proof* is an extraordinary thriller about matters of scholarship and the heart, about the true authorship of a mathematical proof and the passions that coil around it. It is a rare movie that gets the tone of a university campus exactly right and at the same time communicates so easily that you don't need to know the slightest thing about math to understand it. Take it from me.

The film centers on two remarkable performances, by Gwyneth Paltrow and Hope Davis, as Catherine and Claire, the daughters of a mathematician so brilliant that his work transformed the field and has not yet been surpassed. But his work was done years ago, and at the age of twenty-six or twenty-seven he began to "get sick," as the family puts it. This man, named Robert and played by Anthony Hopkins, still has occasional moments of lucidity, but he lives mostly in delusion, filling up one notebook after another with meaningless scribbles. Yet he remains on the University of Chicago faculty, where he has already made a lifetime's contribution; his presence and rare remissions are inspiring. Recently he had a year when he was "better."

Catherine was a brilliant math student, too—at Northwestern, because she wanted to be free of her father. But she returned home to care for him when he got worse, and her life has been defined by her father and the family home. Hal (Jake Gyllenhaal), her father's student and assistant, is hopelessly in love with her; she shies away from intimacy and suspects his motives. Most of the movie takes place after the father's death (flashbacks show him in life and imagination), and Hal is going through the notebooks. "Hoping to find something of my dad's you could publish?" Catherine asks him in a moment of anger.

Claire, the older sister, flies in from New York and makes immediate plans to sell the family home to the university: "They've been after it for years." Catherine is outraged, but the movie subtly shows how Claire, not the brilliant sister, is the dominant one. There is the sinister possibility that she thinks (in all sincerity) that Catherine may have inherited the family illness and should not be allowed to stay alone in Chicago. Claire expresses love and support for her sister in terms that are frightening.

There is a locked drawer in Robert's desk. Catherine gives Hal the key. It contains what may be a revolutionary advance on Robert's earlier work; a new mathematical proof of incalculable importance. Did Robert somehow write this in a fleeting moment of clarity? The authorship of the proof brings into play all of the human dynamics that have been established among Catherine and Claire and Hal, and indeed among all of them and the ghostly presence of the father.

Proof, based on the award-winning Broadway and London play by David Auburn, contains one scene after another that is pitch-perfect in its command of how academics talk and live. Having once spent a year as a University of Chicago doctoral candidate, I felt as if I were back on campus. There is a memorial service at which the speaker (Gary Houston) sounds precisely as such speakers sound; his subject is simultaneously the dead mathematician and his sense of his own importance. There is a faculty party at which all of the right notes are sounded. And when Catherine and Hal speak, they talk as friends, lovers, and fellow mathematicians; they communicate in several languages while speaking only one.

What makes the movie deep and urgent is that Catherine is motivated by conflicting desires. She wants to be a great mathematician but does not want to hurt or shame her father. She wants to be a loyal daughter and yet stand alone as herself. She half-believes her older sister's persuasive smothering. She half-believes Hal loves her only for herself. At the bottom, she only half-believes in herself. That's why the Paltrow performance is so fascinating: It's essentially about a woman whose destiny is in her own hands, but she can't make them close on it.

It would be natural to compare *Proof* with *A Beautiful Mind* (2001), another movie about a brilliant and mad mathematician. But they are miles apart. *A Beautiful Mind* tries to enter the world of the madman. *Proof* locates itself in the mind of the madman's daughter, who loves him and sorrows for him, who has lived in his shadow so long she fears the light and the things that go with it.

Note: It doesn't make the movie any better or worse, but it's unique in that all of the locations match. There are no impossible journeys or nonexistent freeway exits. The trip from Hyde Park to Evanston reflects the way you really do get there. So real do the locations feel that it's a shock to find that most of the interiors were filmed in England; they match the Chicago locations seamlessly.

The Proposition ★ ★ ★ ★

R, 104 m., 2006

Guy Pearce (Charlie Burns), Ray Winstone (Captain Stanley), Danny Huston (Arthur Burns), John Hurt (Jellon Lamb), David Wenham (Eden Fletcher), Emily Watson (Martha Stanley), David Gulpilil (Jacko), Richard Wilson (Mike Burns), Tommy Lewis (Two Bob). Directed by John Hillcoat and produced by Chris Brown, Chiara Menage, Cat Villiers, and Jackie O'Sullivan. Screenplay by Nick Cave.

The Proposition plays like a Western moved from Colorado to hell. The characters are familiar: the desperado brothers, the zealous lawman, his civilized wife, the corrupt mayor, the old coots, the resentful natives. But the setting is the outback of Australia as I have never seen it before. These spaces don't seem wide open because an oppressive sky glares down at the sullen earth; this world is sunbaked, hostile, and unforgiving, and it breeds heartless men.

Have you read *Blood Meridian,* the novel by Cormac McCarthy? This movie comes close to realizing the vision of that dread and despairing story. The critic Harold Bloom believes no other living American novelist has written a book as strong. He compares it with Faulkner and Melville but confesses his first two attempts to read it failed, "because I flinched from the overwhelming carnage."

That book features a character known as the Judge, a tall, bald, remorseless bounty hunter who essentially wants to kill anyone he can, until he dies. His dialogue is peculiar, the speech of an educated man. *The Proposition* has such a character in an outlaw named Arthur Burns, who is much given to poetic quotations. He is played by Danny Huston in a performance of remarkable focus and savagery. Against him is Captain Stanley (Ray Winstone), who is not precisely a sheriff since this land is not precisely a place where the law exists. He is more of an Ahab, obsessed with tracking down Arthur Burns and his brothers Charlie (Guy Pearce) and Mike (Richard Wilson). They are not merely outlaws, desperadoes, and villains but are dedicated to evil for its own sake, and the film opens with a photograph labeled "Scene of the Hopkins Outrage." The Burns boys murdered the Hopkins family, pregnant wife and all, perhaps more for entertainment than gain.

Ray Winstone, who often plays villains, is one of the best actors now at work in movies (see him in *Sexy Beast, Ripley's Game, Last Orders*). Here he plays a man who would be fearsome enough in an ordinary land but pales before the malevolence of the Burns brothers. He lives with Martha (Emily Watson), his fragrant wife from England, who fences off a portion of wilderness, calls it their lawn, plants rosebushes there, serves him his breakfast egg, and behaves, as colonial women did in Victorian times, as if still at "home."

"I will civilize this land," Captain Stanley says. In the 1880s, it is an achievement as likely as Ahab capturing the whale. He is able to capture Charlie and Mike Burns: Mike, a youth like the Kid in *Blood Meridian,* still half-formed but schooled only in desperation, and Charlie, an inward, brooding, damaged man whose feelings are as instinctive as a kicked dog. The captain is not happy with his prisoners because he lacks the real prize. He makes a proposition to Charlie. If Charlie tracks and kills his brother Arthur, the captain will spare both Charlie and Mike.

Charlie sets off on this mission. He feels no particular filial love for Arthur; they are bonded mostly by mutual hatred of others. The captain himself ventures out on the trail, finding such settlers as have chosen to live in exile and punishment. The most colorful—no, "colorful" is not a word for this movie—the most gnarled and cured by the sun is Jellon Lamb, played by John Hurt as if he is made of jerky.

Why do you want to see this movie? Perhaps you don't. Perhaps, like Bloom, it will take you more than one try to face the carnage. But the director, John Hillcoat, working from a screenplay by Nick Cave (the sometime punk rocker and actor in *Johnny Suede*), has made a movie you cannot turn away from; it is so pitiless and uncompromising, so filled with pathos and disregarded innocence, that it is a record of those things we pray to be delivered from. The actors invest their characters with human details all the scarier because they scarcely seem human themselves. In what place within Arthur Burns does poetry reside?

What does he feel as he quotes it? What does Martha, the Emily Watson character, really think as she uncrates a Christmas tree she has had shipped in from another lifetime? If Captain Stanley is as tender toward her as he seems, why has he brought her to live in these badlands?

What of the land itself? There is a sense of palpable fear of the outback in many Australian films, from *Walkabout* to *Japanese Story*, not neglecting the tamer landscapes in *Picnic at Hanging Rock*. There is the sense that spaces there are too empty to admit human content. There are times in *The Proposition* when you think the characters might abandon their human concerns and simply flee from the land itself.

And what of the Aborigines, who inhabit this landscape more or less invisibly and have their own treaty with it? The Stanleys have a house servant named Two Bob, played by Tommy Lewis, who sizes up the situation and walks away one day, carefully removing his shoes, which remain in the garden.

Pure ★ ★ ★

NO MPAA RATING, 96 m., 2005

Molly Parker (Mel), Harry Eden (Paul), Vinnie Hunter (Lee), David Wenham (Lenny), Keira Knightley (Louise), Geraldine McEwan (Nanna), Marsha Thomason (Vicki), Gary Lewis (Detective French). Directed by Gillies MacKinnon and produced by Howard Burch. Screenplay by Alison Hume.

If acting is so hard, why are so many children so good at it? Perhaps they're still in direct touch with emotions that adults have to reach through their art. Consider Harry Eden, who plays ten-year-old boy Paul in *Pure*. In the movie's first scene, he is making breakfast in bed for his mother, Mel (Molly Parker). This involves preparing a hit of heroin. "I told you never to touch my medicine," she says when she sees what he has done. And then: "Are you sure you made it up properly?"

Paul is sure. He has seen his mother do it countless times. He still barely believes the story that the drug is "medicine," and during the movie he will learn the truths that are right there to be seen all around him: His mother is a junkie, her boyfriend, Lenny (David Wenham), is a dealer, her best friend, Vicki (Marsha Thomason), claims she's not an addict because she only smokes crack instead of shooting up. The film's story centers on Paul, and Eden plays him as a good-hearted, frighteningly sincere kid who desperately tries to deal with a situation beyond his understanding. Where the performance comes from, I can't say, but there it is: strong, sure, touching.

Paul and his younger brother, Lee, live with his mother in a London welfare estate. His dad is dead of a heart attack; drugs may have had something to do with that, but we don't know. Lenny was his dad's best friend and is now his mother's lover and supplier. He's a hard man, but not as hard as some drug dealers we've seen; he likes Mel, and he thinks that supplying her addiction is a form of helping her.

Addiction wears down ordinary standards of human conduct until people behave in ways they would have considered unthinkable. Consider Vicki, a hooker whose small child, Rose, is sometimes watched by Mel. Mel is on the bus with the baby, and a man who says he is a doctor tells her the child has an infection and needs immediate attention. What Mel does then makes sense only if you understand that heroin has to come first before anything else in her life can proceed.

Paul is always on the move, running or riding his bicycle, acting as a parent for Lee and in a way for his mother. He makes friends where he finds them. The waitress Louise (Keira Knightley), for example, is nice to him and he confides in her. Like everyone in his world, she's into drugs. Eventually he asks her if he can try some: "I want to know how Mom feels." Her first response: "You can wait until you're eleven."

Always lurking about is a police detective (Gary Lewis) who knows that Lenny is an important supplier in the neighborhood but can't prove it. As the plot plays out, young Paul finds himself involved in the game between Lenny and the detective, in ways he does not understand or even guess.

One scene in the movie is painful almost beyond describing. Mel determines to get off drugs, cold turkey. She will lock herself in her room and Paul is not to listen to her, no matter what she says, until she is clean. To assist in this process, her resourceful son nails her bedroom door shut. This leads to a confrontation between mother and son that no child should ever have to endure, although I have a sad feeling that many do.

Parker is an extraordinary actress of the ordinary. In the strange and daring *Kissed* (1996), she played a necrophiliac employee of a funeral home whose feelings about the dead were not only perverse but, in an inexplicable way, tender and sorrowful as well. Not many actresses could have made the role acceptable, let alone believable, but Parker did. She did it by calmly accepting the reality of her character and never stepping outside it. Here she plays a drug addict whose treatment of her children is cruel and uncaring, and yet she is the best mother it is possible for her to be. She doesn't make Mel into a grotesque caricature; Mel is even more disturbing, really, because she tries to behave better than the drugs will allow her to.

One of the movie's intriguing qualities is that its horrors take place within a world that is not as cruel and painful as we know it could be. Mel's association with Lenny makes the getting of drugs safer and more manageable, and in a way she can kid herself that she leads a normal enough life except for this one area she imagines to be private. Paul has somehow been raised well enough to be capable and self-confident; we sense he will not be destroyed by his childhood. Lenny, like the hero of *Layer Cake* (2005) believes drug dealing can be run like a reasonable business, without unnecessary risk or violence. They are all living in foolishness and self-deception, but there are days that must seem almost normal and happy. After the medicine.

P2 ★ ★ ★

R, 98 m., 2007

Rachel Nichols (Angela Bridges), Wes Bentley (Thomas). Directed by Franck Khalfoun and produced by Alexandre Aja, Gregory Levasseur, Patrick Wachsberger, and Erik Feig. Screenplay by Aja, Khalfoun, and Levasseur.

If you have seen the ads for *P2*, or even heard about them, you know what the movie involves. A woman works late in the office on Christmas Eve, leaves after everyone else, descends to parking level P-2 to get her car, finds it won't start, and then meets the homicidal madman who is the overnight lot attendant. Yes, I know, it sounds like a formula slasher film, but it's actually done well, and in the current climate at least most Women in Danger films end up with Men in Danger. There were elements of *P2* that even reminded me a little of Jodie Foster's *Panic Room*—especially in complexities involving cell phones, alarms, spycams, and doors that are locked or unlocked.

The movie benefits from being played about as straight as it can be, given the material. Rachel Nichols, as the endangered heroine, Angela, doesn't do stupid things or make obvious mistakes. And Wes Bentley, as Thomas, the lonely guy on overnight duty, doesn't froth at the mouth or cackle with insane zeal. Oh, he's insane, all right, but he's one of those insane lonely guys who can't understand why Angela doesn't want to share his Christmas dinner (turkey and trimmings, and even corn muffins!), even though he has stripped her to her negligee, chained her to the furniture, and has a savage dog lunging at her. He's just trying to be friends.

A movie like this depends on invention in the screenplay. You can't merely have the woman running around frantically while the guy pops up in the foreground with a standard horror movie swooshing sound. There has to be a little logic. And Angela thinks of most of the right things to do, even though most of the time she can't do them. In today's high-security climate, if you're locked in, you're locked in. One day when we have more time, I'll tell you about when I went for a winter stroll in London's Hyde Park and didn't know the gates were locked at six, and how it started snowing while I was trying to climb a slushy hill to get to a tree branch that I thought might allow me to drop over a six-foot fence with sharp spikes on the top, and how when I balanced on the tree and called for help to passers-by, they walked a little faster.

It's that kind of an evening for Angela. She does everything right, but it doesn't work. And when she somehow gets out a garbled call for help on 911, two cops turn up and *they* do everything right, too. Often in thrillers the cops are practically standing on a dead body and don't notice anything. But these guys are pros, they follow the ropes, they don't buy Thomas's story at face value, and *still* they don't save Angela. It's a lot more exciting that way.

This is, in case you haven't noticed, the best autumn for movies in years. There are a dozen, maybe two dozen, movies in current release that I would recommend over *P2*. Maybe four dozen. Maybe three dozen. But horror movies routinely *win the weekend* at the box office, and it is no small consolation that the customers who insist on their horror movie this weekend will see a well-made one. It's such a good season that even the slashers are superior.

Q

The Queen ★ ★ ★ ★

PG-13, 97 m., 2006

Helen Mirren (Queen Elizabeth II), Michael Sheen (Tony Blair), James Cromwell (Prince Philip), Sylvia Syms (Queen Mother), Paul Barrett (Trevor Rees-Jones), Helen McCrory (Cherie Blair). Directed by Stephen Frears and produced by Andy Harries, Christine Langan, and Tracey Seaward. Screenplay by Peter Morgan.

The opening shots of Stephen Frears's *The Queen* simply show Helen Mirren's face as her character prepares for it to be seen. She is Queen Elizabeth II, and we know that at once. The resemblance is not merely physical but embodies the very nature of the Elizabeth we have grown up with—a private woman who takes her public role with great gravity.

Elizabeth is preparing to meet Tony Blair (Michael Sheen), the new Labor prime minister who has just been elected in a landslide. We see Blair preparing for the same meeting. His election was a fundamental upheaval of British political life after Thatcherism, and Britain stands on a threshold of uncertain but possibly tumultuous change.

Within months, the queen and Blair will find themselves in a crisis that involves not politics but a personal tragedy that was completely unforeseen—the death of Diana, princess of Wales, in a Paris car crash. *The Queen* tells the story of how her death with her boyfriend, the playboy department store heir Dodi Fayed, would threaten to shake the very monarchy itself. Told in quiet scenes of proper behavior and guarded speech, *The Queen* is a spellbinding story of opposed passions—of Elizabeth's icy resolve to keep the royal family separate and aloof from the death of the divorced Diana, who was legally no longer a royal, and of Blair's correct reading of the public mood, which demanded some sort of public expression of sympathy from the Crown for the "People's Princess."

It was extraordinary, the grief people felt after her death. I was reminded of the weeks after the assassination of Kennedy. Was it out of proportion to Diana's objective importance? She was a young woman almost cynically picked for her marriage, who provided the Crown with its required heirs, who was a photogenic escort for Charles, who found no love from her husband; it was no secret they both had affairs during their marriage. Divorced, her dating choices were peculiar. She died in a late-night crash while being pursued by paparazzi. Yet it was as if a saint had been taken from our midst. Yes, Diana devoted much time to doing good. Yes, I believe she was sincere. But doing good was part of her job description; she signed on for it. In death, the impact was as if a great national hero had died.

The Queen is told almost entirely in small scenes of personal conflict. It creates an uncanny sense that it knows what goes on backstage in the monarchy; the queen, Philip, and the Queen Mother have settled into a sterile domesticity cocooned by servants and civil servants. It shows Tony and Cherie Blair (Helen McCrory) in their own bourgeois domestic environment. Both households, privately, are plainspoken to the point of bluntness, and Cherie is more left-wing than her husband, less instinctively awed by the monarchy, more inclined to dump the institution.

What Tony clearly sees is that the monarchy could be gravely harmed, if not toppled, by the queen's insistence in sticking to protocol and not issuing a statement about Diana. The press demands Elizabeth fly the flag at half-mast as a symbolic gesture at Buckingham Palace. Elizabeth stands firm. The palace will not acknowledge the death or sponsor the funeral.

The Queen comes down to the story of two strong women loyal to the doctrines of their beliefs about the monarchy, and a man who is much more pragmatic.

The queen is correct, technically, in not lowering the flag to half-mast; it is not a national flag, but her own, flown only when she is in residence. But Blair is correct that the flag has become a lightning rod for public opinion. The queen is correct, indeed, by tradition and history in all she says about the affair—but she is sadly aloof from the national mood. Well, maybe queens should be.

Certainly that's what the Queen Mum thinks. Played by Sylvia Syms, she is shown at ninety-plus years still tart and sharp-witted. When at the last minute the palace needs a protocol plan for the funeral, time is so short that the Queen Mum's own funeral plan has to be borrowed and modified. Sylvia Syms has a priceless reaction where she learns that her honor guard, all servicemen, will be replaced by celebrities—even, gasp, Elton John.

The Queen could have been told as a scandal-sheet story of celebrity gossip. Instead, it becomes the hypnotic story of two views of the same event—a classic demonstration, in high drama, of how the Establishment has been undermined by publicity. I think it possible that Thatcher might have supported the queen. That would be impossible to the populist Blair.

Stephen Frears, the director, has made several wonderful films about conflicts and harmonies in the British class system (*My Beautiful Laundrette, Dirty Pretty Things, Prick Up Your Ears*) and *The Queen,* of course, represents the ultimate contrast. No one is more upper-class than the queen, and Tony Blair is profoundly middle-class.

The screenplay is intense, focused, literate, observant. The dynamic between Elizabeth and Philip (James Cromwell), for example, is almost entirely defined by decades of what has not been said between them—and what need not be said. There are extraordinary, tantalizing glimpses of the *real* Elizabeth driving her own Range Rover, leading her dogs, trekking her lands at Balmoral—the kind of woman, indeed, who seems more like Camilla Parker-Bowles than Diana.

Mirren is the key to it all. She finds a way, even in a behind-the-scenes docudrama, to suggest that part of her character will always be behind the scenes. What a masterful performance, built on suggestion, implication, and understatement. Her queen in the end authorizes the inevitable state funeral, but it is a tribute to Mirren that we have lingering doubts about whether, objectively, it was the right thing. Technically, the queen was right to consider the divorced Diana no longer deserving (by her own choice) of a royal funeral. But in terms of modern celebrity worship, she was wrong. This may or may not represent progress.

R

Racing Stripes ★★

PG, 101 m., 2005

Bruce Greenwood (Nolan Walsh), Hayden Panettiere (Channing Walsh), M. Emmet Walsh (Woodzie), Wendie Malick (Clara Dalrymple). And the voices of: Frankie Muniz (Stripes), Mandy Moore (Sandy), Michael Clarke Duncan (Clydesdale), Jeff Foxworthy (Reggie), Joshua Jackson (Trenton's Pride), Joe Pantoliano (Goose), Michael Rosenbaum (Ruffshodd), Steve Harvey (Buzz), David Spade (Scuzz), Snoop Dogg (Lightning), Fred Dalton Thompson (Sir Trenton), Dustin Hoffman (Tucker), Whoopi Goldberg (Franny). Directed by Frederik Du Chau and produced by Broderick Johnson, Andrew A. Kosove, Edward McDonnell, and Lloyd Phillips. Screenplay by David Schmidt.

Racing Stripes is a compromise between *National Velvet* and *Babe,* leading to the inescapable question: Why not see them instead of this? It tells the story of the young girl who has faith in a disregarded animal and rides it to victory in a derby, and it has the barnyard full of cute talking animals. There are kids who will like it, but then there are kids who are so happy to be at the movies that they like everything. Adults are going to find it a little heavy on barnyard humor.

The story: On a night journey, a circus truck breaks down, and when the caravan resumes its journey, a basket has been forgotten by the side of the road. It contains a baby zebra. Horse trainer Nolan Walsh (Bruce Greenwood) and his daughter, Channing (Hayden Panettiere), find the orphan. Nolan wants to trace its owners, but Channing, of course, falls in love with it and wants it for a pet. It wouldn't seem that hard to find the owners of a baby zebra in Kentucky, but Nolan agrees, and the baby is named Stripes.

The Walsh farm occupies high ground above a race track, which absorbs much of the attention of the farm's animals. Walsh himself was a trainer, we learn, until he fell into depression after his wife died in a riding accident. He has forbidden Channing to follow her lifelong dream of being a jockey, but are we all agreed it's only a matter of time until she rides Stripes to victory in the local derby?

The animals in the movie are all real animals, except for the animated flies (voices by Steve Harvey and David Spade). Computer effects are used, however, to synch their mouths with the dialogue—an effect that's a little creepy. Cartoon animals have a full range of facial expressions, but when real animals are given CGI lip movements there often seems to be a disconnect between the lips and the face.

The Walsh farm is that anachronism in these days of agribusiness, a diversified barnyard filled with examples of every farm animal that might show promise as a character. They're voiced by actors who are quickly identifiable (Dustin Hoffman as a short-tempered Shetland, Joe Pantoliano as a goose who seems to be hiding out from the mob, Whoopi Goldberg as a goat, and Mandy Moore as a mare who falls in love with Stripes, although the movie wisely avoids the question of what would happen should they decide to begin a family). Stripes is voiced by Frankie Muniz of *Agent Cody Banks* and the wonderful *My Dog Skip* (an infinitely better movie about a friendship between a kid and his pet).

The racetrack is run by a Cruella DeVille type named Clara Dalrymple (Wendie Malick), reminding us of how reliable Dalrymple is as a movie name for upper-crust snobs. Her own horse, Trenton's Pride (voiced by Joshua Jackson), is favored to win the derby, and she doesn't see any point in letting a zebra enter the race. In a way, she has logic on her side. It's a horse race. There aren't any gazelles or ostriches, either.

I will get the usual feedback from readers who took their children to see *Racing Stripes* and report that the whole family loved the movie. For them, I am happy. It is a desperate thing to be at a movie with children who are having a bad time. But when you think of the *Babe* pictures, and indeed, even an animated cartoon like *Home on the Range,* you realize *Stripes* is on autopilot with all of the usual elements: a heroine missing one parent, an animal missing both, an underdog (or underzebra), cute animals, the big race. This is the kind of movie you might grab at the video store, but it's not worth the trip to the theater.

Rails & Ties ★ ★ ½

PG-13, 101 m., 2007

Kevin Bacon (Tom Stark), Marcia Gay Harden (Megan Stark), Miles Heizer (Davey Danner), Marin Hinkle (Renee), Eugene Byrd (Otis Higgs), Bonnie Root (Laura Danner). Directed by Alison Eastwood and produced by Robert Lorenz, Peer Oppenheimer, and Barrett Stuart. Screenplay by Micky Levy.

Sometimes there's a movie that has better things in it than the underlying material deserves. Alison Eastwood's *Rails & Ties* is a movie like that. I found the opening third tremendously intriguing and involving—I thought the emotions were so real they could be touched—but then the film lost its way and fell into the clutches of sentimental melodrama.

It opens on a railroad engineer going to work. This is Tom Stark (Kevin Bacon), and he not merely loves his job but feels a sense of duty about it that is part of the fiber of his being. He has been told he can take the day off because of bad news he has received about the health of his wife. But he wouldn't think of it. He follows the railroad book on all things, including life and death.

We meet his wife, Megan (Marcia Gay Harden), who is dying of cancer and filled with fear and grief, and she has some moments that are heartbreaking. She needs her husband, or maybe she needs a husband who could be emotionally available to her; Tom is not there for her and hasn't been for years, pouring all of his passion into trains. At work, he's behind the throttle, and at home, he's tinkering with his elaborate model train layout.

We meet another mother and her young son. This is Laura Danner (Bonnie Root), who has big problems and has taken a lot of pills and parked her car on the tracks with her nine-year-old son, Davey (Miles Heizer), belted in next to her. Coming around a bend, Tom sees the car on the tracks but makes a snap judgment that an emergency stop might throw cars off the track and injure passengers. His co-engineer (Eugene Byrd) begs him to brake, but Tom knows the book, the book covers the situation, and the book says not to brake. Davey gets out of the car, tries to pull his mother free, and jumps aside just seconds before he would have been killed along with her.

"He didn't even *try* to stop!" Davey says over and over again. Tom Stark knows there will be a hearing but is confident he will get a pass because he was following the book. And all of that, up to there and for several more scenes, plays immediate and true. But then the movie veers into a more standard storytelling pattern. Because much of it is well done, for what it is, I won't reveal key details. But assume that in one way or another the boy has good reason to escape from a foster home, and that he finds a way to meet Tom and Megan Stark.

Yes, he feels anger toward the man. Perhaps some of it is displaced from his mom, whose decision to park on the tracks remains a troubling mystery to him. The way things work out, his visit to the Starks, which should have been over almost immediately, seems to extend indefinitely. And they begin to love each other.

This in itself is not an unworthy plot development, but somehow the urgency of Megan's early grief and Tom's early emotional stonewalling gets channeled into acceptable, safe, narrative strategies. We can relax. The story will steer us safely past unacceptable despair. There is even a scene involving the model train layout to clear the air because, yes, Davey likes trains about as much as Tom does. And then one development leads to another and everything leads up to a final scene and a final shot that I found myself rejecting emotionally.

I know in the real world that what happens at the end of the movie is likely enough. But other outcomes are possible, and given the places the movie took me and the implicit promises it made, I found no release or closure in the ending. In a movie that detoured into emotional manipulation, I found myself, paradoxically, wanting more manipulation. When a movie jumps the tracks of implacable logic, you may regret it, but you go along with it because you have to. The last thing you want is for it to jump back on the tracks.

That is not to overlook the qualities of *Rails & Ties,* above all in the acting. Marcia Gay Harden has a scene by herself that defines hopelessness and desolation. Kevin Bacon makes it clear, without even seeming to try, why the railroad is his fortress and its rule book is his bible. And young Miles Heizer does such a good job with the nine-year-old that I repeat a recent observation: Have you noticed in a lot of movies how natural, convincing, and pure the performances of the child actors are?

Alison Eastwood (Clint's daughter) must be a good director, because she can place those qualities on the screen. I wish I knew more about the history of the Micky Levy screenplay—whether it went through rewrites, was steered in a wrong direction, was questioned. When the film premiered at Telluride and Toronto, there were some who doubted coincidences involving characters and trains. Those sorts of things go with the territory, and I find it interesting that the screenplay risked them. But there were fundamental decisions to be made about the lives and fates of these characters, and I think somehow the filmmakers lost the way—lost sight of the people inside the plot.

The Rape of Europa ★ ★ ★

NO MPAA RATING, 117 m., 2008

Joan Allen (Narrator). A documentary written, produced, and directed by Richard Berge, Nicole Newnham, and Bonni Cohen, based on the book by Lynn H. Nicholas.

We know the Nazis looted art from the nations they overran. Maybe we've seen *The Train* (1964) and know how one shipment was thwarted. But how many important paintings, sculptures, and other artworks would you say the Nazis made off with? Hundreds? Thousands?

The Rape of Europa, a startling documentary, puts the number rather higher: *one-fifth* of all the known significant works of art in Europe—millions. Incredibly, Hitler maintained shopping lists of art for every country he invaded and dispatched troops to secure (i.e., plunder) the works and ship them back to Germany. He had plans to build a monumental art museum in Linz, his Austrian birthplace, and was working on models of the structure even during his final days in the Berlin bunker. His right-hand man Goering was no less keen as a collector.

That Hitler was mad is well known. That he was mad about art, not so well. He was, in his youth, an ambitious painter and applied to an art school in Vienna but was rejected. The general outline of his early art career, somewhat fictionalized, can be seen in *Max,* a little-noticed 2002 film starring Noah Taylor as Hitler and John Cusack as a one-armed Jewish art dealer in Munich who befriends Hitler, his liquor deliveryman.

Hitler's art was not good (we see some landscape watercolors), and his taste in art was terrible. He had a weakness for heroic Nordic supermen and women in a style of uber-kitsch, and he believed modern art was Jewish and decadent. In addition to the artworks he looted, he ordered the destruction of countless others; not all of those Nazi bonfires consumed only books.

This absorbing documentary begins with one painting, Gustav Klimt's *Gold Portrait of Adele Bloch-Bauer,* which, like countless other paintings, was stolen from Jews, disappeared, and then mysteriously reappeared in galleries and museums in Europe and America with shadowy provenance. Maria Altmann, the niece of the man who commissioned the painting, waged a long legal battle to have possession returned to her and won; when the painting was later sold at auction, its price of $135 million set a record.

But until recently, many possessors of stolen artworks have chosen to ignore claims by their original owners, and only now is an international tracing operation under way. It is believed that countless priceless works languish in the shadows of private homes, discreetly kept out of sight. Work is only beginning on a central clearinghouse of information.

Many other works of sculpture and architecture were destroyed by the bombing raids of both sides, although an occasional exception was made; the city of Venice, for example was spared by American bombers. Much praise is given to the Monument Men, American art experts enlisted into the Army and deployed under the orders of Eisenhower to identify and protect the surviving heritage of liberated nations. In stark contrast, American bombs destroyed museums in Baghdad and throughout Iraq, and others were looted; no effort was made by our commanders to preserve the treasures.

Ratatouille ★ ★ ★ ★

G, 114 m., 2007

With the voices of: Patton Oswalt (Remy), Lou Romano (Linguini), Ian Holm (Skinner), Janeane Garofalo (Colette), Brian Dennehy (Django), Peter O'Toole (Anton Ego), Brad Garrett (Gusteau), Peter Sohn (Emile). Directed by Brad Bird and produced by John Lasseter. Screenplay by Bird, based on an original story by Jan Pinkava, Jim Capobianco, and Bird.

A lot of animated movies have inspired sequels, notably *Shrek,* but Brad Bird's *Ratatouille* is the first one that made me positively desire one. Remy, the earnest little rat who is its hero, is such a lovable, determined, gifted rodent that I want to know what happens to him next, now that he has conquered the summit of French cuisine. I think running for office might not be beyond his reach, and there's certainly something De Gaullean about his snout.

Remy is a member of a large family of rats (a horde, I think, is the word) who ply the trash cans and sewers of a Parisian suburb, just like good rats should. "Eat your garbage!" commands Remy's father, Django, obviously a loving parent. The rats are evicted from their cozy home in a cottage kitchen ceiling in a scene that will have rat haters in the audience cringing (and who among us will claim they don't hate rats more than a little?), and they are swept through the sewers in a torrential flood. Students of Victor Hugo will know that the hero Jean Valjean of *Les Miserables* found the Seine because he knew that every sewer must necessarily run downhill toward it, and indeed Remy washes up near the river, in view of the most famous restaurant in *tout la France.* This is the establishment of Auguste Gusteau, author of the best-seller *Anyone Can Cook,* a title that might not go over very well in France, which is why the book appears to be in English and might well be titled, *Anyone Can Cook Better Than the English.* (Famous British recipe: "Cook until gray.")

Remy (voice by Patton Oswalt) has always been blessed, or cursed, with a refined palate and a sensitive nose, and now he starts skulking around the kitchen of his culinary hero (voice by Brad Garrett). Alas, the monstrous food critic Anton Ego (Peter O'Toole) issues a scathing indictment of Gusteau's recent cooking, the chef dies in a paroxysm of grief, or perhaps it is not a paroxysm, but I like the word, and the kitchen is taken over by the sniveling little snipe Skinner (Ian Holm). Lowest of the low is Gusteau's nephew Linguini (Lou Romano), who must be hired, but is assigned to the wretched job of *plongeur*—literally, one who washes the dishes by plunging them into soapy water.

Linguini and Remy meet, somehow establish trust and communication, and when Linguini gets credit for a soup that the rat has saved with strategic seasonings, they team up. Remy burrows into Linguini's hair, is concealed by his toque, can see through its transparent sides, and controls Linguini by pulling on his hair as if each tuft were a joystick. Together, they astonish Paris with their genius.

All of this begins as a dubious premise and ends as a triumph of animation, comedy, imagination, and, yes, humanity. What is most lovable about Remy is his modesty and shyness, even for a rat. He has body language so expressive that many humans would trade for it. Many animated characters seem to communicate with semaphores, but Remy has a repertory of tiny French hand gestures, shrugs, and physical expressiveness. Does any other nationality have more ways of moving a finger and an eyebrow less than an inch while signaling something as complex as, "I would do anything for you, monsieur, but as you see, I have only two hands, and these times we live in do not permit me the luxury of fulfilling such requests."

Brad Bird and his coproducer John Lasseter pretty clearly take over leadership in the animation field right now. Yes, Bird made *The Incredibles,* but the one that got away was his wonderful *The Iron Giant,* in which a towering robot was as subtle, gentle, and touching as Remy. His eye for detail is remarkable. Every prop and utensil and spice and ingredient in the kitchen is almost tangible, and I for one would never turn off the Food Channel if Remy hosted a program named *Any Rat Can Cook.*

This is clearly one of the best of the year's films. Every time an animated film is successful, you have to read all over again about how animation isn't "just for children" but "for the whole family" and even "for adults going on their own." No kidding!

The Real Dirt on Farmer John ★ ★ ★ ½

NO MPAA RATING, 83 m., 2006

With John Peterson, Anna Peterson, John Edwards, Isa Jacoby, Rosemary Palmer, Jesus Briano, Robert Clothier, Lesley Freeman. A documentary directed by Taggart Siegel and produced by Siegel and Teri Lang. Screenplay by John Peterson.

The filming of *The Real Dirt on Farmer John* essentially began on that day in the 1950s when John Peterson's mother, Anna, brought home a super-8 movie camera. A farmer's wife and schoolteacher from Caledonia, Illinois, she filmed her family working in the fields, her children playing in the yard, the raising of a barn, the changing of the seasons, and the harvest dinners supplied to neighbors who came to help with the threshing.

Her husband died at about the time her son John started to attend nearby Beloit College. By then it was the 1960s, and John and his friends took over the filmmaking; he was a farmer who was also a hippie, and his friends descended on the farm to create their art and, as was said in those days, do their thing. Peterson had his hands full running the farm, a dairy and hog operation, and eventually too many bank loans came due and he had to sell most of it.

That led to a long depression, to trips to Mexico to find himself, and finally, by a meandering route that the movie traces with great love for the meanders, to the present day, when Peterson's farm has been reborn as Angelic Organics, is co-owned with several hundred Chicago and northern Illinois investors, and raises so many organic vegetables, he says, "that I don't know the names of some of them."

The film has been directed and photographed by Taggart Siegel, who has been filming Peterson and his farm for more than twenty years. This is a loving, moving, inspiring, quirky documentary that was made while the lives it records were being lived. We get a sure sense for the gradual death of the American family farm, the auctions of land and farm equipment, the encroachment of suburban housing, and then an almost miraculous rebirth through the introduction of organic gardening. Fruits and vegetables in America have lost half their nutritive value in the past century, and those pretty hothouse tomatoes contain a fraction of the nutrients and phytochemicals in an organic tomato, but visionaries such as Peterson are finding a way back to the land.

Let it be observed, however, that Peterson is a strange man and celebrates his own oddities. He wrote and reads the narration, which is that of a man who has one foot in the counterculture and the other in rich organic soil. He likes to dress strangely, in Dr. Seuss hats or bumblebee costumes. He is taken to dancing wildly in the fields. He is told his speech and body language make him appear to be homosexual, but there is persuasive evidence of heterosexuality in the series of girlfriends who keep him in "relationships" through the decades.

The heroine of the film is his mother, a high-spirited eighty-three-year-old when we meet her, who persuades John not to quit the farm because how could she live without her roadside produce stand? A freethinker who likes Jim Morrison although he didn't "dress nice," she is an articulate life force. Through her we glimpse John's father, his uncles and aunts, and the neighbors of a vanished farm culture.

The miracle of Angelic Organics begins the day in the 1990s some Chicago investors in Community Supported Agriculture buy one of his organic onions, call him up, and offer to go into business with him. Today the Peterson farm is co-owned and -operated with his CSA partners, delivers fresh produce to hundreds of customers every week, has expanded, is working in a way Peterson's father could never have imagined. Oh, and John has finally put to rest those rumors about devil worship, orgies, and drug abuse, which were never true, but if a man is going to wear a Dr. Seuss hat and have hippies living in his barn, he's got to expect that people will talk.

Rebound ★ ★

PG, 103 m., 2005

Martin Lawrence (Roy McCormick), Wendy Raquel Robinson (Jeanie Ellis), Breckin Meyer (Tim Fink), Horatio Sanz (Mr. Newirth), Megan Mullally (Principal Walsh), Oren Williams (Keith

Ellis), Tara Correa (Big Mac), Steven C. Parker (Wes), Steven Anthony Lawrence (Ralph), Gus Hoffman (Goggles). Directed by Steve Carr and produced by Robert Simonds. Screenplay by Jon Lucas and Scott Moore.

Rebound leads us patiently once more through the well-charted formulas of sports movies. We have the team of losers lacking all self-confidence, combined with the hotshot coach who has problems with anger management. Will the team pull itself together and become champions? Will the coach humble himself and take these underdogs seriously? Will he even rehabilitate himself and get his old job back? Can we be made to care?

Movies like this are easy to watch at one level. They usually contain cute kids who are surprisingly effective actors. And they give the grown-up actors opportunities for broad emotion. In *Rebound*, the coach with the temper problem is played by Martin Lawrence, and he looks like a kinder, gentler, happier, and rounder Martin Lawrence than we're accustomed to. He also talks nicer. Lawrence's dialogue may be reduced by 25 percent by the elimination of some of his favorite words, but the PG rating is justified, and the movie is family-friendly.

His character, Roy McCormick, is a big-time college coach who gets into a lot of trouble when he throws a basketball at the opposing team, the Vultures, killing the mascot's pet bird. He's in trouble anyway; he misses the first half of one game because he's doing a photo shoot for *Details* magazine. His endorsement deals seem to cover almost everything offered at retail.

The league threatens him with banishment for life. His agent, Tim Fink (Breckin Meyer), thinks he might be able to rehabilitate himself by doing some pro bono work, and he finds Roy a job coaching a hopeless middle school team. It's at the very school that Roy himself once attended ("I grew up in the mean streets of the suburbs").

If you thought the Vultures was a strange nickname for a team, consider that Roy's team is the Smelters. The team he inherits is so inept, its passing drills look like dodgeball. Tom Arnold, of the *Best Damn Sports Show Period*, finds a second career simply reporting on how bad the Smelters are.

Of the kids on the team, the most endearing, because he's the most like me, is Goggles (Gus Hoffman), who can barely see the ball, let alone pass it. Ralph (Steven Anthony Lawrence) is well named, since he barfs every time he gets nervous. There's a tough girl named Big Mac (Tara Correa), who looks and plays tough but has a sweet spot for the tall, shy Wes (Steven C. Parker). Coach gives him some snarling lessons. And the team starts to come together when Keith Ellis (Oren Williams) joins it. He looks uncannily like a young Dee Brown.

All of this is fun enough in a sweet but predictable way. It bears no resemblance to basketball as it is played and coached in the real world, and it is doubtful if even a school with a teacher played by Horatio Sanz would entrust its thirteen-year-olds with a mad-dog version of Bobby Knight. No matter. We wait complacently until the last second of the last minute of the final game of the season, confident that no matter how grim the situation looks, the underdog tradition of sports movies will be upheld. I can't recommend the movie, except to younger viewers, but I don't dislike it. It's *Coach Carter* lite, and it does what it does.

Recount ★ ★ ★

NO MPAA RATING, 115 m., 2008

Kevin Spacey (Ron Klain), John Hurt (Warren Christopher), Laura Dern (Katherine Harris), Tom Wilkinson (James Baker), Denis Leary (Michael Whouley), Ed Begley Jr. (David Boies), Bob Balaban (Ben Ginsburg). Directed by Jay Roach and produced by Kevin Spacey. Screenplay by Danny Strong.

Katherine Harris was a piece of work. The Florida secretary of state during the 2000 elections is not intended as the leading role in *Recount*, an HBO docudrama about that lamentable fiasco, but every time Laura Dern appears on the screen, she owns it. Watch her stride into a room of powerful men, pick up a little paper packet of sugar for her coffee, and shake it with great sweeping arm gestures as if she were a demonstrator in an educational film.

As much as anyone, Harris was responsible for George W. Bush being declared the winner of the state, and thus of the presidency. In a bewildering thicket of controversy about chads, hanging chads, dimpled chads, military ballots, voting machines, and nearsighted elderly voters, it was her apparent oblivion that prevented a meaningful recount from ever taking place. Don't talk to me about the Florida Supreme Court, the U.S. Supreme Court, or even the hero of the film, a Democratic Party strategist named Ron Klain (Kevin Spacey). They had a great influence on events, but it was Katherine Harris who created a shortage of time that ultimately had a greater effect than anything else.

And this is the fascinating part, the part that Laura Dern exploits until her performance becomes mesmerizing: Harris did it *without seeming to know what she was doing.* Although she was the head of Bush's Florida campaign, she bats her eyes in innocence while announcing a "firewall" isolating her office from anyone, Democrat or Republican, lest they affect her worship of the power of law. After that announcement, it is the merest detail that the film portrays two GOP strategists moving into her office and giving her suggestions. They include her when talking about what "we" have to do.

But even in the privacy of her office, she never quite seems to know what they are doing or why. She signals that her mind is operating in more elevated, more long-range dimensions. She sees it all as an adventure starring herself, and sometimes seems to be thanking her classmates for electing her homecoming queen. "Ten years ago," she tells her minders in a wondering voice, "I was teaching the chicken dance to seniors, and now I've been thrust into a political tempest of historical dimensions."

She sure has. *Recount,* an efficient and relentless enactment of the strategists on both sides of the Florida controversy, shows an accident that was waiting to happen. So confusing was the state's "butterfly ballot" (how such terms resound in memory) that large numbers of senior citizens from liberal districts apparently cast mistaken votes for Pat Buchanan, a right-wing independent. Buchanan himself went on CNN to doubt that his support was quite that strong in Palm Beach County. If their chads alone had been correctly punched, Al Gore might have been elected president. But a chad is a chad. And the film follows all the jaw-dropping developments that kept us so enthralled during that confusing season.

The point of view is largely Klain's, played as a weary and dogged idealist by Spacey. As the film opens and it looks like Gore will win the election, he turns down a job offer from Gore because he thinks he deserves better. Yet soon he is the engine behind the Democrats' legal challenges, persisting even more than Gore himself probably would have. "You know what's funny about all this?" he asks his teammate Michael Whouley (Denis Leary). "I'm not even sure I *like* Al Gore." Klain's GOP opponent is James Baker (Tom Wilkinson), written and played as a man who does what any reasonable politician would have done under the circumstances. Often enough these ultimate insiders seem to get most of their information from CNN; aides frequently run in and tell them to watch the TV, as when both supreme courts drop their bombshells.

You might assume the movie is pro-Gore and anti-Bush, but you would not be quite right. Dave Grusin's almost eerie score evokes a journey into uncharted territories and haunted lands, but that's as close as it comes to making a statement (other than the incredulity voiced by the losers). The Democratic Party figures portrayed in the film have been the loudest in protest, especially Warren Christopher (John Hurt), who was the first head of the Gore team, and is portrayed as a wimp ready to cave in to the GOP. Whether the film is fair to him, I cannot say.

Recount portrays a lot of Democrats as being in favor of an "orderly transition of power" at whatever cost, and a lot of Republicans as being in favor of winning, in an orderly transition or any other kind. At least, as an exhausted Warren Christopher says when all is over and his man has lost: "The system worked. There were no tanks in the streets." Of course, at that time he would not have been thinking of the streets of Baghdad.

Redacted ★ ★ ½

R, 91 m., 2007

Patrick Carroll (Reno Flake), Rob Devaney (Lawyer McCoy), Izzy Diaz (Angel Salazar),

Mike Figueroa (Sergeant Jim Vasquez), Ty Jones (Master Sergeant Jim Sweet), Kel O'Neill (Gabe Blix), Daniel Stewart Sherman (Specialist B. B. Rush). Directed by Brian De Palma and produced by Jennifer Weiss, Simone Urdl, Jason Kliot, and Joana Vicente. Screenplay by De Palma.

The rape and subsequent murders in *Redacted* actually happened, and we are told that director Brian De Palma found out about them on the Internet, in blogs and YouTube postings, and on American and Arabic sites. He fictionalizes them, as he must for legal reasons, but presents them in a way suggesting how he found them; the movie looks cobbled together largely from found Web footage. It's better photographed than much similar material on the Web, and edited to create a relentless momentum, but he wants us to feel as if we're discovering this material for ourselves.

So we would be forced to, if the movie's buried message is clear. *Redacted* is a word simply meaning "edited," and is often used by the military as a way of calling a simple act by an objective, and therefore defused, name. In a similar fashion, a "rendition" can be a kidnapping and torture. The film explains the origin of much of its footage by introducing us to a soldier named Angel Salazar (Izzy Diaz), who carries a digital video camera and thinks maybe he can make a documentary to get him into film school. A good plan, but if you notice that the movie is set in Samarra, you may recall the parable of the man whose best-laid plans went wrong there.

The story comes down to this: The soldiers of Alpha Company are manning a checkpoint. A car speeds past. They open fire, and a pregnant woman and her unborn child are killed. Two more hearts and minds not won over. In retribution, one of the company's members is killed by local militia. In response, the two men who fired on the car (Rush, played by Daniel Stewart Sherman, and the well-named Flake, played by Patrick Carroll) lead a nighttime raid during which a fifteen-year-old girl is raped, her family is murdered, and their house set afire. Company members are informed by Flake and Rush that if they don't keep quiet, they will die. There is no reason to doubt this.

Much of this action mirrors the events in an earlier De Palma film, *Casualties of War* (1989), in which Michael J. Fox played a Vietnam soldier who turned away from a rape. What is different in this film is the visual style, which informs us by its very nature that after the invention of the cheap video camera and the Internet, few actions can be assumed to be secret. De Palma uses the method to demonstrate how good (or neutral) soldiers can be turned into criminals or silent accomplices by a threat of violence from their comrades. How if you put men in a hellhole and arm them, and if they are predisposed to violence, they will not always follow the rules, or even remember them.

Redacted is a metaphor for what De Palma and others believe is the fatal flaw of our Iraq strategy: You cannot enforce "freedom" at gunpoint. Now that some 200,000 Iraqis have died in the war, for whatever reason and at whatever hands, it is hard to see how many of the rest would be as grateful for our presence as we are assured they are. This is something Angel Salazar finds out during the filming of his documentary, although unfortunately his key footage is redacted in a very direct way.

You may be vaguely aware of a controversy involving De Palma and some of his own footage that was "redacted." This involved the montage of "actual" photographs from Iraq that close the film. They were all actual at one point, but now some of them are staged, and others have been altered by having faces obscured by a black marker pen, lest the subjects' privacy be violated. Since they are dead, one doubts they would sue, but perhaps the black smudges make De Palma's point in another way.

The acting is curious. Some of it is convincing, and some of the rest is convincing in a different way: It convinces us that nonactors know they are being filmed and are acting and speaking slightly differently than they otherwise would. That makes some try to appear nicer, and others try to appear tougher or more menacing. That edge of inauthentic performance paradoxically increases the effect: Moments seem more real because they're not acted flawlessly.

The result of the film is shocking, saddening, and frustrating. The latest polls show that the great majority of the American public has withdrawn its approval from the war and its architects. Why should it be a mystery that the Iraqis do not love us? Did our mothers not ask us, "How would you feel if someone did that to you?" Yes, they are killing us, too, but they live there, and we went a great distance for our appointment in Samarra.

The name of the real girl, who was actually fourteen, was Abeer Qasim Hamza al-Janabi.

Redbelt ★ ★ ★

R, 98 m., 2008

Chiwetel Ejiofor (Mike Terry), Alice Braga (Sondra Terry), Emily Mortimer (Laura Black), Tim Allen (Chet Frank), Joe Mantegna (Jerry Weiss), Rodrigo Santoro (Bruno Silva), Max Martini (Joe Collins), Ricky Jay (Marty Brown). Directed by David Mamet and produced by Chrisann Verges. Screenplay by Mamet.

David Mamet's *Redbelt* assembles all the elements for a great Mamet film, but they're still spread out on the shop floor. It never really pulls itself together into the convincing, focused drama it promises, yet it kept me involved right up until the final scenes, which piled on developments almost recklessly. So gifted is Mamet as a writer and director that he can fascinate us even when he's pulling rabbits out of an empty hat.

The movie takes place in that pungent Mamet world of seamy streets on the wrong side of town, and is peopled by rogues and con men, trick artists and thieves, those who believe and those who prey on them. The cast is assembled from his stock company of actors whose very presence helps embody the atmosphere of a Mamet story, and who are almost always not what they seem, and then not even what they seem after that. He is fascinated by the deceptions of one confidence game assembled inside another.

At the center of a story, in a performance evoking intense idealism, is Mike Terry (Chiwetel Ejiofor), a martial arts instructor who runs a storefront studio on a barren city street. His is not one of those glass and steel fitness emporiums, but a throwback to an earlier time; the sign on his window promises jujitsu, and he apparently studied this art from those little pamphlets with crude illustrations that used to be advertised in the back pages of comic books. I studied booklets like this as a boy; apparently one embodies the philosophy of The Professor, a Brazilian martial arts master who is like a god to Mike.

Mike has few customers, is kept afloat by the small garment business of his wife, Sondra (Alice Braga), and is seen instructing a Los Angeles cop named Joe Collins (Max Martini). When you seem to be your studio's only instructor, the impression is fly-by-night, but there's a purist quality to Mike's dedication that has Joe completely convinced, and they both seriously believe in the "honor" of the academy.

Now commences a series of events it would be useless to describe, and which are eventually almost impossible to understand, involving a troubled lawyer (Emily Mortimer), a movie star (Tim Allen), the star's shifty manager (Joe Mantegna), and the world of a pay-TV fight promoter (Ricky Jay). All of these characters seem like marked-down versions of the stereotypes they're based on, and the pay-for-view operation feels more like local access cable than a big-bucks franchise.

In a bewildering series of deceptions, these people entrap the idealistic Mike into debt, betrayal, grief, guilt, and cynical disappointments, all leading up to a big televised fight sequence at the end that makes no attempt to be plausible and is interesting (if you are a student of such things) for its visual fakery. We've seen a lot of crowd scenes in which camera angles attempt to create the illusion of thousands of people who aren't really there, but *Redbelt* seems to be offering a crowd of hundreds (or dozens) who aren't really there. At a key point, in a wildly impossible development, the action shifts out of the ring, and the lights and cameras are focused on a man-to-man showdown in a gangway. The conclusion plays like a low-rent parody of a Rocky victory. The last shot left me underwhelmed.

So now you're wondering why you might want to see this movie at all. It might be because of the sheer art and craft of Mamet himself. For his dialogue, terse and enigmatic, as if in a secret code. For his series of "reveals" in which nothing is as it seems. For his lost world of fly-by-night operators. For his actors like

Ricky Jay, who would be familiar with the term "suede shoe artist." For his bit parts for unexplained magicians. Especially for a sequence when Mike Terry, as baffled as we are, essentially asks for someone to explain the plot to him.

If you savor that sort of stuff, and I do, you may like *Redbelt* on its own dubious but seductive terms. It seems about to become one kind of movie, a conventional combination of con games and action, and then shadowboxes its way into a different kind of fight, which is about values, not strength. It's this kind of film: Some of the characters at the end, hauled in to provide a moral payoff, seem to have been airlifted from Brazil—which, in fact, they were.

Red Eye ★ ★ ★

PG-13, 85 m., 2005

Rachel McAdams (Lisa Reisert), Cillian Murphy (Jackson Rippner), Brian Cox (Joe Reisert), Jayma Mays (Cynthia), Jack Scalia (Charles Keefe). Directed by Wes Craven and produced by Chris Bender and Marianne Maddalena. Screenplay by Carl Ellsworth.

Wes Craven's *Red Eye* is a movie that wants to be a good thriller and moves competently, even relentlessly, toward that goal. It's helped enormously by Rachel McAdams, whose performance is convincing because she keeps it at ground level; thrillers are invitations to overact, but she remains plausible even when the action ratchets up around her. When she's stalking a terrorist with a hockey stick, she seems like a real woman stalking a real terrorist with a real hockey stick. It's not as easy as it sounds.

The terrorist is played by Cillian Murphy, who was the Scarecrow in *Batman Begins* and here plays a young man who seems pleasant and attractive to the heroine, until she asks him what his business is. All the warmth goes out of his eyes as he says, "As fate would have it, my business is all about you."

They meet in the Dallas–Fort Worth airport. She's Lisa, a hotel desk manager, on her way home to Miami. He's the cute guy who helps her put down a jerk, buys her a drink, and ends up with the seat next to hers on the overnight flight.

Murphy is handsome, but, like James Spader, the good looks come with a warning: There are ominous undertones here. Speaking softly, he explains that her father is being held hostage, that her help will be needed in a plot to blow up the deputy secretary of homeland security, and that her job is to call the hotel and have the security guy put him in a suite where he can be more easily assassinated. The encouraging angle is that the deputy secretary is taken that seriously.

What makes this goal worthy of a thriller is that the terrorist plan is of course nine times more complicated than it needs to be and is constructed entirely out of things that could go wrong. It's remarkable that terrorists like these still possess feet they have not shot off.

About the plot I will say no more, except in a general way: The scenes on board the airplane are about as convincing and plausible as they can be, given the situation. And the scenes after the plane lands bring a cool excellence to the standard scenario in which the killer and the victim stalk each other.

Maybe what I like best about the movie is its reticence. After a summer of crashes, bangs, endless chase scenes and special effects that belittle the actors standing in front of them, what a pleasure to see characters in a thriller doing what people like themselves possibly could do. There are no supernatural or superhuman feats in the film, unless you count the piddling detail that a character isn't slowed down by an unexpected tracheotomy. The movie, bless its heart, even tries to make *this* development plausible by providing a doctor who eyeballs the victim and says (I quote from memory), "It's not too bad—only the larynx."

The rise of McAdams has been spectacular, if only because it has been so steep; in 2002, she had eighth billing in *The Hot Chick*. The only thing better would have been ninth billing. But then in 2004 she starred in *Mean Girls*, as the bitchiest girl in Lindsay Lohan's high school. It was a surprisingly good movie. And then came a straight romantic lead in *The Notebook* and a comic romantic lead in *Wedding Crashers*, where Owen Wilson fell in love with her and caught a heartwarming case of sincerity. Now this.

The previous three movies positioned McAdams as a rising star. *Red Eye* will be more important because casting directors, who know what to look for, will see that she brings more presence and credibility to her role than is really expected; she acts without betraying the slightest awareness that she's inside a genre. I wonder if that has anything to do with the fact that she's Canadian and thus culturally trained to avoid calling unnecessary attention to herself. Too many young Hollywood actors, especially in thrillers, think it's all about them. Her performance qualifies her for heavy-duty roles. Murphy is already established and does not need discovering, but here he shows an ability to modulate his character instead of gnashing the scenery. They're very effective together.

Craven, the director, has been making thrillers for a long time and knows how to do it. From *The Last House on the Left* (1972) through *Swamp Thing* (1982), *The Serpent and the Rainbow* (1988), *Wes Craven's New Nightmare* (1994), and the *Scream* movies, he has put stories and characters ahead of *gotcha!* moments. Watching *Red Eye* function so smoothly, doing exactly what it was intended to do, I was reminded of Howard Hawks's definition of a good movie: "Three great scenes. No bad scenes." Craven scores two and one. Not bad.

Reel Paradise ★ ★ ★

R, 110 m., 2005

Featuring John Pierson, Janet Pierson, Georgia Pierson, Wyatt Pierson. A documentary directed by Steve James and produced by Scott Mosier and James.

I know a couple named Jon and Jennifer Vickers, who moved to Three Oaks, Michigan (population 1,829) and bought the local movie theater. It's thirty miles from the closest multiplex. They show first-run art films and after eight years are a solid success. "The audience isn't just the Chicago weekend people," my friend Mary Jo Broderick tells me. She goes every week. "I see the same people I see in the supermarket in February." The Vickerses' theater doesn't show only *March of the Penguins* but also Herzog, Wong Kar Wai, Bergman, Jarmusch. Every summer they have a silent-film festival.

Steve James's new documentary, *Reel Paradise*, is about a couple with similar idealism, who also move to a small town and buy the movie theater. Their theater is the 180 Meridian, on Taveuni, one of the Fiji Islands. They aren't trying to bring art cinema to Fiji. They're trying to bring the movies, period. The audience favorite is *Jackass*, a film so popular it is banned by the local authorities.

The man behind this idea is John Pierson, a producer's rep well-known in indie film circles and crucial to the early success of such directors as Spike Lee (he invested in *She's Gotta Have It*) and Michael Moore *(Roger and Me)*. I've run into him over the years at festivals such as Sundance. He tired of the indie circuit routine and convinced his wife, Janet, and their children, Georgia, sixteen, and Wyatt, thirteen, to join him for a year running a movie theater in Fiji. They do not entirely share his enthusiasm.

Steve James, who made *Hoop Dreams*, arrives in time to chronicle the final month of this experiment. What Pierson proved for sure is that if you show movies for free, you will get an audience. He also proved that a certain kind of great film, such as Buster Keaton's *Steamboat Bill Jr.*, will draw a crowd. It's always claimed that silent comedy is universal in its appeal; here's your proof.

Pierson wanted to show all kinds of movies. He has a hit with *The Hot Chick*. He doesn't do so well with more ambitious films. By the time James arrives with his camera, Pierson has contracted dengue fever and his son, Wyatt, has taken over the day-to-day operations at the 180 Meridian. He may be the son of a legendary art film supporter, but Wyatt keeps his eye firmly on the box office: "If you show *Apocalypse Now* twice," he tells his dad, "I guarantee no one will come the second night." If a fortune is to be made by the Pierson family in the movie business, it may be made by Wyatt.

Fiji seems like a paradise from a distance, but when you live there it turns into a real place with real problems. There is the heat, the humidity, the lack of a power grid (the theater has its own generator). The projectionist tends to get drunk. There is the reality that Georgia is a teenager and interested in boys and, like all teenagers, wants to stay out past her curfew.

There are also two burglaries of the Piersons' home. Suspicion for this crime falls upon people the Piersons like and trust. Considering that the island has only one road, it should not be hard to find their computer, but it is. I am reminded of my visit to Bora Bora when *Hurricane* was being shot there. The movie publicist's Jeep was stolen. The sheriff advised him to stand outside and wait until it came around; the island had one road, which circled the island.

The priests at the Catholic mission disapprove of many of Pierson's movies (especially *Jackass*) and think that by showing them for free, he is undercutting the work ethic. The local teenagers hang out together and sometimes seem up to no good, but that is the nature of teenagers, and the dangers on Taveuni are mild compared to those in New York.

When the experiment ends and the Piersons return to America, the theater closes again. It is hard to say what they accomplished. It's nice to think that if you show people movies, especially good movies, that will somehow change or improve their lives. But movies out of context are a curiosity and may play in unexpected ways. The politically correct might question a Three Stooges movie involving a South Seas cannibal's boiling pot, but the audience explodes with such uncontrolled laughter that you can forget about hearing the dialogue.

The Piersons went, they showed movies, they returned. Taveuni is more or less the same. But by living and coping together for a year, the family is probably stronger and richer: Years from now, Georgia and Wyatt are going to be telling people about how their crazy parents opened a movie theater in Fiji, and in their voices you will hear that although they had their doubts at the time, they now think they were lucky to have such parents. Sometimes it's not whether you succeed, but whether you try.

Rendition ★ ★ ★

R, 120 m., 2007

Jake Gyllenhaal (Douglas Freeman), Reese Witherspoon (Isabella El-Ibrahimi), Omar Metwally (Anwar El-Ibrahimi), Peter Sarsgaard (Alan Smith), Meryl Streep (Corrinne Whitman), Alan Arkin (Senator Hawkins), Igal Naor (Abasi Fawal), Moa Khouas (Khalid El-Emin), Zineb Oukach (Fatima Fawal). Directed by Gavin Hood and produced by Steve Golin and Marcus Viscidi. Screenplay by Kelley Sane.

This is being done in our name. People who are suspected for any reason, or no good reason, of being terrorists can be snatched from their lives and transported to another country to be held without charge and tortured for information. Because the torture is conducted by professionals in those countries, our officials can blandly state "America does not torture." This practice, known as an "extraordinary rendition," was authorized, I am sorry to say, under the Clinton administration. After 9/11 there is reason to believe the Bush administration uses it frequently.

Gavin Hood's terrifying, intelligent thriller *Rendition* puts a human face on the practice. We meet Anwar El-Ibrahimi (Omar Metwally), an Egyptian-born American chemical engineer who lives in Chicago. He and his wife, Isabella (Reese Witherspoon), have a young son, and she is in advanced pregnancy with another child. After boarding a flight home from a conference in Cape Town, Anwar disappears from the airplane, his name disappears from the passenger list, and Isabella hears nothing more from him.

He was taken from the plane by the CIA, we learn. His cell phone received calls from a terrorist, or perhaps from someone else with the same name, or perhaps it was stolen or lost and used by somebody else. His background is clean, and he passes a lie detector test, but is hooded, flown to an anonymous country, and placed in the hands of an expert torturer named Abasi Fawal (Igal Naor). His frantic wife is told he never got on the flight, although she later discovers his credit card was used for an in-flight duty-free purchase.

If there is one thing history and common sense teaches us, it is that if you torture someone well enough, they will tell you what they think you want to hear. As successful interrogation experts have patiently explained to Congress, much more useful information is obtained using the carrot than the stick. Yet Anwar is held naked in a dungeon, beaten, nearly drowned, shocked with electricity, kept sleepless, shackled. Does it occur to anybody that he is more likely to "confess" if he is not a terrorist than if he is?

The movie sets into motion a chain of events caused by the illegal kidnapping. Isabella, played by Reese Witherspoon with single-minded determination and love, contacts an old boyfriend (Peter Sarsgaard) who is now an aide to a powerful senator (Alan Arkin). Convinced the missing man is innocent, the senator intervenes with the head of U.S. intelligence (Meryl Streep). She responds in flawless neocon-speak, simultaneously using terrorism as an excuse for terrorism, and threatening the senator with political suicide. Arkin backs off.

Meanwhile, in the unnamed foreign country, we meet a CIA pencil pusher named Douglas Freeman (Jake Gyllenhaal), who has little experience in fieldwork but has taken over the post after the assassination of his boss. His job is to work with and "supervise" the torturer Abasi. This he does with no enthusiasm but from a sense of duty. He is not cut out for this kind of work, drinks too much, broods, and has discussions with Abasi, who is an intelligent man and not a monster.

How this all plays out has much to do with Abasi's daughter, Fatima (Zineb Oukach), who is secretly in love with a fellow student not approved of by her family. All these human strands, seemingly so separated, eventually weave into the same rope in a film that builds its suspense by the uncoiling of personalities.

It is now so well-established that America authorizes the practices shown in this film that when President Bush goes on television to blandly deny it, with his "Who, we?" little-boy innocence, I feel saddened. He may eventually be the last person to believe himself. What the film documents is that we have lost faith in due process and the rule of law, and have forfeited the moral high ground. Reading some of the reviews after I saw this film at the Toronto festival, I was struck by a comment by James Rocchi on Cinematical.com: "Anytime someone tells you that you can't make an omelet without breaking eggs, immediately demand to see the omelet."

Gavin Hood, the South African director of *Rendition,* first came into wide view with the wonderful *Tsotsi* (2005), which won the Academy Award for best foreign film. Now comes this big, confident, effective thriller with its politics so seamlessly part of its story. Next for him: *Wolverine,* based on the X-Men character. I hope we don't lose him to blockbusters. A film like *Rendition* is valuable and rare. As I wrote from Toronto: "It is a movie about the theory and practice of two things: torture and personal responsibility. And it is wise about what is right, and what is wrong."

Rent ★ ★ ½

PG-13, 128 m., 2005

Rosario Dawson (Mimi Marquez), Taye Diggs (Benjamin Coffin), Wilson Jermaine Heredia (Angel Schunard), Jesse L. Martin (Tom Collins), Idina Menzel (Maureen Johnson), Adam Pascal (Roger Davis), Anthony Rapp (Mark Cohen), Tracie Thoms (Joanne Jefferson). Directed by Chris Columbus and produced by Jane Rosenthal, Robert De Niro, Columbus, Michael Barnathan, and Mark Radcliffe. Screenplay by Columbus and Stephen Chbosky, based on the musical drama *Rent* by Jonathan Larson.

Rent is a stage musical that wants to be a movie musical. Many stage musicals, from *Oklahoma!* to *West Side Story,* feel right at home on the screen. *Rent* on film is missing a crucial element of its life-support system: a live audience. The stage production surrounded the audience with the characters and the production. It lacked the song "We Are Family," but that was the subtext. On film, *Rent* is the sound of one hand clapping.

It is not a bad film. It may be about as good a film as the material can inspire. The performances have a presence and poignancy that can feel surprisingly real, given the contrivances of the story. The film uses many of the same actors who starred in the original 1996 New York production, and the newcomers, Rosario Dawson and Tracie Thoms, earn their roles. But if you stand back from the importance of *Rent* as a cultural artifact and a statement about AIDS, does it stand on its own as a musical?

I don't think so. The song lyrics by Jonathan Larson have an ungainly quality, perhaps deliberate; the words often seem at right angles to the music. I do not demand that lyrics scan, rhyme, and make sense, but I do think they should flow with, or even against, the music; here the words and the music sometimes play as if two radios have been left on at the same time ("My T-cells are low" doesn't strike me as an especially singable line). The music serves the choreography, the words serve the story, but they don't serve each other.

The film left me in a curious state: I felt more respect than affection. From some of the more compelling characters, including Mimi (Dawson) and Angel (Wilson Jermaine Heredia), there are three-dimensional portraits that are convincing on any level. But the roommates in that artist's loft seem just as much of a casting call as they do in Puccini's *La Boheme,* the opera that inspired *Rent.* They're so busy being bohemian and defying authority that they never find time to be themselves.

I no more believe Mark (Anthony Rapp) is a documentary filmmaker and Roger (Adam Pascal) is a musician than I believed Marcello and Rodolfo were an artist and a playwright in the Puccini version. There is not a person reading this review who couldn't make a better film than Mark, who doesn't even know that the handle of his hand-cranked 8 mm camera should not be revolving as he films, and whose footage looks like jerky home movies. To be given $3,000 to supply his sub-Warhol indulgences to TV is about as likely as Ozzy Osbourne getting his own reality show, ho, ho.

When the roommates feed a fire with their screenplays and compositions because it is cold in their unheated loft, I know they are only following Puccini, but I didn't believe it in *La Boheme* and I believe it less now. No matter; the job of the roommates in both versions is to be good friends of Mimi, but careless, so that they misplace her and she risks dying alone in the cold before being hurried onstage for her death scene.

The characters who did convince me have lives apart from the opera (or soap opera) elements in the story. Mimi is played by Dawson as a stripper who shoots drugs and has AIDS because of a tainted needle. She tries to clean up but falls back into drugs and they kill her. Angel (Heredia) is a transvestite who finds Tom Collins (Jesse L. Martin) mugged in an alley and tenderly cares for him as they fall in love. Angel's life force inspires a particularly moving tribute late in the film—one of those scenes that affect us like the real thing might.

There is a romantic triangle involving Mark, whose girlfriend, Maureen (Idina Menzel), dumps him for a girlfriend of her own, Joanne (Thoms). I believed the character of Joanne, but neither Maureen nor Roger. He doesn't seem much depressed by being dumped, and she's so superficial that she flirts with the cute female bartender at her partnering ceremony with Joanne. That Joanne sincerely cares for her and is really hurt I did believe. When she's accused of flirting by Joanne, Maureen sings the showstopper "Take Me for What I Am." I wanted Joanne to reply in her own song: "Okay, You're a Promiscuous Slut, So Take Me for What I Am, Your New Former Partner."

Roger and Mark had a third roommate, Benjamin (Taye Diggs), before he married, moved out, and became their landlord. Benjamin is a character conceived entirely for the convenience of the plot. When needed, he threatens eviction, sics the cops on their rent strike, is partly responsible for the riot after Maureen's performance, does evict them, padlocks the door, confiscates their possessions, and then relents and lets them move back in. All of this is done while he has two poker-faced middle-aged white men (PFMAWM), one of them his father-in-law, hanging around in the background saying nothing and apparently thinking nothing. Their job is to supply poker-faced reaction shots during same-sex dancing. Two guys dance together, PFMAWM see them. Two dolls dance together, PFMAWM see them. What are they thinking? For all I know, they're envious. Why Benjamin would take them to the same club where rent strikers cavort on tabletops is arbitrary if not capricious.

The story is set in 1989, a time when AIDS provided the same kind of death sentence that tuberculosis provided in nineteenth-century novels and operas. Through the story characters remind each other, "take your AZT," but some of them do not, apparently so they can exhibit, I dunno, a death wish, self-hatred, denial, or a desire to supply the playwright with tragedy. This is much the function provided by Puccini's original Mimi, who coughs in Act Three so that she can die in Act Four. More convincing is the treatment of Mimi's drug addiction in the modern version; Dawson plays Mimi as hooked and hopeless, and we believe her.

I think there is an audience for the movie

version of *Rent,* and that would be fans of the stage version. If you came to know and love the material in its original form, this will be a way to see the characters and actors again, and you will bring those memories with you to the movie, as sort of a commentary track. Those who haven't seen *Rent* on the stage will sense they're missing something, and they are.

Note: I gave the movie a marginal thumbs up on Ebert & Roeper *because I felt people might want to see it based on what was good in it, but I am fine-tuning that to a 2.5-star rating because, on the whole, I don't think the movie really works on its own, without reference to the theatrical version.*

Reprise ★ ★

R, 105 m., 2008

Espen Klouman Hoiner (Erik), Anders Danielsen Lie (Phillip), Viktoria Winge (Kari), Odd Magnus Williamson (Morten), Pal Stokka (Geir), Christian Rubeck (Lars). Directed by Joachim Trier and produced by Karin Julsrud. Screenplay by Eskil Vogt and Trier.

If there was ever a movie that seems written and directed by its characters, that movie is Joachim Trier's *Reprise.* Here is an ambitious and romantic portrait of two young would-be writers that seems made by ambitious and romantic would-be filmmakers. In the movie, the young heroes idolize Norway's greatest living writer, who tells one of them his novel is good and shows promise, except for the ending, where he shouldn't have been so poetic. The movie itself is good and shows promise, except for the ending, when Trier shouldn't have been so poetic. Not only does *Reprise* generate itself, it contains its own review.

The twenty-three-year-old heroes are Erik and Phillip. They seem to be awfully nice boys who have some growing-up to do. It opens with the two of them simultaneously dropping the manuscripts of their first novels into a post box. Then an anonymous narrator takes over and describes some possible futures of the characters and their novels. We will be hearing a lot from that narrator, and he, along with Erik and Phillip and Phillip's girlfriend, Kari, remind us inescapably of Francois Truffaut's *Jules and Jim.*

The movie is set in Oslo, with a visit to Paris. I have been to Oslo, and it's nowhere near the gray arrangement of apartment blocks and perfunctory landscaping that we see in the movie. (Nor is it Paris.) I have met Norwegians, who are nowhere near the bland, narcissistic Erik and Phillip. The big problem with the movie is our difficulty in working up much real interest in the characters. They're not compelling. Even when Phillip becomes so obsessed with Kari that he has to be accommodated in a mental institution, and even after (back on the streets) he takes her to Paris on the exact anniversary of their first trip there, it's impossible to see him as passionate. His emotions never seem to be at full volume.

The high point, passion-wise, comes during their Paris trip. His mother has confiscated his photos of Kari, fearing they will trigger a relapse. So in Paris he poses her to take them again, Kari even helpfully hitching up her skirt to more closely match the original. They visit the same café (I think). Then they check into the same hotel and make love in (one assumes) much the same way.

The movie finds it necessary to do something I'm growing weary of: It depicts their love-making at greater length than depth. They're seen in profile, in dim lighting, with a sound track that reminded me of the Hondells ("First gear—it's all right. Second gear—hold on tight").

After their breathing reaches overdrive, they disengage and she soon enough says, "You don't still love me." That word *love* is such a troublemaker. For characters like those in the movie, it represents an attainment like feeling patriotic or missing your dog. It's a state not consuming, not transcendent, but obligatory.

I also wearied of Phillip's countdowns. At a party, he bets himself Kari will turn and look at him at "zero" when he counts down from "ten." He tempts fate on his bicycle, in traffic, by closing his eyes while counting down. It's the kind of numerology that was charming in *Me and You and Everyone We Know,* when the heroine imagines that the sidewalk stretching ahead of her represents the life span of herself and the guy she likes, and they're halfway to the corner. It was fanciful and fetching in that film, but disposable in this one—indeed, bordering on idiotic, because Phillip isn't that kind of person. For him the counting down not only seems to represent (a) something meaningful, but also (b) age-appropriate. If I were Kari, I'd jump ship at "seven," and actually she does tell Phillip, "I can't take it any more." Bonus points for taking it as long as she does.

Erik has a girlfriend, too, the seldom-seen (by his friends) Lillian, whom he pulls apart from because he fears she might not fit in with his friends, who therefore seldom see her. The characters meet in cafés, restaurants, one another's apartments, lakesides, and punk concerts. They take music very seriously, or say they do, but with fans like these, punk audiences would applaud politely.

Then there is the matter of their novels and the title of one of them, *Prosopopeia.* Well, Norway's greatest living writer thinks it's a good title, just as the book is a "good" book. You get the impression that, at his age, "great" would trigger a seizure. I never got any clear idea of what the novels were about, not even during a torturous television chat show that later triggers the greatest living writer's observation that TV is not the ideal medium for discussing literature. The cinema is an ideal medium for considering characters like those in *Reprise,* but you'd have to see *Jules and Jim* to find out why.

Rescue Dawn ★ ★ ★ ½

PG-13, 125 m., 2007

Christian Bale (Dieter Dengler), Steve Zahn (Duane), Jeremy Davies (Gene), Galen Yuen (Y.C.), Abhijati Muek Jusakul (Phisit), Chaiyan Lek Chunsuttiwat (Procet), Teerawat Ka Ge Mulvilai (Little Hitler). Directed by Werner Herzog and produced by Steve Marlton, Elton Brand, and Harry Knapp. Screenplay by Herzog.

When he was a child during World War II, Dieter Dengler had an attic room on a German hillside overlooking a valley. One day an American fighter plane roared past "only feet away," he recalled. The plane's canopy was down; he made eye contact with the pilot for a moment and instantly knew that he wanted to fly.

Werner Herzog's *Rescue Dawn,* based on Dengler's experiences, begins early in the Vietnam War, when Dengler is a U.S Navy pilot stationed on a carrier in the Gulf of Tonkin. At eighteen, he enlisted in order to get American citizenship—and to fly. Assigned to a secret illegal bombing mission over Laos, he is shot down, and the film involves his experiences as a prisoner of war, his escape, and his harrowing fight for survival in the jungle. He was one of only seven Americans to escape from a Viet Cong POW camp and live. Dengler (Christian Bale) scoffs at his flimsy bamboo "cell" until a fellow American tells him, "Don't you get it? It's the jungle that is the prison."

His ordeal includes torture in the camp (he is hung by his heels with an ants' nest fastened to his head) and an agonizing trek through the jungle, at first with a fellow American named Duane (Steve Zahn), then alone. Herzog makes no attempt to pump this story up into a thrilling adventure. There is nothing thrilling about dysentery, starvation, insect bites, and despair. The film heads instead into the trembling fear at Dengler's center.

This feature has been long on the mind of Herzog, who film for film is the most original and challenging of directors. He used the real Dieter Dengler in a 1997 documentary named *Little Dieter Needs to Fly,* in which he took Dengler back to the jungle and together they re-created his escape while Dengler provided a breathlessly intense narration.

Considering that Herzog made both films, it is perhaps not surprising that the "fictional" feature is more realistic than the documentary. With Herzog there is always free trade between fact and fantasy. *Little Dieter* shows Dengler obsessively opening and closing the doors and windows of his house to be sure he is not locked in. Not true, Herzog told me; the director added that detail for dramatic effect. Also in the doc, Dengler imagines himself being followed through the jungle by a bear, who came to represent "death, my only friend." That seems to be a fantasy, yet Herzog says it was real. But there is no bear in *Rescue Dawn.* Too hard to believe, is my guess.

The movie is, indeed, perhaps the most believable Herzog has made. For a director who gravitates toward the extremes of human behavior, this film involves extreme behavior, yes, but behavior forced by the circumstances. There is nothing in it we cannot, or do not, believe. I was almost prepared to compare it to the classic storytelling of a John Huston film when I realized it had crucial Herzogian differences.

One is the use of location. Asked long ago why he went to so much trouble to shoot *Aguirre, the Wrath of God* and *Fitzcarraldo* hundreds of miles into the rain forests of the Amazon, he said it involved "the voodoo of location." He felt actors, directors, cinematographers, and perhaps the film itself absorbed something from where the shooting took place. Even his vampire film *Nosferatu* (1990) sought out the same locations F. W. Murnau used in the silent 1922 original.

In *Rescue Dawn,* filmed in the jungles of Thailand, there is never the slightest doubt we are in the jungle. No movie stars creeping behind potted shrubbery on a back lot. The screen always looks wet and green, and the actors push through the choking vegetation with difficulty. We can almost smell the rot and humidity. To discuss the power of the performances by Bale, Zahn, and Jeremy Davies (another POW) would miss the point unless we speculated about how much of the conviction in their work came from the fact that they were really doing it in the hellish place where it was really done.

The other Herzog touch is the music. Herzog recoils from conventional scores that mirror the action. Here he uses not upbeat adventure music but brooding, introspective, doomy music by Klaus Badelt; classical and chamber performances; and passages by Popol Vuh, the German New Age band that supplied so much of the feeling in *Aguirre* and *Fitzcarraldo.*

Rescue Dawn opened in some markets on July 4. It is about a man who won the Distinguished Flying Cross and the Navy Cross (none of which it mentions). Given the times we live in, is it an upbeat, patriotic film? Not by intention. It is simply the story of this man. When he is finally greeted back aboard his aircraft carrier, there is no "mission accomplished" banner, and when he is asked for his words of advice for the cheering crew, he says: "Empty that which is full. Fill that which is empty. If it itches, scratch it."

Resurrecting the Champ ★ ★ ★

PG-13, 111 m., 2007

Samuel L. Jackson (Champ), Josh Hartnett (Erik), Kathryn Morris (Joyce), Alan Alda (Metz), Teri Hatcher (Flak), Rachel Nichols (Polly), David Paymer (Whitley), Dakota Goyo (Teddy). Directed by Rod Lurie and produced by Lurie, Mike Medavoy, Bob Yari, and Marc Frydman. Screenplay by Michael Bortman and Allison Burnett.

In the news business, there is an intoxication in making a big story your own. In *Zodiac,* a cartoonist strays off his beat and tries to solve a string of serial killings. In Rod Lurie's *Resurrecting the Champ,* a sportswriter stumbles on the story of a skid-row drunk who used to be a contender. Erik (Josh Hartnett) has been told by his editor he is sloppy and lazy, and when he comes upon Champ, it's like a gift from heaven. The former heavyweight boxer (Samuel L. Jackson) has just been beaten up by some young punks but harbors little resentment against them. He's talkative and tells Erik his story.

His real name, he says, is Bob Satterfield. At one time he was ranked number three. He even sparred with Marciano. Now he's a shambling mess, old, homeless, remembering past glories. A lot of boxers with his history would have had their brains scrambled, but Champ remembers the past in detail; alcohol is his problem. Erik senses what we reporters like to assure our editors is a "great story." We are not modest about reviewing our unwritten work.

Erik, separated from his wife (Kathryn Morris), has a son named Teddy (Dakota Goyo) whom he tells about all the celebrities he meets. All reporters meet celebrities, just like all detectives meet murderers, but you know you're a pitiful dad when you try name-dropping to impress a six-year-old. The home life doesn't supply many of the film's best scenes, but I like the newspaper office performance by Alan Alda, as Erik's editor. Have you noticed in recent movies that Alda has *finally* stopped looking so much like Hawkeye Pierce? It frees him up in his characters.

Jackson disappears into his role, completely convincing, but then he usually is. What a fine actor. He avoids pitfalls like making Champ a maudlin tearjerker, looking for pity. He's realistic, even philosophical, about his life and what happened to him. Hartnett is efficient enough in his role, but doesn't have enough edges and angles on him to be a sportswriter. Robert Downey Jr. for sportswriter, Josh Hartnett for movie critic.

There are developments in this movie that I don't want to hint at, especially since they surprised me, and you should have the same pleasure. They call into question, let us say, people's motives for doing things, and what happens when two people have the misfortune to find that their motives are a good fit.

So let us talk about the plight of the former boxer. Jackson obviously gave a lot of thought to the character, and invents him fresh instead of cobbling him together out of leftovers. A punch-drunk stumblebum would have been wearisome here, but you can see the intelligence in Champ's eyes, even despite the hair and makeup that make the sleek Jackson look like Alley Oop. He has a few words with Erik, sizes him up, and takes care of business. Apparently he has a better nose for suckers than for sucker punches.

He made me curious enough that I Wikipediaed Bob Satterfield and found out, yes, he was a real fighter, nicknamed the Bombardier, and was KO'd by the Raging Bull himself in a 1946 fight in Wrigley Field. He was a Chicago boy, Golden Gloves champ in 1941, fought Ezzard Charles and Archie Moore, won fifty, lost twenty-five, with four draws. This is more than Erik knows; he's never heard of Satterfield, but Satterfield is only too happy to fill him in. And Erik is right: It does make a great story. Does he remember everything with perfect accuracy? There is an old newspaper adage, now mostly abandoned: "Never check a good quote twice."

Revolver ½★

R, 115 m., 2007

Jason Statham (Jake Green), Ray Liotta (Dorothy Macha), Vincent Pastore (Zach), Andre Benjamin (Avi), Terence Maynard (French Paul), Andrew Howard (Billy), Mark Strong (Sorter), Francesca Annis (Lili Walker). Directed by Guy Ritchie and produced by Luc Besson and Virginie Silla. Screenplay by Ritchie.

Guy Ritchie's *Revolver* is a frothing mad film that thrashes against its very sprocket holes in an attempt to bash its brains out against the projector. It seems designed to punish the audience for buying tickets. It is a "thriller" without thrills, constructed in a meaningless jumble of flashbacks and flash-forwards and subtitles and mottos and messages and scenes that are deconstructed, reconstructed, and self-destructed. I wanted to signal the projectionist to put a gun to it.

The plot. What is the plot? Jason Statham has spent seven years in jail between a con man in the cell on one side and a chess master on the other. Back on the street, he walks into a casino run by his old enemy Ray Liotta and wins a fortune at the table. Did he cheat or what? I dunno. Liotta sics some hit men on him. Then two mysterious strangers (Vincent Pastore and Andre Benjamin) materialize in Statham's life at just such moments when they are in a position to save it. Who, oh who, could these two men, one of whom plays chess, possibly be?

The movie begins with a bunch of sayings that will be repeated endlessly like mantras throughout the film. Chris Cabin at filmcritic.com thinks these have some connection with the Kabbalah beliefs of Ritchie and his wife, Madonna. I know zilch about the Kabbalah, but if he's right, and if Ritchie follows them, I would urgently warn other directors to stay clear of the Kabbalah. Judging by this film, it encourages you to mistake hopeless confusion for pure reason.

Oh, this film angered me. It kept turning back on itself, biting its own tail, doubling back through scenes with less and less meaning and purpose, chanting those sayings as if to hammer us down into accepting them. It employed three editors. Skeleton crew. Some of the acting is better than the film deserves. Make that all of the acting. Actually, the film stock itself is better than the film deserves. You know when sometimes a film catches fire inside a projector? If it happened with this one, I suspect the audience might cheer.

The Ringer ★ ★ ★

PG-13, 94 m., 2005

Johnny Knoxville (Steve Barker), Brian Cox (Gary Barker), Katherine Heigl (Lynn Sheridan),

Jed Rees (Glen), Bill Chott (Thomas), Edward Barbanell (Billy), Leonard Earl Howze (Mark), Geoffrey Arend (Winston), John Taylor (Rudy), Luis Avalos (Stavi), Leonard Flowers (Jimmy). Directed by Barry W. Blaustein and produced by Peter Farrelly, Bobby Farrelly, John L. Jacobs, and Bradley Thomas. Screenplay by Ricky Blitt.

The Ringer is a comedy about a man who poses as mentally disabled in order to fraudulently enter the Special Olympics. Yes, it's connected to the Farrelly brothers, specialists in bad taste, the same Bobby and Peter who showed the guy's artificial thumb rolling down the alley stuck in his bowling ball; indeed, the same Peter and Bobby who in *There's Something About Mary* gave us the hair gel that could have taken cell cloning research in a new direction. They are the producers of *The Ringer*, which means they came up with the money, and my guess is a lot more than that.

So the movie is in horrible taste and politically incorrect and an affront to all that is decent, right? After all, it stars Johnny Knoxville, whose *Jackass* TV show is probably the Farrellys' idea of *Masterpiece Theater*. But not so fast, Ex-Lax. The movie surprised me. It treats its disabled characters with affection and respect, it has a plot that uses the Special Olympics instead of misusing them, and it's actually kind of sweet, apart from a few Farrellian touches, such as the ex-janitor who gets his fingers chopped off in the lawn mower.

What happens is that the hero, Steve Barker (Knoxville), listens to one self-help tape too many: "Hey, you! Yes, you! I'm talking to you—the loser who bought this tape!" The tape works him into a lather and he demands a promotion. "Sure," says the boss. "You can start now. Fire the janitor."

But, jeez, Stavi the janitor (Luis Avalos) is a nice guy, and a widower with five kids to feed. So Steve fires him and then hires him to mow the lawn at his condo and gives him a raise out of his own salary, and then "Stavi Lose Fingers." Stavi, who always refers to himself in the third person, seems to speak in capitalized words, as in "Stavi's Kids Will Starve," or "HMO Says Stavi Has No Finger-Sewing Insurance."

Steve has an uncle, Gary (Brian Cox), who is wanted by the mob regarding a past-due loan and who knows how he and Steve can raise the money they need. Steve will pose as a Special Olympian, run rings around the other athletes, and Uncle Gary will bet a lot of money on him. Steve is a lot of things, but he is not a Special Actor. He poses as mentally challenged, calls himself Jeffy, forgets his last name and his Uncle Gary suggests Dahmer. The real Special Olympians are not fooled by him for one second: "You talk different," they tell him.

The competition includes Jimmy (Leonard Flowers), the Special Superstar, who arrives in a stretch limo with his agents and trainers, and has a lot of endorsement contracts. Also some regular Special Guys who, once they've blown Jeffy's cover, think it's cool that anyone would be stupid enough to try a stunt like that. And there's a beautiful volunteer named Lynn (Katherine Heigl), whom Steve falls in love with—as Jeffy, leading to complications.

The plot takes care of itself on the level of a competent sitcom. This is not a great movie, but I kinda liked its spirit. It might have been better if the Farrellys had directed instead of Barry W. Blaustein. Some of the Special characters are disabled, some are not, but all are seen as engaging and valuable people.

Although the Farrellys have made a career out of comedies in bad taste, I happen to know they have a sincere interest in mentally challenged people because they have a good friend named Rocket who knows *everything* about the movies. When we were trying out cohosts on the TV show, they called me and pitched Rocket for the job. "For cohost?" I asked. "Or your job," they said. I was tempted but afraid the audition might come across the wrong way.

The Ringer could have been a better movie, but that would have depended more on the screenplay than the cast, which is effective and generates real affection. Knoxville is on target as nothing Special, and Cox demonstrates why he is not only in every movie made, but deserves to be.

Note: Is the movie appropriate for developmentally disabled young people? There is a sincere note on the Internet Movie Database from the mother of a disabled child and Special Olympics participant. I pass along her opinion without comment. She writes:

While you may find the story uplifting, it may elude your students' understanding. It may be painful for them to see the type of teasing and disrespect they experience. Don't assume they will get the same thing out of the movie that you do. You may do a lot more harm than good. . . .

I did not *allow my son to see* Forrest Gump *or* I Am Sam *specifically because he will view these types of films from an entirely different perspective. Because the film is about the disabled, the journey itself is far too personal for many developmentally disabled people to endure and perhaps difficult for them to understand the good intentions.*

The Ring Two ★ ★ ½

PG-13, 111 m., 2005

Naomi Watts (Rachel Keller), David Dorfman (Aidan Keller), Simon Baker (Max Rourke), Sissy Spacek (Evelyn), Elizabeth Perkins (Dr. Emma Temple), Gary Cole (Martin Savide). Directed by Hideo Nakata and produced by Laurie MacDonald, Walter F. Parkes, and Mark Sourian. Screenplay by Ehren Kruger, based on the novel *Ringu* by Koji Suzuki.

I am not sure I entirely understand the deer. In *The Ring Two,* Rachel and her young son, Aidan, visit a farmers' market. Aidan wanders off and observes some deer that emerge from a nearby forest and stare at him. He stares back. Later, as mother and son are driving down a little-traveled road, a deer appears in front of their car. "Keep moving," Aidan says urgently, but his mother hesitates, and soon the car is under attack by a dozen stags, their antlers crashing through the windows. She speeds away and hits another stag, doing considerable damage to the car's front end.

This is in a movie that also involves a mysterious video that brings death to whoever watches it, unless they pass it on to someone else within a week. The video is connected to the death of a young girl named Samara who had a cruel childhood. Samara's ghost is trying to possess Aidan's body. Because she died at the bottom of a well, much water is produced wherever her ghost manifests itself. Usually the water is on the floor, but sometimes it flows up to the ceiling.

Rachel visits the old farm where the girl was mistreated and died. In the basement, she finds antlers. A whole lot of antlers. So maybe the deer sense Samara's ghost's presence in Aidan and are attacking the car in revenge? But Samara was presumably not the deer hunter, being far too occupied as a cruelly mistreated little girl at the time. So is it that the deer are psychic, but not very bright?

One does not know but, oddly, one does not care. The charm of *The Ring Two,* while limited, is real enough; it is based on the film's ability to make absolutely no sense, while nevertheless generating a convincing feeling of tension a good deal of the time. It is like an exercise in cinema mechanics: Images, music, photography, and mood conspire to create a sense of danger, even though at any given moment we cannot possibly explain the rules under which that danger might manifest itself.

We do get some information. Samara, for example, can hear everything Rachel (Naomi Watts) and Aidan (David Dorfman) say to each other, except when Aidan is asleep. So Rachel talks to him a lot while he's asleep, with dubious utility. They also appear in each other's dreams, where they either (a) find a loophole by talking to each other while they're asleep, or (b) are only dreaming.

Meanwhile, the video gimmick, which supported *The Ring* (2002), is retired and the action centers on Samara's assaults on Aidan's body and Rachel's attempts to defend him. At one point this involves almost drowning him in a bathtub, which is the second time (after *Constantine*) that being almost drowned in a bathtub is employed as a weapon against supernatural forces.

The movie has been directed by Hideo Nakata, who directed the two famous Japanese horror films *Ringu* (1998) and *Ringu 2* (1999), although *The Ring Two* is not a remake of *Ringu 2*. It is a new departure, as Rachel, a newspaper reporter, leaves Seattle and gets a job on the paper in the pretty but rainy coastal town of Astoria, Oregon. Here perhaps the tape and its associated menace will not follow them.

Naomi Watts and David Dorfman are always convincing, sometimes very effective, in their roles; in the scene where she's going down into the basement, we keep repeating, "It's only a basement," but I was surprised that the ancient cinematic techniques still worked for me. In all such scenes it is essential for the camera to back into the basement while focused on the heroine, so that we cannot see what she sees, and therefore, through curious movie logic, neither can she.

The scenes involving Aidan's health are also well handled, as his body temperature goes up and down like an applause meter, reflecting the current state of Samara's success in taking over his body. If he becomes entirely a ghost, does he go down to room temperature? Elizabeth Perkins plays a psychiatrist who thinks Aidan may have been abused, and there is a creepy cameo by Sissy Spacek, wearing scary old lady makeup, as Samara's birth mother. Aidan always calls his mother "Rachel," by the way, and when he starts calling her "Mommy" this is not a good sign.

When I say the film defies explanation, that doesn't mean it discourages it. Web sites exist for no other reason than to do the work of the screenwriters by figuring out what it all means. At the end, for example, when Rachel rolls the heavy stone across the top of the well, does that mean Samara is out of business? Rachel seems to think so, but wasn't the stone *always* on top of the well?

Rize ★ ★ ★

PG-13, 85 m., 2005

Featuring Tommy the Clown, Lil Tommy, Larry, Swoop, El Nino, Dragon, Lil C, Tight Eyez, Baby Tight Eyez, Daisy, Big X, Miss Prissy, La Nina, and Quinesha. A documentary directed by David LaChapelle and produced by Marc Hawker, Ellen Jacobson-Clarke, and LaChapelle. Screenplay by LaChapelle.

The footage in this movie has not been speeded up in any way.

We need to be told that, right at the beginning of *Rize*, because krumping, the dance style shown in the movie, looks like life in fast-forward. You haven't heard of krumping? Neither had I. And I didn't know that dressing up like a clown has become an alternative to joining a street gang in the South Central and Watts areas of Los Angeles. When this movie was made, there were more than 50 clown groups; now there are said to be more than 100.

Rize is the rare documentary that plays as breaking news. Krumping and clowning have become so big in L.A. that the fifth annual krumping competition, known as Battle Zone, was held in the Great Western Forum. Yet until this movie was made by *Vanity Fair* photographer David LaChapelle, it was a phenomenon that existed below the radar of the media. It's an alternative to the hip-hop style that is growing a little old; because recording labels and cable TV have so much invested in hip-hop, however, they have been slow to embrace it. Or maybe they just couldn't believe their eyes.

The clowns in these groups are real clowns. Bozo should get royalties. They have rainbow wigs and putty noses and weirdly made-up faces and wildly colored costumes, and they would have floppy shoes except then they couldn't dance. The dance they do, krumping, sometimes looks like a fistfight in fast motion, sometimes borrows moves from strippers, sometimes looks like speeded-up martial arts, sometimes is beyond description.

Borrowing a page from poetry jams, krumpers face off one-on-one and try to out-krump one another, and the final showdown in Battle Zone V is between the two main factions of the movement, the krumps and the clowns. (Just to spell out the difference: While clowns krump, not all krumps are clowns. Krumping was invented by Lil C, Tight Eyez, and Dragon after they left Tommy to start their own school. So now you know.)

This world is the invention, we learn, of Tommy the Clown (Tom Johnson), who as a young man was into drugs and gangs. "Living like that," he says, "you either wind up shot dead or in jail. I was lucky. I wound up in jail." When he was released and unsure what direction his life would take, he was asked to play a clown at a friend's birthday party. He liked the way people responded to him as a clown; they regarded him as if he had dropped out of ordinary categories and lived in a separate world.

Tommy the Clown became "a ghetto celebrity," he tells us, and we see footage of Tommy making unannounced appearances at shopping malls, movie theater lines, and street corners. He takes his first disciple, Lil Tommy ("When my mom was in jail, he took me in"), and soon he's running a clown academy. A key moment comes when the clowns evoke a new kind of dancing; a clown named Larry is a key innovator. Soon there are groups of krump-dancing clowns all over the streets of neighborhoods that were once afire (the film opens with footage from the Watts and Rodney King rioting).

In these neighborhoods to wear the wrong gang colors in the wrong place at the wrong time is to risk being shot dead. But a clown wears every possible color at once, and in a way becomes disqualified. "The gangs sort of leave us alone," one of the clowns says, and there is a sense that joining a clown group may be a way to survive outside the gang culture. It is also a very weird lifestyle.

We see clowns devising elaborate facial makeup, owing more to Batman villains than to Bozo. We witness artistic rivalries between various styles of clowning and dancing. And there are suggestions that not everyone loves clowns; while Tommy is running the face-off at the Forum, his home is trashed. Late in the film, one of the most lovable characters is shot dead by drive-by killers, firing at random. Guns don't kill people; people with guns kill people.

Still, *Rize* on the whole brings good news, of a radical social innovation that simultaneously sidesteps street gangs and bypasses hip-hop. Krumping should turn up any day now on BET and MTV, if it hasn't already; whether the dancers will be dressed as clowns is less likely. There is something a little eerie about clowns, and to see dozens of them at once perhaps inspires even gang members to go elsewhere.

The most remarkable thing about *Rize* is that it is real. I remember hearing vaguely at Sundance about an earlier short subject that LaChapelle made about this phenomenon; was it on the level or a mockumentary? If *Rize* were a fake doc, it would look about the same as it does now, and would be easier to absorb, since the idea of gangs of clowns sounds like a put-on. But it isn't.

Robots ★ ★ ★ ½

PG, 91 m., 2005

With the voices of: Ewan McGregor (Rodney Copperbottom), Halle Berry (Cappy), Greg Kinnear (Phineas T. Ratchet), Mel Brooks (Big Weld), Amanda Bynes (Piper Pinwheeler), Drew Carey (Crank Casey), Jim Broadbent (Madame Gasket), Jennifer Coolidge (Aunt Fanny), Robin Williams (Fender), Stanley Tucci (Herb Copperbottom). Directed by Chris Wedge and Carlos Saldanha and produced by Jerry Davis, John C. Donkin, and William Joyce. Screenplay by David Lindsay-Abaire, Lowell Ganz, and Babaloo Mandel.

The thing that struck me first of all about *Robots* was its pictorial beauty. I doubt that was the intention of the animators, who've made a slapstick comedy set in a futurist city that seems fresh off the cover of a 1942 issue of *Thrilling Wonder Stories.* Towers and skyways and strange architectural constructions look like an Erector set's erotic dreams, and the ideal skyscraper is a space needle ringed by metallic doughnuts.

This world is inhabited by robots who are human in every respect except that they are not human in any respect, if you follow me. They even have babies. As the movie opens, Herb Copperbottom and his wife are unwrapping their new little boy, who has arrived in a shipping crate, some assembly required. This being a PG-rated movie aimed at the whole family, the robots even have the ability to fart, which is a crucial entertainment requirement of younger children.

But look at the design and artistic execution. Each robot is a unique creation, made of nuts and bolts, but also expressing an individual personality, and moving in a way that seems physical and mechanical at the same time. And consider the color palette, which seems to have been borrowed from Fiestaware, which was inspired by the cheap table settings that used to be given away as prizes at Saturday matinees and is now collected by those who inexplicably find it beautiful, such as myself. Even the shapes of some of the robots resemble the plump art deco lines of a Fiestaware teapot or water pitcher.

Like *Finding Nemo,* this is a movie that is a joy to behold entirely apart from what it is about. It looks happy, and more to the point, it looks harmonious. One of the reasons this entirely impossible world works is that it looks like it belongs together, as if it evolved organically.

Of course, organics are the last concern of young Rodney Copperbottom (voice by Ewan McGregor), who is born in Rivet City but dreams of a journey to Robot City, where he hopes that a mysterious tycoon named Big Weld will be amazed by his inventions. Rodney's father (Stanley Tucci) is a dishwasher (the appliance is built right into his midsection), and Rodney has invented a tiny helicopter robot that can whiz around the kitchen, stacking plates and silverware. What is served on the plates I will leave to your imagination.

Encouraged by his father to follow his dream, Rodney takes the train to Robot City. This train apparently uses the same technology as the *Polar Express;* it's pulled by a traditional steam locomotive, which casually takes off and chugs through the air. In Robot City, almost the first robotperson Rodney meets is Fender (Robin Williams), a tourist tout who snaps pictures, sells postcards, and introduces Rodney to the city's public transportation system.

Their trip across town is when we realize how joyously the filmmakers have imagined this world. Chris Wedge and Carlos Saldanha, who worked together on *Ice Age* (2002), create a Rube Goldberg series of ramps, pulleys, catapults, spring-loaded propulsion devices, spiraling chutes, and dizzying mechanical slingshots that hurtle Fender and poor Rodney on a stomach-churning ride, or would if they had stomachs.

Robots has a plot that centers on the availability of spare parts, and uses a lot of them itself, borrowed from other movies. There's a little of *The Wizard of Oz* in the character of Big Weld (Mel Brooks), who does a TV program extolling the virtues and perfection of his vast corporation, but does not seem findable when Rodney visits Big Weld headquarters. Nor are Big Weld's executives interested in Rodney's inventions.

The company is being run day-to-day by Phineas T. Ratchet (Greg Kinnear), who is uninterested in improving the product because a perfect product would be bad for sales. "Upgrades! That's how we make the dough!" he explains, sounding like a consumer electronics executive.

Phineas is dominated by his mother, Madame Gasket, played by Jim Broadbent. Yes, Jim Broadbent, but reflect that in a robot society the genders are elements of design, not function. If you have a screwdriver and swappable attachments, you can come out of the closet as whatever you feel like. Madame Gasket's master plan is to create a shortage of spare parts, so that robots will have to be replaced, instead of being indefinitely repaired like a 1959 Chevy in Havana.

Rodney now meets a sexpot, or would that be an oilpot, named Cappy (Halle Berry), who serves as his guide to some of the secrets of Robot City. She looks great, but of course in a robot society everybody has had some work done. She becomes his sidekick in an invasion of Big Weld headquarters, which leads to a confrontation with the Weld himself.

I have observed before that giant corporations have replaced Nazis as dependable movie villains. Phineas T. Ratchet, who plans an inside takeover of Big Weld's empire, is obviously a student of the theories of conspicuous consumption and planned obsolescence. Such truths of human marketing would presumably have no place in the logical world of robots, but perhaps somewhere in the dim prehistory of Robot City there were human programmers, who added a few lines of code to make the robots endearingly greedy, selfish, and wasteful.

Darwinian processes seem irrelevant in robot society since, as nearly as I can tell, every robot is a unique example of intelligent design, including Aunt Fanny (Jennifer Coolidge), whose enormous derriere would no doubt confer an evolutionary advantage not immediately apparent, if robots reproduced according to the laws of DNA instead of the whims of manufacturers and repairmen. Imagine going to the garage after a breakdown and asking, "How long will it be before I can get myself back?"

Rocket Science ★ ★ ★ ½

R, 101 m., 2007

Reece Daniel Thompson (Hal Hefner), Anna Kendrick (Ginny Ryerson), Nicholas D'Agosto (Ben Wekselbaum), Vincent Piazza (Earl Hefner), Margo Martindale (Coach Lumbly), Stephen Park (Judge Pete), Lisbeth Bartlett (Juliet Hefner), Denis O'Hare (Doyle Hefner). Directed by Jeffrey Blitz and produced by Effie T. Brown and Sean Welch. Screenplay by Blitz.

The high school hero of *Rocket Science* stutters, but all high school kids stutter. It's just that most of them don't do it with their voices. They stutter in the way they don't know how to present themselves, what to say next, how to talk their way out of embarrassment, when to make an approach to someone they have a crush on, or how to perform in class when everybody's looking at them. It's just that Hal Hefner (Reece Daniel Thompson) does it out loud.

That's why he seems to be an odd choice when Ginny Ryerson (Anna Kendrick) talks him into joining the school debate team. The movie opens when she loses her regular debate partner, Ben Wekselbaum (Nicholas D'Agosto). His meltdown is spectacular. In the middle of a debate, he is effortlessly speeding along at a zillion words a second (I learn debaters call this *spreading*) when suddenly he freezes. His mind goes blank and he can't think of a single thing to say. Who can't identify with that?

Ben drops off the team and starts beating himself up psychologically, and that's when Ginny recruits Hal. She has reasons of her own, which are revealed in the fullness of time, but oddly enough they're not the reasons we're expecting. *Rocket Science* is not a formula high school movie, is not about formula kids, and is funny in a way that makes you laugh but it still kinda hurts.

The movie's director, Jeffrey Blitz, must have learned a lot about overachieving kids and their occasional breakdowns while directing his first film, the suspenseful Oscar-nominated documentary *Spellbound* (2002), about the National Spelling Bee. He learned other things, too, like how when adolescent boys of a certain age think about anything but sex, it's a distraction.

Hal has too many hang-ups to develop much of a love life, but the kid who lives next door to Ginny obsesses on her, spies on her, steals her brassiere, and in general makes himself miserable. Meanwhile, does Ginny like Hal, does she feel sorry for him, or is she playing a cruel trick?

Hal has problems beside Ginny. His dad (Denis O'Hare) walks out of his marriage one day, after saying farewell to Hal and his older brother, Earl (Vincent Piazza), in the kind of speech a man might make before leaving for a better job. Then his mom (Lisbeth Bartlett) starts dating a nice Korean judge (Stephen Park), although she lacks certain interethnic instincts. "Is this some kind of an exotic Korean dish?" she asks, "because it has a strange odor." The judge smiles. "It's tuna casserole."

The movie is not a slick repackaging of visual clichés from *Teen Vogue* (that one was *Bratz*) but instead seems to be in a plausible high school filled with students who act and look about the right age, even though they're a little older. The movie was shot in Baltimore, doubling for "Plainsboro High School" in New Jersey, and even spells Plainsboro correctly throughout, unlike "Carry Nation High School" in *Bratz*, which couldn't even spell its title. (This just in: *Carry* is an acceptable spelling for Ms. Nation's first name, but *Bratz* is, of course, a short form of "bratwurst.")

Hold on. I'm drifting back toward my review of *Spellbound*. The thing about *Rocket Science* is that its behavior, even its villainy, is within plausible margins. Ginny is a hateful "popular girl," but she isn't hateful beyond all reason. Hal's mother's new boyfriend is not a stereotyped interloper, but a nice guy who would be an improvement. And a lot of the laughs come in understated asides that reveal character.

The leads, Reece Daniel Thompson and Anna Kendrick (*Camp*), are early in what promise to be considerable careers. Kendrick can make you like her even when you shouldn't, and Thompson fine-tunes the pathos of his dilemma to slip comedy into moments that could be deadly.

I suspect a lot of high school students will recognize elements of real life in the movie (that's why it's rated R, to protect them from themselves) and that the movie will build a following. It may gross as little as *Welcome to the Dollhouse* or as much as *Clueless*, but whichever it does, it's in the same league.

Rock School ★ ★ ★

R, 93 m., 2005

With Paul Green, C. J. Tywoniak, Will O'Connor, Madi Diaz Svalgard, Tucker Collins, Asa Collins, Napoleon Murphy Brock, Eric Svalgard, Andrea Collins, Chris Lampson, Monique Del Rosario, Brandon King, Lisa Rubens, Lisa Green, and Jimmy Carl Black. A documentary directed by

Don Argott and produced by Argott and Sheena M. Joyce.

Paul Green is a great teacher. We have this on the authority of Paul Green. He wanted to be a great rock musician, and when that didn't pan out, he picked something he could be great at, and now, he admits, he is great at it. He is the founder and apparently the entire faculty at the Paul Green School of Rock, a Philadelphia after-school program that takes kids ages nine to seventeen and trains them to be rock musicians. Maybe he would like to start even sooner; at one point he asks his infant son, "Can you say 'Jethro Tull'?"

The school is crammed into a narrow brick building where every classroom seems jammed with kids who do not measure up to Green's standards. He warns them, berates them, shouts at them, waves his arms, issues dire predictions, and somehow gets them to play music. Some of them are pretty good. There is a guitar player named C. J. Tywoniak, who stands about five feet tall and can play better than most of the guitarists you see on *Saturday Night Live.* And a singer named Madi Diaz Svalgard, who comes out of a Quaker background and knows people involved in a group named Quaker Gangsta.

"The whole thing in education now is that you don't compare children," Green says. "Well, I do." It's difficult to figure out what the kids are thinking as they stare at him during his tirades, but he has a certain level of self-mockery that takes the edge off. Green is not an angry jerk so much as a guy playing an angry jerk because he loves rock music and wants these kids to play it well. He is not Mr. Nice Guy, like the Jack Black character in *School of Rock.*

But what does he mean by rock music? "I wanted life as a rock star in 1972," he said. "I'd never want to be a rock star now." His god is Frank Zappa, and he leads the kids through difficult Zappa songs like *Inca Roads,* preparing them for the annual Zappanale Festival in Germany. "We gotta be the best band there," he says, and during his preshow pep talks he sounds uncannily like a coach in a high school sports movie. In Germany they get a chance to play with two Zappa veterans, Napoleon Murphy Brock and Jimmy Carl Black, and Murphy Brock gets down on his knees and bows to young C. J., and is about half-serious.

One of the most intriguing students in the school is Will O'Connor, who provides a description of his rocky beginnings: His was a difficult birth, his head was too large, he had to wear a neck brace for three years, he was misdiagnosed as mentally challenged, he was suicidal, etc., and then he discovered the School of Rock, and while he has not emerged as much of a musician, he no longer thinks of suicide and can even kid about it. Paul Green establishes the school's "Will O'Connor Award for Student Most Likely to Kill Himself," which sounds one way when it's an in-joke in the school corridors and another way when it's quoted in the *Philadelphia Inquirer.* One thing becomes clear when O'Connor is on the screen: Far from being "slow," he talks like the smartest person in the movie. The School of Rock is made for difficult cases like his.

There are scenes showing Lisa, Paul's wife, and his home life, which looks conventional. There are interviews with a few parents, who seem pleased with what their children are learning at school. One even styles her kid's hair in a spiky punk style but draws the line at stenciling pentagrams on his face. Scenes of nine-year-olds rehearsing to sing in a menacing fashion are illuminating, revealing the nine-year-olds inside many rock singers.

Green uses the f-word incessantly, along with all the other words he can think of, and anyone in the conventional educational system would be horrified, I suspect, by moments in this film. What is important is that he doesn't talk down to the students, and he is deadly serious about wanting them to work hard, practice more, and become good musicians. He rants and raves, but at least he doesn't condescend. "By the time I'm thirty," his student Will O'Connor says, evaluating his musical progress, "I think I could be decent. If I live that long."

All very well, but how good a teacher is Paul Green, really? There are no scenes in the movie showing him actually teaching his students to play a guitar. Not a single musical note is discussed. No voice lessons. There are times when the point of the school doesn't seem to be making students into rock stars, but rewriting Green's own lost childhood. There are other times when the students regard him blankly, waiting for his wacky behavior to be over so that they can get back to playing. We see no friendships between the students. Not much school spirit; they're playing for Green's glory, not their own. Green's approach certainly opens up opportunities for his students, and is a refreshing change from the lockstep public school approach, which punishes individualism. But sooner or later, a kid like C. J. Tywoniak is going to have to move on—to Juilliard, maybe.

Roll Bounce ★ ★ ★

PG-13, 107 m., 2005

Bow Wow (Xavier ["X"]), Chi McBride (Curtis Smith), Mike Epps (Byron), Wesley Jonathan (Sweetness), Kellita Smith (Vivian), Meagan Good (Naomi), Khleo Thomas (Mixed Mike), Nick Cannon (Bernard), Rick Gonzalez (Naps), Jurnee Smollett (Tori). Directed by Malcolm D. Lee and produced by Robert Teitel and George Tillman Jr. Screenplay by Norman Vance Jr.

Film by film, the makers of *Roll Bounce* have been creating a new world in American movies. This is a world in which black people live in well-kept homes, have jobs, don't do drugs, don't have guns, aren't in gangs, don't call anybody "bitch," and do not use a famous twelve-letter word. It is sad that I need to write such a paragraph, but relevant: The dominant image of African-Americans in the movies is of the lawless, the violent, and the drugged. This image does not represent the majority of black people, but it works as subtle propaganda in the minds of audiences of all races.

Now consider some titles. The producers of *Roll Bounce,* Robert Teitel and George Tillman Jr., also made *Soul Food, Men of Honor* (with Cuba Gooding Jr. as the first black Navy diver), *Barbershop* and its spin-offs, and *Beauty Shop.* Some of the movies are better than others, but all of them have good hearts. They reflect a reality that is missing in the Friday-night multiplex specials.

Roll Bounce, a nostalgic memory of disco roller dancing in the late 1970s, has warm starring performances from Bow Wow (formerly "L'il") and Chi McBride, who are funny, lovable, and sometimes touching. In their different ways, they're mourning the death of a mother and wife; Xavier (Bow Wow) hangs out with four friends at a Chicago South Side roller rink, and Curtis (McBride) obsesses on repairing his dead wife's car. It is his secret that after ten years as an engineer, he lost his job when his company closed and he is out of work.

Xavier feels his dad is distant. He is right; the father is distracted by his grief and worries. At the Palisades Gardens, "X" and his friends practice synchronized skating routines, but then the rink closes: "There goes our summer." Not quite. On the North Side there's the Sweetwater rink, an establishment so grand that special effects are used to create its facade. Sweetwater is ruled by a showboat dancer named Sweetness (Wesley Jonathan), who has a court of three male backup skaters and three sexy girls who hold his cape and his hat and look at him yearningly.

X is reluctant to go to Sweetwater until he sees Sweetness in action and his competitive spirit is aroused. He and his buddies decide to enter the big $500 skate-off at the end of the summer. Joining them as a mascot is the new girl next door, Tori (Jurnee Smollett), who has braces on her teeth that the boys kid her about—but then the screenplay by Norman Vance Jr. is filled with sharp-edged dialogue in which ritualistic insults are exchanged in language that is colorful precisely because it is not made out of tired vulgarities. Tori's mom, Vivian (Kellita Smith), also lives next door, which eventually becomes of interest to Curtis.

At the rink, X and his friends encounter Naomi (Meagan Good), whom Xavier once almost dated, apparently, before he dropped out because of the loss of his mother and of his self-confidence. She's gotten a lot prettier in the year since he saw her, but she's still nice—too nice to be impressed by Sweetness, for example. It is astonishing Naomi and Tori do not become rivals; instead, Tori encourages X to ask Naomi out, because she thinks they'd be good together. A move like that away from the predictable story line allows all sorts of truth into a situation that would otherwise be on autopilot.

There are two climaxes in the movie: the skate-off, and the inevitable moment of truth between Xavier and his dad. Both are handled well: the skate-off like a reprise of *Saturday Night Fever,* the father-son conversation filled with earnest sentiment. McBride and Bow Wow, who between them have specialized in comedies and music videos, find serious emotion well within their reach. In the skate-off, Sweetness and his gang are so talented that it's unlikely Bow Wow's crowd would be in contention, but there you go.

Roll Bounce is not a great film, but it does a good job of doing exactly what it intends: showing a summer in the lives of ordinary teenagers and their parents, and remembering the roller disco craze that preceded hip-hop. It's based on fact. Chicago black kids in the 1970s really did move between a neighborhood rink and a ritzier North Side rink, and it was kind of a territorial thing. The movie gets something else right (and wrong). Xavier has a paper route, which is right, but he throws the wrong paper.

Romance and Cigarettes ★ ★ ★ ★

R, 115 m., 2007

James Gandolfini (Nick Murder), Susan Sarandon (Kitty), Kate Winslet (Tula), Steve Buscemi (Angelo), Bobby Cannavale (Fryburg), Mandy Moore (Baby), Mary-Louise Parker (Constance), Aida Turturro (Rosebud), Eddie Izzard (Gene), Christopher Walken (Cousin Bo), Elaine Stritch (Mother). Directed by John Turturro and produced by John Penotti and Turturro. Screenplay by Turturro.

How did one of the most magical films of the 2005 festival season become one of the hardest films of 2007 to see? John Turturro's *Romance and Cigarettes* is the real thing, a film that breaks out of Hollywood jail with audacious originality, startling sexuality, heartfelt emotions, and an anarchic liberty. The actors toss their heads and run their mouths like prisoners let loose to race free.

The story involves a marriage at war between a Queens high-steel worker named Nick (James Gandolfini) and his tempestuous wife, Kitty (Susan Sarandon), who has found a poem he wrote to his mistress (Kate Winslet), or more accurately, to that part of her he most treasures. After Kitty calls him a whoremaster (the film is energetic in its vulgarity), they stage a verbal battle in front of their three grown daughters, and then he escapes from the house to do—what? To start singing along with Engelbert Humperdinck's "A Man Without Love," that's what.

He dances in the street and is joined by a singing chorus of garbage men, neighbors, and total strangers. What do I mean by "singing along"? That we hear the original recordings and the voices of the actors, as if pop music not only supplies the sound track of their lives, but they sing along with it. The strategy of weaving in pop songs continues throughout and is exhilarating, reminding me of Woody Allen's *Everyone Says I Love You.*

Gandolfini and Sarandon, who portray a love that has survived but is battered and bitter, are surrounded by their "armies," as Nick describes them to a cop. She has their three young adult daughters (Mary-Louise Parker, Mandy Moore, and Aida Turturro), her cousin Bo (Christopher Walken), and the church choir director (Eddie Izzard). He has his work partner (Steve Buscemi) and of course his mistress, who works in a sex lingerie boutique.

Now that I have made this sound like farce, let me make it sound like comedy, and then romance. The dialogue, by Turturro, has wicked timing to turn sentences around in their own tracks. Notice how Nick first appeals to his daughters, then shouts, "This is between your mother and me!" Listen to particular words in a Sarandon sentence that twists the knife.

Observe a scene in Gandolfini's hospital room. He is being visited by his mother (Elaine Stritch) and Buscemi (eating the Whitman's Sampler he brought as a gift). She tells them both something utterly shocking about her late husband, in a monologue that is off the wall and out of the room and heading for orbit. Then observe Buscemi's pay-off reaction shot, which can be described as an expression of polite interest. I can draw your attention to the way he does that, the timing, the expression, but I can't do it justice. Actors who can give you what Stritch gives you, and who can give you Buscemi's reaction to it, should look for a surprise in their pay packet on Friday.

Now as to Winslet's mistress, named Tula. She is not a tramp, although she plays one in Nick's life. She actually likes the big lug, starting with his belly. She talks her way through a sex romp Russ Meyer would envy, and then is so tender to the big, sad guy that you wanna cry. Although the characters in this movie are familiar with vulgarity, they are not limited to it, and *Romance and Cigarettes* makes a slow, lovely U-turn from raucous comedy to bittersweet regret.

The movie got caught in its own turnaround as MGM and United Artists changed hands, was in limbo for a time, was picked up by Sony for DVD release (2008), and was at one time being distributed by Turturro.

So many timid taste mongers have been affronted by the movie that it's running 33 percent on the TomatoMeter, so let me run my own RebertoMeter, which stands at 100, and includes these quotes: "It's the most original picture by an American director I've seen this year, and also the most delightful" (Andrew O'Hehir, Salon); "More raw vitality pumping through *Romance and Cigarettes* than in a dozen perky high school musicals" (Stephen Holden, *New York Times*); "Turturro's energetic, stylish musical about love, sex, and death is such an outrageous film that it's almost impossible not to adore it" (Geoff Andrew, *Time Out London*); and "Four stars and both of my thumbs way up!" (me).

Roman de Gare ★ ★ ½

R, 103 m., 2008

Dominique Pinon (Pierre Laclos/Louis), Fanny Ardant (Judith Ralitzer), Audrey Dana (Huguette), Cyrille Eldin (Paul). Directed, written, and produced by Claude Lelouch.

Roman de Gare is French for what we call an "airport novel," but it's virtually the opposite. In a good airport novel, the plot plows you through safety-belt demonstrations, five-dollar "snacks," and lists of connecting flights. In *Roman de Gare*, the plot has a way of braking to a halt and forcing us to question everything that has gone before. What can we believe, and when can we believe it? Directed by Claude Lelouch, that inexhaustible middlebrow whose *A Man and a Woman* (1966) monopolized art house screens for months and months, it's so clever that finally that's all it is: clever.

It begins with a flash-forward to the end (or, as it turns out, not quite the end), featuring a famous novelist being questioned by the cops for murder. This is Judith Ralitzer, played by the elegant Fanny Ardant, Francois Truffaut's widow. She's idolized by the next character we meet, Huguette (Audrey Dana). We join her and her boyfriend, Paul (Cyrille Eldin), in a car on an expressway at 3 a.m. They're having a fight that seems to be about her smoking but is actually about their entire relationship, which ends when Paul abandons her at a highway café, taking with him her purse, money, keys, everything. What a lousy trick.

Watching this happen is a man (Dominique Pinon) drinking coffee in the café. He offers her a ride and keeps sipping his coffee until she agrees. The movie hints this is actually Jacques Maury, a pedophile who has escaped from prison. Nicknamed "The Magician," he performs magic tricks to entrance his victims. On the other hand, he may be Judith Ralitzer's ghost writer, as he claims. And what about a worried wife we meet talking to a cop? She thinks her husband, a schoolteacher, has abandoned her. Lelouch constructs a story in which this same man could be one, but not, *I think,* all of the above.

Dominique Pinon is a fascinating actor to watch. With a stepped-on face, a scrawny beard, and a low-key, insinuating manner, he is not blessed by the gods, but he seems able to fascinate women. As he and Huguette drive through the night, he drops the bombshell that he's the ghost writer of her favorite novelist. Then he says things that may synch with news reports of the Magician. All the time, he chews gum in lots of fast little chomps. I was going to say he looks like he's chewing his cud, but he's not like a cow; he's like an insect.

At this point, the movie had me rather fascinated. Turns out Huguette and Paul were driving to the country so she could introduce her parents to Paul for the first time. "Would you do me a huge favor?" she asks her new friend. She wants him to impersonate her fiancé. This leads us into a sly domestic comedy, when Huguette's mother wonders who this little man really is, and Huguette's daughter (who lives on the farm) takes him trout fishing; they're gone for hours, while Huguette reflects she knows nothing about the man except that he said he was a ghost writer and then he said he wasn't. And now the *real* Paul turns up at the farmhouse.

It's here that the movie goes wrong, starting with Huguette's method of facing this situation. Then we learn more about the novelist, her ghost writer, the wife with the missing husband, the cop she's talking to, one of his relatives, and magic tricks. I've invested countless words denouncing plots as retreads! Standard! Obligatory! Here's a plot that double-crosses itself at every opportunity. I should be delighted with it, especially since it visits two of my favorite places, Cannes and Beaune, home of a medieval hospital that made a deep impression on me. Lined up along the walls of an enormous arching room, the patients are bedded in alcoves with a clear view of the altar where Mass is celebrated; the Beaune cure is prayer.

Offshore from Cannes in her luxurious yacht, Judith floats with whomever the hell Dominique Pinon is playing now. He has unexpected plans for her next novel, leading to the question that generates the flash-forward at the beginning. The closing scenes of the movie are dominated by Fanny Ardant, who has the kind of sculptured beauty Truffaut must have recognized when he desired to make her his wife and his star.

When a movie like *Roman de Gare* works, it's ingenious, deceptive, and slippery. When it doesn't, it's just jerking our chains. I think I understand the alternative realities of the plot, and I concede the loose ends are tied up, sort of, but I didn't care. One of the characters played by Pinon would have been enough for this movie. I would have been interested in the escaped pedophile or the ghost writer. But not in both of them interchangeably, and that pesky missing husband. Come on, I'm thinking, give us a place to stand. Do we care about Huguette because her favorite novelist is a fraud, or because her daughter may be sleeping with the fishes?

Rory O'Shea Was Here ★ ★ ★

R, 104 m., 2005

James McAvoy (Rory O'Shea), Steven Robertson (Michael Connolly), Romola Garai (Siobhan), Gerard McSorley (Fergus Connolly), Tom Hickey (Con O'Shea), Brenda Fricker (Eileen). Directed by Damien O'Donnell and produced by James Flynn and Juanita Wilson. Screenplay by Jeffrey Caine.

Don't you want to get drunk, get arrested, get laid?

—Rory to Michael

When Rory O'Shea arrives at the Carrigmore Home for the Disabled, Michael Connolly's life is on hold. Michael's cerebral palsy makes his speech difficult to decipher, except by Rory, who understands every word. Rory himself is exuberantly verbal, but muscular dystrophy has left him with control over two fingers of one hand, and that's it.

Are you still even reading this review? "Marketing challenges don't come much tougher," says *Variety,* the showbiz bible. So I should shift gears and say that *Rory O'Shea Was Here* is funny and moving, and more entertaining than some of the movies you are considering—more than *Son of the Mask* or *Constantine,* that's for sure.

In fact, trying to keep you from tuning out because of the subject matter, I've just gone back and added the quote at the top of this review. That's said by Rory to Michael in his attempt to blast him out of his silent corner at the care home, and get him out in the world—where, Rory is convinced, they both belong.

Rory wears his hair in a weird arrangement of spikes. I didn't notice his shoes, but they were probably Doc Martens. Yes, muscular dystrophy has thrown him a curve, but he's still at the plate and swinging. In no time at all he has Michael following him into a pub, where he tries to pick up girls and at one point seems prepared to start a fight, which with anybody else would be a bad sign but for Rory may actually represent growth.

Rory wants to get out of the institutional world and into independent living. A well-meaning board of supervisors doesn't think he's ready for that yet, not with his disabilities combined with his recklessness. Michael is perfectly prepared to spend forever in the home, until Rory blasts him loose and uses him as his ticket to freedom. He convinces Michael to apply for independent living, and after Michael's application is approved by the board, Rory adds sweetly that of course Michael will need an interpreter.

They'll also need a caregiver, and they interview the usual assortment of hopeless cases. There should be a *Little Glossary* entry about the obligatory scene where a job interview or an audition inevitably involves several weirdly unacceptable candidates, before the perfect choice steps forth.

In this case, they meet Siobhan (Romola Garai) in a supermarket and convince her that life with them will have to be more exciting than stacking toilet tissues. It is more or less inevitable that they'll both get a crush on Siobhan, made more poignant because Rory will have to interpret whatever Michael wants to say to her. How this works out is not predictable and is the occasion for some of the film's best-written and -acted scenes.

James McAvoy plays Rory as a would-be Dublin punk turned into the R. P. McMurphy of the care home. It's a performance combining joy and determination as if they feed off each other. Steven Robertson has more limited opportunities with his character, but let it be said that by the end of the film we can sort of understand what Michael is saying, and we always know what he means. Sometimes, on the other hand, amusingly, a word or two of Rory's Dublin accent slips past undetected.

Both actors are able-bodied in real life. I could not watch the movie without being powerfully reminded of an Australian film that never got theatrical distribution in the United States, Rolf de Heer's *Dance Me to My Song.* It was the first film in my first Overlooked Film Festival, and onstage we greeted Heather Rose, who, like Rory, could control only a finger or two. Yet she wrote the film and starred in it, as a woman with two goals in life, which Rory would have approved of: (1) get revenge on the minder who is mistreating her and stealing from her, and (2) meet a bloke and get laid. Heather Rose was a great and funny woman, who died last year. After the Q&A session, she typed out on her voice synthesizer, in the true Aussie spirit, "Now let's all go out and get pissed."

You can rent *Dance Me to My Song,* and you may want to, after seeing *Rory O'Shea Was Here.* There has been much talk involving the messages about disability sent by two major recent movies. Here is a movie that sends the message that if you want to be a punk and you're in a wheelchair, you can be a punk in a wheelchair. If you're in a chair and want to play rugby, you can, as a documentary named *Murderball* makes perfectly clear. Some are more disabled than others; Rory will not be able to play wheelchair rugby, but he'd make a hell of a coach.

Rumor Has It ★ ★ ★

PG-13, 96 m., 2005

Jennifer Aniston (Sarah Huttinger), Kevin Costner (Beau Burroughs), Shirley MacLaine (Katharine Richelieu), Mark Ruffalo (Jeff Daly), Mena Suvari (Annie Huttinger), Richard Jenkins (Earl Huttinger). Directed by Rob Reiner and produced by Ben Cosgrove and Paul Weinstein. Screenplay by Ted Griffin.

Now here is a curious thing. When I see Jennifer Aniston playing any halfway ordinary character, I have the same reaction: Hey, a friend of mine has somehow gotten into the same movie with all of those stars. I've never actually met Aniston, although once at Sundance I saw paparazzi fight to photograph her with Brad Pitt, in response to a tragic shortage of pictures showing them together. Most of these photos later appeared on the covers of gossip mags with the couple torn in two by a jagged line and Angelina Jolie leering over the bar code, but none of that has anything to do with how I feel when I see Aniston in a movie. It's the damnedest thing. I don't ever want to meet her because then I might lose her as a friend.

In *Rumor Has It,* she plays a character named Sarah Huttinger, who unless she is vigilant may become the *third* woman in her family to sleep with Benjamin Braddock—you remember, the Dustin Hoffman character in *The Graduate.* This, of course, is all based on rumor. In Pasadena, the movie explains, everyone knew the real Charlie Webb, who wrote the novel *The Graduate,* and rumor has it that he based his book on real people who really lived in Pasadena. There really was a bride who ran away with this guy three days before her wedding, and the guy had earlier slept with her mother, who was the original Mrs. Robinson, and so on.

Now another generation has passed. Sarah's mother was the original Elaine Robinson, and a guy named Beau Burroughs (Kevin Costner) was the original Benjamin Braddock, and the original Mrs. Robinson was, therefore, of course, Sarah's grandmother. Can you believe Shirley MacLaine as the original Mrs. Robinson? I can, with no trouble at all.

I could also have believed Anne Bancroft. Sigh. The movie was directed by Rob Reiner, a friend of Anne Bancroft and Mel Brooks since he was a child, and at first I wondered if perhaps the role was intended for her before she become ill. But no: In the film's logic, the characters have *seen* the 1967 movie with Bancroft and Hoffman, and discuss it. It wouldn't make sense for the "real" Mrs. Robinson to be played by the same actress who played the fictional character.

The plot, written by Ted Griffin, sounds like a gimmick. That's because it is a gimmick. But it's a good gimmick. And *Rumor Has It* works for good reasons, including sound construction and the presence of Costner, who is posted sturdily at the balance point between Mrs. Robinson and her granddaughter. We can see him with either one. In fact, at times we seem about to.

As the film opens, Sarah (Aniston) is engaged to marry Jeff (Mark Ruffalo), but they are keeping their engagement a secret until after the wedding of Sarah's sister Annie (Mena Suvari). In "reality," we learn, the original Elaine dumped Benjamin, came back to Pasadena, married Earl (Richard Jenkins), had Sarah and Annie, and then died, which is a neat touch because it sidesteps the Idiot Plot (if their mom is dead, she can't tell them what really happened).

Jeff hears the rumors in Pasadena, does the math, and suggests to Sarah that it's possible she was conceived during the three days her mother ran away with Beau. Obsessed with learning the truth, she tracks down Beau, who is a San Francisco dot-com millionaire, and finds herself attracted to him as a possible dad—and more than a dad, if you see what I mean. Beau is a very attractive guy, but if he's her real father, then that would mean, like, *yeechh!* Try it out loud.

It's for the movie to reveal who does (or doesn't) do what, and with which, and to whom. I will observe that Costner has quietly been reminding us in recent roles *(Open Range, The Upside of Anger)* that when he doesn't play characters who stride astraddle the apocalypse, he is a natural actor with enormous appeal. Ruffalo has a good line in heartfelt sincerity, Richard Jenkins can turn on a dime as good pop/bad pop, and MacLaine plays Mrs. Robinson by just acting naturally.

This is not a great movie, but it's very watchable and has some good laughs. The casting of Aniston is crucial because she's the heroine of this story, and the way it's put together there's danger of her becoming the shuttlecock. Aniston has the presence to pull it off. She has to maybe scuttle her sister's wedding and her own, maybe abandon the guy who loves her, maybe break her official father's heart, maybe (yeechh!) sleep with her (maybe) real dad, yet always retain our sympathy. Well of course she does. She's one of my closest friends.

Running Scared ★ ★ ★

R, 122 m., 2006

Paul Walker (Joey Gazelle), Cameron Bright (Oleg Yugorsky), Vera Farmiga (Teresa Gazelle), Chazz Palminteri (Detective Rydell), Johnny Messner (Tommy "Tombs" Perello), Michael Cudlitz (Sal "Gummy Bear" Franzone), Alex Neuberger (Nicky Gazelle), Ivana Milicevic (Mila Yugorsky), Karel Roden (Anzor Yugorsky), Idalis DeLeon (Divina). Directed by Wayne Kramer and produced by Sammy Lee, Michael A. Pierce, and Brett Ratner. Screenplay by Kramer.

Speaking of movies that go over the top, *Running Scared* goes so far over the top it circumnavigates the top and doubles back on itself; it's the Möbius strip of over-the-topness. I am in awe. It throws in everything but the kitchen sink. Then it throws in the kitchen sink, too, and the combo washer-dryer in the laundry room, while the hero and his wife are having sex on top of it.

I never tire of quoting the French director Truffaut, who said that he was interested only in movies that were about the agony of making cinema or the ecstasy of making cinema. *Running Scared* eliminates the middle man. It's not even about making cinema. It's just about the agony and the ecstasy.

The movie stars Paul Walker. You won't catch him acting in *Running Scared.* The movie never slows down enough. He simply behaves, at an alarming velocity. After an opening flash-forward that features a car crash, the movie flashes back to a drug deal that goes bad. All the crooked cops and drug dealers in the room are killed, except for Joey Gazelle (Walker) and a guy who tells him to take all of the guns and lose them. Actually, maybe some other guys survived, too. This is the kind of movie where the next scene starts before the body count.

Gazelle hides the guns in his basement. His son Nicky (Alex Neuberger) is best friends with Oleg (Cameron Bright), the Russian kid who lives next door. Oleg's father, Anzor (Karel Roden), grew up in Russia watching John Wayne's *The Cowboys* over and over again, maybe a thousand times. But Anzor had only a ten-minute version of the film. So profoundly did it affect him that he had an image of the Duke tattooed on his back. When he came to America and saw the whole movie, he found out Wayne gets shot. This was so traumatic that he turned bitter, beat his wife, and terrorized his son, who steals a gun from the Gazelles' basement and shoots his father, wounding him right about where the sheriff's badge would be.

This is very bad because that is the same gun that killed a cop in the shootout. So Joey Gazelle has to race all over town trying to find the gun and collect the slugs that came out of it (this process involves both impersonating a doctor and chewing gum, although not at the same time). Meanwhile, Oleg runs away, so Joey and Nicky have to find him to get the gun back.

You understand I am giving only the bare bones of the plot. I barely have time to explain why Oleg, who has asthma, is befriended by a hooker (Idalis DeLeon) who gets him a fresh inhaler at gunpoint. And how Oleg is kidnapped by perverts who are so evil they have a body bag in their closet, and how Nicky's mother, Teresa (Vera Farmiga), comes to the rescue, extremely decisively.

Meanwhile, Joey is attacked with an acetylene torch by a mechanic who mistakenly sets himself on fire; Joey delays extinguishing him while screaming, "Where is my gun?" Oh, and there's the scene in the hockey rink where a crime boss has his hockey stars slam pucks at the hero's teeth. Just in case that scene might somehow lack interest, it is shot in black light, so everything glows like a purple necktie at a stag party. Yes, there is extreme material here. The opening sex scene is startling in its exploration of the Midlands. It is certainly a big surprise how the John Wayne tattoo gets shot. The perverts are so creepy they belong in a satanic sitcom. All of this is done using strong characterizations, crisp action, and clear dialogue; this isn't one of those berserk action movies that look like the script was thrown into a fan and the shreds were filmed at random.

Wayne Kramer, the filmmaker, writes and directs with heedless bliss. He's best known for *The Cooler* (2003), that splendid Las Vegas movie about how a casino hired William H. Macy to stand next to lucky gamblers so their luck would turn bad. Kramer is such an overachiever that he actually succeeded in getting *The Cooler* an NC-17 rating for a sex scene starring, yes, William H. Macy. Some would say it starred Maria Bello, but that would be missing the point. The scene had to be trimmed for an R rating, leading to a bitter complaint from the fifty-two-year-old Macy: "I have been working out for thirty years, staying in shape in the dream that someday I would get to play a sex scene. Finally I get one, and they cut it." The Macy specialty they cut out of *The Cooler* ends up in this movie on top of the washer-dryer, in a thrilling combination of sex and the spin cycle.

One of the pleasures of the movie is how supporting characters are given big scenes all for themselves. John Noble has a Tarantinian soliloquy on his childhood obsession with the Duke. Vera Farmiga decisively escapes the cliché of the Thriller Hero's Wife, becomes the Hero's Thrilling Wife, and makes the neatest kills of the movie. Cameron Bright, who played the child containing the reincarnated husband of Nicole Kidman in *Birth,* seems to be a child containing the reincarnated Philip Seymour Hoffman in this one. Chazz Palminteri is such an evil cop that the planes of his face seem to have shifted into a sinister new configuration; I saw him in January at Sundance, where he was pleasant and smiling, and here he looks like a Batman villain who tried to shave with Roto-Rooter.

If you stand way back from *Running Scared*, the plot has certain flaws. For example, close attention to the ending will reveal that Joey Gazelle spent the whole movie risking his life and the lives of his son, his wife, and the neighbor kid in a desperate quest for a gun that *he didn't really need to find*. Don't be depressed if you miss this detail; Joey Gazelle misses it, too. Doesn't matter. The gun is only the MacGuffin. If you don't know what a MacGuffin is, the good news is, you don't need to know.

Rush Hour 3 ★ ★

PG-13, 91 m., 2007

Chris Tucker (Carter), Jackie Chan (Lee), Noemie Lenoir (Genevieve), Hiroyuki Sanada (Kenji), Yvan Attal (George), Jingchu Zhang (Soo Yung), Youki Kudoh (Jasmine), Max von Sydow (Reynard), Roman Polanski (Detective Revi). Directed by Brett Ratner and produced by Arthur Sarkissian, Roger Birnbaum, Jay Stern, Jonathan Glickman, and Andrew Z. Davis. Screenplay by Jeff Nathanson.

I like this movie about as much as it's possible to like a movie with a two-star rating. Given its materials, it couldn't have been much better, but it's every bit as good as it is, if you see what I mean. Once you realize it's only going to be so good, you settle back and enjoy that modest degree of goodness, which is at least not badness, and besides, if you're watching *Rush Hour 3*, you obviously didn't have anything better to do anyway.

The filmmakers didn't either, I guess. It has been six years since *Rush Hour 2*, and unless you believe that director Brett Ratner and his stars, Chris Tucker and Jackie Chan, spent all that time turning down offers for a sequel, it seems fairly likely that this is a case of returning once more with a bucket before the well runs dry. Tucker is again Carter, the motormouth LAPD cop who's always in trouble, and Chan is again Lee, the ace Hong Kong cop called in to partner with him. This is, you realize, a formula. A friend of mine (I think it is me) calls these Wunza Movies. You know, wunza L.A. cop and wunza cop from China, and neither wunza guy you want to mess with.

Curious how Carter is always being hauled in from a punishment gig like traffic cop and being assigned to super-important cases that will require him to investigate backstage at the Folies Bergere in Paris, etc. This time one of Lee's old pals, Ambassador Han, has been shot in L.A., probably by a Chinese Triad gang, who are getting to be as handy as the Mafia for movie plots. Lee, in town as the ambassador's bodyguard, runs after the shooter in one of those impossible Jackie Chan chase scenes; it used to be we were amazed by his stunts, but these days I find myself even more amazed that he can still run that far.

Lee partners with his old friend Carter, and they go to the hospital to question the ambassador's beautiful daughter, Soo Yung (Jingchu Zhang). This produces the movie's funniest line, by Carter: "Let's go to the gift shop and get her a little teddy bear." Soo Yung had possession of an envelope with key evidence her father was going to use in testimony before the World Court. The envelope is, of course, this movie's MacGuffin, and was stolen from Soo Yung at her karate academy.

The cops go there and have a battle with the world's tallest man (Sun Ming Ming). I think he's the same man who got married recently and was about twice as tall as his bride. Or maybe he's another tall guy—naw, it has to be the same guy. Yao Ming, the basketball player, is only seven feet six inches, and Sun Ming Ming is seven feet nine inches. When Jackie Chan engages him in kung fu, he has to call on some of his wall-climbing skills.

Anyway, the chase leads to Paris, where the fragrant Genevieve (Noemie Lenoir) appears. Her function in the film, apart from certain plot details, is—to appear, which she does to great effect. And soon Carter is backstage at the Folies Bergere, and all the time we know, just *know*, that the Eiffel Tower is in the background of so many shots for a reason.

Yes, there is a pursuit up and down the tower, with Jackie Chan doing the usual impossible things, although at fifty-three, he doesn't do all of his own stunts. What difference does it make? In these days of special effects, who can tell anyway? For years, I suspected that the only reason Jackie did the stunts himself was to provide footage for the shots during the closing credits, showing him waving cheerfully as he was taken to the hospital.

All of these events take place efficiently and I was amused, even in a dialogue sequence involving a "Mr. Yu" and a "Mr. Mee," in which "He's Mee" and "I'm Yu," and who's on first? If you are trapped in a rainstorm in front of a theater playing this picture, by all means go right in. You won't have a bad time, will feel affectionate toward Lee and Carter, and stay dry. ☞

RV ★ ★

PG, 98 m., 2006

Robin Williams (Bob Munro), Cheryl Hines (Jamie Munro), Jeff Daniels (Travis Gornicke), Kristen Chenoweth (Mary Jo Gornicke), Joanna "JoJo" Levesque (Cassie Munro), Josh Hutcherson (Carl Munro), Hunter Parrish (Earl Gornicke), Chloe Sonnenfeld (Moon Gornicke), Will Arnett (Todd Mallory). Directed by Barry Sonnenfeld and produced by Bobby Cohen, Lucy Fisher, and Douglas Wick. Screenplay by Geoff Rodkey.

The problem with traveling in a recreational vehicle, Jamie Munro tells her husband, is that you have to spend the night in an RV park with other RV people. "Remember," she tells him, "we're not friendly." The members of the Munro family are not even very friendly with one another. As Bob Munro tells his wife, "We watch TV in four separate rooms and IM each other when it's time to eat dinner." Yet here they are in a gigantic rented RV, traveling cross-country to Colorado and calling it a vacation.

It's almost a genre, the cross-country family vacation movie. In fact, it is a genre. Yellowstone is almost always involved, or at least mentioned. There is trouble with unfriendly animals, reckless driving, and sewage disposal. The genre usually stars Chevy Chase, but this time it's Robin Williams as Pop Munro, Cheryl Hines as his wife, and Joanna "JoJo" Levesque and Josh Hutcherson as their kids, Cassie and Carl. The boy is young enough to still be nice, but Cassie has arrived at that age when parents were put on this earth merely as an inconvenience for her.

Bob had originally thought to take the family to Hawaii, but then his obnoxious boss, Todd (Will Arnett), ordered him to make a presentation in Boulder, Colorado. Afraid to confess the business purpose of his trip, Bob simply rents the giant RV and announces that they'll go camping instead. "But we aren't a camping family," Jamie says. That becomes clear the moment Bob has to perform that least pleasant of RV tasks, emptying the sewage. In real life, this job can theoretically be performed with a minimum of difficulty, but in the movies it always results in the hero being covered by a disgusting substance that oddly never seems to involve toilet paper.

On their first night away, the Munros meet the friendly Gornicke family—Travis and Mary Jo (Jeff Daniels and Kristen Chenoweth) and their kids, Earl, Moon, and Billy (Hunter Parrish, Chloe Sonnenfeld, and Alex Ferris). The Gornickes are mighty friendly. They do country songs as a family. She sells franchise goods from the mobile home. They are masters of sewage, RV lore, route directions, and poking their noses into the business of the Munros, who, as we recall, are not friendly people.

The movie settles down into a rhythm of the road, with the Munros getting into trouble and the Gornickes getting them out of it. There are troublesome raccoons, that emergency brake that doesn't work, and a scene high up on Diablo Pass where Bob gets the RV balanced on a peak and tries to rock it back and forth to get it down onto the road; I was reminded of the tilting cabin in Chaplin's *The Gold Rush,* as I imagine the filmmakers were, too.

All of this is pleasant enough, after a fashion, but it never reaches critical mass. There is nothing I much disliked, but little to really recommend. At least the movie was not nonstop slapstick, and there were a few moments of relative gravity, in which Williams demonstrated once again that he's more effective on the screen when he's serious than when he's trying to be funny.

What else did I like? The good feeling within the Gornicke family. The reptilian loathsomeness of Bob's boss, Todd. Some of the negotiations involving the merger of Bob's giant corporation with a sweet little Boulder beverage company run by the Ben & Jerry of the Rockies. What I didn't much enjoy were extended sequences in which Bob had to run, drive, or pedal desperately. They were intended as comedy but amounted only to behavior.

Now I am going to tell you a strange thing. At one point in the movie, an older man appears on the screen and serves them plates of food. They don't want meat. "It's okay," he says, "it's not meat. It's just organs." The strange thing is: We have never seen this man before, and we never see him again, and no one on screen seems to notice him. Who is he? If there is one thing you should know before driving cross-country in an RV, it is: Never eat organ meats supplied by a man you have never seen before, just because he happens to turn up with a lot of organs.

S

Sahara ★ ★ ★

PG-13, 127 m., 2005

Matthew McConaughey (Dirk Pitt), Steve Zahn (Al Giordino), Penelope Cruz (Eva Rojas), Lambert Wilson (Massarde), Glynn Turman (Dr. Hopper), Delroy Lindo (Carl), William H. Macy (Admiral Sandecker), Rainn Wilson (Rudi), Lennie James (General Kazim). Directed by Breck Eisner and produced by Stephanie Austin, Howard Baldwin, Karen Elise Baldwin, and Mace Neufeld. Screenplay by Thomas Dean Donnelly, Joshua Oppenheimer, John C. Richards, and James V. Hart, based on the novel by Clive Cussler.

Clive Cussler, who wrote the novel that inspired *Sahara,* is said to have rejected untold drafts of the screenplay and sued Paramount over this one. One wonders not so much what Cussler would have left out as what else could have gone in. *Sahara* obviously contains everything that could possibly be included in such a screenplay, and more. It's like a fire sale at the action movie discount outlet.

Do not assume I mean to be negative. I treasure the movie's preposterous plot. It's so completely over the top, it can see reality only in its rearview mirror. What can you say about a movie based on the premise that a Confederate ironclad ship from the Civil War is buried beneath the sands of the Sahara, having ventured there 150 years ago when the region was, obviously, damper than it is now?

Matthew McConaughey plays Dirk Pitt, the movie's hero, who is searching for the legendary ship. Dirk Pitt. Dirk Pitt. Or Pitt, Dirk. Makes Brad Pitt sound like William Pitt. Dirk has a thing about long-lost ships; readers may recall that he was also the hero of *Raise the Titanic* (1980), a movie so expensive that its producer, Lord Lew Grade, observed, "It would have been cheaper to lower the ocean."

Dirk has a sidekick named Al Giordino, played by Steve Zahn in the time-honored Movie Sidekick mode. Was it Walter Huston who explained that movie heroes need sidekicks "because somebody has to do the dance." You know, the dance where the sidekick throws his hat down on the ground and stomps on it in joy or anger? You can't have your hero losing his cool like that.

The two men arrive in Africa to find that a dangerous plague is spreading. The plague is being battled by the beautiful Eva Rojas (Penelope Cruz), and it turns out that Dirk and Eva share mutual interests, since if the plague spreads down rivers and "interacts with salt water," there is a danger that "all ocean life will be destroyed." Actually, I am not sure why that is only a mutual interest; it's more of a universal interest, you would think, although General Kazim (Lennie James), the African dictator, and an evil French zillionaire (Lambert Wilson) don't seem much disturbed. That's because they're getting rich in a way I will not reveal, although there is something grimly amusing about converting pollutants into other pollutants.

The movie, directed by Breck Eisner, son of Michael, is essentially a laundry line for absurd but entertaining action sequences. Dirk, Eva, and Al have an amazing series of close calls in the desert, while Admiral Sandecker (ret.) (William H. Macy) keeps in touch with them by radio and remains steadfast in his course, whatever it is. There are chases involving planes, trains, automobiles, helicopters, dune buggies, wind-propelled airplane carcasses, and camels. The heroes somewhat improbably conceal themselves inside a tank car on a train going toward a secret desert plant (improbably, since the car going in that direction should have been full), and then find themselves one of those James Bondian vantage points inside the plant, from where they can observe uniformed clones carrying out obscure tasks.

There is a race against time before everything explodes, of course, and some bizarre science involving directing the sun's rays, and then what do you suppose turns up? If you slapped yourself up alongside the head and shouted out, "The long-lost Civil War ironclad?" you could not be more correct. Gee, I wonder if its cannons will still fire after this length of time?

I enjoyed this movie on its own dumb level, which must mean (I am forced to conclude) in my own dumb way. I perceive that I have supplied mostly a description of what happens in the film, filtered through my own skewed amusement. Does that make this a real review?

Funny you should ask. As it happens, I happened to be glancing at Gore Vidal's article about the critic Edmund Wilson in a 1993 issue of the *New York Review of Books.* There Vidal writes: "Great critics do not explicate a text; they describe it and then report on what they have described, if the description itself is not the criticism." In this case, I think the description itself is the criticism. Yes, I'm almost sure of it.

Sangre de Mi Sangre ★ ★ ★

NO MPAA RATING, 100 m., 2008

Jorge Adrian Espindola (Pedro), Armando Hernandez (Juan), Jesus Ochoa (Diego), Paola Mendoza (Magda), Eugenio Derbez (Anibal), Israel Hernandez (Ricardo), Leonardo Anzure (Simon). Directed by Christopher Zalla and produced by Benjamin Odell and Per Melita. Screenplay by Zalla.

Sangre de Mi Sangre, the grand jury prize winner at Sundance 2007, gives us wonderful actors struggling in a tangled web of writing. The film is built around two relationships, both touching, both emotionally true. But time after time, we're brought up short by absolute impossibilities and gaping improbabilities in the story. To give one example: A newly arrived Mexican immigrant struggles to find his father in New York City. All he has is the seventeen-year-old information that the man works in (or perhaps owns) a French restaurant. Working his way through the yellow pages listings of French restaurants, he successfully finds his father. Uh-huh.

Let's back up to earlier screenplay questions. We meet the hero, Pedro, as he escapes from Mexico by quickly scaling a fence along the U.S. border. Is it that easy to cross? Never mind; waiting on the other side (not miles away, or hidden) is a truck waiting to take immigrants to New York. Wouldn't U.S. customs patrols notice it, in full view in an urban area? Pedro is hustled inside, the doors are slammed, and the truck begins a 2,500-mile journey that can apparently be survived on half a taco and a small bottle of water. More surprising still is that no effort is made to charge Pedro for the trip. He rides free.

Pedro (Jorge Adrian Espindola) is young, earnest, trusting. On the journey he makes a friend of Juan (Armando Hernandez), and tells him his story: He hopes to find his father in New York and carries a letter to the old man from his mother. When Pedro wakes up at the end of the trip, Juan has already disappeared with the letter.

Juan is enterprising and decides to pose as Pedro; maybe it's true, as Pedro's mother claimed, that the father owned the restaurant where he earned money, which he sent home for several years. But why a French restaurant? Using the address on the envelope, Juan easily finds the shabby apartment of old Diego (Jesus Ochoa), who has never seen him and has no desire to acquire a son. But Juan is ingratiating and tells a convincing story; after all, he has read the letter and Diego refuses to.

Meanwhile, the *real* Pedro wanders the streets, remembering only his father's street address (still accurate after seventeen years). He enlists Magda, a hard-worn Mexican girl who does drugs, makes a living by her wits and her body, and wants nothing to do with Pedro. They nevertheless become confederates, picking up fifty dollars here or there by performing sex for men who want to watch.

At this point you're rolling your eyes and wondering how the grand jury at Sundance, or any jury, could have awarded such a story its prize. But you would have missed what makes the film special: the relationships. Juan does such a good job of playing Pedro that he convinces Diego he really is his son. And the real Pedro gets a quick series of lessons in surviving the mean streets and comes to care about (not for) Magda.

The truest of these relationships, paradoxically, is the false one. Jesus Ochoa, a much-honored Mexican actor, creates a heartbreaking performance as Diego, the "old man," as Juan always calls him. He was once in love in Mexico, left, sent money home, returned, and then (after apparently fathering the real Pedro) returned to New York seventeen years ago. Maybe he told his wife he owned a restaurant, or maybe she lied about that to her son. No matter. He is a dishwasher and vegetable slicer, who earns extra money by sewing artificial roses. He has money stashed away. He is big, burly, very lonely. He comes to care for this "son." And despite Juan's deception, Juan comes to care for him—almost, you could say, as a father.

Magda is a tougher case. She does not bestow her affection lightly, nor is the real Pedro attracted to prostitution as a way for them to earn money. But Zalla, the director, does a perceptive, concise job of showing us how Magda lives on the streets and nearly dies. Magda and Pedro are together as a matter of mutual survival.

Pedro, Juan, and Diego have paths that must eventually cross, we think. See for yourself if they do. And try not to ask why the police, planning to break down a door by surprise, would announce their approach with five minutes of sirens. The story's conclusion is rushed and arbitrary, but so perhaps it has to be. *Sangre de Mi Sangre* (*Blood of My Blood*) is a film that stumbles through a maddening screenplay but nevertheless generates true emotional energy.

Saraband ★ ★ ★ ★

R, 107 m., 2005

Liv Ullmann (Marianne), Erland Josephson (Johan), Borje Ahlstedt (Henrik), Julia Dufvenius (Karin), Gunnel Fred (Martha). Directed by Ingmar Bergman and produced by Pia Ehrnvall. Screenplay by Bergman.

Ingmar Bergman is balancing his accounts and closing out his books. The great director is eighty-seven years old and announced in 1982 that *Fanny and Alexander* would be his last film. So it was, but he continued to work on the stage and for television, and then he wrote the screenplay for Liv Ullmann's film *Faithless* (2000). Now comes his absolutely last work, *Saraband*, powerfully, painfully honest.

Although you can see the film as it stands, it will have more resonance if you remember Bergman's *Scenes from a Marriage* (1973). That film starred Ullmann and Erland Josephson as Marianne and Johan, a couple married twenty years earlier and divorced ten years earlier, who meet again in the middle of the night in a cabin in the middle of the woods. Their marriage has failed, their relationship has faded, and yet on this night it is more real than anything else. I wrote in 1973: "They are in middle age now but in the night still fond and frightened lovers holding on for reassurance."

Now there is no more reassurance to be had. They must be in their eighties now; in real life, Josephson is eighty-two and Ullmann sixty-six. Because Bergman's films can be seen again and again, and because he believes the human face is the most important subject of the cinema, we are as familiar with these two faces as any we have ever seen. I saw Ullmann for the first time in Bergman's *Persona* (1966), which I reviewed seven months after I became a film critic. Now here she is again. When I interviewed her about *Faithless* at Cannes five years ago, I noted to myself that she had not, like so many actresses, had plastic surgery. She wore her age as proof of having lived, as we all must. Now I see *Saraband* and the movie is possible because she did not allow a surgeon to give her a face yearning for its younger form.

As the film opens, she is looking through some old photographs. Marianne and Johan had two daughters together, who are now middle-aged. She never sees them; one lives in Australia, and the other has gone mad. She tells us she has not seen Johan for all of those years but now thinks she will go to visit him. We follow her and find that Johan is now living in misery left over from an earlier marriage. He is rich, lives in the country, owns a nearby cottage that is occupied by his sixty-one-year-old son, Henrik (Borje Ahlstedt), and Henrik's nineteen-year-old daughter, Karin (Julia Dufvenius). Anna—Henrik's wife, Karin's mother—has been dead for two years. She is missed because she was needed, as cartilage if nothing else, to keep her husband and daughter from wearing each other down.

They are not Marianne's problem. But she visits them and witnesses appalling unhappiness. Johan is scornful of his son, who has value in his eyes only as the parent of Karin. Henrik is bitter that his father has money but doles it out reluctantly, to keep his son in constant need and supplication. Karin, who plays the cello, feels trapped because she wants to develop her career in the city and her father possessively hangs onto her (they sleep, Marianne discovers, in the same bed).

The movie is not about the resolution of this plot. It is about the way people persist in creating misery by placing the demands of their egos above the need for happiness—their own happiness and that of those around them. In some sense, Johan and Henrik live in these adjacent houses, in the middle of nowhere, simply so that they can hate each other. If they parted, each would lose a reason for living. Karin is the victim of their pathology.

Oh, but Bergman is sad, as he lives decade after decade on his island of Faro and writes these stories and assembles his old crew, or their children and successors, to film them. His *Faithless* showed an old filmmaker (working in Bergman's office, living in Bergman's house on Bergman's island). He hires an actress to help him think through a story he wants to write. The actress, who is imaginary, is in fact playing a woman he once loved; their love caused pain to her husband, her child, and even to the director. Now in his old age he is working through it, perhaps trying to make amends. We know from Bergman's autobiography that the story is loosely based on fact. We know, too, that Ullmann, who is directing it, was also Bergman's lover and had his daughter.

If *Faithless* was an attempt to face personal guilt, *Saraband* is a meditation on the pathology of selfish relationships. It is filled with failed parents: All three adults lack love in their bonds with their children. It is filled with unsettled scores: Now that Henrik is sixty-one, what does it matter that he has never become as successful as his father? The game is over. It is time to enjoy the success of his daughter—a success he will not permit because he fears losing her. When Marianne, a witness to this triangle of resentment, returns to her own life, she returns to even less—to nothing, to photographs.

The overwhelming fact about this movie is its awareness of time. Thirty-two years have passed since *Scenes from a Marriage.* The years have passed for Bergman, for Ullmann, for Josephson, and for us. Whatever else he is telling us in *Saraband,* Bergman is telling us that life will end on the terms by which we have lived it. If we are bitter now, we will not be victorious later; we will still be bitter. Here is a movie about people who have lived so long, hell has not been able to wait for them.

Sarah Silverman: Jesus Is Magic ★ ½

NO MPAA RATING, 70 m., 2005

Sarah Silverman (Herself), La'vin Kiyano (Tough Guy), Laura Silverman (Herself), Bob Odenkirk (Himself), Brian Posehn (Himself), Brody Stevens (Agent). Directed by Liam Lynch and produced by Heidi Herzon, Randy Sosin, and Mark Williams. Screenplay by Sarah Silverman.

Sarah Silverman: Jesus Is Magic is a movie that filled me with an urgent desire to see Sarah Silverman in a different movie. I liked everything about it except the writing, the direction, the editing, and the lack of a parent or adult guardian. There should have been somebody to stand up sadly after the first screening and say: "Sarah, honey, this isn't the movie you want people to see. Your material needs a lot of work; the musical scenes are deadly, except for the first one. And it looks like it was edited by someone fooling around with iMovie on a borrowed Macintosh."

Apparently the only person capable of telling Sarah Silverman such things is Sarah Silverman, and she obviously did not. Maybe the scene of her kissing herself in the mirror provides a clue. The result is a film that is going to make it hard to get people to come to the second Sarah Silverman film. Too bad, because Silverman is smart and funny, and she blindsides you with unexpected U-turns. She could be the instrument for abrasive and transgressive humor that would slice through the comedy club crap. But here, she isn't.

You have seen her before. She started on *Saturday Night Live* and has been in fifteen movies and a lot of TV shows. She's tall, brunette, and good-looking, and she says shocking things with the precise enunciation and poise of a girl who was brought up knowing how to make a good impression. The disconnect between what she says and how she says it is part of the effect. If she were crass and vulgar, her material would be insupportable: If you're going to use cancer, AIDS, and 9/11 as punch lines, you'd better know how to get the permission of the audience. She does it by seeming to be too well-bred to realize what she's saying. She's always correcting herself. When she uses the word *retards* she immediately registers that it's non-PC and elaborates: "When I say 'retards,' I mean they can do anything."

So that's one of her lines. It would be a cheap shot for me to quote a dozen more and do her act here in the review. Better to stand back and see why she's funny but the movie doesn't work. The first problem is with timing. None of her riffs go on long enough to build. She gets a laugh, and then another one, maybe a third, and then she starts in a different direction. We want her to keep on, piling one offense on top of another. We want to see her on a roll.

That's in the concert documentary parts of the movie. She stands on a stage and does the material and there are cuts to the audience, but curiously not much of a connection; it doesn't seem to be *this* audience at *this* performance, but a generic audience. Then she cuts away from the doc stuff to little sketches. The first one, in which her sister (Laura Silverman) and her friend (Brian Posehn) brag about their recent accomplishments, is funny because she perfectly plays someone who has never accomplished anything and never will, and lies about it. Then we see her in a car, singing a song about getting a job and doing a show, and then she does a show. Fair enough.

But what's with the scene where she entertains the old folks at her grandma's rest home by singing a song telling them they will all die soon? She is rescued by the apparent oblivion of the old folks, who seem so disconnected she could be working in blue screen. Then there's the scene where she angrily shakes the corpse of her grandmother in its casket. Here is a bulletin from the real world: Something like that is not intrinsically funny. Yes, you can probably find a way to set it up and write it to make it funny, but to simply do it, just plain do it, is pathetic. The audience, which has been laughing, grows watchful and sad.

To discuss the film's editing rhythm is to suggest it has one. There are artless and abrupt cuts between different kinds of material. She's on the stage, and then she's at the nursing home. There is a way to make that transition, but it doesn't involve a cut that feels like she was interrupted in the middle of something. And the ending comes abruptly, without any kind of acceleration and triumph in the material. Her act feels cut off at the knees. The running time, seventy minutes including end credits, is interesting, since if you subtract the offstage scenes that means we see less of her than a live audience would.

Now if Silverman had been ungifted or her material had lacked all humor, I would maybe not have bothered with a review. Why kick a movie when it's down? But she has a real talent, and she is sometimes very funny in a way that is particularly her own. Now she needs to work with a writer (not to provide the material but to shape and pace it), and a director who can build a scene, and an editor who can get her out of it, and a producer who can provide wise counsel.

On the basis of this movie, it will be her first exposure as a filmmaker to anyone like that.

Savage Grace ★ ★ ½

NO MPAA RATING, 97 m., 2008

Julianne Moore (Barbara Daly), Stephen Dillane (Brooks Baekeland), Eddie Redmayne (Tony Baekeland), Elena Anaya (Blanca), Unax Ugalde (Jake), Hugh Dancy (Sam Green). Directed by Tom Kalin and produced by Iker Monfort, Katie Roumel, Pamela Koffler, and Christine Vachon. Screenplay by Howard Rodman, based on the book by Natalie Robins and Steven M. L. Aronson.

When a movie's story ends and words appear on the screen telling us what happened then, they are sometimes inspirational, sometimes triumphant, sometimes sad. But I don't think I've ever seen an outcome more pathetic than the one described at the end of *Savage Grace.* They describe the ultimate destiny of Tony Baekeland, whose misfortune it was to be the heir of a great fortune. His fate is all the more appalling because it hardly seems inevitable. He is a very disturbed young man, as who might not be after the life he led? But life took him to tragic extremes.

The movie tells the true story of the marriage of Barbara Daly (Julianne Moore) and Brooks Baekeland (Stephen Dillane), who glittered erratically in the social circles of the 1940s through the 1960s. Brooks's grandfather invented Bakelite, used in everything, we learn, from cooking utensils to nuclear bombs. By the third generation the fortune has produced Brooks, a vapid clotheshorse who nevertheless perhaps deserves better than a wife who is all pose and attitude, all brittle facade, deeply rotten inside. Their son, Tony (Eddie Redmayne), who narrates much of the story, is raised as her coddled darling but feels little real love from either parent and grows into a narcissistic, hedonistic, inverted basket case.

Oh, but they all look so elegant! They know how to dress and how to behave (and misbehave) in the high society watering holes of New York (1950s), Paris (1960s), Majorca and London (into the 1970s). They are known everywhere, loved nowhere, except for a few hangers-on like Sam (Hugh Dancy), a gay "walker" who accompanies Barbara after Brooks has left.

It's not simply that Brooks has left. He left with Blanca (Elena Anaya), the Spanish beauty Tony brought home from the beach one day, only to watch his father seduce her from right under his nose. Tony is of indeterminate sexuality from the beginning and now tilts over into homosexuality, with such friends as Jake (Unax Ugalde), a pot-smoking beach creature. Sam, an art dealer, is also in the mix, and indeed mother, son, and walker all end up in bed together.

The tone of the film is set by Julianne Moore, in what I suppose must be described as a fine performance, although she has little enough to work with. Barbara was so shallow. She was all clothes and hair and endless cigarettes, and conversation that was never really adequate for the level she was aiming for. She also had a nasty habit of saying rude things to break up social events, and you can hardly blame Brooks for leaving—although he, too, was so lacking in ordinary human qualities.

Decadence, of course, is the word to describe this world, but nothing really prepares us for its final descent. I will not describe what happens at the end, except to say nothing has really prepared us for it. It's hard to take. Very hard. And then those stark white letters on the black background.

This is the first film in fifteen years by Tom Kalin, who made *Swoon* in 1992. That was about another famous scandal, the murder of Bobby Franks by Richard Loeb and Nathan Leopold Jr. Both films are about protagonists without ordinary moral values; they find the unacceptable to be thinkable, even a pleasure. Or a compulsion.

But what we miss in the film is insight into Barbara and Brooks and Tony. In his letters and diaries, Tony makes a great effort toward understanding his life but doesn't come up with much. Living these lives, for these people, must have been sad and tedious, and so, inevitably, is their story and, it must be said, the film about it.

The Savages ★ ★ ★ ½

R, 113 m., 2007

Laura Linney (Wendy Savage), Philip Seymour Hoffman (Jon Savage), Philip Bosco (Lenny Savage), Gbenga Akinnagbe (Jimmy), Peter Friedman (Larry). Directed by Tamara Jenkins and produced by Anne Carey, Ted Hope, and Erica Westheimer. Screenplay by Jenkins.

The Savages seems a curious movie to be opening four days before Christmas, but maybe not: Christmas Day itself is said to be the top moviegoing day of the year, as families (a) seek something they can do together without having to talk, or (b) use them as an excuse to escape from the house. Not all holidays are by Norman Rockwell, and maybe some grown children will enjoy this touching, humorous film about an elderly father whose time has come to leave his "retirement community" and move into "assisted living" (which my Aunt Mary referred to as "assisted dying").

Wendy and Jon Savage (Laura Linney and Philip Seymour Hoffman) are sister and brother, she living in New York City, he living in Buffalo, she an aspiring playwright, he a professor and author of books about the theater. They are smart, articulate, and knowledgeable about drama, attributes that do them no good at all when they get a call from Sun City that their dad, Lenny (Philip Bosco), has started to write on the wall with his excrement.

After some reluctance, mostly on Jon's part, they fly to Arizona and find their dad shacked up with Doris, a girlfriend his age. I was reminded of a friend of mine whose eighty-five-year-old dad discovered Viagra and insisted on calling his son with daily reports on his sex life. My friend pleaded with him to spare the details. There are some things children desperately do not want to know. Doris spares them the occasion for such reports, however, by suddenly passing away, and Jon and Wendy decide to move their father to Buffalo so he will be close to them. He is a hostile curmudgeon who probably moved to Arizona in the first place to get away from them, but now he's in no position to resist.

Writer-director Tamara Jenkins (*Slums of*

Beverly Hills) doesn't sentimentalize this material; quite the opposite. Lenny remains Lenny to the best of his ability, which means a short temper, a foul vocabulary, and a constant state of irritation. We gather that he was not a joy to grow up with; indeed, the scars still borne by his children are such that they refer to their childhoods only obliquely. Whatever the relationship between their parents was like, it has left them unable to form liaisons of their own; Wendy is having a joyless affair with a married man, and Jon has a Polish girlfriend he refuses to marry even if it would save her from deportation back to Poland. That he weeps over his inability shows that he is aware of his emotional scars and fears to heal them.

There is a genre of movies set in old-folks' homes that resemble sitcoms, including colorful characters, lots of one-liners, and a pecking order. The nursing home they find for Lenny in Buffalo is the next step after such a place. It is essentially run by the caregivers who treat their clients something like misbehaving children. One who seems to care is a Nigerian immigrant named Jimmy (Gbenga Akinnagbe), who sympathizes with Jon and Wendy and shares lore about caring for the aged. Kristen Thomson played a similar character in Sarah Polley's *Away from Her*—the experienced nurse who knows what the family has gone through and will go through.

A movie like this depends on nuance and performance if it is not to descend entirely into soap opera. Jenkins knows that and is quietly insistent that we observe little moments and dropped words and exchanged glances. The resettling of Jon and Wendy's father causes the resettling of their own lives and forces them to examine memories they hoped were buried. Both Linney and Hoffman are so specific in creating these characters that we see them as people, not elements in a plot. Hoffman in particular shows how many disguises he has within his seemingly immutable presence; would you know it is the same actor here and in two other films this season, *Before the Devil Knows You're Dead* and *Charlie Wilson's War*?

The Savages confronts a day that may come in all of our lives. Two days, actually, the first when we are younger, the second when we are older. *Ballad of Narayama*, a great Japanese film, is about a community that decides when a person has outlived any usefulness and leaves that person on the mountain to die. It seems cruel, but even the dying seem to think it appropriate. Better than to have been healthy and strong once, and reduced to writing on the walls.

Saving Shiloh ★ ★ ★ ½

PG, 90 m., 2006

Scott Wilson (Judd Travers), Jason Dolley (Marty Preston), Gerald McRaney (Ray Preston), Ann Dowd (Louise Preston), Kyle Chavarria (Dara Lynn Preston), Taylor Momsen (Samantha Wallace), Liberty Smith (Becky Preston). Directed by Sandy Tung and produced by Carl Borack and Dale Rosenbloom. Screenplay by Rosenbloom, based on the novel by Phyllis Reynolds Naylor.

Saving Shiloh is the third and final *Shiloh* film, and fully as worthy as the others. It's a family film that deals with real problems and teaches real values, and yet is exciting and entertaining. We come to really care about the young boy Marty, his family and friends, and the ominous presence of their neighbor Judd. Marty, now played by Jason Dolley, has grown up during the series and does some wise thinking in this film.

All three films are based on much-loved novels by Phyllis Reynolds Naylor, and the tension in all three centers on the neighbor, Judd (Scott Wilson), who has a drinking problem, gets in fights, wrecks his car, and as before seems to have no occupation except for shooting squirrels in the trees around his cabin. Wilson plays the character full-bore, not as a villain in a family film, but as a complex and wounded person, earnestly trying to change.

Marty believes in him. His father, Ray (Gerald McRaney), has known Judd most of his life and disliked him until recently. His change of heart came in the first film, after Marty rescued the abused dog Shiloh from Judd, made him his own, and in the process broke into Judd's isolation for the first time. By this third film, Marty has won Judd's confidence to such a degree that the man shares a painful memory of his own father: "Sometimes he beat me when he was sad. Sometimes he beat me when he was happy. Sometimes he was just happy to beat me."

Judd becomes the suspect when a local man disappears after the two men get in a bar fight. Judd is suspected again in a series of thefts. Marty believes in him, and his dad backs him up: Judd is a troubled man, but not a thief and certainly not a killer. Local gossip is quick to blame Judd for everything that goes wrong, but Marty's teacher focuses on the principle that a man is innocent until proven guilty, and Marty puts that into practice. Judd still keeps his dogs chained, but Marty learns from the local vet that chained dogs are unhappy and mean and tells Judd he and his dad will help fence in his yard. In this and other ways, Marty stands true.

All of this may sound too much like an After School Special, so I should add that Marty, his best friend, Samantha (Taylor Momsen), and his sisters, Dara Lynn (Kyle Chavarria) and Becky (Liberty Smith), live ordinary kid lives, have ordinary kid days, fool around, and bring us lots of smiles. His dad and mom (Ann Dowd) are loving and supportive, and that's rare when so many movie parents are wrongheaded or missing.

It's commendable, too, that in this film, growing old and dying are treated respectfully; there's a visit to the grave of Samantha's grandfather Doc Wallace, and a visit to the nursing home where Marty's grandmother is slipping into Alzheimer's. *Saving Shiloh* doesn't overplay its lessons on life, but it contains them, and they give it values many family movies simply ignore. Carl Borack produced and Dale Rosenbloom directed the first film; they coproduced *Shiloh 2: Shiloh Season* (1999) and *Saving Shiloh*, both directed by Sandy Tung.

As for melodrama, there is some business involving the thieves that is fairly exciting but also fairly unbelievable. And a climactic scene where Dara Lynn slips off a bridge into the river, and Marty and Shiloh dive in to save her. The film nicely modulates the danger, making it scary but not traumatizing. Everyone involved with this film obviously had respect for the family audiences they are aiming at, and it's surprising how moving the film is, and how wise, while still just seeming to be about a boy and his dog, his family, and the mean man next door who isn't so mean if you get to know him.

Schultze Gets the Blues ★ ★ ★ ½

PG, 114 m., 2005

Horst Krause (Schultze), Harald Warmbrunn (Jurgen), Karl Fred Muller (Manfred), Ursula Schucht (Jurgen's Wife), Hannelore Schubert (Manfred's Wife), Wolfgang Boos (Gatekeeper), Leo Fischer (Head of Music Club), Loni Frank (Schultze's Mother). Directed by Michael Schorr and produced by Jens Korner. Screenplay by Schorr.

Do they have salt mines in Germany? Or is Schultze's job simply a symbol of a lifetime of thankless toil? Day after day he ventures down into the salt mine until, with a shock, he and three friends are forced to retire. There is a little party at the beer hall, his coworkers singing a lugubrious song of farewell, and Schultze is a retired man. Not married, he passes his days in the sad enjoyment of unwanted freedom. Sometimes he contemplates his retirement present, a lamp made from large block of crystallized salt with a bulb inside. If it ever falls into other hands, will its new owners think to lick it?

Schultze (Horst Krause) is a bulky, stolid, unlovely man who wipes the dust from his garden gnomes, spends as much time as possible napping on his sofa, visits his mother in a nursing home, plays the accordion at a polka club, and plays chess at a club where the level of play is not too high; one should not reach retirement age as a chess player still arguing over applications of the "touch-move" rule. He gets around town on his bicycle, dealing with the delays caused by a rail crossing guard who is distracted by the study of alchemy.

One night Schultze's world changes forever. On the radio he hears zydeco music from Louisiana. I was reminded of *Genghis Blues*, the 1999 film where a blind musician in San Francisco, Paul Pena, hears Tuva throat-singing over the radio, teaches it to himself, and travels to the Republic of Tuva for the annual competition. Schultze becomes a man possessed. He takes up his accordion, begins to pump through a tired song he has played a thousand times, and then gradually increases the tempo and turns up the heat until he is playing, well, zydeco polka.

That is not an impossible musical genre. David Golia, a friend of mine from San Francisco, leads a polka band that explores what he sees as the underlying connection between polka, rock, and Mexican and Brazilian music. It's not all about beer barrels.

Schultze now becomes a man obsessed. His lonely life is filled with fantasies of far-off bayous. He gets a cookbook and prepares jambalaya on his kitchen stove. His polka club listens to his zydeco arrangements and votes to send him to a German music festival in the town's sister city in Texas—not so much to honor him, we suspect, as to get him out of town.

Schultze is not much of a traveler, and speaks perhaps a dozen words of English. Unlike the travelers in many movies, he doesn't magically learn many more. The Texas festival does not nurture his inner man, and he does what any sensible person in Schultze's position would do, which is to purchase a boat and set off across the Gulf and into the waterways of Louisiana.

What may not be clear in my description is that *Schultze Gets the Blues* is not entirely, or even mostly, a comedy, even though it has passages of droll, deadpan humor. It is essentially the record of a man who sets himself into motion and is amazed by the results. I was reminded of Aki Kaurismaki's *The Man without a Past* (2002), the story of a man whose amnesia frees him to begin an altogether different life. The film has also been compared with *About Schmidt* (2002), although Schmidt was a madcap compared to Schultze.

Schultze is not an object of fun, but a focus of loneliness and need, a man who discovers too late that he made no plans for his free time and is deeply bored by his life. His American journey is not travel but exploration—not of a new land, but of his own possibilities. He suddenly realizes that he, Schultze, can move from one continent to another, can medicate his blues with Louisiana hot sauce, and play music that sends his accordion on crazy trills of joy.

He does not, during his journey, meet a soul mate, fall in love, become discovered on *American Idol*, or do anything else than live his new life. He meets people easily because he is so manifestly friendly and harmless, but finds it hard to form relationships because of his handful of words. No matter. We suspect it was the same for him even in Germany, and now he wanders where every single thing he sees is new to his eyes.

The writer and director, Michael Schorr, is making his first film but has the confidence and simplicity of someone who has been making films forever. Unlike many first-timers, he isn't trying to see how much of his genius one film can contain. He begins, I think, not with burning ambition, but with a simple love and concern for Schultze. He creates the character, watches him asleep on the sofa, and then follows a few steps behind as Schultze backs away from the dead-end of retirement. He begins his journey with a single step, as we know all journeys must begin, and arrives at last on a boat in the Gulf of Mexico, where not all journeys end, and where Schultze must be as surprised as his director to find himself.

Self-Medicated ★ ★ ★

R, 107 m., 2007

Diane Venora (Louise Eriksen), Michael Bowen (Dan Jones), Greg Germann (Keith McCauley), Monty Lapica (Andrew Eriksen), Kristina Anapau (Nicole), Matthew Carey (Aaron), William Stanford Davis (Gabe). Directed by Monty Lapica and produced by Tommy Bell and Lapica. Screenplay by Lapica.

The opening scene in Monty Lapica's *Self-Medicated* is a particularly chilling exercise in antisocial behavior. A car filled with out-of-control teenagers cruises the Strip in Las Vegas, shooting at tourists with paint guns. This is the sort of behavior, like using laser pointers illegally, that you hope doesn't leak out to numbskulls at large. One of the kids is Andrew (played by Lapica himself), who is usually high on street drugs, allegedly because he mourns the death of his beloved father.

As most drug counselors will advise you, drug abuse has to be seen separately from the "problems" that "inspire" it. The majority of drunks and druggies use today because they used yesterday, and that's why they will use again tomorrow. I remember a guy in O'Rourke's who said he was drinking "because it's Christmas." Informed that he had missed the mark by three days, he said, "OK, then, I'm drinking because it isn't Christmas."

Whatever his reasons, Andrew is out of control. He has walked out of school, he hates his pill-addicted mom (Diane Venora), and she can't get it together to really talk to him, let alone help him. So she makes a call and attendants from a "treatment center" pounce on him in the middle of the night and haul him away. This is staging an intervention big-time.

The film, said to be somewhat autobiographical, is critical both of Andrew and his treatment. Unlike portrayals you may have seen of the wise and useful Betty Ford or Hazelden centers, this (fictional) outfit in St. George, Utah, treats its patients as prisoners, adopts a good cop/bad cop counseling regime, and apparently plans to send patients to American Samoa to complete their "recovery" as forced labor. I am not making this up; it's inspired, I understand, by an actual treatment center, since shut down, although not the one Lapica attended.

The facility is more realistically portrayed than the one depicted in *One Flew Over the Cuckoo's Nest,* but this is a docudrama, not a fable. Andrew comes up against a counselor named Dan (Michael Bowen), who apparently loathes druggies and thinks his disgust will cure them. Another counselor named Keith (Greg Germann) has a kinder, gentler approach, but if Andrew hated school, it's nothing to how he feels about this place. As he checks in, he's already mentally escaping.

The title is a little misleading. Andrew and his mother are self-medicators, yes (her drugs are prescribed, but a middle-aged woman can often make that happen). But Andrew is also, in a way, self-treating. Alcoholics Anonymous, the most effective means of staying clean and sober, talks about "hitting bottom," and *Self-Medicated* plays like the story of Andrew throwing himself at the bottom and sticking. Eventually, if he's not entirely around the bend, a light will dawn.

Helping him see the light is Gabe, a man who lives on the streets (William Stanford Davis). From the man who has been there, who has nothing and therefore nothing to lose, Andrew senses he is gaining insights without any motive or spin. The same strength sits at the center of an AA meeting, where everyone is in the same boat and there is no captain.

On the basis of this film, Monty Lapica, at twenty-four, has a career ahead of him as a director, an actor, or both. He also has a life ahead of him, which the film does a great deal to make clear.

The Sentinel ★ ★ ★

PG-13, 105 m., 2006

Michael Douglas (Pete Garrison), Kiefer Sutherland (David Breckinridge), Eva Longoria (Jill Marin), Kim Basinger (Sarah Ballentine), Martin Donovan (William Montrose), David Rasche (President Ballentine). Directed by Clark Johnson and produced by Michael Douglas, Marcy Drogin, and Arnon Milchan. Screenplay by George Nolfi, based on the novel by Gerald Petievich.

Michael Douglas is a skilled actor who often works within a narrow range, as he does in *The Sentinel.* Once again, he's a skilled professional who finds himself with problems on two fronts: the romantic and the criminal. Half of his movies, more or less, have involved that formula; the others show a wide variety, as in *Wonder Boys, Traffic, Falling Down,* and *The War of the Roses.* I might object when I see him wearing a suit and tie and juggling adultery and danger, but you know what? He's good at it.

In *The Sentinel,* he is a Secret Service agent named Pete Garrison, who in 1981 took a bullet during the assassination attempt on Ronald Reagan and is still guarding the president twenty-five years later. The movie doesn't identify President Ballentine (David Rasche) as belonging to either major party, although somehow his wife, Sarah (Kim Basinger), looks to me like a Democrat. She also looks like a dish and is having a passionate affair with, yes, Agent Garrison.

As the movie opens, another agent is shot dead after telling Garrison he wanted to talk to him. Did he know something about an assassination attempt? Garrison thinks so after meeting with a seedy informer who tells him there is a mole in the Secret Service—a turncoat agent on the White House detail who will set up the president for assassination. That this informer would know the secrets involved in this particular conspiracy seems unlikely, but then Clay Shaw never seemed like a likely suspect either, maybe because he wasn't one.

Without describing too many plot details, I can say that every agent assigned to the Office of the President is required to take a lie detector test and that only Garrison flunks. We know why: Asked if he has done anything to endanger the president, he naturally thinks of what he has done to endanger the president's marriage, and the needle redlines. That makes him a suspect and brings him into the crosshairs of David Breckinridge (Kiefer Sutherland), an ace investigator who used to be Garrison's best friend until, uh, Garrison apparently had an affair with *his* wife.

With the entire Secret Service looking for him, Garrison busts loose, goes underground, and uses all of his skills as an agent to stay free while trying to contact his informer and single-handedly stop the plot to kill the president. A deadline is approaching because Ballentine is scheduled to attend a summit in Toronto, where he might be a prime target. Since the presidential helicopter was shot down by a rocket while leaving Camp David a few days earlier (not with the president on board), and since the service knows it has a traitor, you might think the wise decision would be to skip Toronto and stay at home, maybe in a panic room. But no: Ballentine goes to Toronto, along with Garrison, Breckinridge, Sarah, the terrorists, and everybody else in the plot.

The Sentinel involves a scenario that is unlikely, I hope. But it's told efficiently and with lots of those little details that make movies like this seem more expert than they probably are. (Did you know that agents are trained to disengage the safety lock on their handguns as they draw them, instead of after, as cops do?) The Douglas character does a lot of quick thinking, and Sutherland is brisk, cold, and efficient as a super-sleuth. Eva Longoria plays Jill, his new assistant, whom he prefers to a veteran agent because she's still fresh and hasn't been worn down by the job. I was able to spot the mole almost the first time he (or she) appears on the screen by employing the Law of Economy of Characters, but his (or her) identity is essentially beside the point.

There comes a point in *The Sentinel,* as there did in Harrison Ford's *Firewall,* when you wonder how a guy in his early sixties can run indefinitely, survive all kinds of risky stunts, hold his own in a fight, and stay three steps ahead of the young guys in his strategy. You wonder, and then you stop wondering, because hey, it's a movie. As I so wisely wrote about the Ford movie, "Nobody can do anything they do in thrillers anyway, so why should there be an age limit on accomplishing the impossible?"

This is the second theatrical feature (after *S.W.A.T.*) directed by Clark Johnson, an actor who has also done a lot of work on television, mostly on shows that would be useful preparation, such as *Homicide, Law & Order, The West Wing,* and *The Shield.* Have I seen movies like *The Sentinel* before? Yes, and I hope to see them again. At a time when American audiences seem grateful for the opportunity to drool at mindless horror trash, it is encouraging that well-crafted thrillers still are being made about characters who have dialogue, identities, motives, and clean shirts.

Separate Lies ★ ★ ★

R, 87 m., 2005

Emily Watson (Anne Manning), Tom Wilkinson (James Manning), Rupert Everett (William Bule), Hermione Norris (Priscilla), John Warnaby (Simon), Linda Bassett (Maggie), John Neville (Lord Rawston), David Harewood (Inspector Marshall). Directed by Julian Fellowes and produced by Steve Clark-Hall and Christian Colson. Screenplay by Fellowes, based on a novel by Nigel Balchin.

Is that what you say when a man dies? How inconvenient?

—*The Third Man*

Separate Lies opens with an event so sudden it is over before it can be registered; only later do we discover that a man was knocked from his bicycle by a speeding car, which didn't pause. The man was killed. It happened on a lane near the country home of a London lawyer, on the afternoon he and his wife invited some neighbors for drinks. The dead man was the husband of their housekeeper.

The movie is not so much about the solution to this crime as about the ethics involved in taking responsibility. If you can, should you get away with murder? What if you did not intend to kill—what if it was an accident? The man is dead. Should you be made to suffer? Many people have one answer to these questions when a stranger is involved, and another when it touches them personally. Not even a hanging judge wants to hang.

Separate Lies stars Tom Wilkinson as James Manning, the lawyer, and Emily Watson as Anne, his wife. Their marriage seems happy enough. He's one of those lawyers who specialize in making powerful clients more powerful. When it comes to matters of right and wrong, he likes to think of himself as inflexible. His wife is accommodating and dutiful and likes the life they lead, the house in London, the Buckinghamshire hideaway.

In the village, a remembered face has reappeared. This is William Bule (Rupert Everett), son of a leading local family, recently returned from America, indolent and insinuating as he plays cricket on the village green. He catches Anne's eye, and it is because of him, really, that she tells her husband they should have neighbors over for drinks.

Everett plays Bule as a man detached and arrogant, dismissive of conventional values, attractive to women because he doesn't seem to care how they feel about him one way or the other. James Manning, on the other hand, is serious and responsible, and we catch glimpses of the idealistic undergraduate. Wilkinson, who often plays ordinary men, here emerges as a sleek London figure, no stranger to the shirtmakers of Jermyn Street; he has the impatience of a man who is always having to explain things to people who do not have his standards. Anne may be one of those people; perfect as she seems, she feels she never quite comes up to his mark.

Now there is the matter of the dead body in the grass beside the lane. There was a witness, as it happens: Maggie (Linda Bassett), whose husband was killed. She saw the car and might be able to identify it. Or perhaps not. Maggie knows William Bule, too; she worked for his family until she was dismissed. It was Anne who gave her a new start in the village. When the police constable comes around, he will want to talk to all of these people, not because they are suspects but because they might (as the British so carefully word it) be able to assist the police in their inquiries. Certainly Anne is not under suspicion: "One person not driving to a party," her husband observes, "is surely the hostess."

The unfolding of the plot I will leave for you to discover. The story, based on a 1950 novel by Nigel Balchin titled *A Way Through the Wood,* could as easily have been told by Agatha Christie, if the focus is on the whodunit aspects, or by Georges Simenon, if we know the whodunit but want to know how they feel about it, and how their feelings change as they discover more details. The movie's director, Julian Fellowes, takes the Simenon approach, although some of his moments of revelation could take place in an Agatha Christie drawing room where a word or two rotates a crime into a new dimension.

Fellowes, who has worked mostly as an actor, won an Academy Award with his screenplay for Altman's *Gosford Park* (2001). There, as here, he is fascinated by the way class lingers on in Britain after its time has allegedly passed, how fierce loyalties and resentments are exchanged between upstairs and downstairs. The way he handles James and Anne is a case study in British manners: There is the sharp outburst, to be sure, and even the f-word, used for effect by a person who doesn't talk that way. But there's none of the screaming and weeping and acting-out of American domestic drama; James and Anne would rather be reasonable than be in love because there's less chance for embarrassment that way. At one point, when a possibility is suggested, James curtly replies: "I'm afraid that's a little too Jerry Springer for me."

Separate Lies reminded me of Woody Allen's *Crimes and Misdemeanors.* Its characters are above reproach—from themselves. Others deserve justice, but we deserve compassion and understanding. This is hypocrisy, but so what? Do unto others as you would not have them do unto you. *Separate Lies* is only seemingly about the portioning of blame. It is actually about the burden of guilt, which some can carry so easily, while for others it is intolerable.

September Dawn no stars

R, 111 m., 2007

Jon Voight (Jacob Samuelson), Trent Ford (Jonathan Samuelson), Tamara Hope (Emily Hudson), Jon Gries (John D. Lee), Taylor Handley (Micah Samuelson), Lolita Davidovich (Nancy Dunlap), Dean Cain (Joseph Smith), Terence Stamp (Brigham Young). Directed by Christopher Cain and produced by Cain, Scott Duthle, and Kevin Matossian. Screenplay by Carole Whang Schutter and Cain.

On September 11, 1857, at the Mountain Meadows Massacre, a group of fanatic Mormons attacked and slaughtered a wagon train of about 120 settlers passing through Utah on their way to California. Can we all agree that the date has no significance? No, we cannot, because *September Dawn* is at pains to point out that on another September 11, another massacre took place, again spawned by religion.

But hold on. Where did I get that word "fanatic"? In my opinion, when anybody believes their religion gives them the right to kill other people, they are fanatics. Aren't there enough secular reasons for war? But there is no shortage of such religions, or such people. The innocent, open-faced Christians on the wagon train were able to consider settling California, after all, because some of their co-religionists participated in or benefited from the enslavement of Africans and the genocide of Native Americans.

Were there fanatics among those who ran the Salem Witch Trials or the Inquisition or the Crusades? Or the Holocaust? No shortage of them. Organized religion has been used to justify most of the organized killing in our human history. It's an inescapable fact, especially if you consider the Nazis and communists as cults led by secular gods. When your god inspires you to murder someone who worships god in a different way or under another name, you're barking up the wrong god. Football teams praying before a game reduce the same process to absurdity: What god worthy of the name cares which team wins?

The vast majority of the members of all religions, I believe and would argue, don't want to kill anybody. They want to love and care for their families, find decent work that sustains life and comfort, live in peace, and get along with their neighbors. It is a deviant streak in some humans, I suspect, that drives them toward self-righteous violence and uses religion as a convenient alibi.

That is true, wouldn't you agree, about Mormons, Christians, Muslims, Jews, Hindus, Buddhists, and so on? No, not all of you would agree, because every time I let slip the opinion that most Muslims are peaceful and nonviolent, for example, I receive the most extraordinary hate mail from those assuring me they are not. And in a Muslim land, let a newspaper express the opinion that most Christians and Jews are peaceful and nonviolent, and that newspaper office is likely to be burned down. The worst among us speak for the best.

Which brings us back to September 11, 1857, when a crazy Mormon zealot named Bishop Jacob Samuelson (Jon Voight) ordered the massacre of the visiting wagon train after first sending his spokesman, John D. Lee (Jon Gries), to lie that if they disarmed, they would be granted safe passage. Whether the leader of his church, Brigham Young (Terence Stamp), approved of this action is a matter of much controversy, denied by the church, claimed by *September Dawn*.

What a strange, confused, unpleasant movie this is. Two theories have clustered around it: (1) It is anti-Mormon propaganda in order to muddy the waters around the presidential campaign of Mitt Romney, or (2) it is not about Mormons at all, but an allegory about the 9/11/01 terrorists. Take your choice. The problem with allegories is that you can plug them in anywhere. No doubt the film would have great impact in Darfur.

My opinion is that there isn't anything to be gained in telling this story in this way. It generates bad feelings on all sides, and at a time when Mormons are at pains to explain they are Christians, it underlines the way that these Mormons consider all Christians to be "gentiles." The Mormons are presented in no better light than Nazis and Japanese were in Hollywood's World War II films. Wasn't there a more thoughtful and insightful way to consider this historical event? Or how about a different event altogether? What about the Donner Party? They may have been cannibals, but at least they were nondenominational.

If there is a concealed blessing, it is that the film is so bad. Jon Voight, that gifted and versatile actor, is here given the most ludicrous and unplayable role of his career, and a goofy beard to go along with it. Terence Stamp, as Brigham Young, comes across as the kind of man you'd find at the back of a cave in a Cormac McCarthy novel. The Christians are so scrubbed and sunny they could have been teleported in time from the Lawrence Welk program.

And isn't it sickening that the plot stirs in some sugar by giving us what can only be described as a horse whisperer? This movie needs human whisperers. And giving us a romance between the bishop's son and a pretty gentile girl? And another son of the bishop who dresses up like an Indian and goes batty at the scent of blood? And real Native Americans who assist the Mormons in their killing, no doubt thinking, well, we can get around to the Mormons later? I am trying as hard as I can to imagine the audience for this movie. Every time I make any progress, it scares me. ☞

Serenity ★ ★ ★

PG-13, 119 m., 2005

Nathan Fillion (Malcolm Reynolds), Gina Torres (Zoe Warren), Adam Baldwin (Jayne), Alan Tudyk (Wash Washburn), Jewel Staite (Kaylee), Morena Baccarin (Inara), Summer Glau (River Tam), Sean Maher (Simon), Ron Glass (Shepherd Book), Chiwetel Ejiofor (The Operative). Directed by Joss Whedon and produced by Barry Mendel. Screenplay by Whedon.

The thrill of a fistfight in a movie was altered for me forever the day I visited a set and watched the sound men beating the hell out of a Naugahyde sofa with Ping-Pong paddles. There was a moment in *Serenity* when I remembered that moment—no, not during a fistfight, but during a battle in interplanetary space. There are so many spacecraft, so large, so close together, it looks as if collision is a greater danger than enemy fire. Imagine spaceships in a demo derby.

As the battle continued and the heroes were hurled about inside their own spaceship, which at times looked curiously like the interior of a loading dock, I made a note: "More banging than in your average space movie." Then something shifted inside my ears and I somehow knew I was hearing sound men, pounding the hell out of garbage can lids, sheets of steel, and big piles of pots and pans.

I say this not with disapproval, but with affection. *Serenity* is an old-fashioned space opera and differs from a horse opera mostly in that it involves space, not horses. It takes place in a solar system of a dozen terraformed planets and "hundreds of moons," and there is a war going on between the Alliance, which runs things and wants everybody to be happy, and a group of rebels who begin to make disturbing discoveries. As the film opens, a psychic named River Tam (Summer Glau) is rescued from Alliance mind-washers by her brother, Simon (Sean Maher), and then we learn that River was unwisely exhibited to a roomful of important Alliance parliamentarians. Because she can read minds, she knows their secrets.

River and Simon are soon enough allied with a team of freelance smugglers on a banged-up old ship named Serenity. Malcolm (Nathan Fillion) is the captain, and his crew includes the pilot, Wash (Alan Tudyk), his wife, Zoe (Gina Torres), the engineer, Kaylee (Jewel Staite), and the tough guy, Jayne (Adam Baldwin). On their trail is the most competent and feared of the Alliance's agents, the Operative (Chiwetel Ejiofor).

Science fiction fans will recognize the plot line and most of the characters from a short-lived Fox series named *Firefly,* which (I learn in a letter from Stephen McNeil of Sydney, Nova Scotia) was canceled in midseason, but not before the episodes were carelessly shown out of proper order. What a crock, especially considering that Joss Whedon, the TV series' author (and writer-director of *Serenity*), earlier created *Buffy, the Vampire Slayer* and so deserved the benefit of the doubt.

Serenity is made of dubious but energetic special effects, breathless velocity, much imagination, some sly verbal wit, and a little political satire. Turns out the Alliance was simply trying to bring contentment to its crowded planetary system by distracting its inhabitants from their problems and making them feel like they had a life. River is in possession of a secret about this process that the Alliance would do anything to suppress. Like *Brave New World* and *1984,* the movie plays like a critique of contemporary society, with the Alliance as Big Brother, enemy of discontent. But as River observes, "Some people don't like to be meddled with."

Some of the dialogue sounds futuristic, some sounds nineteenth century, and some sounds deliberately kooky. (Captain Mal: "Do you want to run this ship?" Discontented crew member: "Yes." Mal: "Well, you can't.") There are also unanticipated scenes of real impact, including a planet where—but see for yourself. I'm not sure the movie would have much appeal for non-sci-fi fans, but it has the rough edges and brawny energy of a good yarn, and it was made by and for people who can't get enough of this stuff. You know who you are.

Sex and the City ★ ★

R, 145 m., 2008

Sarah Jessica Parker (Carrie Bradshaw), Kim Cattrall (Samantha Jones), Kristin Davis (Charlotte York), Cynthia Nixon (Miranda Hobbes), Chris Noth (Mr. Big), Jennifer Hudson (Louise), Candice Bergen (Enid Frick), David Eigenberg (Steve Brady), Evan Handler (Harry Goldenblatt), Jason Lewis (Smith Jerrod). Directed by Michael Patrick King and produced by King, Sarah Jessica Parker, John Melfi, and Darren Star. Screenplay by King, based on the novel by Candace Bushnell and the TV series.

I am not the person to review this movie. Perhaps you will enjoy a review from someone who disqualifies himself at the outset, doesn't much like most of the characters, and is bored by their bubble-brained conversations. Here is a 145-minute movie containing one (1) line of truly witty dialogue: "Her forties is the greatest age at which a bride can be photographed without the unintended Diane Arbus subtext."

That line might not reverberate with audience members who don't know who Diane Arbus was. But what about me, who doesn't reverberate with the names on designer labels? There's a montage of wedding dresses by world-famous designers. I was lucky I knew who Vivienne Westwood was, and that's because she used to be the girlfriend of the Sex Pistols' manager.

The movie continues the stories of the four heroines of the popular HBO series, which would occasionally cause me to pause in my channel surfing. They are older but no wiser, and all facing some kind of a romantic crossroads. New Line has begged critics not to reveal plot secrets, which is all right with me, because I would rather have fun with plot details. I guess I can safely say: Carrie (Sarah Jessica Parker) is in the tenth year of her relationship with Mr. Big (Chris Noth) when they sort of decide to buy a penthouse they name "Heaven on Fifth Avenue." Publicist Samantha (Kim Cattrall) has moved to Los Angeles, where her client Smith (Jason Lewis) has become a daytime TV star. Charlotte (Kristin Davis) and her husband, Harry (Evan Handler), have adopted a Chinese daughter. And Miranda (Cynthia Nixon) is in a crisis with her husband, Steve (David Eigenberg).

What with one thing and another, dramatic developments cause the four women to join each other at a luxurious Mexican resort, where two scenes take place that left me polishing my pencils to write this review. The girls go sunbathing in crotch-hugging swimsuits, and Miranda is ridiculed for the luxuriant growth of her pubic hair. How luxuriant? One of her pals describes it as *the National Forest*, and there's a shot of the offending proliferation that popped the Smith Brothers right into my head.

A little later, Charlotte develops a tragic case of *turista* and has a noisy accident right there in her pants. This is a key moment, because Carrie has been so depressed she has wondered if she will ever laugh again. Her friends say that will happen when something really, really funny happens. When Charlotte overflows, Carrie and the others burst into helpless laughter. Something really, really funny has finally happened! How about you? Would you think that was really, really funny?

Sex and the City was famous for its frankness, and we expect similar frankness in the movie. We get it, but each *frank* moment comes wrapped in its own package and seems to stand alone from the story. That includes (1) a side shot of a penis, (2) sex in positions other than the missionary, and (3) Samantha's dog, which is a compulsive masturbator. I would be reminded of the immortal canine punch line ("because he can"), but Samantha's dog is a female. "She's been fixed," says the pet lady, "but she hasn't lost the urge." Samantha can identify with that. The dog gets friendly with every pillow, stuffed animal, ottoman, and towel, and here's the funny thing, she ravishes them male-doggy-style. I went to AskJeeves.com and typed in "How do female dogs masturbate?" and did not get a satisfactory answer, although it would seem to be: "Just like all dogs do, but not how male dogs also do."

On to Mr. Big, the wealthy tycoon and victim of two unhappy marriages, who has been blissfully living in sin with Carrie for ten years. I will supply no progress report on their bliss. But what about Mr. Big himself? As played by Chris Noth, he's so unreal he verges on the surreal. He's handsome in the Rock Hudson and Victor Mature tradition, and has a low, preternaturally calm voice that delivers stock reassurances and banal clichés right on time. He's so . . . passive. He stands there (or lies there) as if consciously posing as The Ideal Lover. But he's . . . kinda slow. Square. Colorless. Notice how, when an old friend shouts rude things about him at an important dinner, he hardly seems to hear them, or to know he's having dinner.

The warmest and most human character in the movie is Louise (Jennifer Hudson), who is still in her twenties and hasn't learned to be a jaded consumerist caricature. She still believes in True Love, is hired as Carrie's assistant, and pays her own salary on the first day by telling her about a Netflix of designer labels (I guess after you wear the shoes, you send them back). Louise is warm and vulnerable and womanly, which does not describe any of the others.

All of this goes on for nearly two and a half hours, through New Year's Eve, Valentine's Day, and other bonding holidays. The movie needs a Thanksgiving bailout opportunity. But this is probably the exact *Sex and the City* film that fans of the TV series are lusting for. I know some nurses who are going to smuggle flasks of cosmopolitans into the theater on opening night and have a Gal Party. "Do you think that's a good idea?" one of them asked me. "Two flasks," I said.

The Shaggy Dog ★ ★

PG, 98 m., 2006

Tim Allen (Dave Douglas), Kristin Davis (Rebecca Douglas), Spencer Breslin (Josh Douglas), Zena Grey (Carly Douglas), Robert Downey Jr. (Dr. Kozak), Danny Glover (Ken Hollister), Jane Curtin (Judge Whittaker), Shawn Pyfrom (Trey). Directed by Brian Robbins and produced by Tim Allen and David Hoberman. Screenplay by Cormac Wibberley, Marianne Wibberley, Geoff Rodkey, Jack Amiel, and Michael Begler.

This is surely one of the fundamental laws of fiction: When a man and a dog change bodies, it is funnier to see the man act like a dog than to see the dog act like a man. As Dr. Johnson observed so long ago, when a dog stands on its hind legs, "It is not done well, but you are surprised to find it done at all." A dog standing on its hind legs is considerably less convincing than a man on all fours, especially when he lifts his leg near a fire hydrant.

In *The Shaggy Dog,* Tim Allen plays an assistant DA prosecuting a case involving the use of laboratory animals. He is bitten by a three-hundred-year-old dog from Tibet that has been stolen from a monastery. The dog is destined to be used in the DNA research of a scummy longevity researcher in the form of Robert Downey Jr., who plays, as he does so well, a man whose agenda seems not merely buried but decomposing.

There is a special-effects shot of the dog's DNA racing into Allen's veins. The dog DNA looks like lots of little dogs. I suppose we should be relieved that the human DNA doesn't look like a lot of little Tim Allens, although the concept of dog DNA being taken for a walk by human DNA is intriguing.

Allen's rebellious daughter, Carly (Zena Grey), is filled with animal rights fervor after her social studies teacher is accused of setting a fire at a lab where animals were being mistreated. Dave is the prosecutor but finds his courtroom duties increasingly hard to perform as he transmutes into a dog. I think he is supposed to have become the clone of the dog from Tibet, although perhaps he has simply become a new but similar dog. He doesn't go through puppy stage, however, so perhaps he was simply occupied by the other dog, although then does that still leave the original dog behind? Are laws of the conservation of matter involved here? I have extraordinary difficulty in reasoning through the details of plots that are preposterous on principle.

Although he becomes a dog, Dave retains his own mind and tries to behave like a dad would. When Carly gets too friendly with her boyfriend, Trey (Shawn Pyfrom), he jumps on the bed between them. And on his wedding anniversary, as his wife waits forlornly at a table for two in a restaurant, he appears outside the window, wagging his tail, with a bouquet in his teeth. His family is extraordinarily obtuse, I must say, in not quickly realizing that the shaggy dog is their father. How many clues do you need?

For that matter, is the shaggy dog occupied only by a human mind, or by a human mind and a canine mind fighting it out for space? If a human mind, why doesn't the dog need to learn from scratch how to bark, jump, scratch, and fetch? If a canine mind, why does it turn up for the wedding anniversary when so many attractive girl dogs are easily found? Certainly their sexual tastes must be at variance. These are silly questions but might have been promising avenues for the plot to explore.

It says something for Robert Downey Jr. that in a movie where a man becomes a dog, Downey creates the weirdest character. With tics and jerks and strange verbal sorties and a tuft of hair that seems electrified, he plays a scientist who is mad on his good days. To put this man on the witness stand is a foolhardy act by Allen and his boss (Danny Glover), but we are grateful to him, because Downey is entertaining. Maybe they have the wrong actor in the lead. Downey, playing the dog, would have run through a repertory of every canine shtick in *Best in Show*. Even in this movie, you should see him fetch.

At the end of the film, Allen (as the dog) is standing on his hind legs (not well, but one is surprised) and hugging his wife when suddenly he turns back into her husband, and what happens then? The hug continues because, yes, this is the happy ending! Ladies, if a dog turned into your husband while you were hugging it, would you scream? Dial 911? Tell him to roll over and play dead? There is an age above which this movie is unnecessary, and it may be in the low double digits. All through *The Shaggy Dog*, I kept remembering a classic headline in the *Onion:* "Millions of dog owners demand to know: Who's a good boy?" That headline doesn't have anything to do with this movie, but what does?

She's the Man ★ ★ ★

PG-13, 105 m., 2006

Amanda Bynes (Viola), Channing Tatum (Duke), Laura Ramsey (Olivia), Vinnie Jones (Coach Dinklage), Robert Hoffman (Justin), Alex Breckenridge (Monique), David Cross (Principal Gold), Julie Hagerty (Daphne), James Kirk (Sebastian). Directed by Andy Fickman and produced by Lauren Shuler Donner, Jack Leslie, and Ewan Leslie. Screenplay by Ewan Leslie, Jack Leslie, Karen McCullah Lutz, and Kirsten Smith, based on *Twelfth Night* by William Shakespeare.

I didn't for one second believe the plot of *She's the Man,* but I did believe for the entire movie that Amanda Bynes was lovable. She plays a girl who pretends to be a boy in order to play soccer. That this story is recycled from Shakespeare's *Twelfth Night* is something I report right here at the top so that we can work together to put it out of our minds.

Bynes plays Viola, the twin sister of Sebastian (James Kirk), who at the start of the movie conveniently sneaks away to London for two weeks without telling anybody. This is much easier on Viola than the Shakespeare version, in which she fears her brother has perished at sea. But I will not mention Shakespeare again. Viola is the star of the girls' soccer team at Cornwall Prep, a school that seems to have enough money to supply every girl with her own soccer team. She thinks she's good enough to play for the boys' team, but her hopes are scorned, so she takes advantage of Sebastian's absence to take his place at nearby Illyria Prep, named after the country in Shakespeare's play. There she tries out for the soccer team.

Can Bynes convincingly play a boy? Of course not. She plays a cute tomboy with short hair who keeps forgetting to talk low and then nervously clears her throat and talks like she's on the phone to the school office: "Viola is sick today, and this is her mother speaking." Can she play soccer and live with a male roommate and take showers and not be exposed as a girl? Of course not, but at least the movie doesn't make a big deal out of it; she has a few close calls, and thinks fast. When the coach (Vinnie Jones) announces a practice game between shirts and skins, she offers compelling reasons why she should be a shirt.

Viola/Sebastian's roommate at Illyria is Duke, no doubt inspired by Duke Orsino in Shakespeare. But enough about Shakespeare. Duke seems attracted to Olivia (Laura Ramsey), but Olivia is attracted to Sebastian/Viola, who gets a crush on Duke because he speaks with such sensitivity about women even when having a private conversation with her, or him. Duke is played by Channing Tatum, who sounds as if he should be the child of Carol Channing and Tatum O'Neal, which in this movie might be possible, although in real life he was born in Cullman, Alabama.

Tatum is twenty-five, a little old to play a high school kid, but Bynes at nineteen is convincing, and her poise, under the circumstances, is extraordinary. The movie develops interlocking romantic triangles and adds some funny supporting characters, including David Cross as the headmaster, whose exuberance is as boundless as his baldness. Her mother, played by Julie Hagerty, dreams of the day when her little girl will come out as a debutante; while being coached as a deb, Viola is advised to "chew like you have a secret." Does she ever.

Of Bynes let us say that she is sunny and plucky and somehow finds a way to play her impossible role without clearing her throat more than six or eight times. More important, we like her. She first won a following with her show on Nickelodeon, and was funny in *Big Fat Liar* (2002), but in this role, as Shakespeare might say, she achieves greatness, or maybe she has it thrust upon her. The movie is good-natured and silly, and at the end there is a big soccer game between Illyria and Cornwall during which both Viola and the real Sebastian are able to offer proof of their genders, although when the PG-13 rating cites "nudity," I am compelled to report that the movie includes none of the naughty bits. As a famous playwright once wrote in *Twelfth Night*, "Wherefore are those things hid?"

Shine a Light ★ ★ ★ ★

PG-13, 122 m., 2008

Featuring Mick Jagger, Keith Richards, Ron Wood, Charlie Watts, Buddy Guy, Christina Aguilera, Jack White, and Bill Clinton. A documentary directed by Martin Scorsese and produced by Steve Bing, Michael Cohl, Zane Weiner, and Victoria Pearman.

Martin Scorsese's *Shine a Light* may be the most intimate documentary ever made about a live rock 'n' roll concert. Certainly it has the best coverage of the performances onstage. Working with cinematographer Robert Richardson, Scorsese deployed a team of nine other cinematographers, all of them Oscar winners or nominees, to essentially blanket a live September 2006 Rolling Stones concert at the smallish Beacon Theater in New York. The result is startling immediacy, a merging of image and music, edited in step with the performance.

In the brief black-and-white footage opening the film, we see Scorsese drawing up shot charts to diagram the order of the songs, the order of the solos, and who would be where on the stage. This was the same breakdown approach he used with his documentary *The Last Waltz* (1978), which he hoped would enable him to call his shots through the earpieces of the cameramen, as directors of live TV did in the early days. The challenge this time was that Mick Jagger toyed with the song list in endless indecision; we look over his shoulder at titles scratched out and penciled back in, and hear him mention casually that of course the whole set might be changed on the spot. Apparently after playing together for forty-five years, the Stones communicate their running order telepathically.

This movie is where Scorsese came in. I remember visiting him in the postproduction loft for *Woodstock* in 1970, where he was part of a team led by Thelma Schoonmaker that was combining footage from multiple cameras into a split-screen approach that could show as many as three or four images at once. But the footage they had to work with was captured on the run, while *The Last Waltz* had a shot map and outline, at least in Scorsese's mind. *Shine a Light* combines his foreknowledge with the versatility of great cinematographers so that it essentially seems to have a camera in the right place at the right time for every element of the performance.

It helped, too, that the Stones' songs had been absorbed by Scorsese into his very being. "Let me put it this way," he said in a revealing August 2007 interview with Craig McLean of the *London Observer*. "Between '63 and '70, those seven years, the music that they made I found myself gravitating to. I would listen to it a great deal. And ultimately, that fueled movies like *Mean Streets* and later pictures of mine, *Raging Bull* to a certain extent, and certainly *GoodFellas* and *Casino* and other pictures over the years."

Mentioning that he had not seen the Stones in concert until late 1969, he said the music itself was ingrained: "The actual visualization of sequences and scenes in *Mean Streets* comes from a lot of their music, of living with their music and listening to it. Not just the songs I use in the film. No, it's about the tone and the mood of their music, their attitude. . . . I just kept listening to it. Then I kept imagining scenes in movies. And interpreting. It's not just imagining a scene of a tracking shot around a person's face or a car scene. It really was [taking] events and incidents in my own life that I was trying to interpret into filmmaking, to a story, a narrative. And it seemed that those songs inspired me to do that.To find a way to put those stories on film. So the debt is incalculable. I don't know what to say. In my mind, I did this film forty years ago. It just happened to get around to being filmed right now."

The result is one of the most engaged documentaries you could imagine. The cameras do not simply regard the performances; in a sense, the cameras are performers, too, in the way shots are cut together by Scorsese and his editor, David Tedeschi. Even in their sixties, the Stones are the most physical and exuberant of bands. Compared to them, watching the movements of many new young bands on Leno, Letterman, and *SNL* is like watching jerky marionettes. Jagger has never used the mechanical moves employed by many lead singers; he is a dancer and an acrobat and a conductor, too, who uses his body to conduct the audience. In counterpoint, Keith Richards and Ron Wood are loose-limbed and angular, like way-cool backup dancers. Richards in particular seems to defy gravity as he leans so far over; there's a moment in rehearsal when he tells Scorsese he wants to show him something, and leans down to show that you can see the mallet of Charlie Watts's bass drum, visible as it hits the front drumhead. "I can see that because I'm down there," he explains.

The unmistakable fact is that the Stones love performing. Watch Ron lean an arm on Keith's shoulder during one shared riff. Watch the droll hints of irony, pleasure, and quizzical reaction shots, which so subtly move across their seemingly passive faces. Notice that Keith smokes onstage not simply to be smoking, but to use the smoke cloud, brilliant in the spotlights, as a performance element. He knows what he's doing. And then see it all brought together and tied tight in the remarkably acrobatic choreography of Jagger's performance. I've seen the Stones in Chicago in venues as large as the United Center and as small as the Double Door, but I've never experienced them this way, because the cameras are as privileged as the performers onstage.

And the music? What do I have to say about the music? What is there *left* to say about the music? In that interview, Scorsese said, "'Sympathy for the Devil' became this score for our lives. It was everywhere at that time; it was being played on the radio. When 'Satisfaction' starts, the authority of the guitar riff that begins it is something that became anthemic." I think there is nothing useful for me to say about the music except that if you have been interested enough to read this far, you already know all about it, and all I can usefully describe is the experience of seeing it in this film.

Shoot 'Em Up ★ ★ ★ ½

R, 93 m., 2007

Clive Owen (Mr. Smith), Paul Giamatti (Mr. Hertz), Monica Bellucci (DQ), Daniel Pilon (Senator Rutledge). Directed by Michael Davis and produced by Rick Benattar, Susan Montford, and Don Murphy. Screenplay by Davis.

I don't need a lot of research to be confident in stating that never before have I seen a movie open with the hero delivering a baby during a gun battle, severing the umbilical cord with a gunshot, and then killing a villain by penetrating his brain with a raw carrot. Yes, a carrot will do that in this movie. It will do a lot of things.

Shoot 'Em Up, written and directed by the gung-ho Michael Davis, is the most audacious, implausible, cheerfully offensive, hyperactive action picture I've seen since, oh, *Sin City,* which in comparison was a chamber drama. That I liked *Shoot 'Em Up* is a consequence of a critical quirk I sometimes notice: I may disapprove of a movie for going too far and yet have a sneaky regard for a movie that goes much, much farther than merely too far. This one goes so far, if you even want to get that far, you have to start halfway there, which means you have to be a connoisseur of the hard-boiled action genre and its serio-comic subdivision (or subbasement).

The film opens in one of those grimy cityscapes where a little graffiti might brighten things up. A man with a ten o'clock shadow (Clive Owen) sits on a bench eating a carrot. A pregnant woman is chased past him by men intent on murdering her. "Bloody hell," says the man, a phrase I find so much more elegant than, "What the foosball underwater clockmaker kitchen," if you enjoy creating acronyms. He defends the woman in a hail of gunfire, while delivering her baby, ramming the carrot into his victim's cranium, and finding himself on the run with an infant in his arms, which is how Owen spent much of *Children of Men,* also with people shooting at him, so you could say he looks right at home.

The Owen character is named Mr. Smith. The leader of his enemies is Mr. Hertz (Paul Giamatti). No Mr. Brown around anywhere, but Tarantino seems to hover over the action like a guardian skycam. I am not sure why Mr. Smith is so capable during acts of violence, but it may be because Owen practiced up while he was being considered for the role of James Bond. Yes, that might explain the scene where he continues a gun battle while jumping out of an airplane without a parachute.

That was probably one of the scenes Michael Davis drew by hand, thousands of drawings to give the illusion of animation when he made his pitch to the studio. This is a determined guy. I remember ten years ago he wanted me to see his *Eight Days a Week* at the Slamdance film festival. I was covering Sundance, which is itself three full-time jobs, but he kept after me, ominously brandishing a carrot. I made the trek uphill in the snow to a hotel lobby where his film was being shown and found a spot on a sofa. And the movie was a wonderful comedy about a kid so in love with a girl that he sets up camp and lives in her front yard a whole summer before she finally agrees to go out with him. So there's your auteur theory at work: Davis likes movies about men who will go to any lengths for a woman.

Comedy is a tricky genre to give an unknown indie his start, however, so Davis switched to the usual indie port of entry, horror, making among others a movie about roadkill that wants to kill you. That's the kind of movie you want to back up and run over again.

Shoot 'Em Up will become, I suspect, some kind of legend in the murky depths of extreme action. What elevates it from the depraved to the deserving is a sense of style, a sense of warped humor, and the acting. Clive Owen brings what credibility there could possibly be to his character, and makes us believe it as much as we possibly can (not much, in both cases, but points for effort). Paul Giamatti, Hollywood's favorite nerd, is surprisingly, teeth-gnashingly evil. And Monica Bellucci is DQ, the hooker with the heart of gold, who becomes Mr. Smith's partner and the baby's surrogate mother. I thought and thought about what "DQ" could possibly stand for, and finally had my eureka moment: Dairy Queen.

The plot (two words that should be followed by a hollow laugh) involves Mr. Hertz being hired by Senator Rutledge (Daniel Pilon), political party unspecified, who is running for president but learns he is dying and can only be saved by the bone marrow of infants. In the old days, when political campaigns didn't run so long, there would have been no time to impregnate surrogate volunteers and harvest their offspring, another argument against the extended presidential campaign season.

Man, am I gonna get mail from people who hate this picture. I'll fall back on my stock defense: Did I, or did I not, accurately describe the film? You have been informed. Now eat your carrots.

Shopgirl ★ ★ ★ ½

R, 116 m., 2005

Steve Martin (Ray Porter), Claire Danes (Mirabelle Butterfield), Jason Schwartzman (Jeremy), Bridgette Wilson-Sampras (Lisa Cramer), Sam Bottoms (Dan Butterfield), Frances Conroy (Catherine Butterfield), Rebecca Pidgeon (Christie Richards), Gina Doctor (Del Rey). Directed by Anand Tucker and produced by Ashok Amritraj, Jon J. Jashni, and Steve Martin. Screenplay by Martin, based on his novella.

One of the things you cannot do in this life is impose conditions on love. Another impossibility is to expect another's heart to accommodate your own desires and needs. You may think that cleverness, power, or money will work on your behalf, but eventually you will end up feeling the way you really feel, and so will the other person, and there is no argument more useless than the one that begins with the words, "But I thought we had an agreement."

Shopgirl is a tender and perceptive film that argues these truths. It is about an older man named Ray Porter, a millionaire, who sees a young woman named Mirabelle Butterfield standing behind the glove counter at Saks and desires her. He goes through the motions of buying some gloves. Perhaps the gray? "I prefer the black," she says, and so he buys the black, and that night on her doorstep she finds the gloves, neatly gift-wrapped and with a note inside: "Will you have dinner with me? Ray Porter."

Now compare the elegance of this approach with the other man who desires her company. This is Jeremy, who is about her age in years but about twelve in knowledge about the ways of women. You do not honk your horn on a first date and expect the woman to hurry out to your car. You do not pretend you want only to people-watch until she agrees to buy her own ticket to the movies. You do not attempt one of those dreadful snuffling blind approaches to a kiss, the kind where the girl doesn't know if you're trying to kiss her or maybe you just got something caught in your throat while staring at her breasts. I've been around a long time and, young men, if there is one thing I know, it is that the only way to kiss a girl for the first time is to look like you want to and intend to, and move in fast enough to seem eager but slow enough to give her a chance to say, "So anyway . . ." and look up as if she's trying to remember your name.

All of these things and more are known to Ray Porter (Steve Martin). Yes, he is thirty-five years older than Mirabelle (Claire Danes), but we're not talking marriage here; we're talking about a relationship based on shared assumptions and friendly sex, plus a lot of Ray Porter's money, which he is spending not to purchase Mirabelle but simply to provide himself with a woman who dresses, dines, and travels up to his standards. Watch him get shifty when she suggests he stay at her place one night.

"I made myself perfectly clear," he assures his psychiatrist. He is not seeking marriage. He does not want a long-term commitment. Yes, he wants sex, but Mirabelle is not necessary to satisfy that desire, which is so easily solved by a single man of Ray's age and wealth. Mirabelle is necessary because she is young, smart, entertaining, unattached, and there. She is good company. She is a person of character.

Perhaps he shops for her at Saks because anyone working there will understand the finer things and spend a lot of time thinking about the customers who can so easily afford them. He makes the parameters of their relationship perfectly clear, as if he were a surveyor and she a vacant lot. When he says it gives him pleasure to be able to provide her with nice things, it is the truth: He has so much money that cost is irrelevant, and she looks so good wearing that dress, dining in that restaurant, sitting on that airplane.

Mirabelle understands all of these things and accepts them. That's the deal. The Saks job is a dead end, and she wants to work as an artist. She would be wary if Ray came after her with love and sincerity in his eyes. Is she technically a prostitute, since the money all flows in her direction while the sex flows both ways? Not at all. For Ray to spend money is exactly the same thing as for her to receive it. It is of no importance except that it makes their lives together possible.

Now about Jeremy. You know guys who are like him. When he accumulates enough empty pizza boxes, he stacks them up and has himself an end table. Doing the laundry involves sniffing for the most passable T-shirt. He is an artist, too. His art involves stenciling the boxes that amplifiers come in. As his muse, Mirabelle may inspire him to design a new typeface. Shortly after they meet, he conveniently leaves town on an extended road trip with a rock band, which is led by a musician who gets him started on self-help books. He needs a lot of all kinds of help.

No, the movie is not about how Mirabelle realizes that Ray is a phony and Jeremy, for all his faults, is lovable. Ray is not a phony. He really is exactly the man he seems to be, God help him. Jeremy is lovable like a puppy that you are delighted belongs to somebody else. What happens at the end is not tidy like in most romantic comedies, but bittersweet and objective. "I guess I have to choose whether to be miserable now, or miserable later," Mirabelle says. There is an argument to be made for both choices, but when all is said and done she will not be the most miserable person in the movie.

Should I write about the performances, the writing, and the direction? I already have. I just did. That's what you're reading. These are the thoughts they inspired. What thoughts they inspire in you may be entirely otherwise. You may think Ray is a rat, Mirabelle is a victim, and Jeremy cleans up well. If that's what you think, go back and read the first paragraph again, and save yourself some trouble.

Shotgun Stories ★ ★ ★ ★

PG-13, 92 m., 2008

Michael Shannon (Son Hayes), Douglas Ligon (Boy Hayes), Barlow Jacobs (Kid Hayes), Michael Abbott Jr. (Cleaman Hayes), Travis Smith (Mark Hayes), Lynnsee Provence (Stephen Hayes), David Rhodes (John Hayes), Natalie Canerday (Nicole Hayes), Glenda Pannell (Annie Hayes). Directed by Jeff Nichols and produced by David Gordon Green, Lisa Muskat, and Nichols. Screenplay by Nichols.

Jeff Nichols's *Shotgun Stories* is shaped and told like a revenge tragedy, but it offers an unexpected choice: The hero of the film does not believe the future is doomed by the past. If it were, most of the key characters would be dead by the end, an outcome that seems almost inevitable. Here is a tense and sorrowful film where common sense struggles with blood lust.

The movie takes place in a "dead-ass town" where three brothers exist. "Hang out" is the only term for what they do. They were named Son, Kid, and Boy by an alcoholic father and, in Son's words, "a hateful woman." Son (Michael Shannon) sprinkles the feed at a local fish farm and loses all his money trying to perfect a "system" he thinks can beat the local casino. His wife has just walked out, taking their son. His brother Kid (Barlow Jacobs) would like to get married, but "I worry about taking care of her. I mean, I don't have a truck. I don't have a house. I sleep in a damn tent." The youngest, Boy (Douglas Ligon), lives in his van and is struggling to beat the heat by persuading a home air conditioner to run off his cigarette lighter.

If this sounds like the setup for a redneck joke, it isn't. The brothers are quiet, lonely, still suffering from abusive childhoods. And consider the remarkable scene where their mother knocks on the door to tell them their father, now married to another woman and with four more sons, has died.

"When's the funeral?" Son asks.

"You can find out in the newspaper."

"You going?"

"No."

Son, Kid, and Boy attend. Since abandoning them, their father had sobered up in rehab, found Jesus, and started a prosperous middle-class family. Now Son chooses to say a few words over the coffin before spitting on it, and a fight breaks out. This fight will escalate into a blood feud in which lives are lost and blood is shed, and yet the enemies are so unprepared that after one buys a shotgun in a pawn shop, he has to be shown how to assemble and load it.

The film is by no means entirely grim and implacable. There are moments of quiet humor, as when Boy finally figures out a way to run the air conditioner off his car battery, and rigs it to blow at him on a river bank and to run a blender for his margaritas. Annie (Glenda Pannell) is fed up with Son's gambling habit but is a gentle woman who loves him. Son himself has hopes for his own son and wants to break the cycle of violence. So does the oldest son of the other family, although the dead father seems to have done a better job of raising those boys than the first three.

Jeff Nichols, the writer and director, is working in the same world where David Gordon Green sets his films; indeed, Green is a coproducer of this film, which uses his cinematographer, Adam Stone. The photography, of course, is wide-screen; these people live surrounded by distant horizons, the vista broken only by the occasional tree or broken-down tractor. Like Green, Nichols uses sleight of hand to sneak in plot details; *Shotgun Stories* uses the most subtle dialogue I can imagine to reveal, by implication, that Boy has, or had, an African-American wife, or girlfriend.

This film has literally been saved by the festival circuit. After being rejected by major distributors, it found a home in smaller festivals, where word of mouth propelled it into its current wider release. It has qualities that may not come out in a trailer or in an ad, but that sink in when you have the experience of seeing it. Few films are so observant about how we relate with one another. Few as sympathetic.

The film is as spare as the landscape. Classical drama comes condensed to a harshness: "You raised us to hate those boys, and we do. And now it's come to this." In a movie where so much violence obviously takes place, we actually see very little of it. Nichols sidesteps the problem of the intrinsic interest of violence by looking away from it and focusing on its effect. We don't get to know the second family very well, but Son, Kid, and Boy are closed up within their melancholy. Although some orange flowers and gentle music try to do their work at the end, we can only hope Son finds the life he desires for his own son.

Shrek the Third ★ ★ ½

PG, 92 m., 2007

With the voices of: Mike Myers (Shrek), Eddie Murphy (Donkey), Cameron Diaz (Princess Fiona), Antonio Banderas (Puss in Boots), John Cleese (King Harold), Julie Andrews (Queen Lillian), Rupert Everett (Prince Charming), Eric Idle (Merlin), Justin Timberlake (Artie). Directed by Chris Miller and produced by Aron Warner. Screenplay by Jeffrey Price, Peter S. Seaman, and Jon Zack, inspired by the book by William Steig.

Shrek the Third is a damped-down return to the kingdom of Far Far Away, lacking the comic energy of the first brilliant film and not measuring up to the second. From the thrills of dragon slaying and damsel rescuing, Shrek's challenges have been reduced to a career decision: Should he become the king?

The movie is as visually enchanting as the first two in the series, and the big green ogre (voice by Mike Myers) is as gentle and lovable, but the movie settles for action that it trusts is funny, instead of aiming for comedy itself. Another peculiarity is that the plot will probably not be engaging for younger audience members, who understand dragons but don't care that heavy lies the head that wears a crown. Shrek spends too much time in lachrymose conversation with his bride, Fiona (Cameron Diaz), and pondering the challenge of fatherhood, and not enough time being an ogre.

Indeed, Shrek is the only character in the movie who makes a big deal about his ogrehood. The king and queen (John Cleese and Julie Andrews) have long since embraced their son-in-law, and on his deathbed the frog king reveals that Shrek is an heir to the throne—one of two, including the feckless Artie (Justin Timberlake). Shrek demurs, preferring life back in the swamp in what Fiona describes as his "vermin-filled shack."

Why would Fiona, raised as a princess, accept life in such a dreary mire of despond? Recall from *Shrek* (2001) that she was a conventional princess only by day and became an ogre after nightfall. When Shrek's kiss rescued her from marriage to Lord Farquaad, she became an ogre full-time. Before that she was a human, I guess, although her father was a frog. Interspecies reproduction is so common in Far Far Away that it makes irrelevant such questions as whether Kermit and Miss Piggy ever had sex. Remember that the dragon and Donkey fell in love in the first film. For someone like me who has never understood how birds and snakes do it, thoughts of their marital adventures boggle the mind.

Back again this time are the two supporting stars from the earlier films, Donkey (Eddie Murphy) and Puss in Boots (Antonio Banderas). But they're reduced to being friends and traveling partners and are never really "foregrounded." At one point, magically, they switch bodies and talk in each other's voices, but that's what it amounts to: They talk in each other's voices. Such a thing is not intrinsically funny, unless it is plot- or character-driven. Little really depends on it or comes from it, except for a weak little sight gag at the end. Since Murphy's vocal riffs and improvisations have been so inspired earlier in the series, we want more of him this time, not less.

Shrek, Fiona, Donkey, and Puss have to sail to the land of Worcestershire to find Artie, and they encounter Prince Charming (Rupert Everett), who is reduced from princehood to (in an opening scene) performing in dinner theater. Fairly arbitrary developments produce a team of heroines (Cinderella, Snow White, Sleeping Beauty) who are sort of Charlie's Angels, I guess, although they provide the movie with too many characters and not enough for them to do. In the first film, they were a sly DreamWorks dig at Disney and were dumped as obsolete in Shrek's private swamp.

Indeed, the movie practices such economy of characters that the Gingerbread Man and the Three Blind Mice turn up again—unwanted, if you ask me. What's the use of three blind mice if you can't see them run? And although I have been trained to accept talking animals, living pastries fail to engage me.

I learn from *Variety* that there will be a fourth *Shrek* and a Broadway musical, and I hope both turn for their inspiration to the original *Shrek*. That film did so much with the outsider status of an ogre and Shrek's painful uncertainties about his role in non-ogre society. It involved intolerance and prejudice and courage, and had real stakes. And it was funny and had great action scenes, like Shrek's rescue of Fiona. Now everybody in the land of Far Far Away acts as if we (and they) have seen the first two films.

The movie's a pleasure to watch for its skilled animation. But it lacks truly interesting challenges. It makes the mistake of thinking slapstick action is funny for its own sake, a mistake made by a lot of Saturday-morning TV cartoons. True, characters zooming and bouncing around are easy to write because no creative invention is required to set them in motion. But so what?

Shut Up and Sing ★ ★ ★ ½

R, 99 m., 2006

Featuring the Dixie Chicks (Martie Maguire, Natalie Maines, Emily Robison) and Simon Renshaw. A documentary directed by Barbara Kopple and Cecilia Peck and produced by David Cassidy, Claude Davies, Kopple, and Peck.

Maybe Natalie Maines's real problem was with her timing. On March 10, 2003, in the first days of the U.S. invasion of Iraq, she told a London audience, "I'm ashamed that the president of the United States is from Texas." It took two weeks for that wisecrack to make it back home, but then it unleashed a perfect storm: Her group, the Dixie Chicks, had been the most popular female singing group in history, but suddenly disappeared from the playlists of virtually every country radio station in the land. Their number-one single, "Traveling Soldier," dropped 47 percent in sales in one week. Many of their fans were vocal in their opinion that she should not have an opinion. Not long after, George W. Bush staged his premature "Mission Accomplished" photo-op.

As it happens, Barbara Kopple and Cecilia Peck were filming that London concert as part of a proposed film on the Chicks' world tour. Kopple usually chooses weightier subject matter, as with her *Harlan County, USA* doc about a miners' strike, but this was to be a film mostly about music. They stayed aboard to record one of the most revealing episodes in the history of country music, and *Shut Up and Sing* tells the story of how the Dixie Chicks and their manager dealt with the rage of some (not all) of their fans.

Political dissent has an honorable history in country music, just as freedom of speech is the bedrock of our American freedoms, but tell that to the people threatening boycotts of country stations or issuing anonymous death threats against the Dixie Chicks. They're for freedom of speech as long as they agree with what's being said. But listen to Johnny Cash defending the blacklisted Pete Seeger as "the best patriot I know." Or consider these lyrics by John Prine, the best songwriter in modern country history:

Your flag decal won't get you into heaven anymore;
It's already overcrowded by their dirty little war;
And Jesus don't like killin', no matter what the reason for . . .

Or the heartbreak of the great Prine song beginning:

Sam Stone, came home, from the conflict overseas,
With a Purple Heart and a monkey on his back . . .

Of course Prine's songs were about Vietnam, a war that impacted differently because of the draft. Iraq is being fought largely by a volunteer army, if you can call being a National Guardsman in your third tour of duty volunteering. And in those earliest days, the administration was predicting a pacified, peaceful, and democratic Iraq in months if not weeks. As Bush's approval rating has plummeted, the Dixie Chicks have slowly won their way back toward acceptance, and this documentary is a fascinating record of their journey.

Kopple and Peck seem to have free access to the Chicks, backstage and behind closed doors, and we hear them in frank discussions with their manager, Simon Renshaw, about the devastation of their careers. At first, a stunned Maines tries to rationalize: She was just kidding, it was a throwaway line, she supports our troops but not the president's invasion. It becomes clear that Chicks fans are not big on nuance and have zero tolerance for dissent.

Or do they? Were the nation's country stations gutless in caving in to the threats of boycott? Was there not one with the courage to play the most popular country group in the land? On their first American tour after the debacle, the Chicks sell out every arena, are cheered in standing ovations, and are embraced in Greenville, South Carolina, on the very day of "Mission Accomplished." At one concert, Maines tells the audience it's OK to boo: "We believe in freedom of speech. So let's stop right now for fifteen seconds of booing." All she hears are cheers.

The documentary shows what a tight-knit group the Chicks are. Banjo player Emily Robison and fiddler Martie Maguire, sisters who brought in Maines as lead singer, had no idea what Maines was going to say that day in London, but they stand behind her without question. There's no complaining, just shell-shock.

During the course of 2003 to 2006, Robison and Maguire have babies (Emily has twins) after agonizing fertility procedures. They write and record *Taking the Long Way,* a new album in which, far from apologizing, Maines sings "Not Ready to Make Nice." It is some of their best work, freeing them from the confines of country, but the album doesn't sell like their earlier work. Discussing lagging CD and concert sales, they decide to be honest about it. It becomes clear that their careers are less important to them than, for want of a better word, their sisterhood.

The documentary shows an ugly side of the right-wing intimidation they face. Among all of the self-anointed patriots who picket them, there is apparently not a glimmer of a notion of what freedom of speech means. Their opponents live in an Orwellian world in which others are granted only the freedom to agree. Heard in sound bites, seen with hate slogans on signs and T-shirts, they are not a pretty picture.

And there are the chilling backstage preparations for a Dallas concert before which they have received a death threat. To be willing to stand unprotected in front of thousands of people and sing your songs despite such a threat takes courage, and it is a brave defense of American values, although their critics cannot see it that way. *Shut Up and Sing* tells the story of three young women whose belief in America is bred in the bone, and it shames their critics.

As for Natalie Maines's timing, maybe she simply made the mistake of being premature. The country music demographic group is bearing a disproportionate share of the burden of Iraq, with its National Guardsmen husbands, wives, sons and daughters, brothers and sisters absent, wounded, or dead. They are paying a heavy price for a war started on lies, and are perhaps not as angry these days at Natalie for speaking truthfully.

Sicko ★ ★ ★ ½

PG-13, 124 m., 2007

A documentary directed by Michael Moore and produced by Moore and Meghan O'Hara. Screenplay by Moore.

If you heard the story, you remember it. A woman bled to death in an emergency room while her husband and a bystander both called 911 to report she was being ignored. They were ignored. She was already in the ER, wasn't she?

Her death came too late to be included in *Sicko,* Michael Moore's litany of horrors about the American health-care system, which is run for profit, and insurance companies, who pay bonuses to employees who are successful in denying coverage or claims.

But wait a minute. I saw the movie almost a year to the day after a carotid artery burst after surgery and I came within a breath of death. I spent the next year at Northwestern Memorial Hospital, the Rehabilitation Institute of Chicago, and the Pritikin Longevity Center, and I still require the daily care of a nurse.

I mention this to indicate I am pretty deeply involved in the health-care system. In each and every case, without exception, I have been cared for by doctors who are kind, patient, painstaking, and expert, and by nurses who are skilled, wise, and tireless. My insurance has covered a small fortune in claims. My wife and I have also paid large sums from our own savings.

So I have only one complaint, and it is this: Every American should be as fortunate as I have been. As Moore makes clear in his film, some fifty million Americans have no insurance and no way to get it. Many of the insured discover their policies are worthless after insurance investigators reel off an endless list of conditions and procedures that are not covered, or discover "preexisting conditions" the patients "should" have known about. One woman, unconscious when she is put into an ambulance, is billed for the trip because her insurer says it was not preauthorized. How could she get authorization when she was out cold on the pavement?

We also learn a lot about drug companies and HMOs in the film. It is an item of faith in some circles that drug companies need their profits to finance research and development. Out of a dollar of profit, what percentage would you guess goes to R&D, and what percentage goes to advertising and promotion, multimillion-dollar executive salaries, corporate jets, palatial headquarters, bonuses, and stockholders?

Moore plays 1971 tapes from the Oval Office as Nixon discusses the original Kaiser plan for an HMO. "It's for profit," Nixon says admiringly. Have you ever understood exactly what benefit it is that an HMO provides, while it stands between you and the medical care system and acts as a toll bridge? Do its profits not depend on supplying as little health care as possible, at the lowest possible price?

Moore visits the countries of Canada, England, France, and Cuba, all of which have (1) universal health care, and (2) a longer life expectancy and lower infant mortality than America. In France, he drives with one of the many doctors kept on full-time house-call duty. Of course we have heard all about "socialized medicine," which among many evils denies you freedom of choice of hospitals and doctors. Hold on: That's the free-enterprise HMO system.

Moore sails to Cuba with three boatloads of sick people, some of them 9/11 volunteers who have been denied care for respiratory and other problems because they were—well, volunteers. Unlike firemen and policemen, they had no business being there, I guess. One woman is on $1,000-a-month disability, and needs $240 a month for her inhaler medication. Moore's gimmick (he always has one, but this one is dramatic) is to take her to a Cuban hospital where she finds that her $120 medication costs 5 cents in Cuba. At least that R&D money is helping Cubans.

Moore's original purpose in sailing south was to seek medical care for his passengers at the Guantanamo Bay prison base. He is turned away, of course, but not before observing that accused al-Qaeda terrorists get better (free) medical attention than 9/11 volunteers.

It's a different Michael Moore in *Sicko.* He still wears the baseball cap, but he's onscreen less, not so cocky, not going for so many laughs. He simply tells one story after another about Americans who are sick, dying, or dead because we have an undemocratic, profit-gouging health-care system. Moore's films usually make conservatives angry. This one is likely to strike home with anyone, left or right, who has had serious illness in the family. Conservative governments in Canada, England, and France all support universal health care; America is the only developed nation without it.

Yes, nitpickers can find fault with any attack on our system. There are four health-care lobbyists for every congressman. But there's room for irony when the owner of an anti-Moore Web site can't afford to maintain it when his wife gets sick. And room for tears, when a claims investigator for an insurance company tells Congress she knows she was her company's instrument for denying clients care they needed that might have saved their lives. ☞

Silent Hill ★ ½

R, 125 m., 2006

Radha Mitchell (Rose DaSilva), Sean Bean (Chris DaSilva), Laurie Holden (Cybil Bennett), Deborah Kara Unger (Dahlia Gillespie), Kim Coates (Officer Gucci), Tanya Allen (Anna), Alice Krige (Christabella), Jodell Ferland (Sharon DaSilva). Directed by Christophe Gans and produced by Don Carmody and Samuel Hadida. Screenplay by Roger Avary.

I had a nice conversation with seven or eight people coming down on the escalator after we all saw *Silent Hill*. They wanted me to explain it to them. I said I didn't have a clue. They said, "You're supposed to be a movie critic, aren't you?" I said, "Supposed to be. But we work mostly with movies." "Yeah," said the girl in the Harley T-shirt. "I guess this was like a video game that you, like, had to play in order to, like, understand the movie."

I guess. I was out in Boulder, Colorado, the week before on a panel about video games and whether they can be art, and a lot of the students said they were really looking forward to *Silent Hill* because it's one of the best games, and they read on the Internet that the movie was supposed to live up to the game. That was all speculation, of course, because Sony Pictures declined to preview the film for anybody, perhaps because they were concerned it would not live up to the game, or because they were afraid it would. When I told one student that the movie was not being previewed, there was real pain on his face, as if he had personally been devalued.

Not only can I not describe the plot of this movie, but I have a feeling the last scene reverses half of what I thought I knew (or didn't know). What I can say is that it's an incredibly good-looking film. The director, Christophe Gans, uses graphics and special effects and computers and grainy, scratchy film stock and surrealistic images, and makes *Silent Hill* look more like an experimental art film than a horror film—except for the horror, of course. The visuals are terrific; credit also to cinematographer Dan Laustsen, production designer Carol Spier, and the art, set, and costume artists. But what are we to make of dialogue such as I will now describe?

A group of undead citizens of the ghost town of Silent Hill have gathered for some witch-burning. The town was abandoned thirty years ago because of the fumes from mine fires, which still smolder beneath the surface. Gray ash falls like rain. "Something terrible happened here," a character says perceptively. The townspeople pile wood on a bonfire in the center of an abandoned church and tie an alleged witch to a ladder, which is then lowered over the flames until the victim's skin gets extra crispy. Next up: little Sharon (Jodell Ferland), the daughter of the heroine, Rose (Radha Mitchell). She is tied to the ladder and prepared to be lowered and roasted, when her mother bursts into the church and cries out, and I quote, "It's okay, baby. Everything's gonna be okay!"

The people who live in Silent Hill are dead, I guess. Some of them glow like old embers on a fire, which is not a sign of life. They live in abandoned buildings and in the mines and in a Smoke and Flame Factory, which you will recall from my Little Movie Glossary is a factorylike location of uncertain purpose that generates a lot of smoke and flames. Also sharing their space are ratlike little CGI insects, who scurry around thinking they look a lot scarier than they do.

Rose has come here with her daughter, Sharon, because the girl has taken to sleepwalking at night and standing on the edge of high cliffs while saying "Silent Hill" in her sleep. Obviously the correct treatment is to take her to the abandoned town itself. Rose and Sharon race off in the night, pursued by Rose's husband (Sean Bean) and a motorcycle cop (Laurie Holden) who is dressed like a leather mistress. The usual zombielike little girl turns up in the headlights, there is a crash, and then everybody wanders through the town for two hours while the art direction looks great. I especially liked the snakelike wires at the end that held people suspended in midair. I also liked it when Johnny Cash sang "Ring of Fire" on the sound track, since if there was ever a movie in need of a song about a ring of fire, this is that film.

Now here's a funny thing. Although I did not understand the story, I would have appreciated a great deal less explanation. All through the movie, characters are pausing to offer arcane backstories and historical perspectives and metaphysical insights and occult orientations. They talk and talk, and somehow their words do not light up any synapses in my brain, if my brain has synapses and they're supposed to light up, and if it doesn't and they're not, then they still don't make any sense.

Perhaps those who have played the game will understand the movie and enjoy it. Speaking of synapses, another member of that panel discussion at Boulder was Dr. Leonard Shlain, chairman of laparoscopic surgery at California Pacific Medical Center and an author whose book *Art & Physics: Parallel Visions in Space, Time and Light* makes you think that if anyone could understand *Silent Hill,* he could.

Dr. Shlain made the most interesting comment on the panel. He said they took some four- and five-year-olds and gave them video games and asked them to figure out how to play them without instructions. Then they watched the children's brain activity with real-time monitors. "At first, when they were figuring out the games," he said, "the whole brain lit up. But by the time they knew how to play the games, the brain went dark, except for one little point." Walking out after *Silent Hill,* I thought of that lonely pilot light, and I understood why I failed to understand the movie. My damn brain lit up too much.

Silk ★ ★

R, 110 m., 2007

Keira Knightley (Helene Joncour), Michael Pitt (Herve Joncour), Koji Yakusho (Local Overlord), Alfred Molina (Baldabiou), Mark Rendall (Ludovic), Sei Ashina (The Mistress). Directed by Francois Girard and produced by Niv Fichman, Nadine Luque, Domenico Procacci, and Sonoko Sakai. Screenplay by Girard and Michael Golding, based on a novel by Alessandro Baricco.

Silk is a languid, too languid, story of romantic regrets, mostly ours, because romance is expected to carry the film without explaining it. It is told as a mournful flashback, narrated by a man who has been in love with two women, or maybe it was one all the time. He is a young Frenchman as his story begins circa 1860, who falls in love with a local girl, marries her, and then is sent to Japan and falls in love again.

The Frenchman is named Herve, played by Michael Pitt as the passive, soft-spoken plaything of every circumstance he falls into. His complaint seems to be that his life has happened to him. His wife is Helene (Keira Knightley), whom he truly loves, and who truly loves him, but cannot give him a child, although this plays less like a tragedy than just one of those things.

His father is a rich businessman, perhaps the mayor (I could not be sure), who takes the counsel of an entrepreneur, or maybe his employee (I could not be sure), named Baldabiou (Alfred Molina) that they revive the local silk mills. All goes well until disease attacks the silkworms. Then Baldabiou decides to send Herve to Japan to obtain uncontaminated silkworm eggs.

This journey, by carriage, train, ship, caravan, and horseback, takes him to a small Japanese village where the fearsome man in charge (Koji Yakusho) sizes him up, agrees to sell him eggs, and introduces him, in a way, to his beautiful mistress (Sei Ashina). Their eyes meet, and something happens between them, or Herve is sure it does. He returns to France and his wife with the eggs, which make them all rich. But he is obsessed by thoughts of the woman, and that inspires two more trips to Japan and certain undercurrents in his marriage to the wife he still loves.

There are some mysteries in the storytelling, a central one being the night he is told by a Dutch trader that the mistress "is not what she seems." How so? "She is not Japanese." Then what is she? The IMDb has no doubts, reporting that she is "European," which she is certainly not. My guess is Korean or Chinese, but since the question remains unanswered, one wonders why it was introduced. (Find out on the IMDb, which will correct this error the moment they learn about it.)

Another mystery is how long silkworm eggs can survive during a journey back to France, since their fortunes seem to have no relationship to the nature of the journeys. But never mind. Herve's problem is, when he's not with the one he loves, he loves the one he's with, and is sincere about that at all times.

Our problem, on the other hand, is that we don't care. Michael Pitt almost whispers his way through the film, reveals not passion but damp-eyed self-pity, and (given the language barrier) has no reason to be in love with the Japanese woman except for the movie's blatant exoticism, which argues: Why would you be satisfied with a high-spirited, beautiful wife like Helene, who shares jolly tumbles in the sack, when you could have a Japanese woman who kneels submissively before you, takes forever to serve you tea, looks soulfully into your eyes, speaks not a word, and touches you only once (although we know that, not Herve, who is blindfolded at the time).

There are additional unforgivable plot elements that I dare not reveal, meant to be much more stirring than, under the circumstances, they can possibly be. And a piano score that weeps under many a scene. And a lot of beautiful photography. And then everything is brought together at the end in a flash of revelation that is spectacularly underwhelming.

The Simpsons Movie ★ ★ ★

PG-13, 86 m., 2007

With the voices of: Dan Castellaneta, Julie Kavner, Nancy Cartwright, Yeardley Smith, Harry Shearer, Hank Azaria, and A. Brooks. Directed by David Silverman and produced by James L. Brooks, Matt Groening, Al Jean, Richard Sakai, and Mike Scully. Screenplay by Brooks, Groening, Jean, Scully, Ian Maxstone-Graham, George Meyer, David Mirkin, Mike Reiss, Matt Selman, John Swartzwelder, and Jon Vitti.

The Simpsons are fairly surprised to find themselves in a movie; they can't believe "anyone would pay to see what we did on TV for free." But I suspect a lot of people will. Here is a feature-length version of what *Time* magazine, no less, called "the 20th century's best television series." That may say more about *Time* magazine and the twentieth century than it does about the Simpsons, but never mind: The movie is funny, sassy, and intelligent in that moronic Simpsons way.

There is a plot, sort of, involving Homer's role in polluting the lake in Springfield, which calls down the wrath of the federal bureaucracy and leads to dire consequences for his fellow citizens. The Simpsons' guilt is counterbalanced by poor, idealistic Lisa, who goes door-to-door collecting signatures for her environmental crusade, only to get every door slammed in her face. One house even flees.

This story allows room for the sorts of political asides the Simpsons are famous for; not broadsides, but sideswipes. When the feds finally succeed at something in the movie, they're as surprised as everybody else.

For me, the three biggest laughs in the movie (I won't spoil them) were a plug for the Fox network, a skateboarding sequence inspired by *Austin Powers,* and a unique way to go fishing. Those, and the peculiar everyday lives of the closely knit Simpsons, fill in the gaps in the plot, along with a devout neighbor who, considering what Homer puts in his mailbox, is more sinned against than sinning.

The movie sets some kind of record by crediting no less than eleven writers (James L. Brooks, Matt Groening, Al Jean, Ian Maxstone-Graham, George Meyer, David Mirkin, Mike Reiss, Mike Scully, Matt Selman, John Swartzwelder, and Jon Vitti). That's not the usual case of endless tinkering, but an example of devotion; *Variety* says all eleven produced episodes for the TV show at one time or another. The genius of the series is that it has tapped some of the best offbeat comic talent instead of settling for the TV animation groove. Consider James L. Brooks and voice talent A. (for Albert) Brooks. These people work outside the box.

I'm not generally a fan of movies spun off from TV animation. The Flintstones and Ninja Turtles moved me only marginally. But there's something about the Simpsons that's radical and simple at the same time, subversive and good-hearted, offensive without really meaning to be. It's a nice balancing act. And it finally settles the controversy over what state Springfield is in; it is bordered, we learn, by Ohio, Nevada, Maine, and Kentucky. So you can figure it out right there.

If *The Simpsons* is indeed the best television series of one hundred years (almost half of them, to be sure, without television), I guess I shouldn't be surprised to visit the Internet Movie Database and discover that the movie has been voted the 166th best film of all time, seven places above *The Grapes of Wrath* and ten ahead of *Gone with the Wind.*

That's all the more remarkable because it was first screened for critics on July 24, has had no sneak previews I've heard about, and got 81.4 percent perfect "10" votes. Only 4.5

percent voted "9." That's funny, since you'd think more people would consider it really good but not great. Do you suppose somehow the ballot box got stuffed by Simpsons fans who didn't even need to see the movie to know it was a masterpiece? D'oh. ☞

Sin City ★ ★ ★ ★

R, 126 m., 2005

Bruce Willis (Hartigan), Jessica Alba (Nancy), Rosario Dawson (Gail), Benicio Del Toro (Jackie Boy), Clive Owen (Dwight), Mickey Rourke (Marv), Brittany Murphy (Shellie), Nick Stahl (Yellow Bastard), Alexis Bledel (Becky), Devon Aoki (Miho), Jaime King (Goldie), Frank Miller (Priest), Powers Boothe (Senator Roark), Michael Clarke Duncan (Manute), Carla Gugino (Lucille). Directed by Robert Rodriguez, Frank Miller, and Quentin Tarantino and produced by Elizabeth Avellan, Miller, and Rodriguez. Screenplay by Rodriguez and Miller.

If *film noir* was not a genre but a hard man on mean streets with a lost lovely in his heart and a gat in his gut, his nightmares would look like *Sin City.* The movie by Robert Rodriguez and Frank Miller plays like a convention at the movie museum in Quentin Tarantino's subconscious. A-list action stars rub shoulders with snaky villains and sexy wenches in a city where the streets are always wet, the cars are ragtops, and everybody smokes. It's a black-and-white world, except for blood that is red, eyes that are green, hair that is blond, and the Yellow Bastard.

This isn't an adaptation of a comic book; it's like a comic book brought to life and pumped with steroids. It contains characters who occupy stories, but to describe the characters and summarize the stories would be like replacing the weather with a weather map.

The movie is not about narrative but about style. It internalizes the harsh world of the Frank Miller *Sin City* comic books and processes it through computer effects, grotesque makeup, lurid costumes, and dialogue that chops at the language of *noir.* The actors are mined for the archetypes they contain; Bruce Willis, Mickey Rourke, Jessica Alba, Rosario Dawson, Benicio Del Toro, Clive Owen, and the others are rotated into a hyperdimension. We get not so much their presence as their essence; the movie is not about what the characters say or what they do, but about who they are in our wildest dreams.

On the movie's Web site there's a slide show juxtaposing the original drawings of Frank Miller with the actors playing the characters, and then with the actors transported by effects into the visual world of graphic novels. Some of the stills from the film look so much like frames of the comic book as to make no difference. And there's a narration that plays like the captions at the top of the frame, setting the stage and expressing a stark, existential worldview.

Rodriguez has been aiming toward *Sin City* for years. I remember him leaping out of his chair and bouncing around a hotel room, pantomiming himself filming *Spy Kids 2* with a digital camera and editing it on a computer. The future! he told me. This is the future! You don't wait six hours for a scene to be lighted. You want a light over here, you grab a light and put it over here. You want a nuclear submarine, you make one out of thin air and put your characters into it.

I held back, wondering if perhaps the spy kids would have been better served if the films had not been such a manic demonstration of his method. But never mind; the first two *Spy Kids* were exuberant fun (*Spy Kids 3-D* sucked, in great part because of the 3-D). Then came his *Once Upon a Time in Mexico* (2003), and I wrote it was "more interested in the moment, in great shots, in surprises and ironic reversals and close-ups of sweaty faces, than in a coherent story." Yes, but it worked.

And now Rodriguez has found narrative discipline in the last place you might expect, by choosing to follow the Miller comic books almost literally. A graphic artist has no time or room for drifting. Every frame contributes, and the story marches from page to page in vivid action snapshots. *Sin City* could easily have looked as good as it does and still been a mess, if it were not for the energy of Miller's storytelling, which is not the standard chronological account of events, but more like a tabloid murder illuminated by flashbulbs.

The movie is based on three of the *Sin City* stories, each more or less self-contained. That's wise, because at this velocity a two-hour, one-story narrative would begin to pant before it got to the finish line. One story involves Bruce Willis as a battered old cop at war with a pedophile (Nick Stahl). One has Mickey Rourke waking up next to a dead hooker (Jaime King). One has a good guy (Clive Owen) and a wacko cop (Benicio Del Toro) disturbing the delicate balance of power negotiated between the police and the leader of the city's hookers (Rosario Dawson), who despite her profession moonlights as Owen's lover. Underneath everything is a deeper layer of corruption, involving a senator (Powers Boothe), whose son is not only the pedophile but also the Yellow Bastard.

We know the Bastard is yellow because the movie paints him yellow, just as the comic book did; it was a masterstroke for Miller to find a compromise between the cost of full-color reproduction and the economy of two-color pages; red, green, and blue also make their way into the frames. Actually, I can't even assume Miller went the two-color route for purposes of economy, because it's an effective artistic decision.

There are other vivid characters in the movie, which does not have leads so much as actors who dominate the foreground and then move on. In a movie that uses nudity as if the 1970s had survived, Rosario Dawson's stripper is a fierce dominatrix, Carla Gugino shows more skin than she could in *Maxim*, and Devon Aoki employs a flying guillotine that was borrowed no doubt from a circa-1970 Hong Kong exploiter.

Rodriguez codirected, photographed, and edited the movie, collaborated on the music and screenplay, and is coproducer. Frank Miller and Quentin Tarantino are credited as codirectors, Miller because his comic books essentially act as storyboards, which Rodriguez follows with ferocity, Tarantino because he directed one brief scene on a day when Rodriguez was determined to wean him away from celluloid and lure him over to the dark side of digital. (It's the scene in the car with Owen and Del Toro, who has a pistol stuck in his head.) Tarantino also contributed something to the culture of the film, which follows his influential *Pulp Fiction* in its recycling of pop archetypes and its circular story structure. The language of the film, both dialogue and narration, owes much to the hard-boiled pulp novelists of the 1950s.

Which brings us, finally, to the question of the movie's period. Skylines suggest the movie is set today. The cars range from the late 1930s to the 1950s. The costumes are from the trench coat and g-string era. I don't think *Sin City* really has a period, because it doesn't really tell a story set in time and space. It's a visualization of the pulp *noir* imagination, uncompromising and extreme. Yes, and brilliant.

Sir! No Sir! ★ ★ ★

NO MPAA RATING, 85 m., 2006

Narrated by Troy Garity and featuring Edward Asner, Jane Fonda, Donald Sutherland, Terry Whitmore, Donald Duncan, Howard Levy, Oliver Hirsch, Susan Schnall, Randy Rowland, Louis Font, Dave Cline, Bill Short, Dave Blalock, Greg Payton, Darnell Summers, Michael Wong, Terry Whitmore, Joe Bangert, Richard Boyle, Jerry Lembcke, Terry Iverson, Tom Bernard, and Keith Mather. A documentary written and directed by David Zeiger and produced by Evangeline Griego, Aaron Zarrow, and Zeiger.

Quick question: When Jane Fonda was on her "FTA" concert tour during the Vietnam era, who was in her audience? The quick answer from most people probably would be "antiwar hippies, left-wingers, and draft-dodgers." The correct answer would be: American troops on active duty, many of them in uniform.

Sir! No Sir! is a documentary about an almost-forgotten fact of the Vietnam era: Antiwar sentiment among U.S. troops grew into a problem for the Pentagon. The film claims bombing was used toward the end of the war because the military leadership wondered, frankly, if some of their ground troops would obey orders to attack. It's also said there were a few Air Force B-52 crews that refused to bomb North Vietnam. And in San Diego, sailors on an aircraft carrier tried to promote a local vote on whether their ship should be allowed to sail for Vietnam. One of the disenchanted veterans, although he is never mentioned in the film, was John Kerry, who first was decorated for valor and later became a leader of Vietnam Veterans Against the War and testified before Congress.

After the turning point of the Tet offensive in 1968, troop morale ebbed lower, the war seemed lost, and a protest movement encompassed active duty troops, coffeehouses near bases in America, underground GI newspapers, and a modern "underground railway" that helped soldiers desert and move to Canada. According to

Pentagon figures, there were some 500,000 desertions during the Vietnam years.

The film has been written and directed by David Zeiger, who worked in an antiwar coffeehouse near Fort Hood, Texas. In a narration spoken by Troy Garity, the son of Fonda and Tom Hayden, his film says, "The memory has been changed." The GI antiwar movement has disappeared from common knowledge, and a famous factoid from the period claims returning wounded veterans were spit on by "hippies" as they landed at American airports. According to the film, that is an urban legend, publicized in the film *Rambo II: First Blood.*

When we reviewed *Sir! No Sir!* on *Ebert & Roeper,* we cited the film's questions about the spitting story. There is a book on the subject, *The Spitting Image* by Jerry Lembcke, whose research failed to find a single documented instance of such an event occurring in real life. I received many e-mails, however, from those who claimed knowledge of such incidents. The story persists, and true or false it is part of a general eagerness to blame our loss in Vietnam on domestic protesters while ignoring the substantial antiwar sentiment among troops in the field.

Parallels with the war in Iraq are obvious. One big difference is that the Vietnam-era forces largely were supplied by the draft, while our Iraq troops are either career soldiers or National Guard troops, some of them on their second or third tour of duty. The Vietnam-era draft not only generated antiwar sentiment among those of draft age but also supplied the army with soldiers who did not go very cheerfully into uniform. The willingness of today's National Guardsmen to continue in combat is courageous and admirable but cannot be expected to last indefinitely, and the political cost of returning to the draft system would be incalculable.

A group of recent documentaries has highlighted a conflict between information and "disinformation," that Orwellian term for attempts to rewrite history. The archetype of "Hanoi Jane" has been used to obscure the fact that Fonda appeared before about sixty thousand GIs who apparently agreed with her. The Swift Boat Veterans incredibly tried to deny John Kerry's patriotism. The global warming documentary *An Inconvenient Truth* is being attacked by a TV ad campaign, underwritten by energy companies, which extols the benefits of carbon dioxide.

No doubt *Sir! No Sir!* will inspire impassioned rebuttals. No doubt it is not an impartial film, not with Fonda's son as its narrator. What cannot be denied is the newsreel footage of uniformed troops in antiwar protests, of Fonda's uniformed audiences at "FTA" concerts, of headlines citing Pentagon concern about troop morale, the "fragging" of officers, the breakdown of discipline, and the unwillingness of increasing numbers of soldiers to fight a war they had started to believe was wrong.

The Sisterhood of the Traveling Pants ★ ★ ★

PG, 119 m., 2005

Amber Tamblyn (Tibby), Alexis Bledel (Lena), America Ferrera (Carmen), Blake Lively (Bridget), Jenna Boyd (Bailey), Bradley Whitford (Al), Nancy Travis (Lydia Rodman), Rachel Ticotin (Carmen's Mother). Directed by Ken Kwapis and produced by Debra Martin Chase, Denise Di Novi, Broderick Johnson, and Andrew A. Kosove. Screenplay by Delia Ephron and Elizabeth Chandler, based on the novel by Ann Brashares.

Four teenage girls in a clothing store, trying on things, kidding around, giggling. Girls of four different sizes and shapes. What makes them all want to try on the same pair of preowned jeans? And why are the jeans a perfect fit all four times? It's the summer before the girls begin their senior year in high school, and all four have big summer plans. Because the jeans magically fit them all, and perhaps because they all saw *Divine Secrets of the Ya-Ya Sisterhood,* they come up with a plan: Each girl will wear the jeans for a week and then FedEx them to the next on the list.

Along with the solemn vow to forward the jeans on schedule comes a list of rules that must not be violated, of which the most crucial is that the girls must never let anyone else remove the jeans from their bodies. There is, however, a loophole: They can take them off themselves. Here we have a premise that could easily inspire a teenage comedy of comprehensive badness, but *The Sisterhood of the Traveling Pants* is always sweet and sometimes surprisingly touching, as the jeans accompany each girl on a key step of her journey to adulthood.

The movie, like *Mystic Pizza* (1988), assembles a group of talented young actresses who have already done good work separately and now participate in a kind of showcase. America Ferrera (whose *Real Women Have Curves* remains one of the best recent coming-of-age films) plays Carmen, who lives with her Puerto Rican mother and is thrilled to be spending the summer with her absentee non–Puerto Rican father. Alexis Bledel, who struck entirely different notes in *Sin City*, is Lena, off to visit her grandparents and other relatives on a Greek island. Blake Lively plays Bridget, who attends a soccer camp in Mexico and falls in love with one of the hunky young counselors. And Amber Tamblyn (of *Joan of Arcadia*) is Tibby, the one with the sardonic angle on life, who wants to be a filmmaker and takes a low-paying job for the summer at a suburban megastore where she plans to shoot a video documentary about life and work.

The stories of the four girls comes, I learn, from a novel by Ann Brashares, who has written two more in the series. The usefulness of her four-story structure is that none of the stories overstays its welcome, and the four girls aren't trapped in the same dumb suburban teenage romantic plot. They live, and they learn.

Carmen has idealized her father, Al (Bradley Whitford), even though he dumped her mother (Rachel Ticotin) years earlier. She values her Puerto Rican roots and discovers, with a shock, that her dad is planning marriage with a WASP named Lydia (Nancy Travis), who comes equipped with children and a suburban home that her father seems to desire as much as his new bride. Is he ashamed of his golden-skinned daughter whose jeans show off a healthy and rounded but technically overweight body?

Tibby has perhaps been watching IFC too much, and possibly envisions herself at Sundance as she heads off to the Wal-Mart clone with her video camera. She gets a young assistant named Bailey (Jenna Boyd), who is a good soul, open and warmhearted, and with a secret that Tibby discovers one day when Bailey passes out right there on the floor of a store corridor. Tibby's tendency was to look at everything through a lens, objectively; Bailey removes the lens cap on her heart.

In Greece, Lena finds her family living a salt-of-the-earth existence in what are surely outtakes from a tourism commercial. If there really is an island this sun-drenched, with a village this filled with white stucco and deep shade, populated by people who are this jolly and loving and throw a feast on a moment's notice, then I don't know why I'm not there instead of here. Lena's Greek relatives are, however, extremely protective of her chastity, which may exist primarily in their dreams, and she gets a crush on a local teen god.

Meanwhile, in Mexico, Bridget and the counselor know they are violating unbreakable rules by even spending private time together, but Bridget sets her sights on the guy and stages a campaign of attraction and seduction that is more or less irresistible.

The role played by the jeans in all of these stories is, it must be said, more as a witness than as a participant, sometimes from a vantage point draped over a chair near to a bed. But no, the PG-rated movie isn't overloaded with sex, and its values are in the right place. The message for its primary audience of teenage girls is that to some degree they choose their own destinies and write their own stories, and while boys may be an unexplored country, they are not necessarily a hostile one. As for fathers who would like to become Anglo by marriage, and daughters who fiercely resent them, perhaps after all he is still her father and she is still his daughter, and there is hope.

Because the *Ya-Ya Sisterhood* was such a disappointment, I expected even less from what looked, going in, like a teenage retread. But in a world where one pair of jeans fits all, miracles can happen. This *Sisterhood* is real pleasure, a big-hearted movie where a group of gifted actresses finds opportunities most younger movie stars can only dream about.

The Sisters ★ ★

R, 113 m., 2006

Maria Bello (Marcia Prior Glass), Mary Stuart Masterson (Olga Prior), Erika Christensen (Irene Prior), Eric McCormack (Gary Sokol), Chris

O'Donnell (David Turzin), Tony Goldwyn (Vincent Antonelli), Steven Culp (Dr. Harry Glass), Alessandro Nivola (Andrew Prior), Elizabeth Banks (Nancy Pecket), Rip Torn (Dr. Chebrin). Directed by Arthur Allan Seidelman and produced by Judd Payne and Matthew Rhodes. Screenplay by Richard Alfieri, based on his play.

When a classic is transferred to the present time and place, does the material travel well? Can it be reasonably taken from its world and transplanted in ours? Sometimes the transfer works, as when Ian McKellen played Richard III in a fascist 1930s Britain, and Gus Van Sant transmuted *Henry IV* into *My Own Private Idaho.* Sometimes it does not, as in this attempt to take Chekhov's *Three Sisters* out of 1901 Russia and place it in the faculty club of a modern American university.

It could be argued that Shakespeare's characters are more universal and Chekhov's more particular to time and place—which is a strength of both. Because they are interior, the problems of Hamlet can be set anywhere, as Ethan Hawke proved by asking "To be, or not to be?" in the "Action" aisle at Blockbuster. But with Chekhov's *Three Sisters,* we can more easily imagine characters trapped together in a remote country house than believe their timely entrances and exits in a clubroom on campus. Nor do modern families usually work out their problems in general debate, with friends and strangers joining in; the American practice in unhappy families is to choose alienation and limit contact to weddings, funerals, and tortured Thanksgivings.

Arthur Allan Seidelman's *The Sisters,* written by Richard Alfieri and based on his play, assumes that the three sisters and one brother of a dysfunctional family gather in the faculty club after the death of their patriarch. The occasion is the birthday of Irene (Erika Christensen), the middle sister, although this family doesn't seem practiced at birthday parties. The other sisters are the university chancellor Olga (Mary Stuart Masterson), who is the oldest, and Marcia, the youngest (Maria Bello), who is under the spell of the psychologist Harry (Steven Culp). Andrew (Alessandro Nivola) is their brother and brings along his girlfriend, Nancy (Elizabeth Banks). The others think Nancy isn't good enough for him, but if she's sane, she's good enough for this family.

Others who drop in include Irene's fiancé, David (Chris O'Donnell); the sharp-tongued Professor Sokol (Eric McCormack); and a married childhood friend named Vincent (Tony Goldwyn), who is trying to disengage as Marcia's lover. Vincent has known them since childhood and reminds them of events best left to the psychological compost heap. Observing all of this is the sardonic Dr. Chebrin (Rip Torn), who has nothing much to do with anyone and is on the scene because, damn it all, this *is* the faculty club, and he's a member. As an outsider with little stake in the outcome, he makes remarks that uncannily reflect some of our own feelings: "You're too young to be having such thoughts," he tells Irene. "They're all true, of course."

During the course of the birthday party, hurtful truths will be told, lesbianism will be revealed, a drug overdose will take place, a character will require medical attention, and as we watch the mayhem we understand why other faculty members do not seem to flock to the club.

In Laurence Olivier's *Three Sisters* (1970), made for the American Film Theater series, you could tell the players without the program, even though they did seem to bring an extraordinary burden of problems onstage with them. In this version, there are so many cross-purposes to keep straight that the entrance of a character is like a piece being added to the chessboard in the middle of a game. We had it all figured out and, good lord, now the rook is threatened!

Projects like this bring out the best in actors, who take salary cuts to work in Chekhov (even at one remove). What we can guess, watching the film, is that the same players would make a good job of *Three Sisters* but are undermined by the faculty club, which works like a hotel lobby. There's no way to sustain dramatic momentum here. The doorway offers escapes and entrances as required, and the common room plays like a ring for a tag-team match; Chekhovian wrestlers keep climbing over the ropes and pounding on anyone still standing.

16 Blocks ★ ★ ★

PG-13, 105 m., 2006

Bruce Willis (Jack Mosley), Mos Def (Eddie Bunker), David Morse (Frank Nugent), Cylk

Cozart (Jimmy Mulvey). Directed by Richard Donner and produced by Randall Emmett, Avi Lerner, Arnold Rifkin, John Thompson, Jim Van Wyck, and Bruce Willis. Screenplay by Richard Wenk.

Bruce Willis plays Jack Mosley, a tired drunk, in *16 Blocks*. He's a detective who doesn't have the energy to be a cop. As the film opens, he's surrounded by dead bodies and spilled cocaine and is told by an officer, "Sit on this until the uniforms get here." Jack rummages around in the apartment until he finds what he wants: a bottle. He pours himself a drink and sits down to wait for the uniforms. Then he goes back to headquarters, where the receptionist gives him a breath mint.

Jack's shift is over. The last thing he needs is another job. But his boss assigns him to transport a witness sixteen blocks to a grand jury hearing. The witness has to arrive in two hours, before the grand jury's term expires. Jack goes to get the guy, who is named Eddie Bunker and is played by Mos Def as a motormouth who talks all the time, and I mean *all* the time, in a litany of complaints about his treatment, his life, and his fate. Eddie has the kind of voice that makes fingernails on a blackboard sound like Kenny G.

The job looks like a piece of cake. Put a guy in a car and drive sixteen blocks. Jack can't make the sixteen blocks. He makes a pit stop at a liquor store. Coming out again, he sees the wrong kind of guy making the wrong kind of moves on the witness in the car, and he shoots the guy, which is admirable decision-making under the circumstances. He figures out someone wants the witness dead, so he takes him to a friendly saloon and calls his superior officer.

Not a wise decision. Frank Nugent (David Morse), his chief, is the lynchpin of a ring of corruption and drug dealing within the department. He is one of the people who want to prevent Eddie Bunker from testifying. Jack knows this. He's wise to the crooked cops because he's bought into the system. But there's something about Eddie Bunker, something about his innocence, something about his naive trust in Jack, something about the way he won't shut up that somehow gets to Jack. Just when Eddie is about to be killed in the bar, Jack shoots a cop and saves Eddie's life. Now they are both on the same side of the law.

That's the setup for *16 Blocks*, which is a chase picture conducted at a velocity that is just about right for a middle-aged alcoholic. Unlike *Running Scared*, which was pitched a few degrees above manic, *16 Blocks* is more of a character study, a two-hander about how Jack has been fed up with the department for a long time, and Eddie's sweet, goofy nature tilts the balance. Of course, it's a good question whether Eddie is *really* the nutty motormouth he seems to be, but that's not something Jack has the time to determine right now.

The movie has been directed by Richard Donner, a specialist in combining action, chase scenes, and humor (see *Lethal Weapon*, etc.). Here he starts with three good performances: Willis, world-weary and yet with a spark of defiance; Mos Def, whose speaking role is more or less the same as the movie's running time; and David Morse, evil and bureaucratic in equal measure.

The chase scenes involve Chinatown (of course), traffic jams, and a standoff on a bus that may owe something to the 2002 Brazilian film *Bus 174*. None of this is particularly new, but all of it is done well, and Mos Def does the same thing here that Austin Pendleton did in *Dirty Work:* He comes in from left field with a character performance that's completely unexpected in an action movie. At first I found it irritating. Then I began to wonder if something was going on beneath the surface. Eventually I was able to pick up the buried message, which was frightened and sincere, and was hiding behind self-satire. I did not, however, necessarily buy the story about the bakery.

One key scene gave me problems. It involves an ambulance. Actually, it involves two ambulances, which was my problem. I think maybe one additional shot or one more line of dialogue might have oriented me, but there for a moment it seemed as if certain characters had dropped into another dimension. The plot device was explained to me by Dann Gire, president of the Chicago Film Critics Association, which is yet another reason his photograph should be displayed in every post office and schoolroom.

The bedrock of the plot is the dogged determination of the Bruce Willis character. Jack may be middle-aged, he may be tired, he may be balding, he may be a drunk, but if he's played by Bruce Willis, you don't want to bet against him. He gets that look in his eye that says, "It's going to be a pain in the ass for me to do this, but I couldn't live with myself if I didn't." I always believe that more easily than the look that merely says, "I will prevail because this is an action picture and I play the hero."

The Skeleton Key ★ ★ ½

PG, 104 m., 2005

Kate Hudson (Caroline), Gena Rowlands (Violet), John Hurt (Ben), Peter Sarsgaard (Luke), Joy Bryant (Jill), Ronald McCall (Papa Justify), Jeryl Prescott (Mama Cecile). Directed by Iain Softley and produced by Daniel Bobker, Softley, Michael Shamberg, and Stacey Sher. Screenplay by Ehren Kruger.

As I mentally review what happens in *The Skeleton Key,* I think there may be a couple of loopholes, but to describe them would betray too much of the plot, which depends on a series of escalating surprises. Besides, a movie that goes to this much trouble to work out its cosmology must have the answers. I must have missed something.

Doesn't matter. The film depends upon atmosphere, shock, and superstition; the logic of the plot is the last thing on our minds. It takes place in a creepy plantation house in a gloomy Louisiana backwater during a very, very rainy season. The district has something in common with every other horror movie set in the Deep South: a ramshackle backroads gas station operated by degenerates who frighten and repel their customers. In the real world, motorists get their gas at shiny twenty-four-hour travel plazas, many of them incorporating Taco Bells and sales on the latest cassettes by Jeff Foxworthy. Not in horror movies, where the Chainsaw Family lurks in the shadows behind the cash register and cackles unwholesomely about newcomers.

The visitor in this case is Caroline (Kate Hudson), a nurse who grows despondent when a beloved patient dies, and quits her hospital job to sign on as a private caregiver. Her first job pays $1,000 a week, which right there should send up a flare, especially since several earlier employees have quit. She meets a lawyer named Luke (Peter Sarsgaard), and he sends her on to his client, an old lady named Violet (Gena Rowlands). She has lived in the decaying mansion since 1962, "when we came over from Savannah." Now her husband, Ben (John Hurt), has suffered a stroke and can't talk. But he sure can look like he really wants to tell Caroline something.

The big house has rooms Ben and Violet have never used. Caroline is given a skeleton key that opens all of them, except, wouldn't you know, a door in the attic. This door rattles loudly, as if someone is locked inside; the Self-Rattling Door is a variation on the Snicker-Snack Rule, which teaches us that in horror movies a knife will all by itself make a sound like it is being scraped on metal, even when it isn't. All movies with self-rattling doors and/or self-scraping knife sounds also contain Unexpected Foreground Surprises, when the heroine is terrified because a character (or a cat) suddenly leaps up out of nowhere.

The opening scenes of the movie promise a degree of intelligent menace that few movies could live up to, including this one. But it works while it's happening. Rowlands, looking far less elegant than when she played James Garner's fading southern love in *The Notebook,* distrusts Caroline: "She wouldn't understand the house," she tells her lawyer. But then again, who would? And what's to understand?

Old Ben, meanwhile, grabs Caroline's wrist in a deathly grip and really, really has something on his mind. Although he uses a wheelchair, one evening during the nightly monsoon, she finds him missing from his room. He has crawled out of his window and onto the porch, and he falls to the ground, for reasons that seem clearer at the time than they do later. Caroline becomes convinced that Violet is a threat to Ben and tries to help him escape, ramming her VW into the big old iron gates, which are mysteriously locked.

Underlying all of these alarms is a local practice known as hoodoo, not to be confused with voodoo. Hoodoo, we learn, is American folk magic incorporating incantations, conjurations, herbal remedies, and suchlike; voodoo is a religion, Caroline is told, but "God don't have much to do with hoodoo." From Violet, she hears the story of Papa Justify (Ronald McCall) and his wife, Mama Cecile (Jeryl Prescott), who were servants at the plantation ninety years ago, and how their hoodoo practices got mixed up with the rich family that owned the house.

The Skeleton Key is one of those movies that explain too much while they are explaining too little, and it leaves us with a surprise at the end that makes more sense the less we think about it. But the movie's mastery of technique makes up for a lot. Hudson is convincing as the young nurse determined to help her patient, Rowlands is awesome in the Joan Crawford role, and Hurt, who says not a word, semaphores whole dictionaries with his eyes.

There's a kind of moviegoer who likes a movie like this no matter how it ends. It's about the journey, not the destination, even though the ending of *The Skeleton Key* really is a zinger. It's just that—well, what did a lot of the other stuff have to do with anything? How do all the omens and portents and unexplained happenings connect? And what's the deal with hoodoo? It doesn't work unless you really believe in it, we're told, but if you really do, it really does. Considering what happens when you do, I think it's better if you don't. Besides, I believe things either work or don't work regardless of whether you think they can. Especially things that God don't have much to do with.

Sketches of Frank Gehry ★ ★ ★

PG-13, 82 m., 2006

Featuring Frank O. Gehry, Sydney Pollack, Philip Johnson, Bob Geldof, Barry Diller, Michael Eisner, Dennis Hopper, Michael Ovitz, and Milton Wexler. A documentary directed by Sydney Pollack and produced by Ultan Guilfoyle.

From the room he occupied for years in the old Cliff Dwellers Club atop Orchestra Hall, Louis Sullivan could have looked out his window, with the aid of a time machine, and seen Frank Gehry's Pritzker band shell in Chicago's Millennium Park. The man who wrote "form follows function" would have contemplated the work of a man who seems to believe that form *is* function.

Although the band shell functions as a stage for performances, most of its visitors probably regard it first of all as sculpture. By the same token, Gehry's most famous work, the Guggenheim Museum in Bilbao, Spain, has been accused of one-upping the art inside. Certainly when I visited in 2001, the Giorgio Armani career retrospective on the third level was hard-pressed to hold its own against the building containing it.

"Logotecture," one of Gehry's critics calls the Chicago band shell. The charge is that Gehry, having designed some brilliant buildings, is now ripping himself off to provide one city after another with its very own Gehry. This is a cheap shot. Mies van der Rohe attempted as nearly as possible to do the same thing over and over again, only more elegantly. Is there an enormous difference between his residential high-rises at 860 and 880 Lake Shore Drive and his IBM Building? No, but it's not logotecture, and neither is Gehry. An architecture critic has the opportunity to travel widely and become jaded by many Gehry buildings. The average person regarding the band shell is looking at the only Gehry she will see in her lifetime.

Well, not quite the only: Gehry also designed the elegant bridge connecting Millennium Park with the gardens on the east side of Columbus Drive. One day as I was visiting the park, it occurred to me that if Anish Kapoor's vast *Cloud Gate* has been universally renamed the Bean, then obviously Gehry's bridge is the Snake. And what is the band shell? Stand at the south end of the lawn, notice the web of arches that enclose the space and carry the sound, and observe the shell crouching at the other end. The Spider, obviously.

These musings are inspired by *Sketches of Frank Gehry*, an engaging documentary made by Hollywood director Sydney Pollack (*Out of Africa, Tootsie, The Way We Were*). Pollack is not usually a documentarian, and Gehry had never been documented; they were friends, and Gehry suggested Pollack might want to "do something." The result is not a formal doc but an extended chat between two professionals who, as Pollack puts it, search for "a sliver of space in the commercial world where you can make a difference."

Gehry did not begin by designing sculptural buildings. He takes Pollack to look at Santa Monica Place, his conventional 1984 shopping center at the end of the Third Street Mall in Santa Monica. Does Gehry like it? No. We meet his psychiatrist, Milton Wexler, authorized by Gehry to speak about a period in the 1980s when the architect made a breakthrough into his modern work; this process apparently involved, or perhaps even required, divorcing his first wife. All we learn about her from the film is that she pushed for her husband to change his name from Goldberg to sidestep anti-Semitism. Since he then immediately told everyone "my real name is Goldberg," this was less than perfectly functional, but we understand the form.

Gehry's design process could be inspiring for a kindergarten student. First he doodles on sketch pads. A form emerges. He uses construction paper, scissors, and tape to make a three-dimensional model from it. He plays with the model. Eventually it looks about right. His assistants use computer modeling to work out the stresses and supports, and together with his team he works on the interior spaces. Gehry's buildings are so complex that he believes they would have been impossible before computers (which he does not know how to operate). Certainly the math would have been daunting. Computers assure him that his cardboard fancies are structurally sound.

In this connection I remember the first famous architect I met, Max Abramovitz. I was sent as a young reporter to interview him on the site of the University of Illinois Assembly Hall, the largest rim-supported building ever made. Seating 16,000 people in a circle, it had no interior supports and was held together by five hundred miles of steel cable wrapped around the rim where the top bowl rested on the bottom.

"Will this be your greatest achievement?" I asked the man who designed the United Nations complex.

"If it doesn't fall down," he said.

Because Pollack has his own clout and is not merely a supplicant at Gehry's altar, he asks professional questions as his equal, sympathizes about big projects that seem to go wrong, and offers insights ("Talent is liquefied trouble"). Because he is Pollack, and because he has Gehry's blessing, he has access to the architect's famous clients, such as Michael Eisner, who commissioned the Walt Disney Concert Hall in Los Angeles, and Dennis Hopper, who lives in a Gehry home in Santa Monica. He talks to the (late) great architect Philip Johnson, old and secure enough to praise a competitor. There are also a few critics brought in to provide balance, although Pollack's opinion is clear: Gehry is a genius. Having gazed upon the Guggenheim and the Disney and sat happily on the grass beneath the Spider's web, I think so, too. Gehry helped tempt modern architecture out of its well-behaved period.

Sleuth ★ ★ ★

R, 86 m., 2007

Michael Caine (Andrew Wyke), Jude Law (Milo Tindle). Directed by Kenneth Branagh and produced by Jude Law, Simon Halfon, Tom Sternberg, Marion Pilowsky, Branagh, and Simon Moseley. Screenplay by Harold Pinter, based on the play by Anthony Shaffer.

When *Sleuth* premiered at the 2007 Toronto Film Festival, a great many critics (including me), writing in advance about it sight unseen, described it as a "remake" of the 1972 film based on Anthony Shaffer's stage play. The festival program was more accurate, describing it as "a fascinating transformation." So it is. Do not make the mistake of thinking that if you've seen the earlier play or film, you've got this one covered. Yes, one of the plot gimmicks is the same, but be honest: If you saw the original, you'd already heard about the gimmick anyway, hadn't you? Only the London opening night audience *possibly* experienced it as a surprise.

The story isn't about the gimmick, anyway. It's about the vicious verbal duel that two men perform one edgy night. Andrew Wyke (Michael Caine), a millionaire thriller novelist, receives a very late visitor: Milo Tindle (Jude Law), who is having an affair with Wyke's wife. The weathered exterior of his country estate belies the interior, an alarming display of metal, glass, crystal, modernist sculpture, and an advanced spy-cam security system. This is not a house to be lived in but to be shown through. It's hard to say which would be more terrifying, the notion that Wyke did the interior design or that his wife did. I vote for the wife. Every real man needs a La-Z-Boy *somewhere.*

Wyke starts in right at the door, asking Tindle, "Is that your car?" Well, there are only two cars parked in the drive, and since the other is Andrew's, why, yes, it is Milo's. "Your car is smaller than my car," Wyke says. Is this remark juvenile or advanced adult cruelty, a comment so gauche it is intended as an insult to the listener? We ask questions like that all through the movie, which is based on a new screenplay by Harold Pinter, the Nobel laureate playwright. True, Pinter is now seventy-seven, and we know from the journals of his friend Simon Gray that he has been ill, but is the great man now reduced to rewriting old country-house mysteries?

Not at all. He has written a new country-house mystery, which is not really a mystery at all in terms of its plot and eerily impenetrable in its human relationship. What is really at stake between Andrew and Milo? Does either one love the wife? Do both? Would Andrew be just as happy to get her off his hands, or does he want to keep her just to prove there is a reason he has the bigger car? The suspense in the film is not about who gets the wife, but about who wins the conversation. Assume someone who has never heard or seen the original *Sleuth* but is familiar with the work of Pinter. That would include a lot of English professors. Attending only to the dialogue, they would find the film pure Pinter.

And that is what you should do. Cast out all thoughts of wives, adultery, disguises, accents, ploys, surprises, and denouements, and simply listen to the words and watch Caine and Law at work. You will observe the Pinteresque interplay of paradox and contradiction, the answers that didn't quite seem to hear the question, the statements of matters so obviously true that perhaps something else altogether is meant by them. In Pinter, the most banal dialogue can carry disturbing insinuations.

Then try to decide when the characters (not the actors) are acting and when they are not. Do they mean what they say? Do they feel what they do? There is a third act development that is entirely absent in the original. What does it mean? Which man takes it seriously? Both? Neither? Each one calling the other's bluff? When Pinter saw or read the original material, I wonder if he thought: "What this needs is the Pinter touch."

The director is Kenneth Branagh, himself a master of stagecraft and a lover of theatrical gesture. How brilliant he was in his film *Hamlet* (1996) to have the prince address his great soliloquy to his own reflection in a mirror. Look again at his underrated *Dead Again* (1991) and see his joy in dazzling effect. In *Sleuth* what he celebrates is perplexing, ominous, insinuating material in the hands of two skilled actors. Law, interestingly, takes the role played by Caine in 1972, and Caine fills the role played then by Laurence Olivier. Caine, who has never been much for the stage, is a superb screen actor, so good his master classes on acting for the camera are on DVD. Here, dry and clipped, biting and savage, he goes for the kill. Jude Law does a plucky job with Milo Tindle, but isn't it one of the laws of drama that characters named Milo Tindle never have a chance?

Now, all of that said, why do I give the movie three stars, instead of more? Curiously enough, because in its strength is its weakness. It is so much about dialogue and performance that I, at least, found myself thinking more about the actors than the characters. All the same, as exactly what it is, it's fascinating.

Slipstream ★ ★ ★

R, 110 m., 2007

Anthony Hopkins (Felix Bonhoeffer), Stella Arroyave (Gina), Christian Slater (Ray), John Turturro (Harvey Brickman), Michael Clarke Duncan (Bartender), Camryn Manheim (Barbara), Jeffrey Tambor (Geek), S. Epatha Merkerson (Bonnie), Fionulla Flanagan (Bette Lustig), Gavin Grazer (Gavin), Kevin McCarthy (Himself). Directed by Anthony Hopkins and produced by Stella Arroyave and Robert F. Katz. Screenplay by Hopkins.

Leave it to a sixty-nine-year-old actor to make the year's most experimental film. Anthony Hopkins's *Slipstream* is an attempt to represent what goes through the mind of a dying man, although you wouldn't guess that from its official plot summary on the Internet Movie Database, which thinks it's about a screenwriter "on the verge of implosion." So have I revealed a plot point? No, because it's clearly stated in the movie's first line of dialogue and repeated in the last.

I have grown so wise, however, only after viewing the movie a second time. When I wrote my interview with Hopkins, I shared the general opinion: Felix, the writer in the film, I wrote, "is confusing reality with illusion. His characters appear in his life, his life appears in the movie, and mostly he looks on uncertainly while both real and imaginary people do all the loving, living, and dying." All true enough in a way, but beside the point.

There is no direct line through the story, which portrays the way a man might think if he had received a sudden shock, was under heavy sedation, and was combining recent experiences with current ones. He doesn't *confuse* his fictional characters with real people; he sees them interchangeably. Let's say he based a character on his wife (Stella Arroyave). Sometimes the character looks like his wife, sometimes his wife looks like the character, sometimes he thinks she's in the room, sometimes he thinks she's on the set, sometimes he thinks they're together in a third place. It's dream logic, and the movie offers a clue by quoting Edgar Allan Poe:

All that we see or seem,
Is but a dream within a dream.

In the overarching action of the movie, Felix has written a screenplay that is being filmed in the Mojave Desert. Gavin Grazer, who plays the director, is said to have a big-shot producer brother whose shadow he tries to escape. Indeed, Gavin is the brother of big-shot producer Brian Grazer, and that's the kind of connection that might occur in the screenwriter's mind and be assigned as a throwaway line to a character in his fantasy. The movie within the movie involves a couple of tough guys (Christian Slater and Jeffrey Tambor) who terrorize a roadside diner after Slater has put a bullet into the head of a bartender (Michael Clarke Duncan). The diner scene owes much to old crime movies; Felix has lived those movies so intently that one of his favorites, the original *Invasion of the Body Snatchers,* produces the real Kevin McCarthy, whom Felix imagines he is driving with through the desert.

Later imaginations fill his computer screen with a screaming studio boss (John Turturro) who is allegedly inside his hard drive, and there are shots in which Duncan (head still oozing with blood) and the movie's continuity girl (Camryn Manheim) complain to him that their characters have not only been killed but shortchanged on some of their lines. One of the movie's most natural examples of dream logic is when Felix asks a Dolly Parton look-alike her name, and she replies, "Dolly Parton Look-alike." Of all the characters, the only one who doesn't seem to fall into dreaminess is the waitress played by S. Epatha Merkerson, maybe because she is the most like who she really is.

Now is *Slipstream* worth seeing? I think so, if you'll actively engage your sympathy with Hopkins's attempt to do something tricky and difficult. If you want to lie back and let the movie come to you, you may be lying there a long time. But I think Hopkins does an impressive job of creating the kind of dream-drug-reverie state people can go through.

I trust you enough, dear reader, to tell you something I should keep private: During a period after my surgical emergency, when I was on what Mr. Limbaugh so usefully describes as prescription medications, I had dreams more real than my waking moments. Then the fog cleared, my health returned, the medication stopped, and I resumed writing brilliant and lucid reviews like this one. But I know Hopkins gets it right, because I've been there. What he gets right is made clear at the end. No, I do not refer to the last appearance of the red convertible, but to the sequence following that, and then the closing dialogue.

Hopkins himself has wisely declined to "explain" his film, going so far at Sundance as to say, "I did it as a little joke." That's the thing about Brits (and the Welsh, in this case). They tend to be pathologically modest, and understatement is their style. Let's apply the statement "I did it as a little joke" to *Grindhouse,* a film that *was* done as a little joke, and see how the same dialogue would translate into the speech of an American director, such as Quentin Tarantino: "This isn't some *Twilight Zone the Movie* f———g thing. This is not a faux double feature. This is two f———g movies for the price of one! Your ten dollars will be well spent at *Grindhouse,* baby!"

And perhaps as well spent at *Slipstream,* although the two films have been made for altogether different audiences, and I anticipate little overlap.

Slither ★ ★

R, 95 m., 2006

Nathan Fillion (Sheriff Bill Pardy), Elizabeth Banks (Starla Grant), Gregg Henry (Jack MacReady), Michael Rooker (Grant Grant), Tania Saulnier (Kylie Strutemyer). Directed by

James Gunn and produced by Paul Brooks and Eric Newman. Screenplay by Gunn.

Slither is the kind of horror movie where decent citizens are attacked by a nauseating slimy grub from outer space, and the characters watch Troma movies on TV. If the name "Troma" means nothing to you, what are you doing reading a review of *Slither* in the first place? It takes place in a forlorn small town where the mayor screams four-letter words on Main Street. Where the traffic is so slow the cops use the radar gun to time whip-poor-wills. Where the kids in grade school all have acne. Where everybody gets drunk to celebrate the opening of deer-hunting season.

Near this town falls a meteorite that emits a nasty little creature that quickly burrows into the chest of Grant Grant, the richest guy in town. Grant is played by Michael Rooker, from *Henry: Portrait of a Serial Killer*. He is married to Starla (Elizabeth Banks), a poor girl who was trying to escape from poverty and an unhappy family. The funny thing is, she takes her marriage seriously. She takes it way too seriously, if you ask me, when she still talks sweet to Grant after he begins to resemble a rotting version of Jabba the Hutt.

It is difficult to give away too much of the plot; you already know from the ads that the slithering, crawling things leap down the throats of their victims, turning them into beings who still have their human memories but also develop an appetite for raw meat. From their chests spring suction tentacles to suck up your innards. How they reproduce is not a pretty sight.

The action centers around Sheriff Bill Pardy (Nathan Fillion), who runs a fairly incompetent department. He's still in love with Starla from junior high school. When it becomes clear that some kind of slug-tentacle-slime creature is killing the livestock, one of his deputies buys a dime-store octopus to help potential witnesses make an ID. If you see this creature, believe me, you won't need visual aids.

The sheriff, aided by his deputies, Starla, and cute young Kylie Strutemyer (Tania Saulnier), confront the creature(s) during an extended action sequence in which the slugs ooze their way into bathtubs, under doorways, down throats, and so on. Once they've occupied a victim, their prey instantly loses speed and coordination and turns into a lurching example of the zombies so familiar from, well, from all those zombie movies.

So now you know the terrain. What's interesting is that this story sounds so worn-out and yet it works. There is some humor in the plot, effective action, and scenes that entertain us because of how stupidly the characters behave. Consider the possible reconciliation between Starla and her husband, who speaks in that gravelly, placating Michael Rooker voice but looks as if he was absentmindedly left overnight in a cement mixer. She should have suspected something when he padlocked the basement door and told her he was hiding a surprise for her birthday. Her birthday is two months off, and the surprise is getting riper by the hour.

There are better movies. But *Slither* has a competence to it, an ability to manipulate obligatory horror scenes in a way that works. Given my theory of the star rating system, which suggests movies should be rated by their genres, *Slither* gets two if *28 Days Later* gets three. On the other hand, in the genre of slick and classy big-star thrillers, if *Fatal Attraction* gets 2.5 stars, then *Basic Instinct 2* gets 1.5. On the third hand, a lot of people probably would enjoy *Basic Instinct 2* more than *Slither*. One of these days, I'm going to have to take that star rating system and feed it to a meat-eating slime-slug.

Something New ★ ★ ★ ½

PG-13, 100 m., 2006

Sanaa Lathan (Kenya), Simon Baker (Brian), Mike Epps (Walter), Donald Faison (Nelson), Blair Underwood (Mark), Wendy Raquel Robinson (Cheryl), Alfre Woodard (Joyce), Golden Brooks (Suzette), Taraji P. Henson (Nedra), Earl Billings (Edmond). Directed by Sanaa Hamri and produced by Stephanie Allain. Screenplay by Kriss Turner.

Something New opens with cotton-candy titles, arrives in time for Valentine's Day, and is billed as a romantic comedy. Okay, it *is* a romantic comedy, technically, but the romance and the comedy don't arrive easily, and along the way the movie truly is something new: a touching story about a black professional woman facing problems in the workplace and the marriage market. I found myself unexpectedly moved.

Sanaa Lathan stars as Kenya, a Los Angeles accountant who is a workaholic. She's pretty, but the movie doesn't rest on that; Lathan makes Kenya wary, protective, cautious. It's a performance that could have skated the surface but goes more deeply. She's fiercely driven, a child of ambitious parents, a graduate of top schools, a candidate to became a partner in her firm. She doesn't date. She doesn't do much of anything except work, although recently she bought a new house.

That's how she meets Brian Kelly (Simon Baker), who is single, attracted to her, and a landscape architect. And white. They're fixed up on a blind date, but she makes awkward apologies and leaves. She doesn't date white guys. She doesn't seem to date black guys either, but she would in theory, if the IBM (Ideal Black Man) came along. She does hire Brian to landscape her backyard and gradually finds herself drawn to him, against her will. The movie depends on a sudden rain shower, that old Victorian standby, to drive them into the shelter of a tree for an unexpected kiss.

So let's pause and deal with some things you're probably assuming. You probably think *Something New,* like the remake *Guess Who,* approaches interracial romance as a sitcom opportunity. You probably think the cards are stacked in favor of these two people falling in love. But it isn't that simple. The movie is, astonishingly, told from a point of view hardly ever visible in movies: African-American professionals. Kenya's father (Earl Billings) is head of his department at Cedars-Sinai. Her mother (Alfre Woodard) is a pillar of black society, and of course her daughter made her debut at a black-tie cotillion. Her brother is a lawyer for a movie studio. Her family and friends are not thrilled by the notion that she might date a white man.

Neither is Kenya. That is not a prejudice, she tells Brian, but a preference. The movie has frank dialogue about race—not platitudes about how we're all really the same, but realistic observations about race in modern America. There's talk of the "black tax" that requires someone like Kenya to work harder than her white colleagues to overcome doubts about her competence. At work, she advises an important client to stay away from a merger; this is not news the client wants to hear, and he is unhappy hearing it from a black woman who seems better informed than he is.

Kenya and Brian do eventually fall into the first stages of a romance. But they get sidetracked when he asks her to take out her weave and wear her "own hair." She's angry; she thinks this is none of his business (and indeed men of all races would be wise to avoid haircare discussions with women of all races, because it's a touchier subject than a man can possibly realize). In social situations, Brian is aware of coolness from Kenya's brother and her friends, and at a comedy club the black comedienne makes comments about race that land around him like grenades.

They love each other, but are they ready to take on the responsibility of declaring their love and living with it? They have an argument in a grocery store that's real in a way love stories are rarely permitted to be. Kenya breaks up with him. An IBM comes into the picture, a wealthy black professional (Blair Underwood) who says and does all the right things.

How the movie finally ends will not be difficult to guess. It's how it gets there that's compelling. *Something New* doesn't settle for formulas or easy answers. Like its heroine, it knows good reasons for dating within one's race. It knows about social pressure, and how it works both ways. It's able to observe Kenya and Brian in a mostly black social situation, where Brian calls her, correctly, on making "black" comments as a way of holding her white date at arm's length. Interesting, how it gives a fair hearing to both characters.

But the movie knows that if two people truly connect, that is a rare and precious thing and must be respected. And it shows Kenya's family and friends observing the relationship carefully and observing that it seems to work for her, for this driven woman who seemed to be unmarriageable. They size up Brian and like what they see. "The boy's just white," her father tells her mother. "He's not a Martian."

By the end, *Something New* delivers all the usual pleasures of a love story, and something more. The movie respects its subject and characters, and is more complex about race than we could possibly expect. With this film and the completely different but also observant Queen Latifah comedy *Last Holiday*, black women are being paid a kind of attention they deserve but rarely get in the movies. Yes, and it's fun, too: You'll laugh and maybe you'll have a few tears, that kind of stuff.

Son of Rambow ★ ★ ★

PG-13, 96 m., 2008

Bill Milner (Will Proudfoot),Will Poulter (Lee Carter), Jessica Stevenson (Mary), Neil Dudgeon (Brother Joshua), Jules Sitruk (Didier Revol), Ed Westwick (Laurence Carter), Anna Wing (Grandmother). Directed by Garth Jennings and produced by Nick Goldsmith. Screenplay by Jennings.

The two friends in *Son of Rambow* hang out in a backyard shack that rewards close study. It's made of rough lumber, hammered together into not quite parallel lines; it's out of plumb. It could be drawn, but not easily built. Since the eleven-year-old hero, Will Proudfoot (Bill Milner) is himself a cartoonist and sketch artist, his inventions seem to be seeping into his life. He leads an existence that's strictly limited by his family's religious sect, making him a vacuum for fantasy and escapism, and when his friend Lee Carter (Will Poulter) shows him a pirated copy of *First Blood*, the adventures of Rambo ignite him like fireworks whose time have come.

Set in an English village in the early 1980s, *Son of Rambow* is a gentle story that involves a great deal of violence, but mostly the violence is muted and dreamy, like a confrontation with a fearsome scarecrow that looks horrifying but is obviously not real—or real enough, but not alive. The two boys meet one day in the corridor outside their grade school classroom. Will has been sent there because his religion forbids him to watch TV, even educational videos (it also forbids music, dancing, and so on). Lee has been booted out of his classroom, spots Will, and immediately beans him with a hard-thrown tennis ball. This is the beginning of a strange but lasting friendship.

Lee takes Will into his garage, which looks like a toolkit for inventive kids. A rowboat hangs suspended from the ceiling, and there's equipment for pumping out videotape copies of the movies that Lee pirates at the local cinema, while puffing somewhat uncertainly on a filter-tip (yes, you could smoke in the movies in England in those days).

Electrified by his introduction to Rambo, Will joins Lee in making their own home video remake of the film. This involves Will enacting literally death-defying stunts: He's catapulted high into the air, for example, and swings on a rope to drop into a lake, neglecting to tell Lee he can't swim. The special effects are cobbled together from household items, purloined booty, and Will's sketches and flip-book animation.

All is not well at home, where Will lives with his mom (Jessica Stevenson), a sister, and his drooling grandma (Anna Wing). There's an unwelcome visitor in the house most of the time, Brother Joshua (the perfectly named Neil Dudgeon), who covets the role of Will's absent father and enjoys being stern and forbidding to the lad. The intimacy of his relationship with the mother seems limited mostly to significant nods when he says goodbye at the end of the evening.

Will and Lee find their world unsettled when a busload of French exchange students descends on their school, and Didier (Jules Sitruk) captures their admiration. Taller and older, he takes charge of their indie production and their lives. Meanwhile, their stunt work escalates: They steal a life-sized dog from the Guide Dogs for the Blind people, hook it to a parasail, and inadvertently set off fire alarms at their school. And a runaway Jeep causes a load of scrap metal to fall on Will and Lee, with surprisingly limited results.

All of this takes place in a pastoral countryside and a benign city, where the boys move more or less invisibly. They're not simply growing up, but expanding: their horizons, their imaginations, their genius for troublemaking. Since it is made clear at the start that little fatal or tragic is likely to happen, the movie becomes like a fable—maybe too fabulous for its own good. The plot unspools with nothing really urgent at stake, the boys live in innocence and invulnerability, and the settings and action have a way of softening the characters.

I liked *Son of Rambow* in a benign sort of way, but I was left wanting something more.

Drama, maybe? No, that would simply be manufactured. Comedy? It is technically a comedy, although the limited laughs are incredulous. Fantasy? That it is, in a bittersweet way. After the movie, I imagined its writer-director, Garth Jennings (*The Hitchhiker's Guide to the Galaxy*), being more than a little like Will, and the movie uncannily similar to one of Will's comic epics.

Son of the Mask ★ ½

PG, 86 m., 2005

Jamie Kennedy (Tim Avery), Alan Cumming (Loki), Liam Falconer and Ryan Falconer (Alvey Avery), Bob Hoskins (Odin), Traylor Howard (Tonya Avery), Ben Stein (Dr. Arthur Neuman), Bear (Otis the Dog). Directed by Lawrence Guterman and produced by Erica Huggins and Scott Kroopf. Screeplay by Lance Khazei.

One of the foundations of comedy is a character who must do what he doesn't want to do because of the logic of the situation. As Auden pointed out about limericks, they're funny not because they end with a dirty word, but because they have no choice but to end with the dirty word—by that point, it's the only word that rhymes and makes sense. Lucille Ball made a career out of finding herself in embarrassing situations and doing the next logical thing, however ridiculous.

Which brings us to *Son of the Mask* and its violations of this theory. The movie's premise is that if you wear a magical ancient mask, it will cause you to behave in strange ways. Good enough, and in Jim Carrey's original *The Mask* (1994), the premise worked. Carrey's elastic face was stretched into a caricature, he gained incredible powers, he exhausted himself with manic energy. But there were rules. There was a baseline of sanity from which the mania proceeded. *Son of the Mask* lacks a baseline. It is all mania, all the time; the behavior in the movie is not inappropriate, shocking, out of character, impolite, or anything else except behavior.

Both *Mask* movies are inspired by the zany world of classic cartoons. The hero of *Son of the Mask,* Tim Avery (Jamie Kennedy), is no doubt named after Tex Avery, the legendary Warner Bros. animator, although it is *One Froggy Evening* (1955), by the equally legendary Chuck Jones, that plays a role in the film. Their films all obeyed the Laws of Cartoon Thermodynamics, as established by the distinguished theoreticians Trevor Paquette and Lieutenant Justin D. Baldwin. (Examples: Law III: "Any body passing through solid matter will leave a perforation conforming to its perimeter"; Law IX: "Everything falls faster than an anvil.")

These laws, while seemingly arbitrary, are consistent in all cartoons. We know that Wile E. Coyote can chase the Road Runner off a cliff and keep going until he looks down; only then will he fall. And that the Road Runner can pass through a tunnel entrance in a rock wall, but Wile E. Coyote will smash into the wall. We instinctively understand Law VIII ("Any violent rearrangement of feline matter is impermanent"). Even cartoons know that if you don't have rules, you're playing tennis without a net.

The premise in *Son of the Mask* is that an ancient mask, found in the earlier movie, has gone missing again. It washes up on the banks of a little stream and is fetched by Otis the Dog (Bear), who brings it home to the Avery household, where we find Tim (Kennedy) and his wife, Tonya (Traylor Howard). Tim puts on the Mask and is transformed into a whiz-kid at his advertising agency, able to create brilliant campaigns in a single bound. He also, perhaps unwisely, wears it to bed and engenders an infant son, Alvey, who is born with cartoonlike abilities and discovers them by watching the frog cartoon on TV.

Tim won an instant promotion to the big account, but without the Mask he is a disappointment. And the Mask cannot be found, because Otis has dragged it away and hidden it somewhere—although not before Otis snuffles at it until it attaches itself to his face, after which he is transformed into a cartoon dog and careens wildly around the yard and the sky, to his alarm.

A word about baby Alvey (played by the twins Liam and Ryan Falconer). I have never much liked movie babies who do not act like babies. I think they're scary. The first *Look Who's Talking* movie was cute, but the sequels were nasty, especially when the dog started talking. About *Baby's Day Out* (1994), in which Baby Bink set Joe Mantegna's crotch on fire, the less said the better.

I especially do not like Baby Alvey, who behaves not according to the rules for babies, but more like a shape-shifting creature in a Japanese anime. There may be a way this could be made funny, but *Son of the Mask* doesn't find it.

Meanwhile, powerful forces seek the Mask. The god Odin (Bob Hoskins) is furious with his son Loki (Alan Cumming) for having lost the Mask, and sends him down to Earth (or maybe these gods already live on Earth, I dunno) to get it back again. Loki, who is the god of mischief, has a spiky punk hairstyle that seems inspired by the jester's cap and bells, without the bells. He picks up the scent and causes no end of trouble for the Averys, although of course the dog isn't talking.

But my description makes the movie sound more sensible than it is. What we basically have here is a license for the filmmakers to do whatever they want to do with the special effects, while the plot, like Wile E. Coyote, keeps running into the wall.

Sophie Scholl: The Final Days ★ ★ ★

NO MPAA RATING, 117 m., 2006

Julia Jentsch (Sophie Scholl), Gerald Alexander Held (Robert Mohr), Fabian Hinrichs (Hans Scholl), Johanna Gastdorf (Else Gebel), Andre Hennicke (Dr. Roland Freisler). Directed by Marc Rothemund and produced by Christoph Müeller and Sven Burgemeister. Screenplay by Fred Breinersdorfer.

At the heart of *Sophie Scholl: The Final Days* is a long interrogation conducted across a desk in a police headquarters. It is February 1943, in Munich. The questions are asked by Robert Mohr (Gerald Alexander Held), a provincial who has risen in rank under the Nazis and wears a little lapel pin proclaiming his patriotism. The answers come from Sophie Scholl (Julia Jentsch), a student of biology and philosophy. She is accused of helping distribute leaflets on her campus that attack Hitler and his war.

This is not a thriller but a police procedural, in which we have all the information we need, right from the outset. She is guilty. Sophie and her brother, Hans (Fabian Hinrichs), belong to the White Rose, an underground group that mimeographs statements critical of the regime and the continuation of a war that is already lost. In theory their leaflets were to be mailed. Hans gets the idea of distributing them on their campus. This is reckless and stupid, and exactly the sort of grand gesture beloved by idealistic kids. If the Scholls had been communists, party discipline would have mocked them. But they are Catholics carried away by conscience.

Even so, they might have gotten away with it. They put piles of leaflets outside classroom doors, and then Sophie, in a heedless moment, sends a stack of paper swirling down into a central hallway. It is the janitor who turns them in, in part because he is a Nazi toady, in part because they made extra work for him.

Sophie Scholl, an Oscar nominee for best foreign film, contains no artificial suspense or drama. Directed by Marc Rothemund and written by Fred Breinersdorfer, it is based on fact and uses the transcripts of Scholl's actual interrogation and trial, as kept by the Gestapo and liberated when East Germany fell. Most of the words in the questioning are literally what Scholl and Mohr said. He sits behind his desk, impassive and precise, asking her to explain her presence on the campus and her suitcase that is exactly large enough to hold the leaflets. Cool and calm, she answers every question precisely. She has an alibi that is almost good enough.

The effect of this scene is so powerful that I leaned forward like a jury member, wanting her to get away with it so I could find her innocent. But the law moves as the law always does, with no reference to higher justice; even in this Nazi procedure there are carbon copies and paper clips and rubber stamps and a need to see the law followed, as indeed it is. The law underpins evil, but it is observed. When Sophie is found guilty, it is legal enough.

The sentence against her is carried out with startling promptness; because of the movie's title, we are not surprised, but we are jolted. I was reminded of an exchange in *Thank You for Smoking* where the son of a tobacco lobbyist asks him, "Dad, why is the American government the best government?" And his father replies, "Because of our endless appeals system." It is a luxury to be able to joke about such things. One day Sophie Scholl thoughtlessly throws some leaflets off a balcony, and two days later she is dead. Notice how the final sounds of the movie play under a black screen. Does she hear them?

Are the policeman Robert Mohr and the judge Roland Freisler (Andre Hennicke) evil men? Yes, absolutely, but they are doing their duty. I learn from Anthony Lane in the *New Yorker* that Mohr's widow received a state pension after the war. The police and the court are shown to follow the law, and in the law resides either good or evil, depending on what the law says and how it is enforced. That is why it is crucial that a constitution guarantee rights and freedoms, and why it is dangerous for any government to ignore it. There should be no higher priority.

All of these thoughts are made particular in *Sophie Scholl: The Final Days*. Most of the dialogue involves specific questions of where Sophie was, and when, and why the evidence against her is so compelling. Perry Mason–type stuff. The policeman is so passive he is hardly there. Only the judge indulges in speechifying; those who know their actions are wrong are often the loudest to defend them, especially when they fear a higher moral judgment may come down on them. But the most powerful political statement in the film is one of the saddest. Sophie is allowed a few moments with her parents before being taken away forever. "You did the right thing," her father says of Sophie and her brother. "I'm proud of you both."

Sorry, Haters ★ ★ ★

NO MPAA RATING, 83 m., 2006

Robin Wright Penn (Phoebe), Abdellatif Kechiche (Ashade), Elodie Bouchez (Eloise), Aasif Mandvi (Hassan), Sandra Oh (Phyllis MacIntyre), Remy K. Selma (Imam). Directed by Jeff Stanzler and produced by Gary Winick, Karen Jaroneski, Jake Abraham, and Stanzler. Screenplay by Stanzler.

Sorry, Haters is a film that begins in intrigue, develops in fascination, and ends in a train wreck. It goes spectacularly wrong, and yet it contains such a gripping performance by Robin Wright Penn that it succeeds, in a way, despite itself. To see great work is a reason to see an imperfect movie, and to observe how the movie loses its way may be useful even if it's frustrating. My inclination was to give the film a negative star rating, but that would mean recommending you not see this performance by Penn, and that I am unwilling to do.

When I mention Penn, I must also mention Abdellatif Kechiche, who plays the movie's other leading role, and whose anguish is easy to identify with, even if we cannot believe where the plot takes him. He plays a New York cab driver, and she plays a woman who gets into his cab one night—a woman who has been drinking and clutches a child's toy. She has him drive out to New Jersey so they can park across the street and she can look at what was her husband, her child, and their house. Her ex-husband, she says, divorced her, married again, and got the house, custody, everything. Before they leave, she uses her keys to scratch the ex-husband's new car.

Everything about this woman, named Phoebe, feels real, including her mania bordering on madness. There is also the modulation of her gradually growing curiosity about the cab driver, named Ashade. We learn his story: He was a PhD in chemistry in his native Syria. His brother has been a Canadian citizen for ten years and has a French-Canadian wife and a baby. The brother was stopped by U.S. officials on his way through LaGuardia and is now a prisoner at Guantanamo. Appeals have failed, even though the brother (according to Ashade) is completely innocent. Phoebe, an executive for a cable TV company, decides that she would like to help them.

That, in any event, is the surface of the story, the setup. There is a lot more, but as much as I deplore how the movie develops, I will not reveal its secrets, because if you are going to see it, you deserve to see it as I did—going in knowing nothing, and coming out knowing everything and feeling admiration for Penn and something between dissatisfaction and anger for the film. I learn that the producers tried to tell the director, Jeff Stanzler, that his third act didn't work, but he pressed on. And what's the use of making a low-budget film on digital video if you can't make precisely the film you want to make? That's what the low budget buys you: freedom.

With freedom comes responsibility, etc., but never mind. Just watch Penn. She has to move through wide emotional territory in this film, and she does. She has to make a speech explaining her emotions and motivations, and she does that, too. We do not believe it. We believe either that (a) no one would feel as she feels, or (b) if she does, she's too crazy to seem as sane as she does. But perhaps there are forms of self-delusion that can be masked by intelligent psychopaths, and perhaps that's the case here; she drives the taxi driver to an explosion of frustration and desperation.

Certainly Phoebe seems on the level, at least to begin with. She's smart, attractive, articulate, and kind of creepy as she insists on visiting the French-Canadian sister-in-law (Elodie Bouchez) and taking Ashade to her office at the cable company. Later, there is a dinner involving Phyllis MacIntyre (Sandra Oh), her boss at the company, and without going into details, I ask you to observe the dynamic at that restaurant table.

There is (I'm wording this carefully) a surprise that begins to emerge at about the halfway point, but I didn't have a problem with it. I could believe it and consider it consistent with what went before. What I could not accept, where I could not follow, was Phoebe's ultimate purpose and her reasons for it. Perhaps it would have helped if the speech where she explains herself had just been left out altogether. It reminds me too much of the Talking Killer Syndrome—like a T.K., she is compelled to explain and justify herself at a time when only action is called for. I am thinking of the speech involving the word "powerless." Perhaps if we had seen her behavior without explication or complaint, we could have simply followed her actions and then figured out her motivation for ourselves.

It must have taken courage for Penn to commit to *Sorry, Haters*. She must have doubted the ending. And yet like many great actresses, she was willing to give the director the benefit of the doubt, because an ending that raises no questions may also achieve nothing. *Sorry, Haters* is certainly not the kind of movie that should end happily with everything resolved. In its world, and our world, that doesn't happen, not in a case like this.

A Sound of Thunder ★ ★

PG-13, 102 m., 2005

Edward Burns (Travis Ryer),Catherine McCormack (Sonia Rand), Ben Kingsley (Charles Hatton), Jemima Rooper (Jenny Krase), David Oyelowo (Officer Payne). Directed by Peter Hyams and produced by Moshe Diamant, Howard Baldwin, and Karen Baldwin. Screenplay by Thomas Dean Donnelly, Joshua Oppenheimer, and Gregory Poirer, based on a short story by Ray Bradbury.

When I was the president of the Urbana High School Science Fiction Club, this would have been my favorite movie. But the movies have changed and so have I, and today there is something almost endearing about the clunky special effects and clumsy construction of *A Sound of Thunder*. The movie is made with a gee-whiz spirit, and although I cannot endorse it, I can appreciate it. There's a fundamental difference between movies that are bad because they're willfully stupid *(Deuce Bigalow, European Gigolo)* and movies that are bad because they want so much to be terrific that they explode under the strain.

A Sound of Thunder may not be a success, but it loves its audience and wants us to have a great time. The movie is inspired by a famous short story by Ray Bradbury, arguing that to travel back in time and change even one tiny element in the past could completely alter the future. In that it is firmly Darwinian, and indeed, if the common ancestor of all primates had died without reproducing, where would that leave us?

In the movie, a greedy entrepreneur (Ben Kingsley) charges millionaires a small fortune to travel back in time, kill a giant prehistoric reptile, and return with a video of themselves. In theory this will not change the present because (a) frozen liquid nitrogen bullets are used, which will evaporate, making no difference, (b) the targeted beast is selected because in another second it would have died anyway, and (c) the travelers never leave anything behind.

Since the same scenario is played out time and again, it raises the question of why each hunting party doesn't run into the other ones. Subtle dialogue hints suggest that maybe even the "safe" visits are making small changes, but then something happens big time, and the "present" is socked with a series of "time waves," which look like optical tsunamis and leave a different world behind them.

The film's hero is Travis (Edward Burns), a scientist who hopes to re-create ancient DNA. He leads the time expeditions. The heroine is Sonia Rand (Catherine McCormack), who invented the computer that oversees the travel. The heart of the movie involves a series of desperate expeditions into the past to repair or prevent what went wrong, so that the familiar "present" will return. Meanwhile, in alternative realities, a futuristic Chicago becomes a tropical swamp inhabited by giant reptilian bats, saber-toothed eagles, and lots and lots of bugs.

Now about the special effects. The scenes where the giant brontosaurus attacks the travelers looks so precisely like actors standing in front of back projection that it scarcely improves on *King Kong.* In the first time-travel scene, as the travelers walk out of a wormhole and into a shimmering pathway, why do they all look in the same direction? Wouldn't some of them look the other way? Why does the thick rain forest not have any trees in front of a volcano, so we can see it clearly? How can a volcano be so far away that we can see all of it, and yet be so close that its lava arrives in seconds? How can the lava look like dirty shaving cream and not like molten rock? How come if the power is out all over the city, the time machine can work? How can . . .

But what the hell, once you realize the effects are not even going to try to be convincing, you start to enjoy them. Perfect special effects can have a cold detachment to them; lousy ones can be eerie, strange, or fun. The future Chicago in this film, which makes the city in *Batman Begins* look like a documentary, is fantastical and preposterous; seeing the futuristic skyscrapers, the roadways in the sky, the airships, and the cars that all move at exactly the same speed, I was reminded of the covers of old sci-fi pulp magazines. When Travis and Sonia are trapped in a flooded subway with giant eels and the tunnel is caving in, I found it wonderful that they eventually escape through the kind of manhole we see in *The Third Man.*

Some of the dialogue is worth repeating. When Sonia finds the computer incapacitated and says she needs another terminal, someone suggests, "How about Home Depot?" And consider this exchange:

"What's that?"

"The molecular structure of brontosaurus blood."

"No way! Cool!"

The movie was directed by Peter Hyams, who a lifetime ago was an anchor for Channel 2 News in Chicago. He has directed mostly science fiction, including *2010, Capricorn One, Outland, End of Days, Stay Tuned, Timecop,* and *The Relic* (1997), another movie in which creatures in flooded Chicago tunnels played an important role. *A Sound of Thunder* looks cobbled together from a half-baked screenplay and underdone special effects, but it's made with a certain heedless zeal that makes you smile if you're in tune with it.

Southland Tales ★

R, 144 m., 2007

Dwayne Johnson (Boxer Santaros), Seann William Scott (Roland/Ronald Taverner), Sarah Michelle Gellar (Krysta Kapowski/Krysta Now), Curtis Armstrong (Dr. Soberin Exx), Joe Campana (Brandt Huntington), Nora Dunn (Cyndi Pinziki), Michele Durrett (Starla Von Luft), Beth Grant (Inga Von Westphalen). Directed by Richard Kelly and produced by Sean McKittrick, Bo Hyde, Kendall Morgan, and Matthew Rhodes. Screenplay by Kelly.

After I saw the first cut of Richard Kelly's *Donnie Darko* (2002), I was left dazed and confused but somehow convinced that I might have seen *something.* After I saw the director's cut (2004), which was twenty minutes longer, I began to comprehend some of what I had seen, and it became more interesting, even though I still didn't entirely understand it. It even nudged itself up into a favorable review.

After I saw the first cut of Kelly's *Southland Tales* at Cannes 2006, I was dazed, confused, bewildered, bored, affronted, and deafened by the boos all around me at the most disastrous Cannes press screening since, yes, *The Brown Bunny.* But now here is the director's cut, which is twenty minutes shorter, lops off a couple of characters and a few of the infinite subplots, and is even more of a mess. I recommend that Kelly keep right on cutting until he whittles it down to a ukulele pick.

Yes, I admire Kelly's free spirit. In theory. He is a cinematic anarchist, but the problem is, he's throwing bombs at his own work. He apparently has no sympathy at all for an audience unable to understand his plot, and every scene plays like something that was dreamed up with little concern for what went before or would follow after. It's like the third day of a pitch session on speed. What does he imagine an audience feels like while watching this movie? Did his editor ever suggest that he might emerge with a more coherent product if he fed the footage through a revolving fan and spliced it together at random?

The time is the Future: one year from now. By the time the DVD comes out, the time will be the Present. Two Texas towns have been nuked, including Abilene, the prettiest town that I've ever seen. America is in a state of emergency. A left-wing revolution is being masterminded from Venice Beach and the Santa Monica Pier against the oppressive right-wing government. A Schwarzeneggerian actor, related to a political dynasty, has been kidnapped, replaced with a double, and—I give up. A plot synopsis would require that the movie have a plot.

The dialogue consists largely of statements that are incomprehensible, often delivered with timing that is apparently intended to indicate they are witty. All of the actors seem to have generated back stories for their characters that have nothing to do with one another. Only Wallace Shawn emerges intact, because he so easily can talk like that, but a spit curl does not become him. Justin Timberlake is the narrator, providing what are possibly quasi-rational explanations for movies in other time dimensions.

The population of America consists entirely of character actors with funny names. I'm not sure that by the end of the movie they have all met one another, even the ones in the same scenes together. I haven't committed all of *Ebert's Little Movie Glossary* to memory, but I'm pretty sure it contains a Law of Funny Names, which instructs us that funny names are rarely funny in the movies, especially if they are not borne by Groucho Marx or W. C. Fields.

When I tell you I am helpless to describe the plot, perhaps you will have pity on me if I tell you it involves characters named Boxer Santaros; Krysta Kapowski, aka the porn star Krysta Now; Dr. Soberin Exx; Starla Von Luft; Inga Von Westphalen, aka Marion; Dion Warner, aka Dion Element; Nana Mae Frost; Baron Von Westphalen; and Simon Theory. Boxer Santaros is played by Dwayne Johnson, who used to be billed as the Rock and should have led a movement among characters to change their names.

These people mostly seem to have dressed themselves earlier in the day at a used-costume store, although from the Cannes version I particularly miss a character played by Janeane Garofalo, who apparently used the Army surplus store. She was some kind of guerrilla general operating out of what I vaguely recall as a Venice Beach head shop, or maybe it was a bookstore. What a comedown from her great performance in nearby Santa Monica in *The Truth About Cats and Dogs.*

Note to readers planning to write me messages informing me that this review was no more than a fevered rant: You are correct.

Space Chimps ★ ★ ★

G, 80 m., 2008

With the voices of: Andy Samberg (Ham III), Cheryl Hines (Luna), Omid Abtahi (Titan Jagu), Jeff Daniels (Zartog), Kristin Chenoweth (Kilowatt), Stanley Tucci (Senator). Directed by Kirk De Micco and produced by Barry Sonnenfeld and John H. Williams. Screenplay by De Micco and Robert Moreland.

Space Chimps is delightful from beginning to end: a goofy space opera that sends three U.S. chimptronauts rocketing to a galaxy, as they say, far, far away. Although it's aimed at a younger market and isn't in the same science fiction league as *WALL-E,* it's successful at what it wants to do: take us to an alien planet and present us with a large assortment of bug-eyed monsters, not to mention a little charmer nicknamed Kilowatt who lights up when she gets excited, or afraid, or just about anything else.

The story starts with the circus career of the chimp Ham III (voice by Andy Samberg), the grandson of the first chimp launched by NASA into space (and, yes, that first chimp really was named Ham). Ham III works at being shot out of a cannon and never quite landing where he should. Once, when he goes really high, he considers the beauty of the moon and outer space, and has a *Right Stuff* moment, of which there are several. He feels keenly that he hasn't lived up to the family tradition.

Meanwhile, the U.S. space program faces a crisis. One of its deep space probes has disappeared into a wormhole. It is perhaps a measure of the sophistication of younger audiences that no attempt is made to explain what a wormhole is. Perhaps that's because wormholes are only conjecture anyway, and if you can't say there is one, how can you say what it is?

What with one thing and another, Ham III finds himself enlisted in the crew of a space flight to follow the probe into the wormhole and see what happened to it. Joining the mission is a big chimp named Titan (Patrick Warburton) and the cute (in chimp terms) Luna (Cheryl Hines). Hurtling through what looks like a dime-store version of the sound-and-light fantasy in *2001,* they land on a planet where the local creatures are ruled by a big, ugly tyrant named Zartog (Jeff Daniels).

He has commandeered the original NASA probe and uses its extendable arms to punish his enemies by dipping them into a supercold bath so they freeze in an instant. This is a cruel fate, especially since the eyeballs of his victims continue to roll, which means they must be alive inside their frozen shells, which implies peculiarities about their metabolism.

The chimps, of course, have lots of adventures, including being chased through a cave by a monster of many teeth and being rescued by the plucky Kilowatt, who eventually sees more of the monster than she really desires. Then there's a showdown with Zartog, some business about the planet's three suns (night lasts only five minutes), and a most ingenious way to blast off again.

On Earth, there's an unnecessary subplot about an evil senator (Stanley Tucci) who wants to disband the space program and replace it with something you really have to hear to believe. On second thought, maybe the subplot is necessary, just so we get to hear his idea.

I ponder strange things during movies like this. For example, there seem to be only five forms of life on the planet. Zartog is one, his obedient subjects are another, some flying creatures are a third, the toothy monster is the fourth, and Kilowatt is the fifth. I suppose a planet where evolution has produced only five species is possible. But what do they eat? The planet looks like Monument Valley, is covered with sand, and has no flora or fauna. Could they all be silicon-based? And since Zartog, the tooth monster, and Kilowatt each seem to be one of a kind, who do they mate with? Or do silicon beings need to mate? And have they invented the hourglass?

Spider-Man 3 ★ ★

PG-13, 139 m., 2007

Tobey Maguire (Peter Parker/Spider-Man), Kirsten Dunst (Mary Jane Watson), James Franco (Harry Osborn), Thomas Haden Church (Flint Marko/Sandman), Topher Grace (Eddie Brock/Venom), Bryce Dallas Howard (Gwen Stacy), James Cromwell (Captain Stacy), Rosemary Harris (Aunt May), J. K. Simmons (J. Jonah Jameson). Directed by Sam Raimi and produced by Laura Ziskin, Avi Arad, and Grant Curtis. Screenplay by Sam Raimi, Ivan Raimi, and Alvin Sargent, based on the comic books by Stan Lee and Steve Ditko.

The great failing of *Spider-Man 3* is that it failed to distract me from what a sap Peter Parker is. It lingers so long over the dopey romance between Peter and the long-suffering Mary Jane that I found myself asking the question: Could a whole movie about the relationship between these two twenty-somethings be made? And my answer was: No, because today's audiences would never accept a hero so clueless and a heroine so docile. And isn't it a little unusual to propose marriage after sharing only one kiss, and that one in the previous movie, and upside-down?

Faithful readers will recall that I found *Spider-Man 2* (2004) the best superhero movie since *Superman* (1978). But I made the mistake of declaring that was because "the movie demonstrates what's wrong with a lot of other superhero epics: They focus on the superpowers, and short-change the humans behind them." This time, I desperately wanted Peter Parker to be short-changed. If I argued earlier that Bruce Wayne and Clark Kent were boring human beings, I had no idea how Peter would begin to wear on my nerves.

And what's with Mary Jane? Here's a beautiful, (somewhat) talented actress good enough to star in a Broadway musical, and she has to put up with being trapped in a taxi suspended eighty stories in the air by alien spiderwebs. The unique quality of the classic comic books was that their teenagers had ordinary adolescent angst and insecurity. But if you are still dangling in taxicabs at age twenty, you're a slow learner. If there is a *Spider-Man 4* (and there will be), how about giving Peter and Mary Jane at least the emotional complexity of soap opera characters?

Superhero movies and James Bond movies live and die by their villains. Spidey number two had the superb Doc Ock (Alfred Molina), who is right up there with Goldfinger and the Joker in the Supervillain Hall of Infamy. He had a *personality*. In Spidey number three we have too many villains, too little infamy. Take the Sandman (Thomas Haden Church). As an escaped con and the murderer of Uncle Ben, he has marginal interest at best. As the Sandman, he is absurd. Recall Doc Ock climbing buildings with his fearsome mechanical tentacles, and now look at this dust storm. He forms from heaps of sand into a creature that looks like a snowman left standing too late in the season. He can have holes blown into him with handguns but then somehow regains the bodily integrity to hammer buildings. And how does he *feel* in there? Molina always let you know precisely how Doc Ock felt, with a vengeance.

Then there is the black microorganism from outer space, which is not a villain but plays one in the movie. It arrives on Earth in a meteorite that lands, oh, maybe twenty yards from Peter and Mary Jane, but this impact somehow escapes notice by the fabled Spidey-sense. Then it produces little black beasties that look like squids crossed with licorice rope. They not only coat people with a way-cool black, glossy second skin, but specialize in spray-painting Spidey and Spidey wannabes. No ups, no extras.

We know that Spider-Man's powers do not reside in his red suit, which lives in a suitcase under his bed. So how do fake Spideys like Venom gain their powers when they are covered with the black substance? And how does a microorganism from outer space know how to replicate the intricate pattern-work of the Spidey costume, right down to the chest decoration? And to what purpose from an evolutionary point of view? And what good luck that the microorganism gets Peter's rival photographer, Eddie Grace, to infect, so that he becomes Venom! And how does Eddie know who he has become?

Another villain is Harry Osborn, aka the New Green Goblin (James Franco), son of the interesting original (Willem Dafoe), but not a drip off the old gob. While the first GG had the usual supervillain motivations (malevolence, envy, twisted abilities), his son is merely very angry and under the misapprehension that Peter/Spidey murdered his old dad. And *then* Peter and Harry have a *fist fight* when they should be doing Spidey and Goblin stuff.

Yes, there are some nice special effects in the movie. I liked the collapsing construction crane sequence. But the damsel in distress that time was not Mary Jane but Gwen Stacy (Bryce Dallas Howard), the sexy blond lab partner Peter has somehow neglected to mention to Mary Jane, causing her heartbreak because at a civic ceremony he kisses her with "our kiss," i.e., the upside-down one. While Peter goes through a period of microorganism infection, he combs his hair forward, struts the streets, attracts admiring glances from every pretty girl on the street, and feels like hot stuff. Wait until he discovers sex.

Spider-Man 3 is, in short, a mess. Too many villains, too many pale plot strands, too many romantic misunderstandings, too many conversations, too many street crowds looking high into the air and shouting "oooh!" this way, then swiveling and shouting "aaah!" that way. And saints deliver us from another dinner date like the one where Peter plans to propose to Mary Jane. You know a movie is in trouble when the climactic romantic scene of the entire series is stolen by the waiter (Bruce Campbell). And poor Aunt May (Rosemary Harris). An actress of Harris's ability, asked to deliver a one-note performance, and that single note is fretting.

How could Sam Raimi, having gone so right with *Spider-Man 2*, have gone so wrong with *Spider-Man 3*? Did the $250 million budget paralyze him? Has the series grown too heavy on its feet? How many times can we see essentially the same romantic scenario repeated between Peter and Mary Jane? How much dangling in the air can one girl do? And how does Spidey keep his identity a secret anyway, when there are more arrivals and departures through his apartment's window than on a busy day at LaGuardia?

The Spiderwick Chronicles ★ ★ ★ ½

PG, 96 m., 2008

Freddie Highmore (Jared/Simon Grace), Mary-Louise Parker (Helen Grace), Nick Nolte (Mulgarath), Joan Plowright (Aunt Lucinda), David Strathairn (Arthur Spiderwick), Seth Rogen (Hogsqueal), Martin Short (Thimbletack/Boggart), Sarah Bolger (Mallory Grace). Directed by Mark Waters and produced by Karey Kirkpatrick, Mark Canton, Larry Franco, and Ellen Goldsmith-Vein. Screenplay by Kirkpatrick, David Berenbaum, and John Sayles, based on the books by Tony DiTerlizzi and Holly Black.

The Spiderwick Chronicles is a terrific entertainment for the whole family, except those below a certain age, who are likely to be scared out of their wits. What is that age? I dunno; they're your kids. But I do know the PG classification is insane, especially considering what happens right after a father says he loves his son. This is a PG-13 movie for sure. But what will cause nightmares for younger kids will delight older ones, since here is a well-crafted family thriller that is truly scary and doesn't wimp out.

Based on a well-known series of five books, the movie involves a soon-to-be divorced mom and her three children who come to live in a creepy old mansion. This is Spiderwick, named after her great-uncle, Arthur Spiderwick, who disappeared under mysterious circumstances. The house itself is one of the stars of the movie, looking Victorian Gothic with countless nooks and crannies and shadows and scary sounds. Is it haunted? Nothing that comforting. It's . . . inhabited.

The mother is Helen Grace (Mary-Louise Parker), who is battling with the rebellious Jared (Freddie Highmore), one of her twin sons. He doesn't like being away from his dad, is homesick, doesn't want anything to do with this dusty and spiderwebby old ruin that was left to his mom by her aunt. Jared's brainy twin, Simon, looks remarkably identical, no doubt because he is also played by Freddie Highmore, born 1992, a gifted young actor best known for *Finding Neverland, August Rush*, and *The Golden Compass*. The twins' sister is the plucky Mallory (Sarah Bolger), a fencer who seldom goes anywhere without her sword, which is just as well in this movie. You may remember how good she was in *In America* (2002).

Jared is the kind of kid who is always getting blamed for everything. When stuff starts disappearing, for example, he gets the rap. When he hears noises in the wall and punches holes in it, he's being destructive. But he's brave, and when he finds a hidden dumbwaiter, he hauls himself up to a hidden room—his grandfather's study, left undisturbed after all these years. This room fairly reeks of forbidden secrets.

Don't read further unless you already know, as the Web site makes abundantly clear, that he finds a "field guide" to the unseen world left by his great-great-uncle (David Strathairn), and that with its help and a Seeing Stone, Jared can see goblins, sprits, hobgoblins, ogres, trolls, and griffins, which themselves can take many shapes. Some of them are amusing, like Thimbletack (voice by Martin Short), some alarming, like Boggart (Short again), some helpful but undependable, like Hogsqueal (voice by Seth Rogen). And some of the newly visible creatures are truly alarming, like Mulgarath. The credits say his voice is by Nick Nolte, but I gotta say that all of Mulgarath looks a lot like the real Nick Nolte to me.

Anyway, Jared finally convinces his brother, and then his sister and mother, that what he reports is real, and then, after pages from the field guide get into Mulgarath's hands, the Circle of Protection around the house is threatened, and the Graces are faced with dire threats. This is all done with a free mixture of lighthearted action, heavy action, and some dramatic scenes that, as I said, are pretty heavy going for younger imaginations. The movie is distinguished by its acting, not least by the great Joan Plowright as old Aunt Lucinda. Strathairn is completely credible as a spirit-world investigator, although exactly where the sparkling points of light take him, and what he does there, is a little murky.

They say be careful what you ask for because you might get it. I've often hailed back to the really creepy moments in Disney classics, like what happens to Dumbo and Bambi and the witch in *Snow White*, and I've complained that recent family movies are too sanitized. This one, directed by Mark Waters (*The House of Yes, Freaky Friday*), doesn't skip a beat before its truly horrific moments, so if you're under eight or nine years old, don't say you weren't warned.

The Squid and the Whale ★ ★ ★ ½

R, 88 m., 2005

Jeff Daniels (Bernard Berkman), Laura Linney (Joan Berkman), Jesse Eisenberg (Walt Berkman), Owen Kline (Frank Berkman), Halley Feiffer (Sophie), William Baldwin (Ivan), Anna Paquin (Lili). Directed by Noah Baumbach and produced by Wes Anderson, Charlie Corwin, Clara Markowicz, and Peter Newman. Screenplay by Baumbach.

I don't know what I'm supposed to feel during *The Squid and the Whale.* Sympathy, I suppose, for two bright boys whose parents are getting a messy divorce. Both parents are writers and use words as weapons; the boys choose sides and join the war. In theory, I observe their errors and sadness and think, there but for the grace of God go I. In practice, I feel envy.

I would have loved to have two writers as parents, grow up in a bohemian family in Brooklyn, and hear dinner-table conversation about Dickens. These kids have it great. Their traumas will inspire them someday. Hell, the movie was written and directed by Noah Baumbach, whose parents were writers (the novelist Jonathan Baumbach, the film critic Georgia Brown), and look how he turned out. By the time he was twenty-six, he had already directed *Kicking and Screaming* (1995), about sardonic and literate college graduates whose only ambition was to remain on campus. I felt the same way. Left to my own devices, I would still be a student of English literature, entering my forty-fourth year as an undergraduate.

In the movie, the parents, Bernard and Joan Berkman, are played by Jeff Daniels and Laura Linney, and if that's who it takes to play your parents, what are you complaining about? The movie centers on their troubled sons. Joan has been having an affair for four years, their father is moving out, and in theory their divorcing parents will share custody (there is even a plan for time shares of the cat). In practice, Walt (Jesse Eisenberg), who is sixteen, moves in with his father, and Frank (Owen Kline), who is about ten, stays in the family home with his mother.

Both kids have issues with their parents' sexuality. Walt thinks his mother is a "whore" for bringing one of her lovers into their home, but then his father begins an affair with one of his students, and what does that make him? Walt falls into true adolescent love but is compelled to deny it to himself because his father urges him to play the field, and he values his father's opinions more than is wise. "You have too many freckles," he tells Sophie (Halley Feiffer), the girl he likes. I guess he thinks that shows he has high standards. He's so dumb he doesn't know how wonderful too many freckles are.

Frank, his younger brother, has meanwhile discovered masturbation and taken to distributing his semen here and there around his school—on library books, for example. This is an alarming breach of school decorum and leads to a parent-teacher-student conference, during which I kept hoping someone would quote Rodney Dangerfield: "When I was a kid we were so poor, if I hadn't been a boy I wouldn't have had anything to play with."

Bernard, the father, published a good novel some years earlier and is now in a protracted drought season. It doesn't help when his wife sells a story to the *New Yorker.* He is played by Daniels as a man with wise-guy literary opinions that his son remembers and repeats; Bernard says *A Tale of Two Cities* is "minor Dickens," which is correct, and arms Walt with useful terms such as "Kafkaesque." Walt informs Sophie a book is Kafkaesque, and Sophie says, "It's written by Franz Kafka. It has to be." Point, match, and game. Walt's performance in the school talent show is a great success. Everyone is impressed by his songwriting ability except for a fellow student familiar with the lyrics of Pink Floyd. Life lesson: Okay to steal from your father to impress people, not okay to steal from Pink Floyd.

The Squid and the Whale is essentially about how we grow up by absorbing what is useful in our parents and forgiving what is not. Joan may cheat on her husband, but he deserves to be cheated on, and she demonstrates a faith in romance that is, after all, a lesson in optimism. Bernard may be a gold mine of shorthand literary opinions, but in his case he has actually read the books, and sooner or later his son Walt will probably feel compelled to read minor Dickens for himself—and major Dickens, which is so good all you can do is just helplessly stare at the book and turn the pages.

These kids will be okay. Someday Bernard and Joan will be old and will delight in their grandchildren, who will no doubt be miserable about the flaws and transgressions of Walt and Frank, and then create great achievements and angry children of their own. All I know is, it is better to be the whale than the squid. Whales inspire major novels.

Note: Since writing this, I have reread A Tale of Two Cities, *and I no longer agree it is minor Dickens.*

Standard Operating Procedure ★ ★ ★ ½

R, 121 m., 2008

A documentary written and directed by Errol Morris and produced by Morris and Julie Bilson Ahlberg.

Errol Morris's *Standard Operating Procedure,* based on the infamous prison torture photographs from Abu Ghraib, is completely unlike anything I was expecting from such a film—more disturbing, analytical, and morose. This is not a political film or yet another screed about the Bush administration or the war in Iraq. It is driven simply, powerfully, by the desire to understand those photographs.

There are thousands of them, mostly taken not from the point of view of photojournalism, but in the spirit of home snapshots. They show young Americans, notably Lynndie England, posing with prisoners of war who are handcuffed in grotesque positions, usually naked, heads often covered with their underpants, sometimes in sexual positions. Miss England, who was about twenty at the time and weighed scarcely one hundred pounds, often has a cigarette hanging from her mouth in a show of tough-guy bravado. But the effect is not to draw attention to her as the person who ordered these tableaux, but as a part of them. Some other force, not seen, is sensed as shaping them.

This invisible presence, we discover, is named Charles Graner, a staff sergeant Lynndie was in love with, who is more than fifteen years her senior. She does what he suggests. She doesn't question. But then, few questions are asked by most of the Americans in the photographs, who are not so much performing the acts as being photographed performing them.

"Pictures only show you a fraction of a second," says a Marine named Javal Davis, who was a prison guard but is not seen in any of them. "You don't see forward, and you don't see backward. You don't see outside the frame." He is expressing the central questions of the film: Why do these photos exist, why were they taken, and what reality do they reflect? What do we think about these people?

Those are the questions at the heart of many of Morris's films, all the way back to his first, *Gates of Heaven* (1978), in which to this day I am unable to say what he feels about his subjects or what they think of themselves. The answers would be less interesting anyway than the eternally enigmatic questions. Morris's favorite point of view is the stare. He chooses his subjects, regards them almost impassively, and allows their usually strange stories to tell themselves.

There is not a voice raised in *S.O.P.* The tone is set by a sad, elegiac, sometimes relentless score by Danny Elfman. The subject, in addition to the photographs, is Morris's interview subjects, seen in a mosaic of close-ups as they speak about what it was like to be at Abu Ghraib. Most of them speak either in sorrow or resentment, muted, incredulous. How had they found themselves in that situation?

Yes, unspeakable acts of cruelty were committed in the prison. But not personally, if we can believe them, by the interviewees. The torturers seem to have been military intelligence specialists in interrogation. They, too, are following orders and choose to disregard the theory that the information is useless since if you torture a man enough he will tell you anything.

I cannot imagine what it would be like to be suspended by having my hands shackled behind my back so tightly I might lose them. Or feeling I am being drowned. And so on—this need not be a litany of horrors.

More to the point of this film is that the prison wardens received their prisoners after the tortures were mostly committed, and then posed with them in ghastly "human pyramids," in "dog piles," or in scenes with sexual innuendo. Again, why? "For the picture." The taking of the photos seems to have been the motivation for the instants they reveal. And, as a speaker observes in the film, if there had been no photos, the moments they depict would not have existed, and the scandal of Abu Ghraib would not have taken place.

Yes, some of those we see in *Standard Operating Procedure* were paid for their testimony. Morris acknowledges that. He did not tell them what to say. I personally believed what they were telling me. What it came down to was, they found themselves under orders that they did not understand, involved in situations to provide a lifetime of nightmares.

They were following orders, yes. But whose? Any orders to torture would have had to come from those with a rank of staff sergeant or above. But all of those who were tried, found guilty, and convicted after Abu Ghraib were below that rank. At the highest level, results were demanded—find information on the whereabouts of Saddam Hussein (whose eventual capture did not result from any information pried loose by torture). At lower levels, the orders were translated into using torture. But there was a deliberate cutoff between the high level demanding the results and the intermediate level authorizing the violation of U.S. and international law by the use of torture.

At the opening of the film, Defense Secretary Donald Rumsfeld is seen, his blue blazer hooked over one shoulder, his white dress shirt immaculate, "touring" Abu Ghraib. He is shown one cell, then cancels his tour. He doesn't want to see any more.

And so little Lynndie England is left with her fellow soldiers as the face of the scandal. And behind the photos of her and others lurks the enigmatic figure of Sergeant Charles Graner, who was not allowed by the military to be interviewed for this film. I imagine him as the kind of guy we all knew in high school, snickering in the corner, sharing thoughts we did not want to know with friends we did not want to make. If he posed many of the photos (and gave away countless copies of them), was it because he enjoyed being at one remove from their subjects? The captors were seen dominating their captives, and he was in the role, with his camera, of dominating both.

Remember the photo of Lynndie posing with the prisoner on a leash? His name, we learn, was Gus. Lynndie says she wasn't dragging him: "You can see the leash was slack." She adds: "He would never have had me standing next to Gus if the camera wasn't there."

Stardust ★ ★ ½

PG-13. 122 m., 2007

Claire Danes (Yvaine), Charlie Cox (Tristan), Sienna Miller (Victoria), Ricky Gervais (Ferdy the Fence), Jason Flemyng (Primus), Rupert Everett (Secundus), Peter O'Toole (King of Stormhold), Robert De Niro (Captain Shakespeare), Michelle Pfeiffer (Lamia), Ian McKellen (Narrator). Directed by Matthew Vaughn and produced by Vaughn, Lorenzo di Bonaventura, Michael Dreyer, and Neil Gaiman. Screenplay by Jane Goldman and Vaughn, based on a novel by Gaiman.

A fantasy, even a comic fantasy, needs above all to be lean and uncluttered. Only reality is untidy. The classic fantasy structure involves the hero, the quest, the prize, and what stands in the way. It is not a good sign that almost the most entertaining element of *Stardust* is Captain Shakespeare, appearing from the skies in his dirigible pirate ship. Shakespeare, played by Robert De Niro as a transvestite swashbuckler (swishbuckler?), is wonderful, but he should be forced to wear a badge saying, "Hi! I'm the deus ex machina!"

There are lots of other good things in the movie, but they play more like vaudeville acts than part of a coherent plot. It's a film you enjoy in pieces, but the jigsaw never gets solved. I liked it, but *The Princess Bride* it's not.

The plot, by Neil Gaiman, based on his novel: England is separated from the fantasy kingdom of Stormhold by a wall. Outside the wall, in an English village conveniently named Wall, lives a plucky lad named Tristan (Charlie Cox), who is in love with a lass named Victoria (Sienna Miller). He fears to lose her to a rival, but one night they see a shooting star fall beyond the wall, and he vows to retrieve it for her.

It is not very hard to get through the wall,

which is an example of Stormhold's crumbling infrastructure. Tristan's father was once able to bound through a gap in the wall, but Tristan has more trouble with an ancient guard and employs a magic candle which, by definition, works its magic. Inside Stormhold, he discovers that the star is, in fact, a beautiful girl with long blond tresses named Yvaine (Claire Danes). I think her name makes her a sort of vain Yvonne. She possesses such secrets as eternal life, which are worth having, and so there's a rivalry for her powers.

In this corner: Three Macbethesque witches (Gaiman is a fan of Shakespeare), led by Lamia (Michelle Pfeiffer), who believe Yvaine can restore their beauty. In the other corner: The Learesque king of Stormhold (Peter O'Toole), who has three living sons and four dead ones, who appear in black and white as Hamlet's fatheresque ghosts. (Note to editors: Why *can't* that be a word?) The dying king believes Yvaine can restore his throne to his living sons, although let's hope he doesn't try dividing the kingdom among them.

Tristan is on his own among these scoundrels. At least he has Yvaine's sympathy. As the only one who doesn't want to rip out her heart and eat it, he has much to recommend him. Lamia, meanwhile, begins by looking like Michelle Pfeiffer, but the more she employs her black magic, the more she looks like Peter O'Toole, who has already gone about as far as he can go.

Meanwhile, Captain Shakespeare sails in like an outtake from *The Adventures of Baron Munchausen* and hopes to pillage, plunder, and provide comic relief. The movie becomes very busy at this point, and Tristan's quest to win Victoria's heart is upstaged by everybody else's quest to eat Yvaine's.

Still, Gaiman has many admirers, they will be familiar with the material and find their way around, and director Matthew Vaughn lays on the special effects; the movie is not boring, just cluttered and not focused enough. There is a kind of narrative flow that makes you want to be swept along and another that's just one thing after another. *Stardust* is fun enough the first time through, but it doesn't pass the Derek Malcolm Test: "A great movie is a movie I cannot bear the thought of never seeing again."

Starting Out in the Evening ★ ★ ★ ★

PG-13, 111 m., 2007

Frank Langella (Leonard Schiller), Lili Taylor (Ariel Schiller), Lauren Ambrose (Heather Wolfe), Adrian Lester (Casey Davis). Directed by Andrew Wagner and produced by Nancy Israel, Fred Parnes, Wagner, Jake Abraham, and Gary Winick. Screenplay by Fred Parnes and Wagner.

Do you sometimes feel like you're the last serious reader left? Do you remember when the *New York Times* best-selling novels were by Faulkner, Mailer, Updike, Cheever, Welty, or O'Hara? Do you thank heaven when Oprah chooses a great novel like *A Fine Balance*? Have you noticed that people have stopped obsessing about J. D. Salinger's disappearing act? Have you never found a later novelist as entertaining as Dickens? Did you study English in college and carry around Shakespeare a little conspicuously?

Oh, and do you ever wonder if you will ever find a soul mate? Here's a movie made for you. *Starting Out in the Evening* is a film about people who think literature is worth devoting a lifetime to. People who think great novelists are a species of saint. It honors values that seem obsolete in our trashy popular culture, obsessed with the sex lives of vacuumheads.

The story involves a seventy-year-old novelist named Leonard Schiller (Frank Langella) and a twenty-five-ish graduate student named Heather Wolfe (Lauren Ambrose). He wrote four books that were acclaimed as important and still are, although he's not much read anymore. He's been working on a fifth novel for a decade. She plays a graduate student who wants to write her thesis about him and has hopes that she may inspire a revival of interest in his work and maybe blast that fifth novel out of his grip.

They are not alike. He puts on a coat and tie to sit down at his desk and write. He speaks with care and reserve. She is filled with all of the brashness and confidence of youth and believes she's just what the doctor ordered. He almost recoils under her first onslaught, but she is bright and verbal and, let it be said, attractive, and he doesn't send her away.

Soon she is discovering what every interviewer learns from every novelist: He doesn't know what anything in his books "stands for," he doesn't know where he gets his ideas, he doesn't think anything is autobiographical, and he has no idea what his "message" is. I am no novelist, but I am a professional writer, and I know two things that interviewers never believe: (1) the muse visits during, not before, the act of composition, and (2) the writer takes dictation from that place in his mind that knows what he should write next.

Leonard has a forty-ish daughter named Ariel (Lili Taylor). She wants to have a baby and hears her clock ticking. She broke up with a longtime boyfriend named Casey (Adrian Lester) because he had no interest in children, but now they are seeing each other again. They know each other so well, they talk together so readily, that it is tempting to fall into the old ways. Their relationship is portrayed almost as fully as the one between Leonard and Heather, and we realize that everyone in the movie hears a clock ticking for some reason.

The Langella performance deserves an Oscar nomination. This is the man who appeared upside-down outside a window in (the very good) *Dracula* (1979), and here he is as a reserved, solitary intellectual, twenty years a widower, confronted by a maelstrom in his life. And there is another matter, too: the question of whether they will fall in love. No, no, not have an affair: fall in love. Leonard is far past the appetite for affairs. How the movie handles this question is one of the most delicate and subtle things about it, and there is a fully clothed scene of intimacy between them that is as warm as a dozen sex scenes.

Lauren Ambrose's Heather has that superficial charm that masks deep wells of instinct and feeling, and Leonard gradually comes to see that she is more than she seems. Along the way, the film provides unusually intelligent discussion of books and careers, shows some social climbing, and depicts the daughter Ariel as conflicted: She has no objection to her father doing whatever he chooses in theory, but practice is more complicated.

The screenplay, by Fred Parnes and the director, Andrew Wagner, is based on a novel by Brian Morton, unread by me but not for long. Wagner is the man whose first film was the remarkable *The Talent Given Us* (2005), a pseudo-documentary starring his own family in a cross-country trip. One superficial similarity, or perhaps it goes deeper than that, involves the romantic feelings of older men. The movie is carefully modulated to draw us deeper and deeper into the situation and uses no contrived plot devices to superimpose plot jolts on what is, after all, a story involving four civilized people who are only trying, each in a different way, to find happiness.

Star Wars: Episode III — Revenge of the Sith ★ ★ ★ ½

PG-13, 140 m., 2005

Ewan McGregor (Obi-Wan Kenobi), Hayden Christensen (Anakin Skywalker), Natalie Portman (Padme Amidala), Ian McDiarmid (Chancellor Palpatine), Samuel L. Jackson (Mace Windu), Jimmy Smits (Senator Bail Organa), Christopher Lee (Count Dooku), Frank Oz (voice) (Yoda), Anthony Daniels (C-3PO), Kenny Baker (R2-D2). Directed by George Lucas and produced by Rick McCallum. Screenplay by Lucas.

George Lucas comes full circle in more ways than one in *Star Wars: Episode III—Revenge of the Sith*, which is the sixth and allegedly, but not necessarily, the last of the *Star Wars* movies. After *Episode II* got so bogged down in politics that it played like the Republic covered by C-Span, *Episode III* is a return to the classic space opera style that launched the series. Because the story leads up to where the original *Star Wars* began, we get to use the immemorial movie phrase, "This is where we came in."

That Anakin Skywalker abandoned the Jedi and went over to the dark side is known to all students of *Star Wars*. That his twins, Luke Skywalker and Princess Leia, would redeem the family name is also known. What we discover in *Episode III* is how and why Anakin lost his way—how a pleasant and brave young man was transformed into a dark, cloaked figure with a fearsome black metal face. As Yoda sadly puts it in his inimitable word-order: "The boy who dreamed, gone he is, consumed by Darth Vader." Unexplained is how several inches grew he in the process.

As *Episode III* opens, Anakin Skywalker (Hayden Christensen) and his friend Obi-Wan

Kenobi (Ewan McGregor) are piloting fighter crafts, staging a daring two-man raid to rescue Chancellor Palpatine (Ian McDiarmid). He has been captured by the rebel General Grievous (whose voice, by Matthew Woods, sounds curiously wheezy considering the general seems to use replacement parts). In the spirit of all the *Star Wars* movies, this rescue sequence flies in the face of logic, since the two pilots are able to board Grievous's command ship and proceed without much trouble to the ship's observation tower, where the chancellor is being held. There is a close call in an elevator shaft, but where are the guards and the security systems? And why, for that matter, does a deep space cruiser need an observation tower when every porthole opens onto the universe? But never mind.

Back within the sphere of the Jedi Council, Anakin finds that despite his heroism he will not yet be named a Jedi Master. The council distrusts Palpatine and wants Anakin to spy on him; Palpatine wants Anakin to spy on the council. Who to choose? McDiarmid has the most complex role in the movie as he plays on Anakin's wounded ego. Anakin is tempted to go over to what is not yet clearly the dark side; in a movie not distinguished for its dialogue, Palpatine is insidiously snaky in his persuasiveness.

The way Anakin approaches his choice, however, has a certain poignancy. Anakin has a rendezvous with Padme (Natalie Portman); they were secretly married in the previous film, and now she reveals she is pregnant. His reaction is that of a nice kid in a teenage comedy, trying to seem pleased while wondering how this will affect the other neat stuff he gets to do. To say that George Lucas cannot write a love scene is an understatement; greeting cards have expressed more passion.

The dialogue throughout the movie is once again its weakest point: The characters talk in what sounds like Basic English, without color, wit, or verbal delight, as if they were channeling Berlitz. The exceptions are Palpatine and, of course, Yoda, whose speech (voiced by Frank Oz) reminds me of Wolcott Gibbs's famous line about the early style of *Time* magazine: "Backward ran sentences until reeled the mind."

In many cases the actors are being filmed in front of blue screens, with effects to be added later, and sometimes their readings are so flat they don't seem to believe they're really in the middle of amazing events. How can you stand in front of exploding star fleets and sound as if you're talking on a cell phone at Starbucks? "He's worried about you," Anakin is told at one point. "You've been under a lot of stress." Sometimes the emphasis in sentences is misplaced. During the elevator adventure in the opening rescue, we hear, "Did I miss *something*?" when it should be, "Did I *miss* something?"

The dialogue is not the point, however; Lucas's characters engage in sturdy oratorical pronunciamentos and then leap into adventure. *Episode III* has more action per square minute, I'd guess, than any of the previous five movies, and it is spectacular. The special effects are more sophisticated than in the earlier movies, of course, but not necessarily more effective. The dogfight between fighters in the original *Star Wars* and the dogfight that opens this one differ in their complexity (many more ships this time, more planes of action, complex background) but not in their excitement. And although Lucas has his characters attend a futuristic opera that looks like a cross between Cirque du Soleil and an ultrasound scan of an unborn baby, if you regard the opera hall simply as a place, it's not as engaging as the saloon on Tatooine in the first movie.

The lesson, I think, is that special effects should be judged not by their complexity but by the degree that they stimulate the imagination, and *Episode III* is distinguished not by how well the effects are done, but by how amazingly they are imagined. A climactic duel on a blazing volcanic planet is as impressive, in its line, as anything in *The Lord of the Rings.* And Yoda, who began life as a Muppet but is now completely animated (like about 70 percent of the rest of what we see), was to begin with and still is the most lifelike of the *Star Wars* characters.

A word, however, about the duels fought with lightsabers. When they flashed into life with a mighty whizzing "thunk" in the first *Star Wars* and whooshed through their deadly parabolas, that was exciting. But the thrill is gone. The duelists are so well matched that saber fights go on forever before anyone is wounded, and I am still not sure how the sabers seem able to shield their bearers from incoming ammo. When it comes to great movie swordfights, Liam Neeson and Tim Roth took home the gold medal in *Rob Roy* (1995), and the lightsaber battles in *Episode III* are more like isometrics.

These are all, however, more observations than criticisms. George Lucas has achieved what few artists do, and created and populated a world of his own. His *Star Wars* movies are among the most influential, both technically and commercially, ever made. And they are fun. If he got bogged down in solemnity and theory in *Episode II: Attack of the Clones,* the Force is in a jollier mood this time, and *Revenge of the Sith* is a great entertainment.

Note: I said this is not necessarily the last of the Star Wars *movies. Although Lucas has absolutely said he is finished with the series, it is inconceivable to me that 20th Century Fox will willingly abandon the franchise, especially as Lucas has hinted that parts VII, VIII, and IX exist at least in his mind. There will be enormous pressure for them to be made, if not by him, then by his deputies.*

Stay ★ ★ ★ ½

R, 99 m., 2005

Ewan McGregor (Sam Foster), Naomi Watts (Lila Culpepper), Ryan Gosling (Henry Letham), Kate Burton (Mrs. Letham), Elizabeth Reaser (Athena), Bob Hoskins (Dr. Leon Patterson), Janeane Garofalo (Dr. Beth Levy), B. D. Wong (Dr. Ren). Directed by Marc Forster and produced by Arnon Milchan, Eric Kopeloff, and Tom Lassally. Screenplay by David Benioff.

The visual strategy in Marc Forster's *Stay* is so subtle you might miss it, but it provides a clue to the movie's secret. I will describe the strategy but not the secret. It involves transitions from one shot to the next, some subtle, some bold, all of them so agile we're not always sure what we've seen.

On a camera move, for example, an element in one shot becomes the whole of the next shot, but it's not a close-up; it's a new location. Or, as two men walk together, they pass behind pillars and it is possible, although not certain, that while out of sight they do a left-right flip. There is the matter of repeating almost unnoticed elements: Three out-of-focus spheres in the foreground, not lighted so you'd much notice them, turn up in the next shot, also out of focus, also not much noticed. And there are costume details: choices of shoes and socks, the length and style of pants.

The strategy is not underlined. The movie is facile and quick in its editing, and I'm sure another viewing would reveal transitions I missed. Accustomed to fancy footwork in modern movies, we may think Forster, his cinematographer, Roberto Schaefer, and his editor, Matt Chesse, are simply showing off: There are lots of visual flourishes without meaning in movies, and you can see dozens, maybe hundreds, in Tony Scott's *Domino.* True, they are a style and set a pace. But in *Stay,* the visuals are crucial to the movie's point of view and ultimately to its meaning.

Audiences are not always alert to styles, or they may notice them passively, not asking what function they serve. It is possible to watch an Ozu film and not register that he never moves his camera. During a Fred Astaire dance number, you may not notice that he is always shown full frame and in long takes. What Forster is doing in *Stay,* I think, is suggesting we watch the movie on two levels, although the deeper level can be glimpsed only at a tangent, passingly.

There is so much happening on the surface and in the story that we may get entirely involved up there, and Forster, in a departure from his films *Monster's Ball* and *Finding Neverland,* would be pleased if we did. The other level is beavering away in the shadows. Occasionally he'll spring a visual surprise that has a logical explanation; his hero walks through a door, for example, and seems to be undersea, and then we realize he has simply walked into a room where one wall is a very large aquarium.

But who is in this movie and what is it about? No spoilers follow. The film stars Ryan Gosling as Henry, an art student at university, who is in crisis. Asked to put out his cigarette on the subway, he stubs it out on his arm. He is seeing a university psychiatrist, but when he turns up for his appointment, a strange man is in her office. This is Sam (Ewan McGregor), who explains that he is filling in for a few weeks. Henry is angered by the substitution, walks out, returns on another day, and announces that at midnight Saturday he will kill himself.

We see more of Sam's life than Henry's. He plays chess with a blind man (Bob Hoskins). He consults a colleague (B. D. Wong). He visits

Henry's usual psychiatrist (Janeane Garofalo), who is sitting at home with the lights out, depressed. He moves within the geometric architecture of the university campus, which seems to repeat itself, and there is repeating, too, in a curious scene where the corridors and stairways are suddenly populated by twins and triplets.

Sam lives with Lila (Naomi Watts), an artist who was his patient. She's suicidal, too. At various points people make little mistakes. She calls him "Henry" instead of "Sam." Understandable; they were just discussing Henry. Henry thinks the blind chess player is his father, but Henry is clearly going mad. Henry had been dating an actress named Athena (Elizabeth Reaser); Sam visits a rehearsal where she is playing Hamlet. A female Hamlet? No: "I'm just running the lines. I play Ophelia." He follows her down a spiral staircase and trips and falls and loses her. Interesting what happens next.

When the movie is over and we know all that is to be known, it deserves some thought. The ending is an explanation, but not a solution. For a solution we have to think back through the whole film, and now the visual style becomes a guide. It is an illustration of the way the materials of life can be shaped for the purposes of the moment.

The surface story of the film then becomes more interesting than before because we know more about it. Its shape and content mean something. It is the record of how we deal with the fundamental events of life by casting them into terms we can understand: terms like what we did, and what they did, and what we did then, all arranged so they seem to add up and lead somewhere. Maybe they don't. But the mind is a machine for making them seem to. Otherwise, all would be event without form and, therefore, without meaning. How desperately we need for there to be form, and meaning.

Stealth ★ ½

PG-13, 121 m., 2005

Josh Lucas (Lieutenant Ben Gannon), Jessica Biel (Lieutenant Kara Wade), Jamie Foxx (Lieutenant Henry Purcell), Sam Shepard (Captain George Cummings), Joe Morton (Captain Dick Marshfield), Richard Roxburgh (Keith Orbit). Directed by Rob Cohen and produced by Laura Ziskin, Mike Medavoy, and Neal H. Moritz. Screenplay by W. D. Richter.

Stealth is an offense against taste, intelligence, and the noise pollution code—a dumbed-down *Top Gun* crossed with the HAL 9000 plot from *2001*. It might be of interest to you if you want to see lots of jet airplanes going real fast and making a lot of noise, and if you don't care that the story doesn't merely defy logic, but also strips logic bare, cremates it, and scatters its ashes. Here is a movie with the nerve to discuss a computer brain "like a quantum sponge" while violating Newton's laws of motion.

The plot: Navy fliers have been chosen to pilot a new generation of stealth fighter-bombers. They are Lieutenant Ben Gannon (Josh Lucas), Lieutenant Kara Wade (Jessica Biel), and Lieutenant Henry Purcell (Jamie Foxx, who in his speech on Oscar night should have thanked God this movie wasn't released while the voters were marking their ballots).

They're all aboard the aircraft carrier *Abraham Lincoln* in the Philippine Sea, under the command of Captain George Cummings (Sam Shepard, who played the test pilot Chuck Yeager in *The Right Stuff*). In a movie like this, you're asking for trouble if you remind people of *2001*, *Top Gun*, and *The Right Stuff*.

The pilots believe that three is a lucky number, because it is a prime number. One helpfully explains to the others what a prime number is; I guess they didn't get to primes at Annapolis. In a movie that uses unexplained phrases such as "quantum sponge," why not just let the characters say "prime number" and not explain it? Many audience members will assume "prime number" is another one of those pseudoscientific terms they're always thinking up for movies like this.

Captain Cummings has bad news: They're being joined by a "fourth wingman." This is a UCAV (Unmanned Combat Aerial Vehicle) controlled by a computer. The pilots are unhappy, but not so unhappy that Gannon and Wade do not feel a powerful sexual attraction, although pilots are not supposed to fraternize. At one point Gannon visits Wade's cabin, where she has laundry hanging on the line, and is nearly struck by a wet brassiere. "Pardon my C-cup," she says, a line I doubt any human female would use in such a situation.

Suddenly the pilots have to scramble for an emergency: "Three terrorist cells are about to meet in twenty-four minutes in Rangoon," Captain George tells them. Remarkable, that this information is so precise and yet so tardy. The pilots find they not only have time to take off from the aircraft carrier and fly to Burma, but also to discuss their strategy via radio once they get there. The meeting is in a building that is still under construction. Computer simulations show that if it falls over, it will kill a lot of people on the ground. Amazing what computers can do these days. However, if the building is struck from directly above, it may fall down in its own footprint.

Alas, the rocket bombs carried by the planes do not achieve the necessary penetration velocity. Lieutenant Gannon decides that if he goes into a vertical dive, he can increase the velocity. The bomb is released, he pulls out of the dive low enough for everyone in Rangoon to get a good look at his plane, and the building collapses. It looks so much like the falling towers of the World Trade Center that I felt violated by the image.

Whoops! Another emergency. Lightning strikes the UCAV, which goes nuts and starts to download songs from the Internet. "How many?" "All of them." The computer also starts to think for itself and to make decisions that contradict orders. Meanwhile, the three human pilots, having participated in a mission that destroyed a skyscraper in Burma, may be on a worldwide most-wanted list, but they're immediately sent to Thailand for R&R. This gives Gannon a chance to photograph Wade in a bikini under a waterfall, while Purcell picks up a beautiful Thai girl. Soon all four of them are having lunch, and the three pilots are discussing military secrets in front of the Thai girl, who "doesn't speak English." Beautiful Thai girls who allow themselves to be picked up by U.S. pilots almost always speak English, but never mind. It's not that Purcell is too stupid to know that trusting her is dangerous; it's that the movie is too stupid.

How stupid? Nothing happens. The girl *can't* speak English.

Next mission: A nuclear crisis in Tajikistan! A warlord has nuclear bombs. The team flies off to the "former Soviet republic," where a nuclear cloud threatens 500,000 people, and Lieutenant Wade helpfully radios that they're going to need medical attention.

Various unexpected developments lead to a situation in which Lieutenant Wade's plane crashes in North Korea while Lieutenant Gannon is diverted to Alaska (they get such great fuel mileage on these babies, they must be hybrid vehicles). Then Gannon and the UCAV fly an unauthorized mission to rescue Wade, a mission that will succeed if the North Koreans have neglected to plant land mines in the part of the DMZ that Wade must cross.

Now about Newton's laws of motion. Let me try this out on you. A plane is about to explode. The pilot ejects. The plane explodes, and flaming debris falls out of the sky and threatens to hit the pilot and the parachute. If the plane is going at Mach 1, 2, or 3, wouldn't the debris be falling miles away from the pilot's descent path? I'm glad you asked. The parachute sucks up that flaming debris like a quantum sponge.

Steamboy ★ ★

PG-13, 106–126 m., 2005

With the voices of: Anna Paquin (Ray Steam), Alfred Molina (Eddie Steam), Patrick Stewart (Lloyd Steam). Directed by Katsuhiro Otomo and produced by Shinji Komori and Hideyuki Tomioka. Screenplay by Sadayuki Murai and Katsuhiro Otomo.

Steamboy is a noisy, eventful, and unsuccessful venture into Victorian-era science fiction, animated by a modern Japanese master. It's like H. G. Wells and Jules Verne meet *Akira*. The story follows three generations of a British family involved in a technological breakthrough involving steam, which the movie considers the nineteenth-century equivalent of nuclear power. There may be possibilities here, but they're lost in the extraordinary boredom of a long third act devoted almost entirely to loud, pointless, and repetitive action.

The movie opens in 1866 with the collection of water from an ice cave; its extraordinary purity is necessary for experiments by the Steam family, which is perfecting the storage of power through steam under high pressures. Young Ray Steam (voice by Anna Paquin) is the boy hero, whose father, Eddie (Alfred Molina), and grandfather, Lloyd Steam (Patrick Stewart), are rivals in the development of the technology. One day Ray gets a package in the mail from his grandfather, its delivery followed immediately by ominous men dressed in alarming dark Victorian fashions that proclaim, "I am a sinister villain."

The box contains a steam ball, which we learn contains steam under extraordinary pressure. The ball, invented by Lloyd, is either a revolutionary power source or an infernal device that could explode at any moment, take your choice. Ray tries to escape on a peculiar invention that seems to combine the most uncomfortable experiences of riding a unicycle and being trapped in a washing machine, but is captured and taken to the headquarters of the O'Hara Foundation, which wants to control the invention and use it to power new machines of war. It goes without saying, or does it, that the O'Hara family daughter is named Scarlett.

The movie is the result of ten years of labor by Katsuhiro Otomo, whose *Akira* (1988) was the first example of Japanese anime to break through to world theatrical markets. That one created a futuristic Tokyo where a military dictatorship cannot control rampaging motorcycle gangs. The animation was state of the art, the vision was bleak, the tone was a radical departure for American audiences raised to equate animation with cute animals and fairy tales.

Otomo also wrote *Rojin Z* (1991), about a computerized machine that contains elderly patients within an exoskeleton/bed that transports, diagnoses, treats, massages, and entertains its occupants; once installed in the new Z-100 model, owners are expected never to leave, whether or not they want to.

The movie has intriguing ideas about human lives ruled by machines, which is why the technology in *Steamboy* seems promising. Otomo has reportedly been working on the film for ten years, drawing countless animation cells by hand and also using computer resources; why, with all the effort he put into the film's construction, did he neglect to go anywhere interesting with the plot?

We have hope at first, just because Otomo creates Manchester and London at the dawn of the industrial era, when steam power offered limitless possibilities and the internal combustion engine was still impractical. His machines and the interior of the O'Hara Foundation look like the ancestors of pulp sci-fi magazine covers, but without the bright colors. For reasons that don't pay off, Otomo's visuals tend toward the pale and drab. Maybe he's going for period atmosphere. I wondered at first if the movie was being projected on video, but no, Otomo wants it to look washed-out.

His plot holds promise: The evil O'Hara Foundation wants to hijack the Great Exhibition, for which Prince Albert built the Crystal Palace to showcase Britain's leadership of the industrial revolution. But the Great Exhibition was held in 1851, and if the movie is set in 1866, is the chronology off? There may have been an explanation that eluded me, this not being a question that riveted my attention at the time.

The O'Hara people want to jettison the notion of progress for peace and use the exhibition to promote its expensive new engines of war, hoping every country will buy some, go to war, and need to buy more. At this point, when the movie could potentially get its teeth into something, Otomo goes nuts with brainless action sequences in which one retro-futuristic device after another does battle, explodes, dives, surfaces, floats, opens fire, flies, attacks, defends, and so on.

Some of his ideas are promising, including a zeppelin fitted with iron claws that can lift a speeding train car from the tracks. A fearsome strategy indeed, although it would be awkward for the dirigible if the train ever went through a tunnel or under a bridge, or raced past big hard buildings close to the tracks. Other ideas are just collisions of hardware, punctuated by frantic expostulations.

It is a theory of mine that action does not equal interest. Objects endlessly in motion are as repetitive as objects forever at rest. Context is everything. Why are they moving, who wants them to move, what is at risk, what will be gained? By the end of *Steamboy* I was convinced the answers to all of these questions were: Otomo has abandoned the story and, in despair, is filling the screen with wonderfully executed but pointless and repetitive kinetic energy. Action doodles.

Note: The movie is available in a 106-minute English-dubbed version and a 126-minute Japanese version with English subtitles.

Stephanie Daley ★ ★ ★ ½

R, 92 m., 2007

Tilda Swinton (Lydie Crane), Timothy Hutton (Paul Crane), Denis O'Hare (Frank), Jim Gaffigan (Joe), Melissa Leo (Miri), Amber Tamblyn (Stephanie Daley). Directed by Hilary Brougher and produced by Sean Costello, Lynette Howell, Samara Koffler, and Jen Roskind. Screenplay by Brougher.

At a high school ski outing, a trail of blood is visible in the snow. The trail is left by Stephanie Daley, a sixteen-year-old girl, whose stillborn baby is found in a toilet. The girl claims she didn't know she was pregnant, but the "ski mom" case becomes a sensation. She is charged with murder and before her trial is sent for sessions with a forensic psychologist named Lydie Crane.

Stephanie (Amber Tamblyn) has an imperfect understanding of the realities of pregnancy. She had sex only once, at a party, with a young man who told her not to worry; he withdrew in time. Obviously, he did not. Why didn't she realize she was pregnant? It can happen. But confusing evidence suggests the baby may not have been dead at birth, although it was barely long-term enough to live. Did she kill it, or was it already dead?

The psychologist, Lydie Crane (Tilda Swinton), had a miscarriage of her own. Now she is expecting again—about as pregnant as Stephanie was. Their conversations are almost in code, with much silence. The girl is inarticulate, guilt-ridden ("I killed her with my mind"), and confused. The psychologist deals with her personal conflicts over the case. Swinton is an ideal choice for the role, because when she needs to, few actors can be more quiet, empathetically tactful.

There are courtroom scenes, but this is neither a whodunit, a what-was-done, or a moral or political argument from any position. It simply, sympathetically, sees how real life can be too complicated to match with theories.

I personally believe the body of a stillborn infant deserves respect. It should not be found in a toilet. But we learn that the psychologist herself threw away the ashes of her own stillbirth. Heartless? Depends on the thinking at the time. Scattering someone's ashes can be a loving and spiritual act. A libertarian, on the other hand, might reasonably argue that while a living baby has full human rights, a stillborn baby does not, and remains, in a sense, the property of the mother. In this film, that argument grows cloudy because it is unclear when and how the baby died.

We read about cases like this and think the mothers are monsters. If their babies are alive and found in a Dumpster, certainly they exist outside decency and morality, or their values are corrupted. But what led them to that decision? What did they know? What were they taught? What did they fear? I feel it is the responsibility of parents to raise children who know they can tell their parents anything and go to them for help. If a girl cannot tell her parents she is pregnant, something bad is likely to happen.

Yet *Stephanie Daley* goes even deeper: Did she know she was pregnant? As the psychologist struggles with this baffling girl, she feels her own powerlessness. And the movie invites us into her pity and confusion. Written and directed by Hilary Brougher, it has the courage and integrity to refuse an easy conclusion. When I saw it, some audience members said they were unhappy with the ending. What they meant was, they were unhappy about having to think about the ending.

What would a satisfactory ending be? Guilty? Innocent? Forensic revelations? We have been tutored by Hollywood to expect all the threads to be tied neatly at the end. But real life is more like this movie: Frightened and confused people are confronted with a situation they cannot understand, and those who would help them are powerless. Some cases should never come to trial because no verdict would be adequate. You are likely to be discussing this film long into the night.

Stick It ★ ★

PG-13, 105 m., 2006

Jeff Bridges (Burt Vickerman), Missy Peregrym (Haley Graham), Vanessa Lengies (Joanne), Tarah Paige (Tricia Skilken), Nikki SooHoo (Wei Wei), Maddy Curley (Mina), Kellan Lutz (Frank), John Patrick Amedori (Poot). Directed by Jessica Bendinger and produced by Gail Lyon. Screenplay by Bendinger.

Stick It uses the story of a gymnast's comeback attempt as a backdrop for overwrought visual effects, music videos, sitcom dialogue, and general pandering. The movie seems to fear that if it pauses long enough to actually be about gymnastics, the audience will grow restless. It often abandons realism, unless it is possible, which I doubt, that you can do a head-spin on a balance beam.

The movie stars Missy Peregrym as Haley, a once-promising gymnast who disqualified herself by walking away from Team USA during an important final match. She had her reasons for bailing out, but for now she's in disgrace. She spends her time back home in Plano, Texas, hanging out with teenage boys and doing insane stunts with bicycles and skateboards that involve rooftops and empty swimming pools. The cops give chase, and we get the obligatory scene where the mystery character takes off her helmet and lets down her hair, and—gasp!—it's a girl!

Haley did thousands of dollars in damage after crashing her bike through a window and is ordered by the judge to attend, on probation, the Vickerman Gymnastics Academy in Houston. This is a legendary establishment, rumored to be producing "more injuries than champions." Vickerman, played by Jeff Bridges, is a sharp-talking iconoclast with an offhand manner, but then everyone in this movie speaks in a strange, stylized, enigmatic way, and their dialogue sounds like—dialogue.

The story will be familiar to anyone who has ever seen a movie about a troubled athlete and a brilliant coach. It will also be familiar to anyone who has not. We have scenes in which the other students resent Haley for walking off Team USA, scenes where Haley rebels against Vickerman's discipline, scenes of injury and disappointment, moments of heartfelt revelation, some jealousy among the gymnasts, and finally a comeback in which, we sense, Haley probably will not walk off the floor.

All of this is well enough made, although it appears to my untrained eye that some of the better gymnastics stunts are done with CGI effects. Jessica Bendinger, the writer and director, wrote the better *Bring It On* (2000), about competing cheerleading squads.

Here she shows visual mastery but not visual judgment: She can do a lot of stuff that the movie doesn't really require, and it acts like a stylistic barrier between the audience and the emotions. With its stark red and white sets, Vickerman's looks more like a backdrop for an ad than like a working gymnasium. And the characters are rarely so spontaneous they can't find an epigrammatic way of expressing themselves. (By "epigrammatic," I mean smart-ass.)

I liked Peregrym as Haley, in part because she doesn't fit the stereotype of female gymnasts as short and underfed. I shared her anger at bird-brained judges who discount a difficult trick because a bra strap is showing. Bridges does what he can with the Vickerman role but is too good an actor to fit into such a shallow character. All through the movie, I kept thinking of Robert Towne's *Personal Best* (1982), with Mariel Hemingway as an athlete and Scott Glenn as her coach. That film has such honesty and integrity that *Stick It* seems childish by comparison.

The Strangers ★ ½

R, 90 m., 2008

Liv Tyler (Kristen McKay), Scott Speedman (James Hoyt), Gemma Ward (Dollface), Kip Weeks (Man in the Mask), Laura Margolis (Pin-Up Girl), Glenn Howerton (Mike). Directed by Bryan Bertino and produced by Doug Davison, Roy Lee, and Nathan Kahane. Screenplay by Bertino.

My mistake was to read the interview with the director. At the beginning of my review of *The Strangers,* I typed my star rating instinctively: "One star." I was outraged. I wrote: "What a waste of a perfectly good first act! And what a maddening, nihilistic, infuriating ending!" I was just getting warmed up.

And then, I dunno, I looked up the movie on IMDb, and there was a link to an interview with Bryan Bertino, the writer and director, and I went there, read it, and looked at his photo. He looked to be in his twenties. This was his first film. Bertino had been working as a grip on a peanuts-budget movie when he pitched this screenplay to Rogue Pictures and was asked to direct it. He gave a friend his grip tools and thought: "Cool, I'm never going to need this anymore! I'm never using a hammer again." Then he tells the interviewer: "I still had to buy books on how to direct."

So I thought, Bryan Bertino is a kid, this is

his first movie, and as much as I hate it, it's a competent movie that shows he has the chops to be a director. So I gave it 1½ stars instead of one. Still harsh, yes. I think a lot of audience members will walk out really angry at the ending, although it has a certain truthfulness and doesn't cheat on the situation that has been building up. The movie deserves more stars for its bottom-line craft, but all the craft in the world can't redeem its story.

Yes, Bertino can direct. He opens on a dark night in a neighborhood of deserted summer homes with two people in a car. These are Kristen (Liv Tyler) and James (Scott Speedman). They are coming from a wedding reception. They go inside James's summer home. We learn that he proposed to her, but she "isn't ready." The camera focuses on a 33 rpm turntable that, along with their Volvo, are the easiest two props I can imagine to create a 1970s period look.

I am intrigued by these people. Will they talk all night? Will they do things they'll regret forever? Will they . . . *there is a knock on the door!* Not the sound of a human hand hitting wood. The sound of something hard hitting wood. It is very loud, and it echoes. To evoke an infinitely superior film, it creates the same sense of alarm and danger as the planks do, banging against each other in *Le Fils* (*The Son*), by the Dardenne brothers.

They open the door and find a young girl. They tell her she has the wrong house. She goes and stands in the yard. And then, all night long, their sense of security is undercut by more knocks, breaking glass, scraping, smashing. The sound track is the third protagonist. After a time, Bertino creates an empty space in one of his compositions, and it attracts a . . . figure . . . that casually fills it, wearing a mournful, shroudlike mask. We will see the mask again. Also two figures wearing little-doll masks that are not sweet, but ominous. We recall the opening credits telling us, "This film is inspired by true events." Never a good sign.

Is *The Strangers* inspired by other movies? Asked by Moviesonline.ca if he was influenced "by the film" (never named), Bertino answers, as only someone young and innocent could answer: "I don't *necessarily* think that I looked at it, you know." The *necessarily* is a masterstroke. He adds: "I'm definitely influenced by, like, '70s genre stuff in general, structure wise. . . . I read *Helter Skelter* when I was, like, eleven. That was where I first started getting interested in the idea of people just walking into a house that you didn't know. I lived in a house in the middle of nowhere in Texas on this road where you could call out in the middle of the night and nobody would hear you."

There have been great movies about home invasion, like *In Cold Blood*, that made more of it than gruesome events. *The Strangers* is a well-shot film (the cinematographer is the veteran Peter Sova). It does what it sets out to do. I'm not sure that it earns the right to do it. I will say that Bertino shows the instincts and choices of a good director; I hope he gets his hands on worthier material. It's a melancholy fact that he probably couldn't have found financing if his first act had lived up to its promise. There's a market for the kind of movie that inspires the kinds of commercials and trailers that *The Strangers* inspires, ending with a chilling dialogue exchange:

"Why are you doing this to us?"

"Because you were home."

Stranger Than Fiction ★ ★ ★ ½

PG-13, 113 m., 2006

Will Ferrell (Harold Crick), Dustin Hoffman (Dr. Jules Hilbert), Maggie Gyllenhaal (Ana Pascal), Emma Thompson (Kay Eiffel), Queen Latifah (Penny Escher), Linda Hunt (Dr. Mittag-Leffler). Directed by Marc Forster and produced by Lindsay Doran. Screenplay by Zach Helm.

What a thoughtful film this is, and how thought stirring. Marc Forster's *Stranger Than Fiction* comes advertised as a romance, a comedy, a fantasy, and it is a little of all three, but it's really a fable, a "moral tale" like Eric Rohmer tells.

Will Ferrell stars, in another role showing that, like Steve Martin and Robin Williams, he has dramatic gifts to equal his comedic talent. He plays Harold Crick, an IRS agent who for years has led a sedate and ordered life. He lives in an apartment that looks like it was furnished on a fifteen-minute visit to Crate and Barrel. His wristwatch eventually tires of this existence and mystically decides to shake things up.

Harold begins to hear a voice in his head, one that is describing his own life—not in advance, but as a narrative that has just happened. He seeks help from a shrink (Linda Hunt) and, convinced he is hearing his own life narrative, seeks counsel from Jules Hilbert, a literature professor (Dustin Hoffman). Hilbert methodically checks off genres and archetypes and comes up with a list of living authors who could plausibly be writing the "narration." He misses, however, Kay Eiffel (Emma Thompson) because he decides Harold's story is a comedy, and all of her novels end in death. However, Eiffel is indeed writing the story of Harold's life. What Hilbert failed to foresee is that it ends in Harold's death. And that is the engine for the moral tale.

Meanwhile, an astonishing thing happens. Harold goes to audit the tax return of Ana Pascal, a sprightly, tattooed bakery shop owner (Maggie Gyllenhaal), and begins to think about her. Can't stop thinking. Love has never played a role in his life before. Nor does she much approve of IRS accountants.

How rare, to find a pensive film about the responsibilities we have to art. If Kay Eiffel's novel would be a masterpiece with Harold's death, does he have a right to live? On the other hand, does she have the right to kill him for her work? "You have to die. It's a masterpiece."

But life was just getting interesting for Harold. The shy, tentative way his relationship with Ana develops is quirky and sideways and well suited to Ferrell's delicate way of kidding a role. He doesn't *want* to die. On the other hand, after years of dutifully following authority, he is uncertain of his duty—and he is so meekly nice he hates to disappoint Eiffel. Harold himself has never done anything so grand as write a masterpiece.

Although the obvious cross-reference here is a self-referential Charlie Kaufman screenplay like *Adaptation,* I was reminded of another possible parallel, Melville's famous short story *Bartleby the Scrivener,* made into the 2001 movie with Crispin Glover and David Paymer. Bartleby is an office drudge who one day simply turns down a request from his boss, saying, "I would prefer not to." Harold Crick, like Bartleby, labors in a vast office shuffling papers that mean nothing to him, and one day he begins to make a series of gentle but implacable decisions.

He would prefer not to audit any more tax returns. And he would prefer not to die. But he is such a gentle and good soul that this second decision requires a lot of soul searching, and it's fascinating to watch how Hilbert and Ana participate indirectly in it, not least through some very good cookies. And what is Eiffel's preference when she finds what power she has? Her publisher has assigned an "assistant" (Queen Latifah) to force her through her writer's block, so there is pressure there, too. She chain-smokes and considers suicide.

The director, Marc Forster, whose work includes the somber (*Monster's Ball*) and the fantastical (*Finding Neverland*), here splits the difference. He shoots in a never-identified Chicago, often choosing spare and cold Mies van der Rohe buildings, and he adds quirky little graphics that show how Harold compulsively counts and sees spatial relationships.

His work with the actors seeks a low-key earnestness, and Ferrell becomes a puzzled but hopeful seeker of the right thing. Gyllenhaal and Hoffman never push him too hard. And I like the dry detachment with which both Hoffman and Thompson consider literature, which is conceived in such passion and received with such academic reserve. Alas, Forster never finds the right note for Latifah's character, who may not be necessary.

Stranger Than Fiction is a meditation on life, art, romance, and the kinds of responsibility we have. Such an uncommonly intelligent film does not often get made. It could have pumped up its emotion to blockbuster level, but that would be false to the premise, which requires us to enter the lives of these specific quiet, sweet, worthy people. The ending is a compromise—but it isn't the movie's compromise. It belongs entirely to the characters and is their decision. And that made me smile.

Strength and Honour ★ ★ ½

R, 104 m., 2007

Michael Madsen (Sean Kelleher), Vinnie Jones (Smasher O'Driscoll), Patrick Bergin (Papa Boss), Richard Chamberlain (Denis O'Leary), Luke Whelton (Michael Kelleher), Michael Rawley

(Chaser McGrath), Gail Fitzpatrick (Mammy). Directed, produced, and written by Mark Mahon.

Within the first five minutes, we know precisely how *Strength and Honour* is going to end. The rest is in the details, which are sometimes pretty good. The movie is about a boxer named Sean Kelleher who retires forever from the ring after killing his brother-in-law in a sparring match, and returns only to win the money for a $250,000 heart operation for his young son.

Wait, we're not finished yet. How could he win so much money for his first bout? Because he is fighting bare-knuckled for the title of King of the Travelers (also known as gypsies). His arch-foe in the championship bout is a vicious, mean, hard man named Smasher O'Driscoll, played by the British soccer star Vinnie Jones, but what do you think the odds are that Sean will lose his fight and his son will die? I should explain that this all takes place in County Cork and stars Michael Madsen, who is a good deal gentler and more loving than you may remember him from *Kill Bill.*

The movie is much about the travelers on a hilltop outside town. Sean is not a traveler, but after his wife dies and he is forced to sell their house to pay medical bills, he buys a caravan and moves in next door to the earth mother Mammy (Gail Fitzpatrick), whose son Chaser (Michael Rawley) lives nearby and begins to think of Sean as a father figure. Sean's financial crisis in the movie, by the way, should be reported to Michael Moore; Irish medical care seems mighty expensive.

This is melodrama mixed with formula and a great deal of tear-jerking, but Madsen plays the character straight down the center and has considerable authority; he doesn't ask for sympathy, doesn't accept favors lightly, says nothing when the travelers accept his $10,000 deposit on the prizefight, pocket the money, and tell him he's not qualified because he's not of the blood. He needs the $250,000 too much to complain. This and other matters are settled among the gypsies around a small bonfire, which provides warm, flickering light for many a conversation. Eventually he's allowed to fight and in the final bout faces the fearsome, animalistic Smasher, who knocks out people just for knocking at his door.

Sharp eyes among you are wondering how they have dollars in Ireland. They do not. They had the Irish pound (in Gaelic, the punt) until they switched to euros in 2002. Why nobody in the film knows this is a mystery; less so perhaps with Sean, who is an American who moved to Cork with his Irish wife.

There is some nice character work in the movie. Richard Chamberlain plays the manager of a boxing gym and Sean's manager and adviser. Michael Rawley is persuasive as the young acolyte. And Gail Fitzpatrick steals scenes with the sheer ferocity of her passion for justice; it's pretty clear that she and her neighbor Sean may be linking up in a double-wide before long.

But the movie, written and directed by first-timer Mark Mahon, follows so resolutely in the footsteps of so many, many other sporting movies that we're way ahead of the story arc. One novelty is the violence of the bare-knuckle fights, which take place within a ring of savagely shouting men, although it's a puzzle why the prize fight is less well-attended than the opening bouts. If you want to see a predictable boxing movie with a kinder, gentler Michael Madsen who's really quite convincing, here's your movie. But I'd like to see this side of Madsen developed in a better screenplay.

Subject Two ★ ★

NO MPAA RATING, 93 m., 2006

Christian Oliver (Adam), Dean Stapleton (Vick), Courtney Mace (Kate), Jurgen Jones (Hunter), Thomas Buesch (The Professor). Directed by Philip Chidel and produced by Chidel, Christian Oliver, and Dean Stapleton. Screenplay by Chidel.

Having flunked his final exam on medical ethics, a student named Adam gets an e-mail asking him to venture to a remote, snowbound cabin where, his correspondent promises, he will share in revolutionary advances in medical science. Adam (Christian Oliver) takes the bait, is met by a young woman, driven to a remote mountain road, handed cross-country skis, and told he can find the doctor's cabin by following the red ribbons on the trees. After a long, cold journey, he finds the cabin, occupied by young Dr. Vick (Dean Stapleton).

Adam discovers (although not before being choked to death, left outside to freeze, and then brought back to life) that Dr. Vick has invented a serum that offers immortality. Death has no dominion in the mountain cabin, where Adam will be killed several more times (shot, hit by a snowmobile, etc.) and brought back to life several more times. These transitions are necessary because when Vick gets things wrong, it's necessary to kill Adam and leave him dead while making improvements.

I was reminded of *Scream and Scream Again,* in which every time the victim woke up, another body part was missing. In *Subject Two,* it doesn't much matter. There's not even anything special about the brain, apparently, and you don't need it to think. But Adam complains bitterly to Vick that he cannot feel: He lacks both physical and emotional sensations, he says, but since he feels so much anger about that, he must not be quite correct. Still, there's one consolation: He doesn't have those migraines anymore.

Subject Two is a horror film crossed with a workshop on the theory and practice of an earlier doctor, Frankenstein. When you bring the dead to life, what do you have then? Something that is alive? Something that is dead but can walk and talk and think? Would you want to be immortal if you had to keep being killed all the time? Is life worth living for the undead?

These questions play out in a movie that for most of its length involves just the two actors. One problem, for me, is that Vick doesn't seem particularly demented, and Adam doesn't seem particularly disturbed. The usual ramping up of emotions in a horror film doesn't take place; too much of the film consists of the characters using normal speaking voices, however distraught. One promising development, however, is that a man who was apparently Subject One is buried up to his neck out in the yard and apparently is dead. Seeing him planted with tubes going into him, I was reminded for the second time in a month of *Motel Hell,* the movie where Farmer Vincent planted the residents of his motel and used them as a cash crop.

Subject Two, written and directed by Philip Chidel and produced by him along with his two stars, is a good-looking movie, well-acted, but the material seems curiously inert. Even with some surprises at the end, we're left with too little desperation and too much conversation. There are big ideas nibbling around the edges of the screenplay, but the movie seems underwhelmed by its own startling material. There is, however, an idea here that's intriguing: If you had immortality, would you be begging someone to kill you? Can life be too much of a good thing?

Sunshine ★ ★ ★

R, 107 m., 2007

Cillian Murphy (Capa), Chris Evans (Mace), Rose Byrne (Cassie), Michelle Yeoh (Corazon), Hiroyuki Sanada (Kaneda), Cliff Curtis (Searle), Troy Garity (Harvey), Benedict Wong (Trey). Directed by Danny Boyle and produced by Andrew Macdonald. Screenplay by Alex Garland.

As a permanent winter settles upon Earth, a spaceship is sent on a desperate mission to drop a nuclear device into the sick sun and "reignite" it. To name the ship *Icarus I* seems like asking for trouble in two ways, considering the fate of the original Icarus and the numeral that ominously leaves room for a sequel. Indeed, the first ship disappears. As *Sunshine* opens, the *Icarus II,* with seven astronauts on board, is approaching Mercury, protected by a shield that keeps it from incinerating.

Considering that the movie is set only fifty years in the future, the sun seems to be dying several billion years prematurely, especially in a "hard" (i.e., quasi-plausible) science fiction film. Man, am I glad I didn't go off on a rant about that before learning that the film's science adviser, Dr. Brian Cox of CERN (Conseil Europeen pour le Recherche Nucleaire [European Laboratory for Particle Physics]), thought of it, too.

The sun is not "dying in the normal sense," IMDb.com reports, but in the Cox scenario "has instead been 'infected' with a 'Q-ball'—a supersymmetric nucleus left over from the big bang . . . that is disrupting the normal matter. This is a theoretical particle that scientists at CERN are currently trying to confirm—the film's bomb is meant to blast the Q-ball to its constituent parts, which will then naturally decay, allowing the sun to return to normal."

I'll buy that. Blasting a Q-ball to its constituent parts sounds normal to me, but then I read every sci-fi magazine published during my adolescence, and my hero was John W. Campbell Jr., editor of *Astounding/Analog*, who insisted his fiction not be preposterous but sensible and possible, such as a mission to the sun to blast a Q-ball to pieces.

But enough about me. What about the Q-ball? It's a "non-topological soliton," Wikipedia explains before grumbling in a related article that "it is not easy to define precisely what a soliton is." Don't you love this stuff? Isn't it better than a lot of analysis of the psychological interactions among the crew? The movie was written by the sci-fi novelist Alex Garland, whose *28 Days Later* made a scary film, and directed by Danny Boyle, whose work ranges widely from the world's filthiest toilet (in *Trainspotting*) to a young boy who chats with the saints (in *Millions*).

But enough about them. Perhaps I skated too quickly over those psychological interactions. There is a subgenre that assumes that when a crew is shut up in a spaceship in utter isolation, they will start to get on each other's nerves. This would seem to be a waste of time aboard the *Icarus II,* since it's essentially a kamikaze mission; the crew members must presumably share the fate of the Q-ball and be blasted into their own constituent parts, but the difference is, the Q-ball likes it.

The interactions are the weakest elements in *Sunshine,* which is strongest when it focuses on the sheer enormity of the mission and its consequences. Sean Penn is needed on board to utter "Awesome!"

One crew member asks the onboard computer to let him see what the sun really looks like, and the computer's answer is a variation on kids warning each other that staring at the sun can make you go blind.

This is even truer when you are millions of miles closer to the sun, unprotected by an atmosphere and wearing only Ray-Bans.

I don't want to reveal too much of the plot, but there is a nice twist, on the way past Mercury, when they pick up a distress signal from, yes, *Icarus I.* As John W. Campbell Jr. would have known, the *last* thing you want to do while passing Mercury is respond to a distress signal from a ship that should not be there and—well, anyway, they do, which leads to trouble, but also leads to a very effective scene dealing with how long the human body might be able to survive in the cold of outer space (which, as the good doctor Isaac Asimov once explained, is longer than you might think).

The actors (Michelle Yeoh, Cillian Murphy, Chris Evans, Troy Garity, Rose Byrne, Cliff Curtis, Benedict Wong, and Hiroyuki Sanada) are effective by trying not to be too effective; they almost all play professional astronaut/scientists, and not action-movie heroes. The design of the ship itself is convincing; it looks like the inside of a computer used as the bunkhouse at a boys' camp. The special effects in outer space are convincing and remorseless. The drummed-up suspense at the end is not essential, since Boyle and Garland seem more interested in the metaphysics of the voyage; Tarkovsky's *Solaris* demonstrated that if you go all the way with the implications of such a situation, it's more interesting than using plot devices.

So anyway, younger girls won't like this picture, unless they know what happens under an automobile hood. Younger boys won't like it because the only thing that's possibly going to blow up real good is the sun. But science fiction fans will like it, and brainiacs, and those who sometimes look at the sky and think, man, there's a lot going on up there, and we can't even define precisely what a soliton is.

Superbad ★ ★ ★ ½

R, 112 m., 2007

Jonah Hill (Seth), Michael Cera (Evan), Christopher Mintz-Plasse (Fogell), Seth Rogen (Officer Michaels), Bill Hader (Officer Slater), Martha MacIsaac (Becca), Emma Stone (Jules). Directed by Greg Mottola and produced by Judd Apatow and Shauna Robertson. Screenplay by Seth Rogen and Evan Goldberg.

Superbad is a four-letter raunch-a-rama with a heart and an inordinate interest in other key organs. It is autobiographical, I suspect, inspired not just by the lives of the cowriters, Seth Rogen and Evan Goldberg, who named the two leads after themselves, but possibly by millions of other teenagers. The movie is astonishingly foul-mouthed, but in a fluent, confident way where the point isn't the dirty words, but the flow and rhythm, and the deep, sad yearning they represent.

The movie involves best friends Seth (Jonah Hill) and Evan (Michael Cera), who have been inseparable in high school mainly because they were equally unpopular, and now face the ordeal of attending different colleges. It is three weeks until the end of the high school year, bringing to mind the ancient truism that if you haven't had sex yet and you don't have it soon, you will never have had sex in high school. Such deprivation used to be commonplace; I am of the opinion that only about two members of the Urbana High School graduating class of 1960 had experienced sex, but I'll double-check at our next reunion. I will say, though, that at the end of senior year, third base was seeing a lot of traffic.

Seth is the pudgy, curly-haired one, and Evan is thin and has worried eyes. They have a sidekick named Fogell (Christopher Mintz-Plasse), who is so unpopular he is unpopular even with them. They all feel lust for every girl in the school but are so stuck for conversation that sometimes they simply say what time it is, as if they've been asked. To their wonderment, Seth, Evan, and even Fogell are invited to a party on the last night by the uber-popular Jules (Emma Stone), who belatedly explains that it's not a BYO party, but a BYOAEE party (bring your own and everybody else's).

Their attempts to buy booze while underage are more bizarre than some I have witnessed, involving Fogell's production of an ID card claiming he is "McLovin." And they discover that being the guys who bring the booze is a powerful deterrent to unpopularity. (Note: Underage drinking is *wrong.*) Jules is very happy to see the three friends and their brown paper bags, and Evan is amazed that even the fragrant Becca (Martha MacIsaac) has a smile for him and lots else.

To be sure, the lads are not seeking perfect love. They have heard about girls who get drunk and sleep with the wrong guy, and their modest ambition is simply to be the wrong guy. (Note: There is a thin line between being the wrong guy and being a criminal.) Fogell, for that matter, would be happy to even be the *wrong* wrong guy. (Note: Let's stop these notes and make a blanket announcement: This movie was made by professionals. Do not attempt any of this behavior yourself.)

But back to Fogell. What strange ability do teenagers have to always choose the school's future millionaire brainiacs and call them by their last names? For Fogell, poor wretch, there is nothing left in life but to found Microsoft, so to speak. The actor in the role, Christopher Mintz-Plasse, is an actual high-schooler who got the job at a casting call, and it may be a star maker. I am informed by *Superbad* expert David Plummer: "There are already T-shirts being sold with 'I Am McLovin' printed on them."

Anyway, two cops (Bill Hader and coauthor Seth Rogen, in what I assume is a *non*autobiographical role) bust the party, and so original is this film that they are not the usual bullies, but young enough that when a door opens upon the likes of Jules and Becca and the brown paper bags, they begin to lean eagerly over the doorsill.

The movie reminded me a little of *National Lampoon's Animal House,* except that it's more mature, as all movies are. It has that unchained air of getting away with something. In its very raunchiness it finds truth, because if you know nothing about sex, how can you be tasteful and sophisticated on the subject?

In its treatment of adolescent sexual yearning, *Superbad* remembers not only the agony but the complete absence of the ecstasy. I remember in eighth grade, some kid asked how long you could entertain an impure thought before it got upgraded from a venial to a mortal sin. "There aren't rules for things like that," the sister explained, "but I'd say that after five seconds, you're asking for it." The kid and his buddy went down to his basement to study his dad's collection of *Playboys*, and he got a stopwatch and had his buddy punch him in the arm every four seconds.

Superman Returns ★ ★

PG-13, 140 m., 2006

Brandon Routh (Superman/Clark Kent), Kate Bosworth (Lois Lane), James Marsden (Richard White), Frank Langella (Perry White), Eva Marie Saint (Martha Kent), Parker Posey (Kitty

Kowalski), Sam Huntington (Jimmy Olsen), Kevin Spacey (Lex Luthor). Directed by Bryan Singer and produced by Jon Peters and Singer. Screenplay by Michael Dougherty and Dan Harris.

It's no fun being Superman. Your life is a lie, there's nobody you can confide in, you're in love but can't express it, and you're on call twenty-four hours a day. But it can be fun being in a Superman movie. The original *Superman* (1978) was an exuberance of action and humor because Christopher Reeve could play the character straight and let us know he was kidding.

Superman II (1980) was just about as good, but *Superman III* (1983) and *Superman IV* (1987) were disappointments, and then the series disappeared for nineteen years. Now the Man of Steel is back in Bryan Singer's *Superman Returns,* which, like its hero, spends a lot of time dead in the water.

This is a glum, lackluster movie in which even the big effects sequences seem dutiful instead of exhilarating. The newsroom of the *Daily Planet,* filled with eccentricity and life in the earlier movies, now seems populated by corporate drones. Jimmy Olsen, the copy boy, such a brash kid, seems tamed and clueless. Lois Lane (Kate Bosworth) has lost her dash and pizzazz, and her fiancé, Richard White (James Marsden), regards her like a deer caught in the headlights. Even the editor, Perry White (Frank Langella), comes across less like a curmudgeon, more like an efficient manager.

One problem is with the casting. Brandon Routh lacks charisma as Superman, and I suppose as Clark Kent he isn't supposed to have any. Routh may have been cast because he looks a little like Reeve, but there are times when he looks more like an action figure; were effects used to make him seem built from synthetics? We remember the chemistry between Christopher Reeve and Margot Kidder (Lois Lane) in the original Superman movie, and then observe how their counterparts are tongue-tied in this one. If they had a real romance (and they did), has it left them with nothing more than wistful looks and awkward small talk?

It's strange how little dialogue the title character has in the movie. Clark Kent is monosyllabic, and Superman is microsyllabic. We learn Superman was away for five years on a mission to the remains of his home planet, Krypton, and in the meantime Lois got herself a boyfriend and a little son, played by Tristan Lake Leabu, who mostly stares at people like a beta version of Damien, the kid from *The Omen.* Now Superman and (coincidentally) Clark have returned, Clark gets his old job, and Lex Luthor (Kevin Spacey) is out of prison and plotting to rule the earth.

Lex's plan: use crystals from Krypton to raise up a new continent in the mid-Atlantic and flood most of the surface of the populated world. Then he'll own all the real estate. Location, location, location. Alas, the craggy landscape he produces couldn't be loved by a mountain goat and won't be habitable for a million years, but never mind. Spacey plays Luthor as sour and sadistic; he has no fun with the role, nor do we.

As for Superman, he's a one-trick pony. To paraphrase Archimedes: Give me a lever and a place to stand, and I will move the universe. Superman doesn't need the lever or the place to stand, but as he positions himself in midair, straining to lift an airplane or a vast chunk of rock, we reflect that these activities aren't nearly as cinematic as what Batman and Spider-Man get up to. Watching Superman straining to hold a giant airliner, I'm wondering: Why does he strain? Does he have his limits? Would that new Airbus be too much for him? What about if he could stand somewhere?

Superman is vulnerable to one, and only one, substance: Kryptonite. He knows this. We know this. Lex Luthor knows this. Yet he has been disabled by Kryptonite in every one of the movies. Does he think Lex Luthor would pull another stunt without a supply on hand? Why doesn't he take the most elementary precautions? How can a middle-aged bald man stab the Man of Steel with Kryptonite?

Now about Lois's kid. We know who his father is, and Lois knows, and I guess the kid knows, although he calls Richard his daddy. But why is nothing done with this character? He sends a piano flying across a room, but otherwise he just stares with big, solemn eyes, like one of those self-sufficient little brats you can't get to talk. It would have been fun to give Superman a bright, sassy child, like one of the Spy Kids, and make him a part of the plot.

There is, I suppose, a certain bottom line of

competence in *Superman Returns,* and superhero fans will want to see the movie just for its effects, its plot outrages, and its moments of humor. But when the hero, his alter ego, his girlfriend, and the villain all seem to lack any joy in being themselves, why should we feel joy at watching them?

Surfwise ★ ★ ★

R, 93 m., 2008

A documentary directed and narrated by Doug Pray and produced by Graydon Carter, Tommy Means, Matthew Weaver, and Jonathan Paskowitz.

Surfwise sounds, of course, like a surfing documentary. It contains surfers and surfing all right, but in fact it's about the strange and problematical Paskowitz family, "the first family of surfing." We meet Dorian "Doc" Paskowitz at eighty-five years old, doing exercises in the nude and then providing a full body inventory: arthritis, muscular degeneration, but nothing that keeps him from surfing. "And I don't take a single pill!" he boasts. This from a 1940s graduate of the Stanford Medical School.

Young Dr. Paskowitz was on a standard post-college career track, I guess, through two failed marriages. Then he sold everything, went on a quest for meaning, found that he loved surfing more than anything else, introduced the sport to Israel, and took to himself a wife named Juliette, with whom he had eight sons and a daughter. These eleven people lived a nomadic life together in a twenty-four-foot camper during the years when the kids were growing up.

We see the campers—there were three, all purchased used, all the same size. A little crowded for two people. Not for the Paskowitz family. As Doc drove from one surfing mecca to another, they crowded in the back, slept together "like puppies," had to listen to their parents make loud, energetic love every single night, ate a lot of gruel and organic soups, and had just about enough clothing to muster eight clothed children, but not always nine. There was nothing at all like formal education.

What are we to make of this existence? Doc sees himself as a messiah of surfing, clean living, and healthy exercise. We might be more inclined to see him as a narcissistic monster, ruling his big family with an iron fist. Sounds like fun, driving from one beach to another, unless you're crowded in the back of the camper with eight other kids and not much of a view. One son recalls the day he discovered other people had eggs for breakfast.

Doc finally found a more stable way to support his family by starting a surfing camp near San Diego. Graydon Carter, editor of *Vanity Fair* and one of the producers of this film, was an early camper. The Paskowitz Surfing Camp inspired devotion, although one of Doc's children after another drifted away from the camper "home." Doc saw each bail-out as treachery.

Remarkably, the film's director, Doug Pray, has been able to track down each and every Paskowitz child, and he weaves their memories together with old home movies, still photos, and news clippings to create an evocative portrait of their lives. The kids are no more screwed up than any other nine kids—maybe less so. They have survived the absence of formal education. One says, "I love my father, but I don't understand him." And at the end they all bury their differences and gather for a family reunion in Hawaii (staged at least in part for the camera, one suspects). In the center of everything, there's Doc, his weather-beaten skin now a deep bronze, and his wife, Juliette, kissing and hugging and looking completely serene about the lives they built for themselves and their children.

Sweeney Todd: The Demon Barber of Fleet Street ★ ★ ★ ★

R, 117 m., 2007

Johnny Depp (Sweeney Todd), Helena Bonham Carter (Mrs. Nellie Lovett), Alan Rickman (Judge Turpin), Timothy Spall (Beadle Bamford), Sacha Baron Cohen (Adolfo Pirelli), Jayne Wisener (Johanna), Jamie Campbell Bower (Anthony Hope), Edward Sanders (Toby), Laura Michelle Kelly (Beggar Woman). Directed by Tim Burton and produced by John Logan, Walter Parkes, Laurie MacDonald, and Richard D. Zanuck. Screenplay by John Logan, based on the musical by Stephen Sondheim and Hugh Wheeler, adapted from the play by Christopher Bond.

For many a poor orphan lad
The first square meal he ever had
Was a hot meat pie made out of his dad
From Sweeney Todd the Barber.

Tim Burton's film adaptation of *Sweeney Todd: The Demon Barber of Fleet Street* smacks its lips at the prospect of such a meal, and so it should. In telling this story, half-measures will avail him nothing. It is the bloodiest musical in stage history, now become the bloodiest in film history, and it isn't a jolly romp either, but a dark revenge tragedy with heartbreak, mayhem, and bloody good meat pies.

But we know that going in and are relieved that Burton has played true to the material. Here is one scenario that is proof against a happy ending. It has what is much better, a satisfactory mixed ending, in which what must happen, does. Along the way, with merciless performances by Johnny Depp, Helena Bonham Carter, and Alan Rickman; a brooding production design by Dante Ferretti; and the dark shadows of Dariusz Wolski's cinematography, it allows Burton to evoke the nineteenth-century London of Henry Mayhew's *London Labour and the London Poor,* which reported on the dregs of London and greatly influenced Charles Dickens. The worst you've heard about Calcutta would have been an improvement on London poverty in those days.

And yet there is an exhilaration in the very fiber of the film because its life force is so strong. Its heroes, or antiheroes, have been wounded to the quick, its villains are vile and heartless, and they all play on a stage that rules out decency and mercy. The acting is so good that it enlists us in the sordid story, which even contains a great deal of humor—macabre, to be sure. As a feast for the eyes and the imagination, *Sweeney Todd* is—well, I was going to say, even more satisfying than a hot meat pie made out of your dad.

The story: In London years earlier lived a barber named Benjamin Barker (Johnny Depp) and his sweet young wife and child, and he loved them. But the vile Judge Turpin (Alan Rickman) sentenced Barker on trumped-up charges and transported him to Australia, meanwhile capturing the wife and child. Turpin ravishes the wife, destroying her life, and the girl, Johanna (Jayne Wisener), grows up to become the judge's ward and prisoner.

As the film proper opens, Benjamin has escaped from prison down under and sails into London in the company of young Anthony Hope (Jamie Campbell Bower). He races through the streets to his former barbershop, where the landlady is still the dark-eyed beauty Mrs. Lovett (Helena Bonham Carter), who sells the worst meat pies in London. She tells him about the fate of his family. He moves upstairs to his former barbershop, now a ruin, changes his name to Sweeney Todd, and sets up in business again. But so deep is his rage that he makes an architectural improvement: a sliding chute that will drop his customers straight into the basement after he slits their throats, so Mrs. Lovett can cut them up and bake them into her pies. Now she offers the meatiest and most succulent meat pies in London; business booms, and sometimes satisfied customers go upstairs for a haircut and a quick recycling.

Burton fashions his musical in what can almost be described as an intimate style. No platoons of dancers in London squares, as in *Oliver!* This is a London of narrow alleys, streets shadowed by overhangs, close secrets. The Stephen Sondheim songs don't really lend themselves to full-throated performance, although that has been the practice on the stage. They are more plot-driven, confessional, anguished. Depp and Bonham Carter do their own singing, and very well, too, and as actors they use the words to convey meaning as well as melody. There are also star turns by Sacha Baron Cohen, as the rival Italian barber Pirelli, whose singing career ends dramatically rather early in the film. And by Rickman as the judge and the invaluable Timothy Spall as Beadle Bamford, his flunky. And by the barber's daughter, Jayne Wisener, and his fellow traveler, Jamie Campbell Bower, who become lovers and provide some consolation after the last throat has been slit.

To an unusual degree, *Sweeney Todd* works on a quasi-realistic level and not as a musical fantasy. That's not to say we're to take it as fact, but that we can at least accept it on its own terms without the movie winking at us. It combines some of Tim Burton's favorite elements: the fantastic, the ghoulish, the bizarre, the unspeakable, the romantic; he finds a perfect instrument in Johnny Depp, an actor he has worked with since *Edward Scissorhands*. Helena Bonham Carter may be Burton's inamorata, but apart from that, she is perfectly cast, not as a vulgar fishwife type, but as a petite beauty with dark, sad eyes and a pouting mouth and a persistent fantasy that she and the barber will someday settle by the seaside. Not bloody likely.

Syriana ★ ★ ★ ★

R, 126 m., 2005

George Clooney (Robert Barnes), Matt Damon (Bryan Woodman), Jeffrey Wright (Bennett Holiday), Chris Cooper (Jimmy Pope), William Hurt (Stan Goff), Mazhar Munir (Wasim), Tim Blake Nelson (Danny Dalton), Amanda Peet (Julie Woodman), Christopher Plummer (Dean Whiting), Alexander Siddig (Prince Nasir), Akbar Kurtha (Prince Meshal). Directed by Stephen Gaghan and produced by Jennifer Fox, Georgia Kacandes, and Michael Nozik. Screenplay by Gaghan, based on the book by Robert Baer.

Syriana is an endlessly fascinating movie about oil and money, America and China, traders and spies, the Persian Gulf states and Texas, reform and revenge, bribery and betrayal. Its interlocking stories come down to one thing: There is less oil than the world requires, and that will make some people rich and others dead. The movie seems to take sides, but take a step back and look again. It finds all of the players in the oil game corrupt and compromised, and even provides a brilliant speech in defense of corruption by a Texas oil man (Tim Blake Nelson). This isn't about Left and Right but about Have and Have Not.

The movie begins with one of the Gulf states signing a deal to supply its oil to China. This comes as a strategic defeat for Connex, a Texas-based oil company. At the same time, an obscure oil company named Killen signs a deal to drill for oil in Kazakhstan. Connex announces a merger with Killen, to get its hands on the oil, but the merger inspires a Justice Department investigation, and . . .

Let's stop right there. The movie's plot is so complex we're not really supposed to follow it; we're supposed to be surrounded by it. Since none of the characters understands the whole picture, why should we? If the movie shook out into good guys and bad guys, we'd be the good guys, of course. Or if it was a critique of American policy, we might be the bad guys. But what if everybody is a bad guy because good guys don't even suit up to play this game? What if a CIA agent brings about two assassinations and tries to prevent another one, and is never sure precisely whose policies he is really carrying out?

What if . . . well, here's a possibility the movie doesn't make explicit, but let me try it out on you. There is a moment when a veteran Washington oil analyst points out that while Kazakhstan has a lot of oil, none of it is where Killen has drilling rights. Yet Killen is undoubtedly shipping oil. Is it possible the Chinese are buying oil in the Gulf, shipping it to Kazakhstan, and selling it to the United States through Killen?

I bring up that possibility because I want to suggest the movie's amoral complexity without spoiling its surprises. *Syriana* is a movie that suggests Congress can hold endless hearings about oil company profits and never discover the answer to anything, because the real story is so labyrinthine that no one—not oil company executives, not Arab princes, not CIA spies, not traders in Geneva—understands the whole picture.

The movie has a lot of important roles and uses recognizable actors to help us keep everything straight. Even then, the studio e-mailed critics a helpful guide to the characters. I didn't look at it. Didn't want to. I liked the way I experienced the film: I couldn't explain the story, but I never felt lost in it. I understood who, what, when, where, and why, but not how they connected. That was how I wanted to relate to it. It created sympathy for individual characters in their specific situations without dictating what I was supposed to think about the big picture.

Some of the characters I cared about included Robert Barnes (George Clooney), a veteran CIA field agent; Bryan Woodman (Matt Damon), a trader based in Geneva; Jimmy Pope (Chris Cooper), who runs Killen; Dean Whiting (Christopher Plummer), a well-connected Washington lawyer whose firm is hired to handle the political implications of the merger; Bennett Holiday (Jeffrey Wright), assigned by Whiting to do "due diligence" on the deal, by which is meant that diligence that supports the merger; Prince Nasir (Alexander Siddig), who sold the rights to the Chinese; his younger brother Prince Meshal (Akbar Kurtha), who is backed by those who do not want Nasir to inherit the throne; and the mysterious Stan, played by William Hurt as someone who is keeping a secret from the rest of the movie.

Already I regret listing all of these names. You now have little tic-tac-toe designs on your eyeballs. *Syriana* is exciting, fascinating, absorbing, diabolical, and really quite brilliant, but I'm afraid it inspires reviews that are not helpful. The more you describe it, the more you miss the point. It is not a linear progression from problem to solution. It is all problem. The audience enjoys the process, not the progress. We're like athletes who get so wrapped up in the game we forget about the score.

A recent blog item coined a term like "hyperlink movie" to describe plots like this. (I would quote the exact term, but irony of ironies, I've lost the link.) The term describes movies in which the characters inhabit separate stories, but we gradually discover how those in one story are connected to those in another. *Syriana* was written and directed by Stephen Gaghan, who won an Oscar for his screenplay for *Traffic,* another hyperlink movie. A lot of Altman films, such as *Nashville* and *Short Cuts,* use the technique. Also, recently, *Crash* and *Nine Lives.*

In a hyperlink movie, the motives of one character may have to be reinterpreted after we meet another one. Consider the Damon character. His family is invited to a party at the luxurious Spanish villa of the Gulf oil sheik whose sons are Nasir and Meshal. At the party, Damon's son dies by accident. The sheik awards Damon's firm a $100 million contract. "How much for my other son?" he asks. This is a brutal line of dialogue and creates a moment trembling with tension. Later, Damon's wife (Amanda Peet) accuses him of trading on the life of his son. Well, he did take the deal. Should he have turned it down because his son died in an accident? What are Damon's real motives, anyway?

I think *Syriana* is a great film. I am unable to make my reasons clear without resorting to meaningless generalizations. Individual scenes have fierce focus and power, but the film's overall drift stands apart from them. It seems to imply that these sorts of scenes occur, and always have and always will. The movie explains the politics of oil by telling us to stop seeking an explanation. Just look at the behavior. In the short run, you can see who wants oil and how they're trying to get it. In the long run, we're out of oil.

The Syrian Bride ★ ★ ★

NO MPAA RATING, 94 m., 2006

Hiam Abbass (Amal), Makram Khoury (Hammed), Clara Khoury (Mona). Directed by Eran Riklis and produced by Bettina Brokemper, Antoine de Clermont-Tonnerre, Michael Eckelt, and Riklis. Screenplay by Suha Arraf and Riklis.

The Syrian Bride takes place at such a remote corner of the Golan Heights that when an Israeli official refers to it as a "military outpost," a Syrian scoffs at its ramshackle guardhouse and token military contingent. This obscure border crossing is crucial, however, to the future of Mona (Clara Khoury), who hopes to cross from Israel into Syria and be married. Her problem is that Syria considers her to already be in Syria, and Israel considers her to be in Israel. How can she cross from a place one side says does not exist to a place the other side says does not exist?

If *The Syrian Bride* seems vaguely familiar, it is because the same actress, Clara Khoury, starred in the 2004 film *Rana's Wedding,* playing a bride whose wedding is endangered by red tape at the checkpoint between Jerusalem and the Palestinian settlement of Ramallah. Only in the Middle East does a romantic comedy star specialize in border crossings. Odd, too, that in both cases romance has little to do with it; in *The Syrian Bride,* Mona is entering an arranged marriage with a Syrian soap opera star she's never met.

There is a note of gloom in the opening scenes of *The Syrian Bride,* because after Mona crosses into Syria she can never return to Israel and "will never see her family again." True, she will never see them again by crossing into Israel, but there are such things as airplane flights from both Syria and Israel to perfectly pleasant destinations that will welcome them both, and since the soap opera star presumably can afford the tickets, I was not in tears.

What is real is that these personal lives have become unmanageable because of the political positions of the two nations. Mona gets her passport stamped by the Israelis and then crosses to the Syrian checkpoint, which refuses to accept the passport because it has an Israeli stamp even though, the Syrian says, she has not come from Israel at all, but from Syria. Can she get the stamp whited out? No, because the Israelis require it for her to leave the country.

Meanwhile, the soap opera star's intended bride and his relatives wait in the burning sun on one side of the border, and her father and her family wait on the other. Their situation is more complex because her father has just been released by Israel as a political prisoner, and the terms of his parole forbid him to be this close to the border. Theoretically, he could be put back in jail, but an Israeli police official's shrug is the sort of gesture that makes life possible at all in such a situation.

Like many recent films from this part of the world, including *Rana's Wedding* and the 2006 Oscar nominee *Paradise Now, The Syrian Bride* was made by both Israelis and Arabs. *Rana's* director was a Palestinian based in the Netherlands; the director of *Syrian* is Eran Riklis, an Israeli. The crews are drawn from all the populations involved. What is interesting is that *Rana,* by a Palestinian, and *Syrian,* by an Israeli, seem to share exactly the same ideology: We live side by side, we are separated by a history of enmity, we are only people, we deserve to live our lives. Such films, which are said to be popular in Middle Eastern theaters, may assist in the gradual relaxation of tensions, although optimism regarding the Middle East often seems difficult. When *Paradise Now* was nominated for the Oscar, I received indignant e-mails from both sides, charging that the film favored the other side.

As for *The Syrian Bride,* it is difficult to get worked up about a bride and groom who have never met each other. If their marriage does not take place, their hearts will not be broken. That leaves us free to observe the world in which the film takes place, near a remote Druze desert settlement. Not precisely a flash point. It is possible that on some days, the guards on either side have only each other as company.

The real interest in the film enters by the side door, through supporting characters. Mona's family has gathered from far and wide for the ceremony. Her father is just out of jail, one of her brothers is a businessman in Europe, another has moved to Russia with his Russian bride. Most intriguing is Amal (Hiam Abbass), Mona's older sister, who is married, a feminist, has been accepted by the Israeli university at Haifa, and plans to attend despite the objections of her husband. Amal stands between the modern and the traditional, not so much a negotiator as a translator. What gives her intrinsic importance is Hiam Abbass's striking physical presence; if you remember Irene Papas in *Zorba the Greek* (or anything else), you'll get the idea.

Movies like *The Syrian Bride* are not overtly political but nibble around the edges, engaging our tendency to take a big political position and then undermine it with humanitarian exceptions. I am reminded of an appearance by Louis Farrakhan on the Larry King show. King asked him if he was still adamantly opposed to interracial marriages. Farrakhan said he certainly was, and then he shrugged and almost smiled: "But the young people, what can you tell them?"

Take My Eyes ★ ★ ★ ½

NO MPAA RATING, 109 m., 2006

Laia Marull (Pilar), Luis Tosar (Antonio), Candela Pena (Ana), Rosa Maria Sarda (Aurora), Kiti Manver (Rosa), Sergi Calleja (Therapist). Directed by Iciar Bollain and produced by Santiago Garcia de Leaniz. Screenplay by Bollain and Alicia Luna.

I knew a woman who stayed for years with a man who abused her. He couldn't help himself. Neither could she. I think she was addicted to the excitement. She was the center of his world, the focus of his obsessions, the star of his disease. Some of the reviews of Iciar Bollain's *Take My Eyes* can't understand why Pilar returns to Antonio after his violent explosions. That's the point of the movie: Logic becomes irrelevant when she's caught in the drama. Just as he goes to therapy groups to learn how to guard against his anger, she flees to her sister to hear what a bastard Antonio is. Then some dread tidal force draws them together again.

The movie is not neutral. Pilar (Laia Marull) has a problem, but Antonio (Luis Tosar) has a much graver one. He is a sick man whose insecurity and self-hatred boils up into violent outbursts against his wife. Even kicking a soccer ball around with his son, he finds himself kicking it too hard, thinking about his wife and taking it out on the kid. It is clear that Pilar should leave him and never return.

What makes the movie fascinating is that it doesn't settle for a soap opera resolution to this story, with Pilar as the victim, Antonio as the villain, and evil vanquished. It digs deeper and more painfully. The film opens with Pilar desperately waking her young son, grabbing a few clothes, and fleeing in the night to the home of her sister Ana (Candela Pena). In a sane world, this would be the end of the story, with Pilar getting a protection order and Antonio forever out of the picture.

But he pleads to return. He promises to change. He goes into counseling and therapy. He talks sweet. Her deep feelings for the man begin to stir. We saw this process in *What's Love Got to Do With It* (1993), with Tina Turner finally breaking free from Ike. In *Take My Eyes*, which is about middle-class people in Toledo, Spain, the story is less sensational but trickier, because Antonio is a complex man. As we follow his attempts to reform, as we see that he's really serious about controlling his anger, we begin to feel sympathy for him. We even pity him a little as we see how, step by step, his defenses fall, his lessons are forgotten, and rage once again controls him.

Pilar has not asserted herself much in the marriage, but now in a period of independence she gets a job as a volunteer in an art museum, and quickly reveals an aptitude for talking about art. Soon she is a tourist lecturer; Antonio haunts the shadows of the museum, and as his wife describes the passions in paintings, he imagines she is focusing on men in her audience, sending them signals. She isn't, but never mind: The point is that anything Pilar does in the outside world, any skill she demonstrates or independence she shows, is a challenge to him. He cannot bear the possibility that she could live without him, could exist as herself and not as his possession.

The movie doesn't go in for elaborate set pieces of beatings and bloodshed. He is violent toward her, yes, but what's terrifying is not the brutality of his behavior but how it is sudden, uncontrollable, and overwhelming. There is a time, after she has returned to him once again, where his anger grows and grows until finally he strips her down to a brassiere and shoves her out onto the balcony, to be seen by the neighbors, since after all that's what she wants, isn't it? To parade before strange men?

Marull is powerful as Pilar, a woman who slowly, through hard lessons, is learning that she must leave this man and never see him again and not miss him or weaken to his appeals or cave in to her own ambiguity about his behavior. She may think (and some viewers of the film might think) that she is simply a victim, but when she returns to him, she gives away that game. She knows it's insane and does it anyway.

As Antonio, Tosar gives a performance comparable to Laurence Fishburne's in *What's Love Got to Do With It* or Temuera Morrison's in *Once Were Warriors* (1994). He makes his anger absolutely convincing, and that is necessary or this is merely a story. The difference is that Marull's Pilar is less confident, more implicated, than the strong women played by Angela Bassett and Rena Owen in the other two films. That creates a complex response for us. We sympathize at times with both characters, but curiously enough we are more willing to understand why Antonio explodes than why Pilar returns to him. Surely she knows she's making a mistake. Yes, she does. They both know they're spiraling toward danger. If only knowledge had more to do with how they feel and why they act.

The Take ★ ★ ★

NO MPAA RATING, 87 m., 2005

A documentary directed by Avi Lewis and produced by Lewis and Naomi Klein. Screenplay by Klein.

As one documentary after another attacks the International Monetary Fund and its pillaging of the Third World, I wish I knew the first thing about global economics. If these films are as correct as they are persuasive, international monetary policy is essentially a scheme to bankrupt smaller nations and cast their populations into poverty, while multinational corporations loot their assets and whisk the money away to safe havens and the pockets of rich corporations and their friends. But that cannot be, can it? Surely the IMF's disastrous record is the result of bad luck, not legalized theft?

I am still haunted by *Life and Debt* (2001), a documentary explaining how tax-free zones were established on, but not of, Jamaican soil. Behind their barbed-wire fences, Jamaican law did not apply, workers could not organize or strike, there were no benefits, wages were minimal, and factories exported cheap goods without any benefit to the Jamaican economy other than subsistence wages.

Meanwhile, Jamaican agriculture was destroyed by IMF requirements that Jamaica import surplus U.S. agricultural products, which were subsidized by U.S. price supports and dumped in Jamaica for less than local (or American) farmers could produce them for. That destroyed the local dairy, onion, and potato industries. Jamaican bananas, which suffered from the inconvenience of not being grown by Chiquita, were barred from all markets except England. Didn't seem cricket, especially since Jamaican onions were so tasty.

Now here is *The Take*, a Canadian documentary by Avi Lewis and Naomi Klein, shot in Argentina, where a prosperous middle-class economy was destroyed during ten years of IMF policies, as enforced by President Carlos Menem (1989–1999). Factories were closed, their assets were liquidated, and money fled the country, sometimes literally by the truckload. After most of it was gone, Menem closed the banks, causing panic. Today more than half of all Argentineans live in poverty, unemployment is epidemic, and the crime rate is scary.

In the face of this disaster, workers at several closed factories attempted to occupy the factories, reopen them, and operate them. Their argument: The factories were subsidized in the first place by public money, so if the owners didn't want to operate them, the workers deserved a chance. The owners saw this differently, calling the occupations theft. Committees of workers monitored the factories to prevent owners from selling off machinery and other assets in defiance of the courts. And many of the factories not only reopened, but were able to turn a profit while producing comparable or superior goods at lower prices.

A success story? Yes, according to the Movement of Recovered Companies. No, according to the owners and the courts. But after Menem wins his way into a run-off election he suddenly drops out of the race, a moderate candidate becomes president, the courts decide in favor of the occupying workers, and the movement gains legitimacy. The film focuses on an auto parts plant and ceramics and garment factories that are running efficiently under worker management.

Is this sort of thing a threat to capitalism, or a revival of it? The factories are doing what they did before—manufacturing goods and employing workers—but they are doing it for the benefit of workers and consumers, instead of as an exercise to send profits flowing to top management. This is classic capitalism, as opposed to the management pocket-lining system, which is essentially loot for the bosses and bread and beans for everybody else. Sounds refreshing to anyone who has followed the recent tales of corporate greed in North America. Is it legal? Well, if the factories are closed, haven't the owners abandoned their moral right to them? Especially if the factories were built with public subsidies in the first place?

I wearily anticipate countless e-mails advising me I am a hopelessly idealistic dreamer, and explaining how when the rich get richer, everybody benefits. I will forward the most inspiring of these messages to minimum-wage workers at Wal-Mart, so they will understand why labor unions would be bad for them, while working unpaid overtime is good for the economy. All I know is that the ladies at the garment factory are turning out good-looking clothes, demand is up for Zanon ceramics, and the auto parts factory is working with a worker-controlled tractor factory to make some good-looking machines. I think we can all agree that's better than just sitting around.

Take the Lead ★ ★ ★

PG-13, 108 m., 2006

Antonio Banderas (Pierre Dulaine), Rob Brown (Rock), Yaya DaCosta (LaRhette), Alfre Woodard (Augustine James), John Ortiz (Mr. Temple), Laura Benanti (Tina), Dante Basco (Ramos), Jenna Dewan (Sasha), Marcus T. Paulk (Eddie). Directed by Liz Friedlander and produced by Diane Nabatoff and Christopher Godsick. Screenplay by Dianne Houston.

Take the Lead begins with rudeness, ends with good manners, and argues that poor inner-city schools can be redeemed by ballroom dancing. The only thing wrong with this vision, I suspect, is that it works for the ballroom dancers but not for the gang-bangers, who continue on their chosen careers. There is a more pessimistic view of urban high schools in another movie that opened the same day, *American Gun,* and I fear it's closer to the truth. But *Take the Lead* is said to be based on a true story, it tells a heartening fable, and Antonio Banderas is uncommonly charming as a dance teacher who walks into a high school and announces that he will improve it by his very example.

Public manners have degenerated in recent decades. It is now routine to hear obscenities shouted in public, and by all sorts of people, not just in traffic but even in Starbucks. I am as fond of colorful language as anyone, but I try not to inflict it upon strangers. I suspect that many people sense they should have better manners and need only a nudge. In high school I was addressed for the first time in my life as "Mister Ebert" by Stanley Hynes, an English teacher, and his formality transformed his classroom into a place where a certain courtliness prevailed.

In *Take the Lead,* Banderas plays Pierre Dulaine, a Manhattan ballroom dancing instructor who rides the streets, impeccably dressed, on his bicycle. One day he witnesses a student named Rock (Rob Brown) attacking a teacher's car with a golf club. Rock has his reasons, but never mind; instead of calling the cops, Dulaine walks into the school the next day and announces to the principal (Alfre Woodard) that he wants to teach ballroom dancing to the detention class.

She is a take-charge realist who walks the hallways ordering students to take off their hats, pull up their pants, and remove their hands from the netherlands of others, and her impulse is to laugh at Pierre, or throw him out. But he prevails and walks into the detention hall, where the students regard him as a visitor from the moon. They resist him, but he fascinates them, especially when he brings in one of his sexiest ballroom colleagues to show them what is surely true, that the tango is more manly, more feminine, more sexy, and more plain damn hot than any other form of motion requiring clothes.

Having seen the charming documentary *Mad Hot Ballroom* (2005), about New York grade school kids learning to dance, which is based on the same real-life story of Dulaine, I anticipated the general direction of *Take the Lead.* It is not a particularly original movie, and it lacks the impact of such earlier classroom parables as *Stand and Deliver, Lean on Me, Mr. Holland's Opus,* and the similar *Music of the Heart* (1999). The vulgar, rebellious, resentful, potentially criminal students are transformed by dancing as surely as music transforms the hero of *Hustle and Flow.* And of course the film ends in a ballroom dancing competition, with full-court choreography that in real life takes weeks of rehearsal but in the movies springs spontaneously from the souls of the dancers.

The film is more fable than record, and more wishful thinking than a plan of action. Yet the end credits leave me no doubt that the real Pierre Dulaine's programs have spread to many other schools and that thousands of students are now learning the tango, the fox-trot, and other dances that are taught with so much less effect in another movie that opened the same day, *Marilyn Hotchkiss' Ballroom Dancing and Charm School.* Strange, how movies can open simultaneously and cast light on each other.

Still, I felt the Woodard character had something to be said for her dubious realism (the high school principal played by Forest Whitaker in *American Gun* certainly would agree with her) and that the ascendancy of Pierre Dulaine was a little too smooth. I began to suspect that he drew a good hand in that detention class, which is made of basically good and misunderstood kids. One really hard case might have capsized the ship.

That said, Banderas is reason enough to see the movie. There are some people who by their personal style can make us want to be better. "Whenever you're in doubt in a social situation," the director Gregory Nava once assured me, "just ask yourself, what would Fred Astaire do?" Pierre Dulaine must ask himself this question several times a day. He dresses well, carries himself with grace and self-respect, treats everyone politely, and all but shames them into returning his courtesy. By being so resplendent in his bearing and effect, he generates envy: The kids follow him not because they want to improve and reform but because they would like to be that cool.

The Talent Given Us ★ ★ ★ ½

NO MPAA RATING, 97 m., 2005

Judy Wagner (Judy), Allen Wagner (Allen), Emily Wagner (Emily), Maggie Wagner (Maggie), Andrew Wagner (Andrew), Judy Dixon (Bumby), Billy Wirth (Billy). Directed by Andrew Wagner and produced by Wagner, Tom Hines, and Chelsea Gilmore. Screenplay by Wagner.

In some families, certain topics are never discussed. In Andrew Wagner's family, every possible topic is discussed endlessly. It's remarkable that they have the courage (or recklessness) to speak so frankly to each other, and astonishing that they do it in front of a camera. Wagner's *The Talent Given Us* is a brave, funny, affecting film that follows his parents and two sisters as they drive from New York to Los Angeles, picking up a family friend in Iowa. The film rides along with them, stops for meals, eavesdrops in motels, sees the sights.

This is a "fiction film using the materials of documentary," Wagner told me when I met him at Sundance 2005. "My parents, sisters, and friends play my parents, sisters, and friends." They do a convincing job of it; the film feels like cinema verité, even though Andrew is behind the camera while they are allegedly driving to California to visit him. By pretending he's not there, they're acting. Many other details must be fictional.

Consider the family friend nicknamed Bumby (Judy Dixon). In the film we learn she's a publicist who has just been fired from *Field of Dreams 2.* The Internet Movie Database makes no mention of such a film. It must have been invented as an excuse to introduce another character halfway across the country.

Andrew's parents, Judy and Allen, have been married for forty-six years and are still warmly considering divorce. Are we watching them or "characters"? The biographical details match: He was a Wall Street stock specialist and tax consultant; she was a dancer, writer, and technical editor. Both are semi-retired. They wonder if they have been failures as parents, but any family that can make this film has been a success. Maybe their carping at one another is a way of expressing affection.

The cross-country trip happens with all the premeditation of a John Cassavetes plot. Allen, Judy, and their daughter Maggie go to the airport to pick up their daughter Emily, who has flown in from L.A. Both girls are actresses. Leaving the airport, Judy decides on impulse they must all drive as a family *back* to Los Angeles to visit Andrew. Emily reasonably says this is insane, but later she's the one who insists on continuing the trip.

They talk a lot. Allen has apparently had a stroke, which affects his speech, although we understand every word. He keeps a straw in his mouth for reasons never explained; maybe it helps him talk. He's on drugs that have sent his sex life to hell, a fact Judy is unhappy about; her frankness in a motel scene is startling. Emily uses a few drugs, too. She develops alarming symptoms while they're conveniently visiting the Menninger Clinic, and she tells the doctor she has prescriptions for Prozac, Wellbutrin, Synthroid, Xanax, Ativan.

"Any unusual stress in your life right now?" the doctor asks. "I'm driving across the country with my parents," Emily explains.

The Wagners fight about driving skills, the route they should take, where they should stop for meals, what they should eat, and about the years when the children were small. "I'm not in therapy because you were a good mother," Emily tells Judy. Because her mother wouldn't pick her up after school, "I became a compulsive masturbator." Now she compensates with plastic surgery and liposuction. Oh, and sadomasochism. At one point, Emily corners both of her parents and quizzes them about their affairs.

Old Allen, meanwhile, has his eye on Bumby, the curvy family friend, and there is a scene between them where he clearly doesn't think his libido has gone completely to hell. Since Bumby seems to be a character introduced into the film, and Allen is contemplating adultery while being photographed by his son, this scene is probably fictional, wouldn't you say? With the Wagners, you never know. It leads, in any event, to midnight motel room confessions between Allen and Judy that are touching: They have lived together for so long that they no longer have a marriage, they have a condition of life, and sometimes they speculate about other lives they might have lived.

The Wagners look at houses they used to live in. They see the sights. They make hypothetical plans for the future. They meet Andrew, who finally appears in front of the camera, briefly. They meet Andrew's friend, the actor Billy Wirth. Allen and Billy have a heart-to-heart. Ever notice how your friends sometimes like your parents more than you do? That's because they didn't experience them as parents.

All of this somehow adds up, as I wrote from Sundance, to a movie that is "seemingly honest." It's the "seemingly" that fascinates me. Is this a documentary based on truth that has been given shape, like *Nanook of the North,* or a documentary that's fiction in the form of truth, like *Best in Show*? Hard to be sure. I do believe we are really looking at the members of Andrew Wagner's family, and *The Talent Given Us* is a documentary in this sense: It is a record of these people doing these things. Whether they "really" did them is beside the point. They did them for the film, so if they hadn't done them before, they've done them now.

Talk to Me ★ ★ ★ ½

R, 118 m., 2007

Don Cheadle (Petey Greene), Chiwetel Ejiofor (Dewey Hughes), Cedric the Entertainer ("Nighthawk" Bob Terry), Taraji P. Henson (Vernell Watson), Mike Epps (Milo Hughes), Martin Sheen (E. G. Sonderling), Vondie Curtis Hall (Sunny Jim Kelsey). Directed by Kasi Lemmons and produced by Mark Gordon, Sidney Kimmel, Joe Fries, and Josh McLaughlin. Screenplay by Michael Genet and Rick Famuyiwa.

The story of Petey Greene was a movie waiting to be made. Greene came out of prison to become, literally overnight, a popular and influential deejay. He was on WOL, a Washington, D.C., station that was looking for a morning man to connect with its African-American audience and got more than it bargained for. Don Cheadle gives a fascinating performance as a man able to step out of a cell and into a broadcast booth, but not sure where to step next.

The movie, directed by Kasi Lemmons (*Eve's Bayou,* best movie of 1997), remembers a time in the 1960s when the word "Negro" was replaced by "black," when R&B performers like Sam Cooke redefined popular music, when the civil rights movement brought enormous change, and when the assassination of Dr. Martin Luther King Jr. brought despair and anger. The man on the radio in the morning in Washington would stand at the center of these events.

The movie begins with a whirlpool of comedy and manic energy and then grows, as it must, more serious and introspective. Cheadle, that superb actor, embodies the complexities of Petey Greene in a performance that goes from high through second into low (that's harder and more interesting than the usual shifting). When we first meet him, he's a deejay in prison, pumping R&B and his colorful vocabulary out to his fellow inmates. He seems incapable of uttering a boring word.

WOL program director Dewey Hughes (Chiwetel Ejiofor), visiting his brother Milo (Mike Epps) in prison one day, hears Petey and meets him. He casually asks Petey to look him up when he gets out, possibly picturing

Petey sorting a stack of mail or emptying wastebaskets. Petey doesn't see it that way. A self-described con man, he talks his way out of prison and into Dewey's office, demanding the deejay job he thinks (or pretends) he has been offered. Helping him charge over the office staff on his way to the inner sanctum is his girlfriend, Vernell, played by Taraji P. Henson as an unstoppable force and immovable object rolled into one.

Of course Petey is not hired as a deejay. And then of course eventually he is. This happens to the amazement of Sunny Jim, the current morning man (Vondie Curtis Hall), another deejay (Cedric the Entertainer), and WOL's owner (Martin Sheen). Petey's progress provides a roll of high comedy; it's remarkable to see the somber, courageous Don Cheadle of *Hotel Rwanda* take flight here like Chris Rock or Jim Carrey. Picture by picture, he is showing us he can do just about anything.

It would be hard to believe that an ex-con could go to work almost immediately in a coveted time slot, but the movie, based on fact, shows how it happened, and Cheadle is convincing as a man who could win the instant trust and affection of his listeners. Petey was manifestly the real thing, and Cheadle, whether or not he listened to tapes from that time, persuades us. Chiwetel Ejiofor plays a balancing act as Dewey the program director; caught between his cautious, fearful boss (Sheen) and a talent on fire, he improvises with the anarchic situation. Michael Genet, the film's cowriter, is Hughes's son and must be retailing lots of family memories.

The film's turning point comes with the shooting of Dr. King. A wave of disbelief and grief sweeps the land, and the young and angry make a reality of James Baldwin's prediction, "the fire next time." Going on the air the next morning, Petey does not precisely cool the anger of his listeners; he speaks reasonably, from the heart and from his life, of the uselessness of violence. It is his finest moment, a historic one. This unexpected angle on the King assassination, focusing on the pain of the living, is handled by Lemmons with deep feeling. She takes an event of enormous, almost incomprehensible tragedy and focuses it on Petey Greene's personal transformation.

The last third of the film follows Greene's life as Hughes tries to manage him into a career as a standup. It is brave and honest of Lemmons and her writers to follow Petey into deep waters, and there is a television appearance that I felt in the pit of my stomach. When you're lucky enough to do what you're born to do, you can hardly fail. Petey Greene was born to be a talk radio star. But Dewey doesn't understand that it stops there.

The fame of broadcast personalities is by its nature transient. How many people remember Petey Greene? Or, under a certain age, have heard of him? Jay Leno could go on a Jaywalk for miles and not find anybody who has heard of Arthur Godfrey. We labor through life sweeping our memory ahead of us into the dustbin of oblivion. But someone like Petey Greene made a difference and made a mark, and broadcasting is better because of his transparent honesty. He helped transform African-American stations more, probably, than their mostly white owners desired. And talk talents like Howard Stern, whether or not they know who he was, owe him something. ☞

Taxi to the Dark Side ★ ★ ★ ★

R, 106 m., 2008

With Alex Gibney (Narrator), Moazzam Begg, William Brand, Jack Cloonan, Damien Corsetti, Ken Davis, Carlotta Gall, Tim Golden, Scott Horton, Tony Lagouranis, Carl Levin, Alfred McCoy, Alberto Mora, Anthony Morden, Glendale Walls, Lawrence Wilkerson, Tim Wilner, John Yoo. A documentary written and directed by Alex Gibney and produced by Gibney, Eva Orner, and Susannah Shipman.

"We have to work the dark side."

So said Dick Cheney a few days after 9/11, discussing the war on terror. Is this what he meant? In December 2002, an Afghan named Dilawar had scraped together enough money to buy a taxi. He was fingered by a paid informant as a terrorist connected with a rocket attack. Taken to the American prison at Bagram, he was tortured so violently that he died after five days. An autopsy showed that his legs were so badly mauled they would have had to be amputated, had he lived. Later, the informant who collected U.S. money for fingering him was proven to be the terrorist actually responsible for the crime the innocent Dilawar was charged with.

An official report said Dilawar died of "natural causes." The *New York Times* found an autopsy report describing the death as a homicide. After a belated investigation, a few U.S. soldiers were accused of the murder. No officers were involved. Dilawar was the first casualty after we started to work the dark side. In all the torture scandals since, few officers have ever been charged. If all of these crimes took place without their knowledge, they would appear to be guilty of dereliction of duty, if nothing else.

Alex Gibney's horrifying documentary *Taxi to the Dark Side* uses the death of Dilawar as an entry point into a remorseless indictment of the Bush administration's unofficially condoned policy of the torture of suspects, which is forbidden by American constitutional and military law and international agreements, but justified under the "necessity" of working the dark side. Gibney interviews U.S. soldiers who participated in such torture sessions (under orders, they thought, although their superiors claimed innocence, all the way up to Bush, who claimed ignorance of torture even after he had seen official Pentagon and intelligence reports). They seem sorry, sobered, and confused.

The film, one of this year's Oscar nominees for best documentary, has TV footage of administration officials demonstrably lying about what they knew and when they knew it. And it leads to Gibney's conversation with his own father, who was an interrogator of prisoners in World War II, and says not only was such behavior forbidden, but it wouldn't have worked anyway. If you torture a man long enough, he will tell you anything to make you stop. If you act on that "information," you are likely on a fool's errand.

Gibney is the same filmmaker who made the merciless *Enron: The Smartest Guys in the Room* (2005), a documentary where he produced actual tape recordings of Enron operatives *creating* the California "power shortage" by ordering power plants shut down and joking that a few grandmothers might have to die without air conditioning in order for Enron to make more millions. By the same logic, lives may have to be lost to torture to produce intelligence, although there is precious little evidence that the strategy has worked. And besides, is that what we do, as Americans? Are those our values? Then what do we stand for?

Gibney widens the net to include the illegal detainees at Guantanamo, most of whom have never been charged with any crime. He talks with former administration officials and spokesmen who didn't like what they were seeing and resigned. His conversations with the American torturers themselves are the most heartbreaking; young kids for the most part, they thought they were doing their duty. And he includes never-before-seen photos and images of torture at work. One tactic: Prisoners have their hands tied above their heads and are made to balance on boxes in pools of electrified water. Would they really be electrocuted if they fell off? Would you like to try? John McCain, who endured unimaginable torture, is among the most outspoken critics of this strategy.

There are those, their numbers shrinking every day, who would agree we have to "work the dark side." Growing numbers of us are yearning for the light. This movie does not describe the America I learned about in civics class or think of when I pledge allegiance to the flag. Yet I know I will get the usual e-mails accusing me of partisanship, bias, only telling one side, etc. What is the other side? See this movie and you tell me.

Tell No One ★ ★ ★ ½

NO MPAA RATING, 125 m., 2008

Francois Cluzet (Alexandre Beck), Andre Dussollier (Jacques Laurentin), Marie-Josee Croze (Margot Beck), Kristin Scott Thomas (Helene Perkins), Nathalie Baye (Elysabeth Feldman), Francois Berleand (Eric Levkowitch), Jean Rochefort (Gilbert Neuville), Guillaume Canet (Philippe Neuville), Gilles Lellouche (Bruno), Marina Hands (Anne Beck). Directed by Guillaume Canet and produced by Alain Attal. Screenplay by Canet and Philippe Lefebvre, based on a novel by Harlan Coben.

Tell No One will play as a terrific thriller for you if you meet it halfway. You have to be willing to believe. There will be times you think it's too perplexing, when you're sure you're witnessing loose ends. It has been devised that way, and the director knows what he's doing. Even when it's baffling, it's never boring. I've heard of airtight plots. This one is not merely airtight, but hermetically sealed.

The setup is the simple part. We meet a married couple, sweethearts since childhood: Alex (Francois Cluzet) and Margot (Marie-Josee Croze). They go skinny-dipping in a secluded pond and doze off on a raft. They have a little quarrel, and Margot swims ashore. Alex hears a scream. He swims to the dock, climbs the ladder, and is knocked unconscious.

Flash forward eight years. Alex is a pediatrician in a Paris hospital. He has never remarried and still longs for Margot. Two bodies are found buried in the forest where it is believed she was murdered, and the investigation is reopened. Although Margot's case was believed solved, suspicion of Alex has never entirely died out. He was hit so hard before falling back into the water that he was in a coma for three days. How did he get back on the dock?

Now the stage is set for a dilemma that resembles in some ways *The Fugitive.* Evidence is found that incriminates Alex: a murder weapon, for example, in his apartment. There is the lockbox that contains suspicious photographs and a shotgun tied to another murder. Alex is tipped off by his attorney (Nathalie Baye) and flees out the window of his office at the hospital just before the cops arrive. "You realize he just signed his own confession?" a cop says to the lawyer.

Alex is in very good shape. He runs and runs, pursued by the police. It is a wonderfully photographed chase, including a dance across both lanes of an expressway. His path takes him through Clignancourt, the labyrinthine antiques market, and into the mean streets on the other side. He shares a Dumpster with a rat. He is helped by a crook he once did a favor for; the crook has friends who seem to be omnipresent.

Ah, but already I've left out a multitude of developments. Alex has been electrified by cryptic e-mail messages that could only come from Margot. Is she still alive? He needs to elude the cops long enough to make a rendezvous in a park. And *still* I've left out so much—but I wouldn't want to reveal a single detail that would spoil the mystery.

Tell No One was directed and coscripted by Guillaume Canet, working from a novel by American author Harlan Coben. It contains a rich population of characters but has been so carefully cast that we're never confused. There are Alex's sister (Marina Hands), her lesbian lover (Kristin Scott Thomas), the rich senator whose obsession is racehorses (Jean Rochefort), Margot's father (Andre Dussollier), the police captain who alone believes Alex is innocent (Francois Berleand), the helpful crook (Gilles Lellouche), and the senator's son (Guillaume Canet himself). Also a soft-porn fashion photographer, a band of vicious assassins, street thugs, and on and on. And the movie gives full weight to these characters; they are necessary and handled with care.

If you give enough thought to the film, you'll begin to realize that many of the key roles are twinned, high and low. There are two cops closely on either side of retirement age. Two attractive brunettes. A cop and a crook who have similar personal styles. Two blondes who are angular professional women. Two lawyers. One of the assassins looks a little like Alex but has a beard. Such thoughts would never occur during the film, which is too enthralling. But it shows what love and care went into the construction of the puzzle.

One of the film's pleasures is its unexpected details. The big dog Alex hauls around. The Christian Louboutin red-soled shoes that are worn on two most unlikely occasions. The steeplechase right in the middle of everything. The way flashbacks are manipulated in their framing so that the first one shows less than when it is reprised. The way solutions are dangled before us and then jerked away. The computer technique. The tortuous path taken by some morgue photos. The seedy lawyer, so broke his name is scrawled in cardboard taped to the door. Alex patiently tutoring a young child. That the film clocks at only a whisper above two hours is a miracle.

And then look at the acting. Francois Cluzet is ideal as the hero: compact, handsome in a fortyish Dustin Hoffman sort of way, believable at all times (but then, we know his story is true). Marie-Josee Croze, with enough psychic weight she's present even when absent. Kristin Scott Thomas, not the outsider she might seem. Legendary Jean

Rochefort, in a role legendary John Huston would have envied. Legendary Francois Berleand as a senior cop who will make you think of Inspector Maigret. And legendary Andre Dussollier sitting on the bench until the movie needs the bases cleared. Here is how a thriller should be made.

Tell Them Who You Are ★ ★ ★ ½

R, 95 m., 2005

With Mark Wexler, Haskell Wexler, Peter Bart, Verna Bloom, Billy Crystal, Michael Douglas, Conrad L. Hall, Julia Roberts, Jane Fonda, Sidney Poitier, John Sayles, Albert Maysles, Tom Hayden, Studs Terkel, Norman Jewison, Dennis Hopper, Milos Forman, and Paul Newman. Directed and produced by Mark Wexler. Screenplay by Robert DeMaio and Wexler.

I have known Haskell Wexler for thirty-six years. When Haskell had a rough cut of *Medium Cool,* his docudrama shot at the 1968 Democratic Convention, he asked me to see it after Paramount got cold feet about distribution. Like many people since then, I thought it was a powerful and courageous film. Haskell and I became friends over the years. I remember swimming in Jamaica with Haskell and his wife, the actress Rita Taggart. I remember going through *Blaze* a frame at a time with Haskell at the Hawaii Film Festival, and taking apart *Casablanca* with him on Dusty Cohl's Floating Film Festival.

So he is a friend. He is also a great cinematographer. And he is an activist for progressive causes, a sometime director of features and documentaries, and the subject of a new documentary named *Tell Them Who You Are.* The documentary is by his son, Mark, who tells his father very clearly: "I'm not a fan. I'm a son." Mark made a previous doc, *Me and My Matchmaker,* which I found fascinating; he meets a matchmaker, thinks it would be interesting to watch her at work, asks her to find him a wife, and gets involved in a process neither he nor the matchmaker could possibly have anticipated.

Mark's new doc is frankly intended, we learn, as an attempt to get to know his father better. The child of Haskell's second marriage, he has an almost Oedipal rivalry that has, among other things, led him to politics that are the opposite of his father's. Haskell, now in his eighties, agreed to participate with misgivings, and is not very happy with the results.

Two of Haskell's longtime friends, the director John Sayles and producer Maggie Renzi, told me Mark has "issues" with his father and the film doesn't reflect Haskell's bighearted kindness. Then again, they share Haskell's left-wing beliefs. Mark, perhaps not coincidentally, does not. "Haskell gets up every morning and he rants against what's happening in the world," says Haskell's fellow documentarian Pam Yates, with admiration. In the film, he takes Mark along to a peace rally in San Francisco, where he seems to know everybody.

All fathers and sons have issues. If *Tell Them Who You Are* had been a sunny doc about how great the old man was, it wouldn't be worth seeing—and wouldn't be the kind of film Haskell himself makes. What Mark does, better perhaps than either he or his father realizes, is to capture some aspects of a lifelong rivalry that involves love but not much contentment.

Mark remembers his father advising him, "Tell them you're Haskell Wexler's son," which would have done him some good in Hollywood, but Mark has been trying for years to be defined as *not* simply Haskell's son, and this film about his father is paradoxically part of that struggle. This generational thing has been going on for a while with the Wexlers; as a young man, Haskell organized a strike against his own father's factory. And, although he came from a well-to-do family, we learn that Haskell volunteered for the Merchant Marines in World War II and survived a torpedoed ship. This is a man who has been there.

"I don't think there's a movie that I've been on that I wasn't sure I could direct it better," Haskell says in the film. We learn of a few films he was fired from when the directors felt he was making that all too clear; one of them was *One Flew Over the Cuckoo's Nest,* and we get the memories of director Milos Forman ("He was sharing his frustrations with the actors") and producer Michael Douglas ("He reminds me of my own father: critical and judging").

There were also films he walked away from on matters of principle. After one, he told me the director was lazy and didn't treat people with respect. Haskell isn't an obedient hired hand, but a strong-willed artist who gets the admiration of strong directors like John Sayles *(Limbo, The Secret of Roan Inish),* Norman Jewison *(In the Heat of the Night),* Mike Nichols *(Who's Afraid of Virginia Woolf?),* and Hal Ashby *(Bound for Glory).* He won Oscars for his work on *Virginia Woolf* and *Bound for Glory,* and was nominated three other times.

On the other hand, Francis Ford Coppola replaced him on *The Conversation* (after Haskell had finished the legendary opening sequence). Haskell's version: He was working too quickly for Coppola, who wasn't prepared. Coppola's version: unstated. And Haskell believes he shot more than half of Terrence Malick's *Days of Heaven,* which Nestor Almendros won an Oscar for.

After the lights went up at the Toronto Film Festival premiere of the doc, there was Norman Jewison sitting across the aisle and observing, "He could be a son of a bitch." The way he said it, it sounded affectionate.

What Haskell is sure of is that he knows more about making documentaries than Mark does. He tells Mark he should have employed a sound man for some scenes shot at a party, and he turns out to be right. The two men get into a heated argument when Mark tries to set up a shot with his father standing in front of a sunset, and Haskell thinks his son is valuing form over content; forget the sunset, he says, because "I desperately want to say something." On the other hand, he criticizes Mark for having him "say everything" instead of using the technique of telling through showing.

Mark provides a good overview of his father's career: the Academy Awards, the great films, the legendary reputation. He talks to some who love him and some who don't. We learn of Haskell's business partnership and close friendship with Conrad L. Hall, another great cinematographer; Mark sometimes felt closer to Conrad than to his own father, and strangely enough, Conrad's son, also a great cinematographer, felt closer to Haskell.

Then there is the issue of Mark's mother, Marian, Wexler's wife for thirty years, now a victim of Alzheimer's. I've known Haskell only with his third wife, Rita, and I see a couple glowing with love. Mark resents his father for leaving his mother. But then we see probably the film's strongest scene, and it involves Haskell visiting Marian in a nursing home. Marian doesn't recognize him, but Haskell speaks softly to her: "We've got secrets, you, me. We've got secrets. We know things about each other that nobody else in the world knows." There are tears in his eyes.

Certainly only a family member could have had access to such a scene. Possibly Haskell did not expect it to be in the documentary. But it reflects well on him, and on Mark for including it. There is this: Haskell agreed to be in the film, to some degree in order to help his son. And although Mark shows the tension between himself and his father, he also shows a willingness to look beyond the surface of his resentments. Jane Fonda says of them: "Intimacy was not their gift." They are still working at it. This is a film about a relationship in progress.

Thank You for Smoking ★ ★ ★ ½

R, 92 m., 2006

Aaron Eckhart (Nick Naylor), Maria Bello (Polly Bailey), Adam Brody (Jack), Sam Elliott (Lorne Lutch), Katie Holmes (Heather Holloway), Rob Lowe (Jeff Megall), William H. Macy (Senator Finistirre), Robert Duvall (The Captain), Cameron Bright (Joey Naylor), J. K. Simmons (B.R.), David Koechner (Bobby Jay Bliss). Directed by Jason Reitman and produced by David O. Sacks. Screenplay by Reitman, based on the novel by Christopher Buckley.

Here is a satire both savage and elegant, a dagger instead of a shotgun. *Thank You for Smoking* targets the pro-smoking lobby with a dark appreciation of human nature. It stars Aaron Eckhart as Nick Naylor, a spokesman for the Academy of Tobacco Studies. We meet him on the Joan Lunden show, sitting next to bald-headed little Robin, a fifteen-year-old boy who is dying of cancer "but has stopped smoking." Nick rises smoothly to the challenge: "It's in our best interests to keep Robin alive and smoking," he explains. "The antismoking people want Robin to die."

Nick Naylor is a pleasant, good-looking career lobbyist who is divorced, loves his son, Joey (Cameron Bright), and speaks to the kid's class on career day. "Please don't ruin my childhood," Joey pleads, but his dad cross-examines a little girl whose mother says cigarettes can kill you: "Is your mother a doctor?"

Once a week he dines with the MOD Squad, whose other members are alcohol lobbyist Polly Bailey (Maria Bello) and firearms lobbyist Bobby Jay Bliss (David Koechner). They argue over which of their products kills the most people. The initials MOD stand for "Merchants of Death."

The movie was directed by Jason Reitman, now twenty-nine, who warmed up by making short subjects. What's remarkable in his first feature is his control of tone; instead of careening from one target to the next, he brings a certain detached logic to his method. Notice how Nick negotiates with a Hollywood superagent (Rob Lowe) on the challenge of getting movie stars to smoke on-screen once again. Right now, they agree, no one smokes in the movies except for villains and Europeans. The stars would have to smoke in historical pictures, since in a contemporary film other people would always be asking them why they smoke. Or—why not in the future, after cigarettes are safe? Smoking in a space station?

Jason Reitman grew up around movies; his father is Ivan Reitman (*Ghostbusters, Evolution*). But Jason has his own style, sneaky and subtle. Instead of populating his movie with people smoking and coughing and wheezing, he shows not a single person smoking, although the ancient Captain (Robert Duvall), czar of the tobacco industry, holds a cigar like a threat. Eckhart has a good line in plausible corporate villains (see his debut in *In the Company of Men*), and he is smiling, optimistic, and even trusting (as when he tells reporter Katie Holmes things he should know will not be off the record).

Naylor's opponent in the film is Senator Ortolan Finistirre (William H. Macy), a Vermont environmentalist whose office desk is covered with his collection of maple syrup bottles. The senator has introduced legislation requiring a skull and crossbones to be displayed on every cigarette pack, replacing the government health warning. The symbol is better than the words, he explains, because "they want those who do not speak English to die."

Reitman's screenplay is based on a novel by Christopher Buckley (son of William F.) and retains a literary flavor rare in a time when many movies are aimed at people who move their lips when they think. Consider this exchange between Nick and his young son, who wants help on a school assignment:

> Joey: *Dad, why is the American government the best government?*
> Nick: *Because of our endless appeals system.*

Or this nostalgia by Duvall, as the Captain: "I was in Korea shooting Chinese in 1952. Now they're our best customers. Next time we won't have to shoot so many of them."

What I admired above all in *Thank You for Smoking* was its style. I enjoyed the satire, I laughed a lot because it's a very funny movie, but laughs are common, and satire, as we all know, is what closes on *Saturday Night Live.* Style is something modern movies can't always find the time for. I am thinking for some reason of *The Thin Man* (1934), a movie that works in large part because of the way William Powell and Myrna Loy hold themselves, move, and speak; their attitude creates a space between the vulgarities of the plot and the elegance of their personalities, and in that space the humor resides. Their lives are their works of art. Nick Naylor is like them, not egotistical or conceited so much as an objective observer of his own excellence. It is the purpose of the movie to humble him, but he never grovels and even in a particularly nasty situation still depends on his ability to spin anything to his advantage. If you want to remake *The Thin Man,* I say Eckhart and Catherine Keener.

Should the movie be angrier? I lost both of my parents to cigarettes, but I doubt that more anger would improve it. Everyone knows cigarettes can kill you, but they remain on sale and raise billions of dollars in taxes. The target of the movie is not so much tobacco as lobbying in general, which along with advertising and spin control makes a great many evils palatable to the population. How can you tell when something is not good for you? Because of the efforts made to convince you it is harmless or beneficial. Consider the incredible, edible egg. "Drink responsibly." Prescription drug prices doubled "to fund research for better health."

At one point in the movie Nick pays a call on Lorne Lutch (Sam Elliott), a former Marlboro Man now dying of cancer and speaking out bitterly against cigarettes. Nick brings along a briefcase full of hundred-dollar bills. This is not a bribe, he explains. It is a gift. Of course, to accept such a gift and then continue to attack tobacco would be ungrateful. Lorne eyes the money and wonders if he could maybe take half of it and cut back on his attacks. Nick explains with genuine regret that it doesn't work that way. Once you're on board, you're along for the ride.

There Will Be Blood ★ ★ ★ ½

R, 158 m., 2008

Daniel Day-Lewis (Daniel Plainview), Paul Dano (Paul/Eli Sunday), Kevin J. O'Connor (Henry), Ciaran Hinds (Fletcher), Dillon Freasier (H. W. Plainview). Directed by Paul Thomas Anderson and produced by Anderson, JoAnne Sellar, and Daniel Lupi. Screenplay by Anderson, based on the novel *Oil!* by Upton Sinclair.

The voice of the oil man sounds made of oil, gristle, and syrup. It is deep and reassuring, absolutely sure of itself and curiously fraudulent. No man who sounds this forthright can be other than a liar. His name is Daniel Plainview, and he must have given the name to himself as a private joke, for little that he does is as it seems. In Paul Thomas Anderson's brutal, driving epic *There Will Be Blood,* Plainview begins by trying to wrest silver from the earth with a pick and shovel, and ends by extracting countless barrels of oil whose wealth he keeps all for himself. Daniel Day-Lewis makes him a great, oversize monster who hates all men, including, therefore, himself.

Watching the movie is like viewing a natural disaster that you cannot turn away from. By that I do not mean that the movie is bad, any more than it is good. It is a force beyond categories. It has scenes of terror and poignancy, scenes of ruthless chicanery, scenes awesome for their scope, moments echoing with whispers, and an ending that in some peculiar way this material demands because it could not conclude on an appropriate note—there has been nothing appropriate about it. Those who hate the ending, and there may be many, might be asked to dictate a different one. Something bittersweet, perhaps? Grandly tragic? Only madness can supply a termination for this story.

The movie is very loosely based on *Oil!,* Upton Sinclair's 1927 novel about a corrupt oil family—based so loosely you can see the film, read the book, and experience two different stories. Anderson's character is a man who has no friends, no lovers, no real partners, and an adopted son he exploits mostly as a prop. Plainview comes from nowhere, stays in contact with no one, and when a man appears claiming to be his half brother, it is not surprising that they have never met before. Plainview's only goal in life is to become enormously wealthy, and he does so, reminding me of *Citizen Kane* and Mr. Bernstein's observation, "It's easy to make a lot of money, if that's all you want to do, is make a lot of money."

There Will Be Blood is no *Kane,* however. Plainview lacks a "Rosebud." He regrets nothing, misses nothing, pities nothing, and when he falls down a mine shaft and cruelly breaks his leg, he hauls himself back up to the top and starts again. He gets his break in life when a pudding-faced young man named Paul Sunday (Paul Dano) visits him and says he knows where oil is to be found and will share this information for a price. The oil is to be found on the Sunday family ranch, where Standard Oil has already been sniffing around, and Plainview obtains the drilling rights cheaply from old man Sunday. There is another son, named Eli, who is also played by Paul Dano, and either Eli and Paul are identical twins or the story is up to something shifty, since we never see them both at once.

Eli is an evangelical preacher whose only goal is to extract money from Plainview to build his church, the Church of the Third Revelation. Plainview goes along with him until the time comes to dedicate his first well. He has promised to allow Eli to bless it, but when the moment comes, he pointedly ignores the youth, and a lifelong hatred is founded. In images starkly and magnificently created by cinematographer Robert Elswit and set designer Jack Fisk, we see the first shaky wells replaced by vast fields, all overseen by Plainview from the porch of a rude shack where he sips whiskey more or less ceaselessly. There are accidents. Men are killed. His son is deafened when a well blows violently, and Plainview grows cold toward the boy; he needs him as a prop, but not as a magnet for sympathy.

The movie settles down, if that is the word,

into a portrait of the two personalities, Plainview's and Eli Sunday's, striving for domination over their realms. The addition of Plainview's alleged half brother (Kevin J. O'Connor) into this equation gives Plainview, at last, someone to confide in, although he confides mostly his universal hatred. That Plainview, by now a famous multimillionaire, would so quickly take this stranger at his word is incredible; certainly we do not. But by now Plainview is drifting from obsession through possession into madness, and at the end, like Kane, he drifts through a vast mansion like a ghost.

The performance by Day-Lewis may well win an Oscar nomination, and if he wins, he should do the right thing in his acceptance speech and thank the late John Huston. His voice in the role seems like a frank imitation of Huston, right down to the cadences, the pauses, the seeming to confide. I interviewed Huston three times, and each time he spoke with elaborate courtesy, agreeing with everything, drawing out his sentences, and each time I could not rid myself of the conviction that his manner was masking impatience; it was his way of suffering a fool, which is to say, an interviewer. I have heard Peter O'Toole's famous imitation of Huston, but channeled through O'Toole he sounds heartier and friendlier and, usually, drunk. I imagine you had to know Huston pretty well before he let down his conversational guard.

There Will Be Blood is the kind of film that is easily called great. I am not sure of its greatness. It was filmed in the same area of Texas used by *No Country for Old Men*, and that is a great film, and a perfect one. But *There Will Be Blood* is not perfect, and in its imperfections (its unbending characters, its lack of women or any reflection of ordinary society, its ending, its relentlessness) we may see its reach exceeding its grasp. Which is not a dishonorable thing.

The Thing About My Folks ★ ★ ½

PG-13, 96 m., 2005

Peter Falk (Sam Kleinman), Paul Reiser (Ben Kleinman), Olympia Dukakis (Muriel Kleinman), Elizabeth Perkins (Rachel Kleinman), Ann Dowd (Linda), Claire Beckman (Hillary), Mimi Lieber (Bonnie). Directed by Raymond De Felitta and produced by Robert F. Newmyer, Paul Reiser, and Jeffrey Silver. Screenplay by Reiser.

One of the nice things about my job is that I get to enjoy the good parts in movies that aren't really necessary to see. *The Thing About My Folks* travels familiar movie territory: a grown son and his father get to know each other during a journey in, yes, a classic car. They do not discover much they couldn't have learned in screenwriting class, but we discover once again what a warm and engaging actor Peter Falk is. I can't recommend the movie, but I can be grateful that I saw it, for Falk.

He plays a crusty old guy named Sam Kleinman, who descends one day upon his son, Ben (Paul Reiser), with astonishing news: Muriel (Olympia Dukakis), his wife of countless years, has walked out on him. She left a note that essentially said: "I have to go. I have to be alone." Why? Why would she do anything? Why would Sam, who has been married to her for most of his life, expect her to do a crazy thing like that?

Ben is a successful professional, happily married to Rachel (Elizabeth Perkins). There has been talk of moving out of New York and buying a place in the country, and Ben takes Sam along to inspect a property. "This house was built by my grandfather after the Civil War," the owner tells them. Sam is unmoved and wants to know details about the septic tank drainage.

They have car trouble, and when they appeal to a mechanic, they find on his lot a beautifully restored 1940 Ford Deluxe coupe convertible. It reminds Sam of the first cars of his young manhood. They buy it right there on the spot, thereby following two rules of the Little Movie Glossary. One provides that characters drive classic cars whenever possible because modern cars are boring and all look alike; the other calls for ragtops because it makes it easier to see and light the characters. They begin an odyssey through the beautiful scenery and foliage of upstate New York.

The movie is sort of a sideways version of *Sideways*, even down to a scene where the two men join two women for dinner. The difference is, in *Sideways* the guys desperately want to impress the women, and in *The Thing About My*

Folks they want to impress each other. The women excuse themselves to go to the powder room, and somehow we know they won't be coming back. Sam and Ben are so deep in conversation, it's awhile before they realize they've been dumped.

What do they talk about? The early days of Sam's marriage. The meaning of life. Why they never talked about important things. How Sam's job kept him away a lot of the time. All the usual stuff. They also do the usual things. They go on a fishing trip, although they are not fishermen, and play pool, and Sam turns out to know his way around the table.

What will be the result of this trip? Falk has a wonderful speech: "You'll be here when your old man finds himself. While we're at it, we can find you, too. We can find the whole goddamned family. We got a car."

Then a dramatic document emerges: A letter written by Muriel to Sam, two weeks before Ben was born, which has waited in its envelope ever since. What the letter says I will leave for you to discover, but it places the entire marriage in a different light and leads to some closing scenes in which Dukakis has little to do but does it wonderfully; I was reminded a little of her exasperated marriage in *Moonstruck*. Her great discovery about life ("things change, and you make adjustments") is not earthshaking, although it has the advantage of being true.

The movie was written by Reiser, who does an interesting thing with his performance: Instead of going through the usual anger and impatience of a son in this kind of story, he projects a certain protective concern; he humors his old man, sometimes feeds him straight lines, understands about his care and feeding. Old Sam, we feel, has gone at life full-bore for all these years without a lot of introspection, but he is not a monster, and his son feels love for him. Also incredulity.

The film was directed by Raymond De Felitta, whose *Two Family House* is an overlooked treasure. With this film he does what the screenplay requires, with admiration for the actors and sincere acceptance of the material. The problem is that the screenplay doesn't require enough. We have seen situations something like this so often that we need, I dunno, something either stranger or deeper. It would be nice if lifelong problems and questions got solved during a week playing hooky in a 1940 Ford Deluxe coupe, but if it were that easy, you wouldn't need the car.

Things We Lost in the Fire ★ ★ ★

R, 112 m., 2007

Halle Berry (Audrey Burke), Benicio Del Toro (Jerry Sunborne), David Duchovny (Brian Burke), Alison Lohman (Kelly), Omar Benson Miller (Neal), John Carroll Lynch (Howard Glassman), Alexis Llewellyn (Harper Burke), Micah Berry (Dony Burke). Directed by Susanne Bier and produced by Sam Mendes and Sam Mercer. Screenplay by Allan Loeb.

There is one man at the wake who doesn't seem to belong. Scruffy, unshaven, smoking, uncomfortable with himself, he draws aside from the affluent friends of the deceased. Yet he was the dead man's best friend. Jerry Sunborne (Benicio Del Toro) was never approved of by Audrey Burke (Halle Berry), the new widow, but she has invited him to the funeral all the same. She knows her husband would have wanted her to.

As *Things We Lost in the Fire* opens, Audrey was married for eleven years to Brian Burke (David Duchovny, seen in several flashbacks), and they were happy years, giving her two children and a big house in an upscale suburb. Brian was a "genius" at real estate deals, her lawyer tells her, and she has inherited a fortune. But her loneliness haunts her. In a way, it was Jerry's "fault" that her husband died, because Brian visited Jerry's flophouse on his birthday and was killed in a senseless street crime while trying to stop a stranger from beating his wife.

But that was just like Brian, being loyal to his friend and playing a good Samaritan. Jerry and Brian were friends from childhood; Jerry became a lawyer and then a drug addict, and is now trying to get clean and sober at Narcotics Anonymous. And Audrey surprises herself by inviting him to come and live with them, in a room in the garage. No, she's not thinking of falling in love with Jerry—far from it—but she knows her husband would be pleased to see his friend in a safe place, and after all, Audrey and Jerry loved Brian more than anyone else in the world.

The film, directed by the talented Danish filmmaker Susanne Bier, centers on these two damaged people, who do not precisely help each other to recover but at least to not feel so alone. The screenplay by Allan Loeb is a first feature effort, but he has six more films in the works, including one announced by Ang Lee. He is good at following the parallel advances and setbacks of his characters, and especially good at depicting how the children, ten-year-old Harper (Alexis Llewellyn) and six-year-old Dony (Micah Berry, no relation), relate to the newcomer with resentment, then dependence, then uncertainty. The movie also accurately watches how a twelve-step group works, especially in the character of the member Kelly (Alison Lohman), who keeps an eye on Jerry and alerts Audrey to a relapse. Another affecting supporting performance is by John Carroll Lynch, as a tactful neighbor who steers Jerry toward a Realtor's license.

The key performance in the film is by Del Toro, who never overplays, who sidesteps any temptation to go over the top (especially in scenes of his suffering), and whose intelligence as a onetime lawyer shows through his street-worn new reality. He is puzzled and surprised that Audrey invites him into her home, but with his options, it's the best offer he'll ever receive. There is only one scene between them that is ill-advised, and indeed unbelievable, and you'll know the one I mean.

Susanne Bier has made two films I greatly admired, *Open Hearts* (2002) and *Brothers* (2005), but in her American debut she gets a little carried away with style, especially with close-ups, and very especially with close-ups of eyes. I've never see this many great big eyes in a film: Berry's beautiful, Del Toro's bloodshot, the kids' twinkling or doubtful. The human face is the most fascinating subject for the camera, as Ingmar Bergman taught us, but its elements out of context can grow lonely.

I suppose we could be dubious about a great beauty like Halle Berry seeming to be unaware of the strangeness of asking a heroin addict to live in her garage. But I accepted her decision as motivated by a correct reading of what her husband might have wanted her to do. That question settled, the movie is an engrossing melodrama, and it has its heart in the right place.

30 Days of Night ★ ★ ½

R, 113 m., 2007

Josh Hartnett (Eben), Melissa George (Stella), Danny Huston (Marlow), Ben Foster (The Stranger), Mark Boone Junior (Beau). Directed by David Slade and produced by Sam Raimi, Rob Tapert, and Joe Drake. Screenplay by Steve Niles, Stuart Beattie, and Brian Nelson.

A gaunt stranger haunts the streets of Barrow, Alaska, warning: "That cold ain't the weather. That's Death approaching." Since Barrow is said to be the northernmost town in America, three hundred miles of roadless wilderness from its closest neighbor, and thirty days of continuous sunless night are commencing, I expected someone to reply: "You could have fooled me. I thought it was the weather."

But, yes, it is Death, which is very cold. In *30 Days of Night*, Barrow will soon be invaded by vampires, who have apparently trekked across the three hundred miles of roadless ice and snow wearing their street clothes. You'd think they could find easier blood to drink in Fairbanks or Anchorage, but sunlight is fatal to vampires, and so the month of perpetual night in Barrow lures them like Canadians to Florida.

Their method of attack is the standard one in creature features. They move with loud *whooshes* at lightning speed when you can't quite see them and with ungainly lurches when you can. They are a miserable lot. Count Dracula at least had style and a sense of personal destiny; these guys are merely obsessed with their next meal. They don't even speak that elegant Hammer Films English; they talk like a garbled transmission played backward: *"Qwe!nt raqulo*gg brop#sith!"* The movie, which speaks their language, helpfully provides subtitles. It is intriguing to think of newly converted vampires attending language classes at Berlitz, since I do not think Chomsky's theories of speech apply to the Undead.

But I could go on like this all day—or night, that is. Something about vampire movies brings out the one-liners in me, unless they are directed by Dreyer, Murnau, or Herzog. The fact is, David Slade's *30 Days of Night* is a better-than-average example of the genre, even if it follows the time-honored pattern of supplying a macho man who gathers a hardy band in hiding while the vampires snuffle about. Josh Hartnett plays the local sheriff, who teams up with his estranged wife, Stella (Melissa George), another law enforcer, who missed the last flight out of town. (Planes can't land in Barrow at night. Don't ask me why.)

The survivors hide in an attic, plunder a supermarket, and scheme and plot to outwit the vampires; this time, at least, there is no crusty old-timer to say he's going to make a run for it, because of the three hundred miles of snow, etc. The vampires stalk the frigid streets led by Marlow, played by Danny Huston, who is actually quite convincing in the role. I know he is called Marlow because of the movie's credits; in the film I believe he is referred to as *Sxz&vw#ich.*

The most interesting aspect of the movie is Barrow itself. Folks are drawn closer together when they live in such extreme circumstances, although how they support themselves is a mystery to me. No mention of drilling for oil, maintaining the pipeline, guarding against missile attacks, hunting whales, carving scrimshaw, etc. They seem to have settled there out of sheer perversity, and I guess they support themselves by selling stuff to one another. Consider that every knife, fork, spoon, and pickup truck had to come in by air transport.

I award the movie two and a half stars because it is well-made, well-photographed, and plausibly acted, and is better than it needs to be. The director, David Slade, previously made the stunningly good *Hard Candy.* Although his vampires quickly disable the town generators, there seems to be a full moon for all thirty days, bathing the streets in a cold light. Otherwise, this would be a radio play.

I have pretty much reached my quota for vampire movies, but I shouldn't hold that against this one. If you haven't seen too many, you might like it. If you are a horror fanboy, you will love it. And in the interest of equal time for the defense, I close with evocative prose by the critic Undeadmin from his five-dagger (out of five) review on DreadCentral.com: "grabs this hoary monster by the throat, pumps it full of the thick rich blood of life, and shoves it out to greet you, eat you, and coat you in glorious mists of red firing from oh-so-many newly exposed arterial sprays." ☞

39 Pounds of Love ★ ½

NO MPAA RATING, 70 m., 2005

A documentary directed by Dani Menkin and produced by Daniel J. Chalfen and Menkin. Screenplay by Ilan Heitner and Menkin.

When Ami Ankilewitz was born with spinal muscular atrophy, a doctor told his parents he might live for six years; we join him in Tel Aviv at his thirty-fourth birthday party. He is the thinnest human being I have ever seen. The skin on his arm is so tightly wrapped around the bone that only the center of a Harley-Davidson tattoo is visible. His life force is fierce and adamant.

"I just hope I live to fulfill all my dreams," Ami says. So do we all, and we don't want to die then, either. We want to sit around for years having fulfilled them. The documentary *39 Pounds of Love* informs us that Ami's dreams are three: to win the love of his caretaker, Christina, to visit America for a reunion with his brother, and to find that doctor and tell him he was wrong.

Christina is a pretty Romanian, about twenty-one years old, who lifts Ami out of his bath with frightening ease. "She is beautiful, young, alive," Ami says, using a Madonna-style microphone to amplify his fragile voice. "There is nothing in this world I want more than to be with her." Christina says she loves him, "but it is not the love of two lovers." Ami requires more love than that and sends her away: "I can't go on like this. Just tell her to go out of the house." She leaves.

Ami now plans his trip to America, against the urgent advice of his mother, Helene, who argues he is not strong enough to survive the trip. Ami insists on going and enlists his best friend and former caretaker, Asaf, to accompany him, along with Dani Menkin, the director of this film, and no doubt various crew members not seen.

They rent a van and return to his Texas birthplace for a reunion with the brother. In Santa Fe, he visits a church where miracles are said to take place, but none do, or seem about to, or seem to have occurred in the past. A motorcycle club gives him his chance to ride a Harley at last; he is placed in a sidecar, and there is a shot of the wind in his hair and a smile on his face. At the Grand Canyon, Ami passes out and is rushed away in an ambulance. Eventually he finds the elderly and perplexed Dr. Albert Cordova, who listens as Ami explains that he was the child who would die before he was six, that he is thirty-four and did not die, and that the doctor should not presume such confidence about the future. The doctor never says a word during this speech but then gets his own close-up in which he solemnly congratulates Ami on his longevity and wishes him good health.

These are the materials for a touching documentary, but that's what they feel like: the materials, so arranged as to suggest questions that undermine the effect of the film. We know that in most documentaries some casual rearrangement of reality takes place, and events happen at least in part because the camera is there to witness them. But *39 Pounds of Love* feels uncomfortably stage-managed and raises fundamental questions that it simply ignores.

When Ami protests his love for Christina, and she replies, and he sends her away, there is the distinct sensation that all three events were predetermined before they happened in front of the camera. "When was the first time you realized you were completely different?" he is asked, and replies, "When Christina walked out the door." Really? He realized it as late as the events in this film? There's an indefinable scent of reality *actually happening right now* in most documentaries. In this one, we feel that Ami knows Christina will leave before he says he loves her, and that she has already left before we see her leave.

Then the best friend and former caretaker arrives to support the trip to America. But is Asaf along merely as best friend, or has he been hired again as caretaker to make the film possible? It is suggested that the brother has been estranged from the family (there is another brother, never seen, and the Mexican mother's Israeli ex-husband, never dealt with). But when the brother emerges from his American house, it is for a joyous reunion. Was the estrangement settled offscreen? What was its cause? Had it never before occurred to anyone in Israel that Ami could ride in a Harley sidecar? As for poor Dr. Cordova, he seems startled by his role, and there is some question in the film itself about whether this is one and the same man who made the dire prediction about Ami.

Those are questions involving what we see. More perplexing are questions about what we don't see. After Ami collapses and is taken away by ambulance, what happened then? How much time passed before the visit to Cordova? What risks were involved? Was the American visit cut short? The film itself is certainly cut short; it ends after seventy minutes, without any scenes of Ami returning home and without any feeling of closure; it simply stops and the credits begin, at a point when everything we know about storytelling suggests there should be scenes of closure.

How is Ami today? What are his thoughts about his journey? Isn't it ominous that there are no homecoming scenes? Were they not filmed, or were they not happy? "The trip is not going to end well," a friend predicts before it begins. Any experienced documentarian watching this film would be keeping a mental inventory of the missing scenes, realizing that without them, as the saying goes, "we don't have a movie."

None of this is intended to detract from the courage and will of Ami Ankilewitz. His life is extraordinary. But he has not been well-served by the documentarians. Having been assigned by fate to an undeveloped body, he is the victim for reasons unknown of an undeveloped film. That *39 Pounds of Love* was short-listed as an Oscar contender suggests that the short-listers were not knowledgeable about documentaries, or that they were honoring Ami and not his film. That this film but not Werner Herzog's *Grizzly Man* made the cut reflects bad judgment bordering on scandal.

This Christmas ★ ★ ★

PG-13, 120 m., 2007

Loretta Devine (Shirley Ann "Ma Dear" Whitfield), Delroy Lindo (Joseph Black), Idris Elba (Quentin Whitfield), Regina King (Lisa "Sistah" Moore), Sharon Leal (Kelli Whitfield), Lauren London (Mel Whitfield), Columbus Short (Claude Whitfield), Chris Brown (Michael "Baby" Whitfield), Laz Alonso (Malcolme Moore), Keith Robinson (Devean Brooks), Mekhi Phifer (Gerald), David Banner (Mo). Directed by Preston A. Whitmore II and produced by Whitmore and Will Packer. Screenplay by Whitmore.

I'm not going to make the mistake of trying to summarize what happens in *This Christmas.* If you see it, you'll know what I mean. I'm not even talking about spoilers; I'm talking about all the setups as the Whitfield family gathers for the first time in four years. Everybody walks in the door with a secret, and Ma Dear (Loretta Devine), the head of the family, has two: She has divorced her husband and is living with her boyfriend, Joseph (Delroy Lindo). Almost everyone in the family secretly knows her secrets, but nobody knows most of the others'.

That makes *This Christmas* a very busy holiday comedy, where plot points circle and land on an overcrowded schedule. Once I saw what was happening, I started to enjoy it. Preston A. Whitmore II, the writer and director, must have sat up for long hours into the night in front of hundreds of three-by-five-inch index cards tacked to a corkboard to keep all this straight.

Ma Dear has, let's see—a son who is secretly married to a white woman (whoops, forgot to mention the Whitfields are African-American), a daughter who thinks she's better than everyone else, a daughter who thinks she's in love but may be mistaken, a daughter whose husband fools around on her, a son who owes money big-time to a couple of guys who yearn to break his legs, and a youngest son named "Baby" who is afraid to tell her about his deepest dream.

Ma Dear is played by the irreplaceable Loretta Devine (*Grey's Anatomy, Dreamgirls, Down in the Delta*). In order, the children I listed are played by Columbus Short, Sharon Leal, Lauren London, Regina King, Idris Elba, and Chris Brown. A strong cast, and we do begin to feel a sense of family, because for all their problems, they love one another and accept weaknesses they cannot ignore. They all talk so much, though, that they should get extra credit for having any secrets at all. You tell one person something in this family, and you might as well announce it on *Oprah*.

Every single cast member, and a few I didn't mention, such as wives, boyfriends, and hoodlums, has a couple of big scenes as problems are revealed, reach crisis proportions, and are healed in one way or another. There is also a lot of eating going on, which is necessary at Christmastime, although this isn't a movie like *Soul Food* where everyone is a champion cook.

But what I think audiences will enjoy most is the music. Baby Whitfield's big secret from his mother is—don't tell anyone—he wants to be a singer. She already has one musician son, the one being chased by gamblers, and wants her youngest to do something more respectable. Baby is played by Chris Brown, who is only eighteen and has already sold millions of albums, and who is a hip-hop artist who can actually sing a traditional song in a classic and beautiful style, as he proves on the occasion when his mother finds out his big secret. At a church, gospel artist DeNetria Champ has another showstopper. And the sound track is alive.

This is a movie about African-Americans, but it's not "an African-American movie." It's an American movie, about a rambunctious family that has no more problems than any other family but simply happens to discover and grapple with them in about forty-eight hours. What's surprising is how well Whitmore, the director, manages to direct traffic. He's got one crisis cooling, another problem exploding, a third dilemma gathering steam, and people exchanging significant looks about secrets still not introduced. It's sort of a screwball comedy effect, but with a heart.

This Is England ★ ★ ★ ½

NO MPAA RATING, 98 m., 2007

Thomas Turgoose (Shaun), Stephen Graham (Combo), Jo Hartley (Cynth), Andrew Shim (Milky), Vicky McClure (Lol), Joseph Gilgun (Woody). Directed by Shane Meadows and produced by Mark Herbert. Screenplay by Meadows

A burning need is the first thing we see in Shaun's eyes. He needs a father, he needs to be taller and stronger, he needs to dress like the other kids dress, he needs to fit in somewhere. Shaun, played by Thomas Turgoose in one of those performances that seem more like self-discovery than an act of will, is twelve years old and lives at the shabby end of a town in Yorkshire, not far from the sea. It is July 1983, and his father has been killed in the Falklands War; he takes the death as a kind of betrayal.

There isn't much money in the family. His mother (Jo Hartley) throws up her hands when he complains about his lack of Doc Martens shoes, without which a boy his age might as well stay home. She sacrifices to buy him some look-alikes, and when he complains they're not the real thing, she says they're better: "These are from *London*!" All the same.

Shaun is always getting beaten up and picked on, until one day he cuts through an underpass and meets a gang of skinheads led by Woody (Joe Gilgun). Woody is friendly. Cheers him up. Tells him he can come around again. Soon Shaun has a surrogate family and a new social group and a better self-image, especially when one of the gang girls shaves off his curly hair.

His mother is horrified. She marches Shaun down to the café where the gang hangs out, wants to know who did this to her son, and asks, "Don't you think he's a little young to be hanging around with you lot?" Then, curiously, she leaves Shaun in their care. You could spend a lot of time thinking about why she does that.

Shane Meadows's *This Is England* focuses on a specific tipping-point in the history of English skinheads. As we meet the gang, it is somewhat benign and not racist (Milky, played by Andrew Shim, is Afro-Caribbean). Shaun has, in a sense, a new family, and even gets his first kiss from a goth girl who likes him. Then Combo (Stephen Graham) is released from prison, and with the lessons he learned there he teaches them violence, looting, and racism. When the gang splits in two, Shaun makes the mistake of following Combo, maybe because he is more impressed by his strength than Woody's friendship.

All of this takes place nearly twenty-five years ago in England, but it could take place today in any American city. Poverty, absent fathers, and dangerous streets make gang membership seem like a safe haven, and soon Shaun is aping the bigger guys, swaggering around, disregarding his mother, getting in trouble.

Meadows knows this world. The director of such films as *Once Upon a Time in the Midlands* (2003), a portrait of working-class life, he says he was a skinhead at about Shaun's age. Other films, like Alan Clarke's *Made in Britain* (1982), with its early Tim Roth performance, also show the strange attraction to violence that grows in such gangs: Do they hurt and get hurt out of hatred, alienation, fear, or a compulsion to fit into the gang? When two gangs fight, is that essentially a mutual initiation ceremony? In England, certainly at that time, handguns were not easy to own, so at least the body count was low. Guns and cars make accidental drive-by killings common in Chicago, where the gangs have it easy; when you're on foot, it's rare to murder a six-year-old girl when you're really after her neighbor.

The movie is taut, tense, relentless. It shows why Shaun feels he needs to belong to a gang, what he gets out of it, and how it goes wrong. Without saying so, it also explains why skinheads are skinheads: Any threatened group has a tendency to require its members to adopt various costumes, hair, or presentation styles that mark them as members, so they can't deny it or escape it, and the group can exercise authority even at a distance.

What happens at the end is part of history: Skinheads became allied with the neo-Nazi National Front. They became violent toward nonwhites and immigrants. It wasn't so much that they hated them, perhaps, as that they needed an enemy to validate themselves because they felt as worthless as they said their opponents were. Whenever you see one group demonizing another group, what they charge the others with is often what they fear about themselves. For Shaun, this is more than he was looking for. Better to be lonely than to be deprived of the right to be alone.

The Three Burials of Melquiades Estrada ★ ★ ★ ★

R, 121 m., 2006

Tommy Lee Jones (Pete Perkins), Barry Pepper (Mike Norton), Julio Cedillo (Melquiades Estrada), Dwight Yoakam (Sheriff Belmont), January Jones (Lou Ann Norton), Melissa Leo (Rachel). Directed by Tommy Lee Jones and produced by Michael Fitzgerald and Jones. Screenplay by Guillermo Arriaga.

The Three Burials of Melquiades Estrada tells the kind of story that John Huston or Sam Peckinpah might have wanted to film. It begins with a bedrock of loyalty and honor between men and mixes it with a little madness. In an era when hundreds of lives are casually destroyed in action movies, here is an entire film in which one life is honored, and one death is avenged.

The director and star is Tommy Lee Jones, and the story proceeds directly from fundamental impulses we sense in many of his screen appearances. Jones is most at home in characters who mean business and do not suffer fools gladly. Here he plays Pete Perkins, the hard-working operator of a small cattle operation who hires an illegal Mexican immigrant named Melquiades Estrada (Julio Cedillo) to work as a cowboy. When Melquiades is killed in a stupid shooting involving a rookie agent for the Border Patrol, Pete sees that the local sheriff (Dwight Yoakam) is going to ignore the case. So Pete takes justice into his own hands. And not simple justice, which might involve killing the agent, but poetic justice, which elevates the movie into the realm of parable.

All the action takes place in a small border town of appalling poverty of spirit. This is a hard land for men, and a heartbreaking one for women. We meet two in particular. Lou Ann Norton (January Jones) is the wife of Mike, the border patrolman. Rachel (Melissa Leo) is the waitress in the local restaurant, married to Bob the owner but available for afternoons in motel rooms, not because she is a prostitute but because she is friendly and bored.

The story is told in links between the present and the recent past; the writer, Guillermo Arriaga *(21 Grams)*, was honored at Cannes 2005 as best writer, and Jones was named best actor. We see that the Border Patrol agent, Mike Norton (Barry Pepper), is violent and cruel, perhaps as a way of masking his insecurity. He beats up a woman trying to enter the country and is told by his commander, "You were way overboard there, boy." He lives in a mobile home with Lou Ann, who watches soap operas during sex and hangs out at the diner with Rachel because there is absolutely nothing else to do.

The lives of these characters, including Melquiades, are connected in ways that I will not reveal and that show how they all have two avenues of communication: the public and the personal. Some of the hidden connections produce ironies that only we understand, since the characters don't know as much about each other as we do.

The main line of the movie forms as Pete Perkins kidnaps Mike Norton, handcuffs him, and explains to him that Melquiades Estrada, the dead Mexican, was his friend. Melquiades often talked about his village in Mexico, Pete says, and about his wife and family. Now Mike is going to dig up Melquiades's body, and the two men are going to ride into Mexico, return the dead man to his village, and give him a proper burial.

This is a process involving a good deal of gruesome labor. I was reminded of the Peckinpah masterpiece *Bring Me the Head of Alfredo Garcia*, which is also about a journey through Mexico with a dead man—or more exactly, with his head, which suggests that the rest of the man is dead, too, and is quite enough to draw flies. Mike gags as he digs up the body, and Pete is practical about the problems they face: He fills the corpse with antifreeze.

The horseback journey of the two men is a learning experience, shall we say, for Mike the border patrolman. He begins with threats and defiance, tearfully tries to explain how the shooting of Melquiades was a stupid accident, is finally mired in sullen despair. Of their adventures along the way, two are remarkable. One involves an old blind man, living alone, who suspects his son in the city may have died. He welcomes them, offers them what he has, then makes a haunting request. The other comes when Mike is bitten by a snake, and his life is saved by a woman who has no reason to do so. This scene also has a poetic resolution.

The journey and its end will involve more discoveries and more surprises; it traverses the same kinds of doomed landscapes we picture when we read *Blood Meridian* by Cormac McCarthy. What gathers in this story of lonely men and deep impulses is a kind of grandeur; Jones plays Pete Perkins not as a hero but as a man who looks at what has happened to his friend and responds according to the opportunities at hand. He is a man who never puts two and two together without getting exactly four.

There is one word at the end of the film that carries a burden that a long speech could not have dealt with. It is a word that is also used near the beginning of the film. It contains whatever message Jones finds at the end of the journey. As for the rest, the journey of his body and the burials of Melquiades Estrada are an opportunity for all of the characters in the movie to discover who they are and what they are made of. By the end of the film no one is watching TV.

Three Days of Rain ★ ★ ½

NO MPAA RATING, 94 m., 2005

Don Meredith (John), Michael Santoro (Thunder), Joey Bilow (Denis), Peter Falk (Waldo), Merle Kennedy (Tess), Erick Avari (Alex), Blythe Danner (Beverly), Bill Stockton (Michael), Maggie Walker (Jen). Directed by Michael Meredith and produced by Bill Stockton and Robert Casserly. Screenplay by Meredith, based on short stories by Anton Chekhov.

"You're not a kind person," a husband says to his wife of many years, after she won't give a doggie bag to a homeless man who asks for it. This is something he didn't realize and can't live with. There are other people, kind and unkind, in *Three Days of Rain,* and as a storm crouches over Cleveland we wonder if it makes much difference. It is not a kind world.

Consider John (Don Meredith), a taxi driver who has just learned that his son is dead. He runs a red light, is distracted, tells a customer of his loss. The passenger (Blythe Danner) is not sympathetic. "I'm *destined* to hear these things!" she cries out from the backseat. "I'm here to suffer pain. Let me out of this cab!"

There are another father and son in the movie. Waldo (Peter Falk) is a drunk whose charm is so meticulously practiced that we realize his personal style has entirely replaced his self-respect. He asks the bartender for another drink, is told he is out of money, agrees as if relieved to have resolved a great mystery, and then "wonders" if he could have just another "drop or two" to refresh his glass.

Waldo is forever asking his son (Bill Stockton) for an "advance" because his pension check is late, and then charmingly admitting that he has no pension and, therefore, no check. The son is patient with him—and kind, although the only kindness Waldo desires is money for more drinking. Since Waldo is so good at drinking, so courteous and elaborately courtly, would it be a kindness to impose sobriety and leave him with no lies with which to exercise his style?

Another story involves a retarded janitor (Joey Bilow) who is being edged out of his job to make room for a relative of his supervisor. The operation has to be done carefully, the boss observes, because "they don't want the National Association of Forrest Gumps getting on their ass." The janitor may be slow, but as it turns out, he is focused. Still another story involves a judge who with his wife has taken in a foster child. He knows, but his wife does not, that their babysitter (Merle Kennedy) is the baby's birth mother. Is it a kindness to let the mother see her child under those conditions? Is it kind for the judge to keep the secret from his wife?

Kindness and its opposite keep circling around the husband (Erick Avari) and his selfish wife (Maggie Walker). He can't get that homeless man out of his head; he goes back to the neighborhood, quizzes a newsstand guy, wants to do—what? Buy the homeless guy a meal? That would be kind, but what of the next meal?

The movie was written and directed by Michael Meredith (the actor playing the taxi driver is his father, the football star). He based it on six short stories by Anton Chekhov. In the genre of interlocking stories about lonely lives, *Three Days of Rain* is only a sketch compared to the power of Rodrigo Garcia's *Nine Lives,* which continues to grow in my memory. But there is a way in which movies like this create the stage on which we perform our own lives.

Say it is a cold December night and you live in Chicago. You go to Facets Multimedia, known as a home for those who love movies beyond all reason. You watch the movie, with its rain and unkindness and its lonely people, and you are not unhappy to have seen it. It was not made of ugliness and calculation, and it contained certain moments of human perception. Then you linger in the Facets video store and talk casually with someone else just coming out of the movie. You are both the kind of people who would go out into the cold to seek a movie you hope will be better than you expect.

One of you stays in the video store longer than the other, but you nod when you meet again on the Fullerton L platform. At least you are not the only person like yourself. When you get home, you look through Chekhov to see if you can find some of the stories that inspired the movie. It goes without saying that you have Chekhov on your shelf. Somewhere else in the city, the person you met is reading Chekhov, too.

Three . . . Extremes ★ ★ ★ ½
R, 126 m., 2005

"Dumplings"
With: Bai Ling, Miriam Yeung, Tony Ka-Fai Leung. Directed by Fruit Chan and produced by Peter Ho-Sun Chan. Screenplay by Lilian Lee.

"Cut"
With: Lee Byung-Hun, Lim Won-Hee, Gang Hye-Jung. Directed by Park Chan-Wook and produced by Ahn Soo-Hyun. Screenplay by Park.

"Box"
With: Kyoko Hasegawa, Atsuro Watabe. Directed by Takashi Miike and produced by Fumio Inoue, Naoki Sato, and Shun Shimizu. Screenplay by Haruko Fukushima, based on a story by Bun Saikou.

Three . . . Extremes collects directors from Hong Kong, Korea, and Japan to make horror films, each about forty minutes long. The device was common in Europe in the 1960s, where movies like *Boccaccio '70* set assorted directors loose on a vaguely related theme. Here the theme is horror, and by "horror" I don't mean the Hollywood routine of shock, blood, and special effects. These films are deeply, profoundly creepy.

The first one, "Dumplings," may be unwatchable for some people when they figure out what's actually going on. There could be walkouts. Some of those who wait until the end may wish they'd left with the others; the movie's closing image is depraved on a scale that might have shocked the surrealists. I say this not in opposition but simply as an observation.

All three short films are examples of the Extreme Asia movement, which began as a programming category at film festivals and seems to be expanding into a genre. The point is to push beyond the worn-out devices of traditional horror films, to essentially abandon the supernatural and move into horror that has its expression in the dreads and traumas of nightmare. *Three* (2002) was the first Extreme Asia trilogy, and now here are three more.

"Dumplings," directed by Hong Kong's Fruit Chan, takes the debate about stem cells and other recycling of human body material to its ultimate extremity. I don't think the film's science is sound (I sincerely hope not), but the motivation is unassailable: There are some people who will do anything to prolong their youth and beauty.

That's a classic theme in stories of horror and the supernatural, but consider the scenario here. A former TV star (Miriam Yeung) is still attractive but no longer acting. Her husband goes on long trips without her and doesn't even bother with alibis. She turns to a woman (Bai Ling) she has heard about—a perky, cheerful type who works out of a small apartment in a high-rise. This woman cooks and serves dumplings. "How old do I look to you?" she asks her client. The actress guesses—oh, about thirty. I would have said even younger. The cook says she's a lot older than that.

The secret is in her dumplings. The actress pays for an order, looks at them dubiously, eats them, comes back for more. She thinks she looks better. It's not a Dorian Gray situation but, yes, the dumplings do seem to have an effect. The actress wants more dramatic results, faster. That will not be so easy, the cook says, but she will try. What she does in assembling her ingredients is profoundly disturbing. In some cases it may not technically be illegal, on other occasions it is. Depends on the circumstances. I will not describe her secrets, but I will tell you that you may be profoundly disturbed, and that the movie's last scene, sick and evil as it is, doesn't flinch when it comes to confronting the story's ultimate implications.

The second film is "Cut," from Korea, by Park Chan-Wook, whose haunting *Oldboy* made a stir in 2003 with its story of a man kept captive for years for no reason he can imagine. In this story, a horror film director recovers from unconsciousness to find his wife, a pianist, suspended in midair above her piano by an arrangement of piano wires. A young child is bound and gagged on the sofa. The director is tied at the end of a tether allowing him to move only so far.

A laughing, angry man appears. His grudge against the director is interesting: He hates his victim because he is rich, handsome, successful—and a good man. The captor, on the other hand, is poor, ugly, a failure, and not a good man. He wants to force the director to commit evil so that he will realize he is not so good after all—that to be good sometimes means only to have escaped the need to be bad. What the director is asked to do, and whether he does it, and what happens then, you will see for yourself. "Cut" is an effective film but has a certain contrivance that's lacking in the implacable and selfish horror of "Dumplings."

The third film, "Box," is the most complex of all. Made by the Japanese director Takashi Miike, it involves small twin girls who work with their father in a magic act. Their trick is to fold themselves into impossibly small boxes. Their father throws darts at the boxes, which spring open to reveal that the girls have been replaced by flowers.

Backstage, we discover that the father favors one girl over the other, and there is a suggestion of incest. The neglected sister finds her twin rehearsing one day and slams the lid shut on her box. What happens next is horrible enough on the surface level, but there are other levels of possibility here. The story is a recurring nightmare of an adult novelist who may or may not have been one of the two young girls, and may or may not have performed just such an act. The last shot will give you a lot to think about.

What all three of these stories share is the quality found in Edgar Allan Poe, H. P. Lovecraft, and Stephen King: an attention to horror as it emerges from everyday life as transformed by fear, fantasy, and depravity. Here is not a joker in a Halloween mask, scaring screaming teenagers, but adults whose needs and weaknesses turn on them with savage, relentless logic. I imagine *Three . . . Extremes* will attract some customers who thought they wanted to see a horror movie but find they're getting more than they bargained for.

3:10 to Yuma ★ ★ ★ ★

R, 117 m., 2007

Russell Crowe (Ben Wade), Christian Bale (Dan Evans), Logan Lerman (Will Evans), Ben Foster (Charlie Prince), Peter Fonda (Byron McElroy), Vinessa Shaw (Emmy Roberts), Alan Tudyk (Doc Potter), Gretchen Mol (Alice Evans), Dallas Roberts (Grayson Butterfield). Directed by James Mangold and produced by Cathy Konrad. Screenplay by Michael Brandt, Derek Haas, and Halsted Welles, based on a short story by Elmore Leonard.

James Mangold's *3:10 to Yuma* restores the wounded heart of the Western and rescues it from the morass of pointless violence. The Western in its glory days was often a morality play, a story about humanist values penetrating the lawless anarchy of the frontier. It still follows that tradition in films like Eastwood's *Unforgiven,* but the audience's appetite for morality plays and Westerns seems to be fading. Here, the quality of the acting and the thought behind the film make it seem like a vanguard of something new, even though it's a remake of a good movie fifty years old.

The plot is so easily told that Elmore Leonard originally wrote it as a short story. A man named Dan Evans (Christian Bale), who lost a leg in the Civil War, has come to the Arizona territory to try his luck at ranching. It's going badly, made worse by a neighboring bully who wants to force him off his land. The territory still fears Indian raids, and just as much the lawless gang led by Ben Wade (Russell Crowe), which sticks up stagecoaches, robs banks, casually murders people, and outguns any opposition. Through a series of developments that seem almost dictated by fate, Dan Evans finds himself part of a posse sworn in to escort Wade, captured and handcuffed, to the nearby town of Contention, where the 3:10 p.m. train has a cell in its mail car that will transport Wade to the prison in Yuma and a certain death sentence.

Both Dan and Ben have elements in their characters that come under test in this adventure. Dan fears he has lost the confidence of his wife, Alice (Gretchen Mol), and teenage son, Will (Logan Lerman), who doubt he can make the ranch work. Still less does Alice see why her transplanted eastern husband should risk his life as a volunteer. The son, Will, who has practically memorized dime novels about Ben Wade, idealizes the outlaw, and when Dan realizes the boy has followed the posse, he orders him to return home. "He ain't following you," Wade says. "He's following me."

That's an insight into Wade. He plays his persona like a performance. He draws, reads, philosophizes, is incomparably smarter than the scum in his gang. Having spent untold time living on the run with them, he may actually find it refreshing to spend time with Dan, even as his captive. Eventually the two men end up in a room in the Contention hotel, overlooking the street, in earshot of the train whistle, surrounded outside by armed men who want to rescue Ben or kill him.

These general outlines also describe the 1957 version of *3:10 to Yuma,* directed by Delmer Daves, starring Glenn Ford and Van Heflin in the roles of the rancher and the outlaw. The movie, with its railroad timetable, followed the slowly advancing clock in *High Noon* (1952) and was compared to it; when I saw it in 35 mm at Telluride in the 1980s, I thought it was better than *High Noon,* not least because of the personality shifts it involves.

Mangold's version is better still than the 1957 original because it has better actors with more thought behind their dialogue. Christian Bale plays not simply a noble hero, but a man who has avoided such risks as he now takes, and is almost at a loss to explain why he is bringing a killer to justice, except that having been mistreated and feeling unable to provide for his family, he is fed up, and here he takes his stand. Crowe, on the other hand, plays not merely a merciless killer, although he is that, too, but a man also capable of surprising himself. He is too intelligent to have only one standard behavior that must fit all situations, and is perhaps bored of having that expected of him.

Westerns used to be the showcases of great character actors, of whom I was lucky enough to meet Dub Taylor, Jack Elam, Chill Wills, Ben Johnson, and, when she wasn't doing a million other things, Shelley Winters. *3:10 to Yuma* has two roles that need a special character flavor and fills them perfectly. Peter Fonda plays McElroy, a professional bounty hunter who would rather claim the price on Ben Wade's head than let the government execute him for free. And Ben Foster plays Charlie Prince, the second in command of Wade's gang, who seems half in love with Wade, or maybe Charlie's half-aware that's he's all in love. Wade would know which and wouldn't care, except as material for his study of human nature.

Locked in the hotel room, surrounded by death for one or the other, the two men begin to talk. Without revealing anything of the plot, let me speculate that each has found the first man he has met in years who is his equal in conversation. Crowe and Bale play this dialogue so precisely that it never reveals itself for what it really is, a process of mutual insight. One test of a great actor is the ability to let dialogue do its work invisibly, something you can also see in *In the Valley of Elah* with Tommy Lee Jones and Charlize Theron. Too many actors are like the guy who laughs at his own joke and then tells it to you again.

James Mangold first came into view with an extraordinary movie named *Heavy* (1995). His *Walk the Line* (2005) won an Oscar for Reese Witherspoon. To remake *3:10 to Yuma* seems an odd choice after such other modern films as *Girl, Interrupted,* but the movie itself proves he had a good reason for choosing it. In hard times, Americans have often turned to the Western to reset their compasses. In very hard times, it takes a very good Western. Attend well to Ben Wade's last words in this movie, and whom he says them to, and why.

Three Times ★ ★ ★ ★

NO MPAA RATING, 130 m., 2006

Shu Qi (May/Ah Mei/Jing), Chang Chen (Chen/Mr. Chang/Zhen). Directed by Hou Hsiao-hsien and produced by Hua-fu Chang, Wen-Ying Huang, and Ching-Song Liao. Screenplay by Chu Tien-wen.

Three stories about a man and a woman, all three using the same actors. Three years: 1966, 1911, 2005. Three varieties of love: unfulfilled, mercenary, meaningless. All photographed with such visual beauty that watching the movie is like holding your breath so the butterfly won't stir.

The director is Hou Hsiao-hsien, from Taiwan, and this probably will be the first of his seventeen films you've seen. "The movie distribution system of North America is devoted to maintaining a wall between you and Hou Hsiao-hsien," I wrote after seeing this film at Cannes 2005. Here is a factoid from IMDb.com: "Of the ten films that Hou Hsiao-hsien directed between 1980 and 1989, seven received best film or best director awards from prestigious international film festivals. In a 1988 worldwide critics' poll, Hou was championed as one of the three directors most crucial to the future of cinema."

His subject in *Three Times* is our yearning to love and be loved, and the way the world casually dismisses it. His first story, "A Time for Love," set in 1966, involves Chen (Chang Chen), a soldier on his way to the army, who falls in love with the hostess of a pool hall (Shu Qi). The camera perfectly composes the room and the light pouring in from an open door, and the woman, named May, moves gracefully and without hurry to rack the balls, arrange the cues, serve the customers. Does she like Chen? I think she does. When he gets leave, he hurries back to the pool hall, but she is gone. On the sound track, Hou uses the 1959 recording by the Platters of "Smoke Gets in Your Eyes." That is the song that tells us, "They said, some day you'll find, all who love are blind."

In the second story, "A Time for Freedom," set in 1911, the woman is named Ah Mei, and she is a prostitute in a brothel. The man, named Chang, often visits her, and between them a friendship and comfort grows. He is very filled with his own importance and has plans to reform the world, although perhaps he might reflect that his reforms might start by freeing Ah Mei from the brothel. She begins to love him. He loves her, too, I think, but all who love are blind. She never lets him see how she feels. Only we see. The movie is shot like a silent film, although with a fluid moving camera the real films of 1911 certainly lacked. In some sort of accommodation with the rules, Ah Mei cannot be heard to speak in this story, but she can be heard to sing.

The third story, "A Time for Youth," takes place in the present, in modern Taipei. The characters are named Jing and Zhen. She is a pop singer. He works as a photographer. She has a female lover but neglects her while falling in love with the man. In each of the three films, the woman is a professional performer (hostess, prostitute, singer), and the man, in one way or another, is a client. Perhaps the message is that if people meet in a way involving money and their jobs, they are not free to see each other with the perfect clarity required by love. "When your heart's on fire, you must realize, smoke gets in your eyes."

There isn't any deep message in this film. Love never has any deep message. Meryl Streep once said that every good actor knows that the statement "I love you" is a question. We send our love out into the world hoping it will not be laughed at or destroyed. We trust the one we love to accept it. In these stories, acceptance doesn't come with the territory. The pool hall hostess meets a lot of pool players every day. Yes, Chen is nice enough, but when she gets a new job, she doesn't wait for him. The prostitute sees a lot of men. When she falls for Chang, he doesn't notice because he sees himself as her client. And the modern couple are so wrapped up in overlapping relationships and a running parallel life on cell phones that they can barely deal with each other at all.

More than three centuries ago, Andrew Marvell wrote a poem named *To His Coy Mistress*, in which he said they would be free to love, "Had we but world enough, and time." I think these three couples have world enough and time, but the woman in the first, the man in the second, and both in the third are not willing to accept happiness. They can't even see it's there for the having.

This observation is as shallow as a popular song. Maybe there isn't any deeper level. Most of the things we really believe about love are stated most simply and unforgettably in song lyrics. The lives in *Three Times* are not tragedies, unless the tragedy is that they never become the lives they could have been. Hou Hsiao-hsien shows us people who could make each other happy and be happy themselves, and he watches them miss their chance. "And yet today, my love has gone away. I am without my love."

Thumbsucker ★ ★ ★

R, 97 m., 2005

Lou Pucci (Justin Cobb), Tilda Swinton (Audrey Cobb), Vince Vaughn (Mr. Geary), Vincent D'Onofrio (Mike Cobb), Keanu Reeves (Dr. Perry Lyman), Benjamin Bratt (Matt Schraam), Kelli Garner (Rebecca). Directed by Mike Mills and produced by Anthony Bregman and Bob Stephenson. Screenplay by Mills, based on the novel by Walter Kirn.

Sometimes parents act like parents, and sometimes they want to be your best friends. The ideal parents would be both, since either role in isolation can lead to unhappy teenagers. Since teenagers are by their nature unhappy anyway, perhaps this paragraph can end now.

Thumbsucker is about a bright but obscurely discontented seventeen-year-old named Justin (Lou Pucci), who still sucks his thumb. His parents are Audrey and Mike (Tilda Swinton and Vincent D'Onofrio), who like to be called by their first names. Audrey is still channeling her teenager within and has a crush on a TV star named Matt (Benjamin Bratt). She sends in coupons from cereal boxes in hopes of winning a date with him. She may also be way too impressed by a celeb patient at the rehab center where she works. (Her family is intensely curious about her day job: "Who did you see? Matthew Perry? Whitney Houston? Robert Downey Jr.?")

Justin is embarrassed by his thumbsucking, especially when he gets a crush on a girl named Rebecca (Kelli Garner) who, like most girls nowadays, doesn't think it's cool for a thumb to get all the attention. Justin turns not to a shrink but to an orthodontist named Perry (Keanu Reeves). Perry tries hypnosis; when he asks Justin to walk in an imaginary forest and conjure his "power animal," the best Justin can come up with is a fawn. After all these years it's amazing he doesn't need braces, but instead he gets Perry's mantras: "You don't need your thumb, and your thumb doesn't need you." Demonstrably not true.

The school principal prescribes Ritalin, perhaps in hopes that it will unharness Justin's inner power animal, or whatever. It does. Certain other pharmaceuticals occasionally make a contribution. Earlier in the movie Justin was dumbstruck when asked to rebut an argument in the speech class taught by Mr. Geary (Vince Vaughn), but he turns overnight into a confident, persuasive speaker who becomes the star of Geary's debate team. Geary coaches debate the way Mike Ditka coached football ("Be a stone-faced killer"). But even he grows uncomfortable with the inner animal Justin has unleashed, which turns out to be an egotistical monster.

I have focused on Justin, but really the movie is equally about the adult characters, who all seem to have lacked adequate parenting themselves. We talk about the tragedy of children giving birth to children; maybe that can happen at any age. Certainly Justin and Audrey look and behave a lot alike, and certainly Mike distances himself from his wife's obsessions with other men; perhaps having failed in an early dream of playing pro sports, he has felt inadequate ever since.

Then there is the matter of Rebecca, who is willing to go so far and no further with Justin. She has chosen him for sexual foreplay because "I need to educate myself," and Justin seems to have runway skills without all the dangers associated with a pilot's license.

The movie contains many of the usual ingredients of teenage suburban angst tragicomedies, but writer-director Mike Mills, who began with a novel by Walter Kirn, uses actors who can riff; Swinton and D'Onofrio are so peculiarly exact as their characters that we realize Audrey and Mike are supposed to be themselves in every scene and are never defined only as "Justin's parents." She wins the date, and she may be outta here. Or maybe not. In a lot of movies, you'd know one way or the other, but Audrey has free will and Swinton plays her as if neither one of them has looked ahead in the screenplay. Reeves, too, makes more of the orthodontist than what we'd expect. He comes up with a Val Kilmeresque detachment from the very qualities that made him famous, and when he apologizes for "hippie psychobabble," he doesn't even need to smile.

There is some symbology in the movie, involving a construction site and Rebecca's interest in ecology, but the movie is not really interested in saving the environment; it's interested in characters who say they are interested in the environment because, after all, who isn't, or shouldn't be? A subject like that functions as the foreground in suburban angst conversations: You talk about ecology because it shows you are good as a tree and, especially in Justin's case, high as the sky.

Tim Burton's Corpse Bride ★ ★ ★

PG, 75 m., 2005

With the voices of: Johnny Depp (Victor Van Dort), Helena Bonham Carter (Emily the Corpse Bride), Emily Watson (Victoria Everglot), Tracey Ullman (Nell Van Dort), Paul Whitehouse (William Van Dort), Joanna Lumley (Maudeline Everglot), Albert Finney (Finis Everglot), Richard E. Grant (Barkis Bittern), Christopher Lee (Pastor Galswells). Directed by Tim Burton and Mike Johnson and produced by Allison

Abbate and Burton. Screenplay by John August, Pamela Pettler, and Caroline Thompson.

Tim Burton's Corpse Bride is not the macabre horror story the title suggests, but a sweet and visually lovely tale of love lost. In an era when most animated films look relentlessly bright and colorful, *Corpse Bride* creates two palettes, and not the ones we expect.

The world of the living is a drab and overcast place with much of the color drained from it, and the remaining grays and purples and greens so muted they seem apologetic. The world of the dead, on the other hand, is where you'd want to spend your vacation. It's livelier, cheerier, and has brighter colors.

Also, as the hero discovers when he visits there, it *is* true that when your pets die they go to the same place you go: Victor Van Dort is greeted ecstatically by Scraps, the dog he had as a child. Scraps, to be sure, is all bones, but look at it this way: no more fleas. Or maybe skeletal fleas. I'm not sure about all the fine points.

Victor is voiced by Johnny Depp and reflects the current trend in animation by also looking like Johnny Depp. Once cartoons were voiced by anonymous drudges, but now big names do the work and lend their images to the characters. As the movie opens, a marriage is being arranged between Victor's parents and the Everglots. Nell and William Van Dort (Tracey Ullman and Paul Whitehouse) are rich fishmongers; as for Victoria Everglot (Emily Watson), her parents, Maudeline and Finnis (Joanna Lumley and Albert Finney), are poor aristocrats. A marriage would provide her family with money and his with class. Victor and Victoria have never met, except in the title of a Blake Edwards comedy, but when they're finally introduced, they're surprised to find that, despite everything, they love each other.

But is it meant to be? Victor is so shy he cannot blurt out the words of his marriage vow, and he flees to the overgrown graveyard outside the church to practice. Repeating the words to memorize them, he places the wedding ring on a twig that is not a twig but the desiccated finger of Emily (Helena Bonham Carter), whose arm is reaching up from the grave. This marriage, according to the rules of the netherworld, is a legitimate one, and soon Victor is at a wedding celebration where jolly skeletons sing and dance to a score by Danny Elfman, and the wedding cake is made of bones but looks yummy.

The movie's inspiration is to make Emily a figure of sympathy, not horror. She lost her own chance at happiness when she was murdered on the eve of her wedding and wants to be a good wife for Victor. She's rather sexy, in a spectral way, with those big eyes and plump lips, and only a few places where the skin has rotted away to reveal the bone beneath. Long dresses would be a good fashion choice.

A piano is shown at one point in the movie, and we get just a glimpse of its nameplate. It's a Harryhausen. That would be Burton's tribute to Ray Harryhausen, the man who brought stop-motion animation to the level of artistry *(Jason and the Argonauts, The Golden Voyage of Sinbad).* These days most animated movies are computer-generated, creating effortlessly flowing images. But in the days when they had to be laboriously drawn one frame at a time, it was scarcely more trouble to do tabletop animation, building model figures and moving them a tiny bit between each frame.

Famous creatures like King Kong were partly made of stop-frame animation, shot in smaller scale and then combined with live action in an optical printer so that Kong seemed enormous. When you watch *King Kong,* you may notice that his fur seems to crawl or bristle slightly; you are looking at disturbances made by the fingers of the animators between each shot. My own feeling is that the artificiality of stop-motion animation adds a quality that standard animation lacks, an eerie, otherworldly, magical quality that's hard to pin down. Certainly the macabre world of *Corpse Bride* benefits from it, and somehow it is appropriate that a skeleton would move with a subtle jerkiness. The same odd visual quality added to the appeal of Burton's *The Nightmare Before Christmas.*

Meanwhile, aboveground, the blameless Victoria is about to be married off by her heartless parents to a Victorian villain with the Dickensian name Barkis Bittern (Richard E. Grant). She deserves better. It is, after all, not her fault that Victor contracted an unexpected marriage. Nor, really, is it Victor's. Nor, for that matter, the Corpse Bride's. Three young people are unhappy when two of them should be blissful; it's not fair, even if one of them is dead.

As he does in all of his pictures, Burton fills the frame with small grace touches and droll details. He seems to have a natural affinity for the Gothic, and his live-action *Legend of Sleepy Hollow* (also with Depp) remains one of the most visually beautiful films I've seen. He likes moonlight and drear places, trees forming ominous shapes in the gloom, eyes peering uneasily into the incredible, and love struggling to prevail in worlds of complex menace. All of that is a lot for an animated fantasy to convey, but *Corpse Bride* not only conveys it but also does it, yes, charmingly.

Note: The PG *rating is about right, I think, although quite young or impressionable children may be scared by the skeletal characters. Everyone is relatively jolly, however, so maybe not.*

Touch the Sound ★ ★ ★

NO MPAA RATING, 113 m., 2005

Featuring Evelyn Glennie and Fred Frith. A documentary directed by Thomas Riedelsheimer and produced by Stefan Tolz, Leslie Hills, and Trevor Davies.

Evelyn Glennie became aware as a child that she was losing her hearing. It was suggested she attend a school for the deaf. This did not appeal to her. "Hearing or not, she will do what she wants to do," her father declared. She has. Today she is a musician specializing in percussion, and she uses her body as a "resounding chamber" through which she experiences her work.

Touch the Sound is a documentary by Thomas Riedelsheimer that follows Glennie on a musical journey around the world. We visit the Aberdeenshire farm in Scotland where she was raised, and where her father's accordion was her first taste of music. She plays in the center of Grand Central Station, and with improvised devices in a pub, and by running her wet finger across a guitar case, and in the Cologne airport, and beside a rooftop pigeon coop, and with glasses and plates in a Japanese restaurant, and on an ocean shore, and on a marimba, and obtains the sound of space itself unfolding by hurling down from a high place long sheets of graph paper. Her preferred instrument is the snare drum.

"Hearing," she tells us, "is a form of touch." A music teacher in school suggested that while performing she stop using hearing aids and focus on the vibrations picked up by her body through the air and by her bare feet on the floor. "I could hear less through the ears but more through the body," she says. Her body grew more sensitive to the vibrations in the air.

She describes herself not as "deaf," which is an absolute term, but as "profoundly deaf," by which she means she does perceive a very low level of sound. She can lip-read. Her music takes on an eerie quality through the ways of its making; it must feel right to her, and when it does, it sounds slightly uncanny to us, as if appealing to senses we were not aware we possessed. We listen to this film more intensely than is usually the case.

In the closing passages of the film, Glennie records music for a CD she is making with the musician Fred Frith. They occupy a huge abandoned factory, its empty space a sounding board. Frith plays a variety of conventional instruments, and she uses an astonishing variety of percussive ones. There is no doubt she touches the sound, because as they improvise together they develop a musical conversation.

The director, Riedelsheimer, earlier made *Rivers and Tides* (2001), about another artist from Scotland, Andy Goldsworthy, whose art involves materials found in nature. We watch as with infinite patience he builds a geometric structure of flat rocks, or assembles twigs, or directs ice as it thaws and then freezes again. Sometimes his projects collapse in mid-creation. Sometimes they exist in their final perfect form for minutes or hours. They are all doomed eventually to be swallowed up by the indifference of nature.

Glennie and Goldsworthy have in common a profound sensitivity to their environments. They look around wherever they find themselves and begin to discover ways to create the order of art out of the chaos of existence. Their art is intended to be evanescent. It can be recorded on CDs or film, but it exists most fully during its own creation. Both artists seem to live more fully because they are so completely in the moment. There is a kind of bliss about them.

Note: Touch the Sound *is not subtitled, and its words are therefore unavailable to the hearing-impaired. Riedelsheimer is said to oppose subtitles because they would affect his visual compositions. Presumably, he is as entitled to the same control over his art that his subjects exercise, but such directors as Ozu, Bergman, Scorsese, and Welles have lived with subtitles, and I imagine he could have, too.*

The music in the film might, in any case, be out of reach to most in a hearing-impaired audience, so perhaps the DVD will be a better way for them to access it. Volume can be manipulated, the actual speakers can be touched with hands and feet or sat upon, the bass can be boosted, and the experience might approximate what Glennie herself perceives. Almost all DVDs are subtitled even in the language of their making; if the DVD of Touch the Sound *lacks subtitles, then Riedelsheimer will have some explaining to do.*

Trade ★

R, 120 m., 2007

Kevin Kline (Ray), Cesar Ramos (Jorge), Alicja Bachleda-Curus (Veronica), Paulina Gaitan (Adriana), Marco Perez (Manuelo), Kate Del Castillo (Laura). Directed by Marco Kreuzpaintner and produced by Roland Emmerich and Rosilyn Heller. Screenplay by Jose Rivera, based on an article by Peter Landesman.

Trade is a movie about trade in human beings, in this case, a thirteen-year-old Mexican girl who is kidnapped and brought to New Jersey, where her virginity will be auctioned on the Internet for an expected $50,000. Chillingly, the movie is based on fact, on an article by Peter Landesman in the *New York Times Magazine.* And it's not an isolated case.

The girl, named Adriana (Paulina Gaitan), is handed off in a smooth cross-country operation. She finds only one friend along the way, a kidnapped older Polish woman named Veronica (Alicja Bachleda-Curus). Their transportation is handled by Manuelo (Marco Perez), a cruel man with a deeply buried streak of morality that begins to trouble him along the road.

The trip from Mexico to New Jersey turns into a chase, although Manuelo and his captives don't know it. Adriana's seventeen-year-old brother, Jorge (Cesar Ramos), sees her (against all odds) kidnapped in Mexico City and follows Manuelo's car all the way to the border by one means or another (against even greater odds). At a crucial moment near the border, he meets a Texas Ranger named Ray (Kevin Kline), and after some verbal scuffles, they join forces to follow Manuelo, rescue his captives, and penetrate to the heart of the slave-smuggling operation.

A nasty, vile business made more slimy because the director, Marco Kreuzpaintner, doesn't trust the intrinsic interest of his story and pumps it up with chase details, close calls, manufactured crises, and so many scenes of the captives being frightened and abused that they begin to seem gratuitous, even suspect. Yes, it is evil that these heartless gangsters, connected with the Russian Mafia, terrorize young women and sell them as objects. But is it not also evil that the film lingers on their plights with almost as much relish as the camera loved the perils of Pauline tied to the railroad tracks?

My description makes the film sound more urgent than it is. The German director seems to have fallen in love with the American genre of the road picture, and there are altogether too many shots of the trip itself, the land it covers, the roadside civilization, the open spaces.

What is fascinating, in a scary way, are the details of the Internet auction business and how it works and the money made in it. When I watch those TV shows where pedophiles are pounced on by cops, I think "entrapment," but you know what? Some people are asking to be entrapped. How about that Florida federal prosecutor who flew to Michigan hoping to meet a five-year-old girl? Your rights to do what you want in your sex life run into a dead end, I believe, when they involve others doing what they don't want.

All obvious, although not to some deranged creeps. But what is the purpose of this movie? Does it manipulate its subject matter a little too much in its quest to be "entertaining"? Why *should* this material be entertaining? Anything that holds our interest can be entertaining, in a way, but the movie seems to have an unwholesome determination to show us the victims being terrified and threatened. When I left the screening, I just didn't feel right. ☞

Transamerica ★ ★ ★

R, 103 m., 2006

Felicity Huffman (Bree), Kevin Zegers (Toby), Graham Greene (Calvin), Fionnula Flanagan (Elizabeth), Burt Young (Murray), Elizabeth Pena (Margaret), Carrie Preston (Sydney). Directed by Duncan Tucker and produced by Rene Bastian, Sebastian Dungan, and Linda Moran. Screenplay by Tucker.

Transamerica stars Felicity Huffman as a man who feels compelled to become a woman. The surgery is only a week away when Sabrina (Bree, for short) learns that seventeen years ago she fathered a son. Margaret, her therapist, was under the impression that as a man named Stanley, her client was a virgin. "There *was* this one girl in college," Bree muses, "but the whole thing was so tragically lesbian I didn't think it counted." Well, it counts now: Margaret (Elizabeth Pena) insists that Bree must meet the son and come to terms with him before the final surgery.

Bree reluctantly leaves Los Angeles and travels to New York to meet young Toby (Kevin Zegers), a brooding street hustler who wants to improve himself by becoming a porn star. This career choice is distressing to Bree, a ladylike middle-class conservative. Unwilling to reveal her real identity, Bree poses as a Christian caseworker who specializes in converting sex workers to Jesus. Toby agrees to drive back to L.A. with Bree, mostly because he needs the ride.

By this point in the plot description, I have the attention of readers who fired off e-mails about *Brokeback Mountain*, informing me that homosexuality was "a sin promoted by the liberal left." I responded that most people are gay or straight before they can talk, let alone vote. In any event, surely my correspondents would approve of those who go to the length of gender reassignment surgery to be sure their genitals match their orientation.

My own impression is that most transgender people have little interest in homosexuality; if they did, they'd be "pre-op" forever. Bree seems to have had little sex of any kind, working two jobs as she does to save up for her operation. She's not a terrifically exciting person, dresses like Mary Worth, is terribly nice, and needs to get out more. In the early stages of their automobile journey to Los Angeles she spends a lot of time correcting Toby's grammar.

Toby: *I'd probably be, like, disemboweled by a ninja.*
Bree: *You needn't say "like." Probably "disemboweled by a ninja" is sufficient.*

There is a quiet strain of humor throughout *Transamerica*, but this is not so much a comedy as an observation about human nature. I am grateful to Stephanie Zacharek of Salon.com for pointing out something I simply did not notice: The movie assumes a transsexual will be more welcome in a blue state than a red one, and that when a man is attracted to Bree, it is an American Indian named Calvin Two Goats (Graham Greene). "He's allowed to be open-minded," she writes, "because he's a Navajo—in other words, a spiritually open-minded outsider, as opposed to your typical Middle American." (It is significant that Bree works in L.A. as a waitress in a Mexican-American diner; Mexicans, like Indians, apparently have a genetic tendency to open-mindedness.)

Zacharek, who also makes points about lipliner that fell outside my zone of awareness, is correct, and the movie has prejudices about Middle America. How could I have forgotten the documentary *Southern Comfort* (2001), about a group of post-op pipe-smoking, pickup-driving Georgia gun owners? And consider the transsexual support group Bree visits. The only thing that seemed likely to come out was Tupperware.

The movie works, and it does work, because Huffman brings great empathy and tact to her performance as Bree. This is not a person who wants to make a big point about anything. She (we might as well recognize Bree's nature with the pronoun) has spent a lifetime living in a body that does not fit, and just when deliverance seems at hand she is suddenly supplied with an ungrateful son. How ironic, as Wordsworth did not quite observe, that the mother is father to the child.

Bree's original strategy is to keep it a secret that she is a pre-op transsexual and Toby's biological father. Well, it's a lot to spring on a kid. The truth emerges gradually during the trip and would generate more drama if Toby weren't one of those teenagers who cultivates an infuriating detachment. Jeez, kid, you think Bree is a missionary and she turns out to be your father? What does it take to get a rise out of you?

There are, however, personal breakthroughs and discoveries during the journey, especially during a stopover in Phoenix, home to Bree's unpleasant sister (Carrie Preston) and vulgarian parents (Fionnula Flanagan and Burt Young—yes, Rocky's brother-in-law). Bree's mom answers for herself the enigma of pre- or post-op by grabbing Bree's netherlands. No doubt she courted her husband in the same way. Regarding the wide open spaces of his grandparents' minds, Toby perhaps begins to develop some identification with Bree. To escape this family, a child might be willing to change not merely gender but species.

That *Transamerica,* written and directed by Duncan Tucker, works as a film is because Bree is so persistently and patiently herself. If she had been wilder, stranger, more extroverted, the movie might fly off the rails. It is precisely because she is so conventionally sincere that the movie gathers power in deep places while maintaining a relative surface calm. How does she respond to the undeniable interest of Calvin Two Goats? Reader, she blushes.

This is all new for her, too. What Huffman brings to Bree is the newness of a Jane Austen heroine. She has been waiting a long time to be an ingenue, and what an irony that she must begin as a mother. But she is a good person to the bottom of her socks, and at the end of *Transamerica* you realize it was not about sex at all. It was about family values.

Transformers ★ ★ ★

PG-13, 140 m., 2007

Shia LaBeouf (Sam Witwicky), Megan Fox (Mikaela Banes), Josh Duhamel (Sgt. Lennox), Tyrese Gibson (Tech Sgt. Epps), Rachael Taylor (Maggie Madsen), Anthony Anderson (Glen Whitmann), Jon Voight (John Keller), John Turturro (Agent Simmons). Directed by Michael Bay and produced by Steven Spielberg, Bay, Brian Goldner, and Mark Vahradian. Screenplay by Alex Kurtzman and Roberto Orci.

Now I have fans who say, "We are so sorry, Michael Bay, you still suck, but we love you."

That's what the director of *Transformers* told Simon Ang during an interview in Seoul. He could have been speaking for me. I think Michael Bay sometimes sucks (*Pearl Harbor, Armageddon*), but I find it possible to love him for a movie like *Transformers.* It's goofy fun with a lot of stuff that blows up real good, and it has the grace not only to realize how preposterous it is, but to make that into an asset.

The movie is inspired by the Transformer toys that twist and fold and double in upon themselves, like a Rubik's Cube crossed with a contortionist. A yellow Camaro unfolds into a hulking robot, helicopters become walking death monsters, and an enemy named Megatron rumbles onto the screen and, in a voice that resembles the sound effects in *Earthquake,* introduces himself: "I—AM—MEGATRON!!!"

I think that's the first time I've used three exclamation points. But Megatron is a three-exclamation-point kinda robot. He is the most fearsome warrior of the evil Decepticons, enemies of the benevolent Transformers. Both races (or maybe they're brands) of robots fled the doomed planet Cybertron and have been drawn to Earth because Megatron crash-landed near the North Pole a century ago and possesses the Allspark, which is the key to something, I'm not sure what, but since it's basically an alien MacGuffin it doesn't much matter. (Note to fanboys about to send me an e-mail explaining the Allspark: Look up "MacGuffin" on Wikipedia.)

The movie opens like one of those teen comedies where the likable hero is picked on by bullies at school, partly because he didn't make the football team, and mostly because he doesn't have a keen car. Sam Witwicky (Shia LaBeouf) talks his dad into buying him one, and he ends up with an old beater, a yellow Camaro, that is actually the Transformer named Bumblebee and gets so mad when his paint job is insulted that it transforms itself into a shiny new Camaro.

This is more than a hot car. It plays the sound track to Sam's life. It helps Sam become visible to his sexy classmate Mikaela (Megan Fox), who says, "Do I know you?" Sam mentions casually that they take four classes together and have been in the same school since first grade. The high school stuff, which could be a teenage comedy on its own, segues into the battling robot stuff, and there is some low-key political satire in which the secretary of defense (Jon Voight) runs the country, while the president (not even credited) limits himself to a request for a Ding-Dong.

Voight sends the armed services into action, and we see a lot of Sergeant. Lennox (Josh Duhamel) and Tech Sergeant Epps (Tyrese Gibson). They and their men labor during much of the movie under the optimistic impression that a metal robot the size of a ten-story building can be defeated by, or even brought to notice, automatic weapon fire. Sam and Bumblebee are crucial to the struggle, although a Secret Ops guy (John Turturro) asks the defense secretary, "You gonna lay the fate of the world on a kid's Camaro?"

Everything comes down to an epic battle between the Transformers and the Decepticons, and that's when my attention began to wander, and the movie lost a potential fourth star. First let me say that the robots, created by Industrial Light and Magic, are indeed delightful creatures; you can look hard and see the truck windshields, hubcaps, and junkyard stuff they're made of. And their movements are ingenious, especially a scorpion-like robot in the desert. (The little spider robots owe something to the similar creatures in Spielberg's *Minority Report,* and we note he is a producer of this movie.) How can a pickup truck contain enough mass to unfold into a towering machine? I say if Ringling Bros. can get fifteen clowns into a Volkswagen, anything is possible.

All the same, the mechanical battle goes on and on and on and on, with robots banging into each other and crashing into buildings, and buildings falling into the street, and the military firing, and jets sweeping overhead, and Megatron and the good hero, Optimus Prime, duking it out, and the sound track sawing away at thrilling music, and enough is enough. Just because CGI makes such endless sequences possible doesn't make them necessary. They should be choreographed to reflect a strategy and not simply reflect shapeless, random violence. Here the robots are like TV wrestlers who are down but usually not out.

I saw the movie on the largest screen in our nearest multiplex. It was standing room only, and hundreds were turned away. Even the name of Hasbro, maker of the Transformer toys, was cheered during the titles, and the audience laughed and applauded and loved all the human parts and the opening comedy. But when the battle of the titans began, a curious thing happened. The theater fell dead silent. No cheers. No reaction whether Optimus Prime or Megatron was on top. No nothing. I looked around and saw only passive faces looking at the screen.

My guess is, we're getting to the point where CGI should be used as a topping and not the whole pizza. The movie runs 140 minutes. You could bring it in at two hours, by cutting CGI shots, and have a better movie. ☞

The Transporter 2 ★ ★ ★

PG-13, 88 m., 2005

Jason Statham (Frank Martin), Alessandro Gassman (Gianni), Amber Valletta (Audrey Billings), Katie Nauta (Lola), Matthew Modine (Mr. Billings), Jason Flemyng (Dimitri), Keith David (Stappleton), Hunter Clary (Jack Billings). Directed by Louis Leterrier and produced by Luc Besson and Steven Chasman. Screenplay by Besson and Robert Mark Kamen.

Reviewing *The Transporter* in 2002, I expressed doubt that some of the action sequences were possible. *The Transporter 2* sidesteps my complaint by containing action scenes that are even *more* impossible. For example: Seeing the reflection of a bomb in a pool of liquid under his car, and knowing that the bad guys will not explode it while they're standing right next to it, the hero races the car out of a garage and up an incline, spinning the car neatly through the air, so that it makes one complete rotation and the bomb is pulled off by a hook on a crane, exploding harmlessly as the car lands safely. Uh-huh.

I could observe that this is preposterous, but the fact is, I laughed aloud. Other stunts and computer-generated effects were equally impossible, as when Frank Martin (Jason Statham) flies a Jet Ski onto a highway and jumps from it into the back of a school bus. And when he uses a fire hose to immobilize a posse of killers. And when he escapes from a plane that has crashed into the ocean. And when he leads a police pursuit up the ramps of a parking garage and then crashes his car through a wall of the garage and it flies a couple hundred feet through the air to a safe landing.

Either *The Transporter 2* is wall-to-wall with absurd action, or it's not a sequel to *The Transporter.* And in fact the sequel is a better film than the original, as if writer-producer Luc Besson had a clearer idea of what he wanted to do (and didn't want to do); the direction is by Louis Leterrier, whose *Unleashed,* released only three months previously, had that savage chemistry between a gangster (Bob Hoskins) and a fighter (Jet Li) he had raised like a dog. That movie was also written and produced by Besson, who is the hardest-working man in show business. Look him up on IMDb.com if you want to feel tired just reading about his plans.

The Transporter 2 is better for a number of reasons, one of them that it has an ingenious plot that continues to reveal surprises and complications well into the third act; this is not simply a movie where the good guy chases the bad guys, but a movie where the story turns a lot trickier than we expected.

It begins with Frank Martin helping out a friend by filling in for a month as the driver and bodyguard for a cute kid named Jack (Hunter Clary), whose dad (Matthew Modine) heads the U.S. narcotics agency. The kid is kidnapped in a bizarre scheme involving a phony doctor, and then he's recovered too quickly and without the ransom money being picked up, and it turns out the kidnapping—well, you'll see for yourself. Let me just observe that the methods of the kidnappers involve scientific ingenuity raised to evil genius. Not recently have I seen a movie with a better reason why the worst bad guy cannot be allowed to sink to the ocean floor along with the crashed airplane.

But not another word about that. Statham is amusing as a man whose emotions are so well under control that he can barely be bothered to have any. He stars in several martial arts sequences in which he wipes out whole platoons of enemies. They're deployed by Gianni (Alessandro Gassman), a really big, really mean, really smart villain. Modine efficiently plays the role of the sniveling bureaucrat, Amber Valletta is effective as his long-suffering wife, and Kate Nauta plays Lola, a deadly vixen who considers herself dressed after she's troweled on her eye makeup; for Lola, it's run, mascara, run.

There's a development of some interest to students of product placement. The Transporter drives an Audi. The first shots of the titles play like a commercial for the car. It's quite a car, all right, taking full advantage of the all-wheel drive as it survives those incredible stunts. So sturdy is its construction that after it crashes through the concrete wall while jumping to the other building, there's not even a scratch on the shiny silver circles on the front of the car.

There is some history here. In the original film, Frank Martin drove a BMW. Now he drives an Audi. Apparently BMW did not sign on for the sequel. Strange: On the very same day I saw this movie, I saw another thriller, *Memory of a Killer,* in which the characters hate BMWs so much, they urinate into their keyholes. In between, I saw a movie about Truman Capote that mostly featured Chevrolets, which must come as a relief to the home office in Bavaria. It's bad enough when the Transporter switches brands, but when Capote drops you, you're over.

Tristan & Isolde ★ ★ ★

PG-13, 125 m., 2006

James Franco (Tristan), Sophia Myles (Isolde), Rufus Sewell (Lord Marke), David O'Hara (King Donnchadh), Henry Cavill (Melot), J. B. Blanc (Leon), Jamie King (Anwick). Directed by Kevin Reynolds and produced by Moshe Diamant, Lisa Ellzey, Giannina Facio, and Elie Samaha. Screenplay by Dean Georgaris.

Tristan & Isolde begins with bits of the same myth that has inspired works ranging from sword & sorcery movies *(Lovespell)* to operas by Wagner, and transforms them, rather surprisingly, into a lean and effective action romance. The movie is better than the commercials would lead you to believe—and better, perhaps, than the studio expected, which may be why it was on the shelf for more than a year. Distributors who are content with the mediocre grow alarmed, sometimes, by originality and artistry: Is this movie too good for the demographic we're targeting?

The movie dumps the magical love potion that is crucial in most versions of the story. This time, when Tristan and Isolde fall in love, it's because—well, it's because they fall in love. The story takes place in England and Ireland, circa the year 600. The Roman occupiers have withdrawn, leaving a disorganized band of English warlords feuding among themselves while King Donnchadh of the Celts (David O'Hara) rules England from Ireland.

We meet Lord Marke (Rufus Sewell), wisest of the English rulers, who seeks to unite England and repel the Irish. He adopts the young Tristan (James Franco) and raises him as his son. Tristan leads Marke's troops in setting a successful trap for Donnchadh's overconfident raiders but then is poisoned and falls into a coma resembling death. Good thing the early Brits don't believe in burial: They put Tristan's body on a boat and push it out to sea, and a few days later it washes ashore in Ireland and is found by the beautiful Isolde (Sophia Myles), daughter of Donnchadh. Tristan is alive!

All contrived, all melodramatic, yes, but seen in a rugged, muddy, damp, straightforward visual style by director Kevin Reynolds (*The Count of Monte Cristo, Waterworld*), his cinematographer, Artur Reinhart, and the production designer, Mark Geraghty. The knights and ladies don't look like escapees from a Prince Valiant comic strip, but like physical, vulnerable survivors of the conflicts left behind by the Romans. The removal of magic from the story grounds it as a realistic power struggle, and although the device of mistaken identity is used to supply the heart of the plot, we can sort of see how things might have worked out that way.

I don't want to betray details that may come as a surprise. So let me comment on what happens without revealing what it is. Tristan and Isolde, who love each other even though they are the children of bitter enemies, are put into an impossible situation that no one really intended for them. The Irish and English lords don't even realize they know each other. Tristan is entered in a tournament and does not know what the prize is. Isolde thinks she knows what the outcome of the tournament means but is mistaken.

And then, in a decision that is brave of Tristan and Isolde and maybe even braver of the filmmakers, they try to accept the reality they're confronted with. When it is said that "this marriage will end one hundred years of bloodshed," they try to reflect, not without heartbreak, that the problems of two little people don't amount to a hill of beans in this crazy world.

I'm going to remain vague about what happens then, except to say that it all becomes a great deal more involving than you might expect from a movie with castles and swords and horses and secret passageways. There are some fairly delicate scenes involving the deepest feelings of Lord Marke, Tristan, and Isolde, and the actors don't ratchet up the emotions but try for plausibility. They are grown-ups who face an emotional crisis as we think perhaps they might have. The writing of the crucial closing scenes doesn't hurry for easy effects but pays attention to what is meant, and what is felt.

Myles plays Isolde as the daughter of a king, raised by the king's rules, true to her own emotions but true, too, to her duty. She doesn't mistake Isolde for the heroine of a teenage romance. James Franco (the *Spider-Man* movies, *The Great Raid, Annapolis*) is not a larger-than-life comic hero but a vulnerable warrior capable of doubts and schemes. Rufus Sewell (*Dark City*) plays Lord Marke as a statesman in a land of squabbling egos, who, when he discovers a surprising secret, is inspired not so much by jealousy as by the offense to his sense of the rightness of things.

One key to the quality of the movie may be the executive producers, Ridley (*Gladiator*) Scott and Tony (*Top Gun*) Scott. Ridley Scott wanted to direct this movie for fifteen years, and although *Gladiator* may have preempted it on his schedule, it's clear he was intrigued not only by the possibilities for action but also by the impossible personal dilemma that faces Tristan and Isolde. By removing elements of magic and operatic excess from the story, the brothers Scott focus on what is, underneath, a story as tragic (and less contrived) as the one cited in the ads, *Romeo and Juliet.*

Tristram Shandy: A Cock and Bull Story ★ ★ ★ ★

R, 91 m., 2006

Steve Coogan (Tristram Shandy/Walter/Steve), Rob Brydon (Toby Shandy/Rob), Raymond Waring (Corporal Trim), Dylan Moran (Dr. Slop/Dylan), Keeley Hawes (Elizabeth Shandy/Keeley), Gillian Anderson (Widow Wadman/Gillian), Shirley Henderson (Susannah/Shirley),

Jeremy Northam (Mark), Naomie Harris (Jennie), Kelly Macdonald (Jenny). Directed by Michael Winterbottom and produced by Andrew Eaton. Screenplay by Frank Cottrell Boyce and Winterbottom, based on the novel *The Life and Opinions of Tristram Shandy, Gentleman* by Laurence Sterne.

I started reading Laurence Sterne's *The Life and Opinions of Tristram Shandy, Gentleman* in 1965, and I intend to finish it any day now. That is true, and also a joke (a small one) involving a novel about procrastination. *Tristram Shandy* begins with its hero about to be born and becomes so sidetracked by digressions that the story ends shortly after his birth. Perhaps Sterne considered writing a sequel describing the rest of Tristram's life but never got around to it (smaller joke).

Now comes *Tristram Shandy: A Cock and Bull Story,* the movie, which never gets around to filming the book. Since the book is probably unfilmable, this is just as well; what we get instead is a film about the making of a film based on a novel about the writing of a novel. As an idea for comedy, this is inspired, and Michael Winterbottom and his screenwriter, Frank Cottrell Boyce, show the filmmakers constantly distracted by themselves. "But enough about me," Darryl Zanuck once said. "What did *you* think of my movie?"

The film takes place on the set of a movie named *Tristram Shandy.* It involves actors named Steve Coogan, Rob Brydon, Gillian Anderson, and others, played by Steve Coogan, Rob Brydon, Gillian Anderson, and others. The opening scene takes place in a makeup room, where Coogan and Brydon discuss their billing and whether Brydon's teeth are too yellow. Coogan has the lead, playing both Tristram and his father, Walter. Brydon plays Tristram's uncle Toby, who devotes his life to constructing a large outdoor model of the battlefield where, as a young man, he suffered an obscure wound. The Widow Wadman (Anderson), who is considering marrying Toby, wants to know precisely how and, ahem, where he was wounded. "Just beyond the asparagus," Toby explains, pointing to his model landscape.

But I digress. Back to the dressing room. Coogan mentions that he has the lead in the movie. Yes, says Brydon, but Toby is "a featured co-lead." Coogan: "Well, we'll see after the edit." Both actors are competitive in that understated British way that involves put-downs hardly less obscure than Toby's wound. Coogan wants the wardrobe department to build up his shoes so that the "featured co-lead" will not be taller than the leading man. Brydon learns that Gillian Anderson has been hired to join the cast, and he is panic-stricken: He is afraid that in a love scene he might blush or be betrayed by stirrings beyond the asparagus.

There are elements of *This Is Spinal Tap* in the film, and a touch of Al Pacino's *Looking for Richard,* a semidocumentary about actors preparing to play *Richard III.* From *Spinal Tap* come the egos of the artists and the shabbiness of their art; from Pacino the film borrows the device of explaining the material to the viewers while it is being explained to the actors (only one person in *Tristram Shandy,* and possibly nobody in the audience, has read the book).

The art is endearingly shabby. There is a screening of some battle footage in which lackluster foot soldiers wander dispiritedly past the camera, looking like extras on their lunch break. And a scene in which a miniature unborn Tristram is seen inside a miniature womb; I was reminded of Stonehenge in *Spinal Tap.* The explanations of the material include witty dinnertime conversation by Stephen Fry, playing himself playing an actor playing a literary theorist. Coogan picks up enough to lecture an interviewer: "This is a postmodern novel before there was any modernism to be post about." Later it's claimed that *Tristram Shandy* was "No. 8 on the *Observer*'s list of the greatest novels," which cheers everyone until they discover the list was chronological.

Now about that interviewer. He has information about a lap dancer whom the actor met one recent drunken evening. It would be embarrassing to see the lap dancer on the front page of the tabloids, but the interviewer is willing to do a deal: He'll tidy the story in return for an exclusive about Coogan's relationship with his girlfriend, Jenny (Kelly Macdonald), who has just given birth to their baby. It would not be good for Jenny to read about the lap dancer.

Jenny, as it happens, has just arrived on the

set, where Coogan has been having a flirtation with a production assistant named Jennie (Naomie Harris). Jennie is not merely sexy and efficient, but also is a film buff who offers analysis and theory to people who really want only a drink. She compares the ungainly battle scene to Bresson's work in *Lancelot du Lac*, and has a lot to say about Fassbinder, who Coogan vaguely suspects might have been a German director. Not surprisingly, Jennie is the only person on the set who has read the novel, and she tries to explain why the battle scene isn't exactly important.

Because their work is so varied, director Winterbottom and Boyce, his frequent writer, are only now coming into focus as perhaps the most creative team in British film. Their collaborations include films as different as *Butterfly Kiss, Welcome to Saravejo, The Claim, Code 46* and *24 Hour Party People.* That the same director and writer could make such different films is almost inexplicable, and consider, too, that Winterbottom directed *Wonderland* and Boyce wrote Danny Boyle's *Millions.*

Boyce told me *Tristram Shandy* might sound a little like Charlie Kaufman's screenplay for *Adaptation,* but he thinks it's closer to Truffaut's *Day for Night.* (Am I sounding a little like Jennie here?) It wonderfully evokes life on a movie set, which for a few weeks or months creates its own closed society. Wives and lovers visit the set but are subtly excluded from its "family," and even such a miraculous creature as a newborn baby is treated like a prop that is very nice, yes, but not needed for the scene. As the final credits roll, Coogan and Brydon are still engaged in their running duel of veiled insults. They are briefly diverted, however, by imitating Pacino as Shylock. Every actor knows what David Merrick meant when he said, "It is not enough for me to succeed; my enemies must fail."

Tsotsi ★ ★ ★ ★

R, 94 m., 2006

Presley Chweneyagae (Tsotsi), Terry Pheto (Miriam), Mothusi Magano (Boston), Israel Makoe (Tsotsi's father), Percy Matsemela (Sergeant Zuma), Jerry Mofokeng (Morris), Benny Moshe (Young Tsotsi), Nambitha Mpumlwana (Pumla Dube). Directed by Gavin Hood and produced by Peter Fudakowski. Screenplay by Hood, based on the novel by Athol Fugard.

How strange, a movie where a bad man becomes better, instead of the other way around. *Tsotsi,* a film of deep emotional power, considers a young killer whose cold eyes show no emotion, who kills unthinkingly, and who is transformed by the helplessness of a baby. He didn't mean to kidnap the baby, but now that he has it, it looks at him with trust and need, and he is powerless before eyes more demanding than his own.

The movie won the Oscar as best foreign film. It is set in Soweto, the township outside Johannesburg where neat little houses built by the new government are overwhelmed by square miles of shacks. There is poverty and despair here, but also hope and opportunity; from Soweto have come generations of politicians, entrepreneurs, artists, musicians, as if it were the Lower East Side of South Africa. Tsotsi (Presley Chweneyagae) is not destined to be one of those. We don't even learn his real name until later in the film; "tsotsi" means "thug," and that's what he is.

He leads a loose-knit gang that smashes and grabs, loots and shoots, sets out each morning to steal something. On a crowded train they stab a man, and he dies without anyone noticing; they hold his body up with their own, take his wallet, flee when the doors open. Another day's work. But when his friend Boston (Mothusi Magano) asks Tsotsi how he really feels, whether decency comes into it, he fights with him and walks off into the night, and we sense how alone he is. Later, in a flashback, we will understand the cruelty of the home and father he fled from.

He goes from here to there. He has a strange meeting with a man in a wheelchair and asks him why he bothers to go on living. The man tells him. Tsotsi finds himself in an upscale suburb. Such areas in Joburg are usually gated communities, each house surrounded by a security wall, every gate promising "armed response." An African professional woman gets out of her Mercedes to ring the buzzer on the gate so her husband can let her in. Tsotsi shoots her and steals her car. Some time passes before he realizes he has a passenger: a baby boy.

Tsotsi is a killer, but he cannot kill a baby. He

takes it home with him, to a room built on top of somebody else's shack. It might be wise for him to leave the baby at a church or an orphanage, but that doesn't occur to him. He has the baby, so the baby is his. We can guess that he will not abandon the boy because he has been abandoned himself and projects upon the infant all of his own self-pity.

We realize the violence in the film has slowed. Tsotsi himself is slow to realize he has a new agenda. He uses newspapers as diapers, feeds the baby condensed milk, carries it around with him in a shopping bag. Finally, in desperation, at gunpoint, he forces a nursing mother (Terry Pheto) to feed the child. She lives in a nearby shack, a clean and cheerful one. As he watches her do what he demands, something shifts inside of him, and all of his hurt and grief are awakened.

Tsotsi doesn't become a nice man. He simply stops being active as an evil one and finds his time occupied with the child. Babies are single-minded. They want to be fed, they want to be changed, they want to be held, they want to be made much of, and they think it is their birthright. Who is Tsotsi to argue?

What a simple and yet profound story this is. It does not sentimentalize poverty or make Tsotsi more colorful or sympathetic than he should be; if he deserves praise, it is not for becoming a good man but for allowing himself to be distracted from the job of being a bad man. The nursing mother, named Miriam, is played by Terry Pheto as a quiet counterpoint to his rage. She lives in Soweto and has seen his kind before. She senses something in him, some pool of feeling he must ignore if he is to remain Tsotsi. She makes reasonable decisions. She acts not as a heroine but as a realist who wants to nudge Tsotsi in a direction that will protect her own family and this helpless baby, and then perhaps even Tsotsi himself. These two performances, by Chweneyagae and Pheto, are surrounded by temptations to overact or cave in to sentimentality; they step safely past them and play the characters as they might actually live their lives.

How the story develops is for you to discover. I was surprised to find that it leads toward hope instead of despair; why does fiction so often assume defeat is our destiny? The film avoids obligatory violence and actually deals with the characters as people. The story is based on a novel by the great South African writer Athol Fugard, directed and written by Gavin Hood. It won the Oscar one year after the South African film *Yesterday* was the first from that nation to be nominated. There are stories in the beloved country that have cried for a century to be told.

Turtles Can Fly ★ ★ ★ ★

NO MPAA RATING, 95 m., 2005

Soran Ebrahim (Satellite), Avaz Latif (Agrin), Hirsh Feyssal (Henkov). Directed by Bahman Ghobadi and produced by Ghobadi. Screenplay by Ghobadi.

I wish everyone who has an opinion on the war in Iraq could see *Turtles Can Fly.* That would mean everyone in the White House and in Congress, and the newspaper writers, and the TV pundits, and the radio talkers, and you—especially you, because you are reading this and they are not.

You assume the movie is a liberal attack on George W. Bush's policies. Not at all. The action takes place just before the American invasion begins, and the characters in it look forward to the invasion and the fall of Saddam Hussein. Nor does the movie later betray an opinion one way or the other about the war. It is about the actual lives of refugees, who lack the luxury of opinions because they are preoccupied with staying alive in a world that has no place for them.

The movie takes place in a Kurdish refugee camp somewhere on the border between Turkey and Iraq. That means, in theory, it takes place in "Kurdistan," a homeland that exists in the minds of the Kurds even though every other government in the area insists the Kurds are stateless. The characters in the movie are children and teenagers, all of them orphans; there are adults in the camp, but the kids run their own lives—especially a bright wheeler-dealer named Satellite (Soran Ebrahim), who organizes work gangs of other children.

What is their work? They disarm land mines so they can be resold to arms dealers in the nearby town. The land mines are called "American," but this is a reflection of their value and not a criticism of the United States; they were planted in the area by Saddam Hussein, in one of his skirmishes with Kurds and Turks. (Well, technically, they were supplied to Saddam by the United States.) Early in the film, we see a character named Henkov (Hirsh Feyssal), known to everyone as the Boy with No Arms, who gently disarms a mine by removing the firing pin with his lips.

Satellite pays special attention to a girl named Agrin (Avaz Latif), who is Henkov's sister. They have a little brother named Risa, who is carried about with his arms wrapped around the neck of his armless brother. We *think* he is their brother, that is, until we discover he is Agrin's child, born after she was raped by Iraqi soldiers while still almost a child herself. The armless boy loves Risa; his sister hates him, because of her memories.

Is this world beginning to take shape in your mind? The refugees live in tents and huts. They raise money by scavenging. Satellite is the most resourceful person in the camp, making announcements, calling meetings, assigning work, and traveling ceremonially on a bicycle festooned with ribbons and glittering medallions. He is always talking, shouting, hectoring, at the top of his voice: He is too busy to reflect on the misery of his life.

The village is desperate for information about the coming American invasion. There is a scene of human comedy in which every household has a member up on a hill with a makeshift TV antenna; those below shout instructions: "To the left! A little to the right!" But no signal is received. Satellite announces that he will go to town and barter for a satellite dish. There is a sensation when he returns with one. The elders gather as he tries to bring in a signal. The sexy music video channels are prohibited, but the elders wait patiently as Satellite cycles through the sin until he finds CNN, and they can listen for English words they understand. They hate Saddam and eagerly await the Americans.

But what will the Americans do for them? The plight of the Kurdish people is that no one seems to want to do much for them. Even though a Kurd has recently been elected to high office in Iraq, we get the sense he was a compromise candidate—chosen precisely because his people are powerless. For years the Kurds have struggled against Turkey, Iraq, and other nations in the region to define the borders of a homeland the other states refuse to acknowledge.

From time to time the aims of the Kurds come into step with the aims of others. When they were fighting Saddam, the first Bush administration supported them. When they were fighting our ally Turkey, we opposed them. The *New York Times Magazine* ran a cover story about Ibrahim Parlak, who for ten years peacefully ran a Kurdish restaurant in Harbert, Michigan, only to be arrested in 2004 by the federal government, which hoped to deport him for Kurdish nationalist activities that at one point we approved. Because I supported Ibrahim's case, I could read headlines on right-wing sites such as "Roger Ebert Gives Thumbs Up to Terrorism."

I hope Debbie Schlussel, who wrote that column, sees *Turtles Can Fly.* The movie does not agree with her politics, or mine. It simply provides faces for people we think of as abstractions. It was written and directed by Bahman Ghobadi, whose *A Time for Drunken Horses* (2000) was also about Kurds struggling to survive between the lines. Satellite has no politics. Neither does the Boy with No Arms, nor his sister, nor her child born of rape; they have been trapped outside of history.

I was on a panel at the University of Colorado where an audience member criticized movies for reducing the enormity of the Holocaust to smaller stories. But there is no way to tell a story big enough to contain all of the victims of the Holocaust, or all of the lives affected for good and ill in the Middle East. Our minds cannot process that many stories. What we can understand is the Boy with No Arms, making a living by disarming land mines like the one that blew away his arms. And Satellite, who tells the man in the city he will trade him fifteen radios and some cash for a satellite dish. Where did Satellite get fifteen radios? Why? You need some radios?

Twelve and Holding ★ ★ ★ ½

R, 90 m., 2006

Conor Donovan (Jacob and Rudy Carges), Zoe Weizenbaum (Malee Chung), Jesse Camacho (Leonard Fisher), Linus Roache (Jim Carges),

Annabella Sciorra (Carla Chung), Jeremy Renner (Gus Maitland), Marcia DeBonis (Grace Fisher), Tom McGowan (Patrick Fisher). Directed by Michael Cuesta and produced by Leslie Urdang, Jenny Schweitzer, and Brian Bell. Screenplay by Anthony Cipriano.

Michael Cuesta's *Twelve and Holding* weaves together the stories of three families and three children who take desperate measures to try to solve the problems in their lives. All three kids feel let down by their parents—who love them, but not usefully or with much insight. But this isn't one of those films where the kids are filled with wisdom and find wonderful solutions. What they find instead is danger.

The most harrowing story involves twins named Jacob and Rudy, both played by Conor Donovan. They get in a fight with some other kids, who threaten to destroy their tree house. So Rudy and his fat friend Leonard (Jesse Camacho) decide to spend the night in the tree house, and that leads to Rudy's accidental death and to the anguish of Jacob, who refused to come along. Jacob has another problem: a birthmark that covers half his face; sometimes he wears a hockey mask to cover it.

We learn more about Leonard, the fat kid. His family sits around the table gobbling their food, and when he's not eating, he's snacking. A coach gives him books of exercise and nutrition and encourages him to get in shape: "You can play center on my team when you get to high school." Leonard is puzzled. "Why are you doing this for me?" he asks. "Because," says the coach, "I've never met a child so out of shape in my life."

At first Leonard can barely run a block. But the accident that kills Rudy changes his life, too, and as he begins to lose weight, he presents a challenge to his fat mother, Grace (Marcia Debonis). This leads to his attempt to "help" her in a way so ill-advised and hazardous, and yet so ingenious, I will leave it for you to discover.

Quieter, but more heartrending, is the story of Malee (Zoe Weizenbaum), the possibly adopted Asian daughter of a psychiatrist (Annabella Sciorra). Eavesdropping on her mother's therapy sessions, she gets an obsession about a construction worker named Gus (Jeremy Renner). Because she has a lot of inside information about him, she's able to attract his attention and act on the big crush she has for him. But a twelve-year-old girl is clearly playing with fire when she talks about love with a grown man. Weizenbaum is remarkable in the transformations she brings to her character.

Jacob thinks he can make up for the death of his brother. Leonard thinks he can solve his family's obesity. Malee thinks she can find, in a way, a father figure to replace the father she feels abandoned her. The paths these kids take are all wrong, but Cuesta's direction and Anthony Cipriano's screenplay are gentle with them; the movie observes their mistakes and is horrified, but does not blame, and understands how emotions can lead to a failure of common sense. What scars these children may bear as adults we are left to imagine.

Cuesta also directed *L.I.E.* (2001), where the initials stood for, among other things, the Long Island Expressway and the lies of some teenage boys who lived near it. Brian Cox played a pedophile who preyed on them, in a movie of tangled emotional complexity. Here again Cuesta shows a perception for the way young people may observe an adult world, even be familiar with it, and yet completely fail to understand it. *Twelve and Holding* could have been a series of horror stories, but the filmmakers and their gifted young actors somehow negotiate the horrors and generate a deep sympathy.

2 Days in Paris ★ ★ ★

R, 96 m., 2007

Julie Delpy (Marion), Adam Goldberg (Jack), Daniel Bruhl (Lukas), Marie Pillet (Anna), Albert Delpy (Jeannot), Alexia Landeau (Rose), Adan Jodorowsky (Mathieu), Alex Nahon (Manu). Directed by Julie Delpy and produced by Christophe Mazodier and Thierry Potok. Screenplay by Delpy.

I once gave flowers to a French girl and was told they were "flagrant." When Marion, the character played by Julie Delpy in *2 Days in Paris,* makes mistakes like that, she knows what she's doing. If her relationship with her lover, Jack, is coming apart at the seams, that's her with a little thimble and needle, pulling out the stitches. The movie covers the end of a European vacation that was intended to mend their relationship, and the holiday has gone badly. Sometimes when you want to know, really know somebody, you find out that actually you'd rather not.

Jack (Adam Goldberg) had a bad time in Venice. How can that be? Was it Woody Allen who said the worst sex he ever had wasn't that bad? Same with bad trips to Venice. Jack got severe diarrhea and tried Marion's patience by taking photos of everything, apparently, except the diarrhea itself. Has he never heard of Imodium, that word along with "taxi" and "OK" that gets most Americans around the world? And did he think he was needed to remedy the world's tragic shortage of photos of Venice?

But never mind. The last two days of the holiday are to be spent in Paris, Marion's hometown, before they return to New York, where they now live. They move in upstairs from Marion's parents, Anna and Jeannot (played by Delpy's real parents, Marie Pillet and Albert Delpy). Culture shock sets in at the first meal, braised rabbit. You'd think Anna and Jeannot could try the merciful American tactic of calling it "chicken," but perhaps when you serve the rabbit head along with its eyeballs, it looks like a chicken that has been fed too many hormones.

Marion and Jack wander about Paris, talking in that way that lovers have when they're beginning to get on each other's nerves. But, no, this is not a retread of Richard Linklater's *Before Sunset* (2004), in which Delpy and Ethan Hawke walked and talked around Paris. It is a contemplation of incompatibility, as Paris brings out a side of Marion that Jack has never quite seen: Is she a radical political activist and a shameless slut, or does she only act like one? She runs into old boyfriends so often it makes Paris seem like a small town, and attacks one of them in a restaurant for taking a sex vacation to Thailand.

At home, her father quizzes Jack on French culture, and her mother is so eager to wash and press his clothes that he barely has time to get out of them. Both of Delpy's parents are professional actors, and so these are only performances, I hope. In addition to casting her parents, Delpy puts her mark on this film in many other ways: She starred, directed, wrote, edited, coproduced, composed the score, and sang a song. When a woman takes that many jobs, we slap her down for vanity. When a man does, we call him the new Orson Welles.

Delpy in fact has made a smart film with an edge to it; her Jack and Marion reveal things about themselves they never thought they'd tell anybody, and we wonder why they ever went out on a second date. Much has been made of the similarities between Delpy here and Diane Keaton in *Annie Hall,* but if Delpy's character found a spider as big as a Buick in the bathroom, she'd braise it and serve it up for lunch.

Which is an oblique way of saying that Julie Delpy is an original, a woman who refuses to be defined or limited. Her first great roles were in Bertrand Tavernier's *Beatrice* (1987), Agnieszka Holland's *Europa Europa* (1990), and Krzysztof Kieslowski's *White* (1994); she was in Linklater's *Before Sunrise, Waking Life,* and *Before Sunset*; and she dumped Bill Murray at the beginning of Jim Jarmusch's *Broken Flowers* (2005). In between, she studied film at NYU and made herself available for thirty student productions.

What she has done here is avoid all temptation to recycle the usual lovers-in-Paris possibilities and create two original, quirky characters so obsessed with their differences that Paris is almost a distraction. I don't think I heard a single accordion in the whole film.

Two for the Money ★ ★ ★ ½

R, 124 m., 2005

Al Pacino (Walter), Matthew McConaughey (Brandon), Rene Russo (Toni), Armand Assante (Novian), Jeremy Piven (Jerry). Directed by D .J. Caruso and produced by James G. Robinson, David C. Robinson, and Jay Cohen. Screenplay by Dan Gilroy.

In D. J. Caruso's *Two for the Money,* you can see Al Pacino doing something he's done a lot lately: having a terrific time being an actor. At sixty-five he's on a hot streak in one well-written role after another. In *Insomnia, People I Know, Angels in America,* and *The Merchant of Venice* he has given performances vibrating with tension and need, and now here he comes again. George C. Scott used to say when a good actor was in the right role, you could sense the joy of performance. Pacino has moments here when he doesn't quite click his heels.

Matthew McConaughey and Rene Russo are wonderful, too, in a movie with three well-written and fully functional roles, but their characters are by nature more contained than Pacino's. He plays Walter, who runs a sports betting hotline. McConaughey plays Brandon, the Vegas oddsmaker Walter imports to New York, renames, and turns into a star. Walter is a mesmerizer who assaults him with confidence and exuberance. Russo is Toni, Walter's wife, who loves him and despairs of him. He dazzles Brandon and he worries Toni, a recovering junkie. He's recovering from everything: "If it says 'anonymous' at the end, he goes," she tells Brandon.

The nature of Walter's operation is a little hard to grasp, maybe even to Walter. It appears that his offices and home are in the same building, all paneled Prairie-style in dark woods and window partitions. On the ground floor, he has guys manning hotlines where you pay twenty-five dollars and get the early line for your weekend bets. On the second floor, it's bigger business: For the best advice, gamblers are expected to pay a percentage of what they win from their bookies. That way Walter is technically not breaking the law: He's not taking bets; he's taking a percentage at arm's length.

Two for the Money is not about the mechanics of this business but about its emotions. Walter is a promoter who at one point admits his operation is made of smoke and mirrors. He imports Brandon after the kid startles Vegas with the accuracy of his predictions. He gives him a haircut, a wardrobe, a sports car, and a new name, and puts him on TV, and Brandon obliges one weekend by correctly calling twelve games out of twelve.

That's all the plot you need from me. The rest will be observation. Look at the monologue Pacino delivers at a Gamblers Anonymous meeting. It's got the passion, if not quite the language, of his soliloquies in *The Merchant of Venice*. He tells his fellow degenerate gamblers that their problem isn't gambling; it's themselves: "We're all lemons. We need to lose." When they lose everything—the job, the house, the family—they are most fully alive, he says. When they win, they keep gambling until they lose again.

Walter knows this so well he hasn't gambled in years. Brandon has never gambled. Toni has gambled: She gambled when she married Walter. They have a young daughter. The way Walter grabs for the nitroglycerin pills when his angina hits, he shouldn't be in a business that depends on point spreads. But Walter is an optimist: "It was only a small one," he says after one attack.

I won't tell you what happens involving these three people in this movie, but I want you to watch for the way all three change. The screenplay by Dan Gilroy isn't one of those deals where one guy acts out and everybody else watches him. It's about three people who are transformed in relation to one another, as a situation develops that is equally dangerous all the way around. It takes us awhile to understand what Brandon is doing, and then we realize that Walter *knows* what he's doing—and is seeing him and raising him. There are moments here, including one moment before a live TV broadcast, where Walter is pushing his whole stake into the pot, and the game isn't poker; it's life.

Is the movie a realistic portrait of these kinds of people in this kind of business? I'm not an expert, but I doubt it. What I don't understand is how Walter finds out how much his clients bet so he can collect his percentage. Bookies aren't real good at sharing information, especially for the benefit of an operation devoted to out-handicapping them. And besides, there are a lot of bookies. Why can't I get the tips from Walter's company, bet a grand with a bookie he knows about, and ten grand with some guy he doesn't know about?

This is a problem, but it is not a problem that bothers me. It's a classic MacGuffin. The point is that something happens on the second floor that means Walter and Brandon and the telephone guys make a pile of money when Brandon correctly predicts the weekend games, and they do it without placing bets or taking bets. That's what we need to know. Everything else is dialogue, direction, acting, and energy.

I've been watching Pacino a long time. I saw him at the beginning, in 1971, in *The Panic in Needle Park*. Already a great actor. His next movie was *The Godfather*. I could mention *Dog Day Afternoon, Glengarry Glen Ross, Scarface, Carlito's Way, Heat, Donnie Brasco*. I could keep going.

But good as he already was, I think something rotated inside and clicked as he was directing his documentary *Looking for Richard* (1996), which was about how Shakespeare should be acted, and how an actor should play Richard III. Here was an actor in his mid-fifties, asking undergraduate questions, reinventing how he approaches a role, asking what acting is. He chose Richard III, a character who looks in a mirror and asks himself how he should play himself. In his movies since then, Pacino seems to have found something in the mirror.

The Two of Us ★ ★ ★ ★

NO MPAA RATING, 83 m., 1967 (rereleased 2005)

Michel Simon (Pepe), Alain Cohen (Claude), Lucie Fabiole (Meme), Roger Carel (Victor), Charles Denner (Claude's Father), Paul Preboist (Maxime), Jacqueline Rouillard (Teacher). Directed by Claude Berri and produced by Paul Cadeac. Screenplay by Claude Berri, Gerard Brach, and Michel Rivelin.

"I was eight years old and already a Jew."

The famous opening line of Claude Berri's *The Two of Us* (1967) is spoken by an adult voice, the director's own. The film is loosely inspired by his own life. In 1944 in occupied Paris, his parents sent him away to live with Gentiles, who would claim him as one of their own and protect him from deportation and death. In Berri's version of the story, his parents are posing as Alsatians but fear the boy will reveal his true identity in a heedless moment. A friend who is Catholic suggests that young Claude be taught the Lord's Prayer, given a new last name, and sent to live with an old couple on a farm outside Grenoble.

That's the setup for a heartwarming movie that showcases one of the last performances of the great Michel Simon (1895–1975), who began his career by looking old and kept on looking older. He was only thirty-seven in Jean Renoir's *Boudu Saved from Drowning* (1932), and thirty-nine in Jean Vigo's *L'Atalante* (1934), but he looks sixtyish in both films, and by the time he made *The Two of Us*, he was seventy-two, a plump, tottering wreck of a man with a creased face and the subtlety of a bear.

Simon plays Pepe, the old farm owner whose life revolves around his dog, his wife, and his prejudices. He is an anti-Semite who believes World War II was started by an evil conspiracy involving Jews, Masons, communists, and the monster Winston Churchill. He listens to the nightly broadcasts of the BBC, only to rail against them. He has no idea that young Claude, who has come to live with them, is Jewish; he accepts the reasonable explanation that this Catholic child has been sent by his parents to be safe if Paris is bombed.

The small boy has been warned by his parents to be constantly on guard against discovery. For Claude that means keeping his circumcised "birdie" out of view, and there's a harrowing scene where Meme (Lucie Fabiole), the old lady, tries to plunge into the soapy bathwater for a good scrub. But the movie is not really about danger and concealment; it's about how love grows between the boy and the old man, and how the boy, who is "already a Jew," becomes a wiser one.

The heart of the film is in Simon's performance, though young Alain Cohen is convincing and lovable as Claude and would go on to play Berri's autobiographical hero in two more films (their relationship became a little like François Truffaut's with Jean-Pierre Leaud). Simon was a large, shambling fact of life, a man who always seemed too large for the space available. In *L'Atalante,* he is the hired hand on a barge occupied by newlyweds and constantly seems to be in their way. In *Boudu,* which is the story of a drunk "rescued" by a bourgeois couple, he occupies too much space in their lives. In *The Two of Us,* he threatens to overwhelm the little boy with his affection.

They become playmates. That is the only word for it, and it's miraculous how old Pepe chases the boy around the yard, joins in his imaginary games, gets on the swing, puts a knife between his teeth, and pretends to be a dirty Bolshevik about to kill and eat him. The boy squeals with delight and joins Pepe in spoiling the old man's beloved dog. He also has long talks with Pepe about life. One Sunday, after they all go to church and hear a sermon reminding the congregation that Christ was a Jew, he quizzes the old man:

"Was Jesus a Jew?"

"So they say."

"Then God is a Jew, too."

Pepe doesn't think so but is not sure why. The

boy listens to Pepe's descriptions of Jews, but when Pepe says they have big noses, the boy points out that Pepe's nose is enormous. The scene where Simon examines himself in the mirror could have been played for laughs, or ironically, but he plays it as an exercise in mystified curiosity.

A good many of the old man's neighbors oppose the Petain government that rules occupied France on behalf of the Nazis, but Pepe keeps the marshal's portrait framed on the wall, and Meme dusts it every day. When D-Day arrives and it appears the tide of battle has turned, even sympathizers in the district studiously forget their sympathies for Petain, but not Pepe: "In my house, I decide who governs France."

The movie is not so much an argument against anti-Semitism as a demonstration that it feeds on ignorance. The old man has not given much thought to his prejudices, but caught them like a virus in his childhood and has carried them along uncritically into old age. He has no idea that the child he has come to love so much is a Jew. I suspect if he did know, he would make an exception for Claude while continuing to harbor his prejudices against theoretical Jews he has the advantage of knowing nothing about. He is not converted in his thinking by this movie, and one of its strengths is that it ends without him ever becoming enlightened.

Such a scene of discovery would be a sentimental irrelevance, because the movie is concerned not with what Pepe knows but with who Pepe is; the person who learns and grows is Claude. Berri was born in 1934 with the name Claude Beri Langmann, the same name little Claude has in the movie, and so it is fair to conclude that the movie is the result of what the little boy learned during his stay among the Gentiles. He learned that anti-Semitism is an evil, but he learned to forgive some of the Pepes of the world, for they know not what they do. For those who do know, forgiveness is another question, but that is another movie.

2046 ★ ★ ½

R, 129 m., 2005

Tony Leung (Chow Mo Wan), Gong Li (Su Li Zhen), Takuya Kimura (Tak), Faye Wong (Jing Wen Wang), Ziyi Zhang (Bai Ling), Carina Lau (Lulu/Mimi), Maggie Cheung (slz1960). Directed by Wong Kar-Wai and produced by Wong. Screenplay by Wong.

Jam yesterday and jam tomorrow, but never jam today.

—*Alice in Wonderland*

It is always too early or too late for love in a Wong Kar-Wai film, and his characters spend their days in yearnings and regrets. *In the Mood for Love* (2000) brought that erotic sadness to a kind of perfection in its story of a man and a woman who live in hotel rooms next to each other and want to become lovers, but never do because his wife and her husband are lovers, and "for us to do the same thing would mean we are no better than they are." Yes, but no worse, and perhaps happier. Isn't it strange that most of the truths about love are banal?

2046, Wong's new film, is an indirect, oblique continuation of the earlier one. It stars Tony Leung as Chow Mo Wan, also the name of his character in *In the Mood for Love,* and there is a brief role for Maggie Cheung, his costar in that film; they are not necessarily playing the same characters. There was also a Room 2046 in the other film, so there are subterranean connections between the two, but they operate something like the express train to the year 2046 in this one: All memories are there in the future, we are told, but no one has ever returned.

No one, except for the narrator, who tells us about it. We gather that *2046* is the name of a science fiction novel being written by Chow. It is also the room next to his in the hotel where much of this movie takes place—a room lived in by a series of women he loves. Not coincidentally, 2046 is also the year set by China for the expiration of Hong Kong's quasi-independence from the mainland. Does that make the movie *2046* a parable about Hong Kong? You could find parallels, I'm sure, but that doesn't seem to be the point. Chow observes that if he hadn't seen the number 2046 on a room, he wouldn't have started his futuristic novel, and it is just barely possible that Wong is telling us this movie was inspired when he asked himself what happened in Room 2046 after *In the Mood for Love* was over. Or before it began. Whatever.

These speculations are probably of no help in understanding the movie, which exists primarily as a visual style imposed upon beautiful faces; Josef von Sternberg's obsession with Marlene Dietrich is mirrored here by Wong's fascination with the beauty of Ziyi Zhang, Gong Li, Faye Wong, Carina Lau, and Cheung, and in the careworn eyes and tired smile of Leung, his Bogart. Like von Sternberg, he films his actors mostly in close-up and medium shot, with baroque architectural details in the background, and cigarette smoke constantly coiling through the air. There are a lot of foreground screens (doorjambs, draperies, walls, furniture) to add texture and detail while concealing parts of those faces. The film is in lurid colors, a pulp counterpoint to the elegance of the action. Why Nat King Cole's version of "The Christmas Song" is heard two or three times is unclear; his songs were also heard in *In the Mood for Love.*

The story is either briefly summarized, or too complicated to be attempted. Briefly: Chow (Leung) leaves Singapore and Su Li Zhen (Li): "We have no prospects here, so I'll see how things are in Hong Kong." She does not follow. In Hong Kong, he moves into the hotel and meets a series of women: Lulu (Lau), a prostitute whose murder lingers as a troubling mystery throughout the film; Jing (Faye Wong), daughter of the hotel owner; and Bai Ling (Zhang), a prostitute who becomes Chow's confidante as they drown their sorrows, preferring drink to sex. All of these relationships are seen in carefully composed shots that seem to be remembering the characters more than seeing them. One spectacular shot shows Jing from above and behind, smoking a cigarette and listening to an opera. Its composition is really the subject of the shot.

An example of complications: Jing is in love with a Japanese man and earlier in the movie appears as an anime idol in the futuristic story within the story, where she has the same Japanese lover. The Japanese man is the film's original narrator, although later it appears the sci-fi story is being written by Chow, inspired by the present-day Jing and her lover. Whether and why this story is being written, and how the future world of 2046 shares a function with the present Room 2046, is an inviting mystery: Do we define the future as a place in our minds where things can happen later, or be shelved, or be hoped for, or be delayed?

Since it is by Wong Kar-Wai, *2046* is visually stunning. He uses three cinematographers but one style that tries to evoke mood more than meaning. The movie as a whole, unfortunately, never seems sure of itself. It's like a sketchbook. These are images, tones, dialogue, and characters that Wong is sure of, and he practices them, but he does not seem very sure why he is making the movie, or where it should end.

2046 arrived at the last minute at Cannes 2003, after missing its earlier screenings; the final reel reportedly arrived at the airport almost as the first was being shown. It was said to be unfinished, and indeed there were skeletal special effects that now appear in final form, but perhaps it was never really finished in his mind. Perhaps he would have appreciated the luxury that Woody Allen had with *Crimes and Misdemeanors;* he looked at the first cut of the film, threw out the first act, called the actors back, and reshot, focusing on what turned out to be the central story. Watching *2046,* I wonder what it could possibly mean to anyone not familiar with Wong's work and style. Unlike *In the Mood for Love,* it is not a self-contained film, although it's certainly a lovely meander.

U

Uncle Nino ★ ★

PG, 102 m., 2005

Joe Mantegna (Robert Micelli), Anne Archer (Marie Micelli), Pierrino Mascarino (Uncle Nino), Trevor Morgan (Bobby Micelli), Gina Mantegna (Gina Micelli). Directed by Robert Shallcross and produced by David James. Screenplay by Shallcross.

The loudest danger signal for Uncle Nino, after he arrives from Italy to visit his dead brother's family, is that the wine comes from a cardboard box with a spigot. There are other problems. The nephew and his wife are both working too hard, the kids are on the edge of rebellion, and the household has no dog. Obviously, a family in crisis; obviously, Uncle Nino is the solution. He will return them all to their old-world roots and reawaken their sense of family.

And so he does, in *Uncle Nino,* a family movie that some will find wholesome and heartwarming and others will find cornball and tiresome. You know who you are. I know who I am. This is not my kind of movie, and I found myself feeling mighty restless by the end, or even halfway through, or even near the beginning, but objectively I know there are people who will embrace this movie, and my duty as a critic is to tell them about it.

The film goes into national release with an interesting marketing story behind it. Independently financed and made in Chicago, it was rejected by major distributors and festivals. It opened in one theater in Grand Rapids, Michigan, played fifty-five weeks, grossed $170,000, and has ecstatic user comments on the Internet Movie Database. It also has an IMDb "user rating" of 9.1, which is 0.1 higher than *The Godfather.* This rating is interesting because 79.4 percent of everyone voting for it gave it a perfect "10" rating, and because the breakdown of voters into males, females, age groups, U.S. and non–U.S. reveals that the approval rating in each and every group is uncannily close to 9 (every female under eighteen scored it 10, and the hardest to please were males thirty to thirty-four, at 7.4). Does this suggest to you that someone has been force-feeding the database?

Never mind. Let's regard the movie. It stars Joe Mantegna and Anne Archer as Robert and Marie Micelli, a Glenview, Illinois, couple who have moved into an expensive new home and are working hard to keep up. Their son, Bobby (Trevor Morgan), is a fourteen-year-old who belongs to a band that can't find a place to practice, and their twelve-year-old daughter, Gina (Gina Mantegna), spends a lot of time at her best friend's house because nobody is home at her house. She wants a dog, but Robert doesn't want the mess and bother.

Enter Uncle Nino (Pierrino Mascarino), one of those lovable movie ethnic types who speaks no English except for each and every word he requires in a specific situation. He is making a belated visit to America to visit the grave of his late brother. A quick study, he perceives that the Micelli family needs more quality time, more music, wine in bottles, and a dog. In attempting to remedy these needs, he blunders into various episodes of mistaken intentions, mistaken identities, and mistaken mistakes. He is simultaneously saintly and comic, and filled with a wisdom at which American suburbanites can only shake their heads with envy.

The film ends with the high school battle of the bands. Does Bobby's band get enough rehearsal time to qualify? What role do Uncle Nino and his violin play? Is there a scene in which the busy dad is able to tear himself away from the office in order to sit in the audience and make significant eye contact with his son, indicating that a lifelong bond has been forged and that he'll be a better father in the future?

As it happens, Joe Mantegna has appeared in a much better movie about an older Italian man with deep innocence in his heart. That would be David Mamet's wonderful *Things Change* (1988), starring Don Ameche as an old shoeshine man who is mistaken as a Mafia don because of his way of looking mysterious and issuing truisms that sound like profundities. *Uncle Nino* made me wish I was seeing that movie again.

I am quite aware, however, that *Uncle Nino* will appeal to those who seek sunny, predictable, positive family entertainment and do not demand that it also be challenging or have any depth. The success in Grand Rapids was because of word-of-mouth, as people told each other about the film, and if it is allowed to find an audience in its national release, that will probably happen again. It's that kind of movie, for better or worse.

Undead ★ ½
R, 100 m., 2005

Felicity Mason (Rene), Mungo McKay (Marion), Rob Jenkins (Wayne), Lisa Cunningham (Sallyanne), Dirk Hunter (Harrison), Emma Randall (Molly), Noel Sheridan (Chip). Directed, written, and produced by Michael Spierig and Peter Spierig.

Undead is the kind of movie that would be so bad it's good, except it's not bad enough to be good enough. It's, let's see, the sixth zombie movie I've seen in the past few years, after *28 Days Later, Resident Evil,* the remake of *Dawn of the Dead, Shaun of the Dead,* and *George Romero's Land of the Dead.* That is a lot of lurching and screaming and heads blown off.

Undead is the work of two brothers from Australia, Michael Spierig and Peter Spierig, who wrote, directed, edited, and produced it. They are of the kitchen-sink approach to filmmaking, in which zombies are not enough and we must also have aliens and inexplicable characters who seem to have wandered in from another movie without their name tags. It's comedy, horror, satire, and sci-fi, combined with that endearing Australian quality of finding their own country the nuttiest place on Earth. If the Australian cinema is accurate, once you leave the largest cities, the only people you meet are crazies, eccentrics, neurotics, parched wanderers in the outback, and the occasional disc jockey who is actually a fish.

This tradition continues in *Undead,* which even includes some zombie fish. It takes place in the hamlet of Berkeley, in Queensland, a fishing mecca that has just held a beauty pageant to crown Miss Catch of the Day. This is Rene (Felicity Mason), an adornment to any bait store. Excitement such as the crowning of Miss Catch of the Day is interrupted by a meteor shower; rocks from space rain down upon Berkeley, some of them opening up platter-sized holes in the chests of the citizens, who stagger about with daylight showing through them and have become zombies.

In the obligatory tradition of all zombie movies, a few healthy humans survive and try to fight off the zombies and preserve themselves. Rene is on her way out of town when the attack occurs; she has lost the mortgage on the family farm and is fleeing to the big city, or a larger hamlet, when she runs into a traffic jam. All attacks from outer space, natural or alien, immediately cause massive traffic pileups, of course, and the only functioning cars belong to the heroes.

In *War of the Worlds,* for example, Tom Cruise has the only car that works, after he and a friend peer under the hood and say, "It's the solenoid!" And so it is. This moment took me back to my youth, when cars could still be repaired without computers. They just had gas lines and spark plugs and things like that. I never understood anything about engines, but there were always kids in high school who would look under the hood and solemnly explain, "It's the solenoid." The solenoid, always the solenoid. You could impress girls with a line like that. "It's the solenoid." Works every time.

But I digress. Rene hits a traffic jam on the road out of town and meets a bush pilot named Wayne (Rob Jenkins) and his girlfriend, Sallyanne (Lisa Cunningham), who was runner-up to Miss Catch of the Day, which means, I guess, you throw her back in. Sallyanne is preggers, so she can do what all pregnant women in the movies and few pregnant women in life do, and hold her stomach with both hands most of the time. There is also a cop named Harrison (Dirk Hunter), who if you ask me should be named Dirk and played by Harrison Hunter, as Dirk is a better name than Harrison for a cop whose vocabulary consists of four-letter words and linking words.

They wander off the road and into the company of a local gun nut and survivalist named Marion (Mungo McKay), who if you ask me should be named Mungo and played by Marion McKay, as Mungo is a better name than Marion for a guy who has three shotguns yoked together so he can blast a zombie in two and leave its hips and legs lurching around with its bare spine sticking up in the air. For him, every shot is a trick shot; he'll throw two handguns into the air, kill a couple of zombies with a shotgun, and drop the shotgun in time to catch the handguns on the way down and kill some more.

Marion/Mungo hustles them all into his concrete-and-steel underground safe room, where their problems seem to be over until Marion announces, "There is no food or water." He didn't think of everything. Meanwhile, on the surface, the nature of the attack has changed, and some actual aliens appear. Who they are and what they want is a little unclear; I am not even absolutely certain if they were responsible for the meteorite attack that turned people into zombies, or have arrived shortly afterward by coincidence, making this the busiest day in local history, especially if you include the Miss Catch of the Day pageant.

There is a sense in which movies like *Undead* ask only to be accepted as silly fun, and I understand that sense and sympathize with it. But I don't think the Spierig brothers have adequately defined what they want to accomplish. They go for laughs with dialogue at times when verbal jokes are at right angles to simultaneous visual jokes. They give us gore that is intended as meaningless and funny, and then when the aliens arrive they seem to bring a new agenda. Eventually the story seems to move on beyond the central characters, who wander through new developments as if mutely wondering, hey, didn't this movie used to be about us?

Still, the horror genre continues to be an ideal calling card for young directors trying to launch their careers. Horror is the only non-porno genre where you don't need stars, because the genre is the star. *Undead* will launch the careers of the Spierigs, who are obviously talented and will be heard from again. Next time, with more resources, they won't have to repeat themselves. You see one set of hips and legs walking around with a spine sticking up out of them, you've seen them all.

Underclassman ★

PG-13, 95 m., 2005

Nick Cannon (Tracy Stokes), Roselyn Sanchez (Karen Lopez), Shawn Ashmore (Rob Donovan), Angelo Spizzirri (David Boscoe), Cheech Marin (Captain Delgado), Kelly Hu (Lisa Brooks). Directed by Marcos Siega and produced by Peter Abrams, Robert L. Levy, and Andrew Panay. Screenplay by Brent Goldberg and David Wagner.

Underclassman doesn't even try to be good. It knows that it doesn't have to be. It stars Nick Cannon, who has a popular MTV show, and it's a combo cop movie, romance, thriller, and high school comedy. That makes the TV ads a slam dunk; they'll generate a Pavlovian response in viewers conditioned to react to their sales triggers (smart-ass young cop, basketball, sexy babes, fast cars, mockery of adults).

Cannon plays Tracy Stokes, a bike cop who screws up in the title sequence and is called on the carpet by his captain (Cheech Marin), who keeps a straight face while uttering exhausted clichés ("You've got a long way to go before you're the detective your father was"). He gets a chance to redeem himself by working undercover at an exclusive L.A. prep school where a murder has been committed.

Turns out the murder is connected to a student car-theft ring, which is linked to drugs, which is an indictment of the rich students and their rich parents. It is a melancholy fact that a brilliant movie about high school criminals, Justin Lin's *Better Luck Tomorrow* (2002), got a fraction of the promotional support given to this lame formula film. If the teenagers going to *Underclassman* were to see *Better Luck Tomorrow,* they'd have something to think about and talk about and be interested in. *Underclassman* is a dead zone that will bore them silly while distracting them with the illusion that a lot of stuff is happening.

Why couldn't the movie at least have tried to do something unexpected, like making Tracy a good student? It's on autopilot: It makes him into a phenomenal basketball player (so good that most of his shots are special effects) and has him telling a classmate over dinner, "In my old neighborhood, crabs were not something you eat." Another food joke: A popular white student (Shawn Ashmore) mentions Benedict Arnold. "He makes good eggs," Tracy says. If he knows about eggs Benedict, he knows about crab cakes. But never mind. He also gets involved in a linguistic discussion of the difference between "up their asses" and "on their asses."

The movie is multi-ethnic, but guess which ethnic group supplies the stooges, villains, and fall guys. There's a cute Asian cop (Kelly Hu) who helps Tracy a lot, and a sexy Latino teacher (Roselyn Sanchez) he wants to date (he's dying to tell her he's not really a student). And the plot asks us to believe that behind the murder is a conspiracy involving the local white establishment. Uh-huh. The white establishment in a rich Los Angeles neighborhood has ways to make (or steal) lots more money in business, without having to get involved in street crime.

Did anyone at any time during the talks leading up to this film say, "Gee, guys, doesn't it seem like we've seen this a million times before?" Did anyone think to create an African-American character who was an individual and not a wiseass stand-up with street smarts? Was there ever an impulse to nudge the movie in the direction of originality and ambition? Or was everybody simply dazed by the fact that they were making a film and were, therefore, presumably filmmakers?

Underclassman will probably open well, make its money, drop off quickly, go to video in a few months, and be forgotten. The sad thing is that Cannon, who is only twenty-five, showed real promise in *Drumline.* If he thinks *Underclassman* represents the direction his career should be taking, he needs to find himself a mentor.

An Unfinished Life ★ ★ ★

PG-13, 107 m., 2005

Robert Redford (Einar Gilkyson), Morgan Freeman (Mitch Bradley), Jennifer Lopez (Jean Gilkyson), Becca Gardner (Griff Gilkyson), Josh Lucas (Crane Curtis), Damian Lewis (Gary Watson), Camryn Manheim (Nina), Bart (The Bear). Directed by Lasse Hallstrom and produced by Leslie Holleran, Alan Ladd Jr., and Kelliann Ladd. Screenplay by Mark Spragg and Virginia Korus Spragg.

The typical review of *An Unfinished Life* will mention that it was kept on the shelf at Miramax for two years and was released in 2005 as part of the farewell flood of leftover product produced by the Weinstein brothers. It will say that Robert Redford and Morgan Freeman are trying to be Clint Eastwood and Morgan Freeman. It will have no respect for Jennifer Lopez, because she is going through a period right now when nobody is satisfied with anything she does. These reviews will be more about showbiz than about the movie itself.

Sometimes you are either open to a movie, or closed. If you're convinced that *An Unfinished Life* is damaged goods, how can it begin its work on you? If you think Freeman is channeling the relationship he had with Eastwood in *Million Dollar Baby,* reflect that this movie was made a year earlier. And give Lopez your permission to be good again; she is the same actress now as when we thought her so new and fine.

The story takes place on a rundown ranch outside Ishawooa, Wyoming. It has seen better days. So has its owner, Einar Gilkyson (Redford), and his longtime ranch hand Mitch (Freeman), who lives in the little house behind the bigger one. Mitch was mauled a year ago by a bear and is an invalid, given a daily needle of morphine by Einar. These men are essentially awaiting death together when they get visitors: Jean (Lopez) is the widow of Einar's son, who was killed in a car crash a dozen years ago. Griff (Becca Gardner) is Einar's granddaughter.

Einar thinks he hates Jean. He blames her for his son's death. She doesn't want to be at the ranch, but she has no choice; her latest boyfriend, Gary (Damian Lewis), beats her, and she has fled from him. It is a foregone conclusion, I suppose, that Einar will eventually unbend enough to love Griff, who after all is his son's child, and true also that Mitch is the ranch's reservoir of decency. The local sheriff (Josh Lucas) is not indifferent to the arrival in a small town of a good-looking woman.

It's not often noted, but Redford plays anger well. His face gets tight and he looks away. Freeman never seems to be playing anything; he sees what he sees. The four characters seem to be stuck, and then they're budged by the arrival of two predators: The bear comes back, and so does Gary, the boyfriend. The bear (played by Bart, who had the title role in *The Bear*) is more likable, because after all he behaves according to his nature. But he is captured and sold off to a shabby local zoo so that yokels can stare at him through the steel mesh of a cage.

Gary, on the other hand, is a psychopath whose gearbox includes a setting for charm. We can almost see what Jean almost saw in him. Now he lurks around town, intimidated even by the two old men on the ranch, one of them an invalid, because wife-beaters by their nature are cowards. Sooner or later the matter of Gary will have to be settled. Less clear is the fate of the bear.

The unfinished life in the title at first seems to refer to Einar's dead son. Then we realize the death has put Einar, Jean, Mitch, and Griff all on hold. Until they deal with it, they can't get on with things. How they deal with it is not original, but it is sincere, and the actors are convincing. I was not quite as ready for the solution involving the bear, not after seeing *Grizzly Man* and remembering Werner Herzog's scary narration: The "blank stare" of a bear, he says, reveals not wisdom but "only the half-bored interest in food." While it is reasonable for bears to want to be free, it may not be reasonable for humans to want to live close to free bears.

An Unfinished Life was directed by Lasse Hallstrom, who has made a better movie about a dysfunctional family *(What's Eating Gilbert Grape)* and a worse one *(The Cider House Rules)*. This one, based on an original screenplay by Mark Spragg and Virginia Korus Spragg, is modest and heartfelt, dealing directly with straightforward material. We don't expect any twists, and there aren't any, but as Jean tries to put her life back together, her healing makes it possible for the others to get on with things. That is enough.

United 93 ★ ★ ★ ★

R, 90 m., 2006

JJ Johnson (Captain Jason Dahl), Ben Sliney (Himself), Gregg Henry (Colonel Robert Marr), Christian Clemenson (Thomas Burnett), Becky London (Jean Headley Peterson), David Alan Basche (Todd Beamer), Trish Gates (Sandy Bradshaw), Cheyenne Jackson (Mark Bingham), Lewis Alsamari (Saeed Al Ghamdi), Chip Zien (Mark Rothenberg). Directed by Paul Greengrass and produced by Tim Bevan, Eric Fellner, and Lloyd Levin. Screenplay by Greengrass.

It is not too soon for *United 93*, because it is not a film that knows any time has passed since 9/11. The entire story, every detail, is told in the present tense. We know what they know when they know it, and nothing else. Nothing about al-Qaeda, nothing about Osama bin Laden, nothing about Afghanistan or Iraq, only events as they unfold. This is a masterful and heartbreaking film, and it does honor to the memory of the victims.

The director, Paul Greengrass, makes a deliberate effort to stay away from recognizable actors, and there is no attempt to portray the passengers or terrorists as people with histories. In most movies about doomed voyages, we meet a few key characters we'll be following: the newlyweds, the granny, the businessman, the man with a secret. Here there's none of that. What we know about the passengers on United 93 is exactly what we would know if we had been on the plane and sitting across from them: nothing, except for a few details of personal appearance.

Scenes on board the plane alternate with scenes inside the National Air Traffic Control Center, airport towers, regional air traffic stations, and a military command room. Here, too, there are no backstories, just technicians living in the moment. Many of them are played by the actual people involved; we sense that in their command of procedure and jargon. When the controllers in the LaGuardia tower see the second airplane crash into the World Trade Center, they recoil with shock and horror, and that moment in the film seems as real as it seemed to me on September 11, 2001.

The film begins on a black screen, and we hear one of the hijackers reading aloud from the Quran. There are scenes of the hijackers at prayer, and many occasions when they evoke God and dedicate themselves to him. These details may offend some viewers but are almost certainly accurate; the hijacking and destruction of the four planes was carried out as a divine mission. That the majority of Muslims disapprove of terrorism goes without saying; on 9/12, there was a candlelight vigil in Iran for the United States. That the terrorists found justification in religion also goes without saying. Most nations at most times go into battle evoking the protection of their gods.

But the film doesn't depict the terrorists as villains. It has no need to. Like everyone else in the movie, they are people of ordinary appearance, going about their business. *United 93* is incomparably more powerful because it depicts all of its characters as people trapped in an inexorable progress toward tragedy. The movie contains no politics. No theory. No personal chitchat. No patriotic speeches. We never see the big picture.

We watch United 93 as the passengers and crew board the plane and it prepares to depart. Four minutes later, the first plane went into the WTC. Living in the moment, we share the confusion of the air traffic controllers. At first it's reported that a "small plane" crashed into the tower. Then by a process of deduction, it's determined it must have been a missing American flight. The full scope of the plot only gradually becomes clear. One plane after another abandons its flight plan and goes silent. There are false alarms: For more than an hour, a Delta flight is thought to have been hijacked, although it was not. At the FAA national center, the man in charge, Ben Sliney (playing himself), begins to piece things together and orders a complete shutdown of all American air traffic. Given what a momentous decision this was, costing the airlines a fortune and disrupting a nation's travel plans, we are grateful he had the nerve to make it.

As the outline of events comes into focus, there is an attempt to coordinate civilian and military authorities. It is doomed to fail. A liaison post is not staffed. Two jet fighters are sent up to intercept a hijacked plane, but they are not armed; there is discussion of having the fighters ram the jets as their pilots eject. A few other fighters are scrambled but inexplicably fly east, over the ocean. Military commanders try again and again, with increasing urgency, to get presidential authorization to use force against civilian aircraft. An unbearable period of time passes, with no response.

The movie simply includes this in the flow of events, without comment. Many people seeing the film will remember the scene in *Fahrenheit 9/11* in which George W. Bush sat immobile in a children's classroom for seven minutes after being informed of the attack on the WTC. What was he waiting for? Was he ever informed of the military request? The movie does not know, because the people on the screen do not have the opportunity of hindsight.

All of these larger matters are far offscreen. The third act of the film focuses on the desperation on board United 93, after the hijackers take control, slash flight attendants, kill the pilots, and seem to have a bomb. We are familiar with details of this flight, pieced together from many telephone calls from the plane and from the cockpit voice recorder. Greengrass is determined to be as accurate as possible. There is no false grandstanding, no phony arguments among the passengers, no individual heroes. The passengers are a terrified planeload of strangers. After they learn by phone about the WTC attacks, after an attendant says she saw the dead bodies of the two pilots, they decide they must take action. They storm the cockpit.

Even as these brave passengers charge up the aisle, we know nothing in particular about them—none of the details we later learned. We could be on the plane, terrified, watching them. The famous words "Let's roll" are heard but not underlined; these people are not speaking for history.

There has been much discussion of the movie's trailer, and no wonder. It pieces together moments from *United 93* to make it seem more conventional, more like a thriller. Dialogue that seems absolutely realistic in context sounds, in the trailer, like sound bites and punch lines. To watch the trailer is to sense the movie that Greengrass did not make. To watch *United 93* is to be confronted with the grim, chaotic reality of that autumn day in 2001.

The movie is deeply disturbing, and some people may have to leave the theater. But it would have been much more disturbing if Greengrass had made it in a conventional way. He does not exploit, he draws no conclusions, he points no fingers, he avoids "human interest" and "personal dramas" and just simply watches. The movie's point of view reminds me of the angels in *Wings of Desire.* They see what people do and they are saddened, but they cannot intervene.

Unknown White Male ★ ★ ★ ½

PG-13, 88 m., 2006

Featuring Doug Bruce. A documentary directed by Rupert Murray and produced by Beadie Finzi.

Amnesia has a dread fascination because it leaves its victims alive to experience the loss of self. Parents, lovers, photographs, and old letters testify to the existence of a person who lived in the body whose inhabitant now regards them without recognition.

In *Unknown White Male,* that person is named Doug Bruce, or so he is told. He was raised in Britain, immigrated to America, made money in the market, dropped out to study photography, had a girlfriend from Poland named Magda, and has a London pal named Rupert who is now making a documentary about him. All of this he is told, and it goes into his new collection of memories. Everything that happened to him before July 3, 2003, is gone. He is a victim of retrograde amnesia—rare, and total.

Because this documentary may be the inspiration for a fiction film, pause here for a story possibility. What if you awake from amnesia, and those around you, informing you of your earlier life, introducing themselves as parents, lovers, and friends, are lying to you? What if the person you have forgotten was someone other than the person they say you were? Would it make a difference? Does it matter? If a murderer experienced amnesia, would it be ethical to execute the body that formerly harbored his memories?

Such speculations are inspired by this intriguing and disturbing film. Questions have been raised about its truthfulness; is it a fraud? I have interviewed the filmmakers and am convinced of its truthfulness, but what difference does it make? As we watch the film, Bruce exists for us only in the sense that the film transfers him into our memories. Is that person any more or less real to us if the film is truthful or fraudulent?

Rupert Murray, who directed the film, has been asked why it does not contain more "proof" that it is truthful. He says it never occurred to him that anyone would doubt it, and he was more interested in the unfolding of Doug Bruce's new life. Maybe he took the correct path after all, bypassing proof to focus on the question he begins with: "How much is our identity determined by the experiences we have? And how much is already there? Pure us?"

These questions coil around the affable face of Bruce, who found himself on that July morning on a subway train in Coney Island with no idea of who he was or how he got there. A telephone number in his backpack provided a connection to a woman he had been dating, and she collected him from a hospital. There is footage taken less than a week later, as he talks about his complete loss of memory.

Murray hears what has happened to his old friend and starts making this film. Bruce is introduced to Magda, his former girlfriend. They lived together for eight years. She flies back from Poland and moves in (or does she, technically, move in with a person she has never known, and who never knew her?). Bruce travels to London and Spain, and meets his parents and old friends. He does not remember them. They say he is calmer, even nicer, than the old Doug. "Given a new lease on life," Murray tells us in his narration, "Doug seemed to be more articulate than before, more serious, more focused, as if his senses had been sharpened by a rebooting of the system."

Gradually Bruce begins to collect a fresh set of memories. He continues his photography lessons, and his teacher says that "his work has gained enormous depth." He finds Narelle, a new girlfriend. "The longer that it goes on," he says about his current life, "the less I care if my memory comes back." Yes, because if it did, would it invalidate what he now considers to be his identity? Would there be two persons inside his memory, one nicer and more focused, the other burdened with the imperfections of his previous operating system?

The thing about a movie like *Unknown White Male* is that it starts you thinking in the most unsettling ways. Murray, who claims to have met Bruce in London when they were eighteen or nineteen, has been questioned because he knows so little about Doug. If his friend was a stockbroker, what brokerage did he work for? Murray has no idea. "Quite frankly," he told me when I raised this question, "I make films and went to art school. I didn't know or care what firm he worked for. I'd call him up in New York and we'd go out for a drink." Is this plausible? Of course it is. I have friends in London of whom I could say the same thing.

How much of what we know about each other is simply a shared set of words? How much of what we know about ourselves is hearsay? When our parents tell us about our second birthday party, we no more remember that party than Bruce remembers his thirtieth. Yet the party goes into our database. How much is "pure us"? What Doug Bruce seems to have lost is not only his memory but even the "pure us" part—he has a different personality now. Here's an irony: He found that he could still write his signature. But neither he nor anyone else could read it.

Unknown White Male is maddening at times because Murray doesn't ask questions we'd like to shout at the screen: "Magda, if it's not too personal . . . is Doug the same in bed?" "Doctor, is there a way to tell for sure if someone is faking amnesia?" "Doug, do you resent these strangers who make emotional demands because they claim they were your parents?" "Mrs. Bruce, if your son cannot remember you, does it still hurt your feelings if he doesn't call and visit?"

This is not the review I thought I would write. I thought I would describe what is in the film, what happens and is said. But if he meets one set of people who say they were his London friends and not another, what difference does it make? We've never seen them before and neither has he. The real subject of the film is Douglas Bruce sitting on two years of memories and told there is a 95 percent chance that another thirty years may return to him. A lot of people don't want to know when they're going to die. Maybe they wouldn't want to be reborn either.

Unleashed ★ ★ ★

R, 103 m., 2005

Jet Li (Danny), Morgan Freeman (Sam), Bob Hoskins (Bart), Kerry Condon (Victoria). Directed by Louis Leterrier and produced by Luc Besson, Steven Chaseman, and Jet Li. Screenplay by Besson.

The story is familiar. The dog has been raised from infancy as a killer, obedient to its master. When it wears its collar it is passive. When the collar is removed and an order is given, it turns into a savage murder machine. Then a confusing thing happens. The dog experiences kindness for the first time in its life. Does this mean its master is wrong and must be disobeyed?

Luc Besson has produced or written some of the most intriguing movies of the last twenty years *(La Femme Nikita, The Fifth Element, Kiss of the Dragon, Ong-Bak)*. He takes this classic animal story and makes a simple but inspired change: He turns the dog into a human being. Jet Li stars in *Unleashed* as Danny, a lethal martial arts warrior who has been raised in captivity since childhood and is used by Bart, a Glasgow gangster, as a fearsome weapon. Danny lives in a cage under the floor of Bart's headquarters, travels quietly in the gangster's car, and, when his collar is removed, explodes into violent fury and leaves rooms filled with his victims.

This is a story that could have made a laughable movie. That it works is because of the performances of Jet Li and Bob Hoskins, who plays his master. "Danny the dog" is fearful of his owner, passive in captivity, and obedient in action, because he has been trained that way for his whole life. Bart the gangster is another one of those feral characters Hoskins specializes in, a man who bares his teeth and seems prepared to dine on the throats of his enemies. Hoskins, who can be the most genial of men, has a dimension of pitiless cruelty that he revealed in his first starring role, *The Long Good Friday* (1980).

But *Unleashed* would be too simple if it were only about Bart and Danny. Besson's screenplay now adds the character of Sam, a blind piano tuner played by Morgan Freeman. Sam lives in a gentle world of musicians and pianos and his beloved stepdaughter, Victoria (Kerry Condon). Danny falls into their lives by accident, after running away from Bart, as a dog is likely to do when it becomes fed up with its master.

In Danny's early memories, a piano figures somehow. A drawing of a piano triggers some of those old shadows, and when he hears piano music with Sam and Victoria, and when they give him his first simple music lessons, a great cloud lifts from his mind and he knows joy for the first time. He also begins to recall his mother, who was a pianist, and remembers fragments of the events that led to him becoming Danny the dog.

The film is ingenious in its construction. It has all the martial arts action any Jet Li fan could possibly desire, choreographed by Yeun Woo-ping, who is the Gerald Arpino of kung fu and creates improbable but delightful ballets of chops and socks, leaps and twists, and kicks and improvisations. Everything happens in a denatured sepia tone that is not black and white nor quite color, but a palate drained of cheer and pressing down like a foggy day.

Because Hoskins is so good at focusing the ferocity of Bart, he distracts us from the impossible elements in the trained-killer plot. Because Morgan Freeman brings an unforced plausibility to every character he plays, we simply accept the piano tuner instead of noticing how implausibly he enters the story. Freeman handles the role in the only way that will work, by playing a piano tuner as a piano tuner, instead of as a plot device in a martial arts movie. His stepdaughter, Victoria, is invaluable because, as Ann Coulter was explaining when she was so rudely shouted down the other day, women are a civilizing influence on men, who will get up to mischief in each other's company; Victoria's gentleness stirs Danny's humanity more than it inflames his lust.

So many action movies are made on autopilot that I am grateful when one works outside the box. Luc Besson, as producer and writer, almost always brings an unexpected human element to his action stories. *Unleashed* ends with a confrontation between Bart and Danny in which Bart reveals the truly twisted depth of his attachment to the "dog." They say dogs and their owners eventually start to resemble each other, but in this case an actual transference seems to be going on.

The Untold Story of Emmett Louis Till ★ ★ ★

NO MPAA RATING, 70 m., 2005

A documentary directed, written, and produced by Keith Beauchamp.

There is no statute of limitations on murder. Fifty years after the death of Emmett Till, the U.S. Justice Department reopened the case of the fourteen-year-old black boy from Chicago who went to visit his grandfather in Mississippi and was kidnapped, tortured, and killed because he whistled at a white woman.

The case electrified the nation in 1955, not least because Emmett's indomitable mother, Mamie, enlisted Chicago officials in her fight to gain possession of the boy's body, which authorities in Money, Mississippi, wanted to bury as quickly and quietly as possible. In a heartbreaking sequence in *The Untold Story of Emmett Louis Till,* she recalls saying: "I told the funeral director, 'If you can't open the box, I can. I want to see what's in that box.'"

What she found was the already decomposing body of her son, which had spent three days in a bayou of the Tallahatchie River, a heavy cotton gin fan tied to his neck with barbed wire. The mother is deliberate as she describes what she saw. She always thought her son's teeth were "the prettiest thing I ever saw." All but two were knocked out. One eyeball was hanging on his chin. An ear was missing. She saw daylight through the bullet hole in his head. His skull had been chopped almost in two, the face separated from the back of the head.

What Mamie Till did then made history. She insisted that the casket remain open at the Chicago funeral. Thousands filed past the remains. A photograph in *Jet* magazine made such an impression that, fifty years later, *60 Minutes* reporter Ed Bradley remembers seeing it; he discusses it on his program with Keith Beauchamp, director of this film, a much younger man who saw the photo and became obsessed with the case.

It was Beauchamp's nine years of investigation, summarized in the film, that was primarily responsible for Justice reopening the case. In the original trial, two white men, Roy Bryant and J. W. Milam, were charged with the crime. An all-white jury took only an hour to acquit them, later explaining they would have returned sooner, but took a "soda pop break" to make it look better. Only two months later, immune because of laws against double jeopardy, the two men sold their story to *Look* magazine for $4,000 and confessed to the crime.

Both are now dead. But Beauchamp's investigation indicates fourteen people were involved in one way or another in the murder, including five black employees of the white men, as well as the woman Till whistled at. Five of them are still alive.

The film inevitably invites comparison with *4 Little Girls* (1997), Spike Lee's powerful documentary about the 1963 Birmingham church bombing, which includes the long-delayed conviction of Robert ("Dynamite Bob") Chambliss, one of the bombers. Lee is the better filmmaker, with better source materials to work with, and his film is more passionate.

Beauchamp's film, on the other hand, has an earnest solemnity that is appropriate to the material. He has a lot of old black-and-white TV and newsreel footage, including shots of the accused men before, during, and after their trial. He interviews Emmett's young cousins who were in the house on the night the white men took him away. He recounts the courage of Emmett's uncle, who in the courtroom fearlessly pointed out the men who had taken Emmett, when such an act was a death sentence in Mississippi.

It is startling, the way the local sheriff casually tells TV reporters, "We didn't have any problems until our niggers went up north and talked to the NAACP and came back down here and caused trouble." And the way reporter Dan Wakefield recalls, "Everybody in the town knew they did it," even before they confessed in *Look* magazine. The defense attorneys informed the jury their forefathers would "roll over in their graves" if they voted to convict. But the case would not go away, and has not gone away. Mamie Till died in January 2003, just a little too soon to learn that the case was reopened.

Untraceable ★ ★ ★

R, 100 m., 2008

Diane Lane (Jennifer Marsh), Billy Burke (Detective Eric Box), Colin Hanks (Griffin Dowd), Joseph Cross (Owen Reilly), Mary Beth Hurt (Stella Marsh). Directed by Gregory Hoblit and produced by Tom Rosenberg, Gary Lucchesi, Howard Koch Jr., Steven Pearl, and Andy Cohen. Screenplay by Robert Fyvolent, Mark R. Brinker, and Allison Burnett.

Untraceable is a horrifying thriller, smart and tightly told, and merciless. It begins with this premise: A psychopath devises ways to slowly kill people online, in live streaming video. The more hits he gets, the further the process continues, until finally his captive is dead. "You're setting a new record!" he tells one agonized victim, as we see the total growing on a hit counter. Trying to find and stop him are the Cyber Crimes Division of the FBI and the Portland police.

His means of torture and death are sadistic nightmares. Why are so many of us fascinated by horrors in the movies (because, without question, we are)? Maybe it's for the same reason we slow down when we drive past a traffic accident. Maybe because someone else's tragedy is, at least, not ours. It may be hardwired in human nature. I don't have the slightest doubt that if a person were being killed on the Internet, it would draw millions of hits. An FBI spokesman holds a press conference to solemnly warn people that if they log on, they're accessories to murder. Of course that only promotes the site and increases visits.

Diane Lane plays Agent Jennifer Marsh, head of the FBI Portland Cyber Crimes unit. Her partner is Griffin Dowd (Colin Hanks, Tom's son), and her liaison with the Portland police is Detective Eric Box (Billy Burke). They're up against a hacker who uses captive computers of people all over the Net to forward his output and conceal his origins. When you give it a moment's thought, it's sort of a coincidence he's right there in Portland. Maybe that's plot-functional because he can become a threat to Marsh, her daughter, Annie (Perla Haney-Jardine), and her mother (Mary Beth Hurt).

The computer tech jargon in the movie sounds convincing. Whether it's accurate, I have no way of knowing—but that's beside the point, of course. What's ironic is that the key to cracking the case turns out to depend on perhaps our earliest and most basic form of digital communication between remote locations. Diane Lane can play smart, and she does, convincing us she knows her job, while at the same time being a convincing widow, mother, and daughter. The movie is lean and well-acted.

Certain logical questions arise. The killer's ingenuity and unlimited resources are dubious, especially considering what a short turnaround he has between crimes. He has the usual movie villain's ability to know more than he should, move more invisibly than he could, anticipate more than is possible. I think that goes with the territory. Lane's FBI superior is the usual obtuse publicity seeker, making wrong calls. But the through-line of the plot holds firm.

Of course the question occurs: Will the movie inspire copycats? I'm agnostic on this issue. I think a subset of hackers has already demonstrated how ingenious they are at thinking up evil all by themselves, and I doubt a cyber criminal could conceal himself online this successfully: Witness the routine busts of child porn rings.

One detail the movie gets just right. As the current victim dies and the hit-count climbs, we see a scrolling chat room onscreen. The comments are cretinous, stupid, ugly, divorced from all civilized standards. How people with the mentality of the authors of such messages are intelligent enough to get online in the first place is a puzzle. But they do. All you have to do is visit the wrong chat room or bulletin board and see them at their dirty work.

Is there a reason to see this movie? Was there a reason to see *Saw,* or *Se7en*? The purpose and function of the violent movie thriller remains a subject of debate. Yes, I watched fascinated. No, it wasn't art. Its message is visceral. Some people will think: "This is wrong." Others will think: "This is cool." It is the same in countless areas of society.

The movie is made with intelligence and skill. It is a dramatization of the sorts of things that the anonymity of the Internet makes possible, or even encourages. I know that if I learned of a Web site like this one, I, for one, would certainly not log on to it. On the other hand, what did I just do? Type in www.killwithme.com. I found what I expected. But why did I need to find that out? Now what will you do?

Up and Down ★ ★ ★

R, 108 m., 2005

Petr Forman (Martin Horecky), Emilia Vasaryova (Vera), Jiri Machacek (Frantisek Fikes), Natasa Burger (Miluska), Jan Triska (Otakar), Ingrid Timkova (Hana), Kristyna Liska-Bokova (Lenka), Jaroslav Dusek (Colonel). Directed by Jan Hrebejk and produced by Milan Kuchynka and Ondrej Trojan. Screenplay by Hrebejk and Petr Jarchovsky.

In the middle of the night on a back road of the Czech Republic, two truck drivers unload a group of illegal immigrants from India. Then they drive away, unaware that they still have a passenger—a baby, left behind in the confusion. Should they try to return the infant to its mother? No, because they don't know how to find her without risking arrest. Should they dump the baby by the roadside? One thinks that would be a good idea, but the other doesn't, and they end up selling the baby to the owners of a shady pawnshop.

This opening sets up one of the story lines in *Up and Down,* a Czech film about working-class and middle-class characters, former and present wives, infant and grown children, current and retired soccer fans, professors and hooligans, criminals and the police. Director Jan Hrebejk and his cowriter, Petr Jarchovsky, are interested not so much in making a statement about their society as seeing it reflected in specific lives; in this, their film resembles the early work of the Czech director Milos Forman *(The Fireman's Ball),* whose son Petr plays one of the film's leads.

The first couple we meet after the pawnshop are the Fikeses, Miluska and Frantisek (Natasa Burger and Jiri Machacek). They're not very bright, but not bad people. He's a night watchman, sensitive about his cleft palate, grateful to his wife for having dinner with him even though "I eat ugly." He's a member of a soccer team's fanatic group of supporters, who meet to watch the games on TV, get drunk, sing, chant slogans, and go through the emotional yo-yo of victory and defeat.

Miluska desperately wants a baby. She can't conceive. They can't adopt because Frantisek has a police record (he blames the soccer club for leading him into hooliganism). After almost stealing a baby in its carriage, she's afraid: "I'll do something and they'll arrest me." The baby at the pawnshop is a godsend. They buy it, bring it home, and love it. When Frantisek's booster club buddy makes racist remarks about the baby's dark skin, Frantisek boots him out, resigns from the club, and joins his wife in loving the baby.

Then we meet another family, the Horeckys. Martin (Petr Forman) has spent the last twenty years in Australia—a useful explanation for his English-accented Czech, no doubt. He returns home to visit his father, Otakar (Jan Triska), and mother, Vera (Emilia Vasaryova), who have divorced. He is also confronted with the fact that his former girlfriend, Hana (Ingrid Timkova), is now living with his father, and they have an eighteen-year-old daughter, Lenka (Kristana Bokova). No doubt the romance between Otakar and Hana was one of the reasons Martin left for Australia.

Czech movies seem to have some of their finest moments around the dining table, and a Horecky family dinner is funny, sad, and harrowing all at once. So is the uncertain relationship between Martin and his half-sister, Lenka. We learn that Vera is an alcoholic with the kinds of resentments, including racist ones, that drunks often use to deflect anger and attention away from themselves.

These two stories do not so much interact as reflect on each other with notions about families, parents, children, and class. For me, the most affecting character was Franta, the watchman, who is tattooed, muscular, and ferocious, yet so gentle with his wife and baby. He has been under the thumb of the "Colonel" (Jaroslav Dusek), a leader of the booster club, but for a brief moment breaks free into happiness and a content family life. The story of his history with the club is the story of the ups and downs of his life, and his final scene in the movie is heartbreaking in the way it shows the club becoming a substitute family.

There is, of course, the question of the baby's real parents. Can they go to the police without revealing their status as illegal immigrants? Another of the movie's ups and downs is about the way we're simultaneously required to sympathize with the baby's birth mother while witnessing how the baby transforms the marriage of Miluska and Frantisek.

Jan Hrebejk was also the director of *Divided We Fall* (2000), a film about a couple in Prague whose Jewish employers are victims of the Nazis. When the son of the employers appears at their door, they give him shelter in a hidden space within their house. Meanwhile, a local Nazi makes it clear he is attracted to the wife of the couple providing the shelter. He also begins to suspect their secret. What should happen next? Should the wife have sex with the Nazi to protect the man they are hiding?

Such moral puzzles are at the heart of Hrebejk's work, and he has no easy answers. *Up and Down* also lacks any formulas or solutions, and is content to show us its complicated characters, their tangled lives, and the way that our need to love and be loved can lead us in opposite directions.

The Upside of Anger ★ ★ ★ ★

R, 118 m., 2005

Joan Allen (Terry Wolfmeyer), Kevin Costner (Denny Davies), Erika Christensen (Andy Wolfmeyer), Evan Rachel Wood ("Popeye" Wolfmeyer), Keri Russell (Emily Wolfmeyer), Alicia Witt (Hadley Wolfmeyer), Mike Binder ("Shep" Goodman). Directed by Mike Binder and produced by Jack Binder, Alex Gartner, and Sammy Lee. Screenplay by Mike Binder.

Joan Allen and Kevin Costner achieve something in *The Upside of Anger* that may have been harder than costarring in *Macbeth*. They create two imperfect, alcoholic, resentful ordinary people, neighbors in the suburbs, with enough money to support themselves in the discontent to which they have become accustomed. I liked these characters precisely because they were not designed to be likable—or, more precisely, because they were likable in spite of being exasperating, unorganized, self-destructive, and impervious to good advice. That would be true of most of my friends. They say the same about me.

Allen plays Terry Wolfmeyer, suburban wife and mother of four daughters ("One of them hates me and the other three are working on it"). Her husband has walked out of the marriage, and all signs point to his having fled the country to begin a new life in Sweden with his secretary. "He's a vile, selfish pig," Terry says, "but I'm not gonna trash him to you girls." The girls, of college and high school age, dress expensively, are well groomed, prepare the family meals, and run the household, while their mother emcees with a vodka and tonic; her material is smart and bitter, although she sees the humor in the situation, and in herself.

Costner plays her neighbor, Denny Davies, once a star pitcher for the Detroit Tigers, now a sports-talk host who is bored by sports and talk. He spends his leisure time at the lonely but lucrative task of autographing hundreds of baseballs to sell online and at fan conventions. When Terry's husband disappears, Denny materializes as a friend in need. In need of a drinking partner, mostly. Neither one is a sensational *Barfly/Lost Weekend* kind of alcoholic, but more like the curators of a constant state of swizzledom. They are always a little drunk. Sometimes a little less little, sometimes a little more little.

Allen and Costner are so good at making these characters recognizable that we may not realize how hard that is to do. For Allen, the role comes in a season of triumph; she is also wonderful in Campbell Scott's *Off the Map,* and wait until you see her in Sally Potter's *Yes.* Costner reminds us that he is best when he dials down; he is drawn to epic roles, but here he's as comforting as your boozy best pal.

In *The Upside of Anger,* written and directed by Mike Binder, they occupy a comedy buried in angst. The camaraderie between Terry and Denny is like the wounded affection of two people with hangovers and plenty of time to drink them away. The four daughters have sized up the situation and are getting on with their lives in their own ways, mostly competently. Hadley (Alicia Witt) is a cool, centered college student; Andy (Erika Christensen) reacts as second children often do, by deciding she will not be Hadley and indeed will accept an offer to be an intern on Denny's radio show—an offer extended enthusiastically by Shep (Binder), the fortyish producer, who is a shameless letch. Emily (Keri Russell) is at war with her mother; she wants to be a dancer, and her mother says there's no money or future in it. Popeye (Evan Rachel Wood) is the youngest, but maturing way too rapidly, like Wood's character in *13.*

Terry deals imperfectly with events in the lives of her daughters, such as Hadley's impending marriage and Andy becoming Shep's girlfriend. Although Terry is wealthy, stylish, and sexy—a thoroughbred temporarily out of training—she has a rebel streak maybe left over from her teens in the late 1970s. At a lunch party to meet Hadley's prospective in-laws, she tells Denny, "I was like a public service ad against drinking."

It is inevitable that Denny and Terry will become lovers. The girls like him. He is lonely, and Terry's house feels more like home than his own, where the living room is furnished primarily with boxes of baseballs. It is also true, given the current state of the drunk driving laws, that alcoholics are wise to choose lovers within walking distance. So the movie proceeds with wit, intelligence, and a certain horrifying fascination. Sometimes Terry picks up the phone to call the creep in Sweden, but decides not to give him the satisfaction.

And then comes an unexpected development. Because *The Upside of Anger* opened a week earlier in New York than in Chicago, I am aware of the despair about this development from A. O. Scott in the *New York Times* (the ending "is an utter catastrophe") and Joe Morgenstern in the *Wall Street Journal* (the ending is "a cheat").

They are mistaken. Life can contain catastrophe, and life can cheat. The ending is the making of the movie, its transcendence, its way of casting everything in a new and ironic light, causing us to reevaluate what went before, and to regard the future with horror and pity. Without the ending, *The Upside of Anger* is a wonderfully made comedy of domestic manners. With it, the movie becomes larger and deeper. When life plays a joke on you, it can have a really rotten sense of humor.

V

Vanaja ★ ★ ★ ★

NO MPAA RATING, 111 m., 2007

Mamatha Bhukya (Vanaja), Urmila Dammannagari (Rama Devi), Ramachandriah Marikanti (Somayya), Krishnamma Gundimalla (Radhamma), Karan Singh (Shekhar), Bhavani Renukunta (Lacchi), Krishna Garlapati (Ram Babu), Prabhu Garlapati (Yadigiri). Directed by Rajnesh Domalpalli and produced by Latha Rajendra Kumar Domalpalli. Screenplay by Rajnesh Domalpalli.

Vanaja, a beautiful and heart-touching film from India, represents a miracle of casting. Every role, including the challenging central role of a low-caste fourteen-year-old girl, is cast perfectly and played flawlessly, so that it is a renewing pleasure to see these faces on the screen. Then we learn their stories: The actors, naturally and effortlessly true, are all nonprofessionals who were cast for their looks and presence and then trained in an acting workshop set up by the director, Rajnesh Domalpalli. He recalls that his luminous star, Mamatha Bhukya, an eighth-grader, was untrained and had to learn to act and perform classical Indian dances—during a year of lessons set up in his family's basement!

But this movie is not wonderful because of where the actors started. It is wonderful because of where they arrived and who they became. Bhukya is a natural star, her eyes and smile illuminating a face of freshness and delight. And the other characters are equally persuasive, especially Urmila Dammannagari, as the district landlady, who has to negotiate a way between her affection for the girl and her love for her son.

But why are you reading this far? An Indian film? Starring Mamatha Bhukya and Urmila Dammannagari? Lesser readers would already have tuned out, but you are curious. And so I can promise you that here is a very special film. It was made by the director as part of his master's thesis in the film department at Columbia University, shot over a period of years on a $20,000 budget, and all I can say is, $20,000 buys a lot in India, including a great-looking, extraordinary film.

Let me tell you a little of the story. In a rural district of South India, a fourteen-year-old girl named Vanaja (Bhukya) lives with her shambling, alcoholic father. Life is bearable because she makes her own way, and when we first see her she's in the front row of a dance performance with her best friend, Lacchi, where they're giggling like bobby-soxers (a word that will mystify some of my Indian readers, but fair's fair). What beautiful girls these are, and I mean that not in a carnal but a spiritual sense. The sun shines from their skin.

Vanaja's father takes her to the local landlady, Rama Devi (Dammannagari), and asks for a job for her. Rama Devi, in her late forties, is not a stereotyped cruel landowner, but a strong yet warm woman with a sense of humor, who likes the girl's pluck during their interview and hires her—at first to work with the livestock. But Vanaja dreams of becoming a dancer and persuades Rama Devi to give her lessons.

As we know from Satyajit Ray's *The Music Room,* many rural landowners pride themselves on their patronage of the arts; to possess an accomplished dancer in her household would be an adornment for Rama Devi. The lessons go well, and there are dance scenes that show how much the actress learned during her year of basement lessons, but there are no Bollywood-type musical scenes here; indeed, the film industry of this district not far from Hyderabad is known as Tollywood, after the Teluga language. It is also a status symbol to speak English, which Vanaja has never been very good at.

The landlady's twenty-three-year-old son, Shekhar (Karan Singh), returns from study in America, prepares to run for office, and notices the new beauty on his mother's staff. And although you may guess what happens next, I won't tell you, except to observe something that struck me. Although there is usually no nudity or even kissing in Indian films (and there is none here), the screenplay is unusually frank in dealing with the realities of sexual life.

Vanaja becomes fifteen, then sixteen. She grows taller. She will be a great beauty. But her lower-caste origins disqualify her for marriage into Rama Devi's family, her drunken father is a worry and burden, the local post-boy is fresh with her, and although the landlady is very fond of her and covets her dancing, her son will always come first. Vanaja's only real allies are her childhood friend and Radhamma (Krishnamma Gundimalla), the landlady's cook and faithful servant.

In any Indian film many of the pleasures are tactile. There are the glorious colors of saris and room decorations, the dazzle of dance costumes, and the dusty landscape that somehow becomes a watercolor by Edward Lear, with its hills and vistas, its oxen and elephants, its houses that seem part of the land. In this setting, Domalpalli tells his story with tender precision and never an awkward moment.

The plot reminds me of neorealism crossed with the eccentric characters of Dickens. The poor girl taken into a rich family is also a staple of Victorian fiction. But *Vanaja* lives always in the moment, growing from a simple story into a complex one, providing us with a heroine, yes, but not villains so much as vain, weak people obsessed with their status in society. When the final shot comes, we miss the comfort of a conventional Hollywood ending. But *Vanaja* ends in a very Indian way, trusting to fate and fortune, believing that there is a tide in the affairs of men, which—but you know where it leads. Let's hope it does.

V for Vendetta ★ ★ ★

R, 130 m., 2006

Natalie Portman (Evey Hammond), Hugo Weaving (V), Stephen Rea (Finch), Stephen Fry (Deitrich), John Hurt (Adam Sutler), Tim Pigott-Smith (Creedy), Rupert Graves (Dominic). Directed by James McTeigue and produced by Grant Hill, Joel Silver, Andy Wachowski, and Larry Wachowski. Screenplay by the Wachowski brothers.

It is the year 2020. A virus runs wild in the world, most Americans are dead, and Britain is ruled by a fascist dictator who promises security but not freedom. One man stands against him, the man named V, who moves through London like a wraith despite the desperate efforts of the police. He wears a mask showing the face of Guy Fawkes, who in 1605 tried to blow up the houses of Parliament. On November 4, the eve of Guy Fawkes Day, British schoolchildren for centuries have started bonfires to burn Fawkes in effigy. On this eve in 2020, V saves a young TV reporter named Evey from assault at the hands of the police, forces her to join him, and makes a busy night of it by blowing up the Old Bailey courtrooms.

V for Vendetta will follow his exploits for the next twelve months, until the night when he has vowed to strike a crushing blow against the dictatorship. We see a police state that holds its citizens in an iron grip and yet is humiliated by a single man who seems impervious. The state tries to suppress knowledge of his deeds—to spin a plausible explanation for the destruction of the Old Bailey, for example, but V commandeers the national television network to claim authorship of his deed.

This story was first told as a graphic novel written by Alan Moore and published in 1982 and 1983. Its hero plays altogether differently now, and yet, given the nature of the regime, is he a terrorist or a freedom fighter? Britain is ruled by a man named Sutler, who gives orders to his underlings from a wall-sized TV screen and seems the personification of Big Brother. And is: Sutler is played by John Hurt, who in fact played Winston Smith in *Nineteen Eighty-Four* (1984). V seems more like Jack the Ripper, given his ability to move boldly in and out of areas the police think they control. The similarity may have come easily to Moore, whose graphic novel *From Hell* was about the Ripper and inspired a good 2001 movie by the Hughes brothers.

V for Vendetta has been written and coproduced by the Wachowski brothers, Andy and Larry, whose *Matrix* was also about rebels holding out against a planetary system of control. This movie is more literary and less dominated by special effects (although there are plenty), and is filled with ideas that are all the more intriguing because we can't pin down the message. Is this movie a parable about 2006, a cautionary tale, or pure fantasy? It can be read many ways, as I will no doubt learn in endless e-mails.

The character of V and his relationship with Evey (Natalie Portman) inescapably reminds us of the Phantom of the Opera. V and the Phantom are both masked, move through subterranean spaces, control others through the leverage of their imaginations, and have a score to settle. One difference, and it is an important one, is that V's facial disguise does not move (unlike, say, the faces of a *Batman* villain) but is a mask that always has the same smiling expression. Behind it is the actor Hugo Weaving, using his voice and body language to create a character, but I was reminded of my problem with Thomas the Tank Engine: If something talks, its lips should move.

Still, Portman's Evey has expressions enough for most purposes, as she morphs from a dutiful citizen to V's sympathizer, and the film is populated with a gallery of gifted character actors. In addition to Hurt as the sinister dictator, we see Stephen Rea and Rupert Graves as the police assigned to lead the search for V. Tim Pigott-Smith is an instrument of the dictator. These people exist in scenes designed to portray them as secure, until V sweeps in like a whirlwind, using martial arts, ingenious weapons, and the element of surprise. Why the mask does not limit his peripheral vision is a question I will leave for the experts. See the Answer Man entry for this movie.

There are ideas in this film. The most pointed is V's belief: "People should not be afraid of their governments. Governments should be afraid of their people." I am not sure V has it right; surely in the ideal state, governments and their people should exist happily together. Fear in either direction must lead to violence. But V has a totalitarian state to overthrow and only a year in which to do it, and we watch as he improvises a revolution. He gets little support, although Stephen Fry plays a dissident TV host who criticizes the government at his peril.

With most action thrillers based on graphic novels, we simply watch the sound and light show. *V for Vendetta*, directed by James McTeigue, almost always has something going on that is actually interesting, inviting us to decode the character and plot and apply the message where we will. There are times when you think the sound track should be supplying "Anarchy in the U.K." by the Sex Pistols. The movie ends with a violent act that left me, as a lover of London, intensely unhappy; surely V's enemy is human, not architectural.

The film has been disowned by Alan Moore, who also removed his name from the movie versions of his graphic novels *From Hell* and *The League of Extraordinary Gentlemen*, but then any sane person would have been unhappy with the Gentlemen. His complaint was not so much with the films as with the deal involving the use of his work. I have not read the original work, do not know what has been changed or gone missing, but found an audacious confusion of ideas in *V for Vendetta* and enjoyed their manic disorganization. To attempt a parable about terrorism and totalitarianism that would be relevant and readable might be impossible, could be dangerous, and would probably not be box office.

Vicky Cristina Barcelona ★ ★ ★

NO MPAA RATING, 96 m., 2008

Javier Bardem (Juan Antonio), Rebecca Hall (Vicky), Scarlett Johansson (Cristina), Penelope Cruz (Maria Elena), Patricia Clarkson (Judy Nash), Kevin Dunn (Mark Nash), Chris Messina (Doug). Directed by Woody Allen and produced by Letty Aronson. Screenplay by Allen.

The thing about a Woody Allen film is, whatever else happens, the characters are intriguing to listen to. They tend to be smart, witty, not above epigrams. A few days before seeing *Vicky Cristina Barcelona*, I viewed his *Hannah and Her Sisters* again. More than twenty years apart, both with dialogue at perfect pitch. Allen has directed more than forty movies in about as many years and written all of them himself. Why isn't he more honored? Do we take him for granted?

Vicky Cristina Barcelona is typical of a lot of his midrange work. It involves affluent characters at various levels of sophistication, involved in the arts and the intrigues of love. They're conflicted about right and wrong. They're undoubtedly low-level neurotics. In addition, they are attractive, amusing, and living lives we might envy—in this case, during a summer vacation in Barcelona.

Allen's discovery of Europe (of London, Paris, Venice, Barcelona) has provided new opportunities for the poet of Manhattan (and *Manhattan*). In this film we meet two best friends, Vicky (Rebecca Hall) and Cristina (Scarlett Johansson), who decide to spend July and August in the Barcelona home of Vicky's relatives Judy and Mark (Patricia Clarkson and Kevin Dunn). We're briefed by a narrator that Vicky values stable relationships and is engaged to marry Doug (Chris Messina) when she returns. Cristina is more impulsive, more adventurous, not afraid to risk a little turmoil.

Vicki, we learn, is majoring in "Catalan studies," which makes the capital of Catalonia a perfect destination for her. "What will you . . . do with that?" Mark asks over lunch. "Oh," says Vicky, who clearly has no answer. "Maybe teach, or . . . work for a museum?" Her Spanish, it can be observed, could use some work.

They all go to an art gallery show, and Cristina wonders who the man in the red shirt is. Judy explains that he is Juan Antonio (Javier Bardem), an abstract artist, and there was a scandal over his divorce when he tried to kill his wife or she tried to kill him . . . the details are muddled. At midnight in a restaurant (a conventional dinner hour in Barcelona) the two girls see him across the room. "He keeps looking at us!" Cristina says. "That's because you can't take your eyes off of him," says Vicky. He approaches their table, and in quiet, measured tones, offers to fly them in his plane to an interesting city, see the sights, and sleep with him. Both of them.

Vicky is astonished and offended. Cristina accepts, of course, "with no guarantees." Juan Antonio has, in his own words, made a polite, frank, and straightforward offer. And then the film lingers in the complications of the relationships between these three people before introducing a fourth element: the former wife Maria Elena (Penelope Cruz). The tragedy is, she and Juan Antonio are still deeply in love with each other—but they can't live together without violence flaring up. A *ménage à quatre* takes shape—shaky, but fascinating.

Allen is amusing when he applies strict logic to the situation. If everybody knows and accepts what everybody is doing, where's the harm? Cristina is predisposed to such excitement, and Vicky's love for the stable, responsible, absent Doug begins to pale in comparison with this bohemian existence. Judy, the relative, discovers Vicky's secret and urges her to go with her heart, not her prudence. Vicky and Cristina have conversations in which they show they are open-minded, but perhaps not very prudent. There are unexpected arrivals and developments.

And by now we're engrossed in this comedy, which is really a fantasy—beginning with Juan Antonio, who is too cool and good to be true. All the time, Allen gives us a tour of the glories of Barcelona, the city of Gaudi and Miro, the excuse being that Juan Antonio is showing the girls the sights. As Hollywood learned long ago, there's nothing like a seductive location to lend interest to whatever is happening in the foreground.

More surprises than this I must not describe. It is all fairly harmless, although fraught with dire possibilities. Allen has set out to amuse and divert us and discover secrets of human nature, but not tragically deep ones. He is a little like Eric Rohmer here. The actors are attractive, the city is magnificent, the love scenes don't get all sweaty, and everybody finishes the summer a little wiser and with a lifetime of memories. What more could you ask?

Virgin ★ ★ ★

NO MPAA RATING, 113 m., 2005

Robin Wright Penn (Mrs. Reynolds), Elisabeth Moss (Jessie Reynolds), Daphne Rubin-Vega (Frances), Socorro Santiago (Lorna), Peter Gerety (Mr. Reynolds), Stephanie Gatchet (Katie Reynolds), Charles Socarides (Shane). Directed by Deborah Kampmeier and produced by Raye Dowell and Sarah Schenck. Screenplay by Kampmeier.

Jessie Reynolds is not the kind of girl who gets nice things written under her picture in the high school yearbook. She's probably never going to graduate, for one thing. When we see her for the first time in *Virgin,* she's trying to talk a stranger into buying some booze for her, and when he does, he gets a kiss.

Jessie is not bad, precisely. It would be more fair to say she is lost, and a little dim. She clearly feels left behind, even left out, by her family. Her sister, Katie (Stephanie Gatchet), is pretty, popular, and a track star who dedicates her victories to Jesus. Her parents (Robin Wright Penn and Peter Gerety) are fundamentalists, strict and unforgiving. Jessie doesn't measure up and doesn't even seem to be trying.

There is, however, someone she would like to impress: Shane (Charles Socarides), a boy at school. She wanders off from a dance with him, is drunk, is given a date-rape pill, is raped, and wakes up with no memory of the event. When she discovers she is pregnant, there is only one possible explanation in her mind: There has been an immaculate conception, and she will give birth to the baby Jesus.

Jessie is played by Elisabeth Moss, from *West Wing*, as a girl both endearing and maddening. Her near-bliss seems a little heavily laid on, under the circumstances, but director Deborah Kampmeier has ways of suggesting it's the real thing. Whether or not there is a God has nothing to do with whether we believe he is speaking to us, and although in this case there's every reason to believe God has not impregnated Jessie, there's every reason for Jessie to think so. Among other things, it certainly trumps the religiosity of her parents and sister.

Fundamentalists almost always appear in American movies for the purpose of being closed-minded, rigid, and sanctimonious. Anyone with any religion at all, for that matter, tends to be suspect (the priest in *Million Dollar Baby* is the first good priest I can remember in a film in a long time). Movies can't seem to deal with faith as a positive element in an admirable life, and the only religions taken seriously by Hollywood are the kinds promoted in stores that also sell incense and tarot decks. So it's refreshing to see the Robin Wright Penn character allowed to unbend in *Virgin*, to become less rigid and more of an empathetic mother, who intuitively senses that although Jessie may be deluded, she is sincere.

There has, of course, been a great wrong committed here, but it would be cruel for Jessie to learn of that fact. How sad to believe you are bearing the Christ child and then be told, no, you got drunk and were raped. Better, perhaps, to let Jessie bear the child and find out gradually that, like all children, it displays divinity primarily in the eyes of its mother.

But Kampmeier is up to something a little more ambitious here. She uses visual strategies to suggest that Jessie, in the grip of her conviction, enters a state that is just as spiritual as if its cause were not so sad. The performance by Moss invests Jessie with a kind of zealous hope that is touching: Here is a slutty loser touched by the divine and transformed. What has happened to her is more real than the miracles hailed on Sundays by results-oriented preachers. The more you consider the theological undertones of *Virgin*, the more radical it becomes. Must you be the mother of God to experience the benefits of thinking that you are? Can those from a conventional religious background deal with your ecstasy?

There is a wonderful novel named *The Annunciation of Francesca Dunn* by Janis Hallowell, a friend of mine, that tells of a waitress in Boulder, Colorado, whom a homeless man becomes convinced is the Virgin Mary. The novel explores a little more poetically and explicitly than *Virgin* the experience of being blindsided by an unsolicited spiritual epiphany.

Both works are fascinating because in mainstream society, there are only two positions on such matters: either you believe, or you do not (and, therefore, either you are saved or you don't care). Is it not possible that faith is its own reward, apart from any need for it to be connected with reality? I am unreasonably stimulated by works that leave me theologically stranded like that. They're much more interesting than works that, one way or the other, think they know.

Theological footnote: Every once in a while my Catholic grade school education sounds a dogma alarm. Jessie is not a Catholic, which perhaps explains why she thinks the term "immaculate conception" refers to the birth of Jesus, when in fact it refers to the birth of Mary.

The Visitor ★ ★ ★ ½

PG-13, 103 m., 2008

Richard Jenkins (Walter Vale), Haaz Sleiman (Tarek), Danai Gurira (Zainab), Hiam Abbass (Mouna). Directed by Tom McCarthy and produced by Mary Jane Skalski and Michael London. Screenplay by McCarthy.

Richard Jenkins is an actor who can move his head half an inch and provide the turning point of a film. That happens in *The Visitor*, where he plays a man around sixty who has essentially shut down all of his emotions. A professor, Walter has been teaching the same class for years and cares nothing about it. He coldly rejects a student's late paper without even inquiring about the "personal problems" that made it late. He makes an elderly piano teacher figure out for herself why she will not be needed again. His lips form a straight line that neither smiles nor frowns.

He is forced to travel from his Connecticut campus to New York, to present an academic paper he coauthored. At least he is honest. Protesting the assignment, he tells a colleague he agreed to put his name on the paper as a favor, has not read it, is not competent to present it. He has to go anyway.

He keeps an apartment in Manhattan. Lets himself in. The naked African girl in his bathtub screams. Her boyfriend appears from somewhere. The interlopers are ready to call the police when he explains it is *his* apartment. They'd been renting it from a crafty opportunist. These "roomers" are Tarek (Haaz Sleiman), from Syria, and his girlfriend, Zainab (Danai Gurira), from Senegal. They immediately pack to leave. He sees them out, then appears at the top of the stairs to tell them they can stay the night. During the film, he will change his mind and appear at the stair-top three times, each time crucial.

Tarek is a virtuoso on an African drum. Walter's late wife was a famous pianist. He loves music but has failed at learning the piano. One day Walter is walking through Washington Square Park and hears two young black boys drumming on the bottoms of plastic buckets. He stops to listen. After a while his head begins to move side to side, half an inch at a time, in response to the rhythm. There you are.

Of course the film, written and directed by Tom McCarthy, is about a great deal more—about illegal U.S. residents and stupid bureaucrats and drums and love and loss. A fourth major character appears, Mouna (Hiam Abbass), who is Tarek's mother and lives in Michigan. She hopes to help her son after he is arrested in an innocent subway incident and threatened with deportation. Walter has already hired a lawyer. He's no bleeding heart, makes no speeches, barely displays emotion, but now for the first time since his wife died, he is feeling things deeply.

This is a wonderful film, sad, angry, and without a comforting little happy ending. But I must not describe what happens because the whole point of serious fiction is to show people changing, and how they change in *The Visitor* is the film's beauty. So much goes unsaid and unseen. Events in Walter's professorial job happen offscreen. We are left to listen to the silences and observe the spaces.

All four actors are charismatic, in quite different ways. Hiam Abbass is one of those actresses who respects small gestures; she knows that when a good cook is using an unfamiliar salt shaker, she shakes the salt first into her hand, and *then* throws it into the pot. And she has other small gestures here that are much more fraught with meaning. Haaz Sleiman and Danai Gurira, as a musician and a jewelry-maker, are young, in love, and simply nice people. The less complicated they are, the better the characters work. And as Walter, Jenkins creates a surprisingly touching, very quiet character study. Not all actors have to call out to us. The better ones make us call out to them.

Volver ★ ★ ★ ★

R, 120 m., 2006

Penelope Cruz (Raimunda), Carmen Maura (Irene), Lola Duenas (Sole), Blanca Portillo (Agustina), Yohana Cobo (Paula), Antonio de la Torre (Paco), Chus Lampreave (Aunt Paula). Directed by Pedro Almodovar and produced by Esther Garcia. Screenplay by Almodovar.

How would you like to spend the afterlife? Hanging around in a tunnel of pure light, welcoming new arrivals from among your family and friends? It seems to me a dreary prospect. You'd run out of customers in a generation or two. And how boring to smile and beckon benevolently all the time. My Aunt Martha would more likely be cutting the cards for a game of canasta.

In Pedro Almodovar's enchanting, gentle, transgressive *Volver*, a deceased matriarch named Irene (Carmen Maura) has moved in with her sister Paula (Chus Lampreave), who is growing senile and appreciates some help around the house, especially with the baking. They live, or whatever you'd call it, in a small Spanish town where the men die young and the women spend weekends cheerfully polishing and tending their graves, just as if they were keeping house for them. In exemplary classic style, Almodovar uses a right-to-left tracking shot to show this housekeeping carrying us back into the past, and then a centered subtle zoom to establish the past as part of the present.

We meet Raimunda (Penelope Cruz) and Sole (Lola Duenas), Irene's daughters; Raimunda's daughter, Paula (Yohana Cobo); and Paco (Antonio de la Torre), Raimunda's beer-swilling, layabout husband. Two deaths occur closely spaced to upset this happy balance: Aunt Paula keels over, and Young Paula repulses an advance by her stepfather, Paco, using a large, bloody, very Hitchcockian knife. Paco ends up on the kitchen floor, his arms and legs akimbo in an uncanny reminder of the body on the poster of Otto Preminger's *Anatomy of a Murder.*

Where will the ghost of Irene go now? Why, obviously, to the one who needs her most—Raimunda. This is the setup for a confounding gathering of murder, reincarnation, and comedy, also involving Raimunda's almost accidental acquisition of the restaurant where she has one of several part-time jobs.

Almodovar is above all a director who loves women—young, old, professional, amateur, mothers, daughters, granddaughters, dead, alive. Here his cheerful plot combines life after death with the concealment of murder, success in the restaurant business, and the launching of Irene's daughters with completely serendipitous solutions to (almost) everyone's problems. He also achieves a vivid portrait of life in a village not unlike the one where he was born.

Volver is Spanish for "to return," I am informed. The film reminds me of Fellini's *Amarcord,* also a fanciful revisit to childhood that translates as "I remember." What the directors are doing, I think, is paying tribute to the women who raised them—their conversations, conspiracies, ambitions, compromises, and feeling for romance. (What Fellini does more closely resembles revenge.) These characters seem to get along so easily that even the introduction of a dead character can be taken in stride.

Women see time more as a continuum anyway, don't you think? Don't you often hear them speaking of the dead in the present tense? Their lives are a continuum not limited by dates carved in stone.

What a distinctive filmmaker Almodovar has become. He is greatly influenced, we are assured, by Hollywood melodramas of the 1950s (especially if that decade had been franker about its secret desires). But he is equally turned on, I think, by the 1950s palette of bright basic colors and a cheerful optimism that goes without saying. Here the dominant color is red—for blood, passion, and Pedro.

In this connection some mention might be made of Penelope Cruz's cleavage, including one startling shot also incorporating the murder weapon. In an interview at Cannes it seemed impossible not to mention that shot. Almodovar nodded happily. "Yes, I am a gay man," he said, "but I love breasts."

What is most unexpected about *Volver* is that it's not really about murder or the afterlife but simply incorporates those awkward developments into the problems of daily living. His characters approach their dilemmas not with metaphysics but with common sense. A dead woman turns up as a ghost and is immediately absorbed into her family's ongoing problems: So what took her so long?

It is refreshing to see Penelope Cruz acting in the culture and language that is her own. As it did with Sophia Loren in the 1950s, Hollywood has tried to force Cruz into a series of showbiz categories, when she is obviously most at home playing a woman like the ones she knew, grew up with, could have become. For Almodovar, too, *Volver* is like a homecoming. Whenever we are most at ease, we fall easily and gracefully into our native idioms. Certainly as a young gay man in Franco's Spain, he didn't feel at home—but he felt displaced in a familiar way and now feels nostalgia for the women who accepted him as easily as if, well, he had been a ghost.

W

The Wackness ★ ★ ★

R, 95 m., 2008

Josh Peck (Luke Shapiro), Ben Kingsley (Dr. Squires), Olivia Thirlby (Stephanie), Method Man (Percy), Mary-Kate Olsen (Union), Famke Janssen (Kristin), Talia Balsam (Mrs. Shapiro), David Wohl (Mr. Shapiro). Directed by Jonathan Levine and produced by Keith Calder, Felipe Marino, and Joe Neurauter. Screenplay by Levine.

The Wackness, which is set in 1994, contains so many drugs it could have been made in the 1970s, along with *Panic in Needle Park* and other landmarks of the psychotropic generation. The big difference is that drugs have progressed in the years between from cutting-edge material to background music. Both its hero, who has just graduated from high school, and his shrink, forty years his senior, are so constantly stoned that pot and pills are daily, even hourly, fuel.

What saves this from being boring are performances by two actors who see a chance to go over the top and aren't worried about the fall on the other side. Luke Shapiro (Josh Peck) is a college-bound student who deals bushels of marijuana from a battered ice cream pushcart from which no one even attempts to purchase ice cream. Dr. Squires (Ben Kingsley), his psychiatrist, accepts payment in grams and enthusiastically counsels Luke that he needs to get laid. Only when Luke tries to fill the prescription with the doc's stepdaughter Stephanie (Olivia Thirlby, Juno's friend) do ethics come into question.

Peck's performance, for that matter, could have been inspired by Ellen Page's work in *Juno,* assuming he saw the film once and wasn't paying attention. He is cool beyond cool, except when his heart is broken, which happens after he makes the mistake of telling Stephanie he loves her. This is, like, *so* not cool. Meanwhile, Squires's own marriage with Kristin (Famke Janssen) is on the rocks, although both are so spaced out that they don't much care. That leaves space in the story for one meaningful relationship, which is between Luke and Squires.

The Luke character we've seen before, usually not played this well. The psychiatrist is more original. Kingsley, at first unrecognizable with lanky locks and an outdated goatee, is a seriously addicted man, which he must know better than anybody. There's no evidence he has any clients other than Luke, and much of the time he's asking Luke for help. His belief system seems founded on the Beat Generation, and he's acting out his own desires through the younger man. He wants—a laundry list. He wants to be younger, more potent, happily married. He wants to score with hippie chicks (one is played in the movie by Mary-Kate Olsen, who is a superb example of what he has in mind as a hippie chick). He wants to be loved. He wants to love. Everything going wrong in Luke's life right now has been going wrong in the doctor's life for forty years.

It's impossible to not pity this man and carry a reluctant affection for him. He's so screwed up. As a smart, addicted, self-analyzing, secular Jewish intellectual, he could be born of Philip Roth's nightmares. Luke, on the other hand, appears to be a drug-abusing slacker but is, in fact, an *ambitious* drug-abusing slacker, who thinks he might study psychiatry in college. He's in inner turmoil because of problems at home, where the best-laid plans of his father (David Wohl) have run ashore, and the family is being evicted. One motive for Luke's drug-selling spree toward the end of the summer is to bail out his dad, although it appears he would have to turn over the national product of Colombia to succeed.

There's an undeniable pleasure in wallowing in other people's seamy, if entertaining, problems. Even Dr. Squires's descent into despair is accompanied by one-liners and a great sound track (Luke, so retro he's still into cassettes, is always trading custom tracks with both the doctor and his daughter). Toward the end, when Luke summons up the nerve to confess what he truly believes, he has a kind of triumph, heavily laden though it is with qualifiers and apologies. It takes a certain heroism to admit to high feelings and noble instincts of the heart. Drugs are supposed to make that unnecessary, so Luke, I guess, scores more than he realizes. As for the doctor, he achieves all of the benefits of committing suicide, yet suffers none of the drawbacks.

Note: The Wackness *won the audience award at Sundance 2008.*

Wah-Wah ★ ★ ★

R, 97 m., 2006

Gabriel Byrne (Harry Compton), Miranda Richardson (Lauren Compton), Nicholas Hoult (Ralph Compton), Emily Watson (Ruby Compton), Julie Walters (Gwen Traherne), Celia Imrie (Lady Riva Hardwick), Julian Wadham (Charles Bingham), Fenella Woolgar (June Broughton). Directed by Richard E. Grant and produced by Jeff Abberley, Pierre Kubel, and Marie-Castille Mention-Schaar. Screenplay by Grant.

There is a scene early in *Wah-Wah* where the British family drives off in its car and the servants wave after them, smiling happily. The same image could serve at the end of the film, when the British turn Swaziland over to its citizens and leave forever. The only difference would be that in the final scene, the smiles would be sincere.

Wah-Wah takes place just at that moment in the early 1960s when Britain was granting independence to its colonies, one by one, a parade of royals commuting to one distant capital after another to watch the Union Jack being lowered. The movie is of that time, but not about it, and for that it has been criticized in some circles. I think its myopia is accurate.

The colonial Brits, and whites in general, lived within a closed system and were preoccupied with their own lives, ranks, salaries, security, and gossip, to the exclusion of the local population. "How dare you contradict me in front of a servant?" the hero's father asks in *Wah-Wah.* It has escaped his notice that his entire life, and every one of its secrets, is being lived in front of the servants.

The movie is autobiographical, based on the life of its writer-director, Richard E. Grant. We know him as an actor, notably in *Withnail & I* and *How to Get Ahead in Advertising.* He often plays sour and disaffected characters, and on the basis of his early life seen in this movie, no wonder. An early memory involves his mother, Lauren (Miranda Richardson), making love with a man not his father. His father, Harry (Gabriel Byrne), drinks, but then everybody drinks at that time, in that place. His mother leaves with another man. His father's drinking escalates, without affecting his job as Swaziland's minister of education. Young Ralph goes off to boarding school, and when he returns there is a new stepmother, an American stewardess named Ruby (Emily Watson). His father is still drinking.

Life for the Brits revolves around the office, the club, sport, and sundowners (where the drinking begins promptly regardless of the position of the sun). The most excitement in years is when Princess Margaret is announced as the royal visitor who will attend the ceremonies marking the end of British rule. Although their own shining moment was all too brief, the locals decide to stage a performance of *Camelot* in her honor. Ralph (Nicholas Hoult) is involved, and this is essentially his entrance into acting.

Ralph is more of an observer than a participant in the life of his family; his father, nice enough when sober, develops alarming rages when drunk and then cannot remember, when sober again, how reasonable it is for his son to be frightened of him. The key performance in the movie is by Watson, as a good and sensible woman who married too quickly to know what she was getting herself into, and tries to help her husband and protect Ralph. She's the one who says the locals speak "snooty baby talk" that all sounds to her like "Wah-wah-wah-wah-wah." She gives her marriage a brave try, but eventually it's toodle-oo.

What the movie sees clearly is that Harry may have a high post in the colonial administration, but he survives only because of the self-protective colonial system. With independence, his incompetence will make it impossible for him to ever find such a good job again, even if he stops drinking. As a counterpoint to his defeat, we observe the tactics of Lady Riva Hardwick (Celia Imrie), the snooty baby-talking arbiter of British values in the colony, whose word is law in social matters, especially in her own mind. Notice her awkwardness as she adjusts, none too smoothly, to the fact that she will have to address black people in a modulated tone of voice and actually accept them, at least ostensibly, as her equals.

Wah-Wah has a sequence, based on old

newsreels, in which the flag is lowered and the sun sets on another bit of the empire. Odd how many critics have felt the whole movie should be about this. I don't see why. The story is about people who lived closed lives, and a film about them would necessarily give independence only a supporting role.

I admired the movie and was happy to see it but can think of two other films about whites in Africa that do a better job of seeing their roles. *Nowhere in Africa* is about German Jewish refugees who become colonial farmers; their daughter makes African friends and comes to love the continent even as her father grows disillusioned. And *White Mischief* is the classic portrait of life in Kenya's "Happy Valley," where a messy case of adultery and murder interrupts the drinking. The old *Chicago Daily News* had a gossip columnist assigned to O'Hare Airport. Once when former Prime Minister Harold Macmillan was passing through, she asked him if the sun would ever set on the British Empire. His answer was a masterpiece of tact: "Not any more than it already has."

Waiting . . . ★ ½

R, 93 m., 2005

Ryan Reynolds (Monty), Anna Faris (Serena), Justin Long (Dean), Kaitlin Doubleday (Amy), Chi McBride (Bishop), Luis Guzman (Raddimus), David Koechner (Dan), Alanna Ubach (Naomi), Vanessa Lengies (Natasha), John Francis Daley (Mitch), Robert Patrick Benedict (Calvin). Directed by Rob McKittrick and produced by Adam Rosenfelt, Jeff Balis, Robert Green, Stavros Merjos, and Jay Rifkin. Screenplay by McKittrick.

Waiting . . . is melancholy for a comedy. It's about dead-end lives at an early age and the gallows humor that makes them bearable. It takes place over a day at a chain restaurant named Shenaniganz (think Chili's crossed with Bennigan's), where the lives of the waiters and cooks revolve around the Penis Game. The rules are simple: Flash a fellow worker with the family jewels, and you get to kick him in the butt and call him a fag. Ho, ho.

Not long ago the restaurant was in the doldrums, morale was low, customers were rare. "The penis-showing game became a catalyst for change and improvement," says a cook named Bishop (Chi McBride). I dunno; to me it seems more like a catalyst for desperate shock value from a filmmaker who is trying to pump energy into a dead scenario.

I can imagine a good film based on the bored lives of retail workers whose sex lives afford them some relief. *The 40-Year-Old Virgin* is a splendid example, and given the slacker mentality of the waiters in *Waiting* . . . Kevin Smith's *Clerks* leaps to mind. Both of those films begin with fully seen characters who have personalities, possess problems, express themselves with distinctive styles.

The characters in *Waiting* . . . seem like types, not people. What they do and say isn't funny because someone real doesn't seem to be doing or saying it. Everything that the John Belushi character did in *Animal House* proceeded directly from the core of his innermost being: He crushed beer cans against his forehead because he was a person who needed to, and often did, and enjoyed it, and found that it worked for him. You never got the idea he did it because it might be funny in a movie.

The central character in *Waiting* . . . is Monty (Ryan Reynolds), a veteran waiter who justifies his existence in hell by appointing himself its tour guide. He shows the ropes to a new employee named Mitch (John Francis Daley), beginning with the Penis Game and moving on to details about the kitchen, the table rotation, and the cultivation of customers. He also places great importance on the nightly parties where the employees get hammered.

Other staff members include the perpetually snarling Naomi (Alanna Ubach), who could make more money as the dominatrix she was born to play; Dan (David Koechner), the manager who has risen to the precipice of his ability, replacing the Penis Game with the Peter Principle; Serena (Anna Faris), who is way too pretty to be working at Shenaniganz, and knows it; and Raddimus (Luis Guzman), the cook, who is a master at dropping food on the floor and seasoning it with snot, spit, and dandruff. The movie has a lesson for us, and it is: Do not get the food-handlers mad at you.

The hero of sorts is Dean (Justin Long), who is discouraged to learn that while he's been making his seventy dollars a day in tips, a high school classmate has become an electrical engineer. When the supercilious classmate leaves him a big tip, he feels worse than when a stiff leaves another waiter two dollars on a sixty-three-dollar bill. The problem with the customers in both of those scenarios, and with the lady customer who is relentlessly bitchy, is that there's nothing funny about them. They're mean and cruel and do not elevate their hatefulness to the level of satire but sullenly remain eight-letter words (in the plural form) beginning with "a." Even the bitch's dinner companions are sick of her.

A subplot involves Natasha, the restaurant's sexy underage receptionist (Vanessa Lengies), who attracts both Monty and Dan the manager. I am trying to imagine how she could have been made funny, but no: The movie deals with her essentially as jailbait, something Monty is wise enough to just barely know and Dan reckless enough to overlook. I was also unable to see the joke involving Calvin (Robert Patrick Benedict), who (a) can't urinate because he's uptight that some guy may be trying to steal a glimpse of his jewels, but (b) is a champion at the Penis Game. There is a paradox here, but its solution doesn't seem promising.

What it comes down to is that Shenaniganz is a rotten place to work and a hazardous place to eat, and the people on both sides of the counter are miserable sods but at least the employees know they are. Watching the movie is like having one of these wretched jobs, with the difference that after work the employees can get wasted but we can only watch. It can actually be fun to work in a restaurant. Most of the waitpeople I have known or encountered have been competent, smart, and if necessary amusing. All the restaurant's a stage, and they but players on it. Customers can be friendly and entertaining. Tips can be okay. Genitals can be employed at the activities for which they were designed. There must be humor here somewhere.

The Walker ★ ★ ★ ½

R, 108 m., 2007

Woody Harrelson (Carter Page III), Kristin Scott Thomas (Lynn Lockner), Lauren Bacall (Natalie Van Miter), Lily Tomlin (Abigail Delorean), Ned Beatty (Jack Delorean), Moritz Bleibtreu (Emek Yoglu), Willem Dafoe (Larry Lockner). Directed by Paul Schrader and produced by Deepak Nayar. Screenplay by Schrader.

Carter Page III likes to tell his friends: "I'm not naive; I'm superficial." His easy, ingratiating manner is ideal for his vocation, which is to act as the unpaid companion of rich society ladies as they attend events without their husbands. Quietly gay, he adores his ladies as friends and sponsors a weekly canasta game for them, which turns into a gossip fest. Paul Schrader's *The Walker* shows him moving smoothly through Washington, D.C., where his father was a senator who investigated Watergate; his mild southern drawl reflects Carter's heritage as the grandson of a tobacco tycoon and the great-grandson of a slave owner. Apparently supported by an inheritance, he is content to be well-dressed, witty, and good company.

Woody Harrelson, who usually plays much rougher types like the bounty hunter in *No Country for Old Men,* inhabits this character as comfortably as an old shirt. His Carter is a character, but not too much of a character. A star in his circle, but in a supporting role. A man who knows his place and treasures it. Schrader says one inspiration for the character was Jerry Zipkin, an escort for Nancy Reagan, Pat Buckley, and Betsy Bloomingdale. *Women's Wear Daily* coined the term *walker* to describe him, thus identifying a social category. Truman Capote also comes to mind. Unlike the Richard Gere character in Schrader's *American Gigolo,* Carter pleasures his women with company, not sex, and loves doing it.

His three steady "girls," all of a certain age and formidable instincts, are Lynn Lockner (Kristin Scott Thomas), Abigail Delorean (Lily Tomlin), and Natalie Van Miter (Lauren Bacall), who observes that the difficulty with marrying a rich man is that you don't get to have the money, you only get to look at it. Carter is the model of discretion, so much so that Lynn Lockner, the wife of a senator (Willem Dafoe), trusts him to drive her to her weekly meetings with a paid male prostitute in Georgetown. Nobody will recognize his car. He waits outside.

One afternoon she returns to the car almost immediately, trembling. She has discovered her lover stabbed to death. She can't report the murder without involving herself and her husband in scandal. Carter instinctively steps up and takes the hit like a southern gentleman: He tells the police he discovered the body and so becomes their leading suspect. As Carter looks into the crime, the murky undergrowth of Washington corruption begins to exude aromas, and Carter involves his own lover, a young Turk named Emek Yoglu (Moritz Bleibtreu), in their own investigation to save his skin.

The Walker is a quietly enthralling film because it contains the murder and the investigation within Carter's smooth calm. He has practiced for a lifetime at concealing his emotions, first, no doubt, from his father. He is even able to absorb the hurtful fact that his society "friends" drop him like a hot potato. He only wanted to be nice to them; he had no other angle. He enjoyed being on the inside, looking on, overhearing, knowing the real dish. Now he faces murder charges just because he was a good guy.

The Walker is the third of Schrader's "man in a room" films, after *American Gigolo* (1980) and *Light Sleeper* (1992), which starred Willem Dafoe as an upscale drug dealer who tries to get one of his clients off drugs. All three movies involve employment by wealthy older women. Schrader extended the "man in a room" theme to his longtime collaborator Martin Scorsese in his screenplays for *Taxi Driver* and *Raging Bull.* There is always the same signature: the man in his private space, preparing himself to go out into public. Both *Gigolo*'s Richard Gere and *The Walker*'s Woody Harrelson play men who take elaborate pains with their appearance when it is their reality they should be concerned about.

I have heard complaints that the film "drags in" the murder plot. This is nonsense. All three films involve their heroes in a crime they did not commit, and all three show them trapped as a consequence of their occupations. There is a deep morality at work here, as often in Schrader's work. Also, of course, without the crime as a plot engine, the movie might be only a character study ending on a bittersweet minor chord. I found it fascinating to see Carter Page III discovering under fire that he is, after all, a more loyal friend than his famous father, and a better man.

Walk Hard: The Dewey Cox Story ★ ★ ★

R, 96 m., 2007

John C. Reilly (Dewey Cox), Jenna Fischer (Darlene Madison), Tim Meadows (Sam), Kristen Wiig (Edith), Raymond J. Barry (Pa Cox), Harold Ramis (L'Chai'm), Margo Martindale (Ma Cox), Chris Parnell (Theo), Matt Besser (Dave). Directed by Jake Kasdan and produced by Judd Apatow, Kasdan, and Clayton Townsend. Screenplay by Apatow and Kasdan.

John C. Reilly was appearing on stage in Chicago the other night as Dewey Cox, and the act may be something to fall back on if he ever gives up the daytime job. Apart from anything else demonstrated by *Walk Hard: The Dewey Cox Story,* the movie shows that he can do plausible versions of Johnny Cash, Elvis, Bob Dylan, Roy Orbison, and on and on. He's like a kid who locked himself in his room singing along with his record collection and finally made it pay off.

The movie is a spoof of rock-star biopics, most obviously *Walk the Line,* from which it borrows the wife at home and the affair with the backup singer on the road. There's also a lift from *Ray,* who, you may remember, was blamed for letting his little brother drown. Dewey Cox is out in the barn playing with machetes with his own brother one day when he inadvertently slices him in half. Fatally? The doctor observes: "It's a particularly bad case of somebody being cut in half."

Life after that is never quite right for Dewey, whose father turns up at every triumph to remind him, "The wrong brother died." He develops into a musical prodigy who masters an instrument almost as soon as he picks it up, and segues effortlessly from one genre to another in order to stay on top of the charts. Soul music? Bubblegum rock? Acid rock? Surfin' songs? Folk rock? He does it all.

And all the time he's on a downward spiral, tempted by Sam, the drummer in his band (*SNL*'s Tim Meadows). Dewey is forever opening a door and finding Sam behind it with cute backup singers, sampling a drug that Sam warns him he is under no circumstances to ever, ever try. He always tries it and cycles through rehabs like a city inspector. His marriage (with Kristen Wiig) breaks up, he falls in love with his backup singer Darlene (Jenna Fischer), travels to India with the Beatles, crosses paths with Buddy Holly and Elvis Presley, and meets such as Jackson Browne and Lyle Lovett, playing themselves. And all leads to doom because he keeps finding Sam behind another door.

The movie, directed by Jake Kasdan, was cowritten by Kasdan and the producer Judd Apatow (*Superbad*), and they do an interesting thing: Instead of sending everything over the top at high energy—like *Top Secret* or *Airplane!*—they allow Reilly to more or less actually *play* the character, so that, against all expectations, some scenes actually approach real sentiment. Reilly is required to walk a tightrope; is he suffering or kidding suffering, or kidding suffering about suffering? That we're not sure adds to the appeal.

Note: I must mention one peculiar element in the film. As Reilly is having a telephone conversation, a male penis is framed in the upper right corner of the screen. No explanation about why, or whom it belongs to, or what happens to it. Just a penis. I think this just about establishes a standard for gratuitous nudity. Speculate as I will, I cannot imagine why it's in the film. Did the cinematographer look through his viewfinder and say, "Jake, the upper right corner could use a penis?"

Walking to Werner ★ ★ ★

NO MPAA RATING, 93 m., 2007

Featuring Linas Phillips and Werner Herzog. A documentary directed by Linas Phillips and produced by Dayne Hanson.

The free spirit Werner Herzog, whose *Rescue Dawn* is now a considerable success, likes to walk. He has inspired at least two would-be filmmakers to follow in his footsteps. Faithful readers will know that I value Herzog's films beyond all measure and never tire of telling the famous story of the time he learned his dear friend, the film historian Lotte Eisner, was dying in Paris. Thereupon he set off to walk from Munich to Paris, convinced she would not die before his arrival, and he was quite right.

Another time, he walked completely around Albania ("Because at that time, you could not enter Albania"). When I invited him to my film festival a few years ago, he was lowered from a plateau in a South American rain forest, made his way by log canoe and trading skiff to a pontoon plane that took him to a boat, etc. "He came because it was so difficult," his wife, Lena, told me. "If Werner had been in Los Angeles, it would have been too easy, and he might not have made the journey."

His friend Dusan Makavejev tells in the new book, *The Cinema of the Balkans,* that Werner once came looking for an ancestor in Croatia and followed his footsteps up a Serbian mountain, hoping to help end the war raging around him. "The essential things in life," Herzog has said, "I would cover on foot, regardless of the distance."

Herzog, his films, and his walking inspired the filmmaker Linas Phillips to make *Walking to Werner,* the story of his walking 1,200 miles from Seattle to Los Angeles to meet the great man. Another film is by Herzog admirer Lee Kazimir of Chicago, who walked from Madrid to Kiev. In a message to me, Kazimir quoted Herzog: "If you want to make films you should skip film school. Instead, you should make a journey of five thousand kilometers alone, on foot. While walking you would learn more about what cinema truly means than you would in five years of sitting in classrooms."

Herzog doesn't encourage these journeys when he is the destination. He warned Phillips that he would not be at home when the young man arrived, because he would be in Laos, Burma, and Thailand filming *Rescue Dawn.* Phillips persisted. Kazimir wrote asking his blessing, and Herzog told me: "I had instant hesitations, and told him so, as he was going to make his voyage a public event. Traveling on foot was, in my understanding, a thing you had to do as a man exposing yourself in the most direct way to life, to *pura vida,* and this should stay with oneself." Kazimir also persisted.

Walking to Werner is the first of these films to open but doesn't steal the thunder of the second because both will be about the trekkers and not Herzog. The real interest in the film is not the journey or even Linas Phillips (who comes across a little like Timothy Treadwell, the hero of Herzog's *Grizzly Man*), but the people he meets on the way.

Some of them look like you might want to cross the road to avoid them, but with one hostile exception and one sad exception they are all sane, friendly, cheerful, and encouraging. I was particularly moved by Robert, a laid-off Boeing worker in Seattle who sees Phillips in a bar and tells him, "Don't end up like me." Phillips asks him to voice the title of the movie for him and requests his blessing at the start of the walk.

Another, Eli, was walking without food because "he no longer saw the worth of life and was too cowardly to kill himself." Phillips, who discovers "when you travel on foot, there's no small talk," meets another man who tells him, "I have no soul." Five miles down the road, the man catches up with Phillips and corrects himself: "I do have a soul."

These encounters are supplemented by Phillips's narration and by the voice of Herzog, often taken from Les Blank's amazing documentary *Burden of Dreams,* the record of Herzog filming *Fitzcarraldo.* That was the film when Herzog, shunning special effects, hauled a real steamboat over a real hill between two river systems. "Moviegoers have to be able to trust their eyes," he explained.

With his long blond hair flowing from beneath his Tilley hat (the hiker's friend), Phillips is once mistaken for a woman and firmly corrects the impression. His face turns red and weathered, his toes develop blisters, and although he often stays in motels he has a disconcerting tendency to walk late into the night and the rain. He looks exhausted much of the time; did he train for this walk? As gigantic trucks roar past, he calculates the odds of one of them killing him.

One reason for his long hair may be that, in 2003, he performed a one-man show, *Linas as Kinski,* in New York. Having embodied the look and spirit of Klaus Kinski, the temperamental subject of Herzog's documentary *My Best Fiend,* Phillips still seems to be in costume.

He communicates with Herzog by e-mail. "If you want to walk, do it for some other reason," the director advises him. When Phillips speculates about going on to Thailand to film a meeting to end his film, Herzog replies, "An interview would be a cheap end to your film."

Walk the Line ★ ★ ★ ½

PG-13, 135 m., 2005

Joaquin Phoenix (John R. Cash), Reese Witherspoon (June Carter), Ginnifer Goodwin (Vivian Cash), Robert Patrick (Ray Cash), Dallas Roberts (Sam Phillips), Dan John Miller (Luther Perkins), Larry Bagby (Marshall Grant), Shelby Lynne (Carrie Cash), Tyler Hilton (Elvis Presley), Waylon Malloy Payne (Jerry Lee Lewis), Shooter Jennings (Waylon Jennings). Directed by James Mangold and produced by James Keach and Cathy Konrad. Screenplay by Gill Dennis and Mangold, based on *Man in Black* by Johnny Cash and *Cash: The Autobiography* by Cash and Patrick Carr.

Johnny Cash sang like he meant business. He didn't get fancy and he didn't send his voice on missions it could not complete, but there was an urgency in his best songs that pounded them home. When he sang something, it stayed sung. James Mangold's *Walk the Line,* with its dead-on performances by Joaquin Phoenix and Reese Witherspoon, helps you understand that quality. Here was a man whose hard-drinking father blamed him for the death of his older brother, said God "took the wrong son," and looked at Johnny's big new house and all he could say was, "Jack Benny's is bigger." In the movie, you sense that the drive behind a Johnny Cash song was defiance. He was going to sing it no matter what anybody thought—especially his old man.

The movie shows John R. Cash inventing himself. He came from a hardworking Arkansas family and grew up listening to country music on the radio, especially the Carter Family. He wrote his first song while he was serving in the Air Force in Germany. When he came back to the states, he got married and got a regular job but dreamed about being a recording artist. When his first wife, Vivian, complained he was spending more time on music than on her, he referred to his "band" and she said, "Your band is two mechanics who can't even hardly play."

She was just about right. When they finally got the legendary Sam Phillips (Dallas Roberts) of Sun Records in Memphis to let them audition, they sounded like carbon copies of third-rate radio gospel singers. Sam should have shown them the door. Out of kindness, he asked John if he had anything of his own he wanted to play. Cash chose a song he wrote in Germany, "Folsom Prison Blues." One of the key passages in Phoenix's performance comes as Cash learns, while in the process of singing this song, how he should sound and who he should be. You can hear his musicians picking up the tempo to keep pace with him. He starts the song as a loser and ends as Johnny Cash.

Walk the Line follows the story arc of many other musical biopics, maybe because many careers are the same: hard times, obscurity, success, stardom, too much money, romantic adventures, drugs or booze, and then (if they survive) beating the addiction, finding love, and reaching a more lasting stardom. That more or less describes last year's *Ray,* but every time we see this formula the characters change and so does the music, and that makes it new.

What adds boundless energy to *Walk the Line* is the performance by Reese Witherspoon as June Carter Cash. We're told in the movie that June learned to be funny onstage because she didn't think she had a good voice; by the time John meets her she's been a pro since the age of four, and she effortlessly moves back and forth between her goofy onstage persona and her real personality, which is sane and thoughtful, despite her knack for hitching up with the wrong men. Johnny Cash, for that matter, seems like the wrong man, and she holds him at arm's length for years—first because he's a married man, and later because he has a problem with booze and pills.

The film's most harrowing scene shows Johnny onstage after an overdose, his face distorted by pain and anger, looking almost satanic before he collapses. What is most fearsome is not even his collapse, but the force of his will, which makes him try to perform when he is clearly unable to. You would not want to get in the way of that determination. When Cash is finally busted and spends some time in jail, his father is dependably laconic: "Now you won't have to work so hard to make people think you been to jail."

Although Cash's father (played with merciless aim by Robert Patrick) eventually does sober up, the family that saves him is June's. The Carter Family were country royalty ever since the days when their broadcasts came from a high-powered pirate station across the river from Del Rio, Texas. When they take a chance on Cash, they all take the chance; watch her parents as they greet Johnny's favorite pill-pusher.

It is by now well known that Phoenix and Witherspoon perform their own vocals in the movie. It was not well known when the movie previewed—at least not by me. Knowing Cash's albums more or less by heart, I closed my eyes to focus on the sound track and decided that, yes, that was the voice of Johnny Cash I was listening to. The closing credits make it clear it's Joaquin Phoenix doing the singing, and I was gob-smacked. Phoenix and Mangold can talk all they want about how it was as much a matter of getting in character, of delivering the songs, as it was a matter of voice technique, but whatever it was, it worked. Cash's voice was "steady like a train, sharp like a razor," said June.

The movie fudges some on the facts, but I was surprised to learn that Cash actually did propose marriage to Carter onstage during a concert; it feels like the sort of scene screenwriters invent, but no. Other scenes are compressed or fictionalized, as they must be, and I would have liked more screen time for the other outlaws, including Waylon and Willie. Elvis Presley and Jerry Lee Lewis make brief excursions through the plot, but essentially, this is the story of John and June and a lot of great music. And essentially, that's the story we want.

Wallace & Gromit: The Curse of the Were-Rabbit ★ ★ ★ ½

G, 85 m., 2005

With the voices of: Peter Sallis (Wallace), Ralph Fiennes (Lord Quartermaine), Helena Bonham Carter (Lady Tottington), Peter Kay (PC Mackintosh), Liz Smith (Mrs. Mulch), Nicholas Smith (Reverend Clement Hedges). Directed by Nick Park and Steve Box and produced by Claire Jennings, Peter Lord, Park, Carla Shelley, and David Sproxton. Screenplay by Bob Baker, Box, Mark Burton, and Park.

Wallace and Gromit are arguably the two most delightful characters in the history of animation. Between the previous sentence and this one I paused thoughtfully and stared into space and thought of all of the other animated characters I have ever met, and I gave full points to Bugs Bunny and high marks to little Nemo and a fond nod to Goofy, and returned to the page convinced that, yes, Wallace and Gromit are in a category of their own. To know them is to enter a universe of boundless optimism, in which two creatures who are perfectly suited to each other venture out every morning to make the world into a safer place for the gentle, the good, and the funny.

Wallace is an inventor. Gromit is a dog, although the traditional human-dog relationship is reversed in that Gromit usually has to clean up Wallace's messes. No, not those kinds of messes. They're not that kind of movie. In three short subjects and now in their first feature, Wallace sails out bravely to do great but reckless deeds, and Gromit takes the role of adult guardian.

In *Wallace & Gromit: The Curse of the Were-Rabbit,* they face their greatest challenge. Lady Tottington is holding her family's 517th annual Giant Vegetable Fete, and all the gardeners for miles around are lovingly caressing their gigantic melons and zucchinis and carrots and such, and Wallace and Gromit are responsible for security, which means keeping rabbits out of the garden patches.

Their company is named Anti-Pesto. Their methods are humane. They do not shoot or poison the bunnies. Instead, Wallace has devised another of his ingenious inventions, the Bun-Vac, which sucks the rabbits out of their holes and into a giant holding tube, so that they can be housed in comfort at Anti-Pesto headquarters and feast on medium and small vegetables. Their tactics perfectly suit Lady Tottington's humane convictions.

They have a rival, the sniveling barbarian Lord Victor Quartermaine, a gun nut with a toupee heaped on his head like a mess of the sort Gromit never has to clean up. Lord Victor dreams of marrying Lady Tottington and treating himself to the luxuries of her ancestral wealth, and that involves discrediting and sabotaging Anti-Pesto and all that it stands for. Thus is launched the affair of the Were-Rabbit, a gigantic beast (with a red polka-dot tie) that terrorizes the neighborhood and inspires the Reverend Hedges to cry out, "For our sins a hideous creature has been sent to punish us."

I dare not reveal various secrets involving the Were-Rabbit, so I will skip ahead, or sideways, to consider Wallace's new invention, the Mind-o-Matic, which is intended to brainwash rabbits and convince them they do not like vegetables. That this device malfunctions goes without saying, and that Gromit has to fly to the rescue is a given.

Wallace and Gromit are the inventions of a British animator named Nick Park, who codirects this time with Steve Box. In an era of high-tech CGI, Park uses the beloved traditional form of stop-action animation. He constructs his characters and sets out of Plasticine, a brand of modeling clay, and makes minute adjustments to them between every frame, giving the impression not only of movement but of exuberant life and color bursting from every frame. (As a nod to technology, just a little CGI is incorporated for certain scenes that would be hard to do in Plasticine, as when the vacuumed bunnies are in free fall.)

Remarkably, given the current realities of animation, *Wallace & Gromit: The Curse of the Were-Rabbit* was the second stop-motion animated film in two weeks, after *Tim Burton's Corpse Bride.* Both of these films are wonderful, but Wallace and Gromit have the additional quality of being lovable beyond all measure, inhabiting a world of British eccentricity that produces dialogue such as: "This is worse than 1972, when there were slugs the size of pigs."

Speaking of pigs, some of my favorite books are the Blandings Castle novels by P. G. Wodehouse, in which Lord Emsworth dotes on his beloved pig, Empress of Blandings. I have always assumed the Blandings stories to be unfilmable but now realize that Park is just the man for them, with Wallace as Lord Emsworth and Gromit as George Cyrill Wellbeloved, his Lordship's expert pigman. True, Gromit does not speak, but Wellbeloved is a man of few words, and if Gromit can solve the mystery of the Were-Rabbit, he should be able to handle a pig.

WALL-E ★ ★ ★ ½

G, 98 m., 2008

With the voices of: Ben Burtt (WALL-E), Elissa Knight (Eve), Jeff Garlin (Captain), Fred Willard (Shelby Forthright), John Ratzenberger (John), Kathy Najimy (Mary), Kim Kopf (Hoverchair Mother), Garrett Palmer (Hoverchair Son), Sigourney Weaver (Ship's Computer). Directed by Andrew Stanton and produced by Jim Morris. Screenplay by Stanton and Jim Reardon.

Pixar's *WALL-E* succeeds at being three things at once: an enthralling animated film, a visual wonderment, and a decent science-fiction story. After *Kung Fu Panda,* I thought I had just about exhausted my emergency supply of childlike credulity, but here is a film, like *Finding Nemo,* that you can enjoy even if you've grown up. That it works largely without spoken dialogue is all the more astonishing; it can easily cross language barriers, which is all the better, considering that it tells a planetary story.

It is the relatively near future. A city of skyscrapers rises up from the land. A closer view reveals that the skyscrapers are all constructed out of garbage, neatly compacted into squares or bales and piled on top of one another. In all the land, only one creature stirs. This is WALL-E, the last of the functioning solar-powered robots. He (the story leaves no doubt about gender) scoops up trash, shovels it into his belly, compresses it into a square, and climbs on his tractor treads up a winding road to the top of his latest skyscraper, to place it neatly on the pile.

It is lonely being WALL-E. But does WALL-E even know that? He comes home at night to a big storage area, where he has gathered a few treasures from his scavengings of the garbage and festooned them with Christmas lights. He wheels into his rest position, takes off his treads from his tired wheels, and goes into sleep mode. Tomorrow is another day. One of thousands since the last humans left Earth and settled into orbit aboard gigantic spaceships that resemble spas for the fat and lazy.

One day WALL-E's age-old routine is shattered. Something new appears in his world, which otherwise has consisted only of old things left behind. This is, to our eye, a sleek spaceship. To WALL-E's eyes, who knows? What with one thing and another, WALL-E is scooped up by the ship and returned to the orbiting spaceship Axiom, along with his most recent precious discovery: a tiny, perfect green plant, which he found growing in the rubble and transplanted to an old shoe.

Have you heard enough to be intrigued, or do you want more? Speaking voices are now heard for the first time in the movie, although all on his own WALL-E has a vocabulary (or repertory?) of squeaks, rattles, and electronic purrs, and a couple of pivoting eyes that make him look downright anthropomorphic. We meet a Hoverchair family, so known because aboard ship they get around in comfy chairs that hover over surfaces and whisk them about effortlessly. They're all as fat as Susie's aunt. This is not entirely their fault, since generations in the low-gravity world aboard the Axiom have evolved humanity into a race whose members generally resemble those folks you see whizzing around Wal-Mart in their electric shopping carts.

There is now a plot involving WALL-E, the ship's captain, several Hoverpeople, and the fate of the green living thing. And in a development that would have made Sir Arthur Clarke's heart beat with joy, humanity returns home once again—or is that a spoiler?

The movie has a wonderful visual look. Like so many of the Pixar animated features, it finds a color palette that's bright and cheerful, but not too pushy and a tiny bit realistic at the same time. The drawing style is comic-book cool, as perfected in the funny comics more than the superhero books: Everything has a stylistic twist to give it flair. And a lot of thought must have gone into the design of WALL-E, for whom I felt a curious affection. Consider this hunk of tin beside the Kung Fu Panda. The panda was all but special-ordered to be lovable, but on reflection I think he was so fat, it wasn't funny anymore. WALL-E, on the other hand, looks rusty and hardworking and plucky, and expresses his personality with body language and (mostly) with the binocular video cameras that serve as his eyes. The movie draws on a tradition going back to the earliest days of Walt Disney, who reduced human expressions to their broadest components and found ways to translate them to animals, birds, bees, flowers, trains, and everything else.

What's more, I don't think I've quite captured the enchanting storytelling of the film. Directed by Andrew Stanton, who wrote and directed *Finding Nemo,* it involves ideas, not simply mindless scenarios involving characters karate-kicking each other into high-angle shots. It involves a little work on the part of the audience and a little thought, and might be especially stimulating to younger viewers. This story told in a different style and with a realistic look could have been a great science-fiction film. For that matter, maybe it is.

Note: The movie is preceded by Presto Chango, *a new Pixar animated short about a disagreement over a carrot between a magician and his rabbit.*

Wanted ★ ★ ★

R, 110 m., 2008

James McAvoy (Wesley Gibson), Morgan Freeman (Sloan), Terence Stamp (Pekwarsky), Thomas Kretschmann (Cross), Common (The Gunsmith), Angelina Jolie (Fox). Directed by Timur Bekmambetov and produced by Marc Platt, Jim Lemley, Jason Netter, and Iain Smith. Screenplay by Michael Brandt, Derek Haas, and Chris Morgan.

Wanted slams the pedal to the metal and never slows down. Here's an action picture that's exhausting in its relentless violence and its ingenuity in inventing new ways to attack, defend, ambush, and annihilate. Expanding on a technique I first saw in David O. Russell's *Three Kings*, it follows individual bullets (as well as flying warriors) through implausible trajectories to pound down the kills.

The movie is based on comic books by Mark Millar and J. G. Jones. Their origin story involves an anxiety-ridden, henpecked, frustrated office worker named Wesley (James McAvoy), whom you might have glimpsed in a bogus YouTube video trashing his office. In the movie he gets the opportunity to trash a lot more than that. In a plot development that might have been inspired by James Thurber's *The Secret Life of Walter Mitty* (but probably wasn't, because who reads that great man anymore?), Wesley gets the opportunity to find revenge on his tormentors and enter a fantasy world where he can realize his hidden powers as a skilled assassin.

This happens after he is picked up in a bar by Fox (Angelina Jolie), who confides that he is now a member of The Fraternity, a thousand-year-old secret society of assassins who kill bad people. I suppose a lot of people, if they were picked up in a bar by Angelina Jolie, would go along with that story. Although The Fraternity's accuracy rate can be faulted (it missed on Hitler and Stalin, for example), its selection methods must be Really Deep, since orders are transmitted through The Loom of Fate. As demonstrated in the film, if you look at a cloth really, really, *really* closely, you can see that every once in a while a thread is out of line. These threads represent a binary code that is way deeper than my old Lone Ranger Decoder Ring. They also raise questions about the origin, method, and reading of themselves, which are way, way too complicated to be discussed here, assuming they could be answered, which I confidently believe would not be the case.

Never mind. Wesley leaves his office life for a hidden alternative existence in which he masters skills of fighting (by hurtling hundreds of feet) and shooting (around corners, for example). And he is introduced to Sloan (Morgan Freeman), who, the moment I mentioned Morgan Freeman, you immediately knew was deep and wise and in charge of things. He lives in a book-lined library (but Wesley, to my intense regret, never asks him, "Have you really read all these books? Anything by Thurber?"). Sloane explains that Wesley's father was a member of The Fraternity, killed years ago by the man Wesley is now destined to kill. This is Cross (Thomas Kretschmann), who lurks in Europe, where Wesley also meets Pekwarsky (Terence Stamp), another fraternity brother. (Do you suppose The Fraternity's secret handshake is fatal? If brothers give it to each other, do they both die?)

I'd guess there are, oh, ten or fifteen shots in this entire movie without special effects. The rest of the time, we're watching motion-capture animation, CGI, stuff done in the lab. A few of the stunts look like they could not have been faked, but who knows? What do you think your chances are when you run on top of a speeding train? For that matter, if you were assigned to kill someone in Chicago, could you figure out a better way to do it than by standing on top of an El train while it raced past your target's office window? And how did The Fraternity know he would be visible through that window? And how . . . oh, never mind.

Wanted, directed by a hot Russian actionmeister named Timur Bekmambetov, is a film entirely lacking in two organs I always appreciate in a movie: a heart and a mind. It is mindless, heartless, preposterous. By the end of the film we can't even believe the values the plot seems to believe, since the plot is deceived right along with us. The way to enjoy this film is to put your logic on hold, along with any higher sensitivities that might be vulnerable, and immerse yourself as if in a video game. That *Wanted* will someday be a video game, I have not the slightest doubt. It may already *be* a video game, but I'm damned if I'll look it up and find out. Objectively, I award it all honors for technical excellence. Subjectively, I'd rather be watching Danny Kaye in the film version of *The Secret Life of Walter Mitty.*

Note: I learn that The Secret Life of Walter Mitty *will be remade next year and will star Mike Myers. Having seen Myers's* The Love Guru, *I think I can predict one of Walter's big secrets.*

War, Inc. ★★

R, 106 m., 2008

John Cusack (Brand Hauser), Hilary Duff (Yonica Babyyeah), Marisa Tomei (Natalie Hegalhuzen), Joan Cusack (Marsha Dillon), Dan Aykroyd (Ex–Vice President), Ben Kingsley (Walken/Viceroy), Lubomir Neikov (Omar Sharif). Directed by Joshua Seftel and produced by Les Weldon, Danny Lerner, John Cusack, and Grace Loh. Screenplay by Cusack, Mark Leyner, and Jeremy Pikser.

War, Inc. is a brave and ambitious but chaotic attempt at political satire. The targets: the war in Iraq and the shadowy role of Vice President Cheney's onetime corporate home Halliburton in the waging of the war. Dan Aykroyd plays an "ex–vice president," unmistakably Cheney, issuing orders to CIA hit man Brand Hauser (John Cusack) to assassinate a Middle Eastern oil minister (named Omar Sharif, not much of a joke) whose plans to build a pipeline in his own country run counter to the schemes of the supercorporation Tamerlane.

Hauser is an intriguing character, seen chugging shot glasses of hot sauce for reasons that are no doubt as significant as they are obscure. "I feel like a refugee from the island of Dr. Moreau," he confides at one point to the onboard computer on his private plane, a sort of sympathetic HAL 9000. Arriving in the country of Turaqistan, he finds warfare raging everywhere except within a protected area known as the Emerald City, for which of course we are to read Baghdad's Green Zone. Here American corporations are so entrenched that Hauser reaches the secret bunker of the Viceroy (a Tamerland puppet) through a Popeye's Fried Chicken store.

That sort of satire runs through the movie, which is neither quite serious nor quite funny, but very busy with trying to be one or the other. Lots of other brand names (in addition to *brand* Hauser) appear in connection with an expo being staged by public relations whiz Marsha Dillon (Joan Cusack), who becomes Hauser's cynical adviser. Among her plans for the expo: the televised wedding of Middle Eastern pop superstar Yonica Babyyeah (Hilary Duff, but you won't recognize her).

Arriving in Turaqistan at about the same time as Hauser is Natalie Hegalhuzen (Marisa Tomei), a reporter for liberal magazines, whose character and others in the film illustrate my First Law of Funny Names, which teaches us that they are rarely funny. She is a warm, pretty woman who quickly appeals to Hauser, already having second thoughts about his hit-man role. She's smart, too, with an occasional tendency to talk like she's writing (she describes Yonica as "a sad little girl who's been pimped out into a pathetic monstrosity of Western sexuality").

All of the story strands come together into a bewildering series of solutions and conclusions, in which the fictional heritage of the name "Emerald City" plays a prominent role. But the intended satire isn't as focused or merciless as it could be and tries too hard to keep too many balls in the air. The movie's time period is hard to nail down; the opening titles refer to the "21st century," but of course that's the present, and current names are referred to (McLaughlin, Anderson Cooper, Cheney, Katie Couric, 50 Cent, etc). One particularly brilliant invention is Combat-O-Rama, which is a version of a Disney World virtual reality thrill ride allowing journalists to experience battle through what I guess you'd call "virtual embedding."

John Cusack is the power behind the film, as star, top-billed writer, and one of the producers. He deserves credit for trying to make something topical, controversial, and uncompromised. The elements are all here. But the parts never come together. Cusack has made fifty-six films and is only forty-two years old, and his quality control is uncanny. He shies away from unworthy projects and is always available to take a chance. A project like *War, Inc.* must not have been easy to finance, shows a determination to make a movie that makes a statement, and is honorable. Sometimes the best intentions don't pay off. I wanted to like it more than I could.

War of the Worlds ★ ★

PG-13, 118 m., 2005

Tom Cruise (Ray Ferrier), Dakota Fanning (Rachel), Miranda Otto (Mary Ann), Tim Robbins (Harlan Ogilvy), Justin Chatwin (Robbie). Directed by Steven Spielberg and produced by Kathleen Kennedy and Colin Wilson. Screenplay by Josh Friedman and David Koepp, based on the novel by H. G. Wells.

War of the Worlds is a big, clunky movie containing some sensational sights but lacking the zest and joyous energy we expect from Steven Spielberg. It proceeds with the lead-footed deliberation of its 1950s predecessors to give us an alien invasion that is malevolent, destructive, and, from the alien point of view, pointless. They've "been planning this for a million years" and have gone to a lot of trouble to invade Earth for no apparent reason and with a seriously flawed strategy. What happened to the sense of wonder Spielberg celebrated in *Close Encounters of the Third Kind,* and the dazzling imagination of *Minority Report*?

The movie adopts the prudent formula of viewing a catastrophe through the eyes of a few foreground characters. When you compare it with a movie like *The Day After Tomorrow,* which depicted the global consequences of cosmic events, it lacks dimension: Martians have journeyed millions of miles to attack a crane operator and his neighbors (and if they're not Martians, they journeyed a lot farther).

The hero, Ray Ferrier (Tom Cruise), does the sort of running and hiding and desperate defending of his children that goes with the territory, and at one point even dives into what looks like certain death to rescue his daughter. There's a survivalist named Ogilvy (Tim Robbins) who has quick insights into surviving: "The ones that didn't flatline are the ones who kept their eyes open." And there are the usual crowds of terrified citizens looking up at ominous threats looming above them. But despite the movie's $135 million budget, it seems curiously rudimentary in its action.

The problem may be with the alien invasion itself. It is not very interesting. We learn that countless years ago, invaders presumably but not necessarily from Mars buried huge machines all over Earth. Now they activate them with lightning bolts, each one containing an alien (in what form, it is hard to say). With the aliens at the controls, these machines crash up out of the earth, stand on three towering but spindly legs, and begin to zap the planet with death rays. Later, their tentacles suck our blood and fill steel baskets with our writhing bodies.

To what purpose? Why zap what you later want to harvest? Why harvest humans? And, for that matter, why balance these towering machines on ill-designed supports? If evolution has taught us anything, it is that limbs of living things, from men to dinosaurs to spiders to centipedes, tend to come in numbers divisible by two. Three legs are inherently not stable, as Ray demonstrates when he damages one leg of a giant tripod, and it falls helplessly to Earth.

The tripods are indeed faithful to the original illustrations for H. G. Wells's novel *The War of the Worlds,* and to the machines described in the historic 1938 Orson Welles radio broadcast and the popular 1953 movie. But the book and radio program depended on our imaginations to make them believable, and the movie came at a time of lower expectations in special effects. You look at Spielberg's machines and you don't get much worked up, because you're seeing not alien menace but clumsy retro design. Perhaps it would have been a good idea to set the movie in 1898, at the time of Wells's novel, when the tripods represented a state-of-the-art alien invasion.

There are some wonderful f/x moments, but they mostly don't involve the pods. A scene where Ray wanders through the remains of an airplane crash is somber and impressive, and there is an unforgettable image of a train, every coach on fire, roaring through a station. Such scenes seem to come from a different kind of reality than the tripods.

Does it make the aliens scarier that their motives are never spelled out? I don't expect them to issue a press release announcing their plans for world domination, but I wish their presence reflected some kind of intelligent purpose. The alien ship in *Close Encounters* visited for no other reason, apparently, than to demonstrate that life existed elsewhere, could visit us, and was intriguingly unlike us while still sharing such universal qualities as the perception of tone.

Those aliens wanted to say hello. The alien machines in *War of the Worlds* seem designed for heavy lifting in an industry that needs to modernize its equipment and techniques. (The actual living alien being we finally glimpse is an anticlimax, a batlike bug-eyed monster, confirming the wisdom of Kubrick and Clarke in deliberately showing no aliens in *2001*.)

The human characters are disappointingly one-dimensional. Tom Cruise's character is given a smidgen of humanity (he's an immature, divorced hotshot who has custody of the kids for the weekend), and then he wanders out with his neighbors to witness strange portents in the sky, and the movie becomes a story about grabbing and running and ducking and hiding and trying to fight back. There are scenes in which poor Dakota Fanning, as his daughter, has to be lost or menaced, and then scenes in which she is found or saved, all with much desperate shouting. A scene where an alien tentacle explores a ruined basement where they're hiding is a mirror of a better scene in *Jurassic Park* where characters hide from a curious raptor.

The thing is, we never believe the tripods and their invasion are *practical*. How did these vast metal machines lie undetected for so long beneath the streets of a city honeycombed with subway tunnels, sewers, water and power lines, and foundations? And why didn't a civilization with the physical science to build and deploy the tripods a million years ago not do a little more research about conditions on the planet before sending its invasion force? It's a war of the worlds, all right—but at a molecular, not a planetary, level.

All of this is just a way of leading up to the gut reaction I had all through the film: I do not like the tripods. I do not like the way they look, the way they are employed, the way they attack, the way they are vulnerable, or the reasons they are here. A planet that harbors intelligent and subtle ideas for science fiction movies is invaded in this film by an ungainly Erector set.

The Warrior ★ ★ ★

R, 86 m., 2005

Irfan Khan (Lafcadia), Puru Chibber (Katiba, his son), Damayanti Marfatia (Blind Woman), Noor Mani (Thief), Anupam Shyam (Lord), Aino Annuddin (Pursuer), Firoz Khan (Biswas). Directed by Asif Kapadia and produced by Bertrand Faivre. Screenplay by Kapadia and Tim Miller.

The Warrior tells the story of a fierce warrior who changes the direction of his life after a mystical visionary moment.

Lafcadia is an enforcer in the employ of a cruel lord in the far northwest Indian state of Rajasthan. When a village cannot pay its taxes because of a bad harvest, the lord has their leader beheaded and orders the warrior: "Teach them a lesson."

Lafcadia and his men ride out to the village and rape, pillage, and burn—and then the warrior sees a young village girl wearing an amulet given to her earlier that day by Lafcadia's son; he understands that in killing any child he might as well be killing his own. He has an inexplicable image of a snowy mountain vista, and he vows: "I'll never lift a sword again." The lord is enraged: "No one leaves my service. Bring me his head by dawn."

And so now the hunter has become the hunted. And the man who is hunting him, an ambitious warrior who was eager to replace him, faces a death sentence of his own if he does not return with the warrior's head, or one that looks almost like it. This description makes *The Warrior* sound violent, I know, but almost all the violence takes place offscreen, and the action is located primarily in the warrior's mind.

To save his life, and because he is compelled to seek out the source of his snowy vision, he begins a long trek to the mountains of the north. He is accompanied by an orphaned thief (Noor Mani) whose family he may in fact have killed, and by a blind woman (Damayanti Marfatia) who is on a pilgrimage to a holy lake. "There's blood written on your face," she tells the warrior, and he tells the thief, "She's right about me."

The movie won the Alexander Korda Award for Best British Film at the BAFTA Awards and was named Best British Independent Film at the British Indies. Filmed on location near the

Himalayas, it was written and directed by Asif Kapadia, a documentary maker for the BBC.

The film is interesting for what it does not show. Not only is violence offscreen, but so is a lot of motivation; it is only by following the action and then thinking back through the story that we can understand the warrior's thought process. And it is only because he eventually finds the source of his snowy vision that we understand the role it played early in the film. These are not flaws, just curiosities.

What is best in the film is its depiction of the warrior's epic journey, photographed with breathtaking beauty and simplicity by Roman Osin, who filmed the new British version of *Pride and Prejudice*. The lands through which the warrior travels are familiar to my imagination from novels like *The Far Pavilions*, and by not setting the film in a particular period, the story takes on a timelessness. It is about people stuck in an ancient culture of repression, greed, and revenge, and how some are able to escape it by a spiritual path. Parallels with the current eye-for-an-eye ideology of the Middle East are inescapable.

It may be that some American moviegoers will find the film's form unsatisfactory. We are accustomed to closure and completion. If a threat is established at the opening of a film, by the end we expect it to be enforced, or evaded. We do not expect it to be . . . outgrown. Our plots are circular; *The Warrior* is linear. There is a kind of strange freedom in the knowledge that a story has cut loose from its origins and is wandering through unknown lands.

Note: It is hilarious that this elegant and thoughtful film has an R *rating "for some violence," while buildings are destroyed 9/11-style, thousands are killed, and a nuclear cloud poisons a city in the* PG-13*-rated* Stealth.

Wassup Rockers ★ ★ ★ ½

R, 97 m., 2006

Jonathan Velasquez (Jonathan), Francisco Pedrasa (Kiko), Milton Velasquez (Milton/Spermball), Yunior Usualdo Panameno (Porky), Eddie Velasquez (Eddie), Luis Rojas-Salgado (Louie), Carlos Velasco (Carlos), Iris Zelaya (Iris), Ashley Maldonado (Rosalia), Laura Cellner (Jade), Jessica Steinbaum (Nikki). Directed by Larry Clark and produced by Clark, Kevin Turen, and Henry Winterstern. Screenplay by Clark.

You could think of Larry Clark's *Wassup Rockers* as *Ferris Velasquez's Day Off*. In Los Angeles a group of Latino friends, all about fourteen, spend a very long day traveling from South Central to Beverly Hills and back home again, and although they are lighthearted and looking for fun, they don't have Ferris Bueller's good luck. The movie evokes the sense of time unfolding thoughtlessly for kids who have no idea what could happen next.

Clark usually makes movies about teenagers and has a rapport with them that's privileged or creepy, depending on your point of view. His first film was the powerful *Kids* (1995), which launched the acting careers of four first-timers—Rosario Dawson, Chloe Sevigny, Leo Fitzpatrick, and Justin Pierce—and writer-director Harmony Korine. *Bully* (2001) saw how a group dynamic works to drive teenagers toward a murder none of them would have done alone. *Ken Park* (2002) was bold in its frankness about teenage sexuality; a success at Telluride, it was never released commercially in the United States, not because of its content but because, Clark says, a producer never cleared the music rights.

Now comes *Wassup Rockers*, containing one and probably two deaths, a lot of tension between Latinos and African-Americans, and run-ins with cops and homeowners. Perhaps because we hardly meet the first boy who dies, and the second is shot offscreen, the movie is not as fraught as it could have been and, indeed, is Clark's least harrowing work.

The heroes mostly are of Salvadorian descent, although they are routinely mistaken for Mexican-Americans. They come from a poor district; one kid's mother apparently is a lap dancer. But Clark's characters do not carry guns, steal, use drugs, or smoke (anything). At fourteen years old, you're thinking, let's hope not—but Clark's subject often is how children get into sex, drugs, and violence when they are way too young. These kids don't set out looking for trouble, although it finds them.

The movie opens with a monologue by Jonathan (Jonathan Velasquez), who tells us about his friends; he separates each statement with the phrase "and then . . . ." He's the one the others look up to. We meet Kiko (Francisco Pedrasa), Spermball (Milton Velasquez, who keeps asking everyone to call him Milton, not Spermball), Porky (Yunior Usualdo Panameno), and two girls: Iris (Iris Zelaya), Jonathan's girlfriend, and Rosalia (Ashley Maldonado), who wants to be everybody's girlfriend.

They have a band, which plays very loudly, and they hang around and tell stories on each other (one kid tried to commit suicide, not very seriously, by drowning himself in the sink). Kiko "borrows" a car, and they head in the direction of Beverly Hills High School but are stopped by cops on bikes. Since they have no license or ID, they abandon the car, but they've made it to Beverly Hills, and now they practice skateboard jumping on the steps of the high school. Having seen countless skateboarding scenes in the movies, I appreciated Clark's realism: They fall or crash, again and again and again, trying to get a trick right.

They meet two rich 90210 girls, Jade (Laura Cellner) and Nikki (Jessica Steinbaum), and one of them gives them her address: "Come over anytime." They do. Clark has a good feel for how there is no particular tension between these young teens of different race and class. They're curious and talk openly about their differences. But when the Latinos have to leave suddenly, they begin a tour of upper-class backyards in the hills above Sunset; in one, there's a party going on, and the host is a gay man who tells Jonathan, "You'd be a good model." In another, there's a gun owner who shoots one of them and arranges with the cops to "keep it quiet."

With police looking for them, they're taken in by a rich and drunken woman whose maid looks out for them while the drunk gives one a bath and obviously is interested in what could happen next, once he's cleaned up.

The long journey home is by bus, rapid transit, and foot, and they are tired and scared. The fate of their friend who was shot is left unclear, although he obviously was hit and perhaps was killed. The home streets of South Central are not welcoming to them, because the black kids are not friendly. But in the world of a Larry Clark film, they've gotten off relatively easy. Despite its horrors, this is his most easygoing movie, in large part because the young actors are at ease, like each other, and live with delight.

Clark was an honored photographer before getting into movies in his early fifties. The only subject he feels any passion for is, obviously, the private lives of teenagers. Does that make him a pervert? Look at it this way. Hollywood has a cottage industry in Dead Teenager Movies, all devising formulas in which the young characters die in sudden and colorful ways. Clark listens to them and takes them seriously. His films may be the only truthful ones about some aspects of American adolescence, however we might wish that were not so. *Wassup Rockers*, for better and worse, is about lives that might actually be lived.

Water ★ ★ ★

PG-13, 117 m., 2006

Sarala (Chuyia), Seema Biswas (Shakuntala), Lisa Ray (Kalyani), John Abraham (Narayan), Manorma (Madhumati), Raghuvir Yadav (Gulabi). Directed by Deepa Mehta and produced by David Hamilton. Screenplay by Mehta.

Her father asks Chuyia, "Do you remember getting married?" She does not. He tells her that her husband has died, and she is a widow. She is eight years old. Under traditional Hindu law, she will be a widow for the rest of her life. There are two alternatives: marry her husband's brother or throw herself on his funeral pyre.

Deepa Mehta's *Water* is set in 1938. Even then, laws existed in India that gave widows the freedom to marry, but as one character observes, "We do not always follow the law when it is inconvenient." Torn from her father's grasp, crying out for her mother, Chuyia (Sarala) disappears into an ashram controlled by the lifelong widows who live there. Her hair is cut off. She wears a white garment that marks her. The woman in charge is Madhumati (Manorma), fat, indolent, and domineering, who is frightening to the little girl.

Then she makes a friend. This is the beautiful Kalyani (Lisa Ray), who alone among the widows has been allowed to wear her hair long, but for a sad reason. Madhumati has an arrangement with the pimp Gulabi (Raghuvir Yadav) to supply Kalyani to wealthy clients as a source of income for the ashram. Kalyani has a puppy, which they hide and love together. Another friend in the ashram is Shakuntala (Seema Biswas), a wise, thoughtful woman who questions the foundations of the theory of widowhood. It is Narayan

(John Abraham), a follower of Gandhi, who supplies the most pragmatic explanation for the ancient practice: "One less mouth to feed, four less saris, and a free corner in the house. Disguised as religion, it's just about money."

Water is the third film in a trilogy about India by Mehta, whose *Earth* (1998) dealt with the partition of India and Pakistan, and whose *Fire* (1996) dealt with lesbianism among traditional Indian women. She is not popular with Indian religious conservatives, and indeed after the sets for *Water* were destroyed and her life threatened, she had to move the entire production to Sri Lanka. That she is female and deals with political and religious controversy makes her a marked woman.

The best elements of *Water* involve the young girl and the experiences seen through her eyes. I would have been content if the entire film had been her story. But Chuyia meets Narayan, a tall, handsome, foreign-educated follower of Gandhi, and when she brings him together with Kalyani, they fall in love. This does not lead to life happily ever after, but it does set up an ending as melodramatic as it is (sort of) victorious. We're less interested in Kalyani's romantic prospects, however, than with Shakuntala's logical questioning of the underpinnings of her society. It is interesting that the same actress, Biswas, played the title role in the no less controversial *Bandit Queen* (1994).

The film is lovely in the way Satyajit Ray's films are lovely. It sees poverty and deprivation as a condition of life, not an exception to it, and finds beauty in the souls of its characters. Their misfortune does not make them unattractive. In many Indian films it is not startling to be poor, or to be in the thrall of two thousand–year-old customs; such matters are taken for granted, and the story goes on from there. I am reminded of Ray's *The Big City* (1963), in which the husband loses his work and his wife breaks with all tradition and good practice by leaving their home to take employment. The husband is deeply disturbed, but his wife finds that, after all, being a woman and having a job is no big deal.

The unspoken subtext of *Water* is that an ancient religious law has been put to the service of family economy, greed, and a general feeling that women can be thrown away. The widows in this film are treated as if they have no useful lives apart from their husbands. They are given life sentences. They are not so very different from the Irish girls who, having offended someone's ideas of proper behavior, were locked up in the church-run "Magdalene laundries" for the rest of their lives. That a film like *Water* still has the power to offend in the year 2006 inspires the question: Who is still offended, and why, and what have they to gain, and what do they fear?

(The character name "Narayan" is a reminder of R. K. Narayan, the novelist whose works are delightful human comedies about life in India.)

The Water Horse: Legend of the Deep ★ ★ ★ ½

PG, 111 m., 2007

Alex Etel (Angus MacMorrow), Emily Watson (Anne MacMorrow), Ben Chaplin (Lewis Mowbray), David Morrissey (Captain Hamilton), Brian Cox (Old Angus), Priyanka Xi (Kirstie MacMorrow), Marshall Napier (Sergeant Strunk), Joel Tobeck (Sergeant Walker), Erroll Shand (Lieutenant Wormsley). Directed by Jay Russell and produced by Robert Bernstein, Douglas Rae, Barrie M. Osborne, and Charlie Lyons. Screenplay by Robert Nelson Jacobs, based on the book by Dick King-Smith.

If you can't think of three more endearing recent family movies than *My Dog Skip, Babe,* and *Millions,* then here's another title to add to the list. *The Water Horse: Legend of the Deep* is based on a book by the author of *Babe,* made by the director of *My Dog Skip,* and stars the hero of *Millions,* and it fully lives up to its lineage. It opened just in the nick of time on Christmas Day to save parents from having to take the kids to *Alvin and the Chipmunks.*

The movie, set in Scotland but wonderfully photographed in New Zealand, tells the story of a twelve-year-old named Angus (Alex Etel), who finds a curious egg on the beach, brings it home, and is astonished to see it hatch a cute little amphibian with a big appetite. He names it Crusoe and conceals his new pet in the work shed, where it doesn't remain a secret for long, particularly since it seems to double in size every day or so. One day it's terrified by the family bulldog, and a day later the bulldog is terrified by it.

The time is World War II. Angus lives with

his mother, Anne (Emily Watson), and older sister, Kirstie (Priyanka Xi), and keeps a bulletin board with news and memories of his beloved father, who is away fighting the war. He tries his best to be "the man of the family," per his father's final instructions, and there is another man around, Lewis Mowbray (Ben Chaplin), who helps out with barnyard duties and general repairs.

Lewis becomes pals with Angus and Kirstie, and helps them keep the secret of Crusoe from their mother, who might not approve of the pet, especially as it balloons to twice Angus's size, and then three times, and then four times, until it grows so big that there is nothing to be done but move it from the work shed to the nearest large body of water, which is, you guessed it, Loch Ness.

We learn the legend of the water horse. In all the world, only one is alive at a time. Before it dies, it lays an egg, which will produce the next water horse. As it reaches maturity, it looks like a jolly sea serpent with certain characteristics reminding us of Shrek and E.T., especially in its playful nature, humanlike expressions, and inadvertent gift for comedy.

The farm has been commandeered as a posting for a British artillery unit, charged with placing a submarine net across the mouth of the loch. The unit commander, the supercilious Captain Hamilton (David Morrissey), seems certain this is where German U-boats will first land on British soil. Some of his men are equally certain that Hamilton drew this cushy assignment as a way of staying out of action. Anne is courted by the slick officer, who goes out of his way to insult Lewis, the man-of-all-work. But all is sorted out with a vengeance, as Angus gradually comes to accept that his father may not be coming home.

Like most British family films, *The Water Horse* doesn't dumb down its young characters or insult the intelligence of the audience. It has a lot of sly humor about what we know, or have heard, about the Loch Ness Monster and various frauds associated with it, and fills the edges of the screen with first-rate supporting performances. Imagine a family film with actors the caliber of Emily Watson, Ben Chaplin, and Brian Cox as an old-timer who spins stories in the local pub.

Will younger kids be a little scared as Crusoe approaches the dimensions of a whale? Maybe, maybe not. Kids seem harder to scare these days, although I'm afraid some of them will find themselves taken to *Sweeney Todd*, which is definitely not for under-thirteens. What kids will love is Angus's thrilling bareback ride on Crusoe. And viewers of all ages will appreciate that *The Water Horse*, despite its fantasy, digs in with a real story about complex people and doesn't zone out with the idiotic cheerfulness of Alvin and his squeaky little friends.

The Weather Man ★ ★ ★ ½

R, 102 m., 2005

Nicolas Cage (David Spritz), Michael Caine (Robert), Hope Davis (Noreen), Michael Rispoli (Russ), Gil Bellows (Don), Nicholas Hoult (Mike), Gemmenne de la Pena (Shelly). Directed by Gore Verbinski and produced by Todd Black, Jason Blumenthal, and Steve Tisch. Screenplay by Steve Conrad.

We think of tragic heroes outlined against the horizon, tall and doomed, the victims of their vision and fate, who fall from a great height. *The Weather Man* is about a tragic hero whose fall is from a low height. David Spritz (Nicolas Cage) is a Chicago weatherman whose marriage has failed, whose children are troubled, whose father is disappointed, and whose self-esteem lies in ruins. "All of the people I could be," he tells us, "they got fewer and fewer until finally they got reduced to only one—and that's who I am. The weatherman."

There is nothing ignoble about being a weatherman, especially in Chicago, where we need them. David's fatal flaw (all tragic heroes have one) is that he does not value his own work. Perhaps his viewers sense that, which is why they throw fast food at him from passing cars. They sense that he has embraced victimhood and are tempted. To feel inadequate is Dave Spritz's life sentence. His father, Robert (Michael Caine), is a famous novelist who won the Pulitzer Prize and who has always been disappointed in his son—disappointed, we sense, at every stage of Dave's life, and by everything he has done.

In Robert's mind, it's not that Dave is a weatherman but that he is a bad one. He hasn't done the homework. He's not even a meteorologist. He gets the weather off the news service wires. "Do you know," his father asks him, "that the harder thing to do and the right thing to do are usually the same thing?" Dave has made life easy for himself, but Robert tells him, "Easy doesn't enter into grown-up life." Dave's life does indeed seem easy. He does the weather for two hours a day with hardly any preparation and makes the occasional personal appearance; we see him in costume as Abraham Lincoln.

This is one of those Nicolas Cage performances where he seems consumed by worry, depression, and misdirected anger. He often parks his car in front of the house he once shared with his wife, Noreen (Hope Davis), his overweight daughter, Shelly (Gemmenne de la Pena), and his troubled son, Mike (Nicholas Hoult). Noreen is now engaged to Russ (Michael Rispoli), and one day Dave slaps Russ in the face with gloves. Now what in the hell kind of a thing is that to do? Something he saw in a movie? Even Dave's grand gestures are pathetic.

I find myself attracted to movies that are really about somebody. Dave Spritz, whatever his failings, is somebody, he is there, he suffers, he hopes. But he exists, as far as he can see, for no purpose. If his father were cruel in an overt way, that would allow him some focus, but Michael Caine's performance turns Robert into a man who wounds with a thousand little cuts, who is urbane and articulate, and whose words are a rebuke not so much because of what he says as by the tender regret with which he says them. That Robert is dying of lymphoma makes it all the more poignant: Dave's father will not only die but die disappointed, and along the way will attend a "living funeral" in honor of himself. Dave was probably fated to do something inappropriate at his father's funeral; how much more pathetic that he does it while his father is still alive to see him.

Dave's problem is that he is never able to find the right note, the appropriate gesture, the correct behavior, try as he does. Perhaps he tries too hard. Perhaps he is always trying, and people sense it. His wife is not an unreasonable woman and allows Dave access to the children. But she is amazed that, at this point, Dave seriously expects the two of them to remarry. The girl, meanwhile, puts on weight, and the boy's counselor wants the kid to take off his shirt for some photos.

Does all of this make for a good movie? I think so—absorbing, morbidly fascinating. One of the trade papers calls it "one of the biggest downers to emerge from a major studio in recent memory . . . an overbearingly glum look at a Chicago celebrity combing through the emotional wreckage of his life." But surely that is a description of the movie, not a criticism of it. Must movies not be depressing? Must major studios not release them if they are? Another trade paper faults the movie for being released by Paramount, when it "probably should have been made by Paramount Classics. For this is a Sundance film gussied up with studio production values and big stars."

I find this reasoning baffling. Are major stars not allowed to appear in offbeat character studies? Is it wrong for a "Sundance film" to have "studio production values"? What distinguishes Cage as an actor is his willingness to take chances. His previous film, *Lord of War,* was also about an off-the-map character. Should he stick with films like *National Treasure*? Before that he made *Matchstick Men* and *Adaptation,* both brilliant, but *Matchstick* was criticized because it was directed by a big name, Ridley Scott, while *Adaptation* was by the indie Spike Jonze. Both invaluable movies. *The Weather Man* seems to offend some critics because it doesn't know its place and wants to be good even though Paramount made it with a star.

The film was directed by Gore Verbinski, who previously made *Pirates of the Caribbean* and now is making the *Pirates* sequel. How dare he take time off to make an art film? And yet this film has moments of uncommon observation and touching insight. Consider Dave's awkward attempt to bond with his daughter. Shelly unwisely says something about liking archery, and Dave buys her a lot of archery equipment and signs her up for lessons she hates. Has she no sympathy for her old man? Can't she shoot a few arrows? He's trying. The archery episode leads up to a moment of completely unanticipated suspense that concentrates all of Dave's passions and hurts into one moment and one choice.

Yes, *The Weather Man* is a downer, although the sun breaks through from time to time, and there are moments of comedy that are earned, not simply inserted. Do you never want to see a downer? Some time ago, tiring of people telling me, "Oh, I heard that movie was depressing," I started telling them: "Every bad movie is depressing. No good movie is depressing." Sometimes they get it. Sometimes they look at me as if I'm mad. I haven't had any fast food thrown at me yet.

Wedding Crashers ★ ★

R, 119 m., 2005

Owen Wilson (John Beckwith), Vince Vaughn (Jeremy Grey), Christopher Walken (William Cleary), Rachel McAdams (Claire Cleary), Jane Seymour (Kathleen Cleary), Isla Fisher (Gloria Cleary), Bradley Cooper (Sack Lodge), Keir O'Donnell (Todd Cleary), Ellen Albertini Dow (Grandma Cleary), Henry Gibson (Father O'Neil). Directed by David Dobkin and produced by Peter Abrams, Robert L. Levy, and Andrew Panay. Screenplay by Steve Faber and Bob Fisher.

Wedding Crashers is all runway and no takeoff. It assembles the elements for a laugh-out-loud comedy, but it can't make them fly. There are individual moments that are very funny. But it takes a merciless focus to make a good comedy, and the director, David Dobkin, has too much else on his mind. There are sequences involving Vince Vaughn and Owen Wilson where you sense that the actors should have just broken into the cockpit and taken over the controls. There are few lonelier sights than a good comedian being funny in a movie that doesn't know what funny is.

The concept is terrific. The ads will fill the theaters on opening weekend, but people will trail out thinking, gee, I dunno . . . why all the soppy sentiment and whose idea was the potty-mouthed grandmother? And don't they know that in a comedy the villain is supposed to be funny, and not a hateful, sadistic, egotistical monster who when he hits people he really wants to hurt them, and who kicks them when they're down?

Vaughn and Wilson play Jeremy and John, old buddies who crash weddings. They have it all figured out—how to pick up bridesmaids, available girls, unavailable girls, even the occasional straying wife. There's nothing like a wedding to get women feeling romantic. When they debate their seduction theories and go to work on their targets, they're very good, and we sit back expecting the movie to break loose, but the plot makes pointless detours.

Near the beginning, for example, there's a cute montage showing John and Jeremy at a lot of different weddings: Italian, Jewish, Irish, Indian. Different costumes, different food, different dances, great-looking babes. Okay, and then there's *another* montage showing the same stuff, or maybe it's more of the same montage. We feel like we're drifting too far from shore. We need some plot to hang on to.

Jeremy and John's greatest challenge: crashing the yacht club wedding of the daughter of Treasury Secretary Cleary (Christopher Walken). How can this go wrong? Walken can order pizza over the phone and we split a gut. But it goes wrong. Incredibly, the movie never fully exploits Walken's gift for weirdly inspired flights of logical lunacy.

Meanwhile, Jeremy scores down on the beach with the youngest Cleary daughter, Gloria (Isla Fisher), and John falls more seriously in love with the most beautiful Cleary daughter, Claire (Rachel McAdams). Gloria wants her daddy to invite the boys back to the family's shore place, and starts stomping her little feet and throwing a tantrum to get her way—but her tantrum, incredibly, is in long-shot, so we miss the interaction between Walken and his spoiled brat. The movie shows *that* the tantrum happens, as if it needs to explain why her daddy invites the boys to his house. It doesn't need to explain anything; it either has to make it funny, or not show it.

The Clearys are apparently studying to become Kennedys, and on their sprawling lawn Secretary Cleary suggests a game of touch football. That's when we become fully aware of Sack (Bradley Cooper), Claire's fiancé, who tackles with brutality and stares with cold little eyes out of a hard face. He has the charisma of a knife.

There are a lot of ways to make touch football funny, and *Wedding Crashers* misses all of them. Why keep the Walken character so disengaged from the action when it would be funnier for him to get tough than for the hateful Sack, who spreads a cloud of unease in every scene he occupies? I don't blame Cooper for this, by the way; he shows he's very effective. It's just that he should find a movie where he can pound on Vin Diesel.

Formal dining room scenes are often an opportunity for laughter. Remember in *The Party* when Peter Sellers was trying to cut his Cornish game hen, and it flew off his plate and onto the hat of the society lady? In this movie, the dippy daughter slips her hand under the table to rummage among Vaughn's netherlands, and the movie doesn't time the reaction shots and misses the golden opportunity to have someone else at the table realize what's going on—someone like Grandmother Cleary (Ellen Albertini Dow), for example. The actress seems well-chosen to utter sweet little hints of sexual encouragement, but the movie prefers to assign her clanking obscenities about Eleanor Roosevelt.

Toward the end, the movie goes gooey. Too many heartfelt speeches, and a scene at an altar that goes on and on and yet avoids exploiting the reactions of the congregation. Also toward the end, the movie brings in a surprise guest star like a pinch hitter who can clear the bases, but his specialty (picking up girls at funerals) is treated as if it's funny all by itself, and doesn't need to be *made* funny.

Also wandering through this stretch is a priest (the reliable Henry Gibson), who is dealt with mostly in bewildered reaction shots; his most crucial moment in the plot happens offscreen. Thinking of what he must have said offscreen makes me smile. And there is a hapless Cleary brother, Todd (Keir O'Donnell), a stoop-shouldered, spike-haired "artist" who hates his family; the movie keeps starting to do something with him and then misplacing him.

There were probably days on the set of *Wedding Crashers* when everyone thought they had a winner. Vaughn and Wilson do dialogue scenes together that achieve a poetry of comic timing and invention. McAdams is a honey, and Fisher has everything she needs to play a hilarious nymphomaniac except the dialogue and the opportunity.

But how do you misplace Walken in a movie like this? How do you end up with Will Ferrell looking like an afterthought? You know all those horror stories about a cigar-chomping producer who screens a movie and says they need to lose fifteen minutes and shoot a new ending? *Wedding Crashers* needed a producer like that.

The Wedding Date ★ ★ ½

PG-13, 90 m., 2005

Debra Messing (Kat Ellis), Dermot Mulroney (Nick Mercer), Amy Adams (Amy), Jack Davenport (Edward Fletcher-Wooten), Jeremy Sheffield (Jeffrey), Peter Egan (Victor Ellis), Holland Taylor (Bunny Ellis). Directed by Clare Kilner and produced by Jessica Bendinger, Paul Brooks, Michelle Chydzik, and Nathalie Marciano. Screenplay by Dana Fox.

The Wedding Date presents the curious case of two appealing performances surviving a bombardment of schlock. I have so many questions about the movie's premise that it seems, in memory, almost entirely composed of moments when I was shaking my head in disbelief. The character played by Dermot Mulroney is a romance novel fantasy, and yet that doesn't prevent him from also being subtle and intriguing. The character played by Debra Messing not only finds Mulroney through an article in the *Sunday New York Times Magazine,* but seems to have found herself there, too, in the spring fashion issue. But she is nevertheless lovable and touching.

The premise: Kat Ellis (Messing) is a British woman living in New York, who must fly back to London for her sister's wedding. The problem: The groom's best man, Jeff, is Kat's former fiancé, who dumped her. The solution: She hires a male escort named Nick (Mulroney) to go along with her and play the role of her fiancé, so that Jeff will be jealous and she won't look pathetic and single. Nick gets $6,000 plus his airfare on Virgin Upper Class, which is also what he offers: Sex would be extra.

The movie develops the usual assortment of impossible relatives and fun wedding activities; some scenes look like they're posed for snapshots in the *Tatler,* a British society magazine devoted to pretending to like twits. The story expertly compacts *Four Weddings and a Funeral, Pretty Woman,* and *My Best Friend's Wedding* into *One Wedding, an Ex-Best Friend, and a Pretty Man,* with Mulroney (who played the best friend in the original) as the escort with a heart of gold.

Yes, and yet the movie isn't giddy with silliness. There's a melancholy undertow. Mulroney seems to have taken a close look at his character and realized that the less Nick says, the better. His personal thoughts are a closely guarded secret, and he makes a point of separating his role as an escort from his feelings as a man. When there comes, as inevitably there must, a moment when his feelings win out, the movie signals this not with clunky dialogue but with the most romantic use of an anchovy I can recall.

Messing, from TV's *Will & Grace,* makes Kat a character who is dealing with two confusing situations at once. She doesn't know how she feels about hiring an escort, and she doesn't know how she feels about Jeff (Jeremy Sheffield). Does she want Jeff back, or does she just want to make him miserable? Subplots grind away to create last-minute problems for her sister, Amy (Amy Adams), and her fiancé, the forthrightly named Edward Fletcher-Wooten (Jack Davenport). Nick the escort is so handsome, so mysteriously knowledgeable, so at home in every situation, and so wise that Kat forgets everything a grown-up girl like her should know about prostitution, role-playing, and the dangers of STDs, and relates to him as if she were the heroine on the cover of a novel by Jennifer Blake.

"Every woman has the exact love life she wants," Nick believes, according to the *Times* magazine article. It is his job to figure out what that is, and create the illusion that he is supplying it. "It's not about the sex," he says, "it's about what people need." And what does Kat need? Nick says he heard something in her voice on the phone. "Desperation?" she asks. "I think it was hope," he says. Down, boy!

Part of the movie's appeal comes from the way the Nick character negotiates the absurdities of the plot as if he stands outside it. A lesser performance, or one not as skillfully written (by Dana Fox) would have pitched him headlong into the fray. By withdrawing, so to speak, he creates a great curiosity about himself, and the other characters see in him what they need to see. As for Messing, she has an appeal similar to Nia Vardalos's in *My Big Fat Greek Wedding.* We want her to be happy. Whether that happiness will come at the hands of Nick is an excellent question, made simpler by the certainty that Jeff would only make her miserable. The answer to this and other questions, every single one of them, is supplied by one of those romantic comedy endings where false crisis and false hope and real crisis and real hope alternate like a clockwork mechanism. Everyone appears and disappears exactly on cue, driving around in sports cars with the top down and running around in shoes meant only for walking down the aisle.

As for Nick, what makes him happy? Is it also true that every man has the exact love life he wants? Does he want his? When he watches *Five Easy Pieces* and Jack Nicholson says, "I faked a little Chopin, and you faked a big response," does he see himself as the pianist, or the piano?

We Own the Night ★ ★ ★

R, 117 m., 2007

Joaquin Phoenix (Bobby Green), Mark Wahlberg (Joseph Grusinsky), Eva Mendes (Amada Juarez), Robert Duvall (Burt Grusinsky), Antoni Corone (Michael Solo), Moni Moshonov (Marat Bujayev), Alex Veadov (Vadim Nezhinski), Tony Musante (Jack Shapiro). Directed by James Gray and produced by Mark Wahlberg, Joaquin Phoenix, Nick Wechsler, and Marc Butan. Screenplay by Gray.

We Own the Night was the slogan of the New York police in the 1980s, painted on the sides of their squad cars as a promise to take back the night from the drug trade. It might have been premature. In James Gray's new film by the same name, the battle for control of the night is undecided, and brothers from the same family find themselves on opposite sides.

Joaquin Phoenix plays Bobby Green, not his real name, the manager of a thriving Brooklyn nightclub, moving smoothly through the crowds every night, meeting and greeting, keeping an eye on everything, loved by a beautiful girlfriend (Eva Mendes). The club is owned by a Russian émigré named Marat Bujayev (Moni Moshonov), whose smile seems sincere but who is said to control the area's drug traffic. Bujayev's nephew Vadim (Alex Veadov) is a dealer, using the club as his base of operations. Bobby himself is not involved and adopts a don't ask, don't tell position. His job is just to run the club.

Bobby Green's father is Burt Grusinsky (Robert Duvall), the district police chief. His brother is Joseph Grusinsky (Mark

Wahlberg), serving as a top cop under his father. If it were known that Bobby is related to them, his life would be in danger.

Everything comes to a head. Vadim asks Bobby to join him in the drug trade at the same time the chief orders a crackdown. Joseph is the point man for the cops. A police raid busts the club, and there are reprisals involving the near-murder of both the chief and the cop. Bobby's father asks him to work undercover for them, promising, "We'll watch your back." Excellent, but who was watching the chief's back?

This is not precisely original material. James Gray himself has made two earlier films involving Russian crime syndicate members in New York: *Little Odessa* (1994) and *The Yards* (2000, which also starred Phoenix and Wahlberg). The first won the Silver Lion at Venice. The second, and this one, were accepted by Cannes. But *We Own the Night* seems less original than the first two, maybe because Russian gangsters have become the villains du jour (see them portrayed more urgently in David Cronenberg's *Eastern Promises*).

Still, the film is made with confidence and energy and is well-acted by the principals. One unexpected touch is that the very sexy Amada Juarez (Mendes) is in it for the love, not the money, really cares for Bobby, gives him good advice, isn't the standard two-timing dame. Her feelings bring an additional depth to Bobby's danger.

Bobby himself is a puzzle. He likes the recognition and status that comes with his job but doesn't want to accept the consequences. He has severed connections with his family, partly out of prudence, partly out of murky deeper motives. But when his side starts shooting at his father and brother, there is an indelible loyalty that is touched.

I have some questions. In the small world of Brooklyn cops and robbers, wouldn't a lot of people who grew up with them know Bobby was related to Joseph and Burt? Can you just change your name and lose your identity? Don't cops watch their own backs when they know they've been targeted? Elements in the plot are less than plausible.

But this is an atmospheric, intense film, and when it's working it has a real urgency. Scenes where a protagonist is close to being unmasked almost always work. The complexity of Bobby's motives grows intriguing, and the concern of his girlfriend, Amada, is well-used. *We Own the Night* may not solve the question of ownership, but it does explore who lives in the night, and why.

When Did You Last See Your Father? ★ ★ ★

PG-13, 92 m., 2008

Colin Firth (Blake Morrison), Jim Broadbent (Arthur Morrison), Juliet Stevenson (Kim Morrison), Gina McKee (Kathy Morrison), Elaine Cassidy (Sandra), Claire Skinner (Gillian), Matthew Beard (Blake, Teenager), Sarah Lancashire (Auntie Beaty). Directed by Anand Tucker and produced by Elizabeth Karlsen and Stephen Woolley. Screenplay by David Nicholls, based on the memoir by Blake Morrison.

"It's stupid, really," Blake Morrison tells his wife. "You spend a lifetime trying to avoid talking to someone, and then all of a sudden it's too late." He has returned to the Yorkshire town where he was born, and where his father is dying. Surely, his wife says, this is the right time? "He's too doped up."

When Did You Last See Your Father? is based on a 1990s best-seller by Morrison, who redefines the question as, "When did you last *really* see him?" He arrives at an answer for himself, but we're left realizing that he never did really see his father. He was too blinded by anger, and it is only after his death that he forgives him and sees him as a *father*, and not as the focus of resentment.

His father is Arthur (Jim Broadbent), who shares a practice with his wife, Kim (Juliet Stevenson), also a doctor. The son is played by Colin Firth, and it is startling in some scenes how much the two men resemble each other. In an opening where Arthur talks their way into reserved seats at a speedway, Blake tells us his father was a charmer who could talk his way into or out of anything.

The old man does it by bluster, expansive cheerfulness, and bluff. There's a lot of ground to cover. Blake correctly suspects that Arthur is having an affair with his Auntie Beaty (Sarah Lancashire), and even in later years

Arthur is able to out-charm his son in the pursuit of a woman they both covet. Blake hated his father for treating his mother so badly, although there are few scenes showing son and mother as particularly close. The person he does confide in is his first love, the family's maid, Sandra (Elaine Cassidy).

The film moves from the 1950s, when Blake is played by Bradley Johnson, to the 1960s, when he's played as a teenager by Matthew Beard. It's episodic, remembering a time when father and son went camping and found that a stream had overflowed into their tent, and a time when Arthur taught Blake how to drive. They make big circles on a deserted beach in the family's elegant Alvis convertible, and the scene ends with smiles on both men's faces.

We see lots of pairs of faces, but they're rarely smiling. The director, Anand Tucker (*Hilary and Jackie*), uses mirrors repeatedly throughout the movie, perhaps as a way of suggesting there's more than one way to see something or someone. The Arthur we see at least has more vitality than his son and wife, who grow increasingly glum. Poor Blake has his own libidinous feelings constantly interrupted by his father, whom he refers to as the "sex police." Why should his dad get away with everything and he with nothing?

It's a sad movie, with a mournful score, romantic landscape photography, and heartbreaking deathbed scenes (his mother weeps while changing the sheets). But it's not very satisfying. Blake and Arthur never really did talk man-to-man, and Arthur had a strange way of showing affection to "Fathead," as in a scene where he embarrasses his son by switching his drink at a party. "April Fool's!" he chortles, and his laugh grows so harsh it seems to be echoing in memory.

The real Blake Morrison was the literary editor of the *Observer*. Among his resentments were that his father did not respect the literary life and considered it a waste of time and money to study literature at university. His father "never read a single book all the way through," he says. He's been reading *Death on the Nile* for the last forty-two years. That has the sound of an epitaph long rehearsed.

If there is a genre for this sort of film, surely it demands a reconciliation, a moment of truth-telling, an expression of long-delayed love. Although Blake is told by Auntie Beaty that his father worshipped his family, Arthur never says it, and Blake never asks. He has questions still unvoiced near the end of the film, and the way they are finally answered for him is, in a way, perfectly appropriate.

The film did not provide me with fulfillment or a catharsis. Apparently the memoir wouldn't have, either. That's fair enough. How many unanswered questions are we all left with? I have some. This is a film of regret, and judging by what we see of the characters, it deserves to be.

Where the Truth Lies ★ ★ ★

NO MPAA RATING, 107 m., 2005

Kevin Bacon (Lanny Morris), Colin Firth (Vince Collins), Alison Lohman (Karen O'Connor), Rachel Blanchard (Maureen O'Flaherty), David Hayman (Rubin), Maury Chaykin (Sally SanMarco), Sonja Bennett (Bonnie). Directed by Atom Egoyan and produced by Robert Lantos. Screenplay by Egoyan, based on the novel by Rupert Holmes.

Where the Truth Lies is film noir right down to the plot we can barely track; we're reminded of William Faulkner asking Raymond Chandler who did it in *The Big Sleep* and Chandler saying he wasn't sure. Certainly somebody did it in *Where the Truth Lies*, or how would a dead waitress from Miami end up in a bathtub in Atlantic City? The waitress was last seen in the Miami suite of Lanny Morris and Vince Collins, two famous 1950s entertainers. Their alibi: They were on TV, doing their polio telethon, and then got directly on a plane and flew to New York with a lot of other people and had a police escort to their hotel, where the body was awaiting them.

Atom Egoyan, no stranger to labyrinthine plots, makes this one into a whodunit puzzle crossed with some faraway echoes of *Sunset Boulevard*, as an entertainer is confronted with events from the past that might best be left forgotten. The movie takes place in 1957 and 1972, and both of those years involve the crucial participation of beautiful young blondes who want to interview the two stars.

In 1957, Morris (Kevin Bacon) and Collins

(Colin Firth) are at the height of their fame, doing a nightclub act not a million miles apart from Martin and Lewis. The secret of their around-the-clock energy is the use of pills, lots of pills, from their Dr. Feelgood, which give them more urgency than they need in the realm of sex. A college student named Maureen O'Flaherty (Rachel Blanchard) arrives at their suite with room service, and when they suggest another kind of service, she seems sort of willing. She wants to interview them for her school paper.

It is Maureen who is found dead in Atlantic City, leading to a mystery that is never solved and to the breakup of Morris and Collins. Flash forward to 1972, and another would-be reporter, Karen O'Connor (Alison Lohman). Still in her mid-twenties, she negotiates a million-dollar book contract for Collins, who needs the money, but tells him he will have to talk about the murder of Maureen O'Flaherty. What Collins doesn't know is that Karen earlier met Lanny Morris on an airplane, followed him to his hotel room, and was dumped the next morning. What a rotter. What neither man knows is that Karen first met them in 1957, when as a young polio victim she appeared on their telethon. Nor does she know that Morris's tears as he talked to her were inspired not by her plight but by his knowledge that a dead waitress was on the sofa in their hotel suite.

Who killed the waitress and why? It's a classic locked-room mystery; all the relevant doors were locked from the inside, and so either man could have done it. But what if neither did? One imagines Ellery Queen rubbing his hands and getting down to work.

The attempts of Karen O'Connor to get Collins to talk are complicated by his own secrecy, financial need, lust, and general depravity. From his hillside mansion in Los Angeles, he lives in lonely isolation, happy to come and go as he pleases. His former partner, Morris, maintains an office and is apparently more active in showbiz, and both of them have reasons to pressure and mislead the young woman.

Because I have seen *Where the Truth Lies* twice and enjoyed it more when I understood its secrets, I don't understand why several critics have found Alison Lohman wrong for the job of playing the reporter in 1972. Is she too young? If she was nine in 1957, she would be twenty-four in 1972. Would a publisher give her such responsibility? If she can really deliver Collins, maybe one would—and the money depends on delivering. Is it a coincidence that Miss O'Connor looks something like Miss O'Flaherty? No, not if what she represents for both men is an eerie shadow from the past.

The movie departs from film noir and enters the characteristic world of Egoyan in its depiction of sex. Both blondes, and a third one I will not describe, are involved in fairly specific sex scenes with one or both men, and the sad and desperate nature of this sex is a reminder of such Egoyan films as *Exotica*. The MPAA rated the film NC-17 and refused an appeal, so it's being released unrated, but the sex really isn't the point of the scenes in question; it's the application of power, and the way that showbiz success can give stars unsavory leverage with young women who are more impressed than they should be.

Bacon is on a roll right now after several good roles, and here he channels diabolical sleaze while mugging joylessly before the telethon cameras. His relationship with the Firth character involves love and hate and perhaps more furtive feelings. There is a stunning scene in a nightclub where a drunk insults Morris, and Collins invites him backstage for a terrifying demonstration of precisely how those happy pills do not make everyone equally happy.

Alison Lohman has the central role. I've known young reporters like her. Some of them may be reading this review. You know who you are. She is smart, sexy, hungering for a big story, burning with ambition, and (most dangerous of all) still harboring idealistic delusions. Would a young woman like this find herself suddenly inside two lives of secrecy and denial? Yes, more easily than Kitty Kelly would, because she doesn't seem to represent a threat. Her youth is crucial because in some way, the danger Maureen O'Flaherty walked into is still potentially there.

There's another way in which the movie works, and that's through the introduction of an unexpected character, Maureen's mother. Another director might handle the showbiz and the murder and intrigue with dispatch, but Egoyan thinks about the emotional cost to the characters, as he also did in *Felicia's Journey*. The mother and the young reporter have a meeting during which we discover the single good reason why the solution to the murder should not be revealed. It is a flawed reason because it depends on the wrong solution, but that isn't the point: It functions to end the film in poignancy rather than sensation.

The White Countess ★ ★ ★

PG-13, 138 m., 2005

Ralph Fiennes (Todd Jackson), Natasha Richardson (Countess Sofia Belinsky), Vanessa Redgrave (Aunt Sara), Lynn Redgrave (Olga), Madeleine Daly (Katya Belinsky), Hiroyuki Sanada (Mr. Matsuda), Allan Corduner (Samuel). Directed by James Ivory and produced by Ismail Merchant. Screenplay by Kazuo Ishiguro.

The White Countess is a film about a man who dreams of owning the perfect little bar, a place of elegance that finds the delicate balance, as he thinks a woman should, "between the erotic and the tragic." Outside it is Shanghai in 1936, and the world is late for its appointment with war. Inside the bar—well, inside, Mr. Jackson muses, "With a good team of bouncers, you could conduct the place like an orchestra."

Mr. Jackson is a blind man who stands, or sometimes leans, at the center of the last of twenty-eight films to be made together in this life by the director James Ivory and the producer Ismail Merchant. There were two more in preproduction when Merchant died in May 2005. They have been operating their own perfect little bar since 1963. Outside it is Hollywood and the world is hurrying toward commerce and compromise. Inside their bar, cosmopolitan characters, elegant and tragic, have wandered out of the pages of good books; what many share is a personal style employed to conceal wounds, lusts, and disappointments.

Todd Jackson (Ralph Fiennes) is a classic Merchant-Ivory character. He is an exile. He hoped for great things as a young man and now, disillusioned, hopes for smaller victories. He placed great trust in romance, now sees it as a hazard. He has taste. He needs money. He is comfortable with disreputable behavior, as long as it is conducted by the rules. Inside his world, friendships are possible that are otherwise forbidden.

Consider his friend Mr. Matsuda (Hiroyuki Sanada). Everyone knows the Japanese are going to invade China and that Mr. Matsuda is their Shanghai advance man. Mr. Matsuda knows Mr. Jackson was once considered "the last hope of the League of Nations." Mr. Jackson knows that Mr. Matsuda "would like to visit the bar of his dreams."

What would this ideal bar be like? In another bar, which is not the right kind of bar, Mr. Jackson overhears a conversation involving the Countess Sofia Belinsky (Natasha Richardson), once Russian royalty, now supporting her exiled family by working as a taxi dancer. Everyone knows that to make ends meet, taxi dancers must sometimes "fall in love" with their clients. Sofia's Russian family lives on her earnings while insulting her as a whore. Sofia's little daughter Katya (Madeleine Daly) doesn't know what a whore is but defends her mother against her fierce grandmother and aunt (Vanessa and Lynn Redgrave): "If Mama didn't go out to work, then you would have to." Quite so, and at wholesale.

One night Sofia sees a situation developing in the shabby little bar where Jackson drinks, and quietly speaks to the blind man. She warns him he is about to be mugged and advises him to behave as her client. That will get him home unharmed. She wants no payment for this favor. "You're perfect," Jackson tells her. "You're what I need." She will be the hostess in his perfect little bar, talk with the customers, dance with them, decidedly not sleep with them.

The bar, when he wins the money to open it, is called the White Countess, and yes, in its way it *is* perfect. The jazz is good, the clientele is select, and Jackson has the right bouncers. The rest of the movie will involve the approaching collision between this perfect little world and the cataclysm of war.

Merchant and Ivory have never been much concerned with conventional melodrama, excitement, and cheap thrills. Often working with the writer Ruth Prawer Jhabvala, they have adapted works by such as Henry James *(The Golden Bowl),* E. M. Forster *(Howards End, A Room With a View),* and Kazuo Ishiguro *(The Remains of the Day);* Ishiguro wrote this original screenplay. They have catered to a literate minority. If you have read this far, they have catered to you. In the perfect bar, you are likely to meet someone with every taste—even good taste.

Fiennes and Richardson make this film work with the quiet strangeness of their performances; if they insist on their eccentricities, it's because they've paid them off and own them outright. Fiennes's Jackson seems a little shaky for a man long accustomed to being blind, but not if he is also long accustomed to being a little drunk. Richardson's Sofia seems a little too cultivated for a prostitute, and we are reminded of Marlene Dietrich's great line, said by a character who lived in the same time and place: "It took more than one man to change my name to Shanghai Lily." But Sofia was raised as a countess and can hardly shed her elegance when she abandons her morals. These two fallen and needy people are reminded by each other of better times.

What we do is sit and watch them try to live up to their standards in a world that simply doesn't care. I saw my first Merchant and Ivory film, *Shakespeare Wallah,* in 1965, so for forty years I have been watching them live up to their own standards when the world didn't care and, lately, even when it did. Sometimes they have made great films, sometimes flawed ones, even bad ones, but never shabby or unworthy ones. Here is one that is good to better, poignant, patient, moving. In the closing scenes the movie loses its way as Jackson, Sofia, and everybody else get caught up in the chaos of the Japanese invasion, and melodrama is forced upon these reclusive souls. But no matter. No perfect little place lasts forever. The more perfect it is, the more word gets around and the wrong people blunder in and start fights.

The White Diamond ★ ★ ★

NO MPAA RATING, 90 m., 2005

With Graham Dorrington, Mark Anthony Yhap, Werner Herzog, Anthony Melville, Michael Wilk, Jan-Peter Meewes, Jason Gibson, and Red Man (Mark Anthony's rooster). A documentary directed by Werner Herzog and produced by Annette Scheurich, Lucki Stipetic, and Herzog.

Werner Herzog's documentary *The White Diamond* is not about a diamond, but about an airship, one of the smallest ever built, designed to float above the canopy of equatorial rain forests. Every niche in the jungle is exploited by plants, animals, and insects that have evolved to make a living there, and biologists believe that undiscovered species might live their entire lives 80 or 120 feet from the ground.

Herzog introduces us to a London researcher named Graham Dorrington, who dreams of reaching out from his airship to study specimens on the ceiling of the jungle. Like many of Herzog's subjects, he is a dreamer who talks a little too fast and smiles when he doesn't seem to be happy: When a sudden storm threatens to tear his airship to pieces, he says he is philosophical, and we see that he isn't.

Dorrington's airship is shaped like an upside-down teardrop with a tail. It carries a two-man gondola and is powered and steered by small motors. It uses helium gas, which will not burn, unlike hydrogen gas, which caught fire inside the Hindenburg and brought an end to an era when the giant zeppelins served tourist routes between Europe, Brazil, India, and the United States. The zeppelins were cigar-shaped ships that were hard to turn, Dorrington says, unlike his ship, which can pivot in midair. That is the theory, anyway, as he explains his motors and his switches, and we hear Herzog's voice, always filled with apprehension, telling us, "He did not know then that this particular switch would cause a huge problem later."

Dorrington tested an earlier airship in 1993 in Sumatra, and that ended with catastrophe, Herzog tells us. Dorrington describes the death of his cinematographer, Dieter Plage, who fell from a gondola after it was broken on the high branches of a tree by a sudden wind. "It was an accident," Dorrington says, and all agree, but he blames himself every day. Now he is ready to try again.

His airship was built in a huge hangar outside London that once housed dirigibles. Strange, that it cannot be tested there but must be transported to South America and the rain forests of Guyana. Dorrington is a man after Herzog's heart—Herzog, the director who could have filmed *Aguirre, the Wrath of God,* and *Fitzcarraldo* a few miles from cities—but insisted on filming them hundreds of miles inside the rain forest. Herzog has made a specialty of finding obsessives and eccentrics who push themselves to extremes; see his doc

Grizzly Man about Timothy Treadwell, who lived among the bears of Alaska until one killed him.

Now watch what happens during the first test flight. Herzog has an argument with Dorrington. The scientist wants to fly solo. Herzog calls it "stupid" that the first flight might take place without a camera on board. (It might, of course, be the only flight.) Herzog has brought along two cinematographers but insists he must personally take the camera up on the maiden voyage. "I cannot ask a cinematographer to get in an airship before I test it myself," he says. As Herzog buckles himself into the gondola, we reflect that if Dorrington's standards were those that Herzog insists on, *Dorrington* would not allow *Herzog* to get in the airship until he had tested it himself. It is sublimely Herzogian that this paradox is right there in full view.

There are some dicey moments as the ship goes backward when it should go forward, and Herzog observes a motor burning out and pieces of a propeller whizzing past his head. The flight instructor who pilots the expedition's ultralight aircraft says Dorrington has not practiced "good airmanship." Dorrington moans that "seven different systems" failed. We wonder if the catastrophe in Sumatra will be repeated.

There is breathtaking footage of the ship's flights, as it skims the forest canopy and descends to dip a toe in the river. Mournful, vaguely ecclesiastical music accompanies these images. The vast Kaieteur Falls fascinates the party; its waters are golden-brown as they roar into a maelstrom, and countless swifts and other birds fly into a cave behind the curtain of water. Mark Anthony Yhap, a local man employed by the expedition, relates legends about the cave. The team doctor, Michael Wilk, has himself lowered on a rope with a video camera to look into the cave. It is typical of a Herzog project that the doctor would be "an experienced mountain climber." It is sublimely typical of Herzog that he does *not* show us the doctor's footage of the cave, after Yhap argues that its sacred secret must be preserved. What is in the cave? A lot of guano, is my guess.

There are times when this expedition causes us to speculate that the Monty Python troupe might have based its material on close observation of actual living Britons. Consider the "experiment" to determine if the downdraft of the waterfall is so strong it would threaten the airship. Dorrington and Herzog tie together four brightly colored birthday balloons and hang a glass of champagne from them as ballast. Sure enough, the balloons are sucked into the mist.

Yhap is one of the film's riches. Known as "Redbeard," he is a Rastafarian who gives the film its title, saying the airship looks like a "big white diamond floating around in the sunrise." Yhap is fond of his red rooster, a mighty bird that has five wives who present him with five eggs every morning. Toward the end of the film Yhap is given his own chance to ride in the airship and enjoys it immensely, but regrets that he could not take along his rooster.

Although *The White Diamond* is entire of itself, it earns its place among the other treasures and curiosities in Herzog's work. Here is one of the most inquisitive filmmakers alive, a man who will go to incredible lengths to film people living at the extremes. In *La Soufriere,* a 1977 documentary released on DVD in August 2005, he journeys to an island evacuated because of an impending volcanic eruption to ask the only man who stayed behind why he did not leave. What he is really asking, what he is always asking, is why he had to go there to ask the question.

The Whole Shootin' Match ★ ★ ★ ★

NO MPAA RATING, 101 m., 1979 (rereleased 2007)

Lou Perry (Loyd), Sonny Davis (Frank), Doris Hargrave (Paulette), Eric Henshaw (Olan), David Weber (T. Frank), James Harrell (Old Man). Directed by Eagle Pennell and produced by Pennell and Lin Sutherland. Screenplay by Pennell and Sutherland.

Eagle Pennell died a "hopeless drunk," according to a memorial article in the *Austin Chronicle* by his friend Louis Black. His other friends would have sadly agreed with that. He was forty-nine at the time of his death, in 2002. Twenty-three years earlier, in 1979, he wrote and directed a film named *The Whole Shootin' Match* that you may never have heard of, but which had a decisive influence on American independent film.

When Robert Redford saw it at the Park City Film Festival, it awoke him to the possibilities of low-budget indie filmmaking. He started the Sundance Institute, and soon after, the Park City festival became the Sundance festival. When Richard Linklater, then living in Eagle's hometown of Austin, Texas, saw it, he decided to become a filmmaker himself, and his *Dazed and Confused* owes a lot to Pennell.

When I saw the movie at Telluride in 1980, I went for a walk on the mountainside with Eagle and mentioned that he had made a film about alcoholism. He said that had never occurred to him, although he thought I was right. His characters drink in almost every shot of the film. In the last years of his life, Black reports, Eagle spent every dollar he could beg or borrow on booze. He lived on the streets or on the sofas of his shrinking number of friends. He made other films, one of them the very good *Last Night at the Alamo* (1983). It was not about John Wayne's Alamo but about a bar in Austin. The line on the poster read: "Some face the future head on. Tonight the boys at the Alamo face it dead drunk."

Now *The Whole Shootin' Match* is getting an almost miraculous new chance at finding an audience. The few surviving prints were battered and beaten, but a good print turned up a couple of years ago in Germany and has been lovingly restored by Mark Rance of Watchmaker Films.

Rance screened it for a few Chicago film types in the loft of Chicago projection genius James Bond. It was like a reunion of some of those who had loved the film the first time around, including Chicago underground filmmaker Tom Palazzolo and Facets founder Milos Stehlik. The print was so sparkling in crisp black-and-white that it played like a new film, a lovable, low-key tragicomedy about a couple of good ol' boys who live on their pipe dreams. As I wrote the first time the film played at the Film Center, in 1980:

"Loyd and Frank live down around Austin, Texas, where they spend most of their time drinking booze and thinking up new ways to get rich quick. By the time the movie opens, they've already lost small fortunes (very small fortunes) as frog farmers, flying squirrel ranchers, and suppliers of polyurethane to rich hippies. But now they stand on the brink of a really big thing. Loyd has invented something called the Kitchen Wizard, which combines all the worst principles of a mop, a floor polisher, and a vacuum cleaner, and they've sold the rights for $1,000 to a patent attorney: Gray skies are gonna clear up."

That suggests the humor of the film, but not its heart. Played by Lou Perry and Sonny Davis, Loyd and Frank are goofballs, yes, but their struggle has a certain heroism to it, especially since they're drunk or hung over almost all of the time. There is an undertone of unspoken, maybe unrealized, despair beneath their daily adventures.

The film shows that Eagle was a born story spinner and creater of characters. If you Google him and read the tributes and memories in the *Chronicle* and other Texas papers, you'll find that many Texans believe he came closer to capturing the blue-collar spirit of their state than anyone else. I know my friend Molly Ivins thought so. But Eagle *could not* sober up; Louis Black remembers times when he went off to rehab, got drunk on the flight home, turned up at the *Chronicle* to borrow money to pay for the taxi from the airport and more money for another binge. His life must have been torture. But he left behind some lovely work, and *The Whole Shootin' Match* is priceless. I rated it at three stars on its first release. What was I waiting for? Do I ever change a rating? Hell, yes. I'd give it four today, and you'll see why.

Why We Fight ★ ★

PG-13, 98 m., 2006

Featuring Dwight Eisenhower, Wilton Sekzer, Chalmers Johnson, William Solomon, Charles Lewis, Richard Perle, William Kristol, Lieutenant Colonel Karen Kwiatkowski, Joseph Cirincione, Susan Eisenhower, John S. D. Eisenhower, Anh Duong, Gwynne Dyer, Senator John McCain, Gore Vidal, Franklin Spinney. A documentary written and directed by Eugene Jarecki.

I agree with the politics of *Why We Fight*, and I concede it is a skillful assembly of its materials, but as a documentary it's less than compelling. Few people are likely to see this film unless they already agree with its conclusions, and few of those will learn anything new from it. All political documentaries face that dilemma to one degree or another; when one of its distributors said Michael Moore's *Fahrenheit 9/11* would defeat George W. Bush in 2004, he miscalculated, because there was little overlap between those planning to vote for Bush and those planning to see the movie.

The most effective recent political documentaries have focused on reporting rather than opinion. Movies such as *Enron: The Smartest Guys in the Room,* which blames the California energy crisis on deliberate Enron policy, or *Gunner Palace,* which recorded the day-to-day life of American troops in Iraq, added to our knowledge without lecturing us about what to think. The drama *Jarhead* was also effective, because it recorded the daily military routine in the first Gulf War without providing an artificial action structure. I got e-mails from people frustrated that the movie had no payoff—but the payoff for the first Gulf War was, of course, our intervention in Iraq.

Why We Fight compiles archival footage and intercuts it with recent interviews, many conducted for the film, but the movie tells us nothing we haven't heard before. It opens with Dwight Eisenhower warning, in the farewell address of his presidency, of a "vast military-industrial complex" that was placing the nation on a permanent war footing. His prophecy was correct. It is no longer even possible to arouse much indignation when the executives of war industries move freely between their board rooms and government offices. Yes, Vice President Dick Cheney headed a major war supplier and now, in office, backs policies that enrich that supplier; he might have made Ike indignant, but today conflicts of interest are forgiven as a convergence of interests.

Why We Fight is devoted to proving Eisenhower correct. It says, essentially, that we fight because we have constructed a military-industrial complex that needs business. Declaring war opens up markets; from a purely financial point of view, it's like signing free-trade agreements or negotiating tariffs. The documentary, directed by Eugene Jarecki, quotes sources from both sides—conservatives such as Richard Perle, liberals such as Gore Vidal, disillusioned military experts such as Lieutenant Colonel Karen Kwiatkowski, and the descendants of Eisenhower. But after Ike makes his point in the opening minutes, the film itself essentially just elaborates on it.

There is one story thread that stands apart and is compelling. It involves a retired New York cop named Wilton Sekzer. His son died in the 9/11 attacks, and he successfully lobbied the government to put his son's name on one of the first bombs that was dropped in Iraq.

He wanted revenge, and to a degree he felt like he got it. That was before Bush observed (some felt rather belatedly) that Iraq and Saddam Hussein had no direct involvement in the 9/11 attacks. Now Sekzer is bitter: He feels that Bush lied to him and that his patriotism was manipulated and misused. The story of Sekzer is new and is suited to film. Much of the rest of *Why We Fight* says things that can be said as well or better in print, and have been. This doesn't need to be a film.

There are other disillusioned people in the documentary, in particular Kwiatkowski, who resigned from the Pentagon because she witnessed military officers being vetoed by outside consultants whose loyalty was to the defense contractors who employed them. One watches *Why We Fight,* and nods, and sighs, and leaves.

What it says should concern us, but apparently it does not. The film observes that some defense contracts are cleverly planned to spread the government wealth among as many states as possible; some weapons systems have suppliers in all fifty states, and woe to the elected official of either party who votes against them. Shouldn't it be obvious that a legislator who votes against government spending in his own district must have given the matter a lot of thought, and be courageous, and perhaps even correct? That's a useful thought. But it's not news, and when documentaries such as *Enron: The Smartest Guys in the Room* contain fresh and shocking information, a film such as *Why We Fight* is not very necessary.

The Wild ★ ★ ★

G, 94 m., 2006

With the voices of: Kiefer Sutherland (Samson [lion]), Greg Cipes (Ryan [lion cub]), James Belushi (Benny [squirrel]), Janeane Garofalo (Bridget [giraffe]), Richard Kind (Larry [snake]), William Shatner (Kazar [wildebeest]), Eddie Izzard (Nigel [koala]). Directed by Steve "Spaz"

Williams and produced by Beau Flynn and Clint Goldman. Screenplay by Ed Decter, Mark Gibson, Philip Halprin, and John J. Strauss.

When *The Wild* and *Ice Age: The Meltdown* were over, they left me with a question: What did they eat? The animals were awfully chummy, considering that some of them have been known to dine on the others. *The Wild* answers my question, but not very accurately. Some animals, as we know, are carnivores. That would include lions. Others are omnivores. That would include humans. Still others are herbivores, or vegetarians. That would include the mighty wildebeest, also known as the gnu, although "the mighty gnu" lacks a certain je ne sais quoi. Wildebeests move around, we are told, in search of grasslands, not quarry.

Hold that thought. *The Wild* and another recent animated film, *Madagascar,* share the same premise, which is that animals escape from a zoo and find themselves back in the jungle again—Madagascar in the first film, Africa in this one. The premise this time is that little Ryan (voice by Greg Cipes), the lion cub, has wandered off and gotten into a shipping container that is being taken to Africa. His horrified father, Samson (Kiefer Sutherland), races off to save him and ends up chasing Ryan's ship all the way to Africa on a tugboat that gets very good mileage. Along for the ride are such zoo friends as Benny the squirrel (James Belushi), Bridget the giraffe (Janeane Garofalo), Nigel the koala (Eddie Izzard), and Larry the anaconda (Richard Kind).

Benny is in love with Bridget, not realizing he is a squirrel and she is not, which reminds me of the mammoth in *Ice Age: The Meltdown* who thinks she is a possum. The cast continues to grow. On the journey through New York they encounter a couple of alligators in the sewer system, and in Africa they meet other characters, including the undercover chameleons Cloak and Camo (Bob Joles and Chris Edgerly), a vulture (Greg Berg) who I think lacks a name, and then, the earth thundering, the dreaded Kazar (William Shatner), who is king of the wildebeests but can be king of the jungle only if he defeats a lion. That would be Samson, who has a secret in his past he hopes Kazar doesn't discover.

Now, then. Although Samson gets regular T-bones at the zoo, he no doubt would cheerfully eat many of these other animals. But what are we to make of a volcano scene with lots of flowing lava that helps set up a scenario in which it appears that Kazar plans to cook Samson? Is Kazar not a vegetarian, or did I miss something?

The movie has a lot more action than *Ice Age: The Meltdown,* which was essentially one long trek. There are savage beasts (wilde and other), exploding volcanoes, rivers of lava, and so on—some of it may be too intense for the youngest kids. This is the third animated feature in a row (after *Curious George* and *Ice Age: The Meltdown*) that aims at children and has no serious ambition to be all things to all people (i.e., their parents). But for kids, it's okay.

That leaves me with some observations about its technique. I doubt that many audience members will be disturbed by such matters, but I thought the movie's lip-synching was too good. The mouths of the characters move so precisely in time with their words that the cartoon illusion is lost and we venture toward the Uncanny Valley—that shadowy area known to robot designers and animators in which artificial creatures so closely resemble humans that they make us feel kinda creepy. Lip-synching in animation usually ranges from bad to perfunctory to fairly good, and I think fairly good is as good as it should get. In *The Wild,* it felt somehow *wrong* that the dialogue was so perfectly in synch.

I also had some problems with the film's visual strategy. The director, Steve "Spaz" Williams, has a way of cutting to unexpected close-ups. That gives us a subtle feeling that the movie knows in advance what will happen next, when in theory it should seem to find out just when we do. I also think the framing of some of the characters is too close; they hog the foreground and obscure the background. And the fur, hair, and feathers on the creatures look so detailed, thanks to the wonders of CGI, that once again we're wandering toward the Uncanny Valley.

An animated film can approach reality, but it should never arrive there. It must always seem one magical arm's length away. The art is in the style, in the way reality is distorted or heightened. When Miyazaki gives us characters who shout so loudly we can see their tonsils, he knows what he's doing. None of these details will matter to the target audience for *The Wild,* of course, although maybe in some vague, unconscious way they will sense that the movie doesn't have that je ne sais quoi, a phrase I employ again to make you feel vindicated for looking it up in the first place. As French phrases go, it is one of the handiest, and especially useful when you don't know quite what to say.

The Wild Parrots of Telegraph Hill ★ ★ ★

G, 83 m., 2005

A documentary about Mark Bittner, directed and produced by Judy Irving.

Mark Bittner is calm, intelligent, confiding, wise, and well spoken. You would be happy to count him as your friend. He has not worked in thirty years, has lived on the street for fifteen of them, and in recent years has devoted his life to getting to know forty-five wild parrots who formed a flock in San Francisco. It takes a lot of time to get to know forty-five wild parrots as individuals, but as he points out, "I have all the time in the world."

The Wild Parrots of Telegraph Hill, a documentary about Bittner and his birds by Judy Irving, is not the film you think it is going to be. You walk in expecting some kind of North Beach weirdo and his wild-eyed parrot theories, and you walk out still feeling a little melancholy over the plight of Connor, the only blue-crowned conure in a flock of red-crowned conures.

Connor had a mate, Bittner tells us, but the mate died. Now Connor hangs around with the other parrots but seems lonely and depressed, a blue-crowned widower who can sometimes get nasty with the other birds, but comes to the defense of weak or sick birds when the flock picks on them. Picasso and Sophie, both red-crowned parrots, are a couple until Picasso disappears; Bittner begins to hope that maybe Connor and Sophie will start to date and produce some purple-headed babies.

Nobody knows how the parrots, all born in the wild and imported from South America, escaped captivity, found each other, and started their flock. Irving has several North Beach residents recite the usual urban legends (they were released by an eccentric old lady, a bird truck overturned, etc.). No matter. They live and thrive.

You would think it might get too cold in the winter for these tropical birds, but no: They can withstand cold fairly well, and the big problem for them is getting enough to eat. Indeed, flocks of wild parrots and parakeets exist in colder climates; the famous colony of parakeets in Chicago's Hyde Park was evicted from some of their nests in 2005, after fifteen or twenty years, because they were interfering with utility lines.

Oddly, some bird lovers seem to resent trespassers such as wild parrots on the grounds that they are outside their native range. That they are here through no fault of their own, that they survive and thrive and are intelligent and beautiful birds, is enough for Mark Bittner, and by the end of the film that's enough for us, too.

He gives us brief biographies of some of the birds. Sometimes he takes them into his home when they're sick or injured, but after they recover they all want to return to the wild—except for Mingus, who keeps trying to get back into the house. Their biggest enemies are viruses and hawks. The flock always has a hawk lookout posted, and has devised other hawk-avoidance tactics, of which the most ingenious is to fly *behind* a hawk, which can only attack straight ahead and has a wider turning radius than parrots.

Bittner originally came to San Francisco, he tells us, seeking work as a singer. That didn't work out. He lived on the streets, did odd jobs, read a lot, met some of the original hippies (Ginsberg, Ferlinghetti, Gary Snyder). For the three years before the film begins, he has lived rent-free in a cottage below the house of a wealthy couple who live near the parrots on Telegraph Hill. Now he is about to be homeless again, while the cottage is renovated into an expensive rental property. The parrots are threatened with homelessness, too, and Bittner testifies on their behalf before the city council. San Francisco mayor Gavin Newsom vows nothing bad will happen to the parrots; would that we had such statesmen in Illinois.

As Bittner tends and feeds his flock, visitors to the wooded area on Telegraph Hill want to categorize him. Is he a scientist? Paid by the city? What's his story? His story is, he finds the parrots fascinating and lovable. He quotes Gary Snyder: "If you want to study nature, start right where you are." Can he live like this forever? He is about fifty, in good health, with a long red ponytail. He says he decided not to cut his hair until he gets a girlfriend. Whether either Connor the blue-crowned conure or Bittner the red-headed birdman find girlfriends, I will leave for you to discover.

Winter Passing ★ ★ ★ ½

R, 98 m., 2006

Ed Harris (Don Holden), Zooey Deschanel (Reese Holden), Will Ferrell (Corbit), Amelia Warner (Shelly). Directed by Adam Rapp and produced by P. Jennifer Dana and David Koplan. Screenplay by Rapp.

Reese didn't attend her mother's funeral because "she treated me like a mild curiosity all my life," nor she was eager to see her father. Reese lives in New York, works at being an actress, sleeps around, is depressed. Her father, Don Holden, was a famous novelist, then a famous writing teacher, then a famous drunk, and is now a famous drunken recluse. The usual trajectory. Her mother was a writer, too. Did her parents write to each other? An editor offers her money for their correspondence, and Reese needs money. There's nothing to keep her in New York after the death of her cat.

Winter Passing is the story of how Reese (Zooey Deschanel) takes the bus to the Upper Peninsula of Michigan and finds her father (Ed Harris) living in a shack in the backyard. When she knocks on the front door of the big house, it is opened by Corbit (Will Ferrell), who says he wants to see some ID. Later he confides, "I know karate. I've amassed several belts." Corbit is the caretaker, or something. Also living in the house is Shelly (Amelia Warner), a British girl who cooks meals and was Don's writing student at Iowa.

What are the relationships among or between Don, Corbit, and Shelly? Don is mired in a profound alcoholic depression. Corbit and Shelly seem, like Bunuel's dinner guests in *The Exterminating Angel,* to have entered the house only to find themselves unable to leave it. Shelly is maybe an enabler. Corbit is maybe an alien. Reese lives in the house for a few days and begins to understand its desperate chemistry. These people are hanging on by one another's fingernails.

Winter Passing is a sad story told in a cold season about lonely people. Written and directed by the playwright Adam Rapp, it could be inspired by any number of case histories; Frederick Exley (*A Fan's Notes*) comes to mind. There is something about a great author, even in the extremities of alcoholic self-destruction, that exerts a magnetic pull on those who respect his books. Don's house itself is filled with so many books that you wouldn't ask, "Have you really read all of these?" because you'd be afraid of the answer either way. Only one title is clearly visible among the thousands of volumes, but it's the right one: *The Thirsty Muse.*

Rapp's film skirts the edges of humor and love. Approached in a different way, this could be a comedy of eccentricity. Rapp sidesteps temptations for laughter, while nodding to them in passing. Consider the carefully modulated performance of Ferrell, an actor whose presence is an invitation to laughter. Here he finds a way to be peculiar without being silly; he has deep fears, enclosed in a deeper shyness. He can sing and play the guitar but has a phobia about doing both at once in public. That leads to open-mike evening at the local bar and a scene almost impossible to play, but Ferrell and Deschanel find a way. Notice his aborted project to build a sheltered walkway from the shack to the main house. He starts it on impulse, and the impulse fades. Nor does he know much about carpentry.

Ed Harris has played alcoholic artists before; his Oscar-nominated Jackson Pollock is a benchmark. Here he mixes alcoholism with madness. Why does he move his bed, table, and bureau into the yard and sleep under the sky in the deep of winter? The arrival of his daughter seems to awaken him, if only to alert him to let go. Shelly confides in Reese that the old man is still writing, but slowly: "As a teacher, he was always preaching compositional velocity. I've never seen anyone agonize over each sentence the way he does."

Slowly, the old writer surfaces from his slough of despond. His face appears from behind his beard. He talks to Reese, a little, enigmatically. He has been working on a novel. There may indeed be letters between her father and her mother, who could not live together and yet were bound in a terrible need. Watch Don drink and smoke not because he wants to or needs to, but because he has forgotten to stop. Observe the sweetness of the Ferrell character, terrified of being known. Warner, as the former student, is still learning because when you apprentice to a genius you don't bail out. Deschanel, in this film and the dismal *Failure to Launch,* shows the same ability to remain apart, to watch and listen, to move on her own terms. She can love her father or forgive her father, but it will be hard to do both.

This is the kind of movie some people think is too quiet, but it can be more exciting to listen than to hear. It will disappoint those looking for a Will Ferrell comedy. Disappoint, puzzle, maybe enrage. But some Ferrell fans will find a kind of film they may not have seen before. That's how you grow as a filmgoer; your favorite stars lead you by the hand into deep water.

Winter Solstice ★ ★ ★

R, 89 m., 2005

Anthony LaPaglia (Jim Winters), Allison Janney (Molly Ripken), Aaron Stanford (Gabe Winters), Mark Webber (Pete Winters), Ron Livingston (Mr. Bricker), Michelle Monaghan (Stacey), Brendan Sexton III (Robbie). Directed by Josh Sternfeld and produced by Doug Bernheim and John Limotte. Screenplay by Sternfeld.

Oh, what a sad movie this is: Sad not with the details of tragedy, but with the details of life that must go on after the tragedy. *Winter Solstice* is about a family living in emptiness that threatens to become hopelessness. Jim Winters, the father, is a landscape gardener. His boys Gabe and Peter are in high school. Five years ago, Pete was in the car with his mother when there was an accident and she was killed. The family has been broken ever since.

It's conventional in such stories to assign blame to the father, who is seen as distant or bitter. Not here. Jim (Anthony LaPaglia) is filled with desperation as he tries to reach out to his sons. But he doesn't have the tone or the gift, or perhaps they're at that maddening stage in adolescence when they just clam up, taking it out on everybody else that they're angry with themselves.

The movie is not plot-driven, for which we must be thankful, because to force their feelings into a plot would be a form of cruelty. The whole point is that these lives have no plot. The characters and their situation are onstage and waiting for something to happen, but Josh Sternfeld, the writer-director, isn't going to let them off that easily. If this movie ended in hugs it would be an abomination.

Gabe (Aaron Stanford) thinks he will leave town and move to Tampa. He has no firm plans for what he will do in Tampa and only vague reasons for choosing Tampa instead of any other place on the face of the Earth. "What about Stacey?" his father asks. Stacey (Michelle Monaghan) is Gabe's girlfriend, welcome in the house, well liked. "That's my problem and I'm dealing with it," Gabe says. He's dealing with it the way a lot of teenage boys deal with girls: He's dropping her and letting her figure it out. Stacey isn't a weeper; she wisely doesn't answer his phone calls and leaves him without the opportunity for justification, blame, closure, or anything else except a feeling of being lonely on his own.

Pete (Mark Webber) is in trouble at school. His teacher, Mr. Bricker (Ron Livingston), knows he's smart and can do better and rather bravely tries to get around his defenses, but Pete is miserable and punishes himself. The worse he does, the worse he can feel, which is fine with him.

A woman named Molly (Allison Janney) moves in down the street. Jim helps her shift some boxes. She invites them to dinner. Jim has not looked at another woman in five years, and maybe isn't really looking at Molly when he accepts; maybe he just knows it's time to break the pattern. Gabe and Pete fail to turn up for the dinner, and Jim throws their mattresses out onto the lawn and lets them sleep under the stars; this is perceived not as tough love but as anger, which is probably just as well, since these boys are well defended against love.

Josh Sternfeld, like his character Stacey, knows he will have more effect on us if he denies us closure. It would be simple to give this movie a happy ending, but why does the happiness have to come at the end of this particular winter? Maybe it will come five years down the road, with Gabe returning from Tampa with a wife and a kid, and Pete safely in college, and Jim and Molly living together. Or maybe it won't end that way.

The movie knows that life is sometimes very discouraging, and keeps on being discouraging, and sometimes you can't save everybody and have to try to save yourself. Who is to say that it's a bad idea for Gabe to move to Tampa? Sure, his father thinks it is, but is Gabe making any progress in New Jersey? Would it be an answer to marry Stacey? Marrying somebody to solve a problem is never the answer to the problem, just a way to share it. LaPaglia, who often stars in crime movies and comedies, has a sad, resigned tone that is just right for this movie, as it was for the overlooked *Lantana* (2001).

When *Winter Solstice* is over, we sit and look at the screen and wonder what will happen to them all. We don't expect dramatic developments; these lives don't seem on a course for tragedy or happiness, but for a gradual kind of acceptance. Maybe the movies do us no service by solving so many problems, in a world with so few solutions.

The Witnesses ★ ★ ★

NO MPAA RATING, 112 m., 2008

Johan Libereau (Manu), Michel Blanc (Adrien), Emmanuelle Beart (Sarah), Sami Bouajila (Mehdi), Julie Depardieu (Julie). Directed by Andre Techine and produced by Said Ben Said. Screenplay by Techine, Laurent Guyot, and Viviane Zingg.

Michel Blanc is that middle-aged French actor with the round bald head and (often enough) round eyeglasses who has played dozens of engaging roles, most notably in Patrice Leconte's masterpiece *Monsieur Hire.* In Andre Techine's *The Witnesses,* he plays Adrien, a doctor, one of an ensemble of five major characters. They are more or less balanced in importance and screen time, but somehow he draws our attention to himself. He doesn't "steal" scenes; what he does simply seems more urgent, more passionate, more driven.

Early in the film, we see him cruising a Paris late-night rendezvous for gays, picking up a young guy and then stalking away from him in anger when he's asked how old he is. The younger man goes into the shrubbery in search of another partner, but first asks Adrien to hold his coat because he's afraid of it being stolen. "I might steal it myself," Adrien says. "I'd be very surprised," says Manu (Johan Libereau). His instinctive trust generates a connection between the two men, but it doesn't blossom into a sexual coupling. It becomes a friendship that will be greatly tested by the end of the story.

The movie begins in 1984 and has sections set in the following year. This is the time that AIDS begins to be recognized in France, and having sex with strangers in the park will soon lack the illusion of safety. Manu is not sexually interested in Adrien anyway, although Adrien is desperately in love with him. Yet Blanc never turns Adrien's love into something needy and pathetic; he shows Manu around Paris, he confides in him, he glows in his company, they grow close as friends.

Manu lives with his sister, Julie (Julie Depardieu), an aspiring opera singer who has no interest in much of anything beyond her work. We also meet Adrien's friend Sarah (Emmanuelle Beart), a wealthy author of children's books, and her husband, Mehdi (Sami Bouajila), who is a policeman and head of a vice squad that targets prostitution. They've just had a baby; Sarah learns through the experience that, despite her books, she does not like children. Her husband despairs when she neglects the child, does what he can to fill in, and sometimes parks the child with his parents.

Now all the pieces are in place for a momentous weekend when Sarah and Mehdi invite Adrien and Manu to her mother's house at the seaside. The two younger men go swimming in the sea, Manu finds himself in trouble, and he nearly drowns. The policeman saves his life, and in pulling him to shore finds to his surprise that he has an erection. The two men, one of whom has never thought of himself as gay, plunge into a physical relationship that becomes all-consuming.

That Mehdi is being unfaithful to Sarah (whether with a man or a woman) is of little concern to her; they have an "open" marriage, which in her case seems to translate into not caring what anyone else does as long as they leave her alone to write her books. One day Adrien sees telltale lesions on Manu's chest and diagnoses him as a victim of the mysterious new disease he has started to see in his practice. Now consider the ramifications of this infection for all five characters, and you have the driving structure of the story.

I will not reveal details. I would rather focus on the Michel Blanc performance. His Adrien is not a perfect man or a noble doctor, but he is a good man who has the courage to do good, although difficult, things. He has been deeply wounded by Manu's "abandoning" him for Mehdi, and is outraged that Mehdi cheated on his wife with, of all people, the man Mehdi knows the doctor loves. Adrien is even the godfather of the child. This outrage leads to a scuffle that is brief, confusing, violent, and without a "winner," revealing how hurt Adrien really is, and how near his emotional wounds are to the surface of his bland exterior.

Adrien becomes a leader in a gay doctors' crusade against AIDS, meanwhile privately taking on Manu's treatment. Mehdi also doesn't shun his friend when he hears the news, although he is terrified that he has AIDS and cannot bring himself to tell his wife. All of this captures the dread and paranoia of the early AIDS years; none of the characters has the benefit of foresight, and even a kiss or a drink from the same water bottle appears as a possible danger.

Techine tells the story with comic intensity for the first hour, and then aching drama. The possibility of having a disease of this sort, especially when you are married, allegedly straight, and even an anti-gay enforcer for the cops, creates secrecy and shame, and can lead to much worse than simply facing the truth. And it is that pain of the double life that concerns Techine in his later scenes.

Johan Libereau, as Manu, does a completely convincing transformation from an effortless young charmer to a dying man; he wasn't meant to die young like this, he despairingly tells Adrien; in fights at school, he didn't even bruise. Beart is mysterious as a remote, cold woman who likes physical sex but not much else apart from her writing. The cop is deeper and more sensitive than the situation might suggest; when he does the laundry for Manu, it is uncommonly touching, especially when the film notices how staring at an automatic washer can become a form of meditation.

But it is, again, Blanc who fascinates. His face, so often used for comedy or parody, here reflects intelligence, concern, and quiet sadness. His love is real enough, but to no purpose. His attempts to replace Manu are depressing even to himself. *The Witnesses* doesn't pay off with a great, operatic pinnacle, but it's better that way. Better to show people we care about facing facts they care desperately about, without the consolation of plot mechanics.

Wolf Creek no stars

NO MPAA RATING, 95 m., 2005

John Jarratt (Mick Taylor), Nathan Phillips (Ben Mitchell), Cassandra Magrath (Liz Hunter), Kestie Morassi (Kristy Earl). Directed by Greg McLean and produced by McLean and David Lightfoot. Screenplay by McLean.

I had a hard time watching *Wolf Creek.* It is a film with one clear purpose: to establish the commercial credentials of its director by showing his skill at depicting the brutal tracking, torture, and mutilation of screaming young women. When the killer severs the spine of one of his victims and calls her "a head on a stick," I wanted to walk out of the theater and keep on walking.

It has an 82 percent "fresh" reading over at the Tomatometer. "Bound to give even the most seasoned thrill seeker nightmares" *(Hollywood Reporter).* "Will have Wes Craven bowing his head in shame" (Clint Morris). "Must be giving Australia's outback tourism industry a bad case of heartburn" (Laura Clifford). "A vicious torrent of bloodletting. What more can we want?" (Harvey Karten). One critic who didn't like it was Matthew Leyland of the BBC: "The film's preference for female suffering gives it a misogynist undertow that's even more unsettling than the gore."

A misogynist is someone who hates women. I'm explaining that because most people who hate women don't know the word. I went to the Rotten Tomatoes roundup of critics not for tips for my own review, but hoping that someone somewhere simply said, "Made me want to vomit and cry at the same time."

I like horror films. Horror movies, even extreme ones, function primarily by scaring us or intriguing us. Consider *Three . . . Extremes* recently. *Wolf Creek* is more like the guy at the carnival sideshow who bites off chicken heads. No fun for us, no fun for the guy, no fun for the chicken. In the case of this film, it's fun for the guy.

I know, I know, my job as a critic is to praise the director for showing low-budget filmmaking skills and creating a tense atmosphere and evoking emptiness and menace in the outback, blah, blah. But in telling a story like this, the better he is, the worse the experience. Perhaps his job as a director is to make a movie I can sit through without dismay. To laugh through the movie, as midnight audiences are sometimes invited to do, is to suggest you are dehumanized, unevolved, or a slackwit. To read blasé speculation about the movie's effect on tourism makes me want to scream like Jerry Lewis: "Wake up, lady!"

There is a line, and this movie crosses it. I don't know where the line is, but it's way north of *Wolf Creek.* There is a role for violence in film, but what the hell is the purpose of this sadistic celebration of pain and cruelty? The theaters are crowded right now with wonderful, thrilling, funny, warmhearted, dramatic, artistic, inspiring, entertaining movies. If anyone you know says this is the one they want to see, my advice is: Don't know that person no more.

The Woodsman ★ ★ ★ ½

R, 87 m., 2005

Kevin Bacon (Walter), Kyra Sedgwick (Vickie), Mos Def (Sergeant Lucas), Benjamin Bratt (Carlos), David Alan Grier (Bob), Eve (Mary-Kay), Kevin Rice (Candy), Michael Shannon (Rosen), Hannah Pilkes (Robin). Directed by Nicole Kassell and produced by Lee Daniels. Screenplay by Steven Fechter and Kassell.

For the first several scenes of *The Woodsman,* we know that Walter has recently been released from prison, but we don't know the nature of his crime. Seeing the film at Cannes, I walked in without advance knowledge and was grateful that I had an opportunity to see Kevin Bacon establish the character before that information was supplied. His crime has now been clearly named in virtually everything written about the film, and possibly changes the way it affects a viewer.

Walter is a pedophile. The film doesn't make him a case study or an object for our sympathy, but carefully and honestly observes his attempt to reenter society after twelve years behind bars. Maybe he will make it and maybe he will not. He has a deep compulsion that is probably innate, and a belief that his behavior is wrong. That belief will not necessarily keep him from repeating it. Most of us have sexual desires within the areas accepted by society, and so never reflect that we did not choose them, but simply grew up and found that they were there.

Bacon is a strong and subtle actor, something that is often said but insufficiently appreciated. Here he employs all of his art. He seems to have no theory about Walter and no emotional tilt toward his problems, and that is correct, because we do not act out of theories about ourselves, but out of our hopes and desires. Bacon plays the character day by day, hour by hour, detail by detail, simply showing us this man trying to deal with his daily life. Larger conclusions are left to the audience.

He gets an apartment across from a grade school playground. He did not choose the location; he found a landlord who would rent to an ex-con. He gets a job in a lumberyard. No one there knows about his crime, but a coworker named Mary-Kay (Eve) doesn't like him and senses something is wrong. Lucas, his parole officer (Mos Def), visits regularly and is hostile, convinced it is only a matter of time until Walter lapses.

There is a woman at work named Vickie (Kyra Sedgwick), who is tough-talking but has an instinctive sympathy for the newcomer. She's a forklift operator, a realist. They start to date. We know, but she doesn't, that this may be the first normal sexual relationship Walter has had. She is not only his girlfriend but, in a way, an unknowing sex therapist. He eventually feels he has to tell her about his past. How she deals with this, how she goes through a series of emotions, is handled in a way I felt was convincing.

Mary-Kay finds out the truth about Walter and posts a Web site at work. His privacy is gone. There are other developments. Watching the playground through his window, for example, he becomes aware of a pedophile who is obviously hoping to find prey there.

The film has a crucial scene involving Walter and a young girl named Robin (Hannah Pilkes). Without suggesting how the scene develops, I will say that it is so observant, so truthful, that in a sense the whole film revolves around it. There is nothing sensational in this film, nothing exploitative, nothing used for "entertainment value" unless we believe, as I do, that the close observation of the lives of other people can be—well, since entertaining is the wrong word, then helpful. It is easy to present a pedophile as a monster, less easy to suggest the emotional devastation that led into, and leads out of, his behavior. The real question in *The Woodsman* is whether Walter will be able to break the chain of transmission.

The movie is the first film by Nicole Kassell, a recent graduate of the NYU film school, who wrote the screenplay with Steven Fechter, based on his play. It is a remarkably confident work. It knows who Walter is, and to an extent why he is that way, and it knows that the film's real drama exists inside his mind and conscience. This is not a morality play but a study of character—of Walter's character, and of those who instinctively detest him, and of a few, including Vickie and his brother-in-law Carlos (Benjamin Bratt), who are willing to withhold judgment long enough to see if he can find redemption.

The reason we cannot accept pedophilia as we accept many other sexual practices is that it requires an innocent partner whose life could be irreparably harmed. We do not have the right to do that. If there is no other way to achieve sexual satisfaction, that is a misfortune, but not an excuse. It is not the pedophile who is evil, but the pedophilia. That is true of all sins and crimes and those tempted to perform them: It is not that we are capable of transgression that condemns us, but that we are willing.

The Woodsman understands this at the very heart of its being, and that is why it succeeds as more than just the story of this character. It has relevance for members of the audience who would never in any way be even remotely capable of Walter's crime. We are quick to forgive our own trespasses, slower to forgive those of others. The challenge of a moral life is to do nothing that needs forgiveness. In that sense, we're all out on parole.

Wordplay ★ ★ ★

PG, 90 m., 2006

Featuring Will Shortz, Bill Clinton, Jon Stewart, Ken Burns, Mike Mussina, Bob Dole, and the Indigo Girls. A documentary directed by Patrick Creadon and produced by Christine O'Malley.

There are certain things in life you instinctively hold at arm's length, or they will move in with you and put their feet on the furniture. I've spent enough time working crossword puzzles to know I could become addicted. In the documentary *Wordplay,* we observe that to be a crossword champion you have to be incredibly intelligent, be capable of intuitive lateral thinking, know everything, and focus your knowledge into a narrow and ultimately meaningless pursuit. Yes, that makes you an obsessive eccentric, but they're really the only interesting people left, don't you sometimes think?

The movie centers around the twenty-eighth annual American Crossword Puzzle Tournament, hosted every year in Stamford, Connecticut, by Will Shortz, the editor of the *New York Times* crossword puzzles. It also visits fans of the *Times* puzzles (which run in countless other papers). These include Bill Clinton, Bob Dole, Jon Stewart, Ken Burns, Yankee pitcher Mike Mussina, and the Indigo Girls, although they missed my friend Dusty Cohl, who descends into a deep mental well once a day and does not emerge until the puzzle has been completed (I think "filled in" is not the approved terminology).

The film is made with a lot of style and visual ingenuity. Patrick Creadon, the director, uses graphics to show us crossword grids with the problem areas highlighted, and then we see the letters being written in. In one especially ingenious montage, he has all of his celebrities working on the same puzzle in interlocking shots. During the final championship round, with three contenders working on giant crosswords on a stage, he makes their progress easy to follow; I can imagine another film in which it would have been incomprehensible.

You have to be very well-informed to be a crossword puzzle champion. Scrabble and spelling bees require knowledge of a lot of words, but crosswords require unlimited facts, encyclopedic knowledge, and an ability to figure out the author's unstated assumptions about the nature of the clues. The puzzles can be tricky; both Dole and Clinton remember that on the day after their presidential campaign, one clue asked for the name of the winner. Diabolically, the correct seven-letter word could be either CLINTON or BOBDOLE.

All of these people think Merl Reagle is about the best crossword author now active. Mike Mussina, the pitcher, says solving a Reagle puzzle "is like pitching to Barry Bonds." Jon Stewart laments that the *Times* has banished certain words, including those involving bodily functions: "Words like 'urine' and 'enema,'" he says, "are terrific because they pack a lot of vowels in five letters." We meet some of the stars in the crossword world, including a former champ, Trip Payne, and twenty-year-old Tyler Hinman, who is the kid to watch. We also absorb the sense of a family reunion at the crossword tournament; the annual talent show is so democratic it includes baton twirling.

Will Shortz has been the god of this world since he founded the tournament, shortly after taking over as editor of the *Times* puzzles. How do you prepare for such a career? He went to Indiana University, which permits students to design their own majors, and got a degree in "enigmatology." He created the rules for the annual tournament.

The final championship round is incredibly intense. Not only do the finalists stand onstage in front of big boards everyone can see, but they wear headphones that pump music at them, so they can't hear clues or comments from the audience. There is a finalist this time who rips off his headphones, throws them to the ground, and uses a banished word involving a bodily function, and believe me, he has his reasons.

The World ★ ★ ★

NO MPAA RATING, 139 m., 2005

Zhao Tao (Tao), Chen Taishen (Taisheng), Jing Jue (Wei), Jiang Zhongwei (Niu), Huang Yiqun (Qun), Wang Hongwei (Sanlai), Liang Jingdong (Liang), Ji Shuai (Erxiao), Xiang Wan (Youyou), Alla Chtcherbakova (Anna). Directed by Jia Zhangke and produced by Yoshida Takio, Ichiyama Shozo, and Ren Zhonglun. Screenplay by Zhangke.

There is something about a one-ring circus or a run-down theme park that appeals to me. There is a poignancy in the shabbiness of their glory. Once on the Lido in Venice, out of season, I was one of nine people in the audience as an old lady in spangles rode around the ring on a discouraged pony. I ate sugar-coated peanuts and wept inside, perhaps from joy.

The World takes place almost entirely within a theme park in Beijing. "America has lost her Twin Towers," a guide observes, "but we still have ours." Yes, and the Eiffel Tower, Piazza San Marco, St. Peter's Square, the Pyramids, the Taj Mahal, the Leaning Tower of Pisa, and Big Ben. All of these landmarks are about the height of the McDonald's arches; one is reminded of the miniature Stonehenge, descending from above in *This Is Spinal Tap.*

How do you visit these miniature tourist attractions? There is an exhausted two-car monorail that creeps along its elevated track. Or you can board a jet airplane that never leaves the ground, which lends a certain jollity to the instructions about how to use your seat belt and the oxygen masks.

An American documentarian like Errol Morris would visit this world and find easy humor in its stunted grandiosity. But *The World* has been made in China by Jia Zhangke, a director who has been in much trouble with the authorities—not because he embraces the West, but because he mocks modern China for trying to become western in such haste. He doesn't yearn for the days of Chairman Mao, but he doesn't find the emerging China much of an improvement; the nation seems trapped between two sterilities.

His plot keeps most of the tourists at a distance. He is concerned with the people who work in this park, changing their costumes to become now an Italian dancer, now a camel driver. They live in shabby rooms hidden away behind the gaudy attractions and dream of someday visiting the countries whose citizens they impersonate. The dressmaker Qun (Huang Yiqun) is married to a husband she has not seen for years; he was part of a boatload of illegal immigrants to Europe, one of only six to survive. Now he is in Paris, and she hopes for a passport. But passports seem to lead to The World, not away.

Two Russian dancers arrive, and their passports are confiscated by a man who assures them "they will be safer with me."

Later we see Anna (Alla Chtcherbakova) in a club, where she appears to have become a prostitute, probably against her will. Meanwhile, Qun has a sort of affair with Taisheng (Chen Taishen), a security guard. Is she cheating on her husband in Paris, or does he even remember her? Both Taisheng and the dancer Tao (Zhao Tao) come from the same small town and remember it with nostalgia mixed with hopelessness; if The World offers them dubious futures, their childhoods seemed to offer none.

There is a sense that someone is getting rich somewhere in China, but not the owners and operators of The World. There is an irony that foreign tourists are visiting a theme park where poor Chinese wander dubiously among miniatures of a world they will never be able to visit. On New Year's Eve, the park originates a telecast that will be seen "by 1 billion viewers worldwide"—the same mythical billion who also don't really watch the Oscars.

The movie is long and slow. Either you will fall into its rhythm, or you will grow restless. At first I felt like someone who had spent a humid afternoon at The World and wanted to know, "Can I go home now?" Then I became invested in the backstage story, which emerges slowly and in uncertain pieces. There is integrity in a movie that refuses to pump up melodrama where none belongs. This is not a movie about an amusement park threatened by a bomb, or populated by colorful characters, or made into the object of satire. It is a movie about people doing boring and badly paid work day after day while being required to look happy.

In China, the grandparents of these characters no doubt worked in rice fields or garment sweatshops, or as street vendors. Now the young generation wears uniforms and costumes and occupies a replica of the modern world. Zhangke seems to think they are even unhappier than their ancestors were; is hard labor better than pointless labor? Consider the romance between Qun and Taisheng. Where will it lead? What plans can they make? And is China unique in offering this kind of employment as a dead end? Ask a clerk at Wal-Mart.

After the screening, I rode down on the elevator with the great film critic Jonathan Rosenberg. "I've seen it five times," he said. "It's one of my favorite films. I still don't understand the ending." Not only was I afraid to ask him what he didn't understand about the ending, but I also was afraid to ask him what he thought the ending was. In a sense, *The World* is about a story that never really begins.

The World's Fastest Indian ★ ★ ★

PG-13, 127 m., 2006

Anthony Hopkins (Burt Munro), Jessica Cauffiel (Wendy), Saginaw Grant (Jake), Diane Ladd (Ada), Christopher Lawford (Jim Moffet), Aaron Murphy (Sam), Paul Rodriguez (Fernando), Annie Whittle (Fran), Chris Williams (Tina). Directed by Roger Donaldson and produced by Donaldson and Gary Hannam. Screenplay by Donaldson.

The World's Fastest Indian is a movie about an old coot and his motorcycle, yes, but it is also about a kind of heroism that has gone out of style. Burt Munro is a codger in his sixties who lives in Invercargill, New Zealand, takes nitro pills for his heart condition, and has spent years tinkering with a 1920 Indian motorcycle. His neighbors wish he would take a break once in a while to mow the grass.

By 1967, Burt thinks the Indian may be about ready to travel to the Bonneville Salt Flats in Utah and take part in the annual Speed Week. This project involves fund-raising in Invercargill, and a long journey that takes him overland in America, where he meets, among others, an accommodating widow who takes him to visit her husband's grave. In Bonneville, where millionaire drivers are sponsored by big corporations, no one has ever seen anyone like Burt or anything like his ancient machine.

He should have registered weeks ago, but the officials lack the heart to turn him away. They are amazed when they inspect his machine. No braking chute? No brakes? "Where's your fire suit?" Can that be a cork on his gas tank? There is no tread on his tires. Is that mechanical part a—kitchen hinge? Why do they allow this man to risk his life in defiance of every safety standard at Bonneville? I think it is because Burt loves his motorcycle and cannot believe she would harm him; the steadfastness of his trust seduces them. When Burt discusses his motorcycle, which he rhymes with Popsicle, he gets into theories he must have pondered long into the night in his garage in New Zealand: "The center of pressure is behind the center of gravity," he explains, as if that explained anything. Or maybe it does. With Burt you can never be sure.

This is one of Anthony Hopkins's most endearing, least showy performances. The man who created Hannibal Lecter and Richard Nixon is concerned here with the precise behavior of a quiet, introverted man who is simultaneously obsessed and a little muddled. It's as if his fellow racing drivers have been visited by a traveler from the dawn of their sport, when guys tinkered with their machines in the toolshed and roared up and down country roads. Burt Munro is a man for whom the world seems brand new: He is amazed to enter a restaurant and see, for the first time in his life, a menu with photographs. Bonneville involves not racing but time trials. Burt has customized his Indian into a low, streamlined machine that he rides while flat on his stomach. He has a pair of goggles and a battered helmet that looks like Lindy once wore it, and he roars off into the desert sun like a crazy kid.

Burt Munro was a real man, and the film is based on fact. Roger Donaldson, the movie's writer and director, grew up in New Zealand, where Munro was a folk hero. Donaldson wrote the first draft of this script in 1979, after a 1971 documentary, and then life took him to Hollywood and to big-budget thrillers such as *No Way Out*, and now at last he has returned to tell the story of a hero of his youth.

It is also the story of certain New Zealand characteristics, among which is self-effacing modesty. Burt Munro would think it unseemly to call attention to himself, although he is happy for his Indian to get attention. (Before one race, he pops a nitro pill into the gas tank and as he swallows the second, he explains, "One for myself and one for the old girl.") In an era of showboat sports superstars, how strange to see old Burt challenge one of the most durable records in racing and then actually be embarrassed by the attention.

Read no further if you do not want to know how Burt does at Bonneville, although perhaps you have already guessed that *The World's Fastest Indian* is not about the second-fastest Indian. Yes, in 1967 Burt coaxed the Indian to 201.85 mph, even as a muffler was burning the flesh on his leg. That set a record in the category of "streamlined motorcycles under 1,000 cc." It is a record, the film assures us, that stands to this day. Burt returned nine times to Bonneville, becoming a hero, although deflecting attention with his diffidence, his shyness, his way of talking about the Indian instead of about himself. We are reminded that when Lindbergh flew the *Spirit of St. Louis* across the Atlantic, he titled his autobiography *We*—so that it included his airplane. That's how Burt feels about the old girl.

Wristcutters: A Love Story ★ ★ ½

R, 92 m., 2007

Patrick Fugit (Zia), Shea Whigham (Eugene), Shannyn Sossamon (Mikal), Tom Waits (Kneller), Will Arnett (Messiah), Leslie Bibb (Desiree). Directed by Goran Dukic and produced by Tatiana Kelly, Adam Sherman, Chris Coen, and Mikal P. Lazarev. Screenplay by Dukic, based on the short story "Kneller's Happy Campers" by Etgar Keret.

Imagine that after you kill yourself you don't go to heaven or hell but to an industrial wasteland where nothing works right, there are no good jobs, the fast food is generic, and everybody else who lives there committed suicide, too. Oh, and it doesn't look like anyone has sex, either, perhaps for theological reasons: Could a child be born in the land of the dead? How would you like to have a dad with a hole in his head? Think of Parents' Day.

Wristcutters: A Love Story stars Patrick Fugit as Zia, who has evolved from *Almost Famous* to almost dead. He has been forsaken by his girlfriend, Desiree (Leslie Bibb), and slashed his wrists. That'll show her. Apparently fate has designed a macabre punishment for those who commit the sin of suicide: You don't die, but linger forever in a life like the one you had before, but worse, and surrounded by suicidal people.

And what kind of a name is Zia, anyway? A zia is a brachiopod, and Wiki reports that "99 percent of [this] lampshell species are both fossils and extinct." Read that again. *Both* fossils *and* extinct. Sounds like your neighbors in Wristcutterland. Zia makes a friend named Eugene (Shea Whigham), who, as you have probably guessed from his name, was a Russian rock singer. Pissed off at the audience one night, he electrocuted himself onstage. That showed them.

Zia hears from a recent arrival from the Other Side that Desiree killed herself, too. Assuming she must be on This Side somewhere, he convinces Eugene to drive around looking for her, which begins them on a journey like the ones people are always making in Dead Teenager Movies, the ones with gas stations run by Toothless Doom-Mongers. They acquire a cute hitchhiker named Mikal (Shannyn Sossamon), who is looking for someone to complain to because she got a raw deal. She didn't kill herself, but only accidentally overdosed, so I guess at least she should get free laundry.

Along the road to nowhere, they come across a sort of outcast commune (how do you drop out of a society of suicides?). It is run by just the man for the job, Tom Waits, although my vote would have gone to Keith Richards. And they find Desiree, but how much of the story do you need to know, anyway?

This idea of an afterlife for suicides is intriguing. They thought they were ending their misery, and it was just beginning. That'll show them. Zia gets a job at a place called Kamikaze Pizza, which only scratches the surface of the possible jokes. I can't imagine why this movie is opening at Halloween time, although actually it's opening two days after Halloween, which is par for the course in Wristcutterland. But don't get the wrong idea: The movie isn't laugh-out-loud funny, under the circumstances, but it is bittersweet and sort of wistfully amusing; the actors enjoy lachrymosity, and we witness the birth of a new genre, the Post-Slasher Movie.

X

The X-Files: I Want to Believe ★ ★ ★ ½

PG-13, 104 m., 2008

David Duchovny (Fox Mulder), Gillian Anderson (Dana Scully), Amanda Peet (Dakota Whitney), Billy Connolly (Father Joe), Alvin "Xzibit" Joiner (Agent Drummy). Directed by Chris Carter and produced by Carter and Frank Spotnitz. Screenplay by Carter and Spotnitz.

The X-Files: I Want to Believe arrives billed as a "stand-alone" film that requires no familiarity with the famous television series. So it is, leaving us to piece together the plot on our own. And when I say "piece together," trust me, that's exactly what I mean.

In an early scene, a human arm turns up, missing its body, and other spare parts are later discovered. The arm is found in a virtuoso scene showing dozens of FBI agents lined up and marching across a field of frozen snow. They are led by a white-haired, entranced old man who suddenly drops to his knees and cries out that this is the place! And it is.

Now allow me to jump ahead and drag in the former agents Mulder and Scully. Mulder (David Duchovny) has left the FBI under a cloud because of his belief in the paranormal. Scully (Gillian Anderson) is a top-level surgeon, recruited to bring Mulder in from the cold, all his sins forgiven, to help on an urgent case. An agent is missing, and the white-haired man, we learn, is Father Joe (Billy Connolly), a convicted pedophile who is said to be a psychic.

Scully brings in Mulder but detests the old priest's crimes and thinks he is a fraud. Mulder, of course, wants to believe Father Joe could help on the case. But hold on one second. Even assuming that Father Joe planted the severed arm himself, you'll have to admit it's astonishing that he can lead agents to its exact resting place in a snow-covered terrain the size of several football fields with no landmarks. Even before he started weeping blood instead of tears, I believed him. Scully keeps right on insulting him right to his face. She wants *not* to believe.

Scully is emotionally involved in the case of a young boy who will certainly die if he doesn't have a risky experimental bone marrow treatment. This case, interesting in itself, is irrelevant to the rest of the plot except that it inspires a Google search that offers a fateful clue. Apart from that, what we're faced with is a series of victims, including Agent Dakota Whitney (Amanda Peet) and eventually Mulder himself, who are run off the road by a weirdo with a snowplow.

Who is doing this? And why does Father Joe keep getting psychic signals of barking dogs? And is the missing agent still alive, as he thinks she is? And won't anyone listen to Mulder, who eventually finds himself all alone in the middle of a blizzard, being run off the road, and then approaching a suspicious building complex after losing his cell phone? And how does he deal with a barking dog?

I make it sound a little silly. Well, it is a little silly, but it's also a skillful thriller, giving us just enough cutaways to a sinister laboratory to keep us fascinated. What happens in this laboratory you will have to find out for yourself, but the solution may be more complex than you think if you watch only casually. Hint: Pay close attention to the hands.

What I appreciated about *The X-Files: I Want to Believe* was that it involved actual questions of morality, just as *The Dark Knight* does. It's not simply about good and evil, but about choices. Come to think of it, Scully's dying child may be connected to the plot in another way, since it poses the question: Are any means justified to keep a dying person alive?

The movie lacks a single explosion. It has firearms, but nobody is shot. The special effects would have been possible in the era of *Frankenstein*. Lots of stunt people were used. I had the sensation of looking at real people in real spaces, not motion-capture in CGI spaces. There was a tangible quality to the film that made the suspense more effective because it involved the physical world.

Of course, it involves a psychic world, too. And the veteran Scottish actor Billy Connolly creates a quiet, understated performance as a man who hates himself for his sins, makes no great claims, does not understand his psychic powers, is only trying to help. He wants to believe he can be forgiven. As for Duchovny and

Anderson, these roles are their own. It's like they're in repertory. They still love each other and still believe they would never work as a couple. Or should I say they want to believe?

The movie is insidious. It involves evil on not one level but two. The evildoers, it must be said, are singularly inept; they receive bills for medical supplies under their own names, and surely there must be more efficient ways to abduct victims and purchase animal tranquilizers. But what they're up to is so creepy, and the snow-covered Virginia landscapes so haunting, and the wrongheadedness of Scully so frustrating, and the FBI bureaucracy so stupid, and Mulder so brave, that the movie works like thrillers used to work, before they were required to contain villains the size of buildings.

X-Men: The Last Stand ★ ★ ★

PG-13, 104 m., 2006

Patrick Stewart (Charles Xavier), Hugh Jackman (Logan/Wolverine), Ian McKellen (Eric Lensherr/ Magneto), Halle Berry (Ororo Munroe/Storm), Famke Janssen (Dr. Jean Grey/Phoenix), Anna Paquin (Marie/Rogue), Kelsey Grammer (Dr. Hank McCoy/Beast), Rebecca Romijn (Raven Darkholme/ Mystique), Ben Foster (Angel), Michael Murphy (Warren Worthington II), Vinnie Jones (Cain Marko/Juggernaut), Eric Dane (Multiple Man), Cameron Bright (Leech), Shohreh Aghdashloo (Dr. Kavita Rao). Directed by Brett Ratner and produced by Avi Arad, Lauren Shuler Donner, and Ralph Winter. Screenplay by Zak Penn and Simon Kinberg.

The government has a Department of Mutant Affairs in *X-Men: The Last Stand,* and it is headed by the mutant Dr. Hank McCoy (Kelsey Grammer), also known as Beast. The Mutant Community seems on its way into the mainstream, the goal long envisioned by Professor Charles Xavier (Patrick Stewart), head of the school where young X-Men learn to develop and control their powers. The school purrs along proudly with Wolverine (Hugh Jackman) as a role model, but then a kid named Leech surfaces, and all bets are off.

His body produces an antibody to mutation; inject it into X-Men, and their mutant powers disappear. They become regular folks with the same limited powers the rest of us use to scrape by. Leech is played by Cameron Bright, whom you may remember from *Birth,* the movie where he was a child whose body was occupied by the mind of Nicole Kidman's late husband. Bright has large dark eyes and ominously sober features that make you think he might grow up to become chairman of the Federal Reserve, or a serial killer.

He's invaluable to the billionaire Warren Worthington II (Michael Murphy), who lives in shame because his son Warren III (Ben Foster), also known as Angel, has a sixteen-foot wingspan. A flashback shows young Angel in a room full of blood and feathers, having tried to cut the wings from his back. This self-hate is nurtured by Worthington, whose shame about his son translates into hatred of mutants in general. He buys Alcatraz, imprisons Leech, begins to manufacture the antibody and campaigns for a "cure" for mutants.

But what if mutants don't want to be "cured"? What if they're happy the way they are, and cherish their differences? Xavier has always tried to encourage that kind of thinking, but Magneto (Ian McKellen), his archenemy in X-Man land, takes a more direct approach. He wages war against Worthington and all those who would foist a "cure" on the mutants. Although Magneto has always been the villain of the series, this time he makes a good point.

So strong is Leech's anti-mutant power that a mutant need only stand near him to lose his or her abilities; maybe the antibody works through pheromones. Meanwhile, Mutant Cure Clinics spring up around the country and are picketed by pro-mutant militants. Extremists arm themselves with guns that can fire the antibody and go out to shoot themselves some mutants. Beast, as the administration's cabinet minister in charge of mutant affairs, is caught in the middle.

There are so many parallels here with current political and social issues that to list them is to define the next presidential campaign. Just writing the previous paragraph, I thought of abortion, gun control, stem cell research, the "gay gene," and the Minutemen. "Curing" mutants is obviously a form of genetic engineering, and it stirs thoughts of "cures" for many other conditions that humans are born with, which could be loosely defined as anything that prevents you from being just like George or Georgette Clooney. The fact is, most people grow accustomed to the hand they've been dealt, and they rather resent the opportunity to become "normal." (Normal in this context is whatever makes you more like them and less like yourself.)

X-Men: The Last Stand raises all of these questions in embryo form but doesn't engage them in much detail, because it is often distracted by the need to be an action movie. Consider, for example, the lengths Magneto goes to in order to neutralize young Leech. The kid is being held on Alcatraz? Very well then, Magneto will stand on the Golden Gate Bridge and use his powers of industrial-strength levitation to rip loose a whole span of the bridge and rotate it so that it joins Alcatraz with the mainland, and his forces can march on Worthington's fortress. Countless innocent citizens die during this operation, falling from the bridge or otherwise terminating their commute. It seems to me that Magneto in this case is, well, a terrorist. So fanatic is his devotion to mutation that he will destroy the bridge in the service of his belief. Charles Xavier, on the other hand, is like (how does it go?) the vast majority of mutants who are peaceful and responsible citizens.

One of the distractions in all the X-Men movies is that the X-Men are always getting involved in local incidents that have little to do with the big picture. They demonstrate their powers during disagreements and courtships, neighborhood emergencies, psychological problems, or while showing off. After three movies you'd think they would have learned to coordinate their efforts so that Storm (Halle Berry), for example, is not suddenly needed to brew up a last-minute storm and save the neighborhood/city/state/world.

My guess is, there are just plain too many mutants, and their powers are so various and ill-matched that it's hard to keep them all on the same canvas. The addition of Beast, Angel, and Leech, not to mention Multiple Man, Juggernaut, and the revived Dr. Jean Grey (reborn as Dark Phoenix), causes a Mutant Jam, because there are too many X-Men with too many powers for a 104-minute movie. There are times when the director, Brett Ratner, seems to be scurrying from one plotline to another like that guy who had to keep all of his plates spinning on top of their poles. All the same, I enjoyed *X-Men: The Last Stand.* I liked the action, I liked the absurdity, I liked the incongruous use and misuse of mutant powers, and I especially liked the way it introduces all of those political issues and lets them fight it out with the special effects. Magneto would say this is a test of survival of the fittest. Xavier would hope they could learn to live together.

XXX: State of the Union ★ ★ ½

PG-13, 94 m., 2005

Ice Cube (Darius Stone), Willem Dafoe (George Deckert), Samuel L. Jackson (Agent Augustus Gibbons), Peter Strauss (President), Xzibit (Zeke), Robert Alonzo (Guard), Rich Bryant (Man in Trench Coat), Steve Carson (Prisoner). Directed by Lee Tamahori and produced by Gillian Libbert, Neal H. Moritz, and Arne Schmidt. Screenplay by Rich Wilkes and Simon Kinberg.

XXX: State of the Union is theater of the absurd, masquerading as an action thriller. Consider. The president of the United States is giving his State of the Union message, unaware that outside the U.S. Capitol building, storm troopers in black body armor, with little red pinpoints for eyes, are attempting to break in and assassinate him, as well as the vice president and everyone else in the chain of command, until they get to the secretary of defense, who has hired them for his attempted coup.

Opposing them—well, we have an ex-con named Darius (Ice Cube), who has recruited a gang of black street warriors from an upmarket chop shop and outfitted them with supercharged dragsters and heavy-duty weapons. These men have been put into play by a national security agent named Gibbons (Samuel L. Jackson), who is temporarily a prisoner of the secretary of defense (Willem Dafoe), although he will be freed in time to participate in a high-speed chase after the president (Peter Strauss) is spirited out of the Capitol on a secret bullet train.

In the climax of the movie, Darius (now known as XXX) will pursue the bullet train in his 220 mph car, shredding its tires so that it can run on the rails, and so that Darius can leap from his car onto the back of the train, enter it, grab the president, and attempt to swing him to safety via a helicopter before . . . well, before other stuff happens.

How strange to see this movie on the very day when a bullet train in Japan jumped the rails and crashed into a building. And in the very week when Amtrak appealed once again for rescue from its permanent fiscal crisis, caused in part by the lack of adequate rails for bullet trains. As the president's escape train was rocketing along, did he reflect that the tracks were only safe up to about 60 mph? Should have signed that transportation bill! Or was he too busy wondering why he was being rescued from his own secretary of defense by a black dude?

I showed Mario Van Peebles's *Baadasssss* at my Overlooked Film Festival. It is a movie about the making of a 1970 movie by his father, Melvin, about a black man who defies society and yet does not die at the end of the movie. It suggests that there may be corrupt police officers. This movie was very controversial thirty-five years ago. Now we have a movie in which the entire defense establishment is corrupt, and the president is rescued by a posse of baadasssses, who capture a tank and use it to blast their way into the Capitol, at which point I assume but cannot be sure that the media finally notice that all hell is breaking loose.

I am not sure because *XXX: State of the Union* has such a breakneck pace that it doesn't pause for the customary news updates in which the State of the Union Address is interrupted with the information that a war is raging on Capitol Hill. No, there's not even a crawl across the bottom of the screen: *Snows blanket New England . . . Armored vehicles attacking U.S. Capitol . . . Illinois 98, Michigan 91* . . . Just wondering: Are there any kind of security arrangements around the Capitol Building? You know, TV cameras or security guards who might notice when heavily armed bands of warriors dressed like Darth Vader are using rocket launchers?

The premise of the movie is apparently that within the nation's security apparatus there is a deeper, more lethal level of countersecurity agents whose job it is to defeat the regular security guys should they turn traitor. This force is always led by a superwarrior code-named XXX, and now that the original XXX (Vin Diesel) has been killed, Sam Jackson springs Ice Cube from prison to take over the assignment. (Diesel does not appear in the sequel after a salary dispute, which may explain why a Diesel lookalike plays a cameo role as a dead businessman.)

You are eager to know if any of the characters resemble current or former presidents or vice presidents or defense secretaries of the United States. No, they do not. They barely resemble fictional presidents, and so on. The president in the movie believes we must make our enemies our allies. The secretary of defense disagrees, which is why he wants to assassinate the president and half his administration. No political parties are named. There is a moment when the president says something in his speech and everybody on the Republican side of the chamber stands up to applaud, and I thought, a-ha, he's a Republican!—until I saw that all the Democrats stood up, too, and I realized they were all probably applauding praise for themselves.

Did I enjoy this movie? Only in a dumb, mindless way. It has whatever made the original *XXX* entertaining, but a little less of it. Does it make the slightest sense? Of course not. Its significance has nothing to do with current politics and politicians, the threat of terrorism, or the efficiency of bullet trains. It has everything to do with a seismic shift in popular culture.

Once all action heroes were white. Then they got a black chief of police, who had a big scene where he fired them. Then they got a black partner. Then they were black and had a white partner. Now they are the heroes and don't even need a white guy around, although there is one nerdy white guy in *XXX* who steps in when the plot requires the ineffectual delivery of a wimpy speech. So drastically have things changed that when Ice Cube offers to grab the president and jump off a train and grab a helicopter, all the president can do is look grateful.

Oh, and later, in his new State of the Union speech, our nation's leader quotes Tupac, although he doesn't know he does. Well, you can't expect him to know everything.

Y

Yella ★ ★ ★ ½

NO MPAA RATING, 89 m., 2008

Nina Hoss (Yella), Devid Striesow (Philipp), Hinnerk Schoenemann (Ben), Christian Redl (Yella's Father). Directed by Christian Petzold and produced by Florian Koerner von Gustorf. Screenplay by Simone Baer and Petzold.

Yella is a reserved young woman with unrevealed depths of intelligence, larceny, and passion. Their gradual revelation makes this more than an ordinary thriller, in great part because of the performance of Nina Hoss in the title role. Soon after we meet her, she's followed down the street by her former husband, Ben (Hinnerk Schoenemann), who will stalk her throughout the film. Partly to escape him, she leaves her small town in the former East Germany and goes to Hanover to take a job.

Her mistake is to accept a ride to the train station from him. He declares his love, accuses her of betrayal, moans about his business losses. "What time is your train?" he asks. When she says "8:22," he knows her destination. Shortly after, he drives his SUV off a bridge and into a river. Miraculously, they escape. Soaking wet, she runs to the train station and catches the 8:22. Yella has pluck.

That the man who hired her in Hanover has been fired and locked out of his office is the first of her discoveries about the world of business. That night in her hotel lobby, she meets Philipp (Devid Striesow), who sees her looking at his laptop and asks, "You like spreadsheets?" She does. She trained as an accountant.

He asks her to go along with him to a business meeting, carefully coaching her about when to gaze at the spreadsheet, when to gaze at the would-be client, and when to lean over and whisper in his ear—a lawyer's strategy he learned from Grisham movies. She does more than that. She actually reads the spreadsheet and boldly points out deceptions and false assets. She controls the meeting.

Philipp, who now respects her, brings her along to more meetings during which she figures out for herself what he eventually confesses to her: "I cheat." She doesn't mind. And then the film enters more deeply into one particular deal involving shaky patent rights and potential fortunes. Her career seems on an upswing, if it were not that Ben has followed her to Hanover.

All of this time, there are eerie episodes when her ears ring, she hears the harsh cry of a bird, and she seems able to intuitively understand things about people. These episodes remain unexplained until the last minute of the film. And just as well. Nina Hoss is an actress who rewards close observation; she is often seen in profile as a passenger in Philipp's car, her eyes observing him carefully, her expression neutral, then sometimes smiling at what he says, and sometimes only to herself. One of the pleasures of the film is trying to read her mind.

The writer-director, Christian Petzold, uses a spare, straightforward visual style for the most part, except for those cutaways to trees blowing in the wind whenever we heard the harsh bird cry. He trusts his story and characters. And he trusts us to follow the business deals and become engrossed in the intrigue. I did. I could see this being remade as one of those business thrillers with Michael Douglas looking cruel and expensive and finding his female equal. I'm not recommending that, just imagining it.

The male leads have an unsettling similarity in physical presence. You can't say she's attracted to the type, since she's fleeing from Ben and meets Philipp by accident. But they're both ruthless in their way, and Philipp is uncannily effective at imagining things about her that turn out to be pretty accurate. Maybe one thing he senses is that she would be a willing partner in crime. He sets a trap for her, to see if she will return an extra 25,000 euros he entrusted to her. That she would have kept the money angers him at first, but later he apparently decides that by being willing to steal it, she actually passed his test.

There are surprises along the way. One involves the key executive of a company they're dealing with, and is handled with a creepy beginning and a poignant ending. Another surprise in the film I will not even hint at, except to say that I could happily have done without it. It has all the value of the prize in a box of Cracker Jack: worthless, but working your way down to it is a lot of fun.

Yes ★ ★ ★ ★

R, 99 m., 2005

Joan Allen (She), Simon Abkarian (He), Sam Neill (Anthony), Shirley Henderson (Cleaner), Sheila Hancock (Aunt), Samantha Bond (Kate), Stephanie Leonidas (Grace), Gary Lewis (Billy). Directed by Sally Potter and produced by Christopher Sheppard and Andrew Fierberg. Screenplay by Potter.

Sally Potter's *Yes* is a movie unlike any other I have seen or heard. Some critics have treated it as ill-behaved, as if its originality is offensive. Potter's sin has been to make a movie that is artistically mannered and overtly political; how dare she write her dialogue in poetry, provide a dying communist aunt, and end the film in Cuba? And what to make of the housecleaner who sardonically comments on the human debris shed by her rich employers? The flakes of skin, the nail clippings, the wisps of dead hair, the invisible millions of parasites?

I celebrate these transgressions. *Yes* is alive and daring, not a rehearsal of safe material and styles. Potter easily could have made a well-mannered love story with passion and pain at appropriate intervals; or perhaps, for Potter, that would not have been so easy, since all of her films strain impatiently at the barriers of convention. She sees no point in making movies that have been made before. See, for example, *Orlando*, in which Tilda Swinton plays a character who lives for centuries and trades genders.

Yes is a movie about love, sex, class, and religion, involving an elegant Irish-American woman (Joan Allen) and a Lebanese waiter and kitchen worker (Simon Abkarian). They are known only as She and He. She is a scientist, married lovelessly to a rich British politician (Sam Neill). He was a surgeon in Beirut, until he saved a man's life only to see him immediately shot dead. Refusing to heal only those with the correct politics, he fled Lebanon and now uses his knives to chop parsley instead of repairing human hearts.

They meet at a formal dinner. They do it with their eyes. He smiles, she smiles. Neither turns away. An invitation has been offered and accepted. Their sex is eager and makes them laugh. They are not young; they are grateful because of long experience with what can go wrong.

There is a scene in the movie of delightful eroticism. It involves goings-on under the table in a restaurant. The camera regards not the details of this audacity, but the eyes and faces of the lovers. They take their time getting to where they are almost afraid to go. They look at each other, enjoying their secret, he looking for a reaction, she wary of revealing one. Her release is a barely subdued shudder of muffled ecstasy. This is what sex is about: two people knowing each other and using their knowledge. Compared to it, the sex scenes in most movies are calisthenics.

She was born in Belfast, raised in America, is Christian, probably Catholic. He is Arabic and Muslim. Both come from lands where people kill each other in the name of God. They are above all that. Or perhaps not. They have an economic imbalance: "You buy me with a credit card in a restaurant," he says in a moment of anger. And: "Even to pronounce my name is an impossibility." With his fellow kitchen workers he debates the way western women display their bodies, the way their husbands allow them to be looked at by other men. He is worldly, understands the West, and yet his inherited beliefs about women are deeply ingrained, and available when he needs a vocabulary to express his resentment.

She, on the other hand, displays her body with a languorous, healthy pride to him, and to us as we watch the movie. There is no explicit nudity. There is a scene where she goes swimming with her goddaughter, and we see that she is athletic, subtly muscled, with the neck and head of a goddess. To recline at the edge of the pool in casual physical perfection is as natural to She as it is disturbing to He. Their passion cools long enough for them to realize that they cannot live together successfully in either of their cultures.

Now about the dialogue. It is written in iambic pentameter, the rhythm scheme of Shakespeare. It is a style poised between poetry and speech; "to be or not to be, that is the question," and another question is, does that sound to you like poetry or prose? To me, it sounds like prose that has been given the elegance and discipline of formal structure. The characters never sound as if they're reciting poetry, and the rhymes, far from sounding forced, sometimes can hardly be heard at all. What the dialogue brings to the film is a certain unstated gravity; it elevates what is being said into a realm of grace and care.

There is her dying aunt, an unrepentant Marxist who provides us her testament in an interior monologue while she is in a coma. This monologue, and others in the film, are heard while the visuals employ subtle, transient freeze-frames. The aunt concedes that communism has failed, but "what came in its place? A world of greed. A life spent longing for things you don't need." The same point is made by She's housecleaner (Shirley Henderson) and other maids and lavatory attendants seen more briefly. They clean up after us. We move through life shedding a cloud of organic dust, while minute specks of life make their living by nibbling at us. These mites and viruses in their turn cast off their own debris, while elsewhere galaxies are dying; the universe lives by making a mess of itself.

Can She and He live together? Is there a way for their histories and cultures to coexist as comfortably as their genitals? The dying aunt makes She promise to visit Cuba. "I want my death to wake you up and clean you out," she says. You and I know that Cuba has not worked, and I think the aunt knows it, too. But at least in Cuba the dead roots of her hopes might someday rise up and bear fruit. And Cuba has the advantage of being equally alien to both of them. Neither is an outsider when both are.

Potter has said, "I think 'yes' is the most beautiful and necessary word in the English language"—a statement less banal the more you consider it. Doesn't it seem to you sometimes as if we are fighting our way through a thicket of no? When He and She first meet, their eyes say yes to sex. By the end of the film, they are preparing to say yes to the bold overthrow of their lives up until then, and yes to the beginning of something hopeful and unknown.

You Don't Mess with the Zohan ★ ★ ★

PG-13, 113 m., 2008

Adam Sandler (Zohan), John Turturro (The Phantom), Emmanuelle Chriqui (Dalia), Nick Swardson (Michael), Lainie Kazan (Gail), Rob Schneider (Salim), Michael Buffer (Walbridge). Directed by Dennis Dugan and produced by Adam Sandler and Jack Giarraputo. Screenplay by Sandler, Robert Smigel, and Judd Apatow.

The crowd I joined for *You Don't Mess with the Zohan* roared with laughter, and I understand why. Adam Sandler's new comedy is shameless in its eagerness to extract laughs from every possible breach of taste or decorum, and why am I even mentioning taste and decorum in this context? This is a mighty hymn of and to vulgarity, and either you enjoy it or you don't. I found myself enjoying it a surprising amount of the time, even though I was thoroughly ashamed of myself. There is a tiny part of me that still applauds the great minds who invented the whoopee cushion.

Sandler plays an ace agent for the Mossad, the Israeli secret police, who has no interest in counterterrorism and spends as much time as possible hanging out with babes on the beach. Known as The Zohan, he has remarkable physical skills—and equipment, as his bikini briefs and the crotches of all his costumes make abundantly clear. The laws of gravity do not limit him; he can travel through cities like Spider-Man, but without the web strings. He can simply jump for hundreds of feet.

The Zohan harbors one secret desire. He wants to be a hairdresser. His equivalent of pornography is an old Paul Mitchell catalog, and one day he simply cuts his ties with Israel and smuggles himself into the United States in a crate carrying two dogs whose hair he does en route. In America, he poses as an Australian with a very peculiar accent and, asked for his name, combines the names of his airborne flight buddies: Scrappy Coco-man. His auditions in various hair salons are unsuccessful (in a black salon, he attacks a dreads wig as if it were a hostile animal), until finally he is hired by the beautiful Dalia (Emmanuelle Chriqui), a Palestinian.

This plot is simply the skeleton for sight gags. Early on, we saw how much pain he could endure when he dropped a sharp-toothed fish into the crotch of his bikini swimming trunks. Now we see such sights as his sexual adventures with old ladies in the salon. In my notes, I scribbled in the dark: "An angel with the flexibility of a circus freak," adding, "he tells old lady," although maybe the old lady told him. At home with his new friend Michael (Nick Swardson), he effortlessly seduces the friend's mother (the zaftig Lainie Kazan).

His archenemy, the Palestinian agent known as The Phantom (John Turturro), is also in New York, and they make war. The Phantom's training regime is severe. He takes eggs, cracks them, and live chicks emerge. These he puts in a glass and chugs. He punches not only sides of beef but a living cow. Like The Zohan, he is filled with confidence in his own abilities, and with reason (he can cling to ceilings). Their confrontation will be a battle of the Middle Eastern superheroes.

Now creeps in a belated plot, involving a shady developer (Michael Buffer, of "Let's get ready to rumble!" fame). He wants to tear down a street of Arab and Israeli electronics stores and falafel and hummus shops to put up a mall. This would be a terrible thing, particularly given the prominent role that hummus plays in the film. Opposition to the mall unites the Israelis and Arabs, unconvincingly, on the way to peace and brotherhood at the end.

There are scenes here that make you wince. One involves a savage game of hacky-sack using not a hacky-sack bag but a living cat. Only the consolation that it's done with special effects allows us to endure the cries of the cat. Mariah Carey appears, starts to sing "The Star-Spangled Banner," and somehow survives a cameo with the mall builder. (Maybe his contract says Buffer appears in all movies involving the national anthem.) And something must be said about The Zohan's speech, which in addition to the broad comic accent involves the word "no" in a series that can run from two ("no-no!") to his usual five ("no-no-no-no-no!") to the infinite.

Sandler works so hard at this, and so shamelessly, that he battered down my resistance. Like a Jerry Lewis out of control, he will do, and does, anything to get a laugh. No thinking adult should get within a mile of this film. I must not have been thinking. For my sins, I laughed. Sorry. I'll try to do better next time.

Yours, Mine & Ours ★ ½

PG, 90 m., 2005

Dennis Quaid (Frank Beardsley), Rene Russo (Helen North), Rip Torn (The Commandant), Linda Hunt (Mrs. Munion), Jerry O'Connell (Max), David Koechner (Darrell). Directed by Raja Gosnell and produced by Robert Simonds and Michael Nathanson. Screenplay by Ron Burch and David Kidd, based on the 1968 screenplay by Melville Shavelson and Mort Lachman and the book by Helen Eileen Beardsley.

Yours, Mine & Ours has one thing to be thankful for: Frank and Helen realize immediately that they're still in love, all these years after they were the prom king and queen in high school. They see each other, they dance, they talk while dancing, they kiss while talking, and in the next scene they're engaged to be married. That saves us the Idiot Plot device in which they're destined for each other but are kept apart by a series of misunderstandings. In this version, they're brought together by a series of misunderstandings, mostly on the part of the filmmakers, who thought they could remake the 1968 Henry Fonda/Lucille Ball film without its sweetness and charm.

The story: He is a Coast Guard admiral with eight children. She is a fashion designer with ten children. They were in love in high school and darn!—they shoulda gotten married then, if for no other reason than that they'd probably not have eighteen kids, although you never know, and some of hers are adopted. With a little willpower they could be merely starring in a sequel to the remake of *Cheaper by the Dozen.* Too late: *Cheaper by the Dozen 2* opened December 21.

Frank likes everything shipshape. Helen is comfortable with a certain messiness. His kids line up for roll call and mess duty. Her kids are free spirits with a touch of hippie. Her family has a pig for a pet. I think his family has two dogs. That's how many I counted, about forty-five minutes into the movie, although as nearly as I can recall nobody ever claims them. Of course, I may have missed something. I wish I had missed more.

Dennis Quaid can be the most effortlessly charming of actors, but give him a break: It helps when he has effortlessly charming material. Here he has a formula to race through at breakneck speed, as if the director, Raja Gosnell, is checking off obligatory scenes and wants to get home in time for the lottery drawing. Rene Russo can play a convincing and attractive mother of ten, but that's not what this material needs. It needs a ditzy madcap, to contrast with the disciplined Coast Guard man. The earlier casting of Lucille Ball gives you an idea of what the role required, and Russo is simply too reasonable to provide it. If ever there was a role calling out "Goldie! Goldie!" this is the one.

No matter; we never get a sense of a real relationship between Frank and Helen. Their marriage seems like an extended Meet Cute. Gosnell and his writers, Ron Burch and David Kidd, crack the whip while making the characters jump through the obligatory hoops of the plot. We know, because we have seen one or two movies before this one, that it is necessary (a) for the two tribes of kids to become instant enemies, (b) for food fights to erupt on a moment's notice, (c) for there to be a Preliminary Crisis that threatens the marriage, and a Preliminary Solution, followed by (d) a Real Crisis and a Real Solution, and happily ever after, etc., with a farewell sight gag or two involving the pig. There is even a truce among the children, who oppose the marriage and have a plan: "We gotta stop fighting and get them to start."

There's not a moment in this story arc that is not predictable. Consider the outing on the sailboat. The *moment* Admiral Frank warns everybody that the boom can swing around and knock you overboard, I would have given 19-to-1 odds that the person knocked overboard would be—but you already know.

Now about those opening logos before the movie started. This one sets some kind of a record. In no particular order, I counted Columbia Pictures, Nickelodeon Movies, Paramount Pictures, and Metro-Goldwyn-Mayer. Why did no studio in Hollywood want to back a single one of last year's best picture nominees, and every studio in town wanted to get involved with this one? To be sure, Fox, Disney, and Warner Bros. got left out. Too slow off the mark?

Youth Without Youth ★ ½

R, 125 m., 2007

Tim Roth (Dominic Matei), Alexandra Maria Lara (Veronica/Laura), Bruno Ganz (Professor Stanciulescu), Andre Hennicke (Dr. Josef Rudolf), Marcel Iures (Professor Tucci), Alexandra Pirici (Woman in Room 6), Adrian Pintea (Pandit), Florin Piersic Jr. (Dr. Gavrila). Directed and produced by Francis Ford Coppola. Screenplay by Coppola, based on the novella by Mircea Eliade.

Youth Without Youth proves that Francis Ford Coppola can still make a movie, but not that he still knows how to choose his projects. The film is a sharp disappointment to those who have been waiting for ten years since the master's last film. The best that can be hoped is that, having made a film, Coppola has the taste again and will go on to make many more, nothing like this.

His story involves Dominic (Tim Roth), a seventy-year-old Romanian linguist who fears he will die alone and with his life's work unfinished, so he decides to kill himself. Before he can do that, he is struck by a bolt of lightning that should have turned him into a steaming puddle, but instead lands him in a hospital, burned to a crisp. Then a peculiar process begins. He starts to grow younger. His hair thickens and loses its gray. His rotten teeth are pushed out by new ones. His skin heals. His health returns.

It is the eve of World War II, and Dominic becomes of intense interest to the scientists of the Third Reich. Perhaps Hitler thinks his wounded soldiers can be made whole, or that he himself can turn back the march of time. Dominic, now hale and hearty, finds himself in Switzerland being seduced by a sexy German spy, when one day he sees, or thinks he sees, a woman on a mountain hike who resembles Laura, the lost love of his youth. This is Veronica (Alexandra Maria Lara), who is, wouldn't you know, struck by lightning and starts to grow older. In the process, she regresses backward in linguistic time and begins speaking Sanskrit, Babylonian, and perhaps even the Ur language from which all others descended.

This is exciting beyond all measure to Dominic, who has researched the origins of language, but it is also heartbreaking, because he seems to have had his lost love restored to him, only to be taken away by the implacable advance of age. Coppola found this story in a novella by the Romanian Mircea Eliade, for many years a professor of history of religions at the University of Chicago. It is possible to see how it might have been simplified and clarified into an entertainment along the lines of *Time After Time,* but Coppola seems to positively embrace the obscurity and impenetrability of the material.

There is such a thing as a complex film that rewards additional viewing and study, but *Youth Without Youth,* I am afraid, is no more than it seems: a confusing slog through metaphysical murkiness. That it is so handsomely photographed and mounted, and acted with conviction, only underlines the narrative confusion. We know from interviews that the story means a great deal to Coppola, at the same age as his protagonist. But his job is to make it mean a great deal to us. He is a great filmmaker, and I am sure this film is only a deep, shuddering breath before he makes another masterpiece.

Z

Zathura ★ ★ ★

PG, 113 m., 2005

Josh Hutcherson (Walter), Jonah Bobo (Danny), Tim Robbins (Dad), Dax Shepard (Astronaut), Kristen Stewart (Lisa), Frank Oz (Voice of Robot). Directed by Jon Favreau and produced by Michael De Luca, Scott Kroopf, and William Teitler. Screenplay by David Koepp and John Kamps, based on the book by Chris Van Allsburg.

Zathura's opening credits are close-ups of an old science-fiction board game, a game that should have existed in real life and specifically in my childhood but that was created for this movie. In these days of high-tech video games, it's remarkable that kids once got incredibly thrilled while pushing little metal racing cars around a cardboard track: The toy car was *yours*, and you invested it with importance and enhanced it with fantasy and pitied it because it was small, like you were.

Such games were weapons against the ennui of endless Saturdays. In *Zathura,* time hangs heavily on the hands of Walter and Danny Budwing, two brothers, one ten, one six, whose father has left them alone in the house for a few hours. Not quite alone: Their teenage sister, Lisa, is allegedly babysitting, from her vantage point under the covers of her bed with her iPod. Walter and Danny fight, as brothers do; Danny hides in the dumbwaiter (a device that will come as news to many of the kids watching this movie), and Walter lowers him into the basement, which for every six-year-old is a place filled with ominous noises and alarming unseen menaces.

There Danny (Jonah Bobo) discovers the Zathura board game and tries to get Walter (Josh Hutcherson) to play it with him. Walter would rather watch sports on TV. Danny plays by himself. The game is an ingenious metal contraption; you wind it up and push a button and your little car moves around a track and the game emits a card for you to read. Danny has Walter help him read it: METEOR SHOWER. TAKE EVASIVE ACTION. Just about then, the meteors start showering, sizzling through the living room ceiling and drilling through the floor, pulverizing coffee tables and floor lamps.

The game is a portal to an alternative universe of startling adventures; the movie wisely attempts no rational explanation. It resembles the game in *Jumanji* (1995), which ported its players into a world of fearsome beasts and harrowing dangers, and indeed is based on a book by the same author, Chris Van Allsburg, who also wrote the book that inspired *The Polar Express* (2004). The differences between the three movies are fundamental: *Polar Express* is a visionary fable, *Jumanji* is an uneasy thrill ride whose young heroes endure dangers too real to be funny, and *Zathura* is the only board game in history that lives up to the picture on its box.

A key to the film's charm comes during that meteor shower: The living room is pulverized, but Danny and Walter are untouched. They run around as if evading meteors, but actually the meteors evade them. Incredible things will happen while they play Zathura, but they will survive. That helps explain why they can still breathe when they open the front door and discover that their house is now in orbit around Saturn.

Zathura is the third film directed by Jon Favreau, an actor who, like Ron Howard, possibly was born to be a director. His first film was *Made* (2001), his second was *Elf* (2003), and his next will be inspired by Edgar Rice Burroughs's *John Carter of Mars,* a series I have always assumed was unfilmable, but on the basis of these three films, maybe not. Favreau brings a muscular solidity to his special effects; they look not like abstract digital perfection but as if hammered together from plywood, aluminum, and concept cars. By that I don't mean they look cheap; I mean they have the kind of earnest sincerity you can find on the covers of *Thrilling Wonder Stories.* Since you may not know of this publication, I urge you to Google *Thrilling Wonder Stories* magazine and click on "images." You'll find the same kind of breathless pulp absurdity that *Zathura* brings to a boil.

The brothers take turns. The game is inexhaustible. Another card reads, SHIPMATE ENTERS CRYONIC SLEEP CHAMBER. This means that their sister, Lisa, who likes to sleep past noon, has been frozen into immobility in the upstairs bathroom. Other cards produce (a) a fearsome but badly coordinated robot, whose designers spent more time on its evil glowing red eyes than on its memory chips, (b) giant alien lizards who are directly from the pulp sci-fi tradition of bug-eyed monsters, (c) assault fire from spaceships that look like junkyard porpoises, and (d) a descent into a black hole. As the two kids hang on for dear life and lizards get sucked into the black hole, I was reminded of the kind of hubris celebrated by such *Thrilling Wonder Stories* titles as "Two Against Neptune."

What makes this fun is that Danny and Walter obviously are not going to get hurt. Alien fire blasts away whole chunks of their house, but never the chunks they're in, and the giant lizards seem more preoccupied with overacting than with eating little boys. The young actors, Hutcherson and Bobo, bring an unaffected enthusiasm to their roles, fighting with each other like brothers even when threatened with broasting by a solar furnace. Their father, I should have mentioned, is played by Tim Robbins, although his role consists primarily of being absent. Kristen Stewart makes the most of the sister Lisa's noncryonic scenes. And then there is the character of the Astronaut (Dax Shepard), who materializes at a crucial point and helps shield the kids from intergalactic hazards. Lisa's crush on the Astronaut becomes cringy after all is known.

Zathura lacks the undercurrents of archetypal menace and genuine emotion that informed *The Polar Express*, a true classic that was rereleased in 2005. But it works gloriously as space opera. We're going through a period right now in which every video game is being turned into a movie, resulting in cheerless exercises such as *Doom*, which mindlessly consists of aliens popping up and getting creamed. *Zathura* is based on a different kind of game, in which the heroes are not simply shooting at targets but are actually surrounded by real events that they need to figure out. They are active heroes, not passive marksmen. Nobody even gets killed in *Zathura* . . . well, depending on what happens to the lizards on the other side of the black hole.

Zodiac ★ ★ ★ ★

R, 165 m., 2007

Jake Gyllenhaal (Robert Graysmith), Robert Downey Jr. (Paul Avery), Mark Ruffalo (Davd Toschi), Anthony Edwards (Bill Armstrong), Brian Cox (Melvin Belli), Elias Koteas (Jack Mulanax), Chloë Sevigny (Melanie). Directed by David Fincher and produced by Cean Chaffin, Brad Fischer, Mike Medavoy, Arnold Messer, and James Vanderbilt. Screenplay by Vanderbilt, based on the books by Robert Graysmith.

Zodiac is the *All the President's Men* of serial killer movies, with Woodward and Bernstein played by a cop and a cartoonist. It's not merely "based" on California's infamous Zodiac killings, but seems to exude the very stench and provocation of the case. The killer, who was never caught, generously supplied so many clues that Sherlock Holmes might have cracked the case in his sitting room. But only a newspaper cartoonist was stubborn enough, and tunneled away long enough, to piece together a convincing case against a man who was *perhaps* guilty.

The film is a police procedural crossed with a newspaper movie, but free of most of the clichés of either. Its most impressive accomplishment is to gather a bewildering labyrinth of facts and suspicions over a period of years and make the journey through this maze frightening and suspenseful. I could imagine becoming hopelessly mired in the details of the Zodiac investigation, but director David Fincher (*Se7en*) and his writer, James Vanderbilt, find their way with clarity through the murk. In a film with so many characters, the casting by Laray Mayfield is also crucial; like the only eyewitness in the case, we remember a face once we've seen it.

The film opens with a sudden, brutal, bloody killing, followed by others not too long after—five killings the police feel sure Zodiac committed, although others have been attributed to him. But this film will not be a bloodbath. The killer does his work in the earlier scenes of the film, and then, when he starts sending encrypted letters to newspapers, the police and reporters try to do theirs.

The two lead inspectors on the case are

David Toschi (Mark Ruffalo) and William Armstrong (Anthony Edwards). Toschi, famous at the time, tutored McQueen for *Bullitt* and was the role model for Eastwood's Dirty Harry. Ruffalo plays him not as a hotshot but as a dogged officer who does things by the book because he believes in the book. The Edwards character, his partner, is more personally worn down by the sheer vicious nature of the killer and his taunts.

At the *San Francisco Chronicle*, although we meet several staffers, the key players are ace reporter Paul Avery (Robert Downey Jr., bearded, chain-smoking, alcoholic) and editorial cartoonist Robert Graysmith (Jake Gyllenhaal). These characters are real, and indeed the film is based on Graysmith's books about the case.

I found the newspaper office intriguing in its accuracy. For one thing, it is usually fairly empty, and it was true on a morning paper in those days that the office began to heat up closer to deadline. Among the few early arrivals would have been the cartoonist, who was expected to work up a few ideas for presentation at the daily news meeting, and the office alcoholics, perhaps up all night or already starting their recovery drinking. Yes, reporters drank at their desks forty years ago, and smoked and smoked and smoked.

Graysmith is new on the staff when the first cipher arrives. He's like the curious new kid in school fascinated by the secrets of the big boys. He doodles with a copy of the cipher, and we think he'll solve it, but he doesn't. He strays off his beat by eavesdropping on cops and reporters, making friends with the boozy Avery, and even talking his way into police evidence rooms. Long after the investigation has cooled, his obsession remains, eventually driving his wife (Chloë Sevigny) to move herself and their children back in with her mom. Graysmith seems oblivious to the danger he may be drawing into his home, even after he appears on TV and starts hearing heavy breathing over the phone.

What makes *Zodiac* authentic is the way it avoids chases, shoot-outs, grandstanding, and false climaxes, and just follows the methodical progress of police work. Just as Woodward and Bernstein knocked on many doors and made many phone calls and met many very odd people, so do the cops and Graysmith walk down strange pathways in their investigation. Because Graysmith is unarmed and a civilian, we become genuinely worried about his naivete and risk taking, especially during a trip to a basement that is, in its way, one of the best scenes I've ever seen along those lines.

Fincher gives us times and days and dates at the bottom of the screen, which serve only to underline how the case seems to stretch out to infinity. There is even time-lapse photography showing the Transamerica building going up. Everything leads up to a heart-stopping moment when two men look, simply look, at one another. It is a more satisfying conclusion than Dirty Harry shooting Zodiac dead, say, in a football stadium.

David Fincher is not the first director you would associate with this material. In 1992, at thirty, he directed *Alien 3*, which was the least of the Alien movies, but even then had his eye (*Alien 3* is one of the best-looking bad movies I have ever seen). His credits include *Se7en* (1995), a superb film about another serial killer with a pattern to his crimes; *The Game* (1997), with Michael Douglas caught in an ego-smashing web; *Fight Club* (1999), beloved by most, not by me; the ingenious terror of Jodie Foster in *Panic Room* (2002); and now, five years between features, his most thoughtful, involving film.

He seems to be in reaction against the slice-and-dice style of modern crime movies; his composition and editing are more classical, and he doesn't use nine shots when one will do. (If this same material had been put through an Avid to chop the footage into five times as many shots, we would have been sending our own ciphers to the studio.) Fincher is an elegant stylist on top of everything else, and here he finds the right pace and style for a story about persistence in the face of evil. I am often fascinated by true crime books, partly because of the way they amass ominous details (the best I've read is *Blood and Money* by Tommy Thompson), and Fincher understands that true crime is not the same genre as crime action. That he makes every character a distinct individual is proof of that; consider the attention given to Graysmith's choice of mixed drink. ☞

The Best Films of 2006

November 23, 2007—Yes, I know it's a year late, but a funny thing happened to me on the way to compiling a list of the best films of 2006. I checked into the hospital in late June 2006 and didn't get out again until spring of 2007. For a long while, I just didn't feel like watching movies. Then something revolved within me, and I was engaged in life again.

I started writing reviews of the 2006 films, starting with *The Queen,* and screened the Oscar nominees to make my annual predictions. Then I began doubling back to pick up as many promising titles as I could. Am I missing some of the year's worthy entries? No doubt. But even in a good year I'm unable to see everything. And I'm still not finished with my 2006 discoveries. I'm still looking at more 2007 movies, too, and that list will run as usual in late December.

Nothing I am likely to see, however, is likely to change my conviction that the year's best film was *Pan's Labyrinth.*

These were the year's best films:

1. *Pan's Labyrinth*

Guillermo del Toro's *Pan's Labyrinth* tells opposite stories and does both of them full justice. On the one hand, there is an outpost of Franco's fascist army in the forests of Spain, still seeking its holdout enemies in 1944, after the end of the Spanish Civil War. On the other hand, there is the fantastical world of a young girl whose mother is married to the monstrous captain in charge of the unit. She is led into a labyrinth by a fairy and encounters the bizarre and disturbing world of a faun who tells her she is really a princess and must strive to accomplish three tasks to be reunited with her father.

It is universally assumed that this world exists only in the girl's fantasy, but I am not so sure. The film plays as well if it is a real but parallel world, in which she can correct such evils as fascism. The special effects are nightmarish and effective, including the faun and a giant toad, and it takes courage to go into that labyrinth—and to emerge again into a world of politics and cruelty. Del Toro doesn't compromise on the fantasy, or the reality.

2. *Bubble*

Steven Soderbergh's film delicately examines the everyday life of three Ohio factory workers. To cast his film, Soderbergh used actual blue-collar workers from the district; he structured their performances and the plot but remained open to their real lives, and we see the desperation of working poverty, in which you work double shifts, stare at the TV, and collapse. Martha (Debbie Doebereiner), who cares for her father, has enough money to own a car; Kyle (Dustin Ashley), who lives in a mobile home, depends on her for rides to a doll factory. Then Rose (Misty Dawn Wilkins) gets a job in the factory. She's younger and prettier than the fat Martha, but is Martha jealous? No, she doesn't want Kyle's love but his dependency on her. How this pays off is completely unforeseen but sort of inevitable, and illustrates the bleakness and poverty of imagination of their quietly desperate world.

3. *Children of Men*

Children of Men is Alfonso Cuaron's fantasy of the year 2027, when terrorism has rendered the world ungovernable, and no children have been born in eighteen years. When a newborn infant and its mother, Kee (Clare-Hope Ashitey), come into the circle of the hero (Clive Owen), he joins with a former lover (Julianne Moore) and her associate (Chiwetel Ejiofor) in an underground movement to help the young woman find refuge in a rumored haven off the coast of Britain. This involves a journey across the land and a stop at the home of a courageous aging hippie (Michael Caine) who tries to live somewhat outside the system. The view of the deteriorating society they travel through is humbling; is this where we are headed?

4. *The Departed*

The Departed is Martin Scorsese's story of loyalties and deceptions in the worlds of two kids who grow up as impostors: One becomes a gangster (Matt Damon) who goes undercover as a cop, and the other (Leonardo Di Caprio) becomes a cop who goes undercover as a gangster. Each one is assigned to find the other, and each knows things he must conceal; there is a chilling moment when one is given the wrong address and goes to the right one instead. The movie's cross-currents of plot and emotion are terrifying in their application of unforgiving logic. Scorsese, so good for so many years, finally won an Oscar for this film, as best director.

5. *The Lives of Others*

The Lives of Others is a film by Florian Henckel von Donnersmarck, about a member of the Stasi, the East German secret police during the Cold War, and how he spies on a playwright suspected of treason. As he shares the playwright's life through earphones day after day, his own life comes to seem more bleak and friendless than ever, and he makes a certain decision that the film doesn't underline, but simply regards with detached objectivity. The central performance by Ulrich Muehe is a masterpiece of observation about how a man can shut down or open up in reaction to the inhuman requirements of the state.

6. *United 93*

United 93, written and directed by Paul Greengrass, could have been a routine thriller, even an exploitation film, but it is a masterful reconstruction of what happened onboard the 9/11 plane that never did reach its intended target—the one that was brought down in a Pennsylvania field by passengers determined not to cave in to hijackers. Greengrass underlines the impact by making his film entirely in the present tense; at no time do his passengers have any more knowledge than the real ones must have had at the time. That's effective in placing us into the moment.

7. *Flags of Our Fathers* and *Letters from Iwo Jima*

Flags of Our Fathers and *Letters from Iwo Jima* are two paired films by the hugely ambitious Clint Eastwood, who shows the most relentless battle of World War II from the American side, and then, with subtitles, from the Japanese side. Some 44,000 died in a few weeks on a small island in the Pacific, fighting with raw courage and, on the Japanese side, full knowledge that they would die. With masterful production planning, Eastwood is able to make the strategies of both sides clear, and we understand what is happening and how deadly it is, and how the famous photograph of the flag being raised over Iwo Jima does not represent what is assumed, or even show what it seems to show. There is a heartbreaking subplot about Ira Hayes, the Native American who was one of those who raised the flag.

8. *Perfume: The Story of a Murderer*

Perfume: The Story of a Murderer, directed by Tom Tykwer (*Run, Lola, Run*), is based on the portrait of deep evil in Patrick Suskind's mesmerizing novel. A strange little man is born with no body odor of his own (is he the spawn of the devil?) but a nose so sensitive that he lives on a different plane than other people. He grows obsessed with extracting the aromas of beautiful women and becomes a serial killer in the service of his craft. Since neither novel nor movie can impart scents, it would seem they have impossible tasks, but not at all; the film is transgressive in suggesting how much its hero's gift violates the rights and persons of those around him.

9. *Babel*

Alejandro Gonzalez Inarritu's cross-cutting film shows us characters in Morocco, the United States, Mexico, and Japan, all altered by the introduction of a rifle into their matrix. They speak different languages, yes, but more crucially they speak different images and contexts; what is meaningful in one world is inconsequential in another. The linkage is not just a narrative gimmick, but essential to the film's view of cultures in conflicts that are sometimes unconscious.

The inclusion of films in the "best ten" by Inarritu, Alfonso Cuaron, and Guillermo del Toro is emblematic of the stature of the current Mexican cinema; all three have emerged as among the best recent directors.

10. *Man Push Cart*

Man Push Cart, by Ramin Bahrani, is as strong or stronger than anything produced by Italian neorealism, and in the same spirit. The Iranian-American director follows the daily life of an immigrant from Pakistan as he operates a stainless steel coffee and bagel cart on the sidewalks of New York and lives a marginal economic existence. The title reduces his life to his basic element; he was once a rock star at home, but now he pushes a cart. Bahrani's gifts as a filmmaker were evident again at Toronto 2007, when he premiered *Chop Shop,* another unremitting portrait of life on the edge in New York City.

Golden Anniversary Award

The year 2007 was not precisely Robert Altman's fiftieth anniversary as a filmmaker, but *The James Dean Story,* his first feature, was released in 1957, and so the year will serve. This special recognition is given to the great director, who died on November 20, 2006, depriving the film world of one of its most fertile and inspiring geniuses. It goes in particular to his elegiac and bittersweet *A Prairie Home Companion,* which I am convinced is a farewell film of sorts, as the magician lays down his rough magic and a radio show goes off the air.

In terms of its content, it is musical, funny, moving, mysterious. In terms of its function, it is difficult not to see the Garrison Keillor character as standing in for Altman, as he observes that everything must eventually run its course. If this film is a farewell to his career, I wonder if his previous film, *The Company* (2003), was a tribute to his own working style. The largely improvised story of a year in the Joffrey Ballet of Chicago, it stars Malcolm McDowell as "Mr. A," obviously intended as Gerald Arpino, the Joffrey's cofounder and artistic director, but maybe there is another "Mr. A" in view, too, who uses the same directorial method of low-key suggestion, elusive ways of collaboration, a sense of community, an openness to innovation.

I was so ill when Altman died they didn't even tell me. When I finally heard the news, I immediately thought of this film. I watched it again and found myself crying. I miss him so much.

The Special Jury Prize

At many great festivals, including Cannes, this prize essentially means a large minority on the jury strongly feels this is the film that should have won. This year it is shared by ten films, alphabetically:

Akeelah and the Bee, the story of a young girl (Keke Palmer) who is a gifted speller and finds that opens doors to solving problems in her life; *Come Early Morning,* with one of Ashley Judd's best performances as a hard-drinking rural contractor whose life is spinning out of control; *Hard Candy,* starring Ellen (*Juno*) Page as a completely different and astonishingly transgressive young girl who gets revenge on a man; *L'enfant,* by the Dardenne brothers, about two young drifters who have a baby and the callow and heartless husband who decides to sell it; *Little Miss Sunshine,* with Abigail Breslin and a colorful family on a cross-country odyssey to a beauty pageant.

Also, *The Queen,* by Stephen Frears, with Helen Mirren's Oscar-winning performance as Queen Elizabeth II; *Three Burials of Melquiades Estrada,* directed by and starring Tommy Lee Jones as a ranch worker who wants revenge and a proper burial for his murdered friend; *Tristram Shandy, a Cock and Bull Story,* by Michael Winterbottom, about an attempt to film an elusive British classic only one of the filmmakers has read; *Tsotsi,* by Gavin Hood, starring Presley Chweneyagae as a South African township hoodlum, in last year's Oscar winner as best foreign language film; and Pedro Almodovar's *Volver,* with Penelope Cruz and Carmen Maura, about a mother's ghost who returns to tidy up things.

Best Documentaries

Alphabetically: *The Devil and Daniel Johnston,* about an elusive and troubled but legendary singer-songwriter; *49 Up,* the latest chapter of Michael Apted's epic documentary series, tracking the lives of the same British citizens every seven years; the Oscar-winning *An Inconvenient Truth,* containing Al Gore's warning on global meltdown; *Isn't This a Time,* about a final reunion of the legendary folk group the Weavers; *Real Dirt on Farmer John,* about an unconventional Illinois farmer who runs a self-sustaining organic farm; *Shut Up and Sing,* about the Dixie Chicks and their troubles after their lead singer was critical of George W. Bush; and *Unknown White Male,* the strange case of a man who may or may not have had amnesia.

The Tie for Eleventh Place

Every year we traditionally declare a ten-way tie for eleventh place. The distinguished films this year are Eric Byler's *Americanese,* about a tentative romance much entangled with the Asian heritage of the three people involved; Rian Johnson's *Brick,* transposing a hard-boiled detective style to a modern high school; Olivier Assayas's *Clean,* with Maggie Cheung as a drug-addicted fading rock star who wants her child back from her father-in-law (Nick Nolte); Cristi Puiu's *The Death of Mr. Lazarescu,* about an ambulance service in Romania doggedly determined to find a hospital for a dying man; and Bill Condon's *Dreamgirls,* the high-octane musical.

Also Ryan Fleck's *Half Nelson,* with Ryan Gosling as a high school teacher with a drug problem and a student who tries to help; James Marsh's *The King,* with Gael Garcia Bernal as a young man in search of his father; Marc Forster's *Stranger Than Fiction,* with Will Ferrell as a man who hears his own life being narrated in his head; Jason Reitman's *Thank You for Smoking,* a brilliant satire about Big Tobacco; and Michael Cuesta's *Twelve and Holding,* about three kids who take desperate measures to turn around their lives.

The Best Films of 2007

December 21, 2007—It was a time of wonders, an autumn of miracles, one of the best years in recent movie history. One great film after another opened, and movie lovers found there were two or three, sometimes more, must-see films opening on a weekend. I gave up rationing my four-star ratings and went with the flow. The best films of 2007:

1. *Juno*

How can I choose this warmhearted comedy about a pregnant teenager when the year was rich with serious drama? First, because of all the year's films I responded to it most strongly. I tried out other titles in the number-one position, but my heart told me I had to be honest: This was my true love, and I could not be unfaithful. It is so hard to make a great comedy at all, and harder still to make one that is intelligent, quick, charming, moving, and yes, very, very funny. Seeing *Juno* with an audience was to be reminded of unforgettable communal moviegoing experiences, when strangers are united in delight. It was light on its feet, involving the audience in love and care for its characters. The first-time screenplay by Diablo Cody is Oscar-worthy. So is Ellen Page's performance in the title role, which is like tightrope walking: There were so many ways for her to go wrong, and she never did.

2. *No Country for Old Men*

"A perfect movie," I wrote after the premiere at Toronto. And so it is. The Coen brothers supply not a wrong scene or even a wrong moment. A story bleak and merciless, played out by characters who are capable of almost anything except withstanding the relentless evil of its serial killer. Based on the Cormac McCarthy novel, it builds on his eye and ear to create a world in which ordinary assumptions go astray and logic is useless. With spare, wounded performances by Josh Brolin, Tommy Lee Jones, Woody Harrelson, and many others, and Javier Bardem as not a man so much as a force of destruction.

3. *Before the Devil Knows You're Dead*

It was a year for the great character actor Philip Seymour Hoffman, so different and so good in this film, *The Savages*, and *Charlie Wilson's War*. In *Devil*, he and Ethan Hawke play brothers, unalike except in their urgent need for cash, who plan a "victimless" holdup of their family's jewelry store. Everything goes wrong, they feel anguish and panic in the pits of their stomachs, and in the eyes of their father (Albert Finney), the hurt is almost unbearable. They lie and deceive first others and then themselves, and it all turns to ashes. Another masterpiece by Sidney Lumet, who is eighty-three and at the top of his form.

4. *Atonement*

The momentary misunderstanding of a child destroys all possibility of happiness in three lives. Saoirse Ronan plays a young adolescent in a wealthy English family, who sees her older sister (Keira Knightley) and the family groundskeeper (James McAvoy) in a confrontation she misunderstands, which later leads her to telling an unforgivable lie. Against the canvas of World War II, the love of the two older characters is prevented from realizing itself, in a stunning period picture that centers on a tracking shot at Dunkirk that is one of the most elaborate ever staged. Directed by Joe Wright and based on an Ian McEwan novel that saves a final ironic insight until the end.

5. *The Kite Runner*

The beloved best-seller by Khaled Hosseini about two boys in peaceful prewar Kabul, before the Russians, the Taliban, the Americans, and the anarchy destroyed Afghanistan. The boys and their parents are seen in tender detail, then revisited years later after devastation has overthrown their lives. Homayoun Ershadi, who plays the father, has such expressive eyes he makes many of the film's points without speaking. Director Marc Forster, filming in local languages in Afghanistan and the United

States, interlaces the fabric of these lives with a heartbreaking story that leads to a powerfully uplifting ending.

6. *Away from Her*

The Canadian actress Sarah Polley makes her directing debut with a heartbreaking story of the destruction of Alzheimer's. Julie Christie, in one of the year's best performances, plays a woman whose memories are inexorably slipping away. Gordon Pinsent plays her loving husband who cannot comprehend how he could so quickly come to mean so little to her. Based on a story by Alice Munro, the film sees through his eyes the disappearance of love, history, life itself, as he lives on in loneliness.

7. *Across the Universe*

Possibly the year's most divisive film; you loved it or hated it. Julie Taymor brings all of her gifts of visual invention to a story centering on a group of friends living in Greenwich Village and expressing their lives through the Beatles songbook. They encounter people not unlike those in famous Beatles songs or albums, and the music sheds light on their experiences—sometimes unexpectedly, as when "I Want to Hold Your Hand" tenderly expresses the deepest feelings of a lovelorn lesbian cheerleader. The movie captures the best of what the Beatles represented. I want to see it two or three more times, experiencing it like a favorite CD.

8. *La Vie En Rose*

A virtuoso performance by Marion Cotillard as the beloved "Little Sparrow," Edith Piaf, the legendary singer closest to the hearts of the French. Raised in a brothel and then the "property" of a gangster, she was only four feet eight inches tall but had a voice that filled the city. Cotillard portrays her rising from the gutters to international stardom and then dying of an overdose at forty-seven. The title refers to her most famous song, about life through rose-colored glasses. The film ends with "Non, je ne regrette rien (No, I regret nothing)." The period is vividly re-created by director Olivier Dahan. One of the greatest of musical biopics.

9. *The Great Debaters*

Denzel Washington's spellbinding film based on the true story set in 1935 about a debate team from Wiley College, an obscure black institution in Texas, that defeated Harvard for the national championship. Washington plays their coach who demands the highest standards, but the film is not another story about an underdog championship, but a searing reminder of the racist society the team lived in. On a night journey, Washington and his students happen upon a lynching; the horror and danger are overwhelming. With Nate Parker touching as the team researcher who becomes a last-minute substitute, Denzel Whitaker as a debater and future CORE founder James Farmer Jr., Jurnee Smollett as a debater who calls on her deepest feelings, and Forest Whitaker as a local preacher who becomes galvanized. It's a deep, emotional experience.

10. *Into the Wild*

Sean Penn's bleak but sympathetic drama is based on the real story of Christopher McCandless, an idealistic loner who trekked into the Alaskan wilderness and died there. The movie shows him meeting mentors along the way who are concerned about him, especially a rugged individualist (Hal Holbrook) and a spirited hippie (Catherine Keener). Emile Hirsch plays the role to within an inch of his life, somehow expressing without seeming to try how his tunnel vision leads him through his dreams to disaster. Could have been dreary, but Penn's screenplay and direction are compelling.

Special Jury Prize

John Carney's *Once:* At film festivals, the jury sometimes singles out a film for special qualities that especially impressed them. As a jury of one, my award this year goes to the charming, low-key, quietly appealing *Once,* starring Glen Hansard as a Dublin street musician and Marketa Irglova as a Czech immigrant who meet and slowly grow closer while, yes, making beautiful music together. Very little dialogue, but the music and their eyes and silences say it all, in a bittersweet and aching love story.

The Tie for Eleventh Place

In a way, it's silly to rank films in numerical order. I do a top ten because tradition requires it. But here are ten more films for which I have equal affection. Alphabetically: David Cronenberg's *Eastern Promises,* with Naomi Watts, who becomes the protector of an orphaned child, and Viggo Mortensen as a driver for the Russian mafia in London, whose values are challenged by his assignment; Todd Haynes's *I'm Not There,* using six actors to represent aspects of the elusive Bob Dylan (Cate Blanchett is the best); Paul Haggis's *In the Valley of Elah,* with another powerful performance by Tommy Lee Jones, as a father not satisfied with the official explanation of his son's death in Iraq; Tony Gilroy's *Michael Clayton,* with George Clooney as a fixer for a law firm who gets mired in the messiness of truth and conscience; Gavin Hood's *Rendition,* starring Reese Witherspoon as a wife whose Egyptian-American husband "disappears" on a flight from Cape Town, and Jake Gyllenhaal as the CIA temporary station chief who is shocked by discoveries he makes about the outsourcing of torture.

Also, John Turturro's bold, unconventional musical *Romance & Cigarettes,* starring James Gandolfini and Susan Sarandon as a couple at war in Queens, and Kate Winslet as his fiery mistress. The characters sing along with their favorite songs, in a story that starts out rambunctious and grows serious; Andrew Wagner's *Starting Out in the Evening,* with Frank Langella as a seventy-year-old great novelist and Lauren Ambrose as the young student who wants to know why he hasn't published a novel long in progress; Tim Burton's *Sweeney Todd, the Demon Barber of Fleet Street,* a blood-soaked musical starring Johnny Depp as a cut-throat barber and Helena Bonham Carter as the meat-pie baker who recycles his clients; Kasi Lemmons's *Talk to Me,* with its virtuoso performance by Don Cheadle as Petey Greene, who brought an authentic voice to radio in Washington, D.C., at a crucial time; and Paul Thomas Anderson's *There Will Be Blood,* with Daniel Day-Lewis as a single-minded oil well wildcatter who runs roughshod over everyone in his way.

The Best Foreign Films

Julian Schnabel's *The Diving Bell and the Butterfly,* inspired by the extraordinary achievement of French editor Jean-Dominique Bauby (Mathieu Amalric), paralyzed except for his left eye, which he used to blink out a memoir; Cristian Mungiu's *4 Months, 3 Weeks and 2 Days,* about a Romanian girl's attempts to help her friend find an illegal abortion; Ang Lee's *Lust, Caution,* about a passionate sex affair between a spy and her quarry during World War II; Juan Antonio Bayona's *The Orphanage,* about a woman who returns to the orphanage where she was raised and finds it haunted; and Rajnesh Domalpalli's *Vanaja,* about a lower-caste Indian girl who is befriended by a rich woman and learns to be a gifted dancer, only to find caste barriers in the way of her heart.

The Best Animated Films

Robert Zemeckis's *Beowulf,* using motion-capture animation to create a vast warrior-and-monsters epic from the dark ages, with a rich subtext of humor; Vincent Paronnaud and Marjane Satrapi's *Persepolis,* about an Iranian girl who rebels against the rise of the mullahs; and Brad Bird's high-spirited, riotous *Ratatouille,* about rats taking over a kitchen (with excellent results!).

The Best Documentaries

David Sington's *In the Shadow of the Moon,* revisiting many of the surviving astronauts to talk about their great *Apollo* adventures and re-create their triumphs; Seth Gordon's *The King of Kong: A Fistful of Quarters,* about an epic struggle between two competitors for the title of champion of an almost-forgotten arcade game; Tony Kaye's *Lake of Fire,* filmed over a period of seventeen years, about the battle over abortion in America; Charles Ferguson's *No End in Sight,* using first-person testimony from government and military eyewitnesses to document the mismanagement of the Iraq invasion; Jim Brown's *Pete Seeger: The Power of Song,* about the long and productive life of America's folk troubadour; and Michael Moore's *Sicko,* contrasting America's health-care system with the way it's done elsewhere.

Interviews

Michael Apted

September 29, 2006—In 1964, director Michael Apted interviewed a group of seven-year-old British schoolchildren for a BBC television documentary called *7 Up*. Apted, now known for directing such features as *Coal Miner's Daughter* and *Gorillas in the Mist*, has since returned to film these subjects every seven years. They are now forty-nine. I interviewed Apted in London for the release of the latest installment, *49 Up*. The complete interview will be included on the *49 Up* DVD; following is an excerpt.

Roger Ebert: You were a very young man when you got involved in this project. And now here you are. This was a project that would consume all the rest of your life and it still isn't finished.

Michael Apted: It's, in a sense, the perimeters of my life. My work and life. It's the first thing I'll do and it's still going on. Who would've thought that forty-some-odd years later we'd still be doing it, still be talking about it?

RE: That's the remarkable thing, to me, about the film because in a way it's one work, and in another way it's a work that's still being finished.

MA: It's a different perception, isn't it? But it's a whole different rhythm. Now, once you're trapped in it, you have to sit and sit and wait it out. And what effect does it have? Is it as meaningful? I don't know, but for those of us who've grown up with it, it becomes part of our lives.

One thing I've always avoided doing is putting big political signposts. I did it once in *42* and it never worked. I cut it out. It was the year Diana was killed, so I asked them all about that, just to give it some sense of time, but it just seemed trivial. Not that the event was trivial, but the politics of the film are their lives and the way their lives change. They dramatize politics. They don't discuss the abstract of politics. They are political. Their lives are political statements. Like Tony wanting to leave the country, tired of Blair, tired of eight years of Labour government. Fed up with it all. That's a political statement. It isn't him pontificating about it.

RE: There was a person on the Internet who got the box set and started to watch the first film and over the next twenty-four hours, had seen them all. And then posted this notice saying that it was a metaphysical experience for him, that in a way, he had seen not their lives, but life itself.

MA: And it's your own life, too. You know, you must be watching your own life go through, which is the power of film. Everyone can relate to a little bit of it. A piece of memory, a piece of a relationship, something someone says.

RE: The whole crowd in the *49 Up* film seem happier than they had been before, there seems to be a reconciliation with life, an acceptance, a certain serenity in many of them.

MA: It's interesting. One of the interesting things about seeing all the films, about having them all in front of you and not having to wait seven years, is that they're all quite different. The tone of them is quite different, I've always felt. I never know what the tone is until I've shot the film, until I start putting it together.

For example, in *35* a lot of them are losing their parents, so there's a sense of mortality, an awareness that life isn't forever. Things leave you. Things move on. And then at *49*, there's an acceptance, not in a negative way, but really the fact of being comfortable in your own skin.

RE: Which is said by one of the characters. For the first time she says, "I feel comfortable in my own skin."

MA: And then look at *28*. It's very, in a sense, overbearing in the way that they are so full of confidence. And indeed at *21* . . . there's a different atmosphere to each of the films.

RE: And at *21* there's a lot of uncertainty, too. Is it Susie who's the chain smoker? From *21* to *28* it's as dramatic as Neil from *35* to *42*. It's incredible because she flowers into a self-confident, charming woman who's comfortable with herself. And at *21* she looked like she was coming to pieces.

MA: She completely changed from *21* to *28*. She's a strange story because, from all accounts, I've lost her. At *49* she signs off and kind of says, "I'm not doing it anymore." She's one of the great stories of the series. People really like her. People really respond to her in ways that I don't think she quite grasps.

RE: I like her.

MA: She's wonderful, and yet, she, I don't know what it is, she finds it tremendously difficult to do, a great invasion.

RE: Yeah, because this isn't a documentary about these lives so much as it's a documentary about life. And as you sense them at various ages you look at them physically, they've changed. You can still see the face of the child, but nevertheless, hair falls out and their waistlines expand. At the same time, what the tone of their voice tells us is really more important than having another half hour of information about what they did biographically in the past years.

MA: Yes, I agree. I've had an instinct about that, too. I'm always trying to keep it crisp, to keep it moving, not to let it get more and more self-indulgent. You need to keep the thing moving.

There's a lot of information. You're not just absorbing what's happened to them now, you're also absorbing what's happened to them before, all those kind of impulses that you're getting are being fed into your nervous system.

It's interesting, *49*, now, with new technology, is the first one I've done digital, which is a huge advantage to me because I can conduct longer interviews. Before, all the way up to *42*, we were doing them on film, so every ten minutes you'd have to change rolls. It was very hard to keep focused, to try and get after them, get underneath them, when you kept having to stop and start. Now I can shoot for thirty-eight minutes, and all using less equipment, so it's much more intimate between me and them. There's not a large crew around. The change of technology has been very, very interesting and useful to me.

RE: You've said that a couple of things that you did you regretted. There are two characters where you thought that you could predict what would happen in their lives. One of them you were right; the other you were wrong. Tony is a good way to start the film because he is so happy down in Spain with his swimming pool. Asa, the little boy at the beginning of the film who looks like Truffaut's hero in *400 Blows*. He's kind of peering out and baffled. And now he's this 49-year-old confident, expansive, happy man who's got some complaints, but has been able to solve them with his holiday cottage, and he and his wife are working hard and it's incredible.

MA: But he embraces life, doesn't he? He just attacks life. He's so full of everything, so full of ideas. You just have to say "calm down" to him. He tires me out sometimes.

RE: Yet when he was 21, you were convinced he was going to be a criminal.

MA: It's this terrible impulse to play God, which is one of the attractions of the film. It's fun to indulge myself, and you can watch it and say, "Oh, this is going to happen to him." I tried to predict what would happen with Tony. I tried to predict what would happen with the next marriage. Once I was right. Once I was wrong. But just the foolishness of doing that.

RE: You ask some questions occasionally. I guess you have an instinct for what you can ask these people because you asked Neil if he thought he was going mad, and that's an interesting question to ask someone and he answers it very seriously and says, "I think I might be." And we're afraid he might be, too. So we're grateful for having that relationship where you can ask those questions.

MA: There was one question, I think it was *35*, *42*, when I asked Tony when he was giving me another of what he was going to do with his life. And I said, "But you know you failed at everything," and I remember watching it in front of an audience, and they all gasped, and I remember thinking that was a very tough question. Maybe too tough.

I think that's key to really what the film is about. It's my relationship with them, and I know how far I can go with them individually. I know how much I can push them. I know what they're emotional about, but there's a trust between us. I don't think any of them have ever turned their back on me and said, "I'm unhappy with how it's been going." No one's ever complained about it. I think it's because of this unusual relationship. I know these people better than almost anyone alive. I've known them for forty-two years.

RE: No one else in their life has come to them every seven years and asked them how they are doing.

MA: I think, because of that trust, I know what I want to talk about. They're in a very powerful position because as a longitudinal documentarian you have to be on your best behavior. Because if they say, "I don't want to talk about sex," or, "I don't want to talk about money," and you use it, they don't let you back in again.

RE: The first film very definitely sets itself up as being about the British class system. You have rich kids and poor kids, and you later said that you wish you had more middle-class kids than you do. Then, as the years go past, has the class system persisted in their lives? To what degree have some of them moved outside of it?

MA: I think that a lot of them have lived outside it. I think that kind of oppressive class barriers has diminished a lot. It's a very deceptive film because a lot of people ask, Is this a portrait of England? And I say, well, this is a portrait of people who were born in 1956. Had I started the film ten years earlier or ten years later, I think it would have been different.

It's very hard to draw a definitive view of English society. That was the great metamorphosis that the film and I went through. It definitely started out with a political agenda, for this very socialist, left-wing company, Granada Television, working on a very provocative program. And this was a film saying: This is the state of the country. Social barriers shouldn't exist. They're a great waste of people's time and talent. The humanity of the film, I think, came out after *21*. We had kind of grown through that. Those arguments weren't meaningful anymore. What was meaningful was the people.

RE: When you think back to '63, the year the film was shot, the year of the Beatles, for many people, that year represents the difference between people wearing suits and ties and hats, and everything since.

MA: That wasn't an accident.

RE: But when they grew up, especially the East Enders, they were growing up in an East End that was the same as it might have been 20, 30, 100 years earlier.

MA: It was no accident that this film was made in 1963, because people suddenly thought, is England changing? We had the theater. We had *Look Back in Anger*. We had music. We had fashion. So was English society changing? Everybody in England was waking. The war was finally over. And this documentary simply came out of that feeling that maybe there was a brave new world. It was all very well to have the Beatles album, Mary Quant, and John Osborne, but for everyday working people, the class system was very much alive and well. It was the empowered and the unempowered, and the difference between the two was dramatic.

What's so thrilling about the film is the optimism in that generation; it was possible to break through. It was my good luck to be at that time. I could document that awakening. I could record when Britain woke up in the '60s. America woke up after Eisenhower and Kennedy. And I documented that generation who assumed adulthood in that period. It was a very dramatic, very vivid sense of social movement. I hit a period of time when life really did change very dramatically. A whole culture changed dramatically. Culturally. Politically. Economically. Every way.

RE: At the same time that their lives changed dramatically, their personalities didn't much. The thing that struck me the very first one I saw, I think it was *14 Up* or maybe it was *21 Up*, in the faces of those children you see everything you're going to see later, the personality, the slant on life. Now, they may go through little dips and changes along the way. When they're 49, there's the child you saw at 7. Everything that's happened by 7 is going to set the course. Is that true?

MA: The core personality you see at 7 pretty much doesn't change. I mean, you can't predict people's lives. You don't know what is going to be thrown at people. But maybe the Jesuits were right: Show me the child until 7 and I'll show you the man. You can't tell what the man is going to be doing, but you can sense how he's going to react. That look in the eye, that twinkle in Neil's eye that disappeared for generations, is coming back again.

RE: Wasn't he the one that at one point wanted to be a tour bus guide? He wanted to tell people what to look at through the windows. After his period of wandering in the outskirts of society, he gets back on board running the Village Fete in the Shetland Islands, which is, he's making people look at, here look at this. He's still a tour guide. And now as a politician, he's also telling people what to do. He wants to be the supervisor.

MA: One of the most socially mobile people is Bruce, who started out in a very privileged boarding school and then St. Paul's School, and then Oxford and was teaching literature. One of the first things he said at 7 was he wanted to be a missionary. There's a kind of compassion in that 7-year-old face that is never going to leave him, that will be with him his whole life.

RE: And even though he, at the end, is teaching at a school with a better salary and drives a better car, actually a teacher is a missionary, no matter who the students are.

MA: So people say, what are the great lessons we can draw? Can you predict people's lives? There is something at the heart of this film that life is eternal and people's spirit lives on.

RE: With one exception, you've kept with the seven-year rule. But what if you found out one of your subjects was dying?

MA: I would be extremely worried, you know. It's a question now we have to face. There's no one in mind at all, but it now becomes a part of the agenda.

RE: I hope you understand the spirit in which I mean this: I would want to hear their thoughts when they realize the end may be coming.

MA: So you think I should do it.

RE: Well, that's the last chance they'll have.

MA: I think you're right. This has been troubling me since the last twenty years how to handle it. I hope I'll go first and they'll all outlive me.

RE: If you should go first, shouldn't someone else continue on? Shouldn't this project continue on until everyone is . . .

MA: I think it should.

RE: When I became a film critic, I had no idea you could do it for more than five years. And I certainly had no idea that I wanted to spend my life being a film critic. When I look back after forty years, that's what I've done. And so there's reconciliation. And with these people . . . First of all, most of them are happy. Many of them have grandchildren. Do they all? Not quite. But they love their grandchildren and, basically, they're happy with their children. They have a few worries with this one or that one, but essentially there is pride in their voices. And to return to earlier, they're still striving. Now, it's happened. They can see maybe that this film they were in was just really a wonderful opportunity for them that they didn't necessarily love or embrace, but that it happened to them, too.

MA: That's right. Because they behaved with dignity and they've been treated with dignity. And, you know, that's what I love about the film. These are ordinary lives, ordinary stories, ordinary voices, and they're told in such a dignified way that it elevates it to real drama and real dignity. I think they were beginning to realize that. I just got a sense that they took some pride in it.

RE: I've often thought that if we had any piece of film at all from the year 1000 or the year 500 it would be fascinating to see. This project, as it continues and finally concludes and becomes a piece of film, *56 Up, 63 Up, 70 Up,* then 100 years from now, 200 years from now, how fascinating this will be, what a film to show in a classroom 200 years from now.

MA: I think the big contribution that I've made to all of this is just to keep it going. It would have been easy to have stopped it, to have moved on and just carried on doing movies and all that. Sometimes you tear your hair up trying to get them all to agree to do it. It's the most arduous part of actually making the film, that period of ringing them up and saying the time is coming up and they say, oh, well, we're not sure we're going to do it. We kind of just hung in and kept it going.

People say to me, "When are you going to stop?" I think it shouldn't stop. We should just keep it going. But just to see these people, human history at its most simple. And film does that so brilliantly. Because it's so complicated. Much more powerful, dare I say, than a book. There's so much information coming at you out of the corner of your eye. The way their haircuts change or their clothes change or the backgrounds change just gives you a history. And it's not a pushy history, a political history. It's not trying to make points, it's just dealing with these people's lives. It dignifies the ordinary life. This great world of celebrity life which we're living in, which may get worse as time goes on, who knows? It does honor ordinary life.

RE: I think it's the most notable use of film that I've been able to witness as a filmgoer. Noble in its simplicity and its honesty and its directness and its lack of pretension or grandiosity. Just the gaze of an interested observer coming into these lives and saying, "How you doin'?"

MA: Also, it is a family, too. I've kept the same people. George Turner's shot it since *21* and has edited it since *28*. It's like one big family. It's tough stuff we talk about sometimes, but nonetheless, it makes the people who are on it love it. There's a feeling of love about it. It's transmitted. You could do it about anyone. You could take anyone. You could make a film of twelve people and show bad sides and laughter. I think they kind of had a balance, but, nonetheless, underneath it all is an affection, which I think is important in any film. Out of feeling love comes, in any sort of art, I think.

RE: I'm just very happy that there's going to be a *56 Up*.

MA: I'm honored that you should think so.

Michael Caine, Jude Law, and Kenneth Branagh

Toronto, Canada, October 14, 2007—A wealthy novelist named Andrew Wyke is alone in his isolated mansion when he receives a caller. This is Milo Tindle, the man who boldly boasts of being the lover of Wyke's wife. The two engage in a savage verbal duel during the long evening ahead.

This is, of course, the setup for Anthony Shaffer's famous stage play *Sleuth,* made into a movie in 1972, nominated for four Oscars, including Michael Caine and Laurence Olivier as Milo and Andrew. And it is also the setup for a 2007 version with Caine stepping up to the Wyke role and Jude Law as Milo.

But do not make the mistake of calling the film a "remake." The screenplay this time is by Harold Pinter, seventy-seven, the Nobel-winning playwright, and as with most of Pinter's work, the point isn't so much about what happens, as how the characters talk while something is about to happen.

I talked with Caine, Law, and the film's director, Kenneth Branagh, at the Toronto Film Festival, where the film premiered. Good chaps all. Relaxed, kidding one another, pleased to have made an original Pinter.

One question was begging to be asked. Is Law stepping into the former Caine role connected in any way with the fact that he starred in the unsuccessful remake of Caine's famous movie about a romantic scoundrel, *Alfie*?

"We never discussed that," Caine said. "It's one of those things. I've done remakes of films. It's there and you do it and you hope it's going to be all right and sometimes it doesn't turn out right, and that's the end of that."

"You can't regret choices you've made in this business," Law said. "You learn from them and you pick yourself up and dust yourself off and move on. Sometimes you're rewarded. The lesson I learned was that *Alfie* was very much of its time. It didn't work in a modern setting."

"The morality had changed," Caine said. "By the time he made *Alfie,* you could have made Alfie a woman who was going out screwing everybody, and everyone would have believed it. Not in my time, not when I made *Alfie.* Where I came from if you kissed a girl, two brothers came around saying, 'You're gonna get married.' It was a bit like living in Sicily."

And about the 1972 version of *Sleuth*?

"I can't compare them because I haven't seen it since the first time I saw it, and I didn't revisit it," Branagh said.

"We essentially stole the central idea," Caine said. "Two guys playing a deadly game over a woman that we don't see. That was what Pinter took. He read the play twice, he never looked at the film. It was a funny thing, seeing Harold, who came into rehearsals and was around all the time, he was entirely possessive about it. He was excited. And Harold is not an insignificant screenwriter. He may be Mr. Nobel Prize–winning playwright but, you know, he wrote . . ."

Branagh broke in with his credits: *"Accident, The Servant, The French Lieutenant's Woman . . ."*

"The movie told backwards, where they start in misery and end up in happiness," I said.

"*Betrayal,* of course," Branagh said.

Caine: "With Ben Kingsley and Jeremy Irons and Patricia Hodge, directed by David Jones."

I had the impression he could have even told us the cameraman.

"We're not talking about a first-time screenwriter here," Branagh said.

"One of the things I loved about Harold's screenplay, and these two absolutely maximize it, is the question of when they are being genuine. Does Andrew really love his wife, or does he simply want to possess her? And at the end does even that disappear, and is it just about winning?

"I remember an electrifying moment in rehearsal was when you guys did the third act for the first time and we didn't stop, and I got to the bedroom where this strange invitation of Andrew's is made, and I found myself thinking, does he *mean* this?"

The movie is really about performance, not plot, I said. It's about whether they can fake out each other.

"Exactly that," Caine said. "People say, why are you remaking this? I say I'm not. I wouldn't have remade Anthony Shaffer's script because there wasn't any point. I mean, we did a perfectly good job back then, Larry and [director] Joe Mankiewicz and I, I'm sure. But what it was, was Pinter's script took us somewhere else into a whole other movie, and as Jude would tell you, Pinter hadn't seen the movie, and there isn't a single line in this movie that came from the old script. It was as though we stole the plot and the title."

Sir Michael, I asked Caine, were there any moments at all when you thought, this is what Sir Lawrence should have done the first time round?

Caine laughed. "No, no. I haven't seen the movie since. There was no backward reference to him. Larry did what should have been done for that moment. It was an entirely different way of life. When we opened that first picture, it was a lovely, comfortable old English country house. This one, you get inside the country house, and it's suddenly a nightmare. It's brass, it's steel, it's marble, it's glass. And minimal.

"On our set on the first film, there was something everywhere. Stuff, cluttered with stuff. So Larry's performance went with that. My performance goes with this sterile house. That's the way I see it. If I'd been Larry at that time and I saw that room, I'd have given the performance he did. I wouldn't have given it quite so big, but I probably *couldn't* have given it quite so big, because he's such an incredible theater actor."

Law said: "It's like Pinter builds and builds using the devices of the original play, and then you're washed away into his world."

Caine nodded, amused. "With Harold, if you'd say something like, 'Oh, what about the ending, Harold?' he'd say, 'I think it's quite good.' That meant we were not changing this ending under any circumstances."

Law: "He really embraced this idea of men at war. What lengths will they go to? In the end you forget about the prize; it's about domination, and it's in that last chapter they really reveal their hands."

Caine: "Eventually, the woman disappears and is replaced by the two male egos going at each other. These two stags fighting each other, and they've forgotten all about the woman. One of the first lines I say to him is, 'My car is bigger than yours.' Like a seven-year-old. The thin ice of civilization gets cracked quite quickly."

"One of the things I love about what Pinter does in this," Branagh said, "is raise questions without answers. Michael's character says, 'I heard you were a hairdresser.' This issue of whether he is in fact a hairdresser, I still can't answer. Because he screams, 'I'm not a hairdresser!' and then at the end, he goes, 'Here I am, a humble hairdresser,' and I never bloody know, you know. Who is he? Who is this man?"

"It's a Pinter thing to play with you like that," Law said.

"It's a kind of Cockney thing," Caine said. "Harold and I are both Cockneys, where you say something quite ordinary which means something else. For instance, if a Cockney gangster comes to you and says something innocuous like, 'Well, who's been a naughty boy then?' like your mother would say to you, you are probably dead or going to be very severely injured."

They talked on. It occurred to me that *Sleuth* is two men talking about a woman we never see, and our interview was three men talking about a playwright we never see.

Anthony Hopkins

October 21, 2007—Anthony Hopkins has written and directed a very peculiar film. He is the first to say so. It has no continuity. That's what he explained to the continuity girl. It doesn't make logical sense. That's what he told the cast. It's a stream of consciousness. That's what Spielberg told him. It's exactly the film he wanted to make. That's what he told himself. It's the film he had to make. That's what his wife, Stella, told him. "You're next." That's what Kevin McCarthy said in *Invasion of the Body Snatchers,* and he says it again in Anthony Hopkins's very peculiar film.

Its title is *Slipstream.* It played at the Chicago Film Festival, and he thinks it's a thumbnail sketch of his own inner life. "I don't play a big part," he said. "It's not the central showy part. Felix is an observer and a witness of life, which is very much my perception of the world ever since I was a little child. I was a bit slower as a child, and I sat in the back of the class, bemused, with a funny expression on my face, because I couldn't quite fit in anywhere.

"And then I drifted into theater, I became an actor by default, I worked various theaters, and I didn't fit in. I just couldn't hack it. I couldn't get traction on what anyone else was doing. I played Shakespeare and I played Chekhov and so on and so forth. I couldn't get a grip on it; I didn't feel comfortable. I think this movie is me trying to express my feeling of alienation, with no anger or resentment, but a light jab at the acting profession, a kind of tongue-in-cheek poke, saying come on, lighten up, it's only a movie, it's only acting.

"But it's not even meant to be a comment on that, because I broke all the rules. I had no concerns because I'm not a poet or a writer. I can write a letter or write a postcard, but I'm not going to try and prove that I'm a great writer. I'm far from it. I have nothing profound to say. I was just interested in the peculiar randomness of our lives, and my role in the film is exactly what I am, wandering around, interested in the peculiar randomness of our lives. My role is exactly what I am, wandering around in a state of asking, 'What the hell is going on here?'"

Hopkins is a man, you understand, who has been knighted for his services to the acting profession. He won an Oscar for best actor, was nominated three other times. Won two BAFTA best actor awards, British Oscars, nominated for two others. Created Hannibal Lecter, one of maybe a dozen movie characters everybody knows by name.

"I was fascinated by the trick of memory, how memory and the dream world overlap. I think what I was trying to express in this film was that it is all an illusion, that we're just passing through. Goodness knows what's on the other side. The peculiar enigma of life and time. The impermanence. Every minisecond, you can't grab it. Every moment we spend is gone. Not a second can be grasped. There was a nineteenth-century British painter who only painted the backs of people walking away. And I wanted to get the idea of all the actors, walking away. I grabbed as many shots as I could, of actors walking away from the camera as if, well, we're all going to walk away one day."

We were sitting in my living room with our wives. Stella Arroyave, whom Sir Anthony married five years ago, was an antiques dealer who on this picture was a muse (telling him he should write the screenplay), a producer, and an actress, a very good one. Bigger role than her husband.

Hopkins and I once shared a moment neither one of us will ever forget. One night in a Formica restaurant on North Avenue, the waitress said, "Aren't you Hannibal Lecter?" "Why, yes," Hopkins said. "I wish my husband was more like you," she said.

Slipstream centers on a troubled movie being shot in the Mojave Desert. Felix Bonhoeffer, the character Hopkins plays, is the film's writer, who is confusing reality with illusion. His characters appear in his life, his life appears in the movie, and mostly he looks on uncertainly while both real and imaginary people do all the loving, living, and dying. Bonhoeffer, not the most common name, also belonged to Frederick Bonhoeffer, a German theologian who was involved in a plot to assassinate Hitler and was executed. Not the same Bonhoeffer, Hopkins says, although his film is illuminated by flash frames of historical figures who populated the lives of both Bonheffers: Stalin, Roosevelt, Churchill, Hitler.

How can such a famous, respected, and honored actor not "fit in"? I asked him.

"I never really did feel a part of the acting profession," he said, "which I'm very pleased about, because it keeps me detached. I don't mean cold or isolated, but it keeps me detached. When I came to America after leaving the National Theatre, I found myself in movies. I enjoyed the freedom of the movies. But in recent years I thought, well, I've done some passably good films, and I've done some films not that good, and I would like to resurrect my old rebellion or feeling of never belonging and express myself in an experimental way.

"Because the nature of our lives seems so sometimes ridiculous, comical, absurd that I'm almost certain now that I was motivated to do this film to get rid of the irritability in my nature. I thought, I can best express myself through a kind of angst, poke people in the groin, jab them in the eye with ridiculous editing, so that people say, 'You can't do that.'

"Well, I can. What are they going to do? Put me in jail? People are probably gonna sit there and go, 'What was that? Did I just see that? It's like a ghost passing by. Did you see that?' I've sometimes been in situations—I had a concussion once and I've had one or two little things happen to me when I've been overstressed, overworked, tired, overdone, and I get a slight amnesia, which is pretty alarming. So I've learned to calm down and not be so manic. And that's why I wanted to experiment with people's sensibilities. I realize, of course, that it's going to irritate a lot of people.

"But I wanted to stick with the experiment. I knew it was going to be difficult to put together, but Stella was the driving force behind this because she never gave up. She wanted me to make this movie because she believed in it. So we interviewed various producers, and they came up with the usual stuff, like, 'Ah, we wanna talk about final cut.' I said, 'Adios, amigos.' I could understand their problem with it. But I wanted to possess the film.

"And the actors asked me, 'What's it about?' I said, it doesn't matter, really. Christian Slater got it. John Turturro, he said, 'Yeah, I'll do it. OK. What's it about?' One day John had just finished shooting the scene when he's inside the writer's computer screen, complaining about his role, and he said, 'God, it's hot. I'm inside somebody's hard drive.' You know, with those big bug eyes of his. I remember Bill Lucking, who played Inspector Larabee, said, 'What is it about? Beats the hell out of me.' And the continuity person said, 'I'm so thrilled to be on this. But there is no continuity.' I said, well, the theme of it is that there is no continuity.

"Think of life. The mayhem, the carnage and the horror. And then finally the talk, talk, talk. Yalta, Churchill, Roosevelt, Stalin, talk, talk, talk, talk. Yakkity, yakkity, yada, yada, yada. In the meantime, millions of people are just gone to dust."

Why did you choose such a difficult location? I asked. The Mojave, 120 degrees.

"I've always been interested in the desert. When I first came to Los Angeles I drove into the desert a few times, and I loved it. I used to drive up to Bakersfield. I used to get in the car on my own, this was many years ago, and then I saw *Blood Simple*, and I thought that was a wonderful film; Coen brothers filmed *Blood Simple* in the desert. And those peculiar science fiction movies which always have a giant tarantula in the desert. There's that sense of wilderness and spiritual nada, like he's finding this spirit in the nakedness of the desert. Bonhoeffer, wandering through limbo in the desert."

A very peculiar film. He'll tell you so himself.

Darryl Roberts

June 11, 2008—A man from Chicago named Darryl Roberts made *America the Beautiful*, a documentary that nobody wanted. It was about our obsession with being thin and beautiful and perfect. Every distributor in the country turned him down. They told him he was black and the twelve-year-old fashion model at the center of the film was black, and blacks don't go to documentaries. He finally talked it into the American Film Institute's festival in Dallas, where it sold out four shows, "and 99 percent of the audience was white. Not that it means anything."

He had more luck on the festival circuit, and then landed a booking at the Landmark Century in Chicago. It ran for four weeks, three of those the top-grossing film in the 'plex, and on that basis was picked up by First Independent Pictures in partnership with Larry Gleason, former president of Paramount exhibition, and it opened in more than fifty cities, including Chicago again.

That makes me happy. This is a film that deserves to be seen. I said in my review: "It's about a culture 'saturated with the perfect,' in which women are taught to seek an impossible physical ideal and men to worship it. It opens with shots of a pretty girl named Gerren Taylor, who looks terrific in the skimpiest of bikinis and draws admiration at a topless pool party, although she keeps her top on. Gerren is twelve."

Yes, twelve. Roberts was already well into

filming his doc when he attended the first Fashion Week held in Los Angeles.

"This girl comes out on the runway," he remembers, "and I didn't think anything of it; I just saw some twenty-something-year-old girl, and the guy next to me goes, 'I wanna take her home tonight.' But a lady said, 'Well, you better be really careful because she's only twelve years old.' And everybody that heard her say that was like, *oh my God*!

"I went into disbelief. I met her mother; at this time I'd been shooting for about four months. Her mother felt differently, but I felt the industry was sexualizing a twelve-year-old child. I said I wanted to follow them around to see where this ended up going. Her mother agreed to let me go."

So Gerren, a quiet girl with a "model's walk," became Roberts's subject as she became a superstar for a year. Magazine covers, the works.

"There's a law in New York," he said, "that you can't work there unless you're fourteen; no model should be on that runway unless they're fourteen years old. All of them bent the rules. Gerren brought publicity to their shows. She didn't realize she was a gimmick."

By thirteen, after she failed in Europe (she was "too wide" for Milan), her career was over. The movie explains why and contains startling facts about the physical requirements for models; designers like them "the skinnier the better" because the fabric for their costumes is so expensive.

"When she was ten or eleven," Roberts told me, "she was called 'giraffe' and 'stick' and 'beanpole,' and she felt very unattractive. Somebody told her she could model; she got on the runway, and everybody was telling her she was beautiful. But once that was taken away from her, she went right back to how she felt. The gimmick was being twelve. And when she was thirteen and fourteen and the press wasn't paying attention to her anymore, the designers had no need for her, and they threw her away."

Gerren survived. She and her mother now live in Los Angeles, where she's eighteen, a senior in high school, and appearing on a BET reality show.

"So she has aspirations of becoming a movie star," Roberts said, "which could end up just like the modeling thing. It all depends."

Roberts is in his mid-forties, stands an imposing six-four, is soft-spoken, a former party promoter, an entertainment reporter for WMAQ, the Chicago NBC station, directed an earlier film (*How U Like Me Now?*), has shot commercials. Now he finds himself and his film famous among those who are concerned about bulimia, anorexia, and the obsession with perfection. His film contains an astonishing statement: "Three minutes of looking at a fashion magazine makes 90 percent of women of all ages feel depressed, guilty, and shameful."

America the Beautiful is about a lot more than Gerren Taylor. He interviews fashion magazine editors, deconstructs the retouching that went into the famous Dove soap ads about "average" women, explains how most fashion models make hardly any money and are "housed" six to a one-bedroom apartment, and argues "The advertising and beauty industries are on a full-tilt assault against our self-esteem; they want to make us feel bad about ourselves so that we'll buy their products."

I said he was soft-spoken. Yes, but his voice became a little more urgent as he said, "We have to learn to love ourselves just the way we are, just the way we look. We have to do it as a means of survival. Because if we don't, eating disorders are going to get worse. The more they win, the more we suffer. I know I'm on the right track. My principle is that every human being alive has something unique about them. They're beautiful."

John Sayles

January 17, 2008—John Sayles is the living legend of independent film. He and his life partner, Maggie Renzi, have made nineteen features entirely on their own terms. To finance them, Sayles has written, rewritten, or ghost-written screenplays entirely on the terms of others, from *Piranha* to the forthcoming *Jurassic Park* movie. Their new film, *Honeydripper*, is set at the junction of civil rights and rhythm and blues in the 1950s South, and is getting some of his best reviews.

The movie stars Danny Glover as the operator of a club in Harmony, Alabama, Charles S. Dutton as his best friend, the blues singer Mable John, Stacy Keach as the sheriff, and a newcomer named Gary Clark Jr., who impersonates a famous guitar player for Glover's club.

We sat and talked one day. And talked and

talked. The transcript came to 8,400 words, and here are some of the things Sayles told me:

—"There's this rock 'n' roll legend about a guy named Guitar Slim who was an electric guitar player in New Orleans in the early '50s. He was known for two things: He had this long extension cord, and he would go out on the streets and just lure people like the Pied Piper back into his club with his 300-yard-long extension cord. But he would miss gigs because he partied too much. I've heard that Albert King and Albert Collins and BB King would have a club owner say, 'Tonight, you are Guitar Slim,' because nobody knew what he looked like; they just heard his stuff on the jukebox."

—"I found the *Popular Electronics* article where Les Paul describes this new electric guitar that he's made. So the character that Gary Clark in *Honeydripper* plays is a kid who could have been a radio repairman in the Army and could have read this article and, being a guitar player already, say, 'I'm gonna do that.' He would have played acoustic with a pick-up like T-Bone Walker did."

—"We needed an African-American kid who played that kind of stuff, which is rare these days. We were told, 'You gotta come and see this kid Gary Clark Jr. He's an Austin kid.' I think we saw him on the night he turned twenty-one, so his mom no longer had to be the chaperone when he played in clubs that served liquor. He kinda looks like a young Chuck Berry, which was what I had in my head for the character. It took us a year to realize we weren't gonna raise money and that we were gonna have to use our own money again. I had time to write more screenplays. So by the time we shot, he was twenty-two. And just turned out be a great kid to work with. Not a kid anymore."

—"We had stars like Danny Glover and Charles S. Dutton, but everybody gets scale and gets paid according to how many days they work. It's the biggest compliment we get that we ask these well-known actors to be in our movies and they say yes for scale. I think the attraction is (a) they're good parts, (b) all our movies have gotten at least some kind of theatrical release, because now, so many movies get made and not even released theatrically."

—"One of the problems with film schools is so many of the kids coming out of them only know movies. Robert Mitchum was one of the last generation of actors who had a life before he was in movies. You felt it in his performances. Now so many actors and directors, they go right from school. Before they were just watching movies, and then they go right into movies and they have a career right away. I've noticed this with Steven Spielberg. He's growing up. Recently his movies have actually started to deal with stuff out in the real world and not just the movie world. But it took him until he was fifty to feel like he could do that."

—"I think it was ironic when Lars von Trier invented Dogma and started saying, 'Oh, we don't do this, we don't do that.' I said, wait a minute, we've made six Dogma films and we never even had a manifesto! We simply didn't start with any of those things they were giving up. Our movies had no thorny locations or studio stuff. And then he broke almost all of his own rules in his first four movies after he became a Dogma guy. I guess he said, 'Oh, that's inconvenient. I'm not gonna do that.'"

—"People call our movies political, but I think of something Haskell Wexler has said a bunch of times: All movies are political. If you see a comedy made in 1935, there are attitudes about race and class and sex that today we would say, wow, what a political statement that's making! But at the time it was just the status quo. What would offend us today was the air that they breathed back then."

—"*Honeydripper* isn't about race, but it's set in Alabama in 1950, and there are assumptions, because of the apartheid that existed there, that are going to affect people's lives. You can't walk down a road as a black man without a job and not end up on the chain gang. That's gonna create anger and it turns inward, and so always in those juke joints there was this undercurrent of anger and violence, and it's in the music. It's one of the things that Danny Glover's character has to deal with: One of the reasons people go to these places is to see fights or be in them, and he doesn't want them in his club. This is his own past, and it's stupid, senseless violence that's still with us."

—"This one we're releasing ourselves, because of the laziness or the incompetence that's been so disappointing over the years. We've all gotten to be better at making the films, but they haven't gotten any better at distributing. Our independent movies used to get a couple of weeks to build up word-of-mouth. Now they're in the same boat as the studio movies; they live or die in the first weekend. And you can't do that with little movies; they really do need to find their audiences. So either they get lucky like *Sideways* did, and everybody kind of writes about them at once. Or they disappear. The distributors just put it into their system and let it go. They put it on the Landmark chain, and it plays one week and they're fine; they bought it for probably $100,000 and they get $500,000 back and that's it."

I asked Sayles if it changed his life when he won a MacArthur Foundation "genius grant."

"I'm an ex-genius, now. It only lasts five years, and then your IQ drops rapidly. I had never heard of this award. I was in the sound mix for *Baby It's You*, and I got this call from somebody who says, 'You've won this award. It's called the MacArthur Award.' I was a little annoyed that he called because we only had one week to mix this movie. I figure OK, I gotta go get a trophy. He says, 'And there's some money involved.' I picked up a little. And I said, so, what's this money? And he says, 'Well, it's based on your age,' and I was thirty-four at the time, and got $34,000 a year for five years tax-free. I said, that sounds great. Very specifically, we had just made *Brother from Another Planet* on my own nickel and my nickel had run out, so what it meant was I did not have to go back and write another screenplay and was able to pay for the editing room, you know, and just go right ahead and finish the movie and not take a hiatus to write. So that was great."

Paul Schrader

December 16, 2007—Reading over my notes after interviewing Paul Schrader, the writer-director of *The Walker* and many other splendid films, I heard his voice coming through so loudly and clearly that it struck me that the conventional form of an interview ("He paused," "he said," etc.) would only obscure his style. In London, the newspapers sometimes string together quotes and present them as if the subject has written them for publication. I thought I would try something like that.

All you need to know going in is that Schrader's film stars Woody Harrelson as an unpaid gay escort of rich society women in Washington, D.C. One of his friends, a senator's wife, finds the dead body of her lover.

Paul Schrader speaking:

This film started with my *American Gigolo.* I was wondering what that character would be like in middle age, and I realized he would be funny; that his skills would be social. He'd be like a society walker, and that struck me as an interesting occupational metaphor.

All of my man-in-a-room films are occupational service metaphors: a taxi driver, a drug dealer, a gigolo, now a society walker. It fit rather neatly into a kind of age 20, 30, 40, 50 progression. If in *Light Sleeper* I took him out of the front seat and put him in the backseat, in *Walker* I took him out of the closet and put him in Washington, D.C. In my mind those four films are linked.

I don't think I'll do another one. It was too hard to finance this one. It's a character piece, and one of the reasons that I had trouble getting it financed was that everyone wanted me to hype up the Washington thriller aspect. But that's such a set genre, the Washington thriller, that I figured if I went into that, I wouldn't have a character piece anymore. Movies are about things that happen and people who do things, and this guy's mantra is, "I'm not naive; I'm superficial." So he's not the stuff of which movies are financed.

I knew I needed to have some plot because otherwise people would tire of these ladies talking. So I created a kind of a plot, but I tried to keep it far enough in the background so that you wouldn't think, oh, this is all about the plot, because it's really about this guy, Carter Page. It's similar to *Taxi Driver* or *Gigolo* or *Light Sleeper* in that way; they all have a plot, but you don't really remember the plot so much as you remember the character.

Woody Harrelson arrived as a surprise to me because when I wrote it I had sort of financed it with Steve Martin and Julie Christie, and then that fell out. Now I was looking for an actor.

Woody's agent called me up and asked, "Have you thought about Woody?" I said no. I mean, nothing Woody's done would make me think about him for this role. He's not on any list I've ever made up. Jeremy, his agent, said, "Well, I was talking to him. He wants to do something really different. Would you like to meet with him?" I said of course I would, because I've been looking for an actor who could do comedy, and Woody is a good actor despite his public persona of being a kind of a doofus.

And so we met and he was plugged into it and off we went. There was some trepidation; there was a point in preproduction where I felt I might be jumping into an empty pool, but he finally got into it and took off.

He worked out. He really did. I've got a friend in Virginia who this character is based on in some ways. His father was a general and a professor at VMI; his grandfather was in politics in Virginia. He's kind of like this character. I hired him as an associate producer on the film, in London and on the Isle of Man, and he was with Woody a lot, and a lot of what Woody is doing is this guy, and it really helped out.

The term "walker" is fairly new. It was coined by John Fairchild of *W* magazine and *Women's Wear Daily* to describe Jerry Zipkin, who was Nancy Reagan's walker, and Fairchild always used to call him Jerry "The Walker" Zipkin. When Nancy wanted to go to some event, Jerry would take her.

Getting a picture financed, you have a problem with a passive protagonist, you have a problem of a character study, you have a problem of a non-plot-driven film. These films are getting harder and harder to make. One of the ironies of my career is I tend to be working overseas more often. *The Walker,* a solid, all-American film, was financed out of the UK. No money from America. *Adam Resurrected* was financed out of Israel and Germany. *Auto Focus* was financed out of America, but *Affliction* was financed out of Japan. *Touch* was financed out of France.

The role of the independent filmmaker is like an international scavenger dog, scouring the planet for the scraps that have fallen from various tables. And that's what we do. But now with the dollar completely in the toilet, I think opportunities are gonna be better. Canadian films are gonna start shooting here before long.

Working with Lauren Bacall was an experience. Betty is a tough old bird. She has a reputation, which she has earned, as being a tough lady.

My initial response to her was to play her game. She wants a lot of praise, and after a number of days, I realized that there was no praise that was enough, and she wanted to be praised in the presence of other actors so that you got stuck if you had to tell her how great her last take was and there would be Kristin Scott Thomas sitting there, Woody there. And no matter what you said to her, it wasn't quite enough.

So I decided after about a week to just be real professional, basically: "Good, very good, Lauren, thank you, let's move on," and not get into the effusive flattery. She didn't like that, and Kristin told me that I was the main course for dinner on a number of evenings as Lauren launched into me. But I think her work started getting better when it wasn't all this courtship and flattery.

It's interesting about Lauren, because she's just eighty-three now. She is the same age as Sidney Lumet, younger than Arthur Penn, yet you think of her as being older because she was famous so young. She was nineteen when she was married to Humphrey Bogart, so you think of her as somehow an actor from the 1940s, which she was, you know, in a way.

She has some of the best lines. I collected all those bon mots over a period of years. Somebody asked me if I would be interested in writing a TV series based on this character. I said, look, it took me years to collect all those funny lines; you expect me to write a show every week? I'm not that good.

The Woody character genuinely sympathizes with the women. It's not a job. These guys who do this, for the most part, don't do it for money. They may get gifts. They love girl-talk. It's a very ancient profession. I'm sure Versailles was full of them. And the kinds of things that would make a heterosexual man whither in agony, endless talk about fabrics and who's done what, is endlessly entertaining.

What makes Carter interesting is that he's using it as a protection against the legacy of his father and grandfather. He can't compete with them except as a black sheep, so he can become the guy that's whispered about. That's why he's still in Washington, D.C., and that's what makes the character interesting to me, because he shouldn't be in Washington anymore. He should be somewhere else. But he's still there because he's still tied to his father, he's still tied to the notion of being a black sheep.

The essence of the character is contradiction.

Why is he still in Washington? Why is he both in and out of the closet? Then you start to have an interesting character.

When Kristin discovers her lover's body, it's instinctive for him to make that call to the cops. She couldn't afford the scandal. That's the kind of guy he is. Woody was a little uncomfortable with that, and we added a moment when someone sees him, so he sort of has to make the call. But Carter is a well-mannered man, and he realizes that she can't be the one who finds that body, and somebody else should find it. He doesn't think that it'll be a big deal. I walk into my friend's apartment, see a body, call the police. What's the big deal? Well, turns out to be a big deal.

The thing is, you should stand up for your friends even after they desert you. Somebody said to me after seeing the film that his question to Kristin at the end—"Why didn't you stand up for me?"—is one that's unique to movies because you don't usually hear that. Usually a movie makes it clear. Why didn't you stand up for me? She can't understand it.

Jerry Seinfeld

October 28, 2007—Jerry Seinfeld has been known to enjoy the odd bungee jump, but dressing up like a bee and throwing himself off the roof of the Carlton Hotel in Cannes was new for him. This was last May. The studio attached a steel cable to the hotel, 130 feet in the air, and Jerry glided down to the photographers and bee-lovers below. It was a stunt to promote the animated film *Bee Movie.*

"When I got up there to actually do it," he said, "I thought, boy, this could be gruesome. This could be a very ugly scene. Seinfeld thinks he's a bee and falls to his death. What's wrong with this guy?"

He had been talked into it by Jeffrey Katzenberg, one of the co-owners of DreamWorks, who himself once appeared with a real lion on a leash to promote *The Lion King.* I remember the days when everybody thought Debbie Reynolds was a good sport to hop along in a sack race for *Divorce, American Style.*

"It could have been a posthumous work," Seinfeld said. This was during a Chicago visit to promote the movie. "You know, come and see his last unfinished work; we had to use footage of him dying at the end. And then there's absolutely no sequel possibility."

It was another DreamWorks partner, Steven Spielberg, who told him he should make the movie. They were sitting next to each other at dinner somewhere, the Hamptons is my guess.

"I was just trying to make amusing conversation," said Seinfeld, who became richer than anyone on TV except Oprah by making amusing conversation. "It was my first time ever having dinner with him, and I was very excited, and it was really just honestly a lull in the conversation I was trying to fill with this idea that it would be funny to make a movie about bees, and call it a B-movie, and that was it.

"He lit up and went, 'That is the greatest idea! I'm calling Jeffrey out at DreamWorks to see how to do this!' He swept me up in that tornado of enthusiasm he has, and the next thing I was making it."

This was after a decade of almost complete inactivity on TV and in the movies, just some stand-up tours, and suddenly Seinfeld was playing an animated bee.

"You know the DreamWorks logo with the little boy who floats with balloons onto the moon?" he said. "I changed it. I had a bee sting him, and he falls on his face and collapses and lands on the ground, and the bee takes over the moon. I did it as a joke to play on Jeffrey and he loved it, and we actually produced it and it's gonna be on every print. I'm stinging the kid in the logo and he falls to his death." Pause. "Well, not to his death. He just falls and gets hurt."

My next question was obvious, I suppose, but it seemed relevant: Why bees?

"The Discovery Channel has documentaries about different species. They take one animal and that animal becomes the star of the show. You get all into their life, and what they're trying to do to other animals, trying to kill them, trying to eat them, and you become completely involved in their life. Something about the complexity and perfection of bee society was interesting and very human, only more evolved. They have perfected society. They have a product, they have a security system, good living conditions, apartments, offices, streets, everybody employed, everybody happy."

Heroically I did not ask, "Wish you were a bee?"

"To be honest," he said, "I wrote it for adults. I wrote it like the TV show. I just write what I think is funny, and I don't worry about who's gonna get it and what age they are. I think the bee is more present in people's minds than we had realized."

Why, I asked, have you avoided leading roles in feature films? Are you afraid your TV persona will overshadow any movie character?

"I don't feel I do as well trying to become someone else when I do myself. My whole career I have done myself. That's what standup comedians do. We're not known for our ability to disappear into a character. That's the actor's talent. I like to be myself. I don't really wanna be other people. I was myself on the TV show, and I am in this, too, except if I were born as a bee, this is what I would be like."

So you, as Jerry Seinfeld the bee, would jump eight stories off the Carlton Hotel?

"They told me this is the only thing French people understand. You must hurl yourself off a hotel, or they won't go to your movie. That's what Katzenberg told me anyway. He also said Martin Scorsese did the same thing last year when he promoted *The Departed,* but I found out later that was not true."

I pictured Scorsese doing it, dressed not as a bee but in a tailored three-piece suit from his bespoke tailor on Saville Row, shoes from Lobb's on St. James Street, shirt from Turnball & Asser on Jermyn Street, hat from Art Fawcett in Oregon. Not as a bee.

You were just named the number-two TV moneymaker behind Oprah, I observed. Are you amazed at your good fortune?

"I have a satellite dish in my house on Long Island, and you can see the names of all the shows go around. I see my name go by, and it doesn't occur to me you don't see *Alf,* you don't see *Molly Dodd,* you don't see *My Friend, Flicka.* Why is this still going on? Because usually a TV series will get a run on syndication for two or three years, and then the next thing comes along. I think reality television is the number-one reason I'm still around. People want a comedy, and I don't have as much competition as I would normally have."

You are number twelve on Comedy Central's list of the greatest stand-up comics of all time. You might not argue with Richard Pryor, Lenny Bruce, or George Carlin, but what about Roseanne Barr and Chris Rock? Are they funnier than you?

"You haven't lost the sharp edge. I'll tell you, yes, it was quite humiliating to not break into the top ten, but I'm trying. I'm working on my craft, and next time they rate me I can move up the charts a little bit. There are some people on the list that don't have forty minutes of material."

And you?

"I have forty minutes."

That's all I had, too, so it was time to thank Jerry and leave, but he had something on his mind.

"It's hard to be a bee," he said. "They have to work very hard. There's a lot of danger. They're not good fliers. Their weight related to the size of their wings doesn't really work, according to studies they've done."

The bees?

"No, the scientists, of course. It doesn't make sense that they can fly. Their wings are too small for their body mass. That's how the movie begins, about how according to aviation theory bees should not be able to fly. So me, my bee, he gets insulted by the humans. He gets very riled up and inspires the other bees to fight back against this image that they're bad fliers."

They seem pretty good when they're chasing you, I said.

"Recently, Cal Tech solved the puzzle of how bees do it. Their wings flap in a completely different pattern from every other bird and insect. It's totally unique. They actually do a scooping motion, and move their wings at a faster rate."

He smiled. "I'm very intrigued by these little fellows."

Don't worry about my cough, I said. I'm not dying.

"That's great news."

Tarsem

June 4, 2008—Tarsem was talking about how he risked almost everything he owned to make a movie that nobody, nobody at all, was willing to finance for years. The movie is *The Fall,* which will be on my list of the year's best films and is setting box-office records on the art house circuit. It is almost impossible to describe. You can say what happens, but you can't convey the astonishment of *how* it happens.

Tarsem made millions as a director of commercials and gladly spent most of them to make his movie. "Everybody in advertising," he was telling me, "always says one day they'll make a great movie with their own money, blah, blah, blah. They never do it. David Fincher, one of my producers, told me, 'You happen to be the fool that has done it.'"

Tarsem is a thin man of medium height, mercurial in conversation, smiling easily. "Something happened to me that doesn't happen to most people," he said. "Life happens to them. It was happening to me. But at the particular point when I was ready to settle down with a woman and have the babies, the woman moved and had the babies with somebody else. I was freaked out. What happened next was, I had promised myself I would make this film in a heartbeat if I found the right girl. And suddenly I found the little girl."

How would he finance the movie? "I've never known what to do with money. I live quite easily. Ninety-five percent of the time it seems like I'm on airplanes or in airports. I travel making commercials, I have a home that's all paid for, and I'm a prostitute in love with a profession. I had no idea who my money was for. It wasn't for the kids that I didn't have, so I decided to cash in."

The Fall is one of the most extraordinary films I've ever seen. Set in Los Angeles in 1915, it involves a paralyzed stunt man (Lee Pace) and a four-year old Romanian girl named Alexandria (Catinca Untaru) who occupy separate wings in a hospital where most of the beds are empty—waiting, probably, to be filled by victims of the Great War.

The stunt man begins to tell the girl a story. We hear the story in his words, but we see it through her eyes, and she imagines it as a magical vision. After filming all the scenes involving the two characters, Tarsem shot her visions in twenty-eight countries over a period of four years. There are sights in the film you cannot imagine are possible, but Tarsem says he used no computers to create them. They exist.

Who is this Tarsem? Full name, Tarsem Singh Dhandwar. Last name too hard for Americans to say. Millions of Indians have the middle name "Singh." Therefore, Tarsem. Born in India, Tarsem moved to Iran with his family when he was three, but his father was concerned the mullahs would destroy education there, so he sent his two sons to a boarding school in the Himalayas.

"I saw a book in India titled *Guide to Film Schools in America,* and it shell-shocked me," he said. "It changed my life because I thought you went to college to study something that your father loved and you hated. I told my father I wanted to study film, and he said there was no way he was gonna let me do that. I made my way to Los Angeles and made a film that won a scholarship to the Art Center College of Design. My father thought I was headed for Harvard. I called him and said, 'I want to study film,' and he said, 'You don't exist anymore.'"

Tarsem made a music video for Suzanne Vega, another for REM. "The first commercial I did was for Levi's and was based on the movie *The Swimmer,* the Burt Lancaster one, where a guy swims from pool to pool in his neighbors' backyards. The tagline was, 'The more you wash them, the better they get.' That won the Grand Prix in Cannes and so in a way it's been downhill ever since."

The agencies that made commercials, he said, "gave me very good money, and I didn't complain about it. I put it aside like a little squirrel, and at the end I ended up with a project that I wanted to do very badly and threw it all away, so now I'm penniless, but as happy as a pig in poo. I told my brother, 'Sell everything. I'm going on this magical mystery tour. When I finish it, I'll let you know.' I called him when it was almost done. He said the house was almost up for sale. But I was finished."

He has a quick smile and makes his struggle sound like a lark.

"If you think it's hard raising money for a film, try telling people that the script is going to be written by a four-year old. It's going to be dictated to me by a child. For seven years, wherever I would shoot a commercial, I would send people out with a camera to schools, and one day I got a tape of this girl at a school in Romania, in the middle of students talking. I was amazed. She was perfect. She didn't speak English. The penny dropped. She was six, but if she didn't speak the language she would be using, the misunderstanding would buy me the two years that I needed. Because she had to seem four.

"I found a mental asylum in South Africa that gave me a wing. I figured everything for her had to be visual. I explained to her where she lived, where he lived, where everything was. And we taught her the English of her lines, word by word. She would say them, and if she didn't get it right in three or four takes, we changed her dialogue because she needed to sound spontaneous, not rehearsed."

It's true. One of the treasures of the film is the sound of the dialogue by Catinca Untaru. We understand every word, but she sounds as if she's inventing them as she utters them.

Now what about those miraculous locations? I asked him. *No* special effects? What about the zig-zagging, interlocking black-and-white staircases reaching down into the earth?

"It's true. It's Ripley's. What people think is not true in the film is true. The steps that go down, it's a reservoir that has been there for five hundred or six hundred years. It's used for seeing how low the water level is, to determine how to tax people. If the water level is so high, they charge so much tax from the farmers. The problem is most of the time you never see those steps; they're underwater. Somebody showed me these steps and said they went really way down. And I said, well, has anybody seen that?

"They said most Indians think they look cheap. But in fact they look like an inspiration by Escher. So labyrinthine and mad. The problem is, when you see the wide shot, you realize they're not what I'm making them out to be. What matters is how I'm framing it. If you see the wider shots, there are about two thousand Indians on trees watching and wondering why we're shooting in a really crappy well. But since I shot those steps, three Hindi movies have gone and shot there because they figure, if it's good enough for him, it must be beautiful."

And the labyrinth with no escape?

"That is a four-hundred-year-old observatory. The steps line up with one star, the arc lines up with another star, and if you look around the location it's really chaotic and haywire. All I had to do was choose my angle so I could use their shapes without showing their surroundings. I thought, 'I can make a labyrinth out of this if I make it look like it's enclosed.' The fact is, it's a really cheap-looking park in the middle of Jaidpur.

"And as for the blue city . . . I made a contract with the city; we would give them free paint. We knew legally they could only choose blue. So they painted their houses blue, and it looked more vibrant than it ever had before."

Tarsem made it all sound so simple, and when you see the film it all seems literally impossible.

"There are no computer effects. It's just the kind of visual stuff like what I was doing all the time with commercials, where it looks like more than it is. In all these places I had filmed over at least seventeen years, I told the people, this is a paid job, it's a commercial, but I'll come back one day and make this place look magical. To use a line from *The Godfather,* he does them a favor, and one day, 'and that day may never come,' there will be a favor in return. And seventeen years later that day came, I showed up, and some of the favors I could cash in, and some I couldn't."

And then Tarsem made one of the most astonishing films I have ever seen. It is all the more special in this age of computer-generated special effects, because we see things that cannot exist, but our eyes do not lie, and they do exist, yes, they really do.

Essays

I Ain't a Pretty Boy No More

April 24, 2007—My Ninth Annual Overlooked Film Festival opens Wednesday night at the University of Illinois at Urbana, and Chaz and I will be in attendance.

This year I won't be speaking, however, as I await another surgery.

I have received a lot of advice that I should not attend the festival. I'm told that paparazzi will take unflattering pictures, people will be unkind, etc.

Frankly, my dear, I don't give a damn. As a journalist I can take it as well as dish it out.

So let's talk turkey. What will I look like? To paraphrase a line from *Raging Bull,* I ain't a pretty boy no more. (Not that I ever was. The original appeal of *Siskel & Ebert* was that we didn't look like we belonged on TV.)

What happened was, cancer of the salivary gland spread to my right lower jaw. A segment of the mandible was removed. Two operations to replace the missing segment were unsuccessful, both leading to unanticipated bleeding.

A tracheostomy was necessary, so, for the time being, I cannot speak. I make do with written notes and a lot of hand waving and eye rolling. The doctors now plan an approach that does not involve the risk of unplanned bleeding. If all goes well, my speech will be restored.

So when I turn up in Urbana, I will be wearing a gauze bandage around my neck, and my mouth will be seen to droop. So it goes.

I was told photos of me in this condition would attract the gossip papers. So what?

I have been very sick, am getting better, and this is how it looks. I still have my brain and my typing fingers.

Although months in bed after the bleeding episodes caused a lack of strength and coordination, the Rehabilitation Institute of Chicago restored my ability to walk on my own, climb stairs, etc.

I no longer use a walker much, and the wheelchair is more for occasional speed and comfort than need. Just today we went for a long stroll in Lincoln Park.

We spend too much time hiding illness. There is an assumption that I must always look the same. I hope to look better than I look now. But I'm not going to miss my festival.

Why do I want to go? Above all, to see the movies. Then to meet old friends and great directors and personally thank all the loyal audience members who continue to support the festival.

At least, not being able to speak, I am spared the need to explain why every film is "overlooked," or why I wrote *Beyond the Valley of the Dolls.*

Being sick is no fun. But you can have fun while you're sick. I wouldn't miss the festival for anything!

P.S. to gossip rags: I have some back pain, and to make it easier for me to sit through screenings, the festival has installed my very own La-Z-Boy chair.

Photos of me in the chair should be captioned "La-Z-Critic."

No Country for Old Men Thinker

May 22, 2007—Gene Siskel and I came back from our vacations and went to a screening the next morning. It was for a movie named *Fargo.* We knew nothing about it. Sounded like a Western. When the lights came up after that great film, we gasped at the credits: written and directed by Joel and Ethan Coen. It was and it wasn't a "Coen brothers film." It didn't have the deliberate quirkiness and flywheel plot, but it had the intelligence, the humor, the human nature pushed to extremes, the violence raised to the level of classical irony.

Now there is another Coen brothers film you wouldn't know was by them. *No Country for Old Men,* which premiered at Cannes, is a spare, lean, straightforward story, as direct in its way as *The Treasure of the Sierra Madre.* I don't think there's a Coen touch in the movie, unless it's the sheer quality and the plot twisting back on itself, and the plot comes from the Cormac McCarthy novel. The movie has the same kind of deadpan intensity that Tommy Lee Jones, its star, is so good at.

The film's style is pure and uninflected, a series of surprising but, in a way, inevitable developments that are presented with implacable logic. There isn't much we anticipate, but nothing we can't accept. Some of that comes from McCarthy, the heir of Faulkner, who mines the Southwest and Mexico for the way they can break your heart before they kill you.

McCarthy is best known for his Border Trilogy, about men, horses, pain, and loyalty; *All the Pretty Horses* was directed by Billy Bob Thornton. McCarthy's best book is said to be *Blood Meridian,* which Harold Bloom said he hated for its violence so much he threw it across the room twice, and then read it, declared it a masterpiece, and wrote the introduction for the Modern Library edition.

My own favorite is *Suttree,* with its closely woven mosaic of unusual and unknown words and its heartbreaking story. It's about a man fallen from grace, who lives in a houseboat, catches catfish for a living, has hallucinatory alcoholic adventures and episodes of sentiment, pity, and loyalty. In the book, a family of river people die in a way so sudden, arbitrary, and final that you have to read the page again to know for sure what happened. The book's language is such that every page contains words you've never seen before. I have occasionally looked some of them up in the dictionary to find that in every case, they were correctly used. But you don't need to know what they mean; their shape and music do the job.

McCarthy's most recent books are *No Country for Old Men* and *The Road,* for which he just won the Pulitzer Prize. Both are fine, sound books, but not equal to the fierce genius of *Blood Meridian* and *Suttree.* His Pulitzer, in a way, parallels Martin Scorsese's belated Oscar for directing *The Departed.* It's a good film, but where was the Academy after *Raging Bull, Taxi Driver,* or *GoodFellas*?

The Coen brothers may have chosen wisely, however, in selecting *No Country for Old Men* to film. It's filmable. I don't know if audiences could endure *Blood Meridian,* if it were filmed faithfully. As for *Suttree,* imagine *Huckleberry Finn* crossed with *Under the Volcano.*

No Country for Old Men begins with a drug transaction gone so terribly wrong that when a rancher discovers the site in a barren wasteland, all the money and all the cocaine are still there, along with a litter of trucks and corpses. The movie follows the trail of the money and drugs and the rancher (Josh Brolin), and he is followed by a lank-haired, merciless killer named Chigurh (Javier Bardem) while the taciturn local sheriff (Tommy Lee Jones) tries to piece together what happened. Chigurh is a clone, in a way, of the Judge in *Blood Meridian,* who kills as a way of life.

Note: The Road *is a selection of Oprah's Book Club, and McCarthy has agreed to appear on her program. It will be, as far as I am aware, the only television appearance in the history of the mysterious and reclusive author, who is not much given to publicity. This is one program I plan to watch.*

A Bouquet Arrives

May 7, 2007—A beautiful bouquet of flowers was delivered to the house the other day. A handwritten note paid compliments to my work and wished me a speedy recovery.

Who was it from? A friend? A colleague? An old classmate? The card was signed, "Your Least Favorite Movie Star, Rob Schneider."

Saints preserve us.

It will help to establish a context if I mention that my review of Schneider's latest film, *Deuce Bigalow: European Gigolo,* contained three words that provided me with the title of my book *Your Movie Sucks.*

I regard the flowers and intuit they were not sent in the spirit of irony. Despite my review, Rob Schneider was moved to make a kind and generous gesture, one person to another.

The bouquet didn't change my opinion of his movie, but I don't think he intended that. It was a way of stepping back. It was a reminder that in the great scheme of things, a review doesn't mean very much.

Sometimes when I write a negative review, people will say, "I'll bet you can't wait to hammer his next film." Not true. I would far rather praise the next film to show that I maintained an open mind.

When Vincent Gallo's *Brown Bunny* played at Cannes in 2003, I walked out of the screening and declared it "the worst movie in the history of the film festival." This was an unwise thing to do. My policy for years has been to avoid giving a negative review of a festival film until it has a chance to open.

Gallo issued a curse on my colon. I responded that the video of my colonoscopy was more entertaining than his film, and there the matter rested until 2004, when Gallo released a "final cut" of *The Brown Bunny,* which was reedited and thirty minutes shorter. I went to see it, and now I could see better what he was getting at, and I gave it a positive review.

"I'll bet you hated to change your mind," I was told. No, I was happy to. It is a hard and frustrating thing to make a movie, and credit must be give where due.

Now we come back to the flowers. They were a reminder, if I needed one, that although Rob Schneider might (in my opinion) have made a bad movie, he is not a bad man, and no doubt tried to make a wonderful movie, and hopes to again. I hope so, too.

Thanks, Rob.

Pirates of the Caribbean: At World's End

May 25, 2007—Not a review of *Pirates of the Caribbean: Dead Man's Chest.* Just some idle speculation.

1. Does the word "shipshape" mean nothing in the pirate navy? Their ship, the Black Pearl, looks like it should be dipped in Easy-Off Oven Cleaner.

2. By what evolutionary pathway did nature supply Davy Jones (Bill Nighy) with a face of squirming octopus tentacles? What is the advantage? To help him win a hot dog–eating contest?

3. All of Davy's crew members seem to have spent long years in the briny deep, their faces being colonized by lower orders of marine life. They look like the "before" in a before-and-after advertisement when the "after" is scrofula.

4. Is Johnny Depp, that splendid actor, signed up for every movie in the series? Let him take as a cautionary note that Johnny Weissmuller once ranged up and down the aisles of a flight to Cannes uttering the Tarzan yell.

5. Discuss in five hundred words or less: "There is nothing so tedious as nonstop excitement." —Stephanie Zacharek, Salon.com.

6. That's a cute monkey who, like many movie animals, always supplies the correct reaction shot. But with cannon to the left of him and cannon to the right of him, isn't it miraculous that he never has a BM on a sailor's shoulder? Or, given the state of their uniforms, would we be able to see it?

7. Somewhere on that floating sinkhole of decay, Keira Knightley has found a bathtub, a vanity table, a hairdresser, and a wardrobe.

8. In a swordfight, Depp has his sword hacked in two. He thrusts the stump into his scabbard. Later, he pulls his sword again, and is surprised to see it is only a foot long. What kind of pirate forgets that his sword is hacked in two?

9. We learn that at sundown a flash of green sometimes appears on the horizon. What French art film also depends on that phenomenon? Which French author first mentioned it?

10. The movie was inspired by the Pirates of the Caribbean ride at Disney World. If they film It's a Small World, does that mean all those cute little dolls have to die?

Studs Terkel: A Tribute

May 15, 2007—I met Studs Terkel within a few weeks after I arrived in Chicago. I was not a movie critic yet, just a kid who had been hired by the paper, but Studs was always ready to make a friend and give a kid a boost. I've talked with him countless times over the years but only took notes once, in August 2005, over dinner, six days before his open-heart surgery.

He is the greatest living Chicagoan. Through his best-selling oral histories, involving work, World War II, death, and so much more, he has recorded our lives, our thoughts, our fears, our dreams.

Now, as Studs celebrates his ninety-fifth birthday at the Chicago Historical Society, I pulled out those notes. I saw him wondering in 2005 if he'd pull through the surgery. He regarded the possibility of death as he regarded life, with unbounded curiosity.

"It's another adventure!" he said. "The docs say the odds are four to one in my favor. At age ninety-three, those are pretty good odds."

He ordered the whitefish and a glass of wine, and regarded his prospects realistically. "I'm gonna have a whack at it. Otherwise, I'm Dead Man Walking. If I don't have the operation, how long do I have? Six months, maybe. That's no way to live, waiting to die. I've had ninety-three years—tumultuous years. That's a pretty good run.

We were having dinner at the University Club at Michigan and Monroe, chosen not only for the whitefish and crab cakes but because it is quiet, and Studs minced no words: "I'm deaf as a post." His hearing aid worked well in the stillness, however, and besides, Studs did most of the talking. Also at the table: Studs's son Dan, his caregiver J. R., and my wife, Chaz. He produced a signed copy of *And They All Sang: Adventures of an Eclectic Disk Jockey,* which was his twelfth book.

"I've got six thousand or eight thousand tapes of interviews at the Historical Society," Studs said. "If I get through this thing, I have a lot of work to do over there. At least two hundred tapes are missing. I was hopeless with mechanical things. Made a living with a tape recorder and never learned how to work it. I almost erased Bertrand Russell.

"Also, I'd like to stick around long enough to work on my memoirs," he said. "I've got a working title: *The Great American Lobotomy.* I think this country suffers from national Alzheimer's. There was a survey the other day showing that most people think our best president was Reagan. Not Lincoln. FDR came in tenth. People don't pay attention anymore. They don't read the news."

Studs not only reads the news but remembers it. His memory is a limitless storehouse, unaffected by age. Our conversation ranged over a lifetime, over memories of Mahalia Jackson, Paul Robeson, Pete Seeger, Billie Holiday ("She sang at my going-away party for the Army").

"Just the other day," Studs said. "I went to visit Florence Scala. She led the fight to protect the Taylor Street neighborhood when they put up the new University of Illinois. I've been calling on some people who were important to me, in case I don't see them again.

"A lot of my pals are gone. Hank Oettinger, the champion letter-to-the-editor writer. Belongs in the Guinness Book. I was all set to speak at his memorial service, and I was sitting on my bed pulling on my socks, and I woke up three hours later—just fell right to sleep. Old age for you.

"Somebody else I miss, Win Stracke, the troubadour of Old Town."

And Ida. Studs married her in 1939, and they were inseparable until her death from heart surgery on December 23, 1999. In the introduction to his book about death and dying, *Will the Circle Be Unbroken?* (2001), Studs remembered her last words to him, as they wheeled her toward the operating room: "Louis, what have you gotten me into now?"

"The funny thing was," Studs said, "when they unsealed the FBI files about so-called un-American activities, Ida's was thicker than mine. She liked to bring that up to me." He recalled that in her eighties she was advised to use a cane but refused, saying, "I fall over so gracefully.

"When I go, my ashes will be mixed with Ida's and scattered in Bughouse Square," Studs said.

"I had a bad dream last night," he said. "I dreamed I was in London and I couldn't find my passport. I wonder what that symbolized."

"I told him, 'Studs, don't dream any more trips,'" J. R. said.

"Dan and J. R. are taking good care of me," Studs said. "It's not easy being my son. Dan is a man who knows every street and alley in the city. I told him he should have been a wheelman for the mob."

Dan smiled. "It's not easy, but it's been an experience," he said. "You talk about Florence Scala—it wasn't just the Italian neighborhood that got bulldozed. It was also the original Greek Town. It had an informal neighborhood feel. Not just a tourist destination."

There was love around the table. Love for one another, love for life, for the old stories, the memories, the legends.

"O'Rourke's Pub on North Avenue," Studs said. "On a good night, everybody would be there. Mike might be there. Mike Royko. Ben Bradlee, the editor of the *Washington Post,* asked Bob Woodward to write a Royko-style column for the *Post.* Woodward told me he wrote it for two weeks, and then he collapsed. He asked me, 'How does Mike do it? How does he turn it out five days a week?' I told him it was the fire, the fire and the demon. There was a fire inside, in the belly, and a demon, and sometimes the demon won, but usually the fire.

"With Nelson Algren, it was the same. Fire and demons. He was a real Chicagoan, and of course he was nuts. He kept selling people the typewriter he claimed he wrote *The Man with the Golden Arm* on. He had a lot of typewriters. People compared him to Saul Bellow. At Nelson's memorial service, somebody said if Nelson had written about professors at the

University of Chicago and their wives and mistresses, he might have won the Nobel."

Studs admired the whitefish that materialized in front of him. "O'Rourke's," he said, with the tone of voice that meant "those were the days, my friends." "Nelson was always talking about his famous fight with Tom Fitzpatrick. He told me he threw a shot glass of cognac in his face. He said he had never really appreciated cognac until that moment. But I talked to eyewitnesses, and they said what really happened was they threw limes at each other."

He rocked with laughter. "And Riccardo's, especially on Friday nights after work. All the newspaper guys. In the front booth, Bill Mauldin, Royko, John Fischetti. But the history! Fifty years ago, Riccardo's was the only place in the Loop where a black person could be served drinks and a dinner. That place, and one jazz club.

"Ric Riccardo's landlord was P. K. Wrigley, who owned all the land behind the Wrigley Building. He called Ric one day and said he heard he had 'a certain element' among his customers. Ric told him: 'I welcome all customers of good character to my restaurant. What do you plan to do about it?' Nothing. P. K. did nothing. But the reason the Cubs haven't won a World Series since 1908 is that they were the last team in the major leagues to hire a black ballplayer."

Of regrets, Studs said, echoing the cabaret song, he had a few. "I want to tell you a story," he said. "It starts when WFMT, our radio station, was purchased by WTTW, the public station. WFMT was making a nice profit, but the real moneymaker was our magazine, *Chicago* magazine. So WTTW stole our magazine. I was incensed by this, and was composing a very pointed letter to the board of directors, when the phone rang.

"It was Oprah Winfrey. She had just moved here from Baltimore, and she wanted me to be one of the first guests on her show. I was so distracted by the letter I had in my typewriter, so worked up, I wasn't paying attention. I turned her down. I probably sounded distant. I had it in my head that I had to tackle this WFMT problem. It had me all worked up.

"Well, it's only human nature that you remember a rebuff. That was never meant as a rebuff, but I regret it—I regret it to this day. I should have been paying attention. I was never asked on her show again. I knew what that was about. I could picture her thinking about that conversation. I never got a chance to talk to her about it again."

After he told me that story, Studs reached over and patted me on the arm. Now why did he do that? It was a wordless message.

We'd been friends since 1966. We'd seen each other hundreds of times, gone on a cruise together. But when Studs tumbled down the stairs in 2004 and was laid up in the hospital, I didn't come to see him. He took that as a rebuff, as he should have. I was having health problems of my own, but that was no excuse, and he told a friend he was disappointed in me.

I called to apologize. "Forget about it," he said. "There's nothing to talk about." We made dinner plans. Now he had told me a parable. The story wasn't about Studs and Oprah, it was about me and Studs. The pat on the arm was forgiveness.

Since then I have been to see him in the hospital, and he has been to see me in the hospital.

He is a man who embodies the life force more joyfully than anyone else I have ever known. His memory seems to keep his whole life alive at once. Past and present are in the room at the same time. It is not that he is nostalgic; it is that he values the past and respects it. In a sense, everything that has ever happened to him is still happening now.

One day in 1966, only a few weeks after I met him, Studs telephoned. The novelist Doris Lessing was visiting from London. He wanted to show her the town, and because he never learned to drive, he wanted me to drive them around. For three days, Studs showed Chicago to Lessing, and to me. One afternoon we drove through Washington Park.

"Stop here!" Studs said. "You see that tree over there? That's where Studs Lonigan kissed Lucy Scanlon. That's where I got my nickname—from *Studs Lonigan*, the Chicago novel by James T. Farrell."

We got out of the car and walked into the park.

"This is where he kissed her, all those years ago," Studs said.

AFI Top 100 Films: A Few Observations

June 21, 2007—Welles's *Citizen Kane* is still the greatest American film of all time. Coppola's

The Godfather is second. Scorsese's *Raging Bull* and Hitchcock's *Vertigo* have cracked the top 10, booting out *The Graduate* (number 7 to number 17) and *On the Waterfront* (number 8 to number 19). And Ford's *The Searchers* hurtled from number 96 to number 12.

So says the American Film Institute. Its list of the Top 100 American Films, voted on by a group of 1,500 filmmakers, critics, and historians, was revealed Wednesday night on a TV special hosted by Morgan Freeman, star of *The Shawshank Redemption* (number 72).

Lists like these cry out to be disagreed with. Seconds after an advance copy was sent to news outlets, film critic Peter Debruge e-mailed me: "Of all the issues surrounding this list, my biggest question: Where did *Fargo* go?"

What? *Fargo* not on the list? Unthinkable, considering that—well, I was going to name a title that has no business being on the list, but actually they all have a claim, even the few like *High Noon* that I personally don't much like. It's just that—what? No *Fargo*?

In the aftermath of the first list, in 1998, I received enough complaints about missing titles to supply two or three more lists. No doubt most of those 1,500 experts are themselves dismayed by titles that did and didn't make the cut. But such lists serve two functions: (1) The TV special makes money for the AFI, which is a noble and useful institution, and (2) some kid somewhere is gonna rent *Citizen Kane* and have the same kind of epiphany I had when I first saw it as a teenager.

New films become old films so fast. *Raging Bull* came out twenty-seven years ago. It's now older than *Casablanca* (number 3) was when I became a film critic. According to the MPAA, more than 50 percent of moviegoers are under twenty-seven. They are going to find movies on this list that were made before their grandparents were born—and, if judging by the kids I saw Buster Keaton's *The General* (number 18) with, they might love them.

Ah, but there's the problem: Will they find out about them? Too many younger moviegoers are wasting their precious adolescence frying their brains with vomitoriums posing as slasher movies. A list like this can do some good.

During a Google search for "age of average moviegoer," I came across a column by critic T. C. Candler that opened with this quote: "I have here a heartfelt message from a reader who urges me not to be so hard on stupid films, because they are 'plenty smart enough for the average moviegoer.' Yes, but one hopes being an average moviegoer is not the end of the road: that one starts as a below-average filmgoer, passes through average, and, guided by the labors of America's hard-working film critics, arrives in triumph at above-average."

Candler was quoting me, and I cannot agree more. To take a hypothetical possibility, if you were to see all 100 films on the AFI list, by the end of that experience you would no longer desire to see a Dead Teenager Movie. (Yes, there could be a great Dead Teenager Movie. Please send me a list of the 100 greatest.)

To read over the AFI list is to remember spine-tingling moments in movie theaters. The ballet of spaceships in *2001*. The soaking-wet dance in *Singin' in the Rain*. The scary perfection of Astaire and Rogers, the perfect anarchy of the Marx Brothers, the anarchic warfare in *Apocalypse Now*, the warfare of obsession in *Vertigo*. The list will become a retail tool. AOL, Best Buy, and Moviefone have scheduled promotions. You know that Netflix and Blockbuster will push it. The movie channels will feature titles from it. Somebody will find out who James Stewart was, or Ingrid Bergman. So in the last analysis, it doesn't really matter what movies are on the list. What matters is the movies on the list, voted by 1,500 above-average moviegoers who don't think *Citizen Kane* has aged one day.

Debate: Ebert vs. Clive Barker

July 23, 2007—A year or so ago I rashly wrote that video games could not be art. That inspired a firestorm among gamers, who wrote me countless messages explaining why I was wrong and urging me to play their favorite games. Of course, I was asking for it. Anything can be art. Even a can of Campbell's soup. What I should have said is that games could not be high art, as I understand it.

How do I know this? How many games have I played? I know it by the definition of the vast majority of games. They tend to involve (1) point-and-shoot in many variations and plot lines; (2) treasure or scavenger hunts, as in *Myst*; and (3) player control of the outcome. I don't think these attributes have much to do with art and have more in common with sports.

One of the notables taking exception to my opinion was Clive Barker, the British horror novelist, short-story writer, and *Hellraiser* writer-director. Barker studied English and philosophy at Liverpool, is an accomplished artist, and quite possibly knows more about art in its many manifestations than the average gamer does. How can I say that? Only a guess.

Barker was a speaker at the recent Hollywood and Games Summit, and he chose to respond to some of my statements. I have his remarks from www.GamesIndustry.biz and find them stimulating.

CB: It's evident that Ebert had a prejudiced vision of what the medium is, or more importantly, what it can be.

RE: The word "prejudiced" often translates as "disagrees with me." I might suggest that gamers have a prejudiced view of their medium, and *particularly* what it can be. Games may not be Shakespeare quite yet, but I have the prejudice that they never will be, and some gamers are prejudiced that they will.

CB: We can debate what art is, we can debate it forever. If the experience moves you in some way or another—even if it moves your bowels—I think it is worthy of some serious study.

RE: Perhaps if the experience moves your bowels, it is worthy of some serious medical study. Many experiences that move me in some way or another are not art. A year ago I lost the ability (temporarily, I hope) to speak. I was deeply moved by the experience. It was not art.

CB: It used to worry me that the *New York Times* never reviewed my books. . . . But the point is that people like the books. Books aren't about reviewers. Games aren't about reviewers. They are about players.

RE: A reviewer is a reader, a viewer, or a player with an opinion about what he or she has viewed, read, or played. Whether that opinion is valid is up to his audience. Books, games, and all forms of created experience are about themselves; the real question is, do we as their consumers become more or less complex, thoughtful, insightful, witty, empathetic, intelligent, philosophical (and so on), by experiencing them? Something may be excellent *as itself,* and yet be ultimately worthless. A bowel movement, for example.

CB: I think that Roger Ebert's problem is that he thinks you can't have art if there is that amount of malleability in the narrative. In other words, Shakespeare could not have written *Romeo and Juliet* as a game because it could have had a happy ending, you know? If only she hadn't taken the damn poison. If only he'd have gotten there quicker.

RE: He is right again about me. I believe art is created by an artist. If you change it, you become the artist. Would *Romeo and Juliet* have been better with a different ending? Rewritten versions of the play were actually produced with happy endings. *King Lear* was also subjected to rewrites; it's such a downer. At this point, taste comes into play. Which version of *Romeo and Juliet,* Shakespeare's or Barker's, is superior, deeper, more moving, more "artistic"?

CB: We should be stretching the imaginations of our players and ourselves. Let's invent a world where the player gets to go through every emotional journey available. That is art. Offering that to people is art.

RE: If you can go through "every emotional journey available," doesn't that devalue each and every one of them? Art seeks to lead you to an inevitable conclusion, not a smorgasbord of choices. If next time I have Romeo and Juliet go through the story naked and standing on their hands, would that be way cool, or what?

CB: I'm not doing an evangelical job here. I'm just saying that gaming is a great way to do what we as human beings need to do all the time—to take ourselves away from the oppressive facts of our lives and go somewhere where we have our own control.

RE: Spoken with the maturity of an honest and articulate four-year-old. I do not have a need "all the time" to take myself away from the oppressive facts of my life, however oppressive they may be, in order to go somewhere where I have control. I need to stay here and take control. Right now, for example, I cannot speak, but I am writing this. You lose some, you win some.

That said, let me confess I enjoy entertainments, but I think it important to know what they are. I like the circus as much as the ballet. I like crime novels. (I just finished an advance copy of Henry Kisor's *Cache of Corpses,* about GPS geo-caching gamesters and a macabre murder conspiracy. Couldn't put it down.) And

I like horror stories, where Edgar Allan Poe in particular represents art. I think I know what Stan Brakhage meant when he said Poe invented the cinema, lacking only film.

I treasure escapism in the movies. I tirelessly quote Pauline Kael: "The movies are so rarely great art, that if we cannot appreciate great trash, we have no reason to go." I admired *Spider-Man II, Superman,* and many of the Star Wars, Indiana Jones, James Bond, and Harry Potter films. The idea, I think, is to value what is good at whatever level you find it. *Spider-Man II* is one of the great comic superhero movies, but it is not great art.

Barker is right that we can debate art forever. I mentioned that a Campbell's soup can could be art. I was imprecise. Actually, it is Andy Warhol's painting of the label that is art. Would Warhol have considered Clive Barker's video game "Undying" as art? Certainly. He would have kept it in its shrink-wrapped box, placed it inside a Plexiglas display case, mounted it on a pedestal, and labeled it *Video Game.*

In Defense of Ingmar Bergman

August 8, 2007—I have long known and admired the *Chicago Reader*'s film critic, Jonathan Rosenbaum, but his *New York Times* op-ed attack on Ingmar Bergman ("Scenes from an Overrated Career," August 4, 2007) is a bizarre departure from his usual sanity. It says more about Rosenbaum's love of stylistic extremes than it does about Bergman and audiences. Who else but Rosenbaum could actually base an attack on the complaint that Bergman had what his favorites Carl Theodor Dreyer and Robert Bresson lacked, "the power to entertain—which often meant a reluctance to challenge conventional film-going habits"? In what parallel universe is the power to entertain defined in that way?

I love Bresson and respect Dreyer, but what does Rosenbaum mean by their challenges to conventional filmgoing? He continues: ". . . as Dreyer did when constructing his peculiar form of movie space and Bresson did when constructing his peculiar form of movie acting." And what were those peculiar forms? Dreyer built an elaborate set for *The Passion of Joan of Arc* and never revealed it, using close-ups of faces with expressionistic angles and shadows. Bresson would shoot the same take over and over, as many as fifty times, to drain his actors of all emotion; he referred to them, indeed, as "models." I am impressed by the idea and conception of these peculiar forms, but I doubt that they are more "entertaining" than Bergman's less constricted use of sets and actors.

Rosenbaum writes, "Riddled with wounds inflicted by Mr. Bergman's strict Lutheran upbringing and diverse spiritual doubts, these films are at times too self-absorbed to say much about the larger world, limiting the relevance that his champions often claim for them." This statement is perfectly accurate about Dreyer if you substitute his name for Bergman's, and perfectly accurate about Bresson, if you substitute the names and change "Lutheran" to "Catholic." Indeed, Bresson has been called the most Catholic of filmmakers.

Rosenbaum says Bergman is less taught in schools today than Godard and Hitchcock. He carefully avoids saying Bergman is less taught than Dreyer or Bresson. I grant him Hitchcock. He uses Google counts in his argument, so out of curiosity I Googled "film class on Ingmar Bergman" (1,400,000) and "film class on Jean-Luc Godard" (310,000). He says Bergman is "less discussed," so I Googled Web discussion groups and found that Bergman scored 59,000 and Godard 14,400. Of course, these entries cover a multitude of kinds of content, but there you have them.

Curiously, Rosenbaum thinks it is a sign of Bergman's decline that he is hard to find on DVD these days because he had to purchase his copy of *The Magician* in Paris. (Like many of his films, *The Magician* hasn't been widely available here for ages.) Not true. I had to order Welles's *Chimes at Midnight* from Brazil, and his *Magnificent Ambersons* is unavailable in this country, but I find sixty-six DVDs of Bergman's fifty-some titles, including *The Magician,* for sale on Amazon, although some of them are for zones other than ours (an all-zone DVD player now costs less than seventy dollars, something I learned from Rosenbaum before ordering mine). You can find DVDs of all of Dreyer's films from *Joan* onward (five), and ten of the thirteen Bressons.

The most recent of the four Bergmans that Rosenbaum even mentions is *Persona* (1966), except for *Saraband* (2003), his final film. The sin of that film was "his seeming contempt for the medium (digital video) apart from its usefulness as a simple recording device." In other words, at eighty-five, Bergman did not choose to experiment with digital but simply used it. Surely it is also of interest that the film reunited the same two actors, Liv Ullmann and Erland Josephson, who had already played a divorced couple in *Scenes from a Marriage* (1973), and now meet again many years later. As for Bergman's openness to a newer medium, what about his embrace of the lower costs and greater flexibility of Super 16 more than thirty-five years ago? What about him proving with Sven Nykvist in *The Passion of Anna* that a conversation could be shot on 16 mm by the light of a single candle?

I think Rosenbaum gives away the game when he says Bergman's "movies aren't so much filmic expressions as expressions on film." He means form itself is more important (and entertaining, I guess) than narrative, emotional content, and performance. Not everyone would agree.

Rosenbaum complains of "the antiseptic, upscale look of Mr. Bergman's interiors." Would that include the interiors in *The Virgin Spring, The Seventh Seal, The Passion of Anna, The Silence, Wild Strawberries, Hour of the Wolf, Scenes from a Marriage,* and indeed *The Magician* and *Persona?* (I would mention *Fanny and Alexander* and its horror-house Lutheran parsonage, but Rosenbaum says he hasn't seen the film voted number three in the *Sight & Sound* poll of world directors and critics to determine the best films from 1975–2000.)

Finally, Rosenbaum laments how Bergman's "mainly blond, blue-eyed cast members became a brand to be adopted and emulated." Hello? Bergman worked in Sweden! Does he forgive Ousmane Sembene's African exteriors and mainly black-haired, brown-eyed cast members? Or the way Ozu used all those Japanese?

Commentary: The Shaky-Cam

August 23, 2007—"A specter is haunting contemporary cinema: the shaky shot."

So writes David Bordwell, in connection with the growing controversy over the hyperkinetic filming and editing style of such movies as *The Bourne Ultimatum.* This is a specter that will not go away. The quick-cutting of *Ultimatum* (average shot length: two seconds) has inspired a flood of messages to my Answer Man column, and now Bordwell, probably the most-respected film academic, forwards me a post from movies.com in which "sfjockdawg," the writer, says:

"We went to see BU on the IMAX in San Francisco. Near the end, when Webb is having the flashback to when he is forced to show his commitment to the project, the lady next to me spontaneously unleashes a huge amount of vomit all over my leg and all over the floor in front of her! I have never experienced anything like it in my life! Now all the action sequences, the nauseating use of moving cameras, and the relentless score were enough to make anyone dizzy, but to throw up?"

Bordwell tells me he knows the post is accurate because a former student of his was an eyewitness. The "shaky-cam" issue is one on which I have been too slow to react. In years past, the Answer Man got complaints about the hand-held opening sequence of Woody Allen's *Husbands and Wives* and the whole of *Moulin Rouge,* but I guess I considered them the grumblings of an eccentric minority. However, the DVD of *Moulin Rouge* sold like gangbusters, and people wrote me it was because they "could get farther away from it."

Now readers have questioned my sanity after my *Ultimatum* review, in which I wrote that director Paul Greengrass "creates (or seems to create) amazingly long takes, but does it without calling attention to them. Whether they actually are unbroken stretches of film or are spliced together by invisible wipes, what counts is that they present such mind-blowing action that I forgot to keep track."

Well, obviously, they are far from unbroken. The intended illusion worked for me. Even the film's assistant editor, whom I queried, could recall only a twenty-second unbroken take. Readers asked if the editing style didn't bother me. Actually, no, although I was toward the rear of a large theater and not confronted by IMAX.

But it bothers a lot of people. Bordwell has a detailed analysis of the phenomenon on his blog (www.davidbordwell.net/blog/?m=200708), and Jim Emerson, the editor of www.rogerebert.com, has another in his blog (http://blogs.suntimes.com/scanners/). On my Web site, you will find a long collection of reader complaints.

What I conclude is that this phenomenon is real, that many people are disturbed by the vertiginous way that handheld cameras interact with fast cutting, and that it has remained under the radar of many film critics because, perhaps, we are hardened to it. In movies like *Run, Lola, Run,* where it is used with more continuity and control, it can be wonderfully effective. But *Ultimatum,* for many people, is apparently a case of going too far.

In their discussions of "classical style" in film versus the emergence of newer styles such as quick cutting, Bordwell and his equally expert wife, Dr. Kristin Thompson, have been far in front of the curve. It was Bordwell who first armed his students with clickers and sent them to theaters to count the actual shots in a movie, divide them into the running time, and come up with the ASL (average shot length).

Now a whole Web site is devoted to that practice. On www.cinemetrics.lv, you will find the theory, measuring methods, and software so that volunteers can determine the ASL of a film on their home computers. The ASL of John Cassavetes's *Love Streams* is 15.6 seconds, the ASL of *Citizen Kane* is 11.4, the screwball comedy *His Girl Friday* is 15, *Pulp Fiction* is 7.9, and *The Incredibles* is 2.5.

While two seconds is a short shot, remember that an ASL is obtained by averaging all of the shots, long and short; that there are twenty-four frames of film to a second, and that the human eye can actually perceive one frame (as with the satanic face in *The Exorcist*). What is crucial (the "vomiting point," we could call it) is apparently when a film doesn't vary its pace but is largely made of short handheld shots, edited together by quick cuts that ignore spatial continuity.

The shaky-cam, queasy-cam, or whatever you call it, has hardly affected the enormous box-office performances of the *Bourne* pictures, but the phenomenon is real, it has been called to our attention by moviegoers marching in and staggering out, and more research is needed. IMAX, by its nature, provides the phenomenon taken to its extreme.

I remember that in 1993, when I was treated to a tour of a then-new IMAX projection booth, I asked about the future of feature films in the giant process. The IMAX people, I wrote, said their thinking was that a conventional story film wouldn't work in the format, adding that quick dramatic cutting between shots so disorients the audience that some people get nauseous. You don't say.

Siskel & Ebert & Roeper Online Archive

August 2, 2007—The various incarnations of Siskel & Ebert & Roeper represent more than one thousand TV programs, on which the three of us, and various guest critics, reviewed more than five thousand movies. And now at last an online archive exists with all of those reviews.

Visitors can search for and watch all of those past debates, including the film clips that went along with them, plus the "ten best" and other special shows we did. The new archive is at www.atthemoviestv.com and is the Web's largest collection of streaming reviews.

Gene and I knew those old shows would be worth saving, but for a long time nobody agreed with us. In the years before home video, it seemed like a waste of expensive videotape to preserve hundreds of episodes of our earlier incarnations on *Opening Soon at a Theater Near You, Sneak Previews,* or *At the Movies.* After all, the movies we were reviewing weren't going to be opening again, and who'd want to watch a show of old movie reviews? Right?

We began on the air in 1975. Four or five years later, home video first began to attract attention, but in the early years there were format wars, buying a tape could cost $79, and most big recent movies weren't available. Then all of that changed, and the current era of DVDs and Blockbuster and Netflix and streaming online content began to unfold. Today, there *would* be an audience for the original Siskel & Ebert reviews of, say, *Batman* or *Jurassic Park,* or Ebert & Roeper trading opinions on *Crash* or *Brokeback Mountain,* or Martin Scorsese and I picking the best film of the 1990s.

As nearly as I've been able to tell, very few of our programs taped between 1975 and 1985 were preserved. The tapes were erased and reused, or just thrown away to make room. Television lived for today's program, not yesterday's. I remember when Janet LaMonica, an assistant producer for *Siskel & Ebert*, climbed into a Dumpster and rescued most of the work Gene Siskel did locally for WBBM-CBS.

At first we were produced by PBS. Then Tribune Broadcasting. When we went to work for Buena Vista, they started saving the shows. And in a daunting effort over recent months, Buena Vista (now the Disney-ABC Television Group) has digitized hours and hours of those old analog tapes, amounting to more than five thousand reviews.

The archive will be searchable in various ways, but I imagine most users will want to look up reviews of specific movies. For example, the program where Richard Roeper and I went three weeks early with our reviews of *Monster*, and its performance by Charlize Theron. When she won the Oscar, we weren't a bit surprised. Or the entire show that Siskel and I devoted to Spike Lee, and especially his groundbreaking *Do the Right Thing*. Or the show we did in black and white, praising black-and-white movies. Or our early evaluations of laserdisc and DVDs, or our attacks on pan-and-scan and colorizing.

Then there are the memorable disagreements, as when I couldn't believe Gene didn't love *Apocalypse Now*, and he couldn't believe my thumb was down on *Full Metal Jacket*. He said I should have been wearing a Santa suit while giving thumbs-up to *Cop and a Half*. (One day the mail brought an autographed photo of Norman D. Golden II, the eight-year-old costar of *Cop and a Half*, thanking me for helping his career. I thought that was nice of the kid, until I recognized something familiar about his handwriting.) A few years earlier, I told Gene (offscreen) that his praise for the awful family weepers *Six Weeks* and *Table for Five* might indicate sentimentality that was inspired because Gene and his wife, Marlene, were expecting for the first time. He handed me a note, "to be read only when you are on the flight to Cannes," telling me I was right.

After Gene's death in 1999, we used guest critics for a while, and you'll be able to see Peter Bogdanovich debating me about the year's best movies. You can also see Richard's first appearances as a guest, after which we all agreed he was the right guy and should go full-time. After my own illness in 2006, Richard invited guest critics into the guest seat, including *Chicago Tribune* critic Michael Phillips and *New York Times* critic A. O. Scott.

I'm back in action at the *Chicago Sun-Times* and at rogerebert.com, but not on the air; the *Ebert & Roeper* site will provide links to my *Sun-Times* print reviews. Meanwhile, I watch from the other side of the camera. I hope to reclaim that other seat eventually, but I need more surgery to restore my ability to speak. I hope the show, now in its thirty-second year, goes on and on and on. That was another thing Gene and I agreed on.

An Indie Crisis?

November 30,2007—On August 31, 2007, I published a review of a movie titled *Delirious*. I gave it three and a half stars. I liked it a lot. Maybe you remember that it starred Steve Buscemi as Les, a mad-dog paparazzo, scorned by the world. He becomes the hero of a clueless street kid named Toby (Michael Pitt), who begs to hang around with him and learn the ropes. So Les moves Toby into a cupboard of his fleabag apartment and pontificates on the art of catching celebrities off-guard. Alison Lohman plays a Paris Hilton–type starlet who is their quarry. Also in the cast: Gina Gershon and Elvis Costello.

You have not seen this movie. You couldn't have, unless you were one of the few customers who contributed to its depressing $200,000 total national gross. It got enthusiastic reviews from both trade papers, the *New York Times*, Salon.com, the *New Yorker*, and so on, but then it disappeared.

It was written and directed by a legend in the indie film world, Tom DiCillo, who has made other movies I've liked (*Living in Oblivion, Box of Moonlight, The Real Blonde*). Yet it opened in two theaters in both New York and Los Angeles, was supported by pitiful near-zero advertising, went to one theater in each city after a week, had brief one-theater runs here and there, and disappeared. It did have the distinction of inspiring a review by Ray Pride of *New City Chicago* that reads like ol' Ray overdosed on the Mean Pills. To criticize the great Buscemi for having skinny legs that look bad in black socks is overreaching, I would say.

I've never met DiCillo, but after the disappointing release of his movie I got an e-mail from him:

To give you some indication of how disoriented I feel at the moment, I am getting no real, tangible feedback from anyone. And so I'm kind of struggling on my own to make sense of how a film I put my soul into, that Buscemi put his soul into, a film that generated such strong, positive reviews had no life in the market.

I'm not talking about gigantic box office success. I'm simply speaking of a modestly successful run that earned people their money back and, more productively, helped encourage other financiers and studios to invest in another one of my films. Of course I'm extremely proud of the film. Of course I feel a sense of victory in just getting it made. But for a filmmaker to survive, there has to be some form of return.

This is not intended to be a complaint or Whine Fest. I know this is a brutal business, and I'm not asking for, nor expecting, special treatment, babying or sympathy from anyone. I'm just looking for some answers.

In his blog (www.tomdicillo.com), DiCillo pulls no punches in describing the way his film was mistreated and manhandled. I think he may have a book in there somewhere. But my concern is that an entertaining film with a superb Buscemi performance has disappeared and that it never had a chance. In his message, DiCillo went on to employ colorful language about his nightmare, and then he presented me with a list of questions. I don't have the answers, because there probably aren't any, but because they address a crisis in the indie film world, here goes:

1. The film got unusually strong reviews. Why did it not find an audience theatrically?

Reviews work best in connection with a visible opening. When moviegoers have never seen an ad for a movie and it isn't playing in their city, state, or region of the nation, what difference do reviews make?

Apart from that, here's a funny thing: Lots of moviegoers trust a critic less than a brainless ad promising them the sun, the moon, and the stars. They have a certain reluctance to see a movie that might be good. Millions of teenage boys, in particular, flock to the stupid and the brutal, and have no interest in any film that involves words like "paparazzi." (Millions of others are our hope for the future, of course, but opening weekends are driven by horror, superheroes, and comic book and game adaptations, and depend on the fanboys.)

2. Were the U.S. distributors right in passing on it? In other words, is *Delirious* unmarketable?

Because I enjoyed it from beginning to end, I wouldn't call it unmarketable, but it isn't a high-concept (i.e., low-concept) film and needs a chance to be discovered. Let me give you an example.

The second funniest film I've seen in the last ten years is *The Castle* (1997), from Australia. When I showed it at my Overlooked Film Festival, the 1,600 people in the audience almost lost their lunch, they were laughing so hard. It grossed less than a million in North America. It didn't have stars, it wasn't about castles, and hardly anybody went. So it wasn't "marketable."

Because I love movies, it cheers me up when people have a good time at one. This one was released by the old Miramax. "The test audience didn't like it," Harvey Weinstein told me, after he yanked it. OK, either (a) the test audience was wrong, or (b) it was the wrong test audience.

3. If a small film like *Delirious* is judged by its opening weekend gross for survival, what does that say about the state of U.S. independent film? In other words, if an independent film needs a big opening weekend to succeed, how does this make it different from a Hollywood film?

It says indies are being forced out by the Opening Weekend Syndrome. Indie films will rarely have big opening weekends because they don't have the publicity machines to grind out press junkets, talk-show guest shots, celeb magazine profiles, big TV and print campaigns, and fast-food tie-ins. They need a chance to find an audience.

Chariots of Fire (1981) opened in one theater, crept into two or three, tiptoed across the country, had great word of mouth, played for months, and won the Oscar. Today, it would have closed after that first theater.

Here's a hypothesis: Anyone reading this

article is likely to enjoy a movie more if it *doesn't* have free collectibles at McDonald's.

4. If a big opening weekend is the only guarantee of life for an independent film, does this affect the kinds of independent films being made?

Hard to say because so many indie films are labors of love that their makers *had* to make. Consider Miranda July's *Me and You and Everyone We Know* (2005), which had a $2 million budget and grossed less than $4 million. Not so great.

When the lights went up at Sundance, Lisa Schwarzbaum of *Entertainment Weekly* was across the aisle from me. "Whatd'ya think?" she asked me or I asked her, I can't remember which. I remember the reply: "I think it's the best film in the festival." Other person: "Me, too."

How in the hell can a movie that delicate and magical not find a big audience when I *know* there are people starving for films like that?

5. Does independent film exist anymore?

Yes, barely. The irony is that indies are embraced at film festivals, which have almost become an alternative distribution channel. Your film, for example, was invited by San Sebastian, Sundance, San Francisco, Seattle, Avignon, Munich, and Karlovy Vary. All major festivals. But you didn't make *Delirious* to sell tickets for festivals. I frankly think it's time for festivals to give their entries a cut of the box office.

If there is room for hope, it's that good actors are happy to appear in them because the indies are a repository of great roles. Halle Berry has starred in movies budgeted at millions, but won the Oscar for *Monster's Ball.* Robert De Niro top-lined millions of bucks, but won the Oscar for the low-budget *Raging Bull.* Charlize Theron could pull down $1 million to $2 million a picture or more, but won the Oscar for *Monster,* which cost lots less than a million. Actors know that beyond a certain budget level, megaproductions are less likely to contain great acting opportunities. What's being marketed is the spectacle, not the performances.

6. Can any of these questions even be answered? Should I even bother with trying to find the answers? Is the whole thing a Kafkaesque nightmare or can it all be shrugged off simply by saying, "You win some, you lose some"?

I don't know. Maybe DVDs and Netflix and Blockbuster on Demand and cable TV and pay-for-view and especially high-quality streaming on the Internet will rescue you and your fellow independents. I come from an innocent and hopeful time when we went to the Art Theater in Champaign-Urbana to see anything they were showing because we knew it wouldn't have Frankie Avalon in it, and they gave you a free cup of coffee, and we thought that was way cool. It was a movie by Cassavetes or Shirley Clarke? Or DiCillo or Sayles or Jarmusch? How did we get so lucky?

A Letter to Werner Herzog

November 18, 2007

Dear Werner,

You have done me the astonishing honor of dedicating your new film, *Encounters at the End of the World,* to me. Since I have admired your work beyond measure for the almost forty years since we first met, I do not need to explain how much this kindness means to me. When I saw the film at the Toronto Film Festival and wrote to thank you, I said I wondered if it would be a conflict of interest for me to review the film, even though of course you have made a film I could not possibly dislike. I said I thought perhaps the solution was to simply write you a letter.

But I will review the film, my friend, when it arrives in theaters on its way to airing on the Discovery Channel. I will review it, and I will challenge anyone to describe my praise as inaccurate. I will review it because I love great films and must share my enthusiasm.

This is not that review. It is the letter. It is a letter to a man whose life and career have embodied a vision of the cinema that challenges moviegoers to ask themselves questions not only about films, but about lives. About their lives, and the lives of the people in your films, and your own life.

Without ever making a movie for solely commercial reasons, without ever having a dependable source of financing, without the attention of the studios and the oligarchies that decide what may be filmed and shown, you have directed at least fifty-five films or television productions, and we will not count the operas. You have worked all the time because you have depended on your imagination instead of budgets, stars, or publicity campaigns. You have had the visions and made the films and trusted people to find them, and they have. It is safe to say you are as admired and venerated as any filmmaker alive—among those who have heard of you, of course. Those who do not know your work, and the work of your comrades in the independent film world, are missing experiences that might shake and inspire them.

You often say this modern world is starving for images. That the media pound the same paltry ideas into our heads time and again, and that we need to see around the edges or over the top. When you open *Encounters at the End of the World* by following a marine biologist under the ice floes of the South Pole and listening to the alien sounds of the creatures who thrive there, you show me a place on my planet I did not know about, and I am richer. You are the most curious of men. You are like the storytellers of old, returning from far lands with spellbinding tales.

I remember at the Telluride Film Festival, ten or twelve years ago, when you told me you had a video of your latest documentary. We found a TV set in a hotel room, and I saw *Bells from the Deep,* a film in which you wandered through Russia observing strange beliefs.

There were the people who lived near a deep lake and believed that on its bottom there was a city populated by angels. To see it, they had to wait until winter when the water was crystal clear, and then creep spread-eagled onto the ice. If the ice was too thick, they could not see well enough. Too thin, and they might drown. We heard the ice creaking beneath them as they peered for their vision.

Then we met a monk who looked like Rasputin. You found that there were hundreds of "Rasputins," some claiming to be Jesus Christ, walking through Russia with their prophecies and warnings. These people and their intense focus and the music evoking another world (as your sound tracks always do) held me in their spell, and we talked for some time about the film, and then you said, "But you know, Roger, it is all made up." I did not understand. "It is not real. I invented it."

I didn't know whether to believe you about your own film. But I know you speak of "ecstatic truth," of a truth beyond the merely factual, a truth that records not the real world but the world as we dream it. Your documentary *Little Dieter Needs to Fly* begins with a real man, Dieter Dengler, who really was a prisoner of the Viet Cong, and who really did escape through the jungle and was the only American who freed himself from a Viet Cong prison camp. As the film opens, we see him entering his house and compulsively opening and closing windows and doors to be sure he is not locked in. "That was my idea," you told me. "Dieter does not really do that. But it is how he feels."

The line between truth and fiction is a mirage in your work. Some of the documentaries contain fiction, and some of the fiction films contain fact. Yes, you really did haul a boat up a mountainside in *Fitzcarraldo,* even though any other director would have used a model or special effects. You organized the ropes and pulleys and workers in the middle of the Amazonian rain forest, and hauled the boat up into the jungle. And later, when the boat seemed to be caught in a rapids that threatened its destruction, it really was. This in a fiction film. The audience will know if the shots are real, you said, and that will affect how they see the film.

I understand this. What must be true, must be true. What must not be true, can be made more true by invention. Your films, frame by frame, contain a kind of rapturous truth that transcends the factually mundane. And yet when you find something real, you show it. You based *Grizzly Man* on the videos that Timothy Treadwell took in Alaska during his summers with wild bears. In Antarctica, in *Encounters at the End of the World,* you talk with real people who have chosen to make their lives there in a research station. Some are "linguists on a continent with no language," you note, others are "PhDs working as cooks." When a marine biologist cuts a hole in the ice and dives beneath it, he does not use a rope to find his way back to the small escape circle in the limitless shelf above him because it would restrict his research. When he comes up, he simply hopes he can find the hole. This is all true, but it is also ecstatic truth.

In the process of compiling your life's work, you have never lost your sense of humor. Your narrations are central to the appeal of your documentaries, and your wonder at human nature is central to your fiction. In one scene you can foresee the end of life on Earth, and in another show us country musicians picking their guitars and banjos on the roof of a hut at the South Pole. You did not go to Antarctica, you assure us at the outset, to film cute penguins. But you did film one cute penguin, a penguin that was disoriented and was steadfastly walking in precisely the wrong direction—into an ice vastness the size of Texas. "And if you turn him around in the right direction," you say, "he will turn himself around, and keep going in the wrong direction, until he starves and dies." The sight of that penguin waddling optimistically toward his doom would be heartbreaking, except that he is so sure he is correct.

But I have started to wander off like the penguin, my friend. I have started out to praise your work, and have ended by describing it. Maybe it is the same thing. You and your work are unique and invaluable, and you ennoble the cinema when so many debase it. You have the audacity to believe that if you make a film about anything that interests you, it will interest us as well. And you have proven it.

With admiration,
Roger

I Admit It: I Loved *Indy*

May 20, 2008—At noon Sunday, I attended a press screening of *Indiana Jones and the Kingdom of the Crystal Skull.* I returned to my laptop, wrote my review, and sent it off, convinced I would be in the minority. I loved it, but then I'm also the guy who loved *Beowulf,* and look at the grief that got me. Now *Indy*'s early reviews are in, and I'm amazed to find myself in an enthusiastic majority. The Tomatometer stands at 78, and the more populist IMDb user rating is 9.2 out of 10. All this before the movie's official opening.

Why did I think I would be in the minority? Because of what David Poland at the *Movie City News* poetically described as "one idiot." As everybody knows, an exhibitor attended a closed-door screening last week and filed a review with the Ain't It Cool News Web site. This single wrongheaded, anonymous review was the peg on which the *New York Times* based a breathless story of a negative early reaction to the film. That story inspired widespread coverage: Were Spielberg and Lucas making a mistake by showing their film at Cannes? Would it turn out to be a fiasco like showing *The Da Vinci Code* there? *The Code* got terrible reviews and managed to gross only something like $480 million at the box office—suggesting, if not to the *Times,* that even a negative reception at Cannes might not cut Indy off at the knees.

Maybe even Harrison Ford was influenced by Mr. Wrongheaded. "It's not unusual for something that is popular to be disdained by some people," he said at the press conference following the Cannes screening, "and I fully expect it." What he got was a standing ovation in the Palais des Festivals that night. The SO was heralded in all the coverage, even though any Cannes veteran would tell you it meant—nothing. *Every* film gets a standing ovation at the black-tie evening premiere at Cannes, unless it is so bad it transcends awfulness.

There are really two premieres at Cannes: the press screening at 8:30 a.m. and the black-tie, or "official," screening in the evening. Both fill the vast, 3,500-seat Lumiere auditorium. The morning offers a tough audience: critics, festival programmers, people who may have seen hundreds of other movies in this room. They are free with their boos, and if a movie doesn't work for them, they have been known to shout at the screen on their way out.

The black-tie screening, on the other hand, includes many people who have a financial motive for wanting a film to succeed: the worldwide distributors and exhibitors, their guests, and lots of Riviera locals. Or they may have been given tickets and are thrilled to be there. ("I recognized the woman sitting next to me from my hotel," Rex Reed told me one year. "It was my maid.") In some cases, they may simply think it's good manners to cheer movie stars who flew all the way to Cannes. Then, too, the stars are seated in the front row of the balcony. Everybody below stands up after the movie, turns around, and sees them bathed in spotlights. The Standing O creates itself.

Nevertheless, I believe the SO was genuine the other night. It takes a cold heart and a weary imagination to dislike an *Indiana Jones* film, with all of its rambunctious gusto. With every ounce of its massive budget, it strains to make us laugh, surprise us, go over the top with preposterous action. *Kingdom of the Crystal Skull* does those things under the leadership of Spielberg, who knows as much as any man ever has about what reaches the popular imagination. The early reviewer on the Web site, on the other hand, knew as little.

Spielberg at heart will always be that kid who sneaked onto the back lot at Universal and talked himself into a job. He's the kind of man who remains in many ways a boy. He likes neat stuff. He thinks it would be fun to have Indiana and friends plunge over three waterfalls, not one. He knows that we know what back projection is, and he uses it blatantly (Indy arriving in frame as if he had jumped there, while the background rolls past a little out of focus). He knows back projection feels different than perfect digital backgrounds—it feels more like a movie. He likes boldly faked editing sequences: We see the heroes in medium shot at the edge of a waterfall, we see a long shot of their boat falling to what would obviously be instant oblivion below, and then he shows the heroes surfacing together and near the shore (no rapids!) and spitting out a little water. The movie isn't a throwback to the Saturday serials of the 1930s and 1940s. It's what they would have been if they could have been.

Consider another action series, the *Matrix* films. They're so doggedly intense and serious. They seem to think the future of the universe really is at stake. There's a role for serious action, but not when it's hurled at us in a cascade of quick-cutting "queasy-cam" shots that make dramatic development impossible. Even if they are constructed out of wall-to-wall implausibility, the Indy films have characters who aren't frantic. Harrison Ford and Spielberg are wise: They know a pumped-up Indy would seem absurd. Indiana Jones himself is so laid-back he sometimes seems to be watching the movie with us. He's happy to be aboard, just as long, of course, as he can stay in the boat/truck/airplane.

Gidget and the City

June 3, 2008—In an upcoming Answer Man column, I write: "Oddly enough, searching the AM's Google Mail account for questions about *Sex and the City,* I found that all the messages, *every single one,* dealt only with matters of masturbating female dogs." But surely I was mistaken? Surely with such a popular film there would be messages about *something* else, especially since it was a popular movie, my review was negative, and my hit-counting software indicated that tens of thousands had read it? The *only* thing they wanted to write to me about was the leisure activity of Samantha's pet dog? Surely not. Then I had a brainstorm.

Some weeks ago, to rid the Answer Man of tons of spam, I changed its Gmail address. Perhaps there was a glitch, and there would be more broadly based *SATC* messages back at the old address. I went back and looked. That account had piled up an inbox of more than 22,000 messages, but only *one* was about *Sex and the City*! There seemed to be a total disinclination to write me about my review, however widely read it may have been.

The author of that single message deserves recognition. He is Ian Gallaher of Fullerton, California, and he writes to me: "In your review of *Sex and the City,* you wrote, 'But this is probably the exact *Sex and the City* film that fans of the TV series are lusting for,' and, as a twenty-four-year-old straight male who's seen the entire series (but only after my sister already bought it), I can say the movie was a complete letdown.

"To the casual observer, the series was inch-deep raunchy girl talk, but if you give the series time, you get to know each character and their intricate personalities and subtextually honest flaws. The television episodes truly are a work of art, if you can peel back the glossy pink wallpaper and take a look at why the walls and foundation of these girls' lives are deeply flawed.

"But alas, the movie was a disappointment. The girls' pasts were apparently wiped away in favor of cookie-cutter representations of their previously rich selves. My only guess is that the producers got ahold of the script and watered it down in order to appeal to *everybody,* and, in doing so, made it universally unappealing. If you have the opportunity, give the series some time. It is excellent."

I regret, Ian, that I will never have the opportunity. Wild horses could not drag me to the opportunity. *SATC* is so definitely not my cup of tea that, for me, it is not tea at all, and does not come in a cup. As I made clear in the first sentence of my review, "I am not the person to review this movie."

But I found aspects of the movie curious, and one of those aspects was the sight of Samantha's female dog masturbating with great joy and energy in a way that my sadly limited experience had led me to believe was unlikely. I always had male dogs, who went about such matters in a straightforward way. In the Answer Man column you will find how ignorant I was, and I am informed that a great many female dogs masturbate just like male dogs and apparently have no complaints.

Trying to puzzle out this situation, I have concluded: (1) Those who loved *SATC* or hated my review just abandoned me as a hopeless case, but that (2) people love their pets and love to talk about them. So those few shining sentences about Baby, Samantha's dog, stood out for them in a sea of hopelessness, and they sprang to their computers, eager to tell me about Tessa, Timoune, and other beloved lady dogs. The lesson, of course, is that sex is important, but our pets are more important, and have a more direct connection to our daily lives than do the sex lives of four fictional women in The City.

I talked to lots of friends who rushed to the various midnight screenings and Cosmopolitan drink-fests that accompanied the opening of the film, and what I gathered was: (1) Yeah, the movie was OK; (2) it was pretty long; (3) it helped if you've seen the series; (4) the Cosmo is pleasant as a drink, but not as a habit. (The recipe, Wikipedia reports, involves: "vodka, Cointreau or Triple Sec, cranberry juice, and fresh-squeezed lime juice or sweetened lime juice. Informally, it is referred to as a Cosmo." A man named John Caine brought it from the Midwest to San Francisco around 1987 and then faded from the pages of history.)

So I am back where I started. Millions of people watched the series, wanted to see the movie, and have. They are not much moved to defend it or discuss it, at least not on my Web site. But their mother-in-law's beloved Tessa is altogether another matter. I recommend a sequel titled *Tessa and the City.*

The question is, what dog would it star? Here at the movie desk we stop at nothing to inform our readers, and so I can tell you that Baby is played by a dog named Gidget Gormley, who has countless Web pages in her honor, mostly pink. Search as I did, I found no information about how Gidget was trained to masturbate on demand, but since Gidget is billed as "the world's cutest dog," maybe all it took was a mirror.

The Balcony Is Closed

July 24, 2008—I was surprised how depressed I felt all day on July 21, when Richard and I announced we were leaving the *Ebert & Roeper* program. To be sure, our departures were voluntary. We hadn't been fired. And because of my health troubles, I hadn't appeared on the show for two years. But I advised on cohosts, suggested movies, stayed in close communication with Don DuPree, our beloved producer-director. The show remained in my life. Now, after thirty-three years, it was gone—taken in a "new direction." And I was fully realizing what a large, empty space it left behind.

Yes, we're hoping to continue the traditional format in a new venue, and taking the thumbs along with us. I'm involved in that, and it will be a great consolation. But somehow I thought the show Gene Siskel and I began would roll on forever. How many other TV formats had survived so long?

I sat in my chair and daydreamed. I remembered a Saturday afternoon, it must have been the winter of 1975–76, when Gene and I were eating hamburgers in Oxford's Pub on Lincoln Avenue with Thea Flaum, a young woman who would produce the show for WTTW, the Chicago PBS station. You didn't read her name in the news coverage of our departures, but she was the real "creator" of the show, as TV uses that term.

She told us she would build a balcony for us and sit us across the aisle from each other. She told us we couldn't wear suits and ties—no one wore them to the movies. She came up with the idea of Spot the Wonder Dog. The show was monthly at first. On Sunday afternoons before a taping, we would separately sit across her dining room table from her and rehearse our scripts. We had "discussion points" we tried to memorize.

We were bad at that. If one guy dropped a discussion point, the other guy got mad. "We can't remember these points," Gene said, "but we can talk to each other." During that first season (the show was called *Opening Soon at a Theater Near You*), the final format took shape. In the pub that day, Thea told us: "You boys have no idea how far this show is going to go. One day you'll be in national syndication. You'll be making real money. You wait and see."

Her prophecy came true. The day we fully realized it in our guts, I think, was the first time we were invited to appear with Johnny Carson.

We were scared out of our minds. We'd been briefed on likely questions by one of the show's writers, but moments before airtime he popped his head into the dressing room and said, "Johnny may ask you for some of your favorite movies this year."

Gene and I stared at each other in horror. "What was one of your favorite movies this year?" he asked me. "*Gone with the Wind*," I said. The Doc Severinsen orchestra had started playing the famous *Tonight Show* theme. Neither one of us could think of a single movie. Gene called our office in Chicago. "Tell me some movies we liked this year," he said. This is a true story.

We began to catch on. Jack Nicholson told Gene: "Harry Dean Stanton called me and said there were a couple of guys discussing movies on TV, and they didn't even look like they should be on TV." We didn't. Tall and thin, short and fat. Laurel and Hardy. We were parodied on *SNL* and by Bob Hope and Danny Thomas and, the ultimate honor, in the pages of *Mad* magazine.

One thing we never did, apart from an occasional special show, was depart from the format: two critics debating the week's new movies. No "advance looks" at trailers for movies we hadn't even seen. No celebrity interviews. No red-carpet sound bites. Just two guys talking about the movies. At one point, our show and two clones were on the air simultaneously. Then we were left alone again: the only show on TV that would actually tell you if we thought a movie was bad.

There was one improvement: We retired Spot (and his successor, Aroma the Educated Skunk) to free up a segment for another review. I remember when we jumped to commercial syndication at Tribune Entertainment, and our new producer, Joe Antelo, backed us in reviewing movies by Fassbinder, Truffaut, Herzog—"those guys. Where else they gonna hear about them?"

Did Gene and I hate each other? Yes. Did we love each other? Yes. Somehow an outtake from a promo session has found its way onto YouTube, where in a single take you can see us bitterly sniping at one another and then happily joking together. It was like that. "You have the entire staff in terror of you," I told him. "That's funny," he said. "That's what they tell me about you." We were both terrible to work with. And great to work with.

We went to New Orleans for the national convention of syndicated TV. Tribune had been slow in renewing our contract. Leaving our hotel, we ran into Jamie Bennett, an executive Gene knew from Chicago. Jamie asked how we were doing. "Working without a contract," Gene said. "Let's have dinner," Jamie said, and on the spot he talked us into leaving Tribune and becoming the first program of the new Buena Vista syndication division.

Disney was great to work with. Everyone called everyone else by their first name, even the president, Michael Eisner. The wonderful Mary Kellogg was put in charge of our show and was our cheerleader and den mother. Rich Frank was president of the Walt Disney Studio. When he gave a speech, he took along a reel of clips showing Gene and me trashing movies he had produced. Great jollity. Disney never once objected to our negative review of one of its pictures. Great class.

I began to notice that Gene, who had a laser-like intelligence, remembered every phone number he had ever heard, and could do square roots in his head, started getting things out of order. Before a Jay Leno taping in Chicago, he closed himself in a dark room with a splitting headache. But he went to the Bulls game that night. I left the next day for the Cannes festival, where I got a phone call: Gene was sick, was in New York for treatment. He went through the agonies of hell during that final year, but he was heroic and taped a show barely a week before his death. I missed him terribly. I still do.

We carried on, as I believe Gene would have wanted us to do. Many critics filled the other chair, some gifted, some strange. One guy, in introducing himself, couldn't remember where he worked. I agreed with all the staff members that Richard Roeper was our choice. People thought he was chosen because we both worked at the *Sun-Times*. That had nothing to do with it—it worked against him, in fact. When the time came that I had to be replaced, Michael Phillips of the *Tribune* and A. O. Scott of the *New York Times* were my suggestions.

Now the time has come to awake from my daydream. That's all history—treasured history, but past and gone all the same. I remember what Gene said to me in that dressing room before the Carson show: "Roger, we're a couple of kids from the Midwest. We don't belong here."

In Memoriam

Robert Altman

The obituaries for Robert Altman, who died November 20, 2006, all made it a point that he was "preparing a film." Well, of course he was. Preparing a film and making it and releasing it were the conditions of his life.

I remember a day in January 2002 when we visited the set of his *Gosford Park,* shooting outside London. It was a mild and pleasant day, and he was surrounded, as he liked to be, by cast and crew, friends and family. And he confided a personal truth.

"We were out driving one day, looking for a location, and it was time to go and have lunch. We went into a shopping center, and I suddenly realized there wasn't one single person there who would know who I was. We had stepped over into real life. We had gotten lost. There was no assistant director around to do what I wanted him to do.

"Then I realized that if I stopped making movies, I would die, because my entire existence presupposed a movie in production. I don't remember the years when things happened, but I remember the movie I was directing when they happened. The movies are the eras of my life. In fact, the movies are life."

This is literally true. In the thirty-eight years since he stopped working for television, and his career as a movie director started, in 1968, he made thirty-seven movies. He also directed operas for the stage and TV miniseries (*Tanner*).

Altman was in his forties when this act in his life started; before that, he did episode TV, low-budget quickie features, and even industrial films.

*M*A*S*H* in 1970 was his breakthrough, and since then perhaps no other director has made more titles of the first rank, including *McCabe and Mrs. Miller, The Player, Nashville,* and *Short Cuts.*

He liked big casts, overlapping dialogue, a sense of reality as if things are happening spontaneously. He was criticized because Shelley Duvall's skirt kept getting caught in the car door in *Three Women.* The first time, it was an accident. He liked it and kept it in—every time she got in the car.

Altman's range was so wide that sometimes he seemed to be deliberately avoiding patterns and styles. I don't think so—I think he was a youthful adventurer at heart, ready for whatever was next.

I saw him last before the 2006 Academy Awards. He was in a private room with family, friends, colleagues such as Lily Tomlin. Before that I watched him for a day directing *A Wedding* for Chicago's Lyric Opera. In neither case did he seek to be the center of attention. "The actors do it," he said at the Lyric. "My job is to appreciate them."

Yet I saw him subtly adjusting, altering, changing their words, almost without them realizing it. He had a quality of sympathy and empathy that made actors feel free to improvise and experiment.

His last completed film was *A Prairie Home Companion*—ostensibly about the last radio show Garrison Keillor was to record, but more truly (I thought at the time) the last film Altman was to direct. He was not well. He had cancer. He had a transplanted heart.

And yet Keillor's character, in a sense playing Altman, had no regrets. "It is nothing less than an elegy," I wrote in my review, "a memorial to memories of times gone by, to dreams that died but left the dreamers dreaming, to appreciating what you've had instead of insisting on more."

Robert Altman had that quality. I remember when, unable to get a film financed, he filmed his current stage play, *Come Back to the Five and Dime, Jimmy Dean, Jimmy Dean,* on the same set he used for the stage. And had as much fun as he did using his first camera.

Unlike with most directors, you do not look at Altman films one by one. You consider the whole body of work—the mood, the tone, the spirit. There is no director I loved more. When he died, it was at Thanksgiving, surrounded by friends and family, including his devoted wife, Kathryn. I hope he fully realized how much he had given to the world.

A Prairie Home Companion includes "Red River Valley," which for some reason strikes me as the saddest song ever written.

Bob: From this valley they say you are going. We will miss your bright eyes and sweet smile.

Michelangelo Antonioni

Michelangelo Antonioni, the Italian director who perfected a style of languid, weary alienation in a series of influential films mostly made between 1960 and 1970, is dead at ninety-four. He died on Monday, July 30, 2007, the same day as Ingmar Bergman; with Federico Fellini, the three were sometimes thought of as the ruling triumvirate of European art cinema.

Although film lovers endlessly debated his best films, he had only one major international hit, *Blow-Up* (1966). Filmed in London, it starred David Hemmings and Vanessa Redgrave in the story of a photographer who takes a picture of her in a park with a man, and then later, painstakingly enlarging his work, thinks he may have photographed a murder.

The film was popular because of the mystery of the murder, because of its portrait of "swinging London" in a moment of time, and because viewers thought they could see a flash of pubic hair. Those motives were unworthy of a film whose greatness depended much more on an overall tone of uncertainty and dread.

Antonioni's international breakthrough came in 1960, when his film *L'Avventura* was booed at Cannes but inspired a joint statement by critics defending it. For audiences seeking the conventional, it was an affront: Rich people disembark from a yacht on an island, one of them disappears—and never turns up again, the mystery of the vanishing still unsolved at film's end.

Antonioni loved to thwart expectations, showing his often decadent characters afloat in a world without resolution. *L'Avventura* was championed by the young critic Pauline Kael, but with his next film, *La Notte* (1961), she lost patience. In a famous essay titled "The Come-Dressed-as-the-Sick-Soul-of-Europe Parties," she wrote that she had tried to goad people into seeing *L'Avventura,* only to find herself detesting Antonioni's next film:

"*La Notte* is supposed to be a study in the failure of communication, but what new perceptions of this problem do we get by watching people on the screen who can't communicate if we are never given any insight into what they could have to say if they *could* talk to each other?"

In 1964, Antonioni made his first color film, elegantly controlling his palette in *The Red Desert,* and when *Blow-Up* came two years later, he became notorious for color perfectionism in deciding the grass wasn't green enough; he had it painted, and also a road and a building. "Antonioni paints the grass!" he told me in a 1969 interview. "To some degree, all directors paint and arrange or change things on a location, and it amused me that so much was made of it in my case."

Kael observed: "He doesn't tell conventional stories. He uses a seemingly random, peripheral course of development, apparently merely following the characters through inconsistencies and inadvertencies."

She didn't make that as a criticism, and when we spoke in 1969, Antonioni essentially agreed with it: "Until the film is edited, I have no idea myself what it will be about. And perhaps not even then. Perhaps the film will only be a mood, or a statement about a style of life. Perhaps it has no plot at all, in the way you use the word. I depart from the script constantly. I may film scenes I had no intention of filming; things suggest themselves on location, and we improvise. I try not to think about it too much. Then, in the cutting room, I take the film and start to put it together, and only then do I begin to get an idea of what it is about."

I got an insight into how that process worked when in 1999 I received a letter from an actor named Ronan O'Casey, who said he played the "body" in *Blow-Up* and revealed that his character originally had a name, dialogue, and a role in the plot. By reducing him to an indistinct long shot, Antonioni redefined the film and essentially shaped it into a masterpiece.

In 1970, he filmed *Zabriskie Point* in the lowest place in Death Valley, telling the story of two young American hippies disillusioned by the Vietnam era. And in 1975, he made the masterpiece *The Passenger,* with Jack Nicholson as a man who takes a dead man's identity, tries to hide from the world, inherits the man's problems, and finds that only a young hitchhiker (Maria Schneider) cares much about him.

Born in Ferrara in 1912, he worked sometimes as a film critic before attending film school in Rome and later writing for such directors as Visconti. He made seventeen films in Italy, mostly well-received, before *L'Avventura* began his period of fame. Antonioni continued to work with varying success until 2004, although a stroke in the mid-1990s made it necessary to work with collaborators such as Wim Wenders. In 1995, he won an Oscar for lifetime achievement.

He was married twice, most recently in 1986 to Enrica Fico Antonioni, an actress and composer, who survives. He lived for years with the actress Monica Vitti, who starred in many of his films. He had no children.

Speculating on an afterlife, he contrasted himself with Bergman. The London *Telegraph* quoted him that "the Swede was solely concerned with the question of God," while he was just the opposite.

Ingmar Bergman

The solitary, poetic, fearful, creative, brave, and philosophical mind of Ingmar Bergman has been stilled, and the director is dead at eighty-nine. Death was an event on which he long meditated; it was the subject of many of his greatest films, and provided his most famous single image, a knight playing chess with Death in *The Seventh Seal.*

The end came Monday, July 30, 2007, on the remote island of Faro, off the Swedish coast, where he made his home and workshop for many years. During a long and productive career, he made more than fifty films, some of them in longer versions for television, and directed more than two hundred plays and operas.

Woody Allen, who made some films in deliberate imitation of Bergman, said he was "probably the greatest film artist, all things considered, since the invention of the motion picture camera."

And David Mamet has just written me: "When I was young the World Theatre, in Chicago, staged an all-day Ingmar Bergman Festival. I went at 10 o'clock in the morning and stayed all day. When I left the theater it was still light, but my soul was dark, and I did not sleep for years afterward."

Provided with a secure home for decades within the Swedish film industry, working at Stockholm's Film House, which his films essentially built, Bergman had unparalleled freedom to make exactly the films he desired. Occasionally they were comedies, and he made a sunny version of Mozart's *The Magic Flute,* but more often they were meditations on life and death, on the difficulties of people trying to connect, and on what he considered the silence of God. In a film like *Wild Strawberries* (1957), however, he imagined an old man terrified by death, revisiting his memories and finally finding reconciliation.

The son of a strict Lutheran minister, Bergman remembered such punishments as being locked in a cabinet and told mice would nibble at his toes. He resented his father for years, returning to that childhood again near the end of his career in *Fanny and Alexander* (1982), one of his greatest films.

What he saw as God's refusal to intervene in the suffering on Earth was the subject of his 1961–63 Silence of God Trilogy: *Through a Glass Darkly, Winter Light* (a pitiless film in which a clergyman torments himself about the possibility of nuclear annihilation), and *The Silence.* In his masterpiece, *Persona* (1967), an actress (Liv Ullmann) sees a television image of a monk burning himself in Vietnam, and she stops speaking. Sent to a country retreat with a nurse (Bibi Andersson), she works a speechless alchemy on her, leading to a striking image when their two faces seem to blend.

So great was the tension in that film that Bergman made it appear to catch in the projector and burn. Then, from a black screen, the film slowly rebuilt itself, beginning with crude images from the first days of the cinema. These images were suggested by a child's cinematograph, which his brother received as a present; so envious was Ingmar that he traded his brother for it, giving up his precious horde of one hundred tin soldiers.

In the fullness of his career, the director settled into a rhythm. "We've already discussed the new film the year before," Sven Nykvist, his longtime cinematographer, told me in 1975. "Then Ingmar goes to his island and writes the screenplay. The next year, we shoot—usually about the 15th of April. Usually we are the same eighteen people working with him, year after year, one film a year."

Of the eighteen, one was the "hostess," hired to serve coffee and pastries and make the set seem domestic. "How large a crew do you use?" David Lean asked him one year at Cannes. "I always work with eighteen friends," Bergman said. "That's funny," said Lean. "I work with a hundred and fifty enemies."

In 1975 I visited the Bergman set for *Face to Face.* He took a break and invited me to his "cell" in Film House: a small, narrow room filled with an army cot, a desk, two chairs, and on the desk an apple and a bar of chocolate. He said he'd been watching an interview with Antonioni the night before: "I hardly heard what he said. I could not take my attention away from his face. For me, the human face is the most important subject of the cinema."

Nykvist was his collaborator in filming those faces, and in *The Passion of Anna* (1969) did something unprecedented: filmed a conversation by the light of a single candle. "He said it could be done, and he was right," Bergman said.

Bergman was married five times and had eight children, including Liv Ullmann's daughter, the novelist Linn. He was not proud of how he behaved in some of those relationships, and in an extraordinary late film, *Faithless* (2000), written by Bergman and directed by Ullmann, he imagines a director (Erland Josephson) hiring an actress (Lena Endre) to help him "think through" an unhappy affair. It becomes clear that the actress is imaginary, that the affair has some connection with Ullmann and other women, and that the film is a confession. It is all shot on Faro, in Bergman's house.

Other filmmakers spoke in awe of Bergman's methods, which had the luxury of time and complete independence. Haskell Wexler, the great cinematographer, has just written me: "I was good friends with Sven Nykvist, who told me stories about Bergman. They sat in a big old church from very early in the morning until as black as the night gets. They noted where the light moved through the stained glass windows. Bergman planned where he would stage the scenes for a picture they were about to do. This had the practical advantage of minimizing light and generator costs.

"Sven said sitting alone with Ingmar in the church had a profound effect on him. I asked him if it made him more religious. He said he didn't think so, but it did give him some kind of spiritual connection to Ingmar, which helped him deal with the times Bergman became very mean."

There are so many memories crowding in now from the richness of Bergman's work that I know not what to choose. A turning point in his despair occurred, perhaps, in *Cries and Whispers,* a chamber drama in an isolated Swedish estate where Harriet Andersson is a woman dying painfully of cancer and her sisters have come to be with her. After she dies, they find a journal in which she recalls a perfect day in the autumn, when the pain was not so bad, and the women took up their parasols and walked in the garden. "This is happiness. I cannot wish for anything better," she writes. "I feel profoundly grateful to my life, which gives me so much."

When *Faithless* played at Cannes in 2001, Liv Ullmann told me this story:

"When he was sixty years old, he celebrated his birthday on his island, on that beach. And my daughter was there; she was five years old. And he said to her, 'When you are sixty, what will you do then?' She said, 'I'll have a big party, and my mother will be there. She'll be really old and stupid and gawky, but it's gonna be great.' And he looked at her and said, 'And what about me? Will I not be there?' And the five-year-old looked up at him and she said, 'Well, you know, I'll leave the party and I'll walk down to the beach and there on the waves you will come dancing toward me.'"

Dusty Cohl

Nobody ever seemed to know what Dusty Cohl did for a living. He was a lawyer, and it was said he was "in real estate," but in over thirty years I never heard him say one word about business. His full-time occupation was being a friend, and he was one of the best I've ever made.

Yes, he was "cofounder of the Toronto Film Festival." That's how he was always identified in the Toronto newspapers. And he founded and ran the Floating Film Festival, one of the great boondoggles, on which Dusty and 250 friends cruised for ten days while premiering films and paying tributes to actors and directors. There was no reason for the floater except that if you were Dusty's friend, you floated.

But beyond those titles, from which he made not a dollar, he was, simply, a phenomenon of friendship. He didn't want anything from you. He lived to be a friend, and he wanted his friends to know one another, and he liked to put people together so good things would happen. He considered himself at one degree of separation.

"When he was young, he was a social director at a resort in the Canadian Catskills," his wife, Joan, told me once. "I don't think he ever really left the job."

Dusty died about 3 p.m. Friday, January 11, 2008, at Sunnybrook Hospital in Toronto, a victim of liver cancer. He was surrounded at the end by family and friends. He left Joan, his wife of fifty-six years; his children, Karen, Steve, and Robert; five grandchildren; and uncounted happy memories. In 2003, he was given the Order of Canada, the highest civilian honor.

But who was he, and how did I meet him? One day in 1977, when I was a stranger at the Cannes Film Festival, I was crossing the famous terrace of the Carlton Hotel and was summoned by name to the table of a man with a black beard, wearing blue jeans, a Dudley Do-Right T-shirt, and a black cowboy hat studded with stars and pins. How did he know who I was? He knew who everybody was.

Dusty was the nucleus of a group of Canadian and American film people, heavily weighted toward film critics. In those days, his circle included Chuck Champlin of the *Los Angeles Times*, Kathleen Carroll and Rex Reed of the New York *Daily News*, Andrew Sarris of the *Village Voice*, Richard Corliss of *Time*, and his longtime buddy, George Anthony of the *Toronto Sun*. There was a method to his madness. He wanted us involved with the film festival.

A few years earlier, Dusty and Joan had been on holiday on the French Riviera and found a parking space smack dab in front of the Carlton during the Cannes festival. Sitting on the terrace, surrounded by festivalgoers, Dusty asked, "Why doesn't Toronto have a film festival?" Joan replied, "You'll probably start one, Dust." And he did.

In the early years, Toronto was far from its present eminence. We headquartered in a hotel where Dusty and the other organizers held a morning press conference to not announce so much as predict, with fingers crossed, what would happen that day. He almost forced the festival into being, by calling in favors from friends, including the leading Canadian directors Ted Kotcheff and Norman Jewison, young director Atom Egoyan, and actors like Helen Shaver and Donald Sutherland. He raised money from cronies at the morning coffee hour where he presided. He twisted arms to bring in film critics, because he knew press coverage was the key to putting the festival on the map. In the earliest years, the festival was covered more in Los Angeles or New York than it was in Toronto, with the exception of George Anthony's lonely voice at the *Toronto Sun*.

At first the big competition in the autumn was from Montreal and New York. But New York had limited seating, Montreal had political problems, and year by year Toronto grew, until in the 1990s it became the venue of choice for the premieres of the big, new autumn pictures. When Dusty stepped upstairs to his newly created post of "chief accomplice," it was on its way to becoming the most important festival in North America and one of the top five in the world. He was far from retired; one of his bright ideas was for Gene Siskel and me to host annual tributes, which we did for Martin Scorsese, Robert Duvall, and Warren Beatty.

Dusty was not finished with festivals. In the 1990s he created the Floating Film Festival aboard a cruise ship on which everyone had two things in common: They liked movies, and they liked Dusty Cohl. He also kept fingers in other pies. His cousin Michael Cohl owned the company that ran the road tours of the Rolling Stones and other supergroups, and Dusty was often backstage, his cowboy hat serving as his pass. He and Michael were involved in the farewell appearance of the Weavers at Toronto a few years ago. During the week, his "office" was a chair in the office of Eddie Greenspan, the most famous trial attorney in Canada, whose client recently was disgraced press baron Conrad Black. His job? "I gossip with Eddie, and we smoke his cigars."

That left time for other assignments. When I founded my own Overlooked Film Festival at the University of Illinois eleven years ago, it went without question that Dusty and Joan would be in attendance from Year One, bearing the titles "co-accomplices in chief." Most of the festival guests stayed in rooms at the student union, and Dusty posted himself in the coffee atrium to greet them, and, of course, introduce them to one another. He became close friends with such as Werner Herzog, Paul Cox, Scott and Heavenly Wilson, Bertrand Tavernier, Errol Morris, Mario Van Peebles and his father, Melvin, Sturla Gunnarsson, David Bordwell, Lisa Nesselson, and David Poland. That started at 8 a.m. After midnight, he could be found advising on menu choices at the Steak 'n Shake, the official festival restaurant. He and Joan took off one night to attend a Champaign High School production of *Guys and Dolls,* and the next night the cast, now all friends of theirs, turned up at the Steak 'n Shake to serenade the visiting filmmakers.

One way you knew you were a friend was when Dusty honored you with a Dusty Pin, a silver hat with a star on it. Rule was: Wear it at film festivals. At Cannes and Sundance, even on years Dusty wasn't there, I spotted them on studio heads Michael Barker and Harvey Weinstein and half the members of the North American press corps.

Dusty Cohl made an enormous difference in my life, saving a first-time visitor to Cannes from bewilderment, introducing me to everybody, and then plopping me down in the middle of the excitement of creating the Toronto festival. When I got married, he stood up with me, and became Chaz's confidant as well, giving her love, advice, and support during my health crisis. We saw the Cohls three, four, five times a year, and talked on the phone as often as daily. He was devoted to full-time friendship, and he wanted his friends to be friends of one another. So there are hundreds, thousands, of us now.

Just today, I was able to see an advance screening of a film because Dusty pulled some strings from his sickbed in the last few weeks. Chaz and I flew down to Florida to see him over Thanksgiving, where he was weaker but still high-spirited and involved in everything. And we were able to fly to Toronto last Tuesday to say good-bye. When he took a year off from Cannes, the Carlton Hotel took a full-page ad in a festival daily showing only a cowboy hat and a cigar, with the caption, "We miss you." Yes, we all do.

Charlton Heston and Richard Widmark

Recently we lost two American actors who embodied widely different styles, and their passing is a reminder that the very presence of an actor can suggest everything about a film.

Charlton Heston was tall, outward, masculine, exuding bravado, often cast in larger-than-life roles. Richard Widmark was lithe, inward, sardonic. Heston's characters stood on mountaintops and divided the Red Sea. Widmark's often lived in the shadows. Heston played some smaller roles, but there was always the danger he would be too big for them. Widmark often played mainstream roles but was always more interesting when he was an outsider on the run.

Heston made at least three movies that almost everybody eventually sees: *Ben-Hur, The Ten Commandments,* and *Planet of the Apes.* Widmark occupied smaller, darker pieces and embodied film noir. Many filmgoers may not have seen *Night and the City* or *Panic in the Streets* (both 1950) or *Pickup on South Street* (1953), but if they have, they remember him. All the TV obituaries used that same clip of him pushing an old lady in a wheelchair down a flight of stairs in *Kiss of Death* (1947), his first film, but there was so much more than that.

Heston, raised on Chicago's North Shore, wanted to be an actor almost from the get-go and made a 16 mm version of *Julius Caesar* in college. "We used all actual locations," he told me in a 1968 interview. "The steps of the Art Institute, the Elk's Temple, the Field Museum, the beaches of Lake Michigan. You would have sworn it was the real thing, except for the acting."

He was "tabbed for stardom," as they used to say, by Cecil B. DeMille, who cast him as the ringmaster in *The Greatest Show on Earth,* which many argue is the worst movie to ever win the Best Picture Oscar, and in 1956 established himself forever in DeMille's *Ten Commandments.* From then on he was often in epics of the sort called "towering," and began to be the victim of self-parody, even though he was always on pitch and had the heft to carry roles others would have disappeared in. His firm authority makes *Planet of the Apes* (1968) a better film than many, including me, thought at the time.

Widmark's roles were in the middle, not the epic, range. He played cops, robbers, wise guys, military men, horror characters, and cowboys, figuring importantly in some of John Ford's elegiac last films. His characters never saved the world, but they usually saved their own skin, and that was the point. He kept a low public profile, made few statements, endorsed few causes, retired so successfully some people were surprised, at the time of his death, that he was still alive. Why did the Academy never honor his lifetime achievement?

Heston was very public, very political (first liberal, then conservative), a willing spokesman for what he believed. In early days he led the charge against racist Hollywood hiring policies. In later years he was the voice of the National Rifle Association. It is always tragic when someone suffers from Alzheimer's, but his bravery and grace in publicly acknowledging his illness was dignified and touching.

What intrigues me about Heston is what he might have done had he never met the bombastic DeMille. Seek out a little film named *Will Penny* (1968), which he told me was his personal favorite, to see an entirely different side of his abilities. Or see him in Kenneth Branagh's 1996 *Hamlet*, where he embodies the Player King with astonishing invention, transforming conventional ideas about the role.

Probably, DeMille or not, Heston would have found himself in roles of heroic stature; in an industry that focuses on appearances, he looked like the hero, not the best buddy. It took another larger-than-life figure, Orson Welles, to find a channel for that presence, in his *Touch of Evil* (1958).

Widmark stayed within a narrower, more realistic range. He told me in 1968 he treasured his work with the great John Ford in *Cheyenne Autumn* (1964) and *Two Rode Together* (1961). "I'm glad I got him as a director at all," he said almost wistfully. We were speaking at the time of the ascendancy of James Bond, and he defended his own pure, straight-ahead film noir: "I have this kind of nostalgia for crime films," he said. "I think we've about exhausted the fancy angles and trick cigarette lighters. Hollywood developed the crime film almost into an art over the years, and it hurt me to see all that work thrown away on spoofs and put-ons."

If Widmark was guarded and private, Heston was outgoing, good company. I remember drinking with him one night at O'Rourke's, the legendary Chicago newspaperman's saloon. He was introduced to Mike McGuire, the military editor of the *Chicago Tribune*. "Ah, yes," he said. "You supported my policies in the *Ben-Hur* campaign."

Speaking of *Will Penny*, he said: "It's one of my favorite roles because it is real, you see, and not all faked up to make it nice. It even has an unhappy ending." Left unsaid was how many of his films such qualities did not apply to. "I always get the superhero parts," he said. "That's one nice thing about *Will Penny*. I'm just an ordinary cowboy, not Ben-Hur in the saddle."

Compared to today's superstars, who are so cosseted and idolized, actors like Heston and Widmark went at their craft full bore, as solid professionals. They expected to be surrounded by supporting actors, did not monopolize a film, were not marketed as the whole product.

Listen to the gassy profundity of so many of today's stars, analyzing their techniques, and then listen to Widmark describing why John Ford liked making Westerns: "He enjoys working in the fresh air." Or listen to Heston, describing how he mastered the art of Ben-Hur's chariot driving: "Actually, I played it by ear."

Deborah Kerr

She shared a passionate kiss with Burt Lancaster as the surf rolled over them in *From Here to Eternity*. She was *I* in *The King and I*. She crawled through the mud with a marine played by Robert Mitchum in *Heaven Knows, Mr. Allison*. She was a sheep drover's wife in *The Sundowners*, a headmaster's wife in *Tea and Sympathy*, and the wife of Brutus in *Julius Caesar*. She missed an appointment with Cary Grant atop the Empire State Building in *An Affair to Remember*. In three different roles, she represented the colonel's lifelong romantic obsession in *The Life and Death of Colonel Blimp*. And simply by standing up in *Black Narcissus*, she started the young Martin Scorsese thinking about movies in a new way.

Deborah Kerr, the flame-tressed beauty who was one of the most luminous stars of her time, is dead at eighty-six. A victim of Parkinson's disease, she died Tuesday, October 16, 2007, in Suffolk, England, where she had moved from her longtime home in Switzerland to be near her daughters and grandchildren.

Kerr held the record for the most Best Actress Oscar nominations without a win, after getting Academy nods for *Edward, My Son* (1949), *From Here to Eternity* (1953), *The King And I* (1956), *Heaven Knows, Mr. Allison* (1957), *Separate Tables* (1958), and *The Sundowners* (1960). She won an honorary Oscar in 1994, telling the audience, "I've never been so frightened in my life, but it's better now, because I know I am among friends."

Originally trained as a dancer with the Sadler's Wells company, she began appearing in British films in 1940 and caught the eye of Michael Powell, the leading British director of the time, who said in his autobiography that he was always in love with her. In his great film *The Life and Death of Colonel Blimp* (1943), she appears three times in three different characters in the life of the colonel, who ages from a hero into a figure of fun for younger officers.

Four years later, in Powell's *Black Narcissus*, she did something that young Martin Scorsese couldn't figure out. "There was something called the 'Million Dollar Movie' on TV when I was a kid," he told me, "and they played the same movie every day for a week. I watched that one five times. She plays a nun in a convent in the Himalayas, who is told by a British officer that he believes she has sexual feelings. There is a cut to a close-up of her. But not just any close-up. There was a quality of shock and surprise in her face, and another quality I couldn't pin down. What did she do, and how did she do it? I began to look at movies with a more analytical eye."

Years later, Scorsese hired Powell, whose films he hugely admired, as a consultant, and he asked Powell about that shot. "I didn't simply cut to a close-up," Powell said. "I had her stand up in shock, from below frame, and then I edited the shot to begin the moment she arrived in frame. So you sensed that alarmed movement."

Kerr was married twice, first in 1945 to Anthony Bartley, a war hero. They had two daughters, Melanie and Francesca. After they divorced in 1959, Kerr wed the writer Peter Viertel, whose mother was Greta Garbo's best friend, and who was said to be the original for the Robert Redford character in *The Way We Were*. Her husband, daughters, and three grandchildren survive.

Kerr was born in Helensburgh, Scotland, on September 30, 1921. Despite her many down-to-earth roles, she was long seen as a proper English beauty but, the *New York Times* reported, "instructed friends to tell anyone who asked that she preferred cold roast beef sandwiches and beer to champagne and caviar, any day."

Sydney Pollack

Sydney Pollack, who directed some of the best mainstream films of the last forty years and acted in some of the others, is dead at seventy-three. He died Monday, May 26, 2008, of cancer at home, in Pacific Palisades, California, according to a friend.

Born in 1934 in Lafayette, Indiana, the son of Russian immigrants, Pollack was encouraged to try acting by his high school drama teacher in South Bend. "From almost the first time I stepped on a stage," he told me, "I knew that was what I wanted to do."

He went to New York to study acting under the famed teacher Sandy Meisner, taught acting at Meisner's Neighborhood Playhouse, moved into television, and stepped behind the camera. Although his main occupation from the 1960s on would be directing, he never lost his love for acting, and had more credits (thirty) as an actor than as a director (twenty-one). He had top billing in Woody Allen's *Husbands and Wives* and most recently was seen as the powerful, authoritative head of the law firm in *Michael Clayton*; in *Made of Honor* he played Patrick Dempsey's multi-divorced wealthy magnate of a father.

A tall, handsome, immediately charismatic man, he was a director most actors loved to work with because when he talked to them about acting he knew what he was talking about. He and Robert Redford were each other's favorite director and actor, working together seven times. Indeed, in *This Property Is Condemned* (1966), he was instrumental in establishing Redford as a star.

"I am not a visual innovator," Pollack told me shortly before the release of his *Out of Africa* (1985), which won seven Oscars, including Best Picture and Best Director, and was nominated for four more. "I haven't broken any new ground in the form of a film. My strength is with actors. I think I'm good at working with them to get the best performances, at seeing what it is that they have and that the story needs."

To mention the titles of some of his films is to stir smiles, affection, nostalgia, respect: the Depression-era drama *They Shoot Horses, Don't They?* (1969), the epic Western *Jeremiah Johnson* (1972), the Redford-Streisand love story *The Way We Were* (1973), the CIA thriller *Three Days of the Condor* (1975), Robert Mitchum against Japanese mobsters in *The Yakuza* (1975), Redford and Jane Fonda in *The Electric Horseman* (1979), Paul Newman as the maligned son of a gangster in *Absence of Malice* (1981), hungry actor Dustin Hoffman in drag in *Tootsie* (1982), Redford with Meryl Streep in *Out of Africa* (1985), Tom Cruise as a lawyer in *The Firm* (1993).

When I invited the great cinematographer Owen Roizman to join me in analyzing a film using the shot-by-shot approach at the Hawaii Film Festival, he choose Pollack's *Havana,* pointing out the director's instinct for compositions that helped underline the point of a scene. Instead of discussing the film's visuals as representing what he himself did, Roizman often said things like, "Look how Sydney handles this."

Although he got on well with most actors, he had well-publicized differences with Dustin Hoffman during *Tootsie,* for which they both got Oscar nominations. They actually acted together in the movie, with Pollack playing his dubious agent, and Hoffman a desperate actor who says he can play tall, he can play short, and "nobody does vegetables like me. I did an evening of vegetables off-Broadway. I did the best tomato, the best cucumber—I did an endive salad that knocked the critics on their ass."

Hoffman persuaded Pollack that he should cast himself in the role, and they worked on the scene together. "I think it benefited from the experiences both of us have had in that situation," Pollack said, smiling.

He is survived by his wife since 1958, Claire, and two of their three children, Rachel and Rebecca. A son, Steven, died in an airplane crash in 1993.

Toronto Film Festival

Report No. 1: Choices Are Overwhelming at Toronto Festival

Toronto, Canada, September 2, 2007—I have before me a schedule of the 2007 Toronto Film Festival, which runs ten days. I have been looking at it for some time. I am paralyzed. There are so many films by important directors (not to mention important films by unknown directors) that it cannot be reduced to its highlights. The highlights alone, if run in alphabetical order, would take up all my space.

Let me just drop a few names: Eric Rohmer. Carlos Saura. Claude Chabrol. Takeshi Kitano. Ken Loach. Ermanno Olmi. Hector Babenco. Jacques Rivette. Wayne Wang. Volker Schlondorff. Hou Hsiao-hsien. And Portugal's legendary Manoel de Oliveira, who at ninety-nine is probably the oldest director still at work, but with a festival this large, you can't be sure. Well, yes, you can.

Hold on, hold on. I just gave you the wrong list. That's the list of the "Masters" section of the festival, devoted to established directorial superstars. I should have started with the "Gala Presentations," the big premieres held nightly.

OK, here goes. David Cronenberg. Kenneth Branagh. Shekhar Kapur. Julie Taymor. Gavin Hood. Woody Allen. Renny Harlin. Denys Arcand. Paul Schrader. Richard Attenborough. Those are less than half of the Gala directors. The rest are famous to me, but maybe not yet to you.

But then again, how about the "Special Presentations" of films by Sidney Lumet, Neil Jordan, Michael Moore, Gilliam Armstrong, John Sayles, Todd Haynes, Paul Haggis, Sean Penn, Ang Lee, Johnnie To, Jonathan Demme, Noah Baumbach, Guy Maddin, Peter Greenaway, the Coen brothers, Brian De Palma, Julian Schnabel, and Roger Spottiswoode.

Or the "Vanguard, who run ahead of the pack." Gael Garcia Bernal. Harmony Korine. Gus Van Sant. Gregg Araki. Or "Midnight Madness," with Stuart Gordon, Dario Argento, and George Romero. Or "Dialogues: Talking with Pictures," as filmmakers discuss films they made or love (Scorsese on his *Alice Doesn't Live Here Anymore,* Max von Sydow on Bergman's *The Virgin Spring,* Sidney Lumet on Wyler's *The Best Years of Our Lives*). Or "Contemporary World Cinema," with Ramin Bahrani showing his new film after *Man Push Cart,* David Schwimmer with *Run, Fat Boy, Run,* and handheld documentarian Nick Broomfield's film about an alleged U.S. massacre of Iraqi citizens.

This is impossible. I have given you a list of names, and if you are a serious movie lover you know many of them, but Toronto is so much larger than that: 271 features, 352 films including shorts, 85 percent world premieres, 91 percent North American premieres.

I was looking through some old files the other day and found an article of moderate length from the 1970s in which I was able to list and describe most of the interesting films at Toronto. These days, it's necessary to simply describe the enormity of the festival itself. It is the largest and most important in North America, and to Hollywood it is now more important than Cannes (although Hollywood films are only a small percentage of the whole festival). There will be more than five hundred guests appearing with their films, more than one thousand journalists, reps from every distributor, programmers from every other festival.

And you? Toronto is an open, not private, festival, which means a member of the general public stands a fair chance of getting in. Some tickets are actually still on sale. Most of the films are sold out, but year after year I find treasures in the sidebar sections, especially "Discoveries."

It is also possible to take your chances on a "rush line," where they hand you a number, and at the last minute they admit as many people in line as there are empty seats inside. Considering that the films with the highest profiles are shown in the huge Roy Thomson Hall, the

Elgin theater, or the Visa Screening Room, your chances will be fair to middling. Also, it is not unheard of to come across someone outside a theater trying to unload a ticket, although of course that would be wrong.

Say you don't make it into your movie at 7:30 p.m. Tuesday. The Toronto climate is glorious in September, and it is a city vibrating with restaurants, cafés, shops, theaters, concerts, bookstores, and actual movie theaters selling tickets to current attractions. And the festival itself attracts exciting street life around the main projection centers and up and down Yorkville, Yonge, Bloor, King, and Queen streets. You would have to be very determined to have a bad time in Toronto, and it's just not worth the effort.

I feel guilty. I have seen a dozen or more of this year's entries (they screen some titles in advance for critics in big cities), and I could name you some masterpieces. But that would leave out hundreds of other films, many of them maybe just as good.

Descriptions of every film are online, and if you search the Toronto online newspaper sites, you will find that all the papers, mainstream and alternative, have had critics previewing films for weeks and cover the festival the way the *Sun-Times* would cover a Cubs–White Sox World Series. Meanwhile, in my own columns from the festival, I will be balancing between ecstasy and the suspicion that I have just missed the best film in years.

Toronto Report No. 2

September 5, 2007—And now the ecstasy and madness begin. The thirty-second Toronto Film Festival opens Thursday with no fewer than fifteen films, and that's before it gets up to speed. The Trail Mix Brigade is armed with their knapsacks, bottled water, instant snacks, text messengers, and a determination to see, who knows, six, seven, eight films a day. This may be the only city where thousands plan their vacations around movies.

Toronto is now second only to Cannes in size and prestige, and you could get into an interesting argument on the subject of importance. No matter. As we plunge into ten days of movies, all we will be thinking about is how quickly we can get to the next screening and how little sleep we really need.

The opening night gala, *Fugitive Pieces*, is a three-way salute to native sons. Showing in the enormous Roy Thomson Hall and the merely huge Visa Screening Room, it's by director Jeremy Podeswa, a Torontonian who works mostly in TV but made the wonderful film *The Five Senses* in 2000; it's based on an award-winning novel by Canadian writer Anne Michaels, produced by Canadian Robert Lantos (*The Sweet Hereafter, Being Julia*), and follows the saga of a Jewish child who escapes death in Poland and travels to Canada via Greece.

I haven't seen it yet, but one I have seen may gain an Oscar nomination for Frank Langella. It's *Starting Out in the Evening* by Andrew Wagner, starring Langella, Lauren Ambrose, and Lili Taylor. He's an aging professor, once an acclaimed novelist; Ambrose is a gung-ho graduate student who wants to restart his career, and Taylor, without whom Toronto would be unthinkable, is his daughter, who becomes wary of their relationship. I won't say anything else except, well, I loved it.

Persepolis, by Marjane Satrapi and Vincent Paronnaud, is a black-and-white animated film based on her experiences growing up in Iran as it changed from a secular to an Islamic society. Not the kind of film you'd see everywhere, but the buzz is loud.

Neil Jordan's thoughtful *The Brave One*, Jodie Foster's new thriller about a quiet woman who becomes a vigilante, also premieres Thursday night; what's interesting is how Foster's fierce intelligence reawakens the revenge genre. She becomes worried about the changes that are taking place within her. She gets to like shooting people.

Fados, by the great Spanish director Carlos Saura, plays Thursday night and is described as a drama growing out of Spain's Fado music tradition. He is the director of many other music-inspired films, such as *Tango*, and his opening-night slot is promising.

Toronto's "Reel to Reel" documentary section kicks off tonight with *Hollywood Chinese*, Arthur Dong's doc about changing images of Chinese characters in Hollywood movies. It has countless clips and interviews with such as Joan Chen, Nancy Kwan, Ang Lee, Amy Tan, Christopher Lee, Justin Lin, James Hong, B. D. Wong, and Wayne Wang. Christopher Lee? Is he Chinese? No, but he played Fu Manchu, which is the point.

Did I mention madness? That would be "Midnight Madness," the 11:59 p.m. series featuring cult and transgressive films and inaugurated tonight by no less than the Italian horror master Dario Argento with his *The Mother of Tears.* It stars his daughter, Asia, who by accident releases a malevolent witch into the world, according to IMDb, which knows more about it than I do.

The 11:59 p.m. start time, by the way, is a Toronto stroke of genius, short-stopping all conversations about "does that mean 12 p.m. Thursday noon or 12 p.m. early Friday?"

Coming up over the weekend, a torrent of films, of which the most anticipated may be George Clooney as a legal clean-up artist in Tony Gilroy's *Michael Clayton,* Reese Witherspoon and Jake Gyllenhaal in Gavin Hood's CIA thriller *Rendition,* and then, sure to cause crowd-control emergencies even among the polite Canadians, native son David Cronenberg's *Eastern Promises,* with Viggo Mortensen as a Russian gangster in London.

That one may also, finally, have an Oscar nomination tucked inside for Mortensen. Why not? In Hollywood, Toronto is casually referred to as the unofficial opening of Oscar season.

Toronto Report No. 3

September 6, 2007—If there was ever a director who seems in no danger of repeating himself, that director is Ang Lee. None of his films bears the slightest similarity in subject or tone to any of the others. No doubt there is a subterranean link joining them, but it would take a journey to the center of the earth to find it. And he would be your man to film the journey.

Consider his latest and not even most controversial film, *Lust, Caution,* which was a special presentation of the Toronto Film Festival here Friday night. Set in Shanghai during the years of the Japanese occupation of China, it is about politics, students, assassination, mah-jongg, and a great deal of sex. It is also long, languid, and exquisitely beautiful, its camera wandering the world of a privileged class of Chinese who collaborate with the Japanese and profit hugely from the black market.

Let's start with the sex. No, let's start with the mah-jongg. Joan Chen plays the spoiled wife of the secret service boss Mr. Yee (Tony Leung Chiu Wai, the Asian Cary Grant). She and her friends complain that their lives are limited to mah-jongg and shopping; their conversations around the game table include diamonds, nylons, cigarettes, and other black-market bargains.

Into their circle comes Mrs. Mak (Tang Wei), allegedly the wife of a rich merchant, in fact a member of a student revolutionary group that has decided to murder a collaborationist as its summer project. Her assignment: Seduce Mr. Yee and set him up for killing. During a relationship that spans two years, they grow so intimate and passionate that, she observes, for him there is no satisfaction without some blood involved. She doesn't enjoy their sex, exactly, so much as marvel at the intimacy it brings in spite of her hatred for the man.

The sex scenes are not, as had been rumored, hard core. But they make use of positions also employed in Lee's *Brokeback Mountain,* the Kama Sutra, and, I believe, chiropractic. And they show the characters being drawn almost against their will into fearsome intimacy.

Ang Lee's other films have included *Eat Drink Man Woman, The Ice Storm, Sense and Sensibility, Crouching Tiger, Hidden Dragon,* and *The Hulk,* and find if you will the connecting link.

* * *

One of the Galas Friday starred George Clooney as *Michael Clayton,* a polished, sinister, smart business thriller like Michael Douglas used to make. Clayton is the fixer for a law firm, which means he does what is necessary to set things right. But what if things are really wrong, and a partner in the firm has uncovered alarming information about a client, and the firm wonders if it can trust its fixer? I should not say more, except when I see Clooney in a film like this, I wish he had never heard the word *Ocean's.*

* * *

Another film I need not describe is *The Brave One,* Jodie Foster's new vigilante thriller. But it generated one of those ineluctable festival taxicab conversations.

Passenger One: "Look! On the sidewalk! It's Jodie Foster!"

Passenger Two: "No it isn't, it's just a woman who works at the hotel who looks a lot like her."

One: "Any other day of the year you might be right."

Two: "Why not today?"

One: "Because if Jodie Foster has a film in the Toronto festival and she's coming out of the Toronto Four Seasons, it's Jodie Foster and not a woman who works at the hotel who looks a lot like her."

Not a great example of conversational wit, to be sure, but I'll keep my ears open.

Toronto Report No. 4

September 7, 2007—It's not often you see films that are perfect. I have just seen two of them here at the Toronto Film Festival, and two others that are extraordinary, and a documentary that is spellbinding. Do I love everything? Not at all. I have just happened to have an ecstatic period of moviegoing, that's all, and that's enough.

There is no ranking perfection, so I will discuss the perfect films in alphabetical order. The first is *No Country for Old Men,* by the Coen brothers, and the second is *Rendition* by Gavin Hood. The Coens are among our national treasures. Gavin Hood, at forty-four, was the South African director of *Tsotsi,* the masterpiece that won the Oscar for best foreign film of 2005.

Now what do I mean when I say a film is perfect? I described Altman's *McCabe and Mrs. Miller* as perfect, that's what I mean. A perfect film is serious or funny or anything in between, but in its way it owns wisdom about life, and we learn something from it. Our attention is fully engaged by it. If we are movie critics, our notebooks rest forgotten in our hands. It is cast so well that the roles fit the actors like a second skin. It has dialogue that functions to accomplish what is needed and nothing more; it can be poetry, prose, argument, or bullshit, but we believe the characters would say it. There is not an extra or a wrong shot. The compositions make everything clear but not obvious, and they work on an emotional level even if we're not aware of it. And when it's over we know we've seen one hell of a film.

No Country for Old Men, inspired by the Cormac McCarthy novel, follows a million dollars around Texas. That's the MacGuffin. What it does more importantly is give us a character (Josh Brolin) who finds the money, a character (Javier Bardem) who is a homicidal madman who kills with compressed oxygen, a sheriff (Tommy Lee Jones) who tries to protect the first from the second, a private fixer (Woody Harrelson) who is hired to find the money, and the various wives (especially Kelly Macdonald), women, employers, victims, motel clerks, corpses, and deputies in their lives.

Let me just say that Tommy Lee Jones continues to baffle me by concealing so much range behind what seems to be so little, and that Javier Bardem's Anton Chigurh is a character on the level of Anthony Hopkins's Hannibal Lecter, with a precision of dialogue and an insistence on the strict logic of words that is bone chilling and sometimes oddly funny.

Now to *Rendition.* I owe director Gavin Hood an apology for writing in a Toronto festival preview that it is a "CIA thriller." It involves the CIA, and among other things it is a thriller, but it is no more a "CIA thriller" than *Macbeth* is a swashbuckler. It is a movie about the theory and practice of two things: torture and personal responsibility. And it is wise about what is right and what is wrong. The original and tightly coiled screenplay, by Kelley Sane, should get one of several nominations the movie deserves.

The story involves the arrest of an Egyptian-American scientist (Omar Metwally) who is "disappeared" from a flight from Cape Town to Washington. His very pregnant wife (Reese Witherspoon) simply doesn't believe "he was never on the plane" and enlists a former lover (Peter Sarsgaard), now an aide to a senator (Alan Arkin), to investigate through back channels. This runs him up against the head of the CIA (Meryl Streep), who is terrifyingly professional.

Meanwhile, in an unnamed North African country, the new American attaché (Jake Gyllenhaal) is told that the scientist has been brought there to take advantage of its expert torturers, an interesting use of outsourcing. And we meet the country's chief of security, his daughter, her forbidden boyfriend, and others, as several story strands are relentlessly gathered into a conclusion that makes perfect sense and causes us to rethink everything, and no, that doesn't mean what it sounds like it means.

The United States has in recent years been

implicated in torture, official and unofficial, but *Rendition* views the subject in a much deeper and more complex way than you would expect.

The two "extraordinary" films are David Cronenberg's *Eastern Promises,* for which I have already predicted an Oscar nomination for Viggo Mortensen's Russian gangster in London; and Andrew Dominik's *The Assassination of Jesse James by the Coward Robert Ford,* starring Brad Pitt as the outlaw, Casey Affleck as the coward, and James Carville in a supporting presence suggesting he should quit the day job.

The documentary is Amir Bar-Lev's *My Kid Could Paint That,* about a four-year-old girl named Marla Olmstead you may remember from the news. She became famous as a prodigy who created abstract paintings that sold for thousands of dollars, and indeed stand comparison with adult professional work. There is a lot to be said about this film, which inspires great speculation.

Don't get me started. Let me just close by saying that I have seen so many good movies up here I can hardly stand it, and the festival runs for another week.

Toronto Report No. 5

September 7, 2007—I don't know when I've heard a standing ovation so long, loud, and *warm* as the one after Jason Reitman's *Juno,* which I predict will become quickly beloved when it opens at Christmastime, and win a best actress nomination for its twenty-year-old star, Ellen Page.

It's the kind of movie you almost insult by describing the plot, because the plot sounds standard and this is a fresh, quirky, unusually intelligent comedy about a sixteen-year-old girl who wins our hearts in the first scene. Page plays Juno, who gets pregnant, and—no, that's not it at all. Every element in the movie, including her getting pregnant, and her non-boyfriend, and her parents, and the couple that wants to adopt the baby, is completely unlike any version of those characters I have ever seen before. And the dialogue is so quick and funny you feel the actors are performing it on a high-wire.

It was so much fun to sit with a huge audience that laughed not just in good humor, but in appreciation and sympathy. Her boyfriend, played by Michael Cera, is so clueless that Juno translates that as "not being like everyone else." Her father and stepmother, the superb character actors J. K. Simmons and Allison Janney, are older, wiser, and funnier than a teenager's parents are ever allowed to be. The hopeful adoptive couple (Jennifer Garner and Jason Bateman) are the opposite of what you'd expect, and then turn out to be the opposite of that. And the whole story is textured within a school year that focuses on the growing-up that Juno has to do.

This is Reitman's second film, after the also smart and funny but very different *Thank You for Smoking* (2005), and positions the thirty-year-old son of Ivan Reitman (*Ghostbusters*) in the first rank of his generation. It's a nice coincidence that Juno's family nickname is Junebug, reminding us of Phil Morrison's 2005 comedy *Junebug* and its equally lovable heroine. The magical screenplay is Diablo Cody's first, and I won't ask you to believe me, just look up her biography on IMDb.com.

* * *

And now for something completely different, which would certainly be Sean Penn's uncompromising *Into the Wild,* with Emile Hirsch's career-making performance as a young idealist who treks into the Alaskan wilderness to live in harmony with nature, which is not in harmony with him.

Based on the Jon Krakauer best-seller inspired by the real-life experience of Christopher McCandless, Penn's film begins as a road trip. The young man, a dreamer and a loner, meets strangers who become friends, who care for him, mentor him, and worry about him, in a series of self-contained vignettes that are like the last sightings of a boat drifting out to sea. Krakauer and Penn's screenplay takes unremittingly grim material and illuminates it with its hero's idealism, his poetry, and his unwise self-confidence.

* * *

Starting Out in the Evening contains another fascinating performance about a self-confident young woman and pairs it with perhaps Frank Langella's finest work. He plays an aging professor, once considered a great novelist, now long dormant, whose life is upset by a brash young graduate student (Lauren Ambrose), who is doing her thesis on him and decides he needs jump-starting. The professor's daughter

(Lili Taylor) is not pleased with this new person in her father's life, and the prospect of a May-December romance hovers over the story like a storm about to burst.

Director Andrew Wagner's first film was *The Talent Given Us* (2005), a quasi-real documentary about a cross-country trip his family makes to visit him. The fact that he is himself shooting the doc along the way makes it quasi-real, but absolutely everything is real about his family. Now he shows a sure touch for a drama that needs gentle, subtle handling to work as well as it does—and gets it, and deserves it.

Toronto Report No. 6

September 9, 2007—Sometimes in a smaller theater, away from the searchlights and the twenty-four-hour fans making privacy impossible for poor Brad and Angelina, you find an independent film that is miraculous. Such a film is *Chop Shop*, by Ramin Bahrani, the Iran-born American director whose *Man Push Cart* made such a stir three years ago. That film was about an immigrant from Pakistan trying to make a living in New York with a rented coffee-and-bagel cart. It was shot on a shoestring in less than three weeks and won the critics' prize at London and three Independent Spirit Awards, including best first feature. It embodied, I said in my review, the very soul of Italian neorealism.

Now *Chop Shop* is another film about making a hard living in New York City, and—with more time to film and stunning performances by his very young actors—Bahrani has made an even more powerful film. It is set in Willets Point, Queens, and stars a twelve-year-old boy named Alejandro Polanco and a sixteen-year-old girl named Isamar Gonzales, playing a brother and sister who share a tiny room above an auto repair shop. The film is so very real that the shop owner, Rob Sowulski, plays himself, and shares the whole film's feeling of authenticity. For that matter, Alejandro and Isamar attend the same school, and she was a close friend of his sister's.

First a word about Willets Point. Bahrani observes in his notes that this area was the original Valley of the Ashes in F. Scott Fitzgerald's *The Great Gatsby*. Now it is a seventy-five-acre district called "the Iron Triangle," a third-world clone jammed with auto body and parts shops and the population that lives off of them. Alejandro (all the actors use their real names) hustles customers for his boss's shop, learns the auto repair trade, peddles M&M's on the subway, does some hubcap stealing and purse snatching, and dreams that he and his sister will own their own taco-and-beans truck.

He and Isamar, both from Puerto Rico, spontaneously, joyously like each other, and one of the movie's scenes of heartbreaking reality shows them at horseplay—just a couple of kids in a world of unremitting poverty. Bahrani's camera lives in their lives. There is no false sentiment in his story, just a fascination with these characters. The area is across the expressway from Shea Stadium and in the LaGuardia flight path but seems to be in another world than the United States. And yet the ingenuity and improvisation of this brother and sister forces the Iron Triangle to support them, sometimes by any means necessary. Now we have an American film with the raw power of *City of God* or *Pixote*, a film that does something unexpected, and inspired, and brave.

* * *

The big-budget movies playing over the weekend included Andrew Dominik's *The Assassination of Jesse James by the Coward Robert Ford*, starring Brad Pitt as the outlaw and Casey Affleck as the coward, and Shekhar Kapur's *Elizabeth: The Golden Age*, starring Cate Blanchett in a sequel to their *Elizabeth* (1998), nominated for seven Oscars.

The Jesse James saga follows *3:10 from Yuma* as another convincing argument that the Western is far from dead. Pitt embodies the qualities that allowed Jesse James, essentially a low-life murderer, to gain iconic and almost heroic status. Affleck is quietly insidious as James's worshipper, who becomes his murderer, something the outlaw almost seems to expect and invite. Ford is a coward, I suppose, because he shoots James in the back, but what does that make Jesse, whose gang killed helpless stagecoach passengers and bank employees? Once again, the Western demonstrates why it can be such an ideal platform for the scrutiny of character.

The film about Elizabeth begins at the height of her power, as the Virgin Queen enlists Sir Walter Raleigh (Clive Owen), just returned from claiming Virginia and naming it after her, to lead an outgunned British fleet in the humiliating defeat of the Spanish Armada. Once again Blanchett embodies austere queenly and vulnerable human emotions, and Kapur evokes British locations and a royal court that are not only bigger than life but bigger than legend. Samantha Morton, as Mary Queen of Scots, gets as much emotion out of a medium shot of a woman about to be beheaded as I think it is probably possible to extract, and Geoffrey Rush is the fierce, warmongering courtier Sir Francis Walsingham. The word for this film is, I think, sumptuous. Maybe too sumptuous, unless you like that sort of thing, which I do.

* * *

Eran Kolirin's *The Band's Visit* is a charming sleeper of a comedy from Israel, about the mistaken visit of the Alexandria (Egypt) Municipal Policeman's Band to perhaps the smallest hamlet in Israel. The band conductor (Sasson Gabai) is ferocious with an underling who put them on the wrong bus, and Ronit Elkabetz plays Dina, the proprietor of a snack shop that is literally the entire downtown.

During a long, hot day and night, the band members and locals interact (often in English, their common language). Dreams and disappointments are reviewed, truths are told, and romances start out as doomed and go downhill. If you are at all familiar with the uniquely deadpan comedies of the Finnish director Aki Kaurismaki (*The Match Factory Girl, The Man Without a Past*), you will recognize some of the same qualities here, as downbeat characters share misery over Israeli-Egyptian lines. In its sad way, it is very funny.

* * *

Now how does a critic review a film that has been dedicated to him? Werner Herzog has done me the astonishing honor of so dedicating his new documentary about Antarctica, *Encounters at the End of the World*. Yes, it is an awesome film, humbling in the face of a continent so vast it moves beyond human comprehension. But a review from me might seem like a conflict of interest. I've decided the solution is to simply write a letter to this man whose work I have admired beyond measure for more than forty years. It appears in the essays chapter.

Toronto Report No. 7

September 10, 2007—It is probable that Pierre Rissient, a Frenchman, knows more directors, actors, distributors, exhibitors, and critics than any other single person in the film industry. Pierre issues a lot of instructions. I call him Pierre because I have known him for thirty years, and in recent years he has given me my daily instructions every morning in the breakfast room of the Hotel Splendid at Cannes.

But who is he, and what does he do? These are the questions that Todd McCarthy, chief film critic for *Variety*, sets out to answer in his new documentary, *Man of Cinema: Pierre Rissient*. As far as I am concerned, it could also be called *Pierre Rissient: International Man of Mystery*.

These are things we know: Pierre programmed the screenings of American crime movies in Paris that essentially created film noir. Popularized his favorite American directors in Paris, essentially preparing the ground for the auteur theory to be invented. At the birth of the New Wave, was assistant director for Claude Chabrol and on Godard's *Breathless*. Partnered with future director Bertrand Tavernier as "the two best movie publicists in Paris." Resurrected critical respect for Otto Preminger, Joseph Losey, Anthony Mann, Samuel Fuller. Carried a drunken John Ford around Paris for a week. Created the worldwide popularity of King Hu (*A Touch of Zen*) and other martial arts directors. Directed two films of his own, not widely seen.

Went to China and brought back the films of Chen Kaige and Zhang Yimou. Introduced the Filipino director Lino Broca to the world. Single-handedly masterminded Clint Eastwood's embrace by Europe, which in turn elevated his American status. Discovered Australia's Jane Campion, booked her three short subjects at Cannes, and then was responsible for her *Piano* playing at Cannes, which led to the Palme d'Or and three Academy Awards. As the most trusted adviser to Cannes boss Gilles Jacob, led the festival's embrace of Asian cinema. Is the only person in the world who can walk into any screening at Cannes at will, including the evening black-tie events, to which he wears a T-shirt or safari shirt. Just had his own theater, The Pierre, named after him at Telluride.

And . . . I grow breathless. All of these accomplishments and many, many more are covered in McCarthy's doc, which will be fascinating for anyone who has ever meet Pierre (millions, I suppose), but not so much for others, unless you want to see a man obsessed with his lifelong passion for the cinema. (Also a passion for girlfriends, usually young and Asian, which the doc does not neglect to mention.) Pierre lives and breathes the movies, and more than anyone else has influenced the success of the good (key word) films we notice and the directors we admire. You don't believe me, see this documentary and take notes.

Pierre's role in many situations is to "defend," by which he means "support," the films and directors he approves. Telluride once printed a T-shirt quoting him: "It is not enough to like a film. One must like it for the right reasons." Michel Ciment, the famous French film critic, remembers in the film that when Rissient and Tavernier were promoting films as publicists, they used a screening room with a long, narrow corridor so that it was impossible to leave without passing both of them. They wanted to be sure you liked the film and for the right reasons, and if you did not, they would tell you why you were wrong. Uniquely among publicists, they would only handle films they loved—for the right reasons, of course.

One night at Cannes, Pierre used a motorboat to take seven American film critics out to Francis Ford Coppola's yacht, floating in the bay in anticipation of the world premiere of *Apocalypse Now.* It was on this evening that Coppola made his infamous remark that he didn't know if the ending worked, by which he meant dropping the credits on the road-show version, and the world thought he meant the whole Marlon Brando sequence.

Nevertheless, *Apocalypse Now* won the Palme d'Or, although for the only time in history there was a tie for the top award, with Volker Schlondorff's *The Tin Drum.* How did Pierre let that happen? The following December, I was in Los Angeles when the telephone rang in my hotel room (Pierre can find anybody at any time).

"What are you doing in L.A.?" I asked him.

"Handling the Oscar campaign for *The Tin Drum,*" he said.

Toronto Report No. 8

September 11, 2007—Everyone, including me, was under the impression that Kenneth Branagh's new film, *Sleuth,* was a remake of the 1972 film. Same situation: Rich thriller writer is visited in his country house by man who is having affair with his wife. Same outcome: They argue, man is killed. Same visit: Police detective. Same so forth and so on.

But hang on, I thought, watching the film at Monday night's Toronto Film Festival gala, I didn't realize the screenplay was by *Sir Harold Pinter.* What had reduced the Nobel Prize–winning dramatist to adapting old, if good, movies? But then, in the opening moments, as the novelist (Sir Michael Caine) greets his visitor (Jude Law), there was an edgy exchange.

Novelist: Is that your car?

Visitor: On the left, right.

Novelist: Yes, that's my car on the right. My car is bigger than yours.

My memory of the 1972 movie was not crystal clear, but that dialogue didn't ring a bell. Neither did any of the other dialogue. It didn't sound like the Anthony Shaffer play or his screenplay. It sounded—well, Pinteresque. And did the two men go through a little homosexual role-playing the first time around? The earlier movie starred Sir Laurence Olivier as the novelist (apparently you have to be knighted to play the role) and, what do you know, Michael Caine as the visitor. Even after thirty-five years I think I would have remembered Olivier and Caine being gay together.

Talking to Branagh, Caine, and Law on Tuesday afternoon, I got the statistics: Only one line ("It's a game!") from the original screenplay is used in Pinter's. Pinter did not see the movie, read the screenplay once, sat down, and wrote the original situation as a screenplay by Harold Pinter. And what Branagh and his actors have made is a Pinter film, transposing the outline of the original material into an altogether quirkier, weirder, diabolical result. In 1972 we were asked to be absorbed by the plot. In 2007 we are asked to be absorbed by the characters and how they talk and what they say.

What both films share is ambiguity about the material: What do the novelist and the visitor really think about each other? What's really going on here? With Pinter, as always, that's really the question.

* * *

Former President Jimmy Carter is eighty-two years old, but Jonathan Demme's new documentary, *Man from Plains,* shows him with inexhaustible energy. Demme (*The Silence of the Lambs*) watches him in public and backstage as he tours to promote his twenty-first book, *Palestine: Peace Not Apartheid.* He's up at dawn, then still appearing on the late-night shows. He's confronting his critics. He's talking about religion, and we even see him in a pulpit, thinking aloud about how Christians and Darwinians might just have different ways of describing the same process.

We see him on the phone with his wife, Rosalynn, and find out that together or apart, they read a Bible verse every night. We see him driving nails on one of the houses being constructed by Habitat for Humanity. He talks about the Camp David Accords that brought the hope of peace to the Middle East. He is smart, funny, informed, able to think outside the box. This is twenty-seven years after what he calls his "enforced retirement" from the White House.

There was a story the other day about President George W. Bush's plans for retirement, based on the new book *Dead Certain* by Robert Draper. Bush told Draper: "I'll give some speeches, to replenish the ol' coffers. I don't know what my dad gets—it's more than fifty to seventy-five thousand per speech. Clinton's making a lot of money." In another interview, he noted Clinton's recent work with the U.N., and said that after he retired, "You won't catch me hanging around the U.N."

Watching the Jimmy Carter doc, I reflected that everyone should choose the retirement plan that is right for them.

* * *

Woody Allen's new film, *Cassandra's Dream,* is, like his *Match Point,* set in England and deals with murder. It also has certain similarities with his *Crimes and Misdemeanors.* But it's different in one way—the nature of the ending.

The movie costars Colin Farrell and Ewan McGregor as needy brothers whose uncle (Tom Wilkinson) tells them "family is family" and asks them to commit a murder for him. The movie shows them debating this proposition with Allen's usual dialogue of literacy and wit, and there are situations of awkward social irony.

But here's the strange thing. The ending, I thought, was too realistic—just the sort of thing that really could happen. In this movie, at that moment, I thought a little more artifice might have been appropriate. Not that the previous 103 minutes don't work, because they do, but—well, sometimes it's OK, even desirable, to have an ending of contrivance and manipulation.

Toronto Report No. 9

September 12, 2007—*The Walker* is another of Paul Schrader's "man in a room" films, and his best film since *Affliction* (1997). It's a fascinating character study with as fine a performance as Woody Harrelson has given, and certainly the most unexpected. Schrader defined the films as centering on the image of a man in a room, preparing to go out and do something, and then doing it while remaining focused by his preparation. That would define Schrader's *American Gigolo* (1980), with Richard Gere in training for his profession as a professional lover of women. And *Light Sleeper* (1992), with Willem Dafoe as a drug dealer who is also a recovering addict.

And now here is Harrelson as Carter Page III, a paid escort, or "walker," for rich society women in Washington, D.C. Impeccably dressed, charming, kind, friendly, the son and grandson of great men, he is a homosexual who has a lover but genuinely likes the women of a certain age who appear on his arm at social functions. He goes shopping with them, plays in their canasta games, shares gossip, and one day does one favor too many.

Kristin Scott Thomas plays the wife of a senator; she sometimes visits a male prostitute for sex. Page drives her and waits for her, and understands. One day when she arrives at the prostitute's luxurious Georgetown apartment, she finds his throat slashed. To report her discovery would destroy her reputation and her husband's. So Carter drives her home, returns, and calls the police himself.

He immediately becomes the prime suspect in the murder. In *Gigolo* and *Sleeper,* the heroes were also implicated in crimes because of the nature of their work and the goodness of their natures. Harrelson plays Page as a guarded, essentially shy man, soft-spoken, with an amused southern drawl, using a hairpiece to cover his baldness, knowledgeable about the lines of power, money, and sex in the capital, vulnerable because of his profession. The movie surrounds him with ladies of middle and upper ages (Lauren Bacall, Mary Beth Hurt, Lily Tomlin) and portrays his world with a sociologist's precision. It is fascinating.

* * *

Sidney Lumet, at eighty-three, may be one of the oldest directors with a film at Toronto this year, but his films are always sharp-edged and constructed with a taut urgency, and now he has made a crime film as good, in its own way, as his *Dog Day Afternoon, The Verdict, Find Me Guilty,* and *Serpico.*

Like those films, like all of his crime films, *Before the Devil Knows You're Dead* shakes off the conventions of genre and becomes a study of character. It uses, as Lumet likes to do, superb actors: Philip Seymour Hoffman and Ethan Hawke as brothers, Albert Finney as their father, Marisa Tomei as Hoffman's wife, Rosemary Harris as Finney's wife, and Amy Ryan as Hawke's ex-wife. The brothers both face financial emergencies, and Hoffman concocts a plan to stick up their family's suburban jewelry store on a Saturday morning when the staff will be one old lady. His plan: No guns, no muss, no fuss, Dad gets reimbursed by insurance, nobody's a loser, and their problems are over.

The plan does not quite work out. This first screenplay by Kelly Masterson uses interlocking flashbacks to see the plan and the problems gradually swelling toward critical mass. And what is so good about the film is the depth of the characters, of the brothers (one nursing old wounds, the other feckless), the father (Finney sounds the depths of the man's soul), and Tomei (whose marriage is coming apart, and she doesn't know why). Lumet started in TV in 1951. His career directing feature films began with the masterpiece *12 Angry Men* (1957), and he hasn't lost one beat in fifty years.

* * *

And if we're discussing performances, let us now praise *I'm Not There,* a film about a famous man, Bob Dylan. Todd Haynes (*Far from Heaven*) takes an enormous risk and makes a brilliant, if seemingly impossible, film starring six actors as the mysterious cultural icon. Who is Dylan? How many selves does he have? Why are we so fascinated by such questions?

The actors: Christian Bale, Cate Blanchett, Marcus Carl Franklin, Richard Gere, Heath Ledger, and Ben Whishaw. Oddly enough, it is Blanchett who looks and seems the most like Dylan, especially at the time of the documentary *Don't Look Back,* from which it approximates several scenes including a heated exchange with a British journalist. (Extraordinary, to see her in the same Toronto festival playing Bob Dylan and Queen Elizabeth I.)

The more Dylanology you know, the more references you'll catch, although the film mostly works even without expertise on Dylan; the great man authorized use of his songs and performances throughout the movie, and turns up briefly at the end (although, dazzled by so many other Dylans, you may miss the real thing). I liked Haynes's use of a young African-American boy (Marcus Carl Franklin, son of the director Carl Franklin) as the first of the Dylans, who introduces himself as Dylan's idol, Woody Guthrie. The others are effective in one way or another, except for Richard Gere, who appears as Dylan/Billy the Kid, a cross-reference to Kris Kristofferson's famous success in persuading Sam Peckinpah to cast Dylan in *Pat Garrett and Billy the Kid* (1973), although not as Billy.

Look at it this way, though: In addition to all the ways it works and the few ways it doesn't, *I'm Not There* is an experimental Dylan musical in the season that has also given us *Across the Universe* for the Beatles.

Toronto Report No. 10

September 14, 2007—It's the Cinderella story of this year's Toronto Film Festival. Girl is born in Chicago, grows up, graduates from college, moves to Minneapolis to join her boyfriend, Jonny, whom she met on the 'net. Works in advertising, finds it boring. Starts working as a stripper, doesn't find it boring. Changes her name to Diablo Cody. Starts a blog. Works as a phone-sex voice. Writes book, *Candy Girl: A Year in the Life of an Unlikely Stripper.* Quits the sex biz, marries Jonny, moves to suburbs. His daughter is their flower girl at wedding.

That's all boiled down from her bios at IMDb and Amazon. But now we get to the Cinderella part. I am hearing about it from Jason Reitman, the director of *Juno,* which in my guess is the most popular film of the festival, and is written by Diablo Cody.

"She met this guy, he was supposed to be a producer, she wasn't sure, but he tells her she should write a screenplay," Reitman tells me. "It takes her two months. She sends it to Hollywood, where it goes all over town and *everyone* wants to make it. It is one of the best screenplays around."

Reitman, the son of famous director Ivan Reitman, was planning to direct his own screenplay for his second film, after the success of his 2005 written-and-directed *Thank You for Smoking*. But he reads *Juno* and knows he must direct it.

His wonderful, funny movie stars Ellen Page in an Oscar-caliber performance as an intelligent, sassy sixteen-year-old who gets pregnant. Her father and stepmother don't yell and scream at her, but just want to help her out all they can. That, and many other elements of *Juno,* are unlike most films about teenagers. Very unlike. Now back to the Cinderella story.

"Juno and her stepmother (Allison Janney) are very close," Reitman says. "That was Diablo's thinking. She thought stepmothers always got a raw deal in fiction. It was the Cinderella model of the stepmother as a witch. But now Diablo is a stepmother herself, and she and her stepdaughter really like each other."

Reitman says when he read her screenplay he thought, "She really nailed the New Nuclear Family. In the movies, families used to be Mom, Pop, and the kids. In real life today, it's often more complicated. You have stepparents, half-brothers and -sisters, children of single mothers, every kind of family. But she doesn't write about this in a political way, just in an honest light."

The heroine's family, in fact, is one of the most lovable families in recent films. Whatever Diablo Cody's background was, she wrote a positive, human, hilarious story. "Sometimes I just had to trust her," Reitman says. He gave the example of the scene where Juno tries to commit suicide by hanging herself with licorice rope. More I will not reveal. "I didn't understand it," Reitman admits, "but I figured if I loved her screenplay and it was in there, she must have known what she was doing. It gets one of the biggest laughs in the movie."

And Diablo Cody? That's what everyone calls her?

"Even her parents now," Reitman says.

* * *

Speaking of unconventional families and directors who are the children of other directors: *Rails and Ties,* by Alison Eastwood, Clint's daughter, is being well-received at the festival. It stars a childless couple (Marcia Gay Harden and Kevin Bacon). She's dying of cancer; we find out in the first scene, so that's not a spoiler. He's a train engineer whose train slams into the car of a woman who overdosed on pills and parked on the tracks.

The woman's eleven-year-old son (Miles Heizer), angry because the engineer "didn't even *try* to stop," tracks him down and confronts him. But it's more complicated. He's a runaway from a heartless foster home, the engineer and his wife grow to love him, and . . . more I should not reveal.

But the real sadness in the opening third of the movie is visceral and true. We look into the eyes of the woman and see bleak grief, and we look in the eyes of the man, who chooses to drive a train on a day he should be with her, and see a man who lives his life by the book, which is no life at all. And then they are freed from their fixed positions by the lonely need of the boy.

It's a powerful setup, although I found the final shot less than satisfying. Yes, that's what would happen. But more and more I question realism as a complete justification for events in movies. In some movies, yes, maybe a lot of movies; but sometimes what we need is a movie that doesn't turn out like life.

* * *

Toronto closed Saturday night. The general opinion is it was the best Toronto in years. If you see the films I loved, you're going to see some great films this autumn. And I missed about 240 of the films in the festival, including a lot where people looked at me incredulously and said, "You didn't see *that*?"

Ebert's Journal

A Mametian Genre: The Twister

May 4, 2008—David Mamet's recent *Redbelt* is an example of a kind of movie that needs a name. It's not precisely a thriller or a suspense picture or a police procedural, and although it occupies the territory of film noir, it's not a noir. I propose this kind of film be named a twister, because it's made from plot twists, and in a way the twists are the real subject.

A true twister is one twist piled on another. It doesn't qualify if the twist is simply an unanticipated ending, as in *Her Life Before Her Eyes,* when (spoiler alert!) we discover that everything after the confrontation with the killer was imagined in the heroine's dying moments. It was her *future* life that flashed before her eyes. The ending in that film explains and redefines all that went before, and is traditionally called a "twist ending," which is clear enough. It works as a beautiful idea, which comes at the end because that's the only place it belongs. Maybe it's not a twist at all but just the inevitable unfolding of what happened.

Twisters don't twist only at the end. They pull one rug after another out from under our feet, until we're astonished by how many rugs we were standing on. Sometimes it's almost impossible to keep all the versions of reality straight. Sometimes it's a futile exercise, because we realize the film could continue indefinitely. But when a twister is in the hands of a master like Mamet, it can be devilish and ingenious.

Mamet's first film, the great *House of Game,* kept surprising us with the unfolding levels of its con. He's fascinated by con games and loves to use them in his films and plays. In most of his films, you'll see a saturnine, bearded actor named Ricky Jay, one of his friends, who is a consultant on magic and cons. Jay played one of the poker players in *House of Game* and is the pay-for-view TV promoter in *Redbelt.* Mamet even produced a night of Jay's magic, off-Broadway, during which Jay performed the non-Mametian trick of throwing cards at a watermelon so hard they sliced into them.

After the show I went backstage to meet the magician and was told, "Actually, this isn't the first time we've met. We met in college. You published something by me in a little magazine you edited."

I don't remember you, I confessed.

"Don't let the name throw you off," he said. "I wasn't named Ricky Jay then."

What was your name?

"That, my friend, you will never know."

A nice touch. A nicer one is that in searching Jay's various biographies, I could find no mention of him having attended the University of Illinois. You see how it works. But of course it wasn't mentioned, you say, because he attended under another name. Yes, but *he* would have known where he went to college. Perhaps he made up his biography. Why? That, my friends, we will never know.

The difference between *House of Games* and *Redbelt* helps define two kinds of twisters. In *House of Game,* the other characters are in on the con, and Lindsay Crouse, their quarry, represents the film's point of view. In *Redbelt,* while the manager of the martial arts studio (Chiwetel Ejiofor) is the quarry, he becomes a victim on more than one level, and it's hard to see how everyone else could have been in on it, even after some awkward exposition. In every twister, the audience, by necessity, is kept on the outside, but in some of them, the film itself seems to be the confidence game.

The exposition I was referring to in *Redbelt* comes when the studio owner bluntly asks how something happened and is bluntly given the answer. It feels so awkward I almost think Mamet stuck it in after even *he* found the film hard to follow. Reminds me of the story about the Roger Corman film that made no sense. Two bit actors were brought back to stand in front of a backdrop. One asked, "What does this all mean?" and the other told him. Of course, in a twister, it need not mean, but be.

Fanzines

May 4, 2008—Fanzines were mimeographed magazines that were circulated by mail among science fiction fans in the days before the Internet. They still are, for all I know, although now they're generated by computer printers. I first learned about them in a 1950s issue of *Amazing Stories* and eagerly sent away ten or twenty cents to Buck and Juanita Coulson in Indiana, whose *Yandro* was one of the best and longest-running of them all. Overnight, I was a fan, although not yet a BNF (big name fan). It was a thrill for me to have an LOC (letter of comment) published on such issues as the demise of BEMs (bug-eyed monsters), and soon I was publishing my own fanzine named *Stymie*. Then the university intervened, and I found myself publishing the *Spectator* (not precisely an original title), a weekly tabloid of arts and politics at the University of Illinois. I had become too busy for fandom, and found it wise to GAFIA (get away from it all).

I have always been convinced that the culture of SF fanzines contributed heavily to the formative culture of the early Web, and generated models for Web sites and blogs. The very tone of the discourse is similar, and like fanzines, the Web took new word coinages, turned them into acronyms, and ran with them. Think about it. Science fiction fans in the decades before the Internet were already interested in computers, big-time—first with the supercomputers of science fiction myth, and then with the earliest home-built models. Fans tended to be youngish, male, geeky, obsessed with popular culture, and compelled to circulate their ideas. In the reviews and criticism they ran, they slanted heavily toward expertise in narrow pop fields. The *Star Trek* phenomenon was predicted by their fascination years earlier with analysis of *Captain Video, Superman, X Minus One,* and *Sheena, Queen of the Jungle,* and there were learned discussions about how Tarzan taught himself to read.

I was an eyewitness to one of the formative moments in the connection between computers and science fiction. I wrote earlier about going to a speech in Urbana given by Sir Arthur C. Clarke. He spoke about earth satellites, but the key element is: The speech was in *Urbana.* Years later, it was with tingles tangling on my spine that I heard HAL 9000 announce that he had been born in the computer lab at the University of Illinois in Urbana. So far as I know, Clarke had never returned to Urbana, but I assume that while he was there he visited Illiac, one of the first big computers, and its gradually developing successors. When he was writing the *2001* screenplay, the Urbana connection made itself.

That's been my theory. It didn't hold water with Clarke, however. At the university in March 1997 we held a birthday party for HAL 9000 called "Cyberfest," which also considered artificial intelligence in general. For the climax, we screened *2001* in 70 mm and had a cybercast interview with Sir Arthur via the 'net from Sri Lanka. He loomed twenty feet above us, his image and voice dominating the room via a signal carried by one of the satellites he wrote so much about. Of course I asked him about the Urbana connection but alas he did not remember giving a speech in Urbana and doubted it had much to do with the movie.

That took the wind out of my sails. So did a message from Stanley Kubrick. Since HAL clearly says in the movie that he was born in 1992, we came up with the 1997 date because that's HAL's birthday in Clarke's novel. The 1992 date had passed largely ignored, and we were determined not to miss our second chance to gather a roomful of geeks singing him "Happy Birthday."

Him? She? It? "You'll have to ask HAL," Sir Arthur said. What Kubrick said was, if we didn't have a birthday for HAL in 1992, it was too late to have one now. How did the birthday get moved five years between book and movie? Maybe Clarke could see that progress on the AI front was moving more slowly than he anticipated. So was progress in general. As a comment to my Clarke item on this blog noted, Clarke often said he would be aboard the first passenger shuttle to the moon. That date has been pushed *way* back.

There are two heirs to Cyberfest, however. It inspired Ebertfest the following year. And the university is now the home of the National Center for Supercomputing Applications. It houses "the Cave," a room whose walls, floor, and ceiling are created by virtual reality. You can float through outer space. Clarke could have walked on the moon there. I wish he had.

Herd Mentality

May 8, 2008—When a critic votes with a vast majority, I think one reason is that some films are obviously good or bad (in the eyes of most people). But when one lonely critic stands apart from the mob, there may be a message to be learned, and that may be the critic you should make a point of reading, assuming he or she has been interesting in the past. There may be a special expertise or sensitivity coming into view, or a film might have been made with such specialized intent that its qualities are invisible to the majority. Or, sometimes, it may be the auteur theory at work, and the critic may be so invested in the work of that director that he or she sees things that reach specifically to his wavelength.

Example: Harmony Korine's film *Mister Lonely.* It gets a 50 on the Tomatometer, but high praise from Don R. Lewis at *Film Threat.* I understand that. I was one of very few critics who admired Korine's *Julien Donkey-Boy.* In that case I think I responded to the total freedom he granted himself to impose audacious and extreme characters and situations upon us. A lot of people were not willing to take the ride, and I understand them. Another example, close to my heart: It is almost impossible for Werner Herzog to make a film I dislike, but not everybody agrees. I have determined that he is the most creative source of new and visionary imagery in the movies, and I've seen nothing to change that opinion.

The average moviegoer doesn't care about the treasured personal inclinations of a critic on a particular peculiar film. The average moviegoer just wants to walk in, get his movie, and go home. I remember when the Spudnut Shop opened on campus. My friend Paul Tyner went to work there, and noticed a sign behind the counter: "No reading!" He asked the owner what that was about. "I have eighteen stools at my counter," the guy said. "Some guy could come in and start reading some book and never stop. My motto is, get 'em in, give 'em their Spuddies, and get 'em out again."

That is also Hollywood's motive, although they don't care if the Spuddies are studded with nails, as long as people buy them. But there are always some moviegoers who are excited by the experience of the surprising and the new, and realize a film is reaching them in a personal way. Consider the response to my mention of *Joe vs. the Volcano* a week or so ago. I got a lot of comments from readers who have, like me, treasured that rejected and forgotten film for years. One family watches it annually. When I praised the film, I suppose I was writing for those specific readers, although I didn't know it.

Remember that most critics write without benefit of hindsight. The Tomatometer has not yet run up its totals when they review a new film, and they may be astonished to find themselves in a minority of one. They're not running against the herd, because the herd has not yet formed. They are offering an opinion that, it turns out, will be the exception to the rule. When you find a review like that, think about it. Few of us have a desire to see the same damned thing over and again, but Hollywood is never happier than when supplying it. A minority opinion (better still, a majority of critics "surprised," or, one of my favorite words, "blindsided" by a film) are urgently trying to tell you something. And for you, they may be right.

Final example. My review of *Beowulf* was largely alone in the field; I thought it was brilliant, and I thought it was intended not just as action and fantasy spectacle, but as bawdy, audacious humor. Hardly anyone agreed. But the cowriter Roger Avary wrote me that, indeed, it was written as an over-the-top comedy, and he thought it worked that way. See it in that light, and you may see a different movie. Your particular sensibility may discover gold that otherwise washed away in the flood.

Hillary and Bill: The Movie

May 8, 2008—I woke up at about 3:30 a.m. and went online to see if Obama had pulled a victory out of Indiana. He had narrowed Clinton's lead to two points by midnight and later added a few more votes, but the story was basically about the same: Clinton's winning margin was so small that it didn't much count, and Obama would be the likely presidential nominee. Then I started wondering, in the vaporous midnight hours, about how you could make a movie of this primary campaign.

I'm sure there will be documentaries. In the age of the video camera, there cannot be a public moment that goes unrecorded. But I'm thinking of a fiction film. What would the angle be? Like most people I know, the primary went on long past my ability to care about it on a daily basis. It must have been a species of torture for the anchors at CNN, who seemed caught in a *Groundhog Day* loop, with the conclusion of each state election sliding relentlessly into the start of the next, while "panels" of talking heads were badgered to extract meaning when there was only pattern. If CNN had "the best political team on television," would it age and wither before the general election?

But where is the story? Hearing for the first time notes of exhaustion and discouragement in Clinton's voice, I wondered what it had been like for her, month after month, state after state, pumping out the same policies, the same optimism, while she was running on empty. Hotel after hotel, early morning show after late-night show, schools, union meetings, church events, potluck dinners, being introduced by the local clone of the Chairman of Today's Event. For Obama, it was the same, with the difference that for most of the time he seemed to be winning, which must have been a consolation.

The problem with a screenplay based on these events is that there would be a merciless sameness. Where is the drama in the story of a game of forty-eight innings? Each mini-climax, from "Hillary's tears" to the Reverend Wright's display at the National Press Club, was hopefully examined to see if it might "change the direction of the campaign," and it never did; it only prolonged the suffering of that day's CNN "panel." When Wolf Blitzer got out of bed in the morning, were his hand and arm already extended, so that the clipboard had only to be inserted by an aide?

The ideal primary movie was Warren Beatty's *Bulworth* (1998). There were other good films, too, like Mike Nichols's *Primary Colors* (1998), based on a roman à clef about Hillary and Bill. Barry Levinson's *Wag the Dog* (1987) involved Clintonesque moments, had a screenplay by David Mamet, gave a phrase to the language, and was the best of the lot. But *Bulworth* was the ideal, because it had a cutoff point made of drama, not election days. Beatty plays a candidate sick to death of uttering the same clichés. He takes out a contract on his own life, ensuring that he will be assassinated in three days. That gives him the freedom to say exactly what's on his mind—what he, and any sensible person, might be thinking while pretending to believe their own platitudes.

That gave you suspense, comedy, some poignant private moments, and even a possible romance (with the newcomer Halle Berry). It was about transgression, not repetition. But the primary campaign that's now concluding has been a *Groundhog Day* loop, with no cutoff except for a victory, at which point the contest itself becomes yesterday's news.

The commentators Tuesday night spoke of Hillary's tired voice and Bill's dejected body language as if describing the malfunctions of robots. To me, it was humanizing material, like the time Hillary shed those tears. And a few days earlier Bill came close to the truth-telling of *Bulworth* when he told an audience, "I haven't come to ask you to vote for my wife, I've come to ask you to pray for her."

Considering those moments of insight, I thought of another movie that might provide a model for a possible film: *The Queen* (2006). What fascinated me about that film was its uncanny credibility. I could imagine Queen Elizabeth and Prince Philip (and John and Norma Major) sharing their private time much like the characters in the film, with honesty and realism, with exasperation and impatience, carefully modulated to preserve the stability of a long marriage. Even the verbal shorthand was right. These people have been over this ground so many times, they share the same reference points.

Hillary and Bill are both intelligent, experienced political creatures. They've both been running for something since grade school. They are fueled by the desire for high office and public recognition, but fueled also by the process itself. They're good at it. Considering their apparent depression on Tuesday night I realized that, yes, as late as that, they really did still think Hillary could win, even after the CNN "panels" were running out of ways to say farewell. They believed it right up to the end, because they had to, they needed to, in order to keep on running at all.

Yet there must have been private moments of despair. The two realists, as able as anyone to read the trends, must have spoken privately about their shrinking options. And on Tuesday night, as Hillary's double-digit lead in Indiana dwindled to very small single digits, there must have come a time when one of them said, "We've lost this thing."

What were those moments like? What kept them going between themselves? Did they encourage each other, or was there an unspoken pact not to voice the unspeakable? Was there blame when Bill had one of his unwise moments? Did their shared past, of success and scandal, enter into it, or were they absorbed in this moment?

In answering those questions, there you would find the movie. It would be more introspective than audiences would probably prefer, and less sensational. Smarter, too. There would be a limited budget, because you wouldn't need a stadium filled with thousands of people so much as you'd need lots of lonely hotel rooms after midnight. The climaxes would come as one old comrade after another abandoned them for the Obama camp. There would be a desperate, clinging love that had survived all the years, because it was based on shared experience and memories and goals, not so much any longer on passion.

It would be a sad story but a true one, and it might contain more truth than political movies are conventionally allowed to have. It might, like *Bulworth,* say forbidden things. And issues would not be at issue: The campaign was not about political positions, but about sheer desire. Hillary wanted to win, and she ran and ran and ran until there was a kind of heroism to it. Futile heroism after a point, but that's where the story lies.

It's Not What You Do, It's the Way That You Do It

May 8, 2008—My previous blog item, "Hillary and Bill: The Movie," has inspired a lot of comments, and some of them utterly baffle me. They take it for granted that I am pro-Hillary, if not necessarily anti-Obama. I've read the item again and believe it is neutral, as it was intended to be. I'm a political creature, but I intend to keep partisan politics out of this journal, which will, and should, deal only with the movies in various ways. I think those comments do, however, reveal something about how we watch movies.

In the piece, I set out to discuss what sort of a movie might be inspired by the endless 2007–08 primary season. I came up with a backstage drama about the private lives of the Clintons, who, like the Obamas, have found themselves in a Möbius strip of campaigning. It is not natural to be running for office for month after month: to have every public statement and gesture, every shrug of body language, every Freudian slip, pounced on by the attack dogs. If I were forced to live such a life, it would lead me to some species of madness.

I suggested a backstage film that had empathy for the Clintons. It wouldn't involve whether you agreed with them or not, but would center on how these two people, in private, deal with each other and the campaign hell they live in. I imagined weary scenes set late at night in anonymous hotel rooms. The ways they dealt with one piece of bad news after another. The reasons and ways they had to persist in the face of discouragement. I mentioned Stephen Frears's film *The Queen* (2006) as a possible model.

Why the Clintons and not the Obamas? Quite simply, because their story is more interesting. It has a longer history and apparently a bleaker outcome. They seem to be losing the primary season and have seemed so for several months, and they have both been running for something, win or lose, for most of their adult lives. To face this defeat, at the end of the most punishing primary campaign in American history, must be an ultimate test of their relationship and what makes them persist in the face of discouragement. I wrote: "Hillary wanted to win, and she ran and ran and ran until there was a kind of heroism to it. Futile heroism after a point, but that's where the story lies."

Some careless readers thought I was referring to Hillary as heroic. Others argued that she could not be, for one political reason after another. Still more somehow extracted from the essay a defense of Hillary or an endorsement. But the fact is I envisioned a movie *about* the Clintons, not for or against them.

My mail from readers has often assumed that by writing about something, I am endorsing it. Every new documentary about Iraq, for example, inspires a flood of e-mail to the Answer Man. My political views on Bush and Iraq are well known, and I sometimes express them in reviews, but such a documentary's greatest interest is not in what it thinks about the war but what it brings to the table.

Consider Errol Morris's recent doc *Standard Operating Procedure.* Its content centers on the infamous photographs of torture at Abu Ghraib. It interviews many of the American soldiers involved in taking them. That's it. In plain daylight, the film is about why we take photos, how we look at them, why those particular photographs were taken, how they looked to the soldiers at the time, and how they look now. Its political feelings about the war are never stated. Of course, it's implied that the soldiers intensely regret the photos and the military culture that gave birth to their jobs as prison guards, but there is no suggestion they did not support the war in general or that they were not proud to be serving in uniform.

Yet many of my correspondents needed only to see the subject of the review to denounce the movie, and me, as left-wing, antiwar, biased, and so on. I tried in the review to say the movie was about viewing and thinking about the photos, and wondering what the soldiers and the prisoners were thinking and feeling, and asking why they had been posed in the way we were. One of the Marines in the film states, wisely and clearly, that a photo doesn't tell you what happened before or after it was taken. I think Morris makes it clear that the events depicted, with the human pyramids and dog collars and so on, would never have taken place if a camera had not been present. So the film is *about* the photographs, and not about the war, Bush, or anything else.

It's the same, really, about movies about anything. It should be possible to admire a film with subject matter you deplore or positions you despise. The critic can make that clear in a review, but he should acknowledge the qualities of the film. The acid test is Leni Riefenstahl's *Triumph of the Will.* It belongs in my Great Movies Collection, but I've put off reviewing it for years.

The Ultimate Mystery

May 16, 2008—After the release of his *Standard Operating Procedure,* the director Errol Morris writes me: "This movie seems to have incited controversy, almost as if I broke some sort of rule or series of rules. The ultimate mystery is people. They are often mysteries not only to others but to themselves. Almost everyone wants to dismiss the bad apples rather than look at them, as if there is nothing inherently interesting in their stories. Oh well."

The words "to themselves" hold the key.

None of the opinions in the film are owned by Morris. They belong to the people on the screen, who actually appear in the infamous photographs from Abu Ghraib. There are a few very brief offscreen questions by Morris ("That was on your birthday?"), but they're not penetrating, do not suggest opinions, are the sorts of things any attentive listener would say. Most of the reviews of the film get this right. Sampling the reviews linked by IMDb.com, I found little to disagree with. I assume the "controversy" Morris refers to involves message boards, questions at film festivals, people walking up to him in the street, editorial-page bleats, talk radio, those sorts of things.

But listen to the words on the screen. The people in the photographs are as puzzled as we are. They did things they might not have done under other circumstances, and yet were blindsided by this particular set of circumstances. The wisest statement in the film (however obvious) is by the prison guard Javel Davis, who says, "Pictures only show you a fraction of a second. You don't see forward and you don't see backward." You don't see outside the frame. You don't see why these Americans enlisted in the military or the National Guard, you don't see their training, you don't see their experiences, you don't see how Iraq changed them. They seem to wonder about these things themselves. We look at old photos of ourselves and wonder why we ever wore that shirt or combed our hair that way. When did I stop using Brylcreem? Why was I that person? Still more, does Lynndie England wonder how, at twenty, she found herself in photographs from Abu Ghraib, pointing to a man forced (not by herself) to masturbate.

I'm not sure I agree with Morris that the Americans in the photos are even "bad apples." The one who does deserve that description seems to be Charles Graner (not allowed to be interviewed for the movie), who England believes deceived and manipulated her, and held the camera for a lot of the photos and instructed the others in their poses. The others may not have been bad apples but good ones left to spoil too long in the sun of the war in Iraq.

Morris is correct; there is no rule that says he may not simply listen to them speaking. His chief occupation has always been to listen. Perhaps that's why Robert McNamara chose to be interviewed by him; you might think McNamara would go instead for someone like Ken Burns. In his Oscar-winning *The Fog of War: Eleven Lessons from the Life of Robert S. McNamara* (2004), Morris freely used montages and newsreel footage and all sorts of visual material to illustrate McNamara's words, but McNamara didn't squawk, and I think the visuals were fair enough. In *SOP*, on the other hand, although Morris does use some reenactments, all his visuals are based on what might have been seen in that place, at that time.

There is a tradition for films, especially documentaries, that propose merely to look and listen. That *seems* to be the case with Robert Flaherty's *Nanook of the North.* On the other hand, no one would think of Leni Riefenstahl's *Triumph of the Will* as merely looking and listening. We now know, however, that *Nanook* was largely scripted, the locations were constructed, and the film represented a distillation of Flaherty's ideas about the Inuit people. No less was *Triumph* a distillation of Riefenstahl's ideas about the Third Reich, staged and filmed with the resources of the Reich at her disposal. The idea of a purely objective documentary is largely a fantasy, but *SOP* is objective in that it shows these people questioning their own lives and behavior, and it offers no answers.

"The ultimate mystery is people," Morris writes. Yes. That helps explain a kind of film I instinctively admire: one that examines human behavior in minute detail and infinite curiosity, and offers no conventional story structure to "explain" it. Consider *The Son* (*L'Enfant,* 2005), the Cannes winner by the Dardenne brothers. Why is this carpenter instantly so fascinated by the apprentice who has been brought into his shop? Why does he leap onto a cabinet to get a better look at him? Why does he care? The young man has certainly never seen him before. It is their shared mystery that fascinates me, not anything else. And the mystery of Abu Ghraib. And the mysteries that fascinate McNamara, such as that some of the bombing raids against Japan that he participated in might have been considered war crimes if the Japanese had won. Why do we do the things that we do? Must we? Do we have a choice? There is no answer, but the question itself asserts our nature as human beings.

How Studs Helps Me Lead My Life

May 24, 2008—I got caught in the Indiana Jones whirlwind and allowed an important anniversary to pass unremarked: On May 16, 2008, Studs Terkel celebrated his ninety-sixth birthday. One of the great American lives continues to unfold. If I know Studs, the great day passed with calls and visits from friends, and the ceremonious imbibing of one (1) gin martini, very dry. I hope he has eliminated the daily cigar, but I'm not taking odds.

If you don't know Studs, there are few people you can meet more easily in print. He is the greatest conversationalist I've met, the author of a shelf-full of books in which he engages people from all walks of life in thoughtful conversations about their own lives. This life-work began with the best-seller *Division Street: America* (1967), in which he talked to politicians and protestors, firemen and cops, actors and salesmen, saints and thieves.

These talks were engendered by the daily radio program Studs did for decades on WFMT, Chicago's fine arts station, on which morning after morning he would demonstrate that he had actually read an author's book, or seen the play, or attended the performance, or visited the place. Studs has an insatiable appetite for people and the things they do, and may have read as many books as anyone alive. Over the years his attention to the world he lives in has made him a one-man cross-reference. I remember appearing on his program once and mentioning Buster Keaton. Studs paused the tape recorder, rummaged around on a shelf, and produced a tape of Keaton himself, talking about the very same topic.

I met Studs very soon after I moved to Chicago. It was in the Old Town apartment of Herman and Marilu Kogan; Herman was the author and *Chicago Daily News* editor responsible for getting me hired at the *Sun-Times.* The evening was all conversation, nonstop, and all consequential: No small talk or idle chat for these people. I felt as if I'd been put at the same table with the grown-ups.

Not long after, the (now) Nobel Prize–winning novelist Doris Lessing visited Chicago. Studs knew I had read all her books while studying at the University of Cape Town, and, more important, he also knew that I had a car and knew how to drive. Studs has never learned how to drive; he enlisted me as chauffeur and I spent two unforgettable days observing Studs showing Lessing his own Chicago.

I have written about that day and other things Studsian in other articles. My purpose today is not to repeat the same stories, but to tell you how the example of Studs Terkel is helping me live my own life. As you know, I've had a lot of health difficulties over the past few years. After surgery for jaw cancer, I'm told I am cancer-free. But I had operations to repair the cancer's damage, and these surgeries resulted in life-threatening situations. In recovery, I had treatment at the Rehabilitation Institute of Chicago, was restored to health and fitness, was up and about, was even hiking in the foothills at Rancho la Puerta in Mexico. The surgeries failed to restore my ability to speak, but I was healthy and cheerful. I went back to reviewing movies on a full-time schedule.

After the latest restorative surgery in January, I was again very ill, again landed back in the RIC, was restored a third time, and again returned to work. To get into good shape for the Ebertfest in April, my wife and I went to the Pritikin Longevity Institute in Florida, where I've gone for fifteen years or more to benefit from their wise programs. On our second day there, I tripped on a rug, fell, and broke my hip. A stupid accident that could have happened to anyone and was not related to illness. Just one of those things.

I found myself in the rehab institute a *fourth* time. Surely this was enough? Learning to walk after a broken hip is painful, but it must be done and I have done it. I've also returned to my full-time duties at the *Sun-Times* and am pouring myself into the Web site. This new blog is part of that effort.

What influence has Studs had on my life during these years? He has simply continued to live—to talk, read, keep up with the news, see movies, attend events, use e-mail, listen, visit—and write. It is melancholy fact that in the last three years Studs has visited me in the hospital more times than I have visited him. But let me tell you about visiting Studs three days after he had open-heart surgery a few years ago. I expected to find a sick man. I found Studs sitting up in bed, surrounded by books and papers, receiving friends. The author Garry Wills appeared at his door. Studs had just finished reading his new book. He was filled with questions.

In recent years Studs has had open-heart surgery and broken his own bones ("I was walking downstairs carrying a drink in one hand and a book in the other. Don't try that after ninety"). But he has never, ever, not in the slightest degree, retired. He published *Touch and Go: A Memoir* in November 2007, but a memoir could never close the book on this life. In fact, it was his second memoir, after *Talking to Myself.* (1977).

The lesson Studs has taught me is that your life is over when you stop living it. If you can truly "retire," you had a job, but not an occupation. Observing people like Studs and the author Paul Theroux, and the great sports writer William Nack, and directors like Robert Altman and Sidney Lumet, I have seen those whose lifelong occupations absorb them and who are not merely maintaining, but growing. How astonishing it was to learn that Altman made great films after having a heart *transplant*! Nack, having "retired" from *Sports Illustrated,* has coproduced the film *Ruffian* for cable TV, based on his book about the great filly. He is an on-air talent for ESPN and is now one of the producers of a film based on his book *Secretariat: the Making of a Champion.* For the first time in his life, he has an agent. His book *My Turf* has a story in it that has made grown people cry. I know.

Theroux continues among the great writers of fiction and remains a voracious reader. He lives with his wife, Sheila Donnelly, a travel agent, on Oahu. It makes perfect sense for him to be married to a travel agent, since Theroux arguably has seen more of this planet's surface at ground level than anyone else in history, and written about his adventures in famous books about travel. His wanderings continue. We met at the Hawaii Film Festival, began talking, and have kept talking ever since—about books, mostly. It is such a relief to find someone who has read widely among authors you can't discuss with anybody else. We plowed through

George Gissing and on to Mrs. Gaskell. Theroux continues to be *curious.* Not long ago he wrote a long and much-discussed essay for the *Times* (of London) Literary Supplement, seriously comparing the work of Albert Camus and Georges Simenon. He thinks Simenon, the Belgian author of about four hundred novels, mostly about policemen, criminals, and crime itself, deserves comparison with Camus. I agree. But that's another blog entry.

Like Studs himself, I'm free-associating myself away from where I was pointed and toward where my curiosity leads me. That's how he works, too. The point is Studs. Among his books is one about this very subject: *Working: People Talk About What They Do All Day and How They Feel About What They Do.* It became a Broadway musical. And there are *The Good War: An Oral History of World War II* and *Hard Times: An Oral History of the Great Depression.* These books set down eyewitness, first-person accounts of eras in recent history that are already fading in the rearview mirror.

One reason Studs gets people to talk so openly with him is that he's not an academic or a cross-examiner. He comes across as this guy sitting down with you to have a good, long talk. Pick up one of his books, and now you're sitting next to the guy. You can't stop reading. Studs has an interviewing technique I admire: He combines astonishment with curiosity. He can't believe his ears. He repeats with enthusiasm what his subject just said, and the subject invariably continues and expands and wants to make his own story better. So many people have great stories, if only they could find an audience.

It's curious, how only two of Studs's books are technically about himself, but in a way they're all about himself. Reading a novel, we may identify with one of the characters. Reading Studs, we identify with him—with the questions. Through his example, we become inquiring minds. And his subjects range widely. Look at his book *Will the Circle Be Unbroken?: Reflections on Death, Rebirth, and Hunger for a Faith.* He provides not New Age malarkey, but real people having real thoughts about their real lives, and the inevitability of their own real deaths. Some people never articulate such thoughts to themselves, but they should, and in reading the book you are invited to turn inward and interview yourself.

Studs was married for sixty years to a beautiful woman named Ida, who stood by him in the good times (he starred in one of the first sitcoms in network history) and the bad (he lost that job because of the blacklist). He was envious that her FBI file was thicker than his own. When Ida grew older, she refused to use a cane, "because I fall so gracefully." Her death in 1999 inspired him to write *Will the Circle Be Unbroken?* In his introduction, he remembers her last words to him, as she was wheeled into the OR for heart surgery: "Louis, what have you gotten me into now?"

Studs has gotten a limitless number of people into things. I am one of them. He has taught me that if I break my other hip next week, I will simply learn to walk again and continue to do what engages me the most, which is to write about movies. Life might have taken me in many other directions, but this is the one given me, and if I stop following it, I will have lost my way.

True, after all that surgery, I still lack the power of speech. And after all those interviews, Studs is now, in his own words, "Deaf as a post." But I can still write about movies, and thanks to "a nifty little thing-a-ma-jig" device hooked to his hearing aids, Studs can still hear people and write about what they say. You hear about people retiring and then dying a month later, maybe because their life has lost its purpose for them. The lesson Studs teaches me every day is that to live is to live is to live.

Questions for the Movie Answer Man

Alvin and the Chipmunks

Q. In your review of *Alvin and the Chipmunks* you state that the film is "about as good as a movie with these characters can probably be." I don't understand what you mean by this. Aren't you the same person who also said a good movie can be made out of virtually any premise? Surely, a movie starring singing chipmunks could have been wittier, funnier, and more clever than this one.

—Andrew Shuster, Merrick, New York

A. Singing chipmunks, yes. Alvin, Theodore, and Simon, probably not. They need singing lessons.

Armageddon

Q. What do you think has prompted the Criterion Collection to release *Armageddon* on DVD? I've always admired Criterion for their selection of films, but why *Armageddon?*

—Anoop Raj, Philadelphia, Pennsylvania

A. Actually, *Armageddon* is a superb example of its type. I smiled.

Q. I have to agree with Anoop Raj, who wonders why Criterion is releasing *Armageddon.* The movie will be released in editions by other companies eventually. Why not issue movies that can't be found anywhere else? For instance, *Hobson's Choice* with Charles Laughton and *A New Leaf* with Elaine May and Walter Matthau are not yet available on DVD.

—Kathleen Church, Chicago, Illinois

A. Yes, but the Criterion approach allows for an in-depth examination of a genre and style of film that deserves discussion. I agree with your choices and want to know why in the world Bill Forsyth's masterpiece *Housekeeping* (1987) isn't on DVD.

The Assassination of Jesse James . . .

Q. After seeing the title of *The Assassination of Jesse James by the Coward Robert Ford,* I no longer had any desire to see this film, although I am sure it is worth watching. The title for this movie apparently gives away the outcome of its most climactic sequence. Following this logic, *The Sixth Sense* should have been titled *Bruce Willis Is a Ghost.* Why did the producers think it best to reveal the outcome of *Jesse James* in its title?

—Brian A. Peterson, Peoria, Illinois

A. Dunno. For a sequel they're planning *The Assassination of Abraham Lincoln by the Coward John Wilkes Booth.* Who would ever attend a movie about Jesse James or Abraham Lincoln except to find out who killed them?

Atonement

Q. I am a devoted fan of Ian McEwan's novel *Atonement,* one of those books that raises your heartbeat and ignites conflicting emotions and thoughts like fireworks exploding in the sky. So many nights I returned to that book to amuse myself for several hours by just repeating the poetry of McEwan's prose, its words melting over my tongue like butter.

I walked out of the film *Atonement* several hours ago and I am in awe. And I know it's not a fluke—I'm not just exaggerating its greatness because I am still fresh with excitement. One way you can tell this film is surely on the level is that the tracking shot on the beach may be the greatest tracking shot of all time. I do enjoy tracking shots, now more than ever since I have come to realize how nearly impossible they are to film.

The tracking shot in *Atonement* captures so much, so subtly, from the background to the foreground, and touched upon every emotion that I possess—the shot alone could be another film all by itself and worth the price of admission. I was curious if you knew any of the behind-the-scenes facts about that. How long is that shot? Where did they film it? How long did it take them to film? On a budget this low? That whole image, Ferris wheel and all, may be my favorite to ever be captured on film.

—Jonathan D'Ambrosio, Fairfield, Connecticut

A. I wondered whether part of it was CGI. Amazingly, no. The whole thing is one unbroken five-minute take with a handheld camera. Director of photography Seamus McGarvey, who thinks it's the best shot he's ever done, describes how he did it at www.ascmag.com/magazine_dynamic/December2007/Atonement/page1.php.

Awake

Q. My wife and I saw *Awake* with some friends the other night. I knew nothing about the movie and wasn't thrilled when I heard it was a thriller with Jessica Alba. I figured it would be a typical superficial piece of garbage aimed at teenagers. I went anyway to be with my wife. I was very pleasantly surprised. I liked that the twists were delivered with subtlety, and I wasn't able to predict one of them. I also was impressed with the maturity and substance the film carried.

The pace and tone reminded me of David Mamet, especially in how nothing is what it seems. The film kept morphing from thriller to romance to comedy to drama and back to thriller. Usually this means a film has an identity crisis. In this case it's completely intentional and serves the purpose of threading us along on an unknown journey. Or what should be unknown.

As you pointed out, "the trailer and poster ads criminally reveal a crucial plot twist." Now I understand why I liked it and my wife didn't. She had seen the previews and knew what was coming. As a result, I enjoyed the movie more, because I didn't watch the idiotic trailer. Here's my question: Does the director have any say in how his film is presented in the ads and trailers? Is he at fault or is it out of his control? I mean, why would a director make a film that depends on secrets and then let the secrets be revealed in the advertising? Hitchcock would have a cow.

—Justin J. Francis, San Jose, California

A. I am certain that the director, Joby Harold, had a cow or maybe a small herd. The Weinstein Company shot itself in the foot. Too bad it missed.

Away from Her

Q. I saw Sarah Polley's *Away from Her* last night and while it is one of the most beautiful films I have ever seen, I am troubled by one thing. Why is all the credit and Oscar buzz for Julie Christie when the film focuses mainly on Gordon Pinset? Christie's character always seems at a distance and the story is mostly told through his eyes.

—Jerry Roberts, Birmingham, Alabama

A. Studios position their Oscar hopefuls and no doubt correctly believe the best actor category is overcrowded this year, while Christie has a shot at best actress. I agree with you about the excellence of Pinset's performance.

The Band's Visit

Q. In the race for Israel's official Oscar entry, it was a contest between Toronto festival favorite *The Band's Visit* and local box office smash (and Berlin silver bear winner) *Beaufort* (a superb war film). Then *The Band's Visit* swept Israel's Ophir Awards (the equivalent of the Oscars), which means it will be the Israeli submission to the Oscars. But many here in Israel are asking if *The Band's Visit* has enough foreign language in it to qualify as an Oscar nominee? Is there enough Hebrew and Arabic within the English dialogue, or will the film be disqualified?

—Yair Raveh, film critic, *Pnai Plus*, Tel Aviv, Israel

A. I asked Bruce Davis, executive director of the Academy, and he replies: The rule for the Foreign Language category is that more than half of the dialogue (literally 51 percent) must be in a language or combination of languages other than English. As you can imagine, this sometimes leads to some complex measurements, and nearly every year there is a submission whose eligibility is finally determined by Academy staff members sitting in our Goldwyn Theater with stopwatches.

Bathroom Breaks

Q. In regards to your answer regarding the Official Rule of Critic's Conduct on the matter of bathroom breaks: I am astounded at your admission that you leave a movie theater to use the washroom during a screening. I am a lawyer. I am not allowed to simply excuse myself during a court appearance.

Quite apart from my professional responsibility, I know that so many important moments in a trial are fleeting, for example during cross-examination. Properly examining a film,

I would argue, requires the same steadfast attention. And should you argue the feat is impossible, I note that I had previously held my own personal record of never leaving a theater to use the facilities. It lasted from Burton's *Batman* in 1989 to Nolan's *The Prestige* in 2006.

—Ryan Austin, Vancouver, British Columbia

A. What was it about *The Prestige* that made you have to pee? The Chinese Water Torture trick, perhaps?

For an expert opinion, I turned to my college pal Robert Auler, the Goliath-slaying legal giant of Urbana-Champaign, Illinois, and author of the forthcoming novel *Keep and Bear Arms.* He replies:

"In court, a judge is usually old enough to have a bigger prostate than the lawyers do. Also, being a public employee, he is never loath to find an opportunity to stop working if only for a few spurting moments. I've only been denied a pee break once, and that was in my final argument in a major murder case. The judge had heard whispers from more senior colleagues that this defendant was to get no breaks. Guess he interpreted that literally.

"The Canadian lawyer knows damn well that he's comparing sprinklers with fire hoses. Witnesses come and go (pun notice) and so do lawyers. An insider maxim is that a trial lawyer's first loyalty is to his bladder. There are emergency stratagems. Even faking a paroxysm of coughs, hiccups, or heart rhythms can get you a bathroom break. Not so for the Answer Man in these days of automated projection."

Bee Movie

Q. I would like to point out an error in the response to the question about Jerry Seinfeld being a "b-girl." The first part of the answer was spot on about the role of drones. However, in the second part of the answer you cited Frank B. Chavez III of Hayward, California, as claiming that honey is vomit and a waste product. Honey is not a waste product; it is food for the bees. If beekeepers took all their honey, the bees would die. The reason why there can be a honey harvest is because bees make more than they need. And honey is not exactly vomit—at least it is nothing like our vomit. The bees take up nectar into their crop, add enzymes and regurgitate it into wax cells, and evaporate some of the water to create honey.

—Katie Lee, St. Paul, Minnesota

A. That's nothing like our vomit, for sure. I have now allowed Honey-Nut Cheerios back into our kitchen.

Q. Regarding your first question in this week's Answer Man column: Worker bees are not female but neuter. Being "female" is a bit more than the absence of male characteristics.

—Brian Isaacs, Lovington, Illinois

A. The Answer Man is beginning to regret the day he ever let the bees into the column. Not only was *Bee Movie* wrong in everything it said about bees, but the Answer Man was wrong in all his corrections.

Q. I'm a fan; that's why I read your site. However, doesn't it seem odd that you're not exactly raving about *Bee Movie* and yet their ads are all over your site? I understand the importance of advertising space; however, in consideration of the similar industry, perhaps it's a conflict of interest? At a glance, someone may assume that you're promoting this film.

—Nicole Comer, Toluca Lake, California

A. Not if they read my review. Haven't you noticed that movie ads and movie reviews do not always agree? The ads are what make it possible for you to read the site.

Q. You're gonna love this: Sciencedaily.com has an article stating "Worker bees, wasps, and ants are often considered neuter. But in many species they are females with ovaries, who although unable to mate, can lay unfertilized eggs which turn into males if reared. For some species, such as bumblebees, this is the source of many of the males in the species. But in others, like the honeybee, "workers police each other—killing eggs laid by workers or confronting egg-laying workers." You have opened a Pandora's box. Although what just occurred to me is that this article, or even just that paragraph, could have been the genesis for a very interesting movie about bees.

Raymond Ogilvie, Philadelphia, Pennsylvania

A. What I have learned from this whole *Bee Movie* discussion is that bees have very confused and sad sex lives and are much in need of intelligent design.

Before the Devil Knows You're Dead

Q. I can find nowhere (IMDb, etc.) the name of the actor in *Before the Devil Knows You're Dead* who played the part of the old sleazy diamond merchant. He had the best line in the movie, supplying the moral of the story. He had brief scenes with Philip Seymour Hoffman and then Albert Finney.

—Paul McConnell, Albuquerque, New Mexico

A. Mark Urman, president of ThinkFilm, replies: "Leonardo Cimino is the old jeweler. I am my own IMDb!" I agree it is a notable performance, and Cimino is a fabulous character actor. He has played mostly mafioso types, plus the pope, and has been in everything from *Waterworld* to *Penn & Teller Get Killed.*

Beowulf

Q. To me, *Beowulf* was one of the most thrilling movies ever. I can't believe you thought people should have been laughing at it.

—Ronnie Barzell, Los Angeles, California

A. Not at it, with it. You can laugh and still be thrilled (see *Raiders of the Lost Ark*). I thought it was a send-up of itself and asked Roger Avary, the cowriter (who also cowrote *Pulp Fiction*), if he had "a glint in his eye" as he was working on it. He responds: "A glint for sure. I still can't believe we got away with it. I feel like I just pulled off a crazy stunt. You should know by now from my work that I'm always planting tongue firmly in cheek."

After I congratulated him on the film's opening-week gross: "Now I can unleash more weirdness onto the masses. My fiendish plan is nearly complete! All the pieces are in place. . . ."

Q. To fulfill your curiosity about the Geats, the hero's tribe in *Beowulf:* The name of this ancient Germanic tribe is derived from a root word meaning *to pour.* So the Geats are "the Pourers." Pour what, you may ask? There's some academic debate about it; two Wikipedia entries state that the omitted direct object was *men* or *semen* (a third opts for the somewhat tamer *pour, offer sacrifice*).

If true, the first explanation would make the name an ethnic boast—the Geats wanted neighboring tribes to get the idea they couldn't be killed off; they just kept coming. In a similarly warlike vein, the Saxons were literally "the Stone Knife People."

—Ken Cordes, Chicago, Illinois

A. One hesitates to ask what drew the Anglos and Saxons together.

Ingmar Bergman

Q. Even though I am a huge movie fan, I am embarrassed to say that I have yet to see an Ingmar Bergman film. I know *The Seventh Seal* is a must. Can you suggest any other titles I should watch in honor of him?

—Bin Lee, Torrance, California

A. If you admire *The Seventh Seal* you might also like *The Virgin Spring* and *Wild Strawberries.* For a heartbreaking combination of horror, death, fear, and love, there is *Cries and Whispers.* And in a *Sight & Sound* poll of the world's film directors and critics, *Fanny and Alexander* was voted the third best film of the last quarter of the twentieth century (after *Apocalypse Now* and *Raging Bull*).

Best Movies

Q. I read your "Top 10 of 2006" and something caught my eye. You placed *The Departed* (four) ahead of *Babel* (nine). I distinctly remember your Oscar predictions/wishes from earlier this year, and you said that you thought that *Babel* deserved to win best picture. Did you change your mind, or do you sometimes feel that even a better film sometimes doesn't deserve to win best picture? I ask this because I had similar feeling in 2005. Even though I thought that *Crash* was a better movie, I believed that *Brokeback Mountain* deserved the award. The film was much more daring in its presentation and execution.

—Mike Smith, University of Pittsburgh, Pennsylvania

A. Emerson instructs us that "foolish consistency is the hobgoblin of little minds." More to the point, isn't it silly to rank great films in numerical order? I do it only because it is traditional. Jonathan Rosenbaum is much more sensible when he ranks the best films of the twentieth century chronologically. One year I tried listing my "best films" alphabetically, but there was an uproar from readers accusing me of wimping out. I value *The Departed* and *Babel* equally, and that goes for *Man Push Cart,* the number-ten title on my list. I do feel, however, that *Pan's Labyrinth* was the best film of 2006.

Q. Is it actually possible that *Desperately Seeking Susan* was named as 1985's best film of the year by the *New York Times*? That's what Wikipedia says in its entry on the film. Or is this just another case of Wikipedia demonstrating the power of consensus-driven reality?

—Andy Ihnatko, Boston, Massachusetts

A. The *New York Times,* as itself, does not name any film the best of the year. Its critics do. Janet Maslin, who was a *Times* film critic at the time, writes me: "I don't know how it works now, with all three critics making lists. But we used to have a single list from the chief critic, with ten films listed in alphabetical order. Except for the year (this really happened) when Vincent Canby got mixed up and listed only nine. We also had a brief, happy period of being able to make a Ten Worst list. Then it was decided that that was too mean-spirited and un-*Times*ian. I was sorry to see that go."

Canby did include *Susan* on his list of the year's ten best. In alphabetical order: *Desperately Seeking Susan, Kiss of the Spider Woman, Prizzi's Honor, Purple Rose of Cairo, Ran, Secret Honor, 7 Up/28 Up, Shoah,* and *The Trip to Bountiful.* That's only nine, and a later correction says it should also have included *Young Sherlock Holmes.*

Beyond the Valley of the Dolls

Q. Last night I happened to see, for the first time, *Beyond the Valley of the Dolls* on the Fox Movie Channel. You wrote it for Russ Meyer. Watching the film, it seemed obvious that the character "Z Man" was based on Phil Spector. (His name is Ronnie, for God's sake.) He dresses like a girl and shoots an actress in the mouth. What are you guys? A couple of prophets, or something? I ask because of the surprising turn of events regarding Spector, particularly as it relates to the movie.

—G. Brooks Arnold, Los Angeles, California

A. Yes, the character was inspired by Phil Spector, but neither Russ nor I had even met him or knew much about him. In the movie, he's called "the teenage tycoon of rock," which comes from Tom Wolfe's description of him as the "tycoon of teen." Russ and I did not, in fact, know that his wife was named "Ronnie" when we named him Ronnie. I came up with the name "Z-Man" because after Mike Royko bought a Datsun 280-Z some of the guys in O'Rourke's Pub started calling him "Z-Man." For balance, his last name required another *Z* and so I borrowed the last name of Ann Barzel, the legendary dance critic of *Chicago Today.* I cannot explain how the movie seemed to foretell later events. Maybe art influenced life. Did Spector ever see it? I don't know. Would I want to see a rock-horror-exploitation-musical with a character based on me? Yes.

Blade Runner

Q. I am delighted to see you finally list *Blade Runner (The Final Cut)* in the Great Movies collection, as this is my favorite film. But you've made the same mistake that you made in your previous reviews, which is regarding how many replicants Deckard needed to hunt down. Deckard's police superior, Bryant, informs him that, indeed, six did escape; however, as was noted in the final cut (and interestingly, the work print) "two were fried running through an electric field," which nullifies any chance of Deckard being part of the renegade group of Nexus-6s.

However, a few things should be noted. Originally, Deckard was to hunt down five replicants, with only one, named Hodge, getting nailed in the field (as reflected in the original theatrical/international and director releases). The fifth replicant was actually a character named Mary and was to be portrayed by Stacy Nelkin, but her scenes were cut before filming began. This was far enough into production that Bryant made the dialogue mistake. Of course, it is a very valid theory that Deckard is, in fact, a replicant, perhaps even a Nexux-7 (that's not a typo), just not part of Roy's group.

—N. R. Klein, Pomona, New Jersey

A. I am slowly beginning to realize I am a replicant, programmed to spread disinformation to put any loose ones in greater danger.

Blood-Sucking Monkeys of Forest Lawn

Q. I've been enjoying a few of your books lately and I ran across a most unforgettable title in the review for *Assault of the Killer Bimbos*. The title, of course, is *Blood-Sucking Monkeys of Forest Lawn*. I couldn't seem to find any info on *Blood-Sucking Monkeys* at IMDb or Amazon.com, or even eBay. Could you by any chance shed some light on it?

—Jay Wolfe, Oklahoma City, Oklahoma

A. Best as I can recall that title originated with the geniuses at Troma Films, and Lloyd Kaufman may have listed it in an ad in a trade journal at Cannes, but it never got made. It's more commercial, don't you agree, than a title he actually did use: *Rabid Grannies*. Still unused, from a Cannes ad by practical jokesters: *Dig Me a Tunnel to Hitler!*

Q. On the subject of *Blood-Sucking Monkeys of Forest Lawn*, I feel obliged to acknowledge the equally nonexistent *Blood-Sucking Monkeys from West Mifflin, Pennsylvania*, as touted by Count Floyd (Joe Flaherty) on *SCTV*. It promised to be somewhat more scary than the horror disappointments he usually offered, among them *Dr. Tongue's Evil House of Pancakes*.

—Earl Hofert, Chicago, Illinois

A. Don't get me started. Consider the film Lloyd Kaufman is currently shooting, *Poultrygeist: Night of the Chicken Dead*. Or such other titles as *A Nymphoid Barbarian in Dinosaur Hell* and *Pterodactyl Woman from Beverly Hills*.

See the list at www.troma.com/movies.

Josh Brolin

Q. Am I the only one that's noticed Josh Brolin shot a dog in both *American Gangster* and *No Country for Old Men* this year?

—Laurence Yap, Toronto, Ontario

A. Yes. Except Josh Brolin.

The Bourne Ultimatum

Q. Is the movie critic for the *Washington Post* embarrassed that he was the only critic of the "cream of the crop" on Rotten Tomatoes who gave *The Bourne Ultimatum* a negative rating? He's got to be questioning himself.

—Carey Ford, Corsicana, Texas

A. I think it's a badge of honor for Stephen Hunter. When only one review disagrees, read it. I did and understand his point, even if I disagree.

I asked Hunter himself, who replied: "I'm far too shallow to have doubts."

Q. You gave *Bourne Ultimatum* three and a half stars. How much did the studio pay you for that? Not enough to compensate for your lost credibility. I'll never read you again.

—Milt Heft, Colorado Springs, Colorado

A. See above letter. There is now only one major critic in the country you can read.

Casablanca

Q. In your Great Movie review of *Casablanca* you refer to Claude Rains's character as subtly homosexual. I thought that his character was portrayed as a complete, though effete, womanizer.

—William Dienna, Wayne, Pennsylvania

A. He goes trough the motions with young women. He feels nothing for Ingrid Bergman. He'd say yes in a flash to Humphrey Bogart.

Casino Royale

Q. I was glad to read your take on *Casino Royale*. But I have a question. The villain was a terrorism financier (who bled out of his eyes, but that's irrelevant). At the end, Bond begins to go after the terrorist organization. Are they setting this up for SPECTRE?

—Ari Lewis, Charlotte, North Carolina

A. A tantalizing possibility. Health tip: If you start to bleed out of your eyes, it's not irrelevant.

John Cassavetes

Q. I recently saw John Cassavetes's *The Killing of a Chinese Bookie* and was amazed at how good it was. Afterward I thought how much more Cassavetes might have been appreciated by the general public if the production value on his films had been higher. Why was he unable to get more money for his films? Was it simply a matter of choosing artistic freedom? As an actor he must have had good connections within Hollywood.

—Tony Diaz, Austin, Texas

A. The improvised look of his films is the heart and soul of the spontaneous effect and allowed him to make exactly the films he wanted to. It's doubtful the general public would have embraced him even if he'd shot in 3-D IMAX.

Children of Heaven

Q. After watching *Children of Heaven,* I read your review, which supported my opinion of how the film so perfectly captured the innocent nature of the brother and sister. Why does it seem that foreign cinema seems to know more about children than most, if not all, of the films made by American filmmakers? I point out Bruno in *The Bicycle Thief,* the main character of *Pan's Labyrinth,* the sister in *Grave of Fireflies,* and the boys in Del Toro's other masterpiece, *The Devil's Backbone.* These characters seem to be so realistic in capturing the mentality of youth. Why?

I would make the argument that it is our culture of video games and violence—but I was brought up in that culture and I identified with these characters so well. I was just like them. So why does American cinema habitually use child characters, as you so flawlessly put it, "as little stand-up comedians"?

—Jonathan D'Ambrosio, Fairfield, Connecticut

A. Not all American films do. See the recent *Rails and Ties, Bee Season, Akeelah and the Bee,* and even *The Kite Runner,* which is after all, an American film. But most do. It may be because we have so much difficulty in making films about children that are not aimed at children. And most teenagers are represented as demographic group profiles, which makes a film like *Juno* so special. For precisely seen child characters, have a look at *Forbidden Games* in my Great Movies collection. Or consider the British film *Atonement.*

Chimes at Midnight

Q. Are there any plans to restore Orson Welles's *Chimes at Midnight* (aka *Falstaff*) and give the film a proper DVD release in America, or should I just break down and buy one of the overpriced imports?

—Scott Brady, Chicago, Illinois

A. Jonathan Rosenbaum, film critic of the *Chicago Reader* and expert on Welles, tells me: "Michael Dawson, the guy who rejigged the lip-sync on Welles's *Othello,* has been planning for years to do the same thing with *Chimes at Midnight*—only this time, I'm happy to say, without changing the music and sound effects and without turning the sound track into stereo. (My only beef with his ground plan is that he wants to add the sound of neighing horses to one shot! Go figure.) The problem is, until or unless the labyrinthine rights issues get cleared up with the widow of Harry Saltzman, one of the producers, you can't even buy DVDs now from Europe, either, judging from my latest Google search. (When the Locarno film festival had a huge Welles retrospective and conference two years ago, they had to get special permission from her just to show the film once.)"

Ebert again: For my Great Movies piece on the film, I was able to find a decent DVD from Brazil. Probably no longer available.

Control

Q. Regarding the Joy Division biopic *Control*: (1) Is it true that singer Ian Curtis hanged himself either while or after watching Werner Herzog's *Stroszek* on TV? (2) Wasn't one of the ironies behind the name *Joy Division* (besides the joylessness of the music itself) that it's a euphemism used by the Nazis for the brothels in concentration camps?

—Alan Partridge, Manchester, Pennsylvania

A. Yes, to both. You can see Bruno S., the star of *Stroszek,* on the screen in Curtis's house just before he kills himself. But why that film? It doesn't seem terminally depressing to me.

Corpus Christi

Q. Regarding an item in your Answer Man column, there is not a movie but there *is* a play called *Corpus Christi,* about a Christ figure who is gay. It is by Terrence McNally. It has been widely condemned by the sorts of people who typically condemn such things. While it is not McNally's best work, it is certainly relevant artistically. I had the pleasure or displeasure of discussing this play on *The O'Reilly Factor* when it was being presented locally. You can imagine the tone of that.

—Steve Penhollow, arts and entertainment reporter, *Fort Wayne Journal-Gazette*

A. Since it is believed that Jesus never had a sexual experience, isn't it sort of academic (or theological?) that he abstained from both sexes and not just one?

The Darjeeling Limited

Q. I read your review of *The Darjeeling Limited* with interest, and I was hoping that you would point to the fact that a lot of the music of the movie is derived from the music of movies by Satyajit Ray, many pieces composed by the master himself. Is there any other precedent for this: a great director who was a terrifically accomplished music director as well and his music being used as the background for a Hollywood release?

—Santanu Chakrabarti, New Brunswick, New Jersey

A. It's very rare. With the release of the Apu Trilogy on DVD, the master's work is coming into the hands of a new generation, but why have many masterpieces, such as *The Music Room* and *The Big City,* still not been released on DVD?

Dead Teenager Movies

Q. I disagree with your contention that, after having seen all one hundred movies on the American Film Institute's "greatest" list, one would no longer have the desire to see a Dead Teenager Movie. Such a statement does a disservice to the ranks of dedicated horror fans and critics who could intelligently construct arguments for why many of these movies are quite worthwhile.

There is a baseness to them, certainly, but horror's essential function is base—to create a sinister echo in the darkest wells of our psyche. Dead Teenager Films add a layer of exploitation that makes the experience easier to digest, but the chord they strike is necessary. There is room for both the cinematic elite and movie sleaze in the moviegoing experience. To quote the great horror icon Vincent Price, "A man who limits his interests, limits his life."

—Nate Yapp, editor,
Classic-Horror.com, Phoenix, Arizona

A. And to paraphrase Pauline Kael, the movies are so rarely great art that if we cannot appreciate great trash, there is no reason to go. I'd draw a distinction, however, between the classic horror genre, which has produced masterpieces from *Nosferatu* to *Silence of the Lambs,* and the Dead Teenager Movie, which I define as a movie that starts out with a lot of teenagers and kills them all except one, to populate the sequel. On the other hand, DTMs have their defenders; Alex Jackson of Logan, Utah, writes: "There are a handful that I definitely prefer to Hitchcock's cowardly *Vertigo: Friday the 13th,* parts 2, 4, 5, and 8; *A Nightmare on Elm Street* 4 and maybe 5, plus *New Nightmare; Sleepaway Camp; Dr. Giggles;* and *Halloween* (you yourself gave this four stars!).

Ebert again: *Vertigo* is cowardly? I think it is relentlessly brave. I agree that *Halloween* is great but disagree that it is a DTM.

Q. It would be useful to explain what makes a movie like *Halloween* or *Last House on the Left* a step above the DTM. The former is sort of the *Citizen Kane* of DTMs, yet I agree with you entirely that it shouldn't be classified as one. It seems some form of this debate arises every year when you give a negative review to a movie like *Chaos* or *Friday the 13th Part LXII.*

—Jared Glazer, Los Angeles, California

A. There can, of course, be a good Dead Teenager Movie, just as a DTM can escape the genre altogether (*Last House on the Left* recycles the plot of Ingmar Bergman's *The Virgin Spring,* which I don't think anyone has considered a DTM). The horror genre provides a port of entry for many aspiring filmmakers, because the genre is the star and the actors need not be expensive. When I find a film like *Halloween,* I know I am looking at great filmmaking. How do I know? I just know. Great movies teach themselves to you. As Louis Armstrong said in trying to explain jazz, "There are some folks that, if they don't know, you can't tell them."

Deep Voices

Q. Where are all the Hollywood he-men with deep-chested voices such as Peck, Gable, Heston, and Wayne? They were replaced by the baritone smoothies such as Newman and Redford and now we have the soprano-voiced teeny-boppers such as DiCaprio and Pitt, who are laughable as heroes. Your opinion?

—Del Lashbrook, Durham, Oregon

A. Not laughable, and gifted actors. But just on the basis of the actors in three movies I saw on one day last week, I would suggest that deep voices endure, as represented by Morgan Freeman, George Clooney, Tom Wilkinson, Sydney Pollack, Russell Crowe, Christian Bale, Peter Fonda, and Fred Ward.

Digital Decay

Q. *Variety* has a shocking article saying the digital copies of great films like *Taxi Driver* are starting to decay. I thought digital files were forever.

—Greg Nelson, Chicago, Illinois

A. Digital information is timeless, but the storage media may not be. Jeff Joseph, the movie sound guru from Los Angeles, writes me: "Although digital files are 'forever,' the ability to read and interpret them through hardware and software in the future is unknown. Video and computer systems change constantly. So not only do the digital files have to be saved, but so do older computers and software. It can be dicey. On the other hand, I can take a piece of film from one hundred years ago and with a flashlight and magnifying glass, be able to view it."

Documentaries

Q. Why does Michael Moore get so much flak for the editing in his films? All documentaries are edited by someone with an agenda. I've even seen people use quotations around the word *documentary* when describing his films, as if they are not really documentaries.

—Jolon Buchbinder, Cincinnati, Ohio

A. Those people do not know what a documentary is. Many times, it documents opinions and arguments, not "facts" (and yes, there I will use quotation marks). They complain not about what the documentarian did, but what he didn't do that they would have done.

Early Movie Audiences

Q. There are several reports about extreme reactions of early cinema audiences that I find hard to believe. It is said that viewers of the first movies were frightened by what they saw, such as moving images of an oncoming train. Bob Seidensticker writes in *FutureHype*: "[When] the first movies were shown publicly, one presented a scene at the seashore—no monsters, no invading army, just waves rolling in along a beach. The crowd was terrified. They ran from the makeshift movie theater to escape the onrushing water." While this makes a great story, I wonder if film historians can confirm it. It is cited so often that it feels like an urban myth, allowing us modern people to mock our oh-so-naive ancestors.

—Hanno Zulla, Hamburg, Germany

A. Your instincts are correct. I appealed for an authoritative answer from the esteemed film historians David Bordwell and Kristin Thompson of the University of Wisconsin. David replies:

"This is a favorite bête noire of Kristin's and mine. One of my students, Michael Newman, now out teaching on his own, wrote an excellent and thorough blog entry on this sort of myth here: zigzigger.blogspot.com/2007/02/film-history-fakelore.html. In brief, there seem to be no contemporary reports of this happening. People may have ooh'd and ahh'd at seeing moving photographic images projected on a large scale, but panicked? Almost certainly myth mongering."

Newman's blog also demolishes several other fondly held beliefs, some of them passed along as facts by such as me. For example, he questions whether: (1) *The Great Train Robbery* was the first film to tell a story; (2) D. W. Griffith invented or discovered "film language"; (3) *The Jazz Singer* was the first sound film; (4) *Citizen Kane* is the undisputed heavyweight champion of cinematic masterpieces; (5) John Cassavetes (or Sam Fuller, or Andy Warhol . . .) is the "father of independent cinema"; and (6) *Jaws* was the first summer blockbuster and its success killed the more authentic auteur cinema of everyone's beloved early 1970s.

Fan Edits

Q. What is your stand on fan edits? According to Wikipedia.com, a *fan edit* is "a version of a film modified by a viewer that removes, reorders, or adds material in order to create a new interpretation of the film." The largest provider of these fan edits is currently fanedit.org, a site that recently had some legal issues with LucasArts. Do you think it's right by any means for fans to "take justice into their own hands," so to speak?

—Miikka Mononen, Vantaa, Finland

A. The film will be copyrighted, so you have no legal right to do it. However, doing it at home on iMovie, let's say, could be a real learning experience. It's posting it online that's dubious. Some directors, like Kevin Smith, have an anything-goes attitude. Others go ballistic. Michael Moore, who has encouraged piracy of his films, would be enraged if one shot was touched.

Fassbinder

Q. Many years ago, I saw Rainer Werner Fassbinder's masterpiece *Berlin Alexanderplatz.* I would love to see it again. However, as far as I know, it is not available on DVD.

—Mary Margaret, Chicago, Illinois

A. Fassbinder's 941-minute 1980 epic was released by Criterion in November 2007. Based on a classic novel and originally shown on German television, it has been digitally restored shot-by-shot, and the seven-disc edition will add lots of bells and whistles. This is generally considered Fassbinder's best work, a towering achievement. Watch it like you did Kieslowski's *Decalogue,* one episode a day.

Fathers in Movies

Q. Paul Dooley was mentioned in the Answer Man as playing one interesting and funny parent in teenage movies for his part in *Breaking Away.* He also has a touching moment with Molly Ringwald in *Sixteen Candles* after he realizes he had forgotten his daughter's sixteenth birthday. But John Hughes has usually painted his parents as absent (*The Breakfast Club, Ferris Bueller's Day Off*) or needing to be cared for (*Pretty in Pink*). Even in *Home Alone* the parents actually forgot their own kid. What kind of issues does this guy have with his own parents?

—Ricky Duke, North Little Rock, Arkansas

A. Fathers are often missing from teenage movies, as are parents in general. They only complicate the plot; most films in the genre portray teenagers as, for one reason or another, living in a world with absent parents. When parents are around, teenagers are (theoretically) not the masters of their destiny, and teenagers don't spend good money for tickets to be reminded of that.

Fight Club

Q. It's great to see those old debates between you and Siskel and Roeper in the Balcony Archives. While I generally agree with your opinion, there have been films where I think you missed the point. I'd just like to state my (continued) disappointment on your misread of David Fincher's *Fight Club.* This is one of the best films of the 1990s and one of my favorite films of all time, and you completely missed the point.

—Jason Callen, Milwaukee, Wisconsin

A. You know what I did? I took *Fight Club* to the University of Colorado at Boulder for my annual shot-by-shot analysis at the Conference on World Affairs, and went through it over ten hours with about eight hundred students. And I am *still* convinced I was right.

Film Festivals

Q. My girlfriend and I have attended the Chicago International Film Festival for many years (I even once sat a couple rows from you during a special screening of *Gates of Heaven*). We would like to attend another international film festival. Do you have a recommendation?

—Joseph Azazello, Chicago, Illinois

A. Forget about Cannes, Berlin, and Venice: big deals, but expensive and you need credentials. Pick your dates and go online to www.filmfestivals.com. They list 1,400 fests. Near Chicago, the biggest and most user-friendly is Toronto. Montreal is making a comeback. I have had wonderful times at the Hawaii, Virginia, and Savannah festivals. Telluride is magical, but expensive and hard to get to. Here in Chicago we have many festivals, including the Latino, Animation, Reeling (Gay/Lesbian), Underground, Short Film, Future Filmmakers, Asian Animation, Asian-American, Horror, International Children's, Documentary, and Women in the Director's Chair festivals. There's hardly a week of the year without a festival going on here. And in Urbana-Champaign, you might enjoy the Insect Fear Film Festival, and also surf to www.ebertfest.com.

Film Noir

Q. When I recently saw some of the great Coen brothers films again (like *Blood Simple, Fargo, The Big Lebowski,* and *The Man Who Wasn't There*), I was fascinated by their ability to mix elements of classic film noir with their own idiosyncrasies. The constituents of film noir (the atmospheric photography, the labyrinthine plots, the femme fatale, the antihero) seem to be appropriate and popular at almost any time in almost any genre in movie history. Do you think "film noir" is a self-contained genre or should it rather be defined as a special mood or technique?

—Oliver Hahm, Siegen, Germany

A. The genre is defined by mood, look, story, and characters. Classic film noir can be dated to anytime before the French gave a name to the genre, in the 1950s. Modern film noir is by definition more self-aware but can be played very straight (*Red Rock West, Chinatown*) as well as with an angle (*House of Games, After Hours*). Good place for rental ideas: Noiroftheweek.blogspot.com.

Flying Saucers

Q. In my science fiction film class, we were trying to determine the first film to use the "flying saucer" spaceship. The earliest film we could come up with was *The Day the Earth Stood Still* (1951). Any thoughts?

—James Hrivnak, Waterloo, Ontario

A. Two 1950 movies were named *The Flying Saucer* and *The Flying Saucer Mystery.*

The Gates

Q. You recently reviewed *The Gates*, and in doing so shared your appreciation of the Gates themselves (an appreciation I share). I'm curious, though: Given your argument that video games cannot be "high art" because they are open-ended, does this also disqualify the Gates?

—Stephen Eldridge, Landing, New Jersey

A. No more than it would disqualify the Gateway Arch in St. Louis, Stonehenge, or Schubert's *Unfinished Symphony.*

Getting to Third Base

Q. I read your *Superbad* review and agree that it was a fun movie. The only thing is, the times have changed since you were in school and third base no longer means what you think it means. I don't know of a classy way to explain third base now, but "Bill Clinton" should give you a hint. Unless, of course, that's what third base meant back then.

—Jay Aaron, Torrance, California

A. I was thinking of shortstop.

Great Directors

Q. It's going on ten years since we had the last great generation of film directors emerge. Among the directors I am referring to are P. T. Anderson, David Fincher, Darren Aronofsky, Spike Jonze, and Christopher Nolan. With the exception of Michel Gondry, are there any emerging directors that you feel will emerge as the next generation's visionary?

—Neal James, Skokie, Illinois

A. Do we have to stick with Americans? There is a New Mexican Cinema forming around Guillermo del Toro (*Pan's Labyrinth*), Alfonso Cuaron (*Children of Men*), and Alejandro Gonzalez Inarritu (*Babel*).

Q. There was a question posted in the last Answer Man column complaining that there are no new interesting American directors. I would like to counter that. Craig Brewer, Richard Kelly, Rian Johnson, Edgar Wright (admittedly British), and Zack Snyder have all come out recently with creative and unique voices. True, not everyone likes their movies, but as you are fond of saying, good movies aren't for everybody, only mediocre movies are. And, besides, it seems facetious to call the so-called Mexican New Wave *new,* as all three of those filmmakers have been making great films since the midnineties.

—Bryce Wilson, Northridge, California

A. Once in a New Wave, always a New Waver. Godard, Resnais, Chabrol, Herzog, Wenders, they're all still surfing. New American candidates: David Gordon Green, Joey Lauren Adams, Miranda July, Sofia Coppola, Ramin Bahrani, Shane Carruth, Hilary Birmingham, Hadjii, Michael Gilio, Judd Apatow, M. Night Shyamalan, Eric Byler, Jill Sprecher, Ramin Serry, Kerry Conran, but stop me now, because when you start making lists, no one cares except the people you forgot to include.

Q. In your response to the question about promising new directors, you answered, "Do we have to stick with Americans? There is a New Mexican Cinema." Perhaps you have forgotten, but Mexicans *are* Americans. Of course, I realize that the battle against identifying the United States with *America* is already lost, but in the war between the gods and the giants, the giants may win but I fight for the gods.

—Bart Odom, McKinney, Texas

A. Another famous son of McKinney, Haystacks Calhoun, fought for the money. Thanks for the tip about my xenophobia! Of course, Canadians are also Americans. I plan to attend the Toronto Film Festival this year, and meet such leading American directors as Norman Jewison, Denys Arcand, Atom Egoyan, Deepa Mehta, Paul Haggis, Arthur Hiller, David Cronenberg, Guy Maddin, Ted Kotcheff, Patricia Rozema, Alison Maclean, Sturla Gunnarsson, Sarah Polley, and Ivan and Jason Reitman. I'm betting the first one to punch me is Gunnarsson. He was born on the offshore American island of Iceland, and you know how they are.

Harry Potter

Q. What do you think about the decision of some newspapers to break the embargo and run early reviews of *Harry Potter,* just because a few copies got loose?

—Laura Hunt, Chicago, Illinois

A. It's no fair. The papers received their review copies by tacitly agreeing to the embargo date and were grasping at a technicality to excuse the dubious distinction of reviewing the book early. Even worse, they spoiled the delicious suspense of Harry Potter fans, some of whom have become lifetime readers because of the books. With other papers, you're not surprised, but did you ever think the *New York Times* would stoop to using a loophole to be early with a book named *Harry Potter and the Deathly Hallows*? I say it's dirty pool.

By the way, the book, with an initial press run of twelve million copies, has no chance of appearing on the *Times*' best-seller list. Michael Giltz blogs on the Huffington Post:

"[In 2000], the Harry Potter books—a once-in-a-lifetime publishing phenomenon—were dominating the bestseller lists, with three titles ensconced in the Top 15 at the same time. It just wasn't fair, moaned publishers of more serious fiction. It kept more deserving titles off the list, titles that people would never hear about, said bookstore owners. And so in a rash, indefensible decision, the *New York Times* decided to banish children's books solely to their own separate list."

Ebert again: Next step for the *Times* should be to banish crime fiction to a separate category. Currently, all fifteen of its fiction bestsellers involve murder, cops, etc. You'd never guess serious fiction still existed. Of course, what would you do with a book like Michael Chabon's *The Yiddish Policemen's Union,* which considers crime in a (serious) comic novel? Maybe they should simply have a list headed "Best-Selling Books We Think Are Worthwhile."

Headlines

Q. I've been writing movie reviews for the newspaper at the University of Northern Iowa for a little over a year now. I've tended to find that if I don't write my own headlines, I'm usually dissatisfied with what is written by an editor or staff member. As a critic, do you write your own headlines, or do you trust someone to do it for you?

—James Frazier, Cedar Falls, Iowa

A. Editors write the headlines, as they must, because it's a matter of type size and space. Mostly at the *Sun-Times* they're terrific. What bothers me is that occasionally an ad will pull a quote from the headline and attribute it to me. Jim Emerson and I write the heads at rogerebert.com, sometimes indulging in shameless puns. You didn't ask, but my personal favorite, for Jodie Foster's *The Brave One,* was "Silencer of the lamb."

Werner Herzog

Q. Werner Herzog said that if you wanted to make films you should skip film school. Instead, you should "make a journey of five thousand kilometers alone, on foot. While walking you would learn more about what cinema truly means than you would in five years of sitting in classrooms."

Starting in two weeks, I'm taking up Herzog's challenge and setting out from Madrid with a backpack full of basic supplies and a tiny digital video camera. I'm going to walk all the way to Kiev and make a film of my experiences. I have communicated with Herzog and he has given the project his blessing! Check out my Web site at www.madridtokiev.com. Thought you would be interested in this story.

—Lee Kazimir, Chicago, Illinois

A. I received your message on February 14, 2006, filed it, and intended to follow your journey, but only this week did I check your Web site. Despite illness and other troubles, you made it! Congratulations. Now you are editing a film of your trek and write me: "I hope to have a first cut in September to qualify for submission to Sundance and Slamdance. From there it's a crapshoot, so we'll see."

Herzog himself, as you know, once walked entirely around Albania, because "at that time, they would not allow you to enter the country." Another time, he carried a print of one of his films from Munich to Paris to deliver it to the dying film historian Lotte Eisner, correctly convinced she would not die while he was en route. However, I am not sure you received Herzog's unqualified blessing. I asked and he responded:

"Yes, Lee Kazimir asked me for my blessing before he set out on his journey, but I had instant hesitations and told him so, as he was going to make his voyage a public event with constant messages from him on the Internet and a support system of sponsors. Traveling on foot was in my understanding a thing you had to do as a man exposing yourself in the most direct way to life, to *pura vida,* and this should stay with oneself. Anyway, I wished him all the best, but did not accept his offer to walk with him the end of his way and be filmed and interviewed by him."

Horror Porn

Q. I am a twenty-five-year-old middle school teacher always in search of ways to connect to teenage culture in class. Things have changed in the ten-plus years since I was in middle school. Gone are the teen-angst dramas of kids struggling to connect with one another; the movies consumed and talked about now are appropriately dubbed "horror porn" films. What do you make of this? Can you suggest any good teen films of the last few years that aren't disgusting and don't insult teenage intelligence?

—Colleen Young, Eugene, Oregon

A. Many teachers are alarmed. Sarah Adamson, a teacher from Naperville, Illinois, writes: "Please help shield our youth from the emergence of teen horror porn movies."

I am not convinced that a diet of gruesome vivisection, sexual assault, sadistic torture, and hopelessness is a positive contribution to the sponges of many teenage minds. There are superb horror films, but those are ones most kids avoid. I would recommend for them such wonderful non-horror films as *Holes, Millions, Shiloh, Real Women Have Curves, Children of Heaven, George Washington, King of Masks, Maryam, In America, Better Luck Tomorrow, Nowhere in Africa, King of the Hill, Winged Migration, My Family, The Secret of Roan Inish, What's Cooking, The Wild Parrots of Telegraph Hill,* and *Selena.*

Hot Fuzz

Q. I just listened to the commentary on the new DVD of Edgar Wright's *Hot Fuzz.* The filmmakers mention that while writing the screenplay they were reading your *Little Movie Glossary* book, which they referred to as "essential reading." I found this flattering as I am in that book. Just wondering if you have had a chance to see the film.

—John Weckmueller, Milwaukee, Wisconsin

A. Not yet, but I read the book.

I Am Legend

Q. This is growing into a large debate online: Who set the trap for Will Smith's character and left him dangling in *I Am Legend*? The majority believe one of the mutants cleverly copied Robert Neville's traps, and the rest believe he stumbled upon one of his own traps. Did the writers intend on this being ambiguous, or is there an answer from them?

—Jeff Jung, New York, New York

A. The rules are, if the film itself does not contain an answer, one is not allowed to be supplied from outside. Therefore, we do not know which of those two possibilities is the case.

Q. I think you're the only critic who has commented on one of the glaring holes in *I Am Legend,* namely, how did Alice Braga get into (and out of) New York—with a car! There are others: How does Will Smith's apartment still have running water? How can he pump gas for his car if there is no electricity in Manhattan other than the mega-generator we have to assume is powering his apartment? And if there is electricity to pump the gasoline, why aren't the streetlights working to scare away the light-averse mutants? There couldn't be electricity, of course—no one's operating a power plant! They're all dead! Ergo, no gasoline for Will. Then again, with all those dead people, why is he bothering to try to shoot deer? He can go into any supermarket and pick up as much canned food as he and his dog could ever need. These are, of course, quibbles about what was a very scary, fun movie to watch with a terrific performance by Will Smith. This leads to my question: How important do you feel these types of plot holes are to your response to a movie? Do you care?

—Jessica Klein, Los Angeles, California

A. Not very. Since the whole movie is impossible, why quibble? Still, it's distracting to see flaws in the interior logic of the world it creates. The original Richard Matheson novel at least established its reality and stuck to it.

Q. I just sat through *I Am Legend* and have to say that the final act felt like watching a deflating balloon. While it's apparent that Christian groups hold no qualms about denouncing movies that may or may not contain anti-Christian messages (and that they may or may not have seen), I am angered by movies that contain strong Christian messages. *I Am Legend* joins the list as the last movie I felt I should have walked out on as soon as the characters began debating "God's plan."

The end shot of the sanctuary's doors opening up to reveal church bells ringing over a peaceful community threw the entire movie into "allegory" territory, with the sinful New Yorkers banished to the darkness and the staunch God-fearing survivors triumphing by returning to their religious ways. It's sad to ask, but what do you think of adding a "religious content" warning to movies, as in "This movie contains profanity, brief nudity, Christianity?"

—David Young, Ayutthaya, Thailand

A. That'll be the day. More to the point, what does the spiritual status of the survivors and victims have to do with a nondenominational virus? And can Buddhists, Jews, Hindus, Muslims, and agnostics hope for a cure?

Intolerance

Q. I wrote a letter to the American Film Institute about the oddity of D. W. Griffith's *Intolerance* jumping to forty-ninth place from nowhere, replacing his *Birth of a Nation.* I will never believe that enough people went out and rented *Intolerance* over the past ten years to take it from not being on the list to essentially the same spot *Birth of a Nation* held.

When the first list came out, people raised a controversy behind *Birth of a Nation's* racism much the same way as they have since the film's initial release. Griffith made *Intolerance* as a sort of a defense against people accusing him of racial intolerance. Over ten years, some people must have felt guilty enough to decide that when they redo the list, *Intolerance* had to be on it. That would show that they appreciate Griffith's contribution to film history and also that they don't support the message of *Birth of a Nation,* despite its significance as a film.

—Scott Collette, Los Angeles, California

A. I struggled with the *Birth of a Nation* dilemma in my Great Movie piece about it. It is one of the most influential movies ever made, essentially assembling the tools of modern cinema, but it is racist. Still, I agree with you that it's odd that one would replace the other.

I asked Jean Picker Firstenberg, the head of the AFI, if both titles were on the working list of 400 movies sent out to the 1,500 voters (they could also cast write-in votes). "Yes, indeed," she replied. I am confident the votes were counted fairly, and I think it's likely most of those 1,500 filmmakers, critics, etc., would have seen both films. My hunch is that enough voters hesitated this time, thought twice about *Nation,* and saw *Intolerance* as an alternative. Does that make it a better film than *Birth of a Nation?* No.

Juno

Q. You're right about the great performances of J. K. Simmons and Allison Janney as the parents in *Juno.* They're allowed to be smart, funny people who care about their kids. I was immediately reminded of Paul Dooley and Barbara Barrie as the parents in the wonderful *Breaking Away,* a similar movie in many respects. Are there any other examples of great parental roles you can think of?

—Andrew Bradt, New York, New York

A. Well, John Mahoney was a great dad in *Say Anything,* but he turned out to have a guilty secret. Sam Waterston and Tess Harper were great parents in *The Man in the Moon,* the movie where Reese Withersoon had her first kiss. Michael Moriarty and Ann Dowd are loving parents in *Shiloh,* although their son doesn't always see it that way. But Juno's parents are probably the funniest and most lovable.

Killer of Sheep

Q. I read your latest Great Movies essay about Charles Burnett's *Killer of Sheep* and was struck with an enormous desire to see the film. But it seems that the film is simply unavailable on DVD. Do you have any information on where or when the film might be released so the public can once again see it outside of a retrospective or festival screening?

—Mark Adkins, Austin, Texas

A. The film, in a beautiful new print restored by Ross Lipman of the UCLA Film and Television Archive, is being exhibited on the art film circuit, should inevitably come to Austin, and will be released by Milestone on DVD.

Laszlo Kovacs

Q. It's so sad to learn of the death of Laszlo Kovacs. To me, he always seemed Hungarian to the core, yet he's associated with so many films and filmmakers who *are* the American cinema of the last forty years.

—Milos Stehlik, Facets Multimedia, Chicago, Illinois

A. The great Hungarian cinematographer died July 21, 2007, at seventy-five, leaving behind such glorious work as *Say Anything, Ghostbusters, Five Easy Pieces,* and *New York, New York.* He was an artist and an innovator. I remember seeing *Hells Angels on Wheels* (1967), one of his early nonunion shoots, and observing: "There's one shot where the camera moves in and out of focus through a field of green grass and then steals slowly across one of the big, brutal cycles. The contrast has an impact equal to David Lean's similar shots in *Doctor Zhivago* (remember the frosty window fading into the field of flowers?)." I learn from *Movie City News* that ten clips from his best work can be found at: blogs.guardian.co.uk/film/2007/07/laszlo_kovacs_greatest_clips.html.

Lady Chatterley

Q. In your review of *Lady Chatterley,* you said it was based on an earlier version of the D. H. Lawrence classic with the "too perfect" title of *John Thomas and Lady Chatterley.* Why is it too perfect?

—Greg Nelson, Chicago, Illinois

A. Look up *John Thomas* at www.wiktionary.com.

Q. A reader asked you about the spelling of Jean-Louis Coulloc'h's name in *Lady Chatterley.* This kind of spelling with an apostrophe is quite common in the names of people coming from Brittany (Bretagne) in France, *les Bretons.*

—Jean-Pierre Thilges, Luxembourg

A. And Daniel Andre Roy of Montreal, Quebec, adds: "C'H is included in the Breton alphabet, between CH and D. It is pronounced like the Spanish J and German CH."

Lars and the Real Girl

Q. I recently saw *Lars and the Real Girl* and I liked it a lot. However, I was disappointed with how the audience responded to some of the later scenes; they laughed out loud during what I thought were very touching moments. Is this just a matter of people not getting the point of movie? Or was all that stuff near the end funny?

—Craig E. Maddox, Auburn, California

A. Some of it was funny in a deep human-nature sort of way, not laugh-out-loud. I think the problem people have with that wonderful film is that they just can't accept a movie involving a love doll. It embarrasses them, even though there is not the slightest suggestion of sex involved, and Lars is essentially healing himself with the aid of an imaginary friend. One of the critics at *Movie City News* actually suggests Madeleine for best supporting actress, which is not so far-fetched if you contemplate how much we project upon any movie character.

Lazy Actors

Q. I was surprised by Francis Ford Coppola's accusation that De Niro, Pacino, and Nicholson have all become professionally and artistically lazy. "I don't feel that kind of passion to do a role and be great coming from those guys, because if it was, they would do it!" Coppola says in the October 2007 issue of *GQ*. If nothing else, haven't these particular actors painted more than their fair share of the cinematic landscape?

—Jimmy Jacobs, Columbia, South Carolina

A. I think you could say so. In the ten years since Coppola last directed a movie, the three of them have collectively acted in sixty-two films. But I learn through *Movie City News* that Coppola believes he was misquoted. "I was astonished because it wasn't true, and I have nothing but respect and admiration for them," Coppola told the *International Herald Tribune*. "These are the three greatest actors in the world today and they are my friends. So I have nothing but affection for them." To which David Poland of *MCN* footnotes: "A nice opportunity for *GQ* to put the full transcript online?"

The Lives of Others

Q. I, too, loved *The Lives of Others*. While the way the film looks and the acting are both superb, for me it was the subject matter of the story I most admired. However, we had different takes. You referenced current politics while for me, the film resonated because of its accurate depiction of life in a communist country, a subject matter that Hollywood has almost entirely ignored despite the fact that there is over seventy years' worth of material.

Hollywood has produced countless movies about the antiwar movement during the 1960s, McCarthyism, and the evil actions of the U.S. military and CIA. However, where are the movies about Armando Valladares's time in a Cuban prison or Walter Duranty's lies about the Ukrainian famine?

—Jorge A. del Rio, Singer Island, Florida

A. A point well taken. The most effective anticommunist films are made by directors who lived under communism; often, they use codes, as in Istvan Szabo's masterpiece *Mephisto*, which is set during the Nazi occupation of Hungary but could as well be told about the communists.

Q. Additional (sad) information related to the movie *The Lives of Others* that you just reviewed: Ulrich Muehe, the actor playing the lead (Stasi officer Gerd Wiesler) passed away at age fifty-four on July 22, 2007. He suffered from stomach cancer but kept this secret until the week before his death. Maybe this information could be added to the review to honor this extraordinary actor.

—Sven Hader, Wiesloch, Germany

A. That he knew this adds poignancy to every one of his scenes.

Lust, Caution

Q. Ang Lee has dropped some hints that the sex scenes in *Lust, Caution* were not simulated. I'm of the belief that watching actual sex is inherently wrong (but, like, no offense, man; I don't think you're evil or something because you've watched 'em). How exactly does one find out if the sex scenes in a given film were staged or not?

—Christopher Cadworth, Ashton, Ontario

A. As in life, it is hard to tell. Sometimes you have eyewitnesses; both Barbara Hershey and David Carradine have said their sex scenes in Scorsese's *Boxcar Bertha* were the real thing.

Marie Antoinette

Q. The only reason I watched *Marie Antoinette* is that you gave it a four-star rating.

—Cal Ford, Corsicana, Texas

A. Nine times out of ten, when I get an e-mail with a header like this, I ask myself what the message will be. There are usually three choices: (1) How much did they bribe you for that review? (2) I will never read you again, or (3) You suck.

Nevertheless, I opened your message, and here's what I read: "It was worth every star. Thank you. I really enjoyed it."

Thank *you*! Let's all hear it for Cal Ford! It is still possible to be surprised and delighted in this gloomy old world.

Mark Twain

Q. I was on the Web one late lonely evening reading the works of Mark Twain. I found his essay "Fenimore Cooper's Literary Offenses" and immediately thought of you. I was wondering what your thoughts were after reading that?

—Jacob Henderson, Eugene, Oregon

A. Oddly enough, that essay, which I came across in grade school, may have had a greater influence on my critical style (in certain moods) than any other single thing I've read. Mark Twain can make me laugh out loud, as in *The Innocents Abroad,* where an Egyptian guide shows a tour group a mummy that is three thousand years old. An American tourist says: "How calm he is—how self-possessed. Is, ah—is he dead?"

The Martian Child

Q. You write that the film of *The Martian Child* is bland. Here's something that might have saved it. The film is based on a book by openly gay science fiction writer David Gerrold. His book was based on his own experience as a single gay parent who adopted a problem child who was convinced that he was from the planet Mars.

The father's identity as a gay man was a major part of the book but the makers of the new film version seem to have deemed this theme irrelevant and have jettisoned the whole gay angle and made the father straight. In short, they eliminated the very thing that made the original story interesting. Well, I suppose we can't risk getting the evangelicals of this country upset by making a movie that presents gay parenting in a positive way, can we? As always, Hollywood panders to the lowest common denominator. What could have been a groundbreaking film has now been irreparably lessened and that is sad.

—Michael D. Klemm, Buffalo, New York

A. Institutional Hollywood sometimes seems afraid to offend anybody except those with open minds and good taste.

Maxivision 48

Q. I have enjoyed reading your views on the digital versus film issue and was wondering if you had any update on how Dean Goodhill's "Maxivision 48" system has been coming along. Do you know of any directors who are actually considering using it for a feature production? I was sad to read in one of your articles that Eastman House is going digital as well, and lately director Sidney Lumet has mentioned that film is going to be gone within fifty years. I would love to hear if you have any updates about Maxivision 48.

—Ibrahim Shankiti, Baghdad, Iraq

A. Goodhill is still optimistic. The process is so much better than 70 mm or IMAX that it blows them away. The digital revolution is useful for many reasons, including cost, speed, and increasing quality, but a venture capitalist with imagination could transform epics such as comic superhero movies. If fanboys could see *Spider-Man* in Maxivision, you'd never get them down at the multiplex again.

Cormac McCarthy

Q. I've noticed that you're mentioning Cormac McCarthy more and more lately: in your recent article about the Coen brothers movie *No Country for Old Men,* in your review of *The Three Burials of Melquiades Estrada,* in the review of the Australian Western *The Proposition,* and a couple other times I think. And yet his name does not appear in your review of *All the Pretty Horses;* in fact, you attribute the dialogue to Ted Tally. I'm curious. Is it because you had not read McCarthy before viewing the Thornton film?

—Jonathan Glyn, Philadelphia, Pennsylvania

A. Yes. I devoured the McCarthy canon after hearing my sportswriter friend Bill Nack read aloud from *All the Pretty Horses.* Nack is one of the greatest reader-alouders alive, and as an impresario I have "presented" him in two "concerts in words." In my opinion, McCarthy's best book is *Suttree.*

Michael Clayton

Q. In *Michael Clayton,* what was the significance of the three horses in the field, and how did Michael Clayton happen to stop his car there?

—Trish McDonald, Cincinnati, Ohio

A. Weary and depressed, I think he simply saw the horses and wanted to stop and breathe some fresh air. No symbolism. Good timing, though.

Q. The little boy who played Michael Clayton's son was a crucial part of the movie and yet no credit has been given to him. He did a great acting job and the book he was reading was so important to the story.

—Joan Clark, Ketchum, Idaho

A. Praise to Austin Williams, eleven, who also played Timothy Hutton's son in *The Good Shepherd.*

The Mist

Q. I have not seen *The Mist* but understand from reviews that it was set in a small seaport town in Maine, with much of the action taking place in a grocery store. Imagine my surprise when the print ads in today's papers show a scene of two people looking out of a grocery store (note grocery cart at lower right) at the burning ruins of a large city full of ruined skyscrapers. Is the ad grossly misleading, or did the reviews leave out some important details about the plot?

—Tom DeLorey, Blue Island, Illinois

A. Either the ad people did not see the movie, or the characters are looking at a sneak preview of *Mist 2.* The movie also comes from the Weinsteins, whose advertising department has apparently moved on to giving away the ending of the next film.

Moolaade

Q. Some of your readers have been desperately searching for a Region 1 copy of Sembene's *Moolaade.* Look no further than Canada. We've had the movie on DVD for about two years now. Buy a copy online, because it's worth it.

—David Friend, Toronto, Ontario

A. It's also coming out soon from New Yorker Films.

Q. Ousmane Sembene's *Moolaade* was my favorite film at your Overlooked festival this year. I was so saddened to hear of his recent death.

—Greg Nelson, Chicago, Illinois

A. So was I. Sembene, eighty-four, from Senegal, the "father of African cinema," was also a gifted novelist, and his films took strong stands against what he perceived as the Western use of aid to undermine local agricultural communities. In his *Guelwaar* (1992), he was prescient in telling the story of a clash between Catholics and Muslims. But he enriched his politics with humor; the clash comes when a Catholic body is mistakenly buried in a Muslim cemetery, and the Muslims feel that to move it would demean their ancestors.

His last and best film was *Moolaade,* attacking the practice of female circumcision. Not a film you'd like to see, right? My review was a cry from the heart: "Sometimes I seek the right words, and I despair. What can I write that will inspire you to see *Moolaade*? This was for me the best film at Cannes 2004, a story vibrating with urgency and life. It makes a powerful statement and at the same time contains humor, charm, and astonishing visual beauty."

I met Sembene at Cannes, in the company of Daniel Talbot, whose New Yorker Films distributes all his work in the United States. We had a nice chat in the hotel where we were all staying. Afterward, Talbot pulled me aside. "In my opinion, he said, that is the greatest director in the world."

Q. I've been on a quest to see *Moolaade.* This feature is now the basis of a Great Movie article on your Web site but the film is still unavailable on DVD. Is there anyway to see this film? Perhaps a cable station, or a papal decree?

—Mike Hein, Cincinnati, Ohio

A. Dan Talbot tells me his New Yorker Films released *Moolaade* in December 2007. The film remains in local release around the country. Talbot adds: "Sembene's death took me by surprise. When I saw him two years ago at Cannes, he was fit as a fiddle. I really loved that man, and I will miss him mightily."

Movie Phenomena

Q. There are phenomena that exist only in movies and not in real life: telephone numbers beginning 555, cars smashing into fruit carts during chase scenes, the instantaneous dial tone when the offscreen party hangs up, the smoke-and-water factory, characters toting suitcases that are obviously empty, and catastrophes that compel extras to run back and forth in front of the camera instead of out the nearest exit to safety. What are some others? Do these bits have a name?

—Ted Hild, Springfield, Illinois

A. I like to think of them as entries in *Ebert's Little Movie Glossary.*

My "Fifth" Problem

Q. It appears that you have a problem with "fifth." In every great series, it appears that when they get to the fifth film, you are always let down. Such is the case with *Star Trek V, Harry Potter: Order of the Phoenix, Star Wars: Episode II* (the fifth *Star Wars* film made), etc. This is in spite of your appreciation of every other installment of the series. Is this coincidence or do you have something against the number five?

—Samuel Mils, Salt Lake City, Utah

A. I plead the Fifth.

No Country for Old Men

Q. I just saw *No Country for Old Men* the other day and I cannot stop thinking about the character of Anton Chigurh. At first I thought about how much he scared me, and I initially wanted to classify him accordingly. I put him right up there with Jaws and the oil-slick from *Creepshow 2* as one of the all-time scariest creatures to grace the big screen.

But as I thought about it more, Anton seemed less like a monster and more like death personified. This made me think of Bergman's Death and the game of chess he played with von Sydow in *Seventh Seal,* and I thought this somewhat paralleled Anton and the coin-tossing game he played with the gas station owner. Should Anton be considered a monster or is he merely death personified?

—Nathaniel Meek, Los Angeles, California

A. *Merely* death personified? Death gets billing above monsters, in my book. There is something relentlessly supernatural about the way he just keeps coming. We haven't seen the last of him. At least Bergman's Death didn't make the knight risk his life on a coin toss, but had the chess pieces there on the board.

Q. After watching the Coen brothers' wonderful adaptation of *No Country for Old Men,* I was inspired to read the book. After reading the book, I went online and saw a photo of Cormac McCarthy taken in 1972 for the dust jacket of *Child of God.* I was stunned by the resemblance to Josh Brolin in *No Country.* Separated at birth?

—Bruce Burns, Austin, Texas

A. Given the age difference, not separated by birth, probably, but perhaps linked by a blood meridian.

Q. I went to see *No Country for Old Men* with a group of my friends. I was absolutely fascinated and riveted by the film and think that it is the best film I have seen thus far this year. My very good friend, who also happens to be a very smart guy, thought that the film was terrible. I was shocked. Should I debate the merits of the film with him? Is it even worth debating such a wonderful film when the person you are debating with has no appreciation for it, and does it pose a risk to the friendship?

—John Dolores, Chattahoochee, Florida

A. I've said it before and I'll say it again: As Louis Armstrong instructs us, "There are some folks that, if they don't know, you can't tell 'em."

No End in Sight

Q. I have long been a dedicated reader of your reviews. You were responsible for directing me toward the works of Bresson, Bunuel, Bergman, Tarkovsky, and Herzog and thus inspiring my love for the movies (particularly Bresson). I will forever be indebted to you for having changed my life in this regard.

I am also a proud American who enlisted voluntarily in the United States Marine Corps. I served for one and a half years in Iraq. I saw more of the destructive impact of war on the lives of the Iraqi people and those of the men around me than you will ever know. And I am proud to have done so. I know a lot of men and women who were similarly proud to fight what they felt was a just war against a common enemy to all of humanity, a *regime* of mass destruction. Contrary to what you may believe, many serve the American cause because they want to. The soldiers fighting there fight in the name of universal justice that many of the liberal elite take for granted.

Your review of *No End in Sight* deeply wounded me, as one who has come to place tremendous value upon your opinion. I may no longer be in the fight, having served my term and studying now at the University of Chicago. But the message you've sent to your readers is painful all the same for me to receive. I urge you, Roger, to not be so self-possessed in the future, that you presume to know the hearts and minds of men who do not share your worldview.

—Evan Bernick, Chicago, Illinois

A. Thank you for your heartfelt letter. Those who fought and fight in Iraq are brave and patriotic, and risk their lives in the name of their country. My review was not about them. It was about those who sent them into battle. What makes *No End in Sight* unique is that its subjects are almost entirely men and women who served in the U.S government, military, intelligence, and diplomatic corps, and now feel they were lied to and betrayed by their superiors; they all supported the war, but their advice from the ground was ignored by ideologues in Washington. I hope you see the film, which is about your leaders at the time you served. At the least, you will find it provocative.

Ocean's 13

Q. You likened the plans in the caper movie *Ocean's 13* to a Scrooge McDuck scheme. Actually Scrooge was the one with the fortress; it was the Beagle Boys who were always trying to break in.

—Richard Peterson, Burkesville, Kentucky

A. Not always. Surely you have not forgotten McDuck's scheme to float a sunken treasure ship by sending Huey, Louie, and Dewey underwater to pump it full of Ping-Pong balls?

Q. Regarding the *Ocean's 13* machine: In fact, the Department of Energy has one for sale about ninety miles north of Vegas. The DOE used it to bore tunnels at its Yucca Mountain project, and I saw the machine for sale when I visited the mountain last year. So, Ocean's crew would still have to sneak it into Vegas and somehow dig under the strip without suspicion, but at least they wouldn't have to worry about going overseas with the monster machine.

—Rick Michal, Westmont, Illinois

A. You make the plan sound almost plausible, except for a few holes you could drive a six-hundred-ton machine through.

Off the Mainstream

Q. I live in a small city in Tennessee, which means the local theaters get mainstream films almost exclusively. If a movie comes along that I want to watch I have to go alone because my friends aren't interested, or with my wife and hear her snore. As someone with a great love for movies ever since childhood, I feel a sense of melancholy at the thought that the works I love the most might be lost to my generation. What is going to happen to Bergman and Antonioni films now that they've died? Do I belong to an extremely small minority?

—Frank Multari, Cleveland, Tennessee

A. Yes, and you always will. Some people have tastes, most have appetites. But here's encouraging news: Studio Briefing on IMDb.com recently reported, "Theaters showing mainstream movie fare were mostly empty over the weekend, a traditionally slow period at the box office. On the other hand, those showing art-house fare were doing a land-office business."

Q. The latest *Facets Movie Lovers DVD Guide* has a fascinating section where more than one hundred movie-industry people, including many great directors, list ten films about which they are passionate. I'm familiar with most of the listed films. There seemed to be a direct correlation between the types of films that the directors listed and the types of films that they create themselves. For example, those who named films that make you think, such as the works of Bergman, Ozu, Renoir, and Bresson, tended to make films that also make you think. On the other hand, those who cited films that are basically entertainment tended to create that type of film as well. Do you agree?

—Robert Simanski, Sterling, Virginia

A. Facets Multimedia has the world's largest inventory of hard-to-find videos, as well as all the usual ones, and its catalogs are works of art. What surprised me was how some relatively unexpected pairings turned up: *The Bad News Bears* (Ethan Coen), *Cane Toads* (Werner Herzog), *Bring Me the Head of Alfredo Garcia* (Takeshi Kitano), *The Fountainhead* (Jerry Lewis), *Last Year at Marienbad* (Michael Mann), *Auntie Mame* (Camille Paglia), *Trainspotting* (Annie Proulx), *Faster, Pussycat! Kill! Kill!* (John Waters). Info at facets.org.

Q. In a recent debate with some friends, the question of whether it's possible to see all of the "classic" films was raised. I submit that although it may be physically possible, in reality, even the biggest film fans have not seen every single classic film ever made. Am I wrong? Have you seen every classic film from every country, genre, time period?

—Jay Cheel, St. Catharines, Ontario

A. Certainly not. And even those with encyclopedic knowledge, like Martin Scorsese, David Bordwell, Jonathan Rosenbaum, Dave Kehr, Bertrand Tavernier, Michel Ciment, Kevin Brownlow, and the great Pierre Rissient, have not. Too many movies, too little time. A good place to gain a toehold might be my Great Movies books, or *1,001 Movies You Must See Before You Die.* Or start working your way through the DVD catalogs of the Criterion Collection, Kino, Milestone, and Facets Multimedia. Plus, if you have an all-zones DVD player, the British Film Institute.

Oscar Matters

Q. If Cate Blanchett were to win the Oscar for her portrayal of Elizabeth I at next year's Oscars, would Helen Mirren as Elizabeth II give her the Oscar? And do you think the Queen will be watching the Oscars just to see such an event?

—Kathryn Boussemart, Washington, D.C.

A. I think the show comes on too late for Her Majesty. In any event, as the Academy's Bruce Davis reminds me, the best actress award is traditionally given by the previous year's best actor. If Blanchett were to win for Elizabeth I, that would mean she'd receive the award from Forest Whitaker. He won for *The Last King of Scotland.* I hope he doesn't hold the beheading of Mary, Queen of Scots against her.

Q. I really wish people would stop saying that Al Gore has won an Oscar. I admire Gore and am delighted that he has received a Nobel Prize, but he has no Academy Award on his mantle to put it beside. Though he was the host of *An Inconvenient Truth,* the Academy Award is given to the director. Gore is as much the winner of the award as Muhammad Ali was for *When We Were Kings.*

—Jonathan Dunbar, New York, New York

A. Correct. The Oscar went to director Davis Guggenheim.

Ellen Page

Q. You wrote of Ellen Page: "I have seen her in only two films." Rather, you have seen her in three: *Juno, Hard Candy,* and *X-Men 3,* in which she played the role of Kitty Pryde, the girl who got chased through walls by the Juggernaut.

—Jacob Pease, Charlottesville, Virginia

A. She was up to a lot of shenanigans in that movie!

Pan's Labyrinth

Q. As much as I greatly admire *Pan's Labyrinth,* don't you think it's a bit early to add it to your Great Movies list? The fact that it's less than a year old makes me wonder if it should be placed on the same list as so many revered classics that have not only demonstrated what film can do, but have influenced and shaped modern cinema. Shouldn't at least a little time pass before such a recent movie is declared a classic?

—Philip Pangrac, Fort Polk, Louisiana

A. The same thought occurred to me, and Stephen Mack of Washington makes a similar argument. He also noticed how quickly I chose *Moolaade,* but the timing there was inspired by the death of its director, Ousmane Sembene. I missed a lot of movies during my illness, have been catching up with the best or most promising ones, and thought *Pan's Labyrinth* was a masterpiece when I saw it at

Cannes 2006. I have had an informal rule that ten years should pass before a film qualifies as a Great Movie, but illness has caused me to rethink that time span, and so with a few extraordinary recent films I am going to bend the rule a little. Of course I will not neglect older classics: Coming up soon, *El Topo.*

Q. Just read your Great Movie addition of del Toro's *Pan's Labyrinth,* with its discussion of the New Mexican Cinema. Although you didn't mention it, I wanted to point out that Alfonso Cuaron's absolutely superb G-rated film *A Little Princess* from 1995 is a great companion to *Pan's Labyrinth.* They are worlds apart in their execution and yet strikingly similar in many ways, as both follow a young girl escaping to fantasy worlds in the face of the harsh reality of war. Both movies stand on their own, but seeing them again recently in the context of knowing more about the collaboration and friendship of the directors has added greatly to my appreciation of each.

—Kevin Park, Lexington, Kentucky

A. And there's also del Toro's *The Devil's Backbone* (2001), a ghost story set in an orphanage at the time of Franco. Both directors seem interested in younger children faced with a combination of political and supernatural problems. I loved *A Little Princess,* and also don't miss Cuaron's *Great Expectations,* once more, two lonely children in a frightening house.

Paradise Lost

Q. There's a big news story out about the West Memphis Three, subjects of the documentaries *Paradise Lost: The Child Murders at Robin Hood Hills* (1996) and *Paradise Lost 2: Revelations* (2000). They may be exonerated on the basis of DNA evidence. Also, a new movie about them may be in the works.

—Justin Weiss, Tokyo, Japan

A. I've been writing about this case for years. The two documentaries, by Joe Berliner and Bruce Sinofsky, compellingly argue that three young men were railroaded for the crimes because they wore black, liked heavy metal, and fit the local profile of "satanic cult members." The first doc showed us Terry Hobbs, stepfather of one of the victims. Now DNA evidence puts him, but not the three prisoners, at the scene. The full story is at http://observer.guardian.co.uk/world/story/0,,2204901,00.html.

Q. I know that you were greatly moved by the film *Paradise Lost: The Child Murders At Robin Hood Hills* and its sequel, *Paradise Lost 2: Revelations.* I thought you might be interested in this news story.

—William Kane, Brooklyn, New York

A. The films detailed the trial and conviction of three teenagers for the 1993 murders of three eight-year-old boys. All three defendants were found guilty and are still in prison, one on death row, although compelling evidence suggests they are innocent. The films suggested that because the teenagers liked heavy metal music, they were victims of local hysteria about satanic rites. You sent me a link to WMC-TV in Memphis, which reports a new defense team has discovered that DNA evidence available at the time failed to link any of the defendants to any of the victims but did link Terry Hobbs, the stepfather of one of the victims.

Hobbs is not to be confused with John Mark Byers, another stepfather who, I wrote, all but tried to turn himself in during the second film. Bite marks were found on one of the boys; Byers had his teeth extracted after the deaths and told investigators it was done earlier. Now Janice Broach, the WMC-TV reporter on the story, writes me: "Hobbs's ex-wife said he had a partial plate he locked in a box when he got some new teeth. It is all very strange."

Paul Schrader

Q. Your interview with Paul Schrader served as a big-time wake-up call. His *Light Sleeper* was one of the best and most underrated films of the '90s, and the only DVD available is an old and lousy 4:3 DVD from 1998. Does Paul have anything going in revisiting *Light Sleeper* and some of his other past films in comprehensive fashion, with new transfers and features? Other candidates include *The Comfort of Strangers* (like *Atonement,* from an Ian McEwan novel) and the sublime *Mishima: A Life in Four Chapters.*

—Shane Buettner, online editor, HomeTheaterMag.com, Gig Harbor, Washington

A. A DVD of *Mishima,* a Great Movie, is in preparation by the Criterion Collection, with commentary by Schrader. I agree with you about the other titles you praise.

Pauline Kael

Q. In your response to a query you mentioned Pauline Kael. You also wrote an essay about her influence on critics, filmmakers, and filmgoers in your book *Awake in the Dark.* And yet aside from *5,001 Nights at the Movies,* which includes only capsule reviews, none of her books are in print. I fear for the longevity of her work. If someone would only reissue her books, which are regarded as canonical texts by fellow critics and those who still care to remember, I think America's greatest and most important pundit would be discovered for a new generation.

—Paul Babin, Yarmouth Port, Massachusetts

A. I urgently agree. One book to start with would be the mammoth *For Keeps,* her selection of key reviews from all of her other collections. I also think Kael is an obvious candidate for the Library of America series.

Porno Matters

Q. I recently purchased a copy of *Taxi Driver.* Early in the film, Travis visits a porno theater. He walks next to the screen, but the image is blurred. Was it this way when the film was originally released, or was this done for the DVD release? Do you have any way of knowing who's to blame for this idiocy? This is really offensive; this guy walks around taking drugs, buying weapons of all kinds, saying all sort of disturbing things, kills a bunch of people, and we care about sex, the only harmless image in the movie?

—Gabriel Nostel Dominguez, Buenos Aires, Argentina

A. As I recall, it was that way to begin with. There are two ways to look at it. (1) Hardcore porn would have crippled the film's distribution chances; (2) since Travis is in focus, a film in the background would be out of focus unless a deliberate decision was made to use deep focus, which would be a nightmare to light, unless you inserted the background as an optical shot, which would look obvious and distract from the purpose of the scene.

The Producers

Q. I was watching *The Producers* on Turner Classic Movies the other night and afterward Robert Osborne made a comment that I have to tell you about. He said that while he thought it was a great comedy, he found the only flaw was the beatnik character of Lorenzo St. DuBois (L.S.D.) played by Dick Shawn, which he felt dated the picture. He said that while it was funny in 1968, today it seems a little tired in light of other better portrayals of hippies and beatniks that would come along later. I dunno, I think of film as a time capsule of attitudes and images and ideas of the times in which they are made. I think the character puts a stamp on the film so that we understand with clarity that we are watching a movie made in 1968.

—Jerry Roberts, Birmingham, Alabama

A. That's what I think, too. A movie cannot be made outside of time, and is funny on its own terms or not at all.

Queasy Cam

Q. The blogger Brian at goneelsewhere.wordpress.com takes issue with your remarks about Paul Greeengrass's long takes in *The Bourne Ultimatum,* writing: "I don't recall a single take in this movie that was more than about three seconds long." Either Greengrass really does a spectacular job of not calling attention to those long takes, or Ebert saw a different movie. But it's very strange no matter what. Who's right?

—Greg Nelson, Chicago, Illinois

A. This inspired some introspection. I didn't write about long takes in my notes during the movie, but while writing the review they formed in my memory. If Brian is right, perhaps what happened was that sustained stretches of breakneck action, as assembled by editor Christopher Rouse, played like unbroken takes in their effect, especially since so much of the movie follows the action with a Steadicam or handheld camera. Rouse tells me there are *lots* of shots more than three seconds long, and the film's first assistant editor, Robert Malina, writes me: "We have long shots! In reel 2 we have a 20 second steady cam shot going thru the halls of SRD, following the characters Vosen and Wills (Strathairn and Johnson)."

Rush Hour 3

Q. In some of the advertising for *Rush Hour 3*, Jackie Chan has top billing. In some, Chris Tucker has top billing, and in some, Jackie Chan doesn't even appear to be in the movie. How often does the billing for a movie change based upon the specific marketing campaign?

—Harold Hedrick, Silver Spring, Maryland

A. This was probably dictated by the demographic target of each ad.

(1) Jackie top billing: Martial arts fans.

(2) Both equally: *Rush Hour* fans.

(3) Tucker only: A waste of money, if they think African-American audiences don't know and like Jackie Chan.

Scorsese's Short Subject

Q. Have you seen the Scorsese short film paying homage to Hitchcock? Talk about thrilling! Do you think Marty captures the essence of old Hitch? It's at www.scorsesefilmfreixenet.com/video_eng.htm.

—Chase Holland, Tampa, Florida

A. What a discovery! Scorsese begins with three pages purported to be from a lost Hitchcock screenplay (with a page missing), and recreates them in the style of the Master. Yes, he uncannily captures Hitchcock's visual style, pace, tension, and the sound of a Bernard Herrmann score. He speculates (idly?) that this would be a way to "restore" the missing footage from von Stroheim's *Greed,* since its screenplay survives. I immediately thought of the lost ending of Welles's *Magnificent Ambersons.* Well, why not? A profound student of the cinema like Scorsese could make a convincing Wellesian production, and it would be better than the ending we have now, which also isn't by Welles.

Screenplays

Q. Neil Gaiman claims he holds the record for having sold the most screenplays to Hollywood that were never produced. I thought Harlan Ellison was the gold medalist in that event.

—Greg Nelson, Chicago, Illinois

A. Neil Gaiman writes me: "It wasn't me who said it—the *Hollywood Reporter* ran a front-page story in 2003 (when *Coraline* was optioned) saying that I was the person with the most things optioned but never made. They listed lots of them and interviewed various people about how hard it was to make my stuff. Even at the time I thought it was a silly way for them to do an article on me, and I didn't take it seriously. I'm sure there are many more people than me with worse runs of getting things made (and I have three movies coming out in the next twelve months, so I'm definitely off the meter now)."

And Harlan Ellison writes me: "I've no idea what my pal Neil Gaiman claims for a total of unproduced screenplays but (including films intended for TV, as well as theatrical, but not series) I had Susan print out the list and at the moment it stands at a terrifying twenty-seven screenplays written and unproduced. (All were paid for at exorbitant rates, thank goodness.)"

September Dawn

Q. In your zero-star review of *September Dawn,* you stated that there must be a more thoughtful and insightful way to consider the tragedy of the Mountain Meadows Massacre. There is: A film professor of mine at the University of Utah produced a feature-length documentary about the massacre entitled *Burying the Past: Legacy of the Mountain Meadows Massacre,* which has won several awards. The film speaks with descendants of the seventeen children who were spared death that day in 1857, and explores in an intelligent and sensitive manner the deep emotions that continue to haunt them. The Web address is www.buryingthepast.com.

—Aaron Allen, Los Angeles, California

A. Several readers have told me about Brian F. Patrick's film. The film finds that Mormons did indeed commit the massacre, while drawing a line between church teachings and the actions of a fanatic group of fringe dwellers.

The Sex Lives of Jane and Emily

Q. So biographer Jon Spence has discovered a boyfriend for Jane Austen (*Becoming Jane*). I remember when the scholars found first a boyfriend, and then a girlfriend, for Emily

Dickinson. Our society just can't accept the notion of a woman without a sex life, no matter how otherwise extraordinary she may be.

—Mary Shen Barnidge, Chicago, Illinois

A. The experts seem agreed that neither Austen nor Dickinson had actual sexual intercourse. At least Dickinson heard a fly buzz when she died. You have to hand her that.

Sexiest Lips

Q. On Cinematical.com, Eric Davis has written: "If anyone could go up against Angelina Jolie in a Sexiest Hollywood Lips competition, it would be Rosario Dawson." What is your expert opinion?

—Laura Hunt, Chicago, Illinois

A. Rosario Dawson wins. In my review of Ethan Hawke's *Chelsea Walls* (2002), where Dawson plays a poet named Audrey, I wrote, long before Davis: "I do not know how good Audrey's poems are because Dawson reads them in close-up—just her face filling the screen—and I could not focus on the words. I have seen a lot of close-ups in my life but never one so simply, guilelessly erotic. Have more beautiful lips ever been photographed?"

Sicko

Q. I am a former *Fortune* 500 company employee who is one of the fifty million not covered by insurance. My wife and I are in our mid-fifties and are constantly in fear of getting sick and leaving our five kids with unthinkable and unpayable health-care bills.

My wife and I are self-employed and astronomical health insurance payments were sucking us and our credit cards dry. We had to stop. We even tried President Bush's Health Savings Plan only to discover we were never saving anything and always paying for each doctor's visit or emergency. We decided to try to save money ourselves for doctor visits and hope and pray we really didn't get seriously ill. This is no way to live and I think Mr. Moore's movie is a courageous look at this country's failings in this area. My wife and I are seriously thinking of moving to Canada or France to live out our lives.

—Joe Shaw, Detroit, Michigan

A. A leading drawback to the implementation of universal health care is that the medical industries contribute millions to political causes, and sick people don't.

The Simpsons Movie

Q. In your review of *The Simpsons Movie* you mention that it is already voted as the 166th best film of all time on the Internet Movie Database and ask, "Do you suppose somehow the ballot box got stuffed by *Simpsons* fans who didn't even need to see the movie to know it was a masterpiece? D'oh!" Likewise, readers of your own Web site on the morning of the film's release already gave it a four-star rating. Don't you think these are merely fans of the movie showing their contempt for you and all other reviewers, and in fact for any but their own opinions?

—Bill Pierce, Burlington, Ontario

A. Not at all. They simply love *The Simpsons.* By the way, on July 29, 2007, *The Simpsons Movie* had climbed up to the 43rd greatest film of all time, right behind Kubrick's *Paths of Glory* and three ahead of *Chinatown.* Will it knock off *The Godfather* for number one? IMDb.com notes: "For the top 250, only votes from regular voters are considered."

Q. In your review of *The Simpsons Movie,* you noted that *Time* magazine named *The Simpsons* the best TV show of the twentieth century. You sniped that their opinion said more about the magazine and the twentieth century than it did about *The Simpsons.* That was a condescending remark. The Simpsons has been one of the smartest, if not *the* smartest written show, for almost two decades.

You've claimed in the past that you were a better person because you didn't watch TV when you were younger. But there are plenty of people out there who are just as intelligent and cultured as you who do watch television, including shows like *The Simpsons.*

—Leo Flores, Chicago, Illinois

A. Hey, I watched television when I was younger. I do now. That's why I know there were better TV shows. Ever heard of *Omnibus, I Love Lucy, Sesame Street, Ed Sullivan, Jack Benny, 60 Minutes, Fawlty Towers, The Honeymooners, Saturday Night Live, Captain Kangaroo,* or Carol Burnett or Tracey Ullman?

Siskel & Ebert

Q. There is a warm place in my heart for *Sneak Previews* from right around 1980, when I was ten. I used to stay up with my dad to watch the two men argue passionately for or against magical movies that I might or might not be allowed to see some day. When I rent a classic movie that I most likely picked based on your advice, I always look up your review online. I wish I could also see your back-and-forth with Mr. Siskel to complement the review.

—Owen Crow, Houston, Texas

A. I don't think many of the *Sneak Previews* shows were saved by PBS, or *At the Movies* by Tribune, but from 1985 on, *Siskel & Ebert* and *Ebert & Roeper* were syndicated by Disney, and they're streaming the new reviews and digitizing the old ones and making them available on ebertandroeper.tv. Just the other day I came across a raging discussion group debate about whether on an old *Siskel & Ebert* I knew the Sean Young character was a replicant in *Blade Runner.* One person unkindly suggested I didn't. A wiser participant, analyzing my exact words, saw that I was trying to avoid giving away whether she was or not. The debates go on.

Q. As the producer of *Siskel & Ebert* for many years, I am glad to see all the old shows online. But as a writer deeply involved in the current writers' strike, I am wondering—are you being paid for that work? You guys wrote every word yourselves. I should know.

—Nancy de Los Santos, Los Angeles

A. Nope. But I'm happy to see that stuff out there.

Sixth Man in *The Godfather*

Q. I have a *Godfather* question that *no one* can answer. In *The Godfather,* just before Michael leaves to kill Sollozzo and police captain McCluskey, the family is in the Corleone home trying to determine where Michael will have this meeting. There are six people in the room: Michael, Sonny, Tom, Clemenza, Tessio, and an unidentified person wearing a brown suit. He has only seven seconds of screen time, and no dialogue. Who is he? Only the top "family" members would be there, as they are discussing killing a police captain. Even Freddo (a Corleone) is not there. Why would anyone outside of the elite group be there?

—Phil Giordano, Plainfield, New Jersey

A. I am reminded of the great movie line, "And there was another man, a third man." You list all the possible identities for the sixth man and explain why it couldn't be any of them. I asked Tim Dirks, author-manager of filmsite.org, which supplies countless invaluable plot details, and he replies: "It looks like Phil Giordano is searching for some 'logical' answer. And he has already dismissed guesses that may be correct. I don't think there's going to be a definitive answer to his question, because of the way he has made assumptions about who the person must be."

Q. In a recent Answer Man, Phil Giordano asks about a Sixth Man in *The Godfather* who is never identified when the Corleones plan the execution of a police captain. The person he is wondering about is Rocco Lampone, played by Tom Rosqui, who is uncredited in the film, according to the IMDb. Mr. Giordano will remember the earlier scene in the film where Rocco executes Paulie in the car as Clemenza urinates outside (the "leave the gun, take the cannoli" scene). According to the book, this is where Rocco finally makes his bones. He sits in on the meeting as the family waits for news from Sonny's contact at McCluskey's police station to find out where Michael's meeting with Sollozzo will take place. This shows the trust he has earned from the family. He eventually becomes one of Michael's two caporegimes (Al Neri is the other one). Incidentally, it is Rocco, who, in the second film, assassinates Hyman Roth at the airport, only to be shot in the back by a police officer as he tries to flee the scene.

—Ali Arikan, Istanbul, Turkey

A. I received a lot of solutions to the question, only five correct; yours came in first, followed by John Fitzpatrick of Springfield, Illinois, Jorge Gamboa of Tucson, Arizona, Jason Ihle of Seville, Spain, and Glenn Nakachi of Chicago. Some of the other answers refer to an earlier scene discussing the wisdom of the killings. The "sixth man" scene begins at about 1:18:12 and continues until about 1:18:52; it's the man on the far right, drinking from a bottle of beer.

The Sixth Sense

Q. I was watching *The Sixth Sense* with my cousins, and we got into a debate over whether or not Haley Joel Osment's character in the movie knows that the Bruce Willis character is dead. I said he could not possibly know he is dead because he would have been scared to talk to him, but they pointed out that he does know and talks to him because he is not scared of him. Who do you agree with?

—Claudia Cruz, Riverside, California

A. Your cousins. Cole says, "I see dead people." So he knows they're dead. He kindly does not always inform them.

Spoilers

Q. I remember back when *Million Dollar Baby* was in release, you campaigned vehemently against anyone in the media releasing the spoilers. On the other hand, in a recent Answer Man column, you spoiled the ending of *The Sixth Sense* for me, which I understand is a film that's famous for its surprise twist at the end. Even though the film was released seven years ago, I had the film on a rainy-day list and planned on watching it some day.

Was this an error on your part or do you feel that after a certain amount of time, you'd have expected everyone to see *The Sixth Sense*? If so, is there a general expiration date to when movie critics can freely talk about the ending to a film? Does this apply to classic films like *Psycho, Cool Hand Luke, Citizen Kane,* or *Bridge on the River Kwai,* whose twist endings are a big part of the story?

—Orrin Konheim, Arlington, Virginia

A. It's a judgment call. I think the statute of limitations on *Sixth Sense* spoilers has run out. On the other hand, if a film is old enough, it's "new" to many viewers, so I would be shy about revealing too much about *Psycho.*

Star Ratings

Q. When *Eternal Sunshine of the Spotless Mind* came out, I read your review and accepted the three and a half stars. Not that three and a half is anything to sneeze at, but I've seen it several times since and, honestly, it reminds me of the *Vanity Fair* comment on Nabokov's *Lolita*: "The only convincing love story of the twentieth century."

Like many movies it has its flaws, but is this possibly a rare case of the flaws enhancing the wonderful rather than hobbling it? (Another example is *The Big Lebowski,* a three-star wonder on the Ebert-o-Meter.) Would you consider keeping a list of movies you substantially upgrade (or downgrade) upon reflection, including ones like *The Brown Bunny?* It would be a neat way to see how a movie ages in your eyes and mind.

—David Whitehead, Baltimore, Maryland

A. *The Brown Bunny* was upgraded after major changes involving cuts of 25 percent, making it a substantially different movie. But some of my Great Movies began life at 3.5 stars, so there is chance for redemption. I would rather just let original reviews stand, even including my mistakes, than go in for retrospective revisionism.

Q. It seems that your reviews since your return from illness are *nicer.* Are you viewing life and films differently now? I can't remember ever seeing so many three- to four-star reviews from you, week after week, as I have in the past few months. Or do you think that movies are just getting better? What has changed, you or the quality of the films?

—Garry Hasara, Tampa, Florida

A. Maybe I'm just so happy to be writing reviews. Or maybe several other factors are at work: (1) Oscar season began in September, and autumn movies are traditionally superior to other seasons; (2) I no longer automatically review virtually every movie released, and so tend to choose the ones that seem more interesting; (3) Distributors have stopped screening most horror films for critics; (4) I enjoy calling attention to lesser-known indie films and tend to choose those I like; (5) When I double back to review a movie that I missed earlier, of course I don't go looking for lousy ones.

Q. I often find some of my very favorite films are ones you give three-and-a-half-star ratings. I've never read a review where you explain what costs these movies the last half star. *Shoot 'Em Up, Eternal Sunshine, Lord of War,* and *The Incredibles* were all movies I didn't find fault with, but you've been at this longer than I. How do you decide on those?

—William Woody, Columbia, South Carolina

A. I wish I didn't give star ratings at all and every review had to speak for itself. But three and a half is a very good rating, meaning all a movie lacked was an ineffable tingle at the base of my spine.

Steak 'n Shake

Q. In more than one review now, you have cited the slogan of your favorite restaurant chain, Steak 'n Shake, which reads "In Sight, It Must Be Right." After years of puzzling, I still have no idea what that means.

—Michael Miller, Clinton, Connecticut

A. If you can see 'em frying the burgers right there behind the counter, you know there ain't no funny stuff goin's on in the kitchen. This concept of the visible kitchen, introduced in 1934 by S&S founder A. H. "Gus" Belt, was copied decades later by Wolfgang Puck, etc. It is my belief that the motto applies not only to food, but to politics, auto repairs, fresh fish, the cinema, etc.

Surviving in Space

Q. I've just read your review for *Sunshine,* and I'm confused. You say that according to Isaac Asimov, the human body can survive in the cold vacuum of space for longer than I might think. I was under the impression that, in space, a naked human would initially freeze to death, and then summarily explode.

—Ali Arikan, Istanbul, Turkey

A. Asimov and Sir Arthur C. Clarke, both scientists, explored this question in fiction. And damninteresting.com reports: "Though an unprotected human would not long survive in the clutches of outer space, it is remarkable that survival times can be measured in minutes rather than seconds, and that one could endure such an inhospitable environment for almost two minutes without suffering any irreversible damage."

In terms of NASA's experience in a test gone wrong in 1965, a subject in a vacuum remained aware for fourteen seconds.

Q. *Sunshine* is a movie I dreamed about for days after I saw it. I found it interesting that several Answer Man topics focused on the accuracy of the effects of vacuum on a human being, and none on the surprising presence of gravity. Why would such a terrific movie choose to ignore such a fundamental?

—Steve Wierzbowski, Chicago, Illinois

A. True, something was preventing the solarnaughts from floating around, but what? Not likely that gravity will be controlled so soon in the future.

Q. Regarding the question about survival in space: A person exposed to direct sunlight in space would rapidly cook to death, not freeze. If they were in the shade the vacuum would prevent the body temperature from bleeding off very quickly (no wind or air to cool it off, just the body radiating its own heat) and they would die of suffocation instead. Freezing would happen after. Arthur Clarke postulated that to survive you should hyperventilate and fill your bloodstream with as much oxygen as possible before exposure, then vacate the lungs to prevent a pressure imbalance that might create a rupture. So lasting awhile does take a bit of prep time (as shown in *2001*).

—Rob Schwarz, Carlsbad, California

A. I'm gonna stick that to the refrigerator door for when I may need it.

Q. Was the mission in *Sunshine* a "kamikaze" mission, as you say? The characters talk about "getting home," but I don't understand how that is possible if they are meant to jettison their big front shield thingy into the sun to deliver their bomb.

—Gordon Barnard, West Hollywood, California

A. Neither do I. If you're going to fly inside Mercury's orbit and hurl a bomb into the sun to burst its Q-ball (non-topological soliton) into pieces, I suggest that *home* may require a theological definition.

The Stolen Timex

Q. Since you're a movie critic, I don't suppose anyone will ask you about President Bush's "stolen" watch, will they?

—R. Joseph Ebert, Chicago, Illinois

A. You're right. Nobody did. That's why I had to ask myself, because I can't wait to answer. Close scrutiny of photographs and research on the Web reveals that the president and I wear the same watch. It is a Timex Indiglo, with great big numbers on the dial, and it lights up real good. And why does that belong in a movie critic's column? *Because it is the Official Movie Critics' Watch!* Honest. Many years ago, sitting through an endless movie at a film festival, I observed Kenneth Turan, film critic of the *Los Angeles Times*, light up his watch. I asked him about it. "This is the watch a movie critic needs," he said. "In big, bright numbers it tells you instantaneously what time it is, even though you're sitting in the dark." Since then any number of movie critics have adopted it. It is exactly like Bush's, except that ours do not have the presidential seal on the face.

Talk to Me

Q. In your review of *Talk to Me*, you say, "Howard Stern, whether he knew him or not, owes a lot to Petey Greene." In fact, Howard worked in Washington, D.C., during Petey's era, so he got to experience "P-Town" firsthand. Not only has he expressed his admiration for Petey on-air, he even appeared on Petey's television show (in blackface) and traded racial slurs with Petey in a satirical exchange the likes of which may never be seen on public airwaves again. Rest in peace, Petey.

—Daniel Alvarado, Arleta, California

A. I should have known. Problem is, Stern is on satellite radio, our Sirius radio is in the car, and I haven't been driving a lot.

30 Days of Night

Q. Re your review of *30 Days of Night:* The town in Alaska is named Barrow, not Barlow.

—Kristi Kingery, Killeen, Texas

A. So *that* explains why Google hadn't heard of it! I have now located it on a Google map. Just for fun ask for "driving instructions" from Barrow to anywhere.

Q. As for the driving directions to or from Barrow, Alaska, Google has become tame. At one time you could ask it for directions from midtown Manhattan to Paris and it would instruct you to head down to the docks, turn right, and swim 4,000 miles. Now you just get that same bland "could not calculate" message.

—Adam Weintraub, Sacramento, California

A. That's better than wading ashore in New Jersey.

Trade

Q. In your review of *Trade*, about child sexual trafficking, you raise the issue of how or why such a serious subject should be made "entertaining." I believe you answered that question in your last line when you stated that "the movie seems to have an unwholesome determination to show us the victims being terrified and threatened. When I left the screening, I just didn't feel right."

As an adult survivor of these atrocities, I felt that this movie gave a realistic expose of human trafficking. Do you think that a movie like *Trade* needs to try even harder to be entertaining so that viewers can move beyond indifference and allow themselves to be empathically disturbed as you were, yet find enough relief in the lighter entertaining moments to actually leave feeling moved in a sad but wholesome way?

—Nancy F., Chicago, Illinois

A. It's complicated. My friend Gene Siskel had a real issue about movies showing children in danger. I think all depends on the danger, and how it shows the children. Certainly it should not linger on the elements that are the most exploitative.

Transformers

Q. The *Northwest Herald* published this letter from Michael Bay, director of *Transformers:*

"*The Herald*'s movie critic, Jeffrey Westhoff, seems to be woefully out of touch with pop culture. The *Transformers* movie's $155 million seven-day haul is the biggest non-sequel opening in box office history. Numbers like that usually mean positive word of mouth on the film is huge, and people are going back.

"A friend of mine, Steven Spielberg, he's pretty smart about film, said Westhoff's review was idiotic. Westhoff's a critic who actually reviewed his dislike for the director, rather then reviewing the movie, like his job description prescribes. Westhoff talks about the director being an egomaniacal hack. Well I don't believe I've ever had the pleasure of meeting Westhoff, though it sounds like he knows me. If Westhoff actually did know me, he would find me to be a pretty down-to-earth, nice guy.

"I implore the editor to give Westhoff a little relaxation and sunshine, clear his head, let him rediscover that moviegoing is supposed to be a fun experience. Maybe even help him get rid of his hatred."

What do you think of the controversy?

—Charlie Smith, Chicago, Illinois

A. Spielberg, a nice, down-to-earth guy, is more than a friend of Bay's; he's a producer of *Transformers.* I've never had the pleasure of meeting Bay, but I did like his movie more than Westhoff did. I gave it three stars, while it scored only a "rotten" 56 percent on the Tomatometer.

Westhoff's review is smart and funny and wonderfully well-written, although perhaps the words "egomaniacal hack" were incautious. I am glad Bay defended himself against that charge in McHenry County, although he still has a lot of ground to cover.

Q. I noticed that several times you referred to the good Transformers as *Transformers* and not as *autobots.* In the movie, Optimus Prime tells Sam that he can call his group "the autobots" for short. Both the Decepticons and the autobots are Transformers and of the same race, but over time, as Optimus describes, a struggle for power ensued and peace was shattered. I just wanted to clear this up for you.

—Dustin Letkeman, Saskatoon, Saskatchewan

A. Thanks for clearing that up. What is *autobots* short for? Automobile Robots? Robots made of autos? That leads to this question: When Megatron came from space and landed at the North Pole, circa 1900, what was he made from, since he wasn't from Earth and automobiles were presumably unavailable on his home planet?

Aha. I have the answer right here. "Automobiles were reverse-engineered from Transformer technology," according to Peter Debruge, who pays close attention to these things. "That All Spark contains the potential to turn all modern devices back into killer robots (such as the Mountain Dew vending machine we see in the final showdown)." Yes, of course.

Q. I'm not a *Transformers* expert, but I do know that *auto* as a word root is not short for *automobiles,* but rather "for or by oneself or itself." Hence its use in the word *automobiles,* where *mobile* means movement. *Autobots,* I would guess, are bots that perform actions for or by themselves, where *bots* are simply mechanical devices or software programs that carry out tasks. Yes, of course.

—Matt Mercer, Los Angeles, California

A. You are correct. What a coincidence that autobots are made from autos.

Unexplained Penis

Q. After seeing *Walk Hard* and reading your review, I found it curious that you referred to the scene with the unexplained penis as establishing a "standard for gratuitous nudity." I found it actually served to comment on the use of gratuitous nudity. The scene also contains a considerable amount of gratuitous female nudity. But when the male nudity is added, it's so absurd it casts a light on the female nudity. I should also add that I thought it was very funny, as did my wife.

—Glenn Stoops, Astoria, New York

A. And Maria Marella-Kopeck of Lake Villa, Illinois, writes: "This movie and *Superbad* were both produced by Judd Apatow, and *Superbad* had all kinds of drawings of penises in the movie (Seth's character was obsessed with drawing them). Perhaps it was a way for Apatow to link the two movies. Or maybe he thought it was funny."

Ebert again: You guessed right. Apatow has declared, "It's my penis." And he has promised we can look forward to seeing a penis in all of his future films. He told MTV: "It really makes me laugh in this day and age, with how psychotic our world is, that anyone is troubled by seeing any part of the human body."

Video Games as Art

Q. While reading through your essay "Games vs. Art: Ebert vs. Barker," my mind was continually distracted by a single thought. What would Roger Ebert think if a man who, self-admittedly, has never experienced a film, critiqued film as a whole?

—Matthew Schindler, Meadville, Pennsylvania

A. I would value his naivete and learn from his first impressions. During an interview about the movies on his eightieth birthday, in 1908, Leo Tolstoy said: "You will see that this little clicking contraption with the revolving handle will make a revolution in our life—the life of writers." And in a graduate class on Shakespeare's tragedies at the University of Illinois, Professor G. Blakemore Evans, later the editor of the *Riverside Shakespeare* and the world's authority on *Romeo and Juliet,* told us: "I would give anything in the world to read this play for the first time, knowing nothing about it."

Q. In your recent review of *Hitman,* you boldly stated (again) the impossibility of video games achieving the status of "art." I'm sure you again got flooded with e-mails arguing for one side or the other. What I'm wondering is, why bother? There is no universal definition of what art is or isn't. You can't possibly be surprised that a blanket statement that says X "isn't art" will elicit a contrary response. There is no right answer (especially in a world where a can of soup can be "art" if displayed as part of an exhibit). I do have a feeling you enjoy winding people up over this, though.

—Daniel Kozimor, Mississauga, Ontario

A. Well, maybe I do. But it also involves deep love of movies and a regret that millions and millions of life-hours could be invested more fruitfully.

Q. People are trying to change your mind about video games the wrong way. I've designed a simple text-based adventure game that, while I won't claim is great art, should hint at the medium's potential. You are stranded on a desert island with your best friend. As the days go by, you and your friend die slowly of starvation and dehydration. One day, out of desperation, you develop a plan to strangle him and eat the meat from his bones. Your choices are: (a) Go through with the plan, or (b) starve together. I don't think either outcome is less meaningful just because there are two of them.

—Gilbert Smith, Winter Haven, Florida

A. Neither do I.

What Daley Said

Q. Whenever a character immobilizes someone who tried to kill him (or her), the first question is always: "Who sent you?" No one ever assumes that murderers act on their own initiative.

—Alberto Diamante, Toronto, Ontario

A. I wish a character would use the late Mayor Richard J. Daley's classic line. He asked a visitor looking for a job, "Who sent you?" The visitor said, "Nobody." Daley replied: "We don't want nobody nobody sent."

What Did Bill Whisper?

Q. Using digital processing, an intrepid filmgoer has revealed what Bill Murray whispered to Scarlett Johansson at the end of *Lost in Translation!* Here is the proof: www.youtube.com/watch?v=5MV7Sym8bIQ.

—Justin Weiss, Tokyo, Japan

A. I have three reactions: (1) If that's correct, it's a letdown; (2) I felt like Gene Hackman in Coppola's *The Conversation,* trying to decide what I'd heard; (3) I think Sofia Coppola made the right decision artistically by leaving it to our imaginations.

Wilhelm Scream, Etc.

Q. I have been an Indy fan for as long as I can remember; I grew up on the movies. I thought *Indiana Jones and the Kingdom of the Crystal Skull* was a fantastic movie, and I sat through the movie with the biggest grin on my face. And it wasn't just because the movie itself was great. As I was watching, I noticed that the same sound effects were used from the other three movies for the punches in the fights. Also, the same ambient jungle sounds from *Raiders* were used. Hearing these sounds put together with different pictures and sequences made the movie truly special for me. Did you pick up on this reuse as you were watching the film? And if so, did it have a similar effect on you?

—Jonathan Furr, Concord, North Carolina

A. Sound effects experts often recycle existing sounds from other movies. At rogerebert.com, look up "The Wilhelm Scream" in the Answer Man archive for another example of sounds that live on long after they were first used. First used in 1951, the Scream is still being employed today.

Q. Regarding your recent item about the Wilhelm Scream, I must recommend a clip I saw on YouTube, "The Wilhelm Scream Compilation," which plays a long series of film clips containing the scream. Hearing it over and over, in quick succession and in such a diverse variety of films, is hilarious.

—Sarah Jane Herbener, Lexington, Kentucky

A. The Wilhelm Scream is a scream first recorded in 1951 and so beloved by sound effects artists that it has been used in at least 175 movies since. Thanks to you, I viewed the compilation. A scream is worth a thousand words.

Q. I've followed with interest the ongoing Q&A about the "Wilhelm Scream," a sound effect that has appeared in more than 150 movies. Growing up, I enjoyed a children's TV show called *Flipper.* One of the limited special effects was a sound that I've come to call the "Flipper Giggle." This was the sound that Flipper would make whenever it would interact with its human handlers. I think this sound effect is still the only one used to signify human-dolphin interaction in just about any movie where that occurs.

—Matt Robillard, Cary, Illinois

A. My favorite sound effects experts strike out. Maybe a reader will know. The Answer Man would swell with pride thinking the column might have helped identify the Flipper Giggle.

Q. Kudos to your reader who identified the "Flipper Giggle." It came to my attention when the sound clip was used in a segment of "The Simpsons' Treehouse of Horror XI," the segment called *Night of the Dolphin.* It must have been used four or five times; enough to draw attention to itself. Since then, I've noticed the same giggle in other shows and movies.

—Will Seabrook, Baltimore, Maryland

A. Frank Teelucksingh of Port of Spain, Trinidad, offers some history: "I believe that the Flipper Giggle was first recorded by the great Mel Blanc for the TV Show *Flipper.* Dolphins, of course, do not actually make this kind of noise and certainly do not make it with their mouths. They make sounds through the blowhole on top of their heads. Mostly whistles and clicks." And Tom Schwedler of Redlane, California, thinks the Flipper Giggle was also used for the gopher in *Caddyshack.*

Q. Your last Answer Man column mentioned the Flipper Giggle, and that reminded me of a sound effect I've noticed in dozens of TV shows and movies over the years. Very often when there are children playing in the background of a scene, the same sound effect will be used. It originated on *Little House on the Prairie,* and if you listen to the shouts you can clearly hear Melissa Gilbert yell out "Nellie! Noah, catch up!" It's actually a fairly short sound clip, and in a few longer scenes it really distracted me to keep hearing the same shouts at Nellie and Noah every fifteen seconds.

—Joe VanPelt, Richmond, Virginia

A. The Prairie Players, on top of the Wilhelm Scream and the Flipper Giggle, brings a whole dimension of cut and paste to the concept of sound editing.

Q. A wide range of common (probably royalty-free) sounds can turn up in movies. One I've heard a lot is what I call the "Transfusion Crash." The first time I heard it was on the 1956 novelty record *Transfusion,* by Nervous Norvus. Each lyric of the song was punctuated by the sound effect of a few seconds of screeching tire, cut off by a split-second, higher-pitched squeal before the sound of the actual crash. It's from the *Standard Sound Effects Library* owned by many radio stations in the '50s.

—Mark McDermott, Park Forest, Illinois

A. Brian Hagan of Boonton, New Jersey, adds: "In addition to the other stock sound clips you are collecting, there is a stock hospital page that appears in countess movies, TV shows, and soap operas. It's 'Paging Dr. Hamilton. Dr. Jay Hamilton . . .'"

Q. In regard to the Wilhelm Scream, is there a name for the giggle of the little girl or the ah-ah's of the baby heard so often in radio and TV commercials as well as movies?

—Kyle Bright, Joliet, Illinois

A. Steve Lee of hollywoodlostandfound.net, which documents the Wilhelm Scream, tells me: No, I don't believe this particular sound effect has a distinctive name, other than "Baby Coo" or "Baby Laugh." If I am thinking of the same sound that Kyle is, there are several versions. I think the most popular is on a CD library of sounds called *Hollywood Edge,* and it's a small piece of a baby recording on their Premiere Edition series, Disk 14, track 47, 28 seconds in. There, it's called "Baby #10."

But the truth is, it could have been one of many recordings. Babies make similar sounds to this all the time. Many sound editors and commercial houses have their own library of original sounds and have recorded their own children giggling. Loop groups have members who can imitate babies perfectly, and they record original vocals for every new project they work on. And to make sound effects archaeology even tougher, editors trade sound effects with others a lot—making it very difficult to track them all down. But give me some time. I'm on the case!

Writers' Strike

Q. As a member of the Writers' Guild of America, I'd like to get your take on our current strike. Do you think the Internet is a lucrative outlet for films and TV shows? Will it continue to be in the future? Are the writers entitled to a share of the profits made when movies and television are shown on the Internet?

—Nancy de Los Santos, Los Angeles, California

A. Income from video and films streaming on the Internet is currently negligible. But it may become a considerable, even dominant, distribution channel in the future. The studios obviously think so. That's why they're taking a hit of millions of dollars to fight your strike. The studios should do the decent thing and concede that their "product" is created by artists and craftsmen who deserve a fair share of the income.

Zodiac

Q. I recently rented *Zodiac,* which got me thinking about an annoying trend in recent movies. I have noticed that many films in recent years, whether they are science fiction, horror, drama, or comedy, look green. Do directors seriously want their films to look like *The Matrix?* Or is there some other reason behind this new way of shooting films? I don't have a problem with black and white films, which I love, but there is nothing exciting or interesting about all this green we are seeing in films today.

—Christopher Zeidel, San Luis Obispo, California

A. Controlling the palette to tilt toward greens, blues, and sepia are all ways of suggesting B&W and avoiding the unwanted lift from the sun colors. It's a tactic. Having just seen a new film named *Control* that was filmed in black and white, I am reminded that it is a classic and beautiful medium, and less distracting than worlds of green or blue.

Ebert's Little Movie Glossary

These are the year's new contributions to my glossary project. Hundreds of entries were collected in *Ebert's Bigger Little Movie Glossary,* published in 1999. Contributions are always welcome.

* * *

Action-Relationship Clause. Distinguished actors often justify starring in mindless action films by stating that they're actually "relationship" films in disguise. During publicity interviews they say things like, "What attracted me to the script is the relationship between the characters and how it evolves over the course of the film." Said relationship usually consists of two cops who hate each other at the beginning but end up relying on each other in subsequent chase and fight scenes. The paycheck has nothing to do with it.

—Christopher Scharpf, Baltimore, Maryland

All Quiet on the Weather Front. Whenever two characters are free-falling while skydiving, they can carry on a conversation in a normal tone of voice despite the fact that the noise from the rushing wind would prevent them from hearing each other even if they were shouting at the top of their lungs.

—Michael Lieber, Wilmette, Illinois

Anxious Ferry Rule. When film characters have to take a ferry, they inevitably arrive at the dock just as the ferry is leaving and often have to leap onto it as it is pulling away. They never arrive a half hour early and just kill time.

—Michael Lieber, Wilmette, Illinois

The Bathtub Principle. If you have a photo of somebody—anybody—in a bathtub, use it. Movies with bathtub shots in the program always sell lots of tickets!

—Jim Emerson, Seattle, Washington

Behind the Curtain. Whenever a character does something secret or embarrassing behind a curtain during a performance, the finale inevitably has the curtains opening to reveal the person caught in the act. See *Love Actually* and *Moulin Rouge,* etc.

—Kevin Chen, San Mateo, California

The Bungee Shot. Whenever the camera watches someone leave and remains focused on the door through which they left, that person will be back in a moment. This applies to people crawling through windows and cars turning the corner, as well.

—Terry Anastassiou, San Francisco, California

The Bucket List Exception. Except for *The Bucket List,* bathrooms are almost never used in the movies for their primary purpose. Instead, they are for staring into the mirror while hung over, clandestine conversations, quick escapes through the window, secret smoking, stealing drugs from the medicine cabinet, quick sex, concealed cell calls, dumping evidence down the drain, murdering people in the shower, eavesdropping, hiding from angry husbands, getting away so you can scream, and seeing ghosts behind you.

—R.E.

Clean Air Duct Principle. Whenever the protagonist attempts to sneak through a secure building (*Die Hard, The Simpsons*) the air ducts are always clean and dust free, never coating them with dust bunnies or causing so much as a sneeze.

—Darrell Hird, Rolling Meadows, Illinos

Clutchless Shift. During a car chase scene, the protagonist drives a vehicle with manual transmission. The vehicle doesn't have a clutch but viewers get five or ten shots of the hero moving the stick. In *Bourne Supremacy,* Jason commandeers a yellow cab. When he shifted the first time I realized that Europeans have manual transmission BMW taxis. Then he shifted again, and again, and again, and again. I never saw him depress the clutch.

—Troylene Ladner, Jersey City, New Jersey

Collegians Gone Wild. All college freshmen will have sex with someone they met on the first day.

—Jorie Slodki, Arlington Heights, Illinois

The Designated Character Rule. In any movie where two characters arrange a meeting at a bar to exchange valuable information or materials, the person who arrives second will always order a beer. However, once the beer is set down, they won't touch it until they finish explaining the information or giving the person the materials, at which time they will stand up, take one small sip, throw money down, and say one final word of advice before departing. The person left at the bar will usually stare off into space for a second, then say to the bartender, "Give me another one, Johnny," before we cut to the next scene.

—Chris Border, Nashville, Tennessee

Do-It-Yourself Dentistry. If a character complains of a toothache in the first act, they must painfully extract the tooth themselves by the third act. See *Affliction, Cast Away, Bug,* etc.

—Brian Gaul, San Diego, California

Eat Your Food Before It Gets Cold! Characters having dinner never actually try their food. They heap small amounts onto their forks, which dangle in front of their face, but just when they're about to eat they get distracted by the conversation. This practice works especially well if the viewer knows the food has been poisoned or contains something like worms.

—Nick Ostrau, Chapel Hill, North Carolina

Explosion? What Explosion? A major character is seen walking nonchalantly in slow-motion toward the camera and away from a big, napalm-like explosion. Even the Coens use this in *No Country for Old Men.* I believe the granddaddy of all such scenes to be the opening stinger in *Goldfinger* in which James Bond is the only person in a nightclub not reacting to a huge explosion nearby, an explosion for which he, obviously, is responsible.

—Steve Jump, Lawton, Oklahoma

Fire Safety 101. No movie character who catches on fire has apparently heard of Stop, Drop & Roll. They assume the adage to be Panic, Run & Flail. Repeat until burnt to cinder. This is true even for characters whose professions would suggest that they know better, like policemen, firemen, and soldiers.

Joseph Sitek, St. Anthony, Minnesota

The Foresight of Q. Whenever a superhero receives a supply of gadgets from his weapons expert, they are invariably perfectly suited to the exact situations of the ensuing plot. Bond's Q is particularly adept at outfitting James with just the right equipment. In *Casino Royale,* for example, Bond has a handy defibrillator in his vehicle because he will undoubtedly have his heart stopped by the world's slowest poison.

—Walt Freeman, Nashua, New Hampshire

Getting in Shape. In any movie where an athlete must raise himself to another level, there is always a scene in which he/she is seen working out in preposterous ways. This may involve running through crowds that throw fruit at you (*Rocky*), having champagne glasses set up on hurdles (*Chariots of Fire*), or balancing on the bow of a rowboat in the ocean (*The Karate Kid*). A musical corollary is found in *Mr. Holland's Opus,* in which a music student dons a football helmet while the music teacher drums his head with a mallet, an action that would lead to dismissal and litigation in real life.

—Bob Diefendorf, Hong Kong

Grim Reaper's Fertility Clinic. The chances of a heroine conceiving a child with the hero from a one-night stand skyrocket if the hero dies later in the film (see, for example, *The Fly, Terminator, Cold Mountain*).

—Brian Henley, Broomall, Pennsylvania

The Hunk Hypothesis. If the heroine is being courted by a blond hunk, the romance won't last till the end of the movie. The Fabio look never bodes well. The heroine's final choice will be dorkier, scruffier, and most likely have darker hair (see *The Money Pit, Just My Luck, The Devil Wears Prada, Edward Scissorhands*).

—Matthew Stephen Smith, Evanston, Illinois

The *Jeopardy!* IQ Test. Extraordinary intelligence in movie characters is revealed by showing them watching *Jeopardy!* on TV and instantly barking out every answer. See Dustin Hoffman in *Rainman,* Jamal Wallace in *Finding Forrester,* Morgan Freeman in *The Bucket List,* George Constanza in a *Seinfeld* episode, etc.

—Gerardo Valero, Mexico City, Mexico

Law of Friendship and Beauty. No one in a movie has a best friend who is better looking than they are. In the case of posses of high school girls, the leader is always better looking than her sidekicks. The rare exception can take place when it's part of the story line that the main character is nerdy or unattractive (*The Truth About Cats and Dogs*).

—Joe Van Pelt, Richmond, Virginia

Law of Unfinished Movie Beverages. Nobody who is poured a drink in a movie ever comes close to finishing it. This is a curious disconnect with the real world, especially given modern drink prices. Personally, I consider every drink to be good to the last drop.

—Eric Gribbin, Chicago, Illinois

"Let's Get Out of Here." The most common line of dialogue, due to its versatility and applicability to any situation from "We're under attack!" to "I'm in love with you." Noted by Neve Campbell in the film *Three to Tango.*

—Jeff Cross, Marblehead, Massachusetts

Limited Crawl Rule. When locked in a room, a character will escape by opening up a ceiling tile and climbing into the crawl space on top of the tiles (see *The Breakfast Club*, *Die Hard*). In reality, such tiles are extremely easy to break (as a telecom engineer who sometimes installs cabling, I speak from experience) and you'd have to weigh less than a four-year-old kid to actually be able to accomplish this stunt.

—Curtis Burga, Mustang, Oklahmoa

Lonely Girl Häagen-Dazs Rule. When the heroine of a chick flick has her inevitable mid-film breakup with the male lead, we know that she is lonely because she will consume a pint of Häagen-Dazs ice cream in one sitting, often while watching an old black-and-white tear-jerker on the television. The converse of this rule is that when a chick-flick heroine is happily in love, she will lip-synch to Motown tunes, often using a hair brush as a microphone.

—Daniel Fisher, Congers, New York

Name Recognition Rule. The trailer for any movie named after the main character must contain a montage of various characters saying that character's name. (See *Alfie*, *Charlie Bartlett*, *Miss Pettigrew Lives for a Day*, *Charlie Wilson's War.*)

—Isaac Marion, Seattle, Washington

On a Clear Day You Can See the Oranges. In any space film that features a scene in Earth's orbit, the state of Florida will always be visible through a porthole, thus providing the audience with an instantly recognizable reference point.

—Marc Giller, St. Petersburg, Florida

Opposite of "Boy Named Sue Rule." Whenever it is established that a male character is set to meet a person named Chris for the first time, he will always be surprised to find out that Chris is, in fact, a woman.

—Tim Brown, Waterloo, Ontario

The Pepe Le Pew Prerequisite. Comparative device that illustrates the need for a cliché by putting it in terms of the one thing required for any Pepe Le Pew cartoon. For example, "You can't have a main character pregnant in a movie without her giving birth before the credits, any more than you can have a Pepe Le Pew cartoon without spilling a can of white paint."

—Karl Witter, Bloomfield, Connecticut

The Poor Dumb Bastard. This is any secondary character who disregards the hero's wise advice and does the one thing guaranteed to make him die a ghastly death, thereby proving the hero correct. The PDB is often eulogized with the phrase "The Poor Dumb Bastard never had a chance!" In disaster movies, the PDBs tend to travel in packs.

—Merwyn Grote, St. Louis, Missouri

The Requel. This is the practice common among long-running film series to copy plots of previous films in the series while maintaining those films as part of the series continuity. Nearly every James Bond film has been requeled at least once, and *Star Treks* 7 and 10 were both requels of *The Wrath of Khan.*

—Daniel Weissenberger, Ottawa, Ontario

Senseless Devices Rule. Device used in films (especially James Bond films) with a numerical speed/radioactivity/odometer, etc., that inexplicably includes a range (always marked in red) at which the device must never be used or otherwise it will become unstable and kill the user. Why build the device with such capacity at all? (See, for example, the radioactivity pool in *Dr. No* and the astronaut training chamber in *Moonraker.*)

—Gerardo Valero Perez Vargas, Mexico City, Mexico

The Slap That Ends It All. Near the end of any drama about a troubled romance, the couple will have a heated argument and the man (who has always considered himself civilized) will lose control and slap the woman's face in a rage. In that second, as the man marvels at the depths to which he's sunk and the woman ponders what a monster she loved up until a moment ago, they both know it's over.

—Rhys Southan, Brooklyn, New York

Son of Dueling Scar. Any star who is a victim of a crash, explosion, or fight will always have the same cool-looking scratch or abrasion exactly in the same spot: High on the cheekbone near the good side of the face slanted at a forty-degree angle and never more than 2.2 inches long on a female and 3.0 on a male.

—Mick Welsh, Phoenix, Arizona

Sorry, the Auditions Are Over! There's an audition or tryout and everyone fails to measure up. The producers and casting director are disappointed. Then one person shows up late, is told to go home, but pushes onstage, begs for a chance, and ends up dazzling everyone and getting the job (*Mystery Men, The Fabulous Baker Boys,* etc.).

—Alberto Diamante, Toronto, Ontario

Stupid Movie! If there's an exclamation point in the title, it's going to be a bad movie, such as *Mars Attacks!* and *Raise the Titanic!*

—Jeff Cross, Marblehead, Massachusetts

"This Is Not a Movie!" When an actor or actress says, "This is not a movie! This is my life," it's still a movie.

—Nick Coccellato, San Rafael, California

Unfocus, Focus, Unfocus Sequence. Whenever someone is looking through a microscope, we see them put their eyes down to the lens and grab the focus dial. Next, the magnification appears to us onscreen. The object begins out of focus, then transitions into focus and then out again (implying the viewer turned the knob too far in the other direction). Finally we see the object in clear focus.

—Brian Dunn, Alexandria, Virginia

Yes/No Dialogue Trigger Rule. When one character asks another, "Are you scared?" and the answer is no, the first character replies, "Well, you should be." If the answer is yes, the reply is, "Well, you shouldn't be."

—Patrick Imbeau, Val Caron, Ontario

Index

A

B

C

D

E

F

H

I

J

N

O

P

S

T

X

Y